Lecture Notes in Artificial Intelligence 7691

Subseries of Lecture Notes in Computer Science

W0235372

Michael Thielscher   Dongmo Zhang (Eds.)

AI 2012: Advances in Artificial Intelligence

25th Australasian Joint Conference
Sydney, Australia, December 4-7, 2012
Proceedings

 Springer

Volume Editors

Michael Thielscher
University of New South Wales
School of Computer Science and Engineering
Sydney, NSW 2052, Australia
E-mail: mit@cse.unsw.edu.au

Dongmo Zhang
University of Western Sydney
School of Computing and Mathematics
Penrith South DC, NSW 1797, Australia
E-mail: dongmo@scm.uws.edu.au

ISSN 0302-9743   e-ISSN 1611-3349
ISBN 978-3-642-35100-6   e-ISBN 978-3-642-35101-3
DOI 10.1007/978-3-642-35101-3
Springer Heidelberg Dordrecht London New York

Library of Congress Control Number: 2012951926

CR Subject Classification (1998): I.2, H.3-4, F.1, H.2.8, I.4-5, J.3

LNCS Sublibrary: SL 7 – Artificial Intelligence

Typesetting: Camera-ready by author, data conversion by Scientific Publishing Services, Chennai, India

Printed on acid-free paper

Springer is part of Springer Science+Business Media (www.springer.com)

Preface

Welcome to the proceedings of the 25th anniversary of the Australasian Joint Conferences on Artificial Intelligence (AI 2012)! Since its inauguration in Sydney in 1987, this annual conference has become the premier event for artificial intelligence researchers in Australasia and a major international forum on AI worldwide. For its silver anniversary, the conference returned to Australia's iconic and most populous city in December 2012, jointly hosted by the University of Western Sydney and the University of New South Wales.

AI 2012 received 196 submissions with authors from 32 countries. Each submission was reviewed by at least three Program Committee members or external referees. A lively and intense discussion ensued among the reviewers and the dedicated members of the senior Program Committee. After this thorough assessment and rigorous prepublication scrutiny, 76 submissions were finally accepted to be published as full papers in the proceeding. The acceptance rate of less than 39% set a new height of quality for the conference.

AI 2012 featured three exciting keynote speeches by distinguished scientists: Joseph Halpern (Cornell University, USA) talked about decision theory with subjective states and outcomes. Mary O'Kane (New South Wales Chief Scientist and Engineer, Australia) gave an overview of the early days and current impact of AI in Australia. Mamoru Kaneko (University of Tsukuba, Japan) spoke about epistemic logic and inductive game theory.

Four workshops with their own joint proceedings were held on the first day of the conference: the 8th Australasian Ontology Workshop; the second Australian Workshop on Artificial Intelligence in Health; the New Trends of Computational Intelligence in Health Applications Workshop; and the workshop on A Semantic Reasoning Approach to Data Linkage for Optimised Clinical Risk Management. The workshops were complemented by two tutorials: Discrete Non-parametric Methods for Machine Learning and Linguistics by Wray Buntine, and Multimedia Information Extraction: Methods and Applications by Sri Krishnan. Together these tutorials and workshops, which were overseen by the Workshop Chair Hans Guesgen, provided an excellent start to the event.

Two challenges were held during AI 2012: the First General Game Playing International Australian Open and the First Australasian Strategic Trading Game. These two contests each had a purse of $1,000 for the winners.

AI 2012 would not have been successful without the support of authors, reviewers, and organizers. We thank the many authors for submitting their research papers to the conference. We are grateful to the successful authors whose papers are published in this volume for their collaboration during the preparation of final submissions. We thank the members of the Program Committee and the external referees for their expertise and timeliness in assessing the papers. We also thank the organizers of the workshops and tutorials for their commitment and dedication. We are very grateful to the members of the Organizing Committee for their efforts in the preparation, promotion, and organization of the conference, especially David Rajaratnam for his outstanding and tireless service. We acknowledge the assistance provided by EasyChair for conference management, and we appreciate the professional service provided by the Springer LNCS editorial and publishing teams.

December 2012   Michael Thielscher
                                                                Dongmo Zhang

Organization

General Chairs

Simeon Simoff   University of Western Sydney, Australia
Maurice Pagnucco   University of New South Wales, Australia

Program Chairs

Dongmo Zhang   University of Western Sydney, Australia
Michael Thielscher   University of New South Wales, Australia

Local Arrangements Chairs

Yan Zhang   University of Western Sydney, Australia
Abhaya Nayak   Macquarie University, Australia

Award Selection Committee Chair

Toby Walsh   NICTA and UNSW, Australia

Workshop/Tutorial Chair

Hans Guesgen   Massey University, New Zealand

Publicity Chair

Sebastian Sardina   RMIT University, Australia

Sponsorship Chairs

Sumeet Kumar   Telstra Enterprise Government, Australia
Laurence Park   University of Western Sydney, Australia

Conference Coordinator

David Rajaratnam   University of New South Wales, Australia

AI Challenges Coordinator

Anton Bogdanovych   University of Western Sydney

Senior Program Committee

James Bailey	University of Melbourne, Australia
Wray Buntine	NICTA, Australia
Byeong Ho Kang	University of Tasmania, Australia
Reinhard Klette	University of Auckland, New Zealand
Fabio Ramos	University of Sydney, Australia
Mark Reynolds	University of Western Australia
Jussi Rintanen	Griffith University, Australia
Juan A. Rodríguez-Aguilar	IIIA-CSIC, Spain
Abdul Sattar	Griffith University, Australia
Mengjie Zhang	Victoria University of Wellington, New Zealand
Ingrid Zukerman	Monash University, Australia

Program Committee

Hussein Abbass	UNSW Canberra @ ADFA
Quan Bai	Auckland University of Technology
Yun Bai Bai	University of Western Sydney
Jacky Baltes	University of Manitoba
Lubica Benuskova	University of Otago
Partha Bhowmick	Indian Institute of Technology Kharagpur
Wei Bian	University of Technology Sydney
Ivan Bindoff	University of Tasmania
Blai Bonet	Universidad Simon Bolivar
Richard Booth	University of Luxembourg
Rafael H. Bordini	Pontifícia Universidad Católica do Rio Grande do Sul
Sebastian Brand	NICTA and University of Melbourne
Thomas Braunl	University of Western Australia
Tiberio Caetano	NICTA
Longbing Cao	University of Technology Sydney
Lawrence Cavedon	NICTA and RMIT University
Jeffrey Chan	University of Melbourne
Ling Chen	University of Technology Sydney
Songcan Chen	Nanjing University of Aeronautics & Astronautics
Sung-Bae Cho	Yonsei University
Vic Ciesielski	RMIT University
Dan Corbett	Optimodal Technologies
Stephen Cranefield	University of Otago
Xuan-Hong Dang	Aarhus University
Hepu Deng	RMIT University
Grant Dick	University of Otago
Clare Dixon	University of Liverpool

Gerhard Lakemeyer	RWTH Aachen University
Jérôme Lang	LAMSADE Université Paris Dauphine
Maria Lee	Shih Chien University
Jiuyong Li	University of South Australia
Li Li	Southwest University of China
Yuefeng Li	Queensland University of Technology
Fangzhen Lin	Hong Kong University of Science and Technology
Jing Liu	Xidian University
Qing Liu	CSIRO ICT Centre
Wan Quan Liu	Curtin University
Wei Liu	University of Melbourne
Wei Liu	University of Western Australia
Xudong Luo	Sun Yat-sen University
Carsten Lutz	Universität Bremen
Ashesh Mahidadia	University of New South Wales
Eric Martin	University of New South Wales
David Martinez	NICTA and University of Melbourne
Michael Mayo	University of Waikato
Thomas Meyer	CAIR, UKZN and CSIR Meraka
Saeid Nahavandi	Deakin University
Nina Narodytska	NICTA and University of New South Wales
Richi Nayak	Queensland University of Technology
Kourosh Neshatian	University of Canterbury
Vinh Nguyen	Monash University
Kouzou Ohara	Aoyama Gakuin University
Lionel Ott	University of Sydney
Laurence Park	University of Western Sydney
Michal Pěchouček	Czech Technical University in Prague
Laurent Perrussel	IRIT Université de Toulouse
Bernhard Pfahringer	University of Waikato
Duc-Nghia Pham	NICTA and Griffith University
Mikhail Prokopenko	CSIRO ICT Centre
Sarvapali Ramchurn	University of Southampton
Tapabrata Ray	UNSW Canberra @ ADFA
Mark Reid	Australian National University
Jochen Renz	Australian National University
Deborah Richards	Macquarie University
Mariano Rivera	Centro de Investigación en Matemáticas
Ji Ruan	University of New South Wales
Malcolm Ryan	University of New South Wales
Ruhul Sarker	University of New South Wales
Torsten Schaub	University of Potsdam
Daniel Schmidt	University of Melbourne
Rolf Schwitter	Macquarie University
Yanir Seroussi	Monash University

Lin Shang	Nanjing University
Maolin Tang	Queensland University of Technology
Mutsuhiro Terauchi	Hiroshima International University
John Thornton	Griffith University
Andrea Torsello	Università Ca' Foscari Venezia
James Underwood	University of Sydney
Ben Upcroft	Queensland University of Technology
William Uther	NICTA
Jaime Valls Miro	University of Technology Sydney
Pradeep Varakantham	Singapore Management University
Wamberto Vasconcelos	University of Aberdeen
Miroslav Velev	Aries Design Automation
Kristen Brent Venable	University of Padova
Karin Verspoor	NICTA
Meritxell Vinyals	University of Verona
Stephen Wan	CSIRO ICT Centre
Dianhui Wang	La Trobe University
Kewen Wang	Griffith University
Peter Whigham	University of Otago
Wayne Wobcke	University of New South Wales
Brendon Woodford	University of Otago
Shuxiang Xu	University of Tasmania
Bing Xue	Victoria University of Wellington
Roland Yap	National University of Singapore
Jian Yu	Swinburne University of Technology
Lean Yu	Chinese Academy of Sciences
Chengqi Zhang	University of Technology Sydney
Daoqiang Zhang	Nanjing University of Aeronautics and Astronautics
Rui Zhang	University of Melbourne
Shichao Zhang	Guangxi Normal University
Xiuzhen Zhang	RMIT University
Zili Zhang	Deakin University
Yi Zhou	University of Western Sydney
Zhi-Hua Zhou	Nanjing University
Xingquan Zhu	University of Technology Sydney

Additional Reviewers

Abdel-Fatao, Hamidu	Britz, Arina	Gao, Ping
Albathan, Mubarak	Caminada, Martin	Gebser, Martin
Andres, Benjamin	Dai, Qun	Glover, Arren
Beramasco, Filippo	Damigos, Matthew	Guan, Yanyong
Bijaksana, Moch Arif	Du, Jianfeng	Halim, Steven
Braune, Christian	Faber, Wolfgang	Hanna, Nader

He, Hu
Held, Pascal
Huang, Jin
Huang, Xiaowei
Karim, Masud
Kleiner, Alexander
Kwashie, Selasi
Li, Nan
Li, Yun
Liang, Zhenkai
Liu, Jiamou
Manchester, Ian

Moewes, Christian
Moodley, Deshendran
Morgan, Rachael
Morris, Timothy
Mu, Kedian
Newton, M.A.Hakim
Nguyen, Luan
Nofong, Vincent
Peng, Xueping
Pipanmaekaporn, Luepol
Qi, Jianzhong
Rens, Gavin

Rossi, Luca
Sabuncu, Orkunt
Schiffer, Stefan
Schneider, Marius
Shen, Yan
Sim, Terence
Warren, Michael
Wen, Zeyi
Williams, Colin R.
Xie, Feng
Xue, Yuan
Yang, Ming

Sponsoring Institutions

Google Australia
National ICT Australia (NICTA)
New South Wales Trade & Investment
University of New South Wales
University of Western Sydney

Table of Contents

Agents

Applications

Computer Vision

Constraints and Search

Evolutionary Computation

Game Playing

Information Retrieval

Knowledge Representation

Machine Learning

Planning and Scheduling

Robotics

Uncertainty in AI

Measuring the Performance of Online Opponent Models in Automated Bilateral Negotiation

Tim Baarslag, Mark Hendrikx, Koen Hindriks, and Catholijn Jonker

Interactive Intelligence Group, Delft University of Technology,
Mekelweg 4, Delft, The Netherlands
{T.Baarslag,K.V.Hindriks,C.M.Jonker,M.Hendrikx}@tudelft.nl

Abstract. An important aim in bilateral negotiations is to achieve a win-win solution for both parties; therefore, a critical aspect of a negotiating agent's success is its ability to take the opponent's preferences into account. Every year, new negotiation agents are introduced with better learning techniques to model the opponent. Our main goal in this work is to evaluate and compare the performance of a selection of state-of-the-art online opponent modeling techniques in negotiation, and to determine under which circumstances they are beneficial in a real-time, online negotiation setting. Towards this end, we provide an overview of the factors influencing the quality of a model and we analyze how the performance of opponent models depends on the negotiation setting. This results in better insight into the performance of opponent models, and allows us to pinpoint well-performing opponent modeling techniques that did not receive much previous attention in literature.

Keywords: Negotiation, Opponent Model Performance, Quality Measures.

1 Introduction

A negotiation between two agents is a game in which both agents try to reach an agreement better than their status quo. To avoid exploitation, agents often keep their preferences private during the negotiation [6]; however, if an agent has no knowledge about its opponent's preferences, then this can result in a suboptimal outcome [10]. A common technique to counter this is *learning* the opponent's preference profile during the negotiation, which aids in increasing the quality of the negotiation outcome by identifying bids that are more likely to be accepted by the opponent [6,10,21].

If there have been previous negotiations with a similar opponent, the opponent model can be prepared *before* the start of the negotiation; we will refer to these models as *offline* models (for example [6]). Contrastingly, if the agent has to learn the preferences *during* the negotiation it performs *online* modeling (for example [8,10,14]).

In this work we focus on *online* opponent models in a *single-shot* negotiation with *private* preference profiles; i.e., a setting in which an agent has no knowledge about the opponent's preference profile and no history of previous negotiations is available. There has been recent interest in opponent modeling for such settings, for example in the Automated Negotiating Agents Competition (ANAC) [1,4]. Despite ongoing research in this area, it is not yet clear how different approaches compare, and empirical evidence

M. Thielscher and D. Zhang (Eds.): AI 2012, LNCS 7691, pp. 1–14, 2012.

has raised the question whether using an opponent model is beneficial at all in such a setting. To illustrate: state-of-the-art agents, such as the top three agents of both ANAC 2010 [4] and ANAC 2011 [1], do not model the opponent, yet outperformed agents that do. One reason that opponent modeling does not guarantee a better outcome for an agent is that the model can be a poor representation of the opponent's preferences. If the model consistently suggests unattractive bids for the opponent, it may even be preferable to not employ one at all. Secondly, a time-based deadline introduces an additional challenge for online opponent modeling, as learning the model can be computationally expensive and can therefore influence the amount of bids that can be explored. More precisely, the gain in using the model should be higher than the loss in utility due to decreased exploration of the outcome space. We will refer to this as the *time/exploration trade-off*.

Apart from the inherent trade-off in opponent modeling, we are interested whether opponent models are accurate enough to provide gains at all, even when ignoring computational costs. To this end, we evaluate opponent models in two settings: a time-based and round-based negotiation protocol. This paper compares a large set of opponent modeling techniques, which were isolated from state-of-the-art negotiation strategies. We measure their performance in various negotiation settings, and we provide a detailed overview of how the different factors influence the final negotiation outcome.

After discussing related work in Section 2, we introduce the negotiation setting and consider the difficulties in evaluating opponent models in Section 3. In Section 4 we introduce a method to quantify opponent model performance, after which we apply it to a set of models in Section 5. We formulate hypotheses and analyze the results in Section 6; and finally, in Section 7 we provide directions for future work.

2   Related Work

Opponent modeling has received a lot of attention in automated negotiation. There are three groups of related work when considering opponent model evaluation. The first category consists of work that details an agent strategy in which the opponent model is introduced, but the performance is not evaluated. Examples of this type are [8] and [20].

The second category compares a single novel model with a set of baseline strategies. The approaches usually differ in how they define performance. In [10] for example, a model is introduced for the same time-based protocol discussed in this work. The performance of the opponent model is estimated by embedding it in a strategy and comparing the average utility against two baseline strategies. The modeling technique discussed by [16] introduces a model for a similar protocol, but in this case the baseline is set by humans. Zeng and Sycara measure performance in terms of social welfare, but focus on single-issue negotiations in which they compare the performance of three settings: both learn, neither learn, and only the buyer learns [21]. Finally, [5] evaluates the accuracy of a model against simple baseline strategies in terms of the likelihood that the correct class is estimated to which the opponent's preference profile belongs.

The last category is most similar to our work, and consists of literature comparing the performance of a model against other models or against a theoretical lower or upper bound. For example, Coehoorn and Jennings [6] evaluate the performance of their opponent model using a standard bidding strategy that can be used both with and without a model. The performance of the strategy is evaluated in three settings: without knowledge, with perfect knowledge, and when using an offline opponent model. This work is similar to our work, however, it differs in the fact that we focus on *online* opponent modeling. Our setting is especially challenging as it involves the time/exploration trade-off. Another example is the work by [13], which introduces two opponent models for e-recommendation in a multi-object negotiation. Compared to our work, we focus on the more general type of multi-issue negotiations. Finally, [11] defines two accuracy measures and uses these measures to analyze the accuracy of two opponent models. The main differences are that we focus on a larger set of performance measures, and pay more attention to the factors that influence the performance of the model.

Furthermore, as far as we know, our work is the first to compare and analyze such a large set of state-of-the art models of the opponent's preference profile.

3 Evaluating Opponent Models

The main goal of this work is to answer the following research question: *"Under what circumstances is it beneficial to use an online opponent model in a real-time negotiation setting?"*. An answer is not straightforward due to the time/exploration trade-off and potentially poor accuracy of a model. In particular, we want to answer the following:

1. Assuming *perfect* knowledge about the opponent's preferences, is there a significant performance gain in using this information compared with ignoring it?
2. Is there a significant performance gain from using an *online opponent model* in comparison to *not using a model*, assuming no prior knowledge is available?

The main difficulty in finding a conclusive answer to these questions, is that the performance of an opponent model depends on the negotiation setting. Therefore, we study an third, overarching research question:

3. How does the performance of using an opponent model depend on the setting?

3.1 Preliminaries

In this work we focus on a bilateral automated negotiation in which two agents try to reach an agreement while maximizing their own utility. Agents use the widely-employed alternating-offers protocol for bilateral negotiations [17], in which the negotiating parties take turns in exchanging offers. A negotiation scenario consists of the negotiation domain, which specifies the setting and all possible bids, together with a privately-known preference profile for each party. A preference profile is described by a utility function $u(x)$, which maps each possible outcome x in the negotiation domain to a utility in the range $[0, 1]$. In this work we discuss opponent models that attempt to estimate the opponent's utility function $u'(x)$ during the negotiation.

3.2 Influence of the Agent's Strategy

Different agents apply their opponent model in different ways. There are two main factors in which the application of an opponent model by a bidding strategy can differ:

– *Type of information gained from the opponent model.* A bidding strategy can employ an opponent model for different reasons: for example, it can be employed to select the best bid for the opponent out of a set of similarly preferred bids [3,20]; to select a bid that optimizes a weighted combination of both utility functions [8]; or to help estimate the utility of a specific outcome, such as the Nash-point [3].

– *Selecting a bid using an opponent model.* When a model is used to select a bid from a set of similarly preferred bids, the question still remains which one to choose. One can select the *best* bid for the opponent, but this may be suboptimal, as models may be inaccurate. An alternative is to select a bid from the set of n best bids [3].

Even when the factors above are taken into account, still care has to be taken to properly compare different models. Opponent models can only be fairly compared if the other components, such as bidding strategy and acceptance strategy [2] are fixed.

3.3 Influence of the Opponent's Strategy

All opponent modeling techniques make certain assumptions about the opponent, so as to assign meaning to the observed behavior. If the opponent does not adhere to these assumptions, the model may not reflect reality well. The set of strategies against which a model is tested is a decisive factor when measuring its performance. Therefore, a set of opponents should contain both agents that fulfill the model's assumptions to determine its efficacy in optimal conditions; and agents that test the model's robustness by violating its assumptions.

The following assumptions were found by analyzing the models in Section 5.2:

1. *The concession of the opponent follows a particular function.* Some opponent modeling techniques assume that the opponent uses a given time-based bidding strategy. Modeling the opponent then reduces to estimating all issue weights such that the predicted utility by the modeled preference profile is close to the assumed utility.

2. *The first bid made by the opponent is the most preferred bid.* The best bid is the selection of the most preferred value for each issue, and thereby immediately reveals which values are the best for each issue. Many agents start with the best bid.

3. *There is a direct relation between the preference of an issue and the times its value is significantly changed.* To learn the issue weights, some models assume that the amount of times the value of an issue is changed is an indicator for the importance of the issue. The validity of this assumption depends on the distribution of the issue and value weights of the opponent's preference profile and its bidding strategy.

4. *There is a direct relation between the preference of a value and the frequency it is offered.* A common assumption to learn the value weights is to assume that values that are more preferred are offered more often. Similar to the issue weights assumption, this assumption strongly depends on the agent's strategy and domain.

3.4 Influence of the Negotiation Scenario

Three main factors of a scenario influence the quality of an opponent model:

1. *Domain size.* In general, the larger the domain, the less likely a bid is a Pareto-bid. Furthermore, domains with more bids are likely more computationally expensive to model. Therefore, the influence of the time/exploration trade-off is higher.

2. *Bid distribution*. The bid distribution quantifies how bids are distributed. We define bid distribution as the average distance of all bids to the nearest Pareto-bid. The bid distribution directly influences the performance gain attainable by a model.
3. *Opposition*. We define opposition as the distance from the Kalai-point to complete satisfaction $(1, 1)$. The opposition of a domain influences the number of possible agreements, and opponent models may be help in locating them more easily.

4 Measuring the Performance of Opponent Models

As we noted in the previous section, the effectiveness of an agent's opponent model is heavily influenced by the negotiation setting. This work proposes a careful measurement method of opponent modeling performance, and can be interpreted as a first step towards creating a generic performance benchmark for the type of opponent models that we study here. The following sections discuss the four components of the method.

4.1 Negotiation Strategies of the Agents

For the negotiation strategies of the agents in which the opponent models are embedded, we elected a variant of the standard time-dependent tactic [7]. This strategy is chosen for its simple behavior, which elicits regular behavior from its opponents; furthermore, adding a model may significantly increase its performance. Given a target utility, the adapted agent generates a set of similarly preferred bids and then selects a bid using the opponent model. We focus on selecting a bid from a set of similarly preferred bids, as this usage is commonly applied, for example in [20] and [14]. We embedded the models in four time-dependent agents ($e = 0.1; 0.2; 1.0; 2.0$). We opted for multiple agents as we believed that the concession speed can influence the performance gain.

The remaining issue in using an opponent model is which bid to select for the opponent given a set of similarly preferred bids. Given the approaches in Section 3.2, we opted to have the models select the best bid for the opponent, as this approach is most differentiating: it leads to better performance of the more accurate opponent models.

4.2 Negotiation Strategies of the Opponents

This section discusses the opponents selected using the guidelines outlined in Section 3.3. The set of opponent strategies consists of three cooperative agents, which should be easy to model as their concession speed is high, and five competitive agents. The set of conceding agents consists of two *time-dependent agents* with high concession speeds $e \in \{1, 2\}$, and the *offer decreasing* agent, which offers the set of all possible bids in decreasing order of utility. The set of competitive agents contains two *time-dependent agents* with low concession speeds $e \in \{0.0, 0.2\}$, and the ANAC agents *Gahboninho*, *HardHeaded*, and *IAMcrazyHaggler*.

Given the five opponent modeling assumptions introduced in Section 3.3, the first assumption about the opponent's decision function fails in general, as an opponent in practice never completely adheres to the assumed decision function. The second assumption holds for all agents except *IAMcrazyHaggler*, whose first bid is randomly picked. The other three assumptions are typical for the frequency models. It is not possible to adhere to or violate these assumptions completely, as they depend both on the negotiation scenario structure and opponents.

4.3   Negotiation Scenarios

As we explored in Section 3.4, the *domain size*, *bid distribution*, and *opposition* of a negotiation scenario are all expected to influence an opponent model's performance, and therefore we aimed for a large spread of the characteristics of the scenarios, as visualized in Table 1. In total seven negotiation scenarios were selected.

Table 1. Characteristics of the negotiation scenarios

Scenario name	Size		Bid distrib.		Opposition	
ADG [1]	15625	(*med.*)	0.136	(*low*)	0.095	(*low*)
Grocery [1]	1600	(*med.*)	0.492	(*high*)	0.191	(*med.*)
IS BT Acquisition [1]	384	(*low*)	0.121	(*low*)	0.125	(*low*)
Itex–Cypress [12]	180	(*low*)	0.222	(*med.*)	0.431	(*high*)
Laptop [1]	27	(*low*)	0.295	(*med.*)	0.178	(*med.*)
Employment contract [19]	3125	(*med.*)	0.267	(*med.*)	0.325	(*high*)
Travel [4]	188160	(*high*)	0.416	(*high*)	0.230	(*med.*)

4.4   Quality Measures for Opponent Models

The quality of an opponent model can be measured in two ways: a black box approach, in which *performance measures* evaluate the quality of the outcome; and a white box view, which uses *accuracy measures* capable of considering the internal design of a strategy and revealing the accuracy of the estimation of the opponent's preferences.

This work focuses on the performance measures shown in Table 2, as [11] has already compared models using a white box approach, albeit in a more limited setting.

Table 2. Overview of the performance measures

Performance measure	Description
Avg. utility [1,13,10]	Average score of the agents against selected opponents on all negotiation scenarios.
Avg. time of agr. [2]	Average time required to reach an agreement.
Avg. rounds [13,21]	Average rounds a negotiation lasts. In a rounds-based setting, less means more accurate.
Avg. Pareto dist. of agr. [1,9]	Average minimal distance to the Pareto-frontier. Lower is better.
Avg. Kalai dist. of agr. [9]	Average distance to the Kalai-point. Lower means more fair.
Avg. Nash dist. of agr. [9]	Average distance to the Nash-point. Lower means more fair.

5   Experiments

We applied the method described in the previous section to our experimental setup below in order to answer the research questions introduced in Section 3.

5.1   Experimental Setup

To analyze the performance of different opponent models, we employed GENIUS [15], which is an environment that facilitates the design and evaluation of automated negotiators' strategies and their components. The experiments are subdivided into two categories: we use a standard *time-based protocol*, as well as a *round-based protocol*. In total, we ran 17920 matches, which on a single computer takes nearly two months.

Our main interest goes out to the real-time setting, as this protocol features the time/exploration trade-off. We applied our benchmark to the set of models using the time-based protocol. Each match features a real-time deadline set at three minutes.

In the round-based protocol the same approach is applied, but in this case, time does not pass within a round, giving the agent infinite time to update its model. This provides valuable insights into the best *theoretical* result an opponent model can achieve.

5.2   Opponent Models

We compare the performance of the opponent models used in ANAC [1,4], which is a yearly international competition in which negotiating agents compete on multiple domains. Each year, the competition leads to the introduction of new negotiation strategies with novel opponent models. While the domain (i.e., the set of outcomes) is common knowledge to all agents, the utility function of each player is private information and hence has to be learned. The utility functions of the agents are *linearly additive*; that is, the overall utility consists of a weighted sum of the utility for each individual issue. The setting of ANAC is consistent with the preliminaries in this paper.

We specifically opted to use agents that participated in ANAC for the following reasons: the agents are designed for one consistent negotiation setting, which makes it possible to compare them fairly; their implementation is publicly available; and finally, we believe that the agents and opponent models represent the current state-of-the-art. We used modeling techniques from ANAC 2010 [4], ANAC 2011 [1], and a selection of opponent models designed for ANAC 2012. We isolated the opponent models from the agents and reimplemented them as separate generic components to be compatible with all other agents (as in [2]). As discussed in Section 3.2, this setup allows us to equip a single negotiation strategy with various opponent models, which makes it straightforward to fairly compare the different modeling techniques.

Table 3 provides a summary of the online opponent models used in our experiments, with references to the papers in which they are described. We did not include the *Bayesian Model* from [10] and the *FSEGA Bayesian Model* [18], even though they fitted our setup, as both models were not designed to handle domains containing more than a 1000 bids. We are aware that many alternative opponent modeling techniques exist [5,10,16,21]; however, for our negotiation setting, this is currently the largest set available of comparable opponent modeling techniques.

Based on our analysis, we found that in our selection two approaches to opponent modeling are prominent: *Bayesian opponent models* and *Frequency models*.

Bayesian opponent models generate hypotheses about the opponent's preferences [10]. The models presuppose that the opponent's strategy adheres to a specific decision function; for example a time-dependent strategy with a linear concession speed. This is then used to update the hypotheses using Bayesian learning.

Table 3. Overview of the online opponent models and their modeling assumptions (M)

Model	Description	M
No Model	No knowledge about the preference profile.	-
Perfect Model	Perfect knowledge about the preference profile.	-
Bayesian Scalable Model [10]	This model learns the issue and value weights separately using Bayesian learning. Each round, the hypotheses about the preference profile are updated based assuming that the opponent conceded a constant amount.	1
IAMhaggler Bay. Model [20]	Efficient implementation of the *Bayesian Scalable Model* in which the opponent is assumed to use a particular time-dependent decision function.	1
HardHeaded Freq. Model [14]	This model learns the issue weights based on how often the value of an issue changes between turns. The value weights are determined based on the frequency in which they have been offered.	3 4
Smith Freq. Model [8]	Similar to the *HardHeaded Frequency Model*, but less efficient. The issue weights depends on the relative frequency of the most offered values.	3 5
Agent X Freq. Model	This model is a more complex variant of the *HardHeaded Frequency Model* that also takes the opponent's tendency to repeat bids into account.	3 4
N.A.S.H. Freq. Model	In contrast to *HardHeaded Frequency Model*, this model learns the issue weights based on the frequency that the assumed best value is offered.	2 4

Frequency models learn the issue and value weights separately. The issue weights are usually calculated based on the frequency that an issue *changes* between two offers. The value weights are oten calculated based on the frequency of *appearance* in offers.

Both modeling approaches are prone to failure as they rely on a subset of the assumptions introduced in Section 3.3. More specifically, Bayesian models make strong assumptions about the opponent's strategy, whereas frequency models assume knowledge about the value distribution of the issues of a preference profile and place weak restrictions on the opponent's negotiation strategy. Generally, the Bayesian models are far more computationally expensive; however, it is unknown if they are more accurate.

6   Results

Below we analyze the outcomes of the experiment to provide an answer to the research questions in the form of hypotheses **H1–H6**. We first discuss the overall gain in performance when using perfect knowledge versus online opponent modeling. Section 6.2 provides an answer to the final research question on how the negotiation setting influences the performance of an opponent model.

6.1   Overall Performance of Opponent Models

Our experimental results for a selection of the quality measures described in Section 4.4 are shown in Table 4 for both the time-based and round-based protocol. Before we analyze the performance gain of online opponent models, we first answer the question whether perfect knowledge aids in improving the negotiation outcome at all:

H1. *Usage of the perfect model by a negotiation strategy leads to a significant performance gain in comparison to not using an opponent model.*

We expected that perfect knowledge about the opponent's preferences would significantly improve performance of an agent. Our main aim here was not to reconfirm the already widely acknowledged benefits of integrative bargaining, but to analyze whether our experimental setup is a valid instrument for measuring the learning effect in other types of settings. Our expectation is confirmed by the experiment, as the *Perfect Model* yields a significant performance increase on all quality measures (except average rounds) for both protocols. For the real-time protocol, the difference between the best online opponent model (*HardHeaded Frequency Model*) and *No Model* is 0.0135; for the round-based protocol it is 0.0144 (*Smith Frequency Model*). Note that while the gains are small, there are three small domains where opponent modeling does not result in significant gains. If we solely focus on the large *Travel* negotiation scenario, then the gain relative to *No Model* becomes 0.0413 for the *Perfect Model*. Especially note the improvement in distance between the outcome and Pareto-frontier, and the earlier agreements, in Table 4. This leads us to conclude that using an opponent model leads to better performance as it aids in increasing the quality of the outcome.

H2. *Usage of an online opponent model leads to a significant performance gain when time is not an issue. Online opponent modeling does not yield the same benefit in a real-time setting because of the time/exploration trade-off.*

We noted previously that in some cases, ANAC agents that do not model the opponent can outperform agents that do, and such agents have even won the competition. This led us to believe that online modeling does not benefit the agents, either because it misrepresents the preferences, or by taking too much time in a time-sensitive setting.

This is why it came as a surprise that in *both* the time- and round-based protocol, online opponent models performed significantly better on all quality measures. For the time-based protocol the best online opponent models are the frequency models, except for the *Smith Frequency Model* who scores badly in this case. However, for the round-based protocol, the *Smith Frequency Model* is actually best. This is caused by the time/exploration trade-off, because the model is computationally expensive as indicated by the small amount of bids offered in the time-based protocol.

Surprisingly the worst performance on a quality measure is not always made by using *No Model*. For example in the time-based experiment the *Bayesian Scalable Model* has the worst performance. The Bayesian model of *IAMhaggler* however, performs much better, but disappoints in the round-based protocol. We believe this can be attributed to its updating mechanism: only unique bids are used to update the model, which speeds-up updating but can result in poor performance against slowly conceding agents that offer the same bid multiple times.

In conclusion, online opponent model can result in significant gains and surprisingly, frequency models lead to the largest gains, outperforming the Bayesian models. We believe that the winners of ANAC could have performed even better by learning the opponent's preferences with a frequency model. The success of the frequency model can be attributed to its simplicity and hence faster performance, and to the fact that it is more robust by making weaker assumptions about the strategy of the opponent in comparison to the Bayesian modeling approaches.

6.2 Influence of the Negotiation Setting

We will now discuss the influence of each of the three components of the negotiation setting on the quality of an opponent model, following the structure of Section 3.

Table 4. Performance of all models on a set of quality measures for both protocols

Quality Measures	Perfect FM	HH. FM	Agent X FM	Nash FM	IAH. BM	Smith FM	None	Scal. BM
Time-based								
Avg. utility	.7285	.7260	.7257	.7257	.7178	.7156	.7125	**.7077**
Avg. time of agr.	**.4834**	.4865	.4867	.4865	.4958	.4937	.5022	<u>.5055</u>
Avg. rounds	7220	7218	7231	7198	7004	**4745**	<u>7352</u>	4836
Avg. Pareto dist. of agr.	**.0007**	.0017	.0015	.0018	.0069	.0068	.0059	<u>.0071</u>
Avg. Kalai dist. of agr.	**.2408**	.2434	.2447	.2428	.2515	.2474	<u>.2683</u>	.2561
Avg. Nash dist. of agr.	**.2442**	.2471	.2481	.2483	.2541	.2500	<u>.2721</u>	.2594
Rounds-based								
Avg. utility	<u>.7235</u>	.7196	.7191	.7192	.7111	.7199	**.7050**	.7124
Avg. time of agr.	**.4928**	.4975	.4978	.4977	.5058	.4974	<u>.5136</u>	.5038
Avg. rounds	**2508**	2531	2533	2533	<u>2572</u>	2531	2567	2562
Avg. Pareto dist. of agr.	**.0010**	.0029	.0023	.0028	<u>.0073</u>	.0026	.0066	.0063
Avg. Kalai dist. of agr.	**.2332**	.2380	.2395	.2380	.2456	.2369	<u>.2614</u>	.2445
Avg. Nash dist. of agr.	**.2370**	.2403	.2437	.2404	.2516	.2403	<u>.2644</u>	.2472

Influence of the Agent's Strategy. The performance gain of using an opponent model necessarily depends on the strategy in which it is embedded. Table 5 provides an overview of the relative gain in comparison to *No Model* for all opponent models in the time-based experiment. Based on the results, we have tested the following hypothesis:

H3. *The more competitive an agent, the more it benefits from using an opponent model.*

At each turn of a negotiation session, a set of possible agreements can be defined. This is the intersection of two sets: the set of bids that an agent considers for offering, and the set of all bids acceptable to the opponent. The more competitive the agent, the smaller the intersection between the two sets. When an agent concedes, the number of possible agreements increases at the cost of utility. An opponent model can help in finding possible agreements, preventing concession and therefore loss in utility. We therefore expected the gain for competitive agents to be higher, as the set of possible agreements each turn is smaller, and therefore an optimal bid is more easily missed by an agent not employing an opponent model. This is especially decisive in the last few seconds of the negotiation, when many agents concede rapidly to avoid non-agreement.

The hypothesis is confirmed by our experiments. In Table 5 there is a negative correlation between the concession speed and relative gain in performance. If we ignore the results of the three worst performing models, a small – albeit statistically significant – negative correlation of -0.508 is found.

Influence of the Opponent's Strategy. The opponent's behavior also has an important impact on the performance of an opponent model. Based on the results shown in Table 6, we test the three hypotheses below.

H4. *An agent benefits more from an opponent model against competitive agents.*

Intuitively, the more competitive the opponent, the more useful the opponent model as the set of possible agreements is smaller, analogous to hypothesis **H3**. Therefore, we expected the highest gain against the competitive agents *Gahboninho V3*, *HardHeaded*,

Table 5. Utility of each opponent model relative to using *No Model* for each agent

Agents	e = 0.1	e = 0.2	e = 1	e = 2
Perfect Model	0.0180	0.0164	0.0152	0.0144
HardHeaded Freq. Model	0.0156	0.0137	0.0118	0.0128
Agent X Freq. Model	0.0161	0.0137	0.0116	0.0113
N.A.S.H. Freq. Model	0.0166	0.0129	0.0108	0.0121
IAMhaggler Bay. Model	0.0084	0.0055	0.0033	0.0039
Smith Freq. Model	-0.0031	0.0020	0.0071	0.0063
Bayesian Scalable Model	**-0.0050**	**-0.0058**	**-0.0032**	**-0.0053**

and *IAMcrazyHaggler*. However, in Table 6 only the gain for *Gahboninho V3* and *IAMcrazyHaggler* is very high.

For *HardHeaded*, we believe this can be attributed to the agent using an opponent model itself. If the opponent uses a well-performing opponent model, then the performance gain of an opponent model can be expected to be lower, as the opponent is already able to make Pareto-optimal bids. Our experiment appears to the confirm this hypothesis in the case of playing against *HardHeaded*, whose well-performing opponent model seems to diminish the effect of opponent modeling by the other side.

Concluding, given the results of our experiment, we believe that the hypothesis holds, at least for consistently competitive opponents without an opponent model.

H5. *Frequency models are more robust against opponents employing a random tactic than the Bayesian models.*

In order to estimate the opponent's utility of a certain bid, both types of models make certain assumptions about the opponent. The Bayesian opponent models assume that the opponent follows a particular decision function through time (cf. modeling assumption 1 in Section 3.3), while the frequency models assume higher valued bids are offered more often (cf. modeling assumptions 3 and 4). Many opponent strategies do not adhere to these assumptions, which causes the learning models to make wrong predictions when playing against them. For example, opponents such as *IAMcrazyHaggler* who employ a random negotiation strategy, explicitly violate the assumptions of both models. For the Bayesian learning models, this means the opponent preferences will be estimated incorrectly, and more so through time. The frequency models however, are much more robust, not only in the sense that a negotiation tactic has a greater chance to satisfy its assumptions, but more significantly: it is less sensitive to a tactic violating its assumptions. For instance, in the case of *IAMcrazyHaggler*, it will deduce that it equally prefers any bid it has offered so far – which, in this case, is exactly right.

We therefore expected relatively poor performance from the Bayesian models. This hypothesis is confirmed by our experiment: the frequency models have a high performance gain against *IAMcrazyHaggler*, whereas using the Bayesian models is even worse than not using an opponent model at all.

Influence of the Negotiation Scenario. The performance of an opponent model is influenced by the characteristics of the negotiation scenario, such as amount of bids, distribution of the bids, and the opposition of the domain. Table 7 provides an overview of the relative gain of all opponent models in comparison to *No Model* for in the time-based experiment. Based on these results, we formulate the following hypothesis:

Table 6. Utility of each opponent model relative to using *No Model* for each opponent

Opponents	TDT 0	TDT 0.2	TDT 1.0	TDT 2.0	OD	Gah.	HH.	IcH.
Perfect	.0085	.0015	.0008	.0022	.0060	.0676	.0015	.0399
HH. Freq. Model	.0085	.0013	-.0002	.0019	.0060	.0515	.0000	.0388
Agent X Freq. Model	.0085	.0019	.0002	.0036	.0058	.0561	.0009	.0285
N.A.S.H. Freq. Model	.0085	.0005	-.0005	.0020	.0065	.0507	.0037	.0336
IAH. Bay. Model	**.0000**	.0003	-.0021	-.0001	-.0046	.0511	.0039	**-.0066**
Smith Frequency	-.0038	-.0023	-.0019	.0007	-.0113	**.0357**	**-.0224**	.0297
Bay. Scalable Model	**.0000**	**-.0033**	**-.0055**	**-.0058**	**-.0535**	.0458	-.0128	-.0036

H6. *The higher the amount of bids, bid distribution, or opposition of a scenario, the more an agent benefits from using an opponent model.*

We anticipated the bid distribution to be the major factor determining the performance gain of an opponent model. If the bid distribution is high, then the Pareto-frontier is more sparse. This means a higher gain can be expected of utilizing an opponent model to locate bids close to the Pareto-frontier. This hypothesis is confirmed by our experiments, as we found a strong Pearson correlation of 0.778 between the bid distribution and the performance gain of the best four models, and 0.701 if we solely focus on the perfect opponent model. Therefore we confirm this sub-hypothesis.

Another factor is the size of the negotiation domain. If a domain contains more bids, then there are relatively less bids that are Pareto-optimal, so an opponent model can aid more in identifying them. On the other hand, opponent models are more computationally expensive on the larger domains. Despite this effect, we found a strong Pearson correlation between the amount of bids and the performance gain: 0.631 for the best four models, and 0.596 when using the perfect model.

The final factor is the opposition of the scenario. Intuitively, if the opposition is higher, then there are less possible agreements. Opponent models can aid in identifying these rare acceptable bids, thereby preventing break-offs and unnecessary concessions. Nevertheless, if the opposition is high, then the bids are also relatively closer to the Pareto-optimal frontier, which renders it more difficult for an opponent model to make a significant impact on the negotiation outcome. Despite this effect, we expected that higher opposition would lead to higher performance gain. However, in our experiments we noted only a small positive Pearson correlation of 0.256 for the best four models and 0.262 for the perfect model. Based on these results we are unable to draw a conclusion, which leads us to believe the two mentioned effects cancel each other out, making the other two characteristics of the scenario decisive in the effectiveness of a model.

Table 7. Gain of each model relative to using *No Model* for each scenario parameter

	Model	Low	Medium	High
Size	*Perfect*	0.001	0.022	0.041
	Best 4	0.002	0.018	0.039
Bid Distribution	*Perfect*	0.001	0.013	0.035
	Best 4	-0.001	0.010	0.034
Opposition	*Perfect*	0.001	0.023	0.020
	Best 4	-0.001	0.022	0.016

7   Conclusion and Future Work

This paper evaluates and compares the performance of a selection of state-of-the-art online opponent models. The main goal of this work is to evaluate if, and under what circumstances, opponent modeling is beneficial.

Measuring the performance of an opponent model is not trivial, as the details of the negotiation setting affects the effectiveness of the model. Furthermore, while we know an opponent model improves the negotiation outcome in general, the role of time should be taken into account when considering *online* opponent modeling in a real-time negotiation because of the time/exploration trade-off: a computationally expensive model may produce predictions of better quality, but in a real-time setting it may lead to less bids being explored, which may harm the outcome of the negotiation.

Based on an analysis of the contributing factors to the quality of an opponent model, we formulated a measurement method to quantify the performance of online opponent models and applied it to a large set of state-of-the-art opponent models. We analyzed two main types of opponent models: frequency models and Bayesian models. We noted that the time/exploration trade-off is indeed an important factor to consider in opponent model design of both types. However, we found that the best performing models did not suffer from the trade-off, and that most – but not all – online opponent models result in a significant improvement in performance compared with not using a model; not only because the deals are made faster, but also because the outcomes are on average significantly closer to the Pareto-frontier. A main conclusion of our work is that we noted that frequency models consistently outperform Bayesian models. This is not only because they are faster, because the effect remains in a round-based setting. This suggests that frequency models combine the best of both worlds. Surprisingly, despite their performance, frequency models have not received much attention in literature.

Our other main conclusion concerns the effects of the negotiation setting on an opponent model's effectiveness. We found that the more competitive an agent, or its opponent, the more benefit an opponent model provides. In addition, we found that the higher the size or the bid distribution of a scenario, the higher the gain of using a model.

For future work, it would be interesting to examine other uses of opponent modeling, such as opponent prediction. Another direction of future work is to investigate the interaction between opponent model performance and its accuracy through time. We also plan to test a larger set of models derived from literature and ANAC 2012.

Acknowledgments. This research is supported by the Dutch Technology Foundation STW, applied science division of NWO and Technology Program of the Ministry of Economic Affairs. It is part of the Pocket Negotiator project (VICI-project 08075).

References

1. Baarslag, T., Fujita, K., Gerding, E.H., Hindriks, K., Ito, T., Jennings, N.R., Jonker, C., Kraus, S., Lin, R., Robu, V., Williams, C.R.: Evaluating practical negotiating agents: Results and analysis of the 2011 international competition. Artificial Intelligence Journal (accepted)
2. Baarslag, T., Hindriks, K., Hendrikx, M., Dirkzwager, A., Jonker, C.: Decoupling negotiating agents to explore the space of negotiation strategies. In: Proceedings of the 5th International Workshop on Agent-based Complex Automated Negotiations, ACAN 2012 (2012)

3. Baarslag, T., Hindriks, K., Jonker, C.: A Tit for Tat Negotiation Strategy for Real-Time Bilateral Negotiations. In: Ito, T., Zhang, M., Robu, V., Matsuo, T. (eds.) Complex Automated Negotiations: Theories, Models, and Software Competitions. SCI, vol. 435, pp. 231–236. Springer, Heidelberg (2012)
4. Baarslag, T., Hindriks, K., Jonker, C., Kraus, S., Lin, R.: The First Automated Negotiating Agents Competition (ANAC 2010). In: Ito, T., Zhang, M., Robu, V., Fatima, S., Matsuo, T. (eds.) New Trends in Agent-Based Complex Automated Negotiations. SCI, vol. 383, pp. 113–135. Springer, Heidelberg (2012)
5. Buffett, S., Spencer, B.: A bayesian classifier for learning opponents' preferences in multi-object automated negotiation. ECRA 6, 274–284 (2007)
6. Coehoorn, R., Jennings, N.: Learning an opponent's preferences to make effective multi-issue negotiation trade-offs. In: Proceedings of the ICEC 2004, pp. 59–68. ACM (2004)
7. Faratin, P., Sierra, C., Jennings, N.: Negotiation decision functions for autonomous agents. Robotics and Autonomous Systems 24(3-4), 159–182 (1998)
8. van Galen Last, N.: Agent Smith: Opponent Model Estimation in Bilateral Multi-issue Negotiation. In: Ito, T., Zhang, M., Robu, V., Fatima, S., Matsuo, T. (eds.) New Trends in Agent-Based Complex Automated Negotiations. SCI, vol. 383, pp. 167–174. Springer, Heidelberg (2012)
9. Hindriks, K., Jonker, C., Tykhonov, D.: Negotiation dynamics: Analysis, concession tactics, and outcomes. In: IEEE/WIC/ACM International Conference on Intelligent Agent Technology, pp. 427–433. IEEE Computer Society (2007)
10. Hindriks, K., Tykhonov, D.: Opponent modelling in automated multi-issue negotiation using bayesian learning. In: Proceedings of the 7th AAMAS 2008 (2008)
11. Hindriks, K.V., Tykhonov, D.: Towards a Quality Assessment Method for Learning Preference Profiles in Negotiation. In: Ketter, W., La Poutré, H., Sadeh, N., Shehory, O., Walsh, W. (eds.) AMEC 2008. LNBIP, vol. 44, pp. 46–59. Springer, Heidelberg (2010)
12. Kersten, G.E., Zhang, G.: Mining inspire data for the determinants of successful internet negotiations. Central European Journal of Operational Research (2003)
13. Klos, T., Somefun, K., La Poutré, H.: Automated interactive sales processes. IEEE Intelligent Systems 26, 54–61 (2010)
14. van Krimpen, T., Looije, D., Hajizadeh, S.: HardHeaded. In: Ito, T., Zhang, M., Robu, V., Matsuo, T. (eds.) Complex Automated Negotiations: Theories, Models, and Software Competitions. SCI, vol. 435, pp. 225–230. Springer, Heidelberg (2012)
15. Lin, R., Kraus, S., Baarslag, T., Tykhonov, D., Hindriks, K., Jonker, C.M.: Genius: An integrated environment for supporting the design of generic automated negotiators. In: Computational Intelligence (2012)
16. Lin, R., Kraus, S., Wilkenfeld, J., Barry, J.: Negotiating with bounded rational agents in environments with incomplete information using an automated agent. Ai 172, 823–851 (2008)
17. Rubinstein, A.: Perfect equilibrium in a bargaining model. Econometrica: Journal of the Econometric Society 50, 97–109 (1982)
18. Dan Şerban, L., Silaghi, G.C., Litan, C.M.: AgentFSEGA: Time Constrained Reasoning Model for Bilateral Multi-issue Negotiations. In: Ito, T., Zhang, M., Robu, V., Fatima, S., Matsuo, T. (eds.) New Trends in Agent-Based Complex Automated Negotiations. SCI, vol. 383, pp. 159–165. Springer, Heidelberg (2012)
19. Thompson, L.: The Mind and heart of the negotiator, 3rd edn. Prentice Hall Press, Upper Saddle River (2000)
20. Williams, C.R., Robu, V., Gerding, E.H., Jennings, N.R.: IAMhaggler: A Negotiation Agent for Complex Environments. In: Ito, T., Zhang, M., Robu, V., Fatima, S., Matsuo, T. (eds.) New Trends in Agent-Based Complex Automated Negotiations. SCI, vol. 383, pp. 151–158. Springer, Heidelberg (2012)
21. Zeng, D., Sycara, K.: Bayesian learning in negotiation. International Journal of Human-Computers Studies 48(1), 125–141 (1998)

Optimistic Agents Are Asymptotically Optimal

Peter Sunehag and Marcus Hutter

Research School of Computer Science, Australian National University
Canberra, Australia
{peter.sunehag,marcus.hutter}@anu.edu.au

Abstract. We use optimism to introduce generic asymptotically optimal reinforcement learning agents. They achieve, with an arbitrary finite or compact class of environments, asymptotically optimal behavior. Furthermore, in the finite deterministic case we provide finite error bounds.

Keywords: Reinforcement Learning, Optimism, Optimality.

1 Introduction

This article studies a fundamental question in artificial intelligence; given a set of environments, how do we define an agent that eventually acts optimally regardless of which of the environments it is in. This question relates to the even more fundamental question of what intelligence is. [Hut05] defines an intelligent agent as one that can act well in a large range of environments. He studies arbitrary classes of environments with particular attention to universal classes of environments like all computable (deterministic) environments and all lower semi-computable (stochastic) environments. He defines the AIXI agent as a Bayesian reinforcement learning agent with a universal hypothesis class and a Solomonoff prior. This agent has some interesting optimality properties. Besides maximizing expected utility with respect to the a priori distribution by design, it is also Pareto optimal and self-optimizing when this is possible for the considered class. It was, however, shown in [Ors10] that it is not guaranteed to be asymptotically optimal for all computable (deterministic) environments. [LH11a] shows that this is not surprising since, at least for geometric discounting, no agent can be. [LH11a] also shows that in a weaker (in average) sense, optimality can be achieved for the class of all computable environments using an algorithm that includes long exploration phases. Furthermore, it is simple to realize that Bayesian agents do not always achieve optimality for a finite class of deterministic environments even if all prior weights are strictly positive.

We use the principle of optimism to define an agent that for any finite class of deterministic environments, eventually acts optimally. We extend our results to the case of finite and compact classes of stochastic environments. In the deterministic case we also prove finite error bounds. Optimism has previously been used to design exploration strategies for both discounted and undiscounted MDPs [KS98, SL05, AO06, LH12], though here we define optimistic algorithms for any finite class of environments.

M. Thielscher and D. Zhang (Eds.): AI 2012, LNCS 7691, pp. 15–26, 2012.

Related Work. Besides AIXI [Hut05] that was discussed above, [LH11a] introduces an agent which achieves asymptotic optimality in an average sense for the class of all deterministic computable environments. There is, however, no time step after which it is optimal at every time step. This is due to an infinite number of long exploration phases. We introduce an agent, that for finite classes of environments, does eventually achieve optimality for every time step. For the stochastic case, the agent achieves with any given probability, optimality within ϵ for any $\epsilon > 0$. Our very simple agent is relying elegantly on the principle of optimism, used previously in the restrictive MDP case with discounting [KS98, SL05, LH12] and without [AO06], instead of an indefinite number of explicitly enforced bursts of exploration. [RH08] also introduces an agent that relies on bursts of exploration with the aim of achieving asymptotic optimality. The asymptotic optimality guarantees are restricted to a setting where all environments satisfy a certain restrictive value-preservation property. [EDKM05] studied learning general Partially Observable Markov Decision Processes (POMDPs). Though POMDPs constitute a very general reinforcement learning setting, we are interested in agents that can be given any (deterministic or stochastic) class of environments and successfully utilize the knowledge that the true environment lies in this class.

Background. We will consider an agent [RN10, Hut05] that interacts with an environment through performing actions a_t from a finite set $\mathcal{A}$ and receives observations o_t from a finite set $\mathcal{O}$ and rewards r_t from a finite set $\mathcal{R} \subset [0,1]$. Let $\mathcal{H} = (\mathcal{A} \times \mathcal{O} \times R)^*$ be the set of histories and $R : \mathcal{H} \to \mathbb{R}$ the return

$$R(a_1 o_1 r_1 a_2 o_2 r_2 ... a_n o_n r_n) = \sum_{j=1}^{n} r_j \gamma^j$$

with the obvious extension to infinite sequences. A function from $\mathcal{H} \times \mathcal{A}$ to $\mathcal{O} \times \mathcal{R}$ is called a deterministic environment (studied in Section 2. A function $\pi : \mathcal{H} \to \mathcal{A}$ is called a policy or an agent. We define the value function V by $V_\nu^\pi(h_{t-1}) := R(h_{t:\infty}) = \sum_{i=t}^{\infty} \gamma^{i-t} r_i$ where the sequence r_i are the rewards achieved by following π from time step t onwards in environment ν after having seen h_{t-1}.

Instead of viewing the environment as a function from $\mathcal{H} \times \mathcal{A}$ to $\mathcal{O} \times \mathcal{R}$ we can equivalently write it as a function $\nu : \mathcal{H} \times \mathcal{A} \times \mathcal{O} \times \mathcal{R} \to \{0,1\}$ where we write $\nu(o,r|h,a)$ for the function value of (h,a,o,r). It equals zero if in the first formulation (h,a) is not sent to (o,r) and 1 if it is. In the case of stochastic environments, which we will study in Section 3, we instead have a function $\nu : \mathcal{H} \times \mathcal{A} \times \mathcal{O} \times \mathcal{R} \to [0,1]$ such that $\sum_{o,r} \nu(o,r|h,a) = 1 \; \forall h, a$. Furthermore, we define $\nu(h_t|\pi) := \nu(or_{1:t}|\pi) := \Pi_{i=1}^{t} \nu(o_i r_i|a_i, h_{i-1})$ where $a_i = \pi(h_{i-1})$. $\nu(\cdot|\pi)$ is a probability measure over strings or sequences as will be discussed in the next section and we can define $\nu(\cdot|\pi, h_{t-1})$ by conditioning $\nu(\cdot|\pi)$ on h_{t-1}. We define $V_\nu^\pi(h_{t-1}) := \mathbb{E}_{\nu(\cdot|\pi,h_{t-1})} R(h_{t:\infty})$ as the ν-expected return of policy π.

A special case of an environment is a Markov Decision Process (MDP) [SB98]. This is the classical setting for reinforcement learning. In this case the environment does not depend on the full history but only on the latest observation and action and is, therefore, a function from $\mathcal{O} \times \mathcal{A} \times \mathcal{O} \times \mathcal{R}$ to $[0, 1]$. In this situation one often refers to the observations as states since the latest observation tells us everything we need to know. In this situation, there is an optimal policy that can be represented as a function from the state set $\mathcal{S}$ ($:=\mathcal{O}$) to $\mathcal{A}$. We only need to base our decision on the latest observation. Several algorithms [KS98, SL05, LH12] have been devised for solving discounted ($\gamma < 1$) MDPs for which one can prove PAC (Probably Approximately Correct) bounds. They are finite time bounds that hold with high probability and depend only polynomially on the number of states, actions and the discount factor. These methods are relying on optimism as the method for making the agent sufficiently explorative. Optimism roughly means that one has high expectations for what one does not yet know. Optimism was also used to prove regret bounds for undiscounted ($\gamma = 1$) MDPs in [AO06] which was extended to feature MDPs in [MMR11]. Note that these methods are restricted to MDPs and that we do not make any (Markov, ergodicity, stationarity, etc.) assumptions on the environments, only on the size of the class.

Outline. In this article we will define optimistic agents in a far more general setting than MDPs and prove asymptotic optimality results. The question of their mere existence is already non-trivial, hence asymptotic results deserve attention. In Section 2 we consider finite classes of deterministic environments and introduce a simple optimistic agent that is guaranteed to eventually act optimally. We also provide finite error bounds. In Section 3 we generalize to finite classes of stochastic environments and in Section 4 to compact classes.

2   Finite Classes of Deterministic Environments

Given a finite class of deterministic environments $\mathcal{M} = \{\nu_1, ..., \nu_m\}$, we define an algorithm that for any unknown environment from $\mathcal{M}$ eventually achieves optimal behavior in the sense that there exists T such that maximum reward is achieved from time T onwards. The algorithm chooses an optimistic hypothesis from $\mathcal{M}$ in the sense that it picks the environment in which one can achieve the highest reward (in case of a tie, choose the environment which comes first in an enumeration of $\mathcal{M}$) and then the policy that is optimal for this environment is followed. If this hypothesis is contradicted by the feedback from the environment, a new optimistic hypothesis is picked from the environments that are still consistent with h. This technique has the important consequence that if the hypothesis is not contradicted we are still acting optimally when optimizing for this incorrect hypothesis.

Let $h_t^{\pi, \nu}$ be the history up to time t generated by policy π in environment ν. In particular let $h^{\circ} := h^{\pi^{\circ}, \mu}$ be the history generated by Algorithm 1 (policy π°) interacting with the actual "true" environment μ. At the end of cycle t we know $h_t^{\circ} = h_t$. An environment ν is called consistent with h_t if $h_t^{\pi^{\circ}, \nu} = h_t$. Let $\mathcal{M}_t$ be the environments consistent with h_t. The algorithm only needs to check whether $o_t^{\pi^{\circ}, \nu} = o_t$ and $r_t^{\pi^{\circ}, \nu} = r_t$ for each $\nu \in \mathcal{M}_{t-1}$, since previous cycles ensure $h_{t-1}^{\pi^{\circ}, \nu} = h_{t-1}$ and trivially $a_t^{\pi^{\circ}, \nu} = a_t$. The maximization in Algorithm 1 that

Require: Finite class of deterministic environments $\mathcal{M}_0 \equiv \mathcal{M}$
1: $t = 1$
2: **repeat**
3:    $(\pi^*, \nu^*) \in \arg\max_{\pi \in \Pi, \nu \in \mathcal{M}_{t-1}} V_\nu^\pi(h_{t-1})$
4:    **repeat**
5:       $a_t = \pi^*(h_{t-1})$
6:       Perceive $o_t r_t$ from environment μ
7:       $h_t \leftarrow h_{t-1} a_t o_t r_t$
8:       Remove all inconsistent environments from $\mathcal{M}_t$
          $(\mathcal{M}_t := \{\nu \in \mathcal{M}_{t-1} : h_t^{\pi^\circ, \nu} = h_t\})$
9:       $t \leftarrow t + 1$
10:    **until** $\nu^* \notin \mathcal{M}_{t-1}$
11: **until** $\mathcal{M}$ is empty

Algorithm 1. Optimistic Agent (π°) for Deterministic Environments

defines optimism at time t is performed over all $\nu \in \mathcal{M}_t$, the set of consistent hypotheses at time t, and $\pi \in \Pi = \Pi^{all}$ is the class of *all* deterministic policies.

Theorem 1 (Optimality, Finite Deterministic Class). *If we use Algorithm 1 (π°) in an environment $\mu \in \mathcal{M}$, then there is $T < \infty$ such that*

$$V_\mu^{\pi^\circ}(h_t) = \max_\pi V_\mu^\pi(h_t) \ \forall t \geq T.$$

A key to proving Theorem 1 is time-consistency [LH11b] of geometric discounting. The following lemma tells us that if we act optimally with respect to a chosen optimistic hypothesis, it remains optimistic until contradicted.

Lemma 1 (Time-consistency). *Suppose $(\pi^*, \nu^*) \in \arg\max_{\pi \in \Pi, \nu \in \mathcal{M}_t} V_\nu^\pi(h_t)$, that we act according to π^* from time t to time $\tilde{t} - 1$ and that ν^* is still consistent at time $\tilde{t} > t$, then $(\pi^*, \nu^*) \in \arg\max_{\pi \in \Pi, \nu \in \mathcal{M}_{\tilde{t}}} V_\nu^\pi(h_{\tilde{t}})$.*

Proof. Suppose that $V_{\nu^*}^{\pi^*}(h_{\tilde{t}}) < V_{\tilde{\nu}}^{\tilde{\pi}}(h_{\tilde{t}})$ for some $\tilde{\pi}, \tilde{\nu}$. It holds that $V_{\nu^*}^{\pi^*}(h_t) = C + \gamma^{\tilde{t}-t} V_{\nu^*}^{\pi^*}(h_{\tilde{t}})$ where C is the accumulated reward between t and $\tilde{t} - 1$. Let $\hat{\pi}$ be a policy that equals π^* from t to $\tilde{t} - 1$ and then equals $\tilde{\pi}$. It follows that $V_{\tilde{\nu}}^{\hat{\pi}}(h_t) = C + \gamma^{\tilde{t}-t} V_{\tilde{\nu}}^{\hat{\pi}}(h_{\tilde{t}}) > C + \gamma^{\tilde{t}-t} V_{\nu^*}^{\pi^*}(h_{\tilde{t}}) = V_{\nu^*}^{\pi^*}(h_t)$ which contradicts the assumption $(\pi^*, \nu^*) \in \arg\max_{\pi \in \Pi, \nu \in \mathcal{M}_t} V_\nu^\pi(h_t)$. Therefore, $V_{\nu^*}^{\pi^*}(h_{\tilde{t}}) \geq V_{\tilde{\nu}}^{\tilde{\pi}}(h_{\tilde{t}})$ for all $\tilde{\pi}, \tilde{\nu}$. ∎

Proof. **(Theorem 1)** At time t we know h_t. If some $\nu \in \mathcal{M}_{t-1}$ is inconsistent with h_t, i.e. $h_t^{\pi^\circ, \nu} \neq h_t$, it gets removed, i.e. is not in $\mathcal{M}_{t'}$ for all $t' \geq t$.

Since $\mathcal{M}_0 = \mathcal{M}$ is finite, such inconsistencies can only happen finitely often, i.e. from some T onwards we have $\mathcal{M}_t = \mathcal{M}_\infty$ for all $t \geq T$. Since $h_t^{\pi^\circ, \mu} = h_t \ \forall t$, we know that $\mu \in \mathcal{M}_t \ \forall t$.

Assume $t \geq T$ henceforth. The optimistic hypothesis will not change after this point. If the optimistic hypothesis is the true environment μ, we have obviously chosen the true optimal policy.

In general, the optimistic hypothesis ν^* is such that it will never be contradicted while actions are taken according to π°, hence (π^*, ν^*) do not change anymore. This implies

$$V_\mu^{\pi^\circ}(h_t) \;=\; V_\mu^{\pi^*}(h_t) \;=\; V_{\nu^*}^{\pi^*}(h_t) \;=\; \max_{\nu \in \mathcal{M}_t} \max_{\pi \in \Pi} V_\nu^\pi(h_t) \;\geq\; \max_{\pi \in \Pi} V_\mu^\pi(h_t)$$

for all $t \geq T$. The first equality follows from π° equals π^* from $t \geq T$ onwards. The second equality follows from consistency of ν^* with $h_{1:\infty}^\circ$. The third equality follows from optimism, the constancy of π^*, ν^*, and $\mathcal{M}_t$ for $t \geq T$, and time-consistency of geometric discounting (Lemma 1). The last inequality follows from $\mu \in \mathcal{M}_t$. The reverse inequality $V_\mu^{\pi^*}(h_t) \leq \max_\pi V_\mu^\pi(h_t)$ follows from $\pi^* \in \Pi$. Therefore π° is acting optimally at all times $t \geq T$.   ∎

Besides the eventual optimality guarantee above, we also provide a bound on the number of time steps for which the value of following Algorithm 1 is more than a certain $\varepsilon > 0$ less than optimal. The reason this bound is true is that we only have such suboptimality for a certain number of time steps before a point where the current hypothesis becomes inconsistent and the number of such inconsistency points are bounded by the number of environments.

Theorem 2 (Finite error bound). *Following π° (Algorithm 1),*

$$V_\mu^{\pi^\circ}(h_t) \geq \max_{\pi \in \Pi} V_\mu^\pi(h_t) - \varepsilon, \; 0 < \varepsilon < 1/(1-\gamma)$$

for all but at most $|\mathcal{M}| \frac{\log \varepsilon(1-\gamma)}{\gamma - 1}$ time steps t.

Proof. Consider the ℓ-truncated value

$$V_{\nu,\ell}^\pi(h_t) \;:=\; \sum_{i=t+1}^{t+\ell} \gamma^{i-t-1} r_i$$

where the sequence r_i are the rewards achieved by following π from time $t+1$ to $t+\ell$ in ν after seeing h_t. By letting $\ell = \frac{\log \varepsilon(1-\gamma)}{\log \gamma}$ (which is positive due to negativity of both numerator and denominator) we achieve $|V_{\nu,\ell}^\pi(h_t) - V_\nu^\pi(h_t)| \leq \frac{\gamma^\ell}{1-\gamma} = \epsilon$. Let (π_t^*, ν_t^*) be the policy-environment pair selected by Algorithm 2 in cycle t.

Let us first assume $h_{t+1:t+\ell}^{\pi^\circ, \mu} = h_{t+1:t+\ell}^{\pi^\circ, \nu_t^*}$, i.e. ν_t^* is consistent with $h_{t+1:t+\ell}^\circ$, and hence π_t^* and ν_t^* do not change from $t+1, ..., t+\ell$ (inner loop of Algorithm 1). Then

$$\begin{array}{cccccccc}
 & \text{drop terms,} & & \text{same } h_{t+1:t+\ell}, & & \pi^\circ = \pi_t^* \text{ on } h_{t+1:t+\ell}, & & \\
 & \downarrow & & \downarrow & & \downarrow & & \downarrow \\
V_\mu^{\pi^\circ}(h_t) & \geq & V_{\mu,\ell}^{\pi^\circ}(h_t) & = & V_{\nu_t^*,\ell}^{\pi^\circ}(h_t) & = & V_{\nu_t^*,\ell}^{\pi_t^*}(h_t)
\end{array}$$

$$\begin{array}{cccccc}
\geq & V_{\nu_t^*}^{\pi_t^*}(h_t) - \frac{\gamma^\ell}{1-\gamma} & = & \max_{\nu \in \mathcal{M}_t} \max_{\pi \in \Pi} V_\nu^\pi(h_t) - \varepsilon & \geq & \max_{\pi \in \Pi} V_\mu^\pi(h_t) - \varepsilon. \\
\uparrow & & \uparrow & & \uparrow & \\
\text{bound extra terms} & & \text{def. of } (\pi_t^*, \nu_t^*) \text{ and } \varepsilon := \frac{\gamma^\ell}{1-\gamma} & & \mu \in \mathcal{M}_t &
\end{array}$$

Now let $t_1, ..., t_K$ be the times t at which the currently selected ν_t^* gets inconsistent with h_t, i.e. $\{t_1, ..., t_K\} = \{t : \nu_t^* \notin \mathcal{M}_t\}$. Therefore $h_{t+1:t+\ell}^\circ \neq h_{t+1:t+\ell}^{\pi^\circ, \nu_t^*}$ (only) at times $t \in \mathcal{T}_\times := \bigcup_{i=1}^K \{t_i - \ell, ..., t_i - 1\}$, which implies $V_\mu^{\pi^\circ}(h_t) \geq \max_{\pi \in \Pi} V_\mu^\pi(h_t) - \varepsilon$ except possibly for $t \in \mathcal{T}_\times$. Finally

$$|\mathcal{T}_\times| = \ell \cdot K < \ell \cdot |\mathcal{M}| = \frac{\log \varepsilon (1 - \gamma)}{\log \gamma} |\mathcal{M}| \leq |\mathcal{M}| \frac{\log \varepsilon (1 - \gamma)}{\gamma - 1} \qquad \blacksquare$$

We refer to the algorithm above as the conservative agent since it sticks to its model for as long as it can. The corresponding liberal agent reevaluates its optimistic hypothesis at every time step and can switch between different optimistic policies at any time. Algorithm 1 is actually a special case of this as shown by Lemma 1. The liberal agent is really a class of algorithms and this larger class of algorithms consists of exactly the algorithms that are optimistic at every time step without further restrictions. The conservative agent is the subclass of algorithms that only switch hypothesis when the previous is contradicted. The results for the conservative agent can be extended to the liberal one, but we have to omit that here for space reasons.

3   Stochastic Environments

A stochastic hypothesis may never become completely inconsistent in the sense of assigning zero probability to the observed sequence while still assigning very different probabilities than the true environment. Therefore, we exclude based on a threshold for the probability assigned to the generated history. Unlike in the deterministic case, a hypothesis can cease to be the optimistic one without having been excluded. We, therefore, only consider an algorithm that reevaluates its optimistic hypothesis at every time step. Algorithm 2 specifies the procedure and Theorem 3 states that it is asymptotically optimal.

Theorem 3 (Optimality, Finite Stochastic Class). *Define π° by using Algorithm 2 with any threshold $z \in (0, 1)$ and a finite class $\mathcal{M}$ of stochastic environments containing the true environment μ, then with probability $1 - z|\mathcal{M} - 1|$ there exists, for every $\varepsilon > 0$, a number $T < \infty$ such that*

$$V_\mu^{\pi^\circ}(h_t) > \max_\pi V_\mu^\pi(h_t) - \varepsilon \ \forall t \geq T.$$

We borrow some techniques from [Hut09] that introduced a "merging of opinions" result that generalized the classical theorem by [BD62]. The classical result says that it is sufficient that the true measure (over infinite sequences) is absolutely continuous with respect to a chosen a priori distribution to guarantee that they will almost surely merge in the sense of total variation distance. The generalized version is given in Lemma 2. When we combine a policy π with an environment ν by letting the actions be taken by the policy, we have defined a measure, denoted by $\nu(\cdot|\pi)$, on the space of infinite sequences from a finite alphabet. We denote such a sample sequence by ω and the a:th to b:th elements of ω by $\omega_{a:b}$. The σ-algebra is generated by the cylinder sets $\Gamma_{y_{1:t}} := \{\omega | \omega_{1:t} = y_{1:t}\}$

Require: Finite class of stochastic environments $\mathcal{M}_1 \equiv \mathcal{M}$, threshold $z \in (0, 1)$
1: $t = 1$
2: **repeat**
3:     $(\pi^*, \nu^*) = \arg\max_{\pi, \nu \in \mathcal{M}_t} V_\nu^\pi(h_{t-1})$
4:     $a_t = \pi^*(h_{t-1})$
5:     Perceive $o_t r_t$ from environment μ
6:     $h_t \leftarrow h_{t-1} a_t o_t r_t$
7:     $t \leftarrow t + 1$
8:     $\mathcal{M}_t := \{\nu \in \mathcal{M}_{t-1} : \frac{\nu(h_t|a_{1:t})}{\max_{\tilde{\nu} \in \mathcal{M}} \tilde{\nu}(h_t|a_{1:t})} \geq z\}$
9: **until** the end of time

Algorithm 2. Optimistic Agent (π°) with Stochastic Finite Class

and a measure is determined by its values on those sets. To simplify notation in the next lemmas we will write $P(\cdot) = \nu(\cdot|\pi)$, meaning that $P(\omega_{1:t}) = \nu(h_t|a_{1:t})$ where $\omega_j = o_j r_j$ and $a_j = \pi(h_{j-1})$. Furthermore, $\nu(\cdot|h_t, \pi) = P(\cdot|h_t)$.

Definition 1 (Total Variation Distance). *The total variation distance between two measures (on infinite sequences ω of elements from a finite alphabet) P and Q is defined to be*

$$d(P, Q) = \sup_A |P(A) - Q(A)|$$

where A is in the previously specified σ-algebra generated by the cylinder sets.

The results from [Hut09] are based on the fact that $Z_t = \frac{Q(\omega_{1:t})}{P(\omega_{1:t})}$ is a martingale sequence if P is the true measure and therefore converges with P probability 1 [Doo53]. The crucial question is if the limit is strictly positive or not. The following lemma shows that with P probability 1 we are either in the case where the limit is 0 or in the case where $d(P(\cdot|\omega_{1:t}), Q(\cdot|\omega_{1:t})) \to 0$. We say that the environments ν_1 and ν_2 merge under π if $d(\nu_1(\cdot|\pi), \nu_2(\cdot|\pi)) \to 0$.

Lemma 2 (Generalized merging of opinions [Hut09]). *For any measures P and Q it holds that $P(\Omega^\circ \cup \bar{\Omega}) = 1$ where*

$$\Omega^\circ := \{\omega : \frac{Q(\omega_{1:t})}{P(\omega_{1:t})} \to 0\} \quad and \quad \bar{\Omega} := \{\omega : d(P(\cdot|\omega_{1:t}), Q(\cdot|\omega_{1:t})) \to 0\}$$

Lemma 3 (Value convergence for merging environments). *Given a policy π and environments μ and ν it follows that*

$$|V_\mu^\pi(h_t) - V_\nu^\pi(h_t)| \leq \frac{1}{1-\gamma} d(\mu(\cdot|h_t, \pi), \nu(\cdot|h_t, \pi)).$$

Proof. The lemma follows from the general inequality

$$\left|\mathbb{E}_P(f) - \mathbb{E}_Q(f)\right| \leq \sup|f| \cdot \sup_A |P(A) - Q(A)|$$

by inserting $f := R(\omega_{t:\infty})$ and $P = \mu(\cdot|h_t, \pi)$ and $Q = \nu(\cdot|h_t, \pi)$, and using $0 \leq f \leq 1/(1-\gamma)$. ∎

The following lemma replaces the property for deterministic environments that either they are consistent indefinitely or the probability of the generated history becomes 0.

Lemma 4 (Merging of environments). *Suppose we are given two environments μ (the true one) and ν and a policy π (defined e.g. by Algorithm 2). Let $P(\cdot) = \mu(\cdot|\pi)$ and $Q(\cdot) = \nu(\cdot|\pi)$. Then with P probability 1 we have that*

$$\lim_{t \to \infty} \frac{Q(\omega_{1:t})}{P(\omega_{1:t})} = 0 \quad or \quad \lim_{t \to \infty} |V_\mu^\pi(h_t) - V_\nu^\pi(h_t)| = 0.$$

Proof. This follows from a combination of Lemma 2 and Lemma 3.   ∎

The next lemma tells us what happens after all the environments that will be removed have been removed but we state it as if this was time $t = 0$ for notational simplicity.

Lemma 5 (Optimism is nearly optimal). *Suppose that we have a (finite or infinite) class of (possibly) stochastic environments $\mathcal{M}$ containing the true environment μ. Also suppose that none of these environments are excluded at any time by Algorithm 2 (π°) during an infinite history h that has been generated by running π° in μ. Given $\varepsilon > 0$ there is $\tilde{\varepsilon} > 0$ such that*

$$V_\mu^{\pi^\circ}(\epsilon) \geq \max_\pi V_\mu^\pi(\epsilon) - \varepsilon$$

if

$$|V_{\nu_1}^{\pi^\circ}(h_t) - V_{\nu_2}^{\pi^\circ}(h_t)| < \tilde{\varepsilon} \ \forall t, \forall \nu_1, \nu_2 \in \mathcal{M}.$$

Proof. (**Theorem 3**) Given a policy π, let $P(\cdot) = \mu(\cdot|\pi)$ where $\mu \in \mathcal{M}$ is the true environment and $Q = \nu(\cdot|\pi)$ where $\nu \in \mathcal{M}$. Let the outcome sequence (the sequence $(o_1 r_1), (o_2 r_2), ...$) be denoted by ω. It follows from Doob's Martingale inequality [Doo53] that for all $z \in (0, 1)$

$$P(\sup_t \frac{Q(\omega_{1:t})}{P(\omega_{1:t})} \geq 1/z) \leq z \ , \quad \text{which implies} \quad P(\inf_t \frac{P(\omega_{1:t})}{Q(\omega_{1:t})} \leq z) \leq z.$$

This proves, using a union bound, that the probability of Algorithm 2 ever excluding the true environment is less than $z|\mathcal{M} - 1|$.

The limits $\frac{\nu(h_t|\pi^\circ)}{\mu(h_t|\pi^\circ)}$ converge almost surely as argued before using the Martingale convergence theorem. Lemma 4 tells us that any given environment (with probability one) is eventually excluded or is permanently included and merge with the true one under π°. The remaining environments does, according to (and in the sense of) Lemma 4, merge with the true environment. Lemma 3 tells us that the difference between value functions (for the same policy) of merging environments converges to zero. Since there are finitely many environments and the ones that remain indefinitely in $\mathcal{M}_t$ merge with the true environment under π°, there is for every $\tilde{\varepsilon} > 0$ a T such that when following π°, it holds for all $t \geq T$ that

$$|V_{\nu_1}^{\pi^\circ}(h_t) - V_{\nu_2}^{\pi^\circ}(h_t)| < \tilde{\varepsilon} \ \forall \nu_1, \nu_2 \in \mathcal{M}_t.$$

The proof is concluded by Lemma 5 in the case where the true environment remains indefinitely included which happens with probability $z|\mathcal{M} - 1|$.   ∎

4   Compact Classes

In this section we discuss infinite but compact classes of stochastic environments. First note that without further assumptions, asymptotic optimality can be impossible to achieve, even for countably infinite deterministic environments [LH11a]. Here we consider classes that are compact with respect to the total variation distance, or more precisely with respect to

$$\tilde{d}(\nu_1, \nu_2) = \max_{h, \pi} d(\nu_1(\cdot|h, \pi), \nu_2(\cdot|h, \pi))$$

where d is total variation distance from Section 3. An example is the class of Markov Decision Processes (or POMDPs) with a certain number of states. Algorithm 2 does need modification to achieve asymptotic optimality in the compact case. An alternative to modifying the algorithm is to be satisfied with reaching optimality within a pre-chosen $\varepsilon > 0$. This can be achieved by first choosing a finite covering of $\mathcal{M}$ with balls of total variation radius less than $\varepsilon(1 - \gamma)$ and use Algorithm 2 with the centers of these balls. To have an algorithm that for any $\varepsilon > 0$ eventually achieves optimality within ε is a more demanding task. This is because we need to be able to say that the true environment will remain indefinitely in the considered class with a given confidence. For this purpose we introduce a confidence radius inspired by MDP solving algorithms like MBIE [SL05] and UCRL [AO06]. We still use the notation $\mathcal{M}_t$ as in Algorithm 2 and we define Algorithm 3 based on replacing it with a larger $\tilde{\mathcal{M}}_t$. If we do not do this the true environment is likely to be excluded.

Definition 2 (Confidence radius). *We denote all environments within r_t^z from $\mathcal{M}_t$ by*

$$\tilde{\mathcal{M}}_t := \{\nu \in \mathcal{M} \mid \exists \tilde{\nu} \in \mathcal{M}_t : \tilde{d}(\tilde{\nu}, \nu) \le r_t^z\}.$$

Given $z > 0$ we say that $r_t^z(h_t)$ is a p-confidence radius sequence if $r_t^z(h_t) \to 0$ almost surely and if the true environment is in $\tilde{M}_t$ for all t with probability p.

Definition 3 (Algorithm 3). *Given a class of environments $\mathcal{M}$ that is compact in the total variation distance we define Algorithm 3 as being Algorithm 2 with $\mathcal{M}_t$ replaced by $\tilde{\mathcal{M}}_t$*

Definition 4 (Radon-Nikodym differentiable class). *Suppose that the class $\mathcal{M}$ is such that if $\mu \in \mathcal{M}$ is the true environment, then for any policy π it holds with probability one that for all $\nu \in \mathcal{M}$, $X_{t,\nu} := \frac{\nu(h_t|\pi)}{\mu(h_t|\pi)}$ converges as $t \to \infty$ to some random variables X_ν. We call such a class Radon-Nikodym (RN) differentiable. If the property holds with respect to a specific policy π we say that the class is RN-differentiable with respect to π.*

Remark 1. Every countable class is RN-differentiable and so is the class of MDPs with a certain number of states. The MBIE [SL05] and UCRL [AO06] algorithms are based on the fact that one can define confidence radiuses for MDPs, though their bounds need separate intervals for each state-action pair depending on the number of visits. For an ergodic MDP all state-action pairs will almost surely be seen infinitely often and the max length of those intervals will tend to zero. Therefore, one can define a radius based on this maximum length or, alternatively, one can easily allow Algorithm 3 to run with such rectangular sets instead.

Theorem 4 (Optimality, Compact Stochastic Class). *Suppose we use Algorithm 3 with threshold $z \in (0,1)$, a compact (in total variation) RN-differentiable class (with respect to π° is enough) $\mathcal{M}$ of stochastic environments and a p-confidence radius sequence r_t^z for $\mathcal{M}$. Denote the resulting policy by π°. If the true environment μ is in $\mathcal{M}$, then with probability p there is, for every $\varepsilon > 0$, a tim e $T < \infty$ such that*

$$V_\mu^{\pi^\circ}(h_t) \geq \max_\pi V_\mu^\pi(h_t) - \varepsilon \ \forall t \geq T.$$

Lemma 6 (Uniform exclusion). *Let $Q_\nu(\cdot) = \nu(\cdot|\pi^\circ)$ and $P(\cdot) = \mu(\cdot|\pi^\circ)$ where μ is the true environment and π° the policy defined by Algorithm 3. For any outcome sequence ω, let*

$$\mathcal{M}^0(\omega) := \{\nu \mid \frac{Q_\nu(\omega_{1:t})}{P(\omega_{1:t})} \to 0\}.$$

For any closed subset of $\mathcal{M}^0(\omega)$ and for every $z > 0$, there is $T < \infty$ such that for every ν in this subset there is $t \leq T$ such that $\frac{Q_\nu(\omega_{1:t})}{P(\omega_{1:t})} < z$.

Proof. Since $\mathcal{M}$ is compact and the subset in question is closed it follows that it is also compact. Using the Arzelà-Ascoli Theorem [Rud76] we conclude that there is a subsequence t_k such that $Z_k^\nu := \min\{1, \frac{Q_\nu(\omega_{1:t_k})}{P(\omega_{1:t_k})}\}$ converges uniformly to 0 on $\mathcal{M}^0$ which means that there is t_k such that $Z_k^\nu < z$ for all $\nu \in \mathcal{M}^0$ and we can let $t = T = t_k$. ∎

Proof. **(Theorem 4)** The strategy is to use that all environment that will be excluded and does not lie within a certain distance of some environment that merges with the true one, will be excluded after a certain finite time. Then we can say that the remaining environments' value functions differ at most by a certain amount and we can apply Lemma 5.

We can with probability one say that for each $\nu \in \mathcal{M}$, it will hold that $Z_t = \frac{\nu(h_t|\pi^\circ)}{\mu(h_t|\pi^\circ)}$ converges and each environment will be in $\mathcal{M}^0 = \{\nu \in \mathcal{M} \mid Z_t \to 0\}$ or $\bar{\mathcal{M}} = \{\nu \mid d(\nu(\cdot|h_t, \pi^\circ), \mu(\cdot|h_t, \pi^\circ)) \to 0\}$. $\bar{\mathcal{M}}$ is compact (in the total variation distance topology) since it is a closed subset (again in the topology defined by $\tilde{d}$) of the compact set $\mathcal{M}$.

For any $\tilde{\varepsilon}_1 > 0$ we can do the following: For each $\nu \in \mathcal{M}$, consider a total variation ball of radius 2δ where $\delta = (1-\gamma)\tilde{\varepsilon}_1/4$. Note that $|V_\nu^{\pi^\circ}(h_t) - V_{\nu'}^{\pi^\circ}(h_t)| < \tilde{\varepsilon}_1/2$ for all t whenever $\tilde{d}(\nu, \nu') < 2\delta$. The collection of these balls induces an open cover of the compact set $\mathcal{M}$ and it follows that there is a finite subcover. Consider the balls in this finite cover that intersect with $\bar{\mathcal{M}}$. Let $\mathcal{A}$ be the union of these finitely many open balls. Let $\mathcal{B} = \mathcal{M} \setminus \mathcal{A}$. $\mathcal{B}$ is then a closed subset of $\mathcal{M}^0$. We want to say that there is a finite time after which all environments in $\mathcal{B}$ will have been excluded from $\tilde{\mathcal{M}}_t$. This happens if $\tilde{\mathcal{B}}$, defined as the union of the closed balls of radius r_t^z at every point in $\mathcal{B}$, has been excluded from $\mathcal{M}_t$. If t is large enough for $r_t^z < \delta$, then $\mathcal{B}$ is also a closed subset of $\mathcal{M}_0$. Lemma 6 tells us that all of the environments in $\tilde{\mathcal{B}}$ will have been excluded from $\mathcal{M}_t$ after a finite amount of time T_1 and, therefore, all the environments in $\mathcal{B}$ will have been excluded from $\tilde{\mathcal{M}}_t$. Thus $\tilde{\mathcal{M}}_t \subset \mathcal{A}$ $\forall t \geq T_1$ and in particular the optimistic hypothesis ν^* will be in $\mathcal{A}$ when $t \geq T_1$. Let $\nu^*(= \nu_t^*)$ be the optimistic hypothesis at time $t \geq T_1$ and $\pi^*(= \pi_t^*)$ the optimistic policy.

Each parameter in $\mathcal{A}$ (and in particular ν^*) lies within δ of a ball with center ν which lies within δ of a point $\tilde{\nu} \in \bar{\mathcal{M}}$. Hence $\tilde{d}(\nu^*, \tilde{\nu}) < 2\delta$ and $|V_{\nu^*}^{\pi^\circ}(h_t) - V_{\tilde{\nu}}^{\pi^\circ}(h_t)| < \tilde{\varepsilon}_1/2$.

Due to the uniform merging of environments (under π°) on $\bar{\mathcal{M}}$, there is $T_2 \geq T_1$ such that $|V_{\nu_1}^{\pi^\circ}(h_t) - V_{\nu_2}^{\pi^\circ}(h_t)| < \tilde{\varepsilon}_1/2$ $\forall \nu_1, \nu_2 \in \bar{\mathcal{M}}$ $\forall t \geq T_2$. We conclude that $|V_{\nu_1}^{\pi^\circ}(h_t) - V_{\nu_2}^{\pi^\circ}(h_t)| < \tilde{\varepsilon}_1$ $\forall \nu_1, \nu_2 \in \mathcal{A}$ $\forall t \geq T_2$ and since $\tilde{\mathcal{M}}_t \subset \mathcal{A}$

$$|V_{\nu_1}^{\pi^\circ}(h_t) - V_{\nu_2}^{\pi^\circ}(h_t)| < \tilde{\varepsilon}_1 \ \forall \nu_1, \nu_2 \in \tilde{\mathcal{M}}_t \ \forall t \geq T_2.$$

From Lemma 5 we know that if we picked $\tilde{\varepsilon}_1$ small enough we know that for $t \geq T_2$, $V_{\nu^*}^{\pi^\circ}(h_t) \geq V_\nu^\pi(h_t) - \varepsilon/2$ for all $\pi \in \Pi, \nu \in \tilde{\mathcal{M}}_t$. Furthermore, by picking $\tilde{\varepsilon}_1$ sufficiently small we can, for $t \geq T_2$, ensure that there is $\tilde{\nu} \in \tilde{\mathcal{M}}_t$ such that $|V_{\tilde{\nu}}^{\pi^\circ}(h_t) - V_\mu^{\pi^\circ}(h_t)| < \varepsilon/2$. Given that the true environment remains indefinitely in $\tilde{\mathcal{M}}_t$, which happens with at least probability p, it follows that

$$V_\mu^{\pi^\circ}(h_t) \ \geq \ \max_\pi V_\mu^\pi(h_t) - \varepsilon \ \forall t \geq T_2. \qquad \blacksquare$$

5 Conclusions

We introduced optimistic agents for finite and compact classes of arbitrary environments and proved asymptotic optimality. In the deterministic case we also bound the number of time steps for which the value of following the algorithm is more than a certain amount lower than optimal. Future work includes investigating finite-error bounds for classes of stochastic environments.

Acknowledgement. This work was supported by ARC grant DP120100950. The authors are grateful for feedback from Tor Lattimore and Wen Shao.

References

[AO06]   Auer, P., Ortner, R.: Logarithmic online regret bounds for undiscounted
            reinforcement learning. In: Proceedings of NIPS 2006, pp. 49–56 (2006)
[BD62]   Blackwell, D., Dubins, L.: Merging of Opinions with Increasing Informa-
            tion. The Annals of Mathematical Statistics 33(3), 882–886 (1962)
[Doo53]   Doob, J.: Stochastic processes. Wiley, New York (1953)
[EDKM05]   Even-Dar, E., Kakade, S., Mansour, Y.: Reinforcement learning in pomdps
            without resets. In: Proceedings of IJCAI 2005, pp. 690–695 (2005)
[Hut05]   Hutter, M.: Universal Articial Intelligence: Sequential Decisions based on
            Algorithmic Probability. Springer, Berlin (2005)
[Hut09]   Hutter, M.: Discrete MDL predicts in total variation. In: Advances in
            Neural Information Processing Systems, NIPS 2009, vol. 22, pp. 817–825
            (2009)
[KS98]   Kearns, M.J., Singh, S.: Near-optimal reinforcement learning in poly-
            nomial time. In: Proceedings of the 15nd International Conference on
            Machine Learning (ICML 1998), pp. 260–268 (1998)
[LH11a]   Lattimore, T., Hutter, M.: Asymptotically Optimal Agents. In: Kivinen,
            J., Szepesvári, C., Ukkonen, E., Zeugmann, T. (eds.) ALT 2011. LNCS,
            vol. 6925, pp. 368–382. Springer, Heidelberg (2011)
[LH11b]   Lattimore, T., Hutter, M.: Time Consistent Discounting. In: Kivinen,
            J., Szepesvári, C., Ukkonen, E., Zeugmann, T. (eds.) ALT 2011. LNCS,
            vol. 6925, pp. 383–397. Springer, Heidelberg (2011)
[LH12]   Lattimore, T., Hutter, M.: PAC Bounds for Discounted MDPs. In:
            Bshouty, N.H., Stoltz, G., Vayatis, N., Zeugmann, T. (eds.) ALT 2012.
            LNCS, vol. 7568, pp. 320–334. Springer, Heidelberg (2012)
[MMR11]   Maillard, O.-A., Munos, R., Ryabko, D.: Selecting the state-representation
            in reinforcement learning. In: Advances in Neural Information Processing
            Systems (NIPS 2011), vol. 24, pp. 2627–2635 (2011)
[Ors10]   Orseau, L.: Optimality Issues of Universal Greedy Agents with Static
            Priors. In: Hutter, M., Stephan, F., Vovk, V., Zeugmann, T. (eds.)
            Algorithmic Learning Theory. LNCS, vol. 6331, pp. 345–359. Springer,
            Heidelberg (2010)
[RH08]   Ryabko, D., Hutter, M.: On the possibility of learning in reactive environ-
            ments with arbitrary dependence. Theor. C.S. 405(3), 274–284 (2008)
[RN10]   Russell, S.J., Norvig, P.: Artificial Intelligence: A Modern Approach, 3rd
            edn. Prentice Hall, Englewood Cliffs (2010)
[Rud76]   Rudin, W.: Principles of mathematical analysis. McGraw-Hill (1976)
[SB98]   Strehl, A., Littman, M.: A theoretical analysis of model-based interval
            estimation. In: Proceedings of ICML 2005, pp. 856–863 (2005)
[SL05]   Strehl, A., Littman, M.: A theoretical analysis of model-based interval
            estimation. In: Proceedings of ICML 2005, pp. 856–863 (2005)

An Enhanced Multi-Agent System
with Evolution Mechanism
to Approximate *Physarum* Transport Networks

Yuheng Wu[1], Zili Zhang[1,2,*], Yong Deng[1], Huan Zhou[1], and Tao Qian[1]

[1] Faculty of Computer and Information Science,
Southwest University, Chongqing 400715, China
[2] School of Information Technology, Deakin University, VIC 3217, Australia
{zhangzl,wuyuheng,ydeng,iamzhou,taoqian}@swu.edu.cn

Abstract. The primitive unicellular organism slime mould *Physarum Polycephalum* has attracted much attention from researchers of both biology and computer science fields. Biological experiments have revealed that its foraging mechanism can be used to solve shortest path problems, while its foraging process can construct efficient networks among food sources. Oregonator Model and Cellular Automaton have been proposed to simulate the intelligence and morphology of *Physarum*. To better understand the network formation of *Physarum*, a multi-agent system (MAS) model of particles was introduced by Jones, which can simulate many interesting patterns of *Physarum* transport networks. The MAS model is improved in three aspects: the number of sensors of each individual agent is reduced to two, while the function of each sensor is extended to sample both chemical nutrient and trail. A memory module is added to the architecture of an agent, by which the evolution mechanism can be achieved to maintain the population of the system. With such improvements, the system is more flexible and adaptive, and the networks constructed using the MAS model are more approximate to the ones by *Physarum* in biological experiments. All these are verified by constructing stable networks including Steiner's minimum tree, cycle-like and spanning trees.

Keywords: Multi-agent Systems, Population Evolution, *Physarum Polycephalum*, Transport Networks.

1 Introduction

Physarum Polycephalum, or the true slime mould, has been existing and evolving on the planet for millions of years. The multinucleated single-cell protist prefers darksome and moist environment. It feeds with fungal spores, bacteria and other microbes in nature and oat flakes in laboratories. The plasmodium is the most interesting phase in the life cycle of *Physarum*, in which it shows amazing behaviors such as establishing efficient transport networks with low cost and high

---

* Corresponding author.

M. Thielscher and D. Zhang (Eds.): AI 2012, LNCS 7691, pp. 27–38, 2012.

fault tolerance [1,2]. Since Nakagaki found that *Physarum* can find the shortest path to solve maze problem [3], the intelligent behavior of *Physarum* has been the focus of researchers in various fields over the past decade.

Different methods have been proposed to analyze and simulate the intelligence of *Physarum*. Based on Hagen-Poiseuille equation in chemistry and Kirchhoff Law in physics, Nakagaki and Tero et al proposed a mathematical model to describe the feedback between flux and conductivity of the protoplasm tubes [4,5]. The model explains the adaptive feature of *Physarum* in maze-solving. It was also used to simulate the design of the railway network around Tokyo [6]. Inspired by the model, some modified methods are introduced to engineering technology, such as protocol design in Wireless Sensor Network (WSN) [7] and dynamic reconfiguration in service-oriented internet-ware systems [8]. Adamatzky conducted researches on *Physarum* in the perspective of reaction-diffusion. He treats it as a bio-realized unconventional computing substrate called *Physarum* Machine, and uses it to solve maze, graph problems and design logical gates [9]. Through the Oregonator model of Belousov-Zhabotinsky reaction, Adamatzky analyzes the common characteristics between *Physarum*'s foraging behavior and reaction-diffusion [10]. Gunji and Niizatoa et al, utilize Cellular Automatons to simulate *Physarum* solving maze, Stainer minimum tree and spanning tree problems as well as *Physarum*'s motion and morphology [11], and reproduce adaptive and robust transport networks [12]. Jones presents a low-level particle-based agent model to approximate the network formation of *Physarum* [13]. In that model, a population of agents governed by the same rules resulted in their ordered arrangement, which is the emergence of networks in swarm. Other interesting features such as pattern formation of that model are discussed in [14] and [15].

The focus of this paper is mainly on the improvements of Jones' agent model to construct an enhanced multi-agent system. The improvements are in three aspects: 1) The environmental information sensed by the left and the right sensor is enough for an agent to choose its new direction, therefore we get rid of the forward sensor in Jones' model; 2) A Motion Counter is added to establish the evolution mechanism of the system, it actually works as a memory module; and 3) The trail and the chemo-nutrient, two chemo-attractants, are emitted by agents and food sources, respectively. Our sensor is able to distinguish the two chemo-attractants, and different weights are introduced to represent the corresponding influence of each chemo-attractant.

Based on the improvements, the pattern formation and flexibility of population on periodic and fixed boundary conditions are discussed. The enhanced MAS model is then employed to construct stable networks including Steiner's minimum tree, cycle-like and spanning trees. The results are compared with those constructed by *Physarum*. It shows that enhanced MAS can generate better networks – the networks are much closer to the ones constructed by *Physarum*.

In Section 2, the enhanced MAS model is discussed in details. Section 3 presents the approximation of *Physarum* transport networks using the improved MAS model. And finally, Section 4 is concluding remarks.

2   The Enhanced Multi-Agent System Model

This section discusses the improved MAS model in details. The architecture and behavior of individual agent are presented first, followed by other features of the model.

2.1   The Architecture and Behavior of a Single Agent

Our multi-agent system performs on the 2D scenario, which is divided into 200×200 square grids. A grid is a spatial unit, and the chemo-attractants diffuse on the scenario by means of a simple average filter. The agents motion and the range of diffusion by the chemo-attractants are limited in the discretized plane. A time step in our system is finished when all available agents finish one decision in a random sequence. An agent's body occupies one grid and moves no more than one grid at each time step. The agent's sensor samples the chemo-attractants in the grid where the sensor locates. A sensor is a virtual device, which could coexist with other agent body or sensors in the same grid. The emergence pattern of the system is organized by the arrangement of agents' body.

A single agent is composed of three components, i.e. the left sensor, the right sensor and the main body as shown in Fig. 1. The length of the sensor arm is used to represent the distance between the sensor and the body of an agent. The sensor angle formed by the sensor arm and the forward orientation is fixed to 45°. Each sensor is armed with a Trail Sampling module and a Chemo-nutrient Sampling module, which are used to measure the trail and chemo-nutrient concentration of its grid, respectively. The Synthesis Comparator compares the synthetic weighted values of chemo-attractants sampled by the left sensor and the right sensor, and controls the agent to move toward the direction with larger value.

The Motion Counter is simple but effective to record the motion of an agent and balance the amount of the population. A new born agent initializes its motion counter as zero and chooses the forward direction from the eight usual geographical orientations randomly. At each time step, an agent attempts to move forward to the neighbor grid. If the neighbor grid is occupied by another agent, the agent stays at the current grid and changes its forward direction randomly and

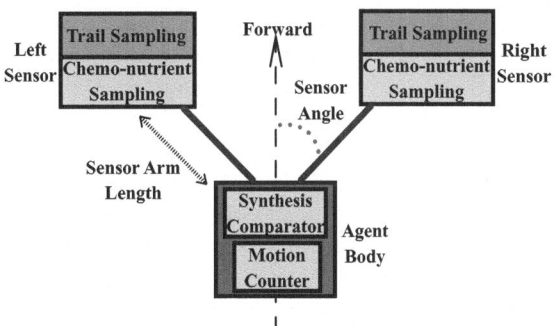

Fig. 1. The architecture and morphology of a single agent

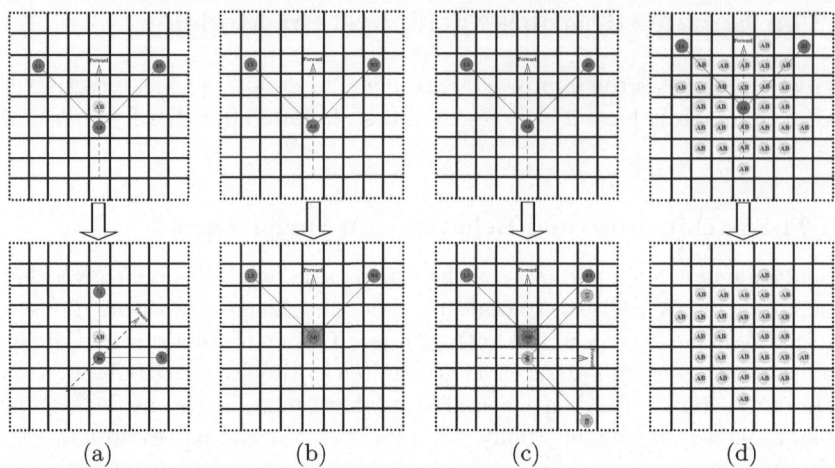

Fig. 2. Four situations that an agent (colored by sky-blue) might confront. (a) Failure to move forward. (b) Success to move forward. (c) Success to move forward and reproduction is triggered. (d) Elimination is triggered by reason of being immovable for a long time.

subtracts one from its Motion Counter. If the neighbor grid is empty, the agent moves to the grid, and deposits certain quantity of trail here, it also adds one to the Motion Counter and rotates to the direction with higher sense value. The number in Motion Counter quantifies the fitness of an agent. The larger the number in Motion Counter is, the more adaptable to the environment the agent is; otherwise, the agent is not fitted for the environment. In consequence, two values (RT and ET, see Table 1) are set to trigger the reproduction and the elimination of an agent. When the number in the Motion Counter is greater than RT, a child agent is born at the last grid where its father agent stayed. If the number is less than ET, the elimination is triggered and leads the forever disappearance of that agent. Fig. 2 gives examples how these situations may take place.

2.2   Basic Parameters of the System

Our enhanced system partially preserves the parameters presented in [13], but the last seven parameters in Table 1 are newly introduced. They are used to distinguish chemo-nutrient and trail, the diffusion and attenuation of chemo-nutrient, and achieve agents' evolution.

An agent calculates the actual value of the sampled chemo-attractant SV by the simple linear weighted method $SV = WT \times TV + WN \times NV$, in which TV and NV denote the trail value and nutrient value in the sensor's grid, respectively. WT and WN are the coefficients to distinguish the different influences of trail and nutrient. To emphasize the function of nutrient, WN is larger than WT. In the scenario, a food source has the shape of square and occupies 3×3 grids. The concentration of chemo-nutrient in these grids occupied by a food source is simulated by the parameter CN. The chemo-nutrient diffuses in the way of

Table 1. Basic parameter setting of the system

Parameter	Value	Explanation
Scenario Size	200×200 grids	The planar area for network formation
Initial Population Density	50%	Initially generating 200×200×50% agents in the scenario randomly
Sensor Arm Length	7 grids	The distance between sensor and its body
depT	5	The quantity of trail deposited by an agent
dampT	0.1	Diffusion damping factor of trail
filterT	3×3	The size of mean filter for trail
WT	0.4	The weight of trail value sensed by an agent's sensor
CN	10	The Chemo-Nutrient concentration of each Node
dampN	0.2	Diffusion damping factor of chemo-nutrient
filterN	5×5	The size of mean filter for chemo-nutrient
WN	1-WT	The weight of chemo-nutrient value sensed by an agent's sensor
RT	15	If the motion counter is greater than RT, the reproduction is triggered
ET	-10	If the motion counter is less than ET, the elimination is triggered

a 5×5 average filter that is a general smoothing operator in image processing. The damping factor $dampN$ controls the attenuation of chemo-nutrient. At each time step, chemo-nutrient in all grids excluding the food source grids updates simultaneously through that filter and decreases to $1 - dampN$ of the previous value. On fixed boundary condition, the system adopts zero as its boundary value. Those grids near the boundary of the scenario require the value to compute its new chemo-attractant through its corresponding filter. As mentioned in Section 2.1, RT and ET are used to maintain the number of agents. And they do not require precise adjustment, but too small values may lead to an unstable mesh-like pattern.

The length of sensor arm is the sampling distance of an agent. On fixed boundary condition, a sensor of an agent might reach out of the scenario. If the left sensor reaches out of the scenario, its agent chooses to turn right 45 degrees; Otherwise, it turns left. However if both sensors are out, its agent turns back. When the length of sensor arm is shorter than the diffusion distance of chemo-attractants, isolated mass may appear in final pattern.

2.3 The Pattern Formation and Population Evolution

After introducing the basic parameters in Table 1, we run the system without the inducing of any food source and observe its self-organized pattern and dynamic population evolution on periodic boundary condition and on fixed boundary condition in this subsection. On either boundary condition, according to the setting of initial population density, 10,000 agents are generated randomly without positional conflict before running the system. Fig. 3 shows the snapshots images of the system running from initial state to stable on periodic boundary condition (Fig. 3(a)) and fixed boundary condition (Fig. 3(b)). A black pixel of Fig. 3 stands for an occupied grid.

In Fig. 3(a), the initial dense irregular little meshes gradually fuse into bigger ones, while the width of each edge is almost the same. Finally, the pattern is stable at the state with five connected straight line segments and without any mesh as shown in bottom middle of Fig. 3(a). By the same operation in [13], the final pattern is tiled to produce a bigger picture in bottom right. The obtained Honeycomb-like mesh here has some differences in angles and edge length from that of [13]. The 120 degrees are not found here, but a closer edge length ratio is observed. The ratio of angles (149.2 degrees vs 105.4 degrees) is 1.42 to 1, and the ratio of the edges length (146 grids vs 102 grids) is 1.43 to 1. The very close ratio of edge length and angle seems to indicate a possible relation between them in this pattern formed by this system.

The pattern formation on fixed boundary condition shown in Fig. 3(b), is significantly different from that on periodic boundary condition. In the stable state (bottom left), all meshes are closed but no strait line survives. The population of agents decreases with the system running. At last, several agents congregate to a little mass in the center of the scenario, which maintains a minimization area of the population. Even though the pattern being stable on the mass, the evolution mechanism of our system keeps both the population and generation dynamically.

The population density, expressing the scale of population, is defined as the percentage of the number of agents to that of grids in the scenario. It is an important feature of population structure. Three different initial population density, 1%, 50% and 90%, are chose to understand the influence of evolution mechanism to the population. Running the system for 20,000 time steps, the curves of the population density at each step on periodic and fixed boundary condition are

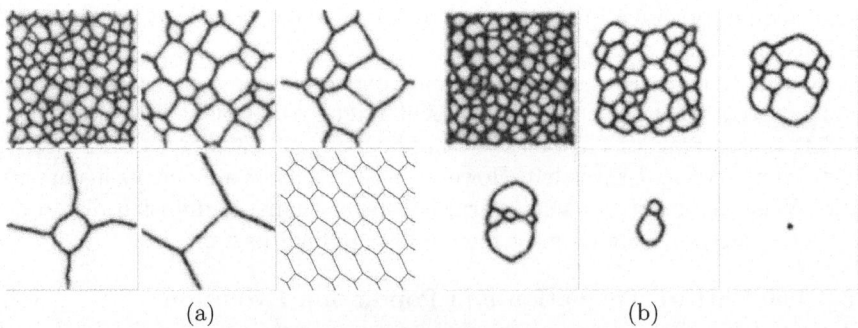

(a)   (b)

Fig. 3. Agent swarm self-organized progress on periodic and fixed boundary conditions

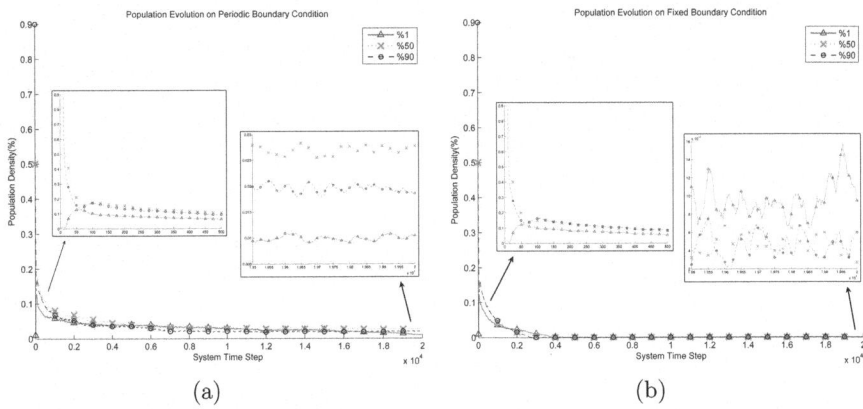

Fig. 4. The population evolutions on periodic and fixed boundary conditions with different initial population density

shown in Fig. 4(a) and 4(b). The three markers, the red delta, the green X and the blue circle in Fig. 4 present the initial population density of 1%, 50% and 90% respectively. The embedded subgraphs in both Fig. 4(a) and 4(b) amplify the detail in the first and last 500 time steps. During the first 500 steps, the three kind curves trend to close the line whose population density is equal to 10%, either suffering a rapid decrease or experiencing a slow increase. A fluctuation of population in a narrow range is observed in all curves in the last 500 steps. The fluctuation of each curve maintains its necessary and different amount of agents to guarantee the persistence of the pattern.

3   The Approximation of *Physarum* Transport Networks

This section describes the situation that all the parameters in Table 1 are used to run the system on fixed boundary condition for simulating the formation of *Physarum* transport networks. In biological experiments, there are two common methods to investigate the evolution of *Physarum* networks. One method is to use the organism of *Physarum* to cover the substrate as well as all food sources, such as in [1] and [2]. The other is inoculating the *Physarum* from one food source, which used in [6] and [10]. The designs of the numerical experiments in this section simulate both methods by consulting some distributions of food sources in those works and other datasets in [13] as well. The videos of all the experiments in this section are available online (http://www.tudou.com/home/_79693894).

3.1   Networks Formation from All Nodes Covered

During the approximation of *Physarum* networks, the scenario could be seen as the substrate cultured the *Physarum*, and the food sources as the nodes.

This section constructs RGB images to show the approximated networks. The purple spots in the images simulate food sources, and the green edges simulate protoplasmic tubes of *Physarum*. The value of Green channel represents the trail in the scenario, however the chemo-nutrient is mapping to both Red and Blue channels.

Fig. 5 shows the network formation of each data set by four images (1-4 from top to bottom) using the basic parameters in Table 1. Initially the randomly generated 20,000 agents cover exactly half grids of the scenario, which has an analogy to the methods using pieces of *Physarum* covering the available agar surface in [1]. By running the system within 20,000 steps, the network of every dataset will be stable as shown in the fourth image of each subfigure. In Fig. 5(a), the final network is analogous to Steiner's minimum tree (SMT) which is similar to the thick tubes of *Physarum* shown in [2]. The network formed by *Physarum* on the six food sources from [1] reveals a half SMT and half cycle-like pattern shown as Fig. 6(a). However the network formed on the same nodes distribution in [13] is of the only feature of SMT shown in Fig. 6(b). The network formation of the six nodes dataset in Fig. 5(b) of this paper, which seems to be a compromise between them, reveals a pattern of SMT on both sides of the nodes as well as a circle in the middle. The network formation in Fig. 5(c) shows a pattern of Delaunay triangulation network mentioned in [1], but the transitory unstable edges in the middle of the circle shown in the second and third images

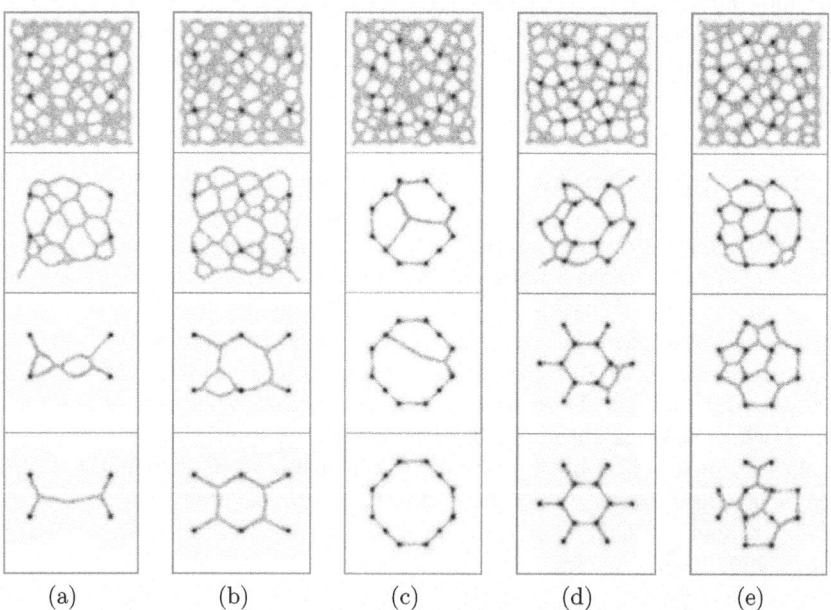

(a)   (b)   (c)   (d)   (e)

Fig. 5. Networks formation on various distributions of nodes completely following the parameters in Table 1. The time-line direction of these snapshots is from top to bottom, and the bottom image is the final stable pattern of each dataset.

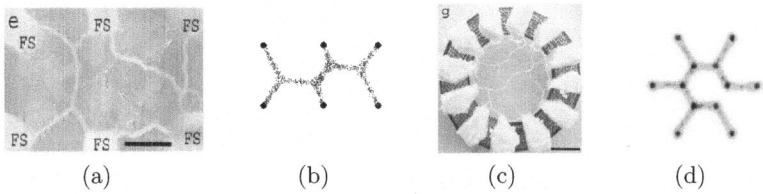

Fig. 6. Figures from [1] and [13] are used to compare with the networks of our system

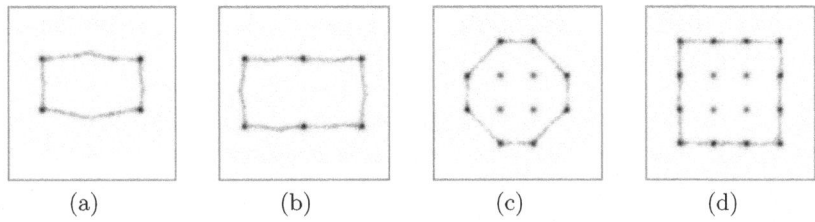

Fig. 7. Outer cycle network formation when the initial population set to 100%

of Fig. 5(c) is more close to the real network of *Physarum* shown in Fig. 6(c). Fig. 5(d) is very similar to that in [13] shown as Fig. 6(d), however ours forms a circle connected the inner nodes. The stable network shown in Fig. 5(e) manifests a more complex structure which blends both the properties of SMT and cycle.

For feather exploring the performance of the system presented in Section 2, we change some parameters to rerun this system on the datasets used above. If the initial population density is set to 100%, there is no empty grid for any agent move forward in this scenario. The population decreases suddenly as the evolution mechanism working, and some agents near the four bounds of the scenario can survive. Then those agents reproduce to form a closed ring and shrink to the center gradually until the ring is adsorb firmly by the outer nodes. That is the interesting pattern shown in Fig. 7. Nodes arrangement in Fig. 7(d) is the supplement of Fig. 7(c) to illustrate how the inner nodes are excluded by the outer cycle. The networks of data set in Fig. 5(c) and 5(d) under the parameter of 100% initial population density are not given because they have the same stable patterns to those in Fig. 5.

Furthermore the dataset, whose three nodes are locating at the vertices of an equilateral triangle, is chosen as the test of approximation. In Fig. 8, the upper of each subfigure is the network formed by our system and the lower is the similar *Physarum* network in [2]. When adopting the basic setting of the system, the SMT pattern formed to connected all the nodes as shown in Fig. 8(a). If the system sets a larger filterN to simulate a further distance of nutrient diffusion, the pattern called cycle (Fig. 8(b)) and analogue of SMT(Fig. 8(c) and 8(d)) in [2] could be observed. The last two patterns are not stable, both of them might transform to SMT. The results of numerical experiment and biological

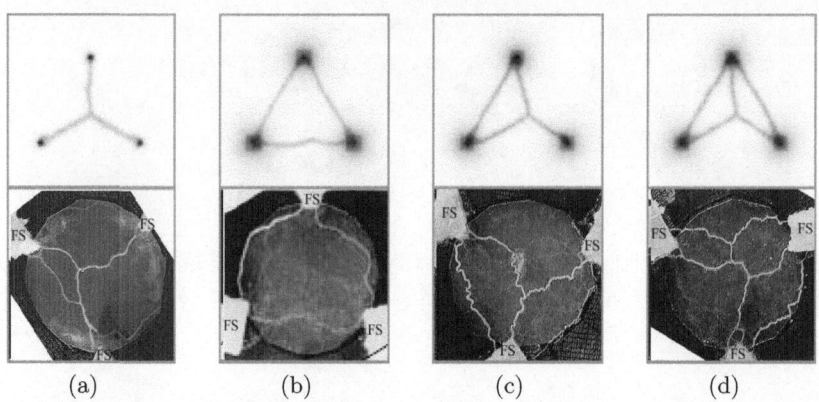

     (a)   (b)   (c)   (d)

Fig. 8. Various networks formation of three nodes located at the vertices of an equilateral triangle. The upper subfigures are from our system ant the lowers from [2](FS is short for Food Source). (a) uses the basic parameter setting. (b) changes the filterN to 19×19. (c) and (d) change the filterN to 17×17.

experiment illustrate the flexibility of our system to form various networks in the same dataset.

3.2 Networks Formation from One Covered Node

When cultured in a nutrient-rich substrate, *Physarum* propagates many branches of protoplasmic tubes. While in a nutrient-poor substrate, it propagates its pseudopodia cautiously to forage for food sources with fewer and tree-like tubes. In [10], a biological experiment is designed to investigate the spanning tree constructed in the nutrient-poor substrate. The distribution of food sources in that experiment is alike the nodes arrangement in the first image of Fig. 10. By inoculating the *Physarum* at the southern food source, the protoplasmic tubes constructs a spanning tree of all food sources finally. In that work, the two component Oregonator Model of BZ reaction is used to explain the building of the spanning tree. Fig. 9 quotes from [10]. The left image of Fig. shows the result of two-variable Oregonator Model after erosion operation on diffusion wave and the right one is the enhanced picture of *Physarum* constructing the spanning tree.

    Inspired by that work, some changes are applied to the system in this paper to simulate the *Physarum*'s behavior to construct spanning tree in nutrient-poor substrate. Firstly, the parameters related to nutrient are adjusted to the suitable values to emphasize the importance of nodes and its gradient in a larger range. Thus these parameters CN, $filterN$, WN and WS are set to 20, 13×13, 0.8 and 0.2, respectively. Secondly, 10 agents are generated manually at the grids of southern node and the system is set up. Then the population of agents develops and gradually covers all nodes. Finally the stable spanning tree is constructed, which is similar to the both trees constructed by the Oregonator Model and

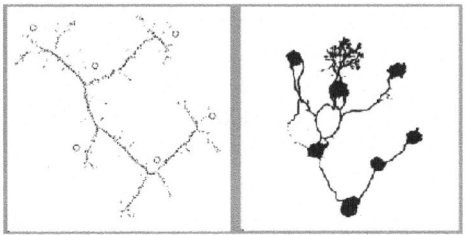

Fig. 9. The spanning trees constructed by Oregonator Model and *Physarum* from [10]

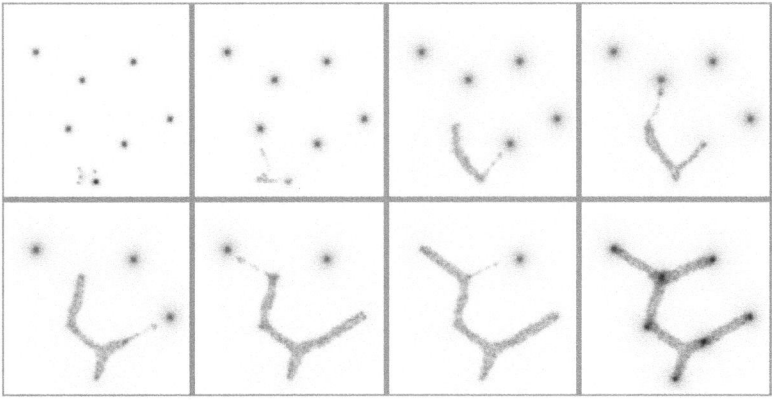

Fig. 10. The process of constructing spanning tree from top to bottom and left to right

the biological experiment in [10]. Fig. 10 records the process of the formation of spanning tree by this system.

4   Concluding Remarks

The enhanced Multi-agent system in this paper approximates the formation of *Physarum* networks in various distributions of food sources. In this system, the diffusion of chemical nutrient is independent from that of trail emitted by agents. Meanwhile, the number of sensors is decreased to two, but the function of a senor is extended to sample both nutrient and trail. The most interesting point of this work is that the Motion Counter as a simple memory module of an agent achieves the complex evolution mechanism. It is a flexible and self-adjusted method to maintain the population to form a stable pattern, comparing with that of utilizing the local population density and probability.

The pattern formation and the variation of population in the system are observed on periodic and fixed boundary conditions. Then some datasets based on the food sources arrangement in biological experiments of other researchers are used to investigate the features of the networks formation by the system. Features, including SMT, cycle-like and spanning-tree, are found in these final networks which are similar to the real networks constructed by *Physarum*. Future works for this system are to explore other possible patterns on various setting of parameters, the construction of efficient networks on more complex data sets and the feature of dynamical reconstruction of the system.

Acknowledgment. This paper is partially supported by Chongqing Natural Science Foundation (Grant No. CSTC, 2010BA2003) and The Key Project of China National Funding of Social Sciences (Grant No. 11AZD57).

References

1. Nakagaki, T., Yamada, H., Hara, M.: Smart network solutions in an amoeboid organism. Biophysical Chemistry 107(1), 1–5 (2004)
2. Nakagaki, T., Kobayashi, R., Nishiura, Y., et al.: Obtaining multiple separate food sources: behavioural intelligence in the *Physarum plasmodium*. In: Proceedings of the Royal Society of London. Series B: Biological Sciences, vol. 271(1554), p. 2305 (2004)
3. Nakagaki, T., Yamada, H., Tóth, Á.: Maze-solving by an amoeboid organism. NATURE 407(6803), 470 (2000)
4. Nakagaki, T., Guy, R.D.: Intelligent behaviors of amoeboid movement based on complex dynamics of soft matter. Soft Matter 4, 57–67 (2007)
5. Tero, A., Kobayashi, R., Nakagaki, T.: A mathematical model for adaptive transport network in path finding by true slime mold. Theoretical Biology 244, 553–564 (2007)
6. Tero, A., Takagi, S., Saigusa, T., et al.: Rules for biologically inspired adaptive network design. Science 327(5964), 439–442 (2010)
7. Li, K., Thomas, K., Torres, C., et al.: Slime mold inspired path formation protocol for wireless sensor networks. Swarm Intelligence, 299–311 (2011)
8. Zhou, H., Zhang, Z., Wu, Y., et al.: Bio-inspired dynamic composition and reconfiguration of service-oriented internetware systems. Advances in Swarm Intelligence, 364–373 (2011)
9. Adamatzky, A.: Physarum machines: computers from slime mould. World Scientific Pub. Co Inc. (2010)
10. Adamatzky, A.: If BZ medium did spanning trees these would be the same trees as Physarum built. Physics Letters A 373(10), 952–956 (2009)
11. Niizato, T., Shirakawa, T., Gunji, Y.-P.: A model of network formation by *Physarum* plasmodium: Interplay between cell mobility and morphogenesis. BioSystems 100, 108–112 (2010)
12. Gunji, Y.-P., Shirakawa, T., Niizato, T., Yamachiyo, M., Tani, I.: An adaptive and robust biological network based on the vacant-particle transportation model. Journal of Theoretical Biology 272, 187–200 (2011)
13. Jones, J.: The emergence and dynamical evolution of complex transport networks from simple low-level behaviours. International Journal of Unconventional Computing 6(2), 125–144 (2010)
14. Jones, J.: Characteristics of pattern formation and evolution in approximations of *Physarum* transport networks. Artificial life 16(2), 127–153 (2010)
15. Jones, J.: Influences on the formation and evolution of *Physarum Polycephalum* inspired emergent transport networks. Natural Computing 10(4), 1345–1369 (2011)

Predicting Shellfish Farm Closures with Class Balancing Methods

Claire D'Este[1], Ashfaqur Rahman[1], and Alison Turnbull[2]

[1] Intelligent Sensing and Systems Laboratory and Food Future Flagship, CSIRO,
Castray Esplanade, Hobart, Australia 7000
[2] Department of Health and Human Services,
GPO Box 125, Hobart, Australia 7001
claire.deste@csiro.au

Abstract. Real-time environmental monitoring can provide vital situational awareness for effective management of natural resources. Effective operation of Shellfish farms depends on environmental conditions. In this paper we propose a supervised learning approach to predict the farm closures. This is a binary classification problem where farm closure is a function of environmental variables. A problem with this classification approach is that farm closure events occur with small frequency leading to class imbalance problem. Straightforward learning techniques tend to favour the majority class; in this case continually predicting no event. We present a new ensemble class balancing algorithm based on random undersampling to resolve this problem. Experimental results show that the class balancing ensemble performs better than individual and other state of art ensemble classifiers. We have also obtained an understanding of the importance of relevant environmental variables for shellfish farm closure. We have utilized feature ranking algorithms in this regard.

1 Introduction

Authorities such as the Tasmanian Shellfish Quality Assurance Program (TSQAP) are responsible for ensuring that shellfish harvested from commercial growing areas are shown to be free of harmful contaminants. Microbial contaminants in particular pose a major risk to public health. The potential presence of such contaminants are continually monitored through a combination of manual sampling and real-time sensors at each of the shellfish growing sites through indicators of salinity, rainfall and river flow, as well as direct water samples of the microbes themselves. When these indicators fall outside the limits provided by the management plan at a particular site, the growing site must be closed. If the shellfish are close to harvesting size and the closure time is lengthy this can result in significant loss of stock. This has economic implications for the individual farms, but can also cause disruptions in the supply of shellfish causing negative impact on the industry statewide.

Management of the TSQAP is hindered by tedious and complex manual processes that are required to obtain the relevant environmental data. This is mainly

M. Thielscher and D. Zhang (Eds.): AI 2012, LNCS 7691, pp. 39–48, 2012.

due to different sensors residing with different organisations that provide the data in different formats through different means; including FTP servers, dial-up communications, web pages etc. This has resulted in a system that relies heavily on the availability of a single expert and has resulted in harmful events being missed when this expert was unavailable. Consequently, we have begun developing a real-time decision support tool for the TSQAP. This tool will deliver all of the proxy indicators of quality assurance from each of the different data custodians in real-time and combine them within a visual interface to provides an overall picture of the water quality at each site. In addition to the initial improvements obtained through data integration, the use of data mining and knowledge discovery may potentially assist with short-term and long-term management decisions.

In this paper we present a classification approach to predict shellfish farm closures. Shellfish farms are closed depending on location, rainfall, salinity and toxicity etc. We have developed a data set where we obtained information on farm closures and corresponding readings of environmental variables. This gives rise to a classification problem. However as the closures are relatively infrequent events, traditional techniques will tend to favour the majority class resulting in a system that always predicts that no event is present. As well as the issues we will face in the future with regards to unreliable inputs from sensors and heterogenous sensors at each of the farm locations, we first need to approach the minority class problem. This will also be relevant when we analyse other potentially harmful events to the aquaculture industry such as algal blooms. We have developed a random class balancing ensemble method to address this problem. We have also presented the results of feature ranking to understand of the relative importance of relevant environmental variables for shellfish farm closure.

2   Related Work

Shellfish farm closure prediction remains to date a novel application of data-driven techniques. In general, data mining/machine learning techniques are rarely applied to aquaculture problems; with the exception of prediction of harmful algal blooms [1].

Ensemble classifiers [2] create complementary base classifiers by manipulating the training set. The idea is to train base classifiers on different subsets of the data. In bagging [3–9] the subsets are randomly drawn (with replacement) from the training set. Boosting [10–13] is a hierarchical process where the first subset is created by randomly drawing patterns from the training set. The patterns that are not correctly classified by the current classifiers are given more importance by the classifiers following passes.

Synthetic Minority Oversampling TEchnique (SMOTE) boosting was developed to address the class imbalance problem. SMOTE not only under samples the majority class, but oversamples the minority class by introducing 'synthetic' examples [14]. These examples are generated by adding a random number to the difference between two neighbouring feature vectors of minority class examples. The amount of oversampling is a tuneable parameter.

3 Random Class Balancing

The class balancing ensemble classifier framework is presented in Figure 1. Given the training data a number of M subsets are produced using random under sampling. This is done to address the class imbalance problem. The under sampling process creates a training set with equal number of instances from every class. When the classifiers are trained on the balanced data set the bias mentioned above is eliminated. We term this method Random Class Balancing (RCB). The random selection process, however, may ignore significant clusters of the majority class. To address this issue we produce M different subsets from the training data using random under sampling. Classifiers are then trained on the M different training subsets.

During testing a sample is classified by all the M classifiers. The decisions produced by the M different base classifiers are merged into a single verdict using majority voting fusion. In this process the class that receives the maximum vote is considered to be the final classification verdict.

The class balancing ensemble classifier framework incorporates balancing to address the unfairness to the minority classes. Use of multiple subsets of the training data improves the overall sampling efficiency. Combined the accuracy of the minority class improves with minimal reduction of accuracy of the majority class.

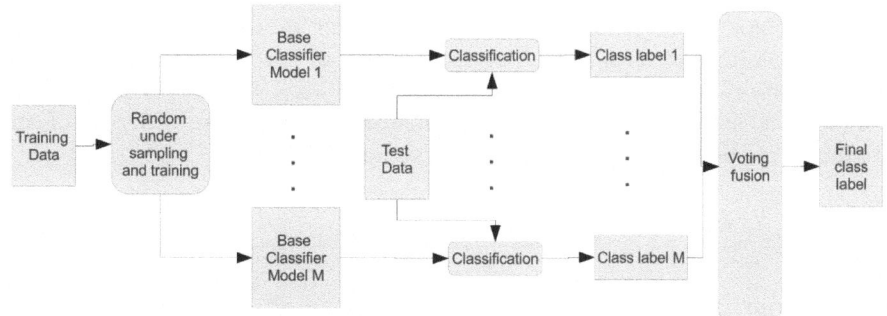

Fig. 1. Class Balancing Ensemble classifier framework

4 Dataset

The dataset is derived from 4543 manual water samples taken by TSQAP between 1988 and 2010. It includes four features:

- **Level of Thermotolerant Coliforms** - Level of faecal bacteria present per 100 millilitres.

- **Location** - 45 shellfish locations all over Tasmania.
- **Rain** - Rainfall in millimetres recorded for last 7 days from the closest weather station.
- **Salinity** - salt level in the water sample in Practical Salinity Units (PSU).

The sample dates have been merged with farm closure dates taken from TSQAP annual reports to create an output class, which is the close/open decision made by the TSQAP manager. We are particularly interested in the examples where the output class is *Closed* as this is when the farmers or the TSQAP manager will want to take action. Unfortunately, over 88% of the samples have the output class *Open*. However, we want to keep as many of the individual samples as we can, even if the farm was kept open, because as much information as possible is necessary to create an accurate model of these kinds of complex environmental processes.

5   Results

5.1   Feature Ranking

Determining which features are most relevant for predicting farm closures will inform our recommendations to farmers regarding what sensors to add. We also wanted to evaluate if learning could be simplified by removing any features that were irrelevant. We have used attribute/feature ranking as the search method to get an ordering of the features. An attribute evaluator method is required to evaluate the strength of an attribute. We have obtained evaluation scores of the attributes from eight different evaluators available in the Weka toolbox [15]. The scores and ranks are presented in Table 1 and Table 2. The average ranks of the attributes are obtained at the end to get an ensemble decision from all the evaluators.

From the average over the eight evaluators the following ordering of the attributes is observed, from most to least significant:

1. Location
2. Salinity
3. Rain
4. Coliforms

5.2   Class Balancing

The shellfish closure dataset was applied to four different classifier types from the Weka Toolbox [15]; Decision Trees (Table 3) with the J48 classifer, Random Forest (4), Multilayer Perceptrons (Table 5), Support Vector Machines (Table 6) using the SMO classifier, and Bayesian Networks (Table 7). The default parameters were used for all of the classifiers and 5-fold cross validation was performed on each. For the ensemble classifiers there were ten classifiers in each ensemble.

Table 1. Attribute score on the Shellfish Farm Closure dataset

Evaluator	Rain	Coliforms	Location	Salinity
Chi-squared Ranking Filter	316.3	307.4	901.3	429.2
Filtered Attribute Evaluator	0.045	0.042	0.1	0.06
Gain Ratio Feature Evaluator	0.02	0.34	0.037	0.04
Information Gain Ranking Filter	0.5	0.04	0.1	0.06
OneR Feature Evaluator	89.1	88.4	88.1	87.7
ReliefF Ranking Filter	0.03	0.001	0.03	0.01
SVM Feature Evaluator	4	3	1	2
Symmetrical Uncertainty Ranking Filter	0.03	0.05	0.07	0.06

Table 2. Attribute/Feature ranking on the Shellfish Farm Closure dataset

Evaluator	Rain	Coliforms	Location	Salinity
Chi-squared Ranking Filter	3	4	1	2
Filtered Attribute Evaluator	3	4	1	2
Gain Ratio Feature Evaluator	4	3	2	1
Information Gain Ranking Filter	3	4	1	2
OneR Feature Evaluator	1	2	3	4
ReliefF Ranking Filter	1	4	2	3
SVM Feature Evaluator	1	2	4	3
Symmetrical Uncertainty Ranking Filter	4	3	1	2
Average	2.5	3.2	1.9	2.8
Ranking	3	4	1	2

In Table 3 to 7 below, Random Class Balancing (RCB) refers to the average of the individual classifiers before they were added to the ensemble. For the Decision Tree tests we implemented three different voting methods. *Average* refers to the average vote over the ensemble, *Majority* is where a majority vote is taken with a random selection taking place on equal numbers of votes, and *Maximum* takes the vote of the classifier whose classification has the highest probability. The

Table 3. Accuracy of decision trees with ensemble and class balancing methods on the Shellfish Farm Closure dataset

Method	Overall %	Closed %	Open %
Default	91.9 (± 1.8)	43.4 (± 4.8)	98.0 (± 0.9)
SMOTE	92.0 (± 2.1)	73.5 (± 3.6)	96.5 (± 2.3)
Ensemble Avg	88.1 (± 0.01)	0.0 (± 0.0)	100.0 (± 0.0)
Ensemble Maj	88.2 (± 0.2)	35.0 (± 48.7)	88.2 (± 0.2)
RCB	78.8 (± 2.5)	90.4 (± 3.3)	77.2 (± 5.1)
RCB Ensemble Average	80.1 (± 1.6)	93.7 (± 2.4)	78.3 (± 1.7)
RCB Ensemble Majority	80.1 (± 1.5)	98.9 (± 2.5)	76.9 (± 4.3)
RCB Ensemble Maximum	75.7 (± 1.5)	93.8 (± 2.5)	73.3 (± 4.3)
AdaBoost	96.6 (± 0.6)	82.0 (± 4.0)	98.5 (± 0.3)
Bagging	95.4 (± 0.8)	72.4 (± 4.8)	98.5 (± 0.4)

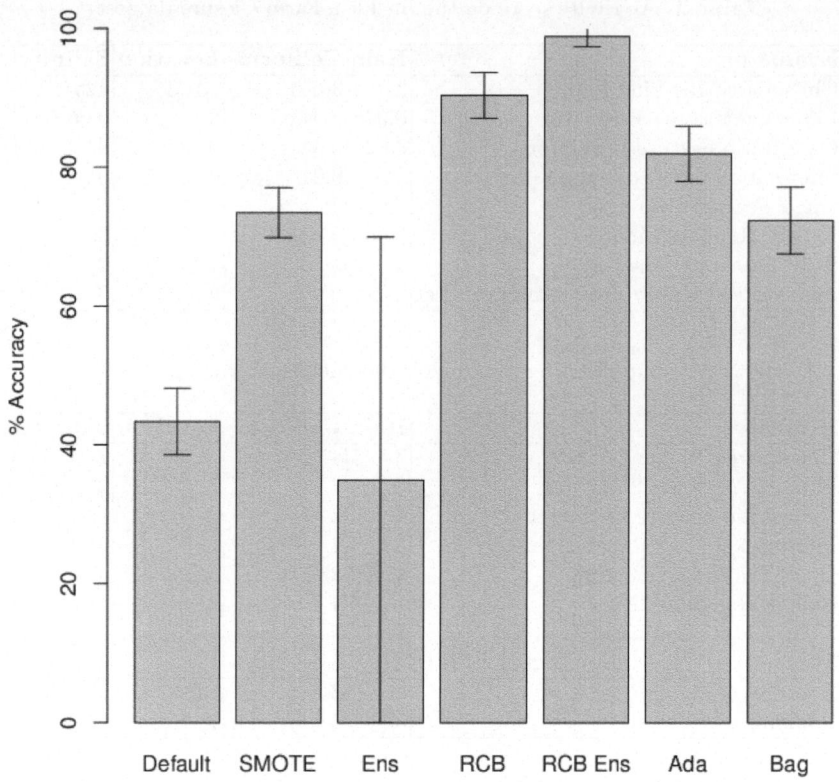

Fig. 2. Accuracy of the minority class, Closed, on the Shellfish Farm Closure dataset using Decision Tree classifiers

Table 4. Accuracy of Random Forest ensemble and class balancing methods on the Shellfish Farm Closure dataset

Method	Overall %	Closed %	Open %
Default	96.1 (± 0.4)	83.0(± 2.5)	97.8 (± 0.3)
SMOTE	95.0 (± 0.1)	83.5 (± 3.6)	96.5 (± 0.6)
RCB	87.6 (± 0.5)	91.6 (± 1.7)	87.0 (± 0.6)
RCB Ensemble	89.7 (± 0.5)	93.3 (± 1.7)	89.3 (± 0.6)

Table 5. Accuracy of Multi-Layer Perceptrons with ensemble and class balancing methods on the Shellfish Farm Closure dataset

Method	Overall %	Closed %	Open %
Default	87.8 (± 0.3)	46.8 (± 10.2)	98.0 (± 0.9)
SMOTE	85.3 (± 1.9)	28.1 (± 10.9)	93.0 (± 3.7)
RCB	67.2 (± 4.1)	72.1 (± 13.1)	66.5 (± 10.0)
RCB Ensemble	75.3 (± 4.1)	60.5 (± 3.8)	71.4 (± 10.3)

Table 6. Accuracy of SVM ensemble and class balancing methods on the Shellfish Farm Closure dataset

Method	Overall %	Closed %	Open %
Default	88.1 (± 0.01)	0.0 (± 0.0)	100.0 (± 0.0)
SMOTE	88.1 (± 0.01)	0.0 (± 0.0)	100.0 (± 0.0)
RCB	81.3 (± 2.8)	42.7 (± 5.2)	86.5 (± 3.6)
RCB Ensemble	81.6 (± 2.1)	45.2 (± 4.0)	86.6 (± 2.8)

Table 7. Accuracy of Bayes Net ensemble and class balancing methods on the Shellfish Farm Closure dataset

Method	Overall %	Closed %	Open %
Default	84.9 (± 0.6)	50.2 (± 3.3)	89.6 (± 0.7)
SMOTE	83.8 (± 0.6)	60.2 (± 3.6)	87.0 (± 0.7)
RCB	75.8 (± 1.4)	69.0 (± 3.3)	76.7 (± 1.7)
RCB Ensemble	75.6 (± 0.6)	70.2 (± 3.4)	76.3 (± 0.4)
AdaBoost	87.6 (± 1.6)	24.4 (± 13.7)	96.1 (± 3.2)
Bagging	85.4 (± 0.9)	46.1 (± 2.6)	90.7 (± 1.2)

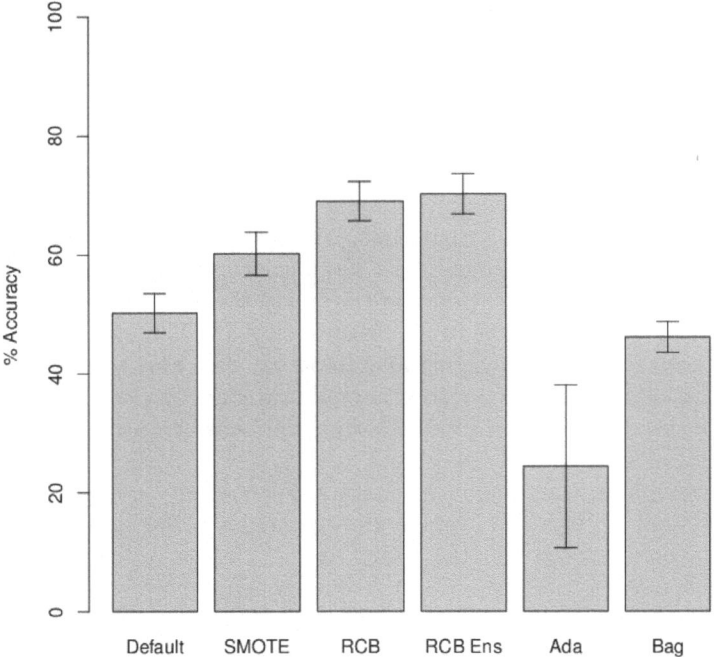

Fig. 3. Accuracy of the minority class, Closed, on the Shellfish Farm Closure dataset using Bayesian Network classifiers

remaining classifier methods use average voting as this is the default in Weka. The Bagging and AdaBoost classifiers were also taken from the Weka toolbox and used with the default parameters.

Figure 3 plots the accuracy on the *Closed* output class of interest for each of the decision tree approaches. Figure 7 plots the accuracy on the *Closed* output class of interest for each of the Bayesian Network approaches.

6   Discussion

The results of the feature ranking emphasise the importance of clustering the farms based on the location. It will not be possible to create a general classifier for every location, but we may be able to cluster the locations to avoid having a separate model for each location. Salinity is the most important environmental variable, followed by rain. It is interesting to note that the direct measures of thermotolerant coliforms are the least relevant when these are the levels we are directly trying to measure. It suggests that closures are carried out in anticipation of drops in thermotolerant coliforms most often, rather than due to high levels of the coliforms themselves. This will be important for our real-time system as the health department and the farmers will want to be forewarned of potential closures so, for example, they can harvest early, instead of closing when it is essentially too late to take appropriate action.

The results of the learning methods show that the classification accuracy can be significantly improved by class balancing techniques. SMOTE shows an improvement over the default method for Decision Trees, Random Forest and Bayesian Networks on the minority class; with the largest increase in accuracy apparent for Decision Trees. The Random Forest proving the best performer using the default method.

The Random Class Balancing Ensembles consistently had the highest accuracy on the minority *Closed* output class. Although it did negatively affect the accuracy on the entire data set and the *Open* output class. We will need to investigate if there is a method that does not decrease the accuracy of the majority class when class balancing. The results suggest that SMOTE also loses accuracy in the majority class. The Bagging and Boosting were able to greater overall accuracy, but significantly lower accuracy on the minority class than the RCB Ensemble method. The Bagging and Boosting methods also had higher variance in accuracy.

There was a small increase in accuracy using majority voting, but similar results were gained from the average and maximum voting methods. For the remaining experiments we left the voting as the average voting default as the accuracy increase was not deemed significant enough.

The accuracy of MLPs and SVMs likely suffer from the format of the location, which has been determined as the most important feature. The location information would not translate well to a single normalised input. It would also not be feasible to have an input node for each of the 45 locations. We believe the neural network learners will respond well to reducing the locations to a much smaller number of clusters before learning. However, these learners still experience a significant increase in accuracy after class balancing.

7 Conclusion

We were successfully able to train classifiers on the Shellfish Farm Closure dataset and produce accurate classifications of farm closures. The application of machine learning techniques in this domain is novel in itself. The classifiers were consistently improved by using class balancing techniques; with 98.9% accuracy on the minority class possible with the RCB Ensemble method described. We also confirmed the importance of salinity as a indictator for farm closure, as well as the importance of the farm location.

We intend to make these classifications with input from real-time data streams to provide an intuitive visualisation tool for the health authority. The probability of closure will be represented by a traffic light colour system on a geographic map. We believe this greatly reduce the workload of the manager as well as the current dependence on her skills.

Acknowledgements. This work is supported by the Food Futures Flagship, CSIRO and the Tasmanian State Government Department of Economic Development, Tourism and the Arts.

References

1. Muttil, N., Chau, K.: Machine-learning paradigms for selecting ecologically significant input variables. Journal Engineering Applications of Artificial Intelligence 20(6), 735–744 (2007)
2. Rahman, A., Verma, B.: Novel layered clustering-based approach for generating ensemble of classifiers. IEEE Transactions on Neural Networks 22(5), 781–792 (2011)
3. Breiman, L.: Bagging predictors. Machine Learning 24(2), 123–140 (1996)
4. Breiman, L.: Random forests. Machine Learning 45(1), 5–32 (2001)
5. Breiman, L.: Pasting small votes for classification in large databases and on-line. Machine Learning 36, 85–103 (1999)
6. Martinez-Munoz, G., Hernandez-Lobato, D., Suarez, A.: An analysis of ensemble pruning techniques based on ordered aggregation. IEEE Trans. on Pattern Analysis and Machine Intelligence 31(2), 245–259 (2009)
7. Chen, L., Kamel, M.: A generalized adaptive ensemble generation and aggregation approach for multiple classifiers systems. Pattern Recognition 42, 629–644 (2009)
8. Nanni, L., Lumini, A.: Fuzzy bagging: a novel ensemble of classifiers. Pattern Recognition 39, 488–490 (2006)
9. Eschrich, S., Hall, L.O.: Soft partitions lead to better learned ensembles, pp. 406–411 (2002)
10. Schapire, R.: The strength of weak learnability. Machine Learning 5(2), 197–227 (1990)
11. Freund, Y., Schapire, R.: Decision-theoretic generalization of on-line learning and an application to boosting. Journal of Computer and System Sciences 55(1), 119–139 (1997)

12. Drucker, H., Cortes, C., Jackel, L., LeCun, Y., Vapnik, V.: Boosting and other ensemble methods. Neural Computation 6(6), 1289–1301 (1994)
13. Garcia-Pedrajas, N.: Constructing ensembles of classifiers by means of weighted instance selection. IEEE Trans. on Neural Networks 20(2), 258–277 (2009)
14. Chawla, N., Bowyer, K., Hall, L., Kegelmeyer, W.: SMOTE: Synthetic minority over-sampling technique. Journal of Artificial Intelligence Research 16, 341–378 (2002)
15. Hall, M., Frank, E., Holmes, G., Pfahringer, B., Reutemann, P., Witten, I.: The weka data mining software: An update. SIGKDD Explorations 11(1) (2009)

Automatic Han Chinese Folk Song Classification Using Extreme Learning Machines

Suisin Khoo, Zhihong Man, and Zhenwei Cao

Faculty of Engineering and Industrial Sciences
Swinburne University of Technology
VIC 3122 Australia
suisin.khoo@gmail.com, {zman,zcao}@swin.edu.au

Abstract. Multilayer feedforward neural networks trained via supervised learning have proven to be successful in pattern recognition. This paper presents the technique of using single hidden layer feedforward neural network as an automatic classifier in music classification. Han Chinese folk songs from five distinct geographical regions in China are studied and encoded using a novel musical feature density map (MFDMap) for machine classification. The extreme learning machine (ELM) and its two variants are employed as the classifiers to categorize the folk songs. Our simulations show that by using a low-pass finite impulse response extreme learning machine (FIR-ELM), we can achieve 80.65% classification accuracy.

Keywords: Musical feature density map, music classification, extreme learning machine, artificial neural network, Han Chinese folk song.

1 Introduction

Automatic music classification has been widely studied in the past decade, but the majority of the works focuses on Western music. Some examples are [1], [2] and [3]. Though Chinese music classification has not been ignored, little effort has been made in this area. An example is the classification of Chinese folk music using Hidden Markov model [4]. Two sets of perceptual features were used for the purpose of classifying Chinese folk music according to the audio taxonomy defined by the authors. As the authors defined Chinese folk music as either vocal or instrumental, they focused mainly on the timbral and rhythmic features.

As far as we are aware, there is only one work for Chinese music classification that involved using an artificial neural network (ANN) as the classifier. Xu, Wang and Yan [5] used a radial basis function neural network to classify Chinese folk songs based on 74 features extracted from the audio signals. The authors achieve 43.208% classification accuracy using Classification Contribution-Ratio Based Selection algorithm for music feature selection.

The single hidden layer feedforward neural network (SLFN) is one of the simplest and most popular types of ANN. Hornik, Stinchcombe and White [6] have proved that a SLFN, using any desired activation function, is a universal approximator. Such

M. Thielscher and D. Zhang (Eds.): AI 2012, LNCS 7691, pp. 49–60, 2012.

SLFN is able to approximate virtually any function if given a sufficient number of hidden neurons and a sufficiently large training set. The extreme learning machine (ELM) [7] is an emerging technology that utilized a SLFN. It has been proved to out-perform conventional SLFNs, especially the gradient-based SLFNs [7]. Nonetheless, ELM technique has limited attention in music classification research. The only research that employs ELM as a music classifier is [8], where a four genre (classical, dance, pop and rock) music classification is performed. Khoo, Man and Cao [9] employed the regularized extreme learning machine (R-ELM) as a geographical based classifier for Han Chinese folk song.

In this paper, we propose using the finite impulse response extreme learning machine (FIR-ELM) as the music classifier for Han Chinese folk songs. The FIR-ELM is a variant of ELM which incorporated two improvements to the ELM. It introduced two balancing parameters to adjust the balance of the empirical risk and the structural risk of the neural network and improved the limitation of the arbitrary characteristic in both ELM and R-ELM by introducing the filtering technique to the input layer of the SLFN. It is more robust especially in solving complex problem such as the one discussed in this paper.

The corpus for our music classification task is the Han Chinese folk songs from five distinct regions in China. There are two distinct approaches for music representation: audio and symbolic. In this paper, we employ a novel symbolic musical feature representation method, the musical feature density map (MFDMap). Unlike audio representation, our MFDMap is very similar to musical notations and hence more appropriately model the human perception of music. In addition, the characteristic of symbolic representation facilitates the possibility of building intelligent systems for music theory teaching and learning.

This paper is organized as follows. In Section 2, we will describe our proposed musical feature density map and the data set used for the simulations. A brief overview of the ELM, the R-ELM and the FIR-ELM will be presented in Section 3. In Section 4, the simulation results will be presented and discussed. Finally, we will conclude our work in Section 5 and propose ideas for further research.

2   Music Representation

In this paper, musical features were extracted from Kern files. There is no particular reason for choosing this format except that the database we employed is coded in Kern format. It is important to note that from a practical perspective, the features discussed in this section could just as easily be extracted from other existing symbolic formats such as MIDI notation.

2.1   Solfege – To Characterize Melody Progression of Notes

One of the main characteristics of folk songs is their method of transmission. Unlike other styles of music, such as classical music, folk songs are transmitted orally. Much existing research that adopts symbolic representation overlooks this important characteristic of folk songs. They usually employ the exact pitch representation of the song melody. As folk songs are transmitted orally, the key of the tune in which a person sings may vary. This means that the tune of a folk song may be sung in many different pitches but the melody progression of all notes remains unchanged. In this case, exact pitch representation will interpret the different versions independently as different songs instead of as the same song, which results in inaccuracy.

Instead of using the exact pitch representation, we proposed using solfege representation of the song melody. Solfege is a solmization technique that is commonly used for sight singing. Each note in a musical scale is assigned to a unique syllable. These syllables are usually written as numerical notations in musical scores of Chinese folk songs. Solfege notation can be easily computed using the available pitch and key information. It is a consistent and robust feature. Despite the different key of each version of the same folk song, the solfege representation always remains the same. The solfege representation can be computed using the following equation:

$$\text{solfege}_i(n) = \text{solfege}(n) + (i \times 7) \tag{1}$$

for $n = 1,2,3,\ldots,N$, where N is the number of notes in a folk song and i is the number of octaves above or below the Middle C.

2.2　Interval – To Characterize Musical Flows

From a broad geographical view, the Han Chinese folk songs can be divided into the northern and southern style, each of which is associated with the two major rivers in China: the Yellow River of the north and the Chang Jiang of the south. In this division, the environment, climate and landscape structure play a significant role in forming the characteristics of the folk songs from the different regions. For example, the cold, dry and windy climate in the north that affects the agricultural activities and lifestyle of the people is reflected by a more intense and disjunct progression of melody in folk songs from that area. Conversely, the folk songs from the southern regions are more lyrical and conjunct. This important characteristic of the musical flow and movement of folk songs is reflected in our encoding scheme through the measurement of the musical interval and changes in duration between adjacent notes.

The musical interval is the measurement of the pitch ratio between two adjacent notes. We measure the interval in terms of the number of semitones between two adjacent notes. The intervals of a folk song melody with N number of notes can be calculated using the following equation:

$$\text{interval}(n) = \text{pitch}(n) - \text{pitch}(n-1) \tag{2}$$

for $n = 2,3,4,\ldots,N$, where N is the number of notes.

2.3　Duration – To Characterize Rhythmic Pattern

Rhythmic patterns define the distinctive identity between music of diverse style and form. For example, a melody with lots of short notes within a short length of time presents an agitated impression but a chunk of lengthy notes usually creates a more graceful feeling. We encoded the duration of each musical note in a folk song to characterize its rhythmic pattern. The numerical notation we employed to represent different lengths of note is the number of crotchets (♩) per measurement. We encoded 19 different note durations that are common in Han Chinese folk songs.

2.4   Duration Ratio – To Characterize Rhythmical Changes

As mentioned previously, the geographical characteristics of the origin of a folk song have significant influences in the texture of the folk song. Duration ratio measures the rhythmical changes. A large ratio reflects a drastic change in rhythmic progression which portrays a rougher, more intense and disjunct texture. On the other hand, a smaller ratio depicts a smooth, more continuous and lyrical texture. The duration ratio can be computed using the following equation:

$$\text{duration ratio}(n) = \frac{\text{duration}(n)}{\text{duration}(n-1)} \tag{3}$$

for $n = 2,3,4,\ldots,N$, where N is the number of notes in each folk song.

2.5   Musical Feature Density Map

In the previous sections, useful musical features are extracted for folk song classification. As the folk songs are of varied length, in order to perform the classification, we need to specify a unified length for all. Most existing research papers, for example both [1] and [5], employ a windowing method. In this method, a window of specific size is defined and a song is sliced into many fragments of the same size. These windows of music fragments are then used as the input to the music classifier.

Although the windowing method is useful, it imposed a few limitations. Firstly, there is no universal value for the window size. Varied window size might result in diverse classification accuracy. Therefore, an exhaustive testing needs to be carried out to determine the most suitable window size. Next, the size of a window determines the amount of information it encapsulates. If a window size is too small, there might not be enough information to define the characteristic of a class. In addition, more than one window might contain the same data. Finally, dividing a song into fragments might result in loss of continuity and integrity of the music.

In this paper, we propose using a musical feature density map which overcomes the above mentioned limitations. MFDMap is a map that portrays the density of each musical feature value in a song. Instead of fragmenting the songs, each song is considered as a whole. The MFDMap consists of 175 map locations: 46 for solfege, 49 for interval, 19 for duration and 61 for duration ratio. The value for each map location is calculated as a percentage:

$$\text{map location}_i = \frac{\text{frequency of musical feature value}_i}{N} \times 100 \tag{4}$$

for $i = 1,2,3,\ldots,175$ and N is the total number of notes in a song. Note that instead of N, we use $N-1$ for interval features and duration ratio features.

One of the advantages of MFDMap is that it preserves the main characteristic of symbolic representations, that is, it closely models the human perception of music. Most musical styles can be differentiated by the high occurrence of certain musical features or the absence of them. This is effectively modelled in the MFDMap. The structure of MFDMap is flexible. It allows all musical features to be encompassed in one map. Any musical features that are not applicable to a particular musical style can be easily removed from the map. MFDMap is also extendable whereby new musical features can be added to it.

By using the occurrence percentage of each musical feature within a song, MFDMap encompasses the complete melody instead of segmenting it into chunks of notes. This is important as music is usually continuous. Each musical note is not an independent object but is closely related to the preceding note(s) and the successive note(s). MFDMap uses the whole song and extracts useful musical features from it, each song has a unique map and the problems of finding a representative segment size can be easily avoided.

2.6   Data Set

We have chosen Chinese folk songs from five regions: Jiangsu, Dongbei, Guangdong, Shanxi and Sichuan as our corpus from the larger database of Han Chinese folk songs from [10]. The melody of each folk song in the corpus is encoded into a MFDMap of its own. There are a total of 312 folk songs in our corpus. 90% of the songs are randomly assigned as the training set and the remaining form the testing set.

3   Machine Classifier

3.1   Extreme Learning Machine

The major bottlenecks of the gradient-based single hidden layer feedforward neural network are the slow learning speed and the convergence issue. These are caused by the learning algorithms that are employed by the SLFN. Gradient-based algorithms suffer from the problem of choosing the learning step that gives good convergence. In addition, the parameters such as the input weights and the hidden layer biases of these learning algorithms need iterative tuning to obtain better learning performance which results in a time consuming and resource consuming process.

The extreme learning machine is proposed by Huang, Zhu and Siew [7] to overcome these drawbacks. ELM algorithm utilizes SLFN architecture but unlike the gradient-based SLFN, ELM randomly chooses the input weights and analytically determines the output weights of a SLFN. In [7], the ELM was theoretically proven to give good generalization performance at an extremely fast learning speed. The brief overview of the ELM algorithm is described as follows.

For a dataset with N distinct samples $\{(X,T) \mid \mathbf{X} = [\mathbf{x}_1,\mathbf{x}_2,\ldots,\mathbf{x}_N], \mathbf{T} = [\mathbf{t}_1,\mathbf{t}_2,\ldots,\mathbf{t}_N]\}$ where $\mathbf{x}_i = [x_{i1},x_{i2},\ldots x_{in}]^T \in \mathbf{R}^n$ is the input vector and $\mathbf{t}_i = [t_{i1},t_{i2},\ldots t_{im}]^T \in \mathbf{R}^m$ is the target vector, the SLFN with $\tilde{N}$ hidden neurons can be written as

$$\mathbf{o}_i = \sum_{j=1}^{\tilde{N}} \boldsymbol{\beta}_j\, g(\mathbf{w}_j \mathbf{x}_i + b_j) \qquad (5)$$

for $i = 1,2,\ldots,N$ where $\mathbf{o}_i = [o_{i1},o_{i2},\ldots,o_{im}]^T \in \mathbf{R}^m$ is the output vector with respect to $\mathbf{x}_i = [x_{i1},x_{i2},\ldots,x_{in}]^T$ the input vector, $\boldsymbol{\beta}_j = [\beta_{j1},\beta_{j2},\ldots,\beta_{jm}]^T$ is the output weights vector connecting the jth hidden neuron and the output neurons, $\mathbf{w}_j = [w_{j1},w_{j2},\ldots,w_{jn}]^T$ is the input weights vector connecting the input neurons and the jth hidden neuron, b_j is the bias of the jth hidden neuron and $g(x)$ is the activation function. This SLFN with $\tilde{N}$ hidden neurons and activation function $g(x)$ is proven to be able to approximate N data samples with zero error, such that

$$\sum_{i=1}^{N} \left\| \mathbf{o}_i - \mathbf{t}_i \right\| = 0 . \tag{6}$$

Therefore, there exist $\boldsymbol{\beta}_j$, $\mathbf{w}_j$ and b_j such that

$$\mathbf{t}_i = \sum_{j=1}^{\tilde{N}} \boldsymbol{\beta}_j \, g(\mathbf{w}_j \mathbf{x}_i + b_j) \tag{7}$$

for $i = 1,2,\ldots,N$. The above (7) can then be written compactly in matrix form $\mathbf{H}\boldsymbol{\beta} = \mathbf{T}$ where

$$\mathbf{H}(\mathbf{w}_1,\mathbf{w}_2,\ldots,\mathbf{w}_{\tilde{N}},\ b_1,b_2,\ldots,b_{\tilde{N}},\ \mathbf{x}_1,\mathbf{x}_2,\ldots,\mathbf{x}_N)$$
$$= \begin{bmatrix} g(\mathbf{w}_1\mathbf{x}_1+b_1) & g(\mathbf{w}_2\mathbf{x}_1+b_2) & \cdots & g(\mathbf{w}_{\tilde{N}}\mathbf{x}_1+b_{\tilde{N}}) \\ g(\mathbf{w}_1\mathbf{x}_2+b_1) & g(\mathbf{w}_2\mathbf{x}_2+b_2) & \cdots & g(\mathbf{w}_{\tilde{N}}\mathbf{x}_2+b_{\tilde{N}}) \\ \vdots & \vdots & \ddots & \vdots \\ g(\mathbf{w}_1\mathbf{x}_N+b_1) & g(\mathbf{w}_2\mathbf{x}_N+b_2) & \cdots & g(\mathbf{w}_{\tilde{N}}\mathbf{x}_N+b_{\tilde{N}}) \end{bmatrix}_{N\times\tilde{N}} , \tag{8}$$

$$\boldsymbol{\beta} = \begin{bmatrix} \boldsymbol{\beta}_1^T \\ \boldsymbol{\beta}_2^T \\ \vdots \\ \boldsymbol{\beta}_{\tilde{N}}^T \end{bmatrix}_{\tilde{N}\times m} \quad \text{and} \quad \mathbf{T} = \begin{bmatrix} \mathbf{t}_1^T \\ \mathbf{t}_2^T \\ \vdots \\ \mathbf{t}_N^T \end{bmatrix}_{N\times m} . \tag{9}$$

The ELM algorithm works by first randomly initializing the input weights and hidden layer biases of the SLFN. Then, the hidden layer output $\mathbf{H}$ is calculated. Finally, the output weights $\boldsymbol{\beta}$ are computed using the Moore-Penrose generalized inverse:

$$\boldsymbol{\beta} = (\mathbf{H}^T\mathbf{H})^{-1}\mathbf{H}^T\mathbf{T} . \tag{10}$$

The major difference between the ELM algorithm and gradient-based learning algorithms is the tuning of the hidden layer. In conventional algorithms, the learning process needs to be repeated many times to tune the input weights but ELM does not require such tuning and its optimal output weights are calculated analytically without any iterative procedure. This results in an extremely fast learning speed and a simpler architecture with fewer parameters to tune. In addition, ELM determines its output weights using the generalized inverse operation which assures a unique solution with the smallest norm. This allows the ELM algorithm to effectively avoid the local minima issue.

Although ELM greatly improved the performance of conventional SLFNs, it still poses a few drawbacks. Firstly, the random assignment of the input weights and hidden layer biases leads to the generation of non-optimal solutions. The arbitrary characteristic of the randomly assigned input weights is similar to the local minima problem in gradient-based algorithm. It results in diverse solutions by an ELM over different trials. Hence, it is difficult to determine the optimal solution in a single run. Repeated trials of testing are required to evaluate the mean classification accuracy of an ELM. In addition, there is no universal value or range of values to set the input weights. Hence, the choice of values is purely empirically based. The next section will further discuss an enhancement to this limitation of ELM.

Next, the design of the output layer weights in ELM gives rise to another issue. ELM uses the generalized inverse of the hidden layer output matrices to determine the output weights. This minimum norm least squares solution of the hidden layer output is an empirical risk minimization (ERM) operation which tends to result in an overfitting model especially if the training set is not sufficiently large. In statistical learning theory, the real prediction risk in learning consists of empirical risk and structural risk. In order to achieve good generalization performance, a model needs to accomplish a good balance between these two risks.

Deng, Zheng and Chen [11] proposed to overcome the drawback in the output weights by introducing a regularization term into the ELM algorithm. A weight factor γ for empirical risk is inserted to regularize the proportion of the empirical risk and the structural risk. Their improved ELM is called the regularized extreme learning machine and it used the following equation to calculate the output weights β:

$$\beta = \left(\frac{I}{\gamma} + H^T H \right)^{-1} H^T T .$$ (11)

3.2   Finite Impulse Response Extreme Learning Machine

As mentioned in the previous section, the ELM poses two major limitations: the robustness issues and the effect of the structural and empirical risks. R-ELM was proposed to enhance the limitation in the output weights by introducing a balancing parameter in the optimization of the error function. However, this improvement does not significantly reduce the structural and empirical risks since the input weights and the hidden layer biases are still randomly assigned. The finite impulse response extreme learning machine proposed by Man et al. [12] served to further improve the ELM algorithm, particularly to overcome the robustness issue of the input weights and the hidden layer biases.

In the FIR-ELM, the input weights are designed such that the hidden layer of the SLFN serves as a pre-processor to remove the effects of the input disturbances. As the output of a linear hidden neuron in a SLFN is the sum of the weighted input data, each of these hidden neurons can be treated as an FIR filter. Hence, based on the FIR filter design techniques in signal processing, the hidden layer of a SLFN can be designed as a group of low-pass, high-pass, band-pass or band-stop filters, or any other types of filter to pre-process input data with disturbance or undesired frequency components. The main advantages of such design are that the input disturbances and undesired frequency components can be removed and that both the empirical and structural risks of the SLFN can be greatly reduced. The output weight matrix in FIR-ELM is designed to further balance the empirical risk and structural risk. It is calculated based on minimizing an objective function that includes both the weighted sum of the output error squares and the weighted sum of the output weight squares of the SLFN.

It should be noted that there is one main difference between FIR-ELM and both the ELM and R-ELM. The SLFN in both ELM and R-ELM uses nonlinear hidden neurons and linear output neurons. However, in FIR-ELM, the SLFN uses both linear hidden neurons and linear output neurons. In order to assure that the SLFN with linear hidden neurons has the capability of universal approximation, an input tapped-delay-line memory with $n-1$ delay units is added to the input layer. Fig. 1 depicts the SLFN architecture of the FIR-ELM, where D is the $n-1$ time-delay element that is added to the input layer to form the tapped-delay-line memory, the input sequence $x(k),x(k-1),...,x(k-n+1)$ represents a time series consisting of the present observation $x(k)$ and the past $n-1$ observations of the process, the hidden layer has $\tilde{N}$ linear neurons and the output layer has m linear neurons.

The definition for the SLFN with $\tilde{N}$ hidden neurons and m output neurons using FIR-ELM algorithm is similar to the ELM from equation (5) to equation (9). However, instead of randomly assigned the input weights, input weights w_{ij} for the ith hidden neuron of the SLFN in FIR-ELM is obtained as follows:

$$w_{i1} = \hat{h}_{id}[0], w_{i2} = \hat{h}_{id}[1],..., w_{in} = \hat{h}_{id}[n-1] \tag{12}$$

where

$$\hat{h}_{id}[k] = \frac{1}{2\pi} \int_{-\omega c}^{\omega c} e^{-j\omega(n-1)/2} e^{j\omega k} d\omega = \frac{\sin[\omega_c(k-(n-1)/2)]}{\pi(k-(n-1)/2)} \tag{13}$$

for $0 \le k < n-1$ is the impulse response of a truncated low-pass filter for the ith hidden neuron and ω_c is the cut-off frequency of the low-pass filter. It is noted that the similar design methods can be used to design the hidden neurons as high-pass,

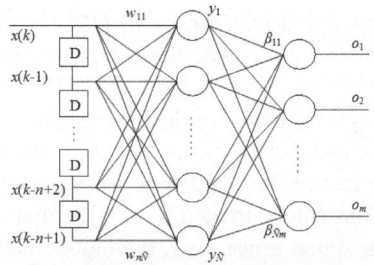

Fig. 1. The FIR-ELM network architecture with linear neurons and time-delay elements

band-pass or band-stop filter, or other types of filter for the purpose of pre-processing the input data.

The output weights for the SLFN is then calculated by minimizing both the weighted sum of the output error squares and the weighted sum of the output weights squares of the SLFN:

$$\text{Minimize } \left\{ \frac{\gamma}{2} \|\varepsilon\|^2 + \frac{d}{2} \|\beta\|^2 \right\} \tag{14}$$

$$\text{subject to } \varepsilon = \mathbf{O} - \mathbf{T} = \mathbf{H}\beta - \mathbf{T} \tag{15}$$

where γ and d are constant balancing parameters for adjusting the balance of the empirical risk and the structural risk. Hence, the output weights of the SLFN in FIR-ELM can be obtained as follows:

$$\beta = \left(\frac{d}{\gamma} \mathbf{I} + \mathbf{H}^{\mathrm{T}} \mathbf{H} \right)^{-1} \mathbf{H}^{\mathrm{T}} \mathbf{T}. \tag{16}$$

4   Simulations and Results

In order to examine the performance of the finite impulse response extreme learning machine as the machine classifier for Han Chinese folk song classification, we conducted our simulations using three classifiers: the ELM, the R-ELM and the FIR-ELM. The maximum number of hidden neurons employed in all classifiers is up to 2000 neurons. As the input weights in both ELM and R-ELM are randomly assigned, each repetition of the simulation will produce a different result. Hence, the simulations using ELM and R-ELM were repeated 50 times for the mean classification accuracy.

In FIR-ELM, the length of the FIR filter is the same as the size of the MFDMap, which is 175. The balancing parameters are set as $\gamma = 1$ and $d = 0.01$ based on empirical studies. The simulations were performed using four different types of FIR filter: low-pass, high-pass, band-pass and band-stop filters, over a range of cutoff frequencies ω_c ranging from 0.1 to 0.9 with a step size of 0.1. A band width of ± 0.05 is used for the band-pass and band-stop filters. The targets for the three classifiers are set using the 1-of-c method by assigning each of the five geographical regions to one target. For a set of targets, the one representing a particular region is assigned '1' and the remaining targets are assigned '0'.

The comparison of the classification accuracy of the three classifiers is presented in Table 1. Since both ELM and R-ELM possess arbitrary characteristics, the simulation was repeated 50 times to obtain the mean classification accuracy and this is shown in Table 1 together with their respective standard deviations. In FIR-ELM simulation, the low-pass filter performs the best among the four different filters. Hence the classification performance for FIR-ELM shown in Table 1 is the low-pass FIR-ELM with cutoff frequency at 0.3.

Table 1. Classification performance of ELM, R-ELM and low-pass FIR-ELM

Number of Hidden Neurons	ELM		R-ELM		FIR-ELM (low-pass)
	Accuracy (%)	Standard Deviation (%)	Accuracy (%)	Standard Deviation (%)	Accuracy (%)
50	51.94	7.96	55.35	6.16	29.03
100	50.77	7.22	60.97	5.80	48.39
200	44.00	7.37	63.29	5.71	61.29
500	45.03	9.15	68.45	5.91	67.74
1000	58.06	7.90	69.03	5.13	74.19
1200	60.84	5.97	70.39	5.28	**80.65**
1500	62.13	6.35	68.71	5.30	**80.65**
2000	64.97	6.29	69.74	5.29	67.74

It is fairly obvious in Table 1 that increasing the number of hidden neurons usually leads to some increase in performance for each classifier. Due to the nature of music, there is great subjectivity that makes music classification a difficult task to accomplish. Although there are differences between folk songs from various geographical regions, the divergence is not easily recognized. In the Han Chinese folk song classification, the differences between the categories are fairly subtle. Sorting these folk songs into regional source is not an obvious task even for humans. The performance shown by these machine classifiers is very encouraging.

In general, the low-pass FIR-ELM is the best classifier among the three. The R-ELM performs slightly better than ELM. The FIR-ELM shows its best performance at 1200 hidden neurons, achieving an accuracy of 80.65% while R-ELM accomplishes 70.39% accuracy and ELM 60.84% accuracy. The performance of the ELM fluctuates a little when the number of hidden neurons is less than 500 but begins to show steady improvement in performance when more hidden neurons are added and reaches 64.97% accuracy with 2000 hidden neurons. The performance of R-ELM on the other hand is fairly steady with a slight drop from 1500 hidden neurons. The low-pass FIR-ELM is the most robust among the three classifiers. Its classification accuracy improves as the number of hidden neurons increases and reaches its saturation point at 1200 hidden neurons. The FIR-ELM manages to maintain this good performance until 1500 hidden neurons before starting to show a hint of deterioration.

The learning time, in number of seconds, required for each classifier to achieve a complete learning of the music classification task is shown in Table 2 to demonstrate the performance speed of each classifier. Overall, these classifiers perform at an extremely fast speed. The maximum time required by a classifier at 2000 hidden neurons is 3.3 seconds. The low-pass FIR-ELM starts off being the fastest but eventually become the slowest among the three classifiers when the number of hidden neurons increases. The learning time required by the R-ELM is about the same as the FIR-ELM while ELM performs at a slightly faster speed than both R-ELM and FIR-ELM between 1000 to 2000 hidden neurons.

Table 2. Learning time in number of seconds for ELM, R-ELM and FIR-ELM classifiers

Number of Hidden Neurons	ELM (sec.)	R-ELM (sec.)	FIR-ELM (low-pass) (sec.)
50	0.0163	0.0049	0.0046
100	0.0270	0.0068	0.0066
200	0.0752	0.0131	0.0113
500	0.2274	0.0812	0.1022
1000	0.2910	0.4454	0.5115
1200	0.3147	0.7212	0.7566
1500	0.3562	1.3228	1.3881
2000	0.4172	2.9797	3.2972

5   Conclusion and Future Work

We have introduced our novel symbolic music encoding method known as the MFDMap. We have demonstrated the feasibility of using our MFDMap in machine classification of Han Chinese folk songs through simulations using the extreme learning machine, the regularized extreme learning machine and the finite impulse response extreme learning machine. Our simulation results have successfully shown that the finite impulse response extreme learning machine using a low-pass filter is the best classifier among the three classifiers. It is more robust especially in solving a complex task such as music classification.

In this paper, our MFDMap employed only symbolic representations of the musical features. One possible enhancement is to extend the versatility and capabilities of our MFDMap to also incorporate musical features extracted from audio signals, especially timbral related features. In addition, the corpus employed by the MFDMap can be extended to include folk songs of other geographical regions in China.

References

1. Tzanetakis, G., Cook, P.: Musical Genre Classification of Audio Signals. IEEE Transactions on Speech and Audio Processing 10, 293–302 (2002)
2. Xu, C., Maddage, N.C., Shao, X., Cao, F., Tian, Q.: Musical Genre Classification Using Support Vector Machines. In: International Conference on Acoustics, Speech and Signal Processing, pp. 429–432 (2003)
3. McKay, C., Fujinaga, I.: Automatic Genre Classification Using Large High-Level Musical Feature Sets. In: 5th International Conference on Music Information Retrieval, pp. 525–530 (2004)
4. Liu, X., Yang, D., Chen, X.: New Approach to Classification of Chinese Folk Music Based on Extension of HMM. In: International Conference on Audio, Language and Image Processing, pp. 1172–1179 (2008)
5. Xu, J., Wang, P., Yan, L.: Feature Selection for Automatic Classification of Chinese Folk Songs. In: Congress on Image and Signal Processing, pp. 441–446 (2008)

6. Hornik, K., Stinchcombe, M., White, H.: Multilayer Feedforward Network Are Universal Approximators. Neural Networks 2(5), 359–366 (1989)
7. Huang, G.-B., Zhu, Q.-Y., Siew, C.-K.: Extreme Learning Machine: Theory and Applications. Neurocomputing 70, 489–501 (2006)
8. Loh, Q.-J.B., Emmanuel, S.: ELM for Classification of Music Genres. In: International Conference on Control, Automation, Robotics and Vision, pp. 1–6 (2006)
9. Khoo, S., Man, Z., Cao, Z.: Automatic Han Chinese Folk Song Classification Using The Musical Feature Density Map. Accepted: 6th International Conference on Signal Processing and Communication Systems (2012)
10. Schaffrath, H.: The Essen Folksong Collection in Kern Format. In: Huron, D. (ed.) Menlo Park, CA (1995)
11. Deng, W., Zheng, Q., Chen, L.: Regularized Extreme Learning Machine. In: IEEE Symposium on Computational Intelligence and Data Mining, pp. 389–395 (2009)
12. Man, Z., Lee, K., Wang, D., Cao, Z., Miao, C.: A New Robust Training Algorithm for a Class of Single-Hidden Layer Feedforward Neural Networks. Neurocomputing 74, 2491–2501 (2011)

People-to-People Recommendation
Using Multiple Compatible Subgroups

Yang Sok Kim, Ashesh Mahidadia, Paul Compton, Alfred Krzywicki,
Wayne Wobcke, Xiongcai Cai, and Michael Bain

School of Computer Science and Engineering
University of New South Wales
Sydney NSW 2052, Australia
{yskim,ashesh,compton,alfredk,wobcke,xcai,mike}@cse.unsw.edu.au

Abstract. People-to-people recommendation aims at suggesting suitable
matches to people in a way that increases the likelihood of a positive interaction. This problem is more difficult than conventional item-to-people recommendation since the preferences of both parties need to be taken into account.
Previously we proposed a profile-based recommendation method that first uses
compatible subgroup rules to select a single best attribute value for each corresponding value of the user, then combines these attribute value pairs into a rule
that determines the recommendations. Though this method produces a significant improvement in the probability of an interaction being successful, it has
two significant limitations: (i) by considering only single matching attribute
values the method ignores cases where different attribute values are closely related, missing potential candidates, and (ii) when ranking candidates for recommendation the method does not consider individual behaviour. This paper
addresses these two issues, showing how multiple attributes can be used
with compatible subgroup rules and individual reply rates used for ranking
candidates. Our experimental results show that the new approach significantly
improves the probability of an interaction being successful compared to our
previous approach.

Keywords: recommender systems, social network analysis.

1 Introduction

Social networks connect people in the world. To extend them, many social network
web sites have been developed. People in online social networks communicate using
messages. To establish a successful social interaction, a user, called here a **sender**,
sends a message to another user, called here a **receiver**, and the receiver should reply
positively to the sender. The success of the interaction depends on **reciprocal interests** between the sender and the receiver. Therefore it is desirable for social networks
to provide sophisticated services that encourage successful social interactions between
users. People-to-people recommenders address exactly this issue. People-to-people
recommenders differ from the conventional item-to-people recommenders since they
need to take into account the preferences of both sender and receiver.

M. Thielscher and D. Zhang (Eds.): AI 2012, LNCS 7691, pp. 61–72, 2012.
© Springer-Verlag Berlin Heidelberg 2012

This research focuses on the problem of recommending suitable matches in an online dating social network. Unlike other social networks, online dating site members usually provide accurate and detailed information about themselves since this is the primary source of information potential partners use to find them. People who have (one or more of) the same attribute values are called here a **subgroup**, and it has been reported that people in the same subgroup usually have similar preference patterns [1]. Our people-to-people recommendation method, called **Compatible Subgroup Rules (CSR)** [2], is based on this property. The term 'compatible subgroup' means that a subgroup is more interested in another subgroup compared to other subgroups, and vice versa. The degree of compatibility is is measured by a **compatibility score**, which is calculated using past interaction data (training data). A rule is defined to suggest a compatible subgroup for a given subgroup containing the active user. Recommendation rules are constructed from training data that contains information for senders, receivers, interaction results (positive or negative), and attribute values of the sender and the receiver, as follows. For a given subgroup defined by an attribute value of the active user, the method finds its compatible subgroup defined by a value of the *same* attribute using the training data. The attribute values of the identified compatible subgroups are incrementally combined together to increase the probability of success interaction. This attribute combination process finishes if there is no significant interaction between a user subgroup and its compatible subgroup in the training data. The most specialised compatible subgroups are used to propose recommendations. This method shows a 26% success rate for the top 10 recommendations and 23% for the top 100 recommendations, considerably greater than the 15% baseline success rate [3].

In spite of its success, this previous method has the following limitations. First, the method only chooses a *single* compatible subgroup for each subgroup defined by the active user's attribute value. It ignores the fact that an attribute may have multiple values that result in very similar compatibility scores to the active user subgroup. Since candidates having the similar (but not best) attribute value are not recommended, many suitable candidates for recommendation may be missed. Second, the method only measures a compatibility score using the sender's interest in the receiver subgroup without considering other possible interest measures. Finally, the method ranks the candidate receivers using the compatibility scores of the *age* and *location* attributes, which does not take into account individual interactions. This paper addresses these limitations and presents several extended CSR methods. The extended CSR methods utilise multiple compatible subgroups based on heuristics for including multiple values for an attribute, include various compatibility score measures, and consider the individual activities of compatible subgroup members to rank the recommended candidates. We conducted experiments to evaluate the extended CSR methods using historical data from a commercial online dating site. Our experimental results show that the best new proposed method significantly improves the probability of successful interactions compared to the CSR method based on single attribute values.

2   Related Work

A recommender system is a system that learns a user's preferences and makes recommendations the user might like. Recommender systems can be classified into item-to-people and people-to-people recommenders [4,5]. Item-to-people recommendation has been studied from the early stages of the Web, and has been applied in various domains. Although there is some non-Web research [6,7], people-to-people recommendation has recently gained attention as social networks become popular on the Web [8–10]. People-to-people recommender systems have been used to recommend experts [7,11,12], friends [10,13] and collaborators [14], etc. Our research has focused on recommending partners in online dating. Methods for people-to-people recommendation can be classified into behaviour-based methods, profile-based methods and hybrid methods. Behaviour-based methods exploit interaction data between users such as contact between users, comments posted on another user's page, following relationships to other users, etc. Typically a collaborative filtering approach is used to identify similar users and generate candidate users using interaction data [15,16]. Profile-based methods use user-supplied data to suggest candidate recommendations [6,11–13,17]. Hybrid methods combine behaviour-based and profile-based methods [8]. We previously proposed a profile-based recommendation method that uses subgroup interaction data to find a compatible subgroup based on a user's profile [2]. We also proposed hybrid methods that combine our interaction-based collaborative filtering approach with our profile-based method [3]. In this paper, our research focuses on extending our previous profile-based approach, but it could easily be combined with interaction-based collaborative filtering in ways similar to those described in [3].

3 Recommendation Methods

3.1 Definitions

Definition 1. A **user** u is a member of the social network website and is described by n distinct attribute values for n different attributes:

$$u = \{u_1, \dots, u_n\}$$

where u_i represents the value of attribute i. The user provides these attribute values when joining the site and can update them at any time. The site allows the user to select only one value for each attribute. Regardless of type, e.g. numeric for number of children or date for date of birth, all values are converted into nominal values before recommendation rules are constructed.

Definition 2. A **subgroup** is a group of users who have the same gender and the same values for one or more attributes. For example, the female postgraduate subgroup consists of the female users who have value *postgraduate* for the *education* attribute.

Definition 3. A **contact** is an action where a user, the **sender,** sends a message to another user, the **receiver.** Such a contact indicates that the sender is interested in the receiver.

Definition 4. An **interaction** between two users is a contact from a sender to a receiver with either a reply from the receiver to the sender or no reply (if the receiver chooses to ignore the contact). An interaction is classified as either positive or negative depending on the receiver's reply message type (which is defined by the system), and if the receiver does not reply to the sender, the interaction is classified as negative. An interaction always shows that the sender is interested in the receiver, but the receiver may or may not be interested in the sender.

Definition 5. A **sender (receiver) subgroup** is the set of senders (receivers) in a set of interactions. Sender subgroups are denoted sg; receiver subgroups are denoted rg.

3.2 Interest Measures

Interest measures show how much the members of one subgroup are interested in the members of another, and are calculated using the number of interactions between them. Interest measures in this work are computed from interaction data for the training period (three months before the time of recommendation). We define four types of interest measure reflecting different intuitions.

Definition 6. Interest in target group measures how much more a sender subgroup sg contacts a receiver subgroup rg compared to all receivers R. This is defined as:

$$P(sg,rg) = \frac{n(sg,rg)}{n(sg,R)}$$

where $n(sg,rg)$ is the number of messages sent from the sender subgroup sg to the receiver subgroup rg and $n(sg,R)$ is the number of messages sent from the sender subgroup sg to all receivers R.

Definition 7. Lift in interest in target group measures how much more a sender subgroup sg, compared to all senders S, is interested in a receiver subgroup rg. This is defined as:

$$L(sg,rg) = \frac{P(sg,rg)}{P(S,rg)}$$

where $P(sg,rg)$ is the sender subgroup sg's interest in the receiver subgroup rg, and $P(S,rg)$ is all sender S's interest in the receiver subgroup rg, as in Definition 6.

Definition 8. Success with target group measures how much more successful a sender subgroup sg is when contacting a receiver subgroup rg compared to all receivers R. This is defined as:

$$P(sg,rg,+) = \frac{n(sg,rg,+)}{n(sg,rg)}$$

where $n(sg,rg,+)$ is the number of messages sent from the sender subgroup sg to the receiver subgroup rg with positive replies from the receivers, and $n(sg,rg)$ is the number of messages sent from the sender subgroup sg to the receiver subgroup rg.

Definition 9. Lift in success with target group measures how much more successful a sender subgroup sg is when contacting a receiver subgroup rg compared to all receivers R, relative to the improvement in success for all senders S. This is defined as:

$$L(sg,rg,+) = \frac{P(sg,rg,+)}{P(S,rg,+)}$$

where $P(sg, rg, +)$ is the sender subgroup sg's success with the receiver subgroup rg and $P(S, rg, +)$ is the success of all senders S with the receiver subgroup rg.

3.3   Compatibility Score

In this research, the term 'compatibility' means that a sender subgroup is interested in a receiver subgroup, and vice versa. The compatibility score measures the degree of compatibility of two subgroups. To dampen significant differences between two subgroup interests in each other, we use the harmonic mean to combine the two reciprocal interest measures.

Definition 10. A **compatibility score** between a sender subgroup sg and a receiver subgroup rg measures how much two subgroups are interested in each other. It is defined as:

$$cs(sg, rg) = \frac{2I_{sg, rg} I_{rg, sg}}{I_{sg, rg} + I_{rg, sg}}$$

where $I_{sg,rg}$ is the interest of sender subgroup sg in the receiver subgroup rg and $I_{rg,sg}$ is the interest of rg in sg. Note that there are different compatibility scores for a sender and receiver subgroup depending on the particular interest measure.

3.4   Learning Compatible Subgroup Rules

Compatible subgroup rules are used to recommend candidate receivers for a given user [2,3]. A compatible subgroup rule has the form:

if $a_1 = u_1$ **and** ... **and** $a_m = u_m$ **then** $a_1 = v_1$ **and** ... **and** $a_m = v_m$

where each a_i is an attribute (e.g. *occupation*) and each v_i is the best matching value of this attribute for candidates to the value u_i of the user. The meaning of the rule is that if a user satisfies the condition part of the rule, the system should recommend candidates satisfying the conclusion part of the rule.

The above approach is, however, limited in that for a given user attribute value, only a **single attribute value** of the candidate is chosen. When the candidate attribute values are closely related, many acceptable candidates are therefore not recommended. As an example, the *occupation* attribute has values *legal*, *accounting* and *consulting*, which the data indicates are all very similar in compatibility for the value of *legal* for the *occupation* attribute of the user. To allow for rules with multiple attribute values, we generalize the form of the compatible subgroup rule as follows:

if $a_1 = u_1$ **and** ... **and** $a_m = u_m$ **then** $a_1 \in V_1$ **and** ... **and** $a_m \in V_m$

where each a_i is an attribute (e.g. *occupation*) and each V_i is a set of compatible **multiple attribute values** of this attribute for candidates to the value u_i of the user (equivalently, we treat each condition $a_i \in V_i$ as a disjunction of equality tests).

Our recommendation algorithm based on compatible subgroup rules is as follows. Let a user have attribute values $\{u_1, ..., u_n\}$ for attributes $\{a_1, ..., a_n\}$. Rules are constructed for each user individually. Rule construction starts with an empty rule (no condition and no conclusion) and produces a sequence of more and more specific rules $R_1, ..., R_m$. At each step, starting with a rule R, an attribute a *with value* u of the user is chosen that has the highest subgroup success rate; $a = u$ is added to the condition of the rule and $a \in V$ is added to the conclusion of the rule, where V is the set of compatible values for the gender (male/female) of the sender (see below). These conditions are added to the rule only if it improves the overall rule success rate $SR(sg, rg)$ defined as follows, and this improvement is statistically significant:

$$SR(sg, rg) = \frac{n(sg, rg, +)}{n(sg, rg)}$$

where sg is the sender subgroup defined by the current rule condition and rg is the receiver subgroup defined by the current rule conclusion.

The two main aspects of the recommendation algorithm are finding multiple compatible subgroups (making use of heuristics to combine single attribute values into sets of compatible attribute values), and generating and ranking candidate receivers.

Finding Multiple Compatible Subgroups. For a user with value u of attribute a, the set of compatible attribute values V is determined as follows. First, for all possible values v_i of a, the compatibility score of v_i with u is calculated using Definition 10, giving a distribution of scores. The mean and standard deviation of this set is calculated. A value is included in the set V if its score is at least 0.5 standard deviations above the mean (this heuristic is based on preliminary experimental analysis).

For example, Figure 1 illustrates compatibility scores of different female age subgroups with the male age 35–39 subgroup. The female age 35–39 subgroup is the most compatible subgroup. However, it also shows that the female age 30–34 subgroup has a very similar compatibility score to the age 35–39 subgroup. Both are included in the set V.

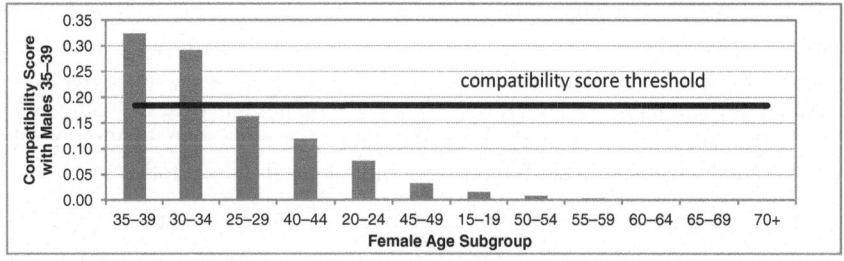

Fig. 1. Multiple Compatible Subgroups: Compatibility scores for male age 35–39 subgroup with female age subgroups. The threshold line shows the mean plus 0.5 standard deviations.

Attribute	Condition (User Value)	Conclusion (Compatible Values)	Rule Success Rate
gender	male	female	14.9%
age	42	35–39 OR 45–49 OR 30–34	14.7%
location	Sydney-North	Sydney-East OR Sydney-North	15.2%
education	Graduate	Graduate OR Diploma	32.7%
smoke	Don't smoke	Don't smoke	37.5%
...	...	...	...
drink	Occasionally	Occasionally	54.5%

Fig. 2. Compatible Subgroup Rules: Each row represents a pair of conditions successively added to the rule where multiple attribute values for each user attribute are chosen. As conditions are added, the rule success rate increases but the number of potential candidates decreases.

Figure 2 illustrates an example rule of rule construction for a hypothetical male user, starting with *gender*. First *age* is considered. Since the user is 42, he is in the age band 40–44; the best set of female age bands are 35–39, 45–49 and 30–34. Accordingly the disjunction of these conditions for the female is added to the rule. Rule construction continues with the *location* attribute, where the male is in Sydney-North. The set of compatible values for the female are Sydney-East and Sydney-North. Continuing this process to define a sequence of rules, the rules become more and more specific, but generate fewer and fewer candidates.

Generating and Ranking Candidate Receivers. Given the sequence of rules $R_1, \ldots, R_m$ generated as above, the potential recommendations are all candidates satisfying the conclusion part of any such rule who were active in the previous 28 days (but only as many candidates as needed are generated, starting with the most specific rule R_m). Candidates satisfying a more specific rule R_i are ranked higher than those only satisfying a rule R_j where $j < i$. However, candidates satisfying the same rule are ranked as follows, using data from the previous 28 days. First, candidates are ordered in terms of positive reply rate (defined as the proportion of contacts received to which the candidate has given a positive reply). Second, if positive reply rates are equal, the number of positive replies is used to order the candidates (those with a larger number are ranked higher). Third, if two candidates are still equally ranked, they are ranked in order of the number of contacts received (again, those who received more contacts are ranked higher). Finally, any ties between remaining candidates are broken randomly.

4   Experimental Design

To evaluate the proposed new methods for defining compatible subgroup rules using multiple attributes with different interest measures and the new way of ranking candidates, we used the same experimental setup previously used for single attribute compatible subgroup rules [3]. In these experiments we used data from a commercial online dating site and generated recommendations once, for March 1, 2010, using only data that would have been available on that date. For evaluation of the recommendation methods, we collected two types of data – interaction data and user profile data. Profile data consists of basic information about the user, such as age, location, marital and family status, plus attributes such as smoking and drinking habits, education and occupation. Each interaction is recorded with a date/time stamp, the type of message and the response message type, which is labelled as either positive or negative, or null if no reply has been received (contacts without reply are classified as negative). We used historical data to evaluate the recommendation methods. The following datasets were collected for the experiment:

— **Rule Learning Data**: This dataset consists of interaction data and user profile data for the users who were the senders and/or receivers of interactions for three months prior to the recommendation construction date.   There were about 5 million interactions by 200,000 users. The collected data was used to learn the recommendation rules.
— **Active User Data**: This dataset consists of active user profiles and their interaction data for 28 days prior to the recommendation construction date. The collected dataset is used to generate candidate receivers using the recommendation rules. There are about 137,000 active users.
— **Test Data**: This dataset consists of interactions from the first three weeks of March 2010 initiated by the active users. The test set consists of around 130,000 users with around 650,000 interactions, of which roughly 15% are positive interactions.

After collecting these datasets, we generated up to 100 candidate receivers for each active user using our recommendation methods, with candidate receivers ranked as defined above. We then examined whether or not the data showed positive or negative test interactions with the candidate receivers. Note that we did not provide users with actual recommendations; the method compares the recommendations with the interactions that occurred in the test set with people who would have been recommended.

The two main metrics are precision and recall for the top N recommendations, where N = 10, 20, ..., 100. **Precision** measures the proportion of recommended interactions that occurred which were positive, so is analogous to the user's success rate when adopting the recommendations. More precisely, if R is the set of recommended interactions and T is the test set, precision is defined as follows, where T^+ is the set of positive interactions in T and $n(S)$ the number of elements in the set S.

$$precision = \frac{n(R \cap T^+)}{n(R \cap T)}$$

A high precision suggests that the recommendations are useful, while a low precision suggests the recommendations are not helpful. Note that this measure can be considered the probability that an interaction resulting from a recommendation is positive. Therefore, we can compare this result with the baseline probability of an interaction being positive (without recommendation).

Recall measures how many of the positive test interactions are included within the top N recommendations, so is analogous to how much the users liked the recommendations. This is measured by the proportion of positive interactions recommended that are positive interactions in the test set.

$$recall = \frac{n(R \cap T^+)}{n(T^+)}$$

This measure indicates whether positive interactions are likely to happen when the recommendations are given to users. If the probability of an interaction being positive (precision) is very high, but such interactions are unlikely to occur, those recommendations are not particularly useful. Therefore, for recommendation methods where the precision is similar, a high recall is a good indicator that the recommendations are better. Even though we have used precision and recall as our evaluation metrics, they differ from the conventional use. Normally such measures are applied to a test set where each item is known to be relevant or irrelevant, but in our experiments we calculate these measures based on the interactions that occurred in historical data. Since these actually occurring interactions are only a very small subset of all possible interactions (around 650,000 out of 4.7 billion), and since we generate only a limited number of recommendations (only up to 100 for each user), the intersection of the recommended interactions and the test set interactions is very small. This results in very small recall results in our experiments. Nevertheless, recall is a useful metric for comparing different methods on how much users like the given recommendations.

5   Results

5.1   Precision and Recall with Candidate Behaviour-Based Ranking

The basic comparison of our methods is shown in Figure 3, which shows precision and recall for the top N recommendations for our previous method based on **single attribute values** [2,3] (ranked using the harmonic mean of the compatibility scores for *age* and *location* under Definition 6), and four new methods based on compatible subgroup rules using **multiple attribute values** with the four different interest measures (Definitions 6–9) and behaviour-based ranking as described in Section 3.4.

The first observation is that all methods based on multiple attributes have a much higher precision (for all values of N) than the previous method based on single attributes. Second, though the methods using interest measures based on successful interactions show the highest precision, recall is very low for these methods, suggesting that the rules used to generate the recommendations are too specific. In other words, the fraction of the candidate receivers that show a high success rate is usually very small, and combining several of those compatible values results in very successful interactions, but these interactions very rarely occur in the historical data.

Thus the methods based on just **multiple attribute values** with **interest in target group** and **multiple attribute values** with **lift in interest in target group** perform best, with similar precision and much higher recall than the methods using interest measures based on successful interactions. The method using **interest in target group** is slightly superior. Moreover, the recall is higher than that based on **single attribute values,** giving evidence that these methods based on **multiple attribute values** with behaviour-based ranking are generating better candidates.

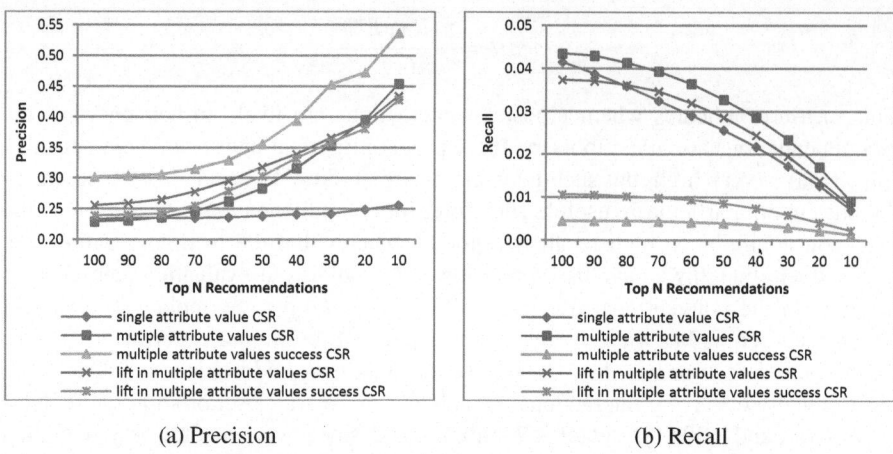

(a) Precision   (b) Recall

Fig. 3. Precision and Recall with Candidate Behaviour-Based Ranking

5.2   Precision and Recall without Candidate Behaviour-Based Ranking

To examine whether the improvement over the previous single attribute method is due to the ranking or to the method of constructing rules by combining multiple attributes, precision and recall for the methods without using behaviour-based ranking are shown in Figure 4. In this case, the candidate receivers are only ranked by the compatible subgroup rules, with ties broken randomly (hence it is expected that precision will be lower). In fact, the precision for the methods based on **multiple attribute values** without success is much lower than in Figure 3, similar to that for **single attribute values**, though slightly higher with **lift in interest in target group.** Recall, however, is comparable to the method based on **single attribute values**. The results show that the ranking method is critical to the increased precision of the methods.

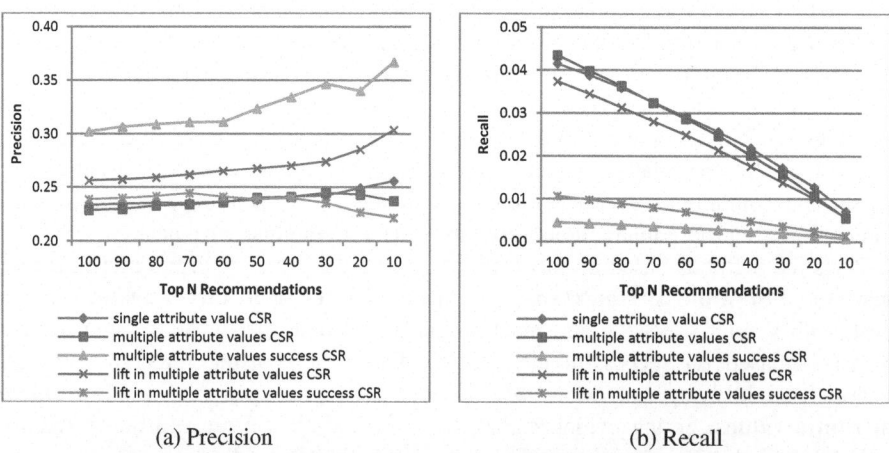

(a) Precision   (b) Recall

Fig. 4. Precision and Recall without Candidate Behaviour-Based Ranking

6   Conclusion

This paper presented several extensions of a profile-based method for people-to-people recommendation based on compatible subgroup rules. We proposed four types of interest measures, and a new way of combining several compatible attribute values in rule construction, and a ranking method based on candidate behaviour. Our experimental results show that a new method based on **multiple attribute values** with **interest in target group** has much higher precision than the other methods and higher recall than our previous method based on **single attribute values,** indicating that the recommendations generates using this method are of higher quality. Our results also show that candidate behaviour-based ranking is very effective in reordering the candidate receivers. In other work [3], we combined single attribute compatible subgroup rule recommendation with interaction-based collaborative filtering [15] and obtained significant improvements in precision and recall. We expect that our new methods are also likely to improve the performance of such hybrid recommendation methods, but this has not yet been evaluated. This will be the subject of further work.

Acknowledgements. This work was funded by Smart Services Cooperative Research Centre. We would also like to thank our industry partners for providing the datasets.

References

[1] McPherson, M., Smith-Lovin, L., Cook, J.M.: Birds of a Feather: Homophily in Social Networks. Annual Review of Sociology 27, 415–444 (2001)

[2] Kim, Y.S., Mahidadia, A., Compton, P., Cai, X., Bain, M., Krzywicki, A., Wobcke, W.: People Recommendation Based on Aggregated Bidirectional Intentions in Social Network Site. In: Kang, B.-H., Richards, D. (eds.) PKAW 2010. LNCS, vol. 6232, pp. 247–260. Springer, Heidelberg (2010)

[3] Kim, Y.S., Krzywicki, A., Wobcke, W., Mahidadia, A., Compton, P., Cai, X., Bain, M.: Hybrid Techniques to Address Cold Start Problems for People to People Recommendation in Social Networks. In: Anthony, P., Ishizuka, M., Lukose, D. (eds.) PRICAI 2012. LNCS, vol. 7458, pp. 206–217. Springer, Heidelberg (2012)

[4] Pizzato, L., Rej, T., Chung, T., Koprinska, I., Kay, J.: RECON: A Reciprocal Recommenderfor Online Dating. In: Proceedings of the Fourth ACM Conference on Recommender Systems, pp. 207–214 (2010)

[5] Pizzato, L., Rej, T., Akehurst, J., Koprinska, I., Yacef, K., Kay, J.: Recommending People to People: The Nature of Reciprocal Recommenders with a Case Study in Online Dating. User Modeling and User-Adapted Interaction (2012)

[6] Belkin, N.J.: Helping People Find What They Don't Know. Communications of the ACM 43(8), 58–61 (2000)

[7] McDonald, D.W., Ackerman, M.S.: Expertise Recommender: A Flexible Recommendation System and Architecture. In: Proceedings of the 2000 ACM Conference on Computer Supported Cooperative Work, pp. 231–240 (2000)

[8] Kazienko, P., Musiał, K.: Recommendation Framework for Online Social Networks. In: Last, M., Szczepaniak, P., Volkovich, Z., Kandel, A. (eds.) Advances in Web Intelligence and Data Mining, pp. 111–120. Springer, Berlin (2006)

[9] Yu, S.J.: The Dynamic Competitive Recommendation Algorithm in Social Network Services. Information Sciences 187, 1–14 (2012)

[10] Naruchitparames, J., Giine, M.H., Louis, S.J.: Friend Recommendations in Social Networks Using Genetic Algorithms and Network Topology. In: Proceedings of the 2011 IEEE Congress on Evolutionary Computation (CEC), pp. 2207–2214 (2011)

[11] Moraes, A., Silva, E., da Trindade, C., Barbosa, Y., Meira, S.: Recommending Experts Using Communication History. In: Proceedings of the 2nd International Workshop on Recommendation Systems for Software Engineering, pp. 41–45 (2010)

[12] Shami, N.S., Yuan, Y.C., Cosley, D., Xia, L., Gay, G.: That's What Friends are For: Facilitating 'Who Knows What' Across Group Boundaries. In: Proceedings of the 2007 International ACM Conference on Supporting Group Work, pp. 379–382 (2007)

[13] Chen, J., Geyer, W., Dugan, C., Muller, M., Guy, I.: Make New Friends, But Keep the Old: Recommending People on Social Networking Sites. In: Proceedings of the 27th International Conference on Human Factors in Computing Systems, pp. 201–210 (2009)

[14] McDonald, D.W.: Recommending Collaboration with Social Networks: A Comparative Evaluation. In: Proceedings of the SIGCHI Conference on Human Factors in Computing Systems, pp. 593–600 (2003)

[15] Krzywicki, A., Wobcke, W., Cai, X., Mahidadia, A., Bain, M., Compton, P., Kim, Y.S.: Interaction-Based Collaborative Filtering Methods for Recommendation in Online Dating. In: Chen, L., Triantafillou, P., Suel, T. (eds.) WISE 2010. LNCS, vol. 6488, pp. 342–356. Springer, Heidelberg (2010)

[16] Pizzato, L.A., Silvestrini, C.: Stochastic Matching and Collaborative Filtering to Recommend People to People. In: Proceedings of the Fifth ACM Conference on Recommender Systems, pp. 341–344 (2011)

[17] Cai, X., Bain, M., Krzywicki, A., Wobcke, W., Kim, Y.S., Compton, P., Mahidadia, A.: Learning to Make Social Recommendations: A Model-Based Approach. In: Tang, J., King, I., Chen, L., Wang, J. (eds.) ADMA 2011, Part II. LNCS, vol. 7121, pp. 124–137. Springer, Heidelberg (2011)

Automatic Scoring of Erythema and Scaling Severity in Psoriasis Diagnosis

Juan Lu[1,*], Ed Kazmiercazk[1], Jonathan H. Manton[2], and Rodney Sinclair[3]

[1] Department of Computing and Information Systems, University of Melbourne
[2] Department of Electrical and Electronic Engineering, University of Melbourne
[3] Department of Medicine(Dermatology), University of Melbourne,
and St. Vincent's Hospital Melbourne
jualu@student.unimelb.edu.au,
{edmundak,jmanton,rodneyds}@unimelb.edu.au

Abstract. Psoriasis is a common skin disease with no known cure. It is both subjective and time consuming to evaluate the severity of psoriasis lesions using manual methods. More objective automated methods are in great demand in both psoriasis research and in clinical practice. This paper presents an algorithm for scoring the severity of psoriasis lesions from 2D digital skin images. The algorithm uses the redness of the inflamed skin, or erythema, and the relative area and roughness of the flaky scaled skin, or scaling, in lesions to score lesion severity. The algorithm is validated by comparing the severity scores given by the algorithm against those given by dermatologists and against other automated severity scoring techniques.

Keywords: Skin image analysis, Severity modelling, Classification, Computer-aided diagnosis, Psoriasis.

1 Introduction

Psoriasis is a chronic skin disease with no known cure. It manifests as lesions consisting of red inflamed and itchy skin (*erythema*) and scaly flaky skin (*scaling*). There are an estimated 125 million people worldwide suffering this disease. In Australia, the percentage of affected people is between 2%-5% [1]. As there is no known cure, a great deal of effort has been expended on finding good treatments for psoriasis symptoms. However, no treatment is generally accepted and different physicians will treat the same symptoms differently. There is a need to compare various treatment methods objectively to determine which treatment is more effective in both psoriasis research and in clinical practice. Psoriasis severity scores are commonly used for comparing treatments [2].

The severity score is a number that is used to classify the severity of psoriasis. A number of severity scores have been proposed in recent decades [3–5]. A widely used severity score is the *Psoriasis Area and Severity Index*, or PASI

---

* Corresponding author.

M. Thielscher and D. Zhang (Eds.): AI 2012, LNCS 7691, pp. 73–84, 2012.

score [6]. The PASI score is calculated by dividing the body into a number of regions and grading the severity of the erythema (the red inflamed skin), and the severity of the scaling (the scaly, flaky skin typically found inside a lesion) within a region [6]. The severity of erythema and scaling in PASI scores are estimated visually often leading to significant inter- and intra- individual variation in scores. Further, PASI scores require that the symptoms of several lesions are estimated which greatly increases the workload of dermatologists. An objective and automatic scoring method will greatly help reduce variation in scoring and help to improve treatment research and clinical outcomes for patients as well as reducing the workload for clinicians.

Table 1 gives the different classes of PASI scores and some examples of lesions that would have the corresponding classification.

Table 1. PASI Erythema and Scaling Severity Intensity Scoring

Scores	Grade	Erythema scoring	Erythema images	Scaling scoring	Scaling images
1	Mild	Light red		Fine scaling covering part of the lesion	
2	Moderate	Red,but not dark red		Fine to rough scaling covering a large part of the lesion	
3	Severe	Dark red		Rough, thick scaling covering a large part of the lesion	
4	Very severe	Very dark red		Very rough, very thick scaling totally covering the lesion	

The aim of this paper is to give a procedure for automatically estimating the severity of erythema and scaling using 2D digital skin images and the PASI severity scale for erythema and scaling.

Computer aided methods for psoriasis severity scoring have been under investigation for a number of decades [7]. In [8] the severity scores for erythema are correlated with the hue (H) value and saturation (S) value in the HSV colour model. The colour differences between psoriasis lesions and normal skin were investigated in [9] which concludes that the distribution of erythema severity is correlated with the difference in hue value.

However, in [8, 9] the colour value is sampled randomly ignoring the variation in lesion and skin colour to assess psoriasis severity. The colours of pigments in lesions are used by [10] to derive mean colour values in RGB colours space and then these are used to grade the severity of lesions using K-Nearest Neighbours.

To the best of our knowledge the only work that attempts to grade the severity of scaling is given in [10], where the severity of scaling is derived by building a decision tree using the area of scaling inside the lesion to determine the lesion severity.

The algorithm presented in this paper differs by deriving a series of features that relate to the redness of erythema, the relative area of scaling and *roughness* of scaling, to evaluate the severity of erythema and scaling in lesions. The features used in this paper are based on a haemoglobin and melanin colour space [11] and the relative scaling area and texture [12]. Haemoglobin is related to the red colour in skin and melanin is related to the yellow and brown colour in skin. The algorithm and the severity features proposed are validated using multivariable analysis and classification evaluation.

2   A Method for Scoring the Severity of Symptoms: Erythema and Scaling in Psoriasis Lesions

2.1   Segmenting Erythema and Scaling in 2D Digital Skin Images

The severity scoring algorithm depends on first being able to identify psoriasis lesions. A typical psoriasis lesion is composed of an area of red inflamed skin (erythema) that surrounds an area of raised, rough scaly skin. Psoriasis lesions can also manifest as just erythema or as patches of scaly skin that are only partially surrounded by erythema. In our previous work an algorithm for segmenting erythema from normal skin is given in [11] and for segmenting scaling from erythema and normal skin is given in [12].

In [11] there are two key steps in the segmentation of erythema: (**1**) the decomposition of skin colour into **melanin** and **haemoglobin** components; and (**2**) erythema classification. Firstly, two independent components are extracted in the log RGB colour space using Independent Component Analysis, which correlates well with the haemoglobin and melanin.

Assuming that the variation in skin colour in the image are caused by melanin and haemoglobin and that melanin and haemoglobin are mutually independent then skin colour can be expressed as a linear combination of the melanin and haemoglobin components. A simple model of skin colour in the RGB colour space in terms of melanin and haemoglobin components is given by:

$$L_{x,y} = c^m q_{x,y}^m + c^h q_{x,y}^h + \Delta \tag{1}$$

where c^m and c^h are the melanin and haemoglobin basis vectors in the RGB colour space, $q_{x,y}^m$ and $q_{x,y}^h$ are the quantities of each pigment for the skin colour $L_{x,y}$ at coordinate (x, y), and Δ is a constant vector that depends on other skin pigments and skin structure. Secondly, a Support Vector Machine (SVM) is then used to separate erythema pixels from normal skin using the erythema features $q_{x,y}^m$ and $q_{x,y}^h$.

Scaling is segmented from normal skin and erythema using a classification algorithm composed of the following steps:

Step 1. A **scaling colour contrast filter** is constructed using the L^* component and the a^* component in the $L^*a^*b^*$ colour space. The filter heightens the contrast between the whiter scaling pixels and the surrounding red erythema pixels.

The filter is a good differentiator of scaling from erythema but does not always give enough contrast to differentiate scaling from normal skin, especially under bright lights or if the skin is pale like scaly skin in a lesion.

Step 2. Scaling, which is rough, can be differentiated from normal skin, which is smooth, based on texture. Gabor filters have proved a useful tool for estimating the degree of 'roughness' and so are used here.

The second step is to derive a set of Gabor responses for each pixel in the image using a bank of Gabor filters tuned for different directions and spatial frequencies. The resulting **Gabor feature** in the image can be displayed using a gray-scale value that captures the degree of *'roughness'* at the pixel.

Step 3. The Gabor features together with the colour contrast features obtained from the scaling colour contrast filter are then used to segment scaling from normal skin using a SVM smoothed by a Markov Random Field (MRF), which properly classifies any pixels that are misclassified by the SVM.

Figure 1 shows the segmentation of erythema and scaling in a psoriasis lesion.

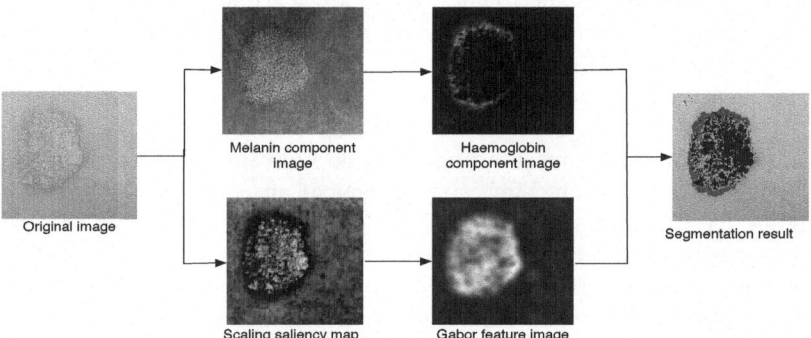

Fig. 1. Segmentation of erythema and scaling: segmented erythema is marked in red, and segmented scaling is marked in blue

2.2 Determining the Severity of the Psoriasis Lesions Using Erythema and Scalingness

In this paper we view erythema and scaling scoring as a multiclass classification problem. The erythema and scaling are can be simply referred as symptom type I and symptom type II respectively.

The input is a 2D digital image of a lesion described by a set F with a series of features depending on the symptom type that is being scored. Ignoring the zero score due to its non-ambiguity in the clinical scoring, the output will be the set $C = \{1 := \text{Mild}, 2 := \text{Moderate}, 3 := \text{Severe}, 4 := \text{Very severe}\}$. The classification function P is built, such that $P : F \rightarrow C$.

The rule of PASI guidelines for scoring the symptom type I erythema is based on the colour of the lesion (as shown in Table 1). The deeper the red colour, the higher the severity score.

The haemoglobin and melanin components are the features used for scoring erythema. Note that dermatologists score erythema by comparing with the surrounding normal skin and so we employ the relative haemoglobin and relative melanin features, $\nabla \overline{q^h}$ and $\nabla \overline{q^m}$, in our classification algorithm. The erythema severity feature set is given by $F = \{\nabla \overline{q^h}, \nabla \overline{q^m}\}$, where $\nabla \overline{q^h}$ is the mean difference of haemoglobin values between erythema and normal skin, and $\nabla \overline{q^m}$ is the mean difference of melanin values between erythema and the normal skin in the lesion.

Scoring of erythema is done by a KNN for its simplicity, where $K = 5$ has been empirically determined. The severity of erythema is decided by the majority training samples in the K nearest neighbourhoods.

The PASI scoring of symptom type II: scaling is also shown in Table 1. The severity scoring rule is based on the roughness of the scaling and the area of scaling relative to the whole lesion.

The features used to differentiate scaling from erythema and normal skin are thus $F = \{\overline{g}, r\}$, where $\overline{g}$ is the mean value of Gabor features describing the degree of roughness and r is the ratio of scaling area to the whole lesion area.

The performance of the C4.5 decision tree used in our algorithm is better than a range of other classification methods which was determined empirically for the scaling severity classification problem. The decision tree is split based on a normalised information gain criterion, followed by post-pruning to avoid the over-fitting [13].

3   Validating the Method

3.1   The Experimental Design

Samples of psoriasis skin images are collected from the Skin & Cancer Foundation Victoria, where the imaging environment is carefully set to ensure controlled illumination. The images used in the comparison were those that were given the same PASI scores by two dermatologists.

The proposed algorithm is validated based linear correlation and classification performance. The linear correlation between the features used in our method with the severity scores given by dermatologists is analysed first. Then the classification accuracy of our scoring method is compared with other scoring systems.

In the linear correlation stage, a t-test is used to measure the correlation based on the hypothesis that the observation of one class is at least as extreme as another class. The resulting p-values and F-values are shown. Moreover, correlation between severity scores and severity features is analysed using correlation coefficients. The analysis shows a linear relationship using a normalised covariance.

In the classification performance evaluation stage, classification accuracy is calculated as the percentage of correctly classified samples. In our experiment, the classification accuracy for each severity degree is evaluated by a 10-fold cross validation. Assuming the accuracy difference between two classifiers is a t-distribution, by setting the confidence level to be 0.95, the confidence interval of true accuracy difference is analysed. If zero is not in the range of the confidence interval, the performance of two classifiers is significantly different.

3.2   Symptom Type I: Erythema Severity Scoring

There are 88 images of erythema lesions spanning a number of different skin types and ethnicities, where 10 samples score 1, 31 samples score 2, 37 samples score 3, and 10 samples score 4.

Linear Correlation Analysis. The result of linear correlation between erythema severity and colour features is shown in Table 2. Table 2 also shows relative hue component $\nabla \overline{H^{ab}}$ used in [9], and relative spectral components $\nabla \overline{R}$, $\nabla \overline{G}$, $\nabla \overline{B}$ from the RGB colour space proposed in [10]. The relative colour component features are defined to be the difference of mean values between erythema and normal skin. Specifically, the hue component in [9] is defined as the arctangent of ratio of a^* component to b^* component in the $L^* a^* b^*$ colour space.

The distribution of the melanin and haemoglobin components with changes to erythema severity intensity is presented with box plots in Figure 2. Notice that though mean values of the melanin component, haemoglobin component and their summation are linearly related with the severity intensity in general, it is hard to distinguish erythema severity by setting thresholding values alone.

Scoring. The result of our erythema scoring method is compared with the results obtained by the Minimum Centre Distance (MCD), where a test sample is grouped into a class in which the mean value of the training samples is closest to the test sample in a feature space [14].

Table 2. Analysis Of Linear Correlation Between Erythema Severity And Colour Features

Features	p-value	F-value	Correlation coefficient
$\nabla \overline{H^{ab}}$	0.299	1.24	0.048
$\nabla \overline{R}$	4.52E-06	10.79	-0.448
$\nabla \overline{G}$	2.18E-10	21.4	-0.63
$\nabla \overline{B}$	6.19E-07	12.72	-0.538
$\nabla \overline{R} + \nabla \overline{G} + \nabla \overline{B}$	2.10E-08	16.22	-0.569
$\nabla \overline{q^m}$	0.048	2.74	0.194
$\nabla \overline{q^h}$	1.44E-09	19.19	0.616
$\nabla \overline{q^h} + \nabla \overline{q^m}$	6.58E-06	10.439	0.456

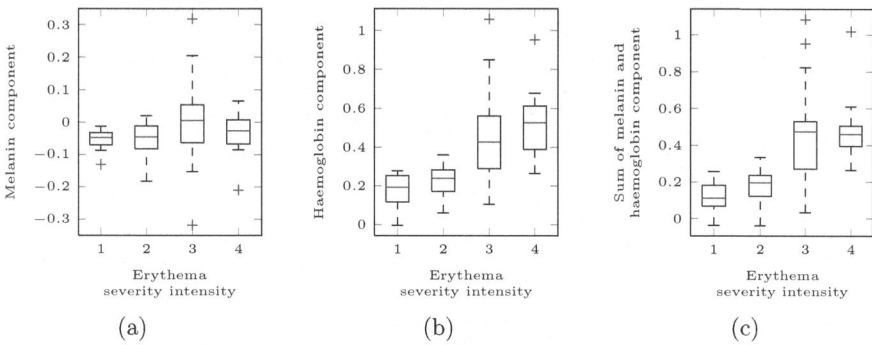

Fig. 2. Box plots of haemoglobin component and melanin component distributions with changes of erythema severity. (a) Box plot of melanin component distribution with changes of erythema severity intensity. (b) Box plot of haemoglobin component distribution with changes of erythema severity intensity. (c) Box plot of summation of haemoglobin component and melanin component distribution with changes of erythema severity intensity.

Figure 3 illustrates the classification accuracy of KNN and MCD clustering samples using features of relative colour component $\nabla \overline{R}, \nabla \overline{G}$ and $\nabla \overline{B}$ in the RGB colour space and the features of relative haemoglobin and melanin component, $\nabla \overline{q^h}$ and $\nabla \overline{q^m}$. KNN clustering method using the relative haemoglobin and melanin components shows the highest accuracy compared with other methods. The mean accuracy in the 10-fold cross validation is 78.85%. Moreover, the performance of KNN is better than MCD in general. For erythema, the accuracy of severity 1 and severity 4 are better than the accuracy for severity 2 and severity 3. This is due to the ambiguity in scoring severity 2 and severity 3 lesions.

Assuming that the accuracy differences in the k-fold cross validation is a t-distribution, the statistical significance of the accuracy difference between the top classifier using KNN with the features used in our algorithm and other severity classifiers are shown in Table 3. The indications are that performance of the top classifier is significantly better that the rest.

Table 3. Accuracy difference between the classifier using KNN in space spanned by haemoglobin component and melanin component and other implemented classifiers

Compared classifier	Colour space	Accuracy difference
MCD	RGB colour space	[-0.097, -0.092]
MCD	Haemoglobin an melanin component	[-0.1, -0.096]
KNN	RGB colour space	[-0.052, -0.05]

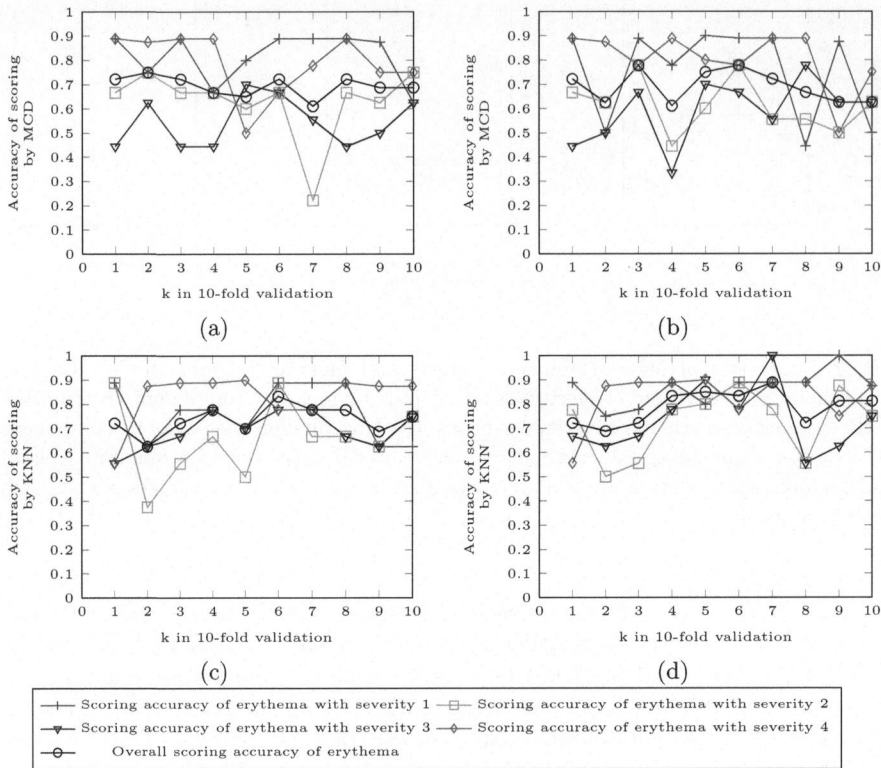

Fig. 3. Accuracy of erythema scoring with 10-fold cross validation for a series of severities and the corresponding classifier. (a) Accuracy of erythema scoring in the RGB colour space using MCD. (b) Accuracy of erythema scoring in the space spanned by the haemoglobin component and melanin component using MCD. (c) Accuracy of erythema scoring in the RGB colour space using KNN. (d) Accuracy of erythema scoring in the space spanned by the haemoglobin component and melanin component using KNN.

3.3   Symptom Type II: Scaling Severity Scoring

In the scaling severity scoring part, 52 images of psoriatic lesion are collected. They are composed of 10 images with scaling severity 1, 17 images with scaling severity 2, 18 images with scaling severity 3, and 7 images with scaling severity 4.

Linear Correlation Analysis. Linear correlation analysis is shown in Table 4. We examined the feature scaling area s, which is considered as a major element related with scaling severity in [10], and the feature set proposed in this paper.

Observe that even though scaling area has a higher correlation coefficient than relative scaling area, it does not possess priority in p-values and F-values, especially when compared to the roughness degree.

Figure 4 shows the distribution of relative scaling area, scaling roughness degree and their summation with changes of scaling severity intensity. We can see

Table 4. Analysis of Linear Correlation Between Scaling Severity And Its Features

Features	p-value	F-value	Correlation coefficient
s	0.023	3.44	0.316
r	0.019	3.61	0.18
$\overline{g}$	8.67E-09	19.81	0.641
$r+\overline{g}$	4.59E-07	14.55	0.58

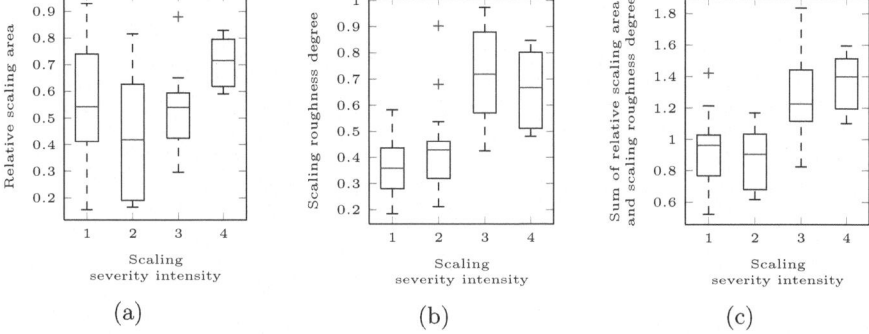

(a)   (b)   (c)

Fig. 4. Box plots of relative scaling area and scaling roughness degree distribution with changes of scaling severity intensity. (a) Box plot of relative scaling area distribution with changes of scaling severity intensity. (b) Box plot of scaling roughness degree distribution with changes of scaling severity intensity. (c) Box plot of summation of relative scaling area and scaling roughness degree distribution with changes of scaling severity intensity.

that ranges of the two features and their summation overlap for different scaling severity intensities. No clear linear relationship exists between the features and the severity intensities.

Scoring. The performance of our scaling scoring method is compared with KNN and the method in [10], where a decision tree is employed to score the severity degree with the scaling area. The result is shown in Figure 5. For KNN and the decision tree, scoring accuracy for severity 1 and severity 4 is generally better than scoring accuracy for severity 2 and severity 3 as with the symptom type I: erythema. Moreover, using the feature set of our method the accuracy is much better than features proposed in [10]. Using features in [10], KNN and the decision tree achieve accuracy of 79.58% and 78.58% respectively, while using our proposed features, an accuracy of 86.75% for KNN and 88.67% for the decision tree are achieved on the samples.

In Table 5, the statistical significance of the accuracy difference between the classifier using the decision tree with the relative scaling area and the scaling roughness degree and other implemented scaling scoring classifiers is shown. All of the difference ranges do not include zero. Thus the accuracy of the decision tree we proposed is significantly different when compared with the other classifiers.

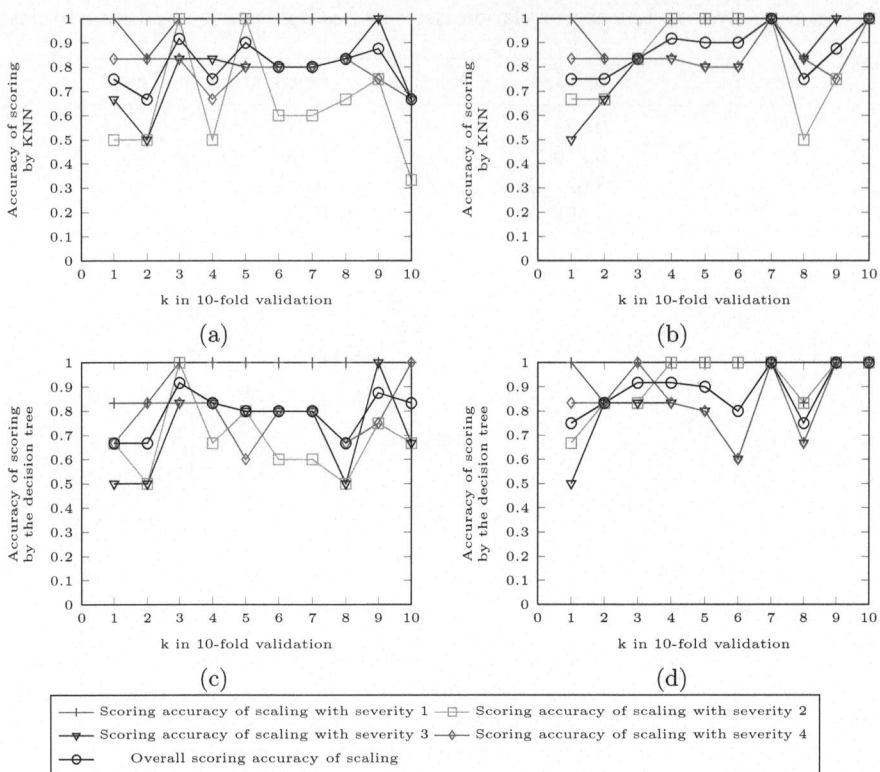

Fig. 5. Accuracy of scaling scoring with 10-fold cross validation for a series of severities and the corresponding classifier. (a) Accuracy of scaling scoring using KNN with the feature proposed in [10]. (b) Accuracy of scaling scoring using KNN with the features of relative scaling area and scaling roughness degree. (c) Accuracy of scaling scoring using the decision tree with the feature proposed in [10]. (d) Accuracy of scaling scoring using the decision tree with the features of relative scaling area and scaling roughness degree.

Table 5. Accuracy difference between the classifier using the decision tree with relative scaling area and scaling roughness degree and other implemented scaling scoring classifiers

Compared classifier	Scaling features	Accuracy difference
KNN	Features in [10]	[0.087, 0.095]
KNN	Relative scaling area and scaling roughness degree	[0.081, 0.02]
Decision tree	Features in [10]	[0.1, 0.102]

4   Discussion

Comparing the erythema scoring method proposed here with [9] shows that our method performs better on the sample. The statistics in Table 2 indicates that our method performs better on the sample, while Figure 3 indicates that scoring performance using the melanin and haemoglobin components is better on the sample than the RGB colours, as suggested in [10]. This can be due to the fact that melanin is distributed in normal skin and is factoring in erythema intensity.

Our scaling severity scoring method outperformed the method in [10], where only scaling area is used. Table 4 indicates that the roughness degree in our model has significantly better statistical correlation values.

Both erythema scoring and scaling scoring give good classification accuracy for the lowest and highest severity, while the classification accuracy for medium severity is a little lower. The severity features derived from segmentation have the obvious advantage in distinguishing symptoms from normal skin, but to further classify the symptom severity, more features closely related to the severity intensities will be explored in future.

Severity 1 erythema may be improperly segmented if the training sets are not chosen carefully. Selecting training sets from individual images will avoid this problem. When it comes to the scaling segmentation, mis-segmentation happened to scaling with severity 1 as well. Shallow redness and shadows are major disturbances in this situation. Determining severity intensity scores in the presence of such disturbance is a topic for future work.

5   Conclusion

In this paper,we proposed automatic scoring methods for erythema and scaling in 2D psoriasis images. Our algorithm is shown to perform better when compared with previous severity models based on the concurrent scores from two dermatologists for a range of different images. In the future, we will continue to focus on the analysis of psoriasis images with the view to determining a wider range of severity scores. More comprehensive models and learning methods will be proposed to achieve this.

Acknowledgments. The authors would like thank to Skin & Cancer Foundation Victoria, Australia and St. Vincent's Hospital Melbourne for support of the research.

References

1. Jenner, N., Campbell, J., Plunkett, A., Marks, R.: Cost of psoriasis: A study on the morbidity and financial effects of having psoriasis in australia. Australasian Journal of Dermatology 43(4), 255–261 (2002)
2. Kreft, S., Kreft, M., Resman, A., Marko, P., Kreft, K.Z.: Computer-aided measurement of psoriatic lesion area in a multicenter clinical trial–comparison to physician's estimations. Journal of Dermatological Science 44(1), 21–27 (2006)

3. Department of Health and Aging Therapeutic Goods Administration. Australian Government: Guideline on clinical investigation of medicinal products indicated for the treatment of psoriasis (2004)
4. Langley, R.G., Ellis, C.N.: Evaluating psoriasis with psoriasis area and severity index, psoriasis global assessment, and lattice system physician's global assessment. Journal of the American Academy of Dermatology 51(4), 563–569 (2004)
5. Puzenat, E., Bronsard, V., Prey, S., Gourraud, P., Aractingi, S., Bagot, M., Cribier, B., Joly, P., Jullien, D., Le Maitre, M., Paul, C., Richard-Lallemand, M., Ortonne, J., Aubin, F.: What are the best outcome measures for assessing plaque psoriasis severity? a systematic review of the literature. Journal of the European Academy of Dermatology and Venereology 2, 10–16 (2010)
6. Fredriksson, T., Pettersson, U.: Severe psoriasis-oral therapy with a new retinoid. Dermatologica 157(4), 238–244 (1978)
7. Savolainen, L., Kontinen, J., Röning, J., Oikarinen, A.: Application of machine vision to assess involved surface in patients with psoriasis. British Journal of Dermatology 137(3), 395–400 (1997)
8. Ahmad Fadzil, M.H., Ihtatho, D.: Modeling psoriasis lesion colour for PASI erythema scoring. In: International Symposium on Information Technology, vol. 2, pp. 1–6 (2008)
9. Ahmad Fadzil, M.H., Ihtatho, D., Affandi, A.M., Hussein, S.: Objective assessment of psoriasis erythema for PASI scoring. In: 30th Annual International Conference of the IEEE Engineering in Medicine and Biology Society, pp. 4070–4073 (2008)
10. Delgado, D., Ersboll, B., Carstensen, J.M.: An image based system to automatically and objectively score the degree of redness and scaling in psoriasis lesions. In: 13th Danish Conference on Image Analysis and Pattern Recognition, pp. 130–137 (2004)
11. Lu, J., Manton, J., Kazmierczak, E., Sinclair, R.: Erythema detection in digital skin images. In: 17th IEEE International Conference on Image Processing, pp. 2545–2548 (2010)
12. Lu, J., Kazmierczak, E., Manton, J., Sinclair, R.: Unsupervised segmentation of scaling in 2d psoriasis skin images (2012), http://repository.unimelb.edu.au/10187/15715
13. Quinlan, J.R.: C4.5: programs for machine learning. Morgan Kaufmann Publishers Inc., San Francisco (1993)
14. Masmoudi, H., Hewitt, S., Petrick, N., Myers, K., Gavrielides, M.: Automated quantitative assessment of her-2/neu immunohistochemical expression in breast cancer. IEEE Transactions on Medical Imaging 28(6), 916–925 (2009)

A Multilayered Ensemble Architecture
for the Classification of Masses in Digital Mammograms

Peter Mc Leod and Brijesh Verma

Central Queensland University
Bruce Highway, Rockhampton QLD 4702, Australia
mcleod.ptr@gmail.com, b.verma@cqu.edu.au

Abstract. This paper proposes a technique for the creation of a neural ensemble that introduces diversity through incorporating ten-fold cross validation together with varying the number of neurons in the hidden layer during network training. This technique is utilized to improve the classification accuracy of masses in digital mammograms. The proposed technique has been tested on a widely available benchmark database.

Keywords: Ensemble classifiers, committee of experts, neural networks, digital mammograms.

1   Introduction

Biomedical diagnostic systems are a real world application where pattern recognition systems have great potential due to their ability to repeatedly process large amounts of data without suffering from fatigue [1,2]. Breast cancer can have a high mortality and morbidity rate with survival directly linked to early detection and appropriate treatment. In the United States alone there are expected to be 39,920 deaths in 2012 due to breast cancer [3]. The Gold standard for detection has long been considered to be screening mammography [4] due to its effectiveness and cost efficiency. Recently a shortage of trained radiologists has increased the need for alternative techniques. Researchers have examined this problem for a number of years with numerous solutions being investigated however due to the similarity between benign and malignant tumors as well as processing constraints no suitable automated solution has been developed. Neural networks on the other hand have demonstrated a capacity to adapt to the medical problem domain and have a proven record [5]. The problem however with neural networks like other techniques in this area has been the variable classification accuracy [6]. Ensemble networks while relatively new on the pattern recognition sphere have shown their capabilities in this sphere as the accuracies obtained are higher than for a standard neural network [7]. The creation of an ensemble however relies on conflict between the constituent classifiers in order to produce a more accurate classifier. This conflict is known as diversity and the ability to create diverse classifiers for ensembles is an area of active research [8, 9].

This research is based on the construction of an ensemble network where the constituent classifiers are neural networks that have been created with a different number of neurons in each hidden layer.

M. Thielscher and D. Zhang (Eds.): AI 2012, LNCS 7691, pp. 85–94, 2012.

The remainder of this paper is organized as follows. Section two presents a review of existing ensemble systems for digital mammograms. The proposed technique is depicted in section three. Experimental results are detailed in section four while an analysis against other techniques is outlined in section five. The conclusions and future directions for this research are presented in section six.

2   Background

In some cases the complexity of a problem means that it is not easily solvable by a single mechanism (classifier), as the capacity to encapsulate the problem cannot be easily bounded by a single model. In the case of mass breast cancer the similarities between the benign and malignant cases make it hard to make an accurate diagnosis between the two, as the resemblance between the diagnostic features is not clear-cut. The use of many networks combined together can provide a better result than a single classifier [7,10,11] as it is better able to model more complex paradigms. Breast cancer in particular has proven to be an area where pattern recognition has struggled due to the similarities between benign and malignant patterns. Due to the nature of the disease and the practical application of pattern recognition techniques this field has received a lot of interest in recent times [10-16]. Due to the similar characteristics between the benign and malignant classes breast cases have low separability in feature space resulting in classification complexity and variable performance of classifiers.

Although the creation of an ensemble has been shown to have higher accuracy than a single classifier [7,10,11] this is dependent on diversity existing in the constituent classifiers. In a group if everyone follows the lead of a figurehead we have an occurrence which is known as "Group Think" where the decision and hence accuracy is really determined by one individual. Disagreement will lead to potentially a better decision. Diversity is this degree of disagreement and is therefore required to have accuracy higher than that of the best performing constituent classifier(s). The creation of an ensemble however does raise several issues. These issues are:

- Selection of the constituent classifiers (types);
- How many classifiers make up the ensemble;
- Membership criteria (accuracy; diversity; computational speed and or memory requirements / restrictions);
- Desired accuracy;
- Time / memory requirements for solution calculation;
- Nature of the classification problem.

Mechanisms for introducing diversity have been a field of active research [8, 9].

Roselin and Thangavel [13] created a metaheuristic ensemble classifier using ant-miner, as they wanted clarity in relation to the output as many classifiers were seen to be too much of a black box approach. Using anomalies from the MIAS database they achieved a classification accuracy of 83%.

Liu et al. [12] contrasted the performance of a random forest technique (ensemble of classification and regression trees) against a Support Vector Machine (SVM) on

236 regions of interest from the Digital Database of Screening Mammography (DDSM) [17]. The random forest ensemble had few tuning parameters and performed more than twice as fast as SVM however it achieved an accuracy of 79% (Az 0.83) compared to 81% (Az 0.86) for SVM.

Gou et al. [10] developed a Partition Based Network (PBN) boosting technique to handle class imbalanced datasets. They paid more attention to the training of classes that were represented less (in this case the malignant condition) in order to convert the network training into a balanced activity. Experiments were performed on the University of California Irvine (UCI) dataset [18] and achieved a higher accuracy value than for standard network boosting. The PBN network achieved a classification rate of 96.50% compared to a network boost accuracy of 96.25%.

Meena, Arya and Kala [14] achieved a classification accuracy of 96.87% on a UCI dataset [18] by implementing a modular neural network where a Self-Organising Map (SOM) selector selected the neural networks that would classify the breast anomalies. Their approach involved the training of the SOM selector, as well as the training of the candidate networks. This was to ensure that the best network possible network was chosen for the classification task.

Huang, Monekosso and Wang [15] utilised a clustered ensemble to reduce the variability and improve the accuracy of clustered classifiers, which they called Clustering Ensembles Based on Multi-classifier Fusion (CEMF) that worked by constructing a number of classifiers that were optimal at classifying a subset of data that had been created through partitioning of the data. They had a 10.5% error rate on their breast cancer dataset.

Luo and Cheng [19] used a Decision Tree (DT) that was bagged to gain a classification rate of 83.4% on mass anomalies. They also used a SVM-SMO (Support Vector Machine Sequential Minimal Optimization) from the Waikato Environment for Knowledge Analysis (WEKA) [20] data mining package. They selected mass anomalies from the UCI machine repository database [18]. During their research they utilised feature selection techniques to reduce the number of input features for the classifier from five to four. They employed four BI-RADS® features and found that the mass margin was the most important feature for mass classification. Luo and Cheng concluded that the ensemble that they created was more effective than using a single classifier.

Zhang, Romuro, Furst and Raicu [21] developed an ensemble classifier where they partitioned a mass dataset from the DDSM [17] into four subsets. The partitioning was based on patient age and mass shape category. A number of classifiers were then evaluated and the best performing classifier on each subset was chosen. The classifiers evaluated were SVM, k-nearest neighbor and a DT. The ensemble achieved a classification accuracy of 72%.

3   Proposed Methodology

Devising mechanisms for generating base classifiers that are diverse for the creation of an ensemble is an active area of research for meta-classifier research [8, 22]. Numerous researchers have utilized techniques on manipulating the training dataset(s) in order to introduce diversity into the ensemble [7,9,22,23]. These techniques have involved training on separate features, training on each classifier on separate datasets as well as other mechanisms. However the number of investigations into using different types of neural networks in ensembles has been low [9] in comparison to manipulation of the training dataset. Neural networks gain their knowledge of the problem domain by being trained on a sufficiently large population sample so that they can then apply that learned knowledge to unseen cases. If the configuration of the classifiers is different the classifier will represent the acquired knowledge in a different way. This is similar to the variation in conceptual understanding that an audience will gain from listening to a lecture. The focus of this research is the demonstration of one mechanism to introduce diversity into the constituent classifiers. Although an explicit diversity inclusion mechanism could have been employed an implicit approach was utilized [9]. Diversity is introduced by varying the number of neurons in the hidden layer. This causes a traversal of feature space that is sufficiently different for each network to result in different weight values that represents the acquired knowledge in the classifier. This introduces diversity into our resultant ensemble [9]. Ten fold cross validation was also utilized as this introduces diversity into the classifier. Partridge and Yates had previously amended the number of neurons to introduce diversity [24] however their research indicated that the impact on diversity and performance was marginal however they only trialed a range of 8 to 12 neurons in the hidden layer. In this research a range from 2 to 150 neurons in the hidden layer has been trialed. This work differs in that the dataset that is utilized also has ten fold cross validation occurring on it, which in itself introduces diversity into the ensemble [9].

The research methodology is represented in Figure 1 below. The process begins with acquiring mammograms. In this research the mammograms have been sourced from a benchmark database called the DDSM [17]. The DDSM provides open access to high quality mammograms that allows for testing of pattern recognition algorithms in order to advance the field of CAD systems for breast cancer diagnosis.

Once the mammograms have been obtained (200 mass type anomalies evenly divided between benign and malignant) the suspicious regions need to be extracted. The process of extracting the anomaly is known as image segmentation and allows a system to more effectively operate as the background noise from normal tissues are removed from the diagnostic or clinical system. Anomalies that are sourced from the DDSM [17] can be extracted by a chain code that exists in order to facilitate the easy extraction of anomalies.

Once the anomalies are extracted it is necessary to obtain the features from the anomalies that are used in feature space to create a mapping to a resultant classification. In this research BI-RADS® are utilised since they have a good diagnostic capability [25-26] and are the same as what a trained radiologist would use to come to a diagnosis. Using the same features helps to increase the utility of this technique for potential clinical usage. The diagnostic features are:

- Density
- Calcification Type / Mass Shape
- Calcification Distribution / Mass Margin

- Abnormality Assessment Rank
- Patient Age
- Subtlety Value

In this research the candidate neural networks that are constructed have six input neurons that correspond directly to the features that are utilised to form a diagnosis.

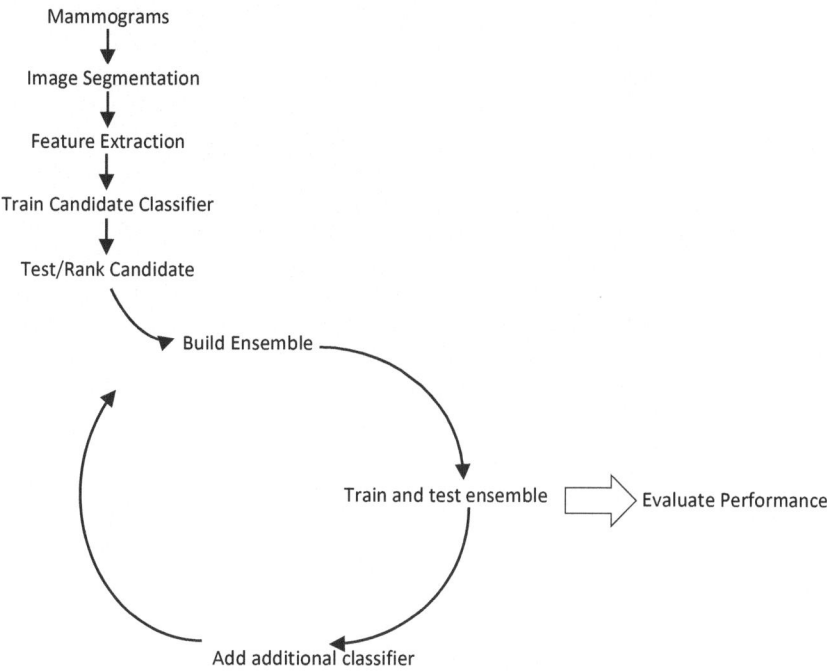

Fig. 1. Proposed research methodology

A number of candidate neural networks were generated for the purpose of this research. These networks were created by varying the number of neurons in the hidden layer from 2 neurons to 150 neurons in order to introduce diversity. The networks were trained and tested using ten-fold cross validation. Once the candidate networks were generated they were ranked based on classification accuracy and then these candidates were utilised to generate our ensemble classifier(s). The ensemble was initially created by using the first three highest performing candidate networks and then was trained and tested (from Table 1 this would be an ensemble that has 24,5 and 15 neurons in each hidden layer). Following this the fourth highest performing candidate classifier was added and then it was trained and tested with the process continuing until a total of the 40 highest performing candidate classifiers had been incorporated into the ensemble and were trained and tested. This was done to evaluate the effect of adding additional classifiers to the ensemble and to attempt to determine the best number of classifiers for the ensemble in terms of achieving a high classification accuracy. The maximum number of constituent classifiers was limited to 40 as the whole process (load data, train and test candidates, generate and evaluate the ensembles) was to occur in only a few minutes.

In accordance with normal scientific practice ten fold cross validation was utilized for all experiments. The stopping condition for network training was a root mean square (rms) error of 0.001 or (a maximum of 3000 iterations). This ensured that the networks were fully trained for the purposes of our experiments. The other parameters were a learning rate of 0.05 and momentum of 0.7.

Table 1. Selection of candidate neural networks for ensemble inclusion

Accuracy	86	85.5	85.5	85.5	85	85	85	84.5	84.5	...	83
Neurons	24	5	15	32	31	43	50	75	38	...	62
Rank	1	2	3	4	5	6	7	8	9	...	40

From Table 1 the best performing network had 24 neurons, the next 5, followed by 15, then 32 in the hidden layer etc.

The proposed system was implemented in MATLAB 7.12.0. MATLAB was running on a 2.66 Ghz Intel Core i7 Mac Book Pro, with 8 Gig of RAM running Mac OX X 10.6.8. The experiments were carried out on a subset from the DDSM [17] utilising only mass type anomalies. The dataset represented 200 anomalies evenly divided between malignant and benign cases.

4   Results

Accuracy of the individual constituent classifiers ranged from 83% to 86% accuracy (Table 1).

Table 2. Ensemble Performance

# Classifiers	Hidden Neurons	TP	TN	Accuracy (%)
4	24,5,15,32	91	95	93.0
14	13,24,5,15,32,31,43,50,75,38,59,68,79,116	98	98	98.0
18	24,5,15,32,31,43,50,75,38,59,68,79,116,146, 14,30,37,95	98	96	97.0
22	24,5,15,32,31,43,50,75,38,59,68,79,116,146, 14,30,37,95,103,104,138,140	98	97	97.5
25	24,5,15,32,31,43,50,75,38,59,68,79,116,146, 14,30,37,95,103,104,138,140,19,29,33	99	97	98.0
35	24,5,15,32,31,43,50,75,38,59,68,79,116,146, 14,30,37,95,103,104,138,140,19,29,33,36,40, 46,48,65,74,84,93,127,22	97	96	96.5

The only condition for inclusion in the ensemble networks was accuracy. The ensemble networks that were constructed had from three to forty constituent classifiers. Table 2 provides a summary of the results obtained for the ensemble classifiers.

5   Discussion

The minimum accuracy that the ensemble achieved was 93% while the maximum accuracy was 98%. Numerous classifiers achieved a classification accuracy of 97%. The improvement in classification accuracy supports the claim by previous researchers that ensembles have higher classification accuracy than their constituents providing that the requirement of diversity is met [27]. Ensembles increase accuracy by reducing the variance in prediction errors [1]. In this research a significant improvement in classification accuracy was achieved by varying the number of neurons in the hidden layer as well as utilizing ten-fold cross validation. In order to determine how significant the results of this research are we need to compare the classification accuracy achieved with that of other researchers and also with the best performance achieved for an individual classifier. Table 3 lists the performance of the proposed technique in comparison to current research. The performance achieved by Verma et al. [28] of 93% is on the same dataset and is directly comparable as it is the same dataset as this research.

Table 3. Comparative performance of proposed technique and current research

Researcher / Reference	Technique	Accuracy [%]
Ensemble technique	Proposed ensemble technique	98.00
Base classifier	Neural network	86.00
Verma et al. [28]	Soft clustered neural network	93.00
Liu et al. [11]	SVM	81.00
Liu et al. [11]	Random forest	79.00
Zhang et al. [20]	Partitioned ensemble classifier	72.00

An ANOVA analysis of variance was performed to determine if the improvement in classification accuracy between the neural network and the ensemble was significant. A 5% confidence level was utilized according to standard scientific methodology.

Table 4. ANOVA Summary

Groups	Count	Sum	Average	Variance
NN	38	3195.5	84.09	0.6197
Ensemble	38	3674	96.68	1.3706

Table 5. ANOVA Analysis

Group Variation						
	SS	df	MS	F	P-value	F crit
Between	3012.66118	1	3012.6612	3027.46475	8.8016E-62	3.97
Within	73.6381579	74	0.9951102			
Total	3086.29934	75				

The p-value (Table 5) is significantly below the required 5% confidence level substantiating that the improvement in performance of the ensemble is statistically significant. Of note is the variance in the ANOVA summary (Table 4.) for the ensemble is much higher than that of the neural network. This is to be expected as the classifiers for the neural network were chosen on the basis of being the highest performers from the candidate classifier pool. The ensemble representatives came from a much smaller candidate pool and the variation was therefore higher as all candidates were chosen.

6   Conclusions

Neural networks have been used extensively to solve many classification dilemmas. The problem with such approaches is that a single neural network has not demonstrated the capacity to solve complex problems where the classification dilemma is not straight forward due to similarities between the distinct classes as occurs in breast cancer diagnosis. This has lead to various authors describing neural networks as a monolithic solution [14] and advocating the usage of ensemble and modular networks. In this solution we utilized redundancy through the creation of an ensemble network that introduced diversity by altering the number of neurons in the hidden layer as well as ten-fold cross validation. The results were fused through the majority vote algorithm. The performance of these networks was then contrasted. The results of this study have demonstrated that ensembles perform better than a single constituent classifier. There is no universal classifier that works best on all given problems. It is not easy to determine a suitable classifier for a given problem, but the use of an ensemble allows for combining the best of multiple classifiers in order to improve accuracy and overcome the limitations of a single classifier. The proposed ensemble approach improved the predictive performance for the mammogram dataset. The improvement in classification accuracy was 12% percentage points (98%-87%) over the best performing single neural network classifier. Our future research will involve the automation of the processes through genetic algorithm pruning of network candidates as well as performance and diversity measures to determine a better performing solution. Our research shall also examine the effects of tuning the momentum and learning rate of the neural network and how this impinges on the creation of an ensemble network.

References

1. Oh, S., Lee, M., Zhang, B.: Ensemble Learning with Active Selection for Imbalanced Biomedical Data Classification. IEEE/ACM Transactions on Computational Biology and BioInformatics 8(2), 316–325 (2011)
2. Doi, K.: Diagnostic imaging over the last 50 years: research and development in medical imaging science and technology. Physics in Medicine and Biology 51(13), R5–R27 (2006)
3. Siegel, R., Naishadham, D., Jemel, A.: CA: A Cancer Journal for Clinicians 62(1) (January/February 2013), doi:10.332/caac.20138
4. Haakinson, D., Stucky, C., Dueck, A., Gray, R., Wasif, N., Apsey, H., Pockaj, B.: A significant number of women present with palpable breast cancer even with a normal mammogram within 1 year. American Journal of Surgery 200(6), 712–717 (2010)

5. Brem, R.: Clinical versus Research approach to breast cancer detection with CAD: where are we now? American Journal of Roentology 188, 234–235 (2007)
6. Abdelaal, M., Sena, H., Farouq, M., Salem, A.: Using Pattern Recognition Approach for Providing Second Opinion of Breast Cancer Diagnosis. In: The 7th International Conference on Informatics and Systems (INFOS 2010), Cairo, pp. 1–7 (2010)
7. West, D., Mangiameli, P., Rampal, R., West, V.: Ensemble strategies for a medical diagnostic decision support system: A breast cancer diagnosis application. European Journal of Operational Research 162, 532–551 (2005)
8. Gou, S., Yang, H., Jiao, L., Zhuang, X.: Algorithm of Partition Based Network Boosting for Imbalanced Data Classification. In: The 2010 International Joint Conference on Neural Networks, pp. 1–6. IEEE, Barcelona (2010)
9. UCI Machine Learning Database, http://archive.ics.uci.edu/ml/%3E
10. Santos, E., Sbourin, R., Maupin, P.: Pareto Analysis for the Selection of Classifier Ensembles. In: Proceedings of the 10th Annual Conference on Genetic and Evolutionary Computation 2008 (GECCO 2008), pp. 681–688 (2008), doi:10.1145/1389095.1389229
11. Liu, J., Chen, J., Liu, X., Tang, J.: An Investigate of Mass Diagnosis in Mammogram with Random Forest. In: Fourth International Workshop on Advanced Computational Intelligence, pp. 638–641. IEEE, Wuhan (2011)
12. Roselin, R., Thangavel, K.: Classification Ensemble for Mammograms Using Ant-Miner. In: Second International conference on Computing, Communication and Networking Technologies, pp. 1–6. IEEE, Karur (2010)
13. Meena, Y., Arya, K., Kala, R.: Classification Using Redundant Mapping in Modular Neural Networks. In: Second World Congress on Nature and Biologically Inspired Computing, pp. 554–659. IEEE, Fukuoka (2010)
14. Huang, Y., Monekosso, D., Wang, H.: Clustering Ensemble Based on Multi-Classifier Fusion. In: 2010 IEEE International Conference on Intelligent Computing and Intelligent Systems (ICIS), pp. 393–397. IEEE, Xiamen (2010)
15. Razavi, A., Gill, H., Åhlfeldt, H., Shahsavar, N.: Predicting metastasis in breast cancer: comparing a decision tree with domain experts. Journal of Medical Systems 31, 263–273 (2007)
16. Oza, N., Tumer, K.: Classifier ensembles: Select real-world applications. Journal of Information Fusion 9, 4–20 (2008), doi:10.1016/j.inffus.2007.07.002
17. Heath, M., Bowyer, K., Kopans, D., Moore, R., Kegelmeyer, P.: The Digital Database for Screening Mammography. In: IWDM 2000. Medical Physics Publishing (2001)
18. Luo, S., Cheng, B.: Diagnosing Breast Masses in Digital Mammography Using Feature Selection and Ensemble Methods. Journal of Medical Systems 36(2), 569–577 (2010)
19. Witten, I.H., Frank, E.: Data Mining: Practical Machine Learning Tools with Java Implementations. Morgan Kaufmann, San Francisco (2000)
20. Zhang, Y., Tomuro, N., Furst, J., Raicu, D.: Building an Ensemble System for Diagnosing Masses in Mammograms. International Journal of Computer Assisted Radiology and Surgery (CARS), 323–329 (2011)
21. Panda, M., Patra, M.: Ensemble of Classifiers for Detecting Network Intrusion. In: International Conference on Advances in Computing, Communication and Control (ICAC3 2009), Mumbai, India, January 23-24, pp. 510–515 (2009)
22. Mc Leod, P., Verma, B.: Clustered Ensemble Neural Network for Breast Mass Classification in Digital Mammography. In: IEEE World Congress on Computational Intelligence, WCCI 2012, June 10-15, Brisbane, Australia, pp. 1266–1271 (2012)
23. Brown, G., Wyatt, J., Harris, R., Yao, X.: Diversity creation methods: a survey and categorization. Journal of Information Fusion 6, 5–20 (2005), doi:10.1016/j.inffus.2004.04.004

24. Partridge, D., Yates, W.: Engineering multiversion neural-net systems. Neural Computing 8(4), 869–893 (1996), doi:10.1162/neco.1996.8.4.869
25. Alto, H., Rangayyan, R., Desautels, J.: Content-based retrieval and analysis of mammographic masses. Journal of Electronic Imaging 14(2), 023016, 1–17 (2005)
26. Andre, T., Rangayyan, R.: Classification of breast masses in mammograms using neural networks with shape, edge sharpness, and texture features. Journal of Electronic Imaging 15, 013019 (2005)
27. Kuncheva, L.: Combining pattern classifiers: methods and algorithms. Wiley-IEEE Press, New York (2004)
28. Verma, B., Mc Leod, P., Klevansky, A.: Classification of benign and malignant patterns in digital mammograms for the diagnosis of breast cancer. Expert Systems with Applications 37(4), 3344–3351 (2010)

Refined Distractor Generation with LSA and Stylometry for Automated Multiple Choice Question Generation

Josef Robert Moser[1,3], Christian Gütl[1,2], and Wei Liu[3]

[1] Institute for Information Systems and Computer Media
Graz University of Technology, Austria
[2] Business School, Curtin University, Australia
[3] School of Computer Science and Software Engineering
The University of Western Australia, Australia
josef.robert.moser@gmail.com,
Christian.Guetl@iicm.tugraz.at,
wei@csse.uwa.edu.au

Abstract. As lifelong learning becomes increasingly important in our society, mechanisms allowing students to evaluate their progress must be provided. A commonly used and widely accepted feedback mechanism is the multiple-choice test. Manual creation of multiple choice questions is often a time consuming process involving many iterations of trail and error. Using text processing and natural language processing techniques, automated multiple choice question generation, in recent years, is getting much closer to reality than ever. However, one of the most difficult tasks in both manual creation and automated generation of this kind of tests is the creation of distractors, because unsuitable distractors allow students to easily guess the correct answer, which counteracts the goal of these questions. In this paper, we investigated the desired properties of distractors and identified relevant text processing algorithms, specifically, latent semantic analysis and stylometry, for distractor selection. The refined distrators are compared with baseline distrators generated by our existing Automated Question Creator (AQC). Our preliminary evaluation shows that this novel combined approach produces distractors with a higher quality than those of the baseline AQC system.

Keywords: Automated Multiple-Choice Question Generation, Distractors, Text Processing, Latent Semantic Analysis, Stylometry.

1   Introduction

Our globalised world demands continuous adaption of knowledge and skills. Consequently, new and improved pedagogical approaches and supportive technologies increasingly attract dedicated research and development efforts. Technology-supported lifelong learning is becoming the key to extend formal education not only in primary and secondary, but also in higher educational

M. Thielscher and D. Zhang (Eds.): AI 2012, LNCS 7691, pp. 95–106, 2012.

learning settings. Specific types of informal learning, such as self-directed learning, become increasingly popular because they enable members of our society to gain knowledge from specialized e-learning repositories, or even from web resources. Especially in these settings, guidance on and information about the learning progress becomes increasingly important, and thus a special focus has to be put on knowledge assessment and feedback methodologies. The creation of test items and the evaluation of tests, however, cannot be performed like in formal settings but requires a creation of test items on the fly [4,6,10].

Our previous work [9,11] and in particular [12] have resulted in a prototype Automatic Question Creator, referred to as AQC hereafter in this paper. The prototype AQC is able to create test items automatically form text corpora [12]. In terms of students' satisfaction of the overall quality of the test items generated, the prototype has demonstrated promising results. However, a deeper investigation highlighted that automatically created *distractors* were perceived by the study participants as being of rather low quality and too easy to detect.

Creating distractors was identified by Haladyna [13] as the most difficult part of the multiple-choice test generation. Furthermore, as our own experience showed, students are exceptionally good at detecting even subtle hints which give away the correct answers. For example,

Q: Which of the following is the term used to describe the task of extracting structured information from unstructured text in natural language?
A) Natural Language Processing
B) Information Extraction
C) Car
D) Insurance

where B) is the correct answer, C) and D) are easily detectable as wrong answers, whereas A) is a reasonable distractor that may confuse students who do not have a clear understanding of the testing concept *Information Extraction*.

Questionnaires containing unsuitable distractors would therefore only grade the students' ability in pattern detection, but not their knowledge or understanding in the subject area. Consequently, improvements in this subfield of automated question generation will not only allow more students to study more effectively in a self-teaching environment, but also contribute in general to the whole field of automated assessment and lifelong learning.

In order to be able to create good distractors, we have to define what a distractor actually is. The first and foremost property of a distractor adopted by this paper is that: *"a distractor is an unquestionably wrong answer"*, as stated by Haladyna [13]. Secondly, these wrong answers are *distractive* in that they should be plausible to students who do not yet understand the course material. Yet however, distractors should be spotted by, and should not confuse, people who already possess the knowledge measured by the multiple-choice test.

In this paper, we developed a novel method for refining distractor generation to ensure that the distractors are plausible yet difficult to detect. The idea of the algorithm reported in this paper is based on the observations by Mitkov et al. [20], who stated that distractors semantically close to the correct answer were the most plausible distractors, and by Haladyna [13], who elaborated that distractors should resemble the grammatical form, style and length of the correct answer.

In addition, we also make use of the weight measures produced by the existing AQC system to improve the distractor quality. Terms receiving a higher weight are considered to represent more important concepts, and substituting one of these concepts for a different, incorrect one should be able to confuse students who only superficially studied the course material.

Consequently, our implementation of the distractor generation process combines the following approaches:

- Latent Semantic Analysis (LSA) which, according to Landauer et al. [18] is able to capture semantic similarities of words and passages, is used as an estimation for semantic closeness.
- Part-of-Speech (POS) tags which are, as Klein and Simmons [17] stated, a set of grammatical codes. These codes can thus be used to ensure that the answer and the distractors have the same grammatical form.
- Stylometry, which was defined by Holmes [16] as *"the statistical analysis of literary style"*. Our proposed method also take the length differences into consideration.
- The existing AQC weight measures, are used in our distractor refinement to identify important concepts.

Our novel approach extracts concepts from some course material, automatically identifies relevant concepts in the material and uses these concepts to generate multiple-choice questions. The system then applies LSA to the course material, calculates style measures, and uses the results from LSA and the style measures to calculate the similarity between the correct answer and possible distractors. The similarity results together with weights calculated by the AQC are used to rank the distractors, and finally, a filter rejects obviously ungrammatical answers.

The remainder of this paper is structured in the following way: Section 2 introduces the framework on which our research is based and describes related research. Section 3 explains how we create the distractors, and Section 4 shows the setup and results of our distractor evaluation experiment. The paper is summed up in Section 5, and this section also provides ideas for future research.

2   Background and Related Work

2.1   Automatic Question Creator

Research focusing on automated test item creation, as stated by Gütl et al [11], uncovered only a small number of already existing approaches and tools. Furthermore, these tools and approaches were also not flexible and extendable enough to address the practical needs of automated question generation. Consequently, in order to alleviate this situation, we initiated the design and implementation of the AQC.

The architecture of the AQC can be segmented into four parts, the *preprocessing*, the *concept extraction* and the *assessment creation* module, and a *graphical user interface*. The modules work in an independent pipelined fashion, where each module accepts the output of the previous one, and each module can also be controlled and influenced via the user interface.

The preprocessing module accepts unstructured or semi-structured text, performs text cleaning and converts the cleaned result into an XML representation. The resulting XML data is in turn processed by the concept extraction module which performs structural, statistical and semantic analysis, calculates weights for phrases present in the text, and uses these weights to extract suitable concepts. This module is described in more detail in Section 3.2. The final module, assessment creation, determines suitable sentences for each extracted concept, and uses these sentences and the concepts to create open ended, single choice, multiple-choice and completion exercises.

AQC's distractors are created in the module responsible for generating multiple-choice exercises, i.e. the assessment creation module. A brief description of how the system creates distractors can be found in Section 2.4, which also introduces the already implemented generation approaches in AQC.

2.2   Latent Semantic Analysis

The aim of Latent Semantic Analysis (LSA) is, according to Landauer et al. [18], to determine how similar the meaning of words or passages is. This similarity measure can be used to rank distractors, where words or phrases highly correlating with the correct answer are assumed to be close enough to the correct one to confuse students not possessing enough knowledge about the specified test item.

LSA is based on performing mathematical operations on a word-by-context matrix. Context can be a sentence, a paragraph or a whole document, and the original matrix counts how often which words appears in what context. This usually high-dimensional but sparsely populated matrix is then normalized and, via singular value decomposition (SVD), transformed into a product of three different matrices. These three matrices are used to calculate a least-square best fit matrix of the original one. The new matrix is understood to better capture the relationship between words and their contexts than the original one.

2.3   Stylometry

Stylometry is, according to Holmes [15] concerned with extracting measurable patterns describing the style of a text. These patterns support us in the task of ensuring that the style of the incorrect answer sentences matches the one of the correct sentence as closely as possible. The most commonly used features, as identified by Abbasi and Chen [1], are:

- Lexical features, which capture word or character based statistics.
- Syntactic characteristics, providing statistics on function words, punctuation and POS tags.

- Structural properties, which consider text organization and layout.
- Content-specific elements, mainly usage statistics over important keywords and phrases.
- Idiosyncratic features, like misspellings, grammatical errors or incorrect usage of words.

However, as we compare sentences which only differ in a small amount of words, not all of these features can be used. Specifically, punctuation, structural properties, phrase usage and the counting of misspellings are not applicable to our distractor sentence style comparison.

2.4 Existing Distractor Generation Approaches

Past and current distractor generators mainly only consider single-word answers, or they use simple algorithms for creating multi-word distractors. Single word term distractors are commonly selected by word frequency (for instance by Brown et al. [5]), by finding semantically related terms via WordNet (like [11] or [20]) and, in the case of grammar tests, by performing rule-based changes to the word form and tense (see [7]). Multi-word distractor generation commonly tries to obtain related multi-word terms via WordNet. However, as this method rarely produces results, Mitkov et al. [20] select noun-phrases with the same head as the answer, and Gütl et al. [11] split the phrase into n-grams and randomly select the longest related n-grams from WordNet, which frequently results in a distractor phrase with only one changed word.

The approach most closely resembling ours was published by Aldabe and Maritxalar [2]. This approach also uses LSA to find distractors, however, the distractors are single-word only, while we focus on important multi-word concepts. Moreover, in contrast to our work, they use manually created blanks, without employing style measures. Furthermore, their published results are only available for the Basque language.

3   Distractor Generation

3.1   System Composition

Figure 1 illustrates our distractor generation process as a pipeline of three independent modules. The system as a whole accepts free-form text documents as input and generates a list of distractors as its output. The individual modules, which are described below, include the Concept Extraction, the Distractor Selection and the Distractor Refinement module. Communication between the modules is also performed in a pipelined fashion, where each module accepts a list of items from the previous module. This communication approach together with the clear segmentation of the system's functionality simplifies the replacement of parts or even whole modules and thus allows us to easily extend and enhance this system.

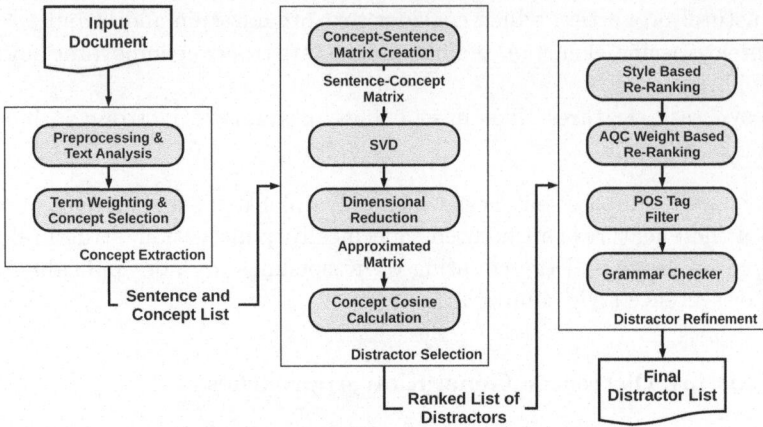

Fig. 1. Overview of the Distractor Generation Process

3.2 Concept Extraction

The concept extraction module, as shown in Figure 1, is actually a part of the AQC, and could be reused without any modification. The most important tasks of this module are the conversion of the input text into a normalized internal representation, the annotation of the text, and the identification of concepts.

The preprocessing and analysis step accepts input texts in various formats, like Microsoft Word, PDF, HTML or plain text, and converts these formats to an internal HTML representation. This internal text is then processed by the General Architecture for Text Engineering (GATE) (see [8]) which performs tasks like tokenisation, named-entity recognition and POS tagging.

Term weights are calculated by performing statistical (like word and term frequencies), semantic (employing WordNet to determine semantic relationships between terms) and structural (for instance if the concept is part of the title, abstract, or chapter heading) analysis of the input text. The numeric values obtained by the analysis are in turn adjusted by user-defined factors and combined into weight measures. Concept selection uses term weights together with weights and annotations provided by XtraK4Me, a module to detect key-phrases in texts (see Schutz [22]), to determine which phrases should be considered to constitute concepts. The most important of these concepts are then used as correct answers for the multiple-choice questions. For a more comprehensive explanation of the details of this module, please see Gütl et al. [11].

3.3 Distractor Selection

After the concept extraction step is finished, lists of sentences and possible concepts are available for this module. The elements of the lists are annotated with POS tags and they contain weight measures provided by AQC. These lists, as can be seen in Figure 1, are used to calculate the semantic similarity between the correct answer and the distractors and to produce a ranked list of distractors. As stated in the introduction, LSA presents itself as a viable approach to this calculation, and the resulting similarity values can be used to estimate if a term could assume the role of a distractor.

The first task of this module is to generate a matrix which can be used for SVD. The matrix in our case is a concept-sentence matrix, where the rows of the matrix are the possible concepts as created by AQC, and the columns state how often the concept appears in a specific sentence. This matrix is high-dimensional yet sparsely populated. Experiments with our system showed that stemming and stop-word removal improved the final distractor quality, and that adjusting the the values by their row entropy, as proposed by Landauer et al. [18], actually decreased the performance of our system.

The concept-sentence matrix is then transformed via SVD into three component matrices, and the dimensionality of the diagonal matrix is reduced by only keeping the highest values of this matrix. The matrix product of the transformed and the reduced matrices provides an approximation of the original concept-sentence matrix, which, as stated above, is able to capture hidden semantic relations between the different concepts. The SVD transformation is implemented by the Lingpipe [3] toolkit, which is used in our system.

The final step of this module takes the correct answer provided by AQC, and selects its row from the approximated concept-sentence matrix. This row, in turn, is used to calculate the cosine between the correct answer and all possible distractor concepts by using the appropriate rows from the approximated matrix. The resulting distractors are then sorted by their respective cosine values, where higher values indicate higher quality distractors. Though many distance measures for determining the relatedness of two vectors are described in literature (like the Euclidean distance, the maximum norm or even correlation between the values of two vectors), experiments showed that the best results were achieved by using the cosine similarity measure.

3.4   Distractor Refinement

Using the ranked list of distractors produced by the distractor selection module, and the POS and weight annotations provided by the concept extraction we are finally performing the last steps of our distractor generation. These steps, as shown in Figure 1, re-rank the distractors and perform filter operations to discard obviously ungrammatical distractors.

As stated above, the conditions imposed by the fact that the amount of different words between distractors and the correct answer is very small, only a selected amount of stylometric features can be feasibly used. These features are:

- Lexical: the number of characters and digits, character and digit uni- and bi-gram counts, the number of words and the average length of words.
- Syntactic: the POS-tag uni-gram count.
- Content-specific: the word frequency.

The style value differences between the correct answer and possible distractors are converted into numeric values and then used to re-rank the list provided by the distractor selection module. These numeric values are obtained by calculating the cosine for uni- and bi-gram counts, and by calculating the difference and normalizing it by the average of the two values for all other style measures.

The next re-ranking step uses the term-weights created by the AQC, to determine the importance of the extracted concepts. Though we initially assumed that important concepts would provide good distractors, our experiments did not provide a clear correlation between the term-weights and the viability of these terms as a distractor. Though this re-ranking step had only a slight impact on the selection process, we nevertheless kept this step and plan to examine its effects in a future study.

A POS tag filter is responsible for ensuring that the grammatical forms of all possible answers match. This filter extracts the POS tag of the head word of the correct answer concept and compares it with the tags of the head word of all distractor concepts. The current implementation of our system performs exact POS matches and rejects the non-matching concepts, however, conversions between similar word forms, like singular and plural, would be possible, and these methods are scheduled for inclusion in a future version of our system.

The concluding refinement step performs a more sophisticated grammar check than the POS filtering step above. Here all blanks generated by the AQC are filled with the correct answer and with possible distractors, and the resulting sentences are examined. As even sentences with the correct answer sometimes contain grammatical errors or are flagged as being not completely correct, we had to relax our rejection criteria, and only discard distractors which would introduce additional errors. The actual checking is performed by the LanguageTool (see [21]) which is provided as open source and written in Java. Furthermore, this tool contains human-editable grammar rule files which allowed us to fine-tune the evaluation algorithm for our needs.

4   Experiment and Results

4.1   Weight Influence Estimation

Different weight measures obviously influence the re-ranking process to a different degree. To estimate these influences, we trained our system based on data obtained from [11], and consequently used the MIT OpenCourseWare lecture on "Project Management for Construction", provided by Hendrickson [14], as source material.

The AQC is responsible for generating the multiple-choice questions and the concepts, which were used by our system to calculate a list of all relevant weight measures. The resulting list was expanded by a column containing distractor-fitness values between 0 and 1000 where 1000 indicated a perfect distractor, and 0 indicated that the concept should not be used. Multiple linear regression was then performed with these fitness values as the dependent variable and with all weight measures as independent variables. Examining the regression results showed that LSA similarity weights had the strongest influence on ranking of the distractor, followed by character-bi-gram differences and POS-tag uni-gram differences.

4.2 Experimental Setting

Evaluation of our distractor generation was performed in the context of the "ISR Natural Language Processing Case Study", which examined the newest version of the AQC based on an introductory text to Natural Language Processing (NLP). Our aim in this experiment was to show that the re-ranking influences obtained for the "Project Management for Construction" were general enough to work even for non-related topics, and thus we did not specifically adapt our distractor generation approach to this new material.

Participants of the experiment had to study an introduction to NLP written in English. They need to summarise this text, answer some questions concerning this text, to extract important concepts and also had to answer some questions intended to evaluate the knowledge of a student concerning the studied text. As the last task, the participants had to rank three distractors created by AQC and three distractors created by our system based on their assessments of each term's suitability as a distractor.

The experiment was conducted by nine tutors and PhD students who served as an expert committee to evaluate the quality of the generated distractors. Two of them are female and seven male with an average age of 33. All of the experts are German native speakers with English as a second language.

We would also like to explain the reasons why we prefer a small but experienced expert panel to the more general approach of conducting real tests among large groups of students. Varying abilities in the students will add noise to the evaluation results. In addition, without running other assessments, it is hard to separate students into distinct groups of those with good conceptual understanding and those with superficial and easily confusable knowledge. The small expert group, who all have good understandings in the subject matter, on the other hand, are more suitable in making informed judgement. Moreover, teaching experiences make them more aware of student common mistakes, which in turn allow them to select distractors that are pedagogically valuable. Having said that, we do plan in the future work to conduct evaluation on students.

4.3 Results

The ranking experiment, as can be seen from Figure 2, shows that our new LSA and stylometry approach (LSA-STY) for creating distractors was indeed able to outperform the base system. This figure displays the rank of each distractor together with the percentage of how many of these ranks were filled by distractors created with the LSA-STY system versus how many of these ranks were from distractors of the base AQC system. The best distractor has a rank of 1, and the worst a rank of 6. Consequently, a good distractor generation approach should

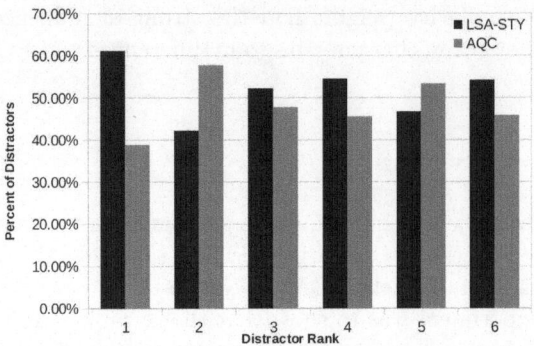

Fig. 2. Result of the distractor ranking. LSA-STY: new system, AQC: base system, lower ranks are better.

posses high percentage values on the low-rank side and low percentages on the high-rank side.

The results for rank 1, the best possible distractor for a question, shows that 61% of these distractors were created by our LSA-STY system versus 39% by the base system. A statistical analysis of this result shows that the two-tailed P-value obtained from the chi-square test equals 0.035, which means that the difference in this distribution can be considered to be statistically significant. Though rank 2 has a high percentage of the second-best distractors generated by the base system (58%), the P-value obtained for this distribution equals 0.14, and thus should not be considered to be statistically significant. The distribution for all other distractors is also not statistically significant.

However, though not significant, the number of the second-best distractors is still high. This indicates, that the WordNet based distractor generation of of the AQC will most probably also create viable distractors and should thus not be completely discarded.

5   Conclusion and Future Work

Our system extends the multiple-choice module of the AQC by providing a sophisticated distractor selection method based on the NLP approaches, namely, LSA and stylometry. The distractor selection considers previously extracted concepts, ranks them via LSA, re-ranks them based on stylometry and AQC-provided weight measures, and uses POS tags and a grammar checker to remove unsuitable candidates. Preliminary experiments performed by nine tutors and PhD students showed that our new approach was able to produce the best distractors for a significant number of questions.

Though our initial experiments showed an improvement in distractor quality, a large scale test in a classroom setting has to be performed. This test should follow the approach provided by [19] and [2], who split the answered questions according to the marks awarded into a high- and a low-achieving group, and checked if the distractors were able to discriminate between these groups. Good question items should confuse low-achieving students more often than high-achieving ones.

Furthermore, due to resource limits, our system was only trained with an excerpt from the "project management in construction" course from MIT Open-CourseWare and tested with an introductory text to Natural Language Processing. The system will be tested with different course material spanning a wide range of subjects. Additionally, when examining these subjects, domain-experts will be employed to manually create some distractors for comparison purposes, and a sub-study should identify how and why these experts select distractors, and might even produce new distractor-weighting techniques.

Another interesting approach would be a combination of the base system and our LSA and stylometry based approach. Though the difference in the number of second-best distractors was not statistically relevant, the WordNet based approach of the base system nonetheless produced a high number of them, and thus also generated viable distractors. This hybrid method could in turn use the distractor-weighting techniques obtained by studying experts to decide which distractor to select.

References

1. Abbasi, A., Chen, H.: Writeprints: A stylometric approach to identity-level identification and similarity detection in cyberspace. ACM Trans. Inf. Syst. 26, 7:1–7:29 (2008)
2. Aldabe, I., Maritxalar, M.: Automatic Distractor Generation for Domain Specific Texts. In: Loftsson, H., Rögnvaldsson, E., Helgadóttir, S. (eds.) IceTAL 2010. LNCS, vol. 6233, pp. 27–38. Springer, Heidelberg (2010), http://dx.doi.org/10.1007/978-3-642-14770-8_5
3. Alias-i: Lingpipe 4.0.0 (2010), http://alias-i.com/lingpipe (access date: December 16, 2010)
4. Bransford, J.D., Brown, A.L., Cocking, R.R. (eds.): How People Learn: Brain, Mind, Experience, and School: Expanded Edition. The National Academies Press (2000)
5. Brown, J.C., Frishkoff, G.A., Eskenazi, M.: Automatic question generation for vocabulary assessment. In: Proceedings of the Conference on Human Language Technology and Empirical Methods in Natural Language Processing, HLT 2005, pp. 819–826. Association for Computational Linguistics, Morristown (2005), http://dx.doi.org/10.3115/1220575.1220678
6. Chang, V., Gütl, C.: Generation y learning in the 21st century: Integration of virtual worlds and cloud computing services. In: Abas, Z.W., Jung, I., Luca, J. (eds.) Proceedings of Global Learn Asia Pacific 2010, pp. 1888–1897. AACE, Penang (2010)
7. Chen, C.Y., Liou, H.C., Chang, J.S.: Fast: an automatic generation system for grammar tests. In: Proceedings of the COLING/ACL on Interactive Presentation Sessions, pp. 1–4. Association for Computational Linguistics, Morristown (2006), http://dx.doi.org/10.3115/1225403.1225404
8. Cunningham, H., Maynard, D., Bontcheva, K., Tablan, V.: GATE: A framework and graphical development environment for robust NLP tools and applications. In: Proceedings of the 40th Anniversary Meeting of the Association for Computational Linguistics (2002)

9. Gütl, C.: Automatic limited-choice and completion test creation, assessment and feedback in modern learning processes. In: LRN Conference 2008, Guatemala (February 2008)

10. Gütl, C., Chang, V.: Ecosystem-based theoretical models for learning in environments of the 21st century. International Journal of Emerging Technologies in Learning (iJET) 3(1) (2008)

11. Gütl, C., Lankmayr, K., Weinhofer, J.: Enhanced approach of automatic creation of test items to foster modern learning setting. In: Proc. of the 9th European Conference on e-Learning, pp. 225–234 (November 2010)

12. Gütl, C., Lankmayr, K., Weinhofer, J., Höfler, M.: Enhanced approach of automatic test item creation to foster modern e-education. Electronic Journal of e-Learning (2011) (to appear)

13. Haladyna, T.M.: Developing and Validating Multiple-Choice Test Items, 3rd edn. Lawrence Erlbaum Associates (2004)

14. Hendrikson, C.: Project management for construction (2000), http://pmbook.ce.cmu.edu/index.html (access date: November 17, 2010)

15. Holmes, D.: Authorship attribution. Computers and the Humanities 28, 87–106 (1994), http://dx.doi.org/10.1007/BF01830689

16. Holmes, D.: The Evolution of Stylometry in Humanities Scholarship. Literary and Linguistic Computing 13(3), 111–117 (1998), http://llc.oxfordjournals.org/content/13/3/111.abstract

17. Klein, S., Simmons, R.F.: A computational approach to grammatical coding of english words. J. ACM 10, 334–347 (1963), http://doi.acm.org/10.1145/321172.321180

18. Landauer, T.K., Foltz, P.W., Laham, L.: An introduction to latent semantic analysis. Discourse Processes 25, 259–284 (1998)

19. Mitkov, R., Ha, L.A.: Computer-aided generation of multiple-choice tests. In: Proceedings of the HLT-NAACL 03 Workshop on Building Educational Applications Using Natural Language Processing, vol. 2, pp. 17–22. Association for Computational Linguistics, Morristown (2003), http://dx.doi.org/10.3115/1118894.1118897

20. Mitkov, R., Ha, L.A., Varga, A., Rello, L.: Semantic similarity of distractors in multiple-choice tests: extrinsic evaluation. In: GEMS 2009: Proceedings of the Workshop on Geometrical Models of Natural Language Semantics, pp. 49–56. Association for Computational Linguistics, Morristown (2009)

21. Naber, D.: A Rule-Based Style and Grammar Checker. Diploma thesis, University of Bielefeld (2003), http://www.languagetool.org/ (access date: January 2011)

22. Schutz, A.: Xtrak4me - extraction of keyphrases for metadata creation. SmILE: Semantic Information Systems and Language Engineering Group (2008), http://smile.deri.ie/projects/keyphrase-extraction (access date: November 17, 2010)

A New Genetic Algorithm
for Simplified Protein Structure Prediction

Mahmood A. Rashid[1,2], Md. Tamjidul Hoque[3], M.A. Hakim Newton[1,2],
Duc Nghia Pham[1,2], and Abdul Sattar[1,2]

[1] Queensland Research Lab, National ICT Australia
[2] Institute for Integrated & Intelligent Systems, Griffith University
[3] Computer Science, University of New Orleans, USA

Abstract. In this paper, we present a new genetic algorithm for protein structure prediction problem using face-centred cubic lattice and hydrophobic-polar energy model. Our algorithm uses *i*) an exhaustive generation approach to diversify the search; *ii*) a novel hydrophobic core-directed macro move to intensify the search; and *iii*) a random-walk strategy to recover from stagnation. On a set of standard benchmark proteins, our algorithm significantly outperforms the state-of-the-art algorithms for the same models.

Keywords: Protein Structure Prediction, Genetic Algorithms, Local Search, Lattice Models, Energy Models, Random-walk.

1 Introduction

Protein Structure Prediction (PSP) is computationally a very hard problem [24]. Given a protein's amino acid sequence, the problem is to find a three dimensional structure of the protein such that the total interaction energy amongst the amino acids in the sequence is minimised. The protein folding process that leads to such structures involves very complex molecular dynamics [4] and unknown energy factors. In the pursuit of addressing this difficulties in a hierarchical way, researchers have considered simplified models [21,17,26] for PSP. However, the complexity of the simplified problem still remains challenging.

There are a large number of existing search algorithms that attempt to solve the PSP problem by exploring feasible lattice-based structures called *conformations*. The state-of-the-art results on face-centred cubic (FCC) lattice based hydrophobic-polar (HP) energy model have been achieved by local search (LS) methods [5,9]. On the other hand, genetic algorithms (GA) [14], and tabu search [3] found promising results on 2D and 3D hexagonal lattice based HP models. In general, the success of GA and LS methods crucially depends on the balance of diversification and intensification of the search. Moreover, these algorithms often get stuck in local minima. As a result, they perform poorly on large proteins. Any further progress to these algorithms require addressing the above issues appropriately.

In this paper, we introduce a population based algorithm (GA$^+$) under the GA framework for simplified PSP. We use HP based energy model on 3D FCC

M. Thielscher and D. Zhang (Eds.): AI 2012, LNCS 7691, pp. 107–119, 2012.

lattice to simplify the problem. In GA$^+$, we use *i*) an exhaustive generation approach to diversify the search; *ii*) a novel hydrophobic core-directed macro move to intensify the search; and *iii*) a random-walk based approach to recover from stagnation. On a set of benchmark proteins, GA$^+$ significantly outperforms the state-of-the-art PSP algorithms in the same models.

The rest of the paper is organised as follows: Sect. 2 reviews background knowledge, Sect. 3 discusses related work on PSP; Sect. 4 describes our new GA for simplified PSP; Sect. 5 presents the experimental results and analyses; and finally, Sect. 6 draws the conclusion and outlines our future research.

2   Preliminaries

Proteins are essentially sequences of amino acids. They adopt specific folded three-dimensional structures to perform specific tasks. The function of a given protein is determined by its *native* structure, which has the lowest possible free energy level. Nevertheless, misfolded proteins cause many critical diseases such as Alzheimer's disease, Parkinson's disease, and Cancer [8]. Protein structures are important in drug design and biotechnology.

Homology modeling, protein threading, and *ab initio* are three computational approaches used in PSP. Prediction quality of *homology modeling* and *protein threading* depend on previously known structures of sequentially similar proteins. Our work is based on the *ab initio* approach that depends only on the amino acid sequence of the target protein. In our simplified PSP model, we use FCC lattice for mapping conformations that satisfy a self-avoiding walk. We also use HP energy model for conformation evaluation, and an enhanced genetic algorithm for conformation search. The self-avoiding walk constraint, FCC lattice, HP energy model, and genetic algorithms are described below.

2.1   Self-avoiding Walk

In lattice based protein representation, the amino acids of a given sequence are mapped on lattice points satisfying a self-avoiding-walk constraint. A self-avoiding walk constraint ensures no revisitation of any lattice point during the sequence mapping.

2.2   FCC Lattice

The FCC lattice has the highest packing density compared to the other existing lattices [10]. In FCC, each lattice point has 12 neighbours (Fig. 1a) with 12 *basis vectors* $(1,1,0)$, $(-1,-1,0)$, $(-1,1,0)$, $(1,1,0)$, $(0,1,1)$, $(0,1,-1)$, $(1,1,0)$, $(1,0,-1)$, $(0,-1,1)$, $(-1,0,1)$, $(0,-1,-1)$, and $(-1,0,-1)$. The hexagonal closed pack (HCP) lattice, also known as cuboctahedron (Fig. 1b), was used in [14]. In HCP, each lattice point has 12 neighours that correspond to 12 basis vertices with real-numbered coordinates, which causes the loss of structural precision for PSP. In simplified PSP, conformations are mapped on the lattice by a sequence of basis vectors, or by the *relative vectors* that are relative to the previous basis vectors in the sequence.

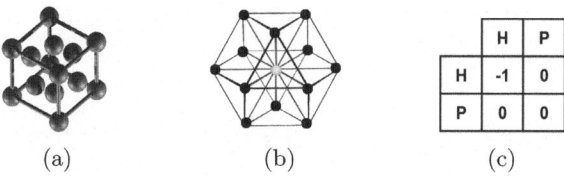

Fig. 1. a) FCC lattice, b) HCP lattice, c) HP energy model [16]

2.3 HP Energy Model

The HP energy model is based on the hydrophobicity of the amino acids. In the HP model [7,16], when two non-consecutive hydrophobic amino acids become topologically neighbours, they release a certain amount of energy, which for simplicity is shown as -1 in Fig. 1c. The total free-energy E (Shown in Equation 1) of a conformation, based on the HP model, becomes the sum of the energy released by all pairs of non-consecutive hydrophobic amino acids.

$$E = \sum_{i<j-1} c_{ij}.e_{ij} \qquad (1)$$

Here, $c_{ij} = 1$ if ith and jth amino acids are non-consecutive in the sequence but are neighbours on the lattice, otherwise 0; and $e_{ij} = -1$ if ith and jth amino acids are both hydrophobic, otherwise 0.

2.4 Genetic Algorithms

GAs are a population-based search for optimisation problems. A genetic algorithm maintains a set of solutions known as population. In each *generation*, it generates a new population from the current population using a given set of genetic operators known as *crossover* and *mutation*. It then replaces inferior solutions by superior newly generated solutions to get a better current population. A typical crossover operator randomly splits two solutions at a randomly selected crossover point and exchanges parts between them (Fig. 2a). A typical mutation operator alters a solution at a random point (Fig. 2b). In the case of PSP, conformations are regarded as solutions of a GA. Below we describe genetic operators used in PSP.

Crossover Operators: The crossover operators are applied on two selected parent conformations to exchange their parts to generate child conformations. In a *single-point crossover*, both parents are splitted at a single point (Fig. 3 a) while in a *multi-point crossover* they are splitted at more than one point. Nevertheless, the crossover operations succeed if they produce conformations that satisfy the self-avoiding walk constraint.

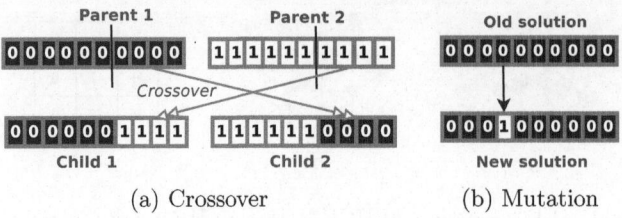

(a) Crossover   (b) Mutation

Fig. 2. Typical (a) crossover and (b) mutation operators

Mutation Operators: The mutation operators are applied on a single conformation. The operators can perform single-point change or multi-point changes.
The mutation operations succeed if the resultant conformation remains a self-
avoiding walk on the lattice. The primitive mutation operators (as shown in Fig
3 (b-e)) are described below:

1. **Rotation:** One part of a given conformation is rotated around a selected
   point (Fig 3 b). This move is mostly effective at the begining of the search.
2. **Diagonal Move:** Given three consecutive amino acids at lattice points A, B,
   and C, a diagonal move at position B takes the corresponding amino acid
   diagonally to a free position (Fig 3 c). Diagonal moves are very effective on
   FCC lattice [5,9] points.
3. **Pull Moves:** The amino acids at points A and B are pulled to the free
   points (Fig 3 d) and the connected amino acids are pulled as well to get a
   valid conformation. Pull moves [18] are local, complete and reversible. Pull
   moves are very effective especially when the conformation is compact.
4. **Tilt Moves:** Two or more consecutive amino acids connected in a straight
   line are moved by a tilt move to immediately parallel lattice positions [12].
   Tilt-moves pull the conformation from both sides until a valid conformation
   is found. In Fig. 3 e), the amino acids at points C and D are moved and
   subsequently other amino acids from both sides are moved as well.

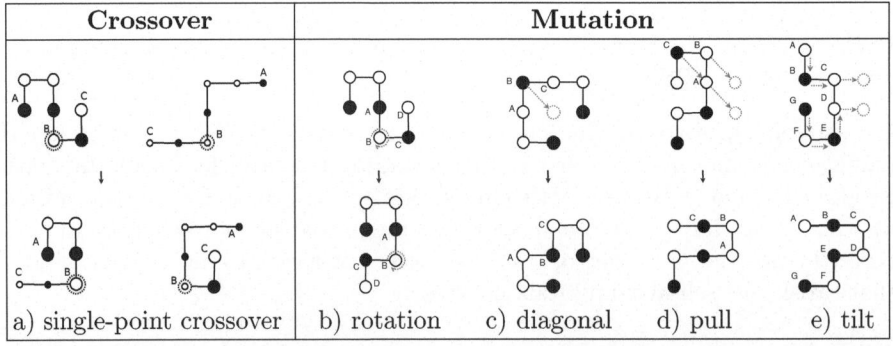

Crossover	Mutation			
a) single-point crossover	b) rotation	c) diagonal	d) pull	e) tilt

Fig. 3. The primitive operators that are used in our GAs on 3D FCC lattice space.
For easy comprehension, the figures are presented in 2D space.

3   Related Work

Different types of metaheuristic have been used in solving the simplified PSP problem. These include Monte Carlo Simulation [23], Simulated Annealing [22], Genetic Algorithms [25,12], Tabu Search with GA [3], Tabu Search with Hill Climbing [15], Ant Colony Optimisation [2], Immune Algorithms [6], Tabu based Stochastic Local Search [5], and Constraint Programming [9]. Below we describe PSP methods that are based on local search and genetic algorithms.

Local Search: Starting from an initial solution, local search algorithms move from one solution to another to find a better solution. Local search algorithms are well known for efficiently producing high quality solutions, which are difficult for systematic search approaches. However, they are incomplete [1], and suffer from revisitation and stagnation. Restarting the whole or parts of a solution remains the typical approach to deal with such situations. In PSP problem, Cebrian et al. [5] used a local search algorithm combined with tabu heuristic. They implemented their method for the 3D FCC lattice and the HP model, and tested its effectiveness on Harvard instances [28]. Later, Dotu et al. [9] extended the work in [5] by using a hybrid method that combines local search and constraint programming together. Overall, these two methods have produced the current state-of-the art results for PSP on FCC lattice and HP energy model.

Genetic Algorithms: Unger and Moult [25] first applied GA to PSP and found their method to be more promising than the Monte Carlo based methods. They used absolute encodings on the square and cubic lattices, and the HP energy model. They only applied single point crossovers, and discarded infeasible solutions. Later, Patton [20] used relative encodings to represent conformations and a penalty method to enforce the self-avoiding walk constraint. In [14], GAs have been used by Hoque et al. for cubic, and 3D HCP lattices. They also introduced a twin-removal operator [13] to remove duplicates from the population and to prevent premature convergence.

4   Our Algorithms

Fig. 4 presents our GA$^+$. The algorithm initialises the current population and evaluates them. At each generation, it selects a genetic operator based on a given probability distribution to use through the generation. This operator is used in an exhaustive way to obtain all conformations in the new population. We ensure that no duplicate conformation is added to the new population. For a given number of generations, if the best conformation in the new population is not better than the best in the current population, our algorithm then resorts to a random-walk procedure to diversify the new population. Nevertheless, after each generation, the new population becomes the current population; and the search continues. Finally, the best conformation found so far is returned.

Procedure gaPlus(opR,rwT)

```
1   op: Operators, c, c′: Conformations
2   opR: Operator selection probabilities
3   curP,newP: Current and new populations
4   rwT: Number of non-improving
5       generations before random walk.
6   //========================
7   initPopulation(curP)
8   foreach Generation until timeout do
9       selectOperator(op, opR)
10      if mutation(op) then
11          foreach c ∈ curP do
12              newP.add(mutConf(c))
13      else //crossover(op)
14          while ¬full(newP) do
15              c, c′ ← randomConfs(curP)
16              newP.add(crsConfs(c, c′))
17      if ¬improved(newP, rwT) then
18          rndWalk(newP)
19      curP ← newP
20  return bestConformation(curP)
```

Procedure mutConf(conf)

```
1   mutants.add(conf)
2   foreach 1 ≤ pos ≤ conf.length() do
3       c ← applyOperator(conf, pos)
4       mutants.add(c)
5   return bestConformation(mutants)
```

Procedure crsConfs(conf,conf′)

```
1   N: Number of iteration
2   // typically N = conf.length()/10
3   crossbred.add(conf, conf′)
4   for i = 1 to N do
5       pos ← random(1, conf.length())
6       c, c′ ← applyOperator(conf, conf′, pos)
7       crossbred.add(c, c′)
8   return best2Conformations(crossbred)
```

Fig. 4. Our new genetic algorithms for PSP

Note that our GA is different from a typical GA in a number of ways. A typical GA *i*) randomly selects an operator every time before generating a new solution; *ii*) selects parent solutions randomly; *iii*) applies the operators on randomly selected points; *iv*) generates only one (for mutation) or two (for crossover) solutions; *v*) does not use any macro-move; *vi*) does not use a random-walk in stagnant situation; and *vii*) does not remove duplicate conformations.

4.1 Exhaustive Generation

For mutation operators, our algorithm adds one resultant conformation to the new population for *each* conformation in the current population. In Fig. 4 Procedure mutConf, notice that the child conformations are generated by applying the genetic operator at *each* position of the parent conformation. The resultant conformation of a mutation operation is either the parent conformation itself or a child depending on the quality of the conformations.

For crossover operators, two resultant conformations are added to the new population from each application of the operator on two randomly selected conformations in the current population. Crossover operators (Procedure crsConfs) generate child conformations by randomly selecting the crossover points on the parent conformations. Note that the child generation method is not strictly exhaustive in crossovers. However, unlike typical GAs, a number of child conformations are generated by our algorithm. The best two conformations from the parents and the children then become the resultant conformations.

4.2 Macro-Move Operator

Protein structures have hydrophobic cores (H-core) that hide the hydrophobic amino acids from water and expose the polar amino acids to the surface to

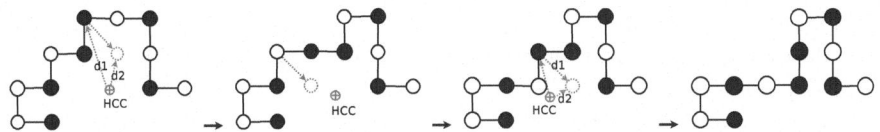

Fig. 5. A macro move operator comprising a series of diagonal moves. For easy understanding, the figures are presented in 2D space. The solid-black circles represent the hydrophobic amino acids and the hollow ones the hydrophilic.

Procedure macroMove(conf)	**Procedure** rndWalk(pop)
1 **for** $i = 1$ **to** Repeat **do**	1 **foreach** conf $\in$ pop **do**
2 $T = $ P **if** bernoulii(p), **else** H	2 **for** $i = 1$ **to** Repeat **do**
3 $A[j]$: jth amino acid in conf.	3 $A[j]$: jth amino acid in conf.
4 **foreach** j : type($A[j]$) = T **do**	4 **foreach** $A[j]$ **do**
5 apply diagonal move at j, **if** $T = $ P	5 apply pull-move move at j.
6 **or** dist($A[j]$,hcc) is non-increaseing.	6 break on first success.
7 break on first success.	
8 **return** conf	7 **return** pop

Fig. 6. Our macro move and random walk algorithms

be in contact with the surrounding water molecules [27]. H-core formation is the main objective of HP based PSP. To achieve this, the total distance of all H-H pairs is minimised in [5]. A predefined motif based segment replacement strategy is applied in [14]. In this paper, we present a macro-move operator to aid forming the H-core. Our macro move performs a series of diagonal-moves on a given conformation to build the H-core around the hydrophobic core centre (HCC). See Fig. 5 for an example. The macro-move squeezes the conformation and quickly forms the H-core. In our implementation, the macro-move is used like any other mutation operators.

In the macro-move (Fig. 6 Procedure macroMove), the HCC is calculated by finding arithmetic means of x, y, and z coordinates of all hydrophobic amino acids. The macro-move for a given number of iterations repeatedly applies the diagonal move either at each P- or at each H-type amino acid positions. Whether to apply the diagonal move on P- or H-type amino acids is determined by using a Bernoulli distribution with probability p (typically $p = 20\%$ for P-type amino acids). For a P-type amino acid, we consider the first successful diagonal move. For a H-type amino acid, we take the first successful diagonal move that does not increase the distance of the amino acids from the HCC. Note that a large number of iterations would prematurely squeeze the conformation to a great extent while a small number of iterations could allow other genetic operators to play their roles in the search. We typically use 10 iterations for the first few hundreds of generations, later we use 5 iterations as the search progresses.

4.3   Stagnation Recovery by Random Walk

When the best conformation found so far remains the same for a number of generations (Fig. 4 Procedure gaPlus Line 14), we term this as a stagnation.

In a stagnation, a random-walk algorithm (Fig. 6 Procedure rndWalk) applies unconditional pull moves on each conformation of the new population. We repeat the process for a number of iterations. A large number of iterations would greatly diversify the population. We typically use a number between 5 to 10 for this.

4.4   Further Implementation Details

Below we describe the other implementation choices of our algorithm in details.

Conformation Representation: We represent conformations by 3D coordinates and relative encodings. While coordinates help us determine whether a point on the lattice is free, relative encodings help apply genetic operators in generating conformations and then eliminate duplicate conformations.

Conformation Generation: For conformation generation, we use the genetic operators listed in Sect. 2 as well as the macro-move operator.

Conformation Evaluation: The fitness function we use in our algorithm to evaluate conformations is the exact energy function for the HP energy model (see Sec. 2). We do not use any other fitness functions such as sum of all H-H pair distances as is used in [5].

Operator Selection: The probability distribution to select operators is chosen intuitively. The single- and multi-point crossovers are selected with 15% and 5% probabilities giving 20% chance to crossovers. The rotation, diagonal-move, pull-move, tilt-move, and macro-move are selected respectively with probabilities 20%, 10%, 30%, 10%, and 10%. For experiments, when macro-moves are not used, diagonal moves are alone given 20% chance. Pull moves are given more chance than tilt moves as the latter tends to make more changes (in both sides) to the conformation than the former (in one side).

Population Size: The number of conformations explored in each generation should be more for a large protein than for a small one. In our algorithm, the number of such conformations are $O(n \times l)$ where n is the population size and l is the protein length. This is because we apply mutation operators at each amino acid position of each conformation in the population. For crossovers, the case is slightly different, but they are selected only with 20% probability. For the time being, we use $n = 100, 80, 60, 50$ for $l >= 50, 100, 200, 400$ respectively.

Population Initialisation: We generate the initial population by randomly selecting the basis vectors between each consecutive pair of amino acids. The generated conformations are all valid and satisfy the self-avoiding walk constraint.

5   Experimental Results

Among the protein instances (Table 1) used in our experiment, the H instances are taken from Harvard benchmarks [28]; F, S, and R instances are taken from Peter Clote laboratory website[1]. Cebrian et al. [5] and Dotu et al. [9] used these instances to test their algorithms. We also use three more large sequences, which are taken from the CASP[2] competition having CASP target IDs: *T0516*, *T0570*, and *T0563*. The CASP targets are converted to HP sequences based on the hydrophobic and polar properties of the constituent amino acids. The lower bounds of free energy (in Column LB-FE of Table 1) are obtained from [5] and also by using the CPSP tool [19]; however, there are some unknown values because CPSP tool cannot find lower bounds of free energy for large sequences.

The main goal of the experiment is to compare the result of our final algorithm GA$^+$ with the state-of-the-art result obtained by LS [5,9]. However, to prove the effectiveness of our new enhancement techniques, we implemented a baseline genetic algorithm denoted by BGA. In BGA, we select one operator for each generation based on the given probability distribution. However, like other typical genetic algorithms, we select parents in BGA by using a *Roulette Wheel* based on the quality of conformations in the current population. Also, we generate only one (for mutations) or two (for crossovers) child conformations from each application of the genetic operators. The points on the conformations, to apply the operators to, are selected randomly as well. Further, inspired by the results of twin-removal in [13], we discard duplicate solutions from new generations. Notice that BGA does not use any of the macro-move, random-walk, and exhaustive generation approaches.

We ran experiments with our algorithm denoted by GA$^+$ and three of its other variants. These variants and BGA all are implemented in Java2 programming language. Nevertheless, these variants allow us to investigate the effect of each

Table 1. Experimental results of GA$^+$, different GA variants, and the local search algorithm in [5]. Column *LB-FE* presents the lower bound of free energies.

Protein Info			Energy Values (-ve) Achieved by Different Algorithms												T
			BGA		RGA		WGA		MGA		GA$^+$		LS [5]		
Seq	Size	LB-FE	Best	Avg	Best	Avg	Best	Avg	Best	Avg	Best	Avg	Best	Avg	mins
H1		69	65	58	=	67	=	68	=	67	=	**69**	68	66	
H2	48	69	63	57	=	67	=	68	=	68	=	**69**	=	65	30
H3		72	64	57	71	69	=	70	=	71	=	**72**	69	66	
F90_1		168	133	119.5	159	144	165	161	165	159	=	**166**	164	160	
F90_2	91	168	132	123.5	155	142	166	161	164	158	=	**165**	165	158	120
F90_3		167	138	124.4	158	146	165	161	163	158	=	**164**	165	159	
S1	135	357	300	279.0	332	313	352	342	344	336	**355**	**348**	351	341	
S2	151	360	298	258.2	332	301	351	339	346	335	**356**	**349**	355	343	120
S3	162	367	290	250.4	322	297	347	336	347	334	**361**	**349**	355	340	
R1		384	249	221.6	295	274	353	331	345	327	**355**	**346**	332	318	
R2	200	383	262	219.4	302	277	351	334	345	327	**360**	**346**	337	324	300
R3		385	250	220.8	299	274	344	331	340	323	**363**	**344**	339	323	
T0516	229	455	274	251.2	340	310	399	384	395	373	**423**	**402**	390	373	
T0570	258	494	288	250.9	359	317	406	388	394	376	**421**	**404**	388	359	480
T0563	279	?	359	315.5	428	390	494	474	482	459	**519**	**490**	491	461	

= denotes the lower bound of free energy is found.   ? denotes unknown.

new aspect of GA$^+$ individually and in a combined way. RGA adds exhaustive generation in the genetic operators (as described in Sect. 4) to BGA. Variants WGA and MGA respectively add random-walk and macro-move methods to RGA. Thus, variants WGA and MGA respectively exclude macro-move and random-walk methods from GA$^+$ while RGA excludes both methods. For the time being, we do not consider other possible combinations that include adding macro-move or random-walk, or their combinations to the BGA.

We also ran the local search algorithm in [5], which is developed in COMET [11]. This algorithm [5] helps us compare our results with the state-of-the-art results of PSP on FCC lattice and HP energy model. We tried to run the algorithm in [9], but unfortunately for most of the proteins, the program aborted on exhausting the memory available. Any effective comparison in this case is therefore not possible.

We ran the experiments on the NICTA^3 cluster. The cluster consists of a number of identical Dell PowerEdge R415 computers, each equipped with 2 x AMD 6-Core Opteron 4184 processors, 2.8GHz clock speed, 3M L2/6M L3 Cache, 64 GB memory and running Rocks OS (a Linux variant for cluster). For each protein, we ran each algorithm 50 times with a time limit specified in Table 1 Column T. In the same table Columns Best and Avg, we report the best and average energy values obtained over 50 runs. Due to space limits, only the magnitudes of the energy values (ignoring the minus signs in all) are shown. Therefore, the larger the number in the table, the better the performance.

From the results in Table 1, we see that the energy values obtained in small proteins by all algorithms are close to the lower bounds. For better comparison, we therefore consider the large proteins, where our RGA significantly outperforms BGA. The differences between RGA and BGA are in the application of the genetic operators. In BGA, genetic operators generate one (for mutations) or two (for crossovers) random conformations. In RGA, an exhaustive generation is used and the best children are returned. These results clearly show the effectiveness of the exhaustive generation.

The results in Table 1 also show that WGA and MGA clearly outperform RGA. These results indicate the importance of our random-walk based stagnation recovery approach and the macro-move operator. Notice that when WGA is compared with MGA, the former significantly outperforms the latter; which means the random walk alone is more effective than the macro-move. This further suggests that given an exhaustive generation approach accompanied by a greedy best child selection method as in RGA, recovery from stagnations is more crucial than intensifying the search.

As noted before, GA$^+$ is the final version of our algorithm. GA$^+$ combines both macro-move and random-walk with RGA. Notice that GA$^+$, benefited from our all three techniques, clearly outperforms BGA, RGA, MGA and WGA. Nevertheless, we observe that the results obtained by GA$^+$ are better than that of LS with wide margins. LS is also outperformed by WGA, but it outperforms RGA and BGA; the results of LS and MGA are very close.

---

^{3} NICTA website: www.nicta.com.au

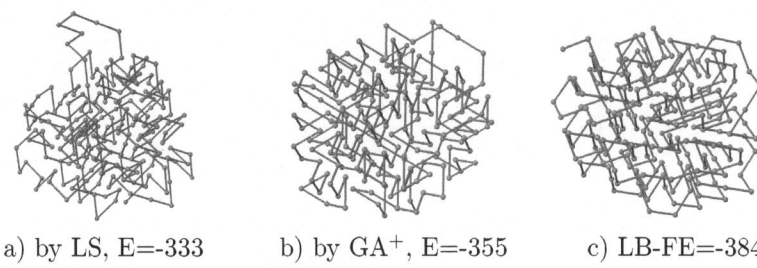

a) by LS, E=-333   b) by GA$^+$, E=-355   c) LB-FE=-384

Fig. 7. 3D structures of Protein R1 obtained by a) LS and b) GA$^+$, and c) the structure with the lower bound free energy

Relative Improvement: In Table 2, we present a comparison of (%) improvements in average conformation quality. We compare GA$^+$ (target) with BGA and LS (references). For each protein, the relative improvement of the target t w.r.t. reference r is $(E_t - E_r)/(E_{lb} - E_r) \times 100$; where E_t and E_r denote the average energy value achieved by t and r respectively, and E_{lb} is the lower bounds of free energy for the protein in the HP model. We present the relative improvements only for the proteins having known lower bounds of free energy. Further, we show the best structures found by GA$^+$ and LS for protein R1 in Fig. 7; the figure also shows the structure of R1 with the lower bound free energy.

Search Progress: We compare the search progresses of different variants of GA and LS over time. Fig. 8 shows the average energy values obtained with times by the algorithms for Protein R1. We observe that MGA achieves very good progress initially, but almost becomes flat later on. WGA and LS perform equally initially but later WGA makes more progress than LS. GA$^+$ combines the positive aspects of MGA and WGA. Initially, it achieves the same progress as MGA does and later it is mostly benefited by random-walk as WGA is.

Table 2. Relative improvements (RI columns) of GA$^+$ over *BGA* and *LS*. The values are calculated using the formula explained in *Relative Improvement* subsection. Column *LB-FE* presents the lower bound of free energies.

Relative improvements of GA^+ w.r.t. BGA and LS							
Protein info			**GA$^+$**	**BGA**		**LS**	
Seq	Size	LB-FE	Avg	Avg	RI	Avg	RI
H1		-69	-69	-58	100%	-66	100%
H2	48	-69	-69	-57	100%	-65	100%
H3		-72	-72	-57	100%	-66	100%
F90_1		-168	-166	-120	96%	-160	75%
F90_2	91	-168	-165	-124	93%	-158	70%
F90_3		-167	-164	-125	93%	-159	63%
S1	135	-357	-348	-279	88%	-341	44%
S2	151	-360	-349	-268	88%	-343	35%
S3	162	-367	-349	-250	85%	-340	33%
R1		-384	-346	-223	76%	-318	42%
R2	200	-383	-346	-219	77%	-324	37%
R3		-385	-344	-221	75%	-323	34%
T0516	229	-258	-402	-251	74%	-373	35%
T0570	258	-494	-404	-251	63%	-359	33%

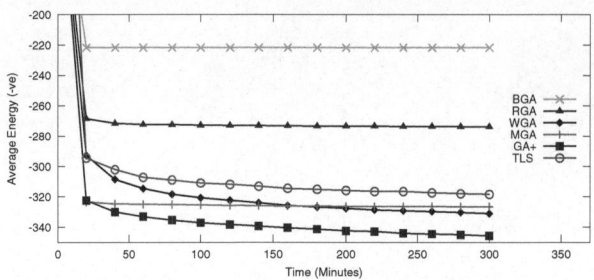

Fig. 8. Search progress of different approaches for Protein R1

The difference between performances of WGA and GA$^+$ roughly remains in the initial boosted progress made by the macro-move i.e. MGA.

6   Conclusion and Future Work

In this paper, we presented five variants of genetic algorithms that individually and in a combined way use three different enhancement techniques: *i*) an exhaustive conformation generation approach; *ii*) a novel hydrophobic-core directed macro-move; and *iii*) a random-walk based stagnanation recovery technique. We compared our results with the state-of-the-art local search algorithm for simplified PSP. We found that our final algorithm GA$^+$ that use a combination of all the three enhancements significantly outperforms all current approaches of simplified PSP. In future, we intend to apply GA$^+$ in high resolution PSP.

Acknowledgments. NICTA is funded by the Australian Government as represented by the Department of Broadband, Communications and the Digital Economy and the Australian Research Council through the ICT Centre of Excellence program.

References

1. Berger, B., Leightont, T.: Protein folding in the hydrophobic-hydrophilic (HP) model is NP-complete. Journal of Computational Biology 5(1), 27–40 (1998)
2. Blum, C.: Ant colony optimization: introduction and recent trends. Physics of Life Reviews 2(4), 353–373 (2005)
3. Böckenhauer, H.-J., Dayem Ullah, A.Z.M., Kapsokalivas, L., Steinhöfel, K.: A Local Move Set for Protein Folding in Triangular Lattice Models. In: Crandall, K.A., Lagergren, J. (eds.) WABI 2008. LNCS (LNBI), vol. 5251, pp. 369–381. Springer, Heidelberg (2008)
4. Bonneau, R., Baker, D.: *Ab initio* protein structure prediction: progress and prospects. Annual Review of Biophysics and Biomolecular Structure 30(1), 173–189 (2001)
5. Cebrián, M., Dotú, I., Van Hentenryck, P., Clote, P.: Protein structure prediction on the face centered cubic lattice by local search. In: Proceedings of the 23rd National Conference on Artificial Intelligence, vol. 1, pp. 241–246 (2008)

6. Cutello, V., Nicosia, G., Pavone, M., Timmis, J.: An immune algorithm for protein structure prediction on lattice models. IEEE Transaction on Evolutionary Computing 11(1), 101–117 (2007)
7. Dill, K.A.: Theory for the folding and stability of globular proteins. Biochemistry 24(6), 1501–1509 (1985)
8. Dobso, C.M.: Protein folding and misfolding. Nature 426(6968), 884–890 (2003)
9. Dotu, I., Cebrián, M., Van Hentenryck, P., Clote, P.: On lattice protein structure prediction revisited. IEEE Transactions on Comp. Bio. and Bioinformatics (2011)
10. Hales, T.: A proof of the kepler conjecture. The Annals of Mathematics 162(3), 1065–1185 (2005)
11. Hentenryck, P., Michel, L.: Constraint-based local search. The MIT Press (2009)
12. Hoque, M.T.: Genetic algorithm for *ab initio* protein structure prediction based on low resolution models. Ph.D. thesis, Gippsland School of Information Technology, Monash University, Australia (September 2007)
13. Hoque, M.T., Chetty, M., Lewis, A., Sattar, A.: Twin removal in genetic algorithms for protein structure prediction using low-resolution model. Transactions on Computational Biology and Bioinformatics 8(1), 234–245 (2011)
14. Hoque, M.T., Chetty, M., Sattar, A.: Protein folding prediction in 3D FCC HP lattice model using genetic algorithm. In: IEEE Congress on Evolutionary Computation, pp. 4138–4145 (2007)
15. Klau, G.W., Lesh, N., Marks, J., Mitzenmacher, M.: Human-guided tabu search. In: The Eighteenth National Conference on Artificial Intelligence, AAAI 2002 (2002)
16. Lau, K.F., Dill, K.A.: A lattice statistical mechanics model of the conformational and sequence spaces of proteins. Macromolecules 22(10), 3986–3997 (1989)
17. Lee, J., Wu, S., Zhang, Y.: Ab initio protein structure prediction. From Protein Structure to Function with Bioinformatics, 3–25 (2009)
18. Lesh, N., Mitzenmacher, M., Whitesides, S.: A complete and effective move set for simplified protein folding. In: Research in Comp. Mol. Biology, RECOMB (2003)
19. Mann, M., Will, S., Backofen, R.: CPSP-tools – exact and complete algorithms for high-throughput 3D lattice protein studies. BMC Bioinformatics 9(1), 230 (2008)
20. Patton, A.L., Punch III, W.F., Goodman, E.D.: A standard GA approach to native protein conformation prediction. In: Int. Conf. on Genetic Algorithms (1995)
21. Rohl, C., Strauss, C., Misura, K., Baker, D.: Protein structure prediction using Rosetta. Methods in Enzymology 383, 66–93 (2004)
22. Tantar, A.A., Melab, N., Talbi, E.G.: A grid-based genetic algorithm combined with an adaptive simulated annealing for protein structure prediction. In: Soft Computing-A Fusion of Foundations, Methodologies and Applications (2008)
23. Thachuk, C., Shmygelska, A., Hoos, H.H.: A replica exchange monte carlo algorithm for protein folding in the HP model. BMC Bioinformatics 8(1), 342 (2007)
24. The Science Editorial: So much more to know. The Science 309(5731), 78–102 (July 2005)
25. Unger, R., Moult, J.: A genetic algorithm for 3D protein folding simulations. In: The 5th International Conference on Genetic Algorithms, p. 581. Morgan Kaufmann Publishers (1993)
26. Xia, Y., Huang, E.S., Levitt, M., Samudrala, R.: *Ab initio* construction of protein tertiary structures using a hierarchical approach. Journal of Mol. Biology (2008)
27. Yue, K., Dill, K.A.: Sequence-structure relationships in proteins and copolymers. Physical Review E 48(3), 2267 (1993)
28. Yue, K., Fiebig, K.M., Thomas, P.D., Chan, H.S., Shakhnovich, E.I., Dill, K.A.: A test of lattice protein folding algorithms. Proceedings of the National Academy of Sciences of the United States of America 92(1), 325 (1995)

Generating Realistic Online Auction Data

Sidney Tsang, Gillian Dobbie, and Yun Sing Koh

The University of Auckland
stsa027@aucklanduni.ac.nz, {gill,ykoh}@cs.auckland.ac.nz

Abstract. To combat online auction fraud, researchers have developed fraud detection and prevention methods. However, it is difficult to effectively evaluate
these methods using commercial or synthetic auction data. For commercial data,
it is not possible to accurately identify cases of fraud. For synthetic auction data,
the conclusions drawn may not extend to the real world. The availability of realistic synthetic auction data, which models real auction data, will be invaluable
for effective evaluation of fraud detection algorithms. We present an agent-based
simulator that is capable of generating realistic English auction data. The agents
and model are based on data collected from the TradeMe online auction site. We
evaluate the generated data in two ways to show that it is similar to the TradeMe
data. Evaluation of individual features show that correlation is greater than 0.9
for 8 of the 10 features, and evaluation using multiple features gives a median
accuracy of 0.87.

1 Introduction

Over a three-month period in 2011, 37% of New Zealanders have purchased at least
one item from an online auction site based in New Zealand called TradeMe [1]. The
popularity of online auction sites such as TradeMe has made them a lucrative target
for dishonest users to commit fraud. There have been several methods proposed by
researchers to identify different types of online auction fraud [2–6]. These methods are
evaluated using synthetic data, or using data collected from commercial sites such as
eBay.

There are disadvantages to using both types of data. One of the drawbacks of synthetic auction data is that it may be dissimilar to data in the real world. Evaluation
performed using this data will be less reliable, since results obtained may not extend to
real auction data. Though it is possible to modify the synthetic data to simulate the real
world, it is difficult to model bidding and selling behaviour because of the large range
of possible actions. This is shown by Shah et al. [7], who found that 88% of users do
not frequently use any of the five bidding strategies described: evaluate, skeptic, snipe,
late bidder and unmask. The advantage of using synthetic data is that the instances and
types of fraud can be controlled.

Evaluation using auction data from commercial sites may give results that are more
representative of the real world than synthetic data. However, it is difficult and time
consuming to manually classify data, in the case of fraud detection, into fraudulent and
non-fraudulent users or auctions. For larger datasets, manual classification is infeasible.
In addition, it is often time-consuming to gather and process data from auction sites, as

M. Thielscher and D. Zhang (Eds.): AI 2012, LNCS 7691, pp. 120–131, 2012.

seen in [3] which used an elaborate system to gather auction data from eBay. Also, data may be selectively missing or removed by operators of the auction site, such as profiles of users that have been identified as fraudsters, or auctions that have been identified afterwards as fraudulent. This complicates the evaluations done using this data.

In this paper, we present an agent-based simulator of an online auction site where agents are modelled on users in real auction data. The resulting simulation can be used to quickly generate realistic auction data. We then validate our simulator by performing quantitative evaluations comparing the generated data to commercial TradeMe auction data, and show that the generated and commercial data shows a high degree of similarity.

The simulator can be easily extended in the future with additional agents to inject fraudulent behaviour. Since the simulator is modelled on a per-user basis, the synthetic data with injected fraud will be valuable for effective evaluation of fraud detection algorithms which often focus on per-user features.

2 Existing Work

Agent-based simulation and modelling has been used in a wide range of complex systems. Macal and North [8] list nine different areas in which agent-based modelling has been applied, including air traffic control, anthropology, and energy analysis. Macal and North propose possible reasons for the widespread use of agent-based modelling. They state that agent-based modelling allows assumptions used in the past for modelling complex systems to be relaxed, such as perfect market or homogeneous agents in economic markets. Collection of data at finer levels of granularity also supports individual-based simulations. We list three reasons that they presented that apply to our work here. First, previous work on formal auction analysis used assumptions such as perfect rationality, perfect market and homogeneous agents, which can be removed in agent-based models. Second, there exists precise bidding and auction information for modelling of individual users. Third, auction users are suitably modelled by agents since they share many similarities; they are both self-contained, autonomous, and have defined ways of interacting with other users.

One of the earliest works in agent-based simulation in auctions was done by Mizuta and Steiglitz [9], who modelled agents of two types: early bidders and snipers, and investigated the effects of the strategies on the probability of winning, auction price increment, and final auction price. More recently, agent-based modelling of bidders has been used to perform evaluations of fraud related algorithms [2, 6], or to investigate the effects of modifying different aspects of the model, such as changing the bid increment [10]. In both [2] and [6], the authors do not evaluate their models against reality.

In [10], Bapna et al. constructed a simulation model of Yankee auctions. They identified three broad types of bidders according to their bidding strategies: evaluators, participators, and opportunists, and created agents that used each strategy. The simulation model is validated by comparing the simulated revenue with the observed revenue from data collected from real auctions. Using this model, they altered the auction bid increment to optimise seller revenue.

We know of no previous work that attempts to accurately model bidder and seller behaviour in commercial online English auctions using agent-based methods without having previously classified bidders.

3   Data Generator Overview

Our data generator is an agent-based simulation of online English auctions, the auction type used in online auction sites such as eBay and TradeMe. For more details on the English auction and other auction types, see [11]. Auction data can be generated by running the simulation and recording the actions of all of the agents, such as auctions submitted and bids made. By carefully specifying the behaviour of the agents, we can generate synthetic auction data that closely approximates real auction data.

The decision to use user-level features instead of auction-level features is because in the future, we plan to inject fraud into the data and use it to evaluate fraud related algorithms which tend to use per-user features instead of per-auction features [2, 3, 6].

We start by giving a brief overview of the stages involved in the implementation of the generator:

Stage 1. Auction and User data is gathered from TradeMe in October 2011 using a web crawler, and stored in a database. A total of 93,179 users and 161,895 auctions were collected.

Stage 2. An agent-based simulator is built in Java with the following characteristics:
   1. Each agent corresponds to a bidder or seller.
   2. Agents communicate with an Auctioneer entity to submit bids or auctions. The Auctioneer also maintains the state of all current auctions and bids and ensures that they conform to the auction rules.

Stage 3. We define the rules that each auction and bid must follow, which are then enforced by the Auctioneer. E.g., auction starting prices must be greater than zero. These rules can be easily changed to model other auction sites, such as eBay.

Stage 4. We specify the behaviour of bidder-agents according to the bidding patterns seen in the TradeMe users. This is done by representing bidders in TradeMe as a set of features, and defining agent rules that gives similar values for those features. Examples of rules is given in Section 4.4.

Stage 5. Next we specify the rules for seller-agents. The two main parameters are rate of auction submission and auction starting price. We match the average rate and distribution of auction submission of the seller-agents to TradeMe users.

Stage 6. We evaluate the synthetic auction data generated using the bidder- and seller-agents by comparing them with the TradeMe user data we have collected. If the synthetic and real data are not sufficiently similar, we modify the agent behaviour, then re-evaluate.

3.1   Generated Auction Example

Table 1 gives an example of an auction generated by the generator. Table 1a lists the bids made for that auction. Table 1b gives information about the auction. *Bid Time*,

Start Time, and *End Time* represent time units since the beginning of the simulator execution, with each unit representing five minutes. *Duration* is the number of time units the auction runs for.

There are 8 bids made for this auction, and User 2285 wins the item for \$40.61 at time 2026. Note that *Duration* is less than the difference between the start and end times because the auction was extended due to a bid submission in the last 3 time units.

Table 1. Example of a generated auction

(a) Auction Bids

BidID	UserID	BidTime	BidAmount (cents)
1	801	871	250
2	1,820	1,710	2,361
3	801	1,735	2,661
4	2,910	1,963	2,761
5	1,820	1,998	3,761
6	2,285	2,014	3,861
7	801	2,025	3,961
8	2,285	2,026	4,061

(b) Auction Information

ListingID	0
StartTime	11
EndTime	2,029
Duration	2,016
ItemValuation (cents)	3,935
itemTypeId	1
startPrice (cents)	100

4 Implementation

In the following section we describe some of the details and difficulties of implementing the generator. First, we describe the method and type of information collected from TradeMe. Second, how this information is represented using a collection of features. Third, how agents were designed using this information. Fourth, what happens during the simulator's execution. And fifth, the limitations of the simulator.

4.1 Data Collection

Data is collected from the TradeMe website [12] using the web crawler Scrapy and stored in a database. Crawling begins at one user's auction history page which contains a list of completed auctions. Completed auctions contain a list of bids which link to the auction history of each bidder. Unvisited pages are placed into a FIFO queue, so that the available auction history for users will be completely collected in the order they were discovered. This is important because the crawler only visits a small percentage of the existing user and auction pages. Using a FILO (first in last out) queue will result in incomplete auction histories for a large number of users.

From user pages, we extracted the number of positive, neutral and negative feedbacks they received, and the number of auctions they participated in. From completed auctions, we extracted bid times and amounts, the winning bid and bidder, item name, seller name and reputation. After cleaning, 56,256 auctions and 53,951 user profiles remained.

There are several limits to the information that cxan be collected. Firstly, only the most recent 20 bids are viewable for a completed auction. Secondly, bid histories for auctions are available only for 60 days after it has completed. Thirdly, some user pages are unavailable. The reason is not given, but one possibility is that those pages belong to identified fraudsters. The last limitation may be an advantage since we currently only wish to simulate legitimate users; removal of suspicious users will improve data quality.

4.2   User Features

It is difficult to identify patterns in bidder behaviour from lists of bids. Therefore, we represent bidders using a set of features that are easier to visualise and interpret. The set of user features used while developing the bidder agents are:

a. **Auction Count** the number of auctions in which the bidder made one or more bids
b. **Reputation** the difference between the number of positive and negative feedback
c. **Bid Amount** the average bid value for all bids the user made
d. **Excess Bid Increment** the average increment over the preceding bid, minus the required minimum increment
e. **Bids Per Auction** the average number of bids made per auction
f. **First Bid Time** the average number of minutes the first bid is made before the end of the auction
g. **Bid Time** the average bid time as a fraction of the auction time that has elapsed
h. **Win Proportion** the number of auctions won divided by Auction Count
i. **Bid Amount Proportion** the average bid value of all bids, with each bid scaled as a proportion of the winning bid
j. **Bid Proportion** the average fraction of bids that are made by this user in an auction

Features a-f are log-transformed so that values are spread out more evenly for clustering, since many values are very similar for some features.

Some features, such as Auction Count, Bids Per Auction, and First Bid Time, can be directly used in rules for bidder-agents. Other features, such as Bid Amount Proportion, Win Proportion, and Bid Proportion, cannot, since their values depend on the behaviour of other agents. However, those features can be used to determine whether synthetic data from the generator is sufficiently similar to the TradeMe data.

4.3   Simulation Execution during 1 Time Unit

Figure 1 shows what happens during one time unit in the simulator. The time unit is split into two stages; the Auctioneer phase (A), and the Agent phase (B). During the Auctioneer phase, only the Auctioneer sends or receives messages, and performs actions; all other agents are inactive. During the Agent phase, this is reversed, and only agents perform actions. Agent actions can be performed in parallel using multiple threads. The Message Store for Agents is simply a hash map, where the key is the agent ID, and the value is the message. The Message Store for Auctioneer is a list.

4.4   Bidder-Agent Behaviour

The TradeMe users are clustered using the features listed in Section 4.2 using the simple k-means algorithm. To select the optimum number of clusters, we use the method proposed by Lange et al. [13] to find the number of clusters that gives the lowest stability value, where a lower value represents a better clustering solution. Stability was calculated for two to ten clusters, and stability was lowest when the number of clusters was four. Therefore, we used four centroids during simple k-means clustering.

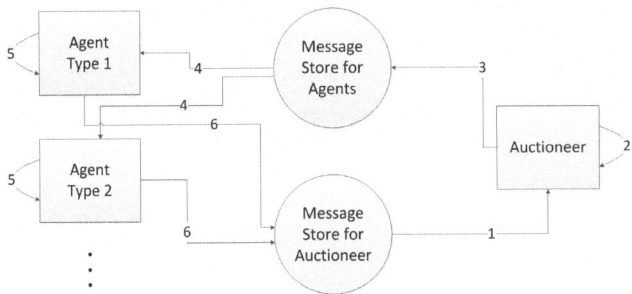

A. Beginning of Auctioneer phase
   1. Retrieve messages from Agents
   2. Process messages
      a. update auction states, terminate finished auctions
      b. ensure auctions and bids have valid states before and after update
   3. Send messages (current time, new auction, end of auction, price change messages)
B. Beginning of Agent phase
   4. Retrieve messages from Auctioneer
   5. Decide on what actions to take, if any
   6. Send messages (new auction, bid messages)

Fig. 1. Events during the execution of the simulator in one time unit

From the clusters we identified patterns, for example: a significant number of users only bid close to the end of the auction and rebid quickly after they have been outbid; users who bid close to the end win more often; and users who bid early and win are often the only bidder in an auction. Bidder agents are given behaviours that allow the synthetic data to contain these same patterns. For example, for the last pattern, the rule may be to increase the likelihood of entering a bid as the number of existing bids in the auction increases, which leaves a fraction of auctions to have only 1 participating bidder.

There are additional rules that determine other aspects of behaviour: the moment a bidder-agent should begin bidding; how often and how much to bid above the minimum required bid; when to stop bidding, etc. These rules generally provide probabilities of whether an action should be taken, and a decision is made using a random number. For instance, an agent will bid, with 10% probability, on an item whose price has reached the agent's perceived value.

4.5 Limitations

A known limitation of this simulator is that it is unable to accurately model the bidding times of bids made close to the end of the auction. This is because the simulator uses time units of five minutes, which means that the fastest speed that an agent can respond to another bid is five minutes. The choice of five minute time units was a calculated trade-off between the simulation performance and precision: it allowed us to quickly generate data while retaining sufficient simulation precision.

As a result, a bidding war close to the auction end time may occur over 30 minutes or more, instead of within minutes. Thus, while the simulator can accurately models user bidding time patterns earlier in the auction, it cannot do so close to the end of the auction and distribution of values for features i and j in Section 4.2 from the simulator will not closely match those from the TradeMe data.

5   Evaluation

In this section we present the method and results for two evaluation techniques to validate our simulation. The method and results for the first evaluation are given Sections 5.1 and 5.2; and those for the second evaluation in Sections 5.3 and 5.4.

5.1   Evaluation Method Using Individual Features

We compared the similarity in the distribution of per-user values, for each feature described in Section 4.2, between the generated and TradeMe data. If the distribution of values from the generated data match those from the TradeMe data, then our model is more likely to be valid. The comparison is done using two correlation measures: Pearson's correlation coefficient and Spearman's rank correlation coefficient [14]. Pearson's correlation is a parametric test, while Spearman's rank correlation is a non-parametric test. The correlation measures are calculated individually for each feature.

For Pearson's correlation coefficient, a value of $+1$ or -1 indicates that a linear equation describes the relationship between the two variables perfectly. For Spearman's rank correlation coefficient, $+1$ or -1 occurs when each of the variables is a perfect monotone function of the other. A value close to $+1$ shows that the TradeMe and synthetic data are similar.

5.2   Evaluation Results Using Individual Features

Figure 2 shows the distribution of values for six features for both the synthetic and TradeMe datasets. To construct the figures, all values from the 30 synthetic datasets were used, giving 111,677 values for each feature. Values are split into 20 equidistant bins using the maximum and minimum values for that feature. The plots reflect the proportion of users that have a value that falls into a particular bin. We see that distribution of values for the 30 synthetic datasets generally match those from the TradeMe dataset.

Table 2 shows the correlation between synthetic and TradeMe data for each feature as measured by Pearson's correlation coefficient and Spearman's rank correlation coefficient. The correlation values for both measures are greater than 0.9 for all features, with the exception of Bid Amount, with a Pearson's correlation of 0.53 and Excess Bid Increment with 0.86. The low similarity for Bid Amounts, and to a lesser extent, Excess Bid Increment, is due to the lack of information on the perceived and actual value of items, making it more difficult to accurately model bid values.

As a whole, the high correlation values show that the value distribution of features from our generated data is similar to TradeMe data.

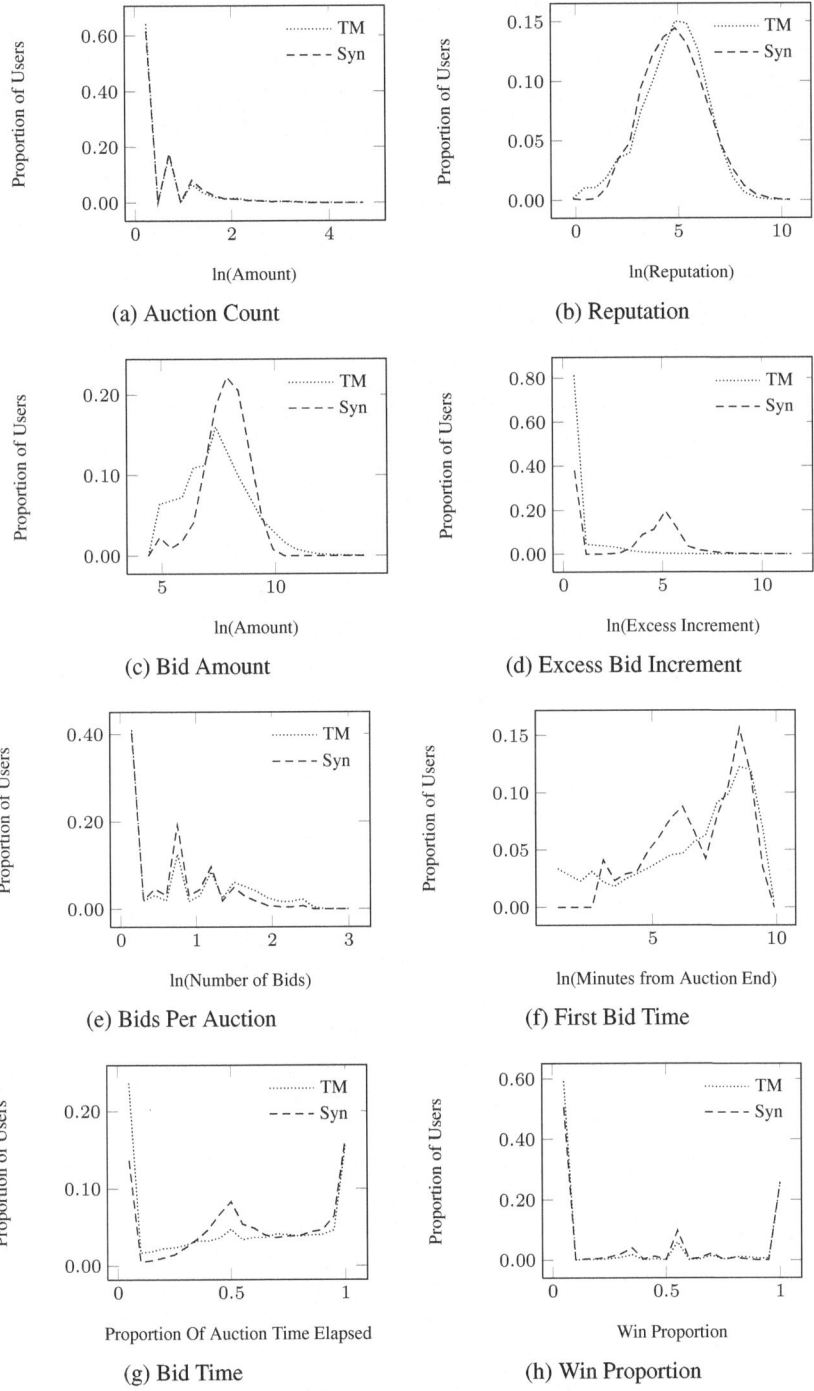

Fig. 2. Value distributions of features

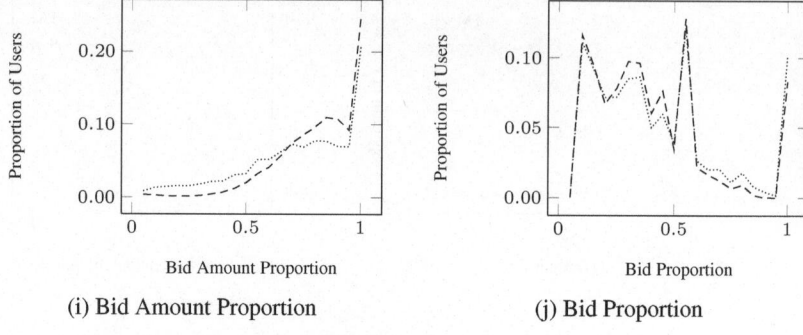

(i) Bid Amount Proportion   (j) Bid Proportion

Fig. 2. (*contiuned*)

Table 2. Correlation results for all features

Feature	Pearson's Correlation		Spearman's Rank
	95% CI	Correlation	ρ
Auction Count	0.9468 - 0.9485	0.9476	0.9625
Reputation	0.9379 - 0.9399	0.9389	0.99997
Bid Amount	0.5207 - 0.5329	**0.5269**	0.9999
Excess Bid Increment	0.8545 - 0.8590	**0.8567**	**0.8497**
Bids Per Auction	0.9702 - 0.9711	0.9706	0.9930
First Bid Time	0.9889 - 0.9892	0.9890	0.99998
Bid Time	0.9701 - 0.9710	0.9706	0.9967
Win Proportion	0.9752 - 0.9760	0.9756	0.9515
Bid Amount Proportion	0.9873 - 0.9877	0.9875	0.9987
Bid Proportion	0.9841 - 0.9846	0.9844	0.9981

5.3   Evaluation Method Using Multiple Features

Lange et al. proposed a method to solve the model order selection problem in cluster analysis; that is, to find a suitable number of clusters k. They state that a cluster solution should be robust: that the cluster analysis should be reproducible using other datasets drawn from the same source, and not depend on the particular sample [13]. The degree to which the cluster solution is reproducible can be used to determine the number of clusters k that should be inferred from a dataset. However, since only one dataset is usually available, the dataset is split into two, and treated as two samples.

Conversely, if the number of clusters for a dataset is given, the degree of reproducibility gives an indication of the similarity of the second dataset to the first. We adapt the method proposed by Lange et al. to evaluate the similarity of TradeMe data with synthetic data. There are two main changes to the method; (1) there is no need to normalise results according to the number of clusters inferred since the number remains unchanged, and (2) two different datasets are used: the TradeMe dataset, and a synthetic dataset.

For evaluating the similarity between datasets, the equation for measuring the normalised Hamming distance between two labelling vectors (in [13]) can be slightly modified to:

$$d(\phi(X'), Y') = \frac{1}{n} \sum_{i=1}^{n} 1\{\phi(X'_i) = Y'_i\} \tag{1}$$

where $1\{\phi(X_i') = Y_i')\} = 1$, if $\phi(X_i') = Y_i'$. This gives the proportion of instances that are given the same labelling via the classifier trained on X (which in our case is the TradeMe dataset) and the clustering solution Y' for X' (the synthetic dataset). Since the corresponding clusters may be assigned different labels in two different clustering solutions even if the datasets are the same, agreement is maximised using the Hungarian method as suggested by Lange et al.

We used the simple k-means algorithm for clustering the TradeMe and synthetic data into four clusters. Clustering the TradeMe dataset X, gives a set of labels Y, one for each instance. Together, (X, Y) is used to construct a closest neighbour classifier ϕ. Clustering the synthetic dataset X' gives a set of labels Y'. The classifier ϕ is then used to classify instances in X', giving the labels $\phi(X')$. With Y' and $\phi(X')$ we can calculate the accuracy using Equation 1.

Features Used. We used four features for evaluating the similarity between the synthetic and TradeMe data: Proportion of Max Bid, Win Proportion, Bids Per Auction, Bid Proportion. These four features were chosen because the others:

1. Have almost the same values for all users, e.g. excess bid increment as shown in Figure 2(d), and are less useful for clustering.
2. Are identically distributed regardless of their cluster assignments, e.g. reputation, bid amount, and are not useful for clustering.
3. Are known not to closely approximate real data (features i and j), as discussed in Section 4.5.

5.4   Evaluation Results Using Multiple Features

We evaluated our simulator using 30 synthetic datasets, each with roughly 3,700 users. We report the results for evaluations using random starting centroids for simple k-means, and using manually defined centroids.

Using 50 sets of random initial centroids for evaluating each synthetic dataset, the average accuracy is 0.745 with a standard deviation of 0.0957. Using the first set of centroids shown in Table 3, the average accuracy is 0.878, an increase of 0.143, with a standard deviation of 0.0282.

Centroid Selection. The k-means algorithm is sensitive to the centroids chosen during initialisation [15], which in turn heavily influences the result given by Equation 1. In our case, this problem may be worsened by characteristics of our dataset. First, clusters are not well defined in the Trade Me data, which means clusters will tend to grow from their initial position. Secondly, the Win Proportion feature is almost binary, where the majority of users have a value of zero or one. Given four initial centroids, there are five configurations the centroids could take for Win Proportion, e.g., all centroids have a Win Proportion of zero. If the configuration of centroids were different for two datasets, the accuracy value will be very low even though the datasets may be very similar. Therefore, it is necessary to manually define the initial centroids so that two will have a value of one, and two with zero. This is similar to the method by Fang et al. [15] to select centroids that maximise inter-centroid distance.

Table 3. Selected centroid centers

	Centroid ID	Bid Amount Proportion	Win Proportion	Bids Per Auction	Bid Proportion
Appropriate Centroids	1	0.8	0.0	0.0	0.2
	2	0.8	0.0	0.0	0.2
	3	1.0	**1.0**	0.0	0.5
	4	1.0	1.0	0.0	1.0
Inappropriate Centroids	1	0.8	0.0	0.0	0.2
	2	0.8	0.0	0.0	0.2
	3	1.0	**0.0**	0.0	0.5
	4	1.0	1.0	0.0	1.0

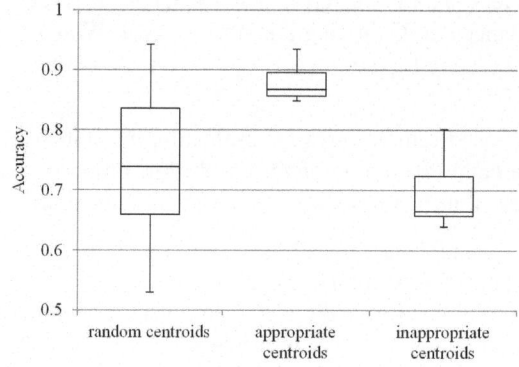

Fig. 3. Accuracy using different centroids for clustering using four features: Bid Amount Proportion, Win Proportion, Bids Per Auction, Bid Proportion

We give evidence of this in Table 3 and Figure 3. Table 3 shows two sets of centroids. The set named "appropriate centroids" have two centroids with the value of 0, and two centroids with the value of 1 for Win Proportion. For the set named "inappropriate centroids", the difference is that the third centroid has as value 0 of instead of 1 as Win Proportion. Figure 3 shows that this change reduces median accuracy by 0.203 and mean accuracy by 0.192.

6   Conclusion

We successfully implemented a agent-based simulator for online auctions. We evaluated the quality of data generated by our simulator in two ways; using two correlation measures, and a modified version of the Stability measure proposed by Lange et al. [13]. The results show that our synthetic data closely matches the TradeMe data. Correlation of individual features compared to TradeMe data exceeds 0.9 for 8 out of 10 features for both measures, and median accuracy as calculated by Equation 1 is 0.87 for user defined centroids.

In the future, we intend to reduce the time unit length from five minutes, so that we can better model bidding at the end of auctions. In addition, we intend to implement additional agents to add fraudulent bids into the auctions. This will allow us to recreate various types of fraud, and test fraud detection algorithms using the generated synthetic data.

References

1. Scherer, K.: Retail store wars move online (2011)
2. Bhargava, B., Jenamani, M., Zhong, Y.: Counteracting shill bidding in online english auction. International Journal of Cooperative Information Systems 14 (2005)
3. Pandit, S., Chau, D.H., Wang, S., Faloutsos, C.: Netprobe: a fast and scalable system for fraud detection in online auction networks. In: Proceedings of the 16th International Conference on World Wide Web, pp. 201–210 (2007)
4. Chae, M., Shim, S., Cho, H., Lee, B.: An empirical analysis of fraud detection in online auctions: Credit card phantom transaction. In: Proceedings of the 40th Annual Hawaii International Conference on System Sciences, p. 155a. IEEE Computer Society
5. Chau, D., Pandit, S., Faloutsos, C.: Detecting Fraudulent Personalities in Networks of Online Auctioneers. In: Fürnkranz, J., Scheffer, T., Spiliopoulou, M. (eds.) PKDD 2006. LNCS (LNAI), vol. 4213, pp. 103–114. Springer, Heidelberg (2006)
6. Trevathan, J., Read, W.: Detecting collusive shill bidding. In: Fourth International Conference on Information Technology, ITNG 2007, pp. 799–808 (2007)
7. Shah, H., Joshi, N., Sureka, A., Wurman, P.: Mining eBay: Bidding Strategies and Shill Detection. In: Zaïane, O.R., Srivastava, J., Spiliopoulou, M., Masand, B. (eds.) WebKDD 2003. LNCS (LNAI), vol. 2703, pp. 17–34. Springer, Heidelberg (2003)
8. Macal, C.M., North, M.J.: Agent-based modeling and simulation. In: Proceedings of the Simulation Conference (WSC), pp. 86–98 (Winter 2009)
9. Mizuta, H., Steiglitz, K.: Agent-based simulation of dynamic online auctions. In: Simulation Conference Proceedings, vol. 2, pp. 1772–1777 (Winter 2000)
10. Bapna, R., Goes, P., Gupta, A.: Simulating online yankee auctions to optimize sellers revenue. In: Proceedings of the 34th Annual Hawaii International Conference on System Sciences, p. 10 (2001)
11. Menezes, F.M., Monteiro, P.K.: Auction Types. In: An Introduction to Auction Theory, pp. 10–11. Oxford University Press, USA (2005)
12. TradeMe (April 17, 2012), http://www.trademe.co.nz/
13. Lange, T., Roth, V., Braun, M.L., Buhmann, J.M.: Stability-based validation of clustering solutions. Neural Comput. 16(6), 1299–1323 (2004)
14. Myers, J.L., Well, A.D.: Research Design & Statistical Analysis, 2nd edn. Lawrence Erlbaum Associates (2003)
15. Haw-ren, F., Saad, Y.: Farthest centroids divisive clustering. In: Seventh International Conference on Machine Learning and Applications, ICMLA 2008, pp. 232–238 (2008)

A Robust Global Motion Estimation for Digital Video Stabilization

Behnam Babagholami-Mohamadabadi, Amin Jourabloo,
and Mohammad T. Manzuri-Shalmani

Department of Computer Engineering, Sharif University of Technology
Tehran, Iran
{babagholami,jourabloo}@ce.sharif.edu, manzuri@sharif.edu

Abstract. This paper proposes a global motion estimation method to remove unintentional camera motions which degrade the visual quality of image sequences. The proposed approach is based on combination of 2D Radon transform, 1D Fourier transform and 1D Scale transform which can accurately estimate scale, rotational and translational distortions of camera motion and is robust to internal moving objects. Our experimental results with real and synthesized videos indicate the effectiveness of our proposed method.

Keywords: Global Motion Estimation, Radon Transform, Fourier Transform, Scale Transform, Similarity Motion Model.

1 Introduction

Digital video stabilization methods try to eliminate unwanted camera motions. These typical high frequency motions such as pan, and jitter, degrade visual appearance quality of videos. Digital video stabilization algorithms can be divided into two main steps, Motion Estimation, and Motion Correction. In motion estimation step, the global motion between consecutive frames is determined. The motion estimation algorithms can be categorized into three main classes, Block matching based methods, Transform domain based methods, and Feature matching based methods. In the block matching based approaches [1,2], the current frame is divided into several blocks. Then, the motion for each block is estimated. Finally, the global motion is calculated using estimated block motions. The main disadvantage of this category is that local movement of internal objects degrades the accuracy of block motion estimation. High time complexity is another problem with this class of algorithms which is due to the exhaustive search for block matching. Feature matching based methods [3,4,5] extract suitable features such as SIFT [6], and SURF [7] from both current and reference frames. After determining the corresponding features, the parameters of global motion is estimated using matched features. Because of handling motions such as rotation and zooming in addition to translational motions, algorithms of this class are more accurate and flexible than block matching approaches which can

M. Thielscher and D. Zhang (Eds.): AI 2012, LNCS 7691, pp. 132–143, 2012.

only deal with translational motions. However, feature based methods have limitation by occlusion which is due to the moving objects. High computational load for feature detection and matching is another drawback of these methods. The algorithms of the last category transform the frames into a new domain and estimate the motion parameters using the information in the transform domain. In phase correlation technique [8], the translation property of Discrete Fourier Transform (DFT) is used in order to obtain the translational motion parameters. Although this method is very fast and is robust to local motion of moving objects, it is not able to estimate rotational motion which is frequent in most shaky videos. Hong et al. [9] utilized polar transform in order to estimate rotation in addition to translation parameter of motion. Although the accuracy of this method is satisfactory, polar transform suffers from nonuniform sampling which makes it unsuitable for videos with moving objects. Being unable to handle scale distortion is another drawback of this algorithm.

The second part of a video stabilization system is motion correction where estimated global motion is filtered to remove unwanted camera movements such that the desired camera motion remains intact. Several techniques [10,11,12] have been proposed to smooth the estimated global motion. Although these methods can fulfill efficient smoothness, sometimes they may have an degrading affect on the intentional motion because of inaccurate tuning of the free parameters of the methods.

In this paper, to improve the accuracy, flexibility, and robustness of the motion estimation, we propose a novel transform domain motion estimation based on combination of 2D Radon transform, 1D Fourier and Scale transforms which can accurately estimate scaling factor in addition to rotation and translation parameters of motion. Since the Radon transform can be computed through 2D Fourier transform with the same complexity by means of the projection-slice theorem [13], and because of calculating motion parameters using 1D projections instead of 2D gray level images, our method is also applicable to realtime applications.

2   Proposed Method

As mentioned in previous section, commonly used motion estimation methods such as block matching, and transform domain based algorithms, can only deal with translational and rotational distortions. These approaches produce poor performance when the image fluctuation contains scale distortion as well as translational and rotational distortions. Although feature based methods can estimate scale parameter in addition to translation and rotation parameters of motion, these approaches are prone to feature mismatching which is due to the internal moving objects or occlusion. So, in this paper, a novel global motion estimation method based on combination of 2D Radon transform, 1D Fourier transform and 1D Scale transform is presented which can estimate the similarity motion model parameters accurately and is robust to internal moving objects and occlusion. The similarity motion model is defined as

$$\begin{pmatrix} x_t^i \\ y_t^i \end{pmatrix} = s \begin{bmatrix} \cos\theta & -\sin\theta \\ \sin\theta & \cos\theta \end{bmatrix} \begin{pmatrix} x_r^i \\ y_r^i \end{pmatrix} + \begin{pmatrix} \Delta x \\ \Delta y \end{pmatrix}, \tag{1}$$

where s is the scale factor, θ is the rotation angle between two correspond-ing points (x_r^i, y_r^i) and (x_t^i, y_t^i) in reference and target frame respectively, and $(\Delta x, \Delta y)$ denotes the displacement in x and y directions respectively.

In this section, we first describe the Radon, Fourier and Scale transforms and their useful properties, then we present our motion estimation algorithm based on combination of these transforms.

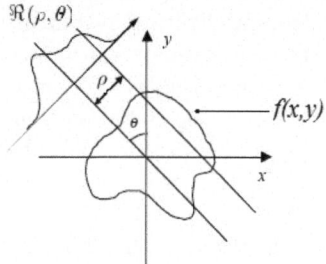

Fig. 1. Geometric illustration of the Radon transform of a 2D function

2.1   Radon Transform

Let $f(x,y)$ be a 2D image. Its Radon transform, denoted $\Re f$ is a 2D function of the real spatial variable ρ and the angular variable θ defined by

$$\Re f(\rho, \theta) = \int_{-\infty}^{+\infty} f\big(\rho\cos(\theta) - t\sin(\theta), \rho\sin(\theta) + t\cos(\theta)\big)\, dt. \tag{2}$$

Geometrically, $\Re f(\rho, \theta)$ is equal to the integral of the function f on the straight line passing through ρ and of direction perpendicular to θ [14]. Figure 1, illus-trates the geometry of the Radon transform. The Radon transform has some properties which is useful for motion estimation. These properties are as follows.

Translation: If we denote the image translated by a vector $\overrightarrow{t}$ with components (t_x, t_y) using $f_{(\overrightarrow{t})}$ we have

$$f_{(\overrightarrow{t})}(x, y) = f(x + t_x, y + t_y). \tag{3}$$

The Radon transform of the translated image becomes

$$\Re f_{(\overrightarrow{t})}(\rho, \theta) = \Re f(\rho + t_x\cos(\theta) + t_y\sin(\theta), \theta). \tag{4}$$

Translating an image in Cartesian domain shifts the spatial variable of its Radon transform. The amount of displacement depends on both translation vector and angular variable. However for a given θ, the Radon transform of the translated image is simply equal to the translation of the Radon transform of the image with respect to the spatial variable [14].

Rotation: Denoting the rotated version of image f by angle ψ using f_ψ, we have

$$f_\psi(x, y) = f(x\cos(\psi) - y\sin(\psi), x\sin(\psi) + y\cos(\psi)). \tag{5}$$

Since the integrand of Equation (2), can be expressed using a rotation matrix, the Radon transform of the rotated image becomes

$$\Re f_\psi(\rho, \theta) = \Re f(\rho, \theta - \psi). \tag{6}$$

It is clear that a rotation in an arbitrary image in the Cartesian domain corresponds to a translation in the angular variable of its Radon transform.

Scale: let f^s be the scaled version of image f with a factor s. Then we have

$$f^s(x, y) = f(sx, sy). \tag{7}$$

The Radon transform of the scaled image is

$$\Re f^s(\rho, \theta) = \frac{1}{s}\Re f(s\rho, \theta). \tag{8}$$

Scaling an image by a factor s corresponds to scaling of its Radon transform and the angular variable ρ by $\frac{1}{s}$ and s respectively.

2.2   Fourier Transform

Let $f(x)$ be a 1D function, its Fourier transform denoted by $F_f(\omega)$ defined as

$$F_f(\omega) = \frac{1}{\sqrt{2\pi}} \int_{-\infty}^{+\infty} f(x)e^{-2j\pi x\omega}. \tag{9}$$

This transform has many properties [15], among which the translation invariance property is suitable for motion estimation. This property can be described as follows.

if we shift a 1D function $f(x)$ by x_0 (displacement value) and denote it by $g(x)$, then we have

$$g(x) = f(x + x_0). \tag{10}$$

If we take the Fourier transform of both sides of above equation, we have

$$F_g(\omega) = \frac{1}{\sqrt{2\pi}} \int_{-\infty}^{+\infty} f(x + x_0)e^{-2j\pi x\omega} dx = e^{2j\pi x_0\omega} F_f(\omega). \tag{11}$$

By taking the magnitude of two sides of equation (11), we have

$$|F_g(\omega)| = |F_f(\omega)|. \tag{12}$$

In other words, the magnitude of Fourier transform of a 1D function is translation invariant.

2.3   Scale Transform

The Scale transform of a 1D function $f(x)$ is defined as

$$\mathcal{D}_f(p) = \frac{1}{\sqrt{2\pi}} \int_0^{+\infty} f(x) x^{-jp-\frac{1}{2}} dx, \tag{13}$$

where $p \in \mathbf{R}$ is the Scale transform parameter. The key property of the Scale transform is the scale invariance. In other words, if we define $g(x) = \sqrt{\alpha} f(\alpha x)$ a scaled version of 1D function $f(x)$ with scale factor α, then,

$$\mathcal{D}_g(p) = \frac{1}{\sqrt{2\pi}} \int_0^{+\infty} g(x) x^{-jp-\frac{1}{2}} dx = \frac{1}{\sqrt{2\pi}} \int_0^{+\infty} \sqrt{\alpha} f(\alpha x) x^{-jp-\frac{1}{2}} dx. \tag{14}$$

By setting $y = \alpha x$,

$$\mathcal{D}_g(p) = \frac{1}{\sqrt{2\pi}} \int_0^{+\infty} \alpha^{jp} f(y) y^{-jp-\frac{1}{2}} dy = \alpha^{jp} \mathcal{D}_f(p). \tag{15}$$

If we take the magnitude of both sides of above equation, we have

$$|\mathcal{D}_g(p)| = |\mathcal{D}_f(p)|. \tag{16}$$

We can see from above equation that the magnitude of Scale transform is scale invariant.

2.4   Parameter Estimation

In this section we propose our motion estimation algorithm base on similarity motion model which is shown in equation (1). Consider $f_r(x,y)$ and $f_t(x,y)$ be the reference frame and target frame respectively and we assume that the target frame is transformed version of the reference frame using similarity motion model. By this assumption, the mathematical relationship between $f_r(x,y)$ and $f_t(x,y)$ is

$$f_t(x,y) = f_r(\alpha_0 cos(\theta_0)x - \alpha_0 sin(\theta_0)y + t_x, \alpha_0 sin(\theta_0)x + \alpha_0 cos(\theta_0)y + t_y), \tag{17}$$

where α_0, θ_0, and (t_x, t_y) are scale, rotation, and translation distortions. By taking the Radon transform of both sides of equation (17), we obtain

$$\Re f_t(\rho, \theta) = \frac{1}{\alpha_0} \Re f_r (\alpha_0 \rho + t_x cos(\theta - \theta_0) + t_y sin(\theta - \theta_0), \theta - \theta_0). \tag{18}$$

From equation (18), it can be seen that for every 1D radial slice $\Re f_t(., \theta)$ of the Radon transform of target frame f_t, there is a corresponding radial slice $\Re f_r(., \theta)$ of the Radon transform of reference frame f_r. Hence, for every constant $\theta' \in [0, \pi]$, if we define $g_{t,\theta'}(\rho) = \Re f_t(\rho, \theta')$ and $g_{r,\theta'}(\rho) = \Re f_r(\rho, \theta' - \theta_0)$, we have

$$g_{t,\theta'}(\rho) = \frac{1}{\alpha_0} g_{r,\theta'}(\alpha_0 \rho + d_0), \tag{19}$$

where $d_0 = t_x cos(\theta' - \theta_0) + t_y sin(\theta' - \theta_0)$ is the amount of displacement in variable ρ. Now, if we take the 1D Fourier transform of both sides of equation (19), we obtain

$$F_{g_{t,\theta'}}(\omega) = \frac{1}{\sqrt{2\pi}} \int_{-\infty}^{+\infty} \frac{1}{\alpha_0} g_{r,\theta'}(\alpha_0\rho + d_0)e^{-2j\pi\rho\omega} d\rho. \tag{20}$$

By seting $t = \alpha_0\rho + d_0$,

$$F_{g_{t,\theta'}}(\omega) = \frac{1}{\sqrt{2\pi\alpha_0^2}} e^{\frac{2\pi}{\alpha_0}j\omega d_0} \int_{-\infty}^{+\infty} g_{r,\theta'}(t)e^{-2\frac{\pi}{\alpha_0}jt\omega} dt = \frac{1}{\alpha_0^2} e^{\frac{2\pi}{\alpha_0}j\omega d_0} F_{g_{r,\theta'}}(\frac{\omega}{\alpha_0}). \tag{21}$$

Taking the magnitude of both side of above equation results in

$$|F_{g_{t,\theta'}}(\omega)| = \frac{1}{\alpha_0^2} |F_{g_{r,\theta'}}(\frac{\omega}{\alpha_0})|. \tag{22}$$

By applying the Scale transform on the two sides of above equation we have

$$\mathcal{D}_{|F_{g_{t,\theta'}}|}(p) = \frac{1}{\sqrt{2\pi}} \int_{0}^{+\infty} \frac{1}{\alpha_0^2} |F_{g_{r,\theta'}}(\frac{\omega}{\alpha_0})|\omega^{-jp-\frac{1}{2}} d\omega = \alpha_0^{-jp-\frac{3}{2}} \mathcal{D}_{|F_{g_{r,\theta'}}|}(p), \tag{23}$$

or

$$|\mathcal{D}_{|F_{g_{t,\theta'}}|}(p)| = \alpha_0^{-\frac{3}{2}} |\mathcal{D}_{|F_{g_{r,\theta'}}|}(p)|. \tag{24}$$

To remove the constant multiplicative factor $\alpha_0^{-\frac{3}{2}}$, we normalize $|\mathcal{D}_{|F_{g_{t,\theta'}}|}(p)|$ and $|\mathcal{D}_{|F_{g_{r,\theta'}}|}(p)|$ by dividing each element of these 1D functions by $|\mathcal{D}_{|F_{g_{t,\theta'}}|}(0)|$ and $|\mathcal{D}_{|F_{g_{r,\theta'}}|}(0)|$ respectively. In other words, if we define $NFD_k(p) = \frac{|\mathcal{D}_{|F_k|}(p)|}{|\mathcal{D}_{|F_k|}(0)|}$, we obtain

$$NFD_{g_{t,\theta'}}(p) = NFD_{g_{r,\theta'}}(p), \tag{25}$$

or in general,

$$NFD_{\Re f_t(\rho,\theta)}(p) = NFD_{\Re f_r(\rho,\theta-\theta_0)}(p) \qquad \forall \theta \in [0, \pi]. \tag{26}$$

In other words, after transforming an image using similarity model, a radial slice of the Radon transform of the original image corresponds to a radial slice of the Radon transform of the transformed image, if the NFD of those radial slices are equal (Figure 2). Using that information, we are able to estimate rotation, scale, and translation parameters of motion with high accuracy. The procedure of estimating motion parameters consists of five steps which are going as followes.

1. The images $\Re I_r(\rho, \theta)$ and $\Re I_t(\rho, \theta)$ are computed by applying Radon transform on reference frame $I_r(x, y)$ and target frame $I_t(x, y)$ for angles between $0°$ and $180°$ respectively.
2. Assuming that the rotational distortion is between $-\theta_{max}$ and $+\theta_{max}$, for each radial slice of $\{\Re I_r(\rho, \theta_r)|\theta_r = 70, 80, 90, 100, 110\}$, its corresponding

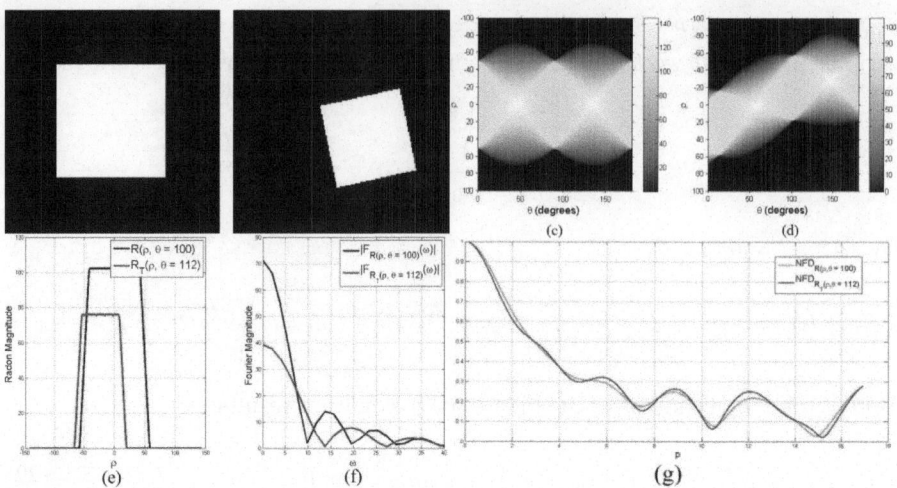

Fig. 2. Illustration of equality between NFD of the two corresponding radial slices of reference and distorted images : (a) reference image; (b) distorted image ($\alpha_0 = 4/3$, $\theta_0 = 12°$, $(t_x, t_y) = (25, 15)$); (c) Radon transform of reference image; (d) Radon transform of distorted image; (e) radial slice $\Re(\rho, \theta = 100)$ of the reference image (blue color) and its corresponding radial slice $\Re_T(\rho, \theta = 112)$ of the distorted image (red color); (f) Fourier Magnitude of two corresponding radial slices; (g) NFD of two corresponding radial slices

radial slice in the range of $\{\Re I_t(\rho, \theta_t) | \theta_r - \theta_{max} \leq \theta_t \leq \theta_r + \theta_{max}\}$ is obtained using Mean Square Error (MSE) criteria. For instance, the procedure for determining the corresponding radial slice of $\Re I_t(., \theta)$ to radial slice $\Re I_r(., \theta = 70)$ is

$$\hat{\theta}_t = argmin_{\theta \in [70-\theta_{max}, 70+\theta_{max}]} \sum_{p=0}^{l} \left(NFD_{\Re_{f_r}(\rho, \theta)}(p) - NFD_{\Re_{f_t}(\rho, \theta=70)}(p) \right)^2, \tag{27}$$

where l is the length of 1D functions $NFD_{\Re_{f_r}(\rho, \theta)}(p)$, and $NFD_{\Re_{f_t}(\rho, \theta=70)}(p)$. After determining the pairs of corresponding radial slices, the mean of difference values $(\theta_t - \theta_r)$ is returned as estimated rotation parameter.

3. for estimating scale factor we utilize equation (22). From that equation we know that the relation between magnitude of Fourier transform of two corresponding radial slices $\Re_r(\rho, \theta - \theta_0)$ and $\Re_t(\rho, \theta)$ is

$$|F_{\Re_t}(\rho, \theta)| = \frac{1}{\alpha_0^2} |F_{\Re_r}(\frac{\rho}{\alpha_0}, \theta - \theta_0)|. \tag{28}$$

Having normalized both sides of above equation by dividing by element zero (DC component), we convert axis to logarithmic scale. Using this, scale factor is reduced to a translational displacement,

$$NF_{\Re_t}(log\rho, \theta) = NF_{\Re_r}(log\rho - log\alpha_0, \theta - \theta_0), \tag{29}$$

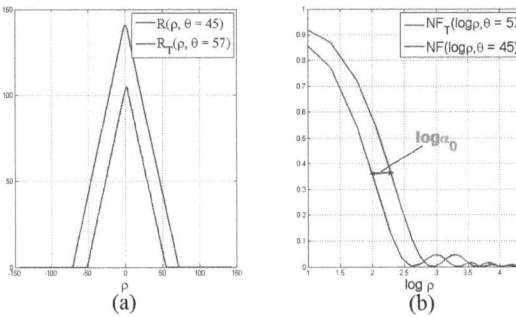

Fig. 3. estimating scale distortion (α_0) using a pair of corresponding radial slices: (a) radial slice $\Re(\rho, \theta = 45)$ of the reference image (purpel color) and its corresponding radial slice $\Re_T(\rho, \theta = 57)$ of the distorted image (green color); (b) NF of two corresponding radial slices

where $NF_\Re(\rho, \theta) = \frac{|F_\Re(\rho,\theta)|}{|F_\Re(0,\theta)|}$ (Figure 3). Hence, the scale factor α_0 can be found by a simple cross correlation technique. Since in step 2, we have determined the corresponding radial slices $\Re_{f_t}(\rho, \theta)$ to radial slices $\Re_{f_r}(\rho, \theta = 70, 80, 90, 100, 110)$, we estimate the scale factor using these five corresponding pairs and return the mean of these five estimations as scale distortion parameter.

4. For calculating the translation parameters, if we replace θ with $\hat{\theta} + 90$ and replace α with $\hat{\alpha}$ ($\hat{\theta}$ is estimated rotation parameter and $\hat{\alpha}$ is estimated scale factor) in Equation (18), then we have

$$\Re f_t(\rho, 90 + \hat{\theta}) = \frac{1}{\hat{\alpha}} \Re f_r(\hat{\alpha}\rho + t_y, 90). \tag{30}$$

Similarly, if we replace θ with $\hat{\theta}$ and $\hat{\theta} + 180$ in Equation (18), then we have

$$\Re f_t(\rho, \hat{\theta}) = \frac{1}{\hat{\alpha}} \Re f_r(\hat{\alpha}\rho + t_x, 0), \tag{31}$$

$$\Re f_t(\rho, 180 + \hat{\theta}) = \frac{1}{\hat{\alpha}} \Re f_r(\hat{\alpha}\rho - t_x, 180). \tag{32}$$

For estimating vertical displacement t_y, between reference and target frame, we choose radial slices $\Re f_r(\rho, 90)$ and $\Re f_t(\rho, 90 + \hat{\theta})$ and after multiplying and scaling radial slice $\Re f_t(\rho, 90 + \hat{\theta})$ by $\hat{\alpha}$ and $\frac{1}{\hat{\alpha}}$ respectively, the location of the maximum cross correlation of these two radial slices is returned as vertical displacement (Figure 4).

5. In the same way, to estimate the horizontal translation parameter, if $\hat{\theta} \geq 0$ then the algorithm selects radial slices $\Re f_r(\rho, 0)$ and $\Re f_t(\rho, \hat{\theta})$, otherwise, the algorithm uses radial slices $\Re f_r(\rho, 180)$ and $\Re f_t(\rho, 180 + \hat{\theta})$ and does the same cross correlation procedure to estimate the horizontal displacement (Figure 4).

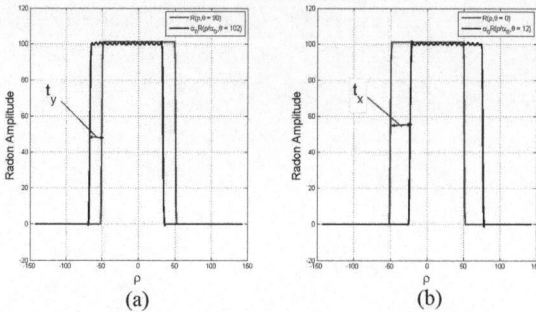

(a)   (b)

Fig. 4. estimating translational distortions (t_x, t_y): (a) estimation of vertical displacement using radial slice $\Re(\rho, \theta = 90)$ of the original image (red color) and radial slice $\Re_T(\rho, \theta = 102)$ of the distorted image (black color); (b) estimation of horizontal displacement using radial slice $\Re(\rho, \theta = 0)$ of the original image (red color) and radial slice $\Re_T(\rho, \theta = 12)$ of the distorted image (black color)

3   Exprimental Results

In this section, robustness of the proposed algorithm is compared to two different methods in spatial and transform domains. We used a Sift based method [16] in spatial domain and a polar transform based method [9] in transform domain. Note that the polar transform method only estimates translational and rotational parameters of camera motion.

3.1   Exprimental Setup

The proposed algorithm is tested against scale, rotational and translational distortions in some videos. We have used one synthesized video where we added random distortion to some of the frames of the video, and one real video where the distortion was due to the camera shake during capturing the video. In synthesized distortions, we have restricted the scale factor to the range of $[0.5, 1.5]$ and rotational distortion to the range of $-15°$ to $+15°$. The translational distortion is also restricted to 30 pixels in both horizontal and vertical direction. The frame resolutions of the synthesized and real sequences are 280×340 and 260×320 respectively.

3.2   Results and Discussion

Figures 5, and 7, show some frames from our test synthesized and real videos before and after stabilization. In this figures we observe that polar based method fails to estimate scale distortion for all sequences. Moreover, due to the large moving objects, the Sift results are not as accurate as our results.

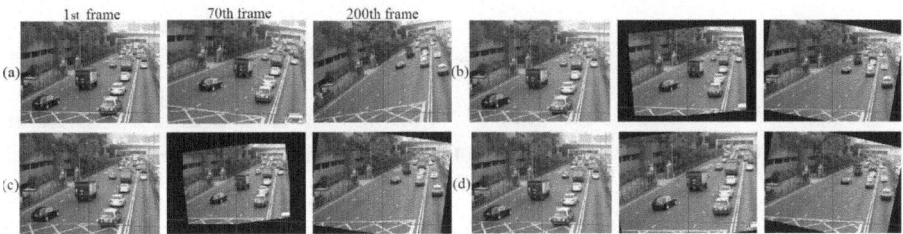

Fig. 5. Stabilization results on some frames of the test synthesized video by different methods: (a) Original frames, (b) Proposed Method, (c) Sift Method, (d) polar based method

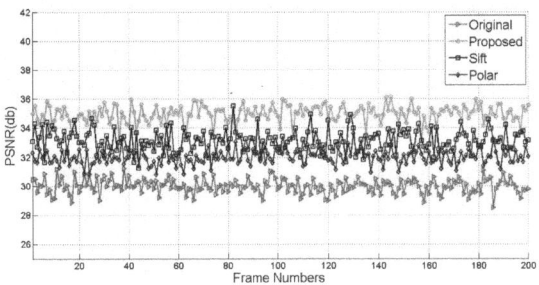

Fig. 6. The graph of PSNR according to equation 33 of the synthesized video

The fidelity of our algorithm is evaluated by the Peak Signal To Noise Ratio (PSNR) between stabilized frames which is defined as

$$PSNR(I_1, I_0) = 10Log\frac{255^2}{MSE(I_1, I_0)}, \tag{33}$$

$$MSE(I_1, I_0) = \frac{1}{wh}\sum_{x=1}^{h}\sum_{y=1}^{w}[I_1(x, y) - I_0(x, y)]^2, \tag{34}$$

where h, and w are the height and width of the image respectively. PSNR quantifies the deviation between the stabilized frame and optimum stabilization result which can be due to various reasons such as inaccurate estimated motion, incorrect motion model, etc. The higher is the PSNR between two frames, the better is their correspondence. Figures 6, and 8, depict the PSNR curves of the sequences. It can be seen from the PSNR curves that the performance of polar transform method is poor due to the scale distortions of the some of the frames. Moreover, the performance of Sift based method is not as well as performance of our method because of existance of large moving objects in videos.

Fig. 7. Stabilization results on some frames of the real video by different methods: (a) Original frames, (b) Proposed Method, (c) Sift Method, (d) polar based method

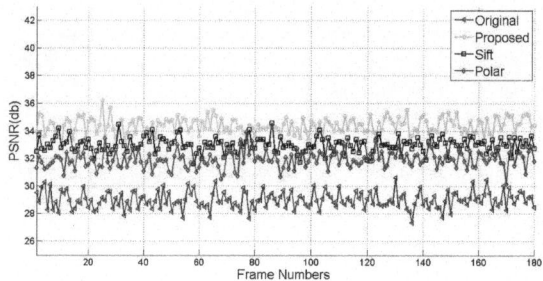

Fig. 8. The graph of PSNR according to equation 33 of the real video

4   Conclusion

In this paper, we have proposed a new transform based global motion estimation method for digital video stabilization. Our method is based on combination of Radon, Fourier and, Scale transforms which can achieve successful stabilization result in the presence of large moving objects which is a big challenge in stabilization framework. Future work will be directed to deal with more complex motion models such as affine and bilinear motion models.

References

1. Ying, Y., Ji-Cheng, H.: Search-length based fast block-matching motion estimation algorithm. Computer Engineering and Design 26(8), 2155–2157 (2005)
2. Xu, L., Lin, X.: Digital image stabilization based on circular block matching. IEEE Transactions on Consumer Electronics 52(2) (May 2007)
3. Yang, A., Schonfeld, D., Mohamed, M.: Robust video stabilization based on particle filtering tracking of projected camera motion. IEEE Transactions on Circuits and Systems for Video Technology 19(7) (July 2009)
4. Pinto, B., Anurenjan, P.R.: Video stabilization using speeded up robust features. In: International Conference on Communications and Signal Processing (ICCSP), pp. 527–531 (2011)

5. Shen, Y., Parthasarathy, G., Thyagaraju, D., Bill, P.B., Kameswara, R.N.: Video stabilization using principal component analysis and scale invariant feature transform in particle filter framework. IEEE Trans. on Consumer Electronics 55(3) (August 2009)
6. Lowe, D.G.: Distinctive image features from scale-invariant keypoints. International Journal of Computer Vision 60(2), 91–110 (2004)
7. Bay, H., Ess, A., Tuytelaars, T., Gool, L.V.: Speeded-up robust features (surf). Journal of Computer Vision and Image Understanding, 346–359 (2008)
8. Erturk, S.: Digital image stabilization with sub-image phase correlation based global motion estimation. IEEE Trans. Consumer Electronics 49(4), 1320–1325 (2003)
9. Zhang, H., Deng, C., Li, J., Yuan, F., Jia, R.: Fast digital image stabilization algorithm based on polar transform and circular block matching. In: IEEE Internationa Conference on Signal Processing Proceeding, ICSP (May 2008)
10. Erturk, S.: Real-time digital image stabilization using kalman filters. Real Time Imaging, 317–328 (2002)
11. Erturk, S., Dennis, T.: image sequence stabilization based on dft filtering. IEEE Proc. Image and Signal Processing (April 2000)
12. Ratakonda, K.: Real-time digital video stabilization for multi-media applications. In: Proceedings of IEEE International Symposium on Circuits and System (May 1998)
13. Averbuch, A., Coifman, R., Donoho, D., Israeli, M., Waldsen, J.: Fast slant stack: A notion of radon transform for data on a cartesian grid which is rapidly computable, algebraically exact, geometrically faithful, and invertible. Stanford University, Tech. Rep. (2001)
14. Peyrin, F., Goutte, R.: Image invariant via the radon transform. In: International Conference on Image Processing and its Applications, pp. 458–461 (1992)
15. Ertürk, S., Dennis, T.: Image sequence stabilization based on dft filtering. In: IEEE Proc. on Image Vision and Signal Processing, vol. 127, pp. 95–102 (2000)
16. Hu, R., Shi, R., Shen, I., Chen, W.: Video stabilization using scale-invariant features. In: International Conference Information Visualization, IV (July 2006)

Automatic Construction of Invariant Features Using Genetic Programming for Edge Detection

Wenlong Fu[1], Mark Johnston[1], and Mengjie Zhang[2]

[1] School of Mathematics, Statistics and Operations Research
[2] School of Engineering and Computer Science
Victoria University of Wellington, PO Box 600, Wellington, New Zealand

Abstract. This paper investigates automatic construction of invariant features using Genetic Programming (GP) for edge detection. Generally, basic features for edge detection, such as gradients, are further manipulated to improve detection performance. In order to improve detection performance, new features are constructed from different local features. In this study, GP is proposed to automatically construct invariant features based on basic invariant features from gradients, image quality (means and standard deviations), and histograms of images. The experimental results show that the invariant features constructed by GP combine advantages from the basic features, reduce drawbacks from basic features alone, and also improve the detection performance.

Keywords: Genetic Programming, Edge Detection, Image Analysis, Feature Construction.

1 Introduction

Edge detection is a well developed area of image analysis, but it is a subjective task [16,19]. Features in edge detection are functions of raw pixel values in an image relative to a local point and are used in the process of classifying pixels as edge points or not. Since there are no formulae to definitely describe the problem of edge detection, various approaches have been developed to extract features for detecting edges [16,4,19].

Generally, one feature for edge detection is not sufficient to fully identify the edges in an image, and multiple features are useful to improve detection performance. For instance, features based on image gradients are not good to detect texture edges [1,16,19]. Since different advantages exist in different features [19], a combination of features may possibly bring the advantages of each basic feature together. Two ways of combining a set of features for edge detection are: (1) to combine different edge detectors to construct features using a fixed model, such as a logistic regression model [16] or the combination of voting consensus ground truth based on a set of features [6]; or (2) to discriminate edge points based on different responses on different parameters in a method, such as multi-scale approaches [1,18]. From these methods, a set of features can improve detection performance [1,16,18,19], but, e.g., the performance of Boosted Edge Learning

M. Thielscher and D. Zhang (Eds.): AI 2012, LNCS 7691, pp. 144–155, 2012.

using approximately 50000 features for natural images is only close to a contour detector *Pb* proposed in [16] with nine local features [4]. In [16], different learned models present very similar detection performance. Therefore, how to efficiently and effectively combine features still needs to be investigated.

Genetic Programming (GP) has been employed for edge detection since at least 1996 [20,12]. In our previous work, GP is employed to evolve low-level edge detectors (based on raw pixels selected automatically with their graylevels) [8,9]. The existing work for constructing edge detectors mainly focuses on low-level edge detectors via choosing raw pixels [24], or a combination of image operators [14]. The work on GP for edge detection for constructing low-level edge detectors shows that GP can evolve good edge detectors [24,14,8], and it is promising to use GP for automatically constructing features for edge detection based on existing features.

Goals. The overall goal of this paper is to investigate automatically constructing invariant features for edge detection using GP from a set of basic features so that the constructed features improve the detection accuracy. Here, invariant features mean that they are not affected by image rotation. The image gradients and histogram gradients [16] are popularly used to train learning contour detectors, so they are used as basic features. In order to enrich the set of features for edge detection, a measure of image quality is also used as a basic feature; it is the first time to use this measure for edge detection. Based on these three basic features, composite features will be constructed automatically by GP. Since invariant features can be directly evaluated, this study is an initial investigation on the construction of invariant features. Specifically, we would like to investigate the following research objectives.

- Whether the features constructed by GP can improve the detection performance, compared with each basic invariant feature alone.
- Whether the constructed features are better than the features constructed by a simple Bayes model.
- What differences between the features constructed by GP and the basic features exist, from an analysis of the characteristics of the detected images.

In the remainder of the paper, Section 2 briefly describes some relevant background. Section 3 presents how GP can be used to construct invariant features for edge detection. After presenting the experimental design in Section 4, Section 5 describes the results with discussion. Section 6 gives conclusions and future work directions.

2   Background

2.1   Edge Detection

Edge detection usually contains three stages: pre-processing, feature extraction and post-processing [17,19]. The pre-processing stage mainly focuses on noise reduction and texture suppression while preserving edges and not blurring boundaries between different areas. The feature extraction stage is the main and necessary stage in edge detection. The purpose of extracting features is to use them

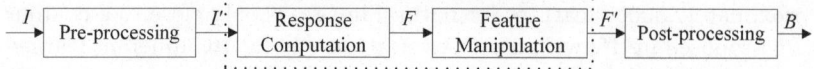

Fig. 1. General edge detection flow

to classify pixels as edge points or not. Post-processing mainly focuses on marking edge points, thinning edges and linking broken edges points. In general, the post-processing techniques can usefully follow most feature extraction approaches. Therefore, the estimation of edge responses is sensitive to the detection performance. The evaluation of the features in edge detection is also important [17] although the performance evaluation usually focuses on final edge maps.

Feature extraction mainly works on local features for the sake of simplicity and ease of implementation. Local features mainly come from gradient computation, such as image gradient [3,11] or local histogram gradient [16]. Based on the difference from different directions, local features are categorised as invariant features and variant features. Variant features are related to a direction, such as the horizontal and vertical derivatives. Invariant features are not affected when the image rotates, such as the outputs of the Laplacian edge detector. However, the local features from gradient computation contain high responses on non-edge points affected by noise or textures. Techniques for manipulating these local features are useful to improve the detection performance. For instance, surround suppression can reduce some texture responses on image gradients [11]. In [11], the features based on gradients and differences of Gaussian filters are used to construct a new feature that suppresses texture responses. Therefore, construction of features from local features has shown promise in improving the detection performance.

Figure 1 shows a general edge detection process flow. For an image I, an intermediate result I' will be obtained after pre-processing. The feature extraction stage is divided into two phases, namely response computation and feature manipulation. In the response phase, the computation can come from gradients, and also statistics [15], and a set of features F is obtained. Note that, some edge detectors combine the pre-processing and response computation together, such as the image gradients after filtering noise by a Gaussian filter in the Canny detector [3]. In the feature manipulation phase, feature selection [4] and further feature construction [16,11] are included, and the output is a set of features F'. After post-processing, a final edge map B is obtained.

2.2   Related Work to GP for Edge Detection

There has not been much previous work done using GP for edge detection. Harris and Buxton [12] designed approximate response detectors in one-dimensional signals by GP, but this is based on a theoretical analysis of the ideal edge detector with raw pixels and the corresponding properties. Poli [20] suggested to use four macros for searching a pixel's neighbours in image process using GP, and Ebner [5] used four shift functions and other functions to approximate the Canny detector. The Sobel detector was approximated by hardware design [13] with the relationship between a pixel and its neighbourhood as terminals. Bolis et al [2] simulated an artificial ant to search edges in image. Zhang and Rockett [24] evolved a 13×13 window filter for comparison with the Canny edge detector. A 4×4 window was employed to evolve digital transfer functions (combination of bit operators or gates) for edge detection by GP [10]. Our previous work [8,9] used GP for edge detection based on ground truth and without using windows. All these GP edge detectors are based on raw pixels and their output can be considered as F in Figure 1.

Also, some image operators have been used to extract features in GP. Wang and Tan [23] used linear GP to find binary image edges, inspired by morphological operators (erosion and dilation) as terminals [21] for binary images. Variant features constructed by image filters with different directions using GP and texture gradients are combined to train a logistic regression classifier for boundary detection [14]. However, only one solution (combined with texture gradients) in their work was presented to compete with other edge and contour detectors. Therefore, their work belongs to the response computation phase, and the detection performance is also dependent on the texture gradients.

To sum up, the existing work has little research for constructing further features based on existing features. Although only one solution in [14] is found in the response computation phase, it still makes automatic feature construction in the feature manipulation phase appealing for edge detection.

3 Constructing Invariant Features Using GP

3.1 Terminal Set

Variant features are dependent on the direction to do extraction, and the number of features are generally large. For further constructing features by GP, the basic features in the terminal set of a GP system only contain invariant features, so that the GP system can easily choose these features to construct a new invariant feature. In this study, only three invariant features are used to construct new features. The three features are image Gaussian filter gradients T_{gg} (approximated by the horizontal and vertical derivatives [3]), a new invariant feature T_{sd} based on image quality (normalised standard deviations [22]), and histogram gradients T_{hg} [16]. Since the three features are totally different, it is possible to construct new features for improving detection performance. Therefore, the terminal set only contains T_{gg}, T_{sd}, T_{hg}, and random constants rnd in the range of $[-100, 100]$. Here, only image grayscales are used.

Image Gaussian Filter Gradients T_{gg}. The Canny edge detector [3] is a very popular edge detector. The features extracted in the Canny edge detector can be represented by the horizontal and vertical derivatives. The Canny detector puts the pre-processing and feature extraction stages together, so the horizontal and vertical derivatives for a Gaussian filter are described in formulae (1) and (2), and the Gaussian filter gradient is defined in formula (3), where u and v are the position relative to a center pixel, and σ is the parameter for Gaussian filter. After doing convolution ($\circledast$) between image $I(x, y)$ with the Gaussian gradient $\nabla g(u, v)$, the image Gaussian filter gradients are obtained (see formula (4)).

$$g_u(u, v) = -\frac{u}{2\pi\sigma^4} \exp\left(-\frac{u^2 + v^2}{2\sigma^2}\right) \tag{1}$$

$$g_v(u, v) = -\frac{v}{2\pi\sigma^4} \exp\left(-\frac{u^2 + v^2}{2\sigma^2}\right) \tag{2}$$

$$\nabla g(u, v) = \sqrt{g_u^2(u, v) + g_v^2(u, v)} \tag{3}$$

$$T_{gg}(x, y) = \nabla g(u, v) \circledast I(x, y) \tag{4}$$

Local Normalised Standard Deviations T_{sd}. Normalised standard deviations are useful for image quality [22], but the normalised standard deviation is seldom used as a feature for edge detection in the literature. The local normalised standard deviation is introduced in this paper, and it is extracted based on a small window as a local invariant feature. The local normalised standard deviation T_{sd} is defined in formula (5), where $SD(x, y)$ and $Mean(x, y)$ are the standard deviation and mean of the pixel (x, y) intensities in a local area around, respectively.

$$T_{sd}(x, y) = \frac{SD(x, y)}{Mean(x, y)} \tag{5}$$

Image Local Histogram Gradients T_{hg}. Local image histogram gradients have shown good performance for detecting edges [16]. The image local histogram gradients are extracted based on different directions. In this paper, the local histogram gradients T_{hg} are combined with the two direction local histogram gradients as one invariant feature. The local histogram gradient in the direction θ is defined in Equation (6), where pixels around pixel (x, y) in a local area are divided into two groups based on the boundary with direction θ, and $l_{\theta,i}$ and $r_{\theta,i}$ are the occurrences for the pixels located in the bin i from the two groups, respectively. Since $h_\theta(x, y) \geq 0$, the local histogram gradient T_{hg} based on all possible directions θ is defined in Equation (7). Being different from T_{gg} (constructed based on the horizontal and vertical directions), T_{hg} is constructed based on $\theta = 45°, 135°$. The other reason for only using the two directions is that our previous work [7] showed that the diagonal derivatives are better than the horizontal and vertical derivatives for detecting edges. For the test image dataset in the Berkeley Segmentation Dataset (BSD) [16], the performance based on T_{hg} with $\theta = 45°, 135°$ is almost the same as T_{hg} based on $\theta = 0°, 45°, 90°, 135°$.

$$h_\theta(x, y) = \tfrac{1}{2} \sum \frac{(l_{\theta,i} - r_{\theta,i})^2}{l_{\theta,i} + r_{\theta,i}} \tag{6}$$

$$T_{hg} = \sum_\theta h_\theta(x, y) \tag{7}$$

3.2   Primitive Functions

The function set contains the four algebraic functions $\{+, -, \times, \div\}$ and three logical operators $\{IF, <, >\}$. Here, $\div$ is protected division, producing a result of 1 for a 0 divisor. IF contains three arguments, the first one is a boolean. IF will return the second argument with a real number when the first is true, otherwise will return the third argument with a real number. It is possible that a feature is better than another feature for some edge responses, but worse than the latter for other responses. Based on the logical operators, two features are combined together, and GP will automatically choose partial responses from one feature. That is why the logical operators are used.

3.3   Fitness Function

We treat the edge detection task as a balanced binary classification task (with the edge pixels as the main class) in the evolutionary training process. For the output (o) of a program, we do not use a threshold for marking edge points, but instead the output is directly evaluated by a simple Bayes model. Since the prior probabilities for the distribution of edge points and non-edge points are the same, the Bayes model is *simplified*, and formula (8) presents the weight value p_j for each class ($j = 0$ for non-edge points, and $j = 1$ for edge points) based on the output o, the estimated mean(s) $\hat{\mu}_j$ and estimated standard deviation(s) $\hat{\sigma}_j$. When p_1 is larger than p_0, the output is considered as an edge point (in a soft edge map), otherwise, a non-edge point. The fitness function is based on the output T_{GP} without post-processing, following the suggestion from [17].

$$p_j = \frac{1}{\hat{\sigma}_j} \exp\left(-\frac{(o - \hat{\mu}_j)^2}{2\hat{\sigma}_j^2}\right) \tag{8}$$

$$T_{GP} = \begin{cases} \frac{p_1}{p_0 + p_1} & \text{if} \quad p_1 > p_0 \\ 0 & \text{otherwise} \end{cases} \tag{9}$$

The aim of new features constructed by GP is that they should detect the number of true edge points as much as possible, so recall r (the number of pixels on the edges correctly detected as a proportion of the total number of pixels on the edges) is a very important indicator. When p_1 is larger than p_0, the discriminated pixel is considered as an edge point ($T_{GP} > 0$). When p_1 is not larger than p_0, the output T_{GP} is considered as very unlikely to be an edge point ($T_{GP} = 0$). However, it is possible that non-edge points are incorrectly detected as edge points, therefore, specificity s (the number of pixels not on the edges correctly detected as a proportion of the total number of pixels not on the edges) is also considered in the fitness function. Therefore, we adopt the fitness function Fit as defined in formula (10) in the training phase.

$$Fit = \frac{2rs}{r + s} \tag{10}$$

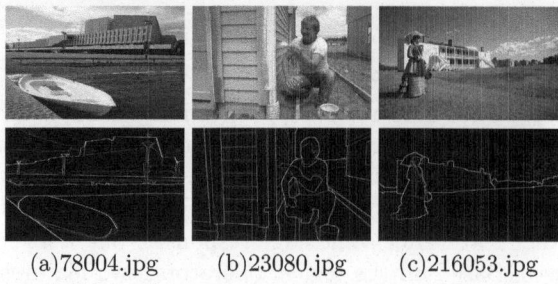

(a)78004.jpg   (b)23080.jpg   (c)216053.jpg

Fig. 2. Training images from BSD dataset and their ground truth

4   Experimental Design

The BSD consists of natural images (of size 481×321 pixels) with ground truth provided. All images are independent and are taken throughout the world. The training dataset contains **200** images and test dataset has **100** images. For fairness of judgement of edges, the ground truth are combined from five to ten persons as graylevel images. Fig. 2 shows three training images and their ground truth. For simplicity, we sample image pixels with the same number of edge points and non-edge points as our training data. Approximately 250 edge points and 250 non-edge points are randomly sampled from each training image. Therefore, the training data is a balanced binary classification dataset, including approximately 100,000 cases and the three invariant features. The window sizes for T_{gg}, T_{sd} and T_{hg} are 7×7, 3×3 and 13×13, respectively.

The parameter values for GP are: population size 200; maximum generations 200; maximum depth (of a program) 7; and probabilities for mutation 0.15, crossover 0.80 and elitism 0.05. These values are chosen based on common settings and initial experiments. There are 30 independent runs.

The evaluation is directly based on one feature, without post-processing. To measure the performance of these features constructed by GP, the F-measure is used in the testing phase [16,4]. The F-measure (used in [16,4] as $F = \frac{2rp}{r+p}$) is the combination of recall r and precision p (the number of pixels on the edges correctly detected as a proportion of the total number of pixels detected as edges). In the F-measure evaluation system, pixels are discriminated as edge points based on the value of their features larger than a threshold, and the predicted edges are simply thinned by the thinning operator [16]. After obtaining thinned prediction, an optimal matching operator will be used to match the prediction and the ground truth. Based on different threshold level indices $k = 0, 1, ..., 51$, a maximum F_{max} ($F_{max} = max\{F_k\}$) will be considered as the measurement for the feature, where F_k is the F value when the threshold level index k is used.

For fair comparison, the F_{max} values of the three basic features (T_{gg}, T_{sd}, T_{hg}) also are given without post-processing, so their values are different from the final performance evaluation in [16]. In the feature performance evaluation, the Sobel edge detector is the same result as the final detection result evaluated in [16], because the Sobel edge detector does not contain special post-processing techniques.

Table 1. Comparison of F_{max} values among constructed features by GP, Image Gaussian Gradients T_{gg}, Normalised Standard Deviations T_{sd}, Histogram Gradients T_{hg}, Sobel Edge Detector and a Bayes Model for the BSD Test Images

	F_{max}
GP	**0.5728** ± 0.0292
T_{gg}	0.5153
T_{sd}	0.4968
T_{hg}	0.5434
Sobel	0.4832
Bayes	0.5302

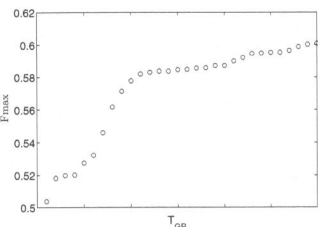

Fig. 3. F_{max} values for the 30 features constructed by GP

5   Results and Discussion

5.1   Overall Results

Table 1 presents the mean and standard deviation of F_{max} values from the 30 features constructed by GP, and F_{max} values from T_{gg}, T_{sd}, T_{hg} and the Sobel edge detector. The training time for each constructed feature is around 3 hours, but the test time can be ignored because the time to extract histogram gradients is far longer than executing a program. Also, an estimated Bayes model based on the sampling dataset is used to extract features (using formulae (8) and (9)) for the test images when T_{gg}, T_{sd}, T_{hg} are considered as independent variables. The bold font means that the results from GP are significantly better than the others using the one sample t-test with significance level 0.05. From the test results, it shows that the features constructed by GP significantly improve the detection performance. However, the combination of the three features by the Bayes model does not improve the detection performance. Therefore, we can see that GP is effective for automatic construction of invariant features.

5.2   Comparison among GP, T_{gg}, T_{sd} and T_{hg}

Figure 3 shows the F_{max} values of the 30 features constructed by GP. The maximum F_{max} is 0.6009, and the lowest F_{max} is 0.5037. From Figure 3, the worst feature in the 30 features is an outlier, and it is worse than T_{gg} and T_{hg} (see Table 1). The number of the 30 features with higher F_{max} than T_{hg} is 24, and

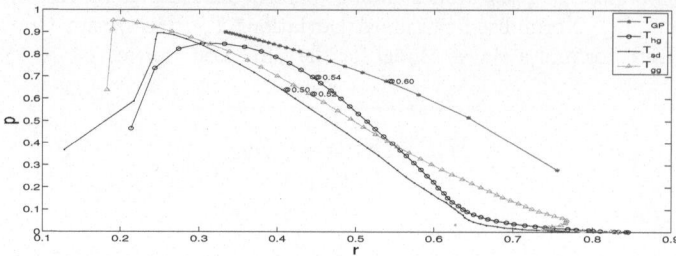

Fig. 4. Details for r and p of T_{gg}, T_{sd}, T_{hg} and the best feature constructed by GP

two thirds of these features are higher than 0.58. Therefore, most of the features constructed by GP are better than the basic features although the training data is not large.

Figure 4 shows the details for r and p with different threshold levels. Here, "@" is the position for the F_{max}. Compared with the three basic features T_{gg}, T_{sd} and T_{hg}, the curve for the best feature constructed by GP (T_{GP}) is obviously better than the three basic curves from T_{gg}, T_{sd} and T_{hg}. Therefore, the r vs p curves also show that GP can construct good features.

5.3   Detected Images

Figure 5 shows four detected images from the BSD test image dataset by T_{gg}, T_{sd}, T_{hg}, the best constructed feature T_{GP}, the Sobel edge detector, and the feature constructed by the simple Bayes model (see formulae (8) and (9)), where "GT" is ground truth. The detected images from T_{gg}, T_{sd}, T_{hg} might be hard to read in print version because of low contrast edge responses. The reason for selecting the four images is that they have edges which are difficult to detect: the graylevels of the top of sail in the first image are similar to the background (dark sky); the texture of the body in the second image is similar to the background (grass covered ground); the middle of the background in the third image has plants with slightly irregular texture in different spaces and their reflection in the water; and the last image includes clouds in different spaces, the graylevels of the left middle of the animal body are almost the same as the clouds, and irregular stone textures.

There are interesting observations from the three basic features. From the detected images, T_{gg} is very good at finding obvious edges without textures, but has only a weak response in low contrast areas, such as the top of the sail in the first image. T_{sd} improves the responses on the edges in low contrast areas (see the detected edges from the sail in the first image), but gives stronger responses on the irregular textures, such as the stone area in the fourth image, compared with T_{gg}. Compared with T_{gg} and T_{sd}, T_{hg} suppresses the responses in the texture areas, however it gives too stronger responses on the discontinuities, such as the responses on the edges for the clouds in different spaces, even the water wave.

The detected images by GP in Figure 5 reveal that the feature constructed by GP weakens the response problems (in T_{gg}, T_{sd} and T_{hg} for some non-edge areas)

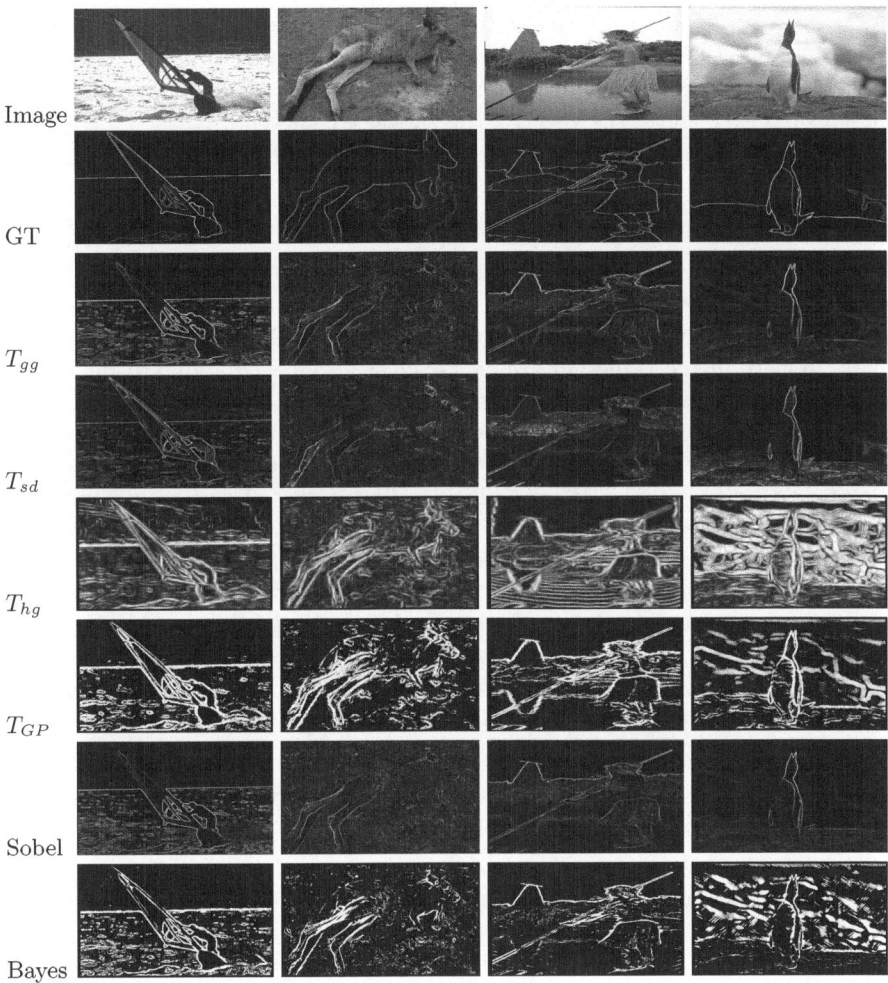

Fig. 5. Detected images based on the different features

and gives clear responses on edges. From the four detected images, it seems that the constructed feature suppresses most of the textures in the four images. From the first image and fourth image, the constructed feature has a good ability to detect edges in low contrast areas, such as the edges of the sail, and the response magnitudes for the boundaries of the clouds (weaker than the response for the contour of the animal). From the third image, the constructed feature avoids the strong response on the water wave. Therefore, the constructed feature combines the advantages from image Gaussian gradients T_{gg}, local normalised standard deviations T_{sd} and image local histogram gradients T_{hg}, and weakens the inappropriate responses existing in the three basic features.

The detected results by the simple Bayes model still have the problem of high responses on low contrast areas, such as the water waves in both sides of the third image and the boundaries of the clouds in the fourth image. The feature constructed by the Bayes model is still not good for texture suppression, such as the water surface in the first image and the grass in the second image. Therefore, these examples confirm the effectiveness of the GP method.

6   Conclusions

The goal of this paper was to investigate using GP to construct invariant features for edge detection to improve the detection performance. Based on the experimental results of the features constructed by GP with three basic features, namely image Gaussian gradients, local normalised standard deviations and image local histogram gradients, the goal was successfully achieved. The constructed features combine the advantages from the three basic features, and reduces their disadvantages. Also, the comparison between GP and a simple Bayes model shows that GP has ability to find a way of efficiently combining different features together.

For future work, we will test this technique on various features and analyse constructed features in order to find useful rules (functions) for combining features to improve detection performance. In addition, other machine learning algorithms will be used to compare with GP. Post-processing techniques will be employed to obtain the final solutions, and the final edge maps will be compared to state of the art edge and contour detectors.

References

1. Basu, M.: Gaussian-based edge-detection methods: a survey. IEEE Transactions on Systems, Man, and Cybernetics, Part C: Applications and Reviews 32(3), 252–260 (2002)
2. Bolis, E., Zerbi, C., Collet, P., Louchet, J., Lutton, E.: A GP Artificial Ant for Image Processing: Preliminary Experiments with EASEA. In: Miller, J., Tomassini, M., Lanzi, P.L., Ryan, C., Tetamanzi, A.G.B., Langdon, W.B. (eds.) EuroGP 2001. LNCS, vol. 2038, pp. 246–255. Springer, Heidelberg (2001)
3. Canny, J.: A computational approach to edge detection. IEEE Transactions on Pattern Analysis and Machine Intelligence 8(6), 679–698 (1986)
4. Dollar, P., Tu, Z., Belongie, S.: Supervised learning of edges and object boundaries. In: Proceedings of IEEE Computer Society Conference on Computer Vision and Pattern Recognition, vol. 2, pp. 1964–1971 (2006)
5. Ebner, M.: On the edge detectors for robot vision using genetic programming. In: Proceedings of Horst-Michael Groβ, Workshop SOAVE 1997 - Selbstorganisation von Adaptivem Verhalten, pp. 127–134 (1997)
6. Fernändez-Garcïa, N., Carmona-Poyato, A., Medina-Carnicer, R., Madrid-Cuevas, F.: Automatic generation of consensus ground truth for the comparison of edge detection techniques. Image and Vision Computing 26(4), 496–511 (2008)
7. Fu, W., Johnston, M., Zhang, M.: Analysis of diagonal derivatives in edge detectors evolved by genetic programming. In: Proceedings of the Twenty-Sixth International Conference on Image and Vision Computing, New Zealand, pp. 345–350 (2011)

8. Fu, W., Johnston, M., Zhang, M.: Genetic programming for edge detection: a global approach. In: Proceedings of the IEEE Congress on Evolutionary Computation, pp. 254–261 (2011)
9. Fu, W., Johnston, M., Zhang, M.: Genetic programming for edge detection based on accuracy of each training image. In: Proceedings of the 24th Australasian Joint Conference on Artificial Intelligence, pp. 301–310 (2011)
10. Golonek, T., Grzechca, D., Rutkowski, J.: Application of genetic programming to edge detector design. In: Proceedings of International Symposium on Circuits and Systems, pp. 4683–4686 (2006)
11. Grigorescu, C., Petkov, N., Westenberg, M.A.: Contour and boundary detection improved by surround suppression of texture edges. Image and Vision Computing 22(8), 609–622 (2004)
12. Harris, C., Buxton, B.: Evolving edge detectors with genetic programming. In: Proceedings of the First Annual Conference on Genetic Programming, pp. 309–314 (1996)
13. Hollingworth, G., Smith, S., Tyrrell, A.: Design of highly parallel edge detection nodes using evolutionary techniques. In: Proceedings of the Seventh Euromicro Workshop on Parallel and Distributed Processing, pp. 35–42 (1999)
14. Kadar, I., Ben-Shahar, O., Sipper, M.: Evolution of a local boundary detector for natural images via genetic programming and texture cues. In: Proceedings of the 11th Annual Conference on Genetic and Evolutionary Computation, pp. 1887–1888 (2009)
15. Lim, D.H., Jang, S.J.: Comparison of two-sample tests for edge detection in noisy images. Journal of the Royal Statistical Society. Series D (The Statistician) 51(1), 21–30 (2002)
16. Martin, D., Fowlkes, C., Malik, J.: Learning to detect natural image boundaries using local brightness, color, and texture cues. IEEE Transactions on Pattern Analysis and Machine Intelligence 26(5), 530–549 (2004)
17. Moreno, R., Puig, D., Julia, C., Garcia, M.: A new methodology for evaluation of edge detectors. In: Proceedings of the 16th IEEE International Conference on Image Processing (ICIP), pp. 2157–2160 (2009)
18. Papari, G., Campisi, P., Petkov, N., Neri, A.: A biologically motivated multiresolution approach to contour detection. EURASIP Journal on Applied Signal Processing, 119 (2007)
19. Papari, G., Petkov, N.: Edge and line oriented contour detection: state of the art. Image and Vision Computing 29, 79–103 (2011)
20. Poli, R.: Genetic programming for image analysis. In: Proceedings of the First Annual Conference on Genetic Programming, pp. 363–368 (1996)
21. Quintana, M.I., Poli, R., Claridge, E.: Morphological algorithm design for binary images using genetic programming. Genetic Programming and Evolvable Machines 7, 81–102 (2006)
22. Rezai-Rad, G., Larijani, H.H.: A new investigation on edge detection filters operation for feature extraction under histogram equalization effect. In: Proceedings of the Geometric Modelling and Imaging, pp. 149–153 (2007)
23. Wang, J., Tan, Y.: A novel genetic programming based morphological image analysis algorithm. In: Proceedings of the 12th Annual Conference on Genetic and Evolutionary Computation, pp. 979–980 (2010)
24. Zhang, Y., Rockett, P.I.: Evolving optimal feature extraction using multi-objective genetic programming: a methodology and preliminary study on edge detection. In: Proceedings of the Conference on Genetic and Evolutionary Computation, pp. 795–802 (2005)

An Abstract Deep Network
for Image Classification

Anthony Knittel and Alan D. Blair

University of New South Wales
{aek,blair}@cse.unsw.edu.au

Abstract. In order to allow more flexible and general learning, it is an
advantage for artificial systems to be able to discover re-usable features
that capture structure in the environment, known as Deep Learning.
Techniques have been shown based on convolutional neural networks
and stacked Restricted Boltzmann Machines, which are related to some
degree with neural processes. An alternative approach using abstract
representations, the ARCS Learning Classifier System, has been shown
to build feature hierarchies based on reinforcement, providing a different
perspective, however with limited classification performance compared
to Artificial Neural Network systems. An Abstract Deep Network is presented that is based on ARCS for building the feature network, and
introduces gradient descent to allow improved results on an image classification task. A number of implementations are examined, comparing
the use of back-propagation at various depths of the system. The ADN
system is able to produce classification error of 1.18% on the MNIST
dataset, comparable with the most established general learning systems
on this task. The system shows strong reliability in constructing features,
and the abstract representation provides a good platform for studying
further effects such as as top-down influences.

1   Introduction

Deep Learning has recently become a significant area of study in machine learning, particularly related to computer vision [1]. The main object of this approach
is the discovery of intermediate features that capture structure in the environment being observed. These features can be re-used and incorporated into other
features, and allow learning based on a deeper network structure than was possible with previous neural network approaches. Deep networks do not always provide better performance than shallow classification techniques, but their ability
to combine and re-use elements in a compositional hierarchy makes them well
suited to certain kinds of tasks, such as object and digit recognition, and gives
them a lot in common with various models of cognitive processing [2–4]. They
may also offer new insights into the functioning of certain learning mechanisms
within the cerebral cortex (although the relationship with cortical structures has
been called into question, and alternative models have been suggested [5]).

One of the established approaches is the use of stacked Restricted Boltzmann
Machines (RBM) [6], which are trained in an unsupervised manner before the

M. Thielscher and D. Zhang (Eds.): AI 2012, LNCS 7691, pp. 156–169, 2012.
© Springer-Verlag Berlin Heidelberg 2012

task-specific training is applied. This allows the system to capture features of the observed environment, and is an important design philosophy as it forces the system to capture structure, rather than just finding the minimal set of features relevant for classification.

One limitation of traditional Artificial Neural Networks (ANN), particularly those with increasing depth, is they can become stuck in local minima, where training ceases to improve performance even though better solutions are available [7]. Neural networks can give very precise solutions, however this depends on the network being initialised in a suitable area of the search space. RBM techniques address this problem, using unsupervised learning to initialise the network according to significant features of the environment, followed by a method to fine-tune performance according to the task, which can be done using back-propagation [6]. This allows initialisation of a deep network that is not likely to give adequate behaviour from random initialisation of weights. However, RBM networks have shown limitations in terms of reliability [8, 9], and a number of attempts have been made to improve discovery of features.

Evolutionary Computation provides an alternative approach to machine learning, usually based on genetic algorithms and reinforcement techniques. Evolutionary systems tend to be very reliable at finding a good solution, however the use of random variation, rather than gradient descent used in ANNs, often does not provide the same precision found with neural networks or kernel methods.

Learning Classifier Systems (LCS) are an evolutionary technique that combine evolutionary processes with reinforcement learning, to maintain a population of classifiers that collectively model the observed system [10]. The Genetic Algorithm used by many LCS approaches follows an evolutionary analogy, however the process of capturing a population of rules based on reinforcement can be viewed as an analogy of cognitive learning processes, with a greater degree of generalisation than Reinforcement Learning. The Activation-Reinforcement Classifier System (ARCS) [11] is a recent LCS approach that bases the design on abstract cognitive features, such as reinforcement of memory traces through use, as seen in cognitive models such as ACT-R [12]. This process is used as a basis for maintaining the rule and feature population. An implementation of this system [13] provides a method for building a feature hierarchy of re-used elements, rather than using a population of discrete rules with redundant building blocks typical of Genetic Algorithm systems. In this feature hierarchy elements are constructed from combinations of other features, producing a deep network related to that found in Deep Learning neural networks.

ARCS has shown reliability in constructing a feature hierarchy on the MNIST visual classification task [13], however the performance level reached is far outside that found by neural networks (10% vs 1% error). Another LCS technique based on Haar-like features has shown better performance, reaching 4% error with the aid of confusion matrices [14], however this is based on pre-defined features and does not build a deep feature hierarchy, and again is well outside the performance level seen by the best neural network and kernel systems.

The principles used for building a feature hierarchy in ARCS are very different to that used in RBM and convolutional neural network systems. ARCS uses an abstract representation, borrowing principles from behavioural psychology which deals with abstract cognitive phenomena. In contrast neural networks relate to localized phenomena such as the interconnection and behaviour of neurons, identified from studies in neuroscience [15]. Providing a different angle on a common problem can be useful for giving a broader perspective. The broader aim of studying the development of a feature hierarchy based on abstract representations, is to use the model to incorporate other important effects in visual perception, such as the role of context in the activation process and related top-down influences. As an example the model by Bar [16, 17] describes a process where the general context of the scene is interpreted first, largely from low spatial frequency information, and this provides a top-down influence on the activation of lower level features that capture details. The use of a more abstract model, which employs a hierarchical part-based representation built in a self-organising manner, gives a good platform for introducing and studying these kinds of effects.

Hinton's model [18] uses unsupervised learning to build the feature network, followed by a fine tuning process to improve classification. ARCS uses a different approach and builds a feature network based on random creation from observations, modified according to reinforcement and selection. This may also benefit from a related fine tuning approach to improve performance. With certain modifications it is possible to introduce back-propagation into the feature network constructed by ARCS, allowing an alternative and reliable manner for constructing features, along with a gradient descent technique to improve performance.

2   Connecting the Reinforcement-Based Feature Network with Gradient Descent

The features used in ARCS are abstract and do not have a direct relationship with individual neurons, but rather represent features that may be captured by a group of neurons or connection weights. The feature network used in ARCS consists of a population of low level atomic features, which can be directly compared with observations, and a network of composite features, that represent common combinations of smaller features. This produces a network of features of increasing field size, each constructed from lower level elements, producing a network related to that in models of the human visual system [3].

Atomic features are represented using a sum of weighted values, created to respond to a section of an observation. Composite features are constructed from approximately 2-8 other features, which may include other composites, and vectors representing the relative positions of the features. When an observation is made, each atomic fragment is tested at each position, producing a map of match values, and each composite is tested according to the match values of each child at their respective positions, producing a match map. Activation values are simplified as binary values according to a threshold, and a composite is activated at a given position if each child is also active.

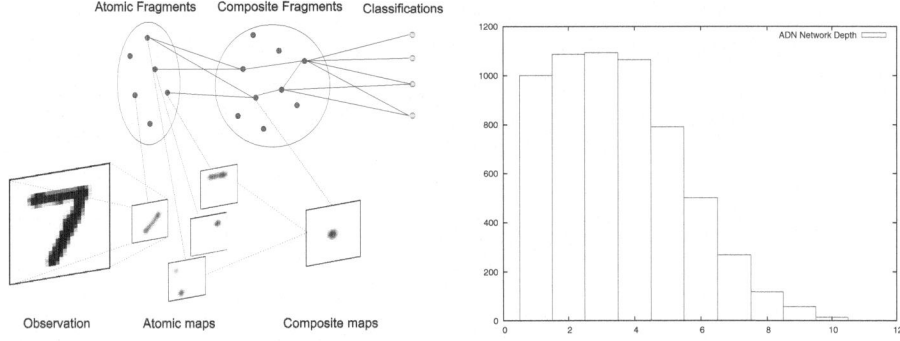

Fig. 1. (L) Connections between atomic and composite fragments, and maps representing match positions of each relative to the observation. (R) Histogram of depth of network produced with the ADN system (Top-BP).

A representation of the connections between fragments and respective match maps used by ARCS is given in Fig. 1(L).

Learning Classifier Systems act by identifying the set of classifiers, or rules, that match the current observation, and each classifier defines an action or classification, along with a value representing the accuracy or expected reward when the classifier matches. In the ARCS system composite features are connected to classifications, using a weight reflecting the probability $P(class|feature)$. Note that this description is a simplification of that used in [13][1]. For each observation a set of active composite fragments is determined, which acts in a similar manner to the set of active rules used in standard LCS systems. From this set the classification is chosen according to the set of Q values captured in the $P(class|feature)$ weights. In exploration/exploitation paradigms this is chosen probabilistically using the Boltzmann distribution $\frac{e^{q_i}}{\sum_j e^{q_j}}$, however in a classification task the maximum value can be used. According to the result the Q value is updated for each class for each active composite feature.

Each fragment also maintains an *accessibility* value, reflecting scalar reinforcement through use, which is used to maintain the feature population. At each time step a value of 1 is distributed amongst the fragments connected to the composite with the highest association with the correct class. This value is derived from models of reinforcement of memory traces such as ACT-R, using a decay function $f_t = \alpha(f_{t-1} + r)$, and provides a ranking amongst features in the population according to the frequency that the feature is significant for classification. This has been modified to use an average function so there is less variation over time for each, while providing ranking amongst the population: $f_t = f_{t-1} + \alpha(r - f_{t-1})$.

---

[1] The previous implementation uses a separate population of rule features to connect composites to classifications, which has the advantage of allowing further sparseness as not all connections between composites and classes are represented, but requires maintenance of another population. This has been removed to reduce complexity, and shows the same performance.

Performance of the feature-based ARCS system reaches approximately 10% error on MNIST [13]. This shows an ability to construct a feature hierarchy using reinforcement methods, and runs with stability and reliability, however classification performance is limited compared to neural network or kernel methods.

2.1   Combining the Feature Network with Neural Network Techniques

While ARCS is able to find a rough solution reliably, back-propagation has many advantages in finding a more precise solution, and can be introduced with appropriate modifications.

ARCS chooses a classification according to the feature with the highest association probability with a class. The classification decision is based on individual features rather than combinations, although combinations can be constructed as new features. One limitation of this approach is that features represent combined positive activation of child elements, and negative weights are not used. Introducing negative weights does not fit the design of the creation process well, as currently new features are constructed from the set of features currently active, emphasising relevance between the features, whereas negative weights would be randomly sampled from the set of all features currently inactive. Introducing this did not improve performance.

The classification step can be modified such that the relationship between composite features and classes acts as a Multi-layered Perceptron (MLP) [15], based on a weighted sum and activation function, modified through back-propagation, along with bias values. These weights replace the $P(class|feature)$ values in the previous design. Given a set of activation values of composite fragments, activation of each class can be determined, and modified according to back-propagation. This only acts on the connections between composites and classes at this stage, not on connections between composites. As the composite network is dynamic, and connections exist between many composites and classification nodes, the network does not have a clear layered structure, but rather contains random or fully connected links between composite fragments at different depths and the classification nodes. This is shown in Fig. 1. The back-propagation method is given in the following equations [15], using a learning rate of 0.01 and no momentum:

$$\delta_k = O_k(1 - O_k)(O_k - t_k) \tag{1}$$
$$\Delta w_{(j,k)} = -\eta \delta_k O_j \tag{2}$$
$$\Delta \theta_k = -\eta \delta_k \tag{3}$$
$$\delta_j = O_j(1 - O_j) \sum_{k \in K} \delta_k w_{(j,k)} \tag{4}$$

where O_x is the activation value, t_x the classification target, $w_{(x,y)}$ the weight, θ_x the bias and $k \in K$ the set of parents of j.

It would be more consistent with the Deep Belief Network model [18] to perform the feature discovery process first and run fine tuning such as back-propagation afterwards, however in ARCS the links between features and classifications use a method based on argmax, rather than summation and sigmoid activation function common in back-propagation systems. As such it is more suitable to change to a system based on summed activation, during the feature discovery process as well as during fine tuning. This requires a modification to the reinforcement method used to maintain the feature population. The important principle followed is allocation of a fixed resource at each time step, which is allocated to features significant to the decision made. This process has shown to be effective in balancing general and specialised rules [11], and ensuring coverage of observations. Instead of reinforcing the feature with highest Q value, the reinforcement is distributed amongst those (top-level) features that are significant in activation of the correct class, as given in Equation 6. As such the reinforcement of the feature population is integrated with the back-propagation process and both are active at the same time, rather than as two separate phases.

$$r_j = e^{\sum_{k \in K} w_{(j,k)} x_k} \tag{5}$$

$$f_j = f_j + \alpha(R \frac{r_j}{\sum_{i \in I} r_i} - f_j) \tag{6}$$

where x_k is 1 for the correct class and -1 for incorrect, R is the reinforcement to be distributed (value 1), and f_j is the accessibility reinforcement for the feature.

To distinguish this design from the Learning Classifier System approach, this system is referred to as an Abstract Deep Network. In summary the first implementation of this system, referred to as Top-BP, uses random creation of atomic and composite fragments, and atom fragments use a weighted product-sum method with sigmoid activation, and a threshold to give a binary activation value, for each position. Composites are active at each position if all child elements are active at their respective positions. The classification layer is a fully interlayer connected network between each composite and each classification node, and back-propagation acts only on the classification layer connections.

2.2   Training and Evaluation on MNIST

The MNIST dataset of handwritten digits [19] is a standard test used by many image classification techniques. The best performing systems are kernel methods and convolutional neural networks using a range of pre-processing and specific transformation techniques [19, 20], and the RBM based Deep Belief Network [18] is one of the best generalised learning systems. A convolutional RBM method [21] provides another approach that captures some of the advantages of both, using unsupervised learning in a convolutional max-pooling based architecture.

Selective training regimes are sometimes used on MNIST, such as training individual classes before introducing wider selections of the training set [18].

Table 1. Summary of results for ARCS and ADN systems, and comparison with existing systems

System	Features	Fine tuning	Error
ARCS	Convolved		10.0%
ADN	Convolved	Top BP	1.57%
ARCS	Full size		12.5%
ADN	Full size	Network BP	2.72%
ADN	Convolved	Network BP	1.39%
ADN	Convolved	Atom BP	1.47%
ADN	Convolved	Top BP, Freeze	1.23%
ADN	Convolved	Atom BP, Freeze	1.18% *
ADN	Convolved, 100	Atom BP, Freeze	1.78%
Ebadi 12	Haar features XCS		4.0%
Hinton 06	Full size RBM		1.25%
Ranzato 07	Convolved NN		0.64%
Lee 09	Convolved RBM		0.82%

To train ARCS and the ADN system a simpler process is used, for each training step a random image is chosen from the MNIST training set (60,000 images). After every 100,000 training steps an evaluation is performed using each of the 10,000 test images, with no adjustments to weights or the population.

Performance of ARCS and the Top-BP implementation of the Abstract Deep Network are shown in Table 1. The use of back-propagation gives greatly improved performance, reaching a level of 1.57% (vs 10%). Analysis of the network topology shows the number of nodes at each depth, approximately half of the 5000 composite nodes are at depth 4 or below, while the network has a maximum depth of 10. The higher depth does not seem necessary for this problem, however analysing the connectivity of the network shows most nodes (4571) have only 2 child elements, and as such the network is very sparse, in a sense representing a clustering representation. The distribution of nodes with 2 children is higher than the creation distribution, indicating a self-organising preference for nodes with limited connectivity.

3   Gradient Descent of the Feature Network

A further advantage may be found by allowing fine tuning to influence the weights of the composite feature network, as well as the classification stage. This however requires a continuous activation function for composite features rather than the existing binary approach. A softer activation function may also handle partial activations in noisy or occluded images in a more reliable way.

A continuous approximation of the AND function used by composites can be found by using a weighted summation method with a sigmoid activation function, and setting the bias such that the feature is 'active' only when each child is also activated. Composite features are created from observations by selecting a number of currently active features. New composites can be created using the continuous activation function by setting the bias of the new composite as $\theta = -\sum_i a_i + \epsilon$, where a_i is the current activation of each feature at the chosen position, ϵ is a margin of tolerance, and it is assumed weights $w_{i,j}$ are initially set to 1.

Using this method the network produced is similar to that of MLPs [15], and the delta values from the classification layer may be passed down through the network. There are however a number of considerations, a) the network is not arranged in fixed layers, which complicates the process of passing delta values through the network, b) the external (classification) layer is connected to nodes at different depths, and c) each feature does not have a single activation value, but rather maintains a map of activation values at various positions.

3.1   Full-Size Features

The evolutionary ARCS system and the Abstract Deep Network described earlier use atomic features with a small receptive field, that are convolved on the observation. In contrast Hinton's RBM method [18] uses features that match the full-size of the image, removing translation invariance but allowing position specific information in the features. Full-size features, which respond to a single position, require less complexity to implement as each feature has a single activation value rather than a map, simplifying the activation process as well as the back-propagation procedure.

An implementation is described that is based on the ARCS system, but uses full-size features, to allow the use of gradient descent with minimum complexity. This is done by generating atomic features that have the same dimensions as the input image, however are defined only in a small region, using the same method used to define the smaller size features. Potential advantages of full-size features are position specificity and reduced processing, however disadvantages are lack of translational invariance, such that a given feature must be identified in each position it is to be used.

The gradient descent algorithm is slightly different to the standard approach used in MLPs, as the network is not defined in fixed layers, and connections between active fragments and the classification layer occur at multiple depths.

The error signal produced from the classification nodes provides a delta value for each top-level feature, as described in Equation 1, and using these values gradient descent can be applied to lower features with a variation of the standard approach. Firstly, from the set of active top-level fragments and all associated child elements, an ordering is constructed such that each child fragment occurs after its parent. Examining each fragment (k) in turn , for each child (j) the respective delta value is adjusted according to Equation 7 below, and the weight of the connection with the parent and bias are modified according to the previous Equations 2 and 3, updating the weights and biases in the feature network.

$$\Delta\delta_j = O_j(1 - O_j)\delta_k w_{(j,k)} \tag{7}$$

3.2   Behaviour with Continuous Feature Activation and Gradient Descent

Behaviour was tested for a number of methods, using full-size features with ARCS, using the continuous-valued feature activation method with full-size features, and using back-propagation, referred to as Network-BP (full-size). Results are given in Table 1. Full-size features show a slightly worse result than convolved features with ARCS of 12.5%, while full-size features using the continuous-valued activation method alone is significantly poorer at 17% error. When back-propagation is used along with continuous-value activation, passing gradient descent adjustments through the weights of the feature network, performance is improved to 2.72%, significantly better than the full-size feature approaches without gradient descent, however with higher error than the convolved system with back-propagation of the top layer.

The continuous activation function operates slightly differently to the AND function previously used by ARCS, and on its own does not support the activation process as effectively, however allows effective learning with gradient descent. Full-size features are not shown to perform as well as convolved features in this domain, however are useful for comparison as they have reduced design complexity and require less processing time.

3.3   Gradient Descent with Convolved Features

Full-size features reduce complexity and processing, however there are conceptual and practical advantages with the convolved method, as individual features can be matched in multiple positions, providing translational invariance. Convolutional methods are also able to scale to larger and more realistic image sizes, and have been shown to be a successful approach [21].

In the convolved system, each feature has a range of activation values according to match positions, however classification nodes are activated from a single value for each connected feature. As such the classification step acts as a bag-of-words model according to the top-most features, while the composition network acts as a part-based model [22]. Back-propagation from classification provides a well defined delta value for each top-level feature, however handling back-propagation through the network must handle a distribution of values for each feature for various match positions.

The activation value of each top-level composite is given by the max value over its match positions, and refers to a single location. Back-propagation can be performed according to the value at this position, and applied to the match position of each child that contributes to this value.

Passing delta values through the network without clearly defined layers, when updates are applied sparsely, would require a complex procedure to combine delta updates according to different match positions of each feature, while at the same time identifying dependencies between nodes to ensure all parents of a given node are updated before its children. For simplification update values can be applied in a distributed manner, at the cost of multiple passes through the network. A distributed approach allows delta updates to refer to different positions of a given node in different passes, as required when receiving back-propagation signals from a number of parent features, which may each relate to different match positions.

The distributed update procedure acts using the delta value of each active top-level fragment, given in Equation 4. The activation value for the fragment is given by its match position with the highest value. For each fragment a distributed top-down pass is run on each child, setting the delta to be used for each child, and subsequently updating the weight to the child, according to Equation 8. The operation recurses to each child, using the activation value at the appropriate position for the child relative to the chosen position in the top level fragment. The weights between composite fragments and between atomic fragments and composites are updated in this manner using a depth-first process.

$$\delta_j = O_j(1 - O_j)w_{(j,k)}\delta_k \tag{8}$$

note that the δ_j value update is not added, but is set once and proceeds in a depth-first pass, with the weight and bias values updated in each pass. In contrast the full-size feature method is breadth-first.

Implementing convolved features with back-propagation (Network-BP) gives improvement over the system based on full-size features, and is comparable to the Top-BP system based on gradient descent of only the top layer, reaching an error rate of 1.39%. Advantages over the Top-BP method are minor in this domain, however it also allows greater flexibility of learning the structure of the feature network.

3.4   Adjustment of Atomic Fragments

Atomic features are created from an observation and remain fixed. Passing the BP updates to the atomic fragments allows them to be modified to better suit the observations matched by the feature, and greater sensitivity. The BP process described previously passes a delta value to each atomic fragment, which can be used to alter the feature. The top-down operation also passes position information about where the feature matches the observation. Adjustment to the feature is performed according to: $\Delta F_{(x,y)} = -\eta\delta_j I_{(x',y')}$, where $F_{(x,y)}$ is the weight value of the feature at a given position, and $I_{(x',y')}$ is the respective observed value. Behaviour (Atom-BP shown in Table 1) shows similar performance on MNIST as with the Network-BP and Top-BP methods of 1.47%, and offers further flexibility with adjusting the feature network to fit observations.

3.5   Fine Tuning

Each of the described approaches act in an online manner, continuously updating the feature population and the weights between features with each new training example. More detailed fine tuning can be performed by freezing the feature population, and allowing the back-propagation to continue independently. This was carried out by running the online system for 10^6 examples, before halting population updates and continuing training of the network weights.

Operation using this approach shows less variation in the result, and gives an improved classification level of 2.26% (vs 2.72%) for full-size features, of 1.23% for convolved features (Top-BP), and 1.18% (vs 1.49%) for convolved features (Atom-BP), taken as the average over four runs. This result shows classification performance equivalent to that shown by the Deep Belief Network used in [18].

3.6   Reduced Feature Set

In the previously described runs, 1000 atomic fragments and 5000 composites have been used. In order to test the influence of a reduced feature set, a population of 100 atoms is used, as shown in Table 1. The full-size system showed a significantly increased error level of 13.53% (from 2.26%), while with convolved features it is able to maintain a level of 1.78% (compared to 1.18% with 1000 atoms). For the convolved system, using a reduced population gives a good compromise, maintaining good performance while reducing processing time.

Fig. 2. Example of atomic features produced in the Atom-BP Abstract Deep Network

4   Discussion and Conclusions

We have described the use of an Abstract Deep Network, that builds a feature network using reinforcement related to Evolutionary Computing, along with a fine tuning step similar to that used by MLPs. This has been applied to the MNIST dataset without pre-processing, and only using spatial assumptions, using vectors to describe relationships between features. In general the system has shown strong reliability, producing similar behaviour with each run and robustness to parameter value changes.

The feature network is self-organising rather than pre-defined. A hierarchical feature network with a depth of 11 was able to be maintained and used for classification, the number of nodes at each depth is shown in Figure 1(R). The large depth is due to the sparseness of the network, with approximately 2-6 child elements for each feature, dominated by 2-child connections, far fewer weights than an equivalent fully connected network. Gradient descent updates were passed through this network to perform fine tuning.

Classification performance is comparable with existing deep learning techniques [18], giving an equivalent classification error rate of 1.18% compared to 1.25%. A careful training routine is not needed, training is performed simply by selecting random examples from the training set, and is able to act in a continuous online manner, without separate feature training and fine-tuning regimes, although a slight improvement to results was produced after freezing the feature population. Specialised approaches have shown lower error rates on MNIST, such as using specific convolutional neural nets [19, 20], although the ADN system is arguably a more general machine learning approach. Convolutional DBNs [21] capture some advantages of both, allowing scalability, accuracy and unsupervised learning, however our approach provides a different design angle, with likely advantages in terms of reliability, and the abstract nature allows more flexibility to capture more complex processes seen in visual perception.

One of the important principles of Deep Learning methods is the use of unsupervised learning [1, 2], as this allows the structure of the observed environment to be captured without training examples. The ADN does not directly follow this approach, as the feature population is modified according to reinforcement. The unsupervised aspect of this system occurs in feature generation, as new atomic features are constructed statistically related to the presence of a feature in observations, and composites are created from features activated from observation. As features are reinforced through use the population becomes biased towards useful features however, diverging from unsupervised learning.

The Abstract Deep Network system produces a sparse neural network based on features found from observations. The abstract representation enables functions such as convolution to be introduced, which allows translation invariance, and activation of a feature in multiple positions. The design also allows further processes to be introduced such as top-down influences resulting from context, which may be more easily incorporated than in systems based on RBMs or convolutional neural nets. In human visual processing, a number of influences can be seen in behavioural and neuroscience studies that play an important role in visual perception, and capturing these effects is important for artificial object recognition and understanding visual cognition. The use of an Abstract Deep Network allows these effects to be explored in a self-organising manner, and provides more freedom to study the big picture of processes involved in visual perception, and their benefits for artificial systems.

References

1. Bengio, Y., Courville, A.C., Vincent, P.: Unsupervised feature learning and deep learning: A review and new perspectives. CoRR abs/1206.5538 (2012)
2. Bengio, Y.: Learning deep architectures for AI. Found. Trends Mach. Learn. 2, 1–127 (2009)
3. Rousselet, G.A., Thorpe, S.J., Fabre-Thorpe, M.: How parallel is visual processing in the ventral pathway? Trends in Cognitive Sciences 8(8), 363–370 (2004)
4. Serre, T., Kreiman, G., Kouh, M., Cadieu, C., Knoblich, U., Poggio, T.: A quantitative theory of immediate visual recognition. In: Paul Cisek, T.D., Kalaska, J.F. (eds.) Computational Neuroscience: Theoretical Insights into Brain Function. Progress in Brain Research, vol. 165, pp. 33–56. Elsevier (2007)
5. Weng, J.: A 5-chunk developmental brain-mind network model for multiple events in complex backgrounds. In: IJCNN, pp. 1–8 (July 2010)
6. Hinton, G.E., Salakhutdinov, R.R.: Reducing the dimensionality of data with neural networks. Science 313(5786), 504–507 (2006)
7. Erhan, D., Bengio, Y., Courville, A., Manzagol, P.A., Vincent, P., Bengio, S.: Why does unsupervised pre-training help deep learning? J. Mach. Learn. Res. 11, 625–660 (2010)
8. Fischer, A., Igel, C.: Empirical Analysis of the Divergence of Gibbs Sampling Based Learning Algorithms for Restricted Boltzmann Machines. In: Diamantaras, K., Duch, W., Iliadis, L.S. (eds.) ICANN 2010, Part III. LNCS, vol. 6354, pp. 208–217. Springer, Heidelberg (2010)
9. Desjardins, G., Courville, A., Bengio, Y., Vincent, P., Delalleau, O.: Tempered Markov Chain Monte Carlo for training of restricted Boltzmann machines. In: Teh, Y.W., Titterington, M. (eds.) Proceedings of the Thirteenth International Conference on Artificial Intelligence and Statistics, Chia Laguna Resort, Sardinia, Italy, May 13-15, pp. 145–152 (2010)
10. Urbanowicz, R.J., Moore, J.H.: Learning classifier systems: a complete introduction, review, and roadmap. J. Artif. Evol. App. 2009, 1:1–1:25 (2009)
11. Knittel, A.: An activation reinforcement based classifier system for balancing generalisation and specialisation (ARCS). In: Proceedings of the 12th Annual Conference on Genetic and Evolutionary Computation, pp. 1871–1878. ACM, New York (2010)
12. Anderson, J.R., Bothell, D., Byrne, M.D., Douglass, S., Lebiere, C., Qin, Y.: An integrated theory of the mind. Psychological Review 111(4), 1036–1060 (2004)
13. Knittel, A.: Learning feature hierarchies under reinforcement. In: IEEE Congress on Evolutionary Computation (CEC). IEEE (2012)
14. Ebadi, T., Zhang, M., Browne, W.: XCS-based versus UCS-based feature pattern classification system. In: Proceedings of the Fourteenth International Conference on Genetic and Evolutionary Computation Conference, GECCO 2012, pp. 839–846. ACM, New York (2012)
15. Haykin, S.: Neural networks and learning machines. Prentice Hall (2009)
16. Bar, M.: A cortical mechanism for triggering top-down facilitation in visual object recognition. J. Cognitive Neuroscience 15(4), 600–609 (2003)
17. Bar, M.: Visual objects in context. Nature Reviews Neuroscience 5(8), 617–629 (2004)
18. Hinton, G.E., Osindero, S., Teh, Y.W.: A fast learning algorithm for deep belief nets. Neural Comput. 18(7), 1527–1554 (2006)

19. Lecun, Y., Bottou, L., Bengio, Y., Haffner, P.: Gradient-based learning applied to document recognition. Proceedings of the IEEE 86(11), 2278–2324 (1998)
20. Ranzato, M., Huang, F.J., Boureau, Y.L., LeCun, Y.: Unsupervised learning of invariant feature hierarchies with applications to object recognition. In: CVPR 2007, pp. 1–8 (June 2007)
21. Lee, H., Grosse, R., Ranganath, R., Ng, A.Y.: Convolutional deep belief networks for scalable unsupervised learning of hierarchical representations. In: ICML, pp. 609–616. ACM, New York (2009)
22. Grauman, K., Leibe, B.: Visual Object Recognition. Synthesis Lectures on Artificial Intelligence and Machine Learning. Morgan & Claypool Publishers (2011)

A Dynamic Approach for Detecting Naturalistic Affective States from Facial Videos during HCI

Hamed Monkaresi, M.S. Hussain, and Rafael A. Calvo

School of Electrical and Information Engineering, University of Sydney, Australia
{hamed.monkaresi,sazzad.hussain,rafael.calvo}@sydney.edu.au

Abstract. Significant progress has been made in automatic facial expression analysis using facial images and videos. The recognition reliability of most current approaches is still poor in naturalistic expressions compared to acted ones. Most of these methods use a static image of each expression that captures the characteristic image at the apex. However, according to psychologists, analyzing a sequence of images in a dynamic manner produces more accurate and robust recognition of facial affect expressions. In this paper, a new dynamic model is proposed for detecting naturalistic affect expressions. The Local Binary Pattern in Three Orthogonal Planes (LBP-TOP) is considered for modeling appearance and motion of facial features. The International Affective Picture System (IAPS) collection was used as stimulus for triggering naturalistic affective states. The dynamic approach produced an improvement of 16% for valence classification and 22% for arousal classification over previous studies.

Keywords: Affective computing, dynamic texture, facial expression recognition.

1 Introduction

It is generally accepted that computing is part of the fabric of our everyday living. We are being increasingly surrounded by cameras, recording our expressions during everyday interactions, whether on a mobile phone, a tablet or a PC. In order to offer the most effective interactions between human and machine, these devices with cameras will need the capacity to perceive and understand human expressions of emotion in realistic scenarios. Facial expression is one of the most cogent, naturally preeminent means for human beings to express emotions, comprehension, agreement or disagreement, and intentions, which regulate interactions with the environment and the people in it [1]. Particularly for the recognition of affective states, humans rely heavily on analyzing facial expressions [2]. While humans routinely extract much of this information automatically in real life situations, the systematic classification and extraction of facial expression information in the laboratory settings has proven to be very challenging. Facial Expression Recognition (FER) systems have been proposed for addressing these challenges [3], [4].

Until not long ago, the most commonly used labels in affect detection were the six basic emotions (fear, sadness, happiness, anger, disgust, and surprise), proposed by

M. Thielscher and D. Zhang (Eds.): AI 2012, LNCS 7691, pp. 170–181, 2012.

Ekman [5], who suggested that these emotions are universally displayed and recognized from facial expressions. He also proposed the Facial Action Coding System (FACS) [6] which is a widely used method for describing facial muscle actions and corresponding expressions.

One of the inherent difficulties with the FACS coding scheme is that it requires a highly trained human expert to manually score each frame of a video. The development of a system that automatically detects the action units (AUs) is a challenging task because the coding system was originally created for static pictures rather than changing expressions over time. Although there has been remarkable progress in this area, the reliability of current automatic AU detection systems do not match the accuracy of humans [7]. This problem is more challenging in spontaneous expression recognition [8].

Two main analytic approaches in FER research considered static images and consequence of images. Most of the research on this area has been based on static images [9] or individual frames of an image sequence [10] and some research efforts toward using temporal models for facial expression recognition [11]. Psychological studies have suggested that facial motion is fundamental clue to the recognition of facial expressions. In addition, Bassili [12] demonstrated that humans are better at recognizing expressions from dynamic images compared to static ones. Few systems attempt to recognize fine-grained changes in the facial expression using dynamic information to analyze facial expression. In the simplest case, the change over consecutive frames or the change with respect to a neutral frame is used to determine the underlying expression [13].

On the other hand, most of the existing datasets focused on posed emotion rather than spontaneous ones [3]. Posed expressions are typically exaggerated and their dynamics are generally much stronger than in spontaneous day-to-day facial expressions, which make them a natural place to start training expression recognition systems. While FER systems should ideally consider spontaneous natural emotion for affect analysis, such approaches have rarely been explored [14].

In our previous study [15], we implemented a geometric-based system to detect valence and arousal through head movement and changes in skin color. Reasonable accuracy was achieved for user-independent analysis. In this study, we have used the same dataset that is used in [15] to compare the performance of our new proposed model. Here, we propose a dynamic texture-based model, which considers the appearance and motion of facial displays simultaneously. The appearance and the motion of facial objects like eyes, eyebrows and mouth during a certain period of time can be valuable sources for detecting spontaneous affective states. These dynamic facial features have been extracted using local binary patterns in three orthogonal planes (XY, XT and YT). The XY plane provides information related to appearance and the XT and YT planes contain the information related to the motion of facial objects. Another novelty of this work is automatic alignment of facial objects. In a similar work [16], the position of eyes had been used for alignment which were set manually. According to the nature of our dataset, which contains rigid head motions, we have implemented an automatic facial object tracker for extracting the facial features.

2   Related Research

Two main approaches have been followed in the area of facial expression analysis; geometric-based and appearance-based approaches. Geometric features include shapes and positions of face components, and the location of fixed facial points [9] such as the corners of the eyes, eyebrows, etc. In most cases, the position of these components and fixed points are detected in the first frame, and motion of these objects are tracked throughout the sequence. A geometric approach that attempts to automatically detect temporal segments of AUs was used by Pantic et al. [17], [18].

Appearance-based methods analyze the deformations of the face skin in both static and dynamic space for recognizing facial expression. Dynamic texture-based method can be seen as a generalization of appearance-based approaches. FER systems which use appearance-based features have been proposed in [10]. Several researchers have used Gabor wavelet coefficients as features [19]. Bartlett et al. [10] have tried different methods, such as explicit feature measurement, Independent Component Analysis (ICA), and Gabor wavelets. Finally they reported that Gabor wavelets provide the best results [20]. Other techniques explored in this field include optical flow [21] and Active Appearance Models [22].

Both geometric-based and appearance-based approaches have advantages and disadvantages. Geometric-based methods mostly rely on the motion of a number of points, and ignore much of the information related to skin texture changes. In contrast, appearance-based methods may be more susceptible to changes in illumination, rigid head motions and differences between individuals [3]. Tian et al. [23]used a combination of geometric-based and appearance-based features (Gabor wavelets) for recognizing facial AUs. They claimed that the former features outperform the latter ones, yet using both yields the best result.

2.1   Dynamic Texture Approach

Dynamic Texture (DT) recognition is an emerging new method of appearance-based activity recognition. Dynamic or temporal textures refer to textures with motion. A DT can be defined as a "spatially repetitive, time-varying visual pattern that forms an image sequence with certain temporal stationarity" [24]. Typical examples of DTs are smoke, fire, sea waves, and talking faces. Many existing approaches for recognition of DTs are based on optical flow [25]. A different approach can be seen in [26], where the system identification techniques are used to learn generative models.

Facial expression recognition can also be defined as one of the most suitable application for the DT recognition techniques. Zhao and Pietikäinen [16] used Volume Local Binary Patterns (VLBPs) for facial expression recognition. VLBPs are a temporal extension of local binary patterns often used in 2-dimentional texture analysis for recognizing facial expressions. In the study [16], the face was divided into overlapping blocks and the extracted features in each block were concatenated into a single feature vector for classification (with SVM). The approach showed promising results, although only the six prototypic emotions were recognized and no temporal segmentation was performed. They normalized the face using the eye position in the first frame, but they ignore any rigid head movement that may occur during the sequence. In addition, they used fixed overlapping blocks distributed evenly over the face instead of focusing on specific regions of the face such as mouth, eyes and eyebrows, which include valuable information about facial expressions. The second attempt at using DT in facial expression analysis was performed by Koelstra et al. [27]. They estimated non-rigid motion between consecutive frames by applying either non-rigid registration using Free-form Deformations (FFDs) or Motion History Images (MHIs). For each AU, a quad-tree decomposition was defined to identify face regions related to the AU. In these regions, orientation histogram feature descriptors were extracted. Finally, a combined Gentle-Boost classifier and a Hidden Markov Model (HMM) were used to classify the sequence in terms of AUs and their temporal segments. However, increasing evidence suggests that deliberate behavior differs in visual appearance, audio profile, and timing from spontaneously occurring behavior.

3   Methodology

3.1   LBP-TOP

The LBP proposed by Ojala et al. [28] is one of the powerful methods for texture description. The LBP operator labels the neighborhood region of each pixel of an image by thresholding the pixels with the central value. Considering P neighborhood-pixels, 2^P different micro-patterns could be addressed. By calculating LBP for all pixels in an image and calculating the distribution of each pattern, a specific histogram could be extracted for each image. This LBP histogram is a powerful indicator of the image, which has been proved to be successful in different pattern recognition applications. By defining different radius (R) and number of neighboring points (P), several types of LBP could be extracted. The best values for R and P depends on the application and general characteristics of image sets. An example of circular 8 neighboring pixels with $R=1$ is presented in Figure 1.

The LBP operator was originally designed for static images. Recently, Zhao and Pietikäinen [16] proposed an extended version of LBP to describe dynamic textures. Usually, a video sequence is thought of as a stack of XY planes in axis T, but it is easy to ignore that a video sequence can also be seen as a stack of XT planes in axis Y and YT planes in axis X, respectively. They divided each video sequence into three orthogonal sets of 2-dimentional planes. The LBP could be computed for each set of planes separately. The Local Binary Pattern in Three Orthogonal Planes (LBP-TOP) [16] descriptor for each video clip is calculated by concatenating three LBP histograms. Figure 2, shows the LBP-TOP procedure. In such a representation, DT is encoded by the XY-LBP, XT-LBP, and YT-LBP, whereas the appearance and motion in three directions of DT are considered, incorporating spatial domain information (XY-LBP) and two spatial temporal co-occurrence statistics (XT-LBP and YT-LBP).

With this approach, the number of bins is only 3×2^P, which makes the extension to many neighboring points easier and also reduces the computational complexity compare with volume-based LBP (VLBP) method [16].

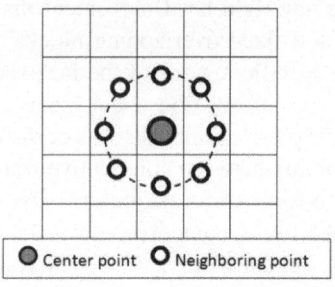

Fig. 1. An example of LBP operator (P=8, R=1)

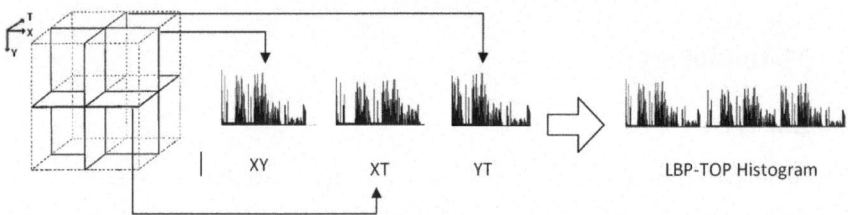

Fig. 2. LBP-TOP procedure: Extracting LBP features from each set of planes and concatenating to a single histogram [16]

Like the LBP representation, the radius in axes X, Y, and T and the number of neighboring points in the XY, XT, and YT planes can also be different, which can be marked as R_X, R_Y , and R_T , P_{XY} , P_{XT}, and P_{YT}. The corresponding feature is denoted as LBP-TOP$_{PXY ;PXT ;PYT ;RX;RY ;RT}$.

3.2   Feature Extraction

An LBP description computed over the whole facial expression sequence encodes only the occurrences of the micro-patterns without any indication about their locations. One solution for this effect is dividing an image to several blocks. The LBP histograms for each block are calculated and concatenated to a single histogram. If the image divides into N blocks, the number of bins in final histogram would be $N \times 3 \times 2^P$. In our proposed model, three fixed blocks correspond to left-eye, right-eye and mouth were considered for each image sequence. So, for each video clip, $3 \times 3 \times 2^P$ features were extracted. These regions were detected and extracted automatically using an extended boosted cascade classifier [29]. Then, deformation of eyes and mouth were monitored during expression of an affective state. In order to have the same size of blocks in each image, the detected objects were resized to fixed sizes. In this study, the size was same for all video clips (10 seconds).

Three variations of LBP-TOP method were used for feature extraction which were different in the radius and the number of neighbor points (LBP-TOP$_{8,8,8,1,1,1,}$

LBP-TOP$_{6,6,6,2,2,2}$ and LBP-TOP$_{8,8,8,3,3,3}$). The classification results for each set of features are shown in the section 5. A total of 2304 features were extracted by LBP-TOP$_{8,8,8,1,1,1}$ and LBP-TOP$_{8,8,8,3,3,3}$ while 576 features were extracted by LBP-TOP$_{6,6,6,2,2,2}$ operator.

Feature selection techniques were applied prior to classification to reduce dimensionality, which automatically removed unnecessary features. To serve the purpose, the correlation based feature selection (CFS) method was used for choosing the best subset of features. This technique evaluates the worth of a subset of attributes by considering the individual predictive ability of each feature along with the degree of redundancy between them [30].

3.3   Classification

All videos were synchronized with time stamps corresponding to the presented IAPS images and their normative ratings. The features extracted from videos for each 10-second widows were labeled using the normative ratings and self-reports (three levels of valence and arousal). A Matlab based computational framework as part of the Siento framework [31], was used for feature selection and classification. The feature selection was implemented in Matlab using the DMML[1] wrapper for Weka. The classification was performed in Matlab using MatlabArsenal[2], a wrapper for the classifiers in Weka. Three machine learning algorithms; k-nearest neighbor ($k=1$), linear support vector machine (SVM) and J48 decision tree were selected for classification. Then, a vote classifier with the average probability rule for combining the classifiers was applied [32]. The training and testing for both types of classes (valence and arousal) was performed separately with a 10-fold cross validation. The classification accuracy was used as the overall classification performance metric. In addition, the F-measure (from precision and recall) was calculated as an indication of how well each affective state was classified. For the classification scores of precision (P) and recall (R), the F-measure ($F1$) is calculated by; $F1=2((P{\times}R)/(P+R))$.

4   Experiment

4.1   Participants and Materials

The participants were 20 undergraduate/postgraduate engineering students at the University of Sydney. The participants' age ranged from 18 to 30 years and there were 8 males and 12 females. Due to major eye occlusion caused by eyeglasses from 7 subjects, results are presented for 13 subjects. This study was approved by the University of Sydney's Human Ethics Research Committee prior to data collection. The participants signed an informed consent prior to the experiment. The experiment, which took approximately an hour was conducted indoors with a varying amount of ambient sunlight entering through windows in combination with normal artificial fluorescent

---

[1]   DMML: featureselection.asu.edu/software.php

[2]   MatlabArsenal: cs.siu.edu/~qcheng/featureselection/index.html

light. Participants were asked to sit in front of a computer and interact normally while their video was recorded by an ordinary webcam (Logitech Webcam Pro 9000). All videos were recorded in color (24-bit RGB with 3 channels, 8 bits/channel) at 15 frames per seconds (fps) with pixel resolution of 640×480 pixels and saved in AVI format.

4.2   Procedure

The participants viewed emotionally charged photos from the IAPS collection. A total of 90 images (three blocks of 30 images each) for 10 seconds each were presented, followed by 6 seconds pauses between the images. The images were selected so that the IAPS valence and arousal scores for the stimuli spanned a 3×3 valence/arousal space (IAPS normative ratings). Participants also self-reported their emotions by clicking radio buttons on the appropriate location of 3×3 valence/arousal grid after viewing each image. In this paper, results are presented using the normative ratings instead of self-reports. Therefore, the computational model was trained and tested using a balanced class distribution, which could be suitable for evaluating accuracies of classification without applying any up or down sampling techniques. The normative ratings are useful because they are standardized scientifically for assessing basic and applied problems in psychology [33]. Moreover, many people do not know how to recognize, express and label/scale their own feelings, therefore self reports sometimes can be unreliable [34]. However, self-reports provide important information and should not be ignored; therefore the collected self ratings will be used as an extension of this work in future studies.

5   Results

The classification for detecting 3-degrees of valence (positive, neutral and negative) and arousal (low, medium, high) are presented in two user models: user-dependent models and combined model. For each set of model, the extracted features from the three methods (LBP-TOP$_{8,8,8,1,1,1}$, LBP-TOP$_{6,6,6,2,2,2}$ and LBP-TOP$_{8,8,8,3,3,3}$) are evaluated and discussed in the following subsections.

5.1   User-Dependent Models

The subsequent analysis focuses on developing user-dependent models. Distinct models were developed and validated for each participant. Figure 3 presents the mean and standard deviation of classification accuracies assessing the overall performance of discriminating 3-degrees of valence and arousal using three proposed methods (LBP-TOP$_{8,8,8,1,1,1}$, LBP-TOP$_{6,6,6,2,2,2}$ and LBP-TOP$_{8,8,8,3,3,3}$). The last set of bars, indicate the best result achieved from our recent method for detecting valence and arousal levels [15]. The new results indicate that the classifier was more accurate in discriminating three levels of valence and arousal for all three dynamic texture-based methods compared to [15]. The accuracy of valence detection was improved by 16% using

LBP-TOP$_{8,8,8,3,3,3}$ features. The 22% improvement was also achieved by LBP-TOP$_{8,8,8,3,3,3}$ features for arousal detection. This finding demonstrate the power of the proposed dynamic texture method in detecting user's affective states compare with the geometric-based method in [15].

According to the results, the number of neighboring points influence the performance of affect detection. LBP-TOP$_{8,8,8,1,1,1}$ and LBP-TOP$_{8,8,8,3,3,3}$ produced almost the same results whereas LBP-TOP$_{6,6,6,2,2,2}$ failed to improve the performance of the classification. This might indicate the importance of the considering number of neighborhood points compare with the radius in the circular LBP-TOP operator. However, considering more neighboring points would increase the computational complexity.

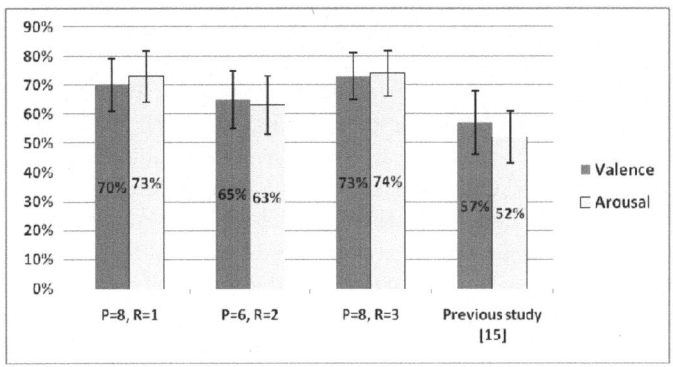

Fig. 3. The mean and standard deviation of the classification accuracy for detecting 3 levels of valence and arousal (User-dependent models)

Next we investigate the classification accuracy of the individual degrees of valence and arousal. Table 1 shows the mean and standard deviation of *F1* as per valence and arousal category across the 13 subjects for the vote classifier.

Table 1. The mean and standard deviation of F1 values for detecting 1-3 degrees of valence and arousal (user-dependent models)

		Valence			*Arousal*		
		Low	Medium	High	Low	Medium	High
LBP-TOP$_{8,8,8,1,1,1}$	Mean	0.76	0.62	0.72	0.75	0.66	0.76
	Std	0.10	0.11	0.15	0.11	0.11	0.10
LBP-TOP$_{6,6,6,2,2,2}$	Mean	0.72	0.57	0.65	0.66	0.53	0.70
	Std	0.14	0.09	0.17	0.16	0.12	0.10
LBP-TOP$_{8,8,8,3,3,3}$	Mean	0.79	0.64	0.76	0.76	0.68	0.78
	Std	0.10	0.11	0.12	0.09	0.10	0.11

The LBP-TOP$_{8,8,8,3,3,3}$ had the highest accuracy for detecting all three degrees of valence and arousal. Among the 3-dergees of valence, low-valence was more predictable followed by high-valence and medium-valence respectively. The same pattern was seen for arousal classification. The performance of all proposed methods for detecting high-arousal showed the best result whereas medium-arousal could not predict well enough using DT based methods.

5.2   Combined Model

Data from individual participants was first standardized (converted to z-scores) to address individual variations of features caused by differences in skin colors or environmental illumination. Then the standardized instances were combined to yield one large data set with 1154 instances. The dimensionality of the data was also reduced by selecting the best features prior to each classification task by using CFS. Figure 4 shows the classification results for 3-degrees of valence and arousal using three variations of LBP-TOP operators for feature extraction. The set of last bars, indicate the best result achieved for the combined model from [15]. The LBP-TOP methods showed better performance than our previous method [15]. The accuracy of three levels of valence detection was raised by increasing the radius (R) of circular LBP-TOP operator. The LBP-TOP$_{8,8,8,3,3,3}$ showed the best performance in detecting valence and arousal. Accordingly for general model we can argue that besides increasing number of neighboring points (P), increasing the radius (R) of the LBP-TOP circular operator could improve the accuracy of affect detection. Achieving the lower accuracy compared to user-dependent models was expected, because there is a mixture of instances from different participants in combined model. This model could be extended to a general (user-independent) model.

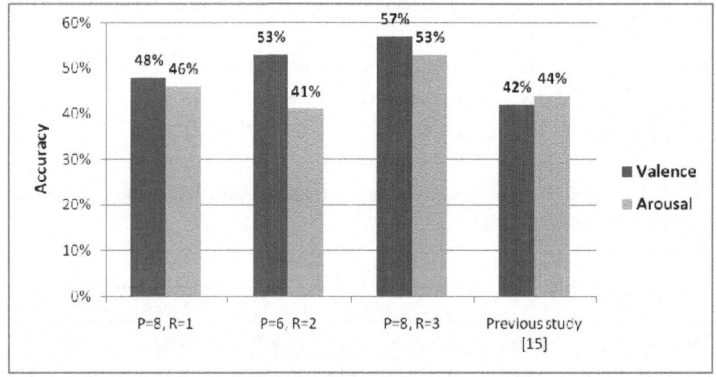

Fig. 4. The classification accuracy for detecting three levels of valence and arousal (Combined model)

Feature Selection Analysis. Analyzing the selected features using CFS gives us a better insight about the important features for detecting affect. Therefore, we investigate the selected features from the combined model. The selected features were divided into two groups; appearance-based features, which were selected from XY planes and motion-based features, which were selected from XT and YT planes.

Figure 5 gives the proportion of features that contribute from each group (appearance-based and motion-based) for valence and arousal. Almost the same proportion of appearance-based features and motion-based features were observed for valence in all three methods. As for arousal, appearance-based features had very high contribution using LBP-TOP$_{8,8,8,3,3,3}$ and motion-based features had very high contribution using LBP-TOP$_{8,8,8,1,1,1}$. Despite the differences in valence and arousal, this analysis reflects that both appearance-based and motion-based features are essential for detecting affective states in naturalistic HCI.

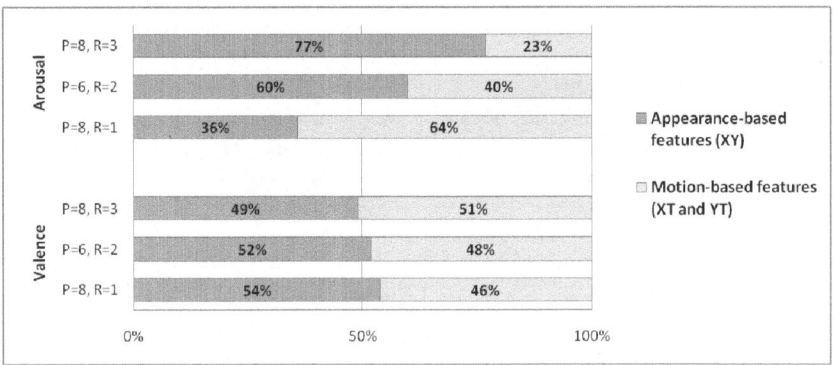

Fig. 5. The percentage of selected features in valence and arousal analysis

6   Conclusion

This study investigated dynamic features of facial expressions for the detection of affective states during naturalistic interactions. Both the user-independent model and a combined model have been evaluated for classifying 3-degeees of valence and arousal.

Results indicate that the best method for extracting dynamic features (LBP-TOP$_{8,8,8,3,3,3}$) can achieve 73% and 74% accuracies for detecting degrees of valence and arousal respectively with the user-dependent model. As for the combined model, 57% and 53% accuracies were achieved valence and arousal respectively. For both models, the dynamic features have shown improvement over our previous study using chromatic and movement features [15].

In this study the correlation based feature selection algorithm and a vote classifier was used. In future work, other machine learning techniques along with other video based or multimodal features can be investigated to improve the accuracy.

References

1. Ekman, P., Rosenberg, E.L.: What the Face Reveals: Basic and Applied Studies of Spontaneous Expression Using the Facial Action Coding System (FACS). Oxford University Press, USA (2005)

2. Picard, R.W.: Affective Computing. The MIT Press (2000)
3. Zeng, Z., Pantic, M., Roisman, G.I., Huang, T.S.: A survey of affect recognition methods: audio, visual, and spontaneous expressions. IEEE Transactions on Pattern Analysis and Machine Intelligence 31, 39–58 (2009)
4. Calvo, R.A., D'Mello, S.: Affect Detection: An Interdisciplinary Review of Models, Methods, and Their Applications. IEEE Transaction on Affective Computing 1, 18–37 (2010)
5. Ekman, P., Friesen, W.V.: Constants across cultures in the face and emotion. Journal of Personality and Social Psychology 17, 124–129 (1971)
6. Ekman, P., Friesen, W.V.: Facial Action Coding System: A Technique for the Measurement of Facial Movement. Consulting Psychologists Press, Palo Alto (1978)
7. D'Mello, S., Graesser, A.: Multimodal semi-automated affect detection from conversational cues, gross body language, and facial features. User Modeling and User-Adapted Interaction 20, 147–187 (2010)
8. Hoque, M.E., el Kaliouby, R., Picard, R.W.: When Human Coders (and Machines) Disagree on the Meaning of Facial Affect in Spontaneous Videos. In: Ruttkay, Z., Kipp, M., Nijholt, A., Vilhjálmsson, H.H. (eds.) IVA 2009. LNCS, vol. 5773, pp. 337–343. Springer, Heidelberg (2009)
9. Pantic, M., Rothkrantz, L.J.M.: Facial action recognition for facial expression analysis from static face images. Systems, Man, and Cybernetics 34, 1449–1461 (2004)
10. Bartlett, M.S., Littlewort, G., Frank, M., Lainscsek, C., Fasel, I., Movellan, J.: Fully Automatic Facial Action Recognition in Spontaneous Behavior. In: 7th International Conference on Automatic Face and Gesture Recognition (FGR 2006), pp. 223–230. IEEE (2006)
11. Cohen, I., Sebe, N., Garg, A., Chen, L.S., Huang, T.S.: Facial expression recognition from video sequences: temporal and static modeling. Computer Vision and Image Understanding 91, 160–187 (2003)
12. Bassili, J.N.: Emotion recognition: the role of facial movement and the relative importance of upper and lower areas of the face. Journal of Personality and Social Psychology 37, 2049–2058 (1979)
13. Michel, P., El Kaliouby, R.: Real time facial expression recognition in video using support vector machines. In: Proceedings of the 5th international conference on Multimodal Interfaces - ICMI 2003, p. 258 (2003)
14. Hoque, M.E., McDuff, D.J., Picard, R.W.: Exploring Temporal Patterns in Classifying Frustrated and Delighted Smiles. IEEE Transaction on Affective Computing (2012)
15. Monkaresi, H., Calvo, R.A., Sazzad Hussain, M.: Automatic natural expression recognition using head movement and skin color features. In: Tortora, G., Levialdi, S., Tucci, M. (eds.) Proceedings of the International Working Conference on Advanced Visual Interfaces (AVI 2012), pp. 657–660. ACM, New York (2012)
16. Zhao, G., Pietikäinen, M.: Dynamic texture recognition using local binary patterns with an application to facial expressions. IEEE Trans. Pattern Analysis and Machine 29, 915–928 (2007)
17. Pantic, M., Patras, I.: Dynamics of Facial Expression: Recognition of Facial Actions and Their Temporal Segments. IEEE Trans. Systems, Man, and Cybernetics 36, 433–449 (2006)
18. Valstar, M.F., Pantic, M.: Combined Support Vector Machines and Hidden Markov Models for Modeling Facial Action Temporal Dynamics. In: Lew, M., Sebe, N., Huang, T.S., Bakker, E.M. (eds.) HCI 2007. LNCS, vol. 4796, pp. 118–127. Springer, Heidelberg (2007)

19. Guo, G., Dyer, C.R.: Learning from examples in the small sample case: face expression recognition. IEEE Transactions on Systems, Man, and Cybernetics, Part B 35, 477–488 (2005)
20. Littlewort, G., Bartlett, M.S., Fasel, I., Susskind, J., Movellan, J.: Dynamics of facial expression extracted automatically from video. Image and Vision Computing 24, 615–625 (2006)
21. Anderson, K., McOwan, P.W.: A real-time automated system for the recognition of human facial expressions. IEEE Transactions on Systems, Man, and Cybernetics, Part B 36, 96–105 (2006)
22. Lucey, S., Ashraf, A.B., Cohn, J.F.: Investigating Spontaneous Facial Action Recognition through AAM Representations of the Face. In: Delac, K., Grgic, M. (eds.) Face Recognition, pp. 275–286. I-Tech Education and Publishing (2007)
23. Tian, Y., Kanade, T., Cohn, J.F.: Evaluation of Gabor-Wavelet-Based Facial Action Unit Recognition in Image Sequences of Increasing Complexity. In: Fifth IEEE International Conference on Automatic Face and Gesture Recognition, pp. 229–234 (2002)
24. Chetverikov, D., Renaud, P.: A brief survey of dynamic texture description and recognition. In: Proc. Conf. Computer Recognition Systems, pp. 17–26 (2005)
25. Polana, R., Nelson, R.: Temporal Texture and Activity Recognition. In: Shah, M., Jain, R. (eds.) Motion-Based Recognition, pp. 87–115 (1997)
26. Saisan, P., Doretto, G., Wu, Y.: Dynamic texture recognition. In: Proc. IEEE Conf. Computer Vision and Pattern Recognition, pp. 58–63 (2001)
27. Koelstra, S., Pantic, M., Patras, I.: A dynamic texture-based approach to recognition of facial actions and their temporal models. IEEE Transactions on Pattern Analysis and Machine Intelligence 32, 1940–1954 (2010)
28. Ojala, T., Pietikäinen, M., Harwood, D.: A comparative study of texture measures with classification based on featured distributions. Pattern Recognition 29, 51–59 (1996)
29. Castrillón, M., Déniz, O., Guerra, C., Hernández, M.: ENCARA2: Real-time detection of multiple faces at different resolutions in video streams. Journal of Visual Communication and Image Representation 18, 130–140 (2007)
30. Hall, M.A.: Correlation-based Feature Selection for Discrete and Numeric Class Machine Learning. In: ICML 2000 Proceedings of the Seventeenth International Conference on Machine Learning, pp. 359–366 (2000)
31. Calvo, R.A., Hussain, M. S., Aghaei Pour, P., Alzoubi, O.: Siento: An Experimental Platform for Behavior and Psychophysiology in HCI. In: D'Mello, S., Graesser, A., Schuller, B., Martin, J.-C. (eds.) ACII 2011, Part II. LNCS, vol. 6975, pp. 307–308. Springer, Heidelberg (2011)
32. Kuncheva, L.I.: Combining pattern classifiers: methods and algorithms. John Wiley & Sons (2004)
33. Lang, P., Bradley, M.: International affective picture system (IAPS): Technical manual and affective ratings. Psychology (1997)
34. Picard, R.: Affective computing: challenges. International Journal of Human-Computer Studies 59, 55–64 (2003)

A Self-adaptive Differential Evolution Algorithm with Constraint Sequencing

Md. Asafuddoula, Tapabrata Ray, and Ruhul Sarker

School of Engineering and Information Technology
University of New South Wales
Northcott Drive, Canberra ACT 2600 Australia
{Md.Asaf}@student.adfa.edu.au,
{t.ray,r.sarker}@adfa.edu.au
http://www.unsw.adfa.edu.au

Abstract. Constrained optimization is an active area of research where attempts are being regularly made to improve the efficiency of the underlying optimization algorithms. While population based stochastic algorithms such as evolutionary algorithms, differential evolution (DE), particle swarm optimization etc. have been the popular choice as the underlying optimization scheme, adaptive strategies are usually employed to deal with constraints. Most of such approaches adopt a complete evaluation policy, i.e., all constraints and objectives corresponding to a solution is always evaluated for every solution under consideration. However, in a typical constrained optimization problem, one or more constraints are often difficult to satisfy and it might be beneficial to evaluate the constraints in a sequence. Evaluation of subsequent constraints and objective function can be skipped whenever a constraint is violated. In this paper, a self adaptive differential evolution algorithm is introduced which maintains multiple subpopulations, each of which is assigned a prescribed constraint sequence based on a ring topology. Solutions are ranked in each subpopulation and a migration scheme is employed to transfer feasible solutions to a subpopulation of feasible individuals. The performance of the proposed scheme is compared with a single sequence approach and other state of the art DE forms using the standard *g-series* test functions having inequality constraints. The results clearly indicate the potential savings in the computational cost. Apart from savings in computational cost, the paper also makes an important contribution as it provides useful physical insights on the search trajectories and their effect in various forms of constrained optimization problems.

Keywords: differential evolution, constraint sequencing, sequence sorting, self-adaptive.

1 Introduction

The performance of all population based stochastic optimization algorithms are affected by the presence of constraints. The nonlinearity, multi-modality and the feasibility associated with each constraint is likely to be different and would vary in different regions of the search space. Various forms of constraint handling schemes have been proposed

M. Thielscher and D. Zhang (Eds.): AI 2012, LNCS 7691, pp. 182–193, 2012.

in literature. Such methods can be broadly categorized in four different types [10,2] i.e. use of penalty functions [3], repair schemes [4], use of decoders [7] and the separation of objective function and constraints [11,5,13]. More recent methods on the other hand, maintain infeasible solutions via stochastic ranking [9], ε based comparisons [14] and adaptive penalty function formulations [12]. However, in all such formulations a full evaluation policy is adopted wherein for an infeasible solution, its constraint violation measure is computed. The term constraint violation (*CV*) is defined as follows:

$$CV = \sum_{i=1}^{p} |min(g_i, 0)| + \sum_{i=1}^{q} max(|h_i - \varepsilon|, 0) \qquad (1)$$

where g and h are the inequality and equality constraints and p is the number of inequality constraints and q is the number of equality constraints. In this work, we have suggested a multi-population based algorithm in the framework of DE where, the population is divided into multiple subpopulations and follow the prescribed constraint sequences. The choice of DE as the underlying optimizer in this work is based on DE's recent success in the winning entries for CEC-2011 competition problems. The performance of the algorithm is subsequently compared with four top performing algorithms include ε-DE [14], JDE [1], COPSO [15] and SaDE [6] in well known *g-series* [8] test problems for inequalities.

Furthermore, since the performance of DE is known to be affected by the choice of its user defined parameters, a self adaptive scheme is employed. The rest of the paper is organized as follows. The proposed approach with an illustrative example is presented in Section 2 while the details of the algorithm is presented in Section 3. The performance of the algorithm is presented in Section 4. The final section summarizes the findings.

2   Proposed Approach

In this work, a population is divided into $p + q$ subpopulations where p and q denotes the number of inequality and equality constraints of the problem. Each subpopulation is assigned a constraint sequence and solutions in the subpopulation are evaluated following the prescribed sequence until it encounters a constraint violation. For any solution in a given subpopulation, the objective function is only computed when it satisfies all its constraints. The solutions are sorted in its subpopulation following a constraint sequence and feasible solutions migrate to a feasible subpopulation. The sequences in each subpopulation follow a ring topology wherein in each subpopulation, solutions tend to approach feasibility from different search directions. Such an approach could be beneficial in two ways i.e. (a) less likely to be trapped at a local optima and (b) save computational cost by avoiding evaluation of infeasible solutions whenever infeasibility is detected. A simple two variable constrained optimization problem is formulated to illustrate the principle.

2.1   An Illustrative Example

To demonstrate the proposed constraint handling method, a simple two variable optimization problem ($T1$) involving three constraints is presented below. The problem has a feasible region bounded by three linear constraints. Since our focus is on handling constraints, our attempt is to show the trajectory of solutions in different subpopulations.

$$\text{Minimize } f_1(x) = x_1^2 + x_2^2 + 2*x_1*x_2$$

Subject to

$$g_1(x) \equiv x_1 + 2*x_2 \geq 0, \tag{2}$$
$$g_2(x) \equiv 10*x_1 - 8*x_2 - 15 \geq 0,$$
$$g_3(x) \equiv -10*x_1 + 2*x_2 - 2 \geq 0,$$

In the proposed approach, three constraint sequences have been considered each of which is assigned to a subpopulation i.e. constraints (g_1, g_2, g_3), (g_2, g_3, g_1) and (g_3, g_1, g_2) are the prescribed sequences for subpopulation, 1, 2 and 3. As an example, let us consider subpopulation 1, containing 4 solutions (S1, S2, S3, S4). The constraint violation matrix would assume a form illustrated in Table 1. Since the prescribed sequence for this subpopulation is (g_1, g_2, g_3), the solutions are sequentially sorted to yield (S3, S2, S4, S1) where S3 is deemed the best and S1 the worst.

Table 1. An example of sequence sorting

Initial order			Final order			
g1	g2	g3	g1	g2	g3	
S1	5	inf inf	0	0	1	S3
S2	0	3	inf	0	3	inf	S2
S3	0	0	1	2	inf inf	S4
S4	2	inf inf	5	inf inf	S1

A small population size of 30 is used to illustrate the behavior. Presented in Fig. 1 is the trajectory followed by the infeasible solutions, if a *CV* based scheme is employed. A *CV* based scheme is often used for population based stochastic algorithms. It is interesting to observe that the solutions tend to be located in a small region of the space satisfying g2 and g3 constraints. With such infeasible solutions, the *CV* based approach will be effective if the optimal feasible solution is close to such infeasible solutions and will be ineffective if the feasible solution is away from such regions.

Presented in Fig. 2, is the same trajectory of the solutions in subpopulations 1, 2 and 3. One can clearly observe that the infeasible solutions in subpopulations clearly are in different regions of the search space and solutions in each subpopulation tend to approach the feasible region from different directions. Such an approach is thus likely to locate optimal solutions as they attempt to enter the feasible search space from different directions.

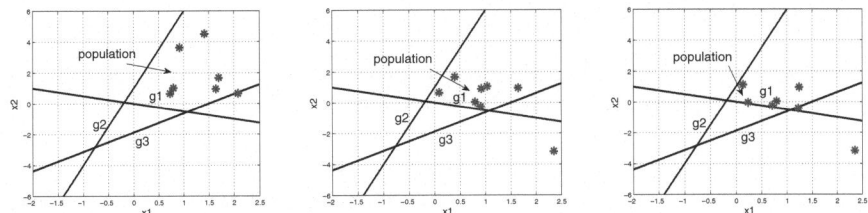

Fig. 1. Progress plots for test problem $T1$ using DE algorithm with constraint violation (DEACV) at generation 5, 10 and 20

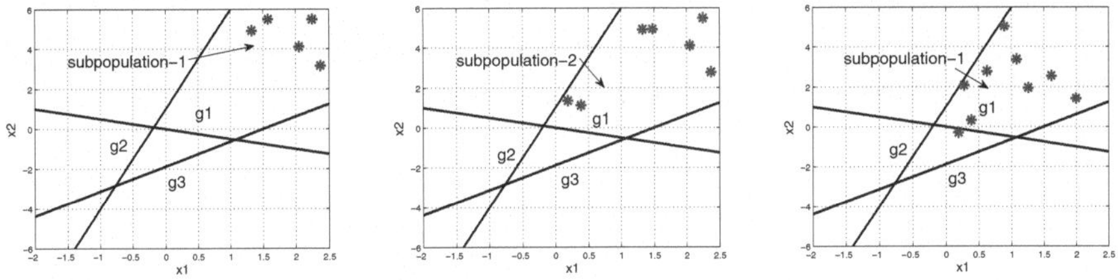

(a) Progress of subpopulation-1

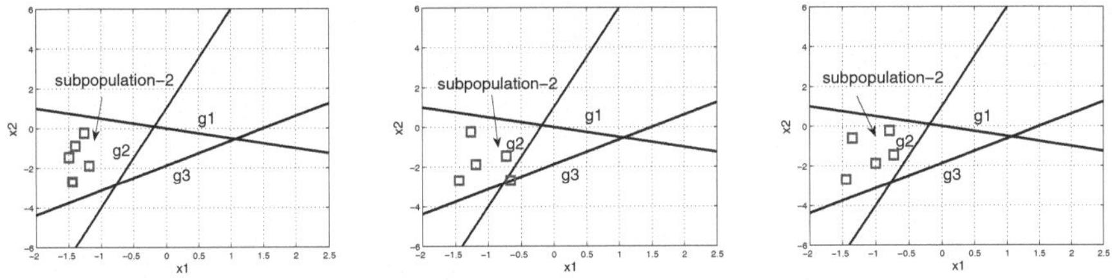

(b) Progress of subpopulation-2

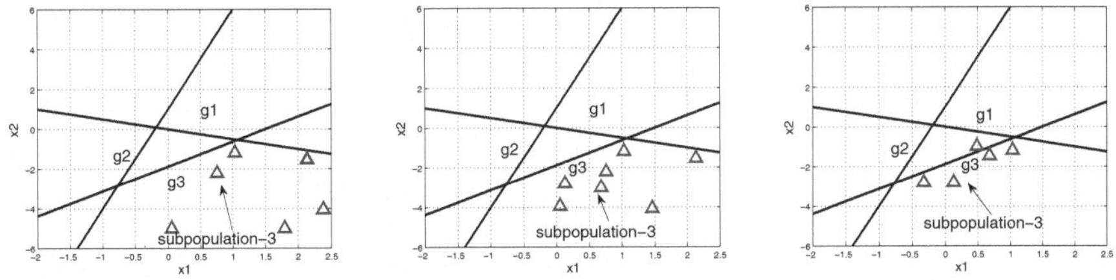

(c) Progress of subpopulation-3

Fig. 2. Progress plots for test problem $T1$ of multiple subpopulations using DE algorithm with constraint sequencing (DEACS) at generation 5, 10 and 20

3 Self-adaptive Differential Evolution Algorithm with Constraint Sequencing (DEACS)

The pseudocode of the proposed algorithm is presented below. A population of N individuals and an archive of $N*2$ are initialized. For each individual in the population the parameters regarding the crossover rate (CR) and mutation factor (F) are assigned randomly in the bounded of $[0,1]$. The population is divided into $p+q$ subpopulations with a prescribed constraint sequence for each subpopulation. In each subpopulation the solutions are ranked using a sequence sort. In order to create a new candidate solution, first parent is selected from the subpopulation itself, the second parent is selected from the entire population and the third parent is selected from the archive.

Algorithm 1. DEACS

SET: NT_{max}{Total number of constraints and objective function evaluation}, M{Size of elite archive}, N{Size of population}, $FeasibleSet = \{\}$, $Evalcount = 0$

1: $Pop = initialize();Archive = initialize()$
2: Assign a random CR and F values from $[0,1]$ for all the individuals
3: Distribute individuals to $(p+q+1)$ subpopulations
4: Assign constraint sequences to subpopulations
5: Evaluate solutions in the subpopulations; $Update(Evalcount)$
6: Rank solutions in each subpopulation using sequence sort
7: Migrate feasible solutions from all the subpopulations to $FeasibleSet$
8: **while** $(((Evalcount \leq NT_{max}))$ **do**
9:     **for** $i=1:p+q+1$ **do**
10:        **if** $!isempty(Subpop_i)$ **then**
11:            **for** $j=1:size(Subpop_i)$ **do**
12:                $p_1 = i, p_2 = rand(M), p_3 = rand(N), p_1 \neq p_2 \neq p_3$
13:                $O = DE_{evolve}(p_1,p_2,p_3)$
14:                $Evaluate(O);Update(Evalcount)$
15:                $Temp = Merge(O,Subpop_{i_j})$
16:                $Rank = SequenceSort(Temp)$
17:                Select best individual from $Temp$ and replace $Subpop_{i_j}$
18:            **end for**
19:        **end if**
20:     **end for**
21:     Migrate feasible solutions from all the subpopulations to $FeasibleSet$
22: **end while**

*$Evalcount$ denotes the sum of objective and all individual constraint evaluations

---

In the DE evolve process, a binomial crossover [6] has been used with the crossover and mutation parameters (i.e. CR and F) from the first parent (i.e. base parent). The new candidate solution is then evaluated and compared with the base parent via sequence sort. If the candidate solution replaces the parent solution, the crossover and mutation parameters of the base parent are retained by the candidate solution else new parameters are randomly assigned to the base parent and candidate solution is moved to archive. In the event a feasible solution is uncovered in any subpopulation, it migrates to the feasible subpopulation. In the event all the infeasible subpopulations are empty, three parents are chosen from the feasible subpopulation.

4 Numerical Experiments

The performance of the algorithm is evaluated using the widely used benchmark problems Table 2 [8]. The selected test problems involve quadratic, nonlinear, cubic, and polynomial objective functions with a number of inequality constraints. For comparison, we have selected five algorithms including the proposed DEACS. These five algorithms are listed as follows: The proposed algorithm (DEACS), $\varepsilon-$DE [14], JDE [1], COPSO [15] ,SaDE [6].

Table 2. Summary of test problems

Problem	D	Search Range	f type	No. of Inequality	Feasibility (ρ)
g01	13	$[0,1]^9[0,100]^3[0,1]^{(D-12)}$	quadratic	6	0.0111%
g02	20	$[0,10]^D$	nonlinear	2	99.971%
g04	5	$[78,102][33,45][27,45]^{(D-2)}$	quadratic	6	52.1230%
g06	2	$[13,100][0,100]$	cubic	2	0.0066%
g07	10	$[-10,10]^D$	quadratic	8	0.0003%
g08	2	$[0,10]^D$	nonlinear	2	0.8560%
g09	7	$[-10,10]^D$	polynomial	4	0.5121%
g10	8	$-$	linear	6	0.0010%
g12	3	$[0,10]^D$	quadratic	1	4.7713%
g18	9	$[-10,10]^8[0,20]^{(D-8)}$	quadratic	13	0.000%
g24	2	$[0,3][0,4]$	linear	2	79.6556%

4.1 Experimental Setup

A population size of 50 is used for the proposed algorithm which is the same used in previous studies. Results of all the problems are computed using 25 independent runs. An archive size of 100 is used for the proposed algorithm across all problems. A self-adaptive approach is used to determine the set of parameters (i.e. CR and F). We also include the results of two other adaptive DE algorithms for a fair comparison.

4.2 Computational Complexity

The algorithm complexity is computed for the selected 11 test problems of CEC-2006 according to [8]. Table 3 shows the complexity of the algorithm by $T1$, $T2$ and $(T2-T1)/T1$ where, $T1$ is the average computing time of 10000 evaluations for all the problems and $T2$ is the average complete computing time for the algorithm with 10000 evaluations for all the problems. We have used Matlab 7.8 to implement the algorithm and the system configuration is as follows: Intel(R) Core(TM)2 Duo 3.00 GHZ, 3.49 GB of RAM, Windows XP Professional Version 2002.

Table 3. Computational Complexity

T1	T2	(T2-T1)/T1
4.8602	5.3359	0.0979

4.3 Results Comparison

One can observe from Table 4 that the proposed algorithm required significantly less number of constraint and objective function evaluations for problems g01, g04, g07, g09, g10, g12 and g18 as compared to the method proposed by Takahama and Sakai [14]. When compared with $\varepsilon-$DE, the proposed algorithm is better in 7 out of 11 test problems using 1e-4 as the measure of merit.

Table 4. Comparison of function evaluations is used by the proposed method, DEACS with other best known algorithms with an accuracy level of $(f(x) - f^*(x)) \leq 0.0001$ and feasible solution, the lowest evaluation in total of function and constraints are in bold face

Proposed Method, DEACS	Function eval.					
Prob.	Best		Median		Worst	
	#func.	#const.	#func.	#const.	#func.	#const.
g01	**6,847**	**10,537**	**11,699**	**16,787**	**16,613**	22,163
g02	**49,176**	**71,438**	105,373	152,686	**108,302**	154,151
g04	**3,691**	**4,857**	**4,234**	**5,592**	**4,777**	**6,110**
g06	**2,426**	6,057	**2,626**	7,820	4,162	9,214
g07	**12,652**	**26,790**	**17,891**	**37,084**	47,587	87,334
g08	138	900	557	1,537	812	1,960
g09	**6,608**	**9,291**	**7,418**	**10,547**	8,109	**11,931**
g10	**13,849**	**32,364**	**20,954**	**46,230**	**38,609**	**77,123**
g12	450	450	**1,000**	**1,000**	**1,200**	**1,200**
g18	**5,674**	**13,206**	**7,554**	**18,240**	34,839	57,641
g24	1,584	2,454	1,867	2,948	2,143	3,559
$\varepsilon-$DE	Function eval.					
Prob.	Best		Median		Worst	
	#func.	#const.	#func.	#const.	#func.	#const.
g01	18,594	18,594	19,502	19,502	19,971	19,971
g02	108,303	108,303	114,347	114,347	129,255	129,255
g04	12,771	12,771	13,719	13,719	14,466	14,466
g06	5,037	**5,037**	5,733	**5,733**	**6,243**	**6,243**
g07	60,873	60,873	67,946	67,946	75,569	75,569
g08	621	621	881	881	**1,173**	**1,173**
g09	19,234	19,234	21,080	21,080	21,987	21,987
g10	87,848	87,848	92,807	92,807	107,794	107,794
g12	2,901	2,901	4,269	4,269	5,620	5,620
g18	46,856	46,856	57,910	57,910	60,108	60,108
g24	**1,959**	**1,959**	**2,451**	**2,451**	**2,739**	**2,739**

The proposed algorithm is also compared against other adaptive DEs (i.e. JDE and SaDE). Table 5 shows the comparison among three different algorithms. Here, the proposed algorithm also shows better result when compared with COPSO, JDE and SaDE for most of the problems. Table 6 shows a one to one comparison with $\varepsilon-$DE including the obtained results. Successful run is shown within 0.1% of the best-known optimum and is feasible.

4.4 Performance Comparison

The same set of problems are used to compare the performance of constraint sequencing. The proposed algorithm is applied with its two variants i.e. with and without constraint sequencing (full evaluation policy). One can see from Fig. 3, that the mean of total number of function evaluations (i.e. summation of number of constraints function evaluations and the number of objective function evaluations) is less when constraint sequencing is used.

Table 5. Comparison of function evaluations is used by the proposed method, DEACS with other best known algorithms with an accuracy level of $(f(x) - f^*(x)) \leq 0.0001$ and feasible solution

COPSO	Function eval.					
Prob.	Best		Median		Worst	
	#func.	#const.	#func.	#const.	#func.	#const.
g01	80,776	80,776	90,343	90,343	96,669	96,669
g02	87,419	87,419	93,359	**93,359**	99,654	**99,654**
g04	**3,147**	**3,147**	103,308	103,308	110,915	110,915
g06	95,944	95,944	109,765	109,765	130,293	130,293
g07	114,709	114,709	138,767	138,767	208,751	208,751
g08	2,270	2,270	4,282	4,282	5,433	5,433
g09	94,593	94,593	103,857	103,857	119,718	119,718
g10	109,243	109,243	135,735	135,735	193,426	193,426
g12	482	482	6,158	6,158	9,928	9,928
g18	97,157	97,157	107,690	107,690	124,217	124,217
g24	11,081	11,081	18,278	18,278	633,378	633,378

JDE	Function eval.					
Prob.	Best		Median		Worst	
	#func.	#const.	#func.	#const.	#func.	#const.
g01	46,559	46,559	50,354	50,354	56,968	56,968
g02	101,201	101,201	138,102	138,102	173,964	173,964
g04	38,288	38,288	40,958	40,958	42,880	42,880
g06	26,830	26,830	29,844	29,844	31,299	31,299
g07	114,899	114,899	126,637	126,637	141,847	141,847
g08	1,567	1,567	3,564	3,564	4,485	4,485
g09	49,118	49,118	55,515	55,515	58,230	58,230
g10	139,095	139,095	144,247	144,247	165,498	165,498
g12	1,820	1,820	6,684	6,684	9,693	9,693
g18	91,049	91,049	101,076	101,076	142,674	142,674
g24	7,587	7,587	10,354	10,354	11,550	11,550

SaDE	Function eval.					
Prob.	Best		Median		Worst	
	#func.	#const.	#func.	#const.	#func.	#const.
g01	25,115	25,115	25,115	25,115	25,115	25,115
g02	76,915	76,915	128,970	128,970	–	–
g04	25,107	25,107	25,107	25,107	25,113	25,113
g06	12,546	12,546	14,404	14,404	18,347	18,347
g07	25,195	**25,195**	101,240	101,240	422,860	422,860
g08	782	782	1,272	1,272	1,775	1,775
g09	12,960	12,960	16,787	16,787	33,166	33,166
g10	26,000	**26,000**	52,000	52,000	153,000	153,000
g12	463	463	1717	1717	2,576	2,576
g18	26,000	26,000	26,000	26,000	–	–
g24	4,280	4,280	4,843	4,843	5,657	5,657

Table 6. Comparison of function evaluations is used by the proposed method, DEACS with an well-known algorithm ε-DE. The results are achieved with an accuracy level of $(f(x) - f^*(x)) \leq 0.0001$ and feasible solution

Proposed method, DEACS

Prob.	Optimum	f^*			Function eval.						Succ.
		Best	Median	Worst	Min		Median		Worst		
					#func.	#const.	#func.	#const.	#func.	#const.	
g01	-15.00000	-15	-15	-15	6,847	10,537	11,699	16,787	16,613	22,163	100%
g02	-0.803619	-0.803619	-0.803619	-0.778310	49,176	71,438	105,373	152,686	108,302	154,151	80%
g04	-30665.538671	-30665.538671	-30665.538671	-30665.538671	3,691	4,857	4,234	5,592	4,777	6,110	100%
g06	-6961.813876	-6961.813876	-6961.813876	-6961.813876	2,426	6,057	2,626	7,820	4,162	9,214	100%
g07	24.306209	24.306209	24.306209	24.306209	12,652	26,790	17,891	37,084	47,587	87,334	100%
g08	-0.095825	-0.095825	-0.095825	-0.095825	138	900	557	1,537	812	1,960	100%
g09	680.630057	680.630057	680.630057	680.630057	6,608	9,291	7,418	10,547	8,109	11,931	100%
g10	7049.248021	7049.248021	7049.248021	7049.248021	13,849	32,364	20,954	46,230	38,609	77,123	100%
g12	-1	-1	-1	-1	450	450	1,000	1,000	1,200	1,200	100%
g18	-0.866025	-0.866025	-0.866025	-0.866025	5,674	13,206	7,554	18,240	34,839	57,641	100%
g24	-5.508013	-5.508013	-5.508013	-5.508013	1,584	2,454	1,867	2,948	2,143	3,559	100%

ε-DE

Prob.	Optimum	f^*			Function eval.						Succ.
		Best	Median	Worst	Min		Median		Worst		
					#func.	#const.	#func.	#const.	#func.	#const.	
g01	-15.00000	-15	-15	-15	18,594	18,594	19,502	19,502	19,971	19,971	100%
g02	-0.803619	-0.803619	-0.803619	-0.803619	108,303	108,303	114,347	114,347	129,255	129,255	100%
g04	-30665.538671	-30665.538671	-30665.538671	-30665.538671	12,771	12,771	13,719	13,719	14,466	14,466	100%
g06	-6961.813876	-6961.813876	-6961.813876	-6961.813876	5,037	5,037	5,733	5,733	6,243	6,243	100%
g07	24.306209	24.306209	24.306209	24.306209	60,873	60,873	67,946	67,946	75,569	75,569	100%
g08	-0.095825	-0.095825	-0.095825	-0.095825	621	621	881	881	1,173	1,173	100%
g09	680.630057	680.630057	680.630057	680.630057	19,234	19,234	21,080	21,080	21,987	21,987	100%
g10	7049.248021	7049.248021	7049.248021	7049.248021	87,848	87,848	92,807	92,807	107,794	107,794	100%
g12	-1	-1	-1	-1	2,901	2,901	4,269	4,269	5,620	5,620	100%
g18	-0.866025	-0.866025	-0.866025	-0.866025	46,856	46,856	57,910	57,910	60,108	60,108	100%
g24	-5.508013	-5.508013	-5.508013	-5.508013	1,959	1,959	2,451	2,451	2,739	2,739	100%

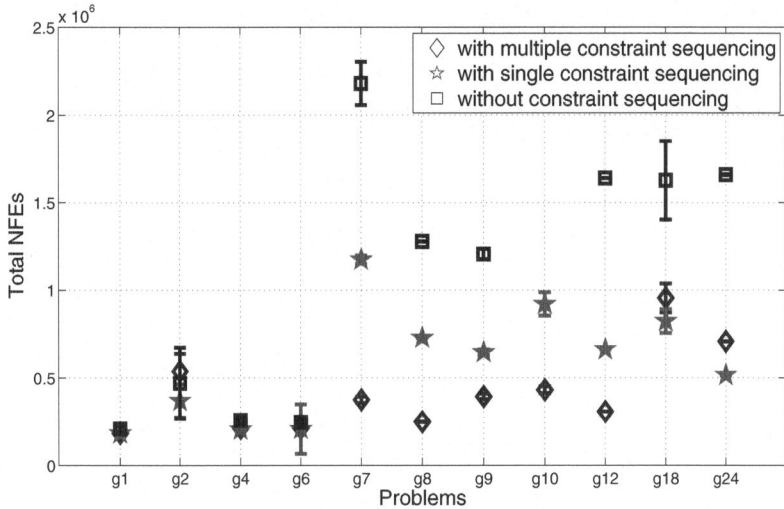

Fig. 3. A comparison of total number of function evaluations without constraint sequencing , with a single constraint sequencing and multiple constraint sequencing

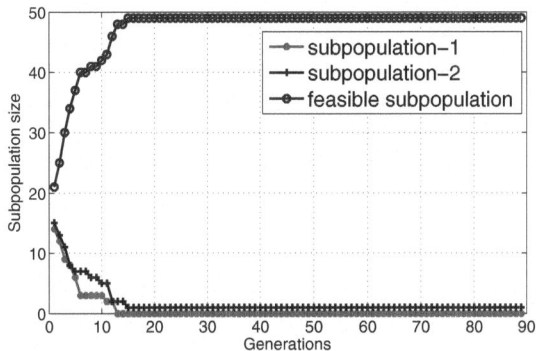

Fig. 4. An example of population migration from infeasible subpopulations to feasible subpopulation

In an another experiment, the comparison is made between the use of a single constraint sequence and multiple constraint sequences following a ring topology. For single constraint sequence, a predefined sequence is assigned to all the subpopulations whereas for the later, different constraint sequences are assigned to each subpopulation. The results in figure 4 illustrate the benefits of multiple sequencing across the subpopulations.

5   Conclusion

In this paper, a novel constraint handling scheme has been introduced within a framework of a self adaptive DE using a scheme of constraint sequencing. The paper presents the idea of constraint sequencing and using a simple example illustrates why such a scheme is likely to improve the efficiency of the search. The study also provides answers to important questions, i.e. when is such a scheme beneficial. The performance of the algorithm is subsequently assessed on 11 well known constrained single objective optimization benchmarks. The results clearly indicate that the approach is efficient when compared with the state of the art algorithms and their underlying schemes for constraint handling. The scheme is generic and can be embedded within other forms of population based stochastic optimization algorithms. The approach is likely to provide significant computational benefits for problems when each of such constraint or objective function evaluation is computationally expensive and can be computed independently. The approach is also efficient for problems where the *CV* function is highly multi-modal where the proposed scheme is less likely to be trapped in local optima. Since the efficiency of the algorithm stems from handling constraints, the approach is likely to be ineffective for some problems with high feasibility ratio as observed for problems g2 and g24.

References

1. Brest, J.: Self-adaptive differential evolution algorithm in constrained real-parameter optimization. In: 2006 IEEE Congress on Evolutionary Computation (CEC 2006), July 16-21, pp. 215–222. IEEE Press, Vancouver (2006)
2. Coello, C.A.C.: Theoretical and numerical constraint handling techniques used with evolutionary algorithms: A survey of the state of the art. Computer Methods in Applied Mechanics and Engineering 191(11-12), 1245–1287 (2002)
3. Coit, D.W., Smith, A.E.: Penalty guided genetic search for reliability design optimization. Computers and Industrial Engineering 30(4), 895–904 (1996)
4. FitzGerald, A., O'Donoghue, D.P.: Genetic Repair for Optimization under Constraints Inspired by *Arabidopsis Thaliana*. In: Rudolph, G., Jansen, T., Lucas, S., Poloni, C., Beume, N. (eds.) PPSN 2008. LNCS, vol. 5199, pp. 399–408. Springer, Heidelberg (2008)
5. Hinterding, R., Michalewicz, Z.: Your brains and my beauty: Parent matching for constrained optimisation. In: Proceedings of the 5th International Conference on Evolutionary Computation, Anchorage, Alaska, pp. 810–815 (May 1998)
6. Huang, V.L., Qin, A.K., Suganthan, P.N.: Self-adaptative differential evolution algorithm for constrained real-parameter optimization. In: 2006 IEEE Congress on Evolutionary Computation (CEC 2006), pp. 324–331. IEEE Press, Vancouver (2006)
7. Koziel, S., Michalewicz, Z.: A Decoder-Based Evolutionary Algorithm for Constrained Parameter Optimization Problems. In: Eiben, A.E., Bäck, T., Schoenauer, M., Schwefel, H.-P. (eds.) PPSN 1998. LNCS, vol. 1498, pp. 231–240. Springer, Heidelberg (1998)
8. Liang, J.J., Runarsson, T.P., Mezura-Montes, E., Clerc, M., Suganthan, P., Coello, C.A., Deb, K.: Problem definitions and evaluation criteria for the cec 2006 special session on constrained real-parameter optimization. Technical Report, Nanyang Technological University, Singapore (December 2005), http://www.ntu.edu.sg/home/EPNsugan/
9. Liu, J., Fan, Z., Goodman, E.: Srde: An improved differential evolution based on stochastic ranking. In: 2009 ACM SIGEVO Summit on Genetic and Evolutionary Computation (GEC 2009), June 12-14, pp. 345–352. ACM Press, Shanghai (2009)
10. Michalewicz, Z., Schoenauer, M.: Evolutionary algorithms for constrained parameter optimization problems. Evolutionary Computation 4(1), 1–32 (1996)

11. Powell, D., Skolnick, M.M.: Using genetic algorithms in engineering design optimization with non-linear constraints. In: Forrest, S. (ed.) Proceedings of the Fifth International Conference on Genetic Algorithms (ICGA 1993), pp. 424–431. Morgan Kaufmann Publishers, San Mateo (1993)
12. Qu, B.Y., Suganthan, P.N.: Constrained multi-objective optimization algorithm with an ensemble of constraint handling methods. Engineering Optimization 43(4), 403–416 (2011)
13. Schoenauer, M., Xanthakis, S.: Constrained GA optimization. In: Forrest, S. (ed.) Proceedings of the Fifth International Conference on Genetic Algorithms (ICGA 1993), pp. 573–580. Morgan Kauffman Publishers, San Mateo (1993)
14. Takahama, T., Sakai, S.: Constrained optimization by the ε constrained differential evolution with an archive and gradient-based mutation. In: 2010 IEEE Congress on Evolutionary Computation (CEC 2010), July 18-23, pp. 1680–1688. IEEE Press, Barcelona (2010)
15. Zavala, A.E.M., Aguirre, A.H., Diharce, E.R.V.: Continuous Constrained Optimization with Dynamic Tolerance Using the COPSO Algorithm. In: Mezura-Montes, E. (ed.) Constraint-Handling in Evolutionary Optimization. SCI, vol. 198, pp. 1–23. Springer, Heidelberg (2009)

On the Violation of Circuits in Decomposable Negation Normal Form

Lucas Bordeaux[1] and Nina Narodytska[2]

[1] Microsoft Research Cambridge, UK
lucasb@microsoft.com
[2] NICTA and University of NSW, Sydney, Australia
ninan@cse.unsw.edu.au

Abstract. Local Search approaches to constraint satisfaction are based on the ability to compute *violation* scores. These estimate 'how far' a given assignment is from satisfying the constraints, and aim at guiding the search towards assignments whose violation will, ultimately, be null. We study the computation of violation functions for Boolean predicates encoded in *Decomposable Negation Normal Form*, an important class of logical circuits that encode interesting constraints. We show that for these circuits an elegant and efficient violation function first proposed by Z. Stachniak is "ideal" in a certain sense. We discuss more broadly the notion of "ideal" violation and discuss the implications of this result.

1   Context and Summary of the Results

Local Search. Local Search (LS) is one of the most useful components in every constraint satisfaction and optimization toolbox. Two recent developments in stochastic local search that relate to this paper are the following:

- In the Constraint Programming (CP) community, Constraint-Based Local Search [19] has emerged as a formalism that integrates LS within a CP approach, clearly separating the *modeling* of a problem from its resolution.
- In the SAT community, most of the recent work on stochastic local search [17,13,14,18,7,8,15,2,3] is based on *circuits*, as opposed to the traditional Conjunctive Normal Form (CNF) representation. This is based on the belief that CNF somehow loses 'structure' compared to a natural modeling with circuits, and that this structure may be needed by the Local Search.

Common to both approaches is the idea to compute, for any assignment, a *violation* (a.k.a. *penalty*, a.k.a. *clash* function) that estimates 'by how much' it violates the constraint.

Violations in SAT. In SAT, the question is to assign a violation to arbitrary Boolean circuits. An elegant scheme for doing so was proposed by [13], following ideas initially proposed by [17] and used futher in e.g. [18,2,3]. The basic idea of [17] is that the violation of an And gate is the *sum* of the violations of its inputs,

M. Thielscher and D. Zhang (Eds.): AI 2012, LNCS 7691, pp. 194–205, 2012.
© Springer-Verlag Berlin Heidelberg 2012

while for an Or gate it is their *minimum*. This follows the obvious intuition, e.g. to satisfy an And gate we have to cumulate the work needed to make both inputs true. To find the violation value of a Boolean circuit we start from the inputs of the circuit and compute the value of the output gate using the sum and minimum rules for And and Or gates, respectively. [13] modified this definition to make it fully *symmetric*[1]: the trick is to use an integer violation score that goes *strictly* positive if the constraint is unsatisfied, and *strictly* negative if it is satisfied (i.e. the violation is always non-zero). The violation of a Not gate is now defined as −[*violation of the input*].

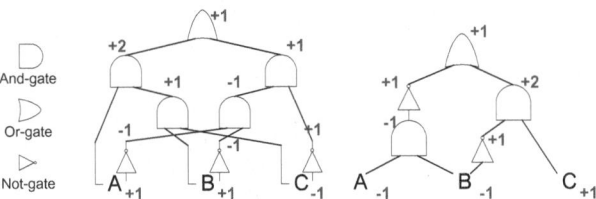

Fig. 1. Violations of circuits, arbitrary (left) and in Negation Normal Form (right)

Fig. 1 illustrates the computation of this violation; the exact definition of the rules we apply for each gate are given in Section 3. In the left-hand side example, the current assignment gives the values *true, true*, and *false*, respectively, to the inputs A, B and C. Seen as violations *true* translates to -1 and *false* to +1.

In this paper, our motivation is to better understand violation functions. These functions are usually seen as purely heuristic indicators in the literature, and little is said about the properties they should respect. For instance, the literature usually defines the violation of a constraint ALLDIFFERENT$(x_1, \ldots, x_n)$ as $\sum_{a \in D} \max(0, \sharp\{h : v(x_h) = a\} - 1)$, where D is the domain of the variables, $v(x_h)$ is the value assigned in the current state v to variable x_h, and $\sharp S$ denotes the cardinality of set S. This definition seems sensible and satisfies the basic correctness property of being > 0 iff the constraint is indeed violated, but so do many alternative definitions—why this one? In the Constraint Programming literature we have a good answer to the question *what is the ideal propagation that can be reached for a constraint?* through the notion of domain-consistency (or "Generalized Arc-Consistency"). From the OR literature, we have a good answer to the question *what is the ideal relaxation of a constraint?* through the notion of convex Hull. We are looking for a similar notion for the third class of constraint solving represented by local search:

What is an ideal violation function for a constraint?

---

[1] This definition is better-behaved, in particular w.r.t. duality: for instance the violations of $\neg(A \land B)$ and of $\neg A \lor \neg B$ are the same. For NNF formulae the initial formulation [17] and the symmetric one [13] are essentially equivalent.

Section 3 proposes an answer to this question. To be fair, although the literature has not asked the question explicitly, partial answers have been pointed to by some authors. We identify 'ideal' properties of violation functions, and observe that it is NP-complete to compute an ideal violation for arbitrary predicates.

Our main contribution is to show that such ideal violation functions can indeed be obtained, in a generic way, for an important class of Boolean circuits. Specifically the violation function described before is shown to be ideal for circuits in Negation Normal Form that have the well-known *Decomposability* property [4]. (Such a circuit is given in Fig. 1, right-hand side). Circuits in Decomposable NNF, or DNNF, are one of the most powerful 'knowledge compilation languages' [5] used in AI. Some properties of this language are: (1) it is *complete* in that it can represent any Boolean function (as for any class of circuits, most Boolean functions nevertheless have an exponential size representation); (2) important reasoning tasks including clausal entailment and model enumeration can be performed in time polynomial in the DNNF size; (3) it generalizes other widely used representations such as OBDDs; (4) it allows to concisely represent a large number of constraints, in particular grammar constraints [16,11].

The violation function of [17,13] seems like a "good" definition of violation for circuits but its properties were not previously well-understood. Our contribution, on the SAT side, is to show that it has indeed strong properties w.r.t. an important and natural class of circuits. We also discuss how, on the CP side, this result gives ideal representations of a number of constraints.

2   Basic Material

Local Minima. We denote by $\{0,1\}^n$ the set of Boolean tuples of dimension n. The n components of a tuple t are written $\langle t_1 \ldots t_n \rangle$. We denote by $\mathcal{D}(t,t')$ the Hamming distance between two tuples $t, t' \in \{0,1\}^n$, which is equal to the number of positions at which the corresponding symbols in these tuples are distinct. We consider functions of signature $\{0,1\}^n \mapsto \mathbb{Z}$ or occasionally $\{0,1\}^n \mapsto \{0,1\}$, in which case the function is called *predicate*. A key LS notion is:

Definition 1. *(Local Minimum) A tuple t is a local minimum of a function $\mathcal{F}$ if any tuple t' at Hamming distance 1 from t is such that $\mathcal{F}(t') \geq \mathcal{F}(t)$.*

A straightforward greedy minimization algorithm[2] converges to a local minimum of any function $\mathcal{F}$ in time $\mathcal{O}(n^2 KR)$, where R is the range of $\mathcal{F}$, defined as $\max_{t \in \{0,1\}^n} \mathcal{F}(t) - \min_{t \in \{0,1\}^n} \mathcal{F}(t)$, and K is the cost of evaluating the violation. It is important to note that the range R can be exponentially large w.r.t. n. There exists no local minimization algorithm of complexity directly polynomial in n and m unless the complexity class PLS is equal to P [10,9].

---

[2] A precise description of this algorithm is found in the Appendix.

Circuits. We focus on circuits with binary gates for notational simplicity (the definitions, techniques and results can be easily adapted to arbitrary gates):

Definition 2. *(**Circuit**) A circuit with n inputs $x_1 \ldots x_n$ is an ordered sequence of gates $\langle g_1 \ldots g_m \rangle$ such that $m \geq n$ and:*

- *The n first gates are the inputs: $g_k := x_k$, for $k \in 1 \ldots n$;*
- *Each gate g_k with $k > n$ is either:*
  - *A negation gate of the form $\neg g_i$ with $i < k$;*
  - *A conjunction gate of the form $g_i \wedge g_j$ with $i, j < k$;*
  - *A disjunction gate of the form $g_i \vee g_j$ with $i, j < k$.*
- *The last gate g_m is called output gate.*

The predicate encoded by a circuit is noted $\mathcal{E}$ (for Boolean evaluation) is defined as follows. Given a tuple of Boolean values $t = \langle t_1 \ldots t_n \rangle$ for the inputs, a value $\mathcal{E}_{g_k}(t)$ is assigned to each gate g_k: for each input $k \in 1 \ldots n$, $\mathcal{E}_{g_k}(t) := t_k$; for non-input gates we apply the definition of the gate, for instance $\mathcal{E}_{g_i \wedge g_j}(t) := \mathcal{E}_{g_i}(t) \wedge \mathcal{E}_{g_j}(t)$. The value $\mathcal{E}(t)$ of the circuit is defined as the value of the output gate $\mathcal{E}_{g_m}(t)$. A tuple t is a *solution* if $\mathcal{E}(t) = 1$.

Definition 3. *(**Dependencies**) When we have a gate g_k of the form $\neg g_i$, $g_i \wedge g_j$ or $g_i \vee g_j$, we say that g_k directly depends on g_i and g_j, which we note $g_i \rightsquigarrow g_k$. We say that g_k depends on g_i if there is a chain of direct dependencies $g_i \rightsquigarrow \cdots \rightsquigarrow g_k$. The set of inputs a gate g_k depends on is called $\mathrm{Vars}(g_k)$.*

Definition 4. *(**Special Forms of Circuit**) The circuit is:*

- *in Negation Normal Form (NNF) if any negation $\neg g_i$ is such that g_i is directly an input, i.e. $i \in 1 \ldots n$.*
- *in Decomposable NNF (DNNF) if it is in NNF and if every conjunction node $g_i \wedge g_j$ of the circuit is such that $\mathrm{Vars}(g_i) \cap \mathrm{Vars}(g_j) = \emptyset$.*

3   Good Violation Functions

Throughout this section $\mathcal{E}$ denotes a predicate of n variables representing a non-empty relation, i.e. if there exists a tuple t that satisfies the relation $\mathcal{E}$ so that $\mathcal{E}(t) = 1$.

Basic Correctness Condition. Following a basic definition, used by e.g. [1], a violation is any poly-time computable function $\mathcal{F}$ that respects the condition:

$$\mathcal{F}(t) > 0 \quad \text{iff} \quad \mathcal{E}(t) = 0 \tag{1}$$

This minimal requirement is needed for correctness. It is weak because it is satisfied by functions that are hard to minimize. For instance a straightforward violation function would define $\mathcal{F}(t)$ as $1 - \mathcal{E}(t)$. It is a correct function in the sense that minimizing this function will lead us to solutions; however the minimization in question won't be easy: if we are not within distance ≤ 1 of a solution, *we have strictly no information on where to move.*

What is a "ideal" Violation Function? Two basic desirable features of a good violation function are the following:

Definition 5. *(Properties of Violation Functions) A function $\mathcal{F}$ is:*

- *plateau-free if all local minima are solutions: whenever we have a non-solution t, there exists a tuple t' at distance 1 from t such that $\mathcal{F}(t') < \mathcal{F}(t)$.*
- *c-bounded if $\mathcal{F}(t) \leq c$, for all tuples t.*

Functions that have plateaus are not ideal because search can get stuck into local minima, where there is no information on where to move next. Functions that are bounded by a c that grows exponentially with the number of variables of the predicate are not ideal because in this case the number of moves needed to reach a local minimum grows exponentially[3]. Functions that are both plateau-free and c-bounded for a polynomially-bounded c are obviously ideal:

Observation 1. *If we have a violation function $\mathcal{F} : \{0,1\}^n \mapsto \mathbb{Z}$ that is plateau-free and c-bounded for a predicate $\mathcal{E}$, then we can find a solution to $\mathcal{E}$ in time $\mathcal{O}(n^2 cK)$, where K is the cost of evaluating $\mathcal{F}$.*

We argue that being (1) efficiently computable, (2) plateau-free, and (3) polynomially-bounded are the properties that characterize an ideal violation function. In fact most definitions of violation function in the constraint-based literature follow this ideal, without necessarily making it clear (see e.g. [6,1,19]). Some remarks:

- This definition basically means that an ideal violation for a constraint should allow a trivial LS (and indeed greedy) search algorithm to find a solution quickly. This is reasonable and follows the approach used for propagation and relaxation: we cannot in general find an ideal propagation / relaxation / violation for an arbitrarily large system of constraints; but reasoning constraint by constraint allows us to do "the best work possible" for each constraint.
- For simplicity our definition is based on the Hamming distance, which is the natural distance for SAT. The notions of local minima and plateau-freeness can obviously be adapted to other distances (e.g. Euclidian distances or distances based on numbers of swaps rather than flips). This captures other notions of "neighborhood".

It is clear that ideal violation functions cannot be defined for all Boolean predicates: notably this cannot be done for some global constraints that are NP-complete, like the Cumulative constraint, that schedules a set of tasks with release times and deadlines so that resource capacity constraints are satisfied. For such predicates the best we can do is to use less-than-ideal violation functions

---

[3] There are well-known optimization problems that are plateau-free but whose violation function has an exponential range, and for which no known method can reach a local minimum in (strongly) polynomial time: some examples are the computation of a stable state in a neural network and other **PLS**-complete problems [10,9].

that satisfy the correctness requirement of Eq. 1 and are 'as close as possible' to the ideal. This is, again, similar to what we do with other constraint processing techniques: propagation methods weaker than arc-consistency, relaxed LP representation.

Distance-Based Violation Functions. An important particular case of ideal violation function is the following:

Definition 6. *The Hamming Violation Function $\mathcal{H}$ is the distance from the current tuple t to the closest solution :*

$$\mathcal{H}(t) = \min_{t' \in \{0,1\}^n} \{\mathcal{D}(t,t') \; : \; \mathcal{E}(t') = 1\}$$

In particular $\mathcal{H}(t) = 0$ for any solution. By convention $\mathcal{H}(t) = \infty$ for every t when the circuit is unsatisfiable. This definition clearly relates to the literature on over-constrained problems, where notions of violation based on (Hamming) distances have been considered, see [20]. The Hamming violation function clearly has ideal properties: it is obviously plateau-free and n-bounded, which means that a local minimum can be found by a greedy algorithm in time $\mathcal{O}(n^3 K)$; and is faithful to the intuition that "the higher the violation, the further-off we are from satisfying the constraint". Unfortunately for general circuits it is easy to see that $\mathcal{H}(t)$ cannot be computed efficiently.

Observation 2. *Given a predicate $\mathcal{E}(t)$ computing $\mathcal{H}$ is NP-hard.*

Proof. Follows from a reduction from the circuit satisfiability problem. We pick an arbitrary point t and ask to compute $\mathcal{H}(t)$. If $\mathcal{H}(t) = \infty$ then the circuit satisfiability problem is unsatisfiable, otherwise it is satisfiable.   □

A Practical Violation Function. Since we cannot in general produce the Hamming violation function or another plateau-free violation for all circuits, it is natural to consider alternatives that are less-than-ideal. We consider the violation function of [13], which generalizes for arbitrary circuits the definition proposed by [17] for NNF and makes it symmetric. We call this function *symmetric* violation function.

Definition 7. *(Symmetric Violation) Given a tuple of Boolean values $t = \langle t_1 \ldots t_n \rangle$, the symmetric violation $\mathcal{V}_{g_k}$ of every gate g_k of the circuit is defined by induction on k as follows:*

- *If $k \le n$ (input gate): $\mathcal{V}_{g_k}(t) := +1$ if $t_k = 0$; $\mathcal{V}_{g_k}(t) := -1$ if $t_k = 1$.*
- *For a non-input gate, i.e. if $k > n$: the definition is by case depending on whether g_k is of the form $\neg g_i$, or $g_i \wedge g_j$, or $g_i \vee g_j$:*

$$\mathcal{V}_{\neg g_i}(t) = -\mathcal{V}_{g_i}(t)$$

$$\mathcal{V}_{g_i \wedge g_j}(t) = \begin{cases} \mathcal{V}_{g_i}(t) + \mathcal{V}_{g_j}(t) & \text{if } \mathcal{V}_{g_i}(t) > 0 \text{ and } \mathcal{V}_{g_j}(t) > 0 \\ \max(\mathcal{V}_{g_i}(t), \mathcal{V}_{g_j}(t)) & \text{otherwise} \end{cases}$$

$$\mathcal{V}_{g_i \vee g_j}(t) = \begin{cases} \mathcal{V}_{g_i}(t) + \mathcal{V}_{g_j}(t) & \text{if } \mathcal{V}_{g_i}(t) < 0 \text{ and } \mathcal{V}_{g_j}(t) < 0 \\ \min(\mathcal{V}_{g_i}(t), \mathcal{V}_{g_j}(t)) & \text{otherwise} \end{cases}$$

– The violation of the circuit is noted $\mathcal{V}(t)$ and is defined as the violation of the output gate: $\mathcal{V}(t) = \mathcal{V}_{g_m}(t)$.

A straightforward induction shows that for every gate g_k, $\mathcal{V}_{g_k}(t) \neq 0$, and the violation $\mathcal{V}_{g_k}(t)$ is positive iff the evaluation of $\mathcal{E}_{g_k}(t)$ is false.

4   Our Main Result and Its Implications

The Symmetric Violation is Ideal for DNNF Circuits. With the context and all required material introduced it is now easy to state our result. The full proof is given in the Appendix.

Proposition 1. *If the circuit is in Decomposable Negation Normal Form (DNNF), the symmetric violation function of Def. 7 is such that, for all $t \in \{0,1\}^n$:*

$$\text{if } t \text{ is not a solution then } \mathcal{V}(t) = \mathcal{H}(t)$$

This result implies that when the considered circuit is in DNNF, (1) $\mathcal{H}(t)$ is equal to $\max(0, \mathcal{V}(t))$ and can be computed in linear time; and (2) the symmetric violation is ideal. In other words: when we have a circuit in DNNF, the violation score used in papers such as [13] is guaranteed to lead greedy or local search algorithms directly to a solution.

Example 1. Consider a Boolean formula $\mathcal{B}$ that is represented by DNNF in Figure 2 (borrowed from [5]). An assignment of A, B, C and D to *false* does not satisfy the Boolean formula $\mathcal{B}$. Fig. 2 shows the computation of the violation function $\mathcal{V}(t)$. The value of $\mathcal{V}(t)$ is 1.

A closest assignment by Hamming distance is A, B, C are *false* and D is *true*. The Hamming distance between these two assignments is one which is the value of the computed violation function $\mathcal{V}(t)$.

We note that for general circuits the symmetric violation is incomparable with the Hamming violation: i.e. can be higher or lower depending on cases. This implies that in this case the violation is a purely heuristic indicator respecting only the weak correctness property. It would be interesting to have useful violation functions that provably *under-approximate* the Hamming distance since these would be *admissible* heuristics in the classical A^* sense.

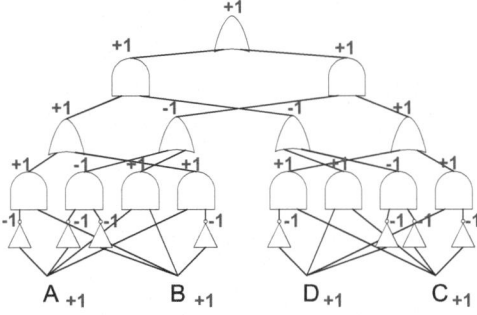

Fig. 2. Computation of the violation function $\mathcal{V}(t)$ for the assignment $[A, B, C, D] = [F, F, F, F]$

Ideal Violation Functions for Global Constraints. The main use of Prop. 1 is that it shows how good violation functions can be defined for a large class of tractable predicates. It has been shown in recent CP work that a large class of constraints can be encoded in DNNF. An example is the TABLE constraint, whose natural Boolean encoding as a disjunction of conjunctions (lines of the tables) is directly in DNNF. A more complex example is the GRAMMAR constraint, for which violation functions were only hinted at in [6]. From these decompositions it is easy to see that Prop. 1 guarantees that the symmetric violation is ideal.

Violation Functions and Weighted Propagators. To conclude on the computation of ideal violation functions for complex constraints, we note that an efficient computation of the Hamming violation for a constraint is implied by the existence of an efficient propagator for the *weighted* version of the constraint, in the sense used by e.g. [12]. In this framework, a function associates a weight to every variable/value pair. A variable is introduced to capture the weight of the assignment, defined as the sum of the weights of the values assigned to all variables. The propagator removes values that are not supported by any assignment with a weight that is less than the cost variable. While initially introduced for SAT, the symmetric violation algorithm can in the case of DNNF be thought of as a specialization of the weighted DNNF constraint propagator of [12]. Being specialized for violations (one value as opposed to two bounds) and purely 'bottom-up', the algorithm is slightly more efficient and incremental.

Proposition 2. *If a constraint has a (polynomially computable) weighted propagator, then its Hamming distance violation can be computed in polynomial time.*

Consider an application of Prop. 2 to the AllDiff constraint.

Example 2. Consider ALLDIFFERENT$[x_1, \ldots, x_4]$ with the following domains: $D(x_1) = [2, 3], D(x_2) = [2, 3], D(x_3) = [1, 4]$ and $D(X_4) = [1, 4]$. Finding a solution of the ALLDIFFERENT constraint corresponds to finding a matching in

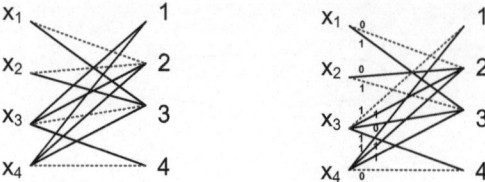

Fig. 3. Computation of Hamming distance violation for the ALLDIFFERENT($x_1, \ldots, x_4$) constraint and the assignment $x = [x_1, x_2, x_3, x_4] = [2, 2, 3, 4]$

a bipartite variable-value graph G. To build the graph G we introduce a vertex for each variable $[x_1, \ldots, x_4]$ and for each value $v \in [1, \ldots, 4]$. We connect a variable-vertex x_i to the value-vertex v iff $v \in D(x_i)$. Fig. 3(left) shows graph G that corresponds to the ALLDIFFERENT constraint.

Consider an assignment $x = [x_1, x_2, x_3, x_4] = [2, 2, 3, 4]$. This assignment does not satisfy the constraint. Hence, it does not correspond to a matching. The set of edges that correspond to the assignment are shown in red dashed line.

To find a solution that has the minimum Hamming distance violation to x we can use the variable-value graph G. We transform G into a weighted graph. We assign cost 0 to all edges that correspond to the assignment and 1 to the remaining edges (Fig. 3, right). The minimum cost matching corresponds to the solution $x = [2, 3, 1, 4]$ that minimizes Hamming distance violation.

5   Future Works

Our main result shows a new facet of the versatile DNNF class of tractable circuits. It was known that any constraint expressible in this language automatically benefits from *ideal propagators*, a meta-result that informs their integration in CP solvers. We showed that predicates expressible in DNNF also benefit from *ideal violation functions*, providing a meta-result that can now be used in constraint-based local search solvers. A third major class of constraint satisfaction tools is Linear Programming, and it would be interesting to study in a similar spirit *ideal (convex Hull) LP relaxations* of DNNF circuits. Another important open question left for future work is the empirical aspect: can we design an efficient circuit-based local search solver in which global constraints are effectively treated by an encoding to DNNF circuits? Lastly, a key question for all solvers is the *combination* of multiple constraints: problems can often be expressed using constraints that have, independently, good propagators / violation functions / relaxations; however by combining these constraints we lose the desired property. For local search it would be interesting to design schemas for combining constraints that are less naive than just summing violations.

Acknowledgements. This work benefitted from discussions with Matthew Kitching and Horst Samulowitz.

References

1. Ågren, M., Flener, P., Pearson, J.: Revisiting constraint-directed search. Information and Computation 207(3), 438–457 (2009)
2. Belov, A., Stachniak, Z.: Improving Variable Selection Process in Stochastic Local Search for Propositional Satisfiability. In: Kullmann, O. (ed.) SAT 2009. LNCS, vol. 5584, pp. 258–264. Springer, Heidelberg (2009)
3. Belov, A., Stachniak, Z.: Improved Local Search for Circuit Satisfiability. In: Strichman, O., Szeider, S. (eds.) SAT 2010. LNCS, vol. 6175, pp. 293–299. Springer, Heidelberg (2010)
4. Darwiche, A.: Decomposable negation normal form. J. ACM 48(4) (2001)
5. Darwiche, A., Marquis, P.: A knowledge compilation map. J. of Artif. Intel. Research (JAIR) 17, 229–264 (2002)
6. He, J., Flener, P., Pearson, J.: Toward an automaton constraint for local search. In: Workshop on LS Techniques for Constraint Satisfaction, pp. 13–25 (2009)
7. Järvisalo, M., Junttila, T.A., Niemelä, I.: Justification-Based Local Search with Adaptive Noise Strategies. In: Cervesato, I., Veith, H., Voronkov, A. (eds.) LPAR 2008. LNCS (LNAI), vol. 5330, pp. 31–46. Springer, Heidelberg (2008)
8. Järvisalo, M., Junttila, T.A., Niemelä, I.: Justification-based non-clausal local search for SAT. In: Euro. Conf. on Artif. Intel. (ECAI), pp. 535–539 (2008)
9. Johnson, D.S.: The NP-completeness column: Finding needles in haystacks. ACM Trans. on Algorithms (TALG) 3(2) (2004)
10. Johnson, D.S., Papadimitriou, C.H., Yannakakis, M.: How easy is local search? J. of Computer and System Sciences 37(1), 79–100 (1988)
11. Jung, J.-C., Barahona, P., Katsirelos, G., Walsh, T.: Two encodings of DNNF theories. In: ECAI Workshop on Inference Methods Based on Graphical Structures of Knowledge (2008)
12. Katsirelos, G., Narodytska, N., Walsh, T.: The weighted grammar constraint. Annals of Operations Research (2010) (to appear)
13. Muhammad, R., Stuckey, P.J.: A Stochastic Non-CNF SAT Solver. In: Yang, Q., Webb, G. (eds.) PRICAI 2006. LNCS (LNAI), vol. 4099, pp. 120–129. Springer, Heidelberg (2006)
14. Pham, D.N., Thornton, J., Sattar, A.: Building structure into local search for SAT. In: Int. Joint. Conf. on Artif. Intel. (IJCAI), pp. 2359–2364 (2007)
15. Pham, D.N., Thornton, J., Sattar, A.: Efficiently exploiting dependencies in local search for sat. In: AAAI Conf. on Artif. Intel. (AAAI), pp. 1476–1478 (2008)
16. Quimper, C.-G., Walsh, T.: Decomposing Global Grammar Constraints. In: Bessière, C. (ed.) CP 2007. LNCS, vol. 4741, pp. 590–604. Springer, Heidelberg (2007)
17. Stachniak, Z.: Going non-clausal. In: Conf. on Theory and Applications of Satisfiability Testing (SAT), pp. 316–322 (2002)
18. Stachniak, Z., Belov, A.: Speeding-Up Non-clausal Local Search for Propositional Satisfiability with Clause Learning. In: Kleine Büning, H., Zhao, X. (eds.) SAT 2008. LNCS, vol. 4996, pp. 257–270. Springer, Heidelberg (2008)
19. Van Hentenryck, P., Michel, L.: Constraint-Based Local Search. MIT Press (2005)
20. van Hoeve, W.-J.: Over-constrained problems. In: Hybrid optimization: the 10 Years of CPAIOR, ch. 6 (2010) (to appear)

t ← (an arbitrary value)
optimal ← **false**
while ¬ optimal **do**
    $n ← t$
    foreach t' at distance 1 from t **do**
        if $\mathcal{F}(t') < \mathcal{F}(t)$ **then** $\{n ← t'; \textbf{break}\}$
    done
    optimal ← $(n = t)$
done

Fig. 4. Greedy local minimization algorithm

A   Appendix

A.1   Greedy Local Minimization Algorithm

A.2   Proof of Proposition 1

Proposition 1. *If the circuit is in Decomposable Negation Normal Form (DNNF), the symmetric violation function of Def. 7 is such that, for all $t \in \{0,1\}^n$:*

$$\text{if } t \text{ is not a solution then } \mathcal{V}(t) = \mathcal{H}(t)$$

Proof. Note that a DNNF is always satisfiable, i.e. represents a non-empty Boolean relation; so we don't have to deal with the case where $\mathcal{H}(t) = \infty$. Given an assignment t we prove by induction on k for all gates g_k that:

$$\text{if } \mathcal{E}_{g_k}(t) = 0 \text{ then } \mathcal{V}_{g_k}(t) = \min\{\mathcal{D}(t,t') : \mathcal{E}_{g_k}(t') = 1\}$$

- if $k \leq n$, i.e. the gate g_k is an input. If g_k is violated by the assignment t then $\mathcal{V}_{g_k}(t) = 1$; the closest tuple t' that satisfies g_k is obtained by flipping the value assigned by t to g_k, and $D(t,t') = 1$.
- if $k > n$, the proof is by case on the type of gate g_k (In all cases the induction hypothesis holds for the inputs g_i, g_j since $i, j < k$):
  - Negation of the form $\neg g_i$. The Negation Normal Form means that g_i is an input. If $\mathcal{E}_{g_k}(t) = 0$ then $\mathcal{V}_{g_k}(t) = -\mathcal{V}_{g_i}(t) = +1$. The closest tuple t' that satisfies g_k is obtained by flipping the value on g_i, and $D(t,t') = 1$.
  - Conjunction of the form $g_i \wedge g_j$. The decomposability property applies, i.e. we have $\text{Vars}(g_i) \cap \text{Vars}(g_j) = \emptyset$. If $\mathcal{E}_{g_k}(t) = 0$, we have the following cases:
    Case 1: $\mathcal{V}_{g_i}(t) > 0$ and $\mathcal{V}_{g_j}(t) > 0$. Both inputs are violated and $\mathcal{V}_{g_k}(t) = \mathcal{V}_{g_i}(t) + \mathcal{V}_{g_j}(t)$.
    By the induction hypothesis there exist (1) a tuple u such that $\mathcal{E}_{g_i}(u) = 1$ and $\mathcal{D}(t,u) = \mathcal{V}_{g_i}(t)$; and (2) a tuple w such that $\mathcal{E}_{g_j}(w) = 1$ and $\mathcal{D}(t,w) = \mathcal{V}_{g_j}(t)$. Consider now the tuple t' whose value on every input $l \in 1 \ldots n$ is defined as follows:

$$t'_l = \begin{cases} u_l & \text{if } l \in \text{Vars}(g_i) \\ w_l & \text{if } l \in \text{Vars}(g_j) \\ t_l & \text{otherwise} \end{cases}$$

(This is well-defined since $\text{Vars}(g_i)$ and $\text{Vars}(g_j)$ are disjoint.) It is easy to show that (1) $\mathcal{E}_{g_k}(t') = 1$; (2) t' is at distance $\mathcal{V}_{g_k}(t) = \mathcal{V}_{g_i}(t) + \mathcal{V}_{g_j}(t)$ from t; (3) any tuple τ at distance $\mathcal{D}(t, \tau) < \mathcal{V}_{g_k}(t)$ is such that $\mathcal{E}_{g_k}(\tau) = 0$. This shows that $\mathcal{V}_{g_k}(t) = \min\{\mathcal{D}(t, t') \;:\; \mathcal{E}_{g_k}(t') = 1\}$.

Case 2: $\mathcal{V}_{g_i}(t) > 0$ and $\mathcal{V}_{g_j}(t) < 0$. (The **Case 3:** $\mathcal{V}_{g_j}(t) > 0$ and $\mathcal{V}_{g_i}(t) < 0$ is symmetric.) g_i is the only input that is violated and $\mathcal{V}_{g_k}(t) = \mathcal{V}_{g_i}(t)$. There exists a tuple u such that $\mathcal{E}_{g_i}(u) = 1$ and $\mathcal{D}(t, u) = \mathcal{V}_{g_i}(t)$. Consider the tuple t' defined for all inputs $l \in 1 \ldots n$ by: $t'_l = u_l$ if $l \in \text{Vars}(g_i)$; otherwise: $t'_l = t_l$. The tuple t' is at distance $\mathcal{V}_{g_k}(t)$ from t and is the closest tuple that satisfies g_k.

- Disjunction of the form $g_i \vee g_j$. If $\mathcal{E}_{g_k}(t) = 0$, then we have $\mathcal{V}_{g_i}(t) > 0$ and $\mathcal{V}_{g_j}(t) > 0$. W.l.o.g. let g_i be the input that is "less violated", i.e. let us assume that $\mathcal{V}_{g_i}(t) \leq \mathcal{V}_{g_j}(t)$. Then $\mathcal{V}_{g_k}(t) = \mathcal{V}_{g_i}(t)$.

  By the induction hypothesis there exists a tuple u such that $\mathcal{E}_{g_i}(u) = 1$ and $\mathcal{D}(t, u) = \mathcal{V}_{g_i}(t) = \mathcal{V}_{g_k}(t)$. It is clear that $\mathcal{E}_{g_k}(u) = 1$. Additionally no tuple t' with $\mathcal{D}(t, t') < \mathcal{V}_{g_k}(t)$ satisfies g_k: if such a tuple did exist it would either satisfy g_i and be at distance $< \mathcal{V}_{g_i}(t)$ from t; or satisfy g_j and be at distance $< \mathcal{V}_{g_j}(t)$. Both cases are contradictory to the induction hypothesis.

A.3   Proof of Proposition 2

Proposition 2. *If a constraint has a (polynomially computable)* weighted *propagator, then its Hamming distance violation can be computed in polynomial time.*

Proof. We show that it is possible to compute the Hamming violation function for many useful global constraints C. Let $C(X)$, $X = [X_1, \ldots, X_n]$ be a global constraint and $C(X, W, z)$ be the weighted version of the constraint $C(X)$. The weight matrix $W(X_i, t_j)$, $t_j \in D(X_i)$ $i = 1, \ldots, n$ of integer values specifies the weight of each variable-value pair, and the cost variable z restricts possible weights of a solution to be less than or equal to z. The weight of a solution $X = t$ is $W(X, t) = \sum_{i=1}^{n} W(X_i, t_i)$. $C(X, W, z)$ holds iff $C(X)$ holds and $W(X, t) \leq z$.

We assume that $C(X, W, z)$ admits a polynomial time propagator that achieves domain consistency on the variables X and bounds consistency on the cost variable z. This is the case for many important global constraints, like ALLDIFFERENT or REGULAR constraints.

We show that we can use $C(X, W, z)$ to compute the Hamming distance function. Suppose t' is the current assignment that violates the constraint $C(X)$. We construct $C(X, W, z)$ in the following way:

$$W(X_i, t_k) = \begin{cases} 0 \text{ if } t_k = t'_i \\ 1 \text{ otherwise} \end{cases}$$

for $t_k \in D(X_i)$, $i = 1, \ldots, n$ and $D(z) = [0, n]$. As the propagator for $C(X, W, z)$ enforces bounds consistency on z, the lower bound of z gives the value of $\mathcal{H}$ and its support $X = t$, such that $W(X, t) = lb(z)$, is the closest, by Hamming distance, solution to t'. This follows from the correctness of the propagator for $C(X, W, z)$.

The RegularGcc Matrix Constraint

Ronald de Haan[1], Nina Narodytska[2], and Toby Walsh[2]

[1] Technische Universität Wien
dehaan.ronald@gmail.com
[2] NICTA and University of NSW, Sydney
{nina.narodytska,toby.walsh}@nicta.com.au

Abstract. We study propagation of a global constraint that ensures that each row of a matrix of decision variables satisfies a Regular constraint, and each column satisfies a Gcc constraint. On the negative side, we prove that propagation is NP-hard even under some strong restrictions (e.g. just 2 values, just 4 states in the automaton, just 5 columns to the matrix, or restricting to limited classes of automata). We also prove that propagation is W[2]-hard when the problem is parameterized by the number of rows in the matrix. On the positive side, we identify several cases where propagation is fixed parameter tractable.

1 Introduction

Constraints are often applied to the rows and columns of a matrix of decision variables [6–8, 17]. For example, the RegularGcc constraint posts a Regular constraint on each row of such a matrix, and a Gcc constraint on each column [1]. The Regular constraints ensure that each row is a sequence of values accepted by a deterministic finite automaton (DFA). The Gcc constraints enforce upper and lower bound on the occurrences of given values down each column. This modelling pattern occurs in nurse scheduling problems. The row constraints ensure shift rules (e.g. two days off after a night shift) whilst the column constraints ensure that sufficient staff are on duty in each shift. This modelling pattern also occurs in call center rostering and related problems.

In this paper, we investigate the computational complexity of propagating the RegularGcc constraint. We provide a detailed picture of the conditions under which propagation is (in)tractable [2–4]. The RegularGcc constraint imposes a special structure on the problem. Such structure in constraints can have a positive impact on the complexity of propagation (e.g. by using the structure of the automaton, the Regular constraint can be propagated in linear time [14, 16]). In our investigation of the complexity of propagating RegularGcc, we will make use of structural properties of the constraint. In particular, we will identify tractable cases by bounding certain structural properties.

2 Background

Constraint Satisfaction Problem A constraint satisfaction problem consists of a set of variables $X = (x_1, \ldots, x_n)$, each with a domain of values $D = (D_1, \ldots, D_n)$,

M. Thielscher and D. Zhang (Eds.): AI 2012, LNCS 7691, pp. 206–217, 2012.

and a set of constraints specifying allowed combinations of values for given subsets of variables. A solution is an assignment of values to the variables satisfying the constraints. A common method to find a solution of a constraint satisfaction problem is backtracking search. Constraint solvers typically prune the backtracking search space by enforcing a local consistency property like domain consistency. A constraint is *domain consistent* (*DC*) iff when a variable is assigned any of the values in its domain, there exist compatible values in the domains of all the other variables of the constraint. Such combination of values is called a *support*. A constraint is *bound consistent* (*BC*) iff when a variable is assigned the minimum or maximum value in its domain, there exist compatible values between the minimum and maximum domain value for all the other variables. Such combination of values is called a *bound support*.

Global Constraints. An automaton $\mathcal{A} = \langle \Sigma, Q, q_0, F, \delta \rangle$ consists of an alphabet Σ, a set of states Q, an initial state q_0, a set of accepting states F, and a transition relation δ defining the possible next states from a state given a symbol. $\mathcal{A}$ is deterministic (DFA) if there is only one possible next state, non-deterministic (NFA) otherwise. A string s is *recognized* by $\mathcal{A}$ iff starting from the state q_0 we can reach an accepting state using the transition relation δ. Both DFAs and NFAs recognize precisely regular languages. The constraint REGULAR($\mathcal{A}, (X_1, \ldots, X_n)$) is satisfied iff X_1 to X_n is a string accepted by $\mathcal{A}$ [14].

The STRETCH($(x_1, \ldots, x_n), \mathcal{A}, [l_{s_1}, \ldots, l_{|\Sigma|}], [u_{s_1}, \ldots, u_{|\Sigma|}]$) constraint, where $s_i \in \Sigma$, is a special case of the REGULAR constraint [9]. The automaton $\mathcal{A}$ defines possible combinations of two consecutive symbols. Parameters l_{s_i} and u_{s_i} restrict the length of a stretch of symbol s_i in a sequence from below and from above, respectively. The GCC($(x_1, \ldots, x_n), [l_1, \ldots, l_m], [u_1, \ldots, u_m]$) constraint ensures that the value i, $i = 1, \ldots, m$ occurs between l_i and u_i times in x_1 to x_n. The SEQUENCE constraint is a conjunction of overlapping AMONG constraints. The AMONG($l, u, (x_1, \ldots, x_k), v$) constraint holds iff $l \leq |\{i|x_i \in v\}| \leq u$. SEQUENCE($l, u, k, (x_1, x_2, \ldots, x_n), v$) holds iff for $1 \leq i \leq n - k + 1$, AMONG($l, u, (X_i, X_{i+1}, \ldots, X_{i+k-1}), v$) holds.

We define the XY constraint over a matrix of variables $\mathcal{M}$ with R rows and C columns where X and Y are two global constraints. XY($\mathcal{M}$) holds iff X holds on each row of M and Y holds on each column of M.

Parameterized Complexity. A problem is fixed parameter tractable (FPT) to compute in a parameter k if it can be solved in $O(f(k)n^c)$ time where f is any computable function, c is a constant, and n is the size of the input. Above FPT, there exists a hierarchy of fixed-parameter *intractable* problem classes: FPT $\subseteq$ W[1] $\subseteq$ W[2] $\subseteq \ldots$. The clique problem is W[1]-complete with respect to the size of the clique, whilst the dominating set problem is W[2]-complete with respect to the size of the dominating set. W[t] is characterized by the depth t of unbounded fan-in gates in a Boolean circuit specifying the problem. There is considerable evidence to suggest that such problem classes are intractable. For example, the halting problem for non-deterministic Turing machines is W[1]-complete with respect to the length of the accepting computation.

3   Intractable Cases

We first prove that propagating the REGULARGCC matrix constraint is NP-hard even under strong conditions. For example, it is NP-hard to enforce even a weak level of local consistency like bound consistency with just a few values.

Theorem 1. *Enforcing BC on* REGULARGCC *is* NP-*hard with just 3 values,* REGULAR *constraints given by a DFA of size 4, and* GCC *constraints specifying only an upper bound on the number of occurrences of one particular value.*

Proof: Reduction from 3-SAT. Let $\varphi = \gamma_1 \wedge \cdots \wedge \gamma_C$ be a 3-CNF formula over Boolean variables $p_1, \ldots, p_R$. We construct an $R \times C$ matrix $\mathcal{M}$ of decision variables taking their values from $\{-1, 0, 1\}$, where each row $1 \leq r \leq R$ corresponds to a propositional variable p_r and each column $1 \leq c \leq C$ corresponds to a clause γ_c. To initialize the domain of variables in the matrix, we do the following for each clause $\gamma_i = l_1^i \vee l_2^i \vee l_3^i$. We set $\mathcal{M}_{r,i} = 0$ for all propositions p_r not occurring in γ_i. For $j \in \{1, 2, 3\}$ we set $\mathcal{M}_{i,k} \in \{0, 1\}$ if $l_j^i = p_k$ and we set $\mathcal{M}_{i,k} \in \{0, -1\}$ if $l_j^i = \neg p_k$. On each column we put the GCC constraint that states that the value 0 occurs at most $R - 1$ times. On each row we put the REGULAR constraint that states that besides 0's either only 1's or only -1's occur. Figure 1 demonstrates that this REGULAR constraint can be enforced by a DFA of size 4. This instance of REGULARGCC has a solution iff φ is satisfiable.

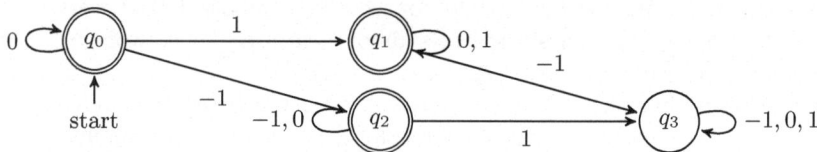

Fig. 1. Deterministic finite automaton used in the proof of Theorem 1

($\Rightarrow$) We create a satisfying assignment I for φ as follows. For each p_r, if in row r occurs at least one 1, we let $I(p_r) = \top$, otherwise we let $I(p_r) = \bot$ (the choice of $I(p_r)$ when only 0's occur in row r is arbitrary). Since in each column c there occur only $R - 1$ many 0's, we know that there exists some p_i for which $\mathcal{M}_{i,c} \neq 0$. By construction of $\mathcal{M}$, this can only happen if $I(l_j^c) = \top$ for some $j \in \{1, 2, 3\}$. Therefore I satisfies γ_c.

($\Leftarrow$) Let I be an assignment satisfying φ. We can instantiate $\mathcal{M}$ as follows. For each clause $\gamma_c = l_1^c \vee l_2^c \vee l_3^c$, for $j \in \{1, 2, 3\}$ we do the following. If $l_j^c = p_k$ and $I(p_k) = \top$, we let $\mathcal{M}_{k,c} = 1$. If $l_j^c = \neg p_k$ and $I(p_k) = \bot$, we let $\mathcal{M}_{k,c} = -1$. Otherwise, we let $\mathcal{M}_{k,c} = 0$. Since I is functional each REGULAR constraint on the rows is satisfied. Also, since at least one literal is satisfied in each clause, each column contains at least one value that is not 0, so the GCC constraints are satisfied. □

In fact, we can strengthen the first condition to show that enforcing BC on REGULARGCC is intractable with a matrix containing just 2 values.

Theorem 2. *Enforcing BC on* REGULARGCC *is* NP-*hard with just 2 values.*

Proof: Reduction from the Exact Cover By 3-Set problem. We are given $F = \{S_1, \ldots, S_n\}$ with $|S_i| = 3$, $\bigcup_i S_i = U$, $|U| = 3m$. We ask if there exists some subset $C \subseteq F$ with $|C| = m$ and $U = \bigcup_{c \in C} c$. W.l.o.g. we assume U contains the integers 1 to $3m$. We construct a $n \times (n + 3m)$ matrix of decision variables ranging over $\{0, 1\}$. The first n columns will indicate which S_j is included in the cover. The first n columns have a GCC constraint to ensures at most one 1 in each column. The next $3m$ columns represent the elements of the chosen set S_j. The REGULAR constraint on each row reads in the first n values. It only accepts those sequences that contain a single 1 in the first n values. Suppose there is a 1 at the jth position for $j \leq n$. Then this row represents the set S_j. Suppose $S_j = \{p, q, r\}$. Then the automaton only accepts those sequences with 1 at positions j, $n+p$, $n+q$ and $n+r$ and 0 everywhere else. To ensure that the m sets form a cover, we have a GCC constraint on the final $3m$ columns that ensures that it contains exactly one occurrence of 1. A solution of this REGULARGCC constraint represents an exact cover.   □

These NP-hardness results hold for very restricted cases, involving only few values or automata with only a few states.

4   Special Cases

We will consider three special cases of the REGULARGCC constraint which turn up frequently in scheduling and rostering problems. These three special cases restrict the REGULAR constraints to a limited class of automaton. We consider these special cases of the REGULARGCC constraint in an attempt to find tractable cases. As we will see, however, just restricting the REGULAR constraints on the rows to these special cases does not yield tractability.

The first special case is the STRETCHGCC constraint in which the REGULAR constraint on each row encodes a STRETCH constraint [9]. This constrains the length of any sequence of consecutive values (e.g. no more than 3 night shifts in a row), as well as the permitted transitions (e.g. a night shift can only be followed by a rest period). Unfortunately, propagation of STRETCHGCC is intractable even under strong conditions. For example, it is NP-hard to enforce a weak level of local consistency like bound consistency with just 3 values.

Theorem 3. *Enforcing BC on* STRETCHGCC *is* NP-*hard with just 3 values.*

Proof: Reduction from the Exact Cover problem. We are given $F = \{S_1, \ldots, S_n\}$ with $\bigcup_i S_i = U$. We ask if there is some subset $C \subseteq F$ with $\bigcup_{c \in C} c = U$ and $c \cap c' = \emptyset$ for all distinct $c, c' \in C$. W.l.o.g. we assume that U contains the integers 1 to $|U|$. We construct a $|F| \times |U|$ matrix $\mathcal{M}$, of decision variables taking their value in $\{-1, 0, 1\}$. For each row $1 \leq r \leq |F|$ and each value $1 \leq i \leq |U|$ we do the following. If $i \in S_r$, we let $\mathcal{M}_{r,i} \in \{0,1\}$. If $i \notin S_r$, we let $\mathcal{M}_{r,i} \in \{-1,0\}$. On each column we put the GCC constraint that states that the value 1 occurs exactly once. On each row we put the STRETCH constraint stating that each stretch of 0's must have a length of at least $|U|$. We show that this instance of STRETCHGCC has a solution iff there exists an exact cover.

($\Rightarrow$) Take a solution for our instance. We let C be the set of all U_r for which row r in the solution contains only -1's and 1's. Obviously $C \subseteq F$. In order to show that $\bigcup_{c \in C} = U$, it suffices to show that $U \subseteq \bigcup_{c \in C}$. Take an arbitrary $i \in U$. Since our solution contains at least one 1 in each column, we know there is some $c \in C$ such that $i \in c$. We also show that all distinct $c, c' \in C$ are disjoint. Take arbitrary $c, c' \in C$ such that $c \neq c'$. Assume $j \in c \cap c'$. This means that column j in the solution would contain two 1's, which contradicts the GCC constraints on the columns.

($\Leftarrow$) Let $C \subseteq F$ be an exact cover. We fill $\mathcal{M}$ as follows. For each row $1 \leq r \leq |F|$, we do the following. If $S_r \in C$, fill the row with -1's and 1's (this can be done only in one way). Otherwise, fill row r with only 0's. Obviously, the STRETCH constraints on the rows are satisfied. Also, since C is an exact cover, we know that for each $1 \leq i \leq |U|$ there is exactly one row r such that $\mathcal{M}_{r,i} = 1$. Thus the GCC constraints on the columns are satisfied. $\square$

The second special case we consider is the SLIDEGCC constraint, in which the REGULAR row constraints encode SLIDE meta constraints [2]. This constrains all subwords of a particular length k to instances of a given k-ary constraint (e.g. directly after two night shifts there must be either a small shift or a rest period). Such SLIDE constraints can be encoded using REGULAR constraints with automata whose number of states depends only on k. Unfortunately, SLIDEGCC propagation is again intractable even under strong conditions.

Corollary 1. *Enforcing BC on* SLIDEGCC *is NP-hard, already for* SLIDE *constraints based on constraints of arity 2 and just 3 values.*

Proof: (Sketch.) The reduction from the proof of Theorem 3 can be adapted for SLIDEGCC by putting on each row a REGULAR constraint accepting only words that contain either only 0's or only -1's and 1's. This can be expressed using a SLIDE constraint with arity 2. $\square$

The third special case of REGULARGCC we consider is the SEQUENCEGCC constraint in which the REGULAR constraint on each row encodes a SEQUENCE constraint [13]. This constrains the repetition of values within a sliding window (e.g. there are at least 2 days off in any 7 day period, and at most 3 night shifts in any 7 day period). Enforcing domain or bound consistency on the SEQUENCEGCC constraint is NP-hard even if the matrix has just a few columns. For the sake of presentation, we firstly give an intractability proof for domain consistency, and then extend this proof to bound consistency.

Theorem 4. *Enforcing DC on* SEQUENCEGCC *is NP-hard with just 5 columns.*

Proof: Reduction from the 3D Matching problem. Given three pair-wise disjoint sets W, Z, Y of equal size q and a set $M \subseteq W \times Z \times Y$, $|M| = m$, we ask if there exists $M' \subseteq M$ such that $|M'| = q$ and no two different elements of M' agree in any coordinate. Assume $M = \{s_1, \ldots, s_m\}$. We create a $m \times 5$ matrix $\mathcal{M}$ of decision variables taking their value in $\{0, t, w_1, \ldots, w_q, z_1, \ldots, z_q, y_1, \ldots, y_q\}$. For each $(w_i, z_i, y_i) = s_i$ we let $\mathcal{M}_{i,1} \in \{0, w_i\}$, $\mathcal{M}_{i,2} \in \{0, t\}$, $\mathcal{M}_{i,3} \in \{0, z_i\}$, $\mathcal{M}_{i,4} \in \{0, t\}$, and $\mathcal{M}_{i,5} \in \{0, y_i\}$. We constrain each row i with the constraint SEQUENCE$(\mathcal{M}_i, 1, 2, 2, \{0\})$, stating that in each sequence of length 2, at least one 0 occurs. On columns 1 (resp. 3 and 5) we put the GCC constraint stating that each value in W (resp. Z and Y) occurs at least once, and that at least $m - q$ many 0's occur. On columns 2 and 4 we put the GCC constraint stating that at least q many t's occur, and at least $m - q$ many 0's. This instance of SEQUENCEGCC has a solution iff there exists a matching.

($\Rightarrow$) Take a solution for SEQUENCEGCC. We know column 2 contains exactly $m - q$ many t's, and q many 0's. For each occurrence of a t in column 2 at row i, columns 1 and 3 contain a 0 at row i (by the SEQUENCE constraint). Then, by the GCC constraint, for all rows j where column 2 contains a 0, columns 1 and 3 contain a non-0 at row j, and thus (by SEQUENCE) column 4 contains a 0 at row j. By a similar argument, we know that in the remaining rows column 4 contains t's. Continuing this argument for column 5, we know that in the solution there are q many rows taking values $(w_i, 0, z_i, 0, y_i)$ and $m - q$ rows taking values $(0, t, 0, t, 0)$. By the GCC constraints, we know that each value $w \in W$ occurs exactly once, as well as each value $z \in Z$ and each $y \in Y$. Since the possible values were chosen by taking elements from M, we know that $M' = \{s_i \mid \mathcal{M}_i \neq (0, t, 0, t, 0)\}$ is a 3D matching.

($\Leftarrow$) Let $M' \subseteq M$ be a 3D matching. We can fill $\mathcal{M}$ as follows. For each $(w_i, z_i, y_i) = s_i \in M'$, we let $\mathcal{M}_i = (w_i, 0, z_i, 0, y_i)$. For each $s_i \in M \backslash M'$ we let $\mathcal{M}_i = (0, t, 0, t, 0)$. Obviously each row satisfies the SEQUENCE constraint. Since $|M'| = q$ and each value $w \in W$ occurs exactly once in the first coordinate of M' (and similarly for values $z \in Z$ and the second coordinate, and $y \in Y$ and the third coordinate), we have that each column satisfies the corresponding GCC constraint.   □

Theorem 5. *Enforcing BC on* SEQUENCEGCC *is NP-hard with just* 5 *columns.*

Proof: The proof is similar to the proof of Theorem 4. Let cw_i (resp. cz_i, cy_i) be the number of occurrences of the value w_i (resp. z_i, y_i) in M. For each value w_i (resp. z_i, y_i) we create $cw_i - 1$ (resp. $cz_i - 1$, $cy_i - 1$) clones of it. We now define the total order on values as $U = [-w_q^1, \ldots, -w_q^{cw_q - 1}, \ldots, -w_1^1, \ldots, -w_1^{cw_1 - 1}, -z_q^1, \ldots, -z_q^{cz_q - 1}, \ldots, -z_1^1, \ldots, -z_1^{cz_1 - 1}, -y_q^1, \ldots, -y_q^{cy_q - 1}, \ldots, -y_1^1, \ldots, -y_1^{cy_1 - 1}, 0, t, y_1, \ldots, y_q, z_1, \ldots, z_q, w_1, \ldots, w_q]$. We create the matrix $\mathcal{M}$ in a similar fashion as in the proof for Theorem 4, with the difference that for each $(w_i, z_i, y_i) = s_i$ we let $\mathcal{M}_{i,1} \in [-w_i^1, \ldots, -w_i^{cw_i - 1}, \ldots, w_i]$, $\mathcal{M}_{i,3} \in [-z_i^1, \ldots, -z_i^{cz_i - 1}, \ldots, z_i]$, $\mathcal{M}_{i,5} \in [-y_i^1, \ldots, -y_i^{cy_i - 1}, \ldots, y_i]$, and $\mathcal{M}_{i,2} \in [0, t]$ and $\mathcal{M}_{i,4} \in [0, t]$. We adapt the constraint on rows to SEQUENCE$(\mathcal{M}_i, 1, 2, 2, [-w_q^1, 0])$, stating that in each sequence of length 2, at least one value in $[-w_q^1, 0]$ occurs. On columns 1 (resp. 3 and 5) we replace the GCC constraint with one stating that each value in $\{-w_q^1, \ldots, -w_q^{cw_q-1}, \ldots, -w_1^1, \ldots, -w_1^{cw_1-1}\} \cup W$ (resp. $\{-z_q^1, \ldots, -z_q^{cz_q-1}, \ldots, -z_1^1, \ldots, -z_1^{cz_1-1}\} \cup Z$ and $\{-y_q^1, \ldots, -y_q^{cy_q-1}, \ldots, -y_1^1, \ldots, -y_1^{cy_1-1}\} \cup Y$) occurs at least once. We do not change the GCC constraints on columns 2 and 4. We show that this instance of SEQUENCEGCC has a solution iff there exists a 3D matching.

($\Rightarrow$) By reasoning similar to the proof of Theorem 4 (replacing '0' with 'a value in $[-w_q^i, 0]$' when reasoning about columns 1, 3 and 5), we know that in the solution there are q many rows taking values $(w_i, 0, z_i, 0, y_i)$, possibly containing clones, and $m - q$ rows taking values (n, t, n', t, n'') where n, n', n'' are either 0 or some clone w_i', z_i', or y_i' (respectively). Furthermore, by the GCC constraint on the odd columns, we know that each value in $\{-w_q^1, \ldots, -w_q^{cw_q-1}, w_q\}$ must occur exactly once. Since these values occur only in the domains of $\mathcal{M}_{i,1}$ for the cw_q many $s_i \in M$ that contain w_q, we know that each of these $\mathcal{M}_{i,1}$ must take a value in $\{-w_q^1, \ldots, -w_q^{cw_q-1}, w_q\}$. Then, by the GCC constraint on the odd columns, we know that each value in $\{-w_{q-1}^1, \ldots, -w_{q-1}^{cw_{q-1}-1}, w_{q-1}\}$ must occur exactly once. These values occur only in the domains of $\mathcal{M}_{i,1}$ for the $s_i \in M$ that contain w_{q-1} or w_q. However, the $\mathcal{M}_{i,1}$ for the $s_i \in M$ that contain w_q must take values in $\{-w_q^1, \ldots, -w_q^{cw_q-1}, w_q\}$. Therefore, the $\mathcal{M}_{i,1}$ for the $s_i \in M$ that contain w_{q-1} must take a value in $\{-w_{q-1}^1, \ldots, -w_{q-1}^{cw_{q-1}-1}, w_{q-1}\}$. Repeating this argument recursively until reaching the value t, we can restrict the effective domain of the odd positions of $\mathcal{M}_i$ for $s_i = (w_i, z_i, y_i) \in M$ to $\mathcal{M}_{i,1} \in \{-w_i^1, \ldots, -w_i^{cw_i-1}, w_i\}$, $\mathcal{M}_{i,3} \in \{-z_i^1, \ldots, -z_i^{cz_i-1}, z_i\}$, and $\mathcal{M}_{i,5} \in \{-y_i^1, \ldots, -y_i^{cy_i-1}, y_i\}$. Therefore, we know that each row $\mathcal{M}_i$ for $s_i = (w_i, z_i, y_i) \in M$ either has the values $(w_i, 0, z_i, 0, y_i)$ or the values (w_i', t, z_i', t, y_i') for some clones w_i', z_i', y_i' of w_i, z_i, y_i. Now, by the GCC constraints, we know that each value $w \in W$ occurs exactly once, as well as each value $z \in Z$ and each $y \in Y$. Since the possible values were chosen by taking elements from M, we know that $M' = \{s_i \mid \mathcal{M}_i = (w, 0, z, 0, y), w \in W, z \in Z, y \in Y\}$ is a 3D matching.

($\Leftarrow$) Let $M' \subseteq M$ be a 3D matching. We can fill $\mathcal{M}$ as follows. For each $(w_i, z_i, y_i) = s_i \in M'$, we let $\mathcal{M}_i = (w_i, 0, z_i, 0, y_i)$. For each $(w_i, z_i, y_i) = s_i \in M \backslash M'$ we let $\mathcal{M}_i = (w_i', t, z_i', t, y_i')$ for some clones w_i', z_i', y_i' of w_i, z_i, y_i that have not been used before in the process of filling $\mathcal{M}$. We know there are enough different clones for this procedure. It is easy to verify that this instantiation of $\mathcal{M}$ satisfies all the constraints. $\qquad\square$

5   Fixed Parameter Tractable Cases

We have seen that propagating the REGULARGCC matrix constraint is NP-hard even under the strong restriction that either the number of values or the number of columns is bounded. We now identify three cases where we obtain tractability by bounding *two* parameters simultaneously. The three cases bound either the number of rows and the size of the automaton, or the number of columns and the product of the upper or lower bounds on the occurrences of values on a column.

Theorem 6. *Enforcing DC on* REGULARGCC *is fixed parameter tractable in* $k = R + |Q|$, *where* R *is the number of rows and* $|Q|$ *the maximum number of states in any row automaton.*

Proof: This follows observing that GCC over a sequence of a fixed size can be encoded in a DFA with polynomially many states, then swapping the rows with the columns, and appealing to Lemma 1 in the Appendix. $\square$

Theorem 7. *Enforcing DC on* REGULARGCC *is fixed parameter tractable in* $k = C + B$, *where* C *is the number of columns, and* B *is the maximum product of upper bounds specified on one column.*

Proof: Let $u_1, \ldots, u_k$ be the upper bounds enforced in a given column on values $v_1, \ldots, v_k$. Note that in the column constraints, for each value either both a lower and upper bound is specified, or neither. We can enforce the cardinality constraints consisting of the lower and upper bounds with a REGULAR constraint of size $u_1 \cdot \ldots \cdot u_k = \mathcal{O}(B)$. The result now follows directly from Lemma 1 in the Appendix. $\square$

Theorem 8. *Enforcing DC on* REGULARGCC *is fixed parameter tractable in* $k = C + B$, *where* C *is the number of columns, and* B *is the maximum product of lower bounds specified on one column, and the* GCC *constraints in* REGULARGCC *only have lower bounds.*

Proof: Let $l_1, \ldots, l_k$ be the lower bounds enforced in a given column on values $v_1, \ldots, v_k$. We can enforce the cardinality constraints consisting of only these lower bounds with a REGULAR constraint of size $l_1 \cdot \ldots \cdot l_k = \mathcal{O}(B)$. The result now follows directly from Lemma 1 in the Appendix. $\square$

We have shown that propagation of REGULARGCC is tractable if certain combinations of parameters of the problem are bounded like the number of rows and the size of the automaton. On the other hand, just bounding the number of rows on its own does not ensure tractability.

Theorem 9. *Enforcing BC on* REGULARGCC *is* W[2]-*hard in* $k = R$ *the number of rows with just 2 values.*

Proof: We reduce from p-HITTING-SET. Let $\mathcal{H} = (V, E)$ a hypergraph, where $V = \{v_1, \ldots, v_{|V|}\}$ and $E = \{e_1, \ldots, e_{|E|}\}$. We ask if there is a hitting set $S \subseteq V$ in $\mathcal{H}$ of cardinality k. We construct an instance $\mathcal{M}$ of REGULARGCC with $|V| + |E|$ columns and k rows on the alphabet $\{0, 1\}$. The REGULAR constraint accepts $|V|$ different words $w^1, \ldots, w^{|V|}$ of length $|V| + |E|$. For any word w^v, the vth value is 1, and the remainder of the first $|V|$ values is 0. Also, for any word w^v and any $1 \le j \le |E|$, the jth value of w^v is 1 if $v \in e_j$, and is 0 otherwise. The GCC constraints we put on the columns are as follows. In the first $|V|$ columns we require exactly one 1. In the remaining columns, we require at least one 1. In this reduction, each row corresponds to one vertex that is being chosen for inclusion in the hitting set, and each column after the first $|V|$ to one hyperedge. The GCC constraints on the first $|V|$ columns ensure that no vertex is chosen in two rows. The constraints on the last $|E|$ columns ensure that each hyperedge contains a vertex chosen for the hitting set. If there is a hyperedge all vertices of which are not included in the hitting set, the column corresponding to this hyperedge will contain 0's only, violating the GCC constraint of that column. We show that there exists a hitting set S in $\mathcal{H}$ of cardinality k iff the REGULARGCC matrix constraint has a solution.

($\Rightarrow$) Assume there exists a hitting set S in $\mathcal{H}$ of size k. We construct an assignment to REGULARGCC by matching one vertex $v \in S$ with each row (in any manner). If row i is matched to vertex v, we assign word w^v to row i. The fact that S contains k different vertices v ensures that k different words w^v are used. Also, since S is a hitting set, we know that for each hyperedge e_j there is at least one $v \in e_j \cap S$, and so each of the last $|E|$ columns contains at least one 1. Thus the GCC constraints are satisfied.

($\Leftarrow$) Suppose the REGULARGCC matrix constraint has a solution. We construct a hitting set S by taking all v such that w^v is a row in the solution. By the GCC constraints we know that the solution contains k different words w^v, so S is of size k. Now, to derive the contrary, assume there exists a hyperedge $e_j \in E$ such that $S \cap e_j = \emptyset$. Then the column corresponding to e_j (column $|V| + j$) contains only 0's. This violates GCC on this column, which is a contradiction. $\square$

6   A Practical Application

We illustrate the usefulness of the tractable cases identified here. In order to do so, we will describe a nurse scheduling problem that can be modelled (partially) using one of the identified tractable cases of REGULARGCC constraints.

Often, medical staff in a hospital are divided into different departments of some bounded size. The schedules of individual departments are mainly constrained by factors independent of other departments (e.g. the minimum number of staff on duty during different time shifts). Of course, there might be constraints expressing dependencies between schedules of different departments. Such constraints, however, are often more complicated than simple number restrictions on the staff on duty (e.g. for certain interdepartmental tasks, staff of different departments with particular skills needs to be on duty at the same time). As a result, these additional constraints need to be expressed by means of constraints separate to the REGULARGCC constraints anyway.

Concretely, we describe an example that corresponds to the result in Theorem 6, where the number of rows and the size of the row automata are bounded. Consider a hospital that can grow arbitrarily large in size, but where the different departments have a fixed maximum size. Since the departments typically have independent requirements on the number of staff on duty, the nurse scheduling problem can be divided into subproblems for every department, expressible by separate REGULARGCC constraints with a bounded number of rows. Also, shift rules typically express constraints on a bounded time window of n days (e.g. weekly or monthly requirements). Then, with row automata of size $\mathcal{O}(n \cdot s)$, for s the number of different shifts, we can express any requirement on (fixed or moving) time windows of n (or less) days, (e.g. minimum and maximum number of working shifts in each calender month, a day off after two night shifts in a row, never more than 5 working days in a row, for every 3 consecutive weekends at least one should be off duty).

Because the maximum time window n and the number of shifts s are typically fixed, we can use instances of the REGULARGCC constraint with bounded row automaton size and a bounded number of rows to solve rostering problems like the example sketched above. Theorem 6 then tells us that propagation for such instances of the REGULARGCC constraint is tractable.

7   Symmetry Breaking

A technique often used to reduce the number of isomorphic solutions and to increase propagation for a given constraint satisfaction problem is the introduction of symmetry breaking constraints [5, 15, 18]. Such constraints eliminate symmetrical solutions. One symmetry breaking constraint that is useful in the case of REGULARGCC requires the rows of the matrix to be lexicographically ordered (with respect to a given ordering on the domain values). Since the column constraints only impose bounds on the number of occurrences of values, swapping rows in any solution results in another solution, symmetric to the first solution. Additional symmetric solutions are often irrelevant, for instance when modelling nurse scheduling problems. Requiring the rows to be ordered eliminates such symmetric solutions, and the constraints that impose this requirement can increase propagation.

The complexity analysis of propagation of the REGULARGCC constraint presented above can be extended to the case where one constraint enforces simultaneously the REGULARGCC constraint and such symmetry breaking constraints [11]. The general NP-hardness and the W[2]-hardness results above can directly be extended to hold for this combined setting as well. The fixed-parameter tractability results can also be extended to the symmetry breaking setting. For the result of Theorem 6, this can be done without modifying the parameter, by constructing an automaton, enforcing lexicographic row ordering, running over the matrix column per column. For the other fixed-parameter tractability results, this can be done when the parameter also includes the maximum domain size, by constructing such an automaton running over the matrix row per row. Further research is needed to extend the complexity analysis of propagating REGULARGCC for combinations with other symmetry breaking constraints.

8   Conclusions

The REGULARGCC constraint is useful to model a range of scheduling and rostering problems. We have provided a detailed picture of the conditions under which propagation of the REGULARGCC constraint on a matrix of decision variables is tractable. On the negative side, we proved that it is NP-hard to enforce even a weak level of consistency like bound consistency with just 2 values, just

4 states in the automaton, or just 5 columns to the matrix. On the positive side, we proved that it is fixed parameter tractable to enforce domain consistency when we bound the number of rows and the size of the automaton, or the number of columns and the product of the upper or lower bounds on the occurrences of values on a column. We note that such FPT results have found practical application recently. For example, Katsirelos, Narodytska and Walsh recently used such a FPT result to break all row and column symmetry [12]. Even more recently, Yip and Van Hentenryck have converted such a FPT result into an effective constraint propagator [19]. In future work, we therefore intend to convert the FPT results identified here into practical algorithms for solving rostering and scheduling problems.

Appendix: Regular^2 Constraint

Some of our fixed parameter tractability results exploit a mapping the REG-ULARGCC constraint onto a closely related global constraint. The REGULAR^2 constraint posts REGULAR constraints on every row and column of a matrix model. When we bound the number of columns and the number of states in the column automaton of such a constraint, propagation is polynomial.

Lemma 1. *Enforcing DC on* REGULAR^2 *is fixed parameter tractable in* $k = C + |Q'|$, *where* C *is the number of columns, and* $|Q'|$ *is the (maximum) size of the column automata.*

Proof: This proof is similar to Observation 2 in [10]. W.l.o.g. we assume that all row constraints are the same, and all column constraints are the same. Let $|Q|$ be the size of the row automaton. We can encode the matrix constraint on an $R \times C$ matrix $\mathcal{M}$ in a single DFA on the matrix stretched out to a single sequence of variables $\mathcal{M}_{1,1}, \ldots, \mathcal{M}_{1,C}, \mathcal{M}_{2,1}, \ldots, \mathcal{M}_{R,C}$. The state set of the automaton is $\{1, \ldots, C\} \times Q \times (Q')^C$. In each state, the automaton keeps track of the column it is in, the current state $q' \in Q'$ for each column c, and the current state $q \in Q$ in the current row. The size of the automaton is $\mathcal{O}(C \cdot |Q| \cdot 2^{C \cdot \log |Q'|})$. Enforcing DC on a REGULAR constraint takes time polynomial in the size of the automaton [14, 16], so our algorithm runs in fixed parameter tractable time. $\qquad\square$

References

1. Beldiceanu, N., Carlsson, M., Flener, P., Pearson, J.: On Matrices, Automata, and Double Counting. In: Lodi, A., Milano, M., Toth, P. (eds.) CPAIOR 2010. LNCS, vol. 6140, pp. 10–24. Springer, Heidelberg (2010)
2. Bessiere, C., Hebrard, E., Hnich, B., Kiziltan, Z., Walsh, T.: SLIDE: a useful special case of the CardPath constraint. In: Proc. of the 18th European Conf. on Artificial Intelligence (ECAI 2008). IOS Press (2008)
3. Bessiere, C., Hebrard, E., Hnich, B., Walsh, T.: The complexity of global constraints. In: Proc. of 19th National Conf. on AI. Association for Advancement of Artificial Intelligence (2004)

4. Bessière, C., Hebrard, E., Hnich, B., Walsh, T.: The Tractability of Global Constraints. In: Wallace, M. (ed.) CP 2004. LNCS, vol. 3258, pp. 716–720. Springer, Heidelberg (2004)
5. Crawford, J., Luks, G., Ginsberg, M., Roy, A.: Symmetry breaking predicates for search problems. In: Proc. of the 5th Int. Conf. on Knowledge Representation and Reasoning (KR 1996), pp. 148–159 (1996)
6. Flener, P., Frisch, A.M., Hnich, B., Kiziltan, Z., Miguel, I., Pearson, J., Walsh, T.: Breaking Row and Column Symmetries in Matrix Models. In: Van Hentenryck, P. (ed.) CP 2002. LNCS, vol. 2470, pp. 462–477. Springer, Heidelberg (2002)
7. Flener, P., Frisch, A., Hnich, B., Kiziltan, Z., Miguel, I., Walsh, T.: Matrix modelling. Tech. Rep. APES-36-2001, APES group (2001); presented at Formul 2001 Workshop on Modelling and Problem Formulation, CP 2001
8. Flener, P., Frisch, A., Hnich, B., Kiziltan, Z., Miguel, I., Walsh, T.: Matrix modelling: Exploiting common patterns in constraint programming. In: Proc. of the Int. Workshop on Reformulating Constraint Satisfaction Problems (2002); held alongside CP 2002
9. Hellsten, L., Pesant, G., van Beek, P.: A Domain Consistency Algorithm for the Stretch Constraint. In: Wallace, M. (ed.) CP 2004. LNCS, vol. 3258, pp. 290–304. Springer, Heidelberg (2004)
10. Katsirelos, G., Narodytska, N., Quimper, C., Walsh, T.: Global matrix constraints. In: Proc. of the Int. Workshop on Constraint Modelling and Reformulation, pp. 27–41 (2011), held alongside CP 2011
11. Katsirelos, G., Narodytska, N., Walsh, T.: Combining Symmetry Breaking and Global Constraints. In: Oddi, A., Fages, F., Rossi, F. (eds.) CSCLP 2008. LNCS, vol. 5655, pp. 84–98. Springer, Heidelberg (2009)
12. Katsirelos, G., Narodytska, N., Walsh, T.: On the Complexity and Completeness of Static Constraints for Breaking Row and Column Symmetry. In: Cohen, D. (ed.) CP 2010. LNCS, vol. 6308, pp. 305–320. Springer, Heidelberg (2010)
13. Maher, M.J., Narodytska, N., Quimper, C.-G., Walsh, T.: Flow-Based Propagators for the SEQUENCE and Related Global Constraints. In: Stuckey, P.J. (ed.) CP 2008. LNCS, vol. 5202, pp. 159–174. Springer, Heidelberg (2008)
14. Pesant, G.: A Regular Language Membership Constraint for Finite Sequences of Variables. In: Wallace, M. (ed.) CP 2004. LNCS, vol. 3258, pp. 482–495. Springer, Heidelberg (2004)
15. Puget, J.F.: On the Satisfiability of Symmetrical Constrained Satisfaction Problems. In: Komorowski, J., Raś, Z.W. (eds.) ISMIS 1993. LNCS, vol. 689, pp. 350–361. Springer, Heidelberg (1993)
16. Quimper, C.-G., Walsh, T.: Global Grammar Constraints. In: Benhamou, F. (ed.) CP 2006. LNCS, vol. 4204, pp. 751–755. Springer, Heidelberg (2006)
17. Walsh, T.: Constraint Patterns. In: Rossi, F. (ed.) CP 2003. LNCS, vol. 2833, pp. 53–64. Springer, Heidelberg (2003)
18. Walsh, T.: General Symmetry Breaking Constraints. In: Benhamou, F. (ed.) CP 2006. LNCS, vol. 4204, pp. 650–664. Springer, Heidelberg (2006)
19. Yip, J., Hentenryck, P.V.: Symmetry breaking via lexleader feasibility checkers. In: Walsh, T. (ed.) Proc. of the 22nd Int. Joint Conf. on Artificial Intelligence (IJCAI 2011). pp. 687–692. IJCAI/AAAI (2011)

A Method to Avoid Duplicative Flipping
in Local Search for SAT

Thach-Thao Duong, Đức Nghia Pham, and Abdul Sattar

Queensland Research Laboratory, NICTA
and Institute for Integrated and Intelligent Systems, Griffith University,
QLD, Australia
{thao.duong,duc-nghia.pham,abdul.sattar}@nicta.com.au

Abstract. Stochastic perturbation on variable flipping is the key idea of local search for SAT. Observing that variables are flipped several times in an attempt to escape from a local minimum, this paper presents a duplication learning mechanism in stagnation stages to minimise duplicative variable flipping. The heuristic incorporates the learned knowledge into a variable weighting scheme to effectively prevent the search from selecting duplicative variables. Additionally, probability-based and time window smoothing techniques are adopted to eliminate the effects of redundant information. The integration of the heuristic and gNovelty$^+$ was compared with the original solvers and other state-of-the-art local search solvers. The experimental results showed that the new solver outperformed other solvers on the full set of SAT 2011 competition instances and three sets of real-world verification problems.

1 Introduction

Stochastic local search (SLS) for Satisfiability (SAT) problems is currently a well-studied and developed research field. Many practical problems (e.g. hardware verification, planning, circuit design) modeled under SAT format have been efficiently solved by local search. Since the prior work of GSAT algorithm [13], there has been a tremendous research on improving local search for SAT such as AdaptNovelty$^+$[3], G2WSAT [6], VW2 [10], gNovelty$^+$ [9], Hybrid [18], TNM [17], Sparrow [1]. While local search is an emerging approach for solving large random instances, it still struggles to solve structured problems because it is mainly based on perturbation and stochastic process of variable flipping [19]. Therefore, minimising duplicative flipping is an important and a challenging issue that need to be addressed.

There are some techniques to improve the performance of local search such as random walk, noise scheme and clause weighting. Random walk technique [8] randomly selects a variable in an unsatisfied clause to escape local minima. This method is significantly developed to the well-known Novelty$^+$ and AdaptNovelty$^+$ [3] methods, which controlled by a probability noise. The probability noise scheme of Novelty$^+$ improves the diversification of the search process by preferring the second best variable within a diversification noise. While

M. Thielscher and D. Zhang (Eds.): AI 2012, LNCS 7691, pp. 218–229, 2012.

Novelty$^+$ retains a constant diversification noise, AdaptNovelty$^+$ adjusts the noise automatically during the search. Clause weighting schemes originated from the work of [12] and have been developed substantially though a series of clause weighting local search algorithms (e.g. DLM [19], SAPS [5], PAWS [15]). In recent SAT competitions, gNovelty$^+$, TNM and Sparrow2011 were respectively the winners of the Random category in 2007, 2009, and 2011. gNovelty$^+$ is a hybrid of a clause weighting scheme from PAWS, Tabu heuristic and AdaptNovelty$^+$. TNM is a combination of G2WSAT and two trap escape heuristics switched by a variable weighting scheme. Sparrow2011 is based on gNovelty$^+$ framework and utilizes its own probability-based scoring function in the stagnation stages instead of applying AdaptNovelty$^+$.

Due to the fact that local search is based on the perturbation of flipping variables to find solutions, flipping the same variables several times in a short period of search steps especially at stagnation stages is a critical drawback of local search. Especially during stagnation stages, some variables are flipped several times in order to escape local minima. This situation is redundant and time-consuming. We call the circumstance that a variable is flipped more than once within a short period at stagnation stages *duplicative flipping*. Currently, there are some methods to reduce duplicative flipping (e.g. Tabu and variable weighting [10]). Tabu search [14] prevents the search from selecting recent variables within a particular tenure. It strictly prohibits duplicative flipping within a given tenure. In addition, variable weighting schemes are used in VW2 [11], Hybrid [18] and TNM [17] for diversification boosting. VW2 employs variable weights to count the number a variable flipped. By preferring the least often selected variables, it aims to minimize duplicative flipping for better diversification in the entire search process. In contemporary local search methods, there is an absence of study on repetitively flipping variables during stagnation stages.

This paper presents a method to minimise duplicative flipping at stagnation stages during the search procedure. The structure of this paper is divided into 4 parts. The introduction provides an overview of contemporary local search methods and their issues. In section two, the approach of duplication avoidance strategy and forgetting techniques are presented. Forgetting techniques (e.g. probability-based smoothing and time window release) are applied to enhance the performance of the heuristic. Afterwards, gNovelty$^+$DL, the integration of the heuristic and the gNovelty$^+$ framework, is clearly explained. Section three reports experiments on some structure test suite and SAT 2011 competition dataset. Finally, section four sums up our conclusions and future work.

2 Duplication Learning Strategy

2.1 Motivation

Avoidance of duplicative flipping is one important issue in local search algorithms for SAT. To investigate duplicative flipping on structured and random instances, we conducted an experiment to compute the duplication ratio in stagnation paths. We define a *stagnation path* as a sequence of consecutively flipped variables back-tracking from a local minimum, and *duplicative variables* are variables that appear more than once within a stagnation path. The *duplication ratio* is the fraction of the number of duplicative variables over the number of variables in stagnation paths. In order to limit collective data for study, a parameter tenure k specifies the length of a stagnation path.

Table 1. Average of duplication ratios on verification benchmarks and SAT 2011 Competition dataset. Stagnation paths have the same length of k=20.

Instances	vw2	gNovelty^{+}	Sparrow2011
cbmc.test (39)	**7%**	38%	27%
swv.test (75)	**4%**	18%	16%
sss-sat-1.0 (100)	**11%**	50%	74%
Application (149)	**2%**	14%	4%
Crafted (150)	24%	30%	**22%**
Random Large (200)	**3%**	38%	6%
Random Medium (400)	**20%**	68%	29%

Table 1 shows the average of duplication ratios of VW2, gNovelty^{+} and Sparrow2011. Experiments were conducted on the verification benchmarks : cbmc, swv, sss-sat-1.0 and the SAT 2011 competition dataset. The experiments on verification benchmarks were conducted 50 times for each instance. SAT 2011 competition dataset experiments were run 10 times for each instance. As seen in Table 1, VW2 had the least duplication ratio compared to gNovelty^{+} and Sparrow2011. This was because VW2 employed variable weighting schemes to avoid duplicative flipping. However, variable weights accumulate information of flipping frequencies during the entire search process rather than specifically during stagnation stages.

According to Table 1, the duplication ratios were high during stagnation stages. This phenomenon increases the duration of the search process by selecting the same variables several times. Additionally, duplicative flipping probably leads to previous local minima or previously visited areas. We hypothesize that variables occurring repeatedly in stagnation paths are sensitive and critical. These variables should not be selected as they are likely to cause stagnation and duplicative flipping in the future. In contemporary literature, there are a few methods that have exploited the duplication information at visited stagnation areas when selecting variables for the next steps. Although Tabu search and variable weighting are methods to minimise duplicative flipping, they do not have a learning mechanism to learn from duplicative variables leading to local minima. In our opinion, there remains a need for an efficient method for learning about duplication in stagnation stages and actively preventing the search from selecting these variables. From that point of view, in the following section we propose a heuristic that combines the advantages of the variable weighting and the duplication learning heuristic.

2.2   Duplication Avoidance Heuristics

As described in the previous section, variables that appear in the bounded stagnation paths are considered important to the learning mechanism. The proposed duplication learning (DL) aims to assist local search algorithms in intelligently avoiding variables that are highly potential to cause duplication in the future by exploiting duplication information at previous stagnations. We associate a duplication weight to each variable and these weights are initially set to 0. At each local minimum, duplication weights of duplicative variables in the stagnation paths are increased by one. Hence, a high value of duplication weight indicates potential likelihood of causing duplicative flipping in trap areas if the variable is chosen to be flipped. In other words, variables whose duplication weight are high have more conflicts with the current solution assignment. For that reason, variables having low duplication weights are preferred to be selected in the next steps. The use of duplication weights and tenure k are inspired by the VW2 algorithm [10] and Tabu search [14]. Compared to VW2, however the weight updating procedure is applied at the stagnation stages and the heuristic does not completely forbid variables in the tenure like Tabu heuristic.

Algorithm 1 describes the proposed duplication learning heuristic in combination with two forgetting techniques. The history of flipped variables during search progress are stored in stack H. Lines 3 - 5 of Algorithm 1 describe the way the stagnation paths are popped from the stack of flipped variables H. At a stagnation stage, variables duplicately flipped in the stagnation path have their weights increased by one (lines 7 - 9). In order to investigate the effectiveness of the learning mechanism, the two forgetting techniques (e.g. the time window release and probability-based smoothing techniques) are applied in duplication prevention heuristic (lines 11 - 19 Alg. 1). These two techniques are explained clearly in the following sections. The parameters time window queue W and its size T are used for time window release strategy; and the duplication smooth probability dp is used for probability-based smoothing mechanism.

2.3   Techniques to Forget Learned Information

As the search visits a large number of local minima, duplication weights may not correctly reflect the duplicative scenarios that are relevant to the current location. It is necessary to apply a mechanism to reduce over-learned duplication weights. For that reason, we integrate a probability-based smoothing technique and a time window mechanism to the heuristic.

Probability-Based Smoothing. The probability-based smoothing mechanism is a simple smoothing technique controlled by a probability parameter dp. Within the smoothing probability dp, duplication weights are reduced by one (Alg. 1 lines 11 - 16). The aim of the probability-based smoothing technique is to reduce over-valued duplication weights which are mostly irrelevant information for selecting variables.

Algorithm 1: Duplication Learning Strategy DL(k,T,dp,H,W)

Input : tenure k, flipped variable history stack H, time window queue W, time window size T, duplication smooth probability dp

1   *stagnation_path* $= \oslash$;
2   *duplication_list* $= \oslash$;
3   **for** $i \leftarrow 1$ **to** T **do**
4 | *var* $\leftarrow$ *pop_stack*(H) ;
5 | *stagnation_path* $\leftarrow$ *var* ;
6   **end**
7   **for** *all var appears more than one time in stagnation_path* **do**
8 | *duplication_weight*[*var*] $+ +$;
9 | *duplication_list* $\leftarrow$ *var* ;
10 **end**
11 **if** $T > 0$ **then**
       | // Using time window release
12 | **if** $Size(W) == T$ **then**
13 | | *further_duplication_list* $=$ *pop_queue*(W);
14 | | **for** *all var in further_duplication_list* **do** *duplication_weight*[*var*] $- -$;
15 | | remove *further_duplication_list* from W;
16 | $W \leftarrow$ *push_queue*(W, *duplication_list*);
17 **if** $dp > 0$ **then**
       | // Probability-based Smoothing
18 | **if** *within probability of dp* **then**
19 | | **for** *all var if duplication_weight*[*var*] > 1 **do** *duplication_weight*[*var*] $- -$;
20 | **end**
21 **end**

Time Window Release. The time window release technique (lines 17 - 19 Alg. 1) resembles a window that moves along-side the search in progress. The aim of this technique is to restrict effects of the duplication weights into limited recent stagnation times. To elaborate, the learned information within the window area is accumulated in duplication weights while the information outside the window is discarded. We define a *duplication list* as a list of duplicative variables occurred in a stagnation path. The time window queue W is an ordered queue of T most recent duplication lists. The size of W are bounded by parameter T. Once a stagnation path is released from the window view, its learned experience has elapsed. In other words, the duplication weights of variables in the corresponding duplication list are decreased by one. The further duplication list is removed from the window and a newly encountered duplication list is pushed into the queue.

2.4   gNovelty$^+$DL: Integration of Duplication Learning into gNovelty$^+$

This section describes the integration of duplication learning heuristic into the gNovelty$^+$ algorithm. gNovelty$^+$ uses a clause weighting scheme while duplication learning employs a variable weighting mechanism. Therefore, gNovelty$^+$DL, an integration of duplication learning into gNovelty$^+$, is a combination of clause weighting and variable weighting focused on duplication avoidance. Algorithm 17 presents the pseudo-code of gNovelty$^+$DL.

As described in [9], gNovelty$^+$ has two parameters: a random walk probability wp and a smooth probability sp. The DL strategy requires three more parameters which are the tenure k, the time window size T and the duplication smoothing probability dp. The parameter dp is used for the probability-based smoothing strategy described in section 2.3. In the initialization phase, duplication weights of variables are set to zero. The variable history H and the time window W are initialized empty. Because gNovelty$^+$ is a clause weighting local search in which the score function is computed based on clause weights, local minima are considered at the steps when there is no promising variable [1]. In this circumstance, the DL strategy is applied (line 11). The criteria of selecting variables is slightly different to gNovelty$^+$. Instead of breaking tie the least recent flipped variable, the heuristic breaks tie by the lowest duplication weight. In lines 8 and 12, the algorithm selects the most promising variable in terms of score value, and then breaks tie by lowest duplication weights. Finally, the selected variable is pushed into the history stack H.

Algorithm 2: gNovelty$^+$DL(k,T,dp,sp)

Input : A formula Θ, random walk probability $wp = 0.01$, smooth probability sp, tenure k, time window size T, duplication smoothing probability dp
Output: Solution α (if found) or TIMEOUT

1 randomly generate a candidate solution α;
2 $W = \oslash$; $H = \oslash$;
3 initialize *duplication_weights* to 0;
4 **while** *not time out* **do**
5   **if** α *satisfies the formula* Θ **then return** α ;
6   **if** *within the probability* wp **then**   Random walk;
7   **else if** *there are promising variables* **then**
8   select the most promising variable, breaking tie by lowest *duplication_weight*;
9   **else**
10   update (and smooth in probability sp) clause weights;
        // Stagnation happens: perform duplication learning
11   **DL**(k,T,dp,H,W);
12   AdaptNovelty$^+$: (breaks tie by lowest *duplication_weight*);
13   **end**
14   flip variable *var*;
15     $H \leftarrow push\_stack(H, var)$;
16 **end**
17 **return** TIMEOUT;

---

3   Experiments

In these experiments, gNovelty$^+$DL was dispersed into 4 variants differentiated by the combination use of the time window release and probability-based smoothing. The list of gNovelty$^+$ variants is shown in Table 2. The intention of these variants was to examine the feasibility of DL heuristic as well as effects of forgetting techniques. By adding both time window release and probability-based smoothing in gNovelty$^+$Rws, we aim to investigate the capabilities of the two forgetting techniques. In the preliminary experiment, the performance of

---

[1] A promising variable is one that improves the objective score [9].

gNovelty$^+$Rp is examined against some common SLS solvers on ternary chains to test the diversification capability. Further experiments were conducted on structured verification benchmarks and the full SAT 2011 competition dataset and compared gNovelty$^+$DL with gNovelty$^+$ (uses clause weighting), VW2 (uses variable weighting), and Sparrow2011 (the winner of the latest SAT competition). Table 5 presents the parameter settings for gNovelty$^+$DL variants. These parameter configurations were optimized by ParamILS [4], a local search optimization tool for parameterized algorithms. The experiments were conducted on the Griffith University's Gowonda HPC Cluster Intel(R) Xeon(R) CPU X5650 2.67GHz.

Table 2. Variants of gNovelty$^+$DL heuristic

Time window release	Probability-based smoothing	
	No	Yes
No	Rp	Rps
Yes	Rw	Rws

3.1   Preliminary Experiments on Ternary Chains

Ternary chain is an artificial problem that deliberately simulates chains of variable dependency in structure problems. It is employed to study the diversification capability of local search algorithms in [10], due to the fact that it has only one solution that assigns all variables to true. Therefore, flipping any variable from true to false is likely to move away from the solution. Given these characteristics, local search algorithms will easily become trapped. The following is the formulation of a ternary chain with N variables.

$$(x_1)\ (x_2)\ (x_1 \wedge x_2 \rightarrow x_3)\ \ldots\ (x_{N-2} \wedge x_{N-1} \rightarrow x_N)$$

Fig 1 depicts a comparison between gNovelty$^+$DL with some popular solvers (e.g. rots - Tabu search [14], adaptG2WSAT [7], PAWS [15], VW2 [11], TNM [17], gNovelty$^+$ [9], Sparrow2011 [1]). It was apparent that VW2, gNovelty$^+$ and gNovelty$^+$Rp performed strikingly better than other solvers. gNovelty$^+$ and VW2 could solve ternary chains successfully due to variable weighting and clause weighting respectively. As a result, gNovelty$^+$DL, which took advantage of both gNovelty$^+$ and VW2, was an improvement over these two algorithms. This indicated that gNovelty$^+$Rp had better diversification than the other solvers in this experiments.

3.2   Experiments on Structural Benchmarks

The real-world problem sets we selected for this experiment are cbmc, swv and sss-sat-1.0. The first two instance sets were software verification problems: (i) 39 cbmc instances generated by a bounded model checking tool and (ii) 75 swv

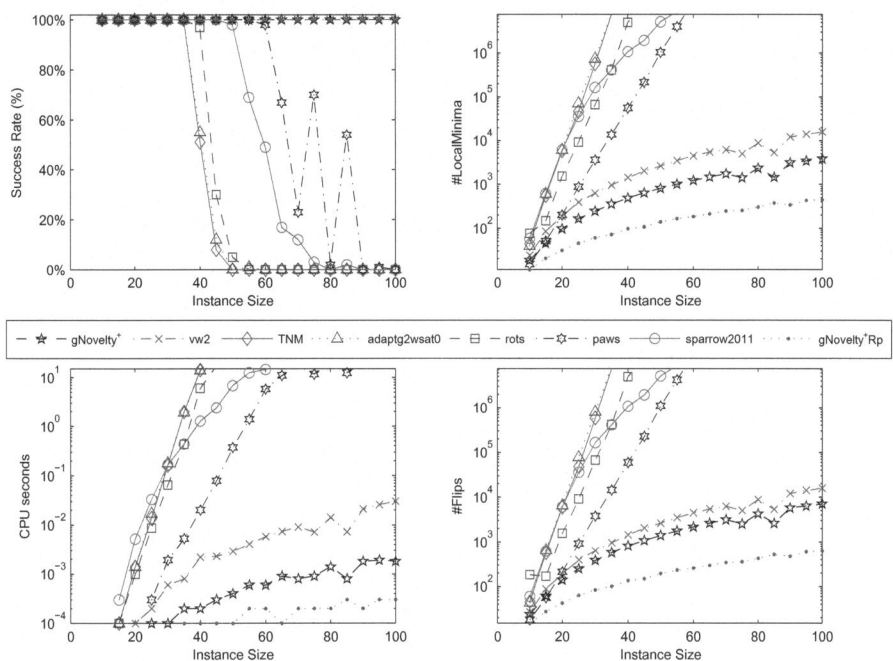

Fig. 1. Experiments on Ternary Chains: size ranging from [10,100]. Based on 100 runs where each run had a 20-second timeout. Methods are compared in terms of success rate, CPU time, the number of local minima and the number of flips. gNovelty$^+$Rp used tenure $k = 20$.

instances generated by the CALYSTO checker [2]. The third one was Velev's sss-sat-1.0 containing 100 instances of encoding verification of super-scalar micro-processors [3]. Even though these instance sets can be easily solved by PICOSAT [2] (a systematic search algorithm), they are currently a remarkable challenges for SLS solvers. Table 3 shows the evaluation of gNovelty$^+$DL variants with gNovelty$^+$, VW2 and Sparrow2011 in terms of success rates, average of median CPU times and number of duplication flipping in thousands of stagnation paths.

Generally speaking, all gNovelty$^+$DL variants performed consistently better than other solvers across the three instance sets. Especially on cbmc and sss-sat-1.0 dataset, the success rate of gNovelty$^+$DL was raised to 100%, which was a significant improvement over the other algorithms. Furthermore, the success rate of swv instances was doubled to 48% compared with other solvers. It was discovered that 50% of swv instances have not been solved consistently by SLS-based solvers [16]. Moreover, all gNovelty$^+$DL variants significantly decreased

---

[2] The test instances of cbmc and swv are available at
http://people.cs.ubc.ca/davet/papers/sat10-dave-instances.zip
[3] Available at http://www.miroslav-velev.com/sat_benchmarks.html

Table 3. Experiments on cbmc, swv, sss-sat-1.0: based on 50 runs with a timeout of 600 seconds per run. Each cell presents the success rate, the average of median CPU times in seconds and the average of duplication times in thousands.

Instances	VW2	Sparrow2011	gNovelty$^+$	gNovelty$^+$DL			
				Rp	Rps	Rw	Rws
cbmc	31%	51%	85%	**100%**	**100%**	**100%**	**100%**
(39)	439.128	384.359	247.997	1.659	2.343	**1.452**	1.774
	6,845	231	3,886	74	69	**40**	72
swv	23%	21%	25%	**48%**	47%	**48%**	44%
(75)	466.002	486.949	459.097	335.343	348.875	**327.477**	350.927
	280	59	1,995	6,036	**232**	1,023	2,903
sss-sat-1.0	24%	7%	50%	**100%**	**100%**	**100%**	**100%**
(100)	481.357	572.993	348.512	2.409	2.729	**2.241**	4.376
	6,700	1,065	2,177	293	**139**	212	522

duplication flipping times in stagnation paths compared with other algorithms. However, there is no clear difference in terms of success rate and CPU times among gNovelty$^+$DL variants.

3.3   Experiments on the SAT 2011 Competition Dataset

The experiment on the SAT 2011 competition dataset was a comparison between gNovelty$^+$DL, Sparrow2011, gNovelty$^+$ and VW2. Figure 2 plots the performance of the best gNovelty$^+$DL variant with Sparrow2011 in 3 categories : Application & Crafted (the structure instances), Random (problems created by randomization), and All (the full SAT 2011 competition dataset). As illustrated in Figure 2, gNovelty$^+$ did not perform as well as Sparrow2011 on the Random category, but it was slightly better than Sparrow2011 in the Application & Crafted category. With the boost from the DL heuristic, gNovelty$^+$DL improved the performance of gNovelty$^+$ on both the Application & Crafted and Random categories. It is evident that the duplication learning heuristic assisted the gNovelty$^+$ in overcoming the limitations on both structure instances and random instances.

Table 4 shows the performance of the algorithms in terms of the success rates and the averages of the minimum, median, maximum CPU times. The data were split into 4 groups [4]: (i) Application: 8 instances; (ii) Crafted: 82 instances; (iii) Random Large: 64 instances (iv) Random Medium: 201 instances. For all categories, most gNovelty$^+$DL variants performed better than other solvers. There were exceptions in the case of Random Large, e.g. gNovelty$^+$Rp (9%) and gNovelty$^+$Rps (17%) had worse results than Sparrow2011 (20%).

---

[4] Because there were many instances cannot be solved at any run, we decided to report instances solved in least one run by any solver. Therefore, the number of instances in Table 4 does not reflect the real number of instances in the original SAT 2011 competition data set.

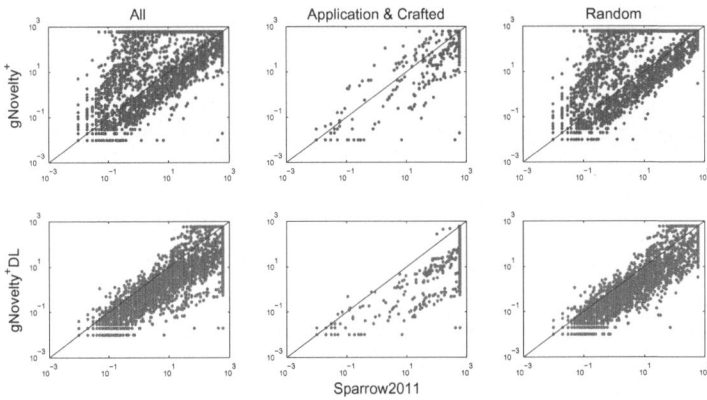

Fig. 2. Experiments on SAT 2011 Competition Benchmark: a comparison of CPU run times between gNovelty$^+$DL and Sparrow2011

Table 4. Experiments on SAT 2011 Competition dataset: based on 10 runs and a timeout of 600 seconds per run. The reported rows are success rates, the averages of the minimum, median, and maximum CPU times (in seconds).

Instances	VW2	Sparrow2011	gNovelty$^+$	gNovelty$^+$DL			
				Rp	Rps	Rw	Rws
Application	12%	25%	12%	**62%**	38%	38%	**62%**
(8)	526.239	461.824	464.149	**131.018**	130.770	55.882	183.981
	526.838	515.799	527.431	**298.067**	397.774	389.998	333.106
	527.603	543.695	527.503	**426.520**	463.189	483.426	456.875
Crafted	37%	56%	62%	**87%**	82%	**87%**	82%
(82)	373.386	237.720	202.872	71.112	53.848	**62.977**	82.665
	390.427	285.159	251.332	111.388	128.326	**110.367**	129.848
	402.716	338.434	285.784	157.880	170.066	**146.968**	161.738
Random	0%	20%	0%	9%	27%	**31%**	17%
Large	600.007	437.202	576.600	426.179	384.403	**334.614**	417.429
(64)	600.010	**509.487**	600.000	566.617	525.684	509.716	550.516
	600.010	**555.076**	600.000	594.413	591.152	579.286	589.425
Random	19%	**100%**	75%	96%	99%	**100%**	99%
Medium	428.007	5.049	130.371	4.017	4.655	**2.169**	2.427
(201)	499.761	40.671	184.698	38.837	21.945	**13.392**	21.432
	527.371	99.540	241.121	102.376	55.434	**48.654**	68.034

Comparing amongst gNovelty$^+$DL variants, gNovelty$^+$Rp was the best performer in the Application & Crafted category while gNovelty$^+$Rw performed best in Random category.

In Random categories (both medium and large), applying at least one forgetting technique improved the performance. For example, in terms of success rate, gNovelty$^+$Rws performed better than gNovelty$^+$Rp in Random Medium categories. However, utilizing both probability-based smoothing and time window

Table 5. gNovelty⁺DL parameters settings

Dataset	Rp		Rw			Rps			Rws			
	k	sp	k	T	sp	k	dp	sp	k	T	dp	sp
cbmc	30	0.4	15	100	0.4	30	0.25	0.4	20	300	0.05	0.4
swv	30	0	15	250	0.05	20	0.2	0.2	30	250	0.4	0.05
sss-sat-1.0	10	0.05	20	200	0.05	10	0.1	0.05	25	200	0.05	0.05
SAT 2011	30	0	25	250	0	10	0.25	0	15	200	0.25	0

release degraded the performance (e.g gNovelty⁺Rws did not perform as good as gNovelty⁺Rw and gNovelty⁺Rs). On large random and medium random, using probability-based smoothing alone improved the results (e.g in Random Large category gNovelty⁺Rps boosted gNovelty⁺Rp from 9% to 26%). However, probability-based smoothing combined with time window decreased the results of time window (for instance in Random Large category, gNovelty⁺Rws degraded the performance of gNovelty⁺Rw from 31% to 17%).

In contrast with Random categories, applying only one forgetting technique did not improve performance in the Application category. For example, the success rates of gNovelty⁺ Rps and gNovelty⁺ Rw were just 38% compared with 62% for gNovelty⁺Rp. In the Crafted category, the results of gNovelty⁺DL variants were not significantly different and they all gained better performance than the other algorithms.

Overall, for structured instances, using forgetting techniques is not recommended because it reduces learned information. In contrast, applying time window release (e.g gNovelty⁺Rw) performed best for random instances. This is due to random instances being more loosely constrained than structure instances. Hence, it is necessary to retain learned information over a limited period of stagnation times for random instances.

4   Conclusion and Future Work

In summary, the duplication learning was feasible and robust for the considered benchmarks when applied to the gNovelty⁺ framework. gNovelty⁺DL performed well on both structured and random instances compared with contemporary SLS solvers. In addition, it was proved to reduce duplication and help search converged quickly to solutions. It can be concluded that duplication learning is a reasonably alternative guidance for local search for the purpose of duplication avoidance.

In addition, the effect of forgetting techniques were examined. Generally, forgetting techniques should not be applied to structured instances. In contrast, to solve random instances efficiently, it is better to adopt forgetting techniques to reduce over-learned stagnation information. To further clarify, gNovelty⁺Rp was a good choice for structured benchmarks while the gNovelty⁺Rw was a good choice for random instances. However, applying both probability-based smoothing and a time window mechanism degraded the performance. Evidently, forgetting techniques are efficient on loosely constrained problems.

According to these results, a further investigation into duplication avoidance using learning mechanisms is worthwhile. Indeed, it is necessary to develop a more intelligent learning strategy and parameter adaptation mechanism. Moreover, in order to examine the generalization of the heuristic, its integration into different SLS solvers should be carefully studied.

References

1. Balint, A., Fröhlich, A.: Improving Stochastic Local Search for SAT with a New Probability Distribution. In: Strichman, O., Szeider, S. (eds.) SAT 2010. LNCS, vol. 6175, pp. 10–15. Springer, Heidelberg (2010)
2. Biere, A.: Picosat essentials. JSAT 4(2-4), 75–97 (2008)
3. Hoos, H.H.: An adaptive noise mechanism for WalkSAT. In: Proceedings of AAAI 2002, pp. 635–660 (2002)
4. Hutter, F., Hoos, H.H., Leyton-Brown, K., Stützle, T.: Paramils: An automatic algorithm configuration framework. J. Artif. Intell. Res. (JAIR) 36, 267–306 (2009)
5. Hutter, F., Tompkins, D.A.D., H. Hoos, H.: Scaling and Probabilistic Smoothing: Efficient Dynamic Local Search for SAT. In: Van Hentenryck, P. (ed.) CP 2002. LNCS, vol. 2470, pp. 233–248. Springer, Heidelberg (2002)
6. Li, C.-M., Huang, W.Q.: Diversification and Determinism in Local Search for Satisfiability. In: Bacchus, F., Walsh, T. (eds.) SAT 2005. LNCS, vol. 3569, pp. 158–172. Springer, Heidelberg (2005)
7. Li, C.-M., Wei, W., Zhang, H.: Combining Adaptive Noise and Look-Ahead in Local Search for SAT. In: Marques-Silva, J., Sakallah, K.A. (eds.) SAT 2007. LNCS, vol. 4501, pp. 121–133. Springer, Heidelberg (2007)
8. McAllester, D.A., Selman, B., Kautz, H.A.: Evidence for invariants in local search. In: AAAI/IAAI, pp. 321–326 (1997)
9. Pham, D.N., Thornton, J., Gretton, C., Sattar, A.: Combining adaptive and dynamic local search for satisfiability. JSAT 4(2-4), 149–172 (2008)
10. Prestwich, S.: SAT problems with chains of dependent variables. In: Discrete Applied Mathematics, vol. 3037, pp. 1–22 (2002)
11. Prestwich, S.D.: Random Walk with Continuously Smoothed Variable Weights. In: Bacchus, F., Walsh, T. (eds.) SAT 2005. LNCS, vol. 3569, pp. 203–215. Springer, Heidelberg (2005)
12. Selman, B., Kautz, H.A.: Domain-independent extensions to gsat: Solving large structured satisfiability problems. In: IJCAI, pp. 290–295 (1993)
13. Selman, B., Levesque, H.J., Mitchell, D.G.: A new method for solving hard satisfiability problems. In: AAAI, pp. 440–446 (1992)
14. Taillard, É.D.: Robust taboo search for the quadratic assignment problem. Parallel Computing 17(4-5), 443–455 (1991)
15. Thornton, J.R., Pham, D.N., Bain, S., Ferreira Jr., V.: Additive versus multiplicative clause weighting for SAT. In: Proceedings of AAAI 2004, pp. 191–196 (2004)
16. Tompkins, D.A.D., Balint, A., Hoos, H.H.: Captain Jack: New Variable Selection Heuristics in Local Search for SAT. In: Sakallah, K.A., Simon, L. (eds.) SAT 2011. LNCS, vol. 6695, pp. 302–316. Springer, Heidelberg (2011)
17. Wei, W., Li, C.M.: Switching between two adaptive noise mechanisms in localsearch. In: Booklet of the 2009 SAT Competition (2009)
18. Wei, W., Li, C.-M., Zhang, H.: Switching among Non-Weighting, Clause Weighting, and Variable Weighting in Local Search for SAT. In: Stuckey, P.J. (ed.) CP 2008. LNCS, vol. 5202, pp. 313–326. Springer, Heidelberg (2008)
19. Wu, Z., Wah, B.W.: Trap escaping strategies in discrete lagrangian methods for solving hard satisfiability and maximum satisfiability problems. In: AAAI/IAAI, pp. 673–678 (1999)

Anytime Algorithms for Biobjective Heuristic Search

Priyankar Ghosh, Partha Pratim Chakrabarti, and Pallab Dasgupta

Indian Institute of Technology Kharagpur, West Bengal, India 721302
{priyankar,ppchak,pallab}@cse.iitkgp.ernet.in

Abstract. Heuristic search algorithms (MOA*, NAMOA* etc) for multiobjective optimization problems, when run with admissible heuristics, typically spend a lot of time and require huge amount of memory for generating the Pareto optimal solution frontier due to the fact that these algorithms expand all nodes/paths whose cost is not dominated by any other optimal solution. In this paper, we present an anytime heuristic search framework for biobjective optimization problems named "Anytime Biobjective Search (ABS)" which quickly finds a set of nondominated solutions and keeps on improving the solution frontier with time. The proposed framework uses the upper and lower limit estimates on one of the objectives to split the search space into a given number of segments and independently runs a particular search algorithm (branch-and-bound, beam search etc.) within each of the segments. In this paper, we present how existing search strategies, branch-and-bound, beam, and beam-stack, can be used within the proposed framework. Experimental results reveal that our proposed framework achieves good anytime performance.

1 Introduction

A large set of optimization problems encountered in real-life applications involve two non commensurate objectives where one typically strives to reach a suitable trade-off between the conflicting objectives. We briefly mention some of the problems below. The operator scheduling problem [1] which is encountered during high level synthesis of digital designs involves two independent objectives – (a) *delay*, and (b) *total number of resources*. For example, with 5 resources the minimum delay schedule may need 8 time units, whereas increasing the number of resources to 7 may allow to have the minimum delay schedule with 6 time units. In finance, a common problem that involves two conflicting objectives are to choose a portfolio [2] where the non commensurate objectives are – (a) *the expected value of portfolio returns* (should be as high as possible), and (b) *the risk factor* (should be as low as possible). Another similar problem arises in connection with macro-economic policy making for central banks [3], where the desired solution tries to achieve a balance between two independent objectives, namely, *inflation* and *balance of trade deficit*. For the domain of traffic/transport information systems, similar problems often arise [4]. For example, in individual route planning for vehicles, *fuel cost* and *delay*, are two conflicting objectives. In the route guidance problem, *the system optimal routing* and *user constraint in the form of delay*, form two conflicting objectives [5].

Heuristic search [6] is often considered for determining optimal/near-optimal solutions for single as well as multiobjective optimization problems [7–9]. The best first

M. Thielscher and D. Zhang (Eds.): AI 2012, LNCS 7691, pp. 230–241, 2012.

heuristic search algorithms, namely, A*, MOA*, and NAMOA* etc., when run with an admissible heuristic, typically spend a considerable amount of time for selecting the best node/path to be explored next. Often the techniques that quickly generate near optimal solutions are preferred. In the context of single objective optimization problems, several such techniques [10–12] are developed. Also combining multiple heuristics [13] and simultaneously searching with multiple setting [14] are studied for the single objective optimization problems. Another popular alternative is to use anytime algorithms which start with generating some sub-optimal solution and keep on generating better quality solution over time [15–19]. However, anytime algorithms are only studied for single objective optimization problems.

For multiobjective optimization problems, several techniques [20–25] have been developed for finding near optimal solutions. These methods typically aim to find a solution frontier which is within a factor of the optimal solution. Several approximation schemes (PTAS, FPTAS, etc.) for multiobjective optimization problems have been proposed [20, 22–24]. In [26], a branch-and-bound based method is presented which uses the notion of *separating hypersurface* for pruning. However, all of these methods work on explicit graphs except the method in [21]. Perny et al. [21] presents an MOA* based ϵ-admissible algorithm for multiobjective search. Although this method works on implicit representation, the proposed algorithm is not an anytime algorithm. There is a significant body of literature [27, 28] on applying evolutionary computing based methods for multiobjective optimization problems for finding near optimal solutions. However, these methods are not evaluated in anytime setting.

In this paper, we present an anytime heuristic search framework named "Anytime Biobjective Search (ABS)" that works on problems with biobjective cost criterion. To the best of our knowledge, this is the first attempt to develop anytime algorithms for optimization problems with more than one objectives. So far, anytime algorithms has been developed for single objective optimization problems only. Our proposed algorithm is particularly useful for biobjective optimization problems whose search space are implicit in nature and typically described using a set of state transformation rules. The proposed framework quickly finds an initial nondominated solution frontier and keeps on improving the solution frontier with time.

We use the idea of splitting the search space using the upper and lower limit estimates on one of the objectives into a given number of non-overlapping segments. Using multiple stacks to expedite the branch-and-bound search for single objective optimization problems had been proposed in [29]. Within each of the segments, ABS independently runs a specific search algorithm (branch-and-bound, beam etc.) and tries to balance the search effort over the segments. We present how existing search strategies, namely, branch-and-bound, beam, and beam-stack etc., can be used within the proposed framework. While using running ABS, the solution found in a particular sub-range is used for further pruning of the other sub-ranges. Experimental results reveal that our proposed framework achieves good anytime performances and sometimes outperforms NAMOA* in terms of finding the optimal solution frontier. In this paper, at first we present the necessary formalisms and definitions required for discussing the proposed method. The proposed algorithm, ABS, is presented in the following section. Then, we present the experimental results followed by the concluding remarks.

2 Definitions

Let $G = \langle V, E \rangle$ be a locally finite directed graph, where V is the set of nodes, $\Gamma \subseteq V$ is the set of goal nodes, and $E \subseteq V \times V$ is the set of directed edges. Every edge $e_{ij} = (v_i, v_j) \in E$ is labeled with a positive 2-dimensional vector, $c(e_{ij}) \in \mathbb{R}^+ \times \mathbb{R}^+$, where c_1 and c_2 are the two cost-components of vector, c. A path in G is a sequence of nodes, $p = \langle v_1, \cdots, v_k \rangle$, such that $(\forall i, 1 \le i < k)$, $(v_i, v_{i+1}) \in E$. The path cost $g(p) = \left(\sum_{i=1}^{k-1} c_1(c(e_{i,i+1})), \sum_{i=1}^{k-1} c_2(c(e_{i,i+1})) \right)$, is the sum of the cost vectors of its component edges. For a path p, we use $c_1(g(p))$ and $c_2(g(p))$ to denote $\sum_{i=1}^{k-1} c_1(c(e_{i,i+1}))$ and $\sum_{i=1}^{k-1} c_2(c(e_{i,i+1}))$, respectively. A solution is a path in G from start node v_s to a goal node $v_t \in \Gamma$. Since the edge costs are 2-dimensional vectors, a set of Pareto optimal solutions can be computed for G. Without loss of generality, we assume that both objectives are to be minimized.

Definition 1. [Dominance] *We define two types of* dominance relations, simple dominance, *denoted using '$\preccurlyeq$', and* strict dominance, *denoted using '$\prec$' as follows.*
1. $\forall g_i, g_j \in \mathbb{R}^2, [g_i \preccurlyeq g_j] \Leftrightarrow [(c_1(g_i) \le c_1(g_j)) \wedge (c_2(g_i) \le c_2(g_j))]$
2. $\forall g_i, g_j \in \mathbb{R}^2, [g_i \prec g_j] \Leftrightarrow [g_i \preccurlyeq g_j] \wedge (g_i \ne g_j)]$ □

Definition 2. [Nondominated Set] *For a set of vectors, $\mathcal{U}$, we define the set of nondominated vectors in $\mathcal{U}$ as* $nd(\mathcal{U}) = \{g_i \in \mathcal{U} \mid \nexists g_j \in \mathcal{U}, g_j \prec g_i\}$.   □

We also use two lexicographical orderings (L_1-*order* and L_2-*order*) which induce a total order among the cost vectors.

Definition 3. [L-ordering] *Let g_i and g_j be two 2-dimensional vectors. Then, based on L_1-ordering, $g_i < g_j$, if either $c_1(g_i) < c_1(g_j)$ or $[c_1(g_i) = c_1(g_j)] \wedge [c_2(g_i) < c_2(g_j)]$. Based on L_2-ordering, $g_i < g_j$, if either $c_2(g_i) < c_2(g_j)$ or $[c_2(g_i) = c_2(g_j)] \wedge [c_1(g_i) < c_1(g_j)]$. The other relational operators ($=$ and $>$) based on L_1-ordering and L_2-ordering can be defined in a likewise manner.*   □

For each node v_i in a graph G, $\mathcal{H}(v_i)$, denotes the set of nondominated heuristic cost vectors at node v_i such that every vector $h(v_i) \in \mathcal{H}(v_i)$ denotes the estimate of cost vector of one or more solution paths from v_i to goal nodes in Γ. Clearly for each goal node, $v_t \in \Gamma$, $\mathcal{H}(v_t) = \{(0,0)\}$.

Definition 4. [Heuristic Evaluation Vector] *For every path, p, in $\mathcal{G}$ starting from v_s to a node v_i, with cost $g(p)$, the set of heuristic evaluation vectors is denoted by* $\mathcal{F}(p) = \mathcal{F}(v_i, g_i) = nd\left(\{f \mid [f = g(p) + h] \wedge [h \in \mathcal{H}(v_i)]\} \right)$ □

Definition 5. [Admissible Heuristics] *A heuristic function is said to be* admissible *if the set $\mathcal{H}(v_i)$ of heuristic vectors computed using that function for each node v_i satisfies that for every solution path, p, from v_i to a goal node having nondominated cost, $h^*(p)$, $\exists h(v_i) \in \mathcal{H}(v_i)$ such that $h(v_i) \preccurlyeq h^*(p)$.*   □

In the rest of the paper we use c_1^l and c_1^u to denote the lower bound and upper bound estimates of the c_1 cost-components of the solutions. Suppose, Σ represents the set of all solutions. Clearly, $(\forall p \in \Sigma)$, $[c_1(g(p)) \ge c_1^l] \wedge [c_2(g(p)) \le c_1^u]$. Such estimates can be computed upfront using some approximate method.

3   Proposed Algorithmic Framework

In this section we present a generic anytime heuristic search framework for biobjective optimization problems named, "Anytime Biobjective Search" (ABS). Our proposed framework uses the lower and upper bound estimates on one of the objectives and divides the entire value range of that objective into a given number of sub-ranges to add a breadth first component to the search effort. Without loss of generality we assume that the lower and upper bound estimate is provided for the first objective function, i.e., c_1^l and c_1^u are given as inputs. The entire range of values, $c_1^u - c_1^l$, is divided into a given number, k, of sub-ranges. The sub-ranges may or may not be equal to each other. Several popular anytime strategies, like branch-and-bound etc. can be used on top of our framework. We denote the ith subrange as an interval $J_i = [r_i, r_i + 1)$ where $1 \le i \le k - 1$. Since $r_{k+1} = c_1^u$ the last subrange is $J_k = [r_k, r_k + 1]$. Each subrange is searched independently using a particular search method and the subrange to be searched next is selected using a given selection policy.

Algorithm 1. Anytime Biobjective Search(ABS)

---

    input   : The start node v_s, c_1^l, c_1^u, the number of ranges k, and strategy σ
    output : Pareto optimal solution frontier
1 Construct the root node of the explicit graph $\mathcal{G}$ with v_s;
2 Invoke strategy specific initialization function, $Init\text{-}\sigma$;
3 **while** $\exists i$, *such that* $1 \le i \le k$ **and** $\delta_i^\sigma \ne \varnothing$ **do**
4   Use a given policy to determine the value of i such that $(1 \le i \le k)$ and $\delta_i^\sigma \ne \varnothing$;
5   Start/Resume the search σ on δ_i^σ using $SearchRange\text{-}\sigma$;
6 **end**
7 Report the solutions in $\mathcal{S}$;

In this paper, we investigate three strategies, namely, (a) Branch-and-bound (denoted as BB) (b) Beam search (denoted as BM), and (c) Beam-stack search (denoted as BmS) on our proposed framework. For each sub-range, J_i $(1 \le i \le k)$, ABS maintains a separate data-structure δ_i^σ. The data-structures depend on the underlying strategy $\sigma \in \{BB, BM, BmS\}$. For example, δ_i^{BB} can be implemented as a queue or stack depending on whether *breadth first* or *depth first* variation of branch-and-bound is used. The major steps of the proposed framework are shown in Algorithm 1.

ABS expands the given implicit graph, G, repeatedly over iterations using state transformation rules to construct and grow the *explicit graph*, $\mathcal{G}$. A *solution frontier*, $\mathcal{S}$, containing the set of nondominated solutions is maintained throughout the course of the algorithm. ABS uses path selection and path expansion as the basic operations. At any point of time ABS maintains the set of *potential solution paths* (the paths that may be extended to reach a solution) corresponding to i^{th} sub-range in δ_i^σ. ABS selects a particular sub-range, say the jth one, using the given selection policy and invokes the strategy specific search routine, $SearchRange\text{-}\sigma$ on δ_j^σ. For our experimentation, we use round-robin selection policy. However, ABS can work with any other selection policies.

We maintain the paths to every node v_d of the explicit graph $\mathcal{G}$ using a list, $\mathcal{P}(v_d)$. Every element of $\mathcal{P}(v_d)$ is a triplet, $\langle v_q, j, \boldsymbol{g}(p) \rangle$, representing a distinct path, p, to node, v_d, where triplet $\langle v_q, j, \boldsymbol{g}(p) \rangle$ denotes that path p is an extension of the jth path to the parent v_q of v_d and have cost $g(p)$. Every *potential solution path* is also represented using a triplet, $\langle v_d, \boldsymbol{g}_d, ptr \rangle$, which denotes that the corresponding potential solution path ends at node v_d and have cost $\boldsymbol{g}_d$. '*ptr*' stores the pointer to the entry representing the corresponding path in $\mathcal{P}(v_d)$.

The individual strategy specific steps are carried out in two different subroutines, namely $Initialize(\sigma)$ and $SearchRange\text{-}\sigma(\delta_i^\sigma)$. However, all the search strategies use the following routine, $UpdateSolutions$, to maintain the current solution frontier $\mathcal{S}$. Whenever a new solution path is found, $UpdateSolutions$ checks whether the new solution, p, is dominated by any of the existing solutions in $\mathcal{S}$ and if the p is a nondominated one, then all the existing solutions in $\mathcal{S}$ that are dominated by p is removed from $\mathcal{S}$. Next, we explain the working of beam search, branch-and-bound, and beam-stack search within ABS framework.

Function UpdateSolutions $(\mathcal{S}, \langle v_q, \boldsymbol{g}_q, ptr_q \rangle)$

/* Suppose, for goal v_q, p_q is the corresponding solution path   */
1 **foreach** $p_i \in \mathcal{S}$ **do if** $g(p_i) \prec \boldsymbol{g}_q$ **then return**;
2 **foreach** $p_j \in \mathcal{S}$ **do**
3   **if** $\boldsymbol{g}_q \prec g(p_j)$ **then** Remove p_j from $\mathcal{S}$;
4 **end**
5 Add p_q to $\mathcal{S}$;

[Branch-and-bound Search] The traditional *branch-and-bound* strategy performs an ordered traversal of a given search space where the pruning is performed based on the cost of current best solution. The traversal is *depth-first* when the underlying list of nodes is implemented as a *stack* and *breadth-first* when that list is implemented as *queue*. In the multiobjective setting, the pruning is performed when the cost of a potential solution is dominated by one of the solutions found so far. ABS framework is used to implement a *multiple-list* variation of the traditional branch-and-bound search, called *multiple-list branch-and-bound (MLBB)* in the context of biobjective costs in the following way. The entire search space is split into a given number of non-overlapping segments based on the value of the c_1 cost-component. Within each of the segments branch-and-bound search is run independently. The entire range of values of c_1 cost-component, $(c_1^u - c_1^l)$, is divided into a given number, k, of equal sub-ranges and for each sub-range a separate list is maintained. δ_i^{BB} denotes the list for i^{th} sub-range.

In each round of the *multiple-list branch-and-bound*, the lists are selected one by one starting from the first list. If the selected list is non-empty, function $SearchRange\text{-}BB$ is invoked on that list. In $SearchRange\text{-}BB$, the list is popped/dequeued (depending on whether the list is implemented as stack or queue respectively) to select the next entry (a potential solution path in the explicit graph $\mathcal{G}$) to be expanded. If a solution is found, function $UpdateSolutions$ is used to update the current solution frontier and the function $SearchRange\text{-}BB$ returns to the main driver function (Algorithm 1) to allow the search to proceed in other segments. Otherwise, $SearchRange\text{-}BB$ expands the selected entry to generate only those successors whose costs are not dominated by the cost of the solutions in the current solution frontier and which are not a candidate for pruning. Each of the generated successors is inserted into the appropriate list (δ_i^{BB}) according to the range to which its c_1 cost-component of the path cost vector g belongs.

We have shown the *SearchRange-BB* function for the *depth-first* version of *multiple list branch-and-bound*. For implementing the *breadth-first* version of *multiple-list branch-and-bound* each list δ_i^{BB} has to implemented using queue.

It may be noted that whenever a new nondominated solution is found, the stacks are pruned using the cost vector of that new solution. Also while generating the successors, it may happen that the cost vector of the newly found path might dominate the cost vector of some of the paths generated earlier. In this case those paths which are dominated are pruned along with their corresponding stack entries.

Function `Initialize-BB`(k)

---

1 $\forall i, 1 \leq i \leq k$, Initialize δ_i^{BB};

2 Insert $\langle v_s, \mathbf{0}, null \rangle$ to δ_1^{BB};

Function `SearchRange-BB`(δ_i^{BB})

---

1 $p_\delta \leftarrow$ Pop(δ_i^{BB}) ; /* **Suppose** $p_\delta = \langle v_q, \mathbf{g_q}, ptr_q \rangle$ */

2 **if** $v_q \in \Gamma$ **then**

3   UpdateSolutions$(\mathcal{S}, \langle v_q, \mathbf{g_q}, ptr_q \rangle)$;

4     $\forall j, i \leq j \leq k$, prune δ_j^{BB}, using $\mathbf{g_q}$;

5   **return**;

6 **end**

7 Expand p_δ and generate the set of valid successors δ_{succ}^{BB} which represent potential solution paths;

8 **foreach** *element p_δ' in δ_{succ}^{BB}* **do**

9   Suppose $p_\delta' = \langle v_d, \mathbf{g_d}, ptr_d \rangle$;

10     $idx \leftarrow \lceil (c_1^u - c_1(\mathbf{g_d}))/k \rceil$;

11   Push$(\delta_{idx}^{BB}, p_\delta')$;

12 **end**

13 **goto** Line-1;

[Beam Search] Typically *beam-search* works with a given beam-width, b. In the ABS framework in the initialization phase (function *Initialize-BM*), NAMOA* is run until the size of δ_{open}^{BM} reaches $k \times b$ where k and b are two parameters of the algorithm. Here, k represents the number of beams to be used and b is the size of an individual beam.

Function `Initialize-BM`(k, b)

---

1 Construct an empty list δ_{open}^{BM};

2 Insert $\langle v_s, \mathbf{0}, null \rangle$ to δ_{open}^{BM};

3 Continue NAMOA* search using δ_{open}^{BM} as $OPEN$ list till $|\delta_{open}^{BmS}| \leq k \times b$;

4 Order the elements of δ_{open}^{BM} according to the c_1 cost component;

5 Split δ_{open}^{BM} into k consecutive sublists where each sublist has no more than b entries;

6 **for** $j \leftarrow 1$ **to** k **do**

7     $\delta_j^{BM} \leftarrow t^{th}$ sublist of δ_{open}^{BM};

8     $r_j \leftarrow$ the c_1 cost component of the first element of δ_j^{BM};

9 **end**

10 $r_{k+1} \leftarrow c_1^u$;

The contents of δ_{open}^{BM} is sorted in L_1-*order* and split into k sublists. We maintain k beams parallelly and function $SearchRange$-BM starts beam search on a given beam δ_i^{BM}. It returns whenever a new solution is found. It may be noted that the k ranges obtained after splitting the contents of δ_{open}^{BM} may not be equal and primarily depends on the search space. Also this method is not complete due to the fact that beam search itself is not complete.

Function SearchRange-BM(δ_i^{BM})

---

1   Expand the deepest layer d of δ_i^{BM} and generate the set of valid successors δ_{succ}^{BM} where each successor represents a potential solution path;

2   **if** *a solution* $\langle v_q, g_q, ptr_q \rangle$ *is generated in the last step* **then**

3   UpdateSolutions($\mathcal{S}, \langle v_q, g_q, ptr_q \rangle$);

4   **return**;

5   **end**

6   **if** $\delta_{succ}^{BM} = \varnothing$ **then**

7   Remove the contents of the all layers of δ_i^{BM};

8   **return**;

9   **end**

10 Sort the elements of δ_{succ}^{BM} in the non-decreasing order the c_1 cost component;

11 Add the first b elements of δ_{succ}^{BM} to the $(d+1)^{th}$ layer of δ_i^{BM};

12 **goto** Line-1;

[Beam-stack Search] In order to make the beam search complete, *beam-stack search* was proposed by Zhou et al. in [10]. The beam-stack search can be applied within our proposed ABS framework in the following way. The initialization phase is identical to *beam search* and in this phase a heuristic breadth first search is run till the size of δ_{open}^{BmS} reaches $k \times b$ where k and b are the same two parameters of the algorithm that are used in beam search. Then the contents of δ_{open}^{BM} is sorted in L_1-*order* and split into k sublists. In the ABS framework k beam-stacks are maintained in parallel where each beam-stack, δ_i^{BmS} ($1 \leq i \leq k$), consists of multiple layers of maximum width b. A $\langle$level-range, slice-index$\rangle$ pair is maintained for each layer. For the layer with depth d of ith beam-stack the *level-range* is denoted as $[\tau_{i,d}^{min}, \tau_{i,d}^{max})$ which denotes the range of the values of c_1 cost-components of successors in the next layer. The successors of a layer are sorted in L_1-*order* for ordered traversal of the search space. Since the width of each layer is limited by the beam-width b, the successors of a layer are explored in an ordered fashion by keeping a slice of b successors only. When the search backtracks to the current layer the next slice of successors (containing at most b elements) is explored. Since the beam-stack search strategy is complete, it is guaranteed to generate optimal solution frontier given sufficient time. However experimental results show that such time for finding the optimal solution frontier may be very large.

4   Experimental Results

Since NAMOA* [9] uses the same underlying path selection and expansion policy and the overall performance of NAMOA* is better than that of MOA* [30], we compare the performance of ABS framework with NAMOA*. Also the the same problem domain

name	t_1	t_2	t_3	t_4	t_5
dim.	61×61	71×71	81×81	91×91	101×101
$\#\mathcal{S}$	61	84	92	98	106
$T(\theta_{100})$	21.94	63.87	113.26	178.85	219.41

name	t_6	t_7	t_8	t_9	t_A
dim.	111×111	121×121	131×131	141×141	151×151
$\#\mathcal{S}$	118	134	146	154	167
$T(\theta_{100})$	362.40	743.82	1869.44	2673.13	4289.72

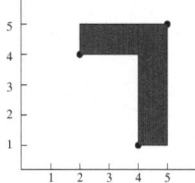

Fig. 1. Average running time (in seconds) for NAMOA*   **Fig. 2.** Hypervolume

which was used in [30, 31], namely randomly constructed $N \times N$ square grids is used for comparison. We have conducted the experiments using a machine with Intel Core i3-2100 cpu, 4GB RAM, running Ubuntu Linux 10.10.

We have constructed 25 grid instances for each N. The average time required for computing the optimal solution frontier for grids with different dimensions using NAMOA* are reported in Table 1. The cost of each edge in a $N \times N$ grid is a two dimensional vector, c, where both the c_1 and c_2 components of c are chosen randomly between 1 and 5. The node at position $(0,0)$ is the source and the node at position (N, N) is the destination. The Manhattan distance heuristic function was used in this problem. We used the hypervolume metric [27] to determine the quality of the solution frontier. In Figure 2 the area of shaded region is the hyper volume of the Pareto frontier $\{(2, 4), (4, 1)\}$ with respect to the point $(5, 5)$. The hypervolume is computed with respect to the point (c_1^u, c_2^u), where c_1^u and c_2^u are the upper bound estimates of the c_1 and c_2 cost-component respectively. The optimality of a solution frontier is defined as :

$$\theta = \frac{\text{hypervolume of the solution frontier}}{\text{hypervolume of the optimal solution frontier}} \times 100$$

The time required in seconds for reaching $x\%$ optimality is denoted using $T(\theta_x)$. Also we use θ_i to denote the optimality measure of the first solution returned by an anytime algorithm. We have deliberately used very large time-out value (5000 seconds) while running NAMOA* in order to generate the actual Pareto optimal frontier so that the anytime performance of the different search strategies under ABS framework can be compared with respect to the exact Pareto optimal frontier.

For evaluating the performance of *multiple list branch-and-bound* using ABS framework, the number of lists, i.e., the value of k is chosen in such a way that the width of the interval represented by an individual subrange does not exceed a certain value, denoted using m, i.e., $r_{i+1} - r_i \leq m$ where $1 \leq i \leq k$. Table 1 and Table 2 report the *average* running time required for reaching different levels of optimality for the *depth-first* and *breadth-first* versions of *multiple list branch and bound* using ABS framework respectively. We have used a time-limit of 600 seconds in order to compare the anytime performance of different search strategies under ABS framework. We have experimented with different values of m (10, 15, 20, 25) and we report the result for $m = 10$ which is the best among the lot. We choose this value based on the results Between the depth-first and breadth-first version of MLBB on ABS, the depth-first version is the clear winner. Also it is interesting to observe that the performance of depth-first MLBB on ABS often beats the performance of NAMOA* for certain valuations of k.

The *average* running time required for *beam* search on ABS framework is reported in Table 3 for square grids with different dimensions. For experimentation we have

Table 1. Running time (in seconds) of depth-first MLBB on ABS framework ('*' denotes timeout after 600 seconds) for different dimensions of grids

	θ_i	$T(\theta_i)$	$T(\theta_{80})$	$T(\theta_{85})$	$T(\theta_{90})$	$T(\theta_{95})$	$T(\theta_{100})$
t_1	76.127%	2.258	4.142	5.375	6.063	7.035	8.677
t_2	75.363%	5.836	9.441	14.384	15.525	16.443	18.142
t_3	76.537%	11.233	18.664	25.457	28.316	31.566	34.480
t_4	74.913%	18.786	31.861	42.193	46.484	53.737	58.871
t_5	76.773%	31.237	52.972	72.567	85.654	96.649	105.565
t_6	75.241%	50.174	83.832	106.852	139.355	158.316	176.789
t_7	74.871%	79.286	121.243	188.393	216.746	244.948	266.635
t_8	77.227%	116.741	187.549	274.408	310.888	338.776	363.426
t_9	75.732%	173.255	303.122	395.732	465.256	512.963	553.989
t_A	76.479%	242.459	442.198	485.941	498.296	*	*

Table 2. Running time (in seconds) of breadth-first MLBB on ABS framework ('*' denotes time-out after 600 seconds) for different dimensions of grids

	θ_i	$T(\theta_i)$	$T(\theta_{80})$	$T(\theta_{85})$	$T(\theta_{90})$	$T(\theta_{95})$	$T(\theta_{100})$
t_1	68.610%	5.634	33.762	52.722	61.048	66.842	72.893
t_2	50.844%	8.040	129.840	184.408	220.631	237.398	258.468
t_3	65.827%	19.602	240.028	290.514	434.276	465.715	480.692
t_4	66.840%	28.326	151.222	330.203	551.338	*	*
t_5	60.499%	48.182	382.505	476.866	*	*	*
t_6	63.124%	75.083	315.121	545.938	*	*	*
t_7	65.058%	126.612	322.617	*	*	*	*
t_8	61.583%	182.997	345.139	*	*	*	*
t_9	67.104%	249.657	344.915	*	*	*	*
t_A	62.441%	348.272	355.810	*	*	*	*

Table 3. Running time (in seconds) of ABS with beam search strategy ('-' denotes that the target value of optimality not reached) for different dimensions of grids

	θ_i	$T(\theta_i)$	$T(\theta_{80})$	$T(\theta_{85})$	$T(\theta_{90})$	$T(\theta_{95})$	$T(\theta_{100})$
t_1	73.545%	0.873	0.655	1.379	3.342	4.723	-
t_2	71.020%	1.072	1.080	3.648	8.572	-	-
t_3	74.363%	1.488	2.472	6.326	12.048	-	-
t_4	72.829%	2.034	4.587	10.707	11.322	-	-
t_5	72.886%	2.537	5.923	12.289	29.034	-	-
t_6	69.072%	3.872	7.241	25.776	-	-	-
t_7	73.666%	3.824	14.655	35.451	-	-	-
t_8	71.922%	5.303	15.818	44.723	-	-	-
t_9	70.554%	6.028	26.375	85.089	-	-	-
t_A	71.802%	7.241	35.893	109.074	-	-	-

Table 4. Running time (in seconds) of ABS with beam-stack search strategy ('*' denotes timeout after 600 seconds) for different dimensions of grids

	θ_i	$T(\theta_i)$	$T(\theta_{80})$	$T(\theta_{85})$	$T(\theta_{90})$	$T(\theta_{95})$	$T(\theta_{100})$
t_1	73.545%	0.429	0.015	2.924	4.533	8.431	272.342
t_2	71.020%	1.465	1.932	5.990	10.092	86.574	287.048
t_3	74.363%	1.273	3.939	7.407	15.319	244.771	482.726
t_4	72.829%	2.031	4.832	12.383	16.877	425.720	*
t_5	72.886%	2.847	5.313	13.827	31.503	*	*
t_6	69.072%	3.587	7.260	27.963	*	*	*
t_7	73.666%	4.098	15.029	36.197	*	*	*
t_8	71.922%	5.829	17.886	45.615	*	*	*
t_9	70.554%	6.357	30.812	88.198	*	*	*
t_A	71.802%	7.290	33.489	112.175	*	*	*

chosen the value of k to be equal to N for an $N \times N$ grid. The value of *beam width*, b, is taken as 20. Table 4 reports the *average* running time requred for *beam-stack* search on ABS framework for square grids with various dimensions. Here also we have chosen the value of k to be equal to the N for an $N \times N$ grid while running the experiments.

Table 5. Running time (in seconds) of depth-first MLBB on ABS framework for different dimensions of knapsacks

#items	θ_i	$T(\theta_i)$	$T(\theta_{75})$	$T(\theta_{80})$	$T(\theta_{85})$	$T(\theta_{90})$	$T(\theta_{95})$	$T(\theta_{100})$
50	81.640%	0.001	0.001	0.001	0.002	0.010	0.046	0.816
52	81.253%	0.001	0.001	0.001	0.004	0.015	0.085	1.221
54	82.170%	0.001	0.001	0.001	0.003	0.015	0.093	1.519
56	81.091%	0.001	0.001	0.002	0.005	0.020	0.095	1.732
58	82.994%	0.001	0.001	0.001	0.003	0.015	0.120	2.638
60	81.918%	0.001	0.001	0.001	0.004	0.017	0.099	2.303

Table 6. Running time (in seconds) of breadth-first MLBB on ABS framework for different dimensions of knapsacks

#items	θ_i	$T(\theta_i)$	$T(\theta_{75})$	$T(\theta_{80})$	$T(\theta_{85})$	$T(\theta_{90})$	$T(\theta_{95})$	$T(\theta_{100})$
50	74.069%	0.009	0.075	0.162	0.484	1.481	4.408	5.651
52	70.215%	0.014	0.105	0.238	0.695	2.720	8.574	11.603
54	68.271%	0.019	0.152	0.234	0.725	2.509	8.815	15.382
56	67.938%	0.021	0.202	0.424	1.326	4.275	9.141	16.024
58	64.251%	0.035	0.181	0.231	0.811	4.446	14.359	23.550
60	63.994%	0.038	0.293	0.519	1.686	6.171	12.677	20.279

Table 7. Running time (in seconds) of ABS with beam search strategy ('-' denotes that the target value of optimality not reached) for different dimensions of knapsacks

#items	θ_i	$T(\theta_i)$	$T(\theta_{75})$	$T(\theta_{80})$	$T(\theta_{85})$	$T(\theta_{90})$	$T(\theta_{95})$	$T(\theta_{100})$
50	92.057%	0.074	0.074	0.074	0.075	0.086	0.109	-
52	90.588%	0.069	0.069	0.069	0.071	0.089	0.129	-
54	90.939%	0.073	0.073	0.073	0.076	0.086	0.148	-
56	90.300%	0.070	0.070	0.070	0.073	0.103	-	-
58	90.090%	0.074	0.074	0.074	0.074	0.109	-	-
60	89.879%	0.073	0.073	0.073	0.074	0.106	-	-

Table 8. Running time (in seconds) of ABS with beam-stack search strategy for different dimensions of knapsacks

	θ_i	$T(\theta_i)$	$T(\theta_{75})$	$T(\theta_{80})$	$T(\theta_{85})$	$T(\theta_{90})$	$T(\theta_{95})$	$T(\theta_{100})$
50	92.057%	0.075	0.075	0.075	0.075	0.086	0.328	1.429
52	90.588%	0.070	0.070	0.070	0.075	0.296	1.193	3.591
54	90.939%	0.070	0.070	0.070	0.071	0.175	0.981	3.893
56	90.300%	0.070	0.070	0.071	0.072	0.123	1.489	4.663
58	90.090%	0.075	0.075	0.075	0.075	0.147	1.852	7.537
60	89.879%	0.072	0.072	0.072	0.072	0.124	1.149	4.625

The value of *beam-stack width*, b, is also taken as 20. On ABS framework, the initial anytime performance of beam-stack search is identical to the performance of beam search. However after a reaching certain level of optimality, beam-stack takes significant time to find the optimal solution. For most of the cases the algorithm encountered time-out after 600 seconds without finding the optimal solution. The overall performance of the depth-first version of MLBB on ABS is better than other strategies.

Apart from the two dimensional grids, we have also experimented with biobjective knapsack problems. We experimented with different number of items $(50, 52, \cdots, 60)$ and randomly constructed 50 instances of knapsacks for each item-count. The capacity of the knapsack is maintained as the half of the total weight of the items. The weights and the profits are chosen as random number between 50 and 100. We report the result for $m = 10$ for ABS with multiple list branch and bound. We use 100 as beam-width and the number of beams used is 10. Table 5 - 8 reports the anytime performance of different strategies on ABS framework. In this test domain the performance of beam-stack search is much better compared to the performance in the grid domain and comparable with the performance of the depth-first version of MLBB on ABS. However the overall performance of the depth-first version of MLBB on ABS is better than other strategies.

5   Conclusion

In this paper, we presented a general anytime framework, ABS, for finding the Pareto optimal solution frontier problems with a biobjective cost criterion. The class of optimization problems considered in this paper is of practical significance and has possible application in problems like *operator scheduling*, *route planning*, *portfolio selection* etc., where two non commensurate objectives are involved and one typically strives to reach a suitable trade-off between the conflicting objectives.

References

1. Gajski, D., Dutt, N., Wu, A., Lin, S.: High-level synthesis: introduction to chip and system design. Kluwer Academic Publishers, Norwell (1992)
2. Elton, E.J., Gruber, M.J., Blake, C.R.: Modern portfolio theory, 1950 to date. SSRN eLibrary (1997)
3. Mishkin, F.S.: The Economics of Money, Banking, and Financial Markets, 7th edn. Addison-Wesley (2004)
4. Müller-Hannemann, M., Weihe, K.: On the cardinality of the Pareto set in bicriteria shortest path problems. Annals OR 147(1), 269–286 (2006)
5. Jahn, O., Möhring, R.H., Schulz, A.S., Stier-Moses, N.E.: System-optimal routing of traffic flows with user constraints in networks with congestion. Operations Research 53(4), 600–616 (2005)
6. Nilsson, N.J.: Principle of artificial intelligence. Tioga Publishing Co. (1980)
7. Stewart, B.S., White III, C.C.: Multiobjective A*. J. ACM 38, 775–814 (1991)
8. Dasgupta, P., Chakrabarti, P.P., DeSarkar, S.C.: Multiobjective heuristic search in AND/OR graphs. Journal of Algorithms 20(2), 282–311 (1996)
9. Mandow, L., Pérez-de-la-Cruz, J.L.: Multiobjective A* search with consistent heuristics. J. ACM 57(5), 27:1–27:25 (2010)
10. Zhou, R., Hansen, E.A.: Beam-stack search: Integrating backtracking with beam search. In: ICAPS, pp. 90–98 (2005)
11. Furcy, D., Koenig, S.: Limited discrepancy beam search. In: IJCAI, pp. 125–131 (2005)
12. Likhachev, M., Gordon, G.J., Thrun, S.: ARA*: Anytime A* with provable bounds on sub-optimality. In: NIPS (2003)
13. Röger, G., Helmert, M.: The more, the merrier: Combining heuristic estimators for satisficing planning. In: ICAPS, pp. 246–249 (2010)

14. Valenzano, R.A., Sturtevant, N.R., Schaeffer, J., Buro, K., Kishimoto, A.: Simultaneously searching with multiple settings: An alternative to parameter tuning for suboptimal single-agent search algorithms. In: ICAPS, pp. 177–184 (2010)
15. Vadlamudi, S.G., Aine, S., Chakrabarti, P.P.: MAWA* - a memory-bounded anytime heuristic-search algorithm. IEEE Transactions on Systems, Man, and Cybernetics, Part B 41(3), 725–735 (2011)
16. Thayer, J.T., Ruml, W.: Anytime heuristic search: Frameworks and algorithms. In: The Third Annual Symposium on Combinatorial Search (2010)
17. Likhachev, M., Ferguson, D., Gordon, G.J., Stentz, A., Thrun, S.: Anytime search in dynamic graphs. Artif. Intell. 172(14), 1613–1643 (2008)
18. Hansen, E.A., Zhou, R.: Anytime heuristic search. J. Artif. Intell. Res. (JAIR) 28, 267–297 (2007)
19. Aine, S., Chakrabarti, P.P., Kumar, R.: AWA* - a window constrained anytime heuristic search algorithm. In: IJCAI, pp. 2250–2255 (2007)
20. Tsaggouris, G., Zaroliagis, C.D.: Multiobjective optimization: Improved FPTAS for shortest paths and non-linear objectives with applications. Theory Comput. Syst. 45(1), 162–186 (2009)
21. Perny, P., Spanjaard, O.: Near admissible algorithms for multiobjective search. In: ECAI, pp. 490–494 (2008)
22. Angel, E., Bampis, E., Kononov, A.: On the approximate tradeoff for bicriteria batching and parallel machine scheduling problems. Theor. Comput. Sci. 306(1-3), 319–338 (2003)
23. Erlebach, T., Kellerer, H., Pferschy, U.: Approximating multiobjective knapsack problems. Manage. Sci. 48(12), 1603–1612 (2002)
24. Papadimitriou, C.H., Yannakakis, M.: On the approximability of trade-offs and optimal access of web sources. In: FOCS, pp. 86–92 (2000)
25. Barichard, V., Hao, J.K.: A Population and Interval Constraint Propagation Algorithm. In: Fonseca, C.M., Fleming, P.J., Zitzler, E., Deb, K., Thiele, L. (eds.) EMO 2003. LNCS, vol. 2632, pp. 88–101. Springer, Heidelberg (2003)
26. Sourd, F., Spanjaard, O.: A multiobjective branch-and-bound framework: Application to the biobjective spanning tree problem. INFORMS Journal on Computing 20(3), 472–484 (2008)
27. Branke, J., Deb, K., Miettinen, K., Slowinski, R.: Multiobjective Optimization. LNCS, vol. 5252. Springer, Heidelberg (2008)
28. Deb, K., Agrawal, S., Pratap, A., Meyarivan, T.: A fast and elitist multiobjective genetic algorithm: NSGA-II. IEEE Trans. Evolutionary Computation 6(2), 182–197 (2002)
29. Sarkar, U.K., Chakrabarti, P.P., Ghose, S., Sarkar, S.C.D.: Multiple stack branch and bound. Inf. Process. Lett. 37(1), 43–48 (1991)
30. Machuca, E., Mandow, L., Pérez-de-la-Cruz, J.L., Ruiz-Sepúlveda, A.: A comparison of heuristic best-first algorithms for bicriterion shortest path problems. European Journal of Operational Research 217(1), 44–53 (2012)
31. Mandow, L., Pérez-de-la-Cruz, J.L.: A multiobjective frontier search algorithm. In: IJCAI, pp. 2340–2345 (2007)

ICHEA for Discrete Constraint Satisfaction Problems

Anurag Sharma and Dharmendra Sharma

Faculty of Information Sciences and Engineering
University of Canberra, ACT, Australia
{Anurag.Sharma,Dharmendra.Sharma}@canberra.edu.au

Abstract. Constraint satisfaction problem (CSP) is a subset of optimization problem where at least one solution is sought that satisfies all the given constraints. Presently, evolutionary algorithms (EAs) have become standard optimization techniques for solving unconstrained optimization problems where the problem is formalized for discrete or continuous domains. However, traditional EAs are considered 'blind' to constraint as they do not extract and exploit information from the constraints. A variation of EA – intelligent constraint handling for EA (ICHEA) proposed earlier models constraints to guide the evolutionary search to get improved and efficient solutions for continuous CSPs. As many real world CSPs have constraints defined in the form of discrete functions, this paper serves as an extension to ICHEA that reports its applicability for solving discrete CSPs. The experiment has been carried on a classic discrete CSP – the N-Queens problem. The experimental results show that extracting information from constraints and exploiting it in the evolutionary search makes the search more efficient. This provision is a problem independent formulation in ICHEA.

Keywords: Constraints, constraint satisfaction problem (CSP), optimization problem, evolutionary algorithm (EA), intelligent constraint handling evolutionary algorithm (ICHEA), N-Queens problem.

1   Introduction

Many engineering problems ranging from resource allocation and scheduling to fault diagnosis and design involve constraint satisfaction as an essential component that require finding solutions to satisfy a set of constraints over real numbers or discrete representation of constraints [4, 5, 21]. EAs are used to solve optimization problem from 1960s. It produces very efficient and robust solutions for unconstrained optimization problems. Even though CSPs are integral part of computer science, little research have been reported on the development of efficient and effective constraint-handling techniques – as compared with a plethora of new methods developed for unconstrained optimization [12]. Traditional EAs are 'blind' towards CSPs as they do not take into account the information from constraints which can reduce the search space; but only heuristically search for the solution in the vast search space. Generally objective functions are designed to use problem dependent penalty functions but some uses error measurements like distance from constraint regions that is applicable to

M. Thielscher and D. Zhang (Eds.): AI 2012, LNCS 7691, pp. 242–253, 2012.

continuous CSPs only. This has been a motivating factor in developing a novel variation of EAs that can extract and exploit information from constraints to produce more efficient solutions for CSPs irrespective of their problem domains. Intelligent constraint handling for EA (ICHEA) has been introduced in [24] to solve continuous CSP that shows promising results when information from constraints are extracted and exploited. In this paper ICHEA is enhanced to solve discrete CSP. Constraint problems are divided into two classes: Constrained Optimizing Problems (COPs) and constraint satisfaction problems (CSPs). The difference between these classes is that in COPs an optimal solution that satisfies all constraints should be found, while for CSPs any solution as long as all the constraints are satisfied is acceptable [9]. This paper has been confined to CSPs only.

Characteristically, CSPs solved by EAs use penalty based functions. A penalty function updates the fitness of chromosomes in EA. A penalty term is used in general for reward and punishment for satisfying and/or violating the constraints [3]. However, its main shortcoming is that penalty factors which determine the severity of the punishment, must be set by the user and their values are problem dependent [16]. Some other constraint handling approaches include expensive *repair* algorithms that promote the local search to transform infeasible solutions to feasible solutions because the feasible parents not necessarily produce feasible progenies [3]. In multi-objective optimization (MOO) constraints are transformed into multiple objectives. Pareto-based selection approaches are currently the most popular multi-objective evolutionary algorithm (MOEA) solution technique. In a typical MOO problem there exists a set of solutions which are superior to the rest of the solution in the search space when all objectives are considered but are inferior to other solutions in the space in one or more objectives. These solutions are known as *pareto-optimal* solutions or non-dominated solutions [25]. (Definition of *pareto* concepts can be found in [26]). There are many established MOO algorithms like MOGA [10], VEGA [20], NSGA and NSGAII [6]. Generally, this type of algorithm requires inequality constraints that can be transformed into many objective functions to be optimized simultaneously. Paredis in [18] has used co-evolution strategies that utilizes *predator-prey* model to keep two populations – one population represents solutions that satisfies many constraints while other population represents those individuals whose constraint(s) is violated by lots of individuals in the first population. This strategy requires extra computational effort to find the intersection of a line with the boundary of the feasible region

The main focus of this paper is to enhance ICHEA to solve CSPs for discrete domains by exploiting information from constraints without making the algorithm problem dependent. The paper is organized as follows: Section 2 briefly discusses the EA techniques used in handling constraints and formalization of discrete CSPs. Section 3 describes changes made in ICHEA to make it compatible for discrete CSPs. Section 4 shows experimental results on N-Queens problems followed by discussion on Section 5. Section 6 concludes the paper by summarizing the results and proposing some further extensions to the research.

2   Constraint Handling through EAs

Traditional EAs are 'blind' to constraint as they do not extract the information from the constraints but search the solution through random heuristic greedy approach [4, 9]. This causes the search engine to spent extra computational effort in searching for the solution into the wider search space without only concentrating in the restricted smaller feasible search space. Constraints can reduce the search space and it can make the heuristic search more efficient by harnessing information from constraint to guide the search engine, search in feasible search space only.

Generally violation count is used as a fitness function for CSPs for discrete domains. Depending on the strengths of constraints, individual weights can be assigned to constraints in a penalty function to calculate the fitness value. To avoid problem dependent penalty functions and to utilize some information from constraints to guide the evolutionary search a distance function is used instead of violation count to indicate how far an individual is from the feasible regions [17]. However this is generally limited to continuous domain only. The main motivation behind developing a novel variation of EA is to avoid using problem dependent penalty based functions for CSPs that can be used for both continuous and discrete domains utilizing only the information from constraints.

ICHEA attempts to solve CSPs by utilizing information from constraints to guide the evolutionary search whether the constraints are given in the form of continuous or discrete functions. It does not use penalty functions, problem dependent formulations or error functions which all of the current EAs do. It does not disregard the information from constraints to produce more efficient results. ICHEA also does not require initial feasible solution and it is also not restricted to produce feasible progenies from feasible parents.

CSP is defined by an input vector $\vec{x} = \{x_1, x_2, \dots x_n\}$ of size n in a finite space S where each variable x_i has a finite domain D_i. A set of m constraints $\{c_1, c_2, \dots c_m\}$ is defined in the form of functions:

$$c_i(x_1, x_2, \dots x_n) = \begin{cases} 1 & , if\ satisfied \\ 0 & , if\ violated \end{cases} \tag{1}$$

Constraint satisfaction sets or feasible regions $\{S_1, S_2, \dots S_m\}$ can also be defined where:

$$S_i = \{\ \vec{x} \in S \mid c_i(\vec{x}) = 1, 1 \leq i \leq m, i \in Z(integer\ set)\} \tag{2}$$

The fitness function of any CSP can be given as:

$$f(\vec{x}) = \sum_{i=1}^{m} c_i(\vec{x}) \tag{3}$$

To incorporate the weighted penalty function Eq. (3) can be redefined as:

$$f(\vec{x}) = \sum_{i=1}^{m} w_i c_i(\vec{x}) \tag{4}$$

where $w_i \geq 0$ are the weighted coefficients representing the relative importance of the constraints. Its main weakness is the difficulty to determine the appropriate weights when there is not enough information about the problem [2]. The solution of a CSP is $s \in S$ when all the constraints c_i are satisfied.

3   ICHEA for Discrete Data

ICHEA is a variation of EA that solves CSPs by extracting information from constraints as described in [24] for continuous domain by realizing *intermarriage* crossover. *Intermarriage* crossover selects two parents from different *constraint satisfaction sets* to make them come closer iteratively towards their corresponding feasible boundary because the CSP solutions lie in the overlapping boundary region of feasible regions that satisfy different constraints. The iterative move for parent P_i and P_j to produce offspring O_i is given as:

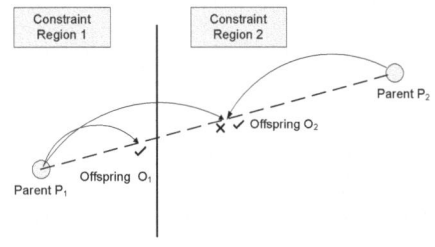

Fig. 1. Intermarriage crossover for continuous CSPs

$$O_i = r^i(P_j - P_i) \qquad (5)$$

where r is a coefficient in the range $(0,1)$ which is generally 0.5. Variable i gets incremented from 1 to a threshold value T in the sequence $\langle 1, 2, \dots, T \rangle$. The intermarriage crossover process is shown in the Fig. 1 where $\checkmark$ mark indicates possible placement for an offspring and $\times$ mark indicate the offspring vector is unacceptable in that particular position. An offspring is accepted if it satisfies equal or more constraints than its corresponding parent. Corresponding parent for offspring O_1 is P_1. So using the Eq. (5) the next i value is used until the offspring

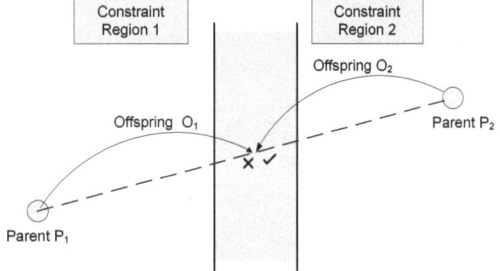

Fig. 2. Intermarriage crossover for discrete CSPs

finds an acceptable place or a threshold value T is reached. This *greedy* approach of crossover might result in generating no offspring at all.

Favouring individuals that satisfy higher number of constraints and the use of feasible regions in *intermarriage* crossover guides the evolutionary search in finding the solution space quickly [24]. When constraint regions are discrete then the *intermarriage* crossover for continuous CSP cannot be used directly to generate progenies as its formulation is based on real numbers for continuous domain. The concept of *intermarriage* crossover is to fuse feasible solutions from two different constraint satisfaction sets together that makes the offspring "generic" that satisfy more constraints because its parents are from two different constraint satisfaction sets. If the fusion of two discrete feasible solutions is represented by $\oplus$ then the *intermarriage* crossover of two parents for discrete CSP transformed from Eq. (5) can be given as:

$$O_i = r^i(P_j \oplus P_i) = (P_j \oplus P_i) \qquad (6)$$

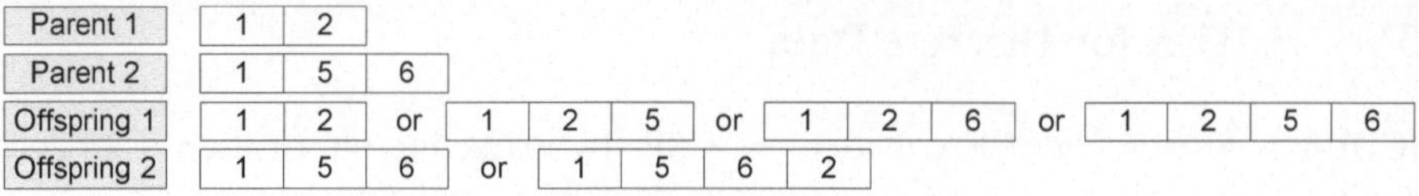

Parent 1	1	2																
Parent 2	1	5	6															
Offspring 1	1	2	or	1	2	5	or	1	2	6	or	1	2	5	6			
Offspring 2	1	5	6	or	1	5	6	2										

Fig. 3. Variable length intermarriage crossover

For discrete *intermarriage* crossover value of r and i is 1 because fusion is non-iterative as shown in Fig. 2 where offspring are accepted if fusion results better chromosome(s). ICHEA uses variable length chromosomes (partial solutions) to accomplish discrete valued *intermarriage* crossover where genotype is used as phenotypes. Variable length chromosome has been used in many applications like [1, 23, 27]. Partial solutions $\vec{p} = \{x_1, x_2, \ldots x_k\}$ where $k \leq n$ are chromosomes that satisfy all the constraints partially i.e. $\sum_{i=1}^{m} c_i(\vec{p}) = m$. Its fitness can be given as:

$$fitness(\vec{p}) = n - |\vec{p}| \tag{7}$$

The partial solutions are fused incrementally considering all constraints at once. For example a CSP problem of size n has parents P_1 and P_2 with partial solutions $\{1, 2\}$ and $\{1, 5, 6\}$ respectively. The generated offspring from these parents either satisfy equal or more constraints as shown in Fig. 3. Each offspring has traits from both parents. The *intermarriage* crossover only tries to append the allele values of other chromosome as shown in Fig. 3. All the allele values that violate the constraints are dropped so the offspring are also feasible chromosomes. An advantage of using variable length chromosome in this manner is reduction in computational time. *Intermarriage* crossover avoids recalculation of objective function because it only requires allele values to be appended. For example an N-Queens problem on chess board of size N requires $N(N + 1)/2$ operations on a single function call and for one complete crossover it requires $N(N + 1)$ operations every time. Its time complexity of *Big-O* order is $O(N^2)$. On the other hand, the *intermarriage* crossover only checks the violation of appended allele value with all other existing feasible values that requires $(l_1 + l_2 + N) + 2l'_1 l'_2$ operations where l_1 and l_2 are the lengths of partial solutions of the parents and l'_1 and l'_2 are length of their non-duplicate allele values. The first expression of time complexity $(l_1 + l_2 + N)$ indicates number of operations required to find the duplicate values. The second expression $2l'_1 l'_2$ indicates the operations required to append the non-duplicate allele values to each other parents. The best time complexity is $2 + N + 2 = N + 4$ operations when lengths of both parents are 1 and the worst time complexity is $(N/2 + N/2 + N) + 2(N/2)(N/2) = 0.5N^2 + 2N$. It is observed that ICHEA's partial solutions quickly attain the size of $N - 1$ or close to it. So two parents with chromosomes of length $N - 1$ is taken for average time complexity which can be calculated as $((N - 1) + (N - 1) + N) + 2(1 \times 1) = 3N$. Hence the average time complexity has the *Big-O* order of $O(N)$. The algorithmic description of ICHEA is given in Appendix (A).

4   Experiments

The motivation behind this research is to show the information extraction and exploitation from constraints can produce the evolutionary solutions more efficiently. We used a toy problem namely N-Queens problem that serves as a classic CSP. Basically, the N-Queens problem can be expressed as placing N queens on N x N chessboard such that no queen is attacked by one another [13]. The first part of the experiment tries to solve N-Queens problem without using any sort of constraints related information/heuristics from the problem. The second part of the experiment does the preprocessing of the chromosomes to work on unique allele values only because same allele value refers to the queens that are in the same row which is a violation of one of the constraints. The idea is to provide as much information about the constraints as possible to the evolutionary search.

4.1   No Exploitation of Information from the Problem

For this test case we compared ICHEA with Differential Evolution (DE), Covariance Matrix Adaptation Evolution Strategy (CMA-ES), standard Genetic Algorithms (GAs) and Non-dominated Sorting GA-II (NSGA-II) [6] that do not use any sort of information from the problem domain. GA is taken from Genetic Algorithms toolbox

Table 1. Comparative test results on no problem specific information extraction

N	CMA-ES [25]	DE [25]	GA	NSGA II	ICHEA
4	456 NFC (SR = 1.00)	134 NFC (SR = 1.00)	367 NFC (SR = 1.00)	93 NFC (SR= 1.00)	39 NFC (SR = 1.00)
5	656 NFC (SR = 1.00)	254 NFC (SR = 1.00)	750 NFC (SR = 1.00)	217 NFC (SR = 1.00)	37 NFC (SR = 1.00)
6	22,013 NFC (SR = 1.00)	1,11,136 NFC (SR = 0.65)	30,086 NFC (SR = 0.75)	694 NFC (SR = 1.00)	51 NFC (SR = 1.00)
7	9,964 NFC (SR = 1.00)	24,338 NFC (SR = 0.95)	1,400 NFC (SR = 1.00)	2631 NFC (SR = 1.00)	34 NFC (SR = 1.00)
8	84,962 NFC (SR = 1.00)	7,576 NFC (SR = 0.75)	3,786 NFC (SR = 0.80)	1273 NFC (SR = 1.00)	41 NFC (SR = 1.00)
9	133,628 NFC (SR = 1.00)	19,296 NFC (SR = 0.50)	18,333 NFC (SR = 0.80)	27,852 NFC (SR = 1.00)	72 NFC (SR = 1.00)
10	263,572 NFC (SR = 0.95)	286,208 NFC (SR = 0.30)	3,300 NFC (SR = 0.30)	1,737 NFC (SR = 1.00)	83 NFC (SR = 1.00)
11	284,382 NFC (SR = 0.95)	68,255 NFC (SR = 0.10)	15,550 NFC (SR = 0.40)	SR = 0.00	132 NFC (SR = 1.00)
12	295,740 NFC (SR = 0.75)	99,120 NFC (SR = 0.25)	23,000 NFC (SR = 0.70)	SR = 0.00	122 NFC (SR = 1.00)
13	376,631 NFC (SR = 0.85)	95,485 NFC (SR = 0.15)	3,400 NFC (SR = 0.10)	SR = 0.00	293 NFC (SR = 1.00)
14	450,654 NFC (SR = 0.85)	160,475 NFC (SR = 0.10)	47,350 NFC (SR = 0.40)	SR = 0.00	308 NFC (SR = 1.00)
15	627,391 NFC (SR = 0.50)	223,425 NFC (SR = 0.10)	95,625 NFC (SR = 0.40)	SR = 0.00	381 NFC (SR = 1.00)

Revision: 1.1.4.2, 2004 available in Matlab 7.0.1 and NSGA II written in C language is taken from [7]. ICHEA has been developed in Java language. The test results for DE and CMA-ES have been taken from [19] where 20 trials for each problem have been taken into account. The test results are based on number of function calls (NFC) and success rate (SR). If the NFC $\geq 2 \times 10^6$ then it is considered that the solution is not found. The experimental set up is discussed below.

— **Fitness Function:** the fitness function is the total violation count and the chromosomes are ranked based on this fitness function. The solution for CSP is to find at least one chromosome with no violation i.e. $fitness(\vec{x}) = 0$.
— **Allele Values:** DE, CMA-ES and GA generate real numbers for allele values but in case of N-queens problem the real numbers are converted into integer values by taking the round off value to calculate the fitness. NSGA II uses binary string representation and ICHEA uses integer values. Candidates can have duplicate allele values.
— **Efficiency Measures:** NFC and SR are used to compare the performance of different algorithms. NFC is simply the total count of objective function invoked by the algorithm. SR is the rate of successful trials for each problem i.e. $SR = successful\ trials / total\ trials$.
— **Parameters:** for all the algorithms population size of 100 is used. Scattered crossover is used for GAs. Mutation rate of 0.1 is used for ICHEA and GAs. All default parametric values are used for NSGA-II.

Table 1 shows the comparative results based on NFC and SR to solve N-queens problem. N denotes the size of the chessboard. It can be observed as the problem size increases the solution quality decreases for all the algorithms except ICHEA. The outcome of the test results clearly shows that ICHEA produces consistent results and dominates other EAs. ICHEA is the most efficient algorithm by getting the lowest NFC and highest success rate (SR = 1.00) for all the problems. GA shows unpredictable results where it usually finds the solution in very few evaluations but if it is stuck in local minima then it is generally not able to find the optimum solution.

Table 2. Comparative test results on after information extraction from the problem

N	SA [19]	TS [19]	GA [19]	GA [10]	PSO [14]	ICHEA (best)	ICHEA (median)	ICHEA (mean)
8	493	182	400	**100**	-	84	119	115
10	948	472	4910	266	-	97	162	**176**
20	-	-	-	2000	5669.7	279	698	**898**
30	2160	4655	91790	2300	-	301	538	**970**
50	2849	22663	1759230	5660	14991.4	729	1190	**2257**
75	6091	81030	571170	6300	-	380	2568	**3393**
100	7873	206910	887770	15600	36199.4	1977	3702	**7595**
200	21708	2399940	2287960	460475	934399	7360	14533	**15489**
300	**24636**	9382620	2774820	-	-	6767	34043	37730

4.2   Information Extraction and Exploitation

The second test case involves utilization of information extraction and exploitation from the N-Queens problem in evolutionary search. Here problem specific chromosomes have been used where only unique integer values are taken into account for chromosomes' allele values. Unique integers ensure that queens are at least in different rows which satisfy a part of constraint for this problem. All the parameter remains same as of the previous experiment. We used Simulated Annealing (SA), Tabu Search (TS), Particle Swarm Optimization (PSO) and GA along with ICHEA for the experiment. The test results of SA, TS and GA is taken from [15] and test results for PSO is taken from [11]. ICHEA does not need to be modified as it has problem independent formulation for its *intermarriage* crossover. Appended allele values are not necessarily unique.

Table 2 shows the comparative test results based on NFC only when some problem specific information has been extracted from the problem. The best, median and mean results for ICHEA have also been shown. There is no changes done in ICHEA and it still performs best in most of the problems (shown in bold). The test results obtained by [8] is also impressive where the authors uses partially matched crossover (PMX) and an unusual selection process where only top two candidates are selected for mating in each generation and rest of the population is replaced by making duplicates of this pair.

5   Discussion

The test results show that EAs can be significantly improved if the chromosomes are designed to be problem specific. The experiment in Section 4.2 shows if only the unique integer value is taken into account for allele values then the solution is converged much earlier for N-Queens problem. Considerable improvement has been seen in GA. The objective here is not to get the best results for N-Queens problem but to show how intelligent an algorithm is. The results in Section 4.1 shows that tested optimization algorithm (DE, CMA-ES, GA and NSGA II) blindly searches for the optimum solution through greedy heuristic search manner without extracting the information from constraints while ICHEA utilizes the information from constraints through its *intermarriage* crossover operator and gets the best results. Test results in Section 4.2 again favor ICHEA. The advantage of ICHEA is that its formulation is problem independent which still extracts enough information from the constraint to solve the problems efficiently. It can be argued that ICHEA also uses problem dependent integer values for N-Queens problem. The novel formulation of ICHEA does not require the generated integer values to be unique. ICHEA works with allele coupling only. So only the definition of constraints and the rules for coupling of two allele values to partially satisfy the constraints need to be provided. It only maintains the population of feasible solutions that drastically reduces the size of the search space.

6   Conclusion

This paper has modeled ICHEA to handle discrete CSPs. It has been demonstrated through N-Queens problem that it outperforms other EAs because it makes use of information from the problems and constraints. The search mechanism of ICHEA is guided by constraints where it concentrates in the feasible regions of constraint satisfaction sets to get the solution without putting extra computational effort in searching through the whole search space. N-Queens is a toy problem that does not have complex constraints structure as in some real world problems like university time tabling, vehicle routing etc. Future work consists of modeling ICHEA to provide problem independent solution for problems that have different constraint strengths. ICHEA will be further tested on mixed CSP where problem domain constitutes both continuous and discrete constraints.

Acknowledgment. We would like to thank Dr. Cecil Schmidt of Washburn University, Topeka for providing the code for GA to solve N-Queens problem from his work in [8].

References

1. Bandyopadhyay, S., Pal, S.K.: Pixel classification using variable string genetic algorithms with chromosome differentiation. IEEE Transactions on Geoscience and Remote Sensing 39(2), 303–308 (2001)
2. Coello, C.A.C.: A Comprehensive Survey of Evolutionary-Based Multiobjective Optimization Techniques. Knowledge and Information Systems 1, 269–308 (1998)
3. Coello Coello, C.A.: Theoretical and numerical constraint-handling techniques used with evolutionary algorithms: a survey of the state of the art. Computer Methods in Applied Mechanics and Engineering 191(11-12), 1245–1287 (2002)
4. Craenen, B.G.W., et al.: Comparing evolutionary algorithms on binary constraint satisfaction problems. IEEE Transactions on Evolutionary Computation 7(5), 424–444 (2003)
5. Craenen, B.G.W.: Solving constraint satisfaction problems with evolutionary algorithms. Phd Dissertation, Vrije Universiteit (2005)
6. Deb, K., et al.: A fast and elitist multiobjective genetic algorithm: NSGA-II. IEEE Transactions on Evolutionary Computation 6(2), 182–197 (2002)
7. Deb, K.: Kanpur Genetic Algorithms Laboratory,
   http://www.iitk.ac.in/kangal/codes.shtml
8. Eastridge, R., Schmidt, C.: Solving n-queens with a genetic algorithm and its usefulness in a computational intelligence course. J. Comput. Sci. Coll. 23(4), 223–230 (2008)
9. Eiben, A.E., et al.: Solving Binary Constraint Satisfaction Problems Using Evolutionary Algorithms with an Adaptive Fitness Function. In: Eiben, A.E., Bäck, T., Schoenauer, M., Schwefel, H.-P. (eds.) PPSN 1998. LNCS, vol. 1498, pp. 201–210. Springer, Heidelberg (1998)
10. Fonseca, C.M., Fleming, P.J.: Genetic Algorithms for Multiobjective Optimization: Formulation, Discussion and Generalization. In: Proceedings of the 5th International Conference on Genetic Algorithms, pp. 416–423. Morgan Kaufmann Publishers Inc., San Francisco (1993)

11. Hu, X., et al.: Swarm intelligence for permutation optimization: a case study of n-queens problem. In: Proceedings of the 2003 IEEE Swarm Intelligence Symposium, SIS 2003, pp. 243–246 (2003)
12. Kramer, O.: A Review of Constraint-Handling Techniques for Evolution Strategies. In: Applied Computational Intelligence and Soft Computing 2010, pp. 1–11 (2010)
13. Letavec, R.: The Queens Problem - Delta. ITE 2(3), 101–103 (2002)
14. Liu, H., et al.: Hybridizing particle swarm optimization with differential evolution for constrained numerical and engineering optimization. Appl. Soft Comput., 629–640 (2010)
15. Martinjak, I., Golub, M.: Comparison of Heuristic Algorithms for the N-Queen Problem. In: 29th International Conference on Information Technology Interfaces, ITI 2007, pp. 759–764 (2007)
16. Mezura-montes, E., Coello, C.A.C.: A Survey of Constraint-Handling Techniques Based on Evolutionary Multiobjective Optimization, Departamento de Computación, Evolutionary Computation Group at CINVESTAV (2006)
17. Michalewicz, Z., Schoenauer, M.: Evolutionary algorithms for constrained parameter optimization problems. Evolutionary Computation 4(1), 1–32 (1996)
18. Paredis, J.: Co-evolutionary Constraint Satisfaction. In: Davidor, Y., Männer, R., Schwefel, H.-P. (eds.) PPSN 1994. LNCS, vol. 866, pp. 46–55. Springer, Heidelberg (1994)
19. Rahnamayan, S., Dieras, P.: Efficiency competition on N-queen problem: DE vs. CMA-ES. In: Canadian Conference on Electrical and Computer Engineering, CCECE 2008, pp. 000033–000036. IEEE (2008)
20. Schaffer, J.D.: Multiple Objective Optimization with Vector Evaluated Genetic Algorithms. In: Proceedings of the 1st International Conference on Genetic Algorithms, pp. 93–100. L. Erlbaum Associates Inc. (1985)
21. Shang, Y., Fromherz, M.P.J.: Experimental complexity analysis of continuous constraint satisfaction problems. Information Sciences 153, 1–36 (2003)
22. Sharma, A.: A new optimizing algorithm using reincarnation concept. In: 2010 11th IEEE International Symposium on Computational Intelligence and Informatics (CINTI), pp. 281–288. Springer, Heidelberg (2010)
23. Sharma, A., Omlin, C.W.: Performance Comparison of Particle Swarm Optimization with Traditional Clustering Algorithms used in Self-Organizing Map. International Journal of Computational Intelligence 5(1), 1–12 (2009)
24. Sharma, A., Sharma, D.: ICHEA – A Constraint Guided Search for Improving Evolutionary Algorithms. In: Huang, T., Zeng, Z., Li, C., Leung, C.S. (eds.) ICONIP 2012, Part I. LNCS, vol. 7663, pp. 269–279. Springer, Heidelberg (2012)
25. Srinivas, N., Deb, K.: Muiltiobjective optimization using nondominated sorting in genetic algorithms. Evolutionary Computation 2, 221–248 (1994)
26. Van Veldhuizen, D.A., Lamont, G.B.: Multiobjective Evolutionary Algorithms: Analyzing the State-of-the-Art. Evolutionary Computation 8, 125–147 (2000)
27. De Weck, O., Kim, I.Y.: Variable Chromosome Length Genetic Algorithm for Structural Topology Design Optimization. Strain. In: AIAA 2004, pp. 1–12 (April 2004)

Appendix

A) ICHEA Algorithm

ICHEA is another variation of EA that has been introduced in [24] adds constraint handling features for continuous CSPs to the standard GAs. Because of space limitations we are only describing the changes in ICHEA accommodated to make it compatible for discrete CSPs. The pseudocode can be given as:

```
chromosomes  = initializeChromosomes();
for each generation
  parents = TournamentSelection();
  offspring = interMarriageCrossover(parents);
  Mutation(offspring);
  chromosomes = chromosomes + offspring;
  SortAndReplace();
  CheckTerminationCriteria();
End for loop;
```

The description of changed subroutines is given below:

InitializeChromosomes: The population of chromosomes is generated using sequence of integer values $\langle 1, 2, ..., |pop| \rangle$ with the modulus operator (mod) as shown below:

$$\vec{x}_i = mod(counter, |pop|) + 1 \tag{8}$$

where $counter$ is initialized with 0 that is always incremented by 1 for each chromosome and $|pop|$ is the population size. The length of initialized chromosome is 1.

TournamentSelection: Here novelty selection is incorporated along with fitness based selection as described in [24] but the selection of chromosomes is based on the following order of preference:
1. Its fitness in the search space
2. If fitness is same then higher novelty value
3. If novelty is same then a chromosome is picked randomly

InterMarriageCrossover: The crossover techniques have been described in Section 3.

Mutation: ICHEA uses *swap* mutation for permutations.

SortAndReplace: According to [14] the lower the individuals' degree of constraint violation, the higher the probability that it clusters together around the current best solution and individuals with lower degrees of constraint violations are very difficult to jump out of current best individual's adjacent region. This may cause the current best individual to stay on the same position for a long time leading to loss of diversity in the population. To avoid this scenario the ICHEA keeps the fair share of all levels of fitness in the population. If the population pop of size $|pop|$ has m constraints in the problem of size n then the whole population is divided into equal sized $\lfloor \sigma n \rfloor$ slots where σ is in the range of (0.1 1.0). $\sigma = 0.1$ is used in the experiments. Slot i

is allocated to individuals based on its fitness value $fitness(\vec{p}) = n - |\vec{p}|$ from Eq. (7) where $i = \lfloor \sigma(n - |\vec{p}|) \rfloor + 1$. If slot i remains empty then its allocated space is evenly distributed to other slots. Let pop_i indicate the population of individuals that belong to slot i so the total population is:

$$pop = \sum_{i=1}^{\lfloor \sigma n \rfloor} pop_i$$

Then pop_i is sorted according to the fitness and the best $|pop|/\lfloor \sigma n \rfloor$ is selected for subpopulation pop_i.

$$\therefore \max (|pop_i|) = |pop|/\lfloor \sigma n \rfloor$$

If after allocation, k slots have $|pop_i| < |pop|/\lfloor \sigma n \rfloor$, then unallocated population of individuals $pop_{unalloc}$ is:

$$pop_{unalloc} = \sum_{i=1}^{m} \begin{cases} |pop|/\lfloor \sigma n \rfloor - |pop_i|, & if \ |pop_i| < |pop|/\lfloor \sigma n \rfloor \\ 0 & , \ otherwise \end{cases}$$

This unallocated population $pop_{unalloc}$ needs to be allocated evenly in the slots that have $|pop_i| > |pop|/\lfloor \sigma n \rfloor$.

Once the chromosomes are sorted a *random death* concept is used defined in [22] to delete some predefined number of chromosomes randomly from the population. The certain top percentage of the population is spared to control the search focus.

CheckTerminationCriteria: The iteration is stopped when:

1. The maximum number of generation is reached or
2. The CSP solution is found or
3. The process is stalled by no improvement in the solution for some generations.

Anytime Column Search

Satya Gautam Vadlamudi[1], Piyush Gaurav[1], Sandip Aine[2],
and Partha Pratim Chakrabarti[1]

[1] Indian Institute of Technology Kharagpur, Kharagpur WB 721302, India
{satya,ppchak}@cse.iitkgp.ernet.in
[2] Carnegie Mellon University, Pittsburgh PA 15213, USA
asandip@andrew.cmu.edu

Abstract. Anytime heuristic search algorithms are widely applied where best-first search algorithms such as A* require large or often unacceptable amounts of time and memory. Anytime algorithms produce a solution quickly and iteratively improve the solution quality. In this paper, we propose novel anytime heuristic search algorithms with a common underlying strategy called Column Search. The proposed algorithms are complete and guarantee to produce an optimal solution. Experimental results on sliding-tile puzzle problem, traveling salesman problem, and robotic arm trajectory planning problem show the efficacy of proposed methods compared to state-of-the-art anytime heuristic search algorithms.

Keywords: problem solving, heuristic search, anytime algorithms.

1 Introduction

Heuristic search is a generic problem solving technique studied in Artificial Intelligence (AI). A* [8] is the most well-known heuristic search algorithm which has been widely used to solve several problems involving path planning and combinatorial optimization. It explores the state space with the help of two lists: OpenList and ClosedList which contain the nodes to be expanded and the nodes that are already expanded respectively. Initially, OpenList comprises of the start node. Each node has a g-value denoting its distance from the start node and an h-value that estimates its distance to a goal node. The promise of a node n called as f-value equals $g(n) + h(n)$. Most promising node from the OpenList is expanded and added to ClosedList by A* till a goal node is found. A* is an optimal algorithm that expands minimum number of nodes to find an optimal solution, when admissible heuristics are used. However, on large problems, the number of nodes which need to be expanded may be exponential in nature, which makes A* ineffective to use in such cases.

Anytime search algorithms are pursued to address this issue. They quickly generate a solution and then produce improved quality solutions with the progress of time. Several anytime algorithms were proposed based on A*. Anytime Weighted A* [6,7] uses weighted heuristics while evaluating f-values of nodes, which helps in converging to suboptimal solutions quickly, and the search is continued to produce results in an anytime manner. Anytime Restricted A* (ARA*) [11] follows similar concept but decreases weights after each iteration to improve the performance.

M. Thielscher and D. Zhang (Eds.): AI 2012, LNCS 7691, pp. 254–265, 2012.

Anytime Nonparametric A* (ANA*) [15] improvises on ARA* by analyzing the theory behind the greedy approach followed by ARA* and gets rid of the weight-parameter tuning.

On the other hand, algorithms that do not rely on heuristic manipulation (via weights, like above) such as depth-first branch and bound (DFBB) [10] are also used as anytime algorithms. Beam search [4] is another such simple algorithm that is widely used which gives an approximate solution. It expands beam-width number of most promising nodes at each level (depth of the search tree) until a solution is found or the depth limit of the search tree is reached, where beam-width is taken as the input parameter. However, it is not complete. Beam-stack search [17] is proposed to complete beam search which also gives anytime performance. It uses a novel data structure called beam-stack to keep track of the nodes being expanded and the ones to be expanded by chronological backtracking, and also works within the given beam-width.

Anytime Window A* (AWA*) [2] is another recent anytime algorithm which uses a window based cutoff for the nodes to be present in open list. It ensures completeness by maintaining a suspend list for nodes that are being removed from open list which are considered for expansion (brought back to open list) at a later point in time. Later, Memory-bounded Anytime Window A* (MAWA*) [14] was proposed based on AWA* and Memory-bounded A* (MA*) [5] to be able to work in restricted memory conditions.

In this paper, we propose a novel yet simple anytime heuristic search algorithm called Anytime Column Search (ACS) that is complete, which takes the column-width as parameter. We also explore several non-parametric versions of the proposed algorithm. The basic idea is to explore column-width number of most promising nodes at each level and put them in closed list, and repeat this until the open lists of all levels become empty. The concept is intuitive and augurs well with anytime objectives such as finding initial solution quickly and improving it with the progress of time.

ACS is similar to beam search up-to an extent, however, we choose a different name from 'beam' as it is traditionally related (and hence expected) to be working within the given beam-width. While beam search can be highly non-monotonic [1], ACS promises to recover from such effect faced in its first iteration as it continues the search in an admissible manner. Most importantly, it does not involve any re-expansions of the same node, which distinguishes it from algorithms such as naive iterative beam search and complete anytime beam search. For example, complete anytime beam search [16] adopts iterative weakening strategy, *restarting* beam search with weaker pruning rules in each iteration, which results in node re-expansions.

Apart from the anytime performance, ACS also has an unique ability of reporting solutions at regular intervals (due to bounded number of node expansions in each iteration). This feature can also be exploited for using it in a contract search environment [3]. Since it looks at nodes at all levels in each iteration, it can be expected to return best possible solution in a given iteration with the corresponding bound on the number of node expansions.

The rest of the paper is organized as follows: In Section 2, we present the proposed methods which includes Anytime Column Search and its non-parametric variants. In Section 3, we present the experimental results of proposed algorithms obtained on the benchmark problems of three different domains compared with various state-of-the-art anytime heuristic search algorithms. We conclude in Section 4.

2   Proposed Methods

In this section, we present the proposed anytime heuristic search algorithms. Firstly, we present the Anytime Column Search (ACS) algorithm which takes column-width w as parameter. Later, we describe its non-parametric variants.

2.1   Anytime Column Search (ACS)

Anytime Column Search is a simple and complete anytime heuristic search algorithm. It takes column-width w as parameter and expands w most promising nodes of *OpenList* at each level in each iteration and puts them in *ClosedList* until a goal node is found. Visually, the set of nodes expanded in each iteration form a *column* (see Figure 1). One may also look at it as a sliding window moving from left to right.

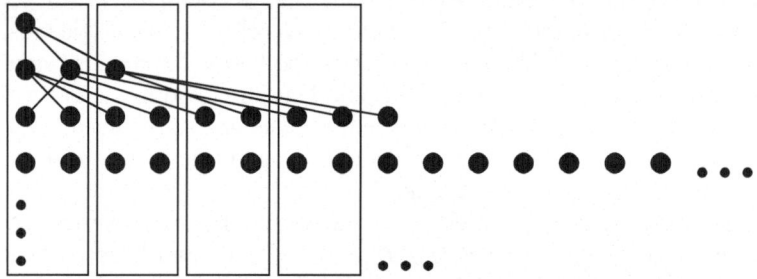

Fig. 1. Progress of ACS_2 on a typical search tree

When using admissible heuristics, the best solution obtained in anytime manner can be used as cutoff as the search progresses (admissible pruning). We denote ACS instance with column-width w as ACS_w. Figure 1 shows the progress of ACS_2 on a typical search tree. Four columns, each of width 2, are shown which are explored from left to right. No edge goes from a given column to any column on its left side on a search *tree* as the right-side columns appear only after the complete exploration of the left-side columns and no node is re-expanded.

ACS_1 is particularly interesting for the following reason: Anytime algorithms are aimed at achieving two main targets, a quick solution, and frequent improved solutions with the progress of time. In this scenario, ACS_1 appears to be a simple base level anytime algorithm which promises both the initial quick solution and frequent solution improvements (even attempted to be regular in time) which looks at the states of all levels in each iteration (hence appearing to be more informed and calculated while trying to produce the next solution in anytime manner).

Algorithm 1. Anytime Column Search (ACS)

1: **INPUT ::** A search graph G, a start node s, and column-width w.
2: $BestSol \leftarrow \infty; g(s) \leftarrow 0$; Calculate $f(s); Level(s) \leftarrow 0$;
   $OpenList(0) \leftarrow \{s\}; OpenList(i) \leftarrow \phi, \forall i (0 < i < MAX\_DEPTH)$;
   $ClosedList \leftarrow \phi$;
3: **while** $\exists i \; OpenList(i) \neq \phi$ **do**
4:   **for** $i = 0$ to $MAX\_DEPTH - 1$ **do**
5:     **for** w number of times **do**
6:       **if** $OpenList(i) = \phi$ **then**
7:         **break**;
8:       **end if**
9:       $n \leftarrow$ least f-valued node from $OpenList(i)$; (for minimization problem)
10:       **if** IsGoal(n) **then**
11:         **if** $BestSol > f(n)$ **then**
12:           $BestSol \leftarrow f(n); Goal \leftarrow n$;
13:         **end if**
14:         Move n from $OpenList(i)$ to $ClosedList$;
15:         **continue**;
16:       **end if**
17:       **GenerateChildren**(n);
18:       Move n from $OpenList(i)$ to $ClosedList$;
19:     **end for**
20:   **end for**
21: **end while**
22: **return** $BestSol, Goal$;

ACS Details: Algorithm 1 presents the proposed method ACS. It maintains different $OpenLists$ for nodes at different levels. As long as there exists a non-empty list, it expands w most promising nodes at each level from depth 0 till the maximum allowed depth. It does not assume that the heuristic being used is admissible. When admissible heuristics are being used, one can perform a check after line 9 as to whether the f-value of node being explored is less than the best solution or not. If the f-value is greater than or equal to that of current best solution (in case of a minimization problem), the node can be pruned admissibly, and the search can be moved to next level.

$GenerateChildren$ routine (Algorithm 2) generates all successors of the input node and checks for their existence already in doing so. If a successor exists with a better path from start node already, then it is not disturbed. When using admissible heuristics, f-value of a child can be checked against $BestSol$ before it is inserted into the corresponding $OpenList$ and the child node can be pruned admissibly if the f-value exceeds $BestSol$.

Algorithm 2. GenerateChildren

1: **INPUT ::** Node n whose children are to be generated, and the lists.
2: **if** $Level(n) = MAX\_DEPTH - 1$ **then**
3:    **return**;
4: **end if**
5: **for** each successor n' of n **do**
6:    **if** n' is not $OpenLists$ and $ClosedLists$ **then**
7:       $Level(n') \leftarrow Level(n) + 1$;
8:       Insert n' to $OpenList(Level(n'))$;
9:    **else if** $g(n') <$ its previous g-value **then**
10:       Update $Level(n'), g(n'), f(n')$;
11:       Insert n' to $OpenList(Level(n'))$;
12:    **end if**
13: **end for**

Theorem 1. *ACS is complete and guarantees terminating with an optimal solution, provided MAX_DEPTH is at least as large as the number of nodes on a minimum-length optimal solution path and the search is not constrained by the memory available.*

Proof. The complete search graph is explored in a column by column manner up-to the maximum depth limit given. Pruning of nodes is only done when using admissible heuristics where the f-values of corresponding nodes are found out to be greater than or equal to that of best solution obtained, which is admissible. Therefore, no potential node exists which is left unexpanded, that can lead to a better solution than that of the final solution.   □

Lemma 1. *ACS does not re-expand any node unless a better path has been found from the start node to that node.*

Note that, the node expansions in the first iteration are same as that of beam search with beam-width w. In that sense, the ACS algorithm can be viewed as another way of making beam search anytime and complete.

Another point to note is that, the ACS algorithm takes column-width w as parameter, and its anytime performance will depend on this input parameter. We present the comparison of ACS instances with different column-widths in Section 3. Column-width can be chosen such that the solutions are reported at required intervals (assuming that goal nodes are found as higher depths are explored, an estimate of the intervals at which a better solution can be expected may be calculated for a particular column-width).

In this paper, we also present non-parametric versions of ACS using simple modifications which are explained next.

2.2   Anytime Column Progressive Search (ACPS)

ACS algorithm expands w nodes from $OpenList$ at each level in each iteration, where w is taken as input parameter. The idea in Anytime Column Progressive

Search (ACPS) is to progressively increase w from an initial value of 1 by a value of 1 in each iteration. It means that the column-width in i^{th} iteration in case of ACPS is i (in contrast to column-width being w in all iterations in case of ACS). The algorithm is clearly a non-parametric version of ACS.

2.3   Anytime Column Scaling Search (ACSS)

Instead of increasing column-width by 1 in each iteration, one may greedily reset the column-width to 1 whenever a solution is found, in the hope of obtaining a better solution with lower number of node expansions next time. We call the algorithm with this idea as Anytime Column Scaling Search (ACSS). It increases its column-width by 1 in each iteration as long as better solution is not obtained and resets the column-width to 1 whenever a better solution is found. Such a reset technique was also used in [13] on top of Anytime Window A*.

2.4   Anytime Column Adaptive Search (ACAS)

Another way of handling column-width is as follows: Initialize column-width to 1; do not change the column-width as long as better solutions are found with that column-width; when a better solution is not found in an iteration using the column-width, increase it by 1. We call the algorithm with this strategy as Anytime Column Adaptive Search (ACAS). The motivation is that, perhaps it is necessary to expand at-least the current number of nodes to get an improved solution, while also hoping that it is sufficient. When it is found to be not sufficient (better solution is not found), the column-width is increased.

Next, we present the experimental analysis of proposed methods and their comparison with some of the state-of-the-art anytime heuristic search algorithms.

3   Experimental Results

In this section, we present the experimental results comparing the proposed algorithms against several existing anytime algorithms, namely, Depth-first Branch and Bound (DFBB) [10], Beam-Stack search [17], Anytime Window A* (AWA*) [2], Anytime Repairing A* (ARA*) [11], and Anytime Non-parametric A* (ANA*) [15]. All the experiments have been performed on a Dell Precision T7500 Tower Workstation with Intel Xeon 5600 Series at 3.47-GHz $\times$ 12 and 192-GB RAM. We display the results in terms of a metric called % *Optimal Closeness*, which is defined as (for a minimization problem, this metric suggests how close the obtained solution is to an optimal solution):

% *Optimal Closeness* = (*Optimal   sol./Obtained   sol.*) $\times$ 100.

3.1   Sliding-Tile Puzzle Problem

For our experiments, we have considered all 50 24-puzzle instances from Korf et al. [9, Table II] which are referred to with the same index number by which they were presented, prefixed with K. Manhattan distance heuristic is used as the heuristic estimation function (which underestimates the actual distance to goal). All algorithms are allowed to explore up-to a maximum depth of 1000.

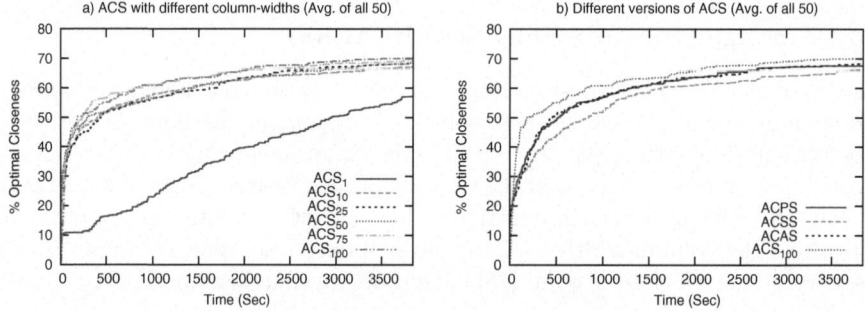

Fig. 2. Comparison of anytime performance of proposed algorithms against each other on the (Sliding-tile) 24-Puzzle instances

Figure 2 presents the comparison of anytime performances of proposed algorithms against each other on the 24-Puzzle instances. This is presented to show the effect of column-width parameter on the performance of ACS as well as to find the best working algorithm for the 24-puzzle domain. From the plots, one can see that ACS_{100} outperforms the other instances. Also note that, performances with column-widths ≥ 10 are very similar which may be due to the low branching factor of the puzzle problem.

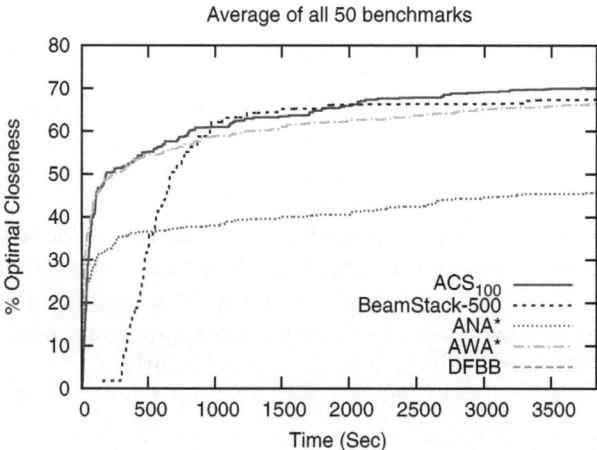

Fig. 3. Comparison of anytime performance of ACS_{100} with some of the existing anytime algorithms on the (Sliding-tile) 24-Puzzle instances. DFBB could not come up with any solution on any of the instances.

Figure 3 presents the comparison of anytime performance of ACS_{100} with some of the state-of-the-art anytime algorithms on the (Sliding-tile) 24-Puzzle instances. At initial stages, ACS outperforms beam stack search and is comparable to AWA* (up-to 1000 Sec.), and at the later stages beam stack search becomes good but ACS remains comparable. Note that, beam stack search is affected by the initial lag due to time taken by beam search with such large beam-width, which is the first step of beam-stack search. When lower beam-widths are used to plug the initial lag of Beam-stack search, it resulted in the degradation of its anytime performance through out the 1 hour window.

Table 1. Comparison of different algorithms on the 50 (Sliding-tile) 24-Puzzle benchmarks

Top Count vs. **Time** (Mins.)									
Algorithm	1	2	4	8	12	16	24	32	48	64
ACS_{100}	22	25	22	18	11	9	10	14	19	17
BeamStack-500	0	0	1	19	30	34	33	29	23	24
ANA*	7	6	4	3	1	0	0	0	2	1
AWA*	19	19	23	12	11	10	10	11	12	14
DFBB	0	0	0	0	0	0	0	0	0	0

Table 1 presents the comparison of different algorithms on Puzzle problem based on the Top count. Top count indicates the number of times an algorithm has produced the best solution in the corresponding column (time) over all 50 24-Puzzle benchmarks of [9]. This measure gives a complementary picture to the plots showing the average values by showing the number of instances on which an algorithm has been found better than others (at different time instants). Note that, the average value of an algorithm may become high if it outperforms other algorithms significantly on a corner case whereas it may be bad in a number of other cases. Such cases can be detected via *Top Count*. Note that, on any instance, multiple algorithms may produce the best solution in a given time. On two instances, none of the algorithms could produce a solution in 1 Minute within the depth of 1000. Clearly, beam stack search outperforms all the other algorithms in this domain once it starts producing the solutions (after 4 Mins.). However, using lower beam-width values to produce the first solution quickly has degraded its anytime performance over the whole window, in which cases ACS came out on top.

3.2   Traveling Salesman Problem

We chose the first 50 symmetric TSPs (when sorted in increasing order of their sizes) from the traveling salesman problem library (TSPLIB) [12] for our experiments. These range from burma14 to gr202 where the numerical postfixes denote the size of the TSPs. Minimum spanning tree (MST) heuristic is used as the heuristic estimation function (which is an under-estimating heuristic). In the initial state, some city c is chosen as the starting point and in each successive state the next city n to be visited is chosen (which is not already visited) till all cities are visited.

TSP was often looked as a tree search problem, however, careful examination suggests that if two states denote paths from c to n through a same set of cities S, then only the best of the two need to be pursued further and the other one can be admissibly pruned. This change resulted in tremendous improvement in terms of search state space as well as the anytime performance and the time taken for termination for all heuristic search algorithms. The results obtained with this procedure are presented here. Note that, this may also be looked as a graph search state-space with the state being represented by $\{c, n, S\}$ rather than the traditional way of using the path as the signature of a state (which can just be maintained as an attribute in the current states).

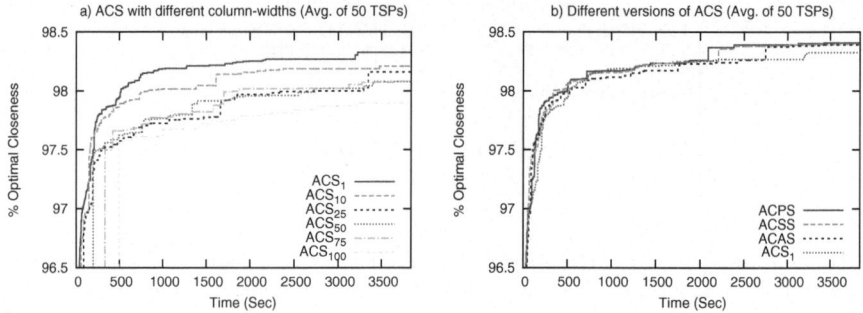

Fig. 4. Comparison of anytime performance of proposed algorithms against each other on various TSP instances

Figure 4 presents the comparison of anytime performance of proposed algorithms against each other on various TSP instances. This is presented to show the effect of column-width parameter on the performance of ACS as well as to find the best working algorithm for the TSP domain. It is interesting to note that ACS_1 outperforms the instances with greater column-widths which shows that in certain cases it is indeed sufficient to expand one column at a time to achieve good anytime performance. From the plots, one can see that all the algorithms are quite effective, and hence we choose ACPS which is the simplest non-parametric algorithm for comparison with the other algorithms.

Figure 5 presents the comparison of anytime performance of ACPS with some of the state-of-the-art anytime algorithms on the TSP instances. Note that, its performance is superior than that of the other algorithms. Only AWA* and Beam-stack search give comparable performances of which Beam-stack algorithm suffers from the initial lag which is explained in Section 3.1. Note that, using larger beam-width for beam-stack algorithm resulted in unacceptable amount of lag at the beginning (delay in producing its first solution).

Table 2 presents the comparison of different algorithms on TSP instances based on the Top count. Top count (whose significance is explained in Section 3.1) indicates the number of times an algorithm has produced the best solution in

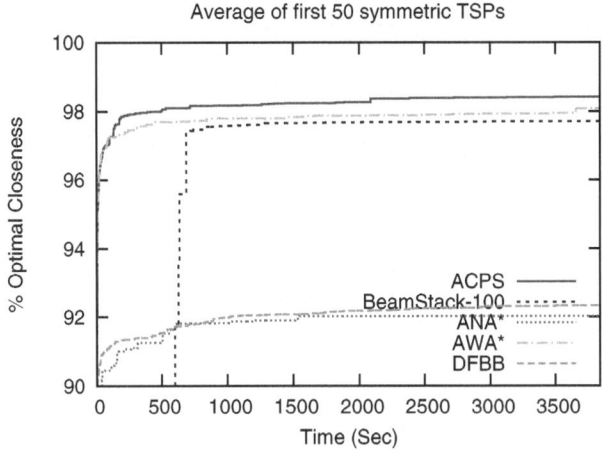

Fig. 5. Comparison of anytime performance of ACPS and the existing search algorithms on various TSP instances

Table 2. Comparison of different algorithms on the 50 TSP benchmarks

Algorithm	Top Count vs. **Time** (Mins.)									
	1	**2**	**4**	**8**	**12**	**16**	**24**	**32**	**48**	**64**
ACPS	**35**	**32**	**35**	**36**	**40**	**41**	**41**	**41**	**42**	**42**
BeamStack-100	21	22	26	26	26	27	28	27	27	27
ANA*	13	11	13	13	12	12	12	13	13	13
AWA*	28	**32**	27	29	29	28	27	27	31	30
DFBB	8	10	10	11	11	11	11	11	11	12

the corresponding column (time) over the 50 TSP benchmarks considered. Note that, on any instance, multiple algorithms may produce the best solution in a given time. Performance of ACPS is clearly better than that of all the other algorithms.

3.3   Robotic-Arm Trajectory Planning

We consider both the 6-degree-of-freedom (DOF) arm instances and the 20-DOF arm instances which are available in Likhachev's software library[1], with fixed base in a 2D environment with obstacles. The objective is to move the end-effector from its initial location to a goal location while avoiding obstacles. An action is defined as a change of a global angle of any particular joint. Cost of each action is taken as one. The environment is discretized into a 50x50 2D grid. Joint angles are discretized so as to never move the end-effector by more than one cell on the 50x50 grid in a single action. The heuristic is calculated as the shortest distance from the current location of the end-effector to the goal location that avoids obstacles (which is an underestimating heuristic).

---

[1] `http://www.cs.cmu.edu/~maxim/software.html`

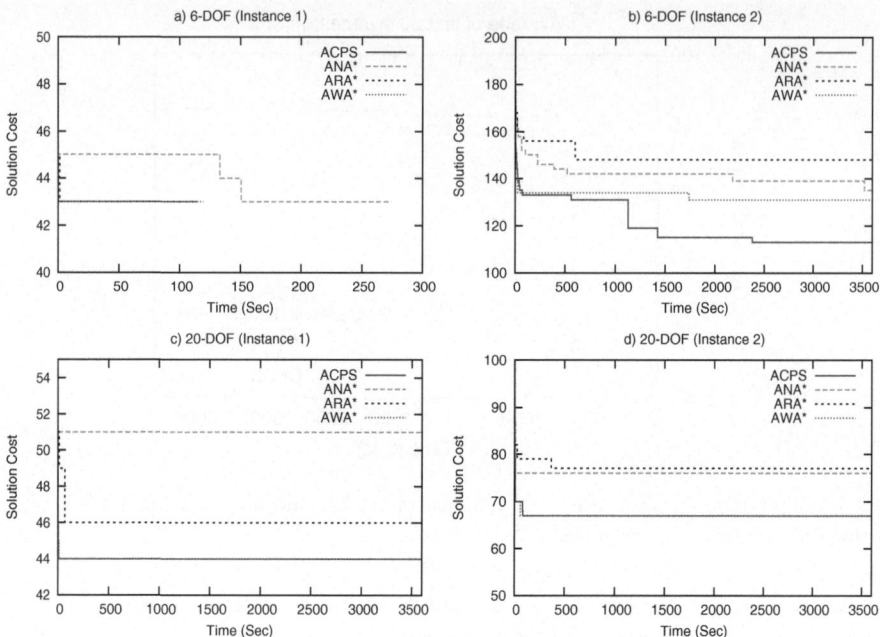

Fig. 6. Comparison of anytime performance of ACPS and the existing search algorithms on various robotic-arm trajectory planning benchmarks

We compared our algorithm ACPS (which gave the best performance in ACS family methods) with the anytime algorithms: ARA*, ANA*, and AWA*, of which ARA* and ANA* implementations came with the software to which we added our implementations of ACS family algorithms and AWA* for comparison. Figure 6 shows the results obtained on the four robotic-arm instances considered (a total of only 5 benchmarks were available out of which the results of a 6-DOF instance are not presented here due to space constraints, which were observed to be similar). Here, the actual cost of the solution is used in the plots instead of % *Optimal Closeness* as the optimal solutions are not available for all instances to compute the closeness. The parameters of ARA*: ϵ_0 and $\Delta\epsilon$ are tuned for best performance. $\Delta\epsilon$ is set to 0.2 as recommended in [11] and ϵ_0 is tested with various values $\in [2, 100]$, out of which the best performance was found at 5, which is used in the plots. Clearly, the performance of ACPS is either comparable or better than that of the other algorithms in this case as well.

4   Conclusion

In this paper, we present a simple and efficient anytime heuristic search algorithm called Anytime Column Search (ACS). ACS takes column-width as parameter for its working and guarantees to find optimal solution. Non-parametric versions of ACS are also presented which also demonstrates how it can be easily tuned as per the working dómain. Experimental results on Sliding-tile puzzle problem, Traveling salesman problem (TSP), and Robotic arm trajectory planning demonstrate that the anytime performance of the proposed methods is either superior or comparable to that of state-of-the-art anytime heuristic search algorithms.

Acknowledgement. S. G. Vadlamudi thanks SAP Labs India for their support through Doctoral Fellowship.

References

1. Aine, S., Chakrabarti, P.P.: An analysis of breadth-first beam search using uniform cost trees. In: The Eleventh International Symposium on Artificial Intelligence and Mathematics (January 2010)
2. Aine, S., Chakrabarti, P.P., Kumar, R.: AWA* - A window constrained anytime heuristic search algorithm. In: Veloso, M.M. (ed.) IJCAI, pp. 2250–2255 (2007)
3. Aine, S., Chakrabarti, P.P., Kumar, R.: Heuristic search under contract. Computational Intelligence 26(4), 386–419 (2010)
4. Bisiani, R.: Beam search. In: Encyclopedia of Articial Intelligence, pp. 56–58 (1987)
5. Chakrabarti, P.P., Ghose, S., Acharya, A., Sarkar, S.C.D.: Heuristic search in restricted memory. Artificial Intelligence 41(2), 197–221 (1989)
6. Hansen, E.A., Zhou, R.: Anytime heuristic search. J. Artif. Int. Res. 28(1), 267–297 (2007)
7. Hansen, E.A., Zilberstein, S., Danilchenko, V.A.: Anytime heuristic search: First results. Technical Report 50, Univ. of Massachusetts (1997)
8. Hart, P.E., Nilsson, N.J., Raphael, B.: A formal basis for the heuristic determination of minimum cost paths. IEEE Transactions on Systems Science and Cybernetics 4(2), 100–107 (1968)
9. Korf, R.E., Felner, A.: Disjoint pattern database heuristics. Artif. Intell. 134(1-2), 9–22 (2002)
10. Lawler, E.L., Wood, D.E.: Branch-and-bound methods: A survey. Operational Research 14(4), 699–719 (1966)
11. Likhachev, M., Gordon, G.J., Thrun, S.: ARA*: Anytime A* with provable bounds on sub-optimality. In: Advances in Neural Information Processing Systems, vol. 16. MIT Press, Cambridge (2004)
12. Reinelt, G.: TSPLIB - A traveling salesman problem library. ORSA Journal on Computing 3, 376–384 (1991)
13. Thayer, J.T., Ruml, W.: Anytime heuristic search: Frameworks and algorithms. In: SOCS (2010)
14. Vadlamudi, S.G., Aine, S., Chakrabarti, P.P.: MAWA*—A memory-bounded anytime heuristic-search algorithm. IEEE Transactions on Systems, Man, and Cybernetics, Part B: Cybernetics 41(3), 725–735 (2011)
15. van den Berg, J., Shah, R., Huang, A., Goldberg, K.Y.: Anytime nonparametric A*. In: AAAI (2011)
16. Zhang, W.: Complete anytime beam search. In: Proceedings of 14th National Conference of Artificial Intelligence AAAI 1998, pp. 425–430. AAAI Press (1998)
17. Zhou, R., Hansen, E.A.: Beam-stack search: Integrating backtracking with beam search. In: Proceedings of the 15th International Conference on Automated Planning and Scheduling (ICAPS 2005), Monterey, CA, pp. 90–98 (2005)

Genetic Programming for Biomarker Detection in Mass Spectrometry Data

Soha Ahmed[1], Mengjie Zhang[1], and Lifeng Peng[2]

[1] School of Engineering and Computer Science
[2] School of Biological Sciences
Victoria University of Wellington, PO Box 600, Wellington 6140, New Zealand
{soha.ahmed,mengjie.zhang}@ecs.vuw.ac.nz, lifeng.peng@vuw.ac.nz

Abstract. Classification of mass spectrometry (MS) data is an essential step for biomarker detection which can help in diagnosis and prognosis of diseases. However, due to the high dimensionality and the small sample size, classification of MS data is very challenging. The process of biomarker detection can be referred to as feature selection and classification in terms of machine learning. Genetic programming (GP) has been widely used for classification and feature selection, but it has not been effectively applied to biomarker detection in the MS data. In this study we develop a GP based approach to feature selection, feature extraction and classification of mass spectrometry data for biomarker detection. In this approach, we firstly use GP to reduce the "redundant" features by selecting a small number of important features and constructing high-level features, then we use GP to classify the data based on selected features and constructed features. This approach is examined and compared with three well known machine learning methods namely decision trees, naive Bayes and support vector machines on two biomarker detection data sets. The results show that the proposed GP method can effectively select a small number of important features from thousands of original features for these problems, the constructed high-level features can further improve the classification performance, and the GP method outperforms the three existing methods, namely naive Bayes, SVMs and J48, on these problems.

1 Introduction

Mass spectrometry (MS) is a method that measures the mass-to-charge ratio (m/z) of charged particles or ions [4]. It is used for the identification of compounds such as peptides and other chemical compounds. The MS main schema works by ionizing chemical compounds to generate charged molecules or molecule fragments and measures their m/z ratios. MS also enables large-scale discovery of candidates for biomarkers which are in terms of machine learning the features selected to discriminate between different categories which indicate biological processes and pharmaceutical or abnormal changes. However, the high dimensionality and small sample size of the data produced by the mass spectrometer make biomarker detection a very challenging task.

M. Thielscher and D. Zhang (Eds.): AI 2012, LNCS 7691, pp. 266–278, 2012.

Many machine learning techniques have been used for classification of mass spectrometry data. For example, the random forest algorithm [16], principal component analysis and linear discriminant analysis (LDA) [13] are used to classify mass spectrometry data. In [18], k-nearest-neighbour, support vector machines (SVMs) with linear kernel, quadric discriminant analysis are used for classification. Genetic algorithms and t-test in conjunction with SVMs [12] are used to select 10 m/z values as features for classification using SVMs. However, most of these machine learning techniques for classification cannot effectively handle a huge number (i.e. thousands) of features, and feature selection and dimensionality reduction of data must take place in advance.

Genetic programming (GP) is an evolutionary algorithm in which computer programs (or functions) are automatically evolved to solve given problems. GP first starts with randomly chosen programs which are modified subsequently by genetic operators such as sexual recombination (crossover) and mutation based on Darwinian natural selection and gene theory [11]. A main advantage of GP is that it is capable of handling a very large number of features as GP has a built-in capability to select features automatically [15]. Therefore GP can be categorized as an embedded approach to feature selection.

Since very recently, there has been a small number of works only using GP for feature selection and classification on bio-data. For example, GP has been used for classifying ^{1}H-NMR data [7] and achieved good results. GP has also been recently used for peptide quantification of MS data and measurement of protein quantities within biological samples [19]. However, GP has been rarely used in the area of biomarker detection in MS data.

Goals. The overall goal of the study is to develop a GP based method for biomarker detection and classification in the very high dimensional MS data. This method has three steps: we first use GP with two fitness functions for feature selection, then develop a fitness function for feature construction, and finally the selected and constructed features are used for classification. This new GP method will be examined and compared with naive Bayes, SVMs, J48 decision trees on two data sets, a full scan MS data set and a tandem LC/MS/MS data set. Specifically, we will investigate:

1. what terminals and functions can be used to construct programs;
2. what measures can be used as fitness functions for feature selection, construction and classification;
3. whether the proposed GP method can do a good enough job for biomarker detection in the MS data and;
4. whether the new GP method can outperform naive Bayes, SVMs and J48 for these problems.

Organisation. The rest of the paper is organised as follows. Section 2 describes the data sets and preprocessing. Section 3 describes the new GP approach. Section 4 presents the experimental results with discussions. Section 5 concludes the paper with future work directions.

2   Data Sets and Preprocessing

2.1   Data Sets

The first benchmark data set used here is the premalignant pancreatic cancer MS data, which has 181 samples. 101 of them are control samples (class 1) and the other 80 samples form the PanIN (pancreatic intraepithelial neoplasias) class (class 2). Control samples are *normal* cases while PanIN samples are the *diseased* cases. This data set was obtained from the FDA-NCI Clinical Proteomics Program[1]. The MS spectra were generated in SELSI-TOF and QSTAR Plusar i systems, which are composed of m/z values on the x axis and the corresponding intensities on the y axis. The number of attributes/features was originally 350,000 for each sample [8], after binning the data the number of features became 6771 per sample.

The second benchmark data set[2] is a liquid chromatography tandem MS (LC/MS/MS) generated from the hybrid Q-TOF mass spectrometer [17]. It consists of the serum of 5 healthy individuals (class 1) and the serum of the same 5 healthy individuals mixed with known concentration of spike-in peptides (class 2). The total number of original features in this dataset is 10,411. Note that human experts found 13 known features (biomarkers) for this data set.

2.2   Preprocessing

The MS data usually consists of two columns which are the m/z and the corresponding intensity or relative abundance of this ion in the sample. Due to the high amount of noise which occurs due to the system measurement errors, preprocessing of such data is an essential step for successfully analyzing the data. There are two levels of preprocessing for the MS data [14], either low level preprocessing which involves baseline adjustment, filtering and normalization, or the high level preprocessing. The high level proprecessing includes *peak extraction*, peaks identification or extraction in each of the samples; *filtering of peak*, removing of noisy peaks; *retention time alignment*, matching peaks with similar retention times across multiple scans, and using the groups of the matched peaks for time alignment; *peak list deisotoping*, converting the data to the ground truth data; *baseline adjustment*, removal of low intensity peaks; *gap filling*, when peak identification initially fails to recognize some peaks, filling in missing peaks or filling in data for peaks that are genuinely missing from a sample, by matching the raw data at the suitable retention time.

Not all steps of preprocessing are compensatory, and some of these steps are chosen according to the kind of the application [14]. However, steps like peak extraction and alignment should be made on raw data for successful interpretation of the results, and other steps can be chosen by the analyst. It is very important to perform these first steps diligently since the accuracy and reproducibility of results from analyzing LC/MS/MS data sets depend in part on careful data preprocessing [6].

---

[1] Available at: http://home.ccr.cancer.gov/ncifdaproteomics/ppatterns.asp
[2] Available at: http://omics.georgetown.edu/massprep.html

2.2.1 Preprocessing of Premalignant Pancreatic Cancer Data

This data set is a binned MS data so it requires low level preprocessing. Based on the framework in [8] which consists of baseline adjustment, filtering and normalization are used here. Baseline adjustment is useful for removal of low intensity peaks, where the baseline was estimated by segmenting the whole spectra into windows with a size of 200 m/z ratio intensities. The mean values of these windows were then used as the estimate of baseline value at that intensity. To perform regression, a piecewise cubic interpolation method is used. After this step, filtering of noise was done using Gaussian kernel filter. Normalization was done to remove the systematic differences between replicates, which was performed using area under curve where the maximum value of intensity for each m/z ratio is rescaled to 100. Figure 1 shows the original spectrogram and the preprocessed one.

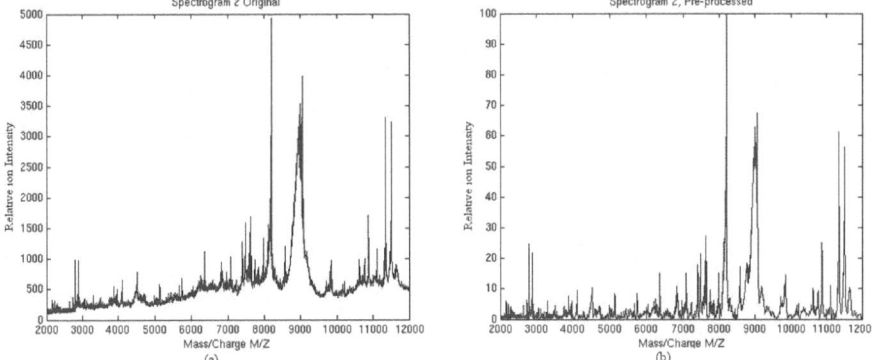

Fig. 1. Premalignant pancreatic cancer data set preprocessing result.Spectrogram 2 is used as an example of the preprocessing. (a) the original spectrogram; (b) the spectrogram after baseline adjustment, noise removal using Gaussian Kernel smoothing and normalization using area under the curve.

2.2.2 Preprocessing of Spike-In Data set

The data set is in its raw form, where the full MS spectra consists of table of values of scan number, LC retention time, ion m/z value and ion intensity. It requires the high level of preprocessing. The first step needed is to extract peaks from the data which is one of the most important steps in MS data analysis. Peptide signals usually appear as local maxima (i.e. peaks) in MS spectra, hence an efficient approach to extracting significant peaks is needed to get meaningful and interpretable results. The peak extraction approach is used based on clustering significant peaks and noisy peaks and removing the noisy peaks. The second step was to filter the peaks to remove noise from each scan, using a percentile of the base peak intensity the filtering is performed, where the base peak is the most intense peak found in each scan. In order to produce the centroid data instead of the raw signal, the peak preserving resampling method is used.

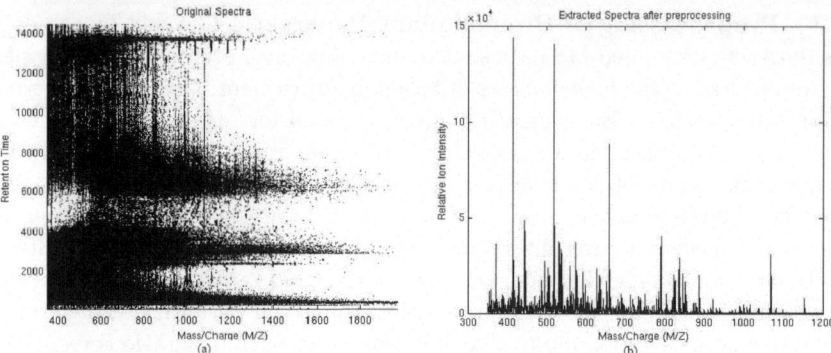

Fig. 2. Spike-in Data set preprocessing. An example of the preprocessing on one of the spectrograms. (a) the original spectrogram; (b) the spectrogram after peak extraction, filtering of peaks, resampling and alignment of peaks.

Finally the alignment of the peaks is used to remove fluctuation of data. The total number of features (scan) was 10,411 and it was reduced to 1252 features per sample after preprocessing. Figure 2 shows an example of the data before and after preprocessing.

3   The GP Method

Although the preprocessing stage has already significantly reduced the number of features, the number of features in MS data sets is still typically very large (too large for most machine learning algorithms to easily cope [8]). So further selection of the important features and construction or generation of new high-level features are still necessary for classification.

In this paper, we use the common tree-based GP [2] for this task. The proposed method has three steps: (1) we use GP's built-in capability for feature selection with the development of two fitness functions; (2) we develop a fitness function for new feature generation/construction; and (3) the selected and constructed features are used in GP for classification. In the rest of this section, we will describe the terminal set, function set, fitness functions, genetic operators and parameter settings for the proposed method.

3.1   Terminal and Function Sets

For n samples, the MS data is typically represented by a $k * (n + 1)$ matrix: $(m/z, Int) = (m/z, Int_1, ..., Int_n)$, where k is the number of m/z ratios (features) observed, m/z is a vector of the measured m/z ratios, and the Int_i are the corresponding intensities for the ith sample. There is also a vector $Y = (y_1, ..., y_n)$ to denote the class label. The main goal is to predict y_i based on the intensity profile $Int_i = (Int_{1i}, Int_{2i}, ..., Int_{ki})$ [21]. For the two data sets in this study, there are two classes, and the class labels y_i can be defined as class1 or class2, respectively.

We used tree based genetic programs [3], each of which is constructed using a terminal set and a function set. The terminal set consists of the features of a data set, plus a randomly generated constant number. The values of the feature terminals are the intensity values of the corresponding features.

The function set consists of the four mathematical operations, the min, max functions, and a conditional operator $ifte$:

$$FuncSet = \{+, -, \times, \%, \min, \max, ifte\}$$

where $+, -$ and $\times$ have the usual meanings while $\%$ is the protected division which is the same division operation except that the result of division by zero returns zero. max and min return the greater and the smaller of the two arguments, respectively. The $ifte$ takes three arguments, and returns the value of the second argument if the first is negative; otherwise it returns the value of third argument. The use of $ifte$ function aims to evolve complex and non-linear functions for feature selection and classification.

3.2 Fitness Functions

To deal with feature selection, construction, and classification, we design three fitness functions as described below.

1. Standard Classification Accuracy: The first fitness function uses the standard classification accuracy on the training set. The classification accuracy is the percentage ratio of the number of examples correctly classified by an evolved genetic program to the total number of examples in the training set.

$$Fit_1 = \frac{\#\text{Correctly Classified Examples}}{\text{Total Number of Examples}} \tag{1}$$

For a particular sample (example), an evolved genetic program will return a single floating point value. If the value is less than or equal to zero (single threshold), then the example is classified as class1; otherwise it is classified as class2. This fitness function will be used for feature selection in the first step and also classification in the third step.

2. Area Under ROC Curve: The first fitness function is generally effective for simple tasks of binary classification. However, it often cannot cope with difficult cases. As the biomarker detection and classification on MS data is a difficult task, we hypothesise that the simple fitness function might not work well. So we use the *area under ROC curve* (AUC) as the second fitness function. Since accurately calculating the AUC of a program is difficult and time consuming, we approximate this value following the approach proposed in [2]. Here multiple threshold values are used, where the program outputs are sorted in ascending order and used as threshold values for classification. Each time the TP (true positive), TN (true negative), FP (false positive), and FN (false negative) values are calculated. The maximum of TP and TN for all thresholds are selected. The fitness function is calculated by the sum of the trapezoids fitted under the ROC points, where the each point of ROC represents the classification accuracy of the two classes at each threshold value [2]. This function will also be used for feature selection and classification.

$$Fit_2 = \sum_{i=1}^{N-1} 0.5(TPR_{i+1} + TPR_i)(FPR_{i+1} - FPR_i) \tag{2}$$

Where the TPR and the FPR are the true positive and false positive rates respectively.

$$TPR = \frac{TP}{TP + FN} \text{ and } FPR = \frac{FP}{FP + TN} \tag{3}$$

3. Linear Discriminant Analysis: Linear discriminant analysis (LDA) and the related Fisher's linear discriminant are methods to find a linear combination of features which separates two or more classes of objects [22]. This measure is used as the third fitness function of GP, which aims to further reduce the number of features by combining the original low-level features into a single high-level feature, as shown below:

$$Fit_3 = \frac{|\mu_i - \mu_j|}{\sqrt{Var_i + Var_j}} \tag{4}$$

The high-level feature is actually the entire genetic program. The means and standard deviations of the program output values with all training examples for a particular class will be calculated. The "middle point" of the means for the two classes normalised by the standard deviations will be used as the threshold value to determine whether an example should be classified as class1 or class2. If the program output value for a given example is less than or equal to this threshold value, this example will be classified as class1; otherwise class2.

This fitness function is used for construction/generation of brand new, high-level features and provides a solution to dimensionality reduction. We expect this fitness function can further improve classification performance for some machine learning algorithms.

3.3   Genetic Operators and Parameters

For generating the programs in the initial population and for the mutation operator, the ramped half and half method [1] is used. The standard subtree crossover and mutation [3] are applied to this method. Elitism is also used here to make sure the best program in the next generation will not be worse than that in the current generation. For feature selection and feature generation/construction, the population size used is 1024, crossover, mutation and elitisim rates are 80%, 19% and 1% respectively. The tournament selection size used is 7. The maximum number of generations is set to 50 or it is terminated if ideal fitness is reached. This number is chosen to avoid overfitting as it can occur if the number of generations is increased. The maximum depth of the tree is set to 8.

For evaluation of the selected and the generated features using GP, some of the parameters selected are changed as the search space is less than the original one. The number of generations is set to 30, the tournament selection size is set to 4, and the maximum depth of the tree is set to 7. All other parameters are kept the same.

4 Results

4.1 Results on Premalignant Pancreatic Cancer Data Set

All the preprocessing framework is done using bioinformatics toolbox in Matlab [5]. ECJ package [20] is used for genetic programming, Weka library [10] is used for classification and evaluation.

4.1.1 Feature Selection

The data set consists of 181 samples with 101 belonging to class Control and 80 samples to class Case. Each sample contains 6771 features. The data set is divided into 50% as a training set and 50% as a test set. Each experiment is repeated 30 independent runs, and the mean and standard deviation of the results, the best result and the number of features selected are shown in Table 1. The number of features are selected from the best evolved program.

Table 1. Test set classification accuracy and the number of selected features by GP the first two fitness functions (STD and AUC). SD: standard deviation.

Fitness Function	Best (%)	Mean±SD (%)	# Features Selected
STD-GP	67.78	53.37± 5.69	367
AUC-GP	71.04	57.52± 6.79	100

As shown in Table 1, GP can at best achieve around 70% of accuracy on the test set using both fitness functions since this problem is difficult. Although the GP results are not as good as expected, the common machine learning algorithms such as decision trees (J48), support vector machines (SVM) and naive Bayes from Weka [10] cannot directly run the experiments since the number of features is too large. Due to the implicitly feature selection capability, the proposed GP method successfully runs the experiments and automatically select a small number from the original 6771 features. While 367 features are selected using the first fitness function (standard accuracy), only 100 features are selected using AUC as the fitness function. Of course, if we increase the search space (population size, number of generations, etc.), we might obtain better results, but the main goal here is to select a small number of features from the huge number (6771) to be used for classification. So we will investigate whether the selected features can be used by GP and other machine learning methods for classification.

4.1.2 Feature Generation/Construction

In the above feature selection stage, GP uses its built-in feature selection ability to significantly reduce the number of features/dimensions over an order of magnitude. However, the number of features is generally over 100, which might still be difficult for common machine learning algorithms. Using the third fitness function, the number of features is further reduced to only a single feature, which is the program output with the largest fitness values among all individuals. The individual with the highest fitness value indicates that the difference between the two classes is large since the magnitude of the Fisher criterion value determines the degree of separation of two classes [9]. The newly generated features for different examples will be tested using GP and compared with naive Bayes, SVMs, J48 algorithms for final classification, which is reported below.

4.1.3 Evaluation and Discussions

Table 2 shows the classification results of GP on the test set using the selected features (by the first two fitness functions) and new constructed features (the third fitness function) with a comparison of Naive Bayes, SVMs and J48. The first line of the table shows the accuracy of different methods using the 367 features selected by GP with the first fitness function (standard accuracy), the second line uses the 100 features selected by GP with the second fitness function (AUC), and the third line uses the constructed feature by GP with the third fitness function (LDA).

Table 2. Test set accuracy of GP and SVM, naive Bayes, J48 tree algorithms using selected and constructed features

Fitness	Accuracy (%)			Best(%)		Mean ±SD (%)	
	Naive Bayes	SVM	J48	AUC-GP	STD-GP	AUC-GP	STD-GP
STD-GP	51.38	56.91	55.80	**78.19**	72.22	70.05±4.89	62.59±5.05
AUC-GP	54.70	55.80	55.80	**69.44**	63.33	58.71±6.03	55.59±4.20
LDA-GP	62.64	62.64	64.84	**68.89**	65.93	66.82±1.51	62.20±2.43

According to Table 2, the features selected and constructed by GP with different fitness functions can be used by the common machine learning algorithms NB, SVM and J48 and lead to comparable or even better results than the original accuracy GP achieved when it was used for feature selection (Table 1). These results suggest that GP can effectively select a small number of features from a huge number of features in MS data for classification. For the three common machine learning methods, the 367 features selected by GP with the first fitness function and the 100 features selected by GP with the second fitness function achieved very similar results. However, the single feature constructed by GP with the third fitness function by the three learning methods achieved considerably better (7-9%) results. This suggests that the single high-level feature (genetic program) captured the regularities for this problem and can be effectively used by all the three learning methods.

For the single constructed feature as input to the GP classifier (line 3), GP with the first fitness function (STD-GP) *on average* achieved very similar performance(62.20%) to the NB and SVM methods, but 2% worse than J48 (64.84%). GP with the second fitness function (AUC-GP) *on average* still achieved better results than all the three commonly learning methods. The best GP run with both STD and AUC as the fitness functions achieved better results than the three commonly used machine learning methods. One noticeable characteristic for the GP method with both fitness functions is that using the 367 or 100 selected features achieved better results than using the single constructed features. This suggests that GP has very strong ability for constructing good classifiers using different combinations of low-level or medium level features, but cannot do much if the feature level is very high and the number of such features is too small (in this case only one).

4.2   Results on Spike-In Data set

This data set has 10 examples each with 1252 features. The small sample size and the huge number of features makes this problem extremely challenging. As the number of examples is so small, we use the one-leave-out cross validation method in our experiments.

4.2.1   Biomaker Detection

On this data set, human experts identified 13 features (biomarkers) that can successfully describe the classification problem. In this subsection, we would like to investigate how many of these 13 features can be detected by GP.

As the AUC fitness function consistently achieved better performance than the standard accuracy fitness function in GP for all the machine learning methods for the first data set, we use the AUC fitness function for feature selection (biomarker detection) and run 30 independent times. The results in Table 3 shows that GP successfully detected 5 of the 13 biomarkers. Using only the 5 detected biomarkers and other features selected by AUC-GP, the proposed GP method achieved **100%** accuracy. This suggests that the 13 biomarkers identified by human experts are not the only best features in the data set, and there exist other combinations of features that should also be considered as biomarkers as they can achieve perfect results. Note that using standard classification accuracy as the fitness function, GP can only detect one of the 13 biomarkers, which suggests that AUC is better than the standard accuracy as the fitness function for feature selection and biomarker detection on this data set.

4.2.2   Classification Results

Table 4 shows the classification results of GP and the three common existing learning algorithms (NB, SVM and J48) using the features selected and constructed by GP with the three fitness functions. Again, the features selected and constructed by GP can be used by these learning algorithms, and all the four methods achieved better results than the first data set, suggesting that the classification task in this data set is easier than that in the first set. In particular, GP with AUC as the fitness function has the potential to achieve 100% accuracy

Table 3. Biomarkers detected by AUC-GP. The highlighted features are the biomarkers successfully detected by GP.

Feature No.	m/z
1	501.25
2	450.23
3a	530.78
3b	354.19
4	523.77
5a	648.84
5b	432.89
6	586.98
7a	624.99
7b	630.35
8	943.43
9a	712.43
9b	570

(the best run), which will open the door of GP to be applied to biomarker detection and classification in MS data. Although GP with the single constructed features achieved a higher average accuracy, the result is not significantly better (by a T-test) than using the selected features.

Table 4. Test set accuracy of GP and SVM, naive Bayes, J48 tree algorithms using selected and constructed features on second data set

Fitness	Accuracy (%)			Best (%)		Mean ± SD (%)	
	Naive Bayes	SVM	J48	AUC-GP	STD-GP	AUC-GP	STD-GP
STD-GP	60.00	70.00	70.00	100.00	100.00	72.66±13.46	63.88±17.87
AUC-GP	50.00	60.00	70.00	100.00	100.00	80.66±3.65	58.33±14.34
LDA-GP	66.67	66.67	100.00	100.00	100.00	86.67±20.57	74±26.34

5 Conclusions

Detection of biomarkers in MS data is a challenge due to the high dimensionality of the data and the small sample size. Selecting the right preprocessing steps of MS data is essential for successful classification and detection of biomarkers. In this study we used GP on two kinds of MS data; the first is a full scan MS data and the second is the tandem LC/MS/MS data. Since GP has a built-in feature selection capability, we used GP for selecting features using two different fitness functions. The first is the standard classification accuracy and the second is the AUC as the fitness function. The results show that GP can be successfully used for feature selection in classification of MS data, and construction of high-level features from low-level existing features can further improve the classification performance. The results also suggest that GP as a classifier outperformed the three common machine learning algorithms on the two data sets.

The results on the second data set show that GP can successfully detect 5 out of 13 biomarkers identified by human experts, and the 5 detected features (with other features selected) can lead to perfect classification accuracy (100%), suggesting that there are far more groups of features that can classify the data. This potential of GP will be further investigated in the future.

Although very preliminary, this paper represents a very first work of GP in biomarker detection, feature selection/construction and classification in MS data. Further investigation in this direction will be carried out in the future.

References

1. Al-Sahaf, H., Neshatian, K., Zhang, M.: Automatic feature extraction and image classification using genetic programming. In: ICARA, pp. 157–162 (2011)
2. Bhowan, U., Johnston, M., Zhang, M.: Developing New Fitness Functions in Genetic Programming for Classification With Unbalanced Data, pp. 406–421 (2012)
3. Bhowan, U., Zhang, M., Johnston, M.: Genetic Programming for Classification with Unbalanced Data. In: Esparcia-Alcázar, A.I., Ekárt, A., Silva, S., Dignum, S., Uyar, A.Ş. (eds.) EuroGP 2010. LNCS, vol. 6021, pp. 1–13. Springer, Heidelberg (2010)
4. Boggess, B.: Mass Spectrometry Desk Reference (Sparkman, O. David). Journal of Chemical Education 78(2), 168 (2001)
5. Cai, J., Smith, D., Xia, X., Yuen, K.-y.: MBEToolbox: a Matlab toolbox for sequence data analysis in molecular biology and evolution. BMC Bioinformatics 6(1), 64 (2005)
6. Cruz-Marcelo, A., Guerra, R., Vannucci, M., Li, Y., Lau, C.C., Man, T.-K.: Comparison of algorithms for pre-processing of SELDI-TOF mass spectrometry data, pp. 2129–2136 (2008)
7. Davis, R.A., Charlton, A.J., Oehlschlager, S., Wilson, J.C.: Novel feature selection method for genetic programming using metabolomic 1H NMR data. Chemometrics and Intelligent Laboratory Systems 81(1), 50–59 (2006)
8. Ge, G., Wong, G.W.: Classification of premalignant pancreatic cancer mass-spectrometry data using decision tree ensembles. BMC Bioinformatics 9(1), 275 (2008)
9. Guo, H., Zhang, Q., Nandi, A.K.: Feature extraction and dimensionality reduction by genetic programming based on the Fisher criterion. Expert Systems 25(5), 444–459 (2008)
10. Hall, M., Frank, E., Holmes, G., Pfahringer, B., Reutemann, P., Witten, I.H.: The weka data mining software: an update. SIGKDD Explorations 11(1), 10–18 (2009)
11. Langdon, W.B., Poli, R., McPhee, N.F., Koza, J.R.: Genetic programming: An introduction and tutorial, with a survey of techniques and applications. In: Computational Intelligence: A Compendium, pp. 927–1028 (2008)
12. Li, L., Tang, H., Wu, Z., Gong, J., Gruidl, M., Zou, J., Tockman, M., Clark, R.A.: Data mining techniques for cancer detection using serum proteomic profiling. Artificial Intelligence in Medicine 32(2), 71–83 (2004)
13. Lin, Q., Peng, Q., Yao, F., Pan, X.-F., Xiong, L.-W., Wang, Y., Geng, J.-F., Feng, J.-X., Han, B.-H., Bao, G.-L., Yang, Y., Wang, X., Jin, L., Guo, W., Wang, J.-C.: A classification method based on principal components of seldi spectra to diagnose of lung adenocarcinoma. PLoS ONE 7(3), e34457 (2012)

14. Listgarten, J., Emili, A.: Statistical and computational methods for comparative proteomic profiling using liquid chromatography-tandem mass spectrometry. Mol. Cell. Proteomics 4, 419–434 (2005)

15. Neshatian, K., Zhang, M., Andreae, P.: Genetic Programming for Feature Ranking in Classification Problems. In: Li, X., Kirley, M., Zhang, M., Green, D., Ciesielski, V., Abbass, H.A., Michalewicz, Z., Hendtlass, T., Deb, K., Tan, K.C., Branke, J., Shi, Y. (eds.) SEAL 2008. LNCS, vol. 5361, pp. 544–554. Springer, Heidelberg (2008)

16. Satten, G.A., Datta, S., Moura, H., Woolfitt, A.R., de Carvalho, M.G., Carlone, G.M., De, B.K., Pavlopoulos, A., Barr, J.R.: Standardization and denoising algorithms for mass spectra to classify whole-organism bacterial specimens. Bioinformatics 20(17), 3128–3136 (2004)

17. Tuli, L., Tsai, T.-H., Varghese, R., Xiao, J.F., Cheema, A., Ressom, H.: Using a spike-in experiment to evaluate analysis of LC-MS data. Proteome Science 13+ (February 2012)

18. Wagner, M., Naik, D., Pothen, A.: Protocols for disease classification from mass spectrometry data. Proteomics 3(9), 1692–1698 (2003)

19. Wedge, D.C., Gaskell, S.J., Hubbard, S.J., Kell, D.B., Lau, K.W., Eyers, C.: Peptide detectability following esi mass spectrometry: prediction using genetic programming. In: Lipson, H. (ed.) GECCO, pp. 2219–2225. ACM (2007)

20. White, D.R.: Software review: the ECJ toolkit, pp. 65–67 (2012)

21. Wu, B., Abbott, T., Fishman, D., McMurray, W., Mor, G., Stone, K., Ward, D., Williams, K., Zhao, H.: Comparison of statistical methods for classification of ovarian cancer using mass spectrometry data. Bioinformatics 19(13), 1636–1643 (2003)

22. Zhu, L., Han, B., Li, L., Xu, S., Mou, H.: Null Space LDA Based Feature Extraction of Mass Spectrometry Data for Cancer Classification. In: BMEI, pp. 1–4 (2009)

An Evolutionary Approach for the Design of Autonomous Underwater Vehicles

Khairul Alam, Tapabrata Ray, and Sreenatha G. Anavatti

School of Engineering and Information Technology,
University of New South Wales,
UNSW Canberra, ACT 2600, Australia
{k.alam,t.ray,s.anavatti}@adfa.edu.au
http://www.unsw.adfa.edu.au

Abstract. Autonomous underwater vehicles (AUVs) are becoming an attractive option for increasingly complex and challenging underwater search and survey operations. To meet the emerging demands of AUV mission requirements, design and tradeoff complexities, there is an increasing interest in the use of multidisciplinary design optimization (MDO) strategies. While optimization techniques have been applied successfully to a wide range of applications spanning various fields of science and engineering, there is very limited literature on optimization of AUV designs. Presented in this paper is an evolutionary approach for the design optimization of AUVs using two stochastic, population based optimization algorithms. The proposed approach is capable of modelling and solving single and multi-objective constrained formulations of the AUV design problems based on different user and mission requirements. Two formulations of the AUV design problem are considered to identify designs with minimum drag and internal clash-free assembly. The flexibility of the proposed scheme and its ability to identify optimum preliminary designs are highlighted in this paper.

Keywords: AUV, MDO, evolutionary algorithm.

1   Introduction

Autonomous underwater vehicles (AUVs) are robotic mobile instrument carriers that have self-contained propulsion, sensors, and 'intelligence', allowing them to successfully complete sampling and survey tasks with little or no human intervention. With significant developments in artificial intelligence, control theory, and computer hardware, totally autonomous underwater vehicles have become a reality [6]. Being untethered and independent, AUVs provide a platform for ocean exploration and fill in the gap left by existing manned submersibles and remotely operated vehicles (ROVs) [14].

Hundreds of different AUVs have been designed over the past 50 or so years [3] to meet the challenges of oceanographic exploration and exploitation programs, but to the best of our knowledge, very limited in-depth systematic study has been

M. Thielscher and D. Zhang (Eds.): AI 2012, LNCS 7691, pp. 279–290, 2012.

done with regards to optimum design, or to use any evolutionary algorithm(s) to find the optimum design of an AUV for specific mission requirements. Most of the previous attempts on AUV designs have focused primarily on functional designs with limited attention directed towards identifying optimum designs.

State-of-the-art evolutionary algorithms for design optimization of AUVs are rarely used in naval architecture because existing design tools are not sufficiently robust and/or fast to be used within an optimization scheme [2]. For this reason, the AUV design process is typically based on previous experience non-optimal designs are often adopted and accepted as an option. However, some recent works have considered the problem of finding the optimum hull form for AUVs that include the works of [2, 5, 11, 12] to minimize drag. Small improvement in drag can result in a substantial saving in thrust requirement. Therefore, much work still needs to be done in terms of optimizing the hull form design to minimize drag and increase propulsion efficiency [10].

While hydrodynamic hull optimization has gained momentum over the years, there is very limited literature on the arrangement strategies within the hull items, i.e. how to optimally place the internal on-board components in a 'clash-free' state while maintaining appropriate clearance among them, and other factors that affect controllability, like the centre of gravity (CG) and the centre of buoyancy (CB) effects. This establishes the need for the development of a framework that is capable of generating optimum design of AUVs by simultaneously considering both internal clash-free arrangement of components and external size and shape for a given design requirements.

This paper presents an optimization framework that is capable of modelling and solving single and multi-objective constrained formulations of the AUV design problems based on user requirements through the use of two population based evolutionary algorithms. Subsequently the algorithms are used to identify optimal AUV designs. The proposed optimization framework is described in Section 2 where the aspects of geometry representation, arrangement strategy, optimization algorithms and hydrodynamic performance estimation methods are discussed. In Section 3, the details of the numerical experiments are given, followed by a discussion of results (optimum designs) obtained. Finally, the findings of this study are summarized in Section 4.

2   Optimization Framework

This work presents an optimization framework for the design of AUVs with minimum drag consideration. The framework incorporates geometry and configuration modules, a hydrodynamics module, several accepted maritime performance and characteristics estimation methods of AUVs and a suite of optimization algorithms. Shown in Fig. 1 is the flowchart of the optimization framework. The framework facilitates the communication of data from one application to the next, producing an automated multidisciplinary design environment.

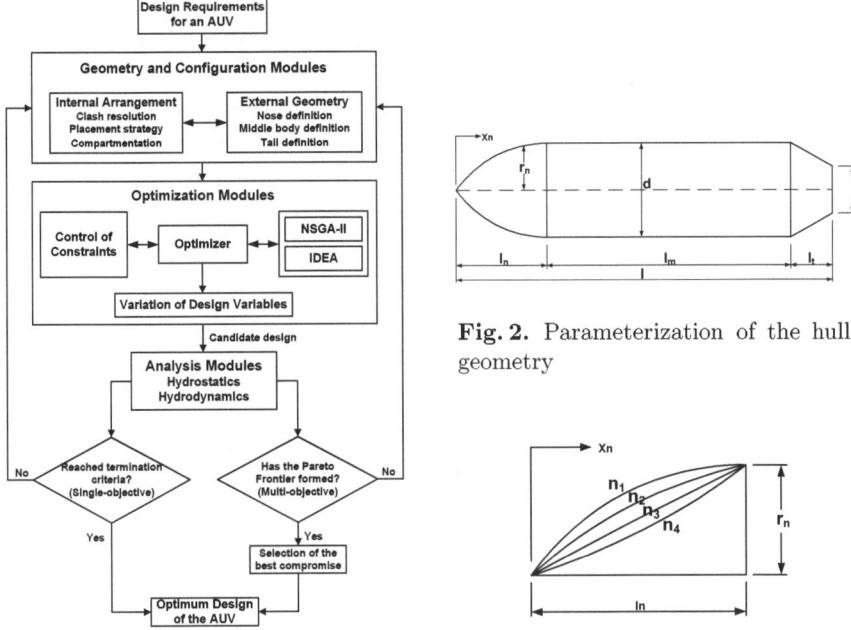

Fig. 1. Detail flowchart of the optimization framework

Fig. 2. Parameterization of the hull geometry

Fig. 3. Parameterization of the nose geometry

2.1 Design Requirements

The basic design concept of the AUV employed herein is based on the development of a small vehicle that can be easily launched, recovered and operated without special handling equipments capable of working at shallow water depth and relies heavily on the use of commercial-off-the-shelf components in an attempt to contain cost. The design requirements used in this study are:

- Operating speed of the AUV is 1 m/s;
- AUV should be able to house a 150 mm cube payload of weighing 10 kg;
- Length of the AUV must be no more than 1.3 m;
- Total weight (including payload) must be less than or equal to 30 kg;
- The AUV is to be propelled by 3 rear jets and 2 jets each for vertical and lateral movements.

2.2 Geometry and Configuration Module

Hull Geometry. The hull size of an AUV is constrained by the space for the onboard instruments that need to be carried, while the hull shape is constrained by the hydrodynamic characteristics. A 'torpedo body' that has a nose cone followed by a parallel cylindrical mid-section and a tapered tail section is considered in this study. The torpedo body exhibits low drag compared to other geometries of similar length to diameter ratios [16]. Illustrations of the family chosen for this study are presented in Fig. 2, where the body is seen to comprise a nose-section of variable length l_n, a mid-section of variable length l_m, and a tail-section of variable length l_t, making up the total body length of l units.

The curve shape of the nose is determined from the Eq. (1).

$$r_n = \frac{1}{2}d\left[1 - \left(\frac{l_n - x_n}{l_n}\right)^n\right] \tag{1}$$

where r_n is the nose radius in m, d is the maximum body diameter in m, which may be varied, and n is the shape variation coefficient of the nose which may also be varied to give different shapes, as shown in Fig. 3.

When it comes to maximizing thrust, there is a requirement to optimize a tail cone shape to direct the three pump nozzle outflows into one single mass flow. While shaped tail cones are a possibility, for ease of fabrication and to direct the three pump nozzle outflows into one single mass flow, a tapered tail cone is more suitable and therefore used in this study. The illustration of the parameterization for the tail geometry is also shown in Fig. 2, where d_t is the smaller diameter of the tail in m and l_t is the length of the tail in m.

Geometry of the Payload Section. The AUVs use on-board computers, power packs, sensors and vehicle payloads for automatic control, navigation and guidance. Therefore, adequate free space should be allocated while designing the AUV hull form. Figure 4 shows the parameterization of the payload section, where a is the edge width and height, and b is the length of the payload box.

Subject to preliminary design requirements, the optimization framework developed herein produces AUV hull shape in a way that can accommodate a variable position payload. Being a relatively heavy system, the capability of adjusting the position of the payload is an important design consideration to account for CG-CB distance manipulations.

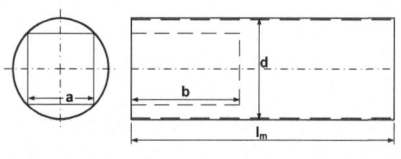

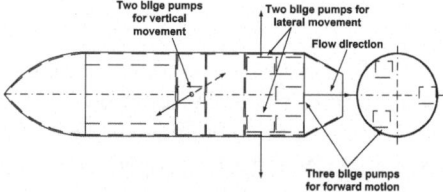

Fig. 4. Parameterization of the payload section

Fig. 5. Configuration of the propulsion system

Propulsion System. Currently available AUVs are predominately propelled by three means: propeller, jet-pump and buoyancy driven (glider) propulsion systems. Although a majority of the current AUVs are equipped with a propeller and rudder mounted at the tail for propulsion and steering, a jet based propulsion system is used in this study. Jet-pumps are more beneficial than propellers in terms of mechanical design, cost realization, robustness with respect to transportation and safety for occasional swimmers.

The propulsion of the AUV under consideration is achieved through the use of bilge pumps. There are seven pumps of three different types mounted inside the vehicle, three of which are used to propel the vehicle forward in the water. The remaining four pumps are used to steer the vehicle left and right, as well as up and down, as illustrated in Fig. 5.

The positions of the bilge pumps for lateral and vertical movements as shown in Fig. 5, are not fixed, but are rather free to move within the entire mid-section. During the optimization process, the optimizer chooses these pumps from a catalogue of ten off-the-shelf different pumps commonly available and also the optimal positions of those pumps while designing the AUV.

Power Source. Unlike tethered vehicles, AUV operations are limited by the on board power they can carry [14]. The power determines the endurance and operating range, and the mission characteristics of the AUV accordingly. The rechargeable high performance Lithium Polymer (LiPo) batteries with nominal cell voltage 3.8 V and energy density of 193 Whr/kg have been selected in this study. These batteries are attractive as they are light and small.

Placement Strategy for the Internal Components. The design optimization framework presented in this paper not only optimizes the hull shape but also arranges its contents avoiding interference while maintaining workable spaces around the components using 'clash-free mechanism'. For efficient utilization of the available internal volume, a careful arrangement needs to be achieved. As the current approach utilizes the optimization modules to iterate, the use of clash-free mechanism is an essential part to obtain a clash-free arrangement of the internal components for every valid design. Details of the clash-free mechanism appear in the authors' earlier work [1].

2.3 Optimization Module

The framework developed here uses two state-of-the-art evolutionary algorithms, NSGA-II and IDEA. It is worth mentioning that any optimization algorithm capable of solving single and multi-objective optimization problems can be used within the framework. The chosen algorithms are written in Matlab and are integrated with CATIA along with VBScript to automate the whole AUV design process. CATIA (Computer Aided Three-dimensional Interactive Application) is a multi-platform computer-aided design (CAD) commercial software suite and widely used for design purposes. VBScript (Visual Basic Scripting Edition) is a tool for scripting the design process of CATIA.

NSGA-II. Non-dominated sorting genetic algorithm II (NSGA-II) was proposed by Deb *et al.* [7], and remains one of the most widely used population based algorithms for evolutionary optimization. It uses Simulated Binary Crossover (SBX) and polynomial mutation for generating off-spring. The ranking of solutions is first done based on non-dominance, followed by the crowding distance. While non-dominance based rank drives the population towards the Pareto Optimal Front, crowding distance based rank aims to preserve the diversity among solutions. For problems with constraints, the feasible solutions are ranked above infeasible solutions. The infeasible solutions are ranked based on their constraint violations. For the single objective formulation, NSGA-II assumes the form of a real coded EA with SBX and polynomial mutation.

IDEA. Infeasibility Driven Evolutionary Algorithm (IDEA) was recently proposed by Singh *et al.* [15]. Since the Pareto optimal solution for a constrained problem usually lies on a constraint boundary, IDEA tries to focus the search near the constraint boundaries by maintaining a set of infeasible solutions (in addition to feasible solutions). During the ranking process, a few marginally infeasible solutions (based on their constraint violations) are ranked above the feasible solutions. The presence of infeasible solutions effectively translates to approaching the constraint boundary from both feasible and infeasible search spaces, which helps in faster convergence, as demonstrated in the earlier study [15].

2.4   Hydrodynamics Module: Drag Estimation

A fundamental interest in the field of hydrodynamics is the reduction of submerged vehicle power requirements and drag minimization is one of the most effective means of achieving this. For drag estimation, the following formula has been used:

$$D = \frac{1}{2}\rho V^2 C_V S \qquad (2)$$

where ρ is the density of the fluid in kg/m^3, V is the velocity in m/s, S is the wetted surface area of the vehicle in m^2, and C_V is the coefficient of viscous resistance for the smooth bare hull and D is the vehicle drag in N.

Three methods: Virginia Tech (VT) [13], MIT [9] and G&J method [8] are employed in this study to measure the coefficient of viscous resistance (C_V) in three different ways to ensure uniformity in drag estimation of the design vehicle.

3   Numerical Experiments

3.1   Problem Formulations

While satisfying the design requirements, optimization of two kinds of objectives are sought. First is the minimization of drag, which is important because minimum drag leads to least power consumption for propulsion, and corresponding savings in the operating costs. Second is to maximize one of the lever arms, as a longer lever arm assists in better diving and turning of the vehicle. The term 'lever arm (LA)' defined here as the longitudinal distance of the pump from the centre of buoyancy of the vehicle. To this effect, two formulations are studied in this paper as described below.

Single Objective Formulation. The single objective optimization problem is posed as the identification of an AUV hull form with minimum drag as well as clash-free optimal placement of the internal objects subject to the constraints on payload (P_l), CG-CB separation (s), length (l) and weight (w) of the vehicle. The objective function, constraints and design variables are listed in the Eq. (3) as Formulation 1.

Minimize:
$$f(1) = D$$

Constraints:
$$g(1) = P_l \geq 15 \ kg; \quad g(2) = P_l \leq 18 \ kg;$$
$$g(3) = a \geq 150 \ mm; \quad g(4) = b \geq 200 \ mm; \quad g(5) = s \leq 10 \ mm;$$
$$g(6) = l \leq 1300 \ mm; \quad g(7) = w \leq 30 \ kg$$

Design variables:
$$1 \leq P_1 \leq 10; \ 1 \leq P_2 \leq 10; \ 1 \leq P_3 \leq 10$$
$$1 \leq O_1 \leq 4; \ 1 \leq O_2 \leq 4; \ 1 \leq O_3 \leq 4$$
$$0 \leq X_{V1} \leq 1 \ mm; \ 0 \leq X_{V2} \leq 1 \ mm$$
$$0 \leq X_{L1} \leq 1 \ mm; \ 0 \leq X_{L2} \leq 1 \ mm$$
$$0 \leq X_{F1} \leq 1 \ mm; \ 0 \leq X_{F2} \leq 1 \ mm; \ 0 \leq X_{F3} \leq 1 \ mm$$
$$0 \leq Y_{V1} \leq 1 \ mm; \ 0 \leq Y_{V2} \leq 1 \ mm$$
$$0 \leq Y_{L1} \leq 1 \ mm; \ 0 \leq Y_{L2} \leq 1 \ mm$$
$$0 \leq Y_{F1} \leq 1 \ mm; \ 0 \leq Y_{F2} \leq 1 \ mm; \ 0 \leq Y_{F3} \leq 1 \ mm$$
$$0 \leq Z_V \leq 600 \ mm; \ 0 \leq Z_L \leq 600 \ mm; \ 650 \leq Z_F \leq 1000 \ mm$$
$$75 \leq r_t \leq 350 \ mm; \ 100 \leq l_t \leq 200 \ mm$$
$$2 \leq n \leq 3; \ 200 \leq l_n \leq 400 \ mm$$

(3)

The constraints and the design variables for the problem formulations are illustrated in Fig. 6 showing exactly which parts of the AUV geometry they define. The design variables are: the type of pump selections for vertical, lateral and forward movements from available catalogue pumps respectively (P_1, P_2, P_3), orientation of the selected pumps for respective movements (O_1, O_2, O_3), position of the selected pumps along X axis (X_V, X_L, X_F), along Y axis (Y_V, Y_L, Y_F) and along Z axis (Z_V, Z_L, Z_F) for respective movements, and the tail and nose parameters.

Multi-objective Formulation. The multi-objective optimization problem is posed as the identification of an AUV hull form with minimum drag and maximum length of one of the lever arms as well as clash-free optimal placement of the internal objects. The objective functions are listed in the Eq. (4) as Formulation 2, while the constraints and variables are the same as in the single objective case.

Minimize:
$$f(1) = D; \quad f(2) = -LA$$

(4)

where $LA = min(LA_1, LA_2)$.

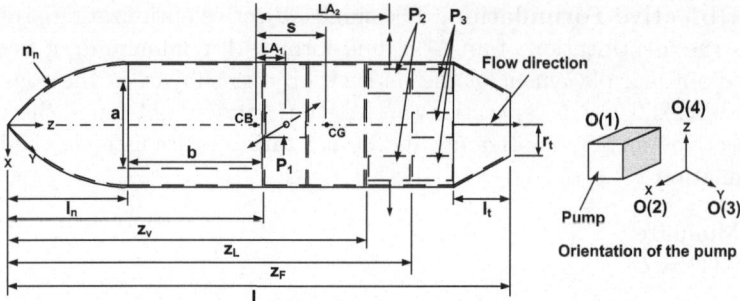

Fig. 6. The constraints and design variables for problem formulations

It can be noted that the optimization algorithms employed in this study are formulated to minimize the objective functions of a problem. Therefore, to maximize the length of lever arm in the Formulation 2, a negative sign has been placed; thereby formulating both the objectives as a minimization problem.

3.2   Computational Setup and Results

For each formulation, thirty independent runs of NSGA-II and IDEA are performed. A crossover probability of 0.9, mutation probability of 0.1, crossover distribution index of 10, mutation distribution index of 20 and an infeasibility ratio (for IDEA) of 0.2 has been used for the algorithms. The number of function evaluations used by each algorithm is kept equal at 40000 for a fair comparison. A population size of 200 has been used for both algorithms. The computing time per evaluation is about 0.05 s on a Intel Xeon processor machine of 3.33 GHz with 6.00 GB memory.

Single Objective Optimization Results. Shown in Fig. 7a is the result of the best run for the single objective drag minimization problem using NSGA-II and IDEA. It is observed that both optimization algorithms are able to minimize the drag in around 30000 function evaluations. The statistics of results computed across 30 runs for each algorithm is reported in Table 1. It is seen that the best, median and the average objective values obtained by IDEA are better than NSGA-II. In addition, the standard deviation across the multiple runs is much less than NSGA-II, indicating that it is able to achieve better objective values more consistently. This is also reflected in the median runs as shown in Fig. 7b, where IDEA is seen to converge faster than NSGA-II.

Results of Optimum AUV Design. Based on the results obtained by carrying out optimization of drag, Fig. 8 shows the optimal shape and internal configuration of the optimized AUV. The resulting performance criteria of the optimized AUV as listed in Table 2, clearly indicate that the design constraints are satisfied while achieving minimum drag.

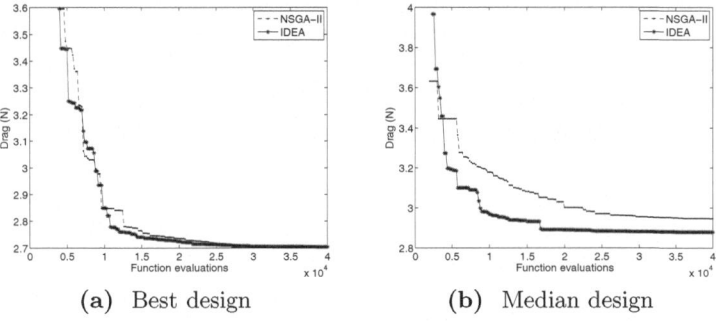

(a) Best design (b) Median design

Fig. 7. Progress plots of the best and median designs using NSGA-II and IDEA

Table 1. Single objective drag minimization results

Design	NSGA-II	IDEA
Best (N)	2.70443	**2.70424**
Mean (N)	3.05906	**2.87254**
Median (N)	2.94658	**2.87850**
Worst (N)	5.65062	2.99905
SD (N)	0.50019	0.05839

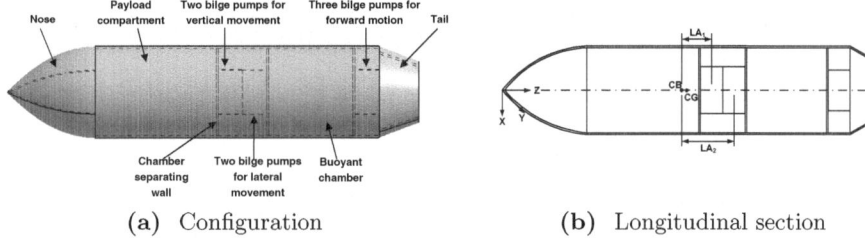

(a) Configuration (b) Longitudinal section

Fig. 8. Hull shape and configuration of the resulting optimized AUV

Table 2. Performance criteria of the resulting optimized AUV

Vehicle particulars	Value	Vehicle particulars	Value
Nose length	294 mm	Length of the second lever arm	155.77 mm
Parallel mid-body length	716 mm	Length of the payload compartment	282 mm
Tail length	100 mm	Length of the buoyant chamber	247 mm
Overall length of the AUV	1110 mm	X-coordinate of CG	0.01254 mm
Outer diameter of the AUV	223 mm	Y-coordinate of CG	0.03201 mm
Length to diameter ratio	4.98	Z-coordinate of CG	524.775 mm
Max. size of the inner square	150 mm	X-coordinate of CB	0
Wetted surface area	0.9897 m^2	Y-coordinate of CB	0
Displacement volume	0.0256 m^3	Z-coordinate of CB	517.162 mm
Mass of the displaced water	25 kg	CG-CB separation	7.613 mm
Mass of the AUV	9 kg	Nominal speed	1 m/s
Payload capacity including batteries	16 kg	Drag (VT method)	2.50177 N
Total mass of the AUV	25 kg	Drag (G&J method)	2.55203 N
Length of the first lever arm	95.44 mm	Drag (MIT method)	2.70424 N

Multi-objective Optimization Results. Multi-objective optimization i.e. minimization of drag and maximization of one of the lever arms is performed using NSGA-II and IDEA. The parameters used are kept the same as that for single objective formulation. Since multi-objective optimization yields a set of non-dominated solutions, the results can not be compared based on objective values obtained (as in single objective optimization). Therefore, a number of performance metrics have been developed in literature to evaluate the quality of the non-dominated set obtained, and to compare the performance of two or more sets. These performance metrics attempt to quantify the convergence and diversity of the obtained non-dominated set. In the present study, two commonly used performance metrics have been used to compare the results obtained using NSGA-II and IDEA: *displacement* [4] and *hypervolume* [17] metrics. A lower value of displacement metric indicates a better non-dominated set. On the other hand, the larger the value of hypervolume, the better is the non-dominated set.

The performance metrics averaged over multiple runs of final solutions obtained using NSGA-II and IDEA are listed in Table 3. It is seen that on average, IDEA is able to achieve lower values of displacement and higher values of hypervolume as compared to NSGA-II. This indicates that IDEA is able to achieve comparatively better non-dominated sets. The best values obtained using IDEA are also better than NSGA-II. The best front (based on displacement metric) obtained using the two algorithms is shown in Fig. 9.

Table 3. Performance metrics for two objectives formulation

	NSGA-II results			
	Best	Mean	Median	Worst
Displacement	0.623945	3.11685	2.39152	7.91698
Hypervolume	772.847	499.548	592.241	58.3212

	IDEA results			
	Best	Mean	Median	Worst
Displacement	0.358976	**1.90145**	1.57697	5.60445
Hypervolume	715.755	**604.82**	642.521	265.639

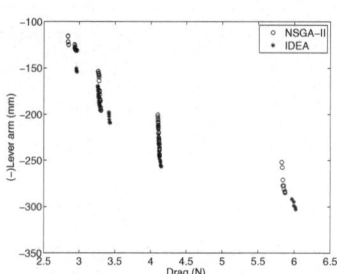

Fig. 9. Best results of the two objectives optimization problem using NSGA-II and IDEA

Once the optimization process is done, then the non-dominated set of solutions can be presented to the decision maker (end user), who can choose a design most suited to his/her needs. For example, in this case the decision maker can choose from a set of optimal designs with minimum drag, or maximum lever arm length, or an intermediate value of both the objectives. Thus the multi-objective formulation can cater to a number of end users, while ensuring that all the basic design criteria are met.

4   Conclusions

In this paper an evolutionary approach for the concept and preliminary design of AUVs is presented. The modular design optimization framework is embedded with a geometry/configuration representation/manipulation module, standard marine performance analysis methods and efficient optimization methods. The seamless integration of the modules allows the designer to identify optimum AUV designs based on a set of user requirements. Both single and multi-objective constrained optimization formulation of the AUV design problems are considered in this paper and solved using two state-of-the-art evolutionary algorithms, NSGA-II and IDEA. The studies highlight the benefits of preserving marginally infeasible solutions in IDEA that accounts for its superior performance over NSGA-II for constrained optimization problems. The modularity and the catalogue driven structure adopted in the framework allows for the design of AUVs for various design requirements and/or with different propulsion and power system options.

The preliminary design obtained from the framework can be further analyzed using a computational fluid dynamics (CFD) tool for more accurate estimates of drag, dynamic performance and controllability. It is also worth highlighting that such performance estimation modules can be easily integrated into the framework and used during the course of optimization.

Acknowledgments. The first author would like to acknowledge the scholarship he received from the University of New South Wales, Canberra, Australia for supporting his research. The second author would like to acknowledge the support of Future Fellowship offered by the Australian Research Council. The authors would like to acknowledge the rigorous suggestions and comments from the anonymous reviewers in improving this work.

References

1. Alam, K., Ray, T., Anavatti, S.G.: A new robust design optimization approach for unmanned underwater vehicle design. Proc. IMechE Part M: J. Engineering for the Maritime Environment 226(3), 235–249 (2012)
2. Alvarez, A., Bertram, V., Gualdesi, L.: Hull hydrodynamic optimization of autonomous underwater vehicles operating at snorkeling depth. Ocean Engineering 36, 105–112 (2009)
3. AUVAC: Autonomous Undersea Vehicle Applications Center (AUVAC) (2012), http://www.auvac.org/ (accessed May 2012)
4. Bandyopadhyay, S., Saha, S., Maulik, U., Deb, K.: A simulated annealing-based multiobjective optimization algorithm: AMOSA. IEEE Transactions on Evolutionary Computation 12(3), 269–283 (2008)
5. Bertram, V., Alvarez, A.: Hydrodynamic aspects of AUV design. In: The Fifth Conference on Computer and IT Applications in the Maritime Industries (COMPIT), Oegstgeest, Netherlands, pp. 45–53 (2006)
6. Chryssostomidis, C., Schmidt, H.: Autonomous underwater vehicles. Center for Ocean Engineering. MIT (2006), http://oe.mit.edu/content/view/126/123/ (accessed on August 7, 2010)

7. Deb, K., Pratap, A., Agarwal, S., Meyarivan, T.: A fast and elitist multiobjective genetic algorithm: NSGA-II. IEEE Transactions on Evolutionary Computation 6, 182–197 (2002)
8. Gillmer, T., Johnson, B.: Introduction to Naval Architecture, 2nd print with revisions edn. US Naval Institute Press (1982)
9. Jackson, H.: MIT Professional Summer Course Submarine Design Trends (1992)
10. Joung, T., Sammut, K., He, F., Lee, S.K.: A study on the design optimization of an AUV by using computational fluid dynamic analysis. In: Proceedings of the Nineteenth International Offshore and Polar Engineering Conference, Osaka, Japan (2009)
11. Lutz, T., Wagner, S.: Numerical shape optimization of natural laminar flow bodies. In: Proceedings of 21st ICAS Congress, Melbourne, Australia (1998)
12. Martz, M., Neu, W.L.: Multi-objective optimization of an autonomous underwater vehicle. Marine Technology Society Journal 43(2) (2009)
13. Martz, M.A.: Preliminary Design of an Autonomous Underwater Vehicle using a Multiple-Objective Genetic Optimizer. Master's thesis, Virginia Polytechnic Institute and State University, Blacksburg, Virginia, United States (May 27, 2008)
14. Shah, V.P.: Design Considerations for Engineering Autonomous Underwater Vehicles. Master's thesis, Massachusetts Institute of Technology (June 2007)
15. Singh, H.K., Isaacs, A., Ray, T., Smith, W.: Infeasibility Driven Evolutionary Algorithm (IDEA) for Engineering Design Optimization. In: Wobcke, W., Zhang, M. (eds.) AI 2008. LNCS (LNAI), vol. 5360, pp. 104–115. Springer, Heidelberg (2008)
16. Wang, W., Chen, X., Marburg, A., Chase, J., Hann, C.: A low-cost unmanned underwater vehicle prototype for shallow water tasks. In: Proceedings of the IEEE/ASME International Conference on Mechatronic and Embedded Systems and Applications, MESA 2008, Beijing, China, pp. 204–209 (2008)
17. Zitzler, E.: Evolutionary Algorithms for Multiobjective Optimization: Methods and Applications. Shaker Verlag, Germany (1999) ISBN 3-8265-6831-1

Unsupervised Learning of Mutagenesis Molecules Structure Based on an Evolutionary-Based Features Selection in DARA

Rayner Alfred, Irwansah Amran, Leau Yu Beng, and Tan Soo Fun

School of Engineering and Information Technology, Universiti Malaysia Sabah, Jalan UMS, 88400, Kota Kinabalu, Sabah, Malaysia
{ralfred,irwansah,lybeng,soofun}@ums.edu.my

Abstract. The importance of selecting relevant features for data modeling has been recognized already in machine learning. This paper discusses the application of an evolutionary-based feature selection method in order to generate input data for unsupervised learning in DARA (Dynamic Aggregation of Relational Attributes). The feature selection process which is based on the evolutionary algorithm is applied in order to improve the descriptive accuracy of the DARA (Dynamic Aggregation of Relational Attributes) algorithm. The DARA algorithm is designed to summarize data stored in the non-target tables by clustering them into groups, where multiple records stored in non-target tables correspond to a single record stored in a target table. This paper addresses the issue of optimizing the feature selection process to select relevant set of features for the DARA algorithm by using an evolutionary algorithm, which includes the evaluation of several scoring measures used as fitness functions to find the best set of relevant features. The results show the unsupervised learning in DARA can be improved by selecting a set of relevant features based on the specified fitness function which includes the measures of the dispersion and purity of the clusters produced.

Keywords: Feature Selection, Data Summarization, Clustering, Genetic Algorithm, Data Reduction.

1   Introduction

Learning relational data is difficult due to the existence of one-to-many relationships between records stored in multiple tables. Structured data such as data stored in a relational database that have one-to-many relationships between records stored in the target and non-target tables can be transformed into a single table. This process is known as propositionalization [1]. DARA (Dynamic Aggregation of Relational Attributes) algorithm is capable to transform relational data that have one-to-many relationships between records stored in the target and non-target tables, into vectors of features [2]. In order to assist the clustering process, a technique borrowed from information retrieval theory has been used to construct vectors of features that represent records stored in non-target tables (see Fig. 1). The approach is based on the idea that,

M. Thielscher and D. Zhang (Eds.): AI 2012, LNCS 7691, pp. 291–299, 2012.

for each unique record stored in non-target tables, there is a vector of patterns that represents this record. With this representation of data, it is possible to compare records in order to cluster them. As a result, clustering can then be applied to summarize data stored in a relational database following the principles of information retrieval theory [3].

The application of feature construction has proved an improvement in the descriptive accuracy of the summarized data from relational domain [22]. However, in this paper, we apply a genetic based feature selection as a pre-processing step in order to further enhance our data summarization method called DARA [2, 23]. It is expected that the predictive accuracy of the classification task for data stored in the target table can be improved by improving the descriptive accuracy of the data summarization for the data stored in the non-target tables, as shown in Fig. 1. We propose that the summarized data to be appended into the list of attributes in the target table as one of the features considered for the classification task as shown in Fig. 1.

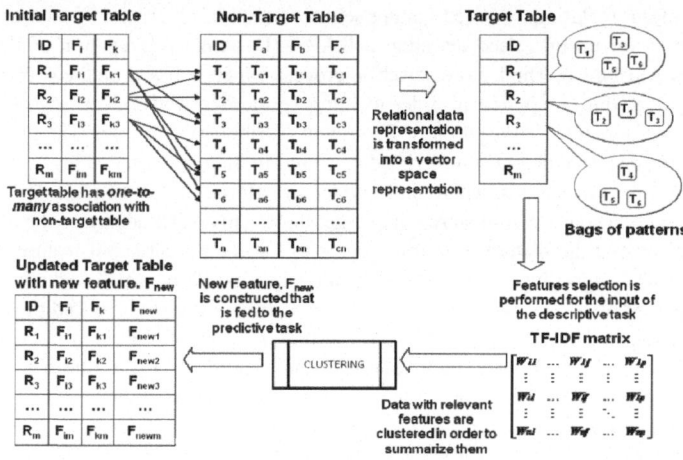

Fig. 1. A data transformation process for data stored in multiple tables with one-to-many relations into a vector space data representation

Section 2 describes the process of transforming a relational data into a vector representation by using the DARA algorithm. Section 3 provides an overview of the more general concept of feature selection that can be applied to improve the accuracy estimations of learning tasks. Section 4 describes a genetic-based (i.e., evolutionary) feature selection algorithm that is applied to reduce the dimensionality of the data for the purpose of summarizing data stored in the non-target tables using the DARA algorithm. This genetic-based feature selection algorithm selects features to characterize each unique object stored in the non-target table. The performance accuracy of the J48 classifier for the classification tasks using these summarized data will be presented in Section 5. Finally, this paper is concluded in Section 6 by presenting some of the findings obtained from the experiments performed in this study.

2 Data Transformation Using DARA

In this section, we first describe the concept of multi-relational setting for data stored in a relational database. Then, we describe how a single object stored in a target table that is associated with many objects stored in a non-target table can be represented in a vector space model.

2.1 Multi-relational Setting

In a relational database, a single record, R_i, stored in the target table can be associated with other records stored in the non-target table, as shown in Fig. 1. Let R denote a set of m records stored in the target table and let S denote a set of n records (T_1, T_2, T_3, ..., T_n), stored in the non-target table. Let S_i be a subset of S, $S_i \subseteq S$, associated through a foreign key with a single record R_a stored in the target table, where $R_a \in R$. Thus, the association of these records can be described as $R_a \leftarrow S_i$. In this case, we have a single record stored in the target table that is associated with multiple records stored in the non-target table. The records stored in the non-target table that correspond to a particular record stored in the target table can be represented as vectors of features. As a result, based on the vector space model [4], a unique record stored in non-target table can be represented as a vector of features. In other words, a particular record stored in the target table that is related to several records stored in the non-target table can be represented as a bag of patterns, i.e., by the patterns it contains and their frequency, regardless of their order. The bag of patterns is defined as follows:

Definition 1. In a bag of patterns representation, each unique record stored in the non-target table is represented by the set of its pattern and the pattern frequencies.

This definition states that a single record data in a multi-relational setting can be described as a collection of individuals and the induced rules generalize over the individuals, mapping them to a class. For instance, individual-centered domains include classification problems in molecular biology where the individuals are molecules.

2.2 Relational Data Representation in a Vector Space Model

In this subsection, we describe the representation of data for objects stored in multiple tables with one-to-many relations. Let DB be a database consisting of n objects. Let $R := \{R_1,...,R_m\}$ be the set of different representations existing for objects in DB and each object may have zero or more than one representation of each R_i, such that $|R_i| \geq 0$, where $i = 1,...,m$. Each object $O_i \in DB$, where $i = 1,...,n$ can be described by maximally m different representations with each representation has its frequency,

$$O_i := \{ R_1(O_i):|R_1(O_i)|:|Ob(R_1)|,...,R_m(O_i):|R_m(O_i)|:|Ob(R_m)| \} \tag{1}$$

where $R_j(O_i)$ represents the j-th representation in the i-th object and $|R_j(O_i)|$ represents the frequency of the j-th representation in the i-th object, and finally $|Ob(R_j)|$ represents the frequency of object with j-th representation. If all different representations exist for O_i, then the total different representations for O_i is $|O_i| = m$ else $|O_i| < m$.

In relational instance-based learning, the distance measures are defined based on the attribute's type [5] and the distance between two objects is based on the minimum distance between pair of instances from the two objects. In our approach, we apply the vector-space model [6] to represent each object. In this model, each object O_i is considered as a vector in the representation-space. In particular, we employed the *rf-iof* term weighting model borrowed from [6], where in which each object O_i, $i = 1,...,n$ can be represented as

$$(rf_1 \cdot \log(n/of_1), rf_2 \cdot \log(n/of_2), \ldots , rf_m \cdot \log(n/of_m)) \qquad (2).$$

where rf_j is the frequency of the j-th representation in the object, of_j is the number of objects that contain the j-th representation and n is the number of objects. To account for objects of different lengths, the length of each object vector is normalized so that it is of unit length ($||o_{rfiof}|| = 1$), that is each object is a vector on the unit hypersphere. In this experiment, we will assume that the vector representation for each object has been weighted using *rf-iof* and it has been normalized so that it is of unit length. In the vector-space model, the cosine similarity is the most commonly used method to compute the similarity between two objects O_i and O_j, $sim(O_i,O_j)$, which is defined as $cos(O_i,O_j) = O_i \cdot O_j/(||O_i|| \cdot ||O_j||)$. The cosine formula can be simplified to $cos(O_i,O_j) = O_i \cdot O_j$, when the record vectors are of unit length. This measure becomes one if the records are identical, and zero if there is nothing in common between them. The idea of our approach is to transform the data representation for all objects in a multi-relational environment into a vector space model and find the similarity distance measures for all objects to cluster them. These objects then are grouped based on the similarity of their characteristics, taking into account all possible representations and the frequency of each representation for all objects.

3   Feature Selection in DARA

Features used to describe instances are not necessarily all relevant and beneficial for inductive learning. In fact, a large number of features may slow down the induction process while giving similar results as obtained with a selected feature subset. The problem of feature subset selection can be considered as an optimization problem, in which the whole search space for optimization contains 2^F possible subsets of features, where F is the number of features.

3.1   Approaches to Feature Subset Selection

There are two main approaches to feature subset selection used in machine learning: the *Filtering* approach [7] and *Wrapper* approach [8]. Filtering approaches for feature subset selection attempt to assess the features and their merits using the data available independently of the learning method that will use the selected features. The decision tree filter, FOCUS, RELIEF and its variants are some of the widely known Filtering algorithms. The main objective of the decision tree filter and FOCUS filter is to find the minimum number of features that can effectively categorize the given objects. The RELIEF algorithm is an instance-based filter that handles instance spaces with no more than two class labels. All these filtering algorithms evaluate the features independently of the classifiers that use them. Some of the statistical and information theoretic measures used such as *information gain* and *cross-entropy* can be used to weigh the relevance of the features [9]. Other measures that capture the relationship of a feature with the target concept include probabilistic distance measure, probabilistic dependence measures, inter-class measures and information theoretic measures such as the *entropy* measure [10].

On the other hand, wrapper approaches for feature subset selection attempt to select a feature subset using the evaluation function based on the same learning algorithm that will be used for learning the domain represented with the selected features. The process is repeated until no improvement is made or addition/deletion of new features reduces the accuracy of the target learner.

3.2   Search Techniques

In the context of search techniques, feature selection algorithms can be divided into two categories: *sequential* algorithms and *randomized* algorithms. The *sequential* algorithm was first introduced by Devijver and Kitler [9] and this algorithm either starts with the full or empty feature set, and proceeds by greedily adding or removing features. *Sequential backward elimination* (SBE) starts with the full set of n features, and considers each of the n subsets of $n - 1$ features by removing each feature once. From these n subsets, the one giving the highest classification performance is chosen. The process is then repeated for the set of $n - 1$ remaining features and so on until some termination criterion is fulfilled. Similarly, *sequential forward selection* (SFS) can be defined, where the initial state is the empty set of features, and features are greedily added. The feature is added at each step that most increases the performance of the learner. It is not clear whether backward elimination or forward selection will perform better on a data set with no prior information on feature correlation.

On the other hand, *randomized* search algorithms differ from sequential algorithms in several aspects. Instead of starting with the full or empty set of features, these algorithms generally start somewhere in between, by generating a random subset of the features. The search then proceeds by randomly adapting the initial solution until a stopping criterion is fulfilled. Techniques based on simulated annealing or hill-climbing start from an initial guess and apply random changes until the solution does not change any more, or a fixed number of iterations have elapsed [11]. However, these methods are prone to getting stuck in local extrema. To solve this disadvantage, Holland [12] introduced population-based techniques, such as genetic algorithms (GA). GA operates on a whole set of possible solutions that are selected from the population instead of one solution. Using an iterative approach that mimics nature's evolutionary principle, new generations of the initial population are created using a set of three operators:

a) **Selection:** A number of good individuals is chosen and copied from one genera-
    tion into the next (survival)
b) **Crossover:** The parameters of two individuals are combined, to produce a new
    individual that is copied to the next generation.
c) **Mutation:** A certain parameter of a chosen individual is adapted (mutated) and
    the resulting individual is copied to the next generation

In this way, a GA can be viewed as a stochastic iterative sampling procedure. GAs
have been particularly useful when faced with complex optimization problems. In the
original GA, individuals were represented as a string of bits, yet later on strings
representing any kind of parameter type have been used [13, 14]. In this paper, we
apply the genetic based filtering approach to select relevant features for the DARA
algorithm to summarize data stored in a relational database.

4   A Genetic Based Feature Selection for Data Summarization

A Genetic Algorithm (GA) is generally a computational abstraction of biological
evolution approach that can be very useful to solve some searching and optimization
problems [12, 15]. GA process applies a series of biological genetic operators such
as selection, crossover and mutation to a population of elements called chromosome.
Chromosomes represent possible solutions to the searching and optimization problem.
Firstly, a random population which represents different points in the search space is
created. An objective and fitness function will be associated with each chromosome
that represents the level of quality of the chromosome. Based on the principle of the
survival of the fittest, several chromosomes are selected and each is assigned a number of copies which will be put into the mating pool. Crossover and mutation which
are biologically inspired operators are applied to these strings to produce a new generation of strings. The combined process of selection, crossover and mutation repeated continuously for a fixed number of generations or till a termination condition
is satisfied.

One of the ways to improve the data summarization results using clustering method
is by identifying and removing the less important features in the dataset. In this paper
we apply the string of bits to represent individual solution for our data summarization
technique. As mentioned in Section 2, DARA algorithm transforms relational data
into vectors of features as shown in Fig. 2. In Fig. 2, W_{if} represents the fth feature for
the ith record. For instance, suppose we have 10 features, $p=10$, for record R_1 as
$\{W_{11}, W_{12}, W_{13}, W_{14}, W_{15}, W_{16}, W_{17}, W_{18}, W_{19}, W_{110}\}$. Then, the possible chromosome that we can have will be $\{1,1,1,1,1,1,1,1,1,1\}$ in order to include all features for
the clustering purposes. However, in case we have a chromosome with a string of bits
as $\{0,1,1,0,1,1,1,0,1,1\}$, then only features $W_{12}, W_{13}, W_{15}, W_{16}, W_{17}, W_{19}$ and W_{110}
will be used for clustering purposes.

$$\begin{bmatrix} W_{11} & \cdots & W_{1f} & \cdots & W_{1p} \\ \vdots & \vdots & \vdots & \vdots & \vdots \\ W_{i1} & \cdots & W_{if} & \cdots & W_{ip} \\ \vdots & \vdots & \vdots & \ddots & \vdots \\ W_{n1} & \cdots & W_{nf} & \cdots & W_{np} \end{bmatrix}$$

Fig. 2. Relational data represented as vectors of features

The genetic algorithm will be used to get the best subset of features based on the cluster's dispersion and purity. In other words, cluster dispersion (e.g., Davies-Boulding Index, DBI [16]) and cluster purity (e.g., Gini Index [17,18]) are used as the fitness function in order to evaluate individual chromosome.

5   Experimental Setup and Results

In this experiment, we employ an algorithm, called DARA that converts the dataset representation in relational model into a space vector model and use a distanced-based method to group objects with multiple representations occurrence. With DARA algorithm, all representations of two objects are taken into consideration in measuring the similarity between these two objects. The DARA algorithm can also be seen as an aggregation function for multiple instances of an object, and is coupled with a few classifiers obtained from WEKA [19] that includes the *C4.5* classifier (J48 in WEKA), *RandomForest*, *HyperPipes*, *LogitBoost* and *SMO*, as induction algorithms that are run on the DARA's transformed data representation. We then evaluate the effectiveness of each data transformation with respect to these classifiers. All experiments with DARA and classifiers were performed using a leave-one-out cross validation estimation. We chose well-known dataset, Mutagenesis [21].

The mutagenesis data [21] describes 188 molecules falling in two classes, mutagenic (active) and non-mutagenic (inactive); 125 of these molecules are mutagenic. The description consists of the atoms and bonds that make up the compound. Thus, a molecule is described by listing its atoms *atom(AtomID, Element, Type, Charge)*, and the bonds *bond(Atom1, Atom2, BondType)* between atoms. In this experiment, we use only one set of background knowledge: B1. In B1, the atoms in the molecule are given, as well as the bonds between them; the type of each bond is given as well as the element and type of each atom. The table for B1 has the schema Molecule(ID, ATOM1, ATOM2, TYPE_ATOM1, TYPE_ATOM2, BOND_TYPE), where each molecule is described over several rows, listing all pairs of atoms with a bond, and the type of each atom, and the type of bond between them.

In the selection process, we apply the roulette-wheel selection in order to select chromosomes which will be used to generate a new population. Other parameters include crossover probability, $p_c = 0.25$, mutation probability, $p_m = 0.10$, population size is set to 20 and the number of generations is set to 50. Table 1 shows the predictive accuracies for *J48*, *RandomForest* and *LogitBoost* classifiers for the transformed data with genetic based feature selection method are higher compared to the transformed data without feature selection.

Table 1. Predictive accuracy results based on 10-fold cross-validation

Classifier	Without Clustering	Clustering Without Feature Selection	Clustering with Genetic Based Feature Selection
J48	78.2 %	80.3 %	**84.0%**
RandomForest	80.9 %	82.4 %	**84.6 %**
HyperPipes	77.1 %	**77.7 %**	**77.7 %**
LogitBoost	83.5 %	83.5 %	**84.6 %**
SMO	84.0 %	**84.6 %**	**84.6 %**

6   Conclusion

In the process of learning a given target table that has a one-to-many relationship with another non-target table, a data summarization process can be performed to summarize records stored in the non-target table that correspond to records stored in the target table. In the case of a classification task, part of the data stored in the non-target table can be summarized based on the class label or without the class label. To summarize the non-target table, a record can be represented as a vector of features. In order to get a better clustering result, a genetic based feature selection method is applied. These objects are then clustered or summarized based on the basis of those selected features. In this work, a genetic-based feature selection algorithm has been proposed to select features that best represent the characteristics of records that have multiple instances stored in the non-target table.

Unlike other approaches to feature selection, this paper has outlined the usage of feature selection to improve the descriptive accuracy of the proposed data summarization approach (DARA). Most feature selection methods deal with problems to find the best set of selected features that can improve the predictive accuracy of a classification task. This paper has described how feature selection can be used in the data summarization process for relational data to get better descriptive accuracy, and indirectly improve the predictive accuracy of a classification task. It is shown in the experimental results that the quality of summarized data is directly influenced by the selected features used to characterize individual record. The results of the evaluation of the genetic-based feature selection algorithm show that the data summarization results can be improved by selecting relevant features.

References

1. Kramer, S., Lavrac, N., Flach, P.: Propositionalisation Approaches to Relational Data Mining. In: Deroski, S., Lavrac, N. (eds.) Relational Data Mining. Springer (2001)

2. Alfred, R., Kazakov, D.: Data Summarization Approach to Relational Domain Learning Based on Frequent Pattern to Support the Development of Decision Making. In: Li, X., Zaïane, O.R., Li, Z.-h. (eds.) ADMA 2006. LNCS (LNAI), vol. 4093, pp. 889–898. Springer, Heidelberg (2006)
3. van Rijsbergen, C.J.: Information Retrieval. Butterworth (1979)
4. Salton, G., McGill, M.: Introduction to Modern Information Retrieval. McGraw-Hill Book Company (1984)
5. Horvath, T., Wrobel, S., Bohnebeck, U.: Relational instance-based learning with lists and terms. Machine Learning 43(1), 53–80 (2001)
6. Salton, G., Wong, A., Yang, C.S.: A vector space model for automatic indexing. Communications of the ACM 18, 613–620 (1975)
7. Bensusan, H., Kuscu, I.: Constructive Induction using Genetic Programming. In: Fogarty, T., Venturini, G. (eds.) Evolutionary Computing and Machine Learning Workshop, ICML 1996 (1996)
8. Aha, D.W., Bankert, R.L.: Feature Selection for Case-Based Classification of Cloud Types. In: Proceedings of the AAAI 1994 Workshop on Case-Based Reasoning. AAAI Press, Seattle (1994)
9. Devijver, P.A., Kittler, J.V.: Pattern Recognition: A Statistical Approach. Prentice Hall (1982)
10. Doak, J.: An Evaluation of Feature Selection Methods and Their Application to Computer Security. Technical report, UC Davis Department of Computer Science (1992)
11. Skalak, D.B.: Prototype and Feature Selection by Sampling and Random Mutation Hill Climbing Algorithms. In: ICML, pp. 293–301 (1994)
12. Holland, J.: Adaptation in Natural and Artificial Systems. University of Michigan Press (1975)
13. Fernando, E.B., Monique, M.S., Freitas, A.A., Nievola, J.C.: Genetic Programming for Attribute Construction in Data Mining. In: Ryan, C., Soule, T., Keijzer, M., Tsang, E.P.K., Poli, R., Costa, E. (eds.) EuroGP 2003. LNCS, vol. 2610, pp. 384–393. Springer, Heidelberg (2003)
14. Kudo, M., Sklansky, J.: Comparison of Algorithms That Select Features for Pattern Classifiers. Pattern Recognition 33(1), 25–41 (2000)
15. Goldberg, D.E.: Genetic Algorithms in Search, Optimization and Machine Learning. Addison-Wesley Publishing Company, Inc. (1989)
16. Davies, D.L., Bouldin, D.W.: A Cluster Separation Measure. IEEE Trans. Pattern Analysis and Machine Intelligence, 224–227 (1979)
17. Breiman, L., Friedman, J., Olshen, T., Stone, C.: Classification and Regression Trees. Wadsworth International, California (1984)
18. Raileanu, L.E., Stoffel, K.: Theoretical Comparison Between the Gini Index and Information Gain Criteria. Annals of Mathematics and Artificial Intelligence 41(1), 77–93 (2004)
19. Witten, I., Frank, E.: Data Mining: Practical Machine Learning Tools and Techniques with Java Implementations. Morgan Kaufman (1999)
20. Quinlan, J.R.: C4.5: Programs for Machine Learning. Morgan Kaufmann, Los Altos (1993)
21. Srinivasan, A., Muggleton, S.H., Sternberg, M.J.E., King, R.D.: Theories for mutagenicity: A Study in first-order and feature-based induction. Artificial Intelligence 85 (1996)
22. Alfred, R.: Feature transformation: A genetic-based feature construction method for data summarization. Computational Intelligence 26(3), 337–357 (2010)
23. Alfred, R.: The Study of Dynamic Aggregation of Relational Attributes on Relational Data Mining. In: Alhajj, R., Gao, H., Li, X., Li, J., Zaïane, O.R. (eds.) ADMA 2007. LNCS (LNAI), vol. 4632, pp. 214–226. Springer, Heidelberg (2007)

Inference of a Phylogenetic Tree: Hierarchical Clustering versus Genetic Algorithm

Glenn Blanchette, Richard O'Keefe, and Lubica Benuskova

Computer Science Department, Otago University, New Zealand
{gblanche,ok,lubica}@cs.otago.ac.nz

Abstract. This paper compares the implementations and performance of two computational methods, hierarchical clustering and a genetic algorithm, for inference of phylogenetic trees in the context of the artificial organism *Caminalcules*. Although these techniques have a superficial similarity, in that they both use agglomeration as their construction method, their origin and approaches are antithetical. For a small problem space of the original species proposed by Camin (1965) the genetic algorithm was able to produce a solution which had a lower Fitch cost and was closer to the theoretical evolution of *Caminalcules*. Unfortunately for larger problem sizes its time cost increased exponentially making the greedy directed search of the agglomerative clustering algorithm a more efficient approach.

Keywords: phylogenetics, genetic algorithm, agglomerative clustering, Caminalcules.

1   Introduction

Phylogenetic trees are a diagrammatic representation of the evolutionary relationships between taxonomic units (TU). They can be inferred using a variety of methods (Cotta 2002, Felsenstein 2004): supervised optimization methods based on cost (Guindon 2003), unsupervised distance methods (Russo 1996) and probability models of evolution.

Recent research has centered on probability models (Sullivan 2005) and clustering. Tamura (2004) has encouraged the use of clustering algorithms even for large taxonomies and these neighbour-joining methods form the basis of an integrated software package 'MEGA' (Tamura 1994). By contrast, genetic algorithms seem to have been neglected or only implemented for small problems (Lewis 1989). Moreover, Hudson and Bryant (2006) have suggested that tree structures do not have the flexibility required to represent complex phylogenies and that networks are better suited.

Joseph Camin invented the *Caminalcules* species in 1965 as a means of evaluating phylogenetic inference methods (Camin 1965). They are used in many universities for teaching phylogenetics (Gendron 2011, Ausich 2011). There are 29 'currently existing' species and 48 'fossil' species. Each individual has 85 morphological characteristics: a variety of Boolean, nominal and ordered numeric attributes. Sokal published an extensive four-part article on the *Caminalcules* in 1983 (Sokal 1983). A cladistic approach to phylogenetic analysis is usually based on evolutionary relationships, which include idiosyncratic heuristic information from the 'fossil' records. However, a

M. Thielscher and D. Zhang (Eds.): AI 2012, LNCS 7691, pp. 300–312, 2012.
© Springer-Verlag Berlin Heidelberg 2012

strict computational approach to the phylogenetic analysis can be applied using just morphological differences (phenetics) between the 'existing' species.

This paper aims to directly compare two different computational methods of inference in the construction of a phylogenetic tree for the *Caminalcules* species. Although other authors have considered which varieties of genetic algorithm are best suited for phylogenetic inference (Cotta 2002), as far as we are aware this is the first direct comparison of a clustering and a genetic algorithm approach for inference of the same *Caminalcules* phylogeny.

2   Implementations

Agglomerative hierarchical clustering was chosen as a distance method and a genetic algorithm as an optimization method. Both applications were implemented using object-oriented design in C++ and share support classes representing a phylogenetic (binary) tree: an abstract parent *TU_Node* class that is extended in its children *OTU_Node* (observed taxonomic unit) and *HTU_Node* (hypothetical taxonomic unit). The data members for each of the *Node* classes include: an identifier and the three tree pointers (parent, left and right child).

The *Caminalcules* data vectors were initially read from a text file of character vectors into bit fields. Non-applicable characteristics 'x' were represented as binary 0001, '0' was represented as binary 0010, '1' was represented as binary 0100, '2' was represented as binary 1000, and so on.

Two methods were implemented for calculating the tree cost metric: the Fitch/Hamming distance and a combined Fitch/Manhattan distance to better adjust for continuous characteristics. The former method measures the minimum number of substitutions required to change one string into the other. The later method finds the difference between two bit fields using intersection and converts the difference into a scaled ordinal distance. The result is a semi-quantitative cost. The advantage of this metric is that continuous measurements such as 'flange-length' are treated as ordinals. The disadvantage is that nominal characteristics such as 'top-of-head' (depressed, flat or crested) may be treated incorrectly if there are more than two values. The cost metric was converted to a fitness metric: fitness = constant – cost. The range of values for the Fitch costing was experimentally determined and a constant value sufficient to maintain a positive value for the fitness was used.

The phylogenetic trees produced by the applications were output in two standard formats: Newick format (wikipedia.org 2012) as text and GraphViz Dot format (graphviz.org 2011) for a diagrammatic tree.

2.1   Agglomerative Clustering

The implementation of bottom-up agglomerative clustering is from O'Keefe [2006]. The algorithm is deceptively simple: starting with the matrix for distances between single OTU clusters it successively merges the closest clusters by forming a tree with an HTU node as the new root, it re-calculates the distances from the new cluster to all the existing clusters and reduces the matrix by moving the last cluster (row/column) up until all the clusters are included in a single tree. The matrix is symmetric around the diagonal, so only one half of the matrix needs to be calculated.

O'Keefe recommends using an average linkage criterion, since this includes a contribution from each of the vectors within a cluster. The maximal and minimal linkage criteria use only one vector difference, which may not be representative of the overall inter-cluster distance. The basis of the clustering algorithm is reported in Sokal [1983] and Murtagh [1984]. A segment of pseudo-code for the clustering agglomeration is shown in Figure 1.

```
Find the two closest existing clusters a & b
    size ab = size a + size b
//Calculate all distances to the new cluster
for every existing cluster x {
    calculate its distance to the new cluster
    based on average linkage: distance ab-x =
    (dist a-x * size a + dist b-x * size b) / size ab
}
//Make new tree from cluster - join a & b with an HTU
tree a = new HTU_Node (HTU_node, tree a, tree b);
//Move last cluster up the matrix, last row/col ->
row/col b

for every column in the matrix {
    make the distance at [col][b] & [b][col] =
    the distance at [col][last]
    and then clear the distance at [col][last]
}
tree b = tree last;
    size b = size last;
```

Fig. 1. Pseudo-code for the Clustering Algorithm agglomeration

2.2   Genetic Algorithm

The base process of any genetic algorithm is identical, it repetitively selects and breeds individuals within the population. Only the individual chromosome representation, which underlies breeding and the fitness/selection metric, are specific to the particular problem.

In this case a chromosome representation outlined by O'Keefe [2009] was used. Here, the chromosome consists of pairs of sub-tree indices. The agglomerative process for building the new subtrees is very similar to the clustering algorithm. Initially Pairs of OTUs are successively merged with a new HTU at the root to form the new sub-trees, as the process continues the indices in the chromosome will apply to progressively larger trees until a single tree is formed. The difference between the algorithms is that the sub-tree indices for agglomeration by the genetic algorithm are chosen randomly on creation of the chromosome, whereas the clustering algorithm chooses clusters dynamically based on shortest distance. A segment of pseudo-code for the tree building is shown in Figure 2. Both the clustering algorithm and the genetic algorithm use the same overloaded constructor in the support class.

```
tree_build() { //method in Phylogeny Class
        //using an array of sub-trees
        //start at the bottom, from the leaves
        bottom = number of OTUs - 1
        for each allele in the chromosome {
        //get the pair of node indices p & q
        p = chromosome->x
        q = chromosome->y
        //combine these as a new sub-tree
        tree p = new HTU_Node (bottom, tree p, tree q)
        //reduce the array
        bottom - 1
        }
        //make a new node at the root
        tree 0 = new HTU_Node (bottom, tree 0, tree 1);
}
```

Fig. 2. Pseudo-code for the Genetic Algorithm agglomeration

The chromosomal representation used is robust and has closure because:

- It is able to represent every tree in the problem space,
- It is well formed and does not require any correction to the chromosome after crossover or mutation
- And it is modular in that changes produced by crossover or mutation are locally limited.

The framework of the genetic algorithm itself is more complex than a single execution of clustering; it requires a separate support class to manage the individuals within the population. The *Phylogeny* class keeps track of the raw and scaled fitness of each individual and its chromosome representation.

Two different selection methods were tried. The more complex method, proportional selection based on scaled fitness over the whole population was not a very strong driver for selection. Most of the random trees created were in the same fitness range, 400 – 800. The simpler method of just sorting the population by fitness and transfering a proportion into the next generation (truncation selection) was more effective. This is a common lay-person's (or 'breeder') method but suffers from the impurity of the attribute selection (Voigt & Muhlenbein, 1996), ie. it may reduce the fitness for some attributes.

Most of the methods in the *Phylogeny* class are just wrappers for methods within the Node classes: Newick and GraphViz Dot print methods and Fitch costing methods are shared with the clustering algorithm. However, the crossover and mutation methods are only required for the genetic algorithm and use an iterative loop to permit multiple crossover or mutation. Both of these methods operate directly on the chromosome, they do not involve any re-arrangement of the constructed trees. They conserve the chromosome structure because of the sound original choice of representation (O'Keefe 2009).

3   Results

3.1   Agglomerative Clustering

Agglomerative clustering using the Fitch metric and the average linkage criterion, produced a constant result, which appeared to have an optimal cost, 277 by Fitch, but 291 by the combined metric. The tree is given in Newick format and GraphViz Dot format, in Figure 3.

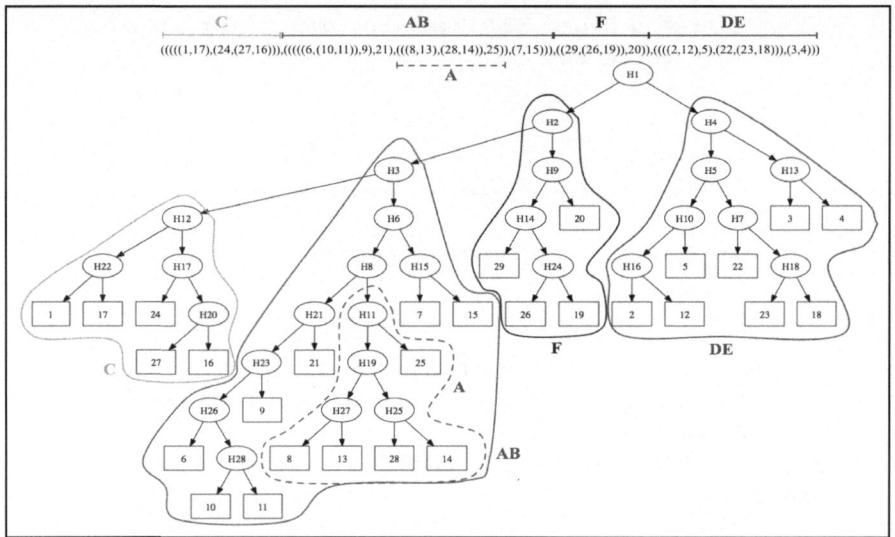

Fig. 3. Phylogenetic tree infered by clustering. Fitch Cost 277

Agglomerative clustering using the combined metric did not produce any marked improvement. There were four major branch groups (Figure 3) as illustrated by their OTUs, which were identical in both trees.

Group AB: (((((6, (10, 11)), 9), 21),
             (((8, 13), (14, 28)), 25)), (7, 15))
Group C: ((1, 17), (24, (16, 27)))
Group DE: (((2, 12), 5), (22, (18, 23)), (3, 4))
Group F: ((29, (19, 26)), 20)

The groups are labeled in this way to match the classification published by Sokal (1983).

3.2   Genetic Algorithm

One of the time-consuming phases of using any genetic algorithm is tuning. The results of trials for tuning the parameters are not presented. However, in summary the optimal values (and range) were:

- Generations: 900 (100 – 18,000)
- Population size: 40 individual trees (20 – 100)
- Selection proportion: 50% (20 – 60)
- Crossover rate: > 0.25 (0.2 – 0.8)
- Mutation rate: >0.35 (0.1 – 0.5)

The low crossover and high mutation rates are unusual. However, there was good propagation of 'beneficial' chromosomes in early generations even at this low crossover rate. A high mutation rate was required to achieve solutions close to the theoretical trees of Sokal (1983) and of lowest Fitch cost. Epistasis may have influenced the high mutation rate. Our mutation algorithm assumed that each attribute was independent of the others; this was in fact not the case. Although Camin and Sokal (1965) have not explicitly defined dependencies within the attributes, implicit dependencies are present in the morphological drawings.

Experiments with two-point crossover and mutation were not beneficial, with a larger number of runs being required to reach a result close to that of agglomerative clustering. So most of the experimental testing was done with just single point mutations and single crossovers.

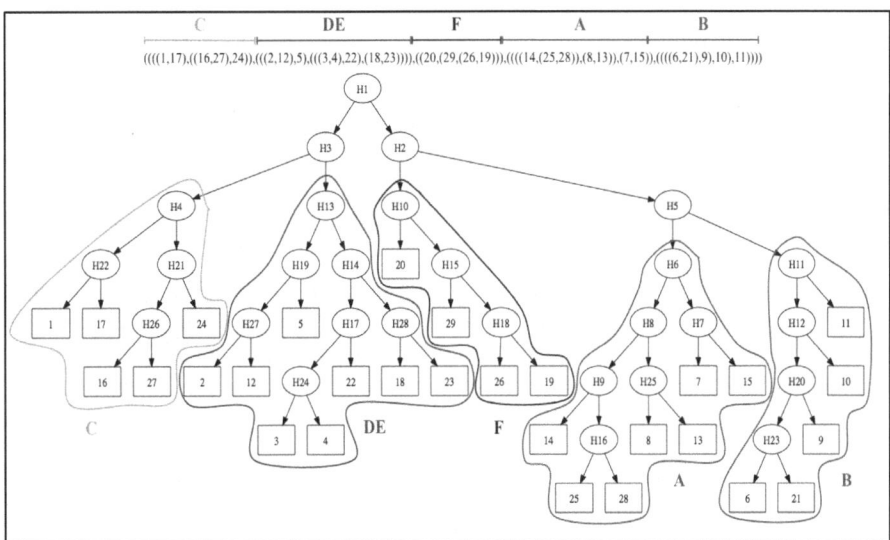

Fig. 4. Phylogenetic tree infered by genetic algorithm. Fitch Cost 266

After much trial and error, a phylogenetic tree with a Fitch cost of 266 was discovered; see Figure 4. This tree was superior to the tree produced by the clustering algorithm. In terms of the previously identified tertiary level branch groupings it is identical for groups C, DE and F but group BA is divided into two subtrees:

Group A: ((8, 13), (25, 28), 14)
Group B: (((((6, 9), 10), (11, 21)), (7, 15))
Group C: (((1, 17), (16, 24)), 27)
Group DE: (((2, 12), 5), ((3, 4), 22), (18, 23))
Group F: (29, (19, (20, 26)))

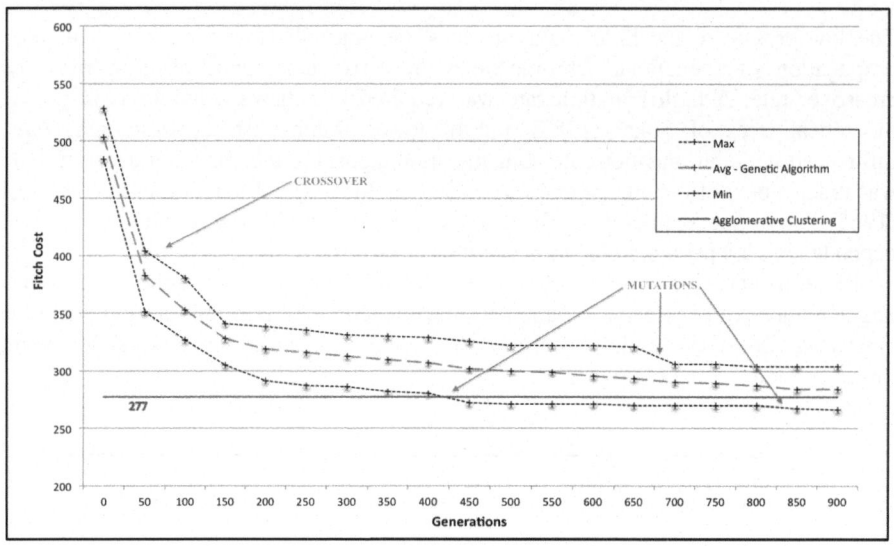

Fig. 5. 'Evolution' of a phylogeny using the genetic algorithm

It is interesting to look at the evolution of this solution over time. Figure 5 shows the data collected from the genetic algorithm compared to the static cost of the agglomerative clustering. Initially it can be seen that the fittest chromosomes are quickly spread through the whole population by crossover and then the process of improvement plateaus at some steady state. Over time 'beneficial' mutations occur and there is a further smaller change in the population. Average solutions for the genetic algorithm are worse than for clustering but the best genetic solution had a lower cost.

4   Discussion

Even for this artificial biological problem: that phylogenetic trees can be inferred by a number of different approaches, phenetic and cladistic, suggests that no single tree is likely to be perfect. A 'history' of the *Caminalcules* has been published by Sokal (1983), which includes the complete cladistic classification.

According to Sokal the *Caminalcules* evolved into five genera over 19 periods, four lines terminating in fossils. The current genera are:

Group A:	(((14, (25, 28)), (18, 13)), (17, 15))
Group B:	((((6, 21), 9), 10), 11)
Group C:	((1, 17), ((16, 27), 24))
Group DE:	(((2, 12), 5), (((3, 4), 22), (18, 23)))
Group F:	(20, (29, (26, 19)))

A binary phylogenetic tree was adapted from Sokal's classification using hypothetical taxonomic units to represent the fossil species and internal node branch points, see Figure 6.

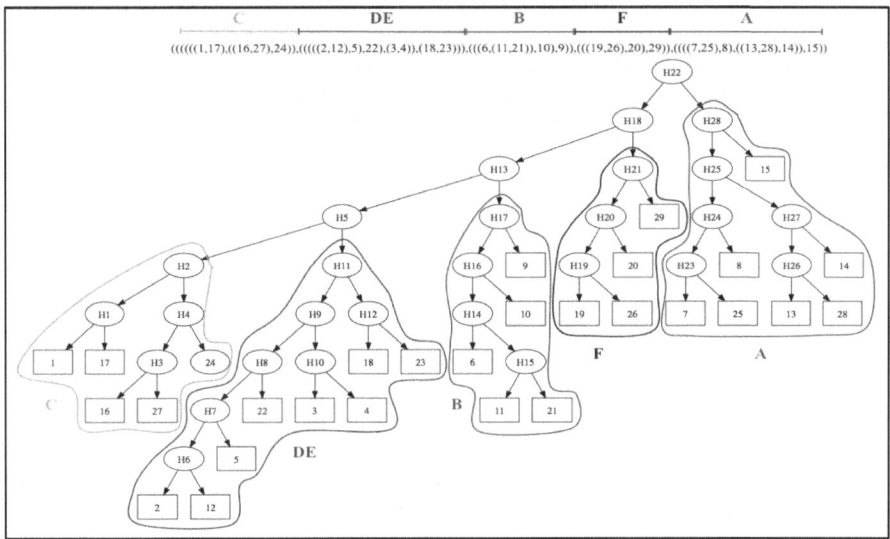

Fig. 6. Phylogenetic tree adapted from Sokal. Fitch Cost 270

It should be noted that the heuristics Sokal used for construction of his cladistic phylogeny are quite different to those used for the current implementations. Sokal's original phylogeny is not a binary tree; it does not require that each pair of OTUs have a common HTU ancestor. In addition Sokal's cladistic tree has current OTUs as branch points and their own leaves. Because the implementations presented are purely computational they have been strictly constructed; as binary trees, with OTUs as leaves and HTUs as internal nodes.

If Sokal's classification is compared to the phenetic tree produced by the genetic algorithm (Figure 4), the distribution of species within each genus is identical. Considering the very different construction of the trees and that the current implementation did not have the evidence of the 48 'fossils' to work with, the results from the genetic algorithm seem very respectable. Why does the agglomerative clustering algorithm fail to find the best solution? One answer could be that it is a greedy algorithm; it chooses only the best current subtrees (at the lower levels). It misses the optimization that occurs at a higher level in the phylogeny.

These two implementations of a phenetic classification (clustering and genetic algorithm) may seem similar, they both construct trees by aggregation of subtrees, but the similarity is superficial because most trees are commonly constructed by aggregation. In fact, the approaches come from entirely different branches of science. Agglomerative clustering is an engineering approach. It aims to provide a single fast concise solution based on an exact as possible mathematical measurement of distance. This exact measurement intentionally drives the process of construction. The genetic algorithm comes from biology. It is inexact; most of its 'solutions' are poor. No plan is applied during construction of the trees. In fact, it is not aiming to find a solution, only explore the problem space. There is no driving force, except chance. It is only after construction that selection and time filter the results; by its nature it is a slow process.

After testing the algorithms on the base *Caminalcules* phylogeny, four ideas emerged for further investigation and comparison of these phylogenetic inference methods.

4.1   Including the Fossil Evidence

The first idea was: could the algorithms be extended to produce a cladistically based phylogenetic tree? Given all the available fossil evidence (48 additional taxons) could the tree published by Sokal (1983) be duplicated exactly? It is perhaps easier to see how the genetic algorithm could be adapted to use this additional information. A separate randomly shuffled array of fossil HTUs could be added to the implementation. As each chromosome pair is aggregated, the next of these random HTUs would be used as the parent node. This would leave 20 terminating fossil lines but still might achieve a result close to Sokal's. Crossover of the chromosome representation would require some structural fix. However, for the agglomerative clustering algorithm, adaption would be more difficult. The fossil HTUs could not just be added to the original distance matrix, as there has to be some distinction between them and the OTUs which cannot be parent nodes. A separate distance matrix for the HTUs as a mid-point between clusters might be needed, but this would greatly increase the complexity of the algorithm.

4.2   Extending the Time for Evolution

The second idea was hinted at previously, in Section 3 Results. If the genetic algorithm was given sufficient time would mutation produce further improvement in the phylogenetic tree? This idea was interesting enough to check immediately. A change was made in the statistical sampling, to look for a particularly 'lucky' run of the algorithm (Fitch cost <= 270) and to continue it for up to 18,000 generations. After hundreds of runs the tree in Figure 7 was discovered. It had a Fitch cost of only 262, thus confirming our hypothesis. The last reduction in the cost of this tree was produced by a mutation after 10,000 generations.

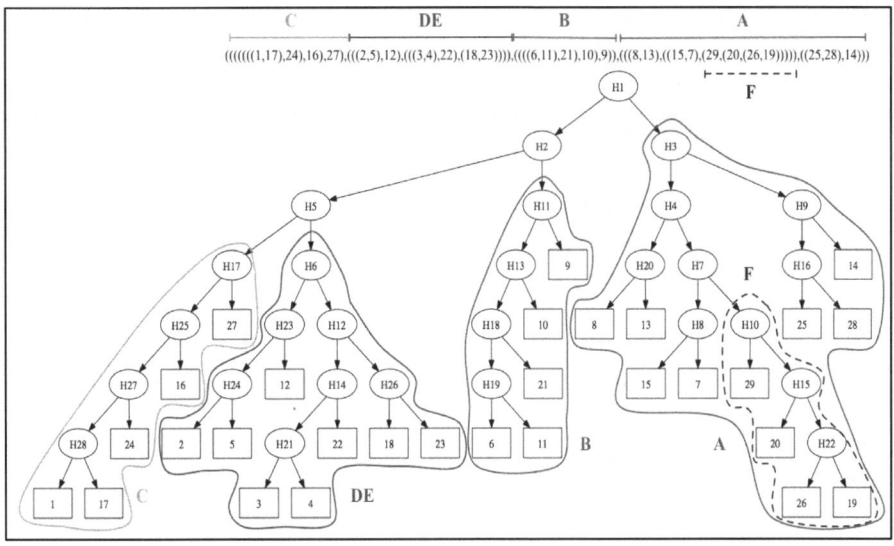

Fig. 7. Phylogenetic tree infered by genetic algorithm. Fitch Cost 262

Surprisingly, this tree had branch groupings, which were quite different from the earlier clustering result (Figure 5) and from the previous results for the genetic algorithm (Figure 6). Particularly genus F was included as a sub-tree of genus A:

Group AF: (((8, 13), ((15, 7),
(F):   (29, (20, (26, 19))))),
((25, 28), 14)))
Group B: (((((6, 11), 21), 10), 9)
Group C: ((((1, 7), 24), 16), 27)
Group DE: (((2, 5), 12), (((3, 4), 22), (18, 23))))

So this tree was not as close to the theoretically correct tree produce by Sokal (1983). Unfortunately, while it is possible to find trees with lower objective morphological cost, they may not always be cladistically as acceptable. It would be difficult to build idiosyncratic cladistic parameters into an objective/fitness function.

4.3   Scaling the Problem Size

The third idea was to examine the complexity of the genetic algorithm, scaling the problem size by inventing further *Caminalcules* species. Considering there are 85 attributes with at least two values; billions of un-utilized combinations are available. A further 50,000 unique *Caminalcules* species were generated. The time cost and solution quality of the inferred phylogenetic trees for both the agglomerative clustering and genetic algorithm were tested against increasing numbers of OTUs, using the optimal tuning parameters for the original problem. Figure 8 shows that while the time complexity of the genetic algorithm is almost linear, it is inferior to the almost constant time cost of the clustering algorithm. Further, Figure 9 shows that the quality of the genetic algorithm solutions were deteriorating in comparison to those of the clustering algorithm because the algorithm was not optimally tuned for these larger problems. Satisfactory tuning of the genetic algorithm for some of these larger problem sizes was attempted, by for example proportionately increasing the population size, in addition to experimenting with the other parameters. This experimentation was unable to improve the quality of the genetic algorithm solutions but did result in an exponential increase in the time cost.

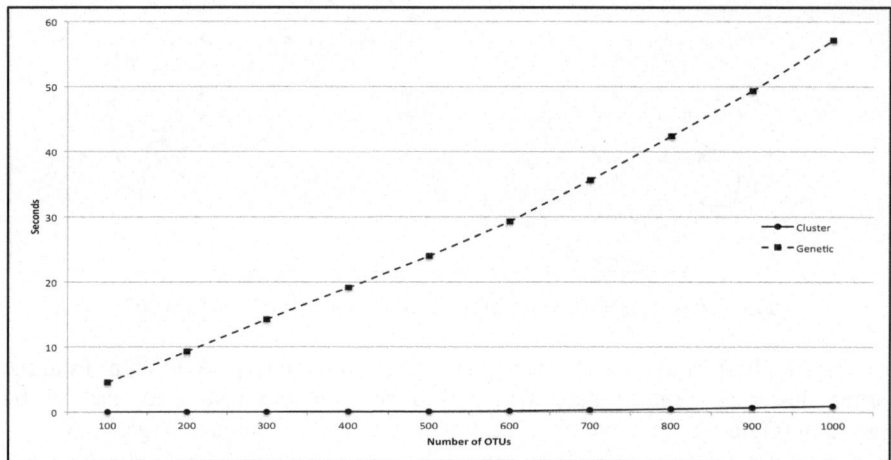

Fig. 8. Comparison of real time costs for the genetic and clustering algorithms

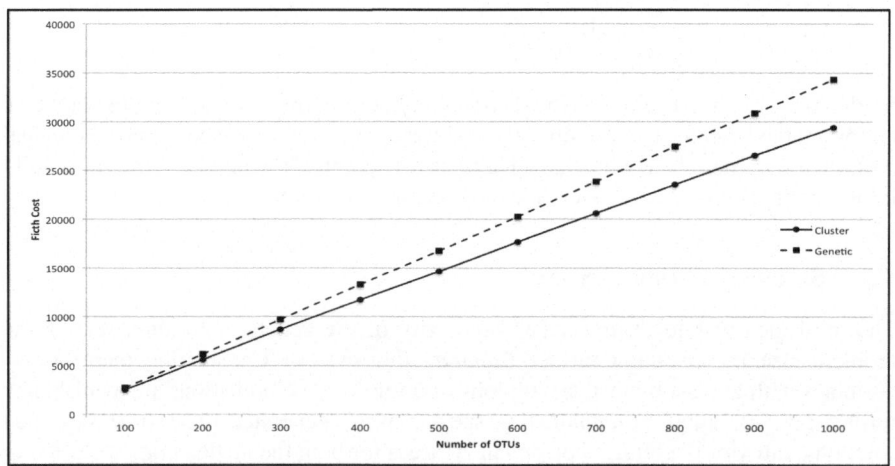

Fig. 9. Comparison of solution quality for the genetic and clustering algorithms

4.4   Extending the Comparisons

If space permitted, it would have been possible to include the results of comparisons for other data sets. However, based on our current experiments, we felt these were likely to show the same difficulties with scaling of the genetic algorithm and would not have altered the conclusion.

Currently, the more modern approaches to phylogenetic inference are based on probabilistic models of evolution; see Ronquist & Huelsenbeck (2003) and Drummond & Rambaut (2007) implemented in the software "MrBayes" and "Beast", respectively. It would be very interesting and informative to compare the phylogeny trees for *Caminalcules* inferred based on a probabilistic model of their evolution, but this work is beyond the scope of the present article.

5   Conclusion

Although these techniques have a superficial similarity, in that they both use agglomeration as their construction method, their origins and approaches are antithetical. The genetic algorithm permits more thorough exploration and for a small problem space, such as the 29 original *Caminalcules* species, it achieves a solution which has a lower Fitch cost and is closer to the theoretical evolution proposed by Sokal (1983). However there is a time cost for this exploration and tuning the algorithm for larger problems is exponentially less efficient than agglomerative clustering. A directed search even though greedy and unable to guarantee an optimal solution, may be advantageous.

References

1. Ausich, W.: Caminalcule Phylogenetic Exercise. Ohio State University (2011), http://www.serc.carleton.edu/NAGTWorkshops/paleo/activities
2. Drumond, A., Rambaut, A.: BEAST: Bayesian Evolutionary Analysis by Sampling Trees. BMC Evolutionary Biology 7, 214–221 (2007)
3. Camin, J., Sokal, R.: A Method for Deducing Branching Sequences in Phylogeny. Evolution 19, 311–326 (1965)
4. Cotta, C., Moscato, P.: Inferring Phylogenetic Trees Using Evolutionary Algorithms. In: Guervós, J.J.M., Adamidis, P.A., Beyer, H.-G., Fernández-Villacañas, J.-L., Schwefel, H.-P. (eds.) PPSN 2002. LNCS, vol. 2439, pp. 720–729. Springer, Heidelberg (2002)
5. Felsenstein, J.: Infering Phylogenies. Sinauer Associates, Sunderland (2004)
6. GraphViz Dot, http://www.graphviz.org/News.php
7. Gendron, R.: Caminalcule Evolution Lab. Indiana University Pennsylvania (2011), http://www.nsm1.nsm.iup.edu
8. Guindon, S., Gascuel, O.: A Simple, Fast, and Accurate Algorithm to Estimate Large Phylogenies by Maximum Likelihood. Systematic Biology 52(5), 696–704 (2003)
9. Hudson, D., Bryant, D.: Application of Phylogenetic Networks in Evolutionary Studies. Molecular Biology and Evolution 23(2), 254–267 (2006)
10. Lewis, P.: A genetic algorithm for maximum likely-hood phylogeny inference using nucleotide sequence data. Molecular Biology and Evolution 15(3), 277–283 (1989)

11. Murtagh, F.: Complexities of Hierarchical Clustering Algorithms: the State of the Art. Computational Statistics Quarterly 1, 101–113 (1984)
12. Newick Format, http://www.wikipedia.org/wiki/Newick_format
13. O'Keefe, R.: Cluster Analysis, notes for Cosc348. Otago University (2006), http://www.cs.otago.ac.nz/cosc348/phylo/phylo5.html
14. O'Keefe, R.: Laboratory 07, notes for Cosc348. Otago University (2009), http://www.cs.otago.ac.nz/cosc348/labs/lab07.html
15. Ronquist, F., Huslsenbeck, J.: MrBayes 3: Bayesian Phylogenetic Inference Under Mixed Models. Bioinformatics 19(12), 1572–1574 (2003)
16. Russo, C., Takezaki, N., Lei, M.: Efficiences of genes and different tree-building methods in recovering a known vertebrate phylogeny. Molecular Biology and Evolution 13(3), 525–536 (1996)
17. Sokal, R.: A Phylogenetic Analysis of the Caminalcules. I. The Data Base. Systematic Zoology 32(2), 159–184 (1983)
18. Sokal, R.: A Phylogenetic Analysis of the Caminalcules. II. Estimating the True Cladogram. Systematic Zoology 32(2), 185–201 (1983)
19. Sokal, R.: A Phylogenetic Analysis of the Caminalcules. III. Fossils and Classification. Systematic Zoology 32(3), 248–258 (1983)
20. Sokal, R.: A Phylogenetic Analysis of the Caminalcules. IV. Congruence and Character Stability. Systematic Zoology 32(3), 259–275 (1983)
21. Sokal, R., Michener, C.: A Statistical Method for Evaluating Systematic Relationships. University of Kanas Science Bulletin 38, 1409–1438 (1985)
22. Sullivan, J., Joyce, P.: Model Selection in Phylogenetics. Annual Review of Ecology, Evolution and Systematics 36, 445–466 (2005)
23. Tamura, K., Nei, M., Kumar, S.: Prospects for infering very large phylogenies by using neighbour-joining method. Procedings of the National Academy of Sciences 101(30), 11030–11035 (2004)
24. Tamura, K., Nei, M., Kumar, S.: MEGA: Molecular Evolutionary Genetics Analysis software for microcomputers. Bioinformatics 10(2), 189–191 (1994)
25. Voigt, H., Muhlenbein, H.: Erroneous Truncation Selection – A Breeder's Decision Making Perspective (1996), http://www.muehlenbein.org/errtrun96.pdf

A Dimension Reduction Approach to Classification Based on Particle Swarm Optimisation and Rough Set Theory

Liam Cervante[1], Bing Xue[1], Lin Shang[2], and Mengjie Zhang[1]

[1] Victoria University of Wellington, PO Box 600, Wellington 6140, New Zealand
[2] State Key Laboratory of Novel Software Technology, Nanjing University,
Nanjing 210046, China
{Bing.Xue,Liam.Cervante,Mengjie.Zhang}@ecs.vuw.ac.nz, shanglin@nju.edu.cn

Abstract. Dimension reduction aims to remove unnecessary attributes from datasets to overcome the problem of "the curse of dimensionality", which is an obstacle in classification. Based on the analysis of the limitations of the standard rough set theory, we propose a new dimension reduction approach based on binary particle swarm optimisation (BPSO) and probabilistic rough set theory. The new approach includes two new specific algorithms, which are *PSOPRS* using only the probabilistic rough set in the fitness function and *PSOPRSN* adding the number of attributes in the fitness function. Decision trees, naive Bayes and nearest neighbour algorithms are employed to evaluate the classification accuracy of the reduct achieved by the proposed algorithms on five datasets. Experimental results show that the two new algorithms outperform the algorithm using BPSO with standard rough set and two traditional dimension reduction algorithms. PSOPRSN obtains a smaller number of attributes than PSOPRS with the same or slightly worse classification performance. This work represents the first study on probabilistic rough set for for filter dimension reduction in classification problems.

Keywords: Dimension reduction, Particle Swarm Optimisation, Filter Approaches, Classification.

1 Introduction

Classification is an important task in machine learning and data mining. However, it often involves a large number of attributes in the datasets. The large attribute dimension causes the problem of "the curse of dimensionality" [1]. Dimension reduction, also called attribute reduction, aims to reduce the unnecessary attributes to reduce the attribute dimension while preserving the classification power of original attributes to maintain the classification performance [2]. By removing the unnecessary attributes, dimension reduction can reduce the training time of a learning algorithm and simplify the learnt classifier [3,4].

Existing dimension reduction algorithms can be broadly classified into two categories: wrapper approaches and filter approaches [3,5]. Wrapper approaches

M. Thielscher and D. Zhang (Eds.): AI 2012, LNCS 7691, pp. 313–325, 2012.

include a learning algorithm as part of the evaluation function to determine the goodness of the reduct. Therefore, wrappers can often achieve better results than filters [6]. Filter approaches are independent of a learning algorithm. Therefore, they are argued to be computationally cheaper and more general than wrappers.

Dimension reduction is a difficult task, where the size of the search space grows exponentially along with the number of attributes in the dataset. Although many different search techniques have been applied to dimension reduction, most of these algorithms suffer from the problems of stagnation in local optima or being computationally expensive [3,7]. In order to better address dimension reduction problems, an efficient global search technique is needed. Evolutionary computation (EC) techniques are well-known for their global search ability. Particle swarm optimisation (PSO) [8,9] is a relatively recent EC technique, which is computationally less expensive than other EC algorithms. Therefore, PSO has been used as an effective technique in dimension reduction [4,10,11].

EC algorithms (including PSO) have been successfully applied to address dimension reduction problems. However, most of the existing EC based dimension reduction algorithms are wrapper approaches. Although wrappers can achieve better classification performance, the use of wrappers is limited in real-world applications because of the high computational cost. The development of EC based filter dimension reduction approaches still remains an open issue. On the other hand, rough set theory has been applied to attribute reduction [12]. However, standard rough set has limitations [13]. Probabilistic rough set can overcome such limitations and from a theoretical point of view, Yao and Zhao [13] have shown that probabilistic rough set can be a good measure in dimension reduction, but its performance has not been reported by experiments.

1.1   Goals

The overall goal of this paper is to develop a PSO based filter dimension reduction approach to classification to reduce the number of attributes and achieve similar classification performance to that of using all original attributes. To achieve this goal, we develop a new filter dimension reduction approach (with three new algorithms) based on PSO and probabilistic rough set theory. The proposed two dimension reduction algorithms will be examined and compared with a filter algorithm using standard rough set theory and two traditional algorithms on five different benchmark datasets. Specifically, we will investigate

- whether using PSO and *standard* rough set theory can reduce the number of attributes and maintain the classification performance,
- whether using PSO and *probabilistic* rough set theory can further reduce the number of attributes without decreasing the classification performance,
- whether considering *the number of attributes* in the fitness function can further reduce the number of attributes and maintain the classification performance.

2   Background

2.1   Particle Swarm Optimisation (PSO)

PSO is an evolutionary computation technique inspired by social behaviours of birds flocking and fish schooling [8,9]. In PSO, each candidate solution is represented as a particle in the swarm and PSO starts with a number of randomly generated particles. All the particles move in the search space to find the optimal solutions. During the movement, each particle (i.e., particle i) has a position and velocity, which are represented by vectors $x_i = (x_{i1}, x_{i2}, ..., x_{iD})$ and $v_i = (v_{i1}, v_{i2}, ..., v_{iD})$, respectively, where D is the dimensionality of the search space. A particle can remember the best positions it visits so far, which is called personal best *pbest*. The best position obtained by the population thus far is called *gbest*, based on which a particle can share information with its neighbours. A particle iteratively updates its position and velocity to search for the optimal solutions based on *pbest* and *gbest* according to the following equations:

$$x_{id}^{t+1} = x_{id}^t + v_{id}^{t+1} \tag{1}$$

$$v_{id}^{t+1} = w * v_{id}^t + c_1 * r_1 * (p_{id} - x_{id}^t) + c_2 * r_2 * (p_{gd} - x_{id}^t) \tag{2}$$

where t represents the tth iteration in the evolutionary process. $d \in D$ represents the dth dimension in the search space. w is the inertia weight, which can balance the local search and global search abilities of the algorithm. c_1 and c_2 are acceleration constants. r_1 and r_2 are random constants uniformly distributed in $[0, 1]$. p_{id} and p_{gd} denote the values of *pbest* and *gbest* in the dth dimension. v_{id}^{t+1} is limited by a predefined maximum velocity, v_{max} and $v_{id}^{t+1} \in [-v_{max}, v_{max}]$.

In order to extend PSO to address discrete problems. Kennedy and Eberhart [14] developed a binary particle swarm optimisation (BPSO). In BPSO, x_{id}, p_{id} and p_{gd} are restricted to 1 or 0. The velocity is still updated according to Equation (2), but it indicates the probability of the position in the corresponding dimension taking value 1. BPSO updates the position of each particle according to the following formula:

$$x_{id} = \begin{cases} 1, & \text{if } rand() <= \frac{1}{1+e^{-v_{id}}} \\ 0, & otherwise \end{cases} \tag{3}$$

where $rand()$ is a random number selected from a uniform distribution in $[0,1]$.

2.2   Rough Set Theory

Rough set theory developed by Pawlak [15] is a mathematical tool, which is able to deal with uncertainty, imprecision and vagueness. The main advantage of rough set theory is that it does not need any prior knowledge about the data.

In rough set theory, an information system can be denoted as $I = (U, A)$, where U is the universe of objects in the system and A is the set of attributes that describe each object. Equivalence relation is a relation that partitions a set so that every element of the set is a member of one and only one cell of the partition. Based on all equivalence relations described by A, the equivalence class relation partitions of U is $U_1, U_2, U_3, ..., U_n$, where n is the number of classes that objects in U may belong to.

For any $P \subseteq A$ and $X \subseteq U$, the equivalence relation is defined as $IND(P) = \{(x, y) \in \mathbb{U}^2 | \forall a \in P, a(x) = a(y)\}$. An equivalence class of $IND(P)$ is denoted as $[x]_P$, which means that $\forall y \in [x]_P$ (x, y) are indiscernible with regards to P. Based on the equivalent classes described by P, rough set theory defines a lower approximation $(\underline{P}X)$ and an upper approximation $(\overline{P}X)$ of X [15], where $\underline{P}X = \{x \in U | [x]_P \subseteq X\}$ and $\overline{P}X = \{x \in U | [x]_P \cap X \neq \emptyset\}$. $\underline{P}X$ contains all the objects, which can be surely classified to the target set X. $\overline{P}X$ contains the objects, which probably belong to the target set X.

An ordered pair $(\overline{P}X, \underline{P}X)$ is called a rough set. The concept of the reduct is fundamental for rough sets theory. A reduct is the essential part of an information system (related to a subset of attributes), which can achieve similar approximation power of classification as all the original attributes A. There can be many different reducts in a rough set and attribute reduction aims to search for the smallest reduct.

In the standard rough set theory [15], $\underline{P}X$ and $\overline{P}X$ were defined as two extreme cases in terms of the relationships between an equivalence class defined by P and the target set X. $\underline{P}X$ requires that the equivalence class is a subset of X while $\overline{P}X$ requires the equivalence class must have a non-empty overlap with X. However, the degree of their overlap is not taken into account, which will limit its applications. Therefore, researchers investigate probabilistic rough set theory to relax the definitions of the lower and upper approximations [13].

In probabilistic rough set theory, $\mu_P[x]$ (See Equation 4) is defined as a way to measure the fitness of a given instance $x \in X$.

$$\mu_P[x] = \frac{|[x]_P \cap X|}{|[x]_P|} \tag{4}$$

The lower approximation is defined as Equation 5.

$$\underline{apr}_P X = \{x | \mu_P[x] \geq \alpha\} \tag{5}$$

where α can be adjusted to restrict or relax the lower and upper approximations. Note that $\underline{apr}_P X = \underline{P}X$ when $\alpha = 1$. $\underline{apr}_P X$ loosens the boundaries of the rough set. In a given equivalence class, if a large number of instances are in the target set X, but a small number of instances are not, $\underline{apr}_P X$ will include them in the lower approximation.

From theoretical point of view, Yao and Zhao have claimed that probabilistic rough set can be a good way for attribute reduction problems [13]. However, it has not been analysed well by experiments.

2.3   Related Work on Dimension Reduction

A number of dimension reduction algorithms have been proposed in recent years [3,1,10]. Typical dimension reduction algorithms are reviewed in this section.

Traditional Dimension Reduction Approaches. A traditional filter dimension reduction approach is principal components analysis (PCA), which constructs a low-dimensional representation of the data by finding a few orthogonal linear combinations of the original variables with the largest variance [16]. Due to its conceptual simplicity and being relatively efficient, PCA has been widely used in practice. However, PCA increases the dimensionality of the data in some cases. Decision trees (DT) use only relevant attributes that are required to completely classify the training set and remove all other attributes. Cardie [17] proposes a filter based dimension reduction algorithm that uses a decision tree algorithm to remove unnecessary attributes for a nearest neighbourhood algorithm.

Two commonly used wrapper methods are SFS [18] and SBS [19]. SFS (SBS) starts with no attributes (all attributes), then candidate attributes are sequentially added to (removed from) the initial attribute subset until the further addition (removal) does not increase the classification performance. However, both SFS and SBS suffer from the problem of nesting effect, because an attribute is selected (eliminated) it cannot be eliminated (selected) later, which is so-called nesting effect [7]. The "plus-l-take away-r" method proposed by Stearns [20] could overcome this limitation by performing l times forward selection followed by r times backward elimination. However, the determination of the optimal values of (l, r) is a difficult problem.

EC Algorithms for Dimension Reduction. Evolutionary computation techniques have been applied to address dimension reduction problems, such as GAs, GP, ant colony optimisation (ACO) and PSO.

Based on GAs, Chakraborty [21] proposes a dimension reduction algorithm using a fuzzy sets based fitness function. However, PSO with the same fitness function in [22] achieve better performance than this GA based algorithm. Kourosh and Zhang [23] propose a dimension reduction algorithm using GP and naïve bayes (NB), where GP is used to combine attribute subsets and a set of operators together to find the optimal attribute subset. Ming [24] proposes a dimension reduction method based on ACO and rough set theory. Experimental results show that the proposed algorithm achieves better classification performance with fewer attributes than a C4.5 based dimension reduction algorithm.

As an EC technique, PSO has recently gained more attention for solving dimension reduction problems. Wang et al. [12] propose a filter dimension reduction algorithm based on an improved BPSO and rough set. However, the classification performance of the reduct was only tested on one learning algorithm, the LEM2 algorithm, which originally is specific used for rough set and has some bias for the proposed algorithm. Meanwhile, only using one learning algorithm can not show the advantage that filter algorithms is more general. Mohemmed et al. [11] propose a hybrid method (PSOAdaBoost) that incorporates PSO with an AdaBoost framework for face detection. PSOAdaBoost aims to search for the best attribute subset and determine the decision threshold of AdaBoost simultaneously, which speeds up the training process and increase the accuracy of weak classifiers in AdaBoost.

Chuang et al. [5] apply the so-called catfish effect to PSO for dimension reduction, which is to introduce new particles into the swarm by re-initialising the worst particles when *gbest* has not improved for a number of iterations. The introduced catfish particles could help PSO avoid premature convergence. Liu et al. [10] introduce a multi-swarm PSO (MSPSO) algorithm to search for the optimal attribute subset and optimise the parameters of SVM simultaneously. Experiments show that MSPSO could achieve higher classification accuracy than grid search, standard PSO and GA. However, MSPSO is computationally more expensive than the other three methods because of the large population size and complicated communication rules between different subswarms. Based on PSO, Unler and Murat [4] propose a dimension reduction algorithm with an adaptive selection strategy, where an attribute is chosen not only according to the likelihood calculated by PSO, but also to its contribution to the attributes already selected. Experiments suggest that the proposed method outperforms the tabu search and scatter search algorithms.

PSO has been shown to be an efficient search technique for dimension reduction by many existing studies. However, most of the existing approaches are wrappers, which are computationally more expensive and less general than filter approaches. Therefore, investigation of an effective PSO based filter dimension reduction algorithm is still an open issue. Probabilistic rough set was claimed to be a good way for dimension reduction problems [13], but its real performance has not been investigated. Therefore, it is thought to investigate the performance of probabilistic rough set and PSO for filter dimension reduction.

3   Proposed Filter Based Methods

Base on rough set theory and BPSO, we will propose a filter dimension reduction approach. Firstly, we use standard rough set theory and BPSO for dimension reduction to see whether it can achieve good results. Then, we will develop a new approach based on probabilistic rough set theory and BPSO to further reduce the dimensionality.

3.1   BPSO and Standard Rough Set Theory for Dimension Reduction(PSORS)

When using rough set theory for dimension reduction, the datasets for a classification problem can be regarded as an information system $I = (U, A)$, where all available attributes can be considered as A in the rough set theory. Based on the equivalence described by A, U can be partitioned to $U_1, U_2, U_3, ..., U_n$, where n is the number of classes in the dataset. After dimension reduction, the achieved reduct can be considered as $P \in A$. Therefore, the fitness of P can be evaluated by how well P represents each target set in U, which is a class in the dataset.

For $U_1 \in U$, let $\underline{P}U_1 = \{x \in U | [x]_P \subseteq U_1\}$ be the lower approximation of P according to U_1 if $[x]_P$ only contains instances in U_1. Let $\overline{P}U_1 = \{x \in U | [x]_P \cap U_1 \neq \emptyset\}$ be the upper approximation of P according to U_1 if $[x]_P$

contains at least one element not in U_1. The rough set, $\overline{P}U_1 - \underline{P}U_1$, contains every instance in U_1, but $\overline{P}U_1$ contains instances from other classes that are indiscernible with instances in U_1. Therefore, the purity of $[x]_P$ according to U_1 can be measured by $\frac{\underline{P}U_1}{\overline{P}U_1}$, which shows how well P represents the target set U_1. Therefore, how well P describe each target in U can be calculated by Equation 6, which is the fitness function in PSORS:

$$Fitness_1(P) = \frac{\sum_{U_i \in U} |PU_i|}{|\mathbb{U}|} \qquad (6)$$

If the dimension reduction algorithm achieves a reduct with $Fitness_1(P) = 1.0$, it means the reduct can completely separate each class from other classes.

3.2 New Dimension Reduction Algorithm 1 (PSOPRS): Based on Probabilistic Rough Set Theory

As discussed in Section 2.2, the definitions of lower approximation and upper approximation limit the application of rough set theory. In classification problems, it may happen that two or more instances might have the same attribute values but be classified in different classes. This is possibly because incorrect values are entered or one instance is an exception to a class. Therefore, it is impossible to achieve the $Fitness_1(P) = 1.0$ in Equation 6. A set of attributes could be adequate, but erroneous or unusual values prevent these attributes being included in a reduct. This problem can be addressed by relaxing the definitions of lower and upper approximations in probabilistic rough set theory. Therefore, we propose a new filter attributes reduction algorithm (PSOPRS) based on BPSO and probabilistic rough set theory [25].

In PSOPRS, for the target set U_1, $\mu_P[x] = \frac{|[x]_P \cap U_1|}{|[x]_P|}$, which quantifies the proportion of $[x]_P$ is in U_1. Here $[x]_P$ does not have to be completely contained in U_1. $\underline{apr}_P U_1 = \{x | \mu_P[x] \geq \alpha\}$ defines the lower approximation of P according to U_1, where α can be adjusted to restrict or relax the lower or upper approximations. When $\alpha = 1.0$, $\underline{apr}_P U_1 = \underline{P}U_1$. The fitness function of PSOPRS is shown by Equation 7.

$$Fitness_2(P) = \frac{\sum_{x=1}^{n} |\underline{apr}_P X_i|}{|\mathbb{U}|} \qquad (7)$$

3.3 New Dimension Reduction Algorithms 2 (PSOPRSN): Based on Probabilistic Rough Set Theory and Size of the Reduct

In PSOPRS, although the use of probabilistic rough can avoid the problems caused by standard rough set, the number of attributes is not considered in the fitness function (Equation 7). For the same α value, if there are more than one reducts that have the same value of $Fitness_2(P)$, PSOPRS will not have the intention to search for the smaller reduct. Therefore, we propose a new algorithm, which searches for a reduct with the two objectives of maximising the

Table 1. Datasets

Dataset	#Attributes	#Classes	#Instances
Lymphography (Lymph)	18	4	148
Spect	22	2	267
Dermatology	33	6	366
Soybean Large	35	19	307
Chess	36	2	3196

representation power of the reduct (represented by $Fitness_2(P)$) and minimising the number of attributes in the reduct. A straightforward way to achieve this goal would be adding one component in fitness function $Fitness_2(P)$ to represent the number of attributes of the reduct, which is shown as Equation 8 and this method is called PSOPRSN:

$$Fitness_3(P) = \gamma * \frac{\sum_{x=1}^{n} |apr_P X_i|}{|U|} + (1 - \gamma) * (1 - \frac{\#attributes}{\#totalAttributes}) \qquad (8)$$

where $\gamma \in (0, 1]$ shows the relative importance of the representation power of the reduct while $(1 - \gamma)$ shows the relative importance of the number of attributes. As the range of $\frac{\sum_{x=1}^{n} |apr_P X_i|}{|U|}$ is in $[0, 1]$, the number of attributes is converted to $(1 - \frac{\#attributes}{\#totalAttributes})$ to make sure the two components in the same ranges.

In PSORS and the two newly proposed algorithms, PSOPRS and PSOPRSN, the dimensionality of the search space is the number of attributes included in the dataset. Each particle is encoded in a binary string, where the "1" means the corresponding attribute is included in the reduct while "0" means the corresponding attribute is removed.

4   Experimental Design

Five datasets in Table 1 are used in the experiments, which were chosen from UCI machine learning repository [26]. They have different numbers of attributes, classes and instances, which are used as representative samples of the problems that the proposed algorithms will address. Note that all the five datasets are categorical data because rough set theory only works on discrete values.

In the experiments, the instances in each dataset are randomly divided into two sets: 70% as the training set and 30% as the test set. The proposed algorithms firstly run on the training set to obtain a reduct. The classification performance of the achieved reduct will be evaluated by a learning algorithm on the unseen test set. As filter algorithms, the learning algorithm only runs on the test set. Almost all learning algorithms can be used here. In order to test the claim that filter dimension reduction methods are general, three different learning algorithms, decision trees (DT), naive Bayes (NB) and K-nearest neighbor algorithms with K=5 (5NN), are used in the experiments to evaluate the classification performance of the achieved reduct on the test set.

In all algorithms, the fully connected topology is used in BPSO, $v_{max} = 6.0$, the population size is 30 and the maximum iteration is 100. $w = 0.7298$, $c_1 = c_2 = 1.49618$. These values are chosen based on the common settings in the literature [9]. Each algorithm has been conducted for 30 independent runs.

In PSOPRS, in order to test how the value of α influence the dimension reduction performance, four different α values are used in the experiments, which are 1.0, 0.9, 0.8, and 0.75. All the α values are larger than 0.5, because the lower approximation in probabilistic rough set should have the majority (at least have half) of the instances that belong to the target set. In PSOPRSN, α is set as 0.75 and five different γ values are used in the experiments, which are 1.0, 0.9, 0.8, 0.75, 0.5, to represent the different relative importance of the number of attributes in the fitness function. When $\alpha = 1$ in PSOPRS and $\gamma = 1$ in PSOPRSN, PSOPRS and PSOPRSN become the same as PSORS. Therefore, the results of PSOPRS $\alpha = 1$ and PSOPRSN with $\gamma = 1$ are not presented in the next section. In order to further examine the performance of the proposed algorithms, two conventional filter feature selection methods (CfsF and CfsB) in Weka [27] are used for comparison purposes in the experiments and the classification performance is calculated by DT.

5   Experimental Results and Discussions

5.1   Experimental Results of PSORS

Tables 2 shows the experimental results of PSOPRS and PSOPRS on the five datasets and DT, NB and 5NN were used for classification. Due to page limit, only the results of using DT for classification are presented here. In Table 2, "All" means that all of the available attributes are used for classification. "AveSize" means the average number of attributes selected in the 30 independent runs. "Ave", "Std" and "Best" represent the mean, the standard deviation and the best classification accuracy achieved by DT across the 30 independent runs.

Table 2. Results of PSORS and PSOPRS with DT as the learning algorithm

Dataset		Chess		Dermatology		Lymph
Method	AveSize	Ave±Std(Best)	AveSize	Ave±Std(Best)	AveSize	Ave±Std(Best)
All	36	0.985	33	0.828	18	0.755
PSORS	30.70	0.983±0.003(0.987)	21.00	0.860±0.048(0.975)	11.73	0.724±0.068(0.796)
PSOPRS						
$\alpha = 0.9$	30.70	0.984±0.002(0.987)	21.00	0.860±0.048(0.975)	11.73	0.724±0.068(0.796)
$\alpha = 0.8$	29.97	0.983±0.003(0.985)	21.00	0.860±0.048(0.975)	11.77	0.723±0.068(0.796)
$\alpha = 0.75$	30.30	0.985±0.001(0.987)	21.00	0.860±0.048(0.975)	11.77	0.723±0.068(0.796)

Dataset		Soybean		Spect		
Method	AveSize	Ave±Std(Best)	AveSize	Ave±Std(Best)		
All	35	0.819	22	0.809		
PSORS	21.53	0.803±0.046(0.872)	21.00	0.860±0.048(0.975)		
PSOPRS						
$\alpha = 0.9$	21.60	0.805±0.044(0.872)	17.30	0.806±0.022(0.843)		
$\alpha = 0.8$	21.67	0.805±0.044(0.872)	17.50	0.800±0.020(0.820)		
$\alpha = 0.75$	21.63	0.804±0.043(0.872)	15.57	0.818±0.008(0.820)		

According to Table 2, it can be seen that in most cases, PSORS reduced around one third of the available attributes. After dimension reduction, the classification performance achieved by DT is still the similar to that of using all attributes. In almost all datasets, the best classification performance achieved by three learning algorithms using the reduct are the better than using all available attributes. The results suggestion that PSORS based on BPSO and standard rough set theory can be successfully used to reduce the dimensionality and also improve the classification performance in many cases.

5.2   Experimental Results of PSOPRS

According to Table 2, it can be seen that in most cases, the number of remained attributes decreases when α in PSOPRS reduces. In terms of the classification performance, for DT, all the reducts can achieve similar classification performance to using all attributes. Although the mean classification accuracy is slightly worse than using all attributes in some cases, the best accuracy is better than using all attributes in all cases. Compared with PSORS, PSOPRS can further reduce the number of attributes and maintain the classification performance, especially when $\alpha = 0.75$. The results suggests that by using probabilistic rough set to evaluate the fitness of the attributes, the algorithm can further reducing the number of remained attributes without reduce its classification performance. A smaller α means more relax on the lower and upper approximations, which usually can slightly remove more unnecessary attributes to further reduce dimensionality of the datasets.

5.3   Experimental Results of PSOPRSN

According to Table 3, with a smaller γ can reduce can achieve a smaller the number of attributes. The reason is that a smaller γ means the number of attributes in PSOPRSN is more important than a relatively large γ. Compared with PSORS and PSOPRS, PSOPRSN can significantly reduce the number of attributes although the classification performance is slightly worse in some cases.

The results also show that when the number of attributes is reduced, the classification performance also decreases in most cases. The reason could be that $Fitness_3$ does not consider the number of equivalence classes in the dataset. In rough set, a small number of attributes (e.g. 12) can describe a large number (2^{12}) of equivalence classes. The problem here is that there could be thousands of small equivalence classes, which only contain one or two instances. If there is another equivalence class, which has slightly more instances, this class will dominate others and the obtained reduct will only contain information that can identify this particular class. Therefore, without considering the size of the equivalence classes, $Fitness_3$ may achieve a small reduct, but it will loss generality and performs badly on unseen test data.

Table 3. PSOPRSN with $\alpha = 0.75$

Dataset	γ	AveSize	DT Ave±Std(Best)	NB Ave±Std(Best)	5NN Ave±Std(Best)
Chess	0.9	12.63	0.977±0.001(0.979)	0.927±0.009(0.945)	0.872±0.054(0.953)
	0.8	8.97	0.972±0.013(0.977)	0.929±0.010(0.953)	0.846±0.062(0.925)
	0.75	7.73	0.961±0.019(0.977)	0.932±0.009(0.953)	0.821±0.114(0.921)
	0.5	4.93	0.931±0.013(0.938)	0.931±0.013(0.941)	0.602±0.198(0.892)
Dermatology	0.9	8.17	0.757±0.068(0.918)	0.816±0.056(0.943)	0.787±0.058(0.877)
	0.8	8.07	0.775±0.078(0.967)	0.799±0.056(0.959)	0.784±0.060(0.918)
	0.75	7.73	0.743±0.085(0.926)	0.786±0.064(0.910)	0.766±0.073(0.893)
	0.5	6.43	0.752±0.093(0.951)	0.783±0.075(0.959)	0.725±0.083(0.943)
Lymph	0.9	5.03	0.667±0.033(0.673)	0.776±0.004(0.796)	0.753±0.011(0.755)
	0.8	5.00	0.661±0.046(0.673)	0.777±0.005(0.796)	0.752±0.010(0.755)
	0.75	5.00	0.673±0.000(0.673)	0.776±0.000(0.776)	0.755±0.000(0.755)
	0.5	4.00	0.714±0.000(0.714)	0.816±0.000(0.816)	0.796±0.000(0.796)
Soybean	0.9	9.70	0.714±0.031(0.767)	0.756±0.036(0.824)	0.675±0.037(0.749)
	0.8	9.00	0.705±0.038(0.780)	0.745±0.041(0.846)	0.665±0.039(0.749)
	0.75	8.77	0.713±0.043(0.775)	0.747±0.031(0.811)	0.668±0.033(0.749)
	0.5	7.47	0.713±0.039(0.802)	0.761±0.042(0.833)	0.670±0.033(0.727)
Spect	0.9	13.97	0.820±0.000(0.820)	0.767±0.010(0.775)	0.818±0.010(0.831)
	0.8	8.97	0.799±0.017(0.820)	0.783±0.024(0.820)	0.834±0.021(0.843)
	0.75	7.07	0.798±0.012(0.831)	0.797±0.029(0.843)	0.805±0.040(0.843)
	0.5	4.63	0.786±0.026(0.843)	0.796±0.025(0.843)	0.739±0.248(0.843)

Table 4. Results of CfsF and CfsB with DT as the learning algorithm

Dataset	Chess		Dermatology		Lymph		Soybean		Spect	
Method	Size	Accuracy	Size	Accuracy	Size	Accuracy	Size	Accuracy	Size	Accuracy
CfsF	5	0.781	17	0.873	8	0.733	12	0.805	4	0.70
CfsB	5	0.781	17	0.873	8	0.733	14	0.854	4	0.70

5.4 Comparisons with Two Traditional Algorithms

Experiments using CfsF and CfsB for dimension reduction have been conducted using Weka and DT was used for classification. The results are shown in Table 4. Comparing the experimental results of the four rough set theory based algorithm in Tables 2 and 3 with the two traditional algorithms, it can be seen that in almost all cases, although CfsF and CfsB can achieve a smaller size of attributes, the classification performance of CfsF and CfsB are smaller or much smaller than the rough set theory based algorithms, PSORS, PSOPRS and PSOPRSN. In terms of the computational time, both our proposed algorithms and two traditional algorithms used a relatively short time (less than 5 minutes in most cases).

6 Conclusions

This paper developed a new approach using *probabilistic* rough set theory and BPSO to remove irrelevant and redundant features and maintain the classification performance achieved by using all features. This new approach includes two new algorithms, which are BPSO and probabilistic rough set theory (*PSO-PRS*) and BPSO with probabilistic rough set theory by adding the number of attributes in the fitness function (*PSOPRSN*). The performance of three new algorithms were examined and compared to BPSO with *original* rough set theory (*PSORS*) and two traditional methods, CfsF and CfsB, on five datasets. In order to test the generality of the proposed algorithms, the achieved reduct was evaluated by three different learning algorithms for classification on the unseen test sets. Experimental results show that in most cases, the three proposed algorithms can be successfully used for dimension reduction and outperform PSORS and the two traditional algorithms. PSOPRSN can significantly reduce the number of attributes in the reduct although the classification performance is slightly reduced in many cases. The reason might be that PSOPRSN does not consider the number of equivalence classes in the dataset.

This work represents the first study that successfully uses BPSO with probabilistic rough set for dimension reduction. In future, we will consider the number of equivalence classes in the dataset to further reduce the number of attributes without decreasing the classification performance and investigate its performance for dimension reduction and attribute selection problems on more datasets with a larger number of attributes. We also intend to investigate multi-objective PSO and rough set based filter algorithms to better explore the Pareto front of non-dominated solutions in dimension reduction and attribute selection to provide more informative solutions for users.

Acknowledgments. This work is supported in part by the National Science Foundation of China (NSFC No. 61170180,61035003), the Key Program of Natural Science Foundation of Jiangsu Province, China (Grant No. BK2011005) and the Marsden Fund of New Zealand (VUW0806) and the University Research Fund of Victoria University of Wellington (200457/3230).

References

1. Gheyas, I.A., Smith, L.S.: Feature subset selection in large dimensionality domains. Pattern Recognition 43(1), 5–13 (2010)
2. Guyon, I., Elisseeff, A.: An introduction to variable and feature selection. The Journal of Machine Learning Research 3, 1157–1182 (2003)
3. Dash, M., Liu, H.: Feature selection for classification. Intelligent Data Analysis 1(4), 131–156 (1997)
4. Unler, A., Murat, A.: A discrete particle swarm optimization method for feature selection in binary classification problems. European Journal of Operational Research 206(3), 528–539 (2010)
5. Chuang, L.Y., Tsai, S.W., Yang, C.H.: Improved binary particle swarm optimization using catfish effect for feature selection. Expert Systems with Applications 38, 12699–12707 (2011)
6. Kohavi, R., John, G.H.: Wrappers for feature subset selection. Artificial Intelligence 97, 273–324 (1997)
7. Yusta, S.C.: Different metaheuristic strategies to solve the feature selection problem. Pattern Recognition Letters 30, 525–534 (2009)
8. Kennedy, J., Eberhart, R.: Particle swarm optimization. In: IEEE International Conference on Neural Networks, vol. 4, pp. 1942–1948 (1995)

9. Shi, Y., Eberhart, R.: A modified particle swarm optimizer. In: IEEE International Conference on Evolutionary Computation (CEC 1998), pp. 69–73 (1998)

10. Liu, Y., Wang, G., Chen, H., Dong, H.: An improved particle swarm optimization for feature selection. Journal of Bionic Engineering 8(2), 191–200 (2011)

11. Mohemmed, A., Zhang, M., Johnston, M.: Particle swarm optimization based adaboost for face detection. In: IEEE Congress on Evolutionary Computation (CEC 2009), pp. 2494–2501 (2009)

12. Wang, X., Yang, J., Teng, X., Xia, W.: Feature selection based on rough sets and particle swarm optimization. Pattern Recognition Letters 28(4), 459–471 (2007)

13. Yao, Y., Zhao, Y.: Attribute reduction in decision-theoretic rough set models. Information Sciences 178(17), 3356–3373 (2008)

14. Kennedy, J., Eberhart, R.: A discrete binary version of the particle swarm algorithm. In: IEEE International Conference on Systems, Man, and Cybernetics. Computational Cybernetics and Simulation, vol. 5, pp. 4104–4108 (1997)

15. Pawlak, Z.: Rough sets. International Journal of Parallel Programming 11, 341–356 (1982)

16. Abdi, H., Williams, L.J.: Principal component analysis. Wiley Interdisciplinary Reviews: Computational Statistics 2(4), 433–459 (2010)

17. Cardie, C.: Using decision trees to improve case-based learning. In: Proceedings of the Tenth International Conference on Machine Learning (ICML), pp. 25–32 (1993)

18. Whitney, A.: A direct method of nonparametric measurement selection. IEEE Transactions on Computers C-20(9), 1100–1103 (1971)

19. Marill, T., Green, D.: On the effectiveness of receptors in recognition systems. IEEE Transactions on Information Theory 9(1), 11–17 (1963)

20. Stearns, S.: On selecting features for pattern classifier. In: Proceedings of the 3rd International Conference on Pattern Recognition, Coronado, CA, pp. 71–75 (1976)

21. Chakraborty, B.: Genetic algorithm with fuzzy fitness function for feature selection. In: ISIE 2002, vol. 1, pp. 315–319 (2002)

22. Chakraborty, B.: Feature subset selection by particle swarm optimization with fuzzy fitness function. In: ISKE 2008, vol. 1, pp. 1038–1042 (2008)

23. Neshatian, K., Zhang, M.: Dimensionality reduction in face detection: A genetic programming approach. In: 24th International Conference Image and Vision Computing New Zealand (IVCNZ 2009), pp. 391–396 (2009)

24. Ming, H.: A rough set based hybrid method to feature selection. In: International Symposium on Knowledge Acquisition and Modeling (KAM 2008), pp. 585–588 (2008)

25. Yao, Y.: Probabilistic rough set approximations. Int. J. Approx. Reasoning 49(2), 255–271 (2008)

26. Frank, A., Asuncion, A.: UCI machine learning repository (2010)

27. Witten, I.H., Frank, E.: Data Mining: Practical Machine Learning Tools and Techniques, 2nd edn. Morgan Kaufmann (2005)

Evolving Plastic Neural Networks for Online Learning: Review and Future Directions

Oliver J. Coleman and Alan D. Blair

School of Computer Science and Engineering
University of New South Wales, Sydney, Australia
{ocoleman,blair}@cse.unsw.edu.au

Abstract. Recent years have seen a resurgence of interest in evolving plastic neural networks for online learning. These approaches have an intrinsic appeal – since, to date, the only working example of general intelligence is the human brain, which has developed through evolution, and exhibits a great capacity to adapt to unfamiliar environments. In this paper we review prior work in this area – including problem domains and tasks, fitness functions, synaptic plasticity models and neural network encoding schemes. We conclude with a discussion of current findings and promising future directions, including incorporation of functional properties observed in biological neural networks which appear to play a role in learning processes, and addressing the "general" in general intelligence by the introduction of previously unseen tasks during the evolution process.

Keywords: plastic neural networks, evolution, online learning, meta-learning.

1 Introduction

Recent years have seen a resurgence of interest in evolving plastic neural networks for online learning. These approaches have an intrinsic appeal – since, to date, the only working example of general intelligence is the human brain, which has developed through evolution, and exhibits a great capacity to adapt to unfamiliar environments. In this paper we review prior work in this area – including problem domains and tasks, fitness functions, synaptic plasticity models and neural network encoding schemes. We conclude with a discussion of current findings and possible future directions.

In this review, a *plastic neural network* is one in which the strengths of synapses may change during the networks operational life. *Online learning* refers to the ability of an agent to discover or learn about some property of its environment, typically by exploration, which it has not been exposed to previously or which changes during its life time, and then exploit this knowledge in order to achieve a goal. *Online adaptation* refers to a robustness or ability to adapt to internal or external perturbations or changes in input and output ranges; in other words, the ability to maintain homeostasis. These latter two definitions are very similar to terms defined by Mouret and Tonelli [19]: an agent is said to possess *behavioural robustness*, which is akin to online adaptation, when it can maintain the same qualitative behaviour despite environmental or morphological changes; and an agent is said to exhibit *behavioural change*, which is akin to online learning, when in a reward-based environment a change in reward causes it to

M. Thielscher and D. Zhang (Eds.): AI 2012, LNCS 7691, pp. 326–337, 2012.

adopt qualitatively new behaviours until a new optimal behaviour has been found. While this review describes progress in evolving plastic neural networks for online learning, work on evolving plastic neural networks for online adaptation has enough similarities to provide useful insights. We include work on online adaptation in the sections on synaptic plasticity, scaling/competition and neuronal excitability regulation. Finally, it should be noted that "adaptive network" is not synonymous with "plastic network": a network may be adaptive without having plastic synapses [11, 18, 25].

2   Problem Domains, Tasks and Fitness Functions

In the evolution of neural networks for online learning, evaluating the fitness of a candidate requires testing the ability of the neural network to learn something about its environment and to then exploit that knowledge to achieve one or more goals. This requires producing environments that are different in some way for each generation and/or change in some way during a fitness evaluation [4, 20, 25, 27].

Initial work on online learning, carried out in the early 1990s, focused on a supervised learning paradigm [3, 4, 13]. Fitness evaluation typically took the form of a training phase during which sets of exemplars are presented to the network, and then an evaluation phase where the network is presented all the input vectors from the training set and the fitness is the percentage of correct corresponding output vectors produced by the network [3, 4]. These studies were largely proof-of-concept in nature and used simple network models and simple, for example single-bit or linearly-separable, binary training examples. The main limitation with this method is that the generalisation performance of the evolved learning algorithms is not tested (not to be confused with the ability to learn all the members of any particular set of exemplars).

Research on evolving neural networks for online learning re-emerged in the early 2000's – this time focusing on reinforcement learning domains. In most reinforcement learning experiments the fitness of an agent has been the amount of reward it received during its lifetime [20, 25, 27] or is at least strongly correlated with the reward received [15, 23]. Use of multiple reward signals, corresponding to multiple goals, has not been explored.

Most tasks studied to date have been designed to provide a simple reinforcement learning environment in order to evaluate the ability of an agent to perform learning. They have required learning a simple association that changes during the agents life time, such as which type of flower provides the most reward in a simple bee foraging task [20, 21, 26], which object types are food or poison in a slightly more complex foraging task [27], or which arm of a T-maze contains a high-value reward [21, 22, 25]. Variations to increase the difficultly of the T-maze task include use of a double T-maze, which has four arms instead of two, or requiring the agent to learn a possibly nonlinear association between the perception of objects and their reward value [22]. Risi and Stanley [23] studied a significantly more difficult version of the T-maze task in wihch the environment was continuous rather than discrete and the controller takes as input only raw output from 5 rangefinder sensors (as well as a reward signal) rather than signals from special sensors indicating arrival at key locations.

Tonelli and Mouret [28, 29] studied a purely associative task, similar to those using a supervised learning paradigm, in which an agent is required to learn associations between each possible input and output pattern. The input and output were vectors of binary values, with a reward signal added to the input. To simplify the task only one bit of the input and output vector each has value 1 while all others have value 0. The difficulty of the task was increased by increasing the size of the vectors. This problem domain is interesting because the number of associations that must be learned can be large, while other problem domains studied have required only learning one or a few associations, and also because it does not require simulation of an environment or learning fixed behaviours for invariant properties of the environment (other than the ability to determine which output to set high for which input, of course). A much more complex task in this problem domain would be to allow arbitrary input and output patterns, instead of setting only one bit high per pattern.

Khan and Miller [15] introduced a modified version of Wumpus world, where pits and the Wumpus only harm rather than kill the agent, as well as a competitive version of Wumpus world where the Wumpus acts as a predator. Rather than a reinforcement signal being provided, the agent can perceive its "energy" level, which is affected by environmental factors and achieving goals.

It has been noted by several authors that most tasks requiring online learning also require some fixed behaviours, and that often the fixed behaviours can be evolved much more easily than the learning behaviours [20, 21]. Indeed, if the goal is to test the ability of an agent to perform online learning, then the experimenter must take care to ensure that the task cannot be solved with purely fixed behaviours [3]. Preventing the evolutionary process from becoming stuck on the local optima of fixed behaviours has typically been addressed by employing specially designed environments and fitness evaluation functions that minimise the advantage of purely fixed behaviours and that strongly favour learning behaviour [3, 21, 23, 29]. In order for the approach of evolving neural networks for online learning to be practical for a wider range of problem domains – where a large number of behaviours may need to be fixed for a successful agent – the minimisation of this requirement represents a significant future challenge.

One novel approach to alleviating the problem of local optima in evolutionary algorithms is novelty search. Novelty search replaces the objective or goal-based fitness function in an evolutionary algorithm with a function that measures the behavioural novelty of an individual with respect to the behaviours exhibited by other individuals in the current and all preceding generations. The main idea behind novelty search is that behaviours that are different in interesting ways from other behaviours collapse to the same objective-based fitness, so objective-based search essentially ignores them even though they may be pathways to a solution. This method has shown promising results in evolving neural networks for online learning [21], where it was able to evolve solutions more quickly than objective-based search on two common benchmark tasks. It has also been used successfully in conjunction with a traditional objective-based fitness function using a multi-objective evolutionary algorithm [29]. However, some studies suggest that novelty search may not scale well to more complex problems [6] and that in some cases it is just as hard to find a good novelty metric as it is to find a good objective-based fitness function [16].

3   Synaptic Plasticity Models

The most common approach to synaptic plasticity in evolved neural networks thus far has been to define either one or four plasticity rules. These may be applied to some or all connections in the network. In the case of a single rule type, this rule has either been evolved [3] or fixed [21]. Floreano and Mondada introduced a set of four rules in 1996 which were then adopted by several subsequent authors [14, 18], with the genome encoding which of the rules is to be used by each connection. From Floreano and Mondada, 1996 [10, pg. 3]: *"The four types of synaptic change are as follows ... The simplest learning mechanism is plain Hebb, whereby synapses can only be strengthened ... The postsynaptic rule is similar to the plain Hebbian rule, but also decreases the synaptic efficacy when the postsynaptic unit is active and the presynaptic unit is not ... in the presynaptic learning rule the decrement takes place when the presynaptic unit is active, but the postsynaptic unit is inactive ... The covariance rule here takes the form of a synchronous-activation detector: if the presynaptic and postsynaptic activity levels differ by more than half the maximum node activation, the synaptic efficacy is reduced in proportion to that difference, otherwise it is increased in proportion to the difference."*

The second most common approach is to use a parameterised weight update rule where the parameters are evolved either for a globally applied rule [25, 26, 30], for a fixed number of rules [27], for each modular grouping of neurons [20], or per connection [8, 9, 22, 23]. No work has compared the effects of these different levels of granularity.

One of the first parameterised rules was introduced by Niv et al. in 2002 [20] and has been used by several subsequent authors [22, 23, 25, 26, 28, 29]. It consists of a correlation term, pre- and post-synaptic terms and a constant term for heterosynaptic updates, with evolved coefficients for each term:

$$\Delta w = \eta(Axy + Bx + Cy + D) \tag{1}$$

where η is the learning rate and x and y are the pre- and post-synaptic activation.

Di Paolo et al. [8, 9] studied spike-timing dependent plasticity (STDP) models. The weight update rule was asymmetric such that if a pre-synaptic spike occurred before a post-synaptic spike then the weight is increased (potentiated), and conversely if a pre-synaptic spike occurred after a post-synaptic spike then the weight is decreased (depressed). Parameters for the time-window and amount of change were evolved per connection.

Di Paolo [8] performed a direct comparison between rate-based and spiking models. It is noted that a direct and fair comparison is not simple; efforts were made to make the comparison as fair as possible, for example by modifying the weight update rule such that the initial direction of weight change in the rate-based model is unbiased by the initial random activation values of neurons, as it is in the spiking model. Evolved rate-based networks had significantly lower performance than spiking networks in the photo-taxis task studied. This was due to the rate-based networks being much slower to converge to the required weight values: *"STDP controllers are rapidly able to define a direction of weight change depending on the relation between the plastic rules and the neural properties ... whereas rate-based plastic controllers take much longer to settle into a given range.*" The practical significance of this result could be questioned: it would be simple to encode initial weight values to overcome this problem. However, in some cases (perhaps developmental network models), such encoding of initial weights may not be possible, thus making the rapid convergence of the spiking networks desirable. Additionally, the STDP rule employed was found to produce more stable networks even in the presence of noise introduced into neuronal activation.

The above approaches all use some kind of relatively fixed rule or rules to change synaptic efficacy, albeit with some evolvable parameters. In contrast there have been two proposed approaches to evolving arbitrary plasticity rules. Khan and Miller [15] evolved genetic programs that controlled changes to synaptic efficacy, as well as several other functional aspects of neurons. While this work is intriguing, and the model developed was demonstrated to be able to evolve solutions to complex tasks, it is not clear to what extent evolving arbitrary rules contributed to the results, positively or negatively. The model developed was very complex and a significant departure from anything that had gone before. The tasks chosen were different from any others used in similar work. The rules that evolved have not been analysed in any studies to date.

Risi and Stanley [22] also developed a novel synaptic plasticity system able to evolve arbitrarily complex rules. They performed a comparison between it and two parameterised rules similar to that introduced by Niv et al. [20] (described above). These models employed the HyperNEAT encoding scheme (see Section 5). The three models of synaptic plasticity compared were:

Plain Hebbian: the update rule is

$$\Delta w = \eta xy \tag{2}$$

where η is the learning rate. The genome function has an output for a synapses existence and for the plasticity learning rate if it exists.

Hebbian ABC: the update rule is

$$\Delta w = \eta(Axy + Bx + Cy) \tag{3}$$

The genome function has an output for each of a synapses existence, the learning rate and the coefficients A, B and C.

Iterated: in this model the genome function is queried throughout the networks life time for each synaptic weight value, instead of only for the initial synapse parameters, and has three inputs additional to the coordinates of the pre- and post-synaptic neurons: the pre- and post-synaptic activation and the current weight value. Thus instead of a fixed Hebbian-type rule, arbitrarily complex weight update rules can be evolved based on location, activation levels and current weight value.

Risi and Stanley tested the networks on a double T-maze task where the complexity of the task could be increased by introducing a non-linearly separable perception and reward value mapping. Evolution using the Plain Hebbian rule could not find solutions for the task at any complexity level, evolution using the Hebbian ABC and Iterated models could find optimal solutions for the linearly separable reward signals task, but only by using the Iterated model could optimal solutions be found for the non-linearly separable reward signals task. For the higher complexity task an optimal solution required a non-linear learning rule which could not be encoded by the Hebbian ABC model. They conclude that although a different network topology may have allowed a less general plasticity rule to solve the non-linear problem in this instance, it is nevertheless risky to make a priori assumptions about which plasticity rules will be suitable. The rules that were evolved with the Iterated model were not analysed.

Both the evolved genetic program and evolved function plasticity rules developed by Khan and Miller and Risi and Stanley, respectively, required significantly more computation time than models using fixed rules, demonstrating a trade-off between computational requirements and generality. While Risi and Stanley demonstrate that in some cases more generality may be required, it is not clear (nor necessarily suggested by the authors) that the level of generality provided by these systems is necessary, or desirable, due to the computational considerations and increased search space in an evolutionary context. Indeed, Risi and Stanley found that the more general model took much longer to find nearly optimal solutions than a parameterised fixed rule model.

Most studies have used either relatively fixed rules, for example the set of four fixed rules popularised by Floreano and Mondada [10] and the parameterised rule introduced by Niv et al. [20], or arbitrarily flexible rules such as the genetic programs introduced by Khan and Miller [15] and the evolved functions studied by Risi and Stanley [22]. While the study performed by Risi and Stanley directly compares simple parameterised rules with arbitrarily flexible rules, a possibly interesting research direction could be to compare plasticity rules that fall between these two extremes. This could especially be the case in plasticity models such as STDP, where evolved parameters could control aspects such as asymmetry, timing-direction, time-frames, plasticity modulation dependent on pre- and post-synaptic firing rates, etc.

Another interesting question is what sorts of synaptic plasticity rules were evolved by the models allowing arbitrary complexity. As noted, the studies performed by Khan and Miller, and Risi and Stanley, did not analyse the evolved rules. Did the same sorts of rules evolve many times? Were there any general properties of these rules that emerged? Did they tend towards simple rules, or unique and/or complex rules for every evolutionary run and/or relatively fit individual in a run? How does modifying the complexity or other properties of the task affect the kinds of rules evolved?

3.1 Synaptic Plasticity Neuromodulation Models

The first model of neuromodulation of synaptic plasticity was introduced by Niv et al. [20]. The topology of the network was fixed and divided up into several modules. The plasticity of synapses between these modules and an output neuron could be gated by evolved dependencies on some of the other modules. If a module had a dependency on another module then synaptic plasticity was only enabled when neurons in the latter fired. They found that this gating of synaptic plasticity was required to evolve networks able to perform a simple reinforcement learning task. While this result is interesting its general applicability is not clear as the allowable dependencies were hand-crafted along with the network topology.

A more general model of neuromodulation of synaptic plasticity was introduced by Soltoggio et al. [26]. In this model there are two neuron types, standard and modulatory. Each neuron maintains values for both standard and modulatory activation, which are the weighted sums of all inputs from the two respective subsets of neurons in the network. Unlike a standard neuron model, the modulatory activation level modulates the plasticity of all synapses leading into the neuron by being used as an overall multiplicative term in the plasticity rule. Evolved solutions using this model outperformed, and could handle more complex environments than, solutions using the model developed by Niv et al. Additionally, solutions using models where neuromodulation was disabled or fixed weights were used either performed very poorly or could not be found at all. Later work showed similar results with a different task (double T-maze with reward moved at random points during trials) [25]: evolution produced solutions with much higher average performance using models incorporating neuromodulation of plasticity compared to models without this neuromodulation.

Similar to the model introduced by Soltoggio, Risi and Stanley [23] developed a model in which some connections, rather than neurons, are modulatory. In this model every neuron has a neuromodulatory activation level (as well as the standard activation) which modulates the plasticity of all synapses leading into the neuron. This model could be considered to more closely mimic biological networks as the same neuron can emit standard signals as well as modulatory signals.

Similar to synaptic plasticity models in general, an open question is what impact more flexible or complex neuromodulation properties would have on the evolution of plastic neural networks for online learning. For example it is known that in biological neural networks neuromodulators can invert the timing-dependency of STDP rules. Specifically, other avenues of potential inquiry include studying the use of multiple neuromodulators affecting different aspects of plasticity, less targeted neuromodulation models such as a neuromodulator that can be dispersed into a region of a network that is defined in some space, and the generation of modulation signals as a by-product of any neuron rather than designated modulatory neurons, similar to the operation of those in biological neural networks.

4   Synaptic Scaling/Competition Models and Neuronal Excitability Regulation Models

Di Paolo [8] studied the effect of explicit activity-dependent synaptic scaling (ADS) and "directional damping" applied to synaptic strength updates (DD). ADS induces homeostasis by actively scaling synaptic strengths in order to maintain post-synaptic firing rates within a pre-defined range. This is achieved by multiplying all weight values by the same factor, introducing heterosynaptic competition. DD adds a factor to the synaptic update rule such that if a change in strength of a synapse that is already near the limit would push the strength closer to the limit then the change is dampened, whereas a change that moves the strength away from the limit is not dampened. This type of damping was chosen for two reasons: it tends to produce a uni-modal distribution of weights centred around the point where potentiation and depression equilibrate, as opposed to other methods that either apply a simple hard limit or non-directional damping and which produce a bimodal distribution where most synapses either become fully potentiated or depressed; and because this model is supported by empirical evidence from studies of biological networks. The study compared the performance of evolved solutions incorporating ADS and/or DD. It was found that DD made no observable difference in the final performance achieved, but that ADS slightly increased it. It is not clear if the difference may have been reduced with longer evolutionary runs as only final performance rather than plots of performance over generations are indicated. Additionally, the reliability of the solutions using different models was assessed by introducing relatively rapid synaptic strength decay factors. Only solutions using ADS were able to perform reliably in this scenario; it is argued that this is a *"consequence of the compensatory nature of the ADS mechanism, which is able to alter synapses as a consequence of longer term changes in neural activity in ways that tend to maintain this activity."*

In later work Di Paolo [30] used another active neuronal excitability regulation mechanism to induce homeostatic firing rates. This mechanism enables synaptic plasticity when neurons are firing outside two pre-defined ranges and modifies the plasticity rule to push the firing rates back into the correct range by modifying the sign of plasticity rule parameters. It was found that non-homeostatic networks made more errors, and that the errors did not follow a predictable pattern, as compared to homeostatic networks which exhibited fewer errors, and for which the errors were more predictable.

Hoinville et al. [14] studied a method of heterosynaptic competition that keeps the squared sum of synaptic strengths equal to unity. Additionally, a symmetric odd activation function – which satisfies the centre-crossing condition and ensures that the operating range of each neuron is centred on the most sensitive region of its activation function [17] – was used to help induce neuronal excitability regulation. The aim was to achieve homeostasis without using active parameter manipulation, that is *"the neuronal activity is not monitored and there is no mechanism that dynamically corrects any parameter. In fact, homeostasis is not ensured to be maintained in the short- or long-term. However ... the chosen constraints would make homeostasis more likely ..."* Unlike the models introduced by Di Paolo, this approach avoids defining ranges for firing rates a priori. Either of these mechanisms in isolation was found to improve the final performance of solutions and the convergence rate during evolution, and especially so when used in tandem. Behavioural stability and robustness, measured by increasing the duration of the task to ten times longer than that used during evolution, was also found to be improved by use of the heterosynaptic competition mechanism and again especially so with both mechanisms. It is concluded that synaptic normalisation supports multistability by *"contributing to a global self-organization of individual plastic rules"* and that *"homeostasis can evolve implicitly without any active homeostatic mechanisms and be implemented through constrained hebbian plasticity."*

Di Paolo and Hoinville et al. have explored several synaptic scaling/competition and neuronal excitability regulation mechanisms in the context of online adaptation. Future research could study these mechanisms in the context of online learning, and explore other mechanisms found in biological neural networks, such as spike adaptation, where the firing threshold of a neuron is increased if high firing rates are maintained.

5   Encoding of Neural Networks in Evolved Genomes

Methods to encode neural networks into genomes for evolution can be broadly categorised into direct and indirect schemes. Direct encoding schemes employ a one-to-one mapping from elements in the genome to components in the phenotype, and include bit-string representations [3, 4, 10], vector-of-values [8, 9, 14, 20, 25, 26, 30], and graph-based schemes [21, 27, 29], where vertices in the graph correspond to neurons and edges to connections between them.

Indirect encoding schemes include a cellular encoding/grammar tree system [13], a matrix rewriting system [11], a "neural map" scheme where a vertex can either become a single neuron or a set of neurons and edges on the map vertex type may describe a one-to-one connection or one-to-all connections [29], HyperNEAT [22] and Evolvable-Substrate-HyperNEAT (ES-HyperNEAT) [23]. In HyperNEAT neurons exist in a geometric space, and a function, which is the genome, maps from the coordinates of a pair of neurons to the parameters of the synapse between them (including whether or not it exists). Thus to decode a network the coordinates of each and every pair of neurons is fed into the function and the outputs are used to determine the properties of the synapse between each pair. In this way the evolved genome function can encode the parameters of the network with respect to the geometry of the network, which can be advantageous when the input and/or output of the network contain geometrically encoded regularities [22, 23]. In ES-HyperNEAT the density and placement of connections, and so neurons, is determined by the amount of information encoded in each region of the hypercube represented by the genome function. Indirect encoding schemes can allow searching a smaller genome space while still creating complex networks [23].

Two developmental schemes have been used to evolve neural networks with plastic synapses. Gruau [13] developed a grammar tree system where the values of weights as determined by plasticity rules could be passed onto new connections created by recursive expansion of the grammar tree during an individuals life. Khan and Miller [15] devised a system where neurons, axons and dendrites situated in a Cartesian space could replicate, migrate, grow/shrink and terminate during an individuals life, partially dependent on environmental input. Each of these developmental functions was controlled by programs evolved using Cartesian genetic programming.

Evolution is the method of choice, and perhaps the only known method, for generating artificial neural networks based on models other than the traditional rate-based, fixed-weight variety (for which there are many methods, the most well known of which is likely back-propagation). There is a wide variety of encoding schemes described here, but relatively little information on the impact of using different encoding schemes on evolving neural networks for online learning.

6   Discussion and Future Directions

While relatively little research has been performed in total over the last couple of decades, advances have been made in tackling increasingly difficult online learning problem domains, by way of increasing the functional capabilities of neural network models and via improvements in methods of artificial evolution as a vehicle to generate neural networks for online learning. Of course, in the context of the goal of creating an agent capable of general intelligence, there is still a long way to go.

Problem domains studied to date have been relatively simple, as compared to many studied in the field of reinforcement learning, and also with respect to the goal of creating agents with some form of general intelligence. The environments typically represent a small state-, percept- and action space, with a small change occurring in the environment during an agents life time (for example, the location of a reward occasionally switches between two places in a fixed maze layout, or stimulus/reward associations are modified). Significantly, this small change is the only kind of change that occurs throughout an entire evolutionary run, and typically an entire set of experiments. These kinds of simple dynamic tasks require evolving a specialised exploration strategy and a specialised memory system to remember which fixed behaviour pattern is the current correct one or to remember a few simple associations. Additionally, all of the studied problem domains using a reinforcement learning paradigm have very clear exploration and exploitation phases: it is clear when exploration can cease and exploitation begin, either initially or upon the environment having changed; thus the specialised exploration strategy is invoked only when the expected reward for the current behaviour pattern or stimulus is not met. These have probably been desirable features, given available computational resources or a focus on other aspects of evolving plastic networks. However, an important question is whether plastic networks can be evolved to operate in more complex environments and, perhaps more importantly, to operate in environments that are significantly different to those seen at any other time during an evolutionary run. In other words, is it possible to evolve plastic neural networks that implement more general exploration strategies and can form and exploit internal models of more complex environments which have not previously been encountered?

As far as the authors are aware there have been no comparative studies on encoding schemes for plastic networks. An open question is what impact encoding schemes have on the ability to evolve plastic networks for the task of online learning.

Several studies have found that introducing functional properties observed in biological neural networks into the neural network models employed for online learning or adaptation, even in a very simplified form, has produced higher quality solutions, enabled new capabilities, and/or improved evolvability in terms of speed and reducing variance in performance. Examples include neuromodulation of synaptic plasticity [25, 26], synaptic scaling/competition [8, 14] and spike-timing-dependent plasticity [8].

Given these findings, and the many functional properties of biological neurons and synapses that have been implicated in learning, memory and information processing, an important question is what functional properties can be introduced to positive effect, particularly in the domain of online learning, for which only a relatively simple form of plasticity neuromodulation has been studied to date. Examples of functional properties for which there is evidence of a role in performing various kinds or aspects of online learning in biological neural networks include spike-timing-dependent synaptic plasticity [2, 5], synaptic scaling and competition [1], stochastic synaptic transmission [24], meta-plasticity [2], and synapto- and neuro-genesis [7].

On a similar note, both the neural map and the HyperNEAT-based schemes aim to allow generating regular structures in the network that map to certain kinds of regularities over multiple inputs and/or outputs [22, 23, 29]. Biological networks achieve this goal by self-organisation processes [7, 12] which can continue to operate throughout the networks life. Thus another interesting open question is whether emulations of these life-time plasticity processes in evolved artificial neural networks can facilitate online learning for such input or output spaces.

A factor of the success in tackling increasingly difficult online learning problem domains is the availability of computational power. Specifically, the availability of increasing computational power has made it possible to simulate more complex neural network models, perform longer evolutionary runs, and simulate more complex environments that require online learning. This factor should not be underestimated: evolution of artificial neural network models can be particularly computationally intensive, especially so for the task of online learning, which by its nature tends to require long fitness evaluation times in the evolutionary algorithm and the simulation of neural network models that are more complex than typical models. We are entering a period where this approach is becoming increasingly practical.

References

1. Abbott, L.F., Nelson, S.B., et al.: Synaptic plasticity: taming the beast. Nature Neuroscience 3, 1178–1183 (2000)
2. Abraham, W.C.: Metaplasticity: tuning synapses and networks for plasticity. Nature Reviews Neuroscience 9(5), 387–399 (2008)
3. Baxter, J.: The evolution of learning algorithms for artificial neural networks. Complex Systems, 313–326 (1993)
4. Chalmers, D.J.: The evolution of learning: An experiment in genetic connectionism. In: Proceedings of the 1990 Connectionist Models Summer School, pp. 81–90 (1990)
5. Cooke, S.F., Bliss, T.V.P.: Plasticity in the human central nervous system. Brain 129(7), 1659–1673 (2006)
6. Cuccu, G., Gomez, F.: When Novelty Is Not Enough. In: Di Chio, C., Cagnoni, S., Cotta, C., Ebner, M., Ekárt, A., Esparcia-Alcázar, A.I., Merelo, J.J., Neri, F., Preuss, M., Richter, H., Togelius, J., Yannakakis, G.N. (eds.) EvoApplications 2011, Part I. LNCS, vol. 6624, pp. 234–243. Springer, Heidelberg (2011)
7. Deng, W., Aimone, J.B., Gage, F.H.: New neurons and new memories: how does adult hippocampal neurogenesis affect learning and memory? Nature Reviews Neuroscience 11(5), 339–350 (2010)
8. Di Paolo, E.: Spike-timing dependent plasticity for evolved robots. Adaptive Behavior 10(3-4), 243–263 (2002)
9. Di Paolo, E.: Evolving spike-timing-dependent plasticity for single-trial learning in robots. Philosophical Transactions of the Royal Society of London. Series A: Mathematical, Physical and Engineering Sciences 361(1811), 2299–2319 (2003)
10. Floreano, D., Mondada, F.: Evolution of plastic neurocontrollers for situated agents. In: Maes, P., Mataric, M., Meyer, J.-A., Pollack, J., Wilson, S. (eds.) From Animals to Animats, vol. 4. MIT Press, MA (1996)
11. Floreano, D., Urzelai, J.: Neural morphogenesis, synaptic plasticity, and evolution. Theory in Biosciences 120(3), 225–240 (2001)

12. Fuerst, P.G., Burgess, R.W.: Adhesion molecules in establishing retinal circuitry. Current Opinion in Neurobiology 19(4), 389–394 (2009)
13. Gruau, F., Whitley, D.: Adding learning to the cellular development of neural networks: Evolution and the baldwin effect. Evolutionary Computation 1(3), 213–233 (1993)
14. Hoinville, T., Siles, C.T., Hénaff, P.: Flexible and multistable pattern generation by evolving constrained plastic neurocontrollers. Adaptive Behavior 19(3), 187–207 (2011)
15. Khan, G.M., Miller, J.F., Halliday, D.M.: Evolution of cartesian genetic programs for development of learning neural architecture. Evolutionary Computation 19(3), 469–523 (2011)
16. Kistemaker, S., Whiteson, S.: Critical factors in the performance of novelty search. In: Proceedings of the 13th annual Conference on Genetic and Evolutionary Computation (GECCO 2011), pp. 965–972 (2011)
17. Mathayomchan, B., Beer, R.D.: Center-crossing recurrent neural networks for the evolution of rhythmic behavior. Neural Computation 14(9), 2043–2051 (2002)
18. McHale, G., Husbands, P.: Quadrupedal locomotion: GasNets, CTRNNs and hybrid CTRNN/PNNs compared. In: Proceedings of the 9th International Conference on the Simulation and Synthesis of Living Systems (Alife IX), pp. 106–112 (2004)
19. Mouret, J.B., Tonelli, P.: Artificial evolution of plastic neural networks: a few key concepts. In: DevLeaNN (2011)
20. Niv, Y., Joel, D., Meilijson, I., Ruppin, E.: Evolution of reinforcement learning in uncertain environments: A simple explanation for complex foraging behaviors. Adaptive Behavior 10(1), 5–24 (2002)
21. Risi, S., Hughes, C.E., Stanley, K.O.: Evolving plastic neural networks with novelty search. Adaptive Behavior 18(6), 470–491 (2010)
22. Risi, S., Stanley, K.O.: Indirectly Encoding Neural Plasticity as a Pattern of Local Rules. In: Doncieux, S., Girard, B., Guillot, A., Hallam, J., Meyer, J.-A., Mouret, J.-B. (eds.) SAB 2010. LNCS, vol. 6226, pp. 533–543. Springer, Heidelberg (2010)
23. Risi, S., Stanley, K.O.: A unified approach to evolving plasticity and neural geometry. In: Proceedings of the International Joint Conference on Neural Networks (IJCNN 2012). IEEE (2012)
24. Seung, S.: Learning in spiking neural networks by reinforcement of stochastic synaptic transmission. Neuron 40(6), 1063–1073 (2003)
25. Soltoggio, A., Bullinaria, J.A., Mattiussi, C., Dürr, P., Floreano, D.: Evolutionary advantages of neuromodulated plasticity in dynamic, reward-based scenarios. Artificial Life 11, 569 (2008)
26. Soltoggio, A., Dürr, P., Mattiussi, C., Floreano, D.: Evolving neuromodulatory topologies for reinforcement learning-like problems. In: IEEE Congress on Evolutionary Computation, CEC 2007, pp. 2471–2478 (2007)
27. Stanley, K.O.: Evolving adaptive neural networks with and without adaptive synapses. In: Proceedings of the 2003 Congress on Evolutionary Computation, vol. 4, pp. 2557–2564 (2003)
28. Tonelli, P., Mouret, J.: Using a map-based encoding to evolve plastic neural networks. In: 2011 IEEE Workshop on Evolving and Adaptive Intelligent Systems (EAIS), pp. 9–16. IEEE (April 2011)
29. Tonelli, P., Mouret, J.-B.: On the relationships between synaptic plasticity and generative systems. In: Proceedings of the 13th Annual Conference on Genetic and Evolutionary Computation, GECCO 2011, pp. 1531–1538. ACM, New York (2011)
30. Wood, R., Di Paolo, E.A.: New Models for Old Questions: Evolutionary Robotics and the 'A Not B' Error. In: Almeida e Costa, F., Rocha, L.M., Costa, E., Harvey, I., Coutinho, A. (eds.) ECAL 2007. LNCS (LNAI), vol. 4648, pp. 1141–1150. Springer, Heidelberg (2007)

A Multimodal Problem for Competitive Coevolution

Philip Hingston, Tirtha Ranjeet, Chiou Peng Lam, and Martin Masek

Edith Cowan University, 2 Bradford St, Mt Lawley 6050 Western Australia
p.hingston@ecu.edu.au

Abstract. Coevolutionary algorithms are a special kind of evolutionary algorithm with advantages in solving certain specific kinds of problems. In particular, competitive coevolutionary algorithms can be used to study problems in which two sides compete against each other and must choose a suitable strategy. Often these problems are multimodal — there is more than one strong strategy for each side. In this paper, we introduce a scalable multimodal test problem for competitive coevolution, and use it to investigate the effectiveness of some common coevolutionary algorithm enhancement techniques.

Keywords: coevolution, multimodal, diversity.

1 Introduction

Competitive coevolutionary algorithms are an important class of evolutionary algorithm, in which there is no externally defined objective fitness function. Instead, fitness is defined in a relative way, based on interactions between several coevolving populations. For this reason, competitive coevolutionary algorithms can suffer convergence "pathologies", and techniques have been developed to address these. In this paper, we focus on multimodality in coevolution, a problem feature that is known to cause convergence problems in evolutionary algorithms.

Coevolutionary algorithms may be either cooperative, in which members of each population combine to solve a problem, or competitive, in which members of each population compete against each other. One class of problem for which coevolutionary algorithms seem especially suited is the problem of determining good strategies for the opposing parties in an adversarial situation. There is one population for each party, in which each member of the population represents a possible strategy for that party. The relative fitness of each strategy in the population depends on the outcomes of conflicts with strategies from the other population(s). Examples of problems that can be approached in this way are games, negotiations and tactical planning. Often these problems appear to be multimodal, i.e. there is more than one strong strategy for each side.

In order to study the effects of multimodality in coevolution, we introduce a scalable multimodal test problem, and use it to investigate the effectiveness of some common coevolutionary algorithm enhancement techniques in improving an algorithm's ability to solve multimodal problems.

M. Thielscher and D. Zhang (Eds.): AI 2012, LNCS 7691, pp. 338–349, 2012.

In the next section, we briefly review related work, before introducing our test problem. We then describe a simple coevolutionary algorithm and some commonly used enhancement techniques. In the following section, we describe our experiments, in which we test the simple version of the algorithm as well as variations that use these enhancements. Finally, we present a series of plots summarising the results of our experimentation and draw our conclusions.

2   Related Work

With regard to evolutionary algorithms, multimodality has long been recognised as an important issue, and something that often occurs in real world problems. Accordingly, there have been many studies testing various evolutionary algorithms on a range of multimodal test problems (e.g. [9,17,13,22,18,28,29]). Techniques have been developed to enhance evolutionary algorithms for multimodal problems, such as crowding [25], fitness sharing [23], derating [2] and speciation [15]. However, we have been unable to locate any similar work on multimodal test problems for competitive coevolution, or on testing the effectiveness of these special techniques in the context of competitive coevolution.

Coevolutionary algorithms have been used to solve multimodal function optimisation problems (e.g. [10,16,27]), generally by subdividing the problem, assigning subpopulations to different subproblems. Our interest here is different – there is no external objective function to optimise, instead, the multimodality arises from the interaction between two competing, coevolving populations. There are many examples of competitive coevolution being used to solve such problems, for example in game playing (e.g. [20,12,5]) and red teaming (e.g. [24,14]), but we have not located any work specifically addressing multimodality in these applications.

3   A Multimodal Test Problem

In this section, we introduce a multimodal test problem for coevolutionary algorithms with two competing sides. What does multimodality mean in an adversarial problem? Intuitively, the idea is that a problem is multimodal if there is more than one strong strategy for each side, but how can this idea be operationalised? For an evolutionary algorithm, multimodalty means that there is more than one local optimum in the fitness landscape. But in a coevolutionary algorithm, fitness landscapes are constantly changing as the compositions of the populations change.

For the purposes of this study, we replace the usual fitness landscape with what we will call a *generalisation landscape*. The *generalisation performance* of a solution is based on its expected performance against a randomly selected opponent. This notion has been formalised by Chong et al. [6,7], who proposed a suitable set of related measures for generalisation performance, and provided methods to estimate the values of these measures. We discuss these measures in more detail in Section 5. A generalisation landscape is then defined as the surface generated by mapping generalisation performance over a search space. We will consider a problem to be multimodal if its generalisation surface has multiple local optima.

We will call our multimodal test problem an *n-peaks* problem, as there are n equally good strategies (corresponding to n peaks in the generalisation landscape) for each side. The challenge for a coevolutionary algorithm is to locate as many of these peaks as possible.

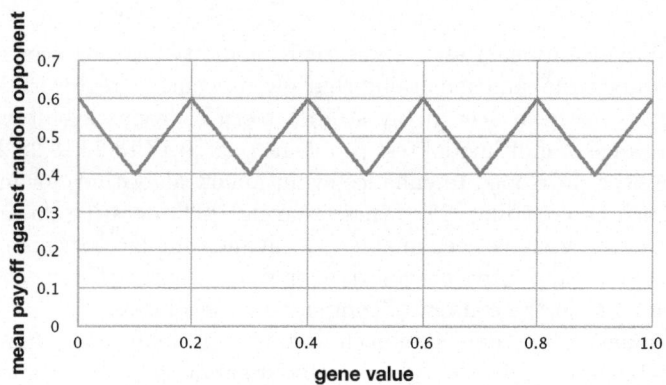

Fig. 1. Mean payoffs against random opponents for solutions to the 5-peaks problem with H= 1 and L = 1. An individual near 0, for example, will get a payoff of H (i.e. 1) against most opponents in the first interval (0 to 0.2), the third interval (0.4 to 0.6), and the fifth interval (0.8 to 1.0), and a payoff of L (i.e. also 1) against only a few opponents, in the second and fourth intervals, giving a mean payoff of nearly 0.6.

The problem is symmetric (the domain and task are the same for both sides). The domain for each side is the interval $[0, 1]$. The problem is parameterised by n, and by two payoff values $H > 0$ and $L > 0$. When two individuals x and y compete, the outcome is determined as in Equations (1)–(6).

$$i_x = \lfloor (x \times n) \rfloor \tag{1}$$

$$i_y = \lfloor (y \times n) \rfloor \tag{2}$$

$$v_x = |0.5 - (x \times n) + i_x| \tag{3}$$

$$v_y = |0.5 - (y \times n) + i_y| \tag{4}$$

$$gap = \mathrm{mod}(i_x - i_y, n) \tag{5}$$

$$score(x, y) = \begin{cases} H, \ if & gap\%2 = 0 \ and \ v_x > v_y \\ L, \ if & gap\%2 = 1 \ and \ v_x < v_y \\ 0 & otherwise \end{cases} \tag{6}$$

Intuitively, we picture the domain as divided into n equal intervals. Figure 1 illustrates the case $n = 5$, $H = L = 1$. When x and y compete, the outcome depends on which intervals they belong to (Equations 1 and 2), and on the distances from the centres of their intervals (Equations 3 and 4). If x and y are in the same interval, then x gets a payoff of H if it is *further from* the centre of the interval than y is (otherwise 0). If y is in the next interval to the right of x, then x gets a payoff of L if it is *closer to* the centre of its interval than y is to the centre of its interval. For this purpose, the "next interval to the right" of the rightmost interval is considered to be the leftmost interval - i.e. the domain wraps around. If y is two intervals to the right of x, then x gets a payoff if it is furthest from the centre of its interval. This pattern continues, with wrapping if necessary, so that the domain is actually circular, rather than linear. If y is an even number of intervals to the right of x, then it is good for x to be nearer its boundary (for a payoff of H), while if y is an odd number of intervals to the right, then it is good for x to be nearer the centre of its interval (for a payoff of L).

In the case of the problem in Figure 1, those individuals close to the interval boundaries get a high payoff against about 60% of opponents randomly selected from the domain (for an average payoff of 0.6), while those near the middle of their interval only get a high payoff against about 40% of opponents (average payoff 0.4). Thus, there are n local optima or peaks in the generalisation landscape (counting 0 and 1 as the same individual, so that there is half a peak near 0 and the other half of it is near 1).

Although, in this paper, we study only the 5-peaks problem in Figure 1, the picture is similar for other values of n. By setting the values of H and L, the difference between peak and trough values can be manipulated. By changing the definition slghtly and using more than one H and/or L value, the heights of individual peaks could also be controlled. It is also straightforward to extend the idea to higher dimensions, by subdividing a hypercube into cells, and using a kind of Manhatten distance between cells in place of the *gap* value.

4   Algorithm and Variations

In order to illustrate the difficulties posed by multimodality, we carried out experiments to test the performance of a simple competitive coevolutionary algorithm, along with some popular variations, on an *n-peaks* problem. In this section we describe the algorithm and variations that we used.

4.1   CEAN - A Naïve Coevolutionary Algorithm

As a base case, we use a simple, naïve, competitive coevolutionary algorithm which we call *CEAN*. We then define variations on *CEAN* which include a fitness sharing mechanism, or a Hall of Fame, or both, and we also vary the mutation rate. Algorithm 1 describes the algorithm in pseudocode. Note that we have not included crossover (but it could easily be added) − we don't use crossover here because the genome for our problem is a single real number. The parameter μ is the mutation rate and the procedure *Mutate* mutates an individual population member. The procedure *Select* selects one individual from a population, based on the fitness values of the population members. Finally, the procedure *CalculateFitness* assigns fitness values to the members of both populations, based on competition between members of the two populations.

Input: Two initial populations P_1^0 and P_2^0
Output: Two final populations P_1^f and P_2^f
1 begin
2     $t \leftarrow 0$;
3   while $t < f$ do
4   CalculateFitness(P_1^t, P_2^t);
5   for $i \in 1..2$ do
6           $P_i^{t+1} \leftarrow \{\}$;
7   while P_i^{t+1} *is not full* do
8              $s \leftarrow Select(P_i^{t+1})$;
9   with probability μ, $s \leftarrow Mutate(s)$;
10              $P_i^{t+1} \leftarrow P_i^{t+1} \cup \{s\}$;
11   end
12   end
13        $t \leftarrow t + 1$;
14   end
15 end

Algorithm 1: CEAN

For the naïve algorithm, *CalculateFitness* assigns a fitness value for each population member as the mean payoff achieved in competition with the members of the other population. This is presented in pseudocode in Algorithm 2.

4.2 Variants

Even when solving unimodal problems, we know that coevolutionary algorithms often need special care to avoid coevolutionary pathologies such as cycling, loss of gradient, and so on [1,11,23,8,3]. Two common remedies are the use of an archive (to prevent evolutionary forgetting), and diversity maintenance techniques (to prevent loss of diversity). We therefore created variations on CEAN that include an archive and/or a diversity maintenance mechanism.

First let us consider diversity maintenance. A simple, explicit way to maintain diversity is to use a high mutation rate, but this also has the disadvantage of disrupting evolutionary learning in a random, uncontrolled way. Among the available implicit diversity maintenance techniques, we chose to use competitive fitness sharing [23]. This works by penalising population members that are similar to others in the population. The simple fitness of an individual is calculated in the normal way, and is then divided by a quantity called the *niche count* to determine its *shared fitness*. Selection is then carried out using shared fitness rather than simple fitness. Modifying CEAN to use this selection procedure gives an algorithm variant we call CEAFS.

Input: Two populations P_1 and P_2

```
1  begin
2  |   for x ∈ P₁ do
3  |   |   f ← 0;
4  |   |   for y ∈ P₂ do
5  |   |   |   f ← f + score(x, y);
6  |   |   end
7  |   |   fitness(x) = f/|P₂|;
8  |   end
9  |   for y ∈ P₂ do
10 |   |   f ← 0;
11 |   |   for x ∈ P₁ do
12 |   |   |   f ← f + score(y, x);
13 |   |   end
14 |   |   fitness(y) = f/|P₁|;
15 |   end
16 end
```

Algorithm 2: Calculating fitness for CEAN

Equations 7 and 8 are used to calculate the niche count, where x_i is the ith individual in the population, and u is the genome length (so $d_{i,j}$ is the Euclidean distance between x_i and x_j). c_i is the niche count for x_i, τ is a constant that determines the shape of the sharing function, n_r is a constant (*niche radius*) and N is the population size.

$$c_i = \sum_{j=1}^{N} \begin{cases} 1 - (\frac{d_{i,j}}{n_r})^\tau & \text{if } d_{i,j} \leq n_r \\ 0 & \text{otherwise} \end{cases} \tag{7}$$

$$d_{i,j} = \sqrt{\sum_{m=1}^{u} (x_{i,m} - x_{j,m})^2} \tag{8}$$

As an archive mechanism, we implemented a Hall of Fame (HOF) [23]. For each population, we maintain an archive, known as a Hall of Fame, consisting of fittest individuals from each earlier generation. In this CEAHOF variant of CEAN, the fitness calculation given in Algorithm 2 is modified to calculate the average payoff of the individual in question against members of the opposing population *as well as* the members of the archive. After each generation, the fittest individual from each population is added to the archive.

Thus we have three variants: the naïve algorithm, CEAN, a variant that uses fitness sharing, CEAFS, and a variant that uses a Hall of Fame, CEAHOF. Finally, we also created a fourth variant which uses both fitness sharing and a Hall of Fame, CEACFH. In this variant, fitness values are calculated using the Hall of Fame as for CEAHOF, and then these values are adjusted to obtain shared fitness values as for CEAFS.

5   Performance Measures

One aspect of performance is generalisation performance - that is, how well do solutions found for one side in a contest, learned via a coevolutionary algorithm, generalise to compete well against arbitrary strategies for the other side?

We use Chong et al.'s notion of generalisation performance [6,7]. They describe their methods in terms of a population attempting to learn general solutions to perform well against a large space of test cases. They begin by defining generalization performance as the mean score of a solution in all possible test cases. This intuitively appealing definition poses several practical difficulties. First, for many problems of interest, the space of possible test cases could be very large, or even infinite, and there may be no way to compute a mean score analytically. Therefore, they propose a statistical approximation approach, in which a mean score is computed for a suitable sample of test cases. The second difficulty is to decide what probability distribution should be used over the space of test cases. In many cases, scores against "high quality" test cases might be considered more important, as they would be more likely to be chosen by an opponent, for example. Chong et al. therefore propose two different methods for sampling the space of test cases: unbiased sampling (which is purely random) and biased sampling (which favours higher quality test cases). In this paper, we use biased sampling to measure algorithm performance. The procedure to obtain a biased sample for testing is described in detail in [6,7].

In addition, they consider several different summary values to describe the overall generalisation performance of a population of solutions: average, best and ensemble. We consider only the "best" figure. Equations 9 and 10 describe how this is calculated. Here *TestSet* is a biased sample of test cases, P is a population of solutions, and $best(P, k)$ is the set consisting of the k members of P with the highest simple fitness values. Intuitively, $best(P, k)$ is what the coevolutionary algorithm "thinks" is the best k solutions found, and $BestGP(P)$ is the generalisation performance of the best generaliser amongst them.

$$GP(x) = \frac{1}{|TestSet|} \sum_{y \in TestSet} score(x, y) \tag{9}$$

$$BestGP(P) = \max_{x \in best(P,k)} GP(x) \tag{10}$$

In the case of a multimodal problem, another relevant aspect of performance is how well an algorithm does at locating *as many peaks as possible* – that is, can the algorithm locate many different representative solutions with high generalisation performance, rather than simply *any of them*.

One way to quantify this aspect of performance is to calculate what proportion of peaks the algorithm finds on average, and how often it succeeds in finding all peaks. These are summarised by the two measures *peak ratio* (Equation 11) and *success ratio* (Equation 12) [26].

$$\text{peak ratio} = \frac{\text{total peaks found}}{\text{number of peaks} \times \text{number of runs}} \tag{11}$$

$$\text{success ratio} = \frac{\text{number of times all peaks found}}{\text{number of runs}} \qquad (12)$$

In addition to these ratios, we also calculated the *circular earth mover's distance* (CEMD). CEMD was introduced by Rabin et al. [21] for comparing two histograms, and has been widely used in image processing for comparing images. Since we know the true location of the peaks in our test problem, we can construct an "ideal" distribution for an evolved population, in the form of a histogram in which all buckets not containing a peak are empty, and all buckets containing a peak contain equal numbers of solutions. We can then compare the actual histogram with this ideal histogram. *Earth mover's distance* is the minimum total amount of movement that would be required to make the two histograms identical. For the case of a circular domain, there is a simple way to calculate this, given in Equation 13.

Here the two histograms are F and G, and N is the number of buckets. F_k is the cumulative histogram derived from F, starting at bucket k and wrapping at the right hand edge of the domain (and likewise for G_k). In our experiments we used 40 equally spaced buckets for this calculation.

$$CEMD = \min_{k \in \{1,2,\dots,N\}} \{ \frac{1}{N} \sum_{i=1}^{N} |F_k[i] - G_k[i]| \} \qquad (13)$$

6 Experiments and Results

To investigate the effects of diversity maintenance via fitness sharing and/or mutation, and of an archive in the form of a Hall of Fame, on the 5-peaks problem, we executed each algorithm 60 times for each mutation rate from 2.5% to 100% in steps of 2.5%. In each case we used the fixed parameter settings as in Table 1. The values of niche radius and τ were set on the basis of preliminary empirical tests. For each execution, in each generation, we recorded diversity (genotypic diversity), generalisation performance (best GP), and peak finding ability (CEMD, peak ratio and success ratio).

Table 1. Fixed Algorithm Parameters

Parameter	Value
Mutation	Gaussian, with wrapping, $\sigma = 0.1$
Selection	Stochastic universal sampling
Population size	50 in each population
Generations	300
Niche radius	0.2
τ	1.0
HOF size	50

Figures 2 to 4 present the results in the form of a series of profile plots. Each data point is an average over 60 executions of the mean value for the figure in question over the final 60 generations. There is a data point for each algorithm variant and mutation rate. (Here we report data for the first side, but the problem is symmetric and the data for the other side is entirely similar, as expected.)

For example, in terms of diversity, in Figure 2(a), we see that the variants that use fitness sharing have the highest diversity, and that this diversity is not sensitive to the mutation rate (with a slight peak at a mutation rate of about 12.5%). The two variants without fitness sharing have lower diversity, increasing with mutation rate, with CEAHOF performing worst in terms of diversity.

Turning next to generalisation performance, Figure 2(b) shows the equivalent plot for best generalisation performance. For reference, assuming that both populations are reasonably diverse, generalisation performance should be in the range 0.4 to 0.6. We can see from the figure that CEAN, the naïve algorithm, is the worst performer, with a maximum of only about 0.56, for mutation rates above 27.5%. Fitness sharing improves performance to about 0.58 for CEAFS with mutation rates between about 7.5% and 12.5%, which is also the range that gives slightly better diversity with this variation. CEAHOF achieves almost the same level for mutation rates between about 17.5% and 57.5%. But the best performance is for the combined variant CEACFH, with above 0.59 for mutation rates between 5% and 12.5%.

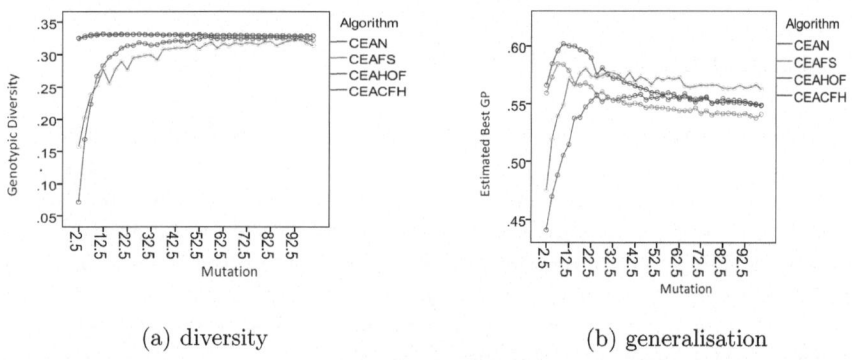

(a) diversity   (b) generalisation

Fig. 2. Profile plots of diversity and best generalisation performance (mean over the final 60 generations) versus mutation rate for each of the 4 algorithm variants.

From this, we draw a tentative conclusion that Hall of Fame provides a benefit to generalisation performance, but this may be limited by the drawback that it reduces diversity. Combining a Hall of Fame with a diversity mechanism solves the diversity loss problem, and fitness sharing is a more effective mechanism for this than simply increasing the mutation rate.

The last three plots address the question of the ability of the algorithm variants to find the multiple peaks of our multimodal problem. Figure 3 shows this in terms of the circular earth mover's distance. Recall that this measures how similar the distribution of the population is to an 'ideal' distribution, so smaller values are considered better. Clearly the minimum value is achieved by the combined variant (closely followed by the fitness sharing one), with low mutation rates of about 2.5% to 12.5%. This picture is confirmed by the results for peak ratio (Figure 4(a)) and success ratio (Figure 4(b)). The two fitness sharing variants with low mutation rates are clearly superior, with the combined variant slightly shading the plain fitness sharing variant. For mutation rates above about 35%, all the variants perform equally poorly.

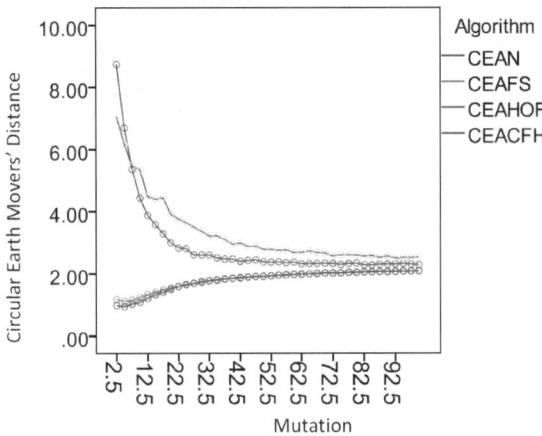

Fig. 3. Profile plot of the circular earth mover's distance (mean over the final 60 generations) versus mutation rate for each of the 4 algorithm variants

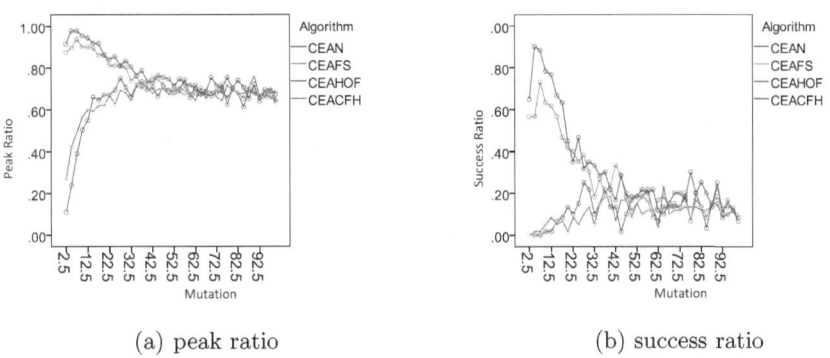

(a) peak ratio   (b) success ratio

Fig. 4. Profile plots for peak finding performance (mean over the final 60 generations) versus mutation rate for each of the 4 algorithm variants

7   Conclusion

In this paper, we have examined the performance of a competitive coevolutionary algorithm on a multimodal problem. We created the *n-peaks* problem, a scalable multimodal test problem in which the number and amplitude of the peaks in the fitness landscape can be manipulated.

We then used an instance of the problem to test a naïve competitive coevolutionary algorithm, as well as several variants incorporating an archive (Hall of Fame) and a diversity maintenance mechanism (competitive fitness sharing), in terms of their generalisation ability, and peak finding ability. We found that, for this problem, best results in terms of both criteria were obtained with the combination of an archive and diversity maintenance, with a moderately low level of mutation.

In future work, it remains to investigate other instances of the problem with different generalisation landscapes, and in higher dimensions. In addition, other methods for handling multimodality can be tested.

References

1. Watson, R.A., Pollack, J.B.: Coevolutionary dynamics in a minimal substrate. In: Proceedings of the 2001 Genetic and Evolutionary Computation Conference (GECCO 2001), pp. 702–709 (2001)
2. Beasley, D., Bull, D.R., Martin, R.R.: A sequential niche technique for multimodal function optimization. Evolutionary Computation 1(2), 101–125 (1993)
3. Cartlidge, J., Bullock, S.: Combating coevolutionary disengagement by reducing parasite virulence. Evolutionary Computation 12(2), 193–222 (2004)
4. Chellapilla, K., Fogel, D.: Evolving neural networks to play checkers without expert knowledge. IEEE Transactions on Neural Networks 10(6), 1382–1391 (1999)
5. Chiong, R., Kirley, M.: Iterated N-Player games on small-world networks. In: Proceedings of the Genetic and Evolutionary Computation Conference (GECCO 2011), Dublin, Ireland, pp. 1123–1130 (July 2011)
6. Chong, S., Tino, P., Yao, X.: Measuring generalisation performance in coevolutionary learning. IEEE Transactions on Evolutionary Computation 12(4), 479–505 (2008)
7. Chong, S., Tino, P., Yao, X.: Relationship between generalization and diversity in coevolutionary learning. IEEE Transactions on Computational Intelligence and AI in Games 1(3), 214–232 (2009)
8. de Jong, E.D., Pollack, J.B.: Ideal evaluation from coevolution. Evolutionary Computation 12(2), 159–192 (2004)
9. Deb, K., Goldberg, D.: An investigation of niche and species formation in genetic function optimization. In: Proceedings of the Third International Conference on Genetic Algorithms, pp. 42–50 (1989)
10. Drezewski, R.: A co-evolutionary multi-agent system for multi-modal function optimization. In: Proceedings of the International Conference on Computational Science, Krakow, Poland, pp. 654–661 (2004)
11. Ficici, S.G.: Solution concepts in coevolutionary algorithms. PhD thesis, Brandeis Univ., Waltham, MA (2004)

12. Fogel, D.: Blondie24: playing at the edge of AI. Morgan Kaufmann Publishers Inc. (2002)
13. Hansen, N., Kern, S.: Evaluating the CMA Evolution Strategy on Multimodal Test Functions. In: Yao, X., Burke, E.K., Lozano, J.A., Smith, J., Merelo-Guervós, J.J., Bullinaria, J.A., Rowe, J.E., Tiňo, P., Kabán, A., Schwefel, H.-P. (eds.) PPSN 2004. LNCS, vol. 3242, pp. 282–291. Springer, Heidelberg (2004)
14. Hingston, P., Preuss, M.: Red teaming with coevolution. In: 2011 IEEE Congress on Evolutionary Computation (CEC), pp. 1155–1163 (June 2011)
15. Li, J.P., Balazs, M.E., Parks, G., Clarkson, P.J.: A species conserving genetic algorithm for multimodal function optimization. Evolutionary Computation 10(3), 207–234 (2002)
16. Liu, Y., Yao, X., Zhao, Q.: Scaling up fast evolutionary programming with cooperative coevolution. In: Proceedings of the 2001 Congress on Evolutionary Computation, Seoul, Korea, pp. 1101–1108 (2001)
17. Miller, B., Shaw, M.: Genetic algorithms with dynamic niche sharing for multimodal function optimization. In: Proceedings of IEEE International Conference on Evolutionary Computation (1995)
18. Parsopoulos, K., Vrahatis, M.: A generator for multimodal test functions with multiple global optima. IEEE Transactions on Evolutionary Computation 8(3), 211–224 (2004)
19. Petrowski, A.: A clearing procedure as a niching method for genetic algorithms. In: Proceedings of the 3rd IEEE International Conference on Evolutionary Computation, pp. 798–803 (1996)
20. Pollack, J., Blair, A.: Co-evolution in the successful learning of backgammon strategy. Machine Learning 32, 225–240 (1998)
21. Rabin, J., Delon, J., Gousseau, Y.: Circular earth mover's distance for the comparison of local features. In: Proceedings of the International Conference on Pattern Recognition (2008)
22. Rönkkönen, J., Li, X., Kyrki, V., Lampinen, J.: A framework for generating tunable test functions for multimodal optimization. Soft Computing 15(9), 1689–1706 (2011)
23. Rosin, C., Belew, R.: New methods for competitive coevolution. Evolutionary Computation 5(1), 1–29 (1997)
24. Seng, C.C., Lian, C.C., Spencer, L.K.M., Darren, O.W.S.: A co-evolutionary approach for military operational analysis. In: Proceedings of the first ACM/SIGEVO Summit on Genetic and Evolutionary Computation, GEC 2009, pp. 67–74. ACM, New York (2009)
25. Mahfoud, S.W.: Crowding and preselection revisited. In: Proceedings of Parallel Problem Solving from Nature 2, pp. 27–36 (1992)
26. Thomsen, R.: Multimodal optimization using crowding-based differential evolution. In: Proceedings of the IEEE Congress on Evolutionary Computation, pp. 1382–1389 (2004)
27. Xuhua, S., Haizhen, Y.: An exploring coevolution multi-agent system for multimodal function optimization. In: International Workshop on Intelligent Systems and Applications, ISA 2009, pp. 1–4 (May 2009)
28. Weise, T., Niemczyk, S., Skubch, H., Reichle, R., Geihs, K.: A tunable model for multi-objective, epistatic, rugged, and neutral fitness landscapes. In: Proceedings of the Genetic and Evolutionary Computation Conference (GECCO 2008), Atlanta, GA, USA, pp. 795–802 (July 2008)
29. Yu, E., Suganthan, P.: Ensemble of niching algorithms. Information Sciences 180, 2815–2833 (2010)

XCSR with Computed Continuous Action

Muhammad Iqbal, Will N. Browne, and Mengjie Zhang

Evolutionary Computation Research Group,
School of Engineering and Computer Science,
Victoria University of Wellington,
PO Box 600, Wellington 6140, New Zealand
{muhammad.iqbal,will.browne,mengjie.zhang}@ecs.vuw.ac.nz

Abstract. Wilson extended XCS with interval based conditions to XCSR to handle real valued inputs. However, the possible actions must always be determined in advance. Yet domains such as robot control require numerical actions, so that neither XCS nor XCSR with their discrete actions can yield high performance. In the work presented here, genetic programming-based representation is used for the first time to compute continuous action in XCSR. This XCSR version has been examined on a simple one-dimensional but non-linear testbed problem – the "frog" problem – and compared with two continuous action based systems, GCS and XCSFCA. The proposed approach has consistently solved the frog problem and outperformed GCS and XCSFCA.

Keywords: Learning Classifier Systems, XCS, XCSR, Code Fragment, Computed Action, Continuous Action.

1 Introduction

A learning classifier system (LCS) represents a rule-based agent that incorporates evolutionary computing and machine learning to solve a given task by interacting with the environment. The rules are of the form "if *state* then *action*". Usually the possible number of actions are known in a learning classifier system, but for problems requiring continuous real valued outputs, it is not possible. Therefore discrete action based systems like XCS and XCSR show some limits. A solution is to use a generalized classifier system (GCS) [20] in which the input x is linked to the action a in the process of matching the environmental instance. The difficulty of GCS is to evolve a condition form $t(x, a)$ so that the action is continuous. Tran et al. [14] implemented XCSF [19] having computed continuous actions, named as XCSFCA, where the action is computed directly as a linear combination of the input state and a vector of action weights. XCSFCA has outperformed GCS and produced very promising results for the frog problem, but could not achieve the 100% performance.

In this paper, a new approach will be investigated in which the discrete action in XCSR is replaced by a code fragment. A code fragment is a tree-expression, similar to a tree generated in genetic programming. The action value is determined using the input state values as terminals of the code fragmented action.

M. Thielscher and D. Zhang (Eds.): AI 2012, LNCS 7691, pp. 350–361, 2012.

Thus the action is continuous with respect to the input state in this version of XCSR, named XCSRCFA (*XCSR with Code Fragmented Action*). The proposed approach will be examined and compared with GCS and XCSFCA on the frog problem described in [20].

The rest of the paper is organised as follows. Section 2 describes genetic programming, learning classifier systems, accuracy based learning classifier systems (XCS), and real valued XCS (XCSR). In section 3 the novel implementation of XCSR using code fragmented actions is detailed. Section 4 describes the frog problem and experimental setup used in the experimentation. In section 5 experimental results are presented and compared with GCS and XCSFCA. In the last section this work is concluded and the future work is outlined.

2   Background

2.1   Genetic Programming

Commonly, genetic programming (GP) uses a rich alphabet to encode the solution, i.e. symbols that can express functions as well as numbers. A GP like alphabet to describe the problem is used in the LCS developed here, so the GP technique is described to aid understanding.

GP is an evolutionary approach to generating computer programs for solving a given problem automatically [10]. The task to be solved is represented by a primitive set of operations, known as the *function set*, and a set of operands, known as the *terminal set*.

The GP generated computer program is normally represented as a tree, which may contain unnecessary terms (bloat). The bloat problem in GP is usually addressed by limiting maximal allowed depth for an individual tree and/or using a fitness measure that punishes excess sized individuals [12], or using specific bloat control operators [2]. LCSs are a well structured rule-based learning technique that have various evolutionary pressures [4] to produce maximally general, optimal and accurate classifier rules, implicitly avoiding bloat.

A GP system produces a tree as a 'single' solution, rather than a co-operative set of rules as in an LCS. It generally requires supervised learning with the whole training set, rather than on-line, reinforcement learning as in LCS.

2.2   Learning Classifier Systems

Traditionally, an LCS represents a rule-based agent that incorporates evolutionary computing and machine learning to solve a given task, enacting in an unknown environment via a set of sensors for input and a set of effectors for actions. The rules are of the form "if *state* then *action*". After observing the current state of the environment, the agent performs an action, and the environment provides a reward, as depicted in Figure 1.

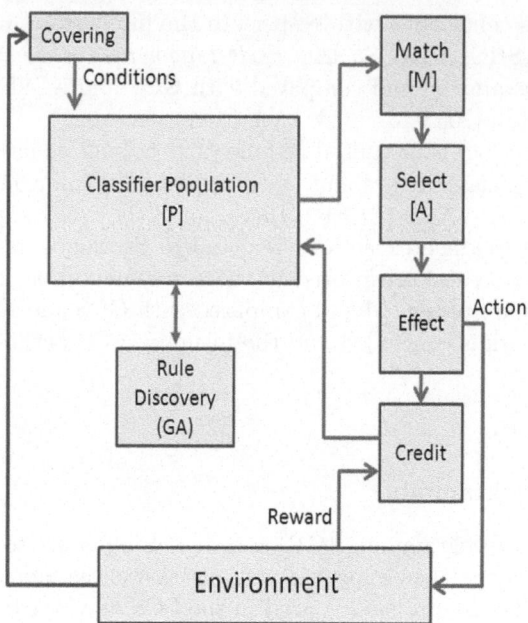

Fig. 1. Schematic depiction of a learning classifier system. In the proposed approach of computed continuous action, a classifier will become a member of M if its condition part matches the input as usual and its action belongs to the allowed action range. The action set $[A]$ is governed by the classifiers in $[M]$ that have the highest fitness-weighted average prediction value, see section 3.

Accuracy Based Learning Classifier System. XCS is a formulation of LCS that uses accuracy-based fitness to learn the problem by forming a complete mapping of states and actions to rewards.[1] In XCS, the learning agent evolves a population $[P]$ of classifiers, where each classifier consists of a rule and a set of associated parameters estimating the quality of the rule. Each rule is of the form 'if *condition* then *action*', having two parts: a condition and the corresponding action. Commonly, the condition is represented by a fixed length bitstring defined over the ternary alphabet $\{0, 1, \#\}$, and the action is represented by a numeric constant.

Each classifier has three main parameters: (1) prediction p, an estimate of the payoff that the classifier will receive if its action is selected, (2) prediction error ϵ, which estimates the error between the classifier's prediction and the received payoff, and (3) fitness F, computed as an inverse function of the prediction error. In addition, each classifier keeps an experience parameter exp, which is a count of the number of times it has been updated, and a numerosity parameter n, which is a count of the number of copies of each unique classifier.

---

[1] For a detailed review of different types and approaches in LCS refer to [15].

The agent has two modes of operation, explore (training) and exploit (application). In the following, XCS operation is concisely described. For a complete description, the interested reader is referred to the original XCS paper by Wilson [16], and to the algorithmic details by Butz et al. [5].

In the explore mode the agent attempts to obtain information about the environment and describe it by creating the decision rules:

1. observes the current state of the environment, $s \in S$ where S is the set of all possible environmental states. The current state s is usually represented by a fixed length bitstring defined over the binary alphabet $\{0, 1\}$.
2. selects classifiers from the classifier population $[P]$ that have conditions matching the state s, to form the match set $[M]$.
3. performs covering: for every action $a_i \in A$ in the set of all possible actions, if a_i is not represented in $[M]$ then a random classifier is generated with a given generalization probability such that it matches s and advocates a_i, and added to the population (termed covering)[2].
4. forms a system prediction array $P(a_i)$ for every $a_i \in A$ that represents the system's best estimate of the payoff should the action a_i be performed in the current state s. Commonly, $P(a_i)$ is a fitness weighted average of the payoff predictions of all classifiers advocating a_i.
5. selects an action a to explore (probabilistically or randomly) and selects all the classifiers in $[M]$ that advocated a to form the action set $[A]$.
6. performs the action a, records the reward r from the environment, and uses r to update the associated parameters of all classifiers in $[A]$.
7. when appropriate, implements rule discovery by applying an evolutionary mechanism, commonly a genetic algorithm (GA), in the action set $[A]$ to introduce new classifiers to the population.

Additionally, the explore mode may perform subsumption, to merge specific classifiers into any more general and accurate classifiers.

In contrast to the explore mode, in the exploit mode the agent does not attempt to discover new information and simply performs the action with the best predicted payoff. The exploit mode is also used to test learning performance of the agent in the application.

Various GP-based representations have been investigated to represent high level knowledge in LCS in an attempt to obtain compact classifier rules [6], to reach the optimal performance faster [11], to develop useful feature extractors [1], and to extract building blocks of knowledge [8,7]. In the work presented here, GP-based representation is used for the first time to compute continuous action in LCS.

Real Valued XCS (XCSR). The changes to XCS for real inputs were as follows [17,18]. The classifier condition was changed from a string from $\{0, 1, \#\}$

---

[2] If the classifier population size grows larger than the specified limit, then one of the classifier rules has to be deleted so that the new rule can be inserted.

to a concatenation of interval predicates, $int_i = (l_i, u_i)$, where l_i("*lower*") and u_i("*upper*") are real values. A classifier matches an input message x if each element x_i belongs to the corresponding interval predicate, i.e. $l_i \leq x_i \leq u_i$. When a new covered classifier is created, each interval predicate $int_i = (l_i, u_i)$ is generated as $l_i = x_i - rand(r_0)$ and $u_i = x_i + rand(r_0)$, where $rand(r_0)$ is a value uniform randomly from $[0, r_0]$ and r_0 is a real constant.

The GA works as in XCS. Crossover (with probability χ) permutes alleles of two parents between two crossover points. Since an allele is a real value, a new mutation operator is introduced. Mutation (with probability μ) modifies an allele by adding an amount $\pm rand(m_0)$ where m_0 is a real constant. A classifier *clfr1* can subsume another classifier *clfr2* if every interval predicate in *clfr1*'s condition is more general than the corresponding predicate in *clfr2*'s condition.

Covering and mutation operators can generate intervals out of the condition range. If it happens, l_i and u_i of an interval predicate int_i are brought back to the extremes of the condition range and they are possibly permuted in order to respect the predicate constraint $l_i \leq u_i$.

XCSR can handle real valued inputs using interval based conditions, but the possible actions still need to be determined in advance. Yet domains such as robot control require numerical actions, so that neither XCS nor XCSR with their discrete actions can yield high performance. In the work presented here, the discrete action in XCSR is replaced by a continuous action represented as a genetic programming-tree like code fragment. We have also implemented a discrete code fragmented action in XCS (while using the ternary alphabet based conditions in the classifier rules), to successfully evolve compact and optimal populations for multiplexer domain problems [6].

3   XCSR with Code Fragmented Action (XCSRCFA)

In the work presented here, the discrete action in XCSR is replaced by a continuous action represented as a code fragment while using the interval based conditions in the classifier rules. Each code fragment is a binary tree of depth up to two, which was set to limit the tree size. A binary tree of depth two can have maximum seven nodes. The function set for the tree is problem dependent such as $\{+, -, *, /...\}$ for linear regression problems, and $\{AND, OR, NAND, NOR...\}$ for binary classification problems as is the simple standard set in GP domain [10]. The terminal set is $\{ERC, D0, D1, D2, ..., Dn - 1\}$ where ERC is an ephemeral random constant and n is the length of condition in a classifier rule.

The action value of a classifier is determined by evaluating the action code tree. The action code tree is evaluated by replacing the terminal symbols with the corresponding environmental instances' values. Thus the action is continuous with respect to the input state in XCSRCFA. For example, consider the code fragmented action shown in Figure 2. The internal nodes of the tree are functions and leaves are the terminals. In this action tree, 1.0 is an ERC and $D0$ is the environmental input. If the input value is 0.4 then the action value will be 0.6 for this code fragmented action.

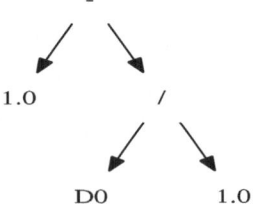

Fig. 2. A sample code fragmented action. Here 1.0 is an *ERC* and *D*0 is the environmental input. If the input value is 0.4 then the action value will be 0.6 for this code fragmented action.

A classifier will become a member of the match set [*M*] if its condition part matches the input as usual and its computed action belongs to the allowed action range. A pure random exploration is usually used for exploring actions of the environment, but in XCSRCFA it is replaced by a deterministic strategy, i.e. the action with the highest fitness-weighted average prediction value is selected. The classifiers advocating the best action will survive while GP-based crossover and mutation operations will allow the system to explore actions.

If the match set [*M*] is empty then a new covered classifier is generated with a random code fragmented action that outputs an allowed action value against the current environmental input state *s*.

When the GA is applied in the action set [*A*] to produce two offspring, action trees of the offspring are generated by crossing over the action trees of the parents. Then the action trees of the offspring are mutated with a given probability, to replace a subtree of the action with a randomly generated subtree of depth up to 1. The prediction of the offspring is set to the average of the parents' values whereas the prediction error and fitness of the offspring are set to the average of the parents' values reduced by constants *predictionErrorReduction* and *fitnessReduction* respectively, as in [3].

As the frog problem is one-dimensional, therefore the recombination of alleles of two parents does not generate new values of alleles. The system cannot explore values near the parents values, and thus appropriate conditions are not generated. To solve this problem, a mix crossover [14] is used.

It is to be noted that advantages of subsumption deletion are lost due to genotypic differences resulting in subsumption not occurring despite phenotypically similar behaviour. Subsumption deletion is made possible, albeit still problematic, by matching the action code on a character by character base.

4   The Problem Domain and Experimental Setup

4.1   The Frog Problem

In the frog problem, a system (frog) senses an object (fly) via a signal that monotonically decreases with the distance between them [20]. The frog should learn to catch the fly in one jump. Let d ($0.0 \leq d \leq 1.0$) be the frog's distance from the fly. For simplicity, it is assumed that the frog's sensory input x, falls linearly with distance d, as given in Equation 1:

$$x(d) = 1 - d \tag{1}$$

On receiving the signal input x, the frog jumps a certain distance a as an action. A jump can be over or under the fly. Then the frog receives a payoff related to the remaining distance, as given in Equation 2:

$$P(x, a) = \begin{cases} x + a & if \ x + a \leq 1 \\ 2 - (x + a) & otherwise \end{cases} \tag{2}$$

It is to be noted that the payoff function is continuous and nonlinear – albeit composed of two linear planes. To solve the frog problem, a system must learn to choose, given x, the value of a corresponding to maximum payoff.

4.2   Experimental Setup

The system uses the following, commonly used in the literature, parameter values as suggested by Butz et al. in [3,5]: fitness fall-off rate $\alpha = 0.1$; prediction error threshold $\epsilon_0 = 0.01$; fitness exponent $\nu = 5$; learning rate $\beta = 0.2$; threshold for GA application in the action set $\theta_{GA} = 25$; experience threshold for classifier deletion $\theta_{del} = 20$; fraction of mean fitness for deletion $\delta = 0.1$; classifier experience threshold for subsumption $\theta_{sub} = 20$; crossover probability $\chi = 0.8$; mutation probability $\mu = 0.04$; $r_0 = 0.1$; $m_0 = 0.1$; initial prediction $p_I = 0.01$; initial prediction error $\epsilon_I = 0.0$; initial fitness $F_I = 0.01$; reduction of the prediction error $predictionErrorReduction = 0.25$; reduction of the fitness $fitnessReduction = 0.1$; and the selection method is tournament selection with tournament size ratio 0.4. The action of a newly created classifier by GA invocation is mutated with probability 0.2. Both GA-subsumption and action set subsumption are activated. The range of ERC is [-2, 2] and the function set is {+, -, *, /}. The allowed action range is [0, 1]. The number of micro classifiers used is $N = 2000$. Explore and exploit problems are alternated with probability 0.5. All the experiments have been repeated 30 times with a known different seed in each run. One run is stopped after $100,000$ explore problems.

5   Results

5.1   Performance

The results of the frog problem using GCS, XCSFCA, and the proposed approach XCSRCFA are shown in Figure 3[3]. The system error measures the difference between the prediction of the expected payoff and the payoff received. The payoff and system error curves are plotted by using a 50-point running average from

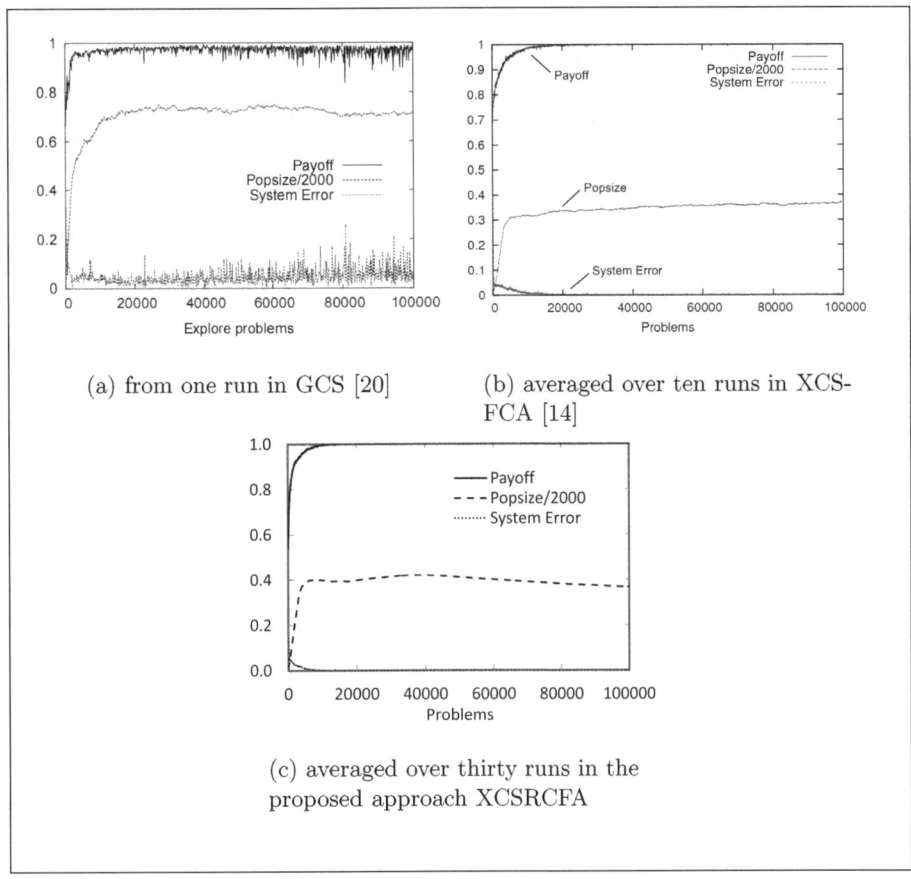

(a) from one run in GCS [20]

(b) averaged over ten runs in XCS-FCA [14]

(c) averaged over thirty runs in the proposed approach XCSRCFA

Fig. 3. Results of the frog problem in terms of payoff, system error, and population size using GCS, XCSFCA, and the proposed approach XCSRCFA (curve order same as in legend). (a) one run in GCS [20], (b) averaged over ten runs in XCSFCA [14], and (c)averaged over thirty runs in XCSRCFA.

exploit problems. In each problem of an experiment, the fly was placed at a random distance d $(0.0 \leq d \leq 1.0)$ from the frog.

The payoff curve in Figure 3(a) shows that the performance of GCS was volatile. Although the performance did rise quickly to receive payoff greater than 0.95, it did not reach optimal performance (payoff 1.0). The system error curve approximately complements the payoff curve, so the system error for GCS is approximately 0.05 throughout the learning process. The population size curve for GCS rises to about 70% of N and then declines very gradually. The payoff curve in Figure 3(b) shows that the performance of XCSFCA is greater than 99% after an averaged number of 30,000 problems, but could not acheive stabilized

---

[3] The results of GCS and XCSFCA were taken from [20] and [14] respectively, with permission from authors and copyright holders.

100% performance. The system error drops to smaller than 1%. The population size of classifiers is about 37% of N. The payoff curve in Figure 3(c) shows that the performance of the proposed approach XCSRCFA reached 100% after an averaged number of 18,000 problems and did not decline after that. The population size of classifiers is about 37% of N.

Preen et al. [13] conducted experimentation on the frog problem using fuzzy dynamical genetic programming in XCSF and reported greater than 99% performance after an averaged number of 4,000 problems, but could not acheive stabilized 100% performance. The reported population size of classifiers is around 0.08% of N.

5.2   Best Action

If the frog wants to catch the fly at d, it must jump a distance $a = d = 1-x$. Since d is generated randomly from $[0,1]$, the sensory input x received by Equation 1 gives the value from $[0,1]$. As a direct indication of the system's ability to choose the best action a^* and to gauge a^*'s continuity with respect to x, at the end of each run x was scanned from 0 to 1 with increment 0.001 and the resulting a^* plotted in Figure 4[4]. The plot for GCS, Figure 4(a), lies close to the diagonal but has discontinuities. The plot for XCSFCA, Figure 4(b), is nearly coincident with the diagonal '$1 - x$', but is *slightly broken* at some inputs x. The plot for the proposed approach XCSRCFA, Figure 4(c), is exactly the diagonal with *no broken points*.

5.3   Analysis of Evolved Rules

The proposed approach evolved maximally general and accurate classifiers by exploiting the generalization ability of LCS (to create a maximally general condition) and the rich GP-based representation (to create the corresponding accurate action in the classifier). The experienced (i.e. $exp \geq 1/\beta$) and accurate (i.e. $\epsilon \leq \epsilon_0$) classifier rules from the final population of a run are shown in Table 1. The code fragmented action is shown in postfix form, where $D0$ represents the sensory input x. Here F, n, p, ϵ, and exp denote fitness, numerosity, prediction, prediction error, and experience of a classifier respectively, and as denotes the average size of the action sets this classifier has belonged to.

The proposed XCSRCFA has successfully solved the frog problem evolving maximally general and accurate classifier rules like $9 - 16$ and $19 - 23$, shown in Table 1, that have the optimal payoff value of 1.0. Each of these maximally general classifier covers the whole input space ranging from 0.0 to 1.0 and has the accurate action that is equivalent to the diagonal '$1 - x$', therefore each of them is able to solve the frog problem individually.

Subsumption deletion was made possible by comparing the code fragmented action on a character by character base, but due to the multiple genotypes to a

---

[4] The results of GCS and XCSFCA were taken from [20] and [14] respectively, with permission from authors and copyright holders.

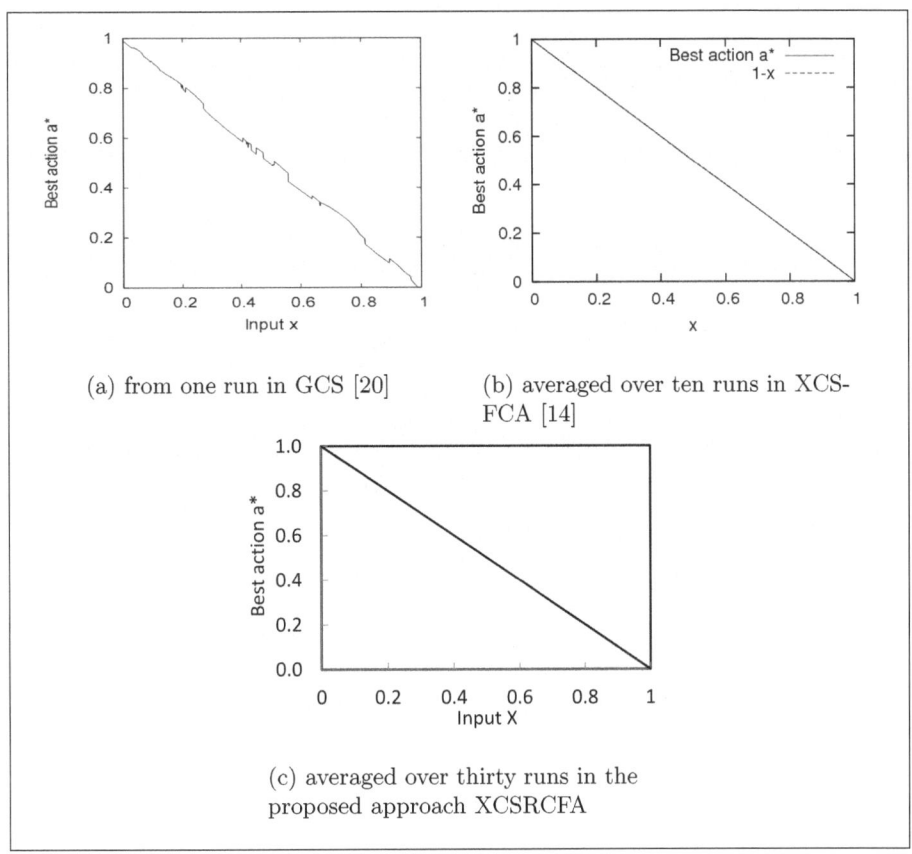

(a) from one run in GCS [20]

(b) averaged over ten runs in XCS-FCA [14]

(c) averaged over thirty runs in the proposed approach XCSRCFA

Fig. 4. Best action a^* of the frog problem is plotted by scanning the values of x from 0 to 1 increased by 0.001 using GCS, XCSFCA, and the proposed approach XCSRCFA. (a) The plot for GCS [20] has discontinuities. (b) The plot for XCSFCA [14] is nearly coincident with the diagonal '$1 - x$', but is *slightly broken* at some inputs x. (c) The plot for the proposed approach is coincident with the diagonal and have *no broken points*.

single phenotype issue code fragmented XCSR could not combine the phenotypically similar classifiers, like $9 - 16$ and $19 - 23$, into a single macro-classifier while evolving the population. So, the final population contains redundant classifier rules.

The average size of the action sets as classifiers $1 - 8$ and $17 - 18$ have belonged to is very small as compared with that of classifiers $9 - 16$ and $19 - 23$ due to the corresponding range of input space covered by them. As as is smaller for classifiers $1 - 8$ and $17 - 18$ so higher proportionate fitness F, but low numerosity n and experience exp highlight lack of worth.

Table 1. The experienced (i.e. $exp \geq 1/\beta$) and accurate (i.e. $\epsilon \leq \epsilon_0$) classifier rules, obtained in a typical run for the frog problem, using XCSR with code fragmented actions. The code fragmented action is shown in postfix form, where $D0$ represents the sensory input x. Here F, n, p, ϵ, and exp denote fitness, numerosity, prediction, prediction error, and experience of a classifier respectively, and as denotes the average size of the action sets this classifier has belonged to.

Sr. No.	Condition	Action	F	n	p	ϵ	exp	as
1	0.465356, 0.595225	D0 D0 *	0.907365	10	0.921854	0.006570	52	63.282196
2	0.000000, 0.064200	D0 2.0 /	0.893442	4	0.022754	0.005511	10	3.148032
3	0.133880, 0.279742	D0 D0 /	0.614114	10	0.834261	0.005719	72	41.985043
4	0.610654, 0.820274	D0 D0 *	0.612922	12	0.987231	0.009383	43	35.619358
5	0.673753, 0.881177	D0 2.0 / 0.0 -2.0 * +	0.498389	6	0.977880	0.008186	288	78.365341
6	0.891880, 0.943779	D0 D0 0.0 - -	0.497211	3	0.907607	0.003826	128	51.026615
7	0.891880, 0.943779	0.0	0.390534	3	0.907607	0.003826	128	51.026615
8	0.374393, 0.380699	D0 0.0 + 2.0 D0 * /	0.245285	1	0.877544	0.007733	5	22.799999
9	0.000000, 1.000000	D0 D0 / D0 -	0.153247	59	1.0	0.0	62585	384.999939
10	0.000000, 1.000000	0.0 -1.0 - D0 -	0.135065	52	1.0	0.0	58435	384.999939
11	0.000000, 1.000000	1.0 1.0 D0 * -	0.122078	47	1.0	0.0	50335	384.999939
12	0.000000, 1.000000	-2.0 -2.0 / D0 -	0.119481	46	1.0	0.0	67660	384.999939
13	0.000000, 1.000000	1.0 D0 0.0 + -	0.116883	45	1.0	0.0	49710	384.999939
14	0.000000, 1.000000	1.0 D0 -	0.111689	43	1.0	0.0	71558	384.999939
15	0.000000, 1.000000	-2.0 -2.0 / 1.0 D0 * -	0.100853	39	1.0	0.0	62710	384.999939
16	0.000000, 1.000000	-2.0 -2.0 / D0 0.0 + -	0.096548	37	1.0	0.0	53760	384.999939
17	0.680369, 0.895523	0.0 -2.0 * D0 / +	0.052886	1	0.884182	0.006870	20	43.390942
18	0.641876, 0.825135	D0 2.0 / 0.0 D0 / +	0.037919	1	0.985085	0.006275	5	64.599998
19	0.000000, 1.000000	2.0 1.0 - D0 1.0 / -	0.033766	13	1.0	0.0	28460	384.999939
20	0.000000, 1.000000	-2.0 -2.0 / D0 1.0 / -	0.002597	1	1.0	0.0	736	384.999939
21	0.000000, 1.000000	1.0 0.0 - D0 0.0 + -	0.002597	1	1.0	0.0	5161	384.999939
22	0.000000, 1.000000	1.0 0.0 - D0 -	0.002597	1	1.0	0.0	12761	384.999939
23	0.000000, 1.000000	-2.0 -2.0 / 0.0 D0 + -	0.002597	1	1.0	0.0	34235	384.999939

6   Conclusions

This paper presented an extension to XCSR in which the discrete action has been replaced by a code fragmented action that is continuous with respect to the input state. The proposed XCSRCFA has successfully solved the frog problem, consistently producing the optimum rules with the maximum predicted payoff.

The investigation of code fragments shows that the multiple genotypes to a single phenotype issue in XCSRCFA disables the subsumption deletion function. Due to this loss of subsumption deletion, the final population contains optimal, but redundant classifier rules.

The next stage is to introduce a mechanism for treating two phenotypically similar code fragments as a single code fragment during the learning process, by simplifying the code fragment trees using algebraic and numerical simplification methods [9], in an attempt to reduce the number of classifiers in the final population. The XCSRCFA will be tested for more continuous state space problems from the reinforcement learning domain.

Acknowledgments. We would like to thank the authors and copyright holders of [20] and [14] for granting permission to re-use the figures.

References

1. Ahluwalia, M., Bull, L.: A Genetic Programming Based Classifier System. In: Proceedings of the Genetic and Evolutionary Computation Conference, pp. 11–18 (1999)
2. Alfaro-Cid, E., Merelo, J.J., de Vega, F.F., Esparcia-Alcázar, A.I., Sharman, K.: Bloat Control Operators and Diversity in Genetic Programming: A Comparative Study. Evolutionary Computation 18(2), 305–332 (2010)
3. Butz, M.V.: XCSJava 1.0: An Implementation of the XCS Classifier System in Java. Technical Report 2000027, Illinois Genetic Algorithms Laboratory (2000)
4. Butz, M.V.: Rule-based Evolutionary Online Learning Systems: A Principal Approach to LCS Analysis and Design. Springer (2006)
5. Butz, M.V., Wilson, S.W.: An Algorithmic Description of XCS. Soft Computing - A Fusion of Foundations, Methodologies and Applications 6(3-4), 144–153 (2002)
6. Iqbal, M., Browne, W.N., Zhang, M.: Evolving Optimum Populations with XCS Classifier Systems. Soft Computing (2012), http://dx.doi.org/10.1007/s00500-012-0922-5, doi:10.1007/s00500-012-0922-5
7. Iqbal, M., Browne, W.N., Zhang, M.: Extracting and Using Building Blocks of Knowledge in Learning Classifier Systems. In: Proceedings of the Genetic and Evolutionary Computation Conference, pp. 863–870 (2012)
8. Iqbal, M., Zhang, M., Browne, W.N.: Automatically Defined Functions for Learning Classifier Systems. In: Proceedings of the Genetic and Evolutionary Computation Conference (Companion), pp. 375–382 (2011)
9. Kinzett, D., Johnston, M., Zhang, M.: Numerical Simplification for Bloat Control and Analysis of Building Blocks in Genetic Programming. Evolutionary Intelligence 2(4), 151–168 (2009)
10. Koza, J.R.: Genetic Programming: On the Programming of Computers by Means of Natural Selection. The MIT Press (1992)
11. Lanzi, P.L.: XCS with Stack-Based Genetic Programming. In: Proceedings of the Congress on Evolutionary Computation, pp. 1186–1191 (2003)
12. Luke, S., Panait, L.: A Comparison of Bloat Control Methods for Genetic Programming. Evolutionary Computation 14(3), 309–344 (2006)
13. Preen, R.J., Bull, L.: Fuzzy Dynamical Genetic Programming in XCSF. In: Proceedings of the Genetic and Evolutionary Computation Conference (Companion), pp. 167–168 (2011)
14. Tran, T.H., Sanza, C., Duthen, Y., Nguyen, D.T.: XCSF with Computed Continuous Action. In: Proceedings of the Genetic and Evolutionary Computation Conference, pp. 1861–1869 (2007)
15. Urbanowicz, R.J., Moore, J.H.: Learning Classifier Systems: A Complete Introduction, Review, and Roadmap. Journal of Artificial Evolution and Applications 2009(1), 1–25 (2009)
16. Wilson, S.W.: Classifier Fitness Based on Accuracy. Evolutionary Computation 3(2), 149–175 (1995)
17. Wilson, S.W.: Get Real! XCS with Continuous-Valued Inputs. In: Lanzi, P.L., Stolzmann, W., Wilson, S.W. (eds.) IWLCS 1999. LNCS (LNAI), vol. 1813, pp. 209–219. Springer, Heidelberg (2000)
18. Wilson, S.W.: Mining Oblique Data with XCS. In: Lanzi, P.L., Stolzmann, W., Wilson, S.W. (eds.) IWLCS 2000. LNCS (LNAI), vol. 1996, pp. 158–174. Springer, Heidelberg (2001)
19. Wilson, S.W.: Classifiers that Approximate Functions. Natural Computing 1, 211–233 (2002)
20. Wilson, S.W.: Three Architectures for Continuous Action. In: Kovacs, T., Llorà, X., Takadama, K., Lanzi, P.L., Stolzmann, W., Wilson, S.W. (eds.) IWLCS 2003. LNCS (LNAI), vol. 4399, pp. 239–257. Springer, Heidelberg (2007)

A Memetic Algorithm for Efficient Solution of 2D and 3D Shape Matching Problems

Mohammad Sharif Khan and Tapabrata Ray

School of Engineering and Information Technology,
University of New South Wales, Northcott Drive, Canberra, Australia
Mohammad.Khan2@student.adfa.edu.au, T.Ray@adfa.edu.au

Abstract. Shape representation and the associated morphing (repair) operators play a vital role in any shape optimization exercise. This paper presents a novel and an efficient methodology for morphing via smart repair of control points, wherein a repaired sequence of control points are generated. The repaired set of control points are then used to define the curve or the surface using a B-spline representation, while the control points themselves are optimized using a memetic algorithm. While the authors have already proposed the approach for 2D shape matching, this paper extends the approach to deal with 3D shape matching problems. Two 2D and one 3D examples have been presented to illustrate the performance of the proposed approach.

Keywords: shape representation, design optimization, shape matching.

1 Introduction

Shape representation and optimization is a key element in any product design process. Shape representation schemes are required for the generation of shapes which in turn facilitates the design of functional articles. For example, aerofoils, converging-diverging nozzles, ship-hulls, medical prosthesis, structural elements, and many other functional articles require shape generation and shape modification to achieve the desired performance. The performance parameters may vary from an application to another depending on the intended use of the object. In a shape optimization exercise, the shapes are generally modified using an optimization algorithm. Efficiency of the optimization process and flexibility of shape representation scheme are the two major issues requiring serious attention. A lack of flexibility in shape representation will limit the evolution of various shapes whilst an inefficient optimization algorithm will require evaluation of numerous shapes prior to its convergence, both of which are not desirable. Several methods for shape representation have been proposed over the years such as implicit polynomials [9, 16], cubic splines [26, 28], Bezier curves [26, 31] and B-splines [5, 25]. A B-spline representation has been used in the present study wherein the control points of the curve or surface are identified through an optimization algorithm. In a B-spline representation, a small number of control points are able to represent a wide variety of complex geometries and a change in the position of the control points are known to affect the shape locally. The B-spline basis also allows the order of the basis function and hence the degree of the resulting curve to be changed without changing the number

M. Thielscher and D. Zhang (Eds.): AI 2012, LNCS 7691, pp. 362–372, 2012.

of defining polygon vertices [26]. Its strong convex-hull property, variation diminishing and affine invariance properties are also attractive in the realm of shape optimization.

Evolutionary design optimization has been an active area of research in the last two decades [1–3, 8, 12, 13, 15]. Several applications span across a range of domains such as aerodynamic design [27], hydrodynamic design [3], structural design [13, 19, 21], and electromagnetic component design [2, 17, 32]. Shape matching is often a pre-cursor to a shape optimization exercise, where the efficiencies of the underlying shape representation scheme and the performance of the optimization algorithm is investigated in depth. An efficient optimization algorithm coupled with a flexible and effective shape representation scheme is the key to a successful approach that requires limited number of design evaluations to arrive at the optimum shape [14].

A number of approaches have also been reported in literature that attempts to solve 2D and 3D shape matching problems [4, 18, 20, 29, 30, 34–37]. A genetic algorithm with multi-parent recombination using latin square crossover operator was adopted in [35], whereas an individual mutative evolution strategy (iES) with covariance matrix adaptation evolution strategy (CMA) was used over a B-spline representation in [36]. An effective genetic algorithm with an enhanced geometry representation scheme was also presented by Wang in [34] and an adaptive constraint concept was used to direct search in regions of interest. A mixed integer quadratic approach was suggested using 3D shape constraints to guide shape matching [30] whereas, an unconstrained quadratic optimization problem formulation was proposed instead of handling a large set of complicated SOCP constraints by Zhu in [37] for 3D deformable surface tracking. Three different morphing methods were introduced and employed within a standard evolution strategy in [20]. A method for the automatic construction of control volumes was proposed in [18] based on the concept of evolvability as a potential capacity of representations. In [4], an incremental abstraction of control points was embodied into evolution strategies with a modified 1/5 rule. It is important to highlight that the computational cost involved in the above studies are still significant and often restricted bounds were used to limit the search space.

In summary, population based optimization algorithms have had limited success for 2D shape matching problems and their performance for 3D shape matching problems were far from satisfactory. Such approaches in principle allowed the connectivity and location of control points to evolve within the course of optimization. Such an attempt is likely to yield a number of impractical shapes with crossings which in turn results in a significant computational cost. In this paper, we alleviate the problem via repair, wherein the set of control points are repaired and sorted. While the sequence of control points are generated via repair, their locations are evolved using the memetic algorithm.

Rest of the paper is organized as follows. Aspects of shape matching metrics and the proposed method are discussed in Section 2 and 3 respectively. The results are reported in Section 4. Finally Section 5 concludes the paper.

2   Shape Matching Metrics

Shape matching usually refers to transforming a shape, and measuring its resemblance with a target shape using some similarity measures. In the present study, we assume that the length, width and height of the box enclosing the target shape is known along with its location of centroid. Two commonly used shape matching metrics include Euclidean distance and Hausdorff distance. For two finite point sets $A = \{a_1, a_2, \cdots, a_m\}$ and $B = \{b_1, b_2, \cdots, b_m\}$ (where, m indicates the total number of points in a particular point set), the distance is defined as $L_j(A, B) = (\sum_{i=0}^{m} |a_i - b_i|^j)^{\frac{1}{j}}$. For $j = 2$, this yields the Euclidean distance L_2 [24]. Hausdorff distance is a classical non correspondence-based shape matching metric [10, 11, 33]. The Hausdorff distance between A and B is defined as

$$H(A, B) = max\,\{h(A, B), h(B, A)\} \tag{1}$$

where,

$$h(A, B) = \underset{a \in A}{max}\, \underset{b \in B}{min} \, \|a - b\| \tag{2}$$

and $\|.\|$ is the underlying norm on the points of A and B, usually Euclidean distance. $h(A, B)$ in effect ranks each point of A based on its distance to the nearest point of B and then uses the largest ranked of such point as the distance (the most mismatched point of A) [10]. The Hausdorff distance $H(A, B)$ is the maximum of $h(A, B)$ and $h(B, A)$.

3   Proposed Method

In the proposed method, the number of control points required to represent the shape, the dimensions of the box enclosing the shape and the centroid of the shape are assumed to be known. The variables of the optimization problem are the x, y and z coordinates of the control points, the range of which are the same as the dimensions of the enclosing box. Every solution generated through the process of initialization or recombination is repaired, wherein the sequence of the control points are changed to obtain a non-intersecting control polygon net while maintaining the specific values of its coordinates. The concept is illustrated using Fig. 1a, 1b and 1c, where the original randomly generated control polygon net and the convex-hull are presented alongside its repaired form. The repaired solution (ordered set of vertices in the control polygon net) is used to create the shape using B-splines and compared with the target shape based on the metrics described above. For the 3D shape optimization problem, the shape is assumed to be disintegrated to several 2D shape optimization problems (cross-sections of 3D shape) termed as stations, wherein the set of control points representing the 2D shape in each station are repaired.

3.1   Initialization and Repair Strategy

The number of control points (N) used to describe a shape is a user defined parameter. Since the limits of x, y and z coordinates i.e. the space enclosing the target shape is known, a random solution is created and repaired during the phase of initialization of 2D shape. Firstly, a convex-hull is generated using a set of control points (Fig. 1b). Thereafter, the points (lying inside the convex-hull) nearest to their adjacent edges are inserted to generate the non-intersecting control polygon net (Fig. 1c). In order to avoid

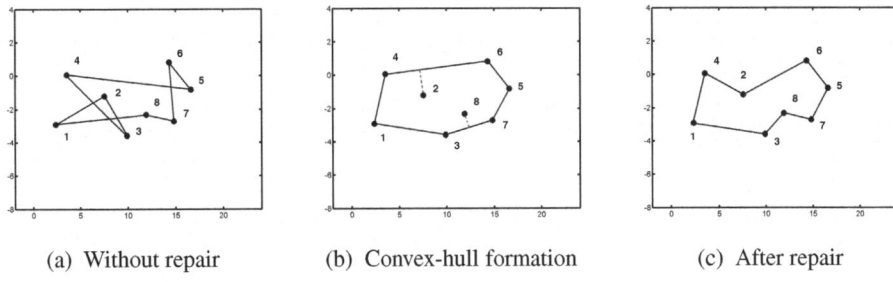

(a) Without repair   (b) Convex-hull formation   (c) After repair

Fig. 1. Effect of repair scheme on the position of initial control points

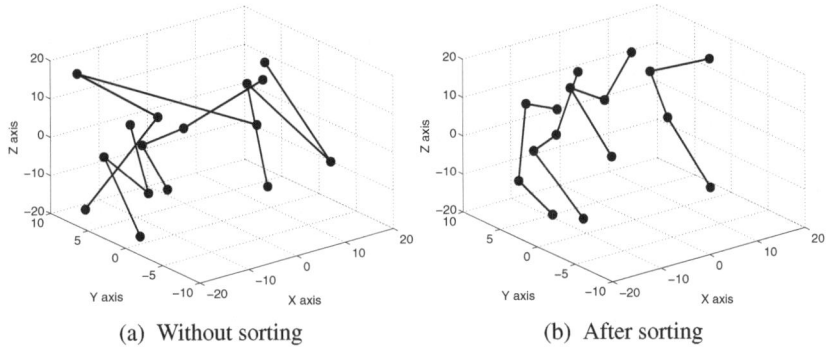

(a) Without sorting   (b) After sorting

Fig. 2. Effect of sorting on the position of control points

entangling or crossings of control points between two neighbouring stations, every set of x coordinates of control points spanning the shape in x direction is sorted in ascending order during the optimization process. The effect of sorting on the position of control points is illustrated in Figure 2a and Figure 2b.

3.2 Matching Error

Since the centroid of the target shape is known, the shape generated using the repaired solution (reordered set of control points) is shifted such that its centroid matches the centroid of the target shape. The maximum of Euclidean and Hausdorff distance is computed using the generated shape and the target shape.

3.3 Optimization Algorithm

Evolution: The pseudo-code of the proposed optimization is presented in Algorithm 1. In the proposed algorithm, two different evolution strategies are used for generating the offspring population. These are:

1. *EA-like evolution* – This includes simulated binary (SBX) crossover and polynomial mutation [7].

Algorithm 1. Proposed Algorithm

Require: Population size (S), Number of generations (S_g), Crossover and mutation parameters, Target shape (s_T)

1: Initialize (pop_1) {Assumed number of control points}
2: Repair (pop_1) {Create the sequence of control points}
3: CS_{pop_1} = Centroid_Shift (pop_1, s_T) {Shift all pop_1 solutions such that the centroids of those solutions match the centroid of the target shape}
4: $Matching\_Error_{pop_1}$ = Max (E_dist, H_dist) {For all pop_1 evaluate the maximum of Euclidean and Hausdorff distances as matching error between target and generated shape}
5: **for** $i = 2$ to S_g **do**
6:     **if** rand (0,1) ≤ 0.5 **then**
7:         $childpop_i$ = Evolve_EA (pop_{i-1})
8:     **else**
9:         $childpop_i$ = Evolve_DE (pop_{i-1})
10:     **end if**
11:     $childpop_i$ = Repair ($childpop_i$)
12:     $CS_{childpop_i}$ = Centroid_Shift ($childpop_i, s_T$)
13:     Evaluate ($childpop_i$)
14:     R = Rank ($pop_{i-1} + childpop_i$)
15:     pop_i = Reduce (R) {Selecting best S solutions for the next generation}
16:     $\mathbf{x_{best}} \leftarrow$ Local_ search ($\mathbf{x}$) {$\mathbf{x_{best}}$ is the best solution found using local search from $\mathbf{x}$}
17:     Replace worst solution in pop_i with $\mathbf{x_{best}}$
18:     pop_i = Rank (pop_i) {Rank the solutions again in pop_i}
19: **end for**

---

2. *DE-like evolution* – This includes the DE exponential crossover and mutation, as described in [6, 23].

Ranking and Reduction: Since the test problems studied in the paper are formulated as single-objective, unconstrained minimization problems, the ranking is done by sorting the objective values in ascending order. The best N solutions from the (parent+child) population form the population for the next generation.

Local Search: At each generation, in addition to generation of new solutions using recombination and mutation, a local search is used for further improvement. Sequential quadratic programming (SQP) [22] is used for the local search in the present study. After performing the local search, the worst solution in the population is replaced by the best solution found from the local search.

4   Results

Two 2D shape and one 3D shape examples have been used to test the performance of the proposed approach. The parameters used for the algorithm are the same for each shape matching exercise and listed in Table 1.

4.1   2D Shape Example

From the two 2D examples, the target shapes i,e the damselfly-wing data contains 516 points whereas the stingray data contains 740 points. A population size of 40 and a maximum of 5,000 function evaluations are set for both the examples. For both the problems, we have assumed that the shapes can be represented using 16 control points which render to a 32 variable optimization problem. The results after 5,000 function evaluations for both examples are shown in Table 2.

4.2   3D Shape Example

A flower vase shape (or a converging-diverging nozzle) is considered for the 3D case. The target flower vase data consists of 676 points. A population size 400 and a maximum of 100,000 function evaluations are set for this problem. The flower vase shape has been assumed to be represented using 10X8 control polygon net (a total 80 control points) which translates to a 240 (3X80) variable optimization problem. The results after 100,000 function evaluations for the flower vase shape example are reported in Table 2.

For all the problems the best and worst values are reported as the minimum and maximum errors across 20 runs, respectively. The median value reported is the average of 10th and 11th values in the sorted list of matching errors obtained across 20 runs. The small values of standard deviations of all the shape examples reflect the consistency in terms of convergence of the algorithm. Various states of evolution of generated shape towards the target or original shape are shown in Fig. 4, 5 and 6. The average computational time for repairing a solution is around 0.0014 seconds (averaged over 1000 solutions) whereas the average computational cost of computing shape matching error is 0.0053 seconds (averaged over 1000 instances) for a problem involving 16 control points. In case of 3D flower vase problem, the average computational cost of

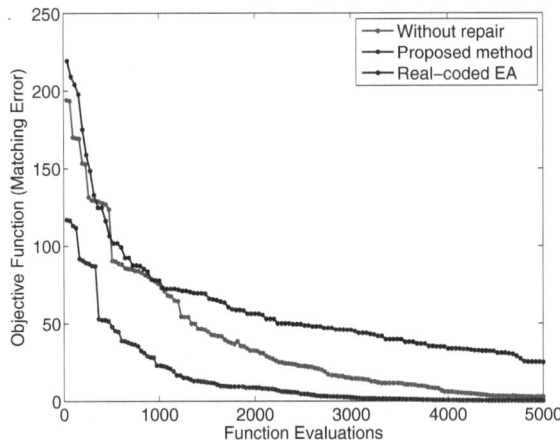

Fig. 3. Progress plot of the best shape of stingray for single objective matching error minimization

Table 1. Parameters used for the proposed algorithm

Parameter	Value
Population size	40/400
Max. function evaluations	5000/100000
Crossover probability (for both SBX/exponential)	1.0
Crossover index	10
Mutation probability	0.05
Mutation index (polynomial)	20
Scale factor F (for DE mutation)	0.9

Table 2. Results with repair and centroid shift using hybrid evolutionary algorithm

Shapes	Error	Best	Worst	Mean	Median	Std.
Damselfly-wing	Max(Eucli,HD)	1.4e-05	3.2e-04	8.3e-05	6.1e-05	8.1e-05
Stingray	Max(Eucli,HD)	0.067	1.863	0.706	0.589	0.518
Flower vase	Max(Eucli,HD)	0.848	1.553	1.244	1.264	0.166

Table 3. Results without repair and centroid shift using hybrid evolutionary algorithm

Shapes	Error	Best	Worst	Mean	Median	Std.
Damselfly-wing	Max(Eucli,HD)	4.6e-03	7.6e-03	5.1e-03	4.8e-03	7.1e-04
Stingray	Max(Eucli,HD)	2.578	11.668	4.947	4.590	2.176
Flower vase	Max(Eucli,HD)	2.367	3.817	3.091	3.081	0.333

Table 4. Results without repair and centroid shift using real-coded evolutionary algorithm

Shapes	Error	Best	Worst	Mean	Median	Std.
Damselfly-wing	Max(Eucli,HD)	3.026	6.958	5.132	5.202	1.210
Stingray	Max(Eucli,HD)	24.665	50.710	40.771	42.092	6.677
Flower vase	Max(Eucli,HD)	44.694	51.002	48.324	48.043	1.627

computing its error is 0.0820 seconds and the average computational cost of repairing a solution is 0.0066 seconds. All the computations are performed on a computer with the following configuration.

- Processor - Intel Core2Duo E8400 @ 3.00GHz, 2.99GHz.
- RAM - 4GB.
- Operating System - Microsoft Windows XP .

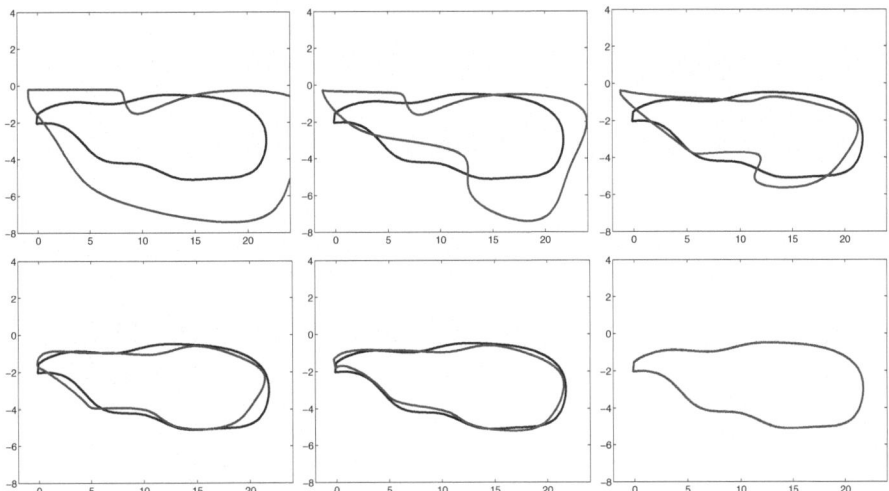

Fig. 4. Evolutions of generated damselfly-wing (red) towards the target damselfly-wing (blue) for matching

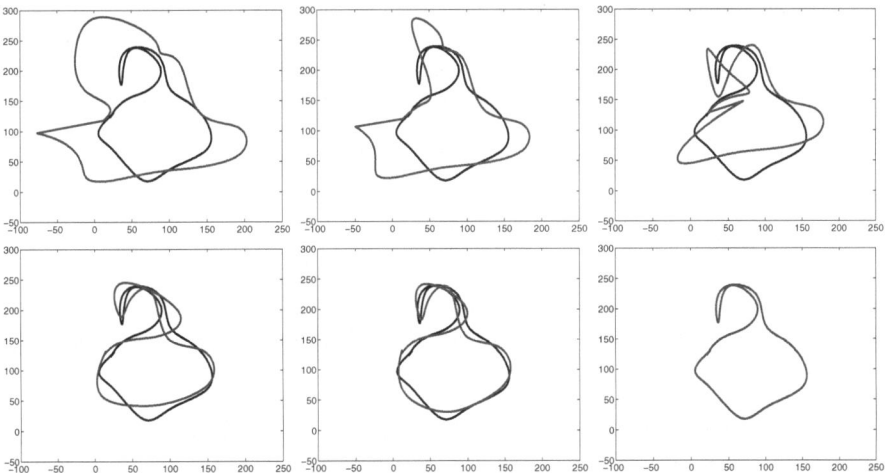

Fig. 5. Evolutions of generated stingray (red) towards the target stingray (blue) for matching

In an attempt to observe the performance of the repair scheme and the centroid shift mechanism, the same exercise was conducted with the same parameter setting without the reordering of the control points (without repair) and centroid shift. The performance statistics are presented in Table 3. It is clear from Table 2 and Table 3, that a significant improvement in performance has been achieved through the use of repair and centroid shift strategy. For the sake of comparison, results of using a real-coded evolutionary

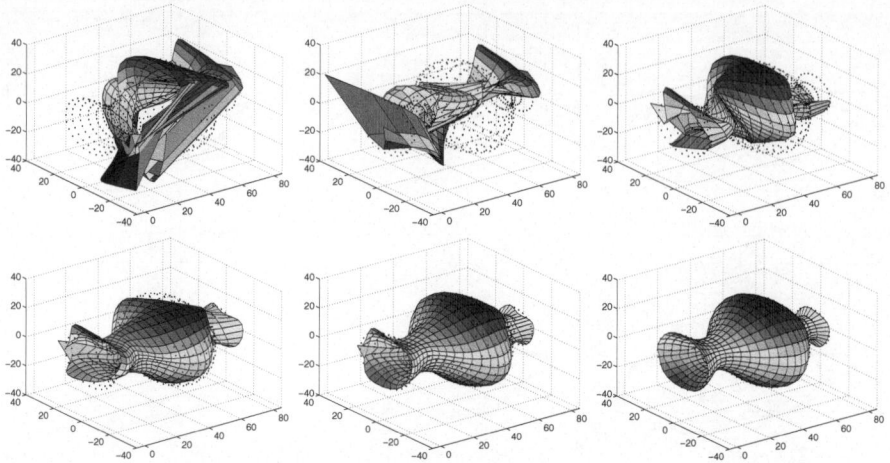

Fig. 6. Evolutions of generated flower vase (evolving surface) towards the target flower vase (point cloud) for matching

algorithm without repair and centroid shift are also presented in Table 4. The parameter setting for the runs are the same as listed in Table 1. Progress plot of the best shape of stingray shape example is presented in Figure 3, where the results for the three different cases are compared. It is interesting to observe that the best results of the proposed algorithm for the two shape examples are more than 100 times better than the results of the real-coded evolutionary algorithm.

5   Conclusion

In the present paper, an efficient method is introduced that is capable of solving 2D and 3D shape matching problems. The control points of the underlying B-spline representation are optimized using a memetic algorithm, while the presence of repair or morphing operation ensures generation of valid shapes. The memetic algorithm is embedded with multiple recombination strategies (EA and DE) and a local search to improve its efficiency. Two commonly used measures (Euclidean and Hausdorff distance) have been considered as the measure of similarity between the generated and the target shape. The proposed method has been tested using two 2D examples of varying complexity, each of which was solved to desired accuracy within 5,000 evaluations, while for the complex 3D example, 100,000 evaluations were required. The performance of the repair strategy has been studied for both 2D and 3D examples to highlight the benefits. Such a capability is the first step towards a cutting edge shape optimization approach, where one is interested to uncover novel shapes with extreme performance characteristics.

Acknowledgement. The second author would like to acknowledge the support of Future Fellowship offered by the Australian Research Council.

References

1. Arabnia, M., Ghaly, W.: A strategy for multi-point shape optimization of turbine stages in three-dimensional flow. In: Proceedings of the 12th AIAA/ISSMO Multidisciplinary Analysis and Optimization Conference, June 8-12. ASME, Orlando (2009)
2. Barba, P.D.: Evolutionary multiobjective optimization methods for the shape design of industrial electromagnetic devices. IEEE Transactions on Magnetics 45(3), 1436–1441 (2009)
3. Calcagni, D., Salvatore, F., Bernardini, G., Miozzi, M.: Automated marine propeller design combining hydrodynamics models and neural networks. In: Proceedings of the First International Symposium on Fishing Vessel Energy Efficiency, May 18-20, INSEAN, E-Fishing, Vigo, Spain (2010)
4. Chang, W., Chung, C., Sendhoff, B.: Target shape design optimization with evolutionary computation. In: Proceedings of the IEEE Congress on Evolutionary Computation, December 8-12, vol. 3, pp. 1864–1870 (2003)
5. Cox, M.: The numerical evaluation of B-splines. IMA Journal of Applied Mathematics 4(10), 134–149 (1971)
6. Das, S., Suganthan, P.: Differential evolution: A survey of the state-of-the-art. IEEE Transactions on Evolutionary Computation 15(1), 1–28 (2010)
7. Deb, K., Agarwal, S.: Simulated binary crossover for continuous search space. Complex Systems 9, 115–148 (1995)
8. Garcia, M., Boulanger, P., Giraldo, S.: CFD based wing shape optimization through gradient-based method. In: Proceedings of the International Conference on Engineering Optimization. EngOpt, Rio de Janeiro, Brazil, June 1-5 (2008)
9. Helzer, A., Barzohar, M., Malah, D.: Stable fitting of 2D curves and 3D surfaces by implicit polynomials. IEEE Transactions on Pattern Analysis and Machine Intelligence 26(10), 1283–1294 (2004)
10. Huttenlocher, D., Kedem, K.: Efficiently computing the hausdorff distance for point sets under translation. In: Proceedings of the Sixth Annual Symposium on Computational Geometry, New York, USA (1990)
11. Huttenlocher, D., Klanderman, G., Rucklidge, W.: Comparing images using the hausdorff distance. IEEE Transactions on Pattern Analysis and Machine Intelligence 15(9), 850–863 (1993)
12. Jinya, Z., Hongwu, Z., Yan, L., Chun, Y.: Shape optimization of helico-axial multiphase pump impeller based on genetic algorithm. In: Proceedings of the Fifth International Conference on Natural Computation, August 14-16, pp. 408–412. IEEE, Tianjin (2009)
13. Jolgaf, M., Sulaiman, S., Ariffin, M.A., Faieza, A.: Billet shape optimization for minimum forging load. European Journal of Scientific Research 24(3), 420–427 (2008)
14. Khan, M.S., Ayob, A.F.M., Isaacs, A., Ray, T.: A smart repair embedded memetic algorithm for 2D shape matching problems. Engineering Optimization (2011)
15. Kim, Y.S., Park, H.: Topology optimization of rotor in synchronous reluctance motor using level set method and shape design sensitivity. IEEE Transactions on Applied Superconductivity 20(3), 1093–1096 (2010)
16. Landa, Z., Malah, D., Barzohar, M.: 2D object description and recognition based on contour matching by implicit polynomials. In: Proceedings of the 18th European Signal Processing Conference, EURASIP, Aalborg, Denmark, August 23-27 (2010)
17. Makinen, R.A.E., Periaux, J., Toivanen, J.: Multidisciplinary shape optimization in aerodynamics and electromagnetics using genetic algorithm. International Journal for Numerical Methods in Fluids 30(2), 149–159 (1999)
18. Menzel, S.: Evolvable free-form deformation control volumes for evolutionary design optimization. In: Proceedings of the IEEE Congress on Evolutionary Computation, pp. 1388–1395 (2011)

19. Nadir, W., Kim, Y., de Weck, O.L.: Structural shape optimization considering both performance and manufacturing cost. In: Proceedings of the Multidisciplinary Analysis and Optimization Conference, August 27. AIAA (2004)

20. Nashvili, M., Olhofer, M., Sendhoff, B.: Morphing methods in evolutionary design optimization. In: Proceedings of the Conference on Genetic and Evolutionary Computation, Washington DC, USA, June 25-29, pp. 897–904 (2005)

21. Ozakea, M., Taysi, N.: Analysis and shape optimization of variable thickness box girder bridges in curved platform. Electronic Journal of Structural Engineering 3 (2003)

22. Powell, M.: A fast algorithm for nonlinearly constrained optimization calculations, vol. 630. Springer (1978)

23. Price, K., Storn, R., Lampinen, J.: Differential evolution- A practical approach to global optimization. Springer, Berlin (2005)

24. Remco, C.: Shape matching: Similarity measures and algorithms. In: Proceedings of the International Conference on Shape Modeling and Applications, May 7-11, pp. 188–197. IEEE, Genova (2001)

25. Riesenfeld, R.: Application of B-spline approximation to geometric problems of computer aided design. Ph.D. thesis, Syracuse University (1972)

26. Rogers, D., Adams, J.: Mathematical elements for computer graphics. McGraw-Hill, New York (1990)

27. Samareh, J.A.: Aerodynamic shape optimization based on free-form deformation. In: Proceedings of the 10th AIAA/ISSMO Multidisciplinary Analysis and Optimization Conference (2004)

28. Sarfraz, M., Habib, Z.: Conic representation of a rational cubic spline. In: Proceedings of the IEEE International Conference on Information Visualization, July 14-16. IEEE, London (1999)

29. Sederberg, T.W., Parry, S.R.: Free-form deformation of solid geometric models. Computer Graphics 20(4), 151–160 (1986)

30. Shaji, A., Varol, A., Torresani, L., Fua, P.: Simultaneous point matching and 3D deformable surface reconstruction. In: Proceedings of the IEEE Conference on Computer Vision and Pattern Recognition, pp. 1221–1228 (2010)

31. Sohel, F., Karmakar, G., Dooley, L., Bennamoun, M.: Bezier curve-based generic shape encoder. Image Processing 4(2), 92–102 (2010)

32. Toivanen, J.I., Makinen, R.A.E., Jarvenpaa, S., Oijala, P., Rahola, J.: Electromagnetic sensitivity analysis and shape optimization using method of moments and automatic differentiation. IEEE Transactions on Antennas and Propagation 57(1), 168–175 (2009)

33. Vivek, E., Sudha, N.: Robust hausdorff distance measure for face recognition. Pattern Recognition 40(2), 431–442 (2007)

34. Wang, N., Tai, K.: Target matching problems and an adaptive constraint strategy for multiobjective design optimization using genetic algorithms. Computers and Structures 88(19-20), 1064–1076 (2010)

35. Wu, A., Tsang, P., Yuen, T., Yeung, L.: Affine invariant object shape matching using genetic algorithm with multi-parent orthogonal recombination and migrant principle. Applied Soft Computing 9(1), 282–289 (2009)

36. Zhang, P., Yao, X., Jia, L., Sendhoff, B.: Target shape design optimization by evolving splines. In: Proceedings of the IEEE Congress on Evolutionary Computation, September 25-28. IEEE, Singapore (2007)

37. Zhu, J., Hoi, S.C.H., Xu, Z., Lyu, M.R.: An Effective Approach to 3D Deformable Surface Tracking. In: Forsyth, D., Torr, P., Zisserman, A. (eds.) ECCV 2008, Part III. LNCS, vol. 5304, pp. 766–779. Springer, Heidelberg (2008)

Local Search in Parallel Linear Genetic Programming for Multiclass Classification

Aaron Scoble[1], Mark Johnston[2], and Mengjie Zhang[1]

[1] School of Engineering and Computer Science
[2] School of Mathematics, Statistics and Operations Research
Victoria University of Wellington, P.O. Box 600, Wellington, New Zealand
{aaron.scoble,mengjie.zhang}@ecs.vuw.ac.nz, mark.johnston@msor.vuw.ac.nz

Abstract. Parallel Linear Genetic Programming (PLGP) is an architecture that addresses instruction dependencies in Linear Genetic Programming (LGP). The Co-operative Coevolution (CC) methodology has previously been applied to PLGP but implementations have not been able to improve performance over vanilla PLGP. In this paper we present Hill Climbing Parallel Linear Genetic Programming (HC-PLGP) which uses a local search to discover effective combinations (blueprints) of partial solutions that are evolved in subpopulations. By introducing a new caching technique we can efficiently search over the subpopulations, and our improved fitness function combined with normalisation and blueprint elitism address some of the weaknesses of the previous approaches. HC-PLGP is compared to three PLGP architectures over six datasets, and significantly outperforms them on two datasets, is comparable on three, and is slightly worse on one dataset.

1 Introduction

Classification tasks involve classifying a set of instances as one of a number of potential classes. Each instance is typically represented by a set of features, and a machine learning classifier will use the features as input and attempt to learn some relationship between them that allows it to correctly classify each instance. The *classifier* is first fed training data in which each item is already labeled with the correct class, and creates models that can then be used to classify similar, previously unseen, data.

Genetic Programming (GP) seeks to evolve useful programs in a *population* which evolves over a number of *generations* by applying evolutionary operations analogous to those found in nature [12][13]. Individual programs have their *fitness* measured to determine their suitability as donors for the next generation. *Mutation* and *crossover* operations are performed, and *elitism* preserves the best solutions. The original and most widely used form of GP is Tree Based GP (TGP) [12] where operations are performed on subtrees of operations.

Linear Genetic Programming (LGP) uses a linear sequence of instructions using a set of registers that are re-used during execution of the program and give multiple outputs upon completion [1]. Similar to assembly language, each

M. Thielscher and D. Zhang (Eds.): AI 2012, LNCS 7691, pp. 373–384, 2012.

instruction may use up to two registers as input, and a single register as output. The strength of LGP is that values that have been computed by one instruction can be used by another instruction later in the program execution. This makes LGP a powerful problem solving technique that has been shown to outperform TGP in multiclass classification [15][6]. However, every time a result is reused an *instruction dependency* is introduced, which means that a relatively minor modification to one instruction may then cascade throughout the program by altering the value in a register that is used by multiple subsequent instructions. As large and random changes are known to disrupt the performance of GP, the strength of LGP is also a potential shortcoming. To reduce the effect of instruction dependencies, Downey and Zhang [4] proposed the Parallel Linear Genetic Programming (PLGP) architecture, in which a program is separated into independent sub-programs, or *factors*. Each factor is executed with its own set of registers, and the register values from all factors are summed to give an overall *result vector*.

LGP can easily be applied to classification problems by providing an output register for each of the class labels. When execution is complete, the register with the highest value is selected as the result of classification. For example, the highest value in a result vector of $[-1, 4, 0]$ for a three class problem is that of the second register, so the instance is classified as class two.

Co-operative Coevolution (CC) considers several subpopulations, each of which evolves in parallel and optimises one aspect of the final solution [17][16][18]. This technique is applied in Downey and Zhang's Co-operative Coevolution Parallel Linear Genetic Programming (CC-PLGP) and Blueprint Search Parallel Linear Genetic Programming (BS-PLGP) which introduce a two level solution into the PLGP architecture. The CC architecture is implemented by first evolving *individual* factors in subpopulations, and then searching for the best *combinations* of those factors [3].

CC-PLGP has not so far proven to be as effective as PLGP or the state-of-the-art BS-PLGP. The goal of this paper is to refine CC-PLGP to further exploit caching techniques, as well as introducing a new approach to blueprint evolution using local search. We discuss some of the obstacles to effective evolution when using a CC design, and propose solutions to them.

The rest of the paper is organised as follows. Section 2 provides some background, and Section 3 describes our approach to addressing some of the shortcomings of current solutions. Section 4 describes our experimental setup, and Section 5 provides results and analysis. Conclusions are presented in Section 6.

2   Background

2.1   Classification

Supervised learning methods, such as GP, require a labelled data set, in which each *instance* consists of a set of features that describe the real-world object as well as a class label which denotes the desired output from the classifier for that instance [12]. The data set is divided into three subsets: training, validation, and testing.

A GP program iterates through each instance in the training set, using features as input, and produces an output which represents the classification that has been made. The *fitness* of that program is typically calculated from the number of correct classifications. Programs are checked periodically (every few generations) by executing them on the validation set so that the problem of *overfitting* is addressed, i.e., where programs fail to generalise by memorising the training set rather than learning how to identify them. Finally, after a predefined number of generations, the best program that has been evolved is executed on the test set, which is an entirely unseen set of instances, and the true effectiveness of the best program is evaluated.

2.2   Linear Genetic Programming

The use of registers is the key motivation behind LGP, as it allows the reuse of computational results by instruction sequences later in the program [1]. This makes it possible to express complicated solutions, but a genetic operation may be propagated throughout the program by making even a small modification. If an instruction is modified and that changes the value in a register that is subsequently reused many times, the result may be much larger and less controlled than was intended. The value in the register r that holds the output from an instruction i may be modified if instruction i is altered by genetic operations, and any subsequent instruction that uses register r as input is said to have an *instruction dependency* on instruction i.

line	instruction	depends on
1	$r[1] = 3.1 + f1;$	–
2	$r[3] = f2/r[1];$	1
3	$r[2] = r[1] * r[1];$	1
4	$r[1] = f1 - f1;$	–
5	$r[1] = r[1] - 1.5;$	4
6	$r[2] = r[2] + r[1];$	3,5

Fig. 1. An example of instruction dependency, adapted from [3]

An example of instruction dependencies is given in Figure 1. The registers are denoted as $r[i]$, and the features are denoted as fi. Here, e.g., instructions 2 and 3 will both read from $r[1]$, so they have a dependency on instruction 1.

2.3   Parallel Linear Genetic Programming

Downey and Zhang [4] developed PLGP to limit instruction dependencies between instructions by controlling the interaction between them. Here, n instruction sequences, called *factors*, are evaluated independently to give n register vectors which are then summed to give a single result vector. Each program factor has its own set of registers which are initialised to zero before execution and are not passed to the following factor. This prevents instruction dependencies between factors, and limits the potential number of instruction dependencies to the number of instructions in each factor. Each generation, evolutionary operations are applied to a single program factor, and mutation is restricted to operate on instructions *within a single factor*. By regarding each program as an *ordered list* of factors, crossover is limited to *equivalent factors*, i.e., those that occupy the same list position in both programs. Crossover is performed by exchanging contiguous blocks of instructions between equivalent factors. This creates Enforced Sub-Populations (ESP) [8] where genetic material may flow within subpopulations but not between them.

A PLGP program *topology* specifies the number of factors in a program and the number of instructions in each of those factors. A large number of small factors will allow few dependencies and produce simple solutions, while a small number of large factors may produce a large number of dependencies, although allow for greater complexity.

The structure of PLGP makes it possible to exploit caching of registers, and *difference caching* [5][3] significantly reduces execution time. The evolutionary process is faster when three or more factors are used, and efficiency improves as the number of factors increases. In PLGP, program result vectors are retained from one generation to the next, and when a factor is selected for modification, the difference in output for that factor before and after modification is simply added to the overall evaluation.

2.4   Co-operative Coevolution

A CC framework consists of n subpopulations where each individual is a *partial solution*. A *complete solution* will consist of n partial solutions, with one candidate from each subpopulation. Each subpopulation performs evolutionary operations in isolation and components are encouraged to specialise and evolve within a *niche* consisting of similar individuals.

Symbiotic Adaptive Neuroevolution (SANE) applies this approach to evolving neural networks [14] and describes complete solutions as *blueprints*, which contain pointers to neurons (partial solutions) and act as a mechanism for discovering and remembering high quality *combinations* of neurons. In CC-PLGP, the principles of SANE are applied to the PLGP architecture [3][14]. The notion of equivalent factors is extended to the creation of subpopulations, and a PLGP program is replaced by a list of pointers, or blueprint. After the factor subpopulations perform their evolutionary operations, the blueprints undergo a further evolutionary process to create new combinations of factors.

In the first phase of a generation, factors are executed against all instances and their register values are cached. A blueprint is evaluated by summing the register values for each factor that contributes to that blueprint, relative to each instance. The index of the register with the highest value for each instance is compared to the class label for that instance, and the number of incorrect classifications is assigned as that blueprint's fitness value. The fitness measure of a factor is calculated as the average fitness of all the blueprints that factor contributes to. If a factor does not contribute to any blueprint, it is assigned a *No Fitness Information (NFI)* fitness value which is the average fitness of all blueprints. Blueprint evolution in CC-PLGP is performed by applying a set of evolutionary operations to the blueprints. Mutation changes a pointer into a new random pointer, and crossover exchanges randomly selected pointers between two blueprints.

Using outdated factor information when selecting combinations for blueprints is a flawed approach to fitness evaluation [3]. In CC-PLGPs factor evolution phase, factors may be modified by evolutionary operations regardless of whether they contributed to blueprints. Any assumptions made in finding effective blueprints based on improving existing blueprints are therefore undermined. A blueprint that had high fitness in generation g could conceivably have every factor modified in generation $g + 1$, making the search for solutions through gradual modification more difficult. The ability of a blueprint to make changes to several pointers in the same generation may also have presented problems, as blueprints quickly attained a reasonable fitness in early generations, but seemed unable to be refined in sufficiently accurate steps during later generations.

BS-PLGP is another approach to CC, but with a different approach to blueprint evolution. Particle Swarm Optimisation (PSO) [11] is used to select combinations of factors [3].

The improved accuracy attained by BS-PLGP suggests that the CC concept has its merits in PLGP, but the evolutionary operations CC-PLGP applies to blueprints are ineffective. Although BS-PLGP and CC-PLGP have not provided significant improvement over PLGP with regard to classification accuracy, it is suggested that a more thorough investigation of the interaction and cooperation between subpopulations could enable further improvements.

3 Hill Climbing Parallel Linear Genetic Programming

We propose Hill Climbing Parallel Linear Genetic Programming (HC-PLGP) as a CC framework where factors are evolved in subpopulations and hill climbing search is used for blueprint evolution. We extend the use of register caches to enable a complete search through the factor combinations, allowing us to develop a fitness function that is not dependent on the NFI values. The hill climbing blueprint search searches for a better candidate from each subpopulation in turn while the rest of the blueprint remains unchanged, to find the best candidate factor to cooperate with the existing factor combination, if one can be found in the current generation. The goal is to develop a method that is comparable to PLGP in accuracy and efficiency, while strengthening the CC architecture.

Overview of HC-PLGP

A *Register Vector* rv_i is a set of registers that are used to store the output for a factor after it has been executed on an instance i. A register vector will contain c

registers, where c is the number of classes in the classification problem. A *Register Collection* rc_j is a set of k register vectors, one for each of the k instances in the dataset. Each factor j will have a register collection that stores the register vector after execution on each instance, i.e., rc_j will contain $rv_0, rv_1, \ldots, rv_k$ which are the results for executing factor j on instances $0, 1, \ldots, k$.

In the same manner as the previous CC designs, n subpopulations are evolved in isolation from each other. In addition to this, a blueprint population undergoes a separate process in which combinations of factors are selected and evaluated.

At the beginning of each generation, factors are evolved within their subpopulations using standard evolutionary operations. Any factors that contribute to blueprints will be retained in the child population, and the remaining child factors are generated. Once factor evolution is complete, the factors are executed on all training examples. The Training Register Cache (TRC) is filled with a set of register collections, one for each factor. Factor combinations are then searched using the TRC, giving a value for classification fitness for every combination of factors, which are stored in the Fitness Cache (FC). Once the classifications have been made, the hill climbing blueprint search will determine whether the replacement of any single factor can improve that blueprint's fitness by searching through the FC. The algorithm is divided into four main stages as follows.

Execution. Here, factor output is calculated, similar to the execution stage in CC-PLGP, i.e., every instance is presented in turn and executed by all factors. Register vectors for each instance are stored as the register collection of each factor.

Classification. For each training instance i, we consider every blueprint b in turn. We sum the register vectors rv_i for each factor that contributes to this blueprint b, giving the *reference vector* for b. Classification accuracy can be observed here by comparing the index of the highest register value against the class label for i. Iterate through each subpopulation s to cache the classification accuracy for each factor in the subpopulation, with the other factors in b remaining unchanged. To achieve this, subtract the output vector rv_i of the factor that currently represents subpopulation s in blueprint b to obtain a *base vector*, or a result vector for b that does not include a factor from s. Then iterate through s and test the other factors in turn by adding their register vector rv_i to the *base vector*, and comparing the index of the highest register value against the class label for instance i. An incorrect classification will result in the FC for that combination being incremented, and after all instances have been presented the FC will represent the classification accuracy for that combination over all instances. Of note here is that only the factors being searched are assigned classification accuracies in the FC, not the 'locked' factors that the search aims to compliment when searching for replacement factors. Also of importance is that the order of execution specifies that all factor combinations are checked against each instance before moving on to the next.

Hill Climbing Blueprint Search. The hill climbing blueprint search is performed by searching through the FC to find the best single modification for each blueprint, if an improvement is possible. The FC is used for these calculations, and by adding the errors for all the factors that contribute to b, we can search each subpopulation for a viable replacement for any of them. We record the best factor for each subpopulation with the other pointers locked, and after all subpopulations have been investigated the best overall improvement is selected. If that will give an improvement over the original combination, a single factor is exchanged.

To help prevent the search from becoming trapped in local optima, *Blueprint mutation* provides a stochastic element to HC-PLGP. With a probability p one of the following types of mutation are applied. *Micro mutation* chooses a subpopulation at random and then searches it in the normal way, and *macro mutation* selects a random subpopulation and then a random factor from that subpopulation.

Conditional Validation. The final step is to execute the newly selected blueprints on the validation dataset. By performing this step after blueprint combinations have been finalised, we avoid executing redundant factors, or those that will not contribute to any blueprints. If 5 blueprints are used with a subpopulation size of 100 (10×10 topology), at least 95 factors per subpopulation will not need to be validated.

Factor	r1	r2	r3	r4
1	0.3	0.5	−1.2	3.4
2	−0.8	−2.4	1.1	2.2
3	1.2	40	−5.2	−0.3
4	4.6	0.8	−1.2	0.1
Total	5.3	[38.9]	−6.5	5.4

(a) non-normalised registers

Factor	r1	r2	r3	r4
1	0.23	0.33	−0.54	0.77
2	−0.44	−0.70	0.52	0.68
3	0.54	0.97	−0.83	−0.23
4	0.82	0.44	−0.54	0.09
Total	1.15	1.04	−1.39	[1.31]

(b) $h(x)$ normalised registers

Fig. 2. Normalisation of registers

Register Normalisation. Figure 3 represents a blueprint that consists of four factors, each with four registers. In Figure 3(a) the registers have not been normalised, and in (b) they have been normalised with the function $h(x) = \frac{x}{1+|x|}$. It can clearly be seen that in (a) factor 3 has greatly influenced the classification from the blueprint with a single large value for register $r2$. In (b), we can see that normalisation has mitigated this effect by reducing the range of register values to $[-1, 1]$. This normalisation may encourage factor specialisation by preventing a single large register value from dominating factors that may otherwise have combined to form an effective classifier.

Improved Fitness Function. A new fitness function is derived from the values retained in the FC and does not distinguish between factors that contribute to a blueprint and those that do not. As each factor is checked once for every blueprint during the classification phase, the FC will hold a number of classification values for that factor. The average of those classification values is assigned as the fitness for that factor, providing a function with a much better ability to discern between factors than one that assigns an NFI fitness value.

Factor Elitism. A critical shortcoming of CC-PLGP was the problem of factor evolution undermining blueprint composition by modifying the components that had been selected during the blueprint evolution phase. To address this, any factors that are selected to contribute to a blueprint are added to a set of *elite* factors that are preserved during the evolutionary process, where they are eligible as parents but will not be replaced.

4   Experimental Setup

A series of experiments were performed and results were averaged over 30 replications. Execution time and classification accuracy of HC-PLGP were compared with PLGP, CC-PLGP, and BS-PLGP using six datasets. Eight program topologies were used, although space limitations have necessitated that comparisons from only one topology are presented here. PLGP, CC-PLGP, and BS-PLGP were run with 500 blueprints, and HC-PLGP was run with 5. Preliminary experimentation was performed with the number of HC-PLGP blueprints ranging from 1 to 40, and although reducing the number of blueprints to less that 5 had a negative effect on accuracy, increasing to more than 5 did not improve accuracy sufficiently to justify the extended execution time.

Datasets. Six data sets are used that provide classification problems of varying complexity. Artificial Characters, Hand Written Digits, and Yeast were used in order to compare directly with [4][3], and the others were chosen so that their characteristics would give a good range of observations. The large number of classes was the selection criterion for Letters, and USPS was introduced due to the large number of features. The datasets are summarised in Table 1, and were divided equally into training, validation, and test sets.

The following datasets are from the UCI machine learning repository [7]. *Hand written digits* consists of 3750 hand written digits with added noise. There are 10 classes of 64 attributes. *Artificial characters* consists of vector representations of the English letters {A,C,D,E,F,G,H,L,P,R}. There are 5000 instances, 10 classes, and 56 features. The *Yeast* dataset represents protein localisation sites and has 1484 instances, 10 classes and 8 attributes. *USPS* contains alphanumeric characters and codes extracted from handwritten addresses, gathered as part of a research project sponsored by the United States Postal Service [10]. It has 4863 instances, 10 classes, and 256 features. *Cardiotocography* contains 2126 instances where diagnostic features processed from foetal cardiograms. There are 10 classes, and 22 features. It was obtained from [2]. *Letters* consists of all 26 English capital letters using different fonts on black and white rectangular displays. There are 2126 instances, 26 classes, and 16 features, also obtained from [2].

GP Parameters. The GP parameters are constant across all experiments. We use terminal constants in the range $[-1, 1]$, and a function set that consists of addition, subtraction, multiplication, protected division, and $if < 0$. Protected division returns a value of one if the denominator is zero. $if < 0$ takes three arguments and returns the second if the first is negative, otherwise it returns the third. Population size is 1000 and evolution is performed over 400 generations.

Table 1. Datasets

Dataset	type	instances	features	classes
(a) Artificial Characters	real	5000	56	10
(b) Cardiotocography	real	2126	22	10
(c) Letters	real	2226	16	26
(d) Hand Written Digits	real	3750	64	10
(e) USPS	real	4863	256	10
(f) Yeast	real,binary	1484	8	10

The parameters for factor evolution are as follows: mutation 30% crossover 60%, elitism 10%. Tournament size is 5. Of note here is the elitism parameter, which in the case of HC-PLGP, is equal to the number the blueprints, and is therefore set at a constant 5 for all experiments. For CC-PLGP, blueprint evolution is performed with equal weighting to the operators mutation, crossover, and new random blueprint. HC-PLGP blueprint mutation probability p was set to 0.30.

Table 2. Program topologies

	2x5	4x5	5x7	5x10	10x10	10x20	20x20	30x20
Instructions	10	20	35	50	100	200	400	600
Factors	2	4	5	5	10	10	20	30
Instructions per factor	5	5	7	10	10	20	20	20

PLGP Program Topologies. Program topologies are selected to give a reasonable diversity of factor sizes and number of factors. Table 2 shows the eight program topologies that were used to evaluate the methods. Due to space constraints, we have only included results for the 10x10 program topology. This particular topology was overall the most effective for all methods and has therefore been selected as the best representative topology.

5   Results and Analysis

Table 3 shows the classification accuracy of the four methods for each problem. The results are averaged over 30 replications and are as follows: *Fac* and *Ins* are the number of factors in a program and the number of instructions in a factor, respectively; *Time* is the total execution time, in seconds, for 400 generations; *BstGen* is the generation at which the best validation accuracy was achieved, and at which point the best program was selected to perform the test; *Train* and *Test* represent the classification accuracies for the different procedures; and standard deviations of training and test accuracy are given in *TrainSD* and *TestSD*.

In general, PLGP and BS-PLGP have similar test accuracy over all the problems, and CC-PLGP does not perform as well. Although the execution time of HC-PLGP is longer than that of CC-PLGP, it is much faster than BS-PLGP and comparable to that of PLGP, being faster on (c),(e), and (f) but slower in (a),(b), and (d). The Test SD for HC-PLGP is the lowest of all the architectures in (a),(b),(d),and (e). Performance in (f) is much worse for HC-PLGP, and although the SD is high for both training and testing, it has been consistently

Table 3. Experiment Results for 10x10 topology

(a) Artificial Characters

Method	Fac	Ins	Time	BstGen	Train	Test	TrainSD	TestSD
BS-PLGP	10	10	6148.22	322.43	95.30	94.60	2.71	2.64
CC-PLGP	10	10	983.17	333.67	85.44	84.54	5.81	5.93
PLGP	10	10	1348.15	311.10	95.46	94.56	2.89	2.90
HC-PLGP	10	10	1556.97	260.430	96.74	97.16	4.20	1.76

(b) Cardiotocography

Method	Fac	Ins	Time	BstGen	Train	Test	TrainSD	TestSD
BS-PLGP	10	10	2137.54	265.30	58.54	40.12	4.49	9.07
CC-PLGP	10	10	491.40	253.13	53.39	38.82	5.27	9.61
PLGP	10	10	713.16	276.07	62.94	46.05	4.99	6.96
HC-PLGP	10	10	781.67	276.74	60.11	37.46	8.27	4.80

(c) Letters

Method	Fac	Ins	Time	BstGen	Train	Test	TrainSD	TestSD
BS-PLGP	10	10	3800.41	359.53	36.59	30.72	2.67	2.35
CC-PLGP	10	10	1440.35	326.63	31.19	26.27	2.25	2.13
PLGP	10	10	1578.88	353.00	40.44	31.72	2.77	3.10
HC-PLGP	10	10	1312.09	347.20	41.30	34.66	3.57	2.93

(d) Hand Written Digits

Method	Fac	Ins	Time	BstGen	Train	Test	TrainSD	TestSD
BS-PLGP	10	10	3928.20	372.60	82.40	80.07	3.56	3.87
CC-PLGP	10	10	783.03	359.37	71.04	69.33	2.89	2.98
PLGP	10	10	1155.97	374.70	85.68	81.61	2.55	3.00
HC-PLGP	10	10	1499.29	355.55	84.22	82.17	1.87	1.79

(e) USPS

Method	Fac	Ins	Time	BstGen	Train	Test	TrainSD	TestSD
BS-PLGP	10	10	3777.47	374.43	80.09	78.49	3.78	3.93
CC-PLGP	10	10	982.70	356.93	69.01	68.03	6.47	6.40
PLGP	10	10	2131.17	346.93	82.59	79.20	3.81	3.77
HC-PLGP	10	10	1958.34	357.40	84.52	78.10	2.10	2.15

(f) Yeast

Method	Fac	Ins	Time	BstGen	Train	Test	TrainSD	TestSD
BS-PLGP	10	10	1277.93	300.20	56.03	56.07	2.38	2.87
CC-PLGP	10	10	371.01	268.27	50.45	50.82	4.71	4.74
PLGP	10	10	591.68	242.40	58.77	55.61	2.96	3.54
HC-PLGP	10	10	521.65	287.10	52.64	48.57	5.46	4.14

outperformed across all experiment replications. Of note with this dataset is that it has the least number of both instances and classes. There is very pronounced overfitting apparent on (b) for all architectures, and the SD for HC-PLGP here is much higher for training than the other methods, yet lower for testing.

Test accuracy of HC-PLGP was compared to that of all other methods. Significance testing was performed using two-sided t-tests and summarised in Table 4.

Table 4. Significance of results : HC-PLGP vs PLGP, CC-PLGP, and BS-PLGP

	PGLP	CC-PLGP	BS-PLGP
(a) Artificial Characters	0.00002 △	0.00000 △	0.00004 △
(b) Cardiotocography	0.00000 ●	0.49458	0.13854
(c) Letters	0.00318 △	0.00000 △	0.00002 △
(d) Hand Written Digits	0.37313	0.00000 △	0.02032 △
(e) USPS	0.16684	0.00000 △	0.68146
(f) Yeast	0.00000 ●	0.07793	0.00000 ●

The columns represent the p-values of the comparison between HC-PLGP and each method in turn, where the p-values are corrected using Holm's method with an overall significance level of 0.05 for each row [9]. Here, △ denotes that the performance of HC-PLGP is significantly better, while ● indicates that it is significantly worse. The results show that HC-PLGP significantly outperforms all methods on (a) and (c), and outperforms CC-PLGP and BS-PLGP on (d). However, it is outperformed by PLGP on (b), and by both BS-PLGP and PLGP on (f).

6   Conclusions

Hill Climbing Parallel Linear Genetic Programming (HC-PLGP) has been implemented as a complete search through the subpopulations where all factors are examined, and the best improvement is selected. Blueprint mutation provides a stochastic element to help prevent the search from becoming trapped in local optima. Five blueprints was found to be effective, providing a good balance between execution time and classification accuracy. This number was small enough to retain factor diversity in the subpopulations once elitism had prevented selected factors from being modified by evolution. Output registers were normalised and a new fitness function was used that exploited existing classification information from the Fitness Cache (FC). Classification accuracy of HC-PLGP compares well against the existing Parallel Linear Genetic Programming (PLGP) architectures, significantly outperforming them all on a number of datasets, with a comparable execution time.

Future work. In general, all implementations of the PLGP architecture performed best with the 10x10 topology. It is not clear whether the difference in performance has been affected directly by the structure of the complete program, or the effect on diversity by a changing subpopulation size. A set of experiments where the subpopulation size remains constant and the number of factors and instructions changes will be performed to investigate this further.

There are three datasets, Cardiotocography, Letters, and Yeast, where none of the PLGP methods were very effective and some overfitting was apparent. As these are the datasets with the least number of instances, cross-validation will be used to re-evaluate performance of these methods. The vast difference in training and test accuracy in the Cardiotocography dataset for all architectures is certainly a subject for closer investigation. Simple metaheuristics, e.g., Iterated

Local Search, may be used to prevent becoming stuck in local optimum, so HC-PLGP is potentially very promising as an architecture.

References

1. Brameier, M., Banzhaf, W.: A comparison of linear genetic programming and neural networks in medical data mining. IEEE Transactions on Evolutionary Computation 5(1), 17–26 (2001)
2. Chang, C.C., Lin, C.J.: LIBSVM: A library for support vector machines. ACM Transactions on Intelligent Systems and Technology 2, 27:1–27:27 (2011), software available at http://www.csie.ntu.edu.tw/~cjlin/libsvm
3. Downey, C.: Explorations in Parallel Linear Genetic Programming. Master's thesis, Victoria University of Wellington, New Zealand (2011)
4. Downey, C., Zhang, M.: Parallel Linear Genetic Programming. In: Silva, S., Foster, J.A., Nicolau, M., Machado, P., Giacobini, M. (eds.) EuroGP 2011. LNCS, vol. 6621, pp. 178–189. Springer, Heidelberg (2011)
5. Downey, C., Zhang, M., Liu, J.: Parallel linear genetic programming for multi-class classification. Genetic Programming and Evolvable Machines 13(3), 275–304 (2012)
6. Fogelberg, C., Zhang, M.: Linear Genetic Programming for Multi-class Object Classification. In: Zhang, S., Jarvis, R.A. (eds.) AI 2005. LNCS (LNAI), vol. 3809, pp. 369–379. Springer, Heidelberg (2005)
7. Frank, A., Asuncion, A.: UCI machine learning repository (2010), http://archive.ics.uci.edu/ml
8. Gomez, F., Miikkulainen, R.: 2-d pole balancing with recurrent evolutionary networks. In: Proceedings of the International Conference on Artificial Neural Networks, pp. 425–430 (1998)
9. Holm, S.: A simple sequentially rejective multiple test procedure. Scandinavian Journal of Statistics, 65–70 (1979)
10. Hull, J.J.: A database for handwritten text recognition research. IEEE Transactions on Pattern Analysis and Machine Intelligence 16, 550–554 (1994)
11. Kennedy, J., Eberhart, R.: Particle swarm optimization. In: Proceedings of the IEEE International Conference on Neural Networks, vol. 4, pp. 1942–1948 (1995)
12. Koza, J.R.: Genetic Programming: On the Programming of Computers by Means of Natural Selection. MIT Press, Cambridge (1992)
13. Koza, J.R., Streeter, M.J., Keane, M.A.: Routine high-return human-competitive automated problem-solving by means of genetic programming. Information Sciences 178(23), 4434–4452 (2008)
14. Moriarty, D.E., Miikkulainen, R.: Forming neural networks through efficient and adaptive coevolution. Evolutionary Computation 5, 373–399 (1997)
15. Olague, G., Romero, E., Trujillo, L., Bhanu, B.: Multiclass Object Recognition Based on Texture Linear Genetic Programming. In: Giacobini, M. (ed.) EvoWorkshops 2007. LNCS, vol. 4448, pp. 291–300. Springer, Heidelberg (2007)
16. Potter, M., Jong, K.: Cooperative coevolution: An architecture for evolving coadapted subcomponents. Evolutionary Computation 8(1), 1–29 (2000)
17. Potter, M., De Jong, K.: A Cooperative Coevolutionary Approach to Function Optimization. In: Davidor, Y., Schwefel, H.P., Milnner, R. (eds.) PPSN 1994. LNCS, vol. 866, pp. 249–257. Springer, Heidelberg (1994)
18. Yang, Z., Tang, K., Yao, X.: Large scale evolutionary optimization using cooperative coevolution. Information Sciences 178(15), 2985–2999 (2008)

Opponent's Style Modeling Based on Situations for Bayesian Poker

Ruobing Li[1], Wenkai Li[1], Lin Shang[1], Yang Gao[1], and Mengjie Zhang[2]

[1] State Key Laboratory for Novel Software Technology,
Nanjing University, China
{l.ruobing,easerene}@gmail.com, {shanglin,gaoy}@nju.edu.cn
[2] School of Engineering and Computer Science,
Victoria University of Wellington, New Zealand
Mengjie.Zhang@ecs.vuw.ac.nz

Abstract. In a real poker game, one player can take actions of different styles in different situations. In this paper, a novel method is proposed to quantify and model the opponent's style in corresponding situation of a hand. Based on the proposed representation of Action Pair, the value of the style can be calculated and stored as "experience". When making a decision, the specific style will be obtained from the "experience". The style and the observable information will be used to estimate the value of the opponent's hand. In experiments, the obtained "experience" validates the correctness of our assumption that a player does not show an invariable style in all situations. The experimental results show that the agent player using our method can predict the value of the opponent's hand and earn more money in fixed hands comparing with the original agent.

Keywords: Style Modeling, Bayesian Poker, Hold'em Poker.

1 Introduction

Poker is essentially a process of reasoning under uncertainty. It provides a good platform for testing new ideas and approaches to dealing with uncertainty. In a poker game, the opponent's cards are unobservable. Thus, the value of the opponent's hand is unknown. The information which can be obtained from the opponent is only his action. If the opponent's style or other useful features can be effectively modeled, we will have a better understanding of the opponent's action. If we want to win more money in a poker game, we have to model the opponent's style, habits, characters or other features. These hidden information can help us better grasp the opponent's motivation. The opponent may show an obvious tendency in a number of hands. However, specific to each decision, a good player is likely to be inconsistent with his style. For example, a player may bluff in order to disrupt his opponent's thinking and make himself unpredictable. Thus, there is a strong need to adapt to the opponent well. Opponent modeling is then considered important in poker [1,2,3]. Researchers have been committed to find a reasonable and effective model to adapt poker agents to its opponents.

M. Thielscher and D. Zhang (Eds.): AI 2012, LNCS 7691, pp. 385–396, 2012.

Opponent modeling in poker is mainly led by two ideas in current research [4]. In essential, both ideas are based on analyzing the opponent's action.

The first idea aims to classify the opponent into one of styles. As we know from [5], there are four recognized styles which are conservative-loose, conservative-tight, aggressive-loose and aggressive-tight in poker.

- **Conservative-Loose.** Players who over value their hands, but rarely raise, being fearful of large pots.
- **Conservative-Tight.** Players who play few hands, usually with a high probability of winning, but rarely raise, being fearful of large pots.
- **Aggressive-Loose.** Players who over value their hands, and who often raise to increase potential winnings.
- **Aggressive-Tight.** Players who play few hands, usually with a high probability of winning, and often raise to increase potential winnings.

Baker defines the opponents as above four distinctive styles and develops customized tactics to defeat each of the styles [6]. By analyzing the opponent's past actions, he classifies the opponent's style into one of four styles. After that, he chooses the most threatening opponent to play against and adopt that corresponding tactic when facing all the opponents of other styles. However, a player with a determinate style may act with an inconsistent style in a certain situation. Then the single style will be ineffective.

The second idea aims to model the distribution over the opponent's future actions or current state. The predictive model can be used to estimate hidden state in situations where the opponent has access to information only available to the observer through his actions.

Some researchers count the times of each player folded, called, or raised [7,8]. Then the distribution of the opponent's actions is constructed. Given the observed action and the board cards, the obtained distribution can be used to estimate the value of the opponent's hand.

Researchers have also studied on modeling the opponent's next actions. Billings [9,10] creates a statistics-based opponent modeling system. In this system, a probability distribution of actions is generated with each of the opponent's action. The opponent's next action is then predicted. The question is that the predictions of the next action are not so accurate in particular situations.

Most existing contributions of above two ideas are giving a representation of style and revealing the relation between the action and style. However, it is insufficient to represent the opponent's styles in all situations. There has been no work conducted to consider the diverse styles showed by opponents in various situations of a hand. In this paper, we work on 2 Players Limit Texas Hold'Em. Bets are predefined at a fixed size in this form. Therefore, we can be focused on opponent's style modeling in this form of Texas Hold'Em Poker. We propose a novel method aiming to model the opponents style based on situations. We first propose Action Pair to describe the relation between actions and styles. Based on Action Pair, we will define some formulas to quantify and determine the opponent's style in various situations of a hand. The style model will then be used to estimate the opponent's hidden information, which plays the decisive role in playing poker. Specifically, we intend to investigate:

- properly provide an objective and exact perception of the value of a hand,
- accurately model the style of the opponent in all situations,
- effectively use the modeled style of opponent.

The remainder of the paper is organized as follows. Section 2 introduces the new method. Section 3 describes the experiments and results with discussions. Section 4 presents the conclusions and future work.

2   The New Method

Understanding the opponent is the key to win in poker game. In order to make our agent better adapt to the opponent, we propose a method to quantify and determine the opponent's style based on situations. With the modeled style, the value of the opponent's full hand can be estimated.

The flow chart of the method is shown in Fig. 1, which has three modules.

The first module is **Inference**. Bayesian network [11,12] is used to model the probability distribution of win, lose and tie in this module. The distribution will provide us an objective and exact understanding of a hand. Korb has done much work in this field [9].

The second module is **Learning**. In this module, the opponent's style will be modeled for each situation of a hand.

The third module is **Tactic**. The modeled style will be used in the **Learning** module to help make decisions.

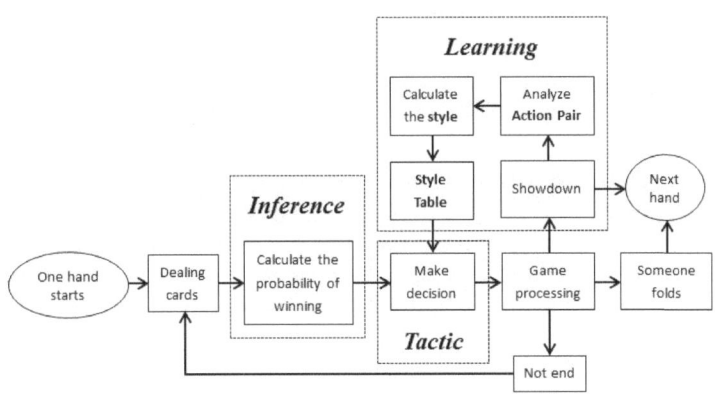

Fig. 1. The flow chart of the method

When a human player is dealing with a hand, he probably has two problems to consider: One is what the real value of a hand is, at least a relatively accurate estimate given observable information. The other problem is how to understand the opponent's last action given the history of the opponent's actions. When a hand is over, he will start thinking again how the opponent plays. Reviewing last hand will provide experience for his future playing. The method we propose in this paper will follow such process.

In our method, Bayesian network is used to construct the probability distribution of win, lose and tie of a hand. After each showdown hand, Action Pair and the probability of winning are employed to calculate the style based on situations. The new style value is then merged with the historical data of the style. Style functions are designed to accomplish the style calculation. Then the decisions are made according to the opponent's style value. The details will be presented in the following subsections.

2.1   The Probability Distribution of Win, Lose and Tie

Firstly, we will model the probability distribution of win, lose and tie given the current information of a hand. With the observable information such as round, board cards and our hole cards, although it is possible to compute the probability distribution exactly under the assumption of a uniform probability over the cards on a fair deck, the high computational cost is still unbearable [13]. So the distribution can only be estimated. The distribution in this paper is inferred by a Bayesian network. It is the *Inference* module in Fig. 2.

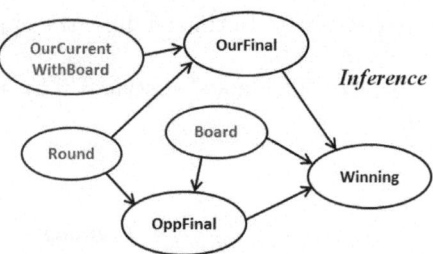

Fig. 2. The structure of the Bayesian network which is used to infer the probability distribution of win, lose and tie

Based on previous research [9], we refine the factors that remarkably influence the probability distribution of win, lose and tie given each hand. These factors are used to construct the Bayesian network. *OurCurrentWithBoard*, *OppFinal*, *OurFinal* and *Board* are the nodes which represent the types of corresponding hand. All the hand types are refined into 22 types as the nodes' states which are shown in Table 1.

The nodes *Round*, *OurCurrentWithBoard* and *Board* in Bayesian network are observed in Fig. 2. *Round* indicates the current round in a hand. *Board* indicates the current board cards on the table. *OurCurrentWithBoard* indicates the type of our hand including the board cards. *OurFinal* indicates our probability distribution of hand types inferred by *Round* and *OurCurrentWithBoard*. *Opp-Final* indicates the opponent's probability distribution of hand types inferred by

Table 1. The 22 Types of Hand Cards. Low means the top rank $2 \sim 8$(in Busted Low means lower than Q). Medium means top rank $9 \sim J$. High means top rank $Q \sim A$. L is short for Low. M for Medium and H for High.

Type	Example	Type	Example
Busted Low	♢J ♡10 ♠8 ♣4 ♡2	Pair H Second M	♢K ♡K ♠J ♣4 ♡2
Busted Q	♣Q ♢2 ♡10 ♠7 ♢4	Pair H Second H	♣A ♢A ♡K ♠7 ♢4
Busted K	♠K ♣4 ♡7 ♣Q ♢6	Two Pair Low	♠7 ♣7 ♡6 ♣6 ♢3
Busted A	♡A ♠K ♣10 ♡8 ♣2	Two Pair Medium	♡J ♠J ♣8 ♡8 ♣2
Pair L Second L	♠6 ♣6 ♡3 ♢7 ♣5	Two Pair High	♠A ♣A ♡7 ♢7 ♣K
Pair L Second M	♠5 ♡5 ♢2 ♣10 ♢9	Triple	♠5 ♡5 ♢5 ♣10 ♢9
Pair L Second H	♣3 ♡3 ♠A ♣10 ♠9	Straight	♣K ♡Q ♠J ♣10 ♠9
Pair M Second L	♡J ♣J ♡8 ♠3 ♢2	Flush	♡K ♡10 ♡8 ♡3 ♡2
Pair M Second M	♡J ♠J ♣10 ♣9 ♢3	Full House	♡K ♠K ♣K ♣9 ♢9
Pair M Second H	♡10 ♠10 ♣K ♢6 ♣5	Four of a Kind	♡6 ♠6 ♣6 ♢6 ♣K
Pair H Second L	♢A ♠A ♣3 ♠5 ♡6	Straight Flush	♠A ♠K ♠Q ♠J ♠10

Round and *Board*. *Winning* indicates the probability distribution of win, lose and tie. It is inferred by *OppFinal*, *OurFinal* and *Board* together.

To obtain the conditional probability table, 100,000,000 hands are randomly generated to be used to conduct statistics.

2.2 Model the Opponent's Style Based on Situations

Poker does not merely concern the probability of which hand can win. It is psychological warfare between players. The better we know the opponent, the more money we win. Different from existing work [7], it is limited to classify an opponent into one of styles. A player will not always take actions of an invariable style. Having studied match logs of some players of different styles, we find that a player will show different styles in different situations. While in similar situations the player will show a similar style. We assume that the player's style will be consistent in a similar situation. Then there comes two problems: we need a method to quantify the style; we need to define what "a similar situation" is.

As mentioned in Section I, there are four main styles of players which are recognized: *conservative-loose*, *conservative-tight*, *aggressive-loose* and *aggressive-tight*. In order to get rid of the constraints of limited style, we quantify the style and map them to a continuous interval $[0, 1]$. When the value of the style tends to be 0, the style tends to be aggressive. When the value of the style tends to be 1, the style tends to be conservative. Of course, when the value of style tends to be 0.5, the middle of $[0, 1]$, the style tends to be normal.

When analyzing the opponent's style, we are finding the opponent's motivation behind his actions. We generalize the factors related with opponents' actions: our action before the opponent, the opponent's hand(hole cards and board cards) and round. These factors together form the opponent's style. We call the process **Learning**.

In this module, we propose the notion Action Pair. It consists of our agent's action and the opponent's action, which are contextual. For example, "rc" means the opponent checks after our agent's raise action. Leaving aside the hand, we can intuitively find interesting information hidden in the Action Pair.

If the opponent raises after our agent's raise action, we assume that the opponent has a strong tendency of aggressiveness. If the opponent checks after our agent's check action, we assume that the opponent has no particular tendency. Following this principle, we sort all types of Action Pair according to the order which is from "Aggressive" to "Conservative". We conclude the Action Pair order in Fig. 3.

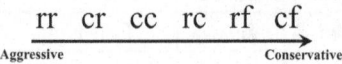

Fig. 3. The Action Pairs in the order of the style

We assume that if the opponent's hole cards are unobservable, any analysis of the opponent's style is unconvincing because we do not have enough exact information to infer the opponent's motivation behind. Therefore, we only analyze the opponent's style after a showdown hand when the opponent's hole cards are observable.

In addition, *Round* is an important factor, which affects the thinking of an opponent. A player will have different considerations in different rounds. It can be easily understood that it is totally different when we have one pair in the first round from the last round.

With the three factors *Action Pair*, *Opponent's Hand Cards* and *Round* above, the opponent's style can be modeled.

We propose a method to compute the value of the opponent's style. The Action Pair and the probability distribution of win, lose and tie are used to map the value of the style to the a continuous interval [0, 1] as shown in Fig. 4.

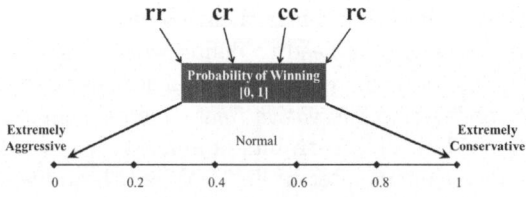

Fig. 4. The graphical representation of the mapping process

Corresponding to each Action Pair, a function $Style(WinP)$ is defined as follows to compute the value of the style:

- For Action Pair "rr" : $Style(winP) = 0.5 \times winP^{\frac{1}{3}}, \quad winP \in [0, 1]$.
- For Action Pair "cr" : $Style(winP) = 0.5 \times winP^{\frac{1}{2}}, \quad winP \in [0, 1]$.
- For Action Pair "cc" : $Style(winP) = winP, \quad winP \in [0, 1]$.
- For Action Pair "rc" : $Style(winP) = \frac{1}{1+e^{-8\times(-winP+0.5)}}, \quad winP \in [0, 1]$.

It can be deduced that if the opponent has a high probability of winning, but he chooses to check, there is a good reason to assign a value representing a conservative tendency as his style. There are still some rules in defining style functions:

- If the opponent has a high probability to win and he raises, the value of style should be tended to be Normal.
- A small probability of winning and a nonconservative Action Pair produce aggressive style. This aggressiveness will be intensified as the Action Pair tends to be more aggressive.
- A big probability of winning and a nonaggressive Action Pair produce conservative style. This conservativeness will be intensified as the Action Pair tends to be more conservative.

When the opponent folds, his hole cards will be unobservable. Then such case of fold will not be considered.

Given the style functions, the calculations will only be operated after showdown. Such information for each style calculation should be ready: Action Pair, Current Round, Opponent's Hole Cards, Board Cards. $Style(winP)$ can be calculated by above information. E.g., $winP$ (the probability of winning) can be obtained in previous **Inference** module using *Round, Opponent's Hole cards* and *Board cards*. Then we can calculate the style of the opponent according to $Style(winP)$. This style is what the opponent shows in the current situation of a hand. It satisfies the distribution of the current information of a hand. The current situation consists of information which are observable by both the opponent and ourselves. *Round* and *Board cards* are obviously the most appropriate information within the situation. The table *StyleTable*, which is indexed by *Round* and *BoardCardsType*, is created to store the values of styles as "experience". Each obtained value will be put in the position where is indexed by the combination of corresponding *Round* and *Board cards type* and calculated with the historical data together in a statistical way. The greatest advantage is that it's an online learning which can learn the opponent's style while in the play.

2.3   Make Decisions with Modeled Style

We call this process the **Tactic** module in Fig. 1. When estimating the value of the opponent's hand cards in a certain stage of a hand, information such as *Round, Board cards* should be first observed. Meanwhile, the historical style will be obtained from *StyleTable*. The style is what the opponent shows in the similar situation based on "experience". Given the latest Action Pair in the same round, we can restore the opponent's approximate probability of winning. The approach is almost the inverse process of obtaining the style of opponent. Following functions are designed to map the style to the probability of winning:

- For Action Pair "rr" or "cr" : $EWinP(style) = style^{\frac{2}{3}}, \quad style \in [0,1]$
- For Action Pair "cc" : $EWinP(style) = style, \quad style \in [0,1]$
- For Action Pair "rc" : $EWinP(style) = 4 \times (x - 0.5)^3 + 0.5,, \quad style \in [0,1]$

Note that all the calculations can only be operated when all the required information comes from the same round of a hand. This is consistent with what we have always emphasized that the opponent will show a similar style in a similar situation.

After having obtained the estimated opponent's probability of winning, we can have many ways to adaptively change our action. The simplest way is that if the estimated value is very high, the opponent may have a very good hand. Because the value of the style is an average calculated in a number of hands, we do not need to consider whether the opponent is bluffing this time.

3   Experiments and Analysis

There are two issues to be verified in the experiments. The first is whether the style shows a significant difference in different situations. The second is whether style modeling can improve the performance of an agent. These two issues guide the experiments. To compare the results, we use three agents as opponents with different styles, which will be described in the following section.

3.1   Contrast Agents and Opponents

Contrast agents. The contrast agent bases on previous *Inference* module. 100,000,000 hands are randomly generated to train its Bayesian network. It raises when its probability of winning is over 0.6 and folds when its probability of losing is over 0.6. It is designed to carry normal style.

Rule-Based Opponents. By adjusting the threshold of the probability of winning to take actions, we simulate the aggressive and conservative opponents based on previous *Inference* module. The aggressive agent raises when its probability of winning is over 0.4 and folds when its probability of losing is over 0.8. The conservative agent raises when its probability of winning is over 0.8 and folds when its probability of losing is over 0.4.

Monash BPP(Bayesian Poker Player) Opponent. We introduce the Monash BPP of *ACPC*(Annual Computer Poker Competition) 2006 version as another opponent [14]. Its complete version got the third prize in the competition. For simplification, we do not include its opponent modeling part.

3.2   Results and Analysis

Each experiment is performed in 100, 200, 500 and 1,000 hands. The performance of the agents with and without style modeling are compared by the winning money after each experiment. After each opponent's experiments, the corresponding *StyleTable* will be analyzed. The experiments are carried on the *ACPC* Server.

The Opponent with Aggressive Style. As mentioned before, the threshold adjustment will make the opponent tend to take more risks to play more hands. Thus, the opponent will act aggressively even if it has no big hand in many situations of a hand. The performances of the agent with and without style modeling are then observed. A tactic is tried so that if the estimated opponent's probability of winning is larger than the agent's, we assume that the opponent has a larger hand than our agent and it will not raise in any way.

Note that the value of the style is 0.5 in some situations. The reason is that, in the first round, two board cards cannot form the combination of some hand types. In the following round, some hand types with a low probability cannot appear. Thus, a priori value 0.5 has to be assigned to this situation.

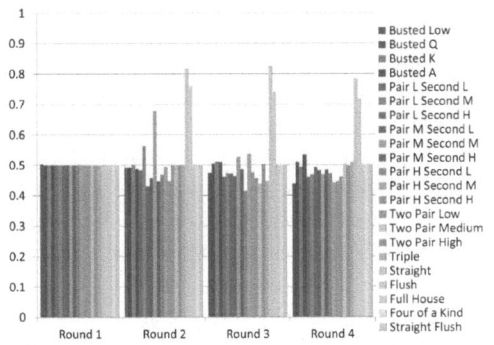
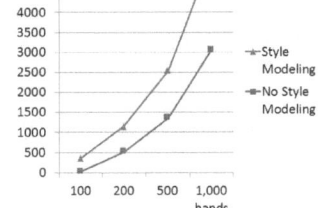

(a) The *StyleTable* for the aggressive opponent. The vertical axis indicates the scale of the style.

(b) The result of comparison with style modeling against the aggressive opponent.

Fig. 5. Experiments for the aggressive opponent. In (b), the vertical axis indicates the scale of money won by the agents. The abscissa indicates the scale of the number of hands the agents play.

In Fig.5(a), the opponent shows an obvious aggressive style in most of situations. The values of styles are generally less than 0.5. In addition, the style is variable in all situations. It can be justified by the experiments that the opponent shows various styles in different situations.

According to Fig.5(b), a big advantage is shown to the aggressive opponent. Although the aggressive opponent loses money more easily, the agent with style modeling wins averagely more than 50% of the agent without style modeling in each match. By analyzing the log of matches, we find that the agent with style modeling does well in reducing its threshold of raising to adjust itself to the opponent's aggressive style and win more.

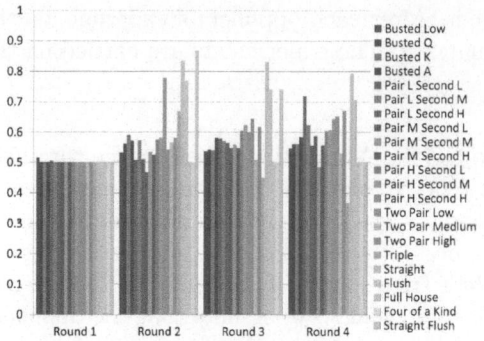

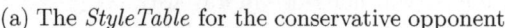

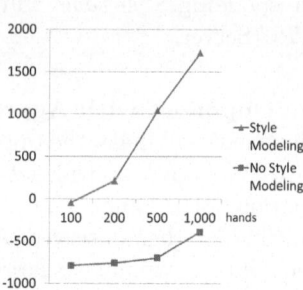

(a) The *StyleTable* for the conservative opponent.

(b) The result of comparison with style modeling against the conservative opponent.

Fig. 6. Experiments for the conservative opponent

The Opponent with Conservative Style. The conservative opponent tends to take fewer risks so that it will play only sure hands and raise only when it has a greater assurance. We make slight adjustment that if the estimated opponent's probability of winning is larger than the agent's, the agent will directly fold.

In Fig.6(a), the conservative opponent clearly shows the opposite tendency from aggressive opponent. The values of styles are generally greater than 0.5. It indicates that the opponent shows an obvious conservative style in most of situations. The obtained style from the style model is able to reasonably demonstrate the tendency of the opponent. Furthermore, we find that again the style in different situations of a hand is variable as in last experiment.

In Fig.6(b), the compared agent loses all the matches. In contrast, the agent with style modeling wins money at a steady rate along with the increase of the hands. By analyzing the log, we conclude that the conservative opponent gives no chance to us since it only plays a good hand. So the compared agent with no style modeling has no advantages. When it raises, the opponent either folds or has a greater hand. However the agent with style modeling will fold once the estimated opponent's probability of winning is greater than its hand. Thus, it is not difficult to explain why the agent with style modeling performs better.

The Opponent Monash BPP. Based on Bayesian network, it first infers the probability of winning through belief propagation. Combining the probability and its next action, the final decision is made. In addition, it adds randomization to make itself unpredictable.

In Fig.7(a), the opponent shows no clear general style. In this case, a single style modeling will not work. Considering that the styles in different situations are variable, style modeling will take effect.

In Fig.7(b), the agent with style modeling begins to show significant advantage from 500 hands match. Based on the analysis of the log of matches, the "experience" *StyleTable* does not help much in the first 200 hands. Since the statistical effect is not obvious at the very beginning. After that, the agent with

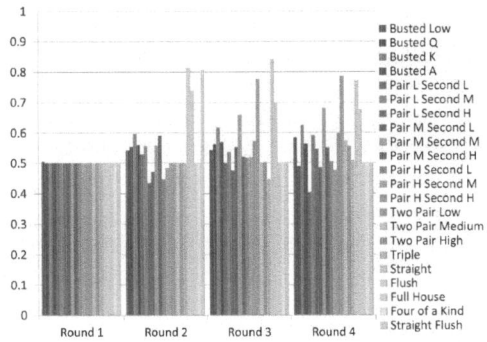

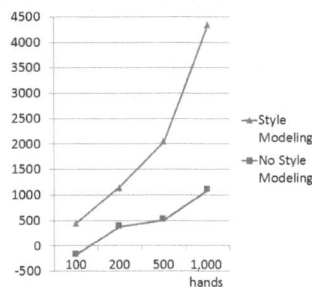

(a) The *StyleTable* for the Monash BPP opponent.

(b) The result of comparison with style modeling against the Monash BPP opponent.

Fig. 7. Experiments for the Monash BPP opponent

style modeling successfully avoids to raise when facing the Monash BPP's larger hand. Meanwhile, it succeeds in finding the opponent's poor hand and stays close to it even if the hand of the agent with style modeling is also poor.

3.3 Discussion

Even if the opponent has a distinct style, it is hard for him to avoid showing inconsistent styles in different situations of a hand. As a result, we cannot use his single style to guide all of our actions. This is why we propose the method to model the style in all situations. The obtained *StyleTable* and the estimated opponent's probability of winning effectively help the agent improve the performance. The improved agent adapts to the opponent and performs better than its original version, which is very encouraging.

Additionally, the agent with style modeling will adjust with the increase of the hands. We find that the *StyleTable* tends to be a stable distribution after 1000 hands. It indicates that the opponent's style modeling based on situations will not change much after that.

4   Conclusions and Future Work

This paper proposed a novel method to model the opponent's style based on situations and a detailed procedure centered at the modeled style. In order to achieve this goal, a notion of Action Pair and a calculation method are first given to obtain the value of the style and known as "experience". The specific style will be obtained from the "experience" according to the current situation of the hand. Then the style was used to help estimate the value of the opponent's hand. In this way, the final decision can be made by some tactics.

The experimental results show that the modeled style validates the correctness of our assumption that a player does not always show an invariable style in situations. This style modeling subdivides the style into different situations. Having obtained the style values in all situations, we can have an insight into the opponent's style in detail, which cannot be easily observed by existing methods. It's encouraging to find that the obtained style and the estimated opponent's probability of winning can effectively improve the performance of the original agent. They jointly help the agent predict the hidden information of the opponent's hand and earn more money in fixed hands.

Future work will pay attention to building the style quantifying process more accurately. The method will also be extended to No-Limit Hold'Em Poker where the pot is an important factor which has a great impact on player's decision.

Acknowledgments. We would like to acknowledge the support for this work from the National Science Foundation of China(Grant Nos.61035003, 61170180, 61175042, 61021062), and Program for New Century Excellent Talents in University(Grant No. NCET-10-0476).

References

1. Billings, D., Papp, D., Schaeffer, J., Szafron, D.: Opponent modeling in poker. In: Proceedings of the Fifteenth National AAAI Conference, pp. 493–499 (1998)
2. Davidson, A.: Opponent modeling in poker: Learning and acting in a hostile and uncertain environment. Master's thesis, University of Alberta (2002)
3. Machado, M., Fantini, E., Chaimowicz, L.: Player Modeling: Towards a Common Taxonomy. In: 16th International Conference on Computer Games, pp. 50–57 (2011)
4. Lockett, A.J., Miikkulainen, R.: Evolving opponent models for Texas Hold'Em. In: IEEE Symposium on Computational Intelligence and Games, pp. 31–38 (2008)
5. Barone, L., While, L.: Adaptive learning for poker. In: Proceedings of the Genetic and Evolutionary Computation Conference, pp. 566–573 (2000)
6. Baker, R.J.S., Cowling, P.I.: Bayesian Opponent Modeling in a Simple Poker Environment. In: IEEE Symposium on Computational Intelligence and Games, pp. 125–131 (2007)
7. Davidson, A., Billings, D., Schaeffer, J., Szafron, D.: Improved opponent modeling in poker. In: International Conference on Artificial Intelligence, pp. 1467–1473 (2000)
8. Billings, D., Davidson, A., Schaeffer, J., Szafron, D.: The challenge of poker. Artificial Intelligence 134, 201–240 (2002)
9. Korb, K.B., Nicholson, A.E., Jitnah, N.: Bayesian poker. In: Proceedings of the Fifteenth Conference on Uncertainty in Artificial Intelligence, pp. 343–350 (1999)
10. Billings, D., Castillo, L., Schaeffer, J., Szafron, D.: Using probabilistic knowledge and simulation to play poker. In: Proceedings of the 16th National Conference on Artificial Intelligence, pp. 697–703 (1999)
11. Russell, S., Norvig, P.: Artificial Intelligence: A Modern Approach. Prentice Hall (2006)
12. Korb, K.B., Nicholson, A.E.: Bayesian Artificial Intelligence. Chapman and Hall/CRC, Boca Raton (2004)
13. Tretyakov, K., Kamm, L.: Modeling texas hold'em poker strategies with bayesian networks (2009)
14. Annual Computer Poker Competition,
    http://www.computerpokercompetition.org/

Game Designers Training First Person Shooter Bots

Michelle McPartland and Marcus Gallagher

University of Queensland
{michelle,marcusg}@itee.uq.edu.au

Abstract. Interactive training is well suited to computer games as it allows game designers to interact with otherwise autonomous learning algorithms. This paper investigates the outcome of a group of five commercial first person shooter game designers using a custom built interactive training tool to train first person shooter bots. The designers are asked to train a bot using the tool, and then comment on their experiences. The five trained bots are then pitted against each other in a deathmatch scenario. The results show that the training tool has potential to be used in a commercial environment.

Keywords: Reinforcement learning, interactive training, first person shooters, game artificial intelligence.

1   Introduction

Over the past decade there has been a dramatic increase in using computer games for Artificial Intelligence (AI) research. In particular, first person shooter (FPS) games are an increasing popular environment in which to test traditional machine learning techniques due to their similarities to robotics and multi-agent systems (MAS). For example, FPS game agents, termed bots, are able to sense and act in their environment, and have complex, continuous movement spaces. FPS bot AI generally consists of hard-coded techniques such as finite state machines, rule-based systems, and behaviour trees [1][2]. These techniques are generally associated with drawbacks such as predictable behaviours [3] and time consuming tuning of parameters [4].

Reinforcement Learning (RL) is a class of machine learning algorithms which allow the agent to build a map of behaviours by sensing and receiving rewards from the environment. An extension to the standard RL algorithm is interactive RL, or interactive training, a method that allows human users to interact with the learning algorithm by providing rewards or punishments instead of using a fixed reward function.

While there is an increasing amount of research into using machine learning techniques for FPS bot AI [5-7], this research removes the game designers from the development loop. While automating the learning of AIs may appear to be an advantage, it is hard to control the direction the algorithm learns in [8], and is also hard to fine tune to commercial standards. This research attempts to bridge this gap by allowing game designers to interact with the underlying learning algorithm in order to direct what behaviours the bot learns. There are a number of advantages of using

M. Thielscher and D. Zhang (Eds.): AI 2012, LNCS 7691, pp. 397–408, 2012.
© Springer-Verlag Berlin Heidelberg 2012

interactive training for FPS bot AI. It gives designers control over the types of bots that are made. The underlying code of the behaviours can be modularised and reused thereby decreasing bugs and coding time. Finally, iteration time designing bots is decreased as the designers can see in real-time the effects of the bot behaviours while the game is being played.

This paper extends previous work in interactive training [9] with the aim of further investigating its suitability for commercial first person shooter games. The research is continued through experiments involving commercial computer game designers using the tool to train a bot. This aim will be achieved by examining the results from the training session, to see if they match the intention of the designers. The secondary aim is to prove that diverse types of bots can be created by different users.

The contribution of this paper is twofold. Investigating how human users interact with learning algorithms is an interesting and novel idea, and may provide insight into the underlying algorithm itself. The results from the paper also benefit the game industry as a new method for designing and training bot AIs may be established.

This paper is organized as follows. Section 2 will provide background on FPS games and relevant research. An introduction to RL and interactive training will then be given. Section 3 will outline the game test bed used for the research, including the interactive training tool interface. Section 4 presents the data gathered from game designers' training sessions and results from playing the trained bots against each other. The final section concludes the paper with ideas on future work.

2   Background

FPS games are one of the most popular types of game being played in the current market [10]. FPSs are categorized for their combat nature and fast paced action. These games are generally made up of bots that navigate the environment, shoot at enemies, and pick up items of interest. AI research using FPS games has gained considerable attention in the research [6][11].

During the last decade, research into FPS games has continued to increase. A Neural Network (NN) was used to train the weapon selection module of Unreal Tournament bots [5]. The results showed that the bots trained against the base AI had improved performance, and the bots trained against the harder AI were not as competitive, but had improved slightly. In a similar environment an evolutionary NN was used to train hierarchical controllers for FPS bots [6]. Three controllers for shooting, exploring and path following were evolved individually, and then an evolutionary algorithm (EA) was trained to decide when to use each of the controllers. The results showed that bots using the evolved controllers were not able to outperform the hard-coded full knowledge bots, but they were able to play the game quite well. A NN was also used to learn sub-controllers for the movement of an FPS bot and found that it was able to outperform controllers using decision trees and Naïve Bayes classifiers [11].

Game AI has many parameters which are usually balanced or fine tuned by developers once all the features of the game are complete. The job of tuning parameters can be time consuming due to the large number of them. Some researchers have attempted to tune these parameters using genetic algorithms [4][7][12][13]. An FPS environment was used with the parameters being the behaviour of the bots [12][13][4]. Bots were tuned from Unreal Tournament (Epic Games) and found the tuned bots were better, in terms of kills, than the standard AI in the game [12]. The popular Counter Strike (Valve) game has been used as a test bed for FPS research [13]. They found that evaluation times were extremely long as the rendering could not be "turned off", and therefore only 50 generations were completed. Results showed that after only 50 generations the evolved bots had a slight advantage. Other research evolved the behaviour of bots in an open sourced FPS engine called Cube [4]. Evaluation was performed by the author manually playing against the bots with an evaluation function consisting of the bots health, kills and deaths. Results showed that the bots evolved into capable enemies from initial useless ones.

Reinforcement learning (RL) is a type of action selection mechanism where an agent learns through experience interacting with the environment [14]. The field of RL is widespread but is mainly focused in robotics and multi agent systems [15][16]. Sarsa(λ) is a type of RL algorithm where the policy is updated after the next action is selected using the rewards obtained from the current and next action. The Sarsa(λ) algorithm has been successfully applied to multi-agent systems using a computer game environment [17][18].

Previous work has been performed in using RL for learning individual bot behaviors in a shooter style environment [8][19]. Both of these research papers show that RL can successfully be used to learn navigation, item collection and combat behaviors. A simplified FPS test bed has also been used in other research, where the map was broken into square areas, and each area represented one of the states, along with enemy visible and a set of plans which denoted a planned path through the areas [19]. This work looked at using RL for learning bot behaviours in FPS team scenarios.

Interactive RL is an extension to the standard RL algorithm as it allows a human user to interact with the reward process and the action selection process. There is little research in the literature on interactive RL, and none in an FPS environment. An interactive RL algorithm was used in a simple 2d environment to train a synthetic dog how to behave [20]. The user was able to guide the dog by using the mouse to lure the dog into positions such as sitting or begging. An extension to this work is seen in [21] which used a more complex environment to teach a virtual character how to make a cake. Reward values were represented with a sliding bar, and guide actions were used in the form of clicking an object in the environment. The research presented here extends previous work on interactive RL [9], which performed a preliminary investigation into using the algorithm in an FPS environment. From the success of the previous work, this paper will test the interactive training tool on five commercial game designers, and will compare the results of the trained bots.

3   Method

A purpose built FPS game environment was used for the interactive training experiments as full control was needed over the game update loop, the user interface and the

CPU cycles. The game environment consisted of the basic components of an FPS game: bots that can navigate the environment at different speeds, shoot weapons, pick up items, strafe, and duck behind cover. See Figure 1 for a screenshot of the game environment with four bots currently in combat. For more details on the game environment refer to [9].

Fig. 1. Screenshot of game environment with bots playing against each other

The state sensors of the bot were designed to capture local information that the bot can use to sense the environment. The input states for the bot are as follows:

- Health: Low (0), Medium (1), High (2)
- Ammo: Low (0), Medium (1), High (2)
- Enemy: NoEnemy (0), Melee Range (1), Ranged (2), Out of Attack Range (3)
- Item: None (0), Health (1), Ammo (2)

The output states were the actions the bot can perform in the world as follows: Melee (0), Ranged (1), Wander (2), Health Item (3), Ammo Item (4), Dodge (5), and Hide (6). Therefore the number of state action pairs in the policy table is 756.

The ITRL algorithm used in this paper was loosely based on the work on interactive synthetic dog [20], and human training [21]. The algorithm runs as normal when no human input is recorded using a pre-defined reward function. The reward function can be modified by the user at any stage of the training through edit boxes in the User Interface (UI) (see Figure 2). A button was also available to clear all reward values, which will disable the pre-defined reward function and only user rewards are used.

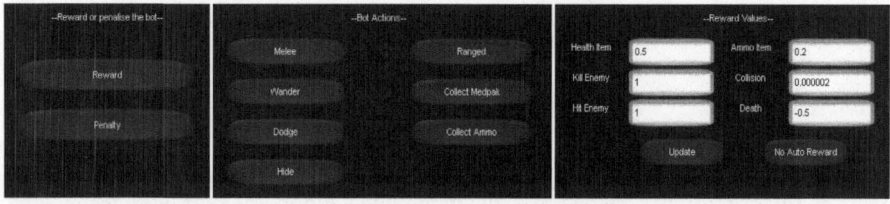

Fig. 2. User Interface design for the interactive training tool

Table 1 lists the steps of the interactive training algorithm. If the user selected a guide action, the algorithm will use this input to override the RL action selection method. For a complete description of the algorithm and user interface design see [9]. The learning rate was represented by $\alpha = 0.1$, reduced over time to 0.05. The decay factor was $\gamma = 0.4$, the eligibility trace was $\lambda = 0.8$, and the exploration rate was $\varepsilon = 0.2$. The end game condition is the terminal state which was decided by the designers at any point during the training. Trained bots can be saved and loaded for continuation of training as well.

Table 1. Interactive Sarsa(λ) Algorithm

1:	Initialize $Q(s,a)$ arbitrarily, set $e(s,a)=0$ for all s, a
4:	Repeat for each update step t in the game
5:	$g \leftarrow$ guidance object
6:	If guidance received then
7:	$a \leftarrow g$
8:	Else
9:	$a \leftarrow$ action select a from policy, Q, using ε-greedy selection
10:	End if
11:	Execute a
12:	$hr \leftarrow$ user reward or penalty
13:	If user reward received then
14:	$r \leftarrow g$
15:	Else
16:	Observe r
17:	End if
18:	$\delta \leftarrow r + \gamma Q(s',a') - Q(s,a)$
19:	$e(s,a) \leftarrow 1$
20:	For all s, a:
21:	$Q(s,a) \leftarrow Q(s,a) + \alpha \delta e(s,a)$
22:	$e(s,a) \leftarrow \gamma \lambda e(s,a)$
23:	$s \leftarrow s'$, $a \leftarrow a'$
24:	Until s is terminal

The interactive training algorithm updates when a state change occurs and when the user has selected a guide action or reward. When the user selects a guide action, it immediately overrides the current action. The user chosen action continues until it either succeeds or fails, or the user selects another action.

Emails were sent to five game designers working in the computer games industry that have worked on commercial shooter games. The designers were asked to train a bot using the supplied training tool, and to email the results back along with answers to some questions regarding their training experience. Data was recorded for all user actions, including reward and penalty frequencies, and whether the guide actions failed or succeeded after the action was pressed.

4   Results

This section looks at the results from the five game designers using the interactive training tool to train bots to play a first person shooter game. Feedback was gathered from the users to find out what type of bot they tried to train. The first section will compare the feedback with the data from the training phase. The second section will investigate the results from the five user trained bots playing against each other.

4.1   Training Phase

Figure 3 displays the state-action value functions represented by a colour scale visualisation to show the similarities and differences between the trained bots. User 3 clearly has the most active policy with the majority of states having adjusted values, and very few areas where the state action pairs have not been visited. This activity

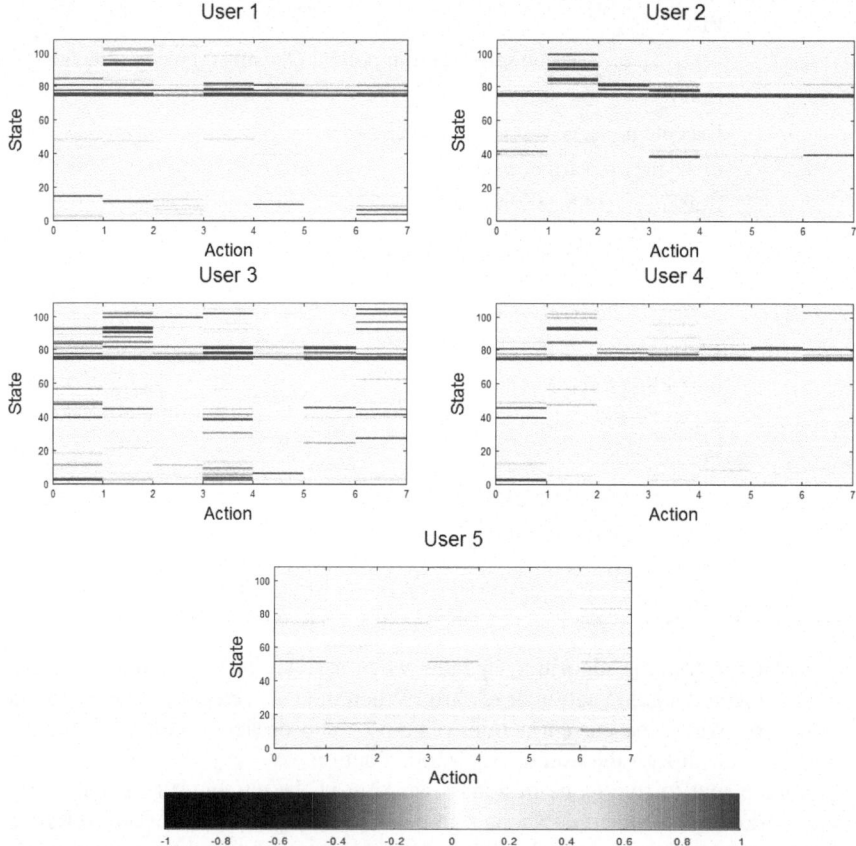

Fig. 3. Clockwise from top left to bottom right, the state-action value functions represented with a colour scale for user 1, user 2, user 3, user 4 and user 5

indicates that user 3 spent a lot of time training the bot and therefore the bot, in theory, should be more experienced at playing the game than the other bots. The next most active landscape is from user 5, although this is not immediately clear from Figure 3 as it appears very flat all over. The reason for the decrease in values is that user 5 turned off the automatic reward distribution at the beginning of the training session. Therefore all reward values were manually given by the user causing the smaller values. However, despite the small values, a good spread of clusters are seen in the landscape, with some flat areas but less than seen in the policies of users 1, 2 and 4.

Users 1, 2 and 4 have similar clusters; although their values are varied over the three users. For example, user 2 has higher peaks in the states over 100, and very low peaks in the states less than 20. Whereas, user 1 had high values in states less then 20, and small peaks in the ones greater than 100. User 4 generally had lower values, but across more state-actions, indicating a broader training experience with less repetition on similar states than other uses.

Table 2. Guide actions successes (S) and failures (F) for user training

Action	S1	F1	S2	F2	S3	F3	S4	F4	S5	F5
Melee	6	1	3	21	15	13	4	2	9	0
Ranged	2	8	2	3	3	1	3	5	6	15
Wander	0	0	0	0	0	0	1	0	0	0
Health Item	11	1	16	5	64	6	9	0	31	0
Ammo Item	6	0	1	3	0	0	2	2	14	0
Dodge	8	0	0	0	0	0	3	0	0	0
Hide	1	2	0	0	0	0	0	1	6	2
TOTAL	*34*	*12*	*22*	*32*	*82*	*20*	*22*	*10*	*66*	*17*

User 1 tried to create an item collecting bot that shot at range then moved into melee. Table 2 shows an even number of ranged and melee actions being used, with melee (six actions) being more successful than the ranged action (two successes). The health and ammo item actions were also evenly used with 11 health and six ammo item successes. Therefore, overall a general type bot was attempted to be trained.

User 2 tried to create an aggressive melee combatant and this can clearly be seen by the number of melee actions that were selected. Unfortunately a very high number of these guide actions failed, indicating that either the failure condition for the melee action was unreasonable (i.e. having to kill the opponent), or that the range for using the melee action was not clear to the user.

User 3 attempted a health collecting ranged/melee combination bot that favoured melee. The figures in Table 2 reflect what the user attempted to do. The melee action was focussed on with 15 successes and 13 failures, and the ranged action was selected less frequently with three successes and one failure. The health item action was used as a guide 64 times successfully, and six times unsuccessfully. These figures show that user 3 performed more interactive training than all the other users, which were also seen by the height field representation of the policy in Figure 3 as the landscape was more active, compared to the others.

User 4 aimed to create a bot that fled the stronger enemies but attacked the weak ones. The data does not reflect this training as the hide action was only selected once

by the user. However, this failure may be an indication of why the user felt the training did not work well for them. Improvements need to be made on the hide behaviour
so that it is useful for the intended purpose as user 4 assumed.

The user with the second most active training session was user 5. Their feedback
quoted them trying to create a bot that was primarily ranged but also used melee attacks, and attempted to collect health and ammo items. The guide action data back up
this statement as the ranged attack was focused on with nine successes and 15 failures, while the melee attack was used nine times successfully. Health and ammo
items were selected 31 and 14 times successfully successively. User 5 tried training
the hide action more than the rest of the users with six successful attempts and two
failures.

This section has shown that the users were able to use the interactive training tool
to train the types of bots they wanted. The policy visualisations showed that there
were three distinct types of bots that were trained, where user 1, 2 and 4 had similar
trends, and user 3 and 5 had distinctly different trends. The next section will continue
investigating the varied nature of the bots from the different users.

4.2   Simulation Phase

This section looks at the results from a game played with five trained bots, one from
each user, fighting against each other. No AI controlled bots were included in the
games. The simulations were run for 12000 game ticks or iterations. An iteration was
a complete update cycle of the game and was used to be consistent over all replays.
Due to there being multiple RL bots, using RL iterations would only be relevant to
one of the five bots. 50 games were played and the results averaged. Figure 1 shows
the five user trained bots playing against each other.

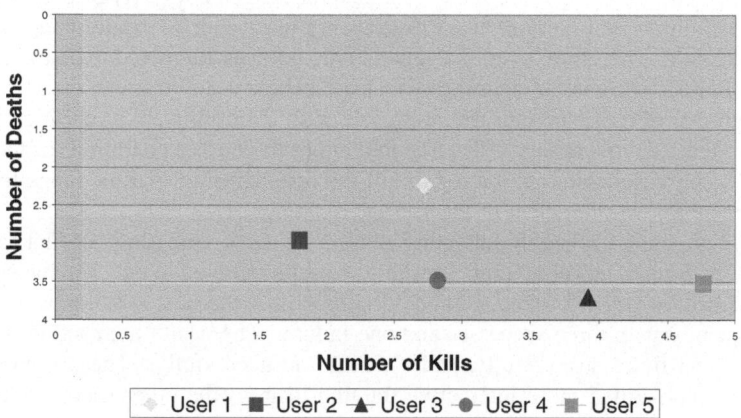

Fig. 4. Number of kills versus deaths for each user

Figure 4 maps the number of kills versus deaths to represent an overall combat strategy based on maximising kills and minimising deaths. The number of deaths scale on the Y axis was reversed as the best strategy has the lowest death count. The figure indicates that user 5 has the best combat strategy bot, being the only one in the first wave on the Pareto front. User 5 had the highest number of average kills of 4.8, and although they did not have the lowest number of deaths of 3.5, they were still able to dominate the other bots in combat. The next front had user 3 in it with an average of 3.9 kills and 3.7 deaths, with user 1 in the next front with 2.7 kills and the lowest number of deaths of 2.2. Users 2 and 4 were dominated by the other three bots with average kills of 1.8 and 2.8, and deaths of 3.0 and 3.5 respectively.

Observation of the games showed that user 1 was extremely competent in health item collection, and often avoided ammo items in favour of health. This behaviour is also reflected in the values recorded for health and ammo collection. User 1 was the second best at collecting health items with an average of 18.0 health items per game, whereas they were the second lowest in ammo collection at 8.7 items per game (see Figure 5a). This bot rarely used the wander behaviour, which corresponds to feedback from user 1 that they wanted their bot to always try to move with an intention.

User 3 followed a similar strategy to user 1 of favouring health items over ammo items. They were successful in this goal, and achieved the highest health collecting bot with an average of 23.0 health items per game. User 3 not only trained a very good health item collecting bot, but also a competitive combat bot, proving that the extensive training they did produced a bot that was well rounded in all the game objectives.

Users 2, 4 and 5 produced bots with a similar health collecting ability with averages of 6.0, 10.7 and 7.7 respectively. While these bots were capable at health item collection, they frequently chose different actions during non-combat states such as wander, and ammo collection.

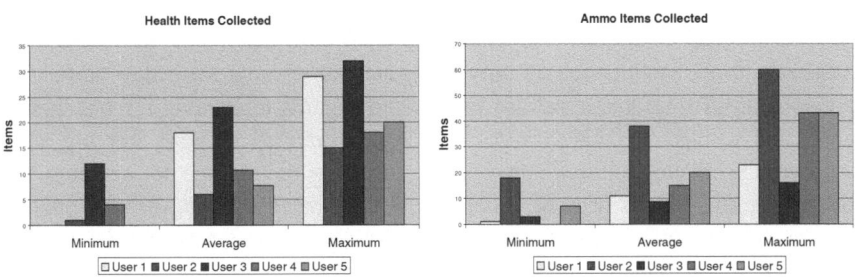

Fig. 5. (a) Average health items collected for user trained bots and (b) Average ammo items collected for user trained bots

Although user 2 had the lowest health collection rate, they scored extremely high in the ammo item collection task with an average of 38.1, almost double that of the next highest scoring bot from user 5 who had an average of 19.9 (see Figure 5b). Observation of one game showed user 2 spending a lot of time wandering around an area of the map with number of ammo items, which could be attributed to this very high number.

The increased activity seen in the policy height field representations of user 3 and 5, seemed to have paid off as these bots stood out in combat. Observation of the combat strategy of user 3 and 5's bots showed intelligible behaviours, and they would only break out of combat to collect health items. Bots from users 1, 2 and 4 had more erratic behaviour with rapid state changes and selection of strange actions during combat. For example, in the replay, user 1 is fighting user 2 and user 1 breaks out of the combat and wanders away even though the enemy is still in sight. They re-engage in combat after a time, but the behaviour looks erratic and is not what would be expected of a commercial FPS bot.

5   Discussion

The user trained bots have shown greater diversity in their policy landscapes and behaviours than in previous research of automatically trained bots [8]. The policy landscapes were especially varied in user 3 and 5's bots, both of which spent more time training than the other three users. The bots produced from the varied policies appeared better in their behaviours than the other three bots. An example of the diversity in bots can be seen by the bot user 1 trained, which was very good at health collection but not as competitive in combat, whereas user 3 also produced a very good health collecting bot and was also very good in combat.

One of the major concerns with the combat system was that the bots did not have the ability to shoot and move to a designated position at the same time. User 4 was not able to train the type of bot that they wanted to due to this restriction and the limited actions that could be performed in combat. A solution to this issue is to add guide actions which are able to add to the combat experience. These actions could include a flee to health item action, an action which allowed the bot to kite by staying in ranged attack distance, and a separate ranged action which moved into melee range.

The results showed that user 5 only using manual rewards seemed to perform better than using the automatic reward function in regards to training the bot that they wanted and seeing immediate feedback during the training session. Forcing manual rewards only should improve some of the issues with training not seeming to be working for some types of bots, especially those that differ from the path the automatic reward system steered them towards. This issue is clearly seen in the policy landscapes of the trained bots. Users 1, 2 and 4 did the least amount of training (as seen in the training results listed in Table 2) and the policy landscapes were all very similar. User 3 performed extensive training using automatic rewards, and was able to produce a more varied landscape for their trained bot. User 5 had an extremely different policy landscape to the other users due to only manual rewards being used, and they were the most successful in creating a bot that they wanted in accordance to their feedback. These results imply that the automatic training reward feature is too forceful for allowing full customisation for user guided training.

6   Conclusion

This paper has clearly shown that interactive training is a viable option for designing bots in an FPS game. All the users, who have experience working on big budget, high quality FPS games, felt that the tool had potential to be used during the development of a FPS game. The secondary aim of this paper was to show that a diverse set of bot types could be trained by different users. The results showed that the bots were all different from each other, and particularly the bot which was trained with manual rewards only was unique from the others and performed well in the game objectives.

A number of improvements have been identified based on the feedback from the users which will make the tool more suitable for commercial FPS game needs. A number of the users made points about the inadequacy of the wander behaviour, and commented on how it is not what bots should be doing, rather they should be moving with intention around the level to known item positions and known pathways. To address this issue bot patrol paths will replace the wander behaviour.

The difference between what the bot knows and what the user knows caused some frustration with one of the users. To address this issue, items and enemies that are visible will be marked so that the user can immediately see what the bot can see. Also the bot's vision will be modified from a distance based system to a line of sight based system to be closer to what a human player could see. Similarly the ranges for the ranged and melee attack behaviours were not obvious. Some of the users failed the melee action many times during training and this could be improved by having clear ranges visible on screen. In addition to this visual feedback, the actions that are not available (i.e. would fail due to parameter constraints) will be disabled on the UI. Further improvements will also be made to allow the designers to hand initialise the policy before training commences.

References

1. Sanchez-Crespo Dalmau, D.: Core Techniques and Algorithms in Game Programming. New Riders, Indianapolis (2003)
2. Isla, D.: Handling Complexity in the Halo 2 AI. In: Proceedings of the Games Developers Conference. International Game Developers Association, San Francisco (2005)
3. Jones, J.: Benefits of Genetic Algorithms in Simulations for Game Designers. School of Informatics. University of Buffalo, Buffalo (2003)
4. Overholtzer, C.A., Levy, S.D.: Adding Smart Opponents to a First-Person Shooter Video Game through Evolutionary Design. In: Artificial Intelligence and Interactive Digital Entertainment. AAAI Press, USA (2005)
5. Petrakis, S., Tefas, A.: Neural Networks Training for Weapon Selection in First-Person Shooter Games. In: Diamantaras, K., Duch, W., Iliadis, L.S. (eds.) ICANN 2010, Part III. LNCS, vol. 6354, pp. 417–422. Springer, Heidelberg (2010)
6. van Hoorn, N., Togelius, J., Schmidhuber, J.: Hierarchical Controller Learning in a First-Person Shooter. In: Computational Intelligence and Games, pp. 294–301. IEEE Press, Milano (2009)
7. Spronck, P.: Adaptive Game AI. Dutch Research School of Information and Knowledge Systems. University of Maastricht, Maastricht (2005)

8. McPartland, M., Gallagher, M.: Reinforcement Learning in First Person Shooter Games. In: Computational Intelligence and AI in Games, pp. 43–56. IEEE Press, Perth (2011)

9. McPartland, M., Gallagher, M.: Interactive Training For First Person Shooter Bots. In: Computational Intelligence in Games. IEEE Press, Granada (2012)

10. First-Person Shooter Games Prove to be Most Popular at MTV Game Awards. Entertainment Close - Up (2011)

11. Geisler, B.: An Empirical Study of Machine Learning Algorithms Applied to Modelling Player Behavior in a First Person Shooter Video Game. University of Wisconsin, Madison (2002)

12. Mora, A.M., Montoya, R., Merelo, J.J., Sánchez, P.G., Castillo, P.Á., Laredo, J.L.J., Martínez, A.I., Espacia, A.: Evolving Bot AI in Unreal^{TM}. In: Di Chio, C., Cagnoni, S., Cotta, C., Ebner, M., Ekárt, A., Esparcia-Alcazar, A.I., Goh, C.-K., Merelo, J.J., Neri, F., Preuß, M., Togelius, J., Yannakakis, G.N. (eds.) EvoApplicatons 2010, Part I. LNCS, vol. 6024, pp. 171–180. Springer, Heidelberg (2010)

13. Cole, N., Louis, S.J., Miles, C.: Using a Genetic Algorithm to Tune First-Person Shooter Bots. In: Congress on Evolutionary Computation, pp. 139–145. IEEE Press, Portland (2004)

14. Sutton, R.S., Barto, A.G.: Reinforcement Learning: An Introduction. MIT Press, Cambridge (1998)

15. Busoniu, L., Babuska, R., De Schutter, B.: A Comprehensive Survey of Multiagent Reinforcement Learning. Systems, Man and Cybernetics Part C: Applications and Reviews, 156–172 (2008)

16. Suh, I.H., Lee, S., Young Kwon, W., Cho, Y.-J.: Learning of Action Patterns and Reactive Behaviour Plans via a Novel Two-Layered Ethology-Based Action Selection Mechanism. In: International Conference on Intelligent Robot and Systems, pp. 1799–1805. IEEE Press, Edmonton (2005)

17. Bradley, J., Hayes, G.: Group Utility Functions: Learning Equilibria Between Groups of Agents in Computer Games By Modifying the Reinforcement Signal. In: Congress on Evolutionary Computation, pp. 1914–1921. IEEE Press, Edinburgh (2005)

18. Nason, S., Laird, J.E.: Soar-RL: Integrating Reinforcement Learning with Soar. Cognitive Systems Research 6(1), 51–59 (2005)

19. Patel, P.G., Carver, N., Rahimi, S.: Tuning Computer Gaming Agents using Q-Learning. In: Computer Science and Information Systems, pp. 581–588. IEEE Press, Szczecin (2011)

20. Blumberg, B., Downie, M., Ivanov, Y.A., Berlin, M., Johnson, M.P., Tomlinson, B.: Integrated Learning for Interactive Synthetic Characters. ACM Transactions on Graphics 21(3), 417–426 (2002)

21. Thomaz, A.L., Breazeal, C.: Reinforcement Learning with Human Teachers: Evidence of Feedback and Guidance with Implications for Learning Performance. In: Proceedings of the 21st National Conference on Artificial Intelligence, pp. 1000–1005. AAAI, USA (2006)

Games with Ambiguous Payoffs and Played by Ambiguity and Regret Minimising Players

Wei Xiong, Xudong Luo*, and Wenjun Ma

Institute of Logic and Cognition, Sun Yat-sen University, Guangzhou, 510275, China

Abstract. In real life games, a player's belief about the consequence of a strategy is often ambiguous due to out-of-control factors in the environment where the games are played. However, existing work cannot handle this situation. To address the issue, we introduce a new kind of games, called ambiguous games, and incorporate human cognitive factors of ambiguity aversion and minimising regret to propose a concept of solution to such a game. Moreover, we also study how ambiguity degrees of belief about payoffs impact the outcomes of a game, and find the condition under which a player should release more or less ambiguous information to his opponents.

1 Introduction

Game theory is a powerful tool for analysing the interactions between decision-makers in many domains, such as voting, biology, economics, management science, and artificial intelligence [5,18]. In game theory, it is assumed that a player's belief about the consequences of a strategy taken is accurate. However, in real world, it is not always the case [2,10]. For example, two competitive cell phone retailers can choose two different brands, which are their pure strategies. In real llife, the payoffs of each retailer are often impacted by some uncontrol and uncertain factors [14], such as buyers' tastes and economical environments, and so it is impossible to assign a precise payoff to a single consequence of a strategy profile. This kind of uncertainty about consequence of a strategy is so called ambiguity. That is, in a game the possible consequence of each strategy profile is in a set, and we do not have a precise probability for each of all possible consequences of a strategy but could have for their subsets [14,22,24].

Although the ambiguity cannot be avoidable in games played in real world, existing work cannot handle properly the situation. In fact, there are mainly two kinds of games (the more detailed discussion can be founded in related the work section). One is based on the assumption that the precise probabilities can be estimated for each single possibility of the consequences of a strategy, including Bayesian games [8] as well as the concepts of trembling hand perfect equilibrium [20] and proper equilibrium [16]. The another is fuzzy game [2,10,12,13], which assumes that the payoffs are fuzzy. However, it is also assumed each possibility of a fuzzy payoff can be estimated accurately.

---

* Corresponding author.

M. Thielscher and D. Zhang (Eds.): AI 2012, LNCS 7691, pp. 409–420, 2012.
© Springer-Verlag Berlin Heidelberg 2012

The aim of this paper is to address the problem. The main tool to handle ambiguity is D-S theory [21]. In [24], based on the theory we construct a decision model, in which we use cognitive factors of ambiguity-avoiding and regret minimising to set a proper preference ordering over strategies with interval-valued expected utilities. In [24], we show that our model can solve classic Ellsberg paradox [4] under ambiguity, and the preference ordering is a pre-order (i.e., complete and transitive). So, it is proper to employ the model for choosing the best response problem of games under ambiguity.

The main contributions of this paper are: (i) we can solve games with ambiguous payoffs; and (ii) we discover the rule of how ambiguity degrees of the players' beliefs about consequences impact the outcome of an ambiguous game.

The remainder of this paper is organized as follows. Section 2 briefs D-S theory and our ambiguity decision model. Section 3 defines static games under ambiguity and introduces the solution concept to the games. Section 4 studies how the ambiguity degrees of belief about possible consequences influence the outcome of an ambiguous game. Section 5 relates our work to others'. Finally, Section 6 concludes the paper and points out the future work.

2   Preliminaries

This section recaps D-S theory [21] and our decision model under ambiguity [24].

2.1   Basics of D-S Theory

Definition 1. *Let Θ be a frame of discernment. (i) Function $m : 2^\Theta \to [0,1]$ is called a basic probability assignment or a mass function over Θ if $m(\emptyset) = 0$ and $\sum_{A \subseteq \Theta} m(A) = 1$. (ii) Let $A \subseteq \Theta$, mass function m is called a simple support function if $m(A) = s$, and $m(\Theta) = 1 - s$; we also say the mass function is focused on A, and s is the focused mass.*

D-S theory is different from probability theory. For example, a student lost his keys. Unfortunately, he has no ideas where he lost exactly, and locations a, b, and c are all possible. In D-S theory, it can be modeled by a mass function: $m(A) = 0$ if $A \neq \Theta$, and $m(\Theta) = 1$, where $\Theta = \{a, b, c\}$. While in probability theory, we have to find a probability function p such that $p(a) = s_1$, $p(b) = s_2$, and $p(c) = s_3$, where $s_1 + s_2 + s_3 = 1$. And this probability function p needs to be justified by lots of evidence. Obviously, this is much harder than the treatment of D-S theory. Another difference between D-S theory and probability theory is that mass function does not have to be additive, while probability one has to. Actually, probability function is a special case of mass function. In fact, if $m(A) > 0$ and $\sum m(A) = 1$, where A is a singleton (i.e., $|A| = 1$), then m is a probability function.

Generally speaking, a mass function represents a piece of ambiguous evidence. Intuitively, the bigger the cardinality of set A the more ambiguous in a simple support function focused on A. The concept of ambiguity degree of a mass function is formally defined as follows [3]:

Definition 2. *Let m be a mass function over Θ and $|A|$ be the cardinality of set A. Then the ambiguity degree of m, denoted as δ_m, is given by*

$$\delta_m = \frac{\sum\limits_{A \subseteq \Theta} m(A) \log_2 |A|}{\log_2 |\Theta|}. \tag{1}$$

For the key missing example that we mentioned above, a mass function can model complete ignorance (absolute ambiguity), i.e., $m(A) = 0$ if $A \neq \Theta$, and $m(\Theta) = 1$. By Definition 2, we have $\delta_m = 1$. On the other side, if we have sufficient evidence to obtain a mass function, denoted as m, such that $m(\{a\}) = s_1$, $m(\{b\}) = s_2$, and $m(\{c\}) = s_3$, where $s_1 + s_2 + s_3 = 1$. In this case, m is a probability function and by formula (1) we have ambiguity degree $\delta_m = 0$.

2.2   The Ambiguity and Regret Aversion Model

Given a decision problem, assume that the decision maker knows the utility of each single consequence, but he is unsure which consequence that an action could cause. In other words, he only knows a mass function over the power set of consequences. Formally, such a problem can be defined as follows [24]:

Definition 3. *A decision problem under uncertainty of ambiguity (or call an ambiguity decision problem) is a 4-tuple of (C, S, U, M), where:*

(i) C is the set of all choices;
(ii) S is the set of all consequences of choices;
(iii) $U = \{u_c \mid c \in C, \forall s \in S, u_c(s) \in \mathbb{R}\}$, i.e., the utility of consequence $s \in S$ that be caused by strategy choice $c \in C$ is $u_c(s) \in \mathbb{R}$ (real number); and
(iv) $M = \{m_c \mid c \in C\}$, i.e., the decision maker's uncertainty about the consequences that strategy choice c could cause is represented by mass function m_c over the discernment frame $\Theta = \{s_1, \ldots, s_n\}$, where $s_1, \ldots, s_n \in S$.

Based on the concept of mass function, the point-valued expected utility formula can be extended to the expected utility interval [23]:

Definition 4. *Given ambiguity decision problem (C, S, U, M), for choice c that is specified by mass function m_c over Θ, its expected utility interval is $EUI(c) = [\underline{U}(c), \overline{U}(c)]$, where:*

$$\underline{U}(c) = \sum_{A \subseteq \Theta} m_c(A) \min\{u_c(s) \mid s \in A\}, \tag{2}$$

$$\overline{U}(c) = \sum_{A \subseteq \Theta} m_c(A) \max\{u_c(s) \mid s \in A\}. \tag{3}$$

Let $EUI(c_1) = [\underline{U}(c_1), \overline{U}(c_1)]$ and $EUI(c_2) = [\underline{U}(c_2), \overline{U}(c_2)]$ be the expected utility intervals, then according to [13],

$$EUI(c_1) + EUI(c_2) = [\underline{U}(c_1) + \underline{U}(c_1), \overline{U}(c_1) + \overline{U}(c_2)]. \tag{4}$$

Then, how to make a choice with interval-valued expected utility? We have the following [24]:

Definition 5. *Let $EUI(x) = [\underline{U}(x), \overline{U}(x)]$ be the expected utility interval of choice $x \in \{c_1, c_2\}$, and $\delta_{m'}$ be the ambiguity degree of mass function m' corresponding to c_2. Then the ambiguity-avoiding maximum regret of choice c_1 against choice c_2 is*

$$\Re^{c_2}_{c_1} = \overline{\varepsilon}(c_2) - \underline{U}(c_1), \tag{5}$$

where

$$\overline{\varepsilon}(c_2) = \underline{U}(c_2) + (1 - \delta_{m'})(\overline{U}(c_2) - \underline{U}(c_2)), \tag{6}$$

called the ambiguity-discounted upper bound of the expected utility of choice a'. The preference ordering $\succeq$ over choices is defined as follow:

$$c_1 \succeq c_2 \Leftrightarrow \Re^{c_2}_{c_1} \leq \Re^{c_1}_{c_2}. \tag{7}$$

By Definition 5, we have

$$c_1 \succeq c_2 \Leftrightarrow \overline{\varepsilon}(c_2) - \underline{U}(c_1) \leq \overline{\varepsilon}(c_1) - \underline{U}(c_2) \Leftrightarrow \underline{U}(c_1) + \overline{\varepsilon}(c_1) \geq \underline{U}(c_2) + \overline{\varepsilon}(c_2). \tag{8}$$

3   Game Definition

This section will define the ambiguous game and its solution concept.

Definition 6. *An ambiguous game G is a 5-tuple of (N, S, Θ, M, U), where:*

(i) N is a set of natural numbers, to denote the set of players of the game;
(ii) $S = \{S_i\}_{i \in N}$, where S_i is the finite set of all pure strategies of player i;
(iii) Θ is the set of all possible consequences for all strategy profiles.
(iv) $M = \{M_i\}_{i \in N}$, where $M_i = \{m_{i,j} \mid \forall \rho_j \in \times_{k \in N} S_k, m_{i,j}(B_{i,j}) = \xi, m_{i,j}(\Theta) = 1 - \xi, B_{i,j} \subset \Theta\}$;
(v) $U = \{u_i\}_{i \in N}$, where u_i is the payoff function from the set of consequences to the set of real numbers.

In the above definition, item (iv) means that for a pure-strategy profile each player has *a simple support function* over the power set of the consequence set.

Given an ambiguous game, suppose each player calculates the expected payoff interval of a pure-strategy profile by formulas (2) and (3). Then we can transfer it to a normal static game in classic game theory [5,17]. In particular, we have the following theorem, which provides the way to calculate the sum, denoted as $\Xi_i(\rho_j)$, of the lower and ambiguity-discounted upper expected payoffs (see Definition 5) to any pure-strategy profile ρ_j for a specific ambiguous game.

Theorem 1. *Given game (N, S, Θ, M, U), suppose for any pure-strategy profile ρ_j, $m_{i,j}(B_{i,j}) = \xi_{i,j}$, and $m_{i,j}(\Theta) = 1 - \xi_{i,j}$, $B_{i,j} \subset \Theta$, $j = 1, 2, \ldots, n$ ($n = |\times_{k \in N} S_k|$). Let $t_{i,j} = \min\{u_i(s_i), \ldots, u_i(s_j)\}$, $T_{i,j} = \max\{u_i(s_i), \ldots, u_i(s_j)\}$, $s_i, \ldots, s_j \in B_{i,j}$, $y = \min\{u_i(s_1), \ldots, u_i(s_n)\}$, and $Y = \max\{u_i(s_1), \ldots, u_i(s_n)\}$, $s_1, \ldots, s_n \in \Theta$. Then*

$$\Xi_i(\rho_j) = \underline{U}_i(\rho_j) + \overline{\varepsilon}_i(\rho_j), \tag{9}$$

where

$$\underline{U}_i(\rho_j) = \xi_{i,j}t_{i,j} + (1 - \xi_{i,j})y, \tag{10}$$

$$\overline{\varepsilon}_i(\rho_j) = \xi_{i,j}t_{i,j} + (1 - \xi_{i,j})y + \xi_{i,j}(1 - log_{|\Theta|}|B_{i,j}|)((T_{i,j} - t_{i,j})\xi_{i,j} + (1 - \xi_{i,j})(Y - y)). \tag{11}$$

Proof. Since player i has simple support function $m_{i,j}$, by formulas (2) and (3), for player i the lower and upper expected payoffs of profile ρ_j to mass function $m_{i,j}$ are as follows:

$$\underline{U}_i(\rho_j) = \xi_{i,j}t_{i,j} + (1 - \xi_{i,j})y, \quad \overline{U}_i(\rho_j) = \xi_{i,j}T_{i,j} + (1 - \xi_{i,j})Y.$$

By formula (1), discounting factor $\delta_{i,j}$ to the upper expected payoff of profile ρ_j is

$$\delta_{i,j} = \frac{\xi_{i,j}log_2|B_{i,j}| + (1 - \xi_{i,j})log_2|\Theta|}{log_2|\Theta|}.$$

Thus, by formula (6), we can obtain the ambiguity-discounted upper expected payoff of profile ρ_j for player i as formula (11). Then, the expected payoff interval of profile ρ_j is $[\underline{U}_i(\rho_j), \overline{\varepsilon}_i(\rho_j)]$. So, we have $\varXi_i(\rho_j) = \underline{U}_i(\rho_j) + \overline{\varepsilon}_i(\rho_j)$.   □

Theorem 1 shows that a point-valued $\varXi_i(\rho_j)$ can be derived given any pure-strategy profile ρ_j by formula (9). So, we can obtain a normal game matrix with precise numbers. That is, we can obtain a traditional static game [5,17].

Definition 7. *Given ambiguous game $G = (N, S, \Theta, M, U)$, a static game, denoted by $G' = (N, S, U')$, is called an induced game of G if the element of its payoff matrix is obtained by using formula (9) from game G.*

A mixed strategy α_i for player i is a probability distribution over set S_i. Let $\varXi_i(\alpha_i, \alpha_{-i})$ be the sum of the lower expected payoff and ambiguity-discounted upper expected payoff to mixed-strategy profile $\alpha = (\alpha_i, \alpha_{-i})$.

Given an ambiguous game, the following lemma provides the way to calculate the sum of the lower and ambiguity-discounted upper expected payoffs to any mixed-strategy profile of α.

Lemma 1. *Given game (N, S, Θ, M, U) and its mixed-strategy profile α, suppose for any pure-strategy profile ρ_j, $m_{i,j}(B_{i,j}) = \xi_{i,j}$, and $m_{i,j}(\Theta) = 1 - \xi_{i,j}$, $B_{i,j} \subset \Theta$, $j = 1, 2, \ldots, n$ $(n = | \times_{k \in N} S_k|)$. Let $t_{i,j} = \min\{u_i(s_i), \ldots, u_i(s_j)\}$, $T_{i,j} = \max\{u_i(s_i), \ldots, u_i(s_j)\}$, $s_i, \ldots, s_j \in B_{i,j}$, $y = \min\{u_i(s_1), \ldots, u_i(s_n)\}$, and $Y = \max\{u_i(s_1), \ldots, u_i(s_n)\}$, $s_1, \ldots, s_n \in \Theta$. Then*

$$\varXi_i(\alpha) = \sum_j \left(\prod_i \alpha_i(\rho_j) \right) \varphi(\xi_{i,j}), \tag{12}$$

where

$$\varphi(\xi_{i,j}) = 2\xi_{i,j}t_{i,j} + 2(1 - \xi_{i,j})y + \xi_{i,j}(1 - log_{|\Theta|}|B_{i,j}|)((T_{i,j} - t_{i,j})\xi_{i,j} + (1 - \xi_{i,j})(Y - y)). \tag{13}$$

Proof. By Theorem 1, the expected payoff interval of profile ρ_j is $[\underline{U}_i(\rho_j), \overline{\varepsilon}_i(\rho_j)]$. So, by formula (4), we have

$$\Xi_i(\alpha) = \sum_j \left(\prod_i \alpha_i(\rho_j) \right) (\underline{U}_i(\rho_j) + \overline{\varepsilon}_i(\rho_j)) = \sum_j \left(\prod_i \alpha_i(\rho_j) \right) \varphi(\xi_{i,j}),$$

where $\varphi(\xi_{i,j})$ is given by (13). □

Definition 8. *Mixed-strategy profile α^* in game $G = (N, S, \Theta, M, U)$ is an ambiguous equilibrium of mixed strategy if $\forall i \in N$, for every mixed-strategy α_i of player i, $\Xi_i(\alpha_i^*, \alpha_{-i}^*) \geq \Xi_i(\alpha_i, \alpha_{-i}^*)$, where $(\alpha_i^*, \alpha_{-i}^*) = \alpha^*$.*

Given game $G = (N, S, \Theta, M, U)$, suppose $G' = (N, S, U')$ is its induced game. By Definitions 7 and 8, we have $E_i(\alpha_i^*, \alpha_{-i}^*) \geq E_i(\alpha_i, \alpha_{-i}^*) \Leftrightarrow \Xi_i(\alpha_i^*, \alpha_{-i}^*) \geq \Xi_i(\alpha_i, \alpha_{-i}^*)$. So, mixed-strategy profile α^* is an ambiguous equilibrium of G if and only if it is a mixed-strategy Nash equilibrium of G'. However, it should be noted that our model does not assume that we could have that all the payoffs are precise under ambiguity, and the point-valued payoffs in the induced game in our model is calculated from an interval that carries the factor of ambiguity.

In the following, we will give an example to illustrate our model. Suppose two competitive retailers 1 and 2 sell cell phones and can choose two different brands, C and D, which are their pure strategies. Since buyers' tastes, economical environments, and other factors are often uncertain and out of sellers' control, sellers' belief about the consequences of their choices are ambiguous. For example, they can only know that the possible consequence of each pure-strategy profile is: bad sales and high costs (s_1), bad sales and low costs (s_2), good sales and high costs (s_3), or good sales and low costs (s_4). Then, what is the outcome of this game?

Then this game can be modeled as $G = (N, S, \Theta, M, U)$, where $N = \{1, 2\}$, $S = \{S_1, S_2\}$, $S_1 = S_2 = \{C, D\}$, $\Theta = \{s_1, s_2, s_3, s_4\}$ and $u_1(s_i) = u_2(s_i) = i$ ($i = 1, 2, 3, 4$). Since the players are ambiguous about the payoffs of pure-strategy profiles, for retailer 1, with respect to four pure-strategy profiles $\rho_1, \ldots, \rho_4$, suppose there are four simple support functions over Θ,[1] respectively, as follows:

$$\rho_1 = (C, C) : m_{1,1}(B_{1,1}) = m_{1,1}(\{s_4\}) = 0.7, \ m_{1,1}(\Theta) = 0.3;$$
$$\rho_2 = (C, D) : m_{1,2}(B_{1,2}) = m_{1,2}(\{s_1\}) = 0.6, \ m_{1,2}(\Theta) = 0.4;$$
$$\rho_3 = (D, C) : m_{1,3}(B_{1,3}) = m_{1,3}(\{s_1\}) = 0.5, \ m_{1,3}(\Theta) = 0.5;$$
$$\rho_4 = (D, D) : m_{1,4}(B_{1,4}) = m_{1,4}(\{s_2\}) = 0.6, \ m_{1,4}(\Theta) = 0.4.$$

Similarly, for retailer 2, with respect to four pure-strategy profiles, suppose there are four simple support functions over Θ, respectively, as follows:

$$\rho_1 = (C, C) : m_{2,1}(B_{2,1}) = m_{2,1}(\{s_1\}) = 0.8, \ m_{2,1}(\Theta) = 0.2;$$

---

[1] The mass function of $m_{1,1}(B_{1,1}) = 0.7$ and $m_{1,1}(\Theta) = 0.3$ implies $Bel(B_{1,1}) = 0.7$ and $Pl(B_{1,1}) = 1$ according to [21]. In other words, since $Bel(B_{1,1}) \leq P(B_{1,1}) \leq Pl(B_{1,1}) = 1$, actually the mass function means that we can only estimate the lower bound probability of $B_{1,1}$ (a kind of imprecise probability). Similarly, we can understand other similar mass functions in this paper.

$$\rho_2 = (C,D) : m_{2,2}(B_{2,2}) = m_{2,2}(\{s_2\}) = 0.6, \ m_{2,2}(\Theta) = 0.4;$$
$$\rho_3 = (D,C) : m_{2,3}(B_{2,3}) = m_{2,3}(\{s_3\}) = 0.8, \ m_{2,3}(\Theta) = 0.2;$$
$$\rho_4 = (D,D) : m_{2,4}(B_{2,4}) = m_{2,4}(\{s_1\}) = 0.5, \ m_{2,4}(\Theta) = 0.5.$$

Let $((p, 1-p), (q, 1-q))$ be a mixed-strategy profile. By formula (12), we have

$$\Xi_1 = 3.1pq + 3.73pq + p(1-q) + 1.72p(1-q) + q(1-p)$$
$$+ 1.75q(1-p) + 1.6(1-p)(1-q) + 2.32(1-p)(1-q); \quad (14)$$
$$\Xi_2 = pq + 1.48pq + 1.6p(1-q) + 2.32p(1-q) + 2.60q(1-p)$$
$$+ 3.08q(1-p) + (1-p)(1-q) + 1.75(1-p)(1-q). \quad (15)$$

Thus, we have $\frac{\partial \Xi_1}{\partial p} = 5.28q - 1.2$ and $\frac{\partial \Xi_2}{\partial q} = 2.93 - 4.37p$. Let $\frac{\partial \Xi_1}{\partial p} = 0$ and $\frac{\partial \Xi_2}{\partial q} = 0$, then we obtain $p = 0.6705$ and $q = 0.2273$. Thus, $\alpha^* = ((0.6705, 0.3295), (0.2273, 0.7727))$ is the ambiguous equilibrium of mixed strategy of the game. And at this equilibrium point, by formulas (14) and (15) we can obtain $\Xi_1(\alpha^*) = 3.6541$ and $\Xi_2(\alpha^*) = 3.5345$.

4   Properties

In above example, each focused mass $\xi_{i,j}$ is a constant. This section will discuss what if the focused masses are variables. Then we study how the ambiguity degrees in beliefs about possible consequences affect the outcome of an ambiguous game.

The following theorem studies the monotonicity of function $\Xi_i(\xi_{i,1}, \ldots, \xi_{i,m})$, and finds the maximum value of this function.

Theorem 2. *Given game* (N, S, Θ, M, U), *suppose* α *is a mixed-strategy profile, and* $m_{i,j}(B_{i,j}) = \xi_{i,j}$, *and* $m_{i,j}(\Theta) = 1 - \xi_{i,j}$, $B_{i,j} \subset \Theta$, $j = 1, 2, \ldots, n$ ($n = | \times_{k \in N} S_k |$). *Let* $t_{i,j} = \min\{u_i(s_i), \ldots, u_i(s_j)\}$, $T_{i,j} = \max\{u_i(s_i), \ldots, u_i(s_j)\}$, $s_i, \ldots, s_j \in B_{i,j}$, $y = \min\{u_i(s_1), \ldots, u_i(s_n)\}$, $Y = \max\{u_i(s_1), \ldots, u_i(s_n)\}$, $s_1, \ldots, s_n \in \Theta$, *and*

$$a_{i,j} = \frac{2t_{i,j} - 2y + (1 - log_{|\Theta|}|B_{i,j}|)(Y - y)}{2(1 - log_{|\Theta|}|B_{i,j}|)(Y - y - T_{i,j} + t_{i,j})}.$$

Then player i *has the maximum value of* $\Xi_i(\xi_{i,1}, \ldots, \xi_{i,m})$ *at* $(\hat{\xi}_{i,1}, \ldots, \hat{\xi}_{i,m})$, *where*

$$\hat{\xi}_{i,j} = \begin{cases} a_{i,j} & \text{if } a_{i,j} < 1, \\ 1 & \text{if } a_{i,j} \geq 1. \end{cases}$$

Proof. Let focused masses $\xi_{i,1}, \ldots, \xi_{i,m}$ be variables in the assumption of Lemma 1. Then for any mixed-strategy profile α, by formula (12) we have

$$\frac{\partial \Xi_i}{\partial \xi_{i,j}} = \sum_j \left(\prod_i \alpha_i(\rho_j) \right) \frac{d\varphi}{d\xi_{i,j}}, \quad (16)$$

where

$$\frac{d\varphi}{d\xi_{i,j}} = 2t_{i,j} - 2y + 2\xi_{i,j}(1 - log_{|\Theta|}|B_{i,j}|)((T_{i,j} - t_{i,j} - Y + y) + (1 - log_{|\Theta|}|B_{i,j}|)(Y - y)).$$

Let $\frac{\partial \Xi_i}{\partial \xi_{i,j}} = 0$, by formula (16), $\frac{d\varphi}{d\xi_{i,j}} = 0$. Then we have $\xi_{i,j} = \hat{\xi}_{i,j} = a_{i,j}$.
Since $B_{i,j} \subset \Theta$, we have $y \le t_{i,j} \le T_{i,j} < Y$ and $1 \le |B_{i,j}| < |\Theta|$. Thus,
$0 < 1 - log_{|\Theta|}|B_{i,j}| \le 1$. So, $\hat{\xi}_{i,j} > 0$, and by the definition of mass function, $\hat{\xi}_{i,j}$
should be in $(0, 1]$. For any $\hat{\xi}_{i,j}$, if $0 < \hat{\xi}_{i,j} < 1$, then $(\hat{\xi}_{i,1}, \ldots, \hat{\xi}_{i,m})$ is a critical
point.

Further, we have

$$\frac{\partial^2 \Xi_i}{\partial^2 \xi_{i,j}}(\hat{\xi}_{i,1}, \ldots, \hat{\xi}_{i,m}) = 2(1 - log_{|\Theta|}|B_{i,j}|)(T_{i,j} - t_{i,j} - Y + y),$$

$$\frac{\partial^2 \Xi_i}{\partial \xi_{i,j} \partial \xi_{i,k}}(\hat{\xi}_{i,1}, \ldots, \hat{\xi}_{i,m}) = 0, j \ne k.$$

Let $r_{i,j} = 2(1 - log_{|\Theta|}|B_{i,j}|)(T_{i,j} - t_{i,j} - Y + y) < 0$. So, the Hessian of function Ξ_i
at the critical point, the matrix formed from the second-order partial derivatives
of the function [25], is a diagonal matrix as follows:

$$A_m = \begin{pmatrix} 2r_{i,1} & 0 & \cdots & 0 \\ 0 & 2r_{i,2} & 0 & 0 \\ \vdots & \vdots & \ddots & \vdots \\ 0 & 0 & \cdots & 2r_{i,m} \end{pmatrix}.$$

Since for any $r_{i,j}$, $2r_{i,j} < 0$, the characteristic value of A_m is negative, which
means A_m is negative definitely. Consequently, player i has an extremum of
$\Xi_i(\xi_{i,1}, \ldots, \xi_{i,m})$ at the critical point.

For any $\tilde{\xi}_{i,j}$, if $0 \le \tilde{\xi}_{i,j} < \hat{\xi}_{i,j}$, since Ξ_i is differentiable at point $(\tilde{\xi}_{i,1}, \ldots, \tilde{\xi}_{i,m})$,
we have

$$\frac{\partial \Xi_i}{\partial v}(\tilde{\xi}_{i,1}, \ldots, \tilde{\xi}_{i,m}) = \sum_j \frac{\partial \Xi_i}{\partial \tilde{\xi}_{i,j}} \cos \beta_{i,j},$$

where $v = (v_{i,1}, \ldots, v_{i,m})$ is a direction, $v_{i,j} = \cos \beta_{i,j}$ is the angle between v
and the positive direction of coordinate $\xi_{i,j}$ in a Cartesian coordinate system,
and $\frac{\partial \Xi_i}{\partial v}$ is the directional derivative in direction v. So, we have

$$\frac{\partial \Xi_i}{\partial v}(\tilde{\xi}_{i,1}, \ldots, \tilde{\xi}_{i,m}) = \sum_j \left(\prod_i \alpha_i(\rho_j) \right) \varphi'(\tilde{\xi}_{i,j}) \cos \beta_{i,j}$$

$$> \sum_j \left(\prod_i \alpha_i(\rho_j) \right) \varphi'(\hat{\xi}_{i,j}) \cos \beta_{i,j} = 0.$$

Similarly, for any $\tilde{\xi}_{i,j}$, if $\hat{\xi}_{i,j} \le \tilde{\xi}_{i,j} \le 1$, then we have $\frac{\partial \Xi_i}{\partial v}(\tilde{\xi}_{i,1}, \ldots, \tilde{\xi}_{i,m}) < 0$.
Thus, function $\Xi_i(\tilde{\xi}_{i,1}, \ldots, \tilde{\xi}_{i,m})$ is strictly increasing on the any direction v if

$\tilde{\xi}_{i,j} \in [0, \hat{\xi}_{i,j})$, and is strictly decreasing on the any direction v if $\tilde{\xi}_{i,j} \in [\hat{\xi}_{i,j}, 1]$. Hence, for any $a_{i,j}$, $a_{i,j} < 1$, player i has the maximum value of $\Xi_i(\xi_{i,1}, \ldots, \xi_{i,m})$ at point $(\hat{\xi}_{i,1}, \ldots, \hat{\xi}_{i,m})$, i.e., $(a_{i,1}, \ldots, a_{i,m})$.

If $\hat{\xi}_{i,j} \geq 1$, as shown as above, function Ξ_i is strictly increasing on the any direction if $\tilde{\xi}_{i,j} \in [0, \hat{\xi}_{i,j})$, and so the function is also strictly increasing on $\hat{\xi}_{i,j} \in [0, 1]$. Hence, the function has the maximum value at point $(\hat{\xi}_{i,1}, \ldots, \hat{\xi}_{i,m})$, where $\hat{\xi}_{i,j} = a_{i,j}$ if $a_{i,j} < 1$, or $\hat{\xi}_{i,j} = 1$ if $a_{i,j} \geq 1$.   □

If function Ξ is a univariate function, then we can derive the following corollary by Theorem 2.

Corollary 1. *Under the assumption of Theorem 2, let $\xi_{i,j}$ be a variable, and any $\xi_{i,k}$ $(j \neq k)$ a constant. Then,*

(i) Player i has the maximum value of Ξ_i under the following condition:

$$\xi_{i,j} = \begin{cases} \hat{\xi}_{i,j} = \frac{2t_{i,j} - 2y + (1 - log_{|\Theta|}|B_{i,j}|)(Y-y)}{2(1 - log_{|\Theta|}|B_{i,j}|)(Y - y - T_{i,j} + t_{i,j})} & \text{if } \hat{\xi}_{i,j} < 1, \\ 1 & \text{if } \hat{\xi}_{i,j} \geq 1. \end{cases}$$

(ii) If $B_{i,j} = \{b_{i,j}\}$ $(b_{i,j} \in \Theta)$, then player i has the maximum value of Ξ_i under the following condition:

$$\xi_{i,j} = \begin{cases} \hat{\xi}_{i,j} = \frac{2u_i(b_{i,j}) + Y - 3y}{2(Y - y)} \geq \frac{1}{2} & \text{if } u_i(b_{i,j}) < \frac{Y+y}{2}, \\ 1 & \text{if } u_i(b_{i,j}) \geq \frac{Y+y}{2}. \end{cases}$$

Proof. Item (i) of this corollary can be derived by Theorem 2 directly. Now we check item (ii) of the corollary. Since $|\{b_{i,j}\}| = 1$, we have $log_{|\Theta|}|B_{i,j}| = 0$ and $t_{i,j} = T_{i,j} = u_i(b_{i,j})$. So, we have

$$\hat{\xi}_{i,j} = \frac{2t_{i,j} - 2y + (1 - log_{|\Theta|}|B_{i,j}|)(Y - y)}{2(1 - log_{|\Theta|}|B_{i,j}|)(Y - y - T_{i,j} + t_{i,j})} = \frac{2u_i(b_{i,j}) + Y - 3y}{2(Y - y)}.$$

Since $u_i(b_{i,j}) \geq y$, we have $2u_i(b_{i,j}) + Y - 3y \geq Y - y$. Thus, $\hat{\xi}_{i,j} \geq \frac{1}{2}$. If $\hat{\xi}_{i,j} < 1$, that is, $\frac{Y+y}{2} > u_i(b_{i,j})$. In this case, by the first part of this corollary, Ξ_i has the maximum at point $\hat{\xi}_{i,j} \in [\frac{1}{2}, 1)$. If $\hat{\xi}_{i,j} \geq 1$, that is, $\frac{Y+y}{2} \leq u_i(b_{i,j})$. So, Ξ_i has the maximum at point $\hat{\xi}_{i,j} = 1$.   □

Corollary 1 explores the maximum of function Ξ_i in the case of if focused mass $\xi_{i,j}$ is the only one variable. In particular, item (ii) of Corollary 1 shows that for any player i if $u_i(b_{i,j}) \geq \frac{Y+y}{2}$, the bigger the focused mass $\xi_{i,j}$ the bigger the sum of the lower and ambiguity-discounted upper payoffs. So, the less ambiguity degree the better for player i. In this case, function Ξ_i has a maximum if $\xi_{i,j} = 1$ (the degree of ambiguity is zero). If $u_i(b_{i,j}) < \frac{Y+y}{2}$, Ξ_i is strictly increasing when $\xi_{i,j}$ is in $[0, \hat{\xi}_{i,j}]$, and is strictly decreasing when $\xi_{i,j}$ is in $(\hat{\xi}_{i,j}, 1]$. That is, if ξ is in $[0, \hat{\xi}_{i,j}]$, the bigger ambiguity degree the better for player i; if $\xi_{i,j}$ is in $(\hat{\xi}_{i,j}, 1]$, the smaller ambiguity degree the better for player i.

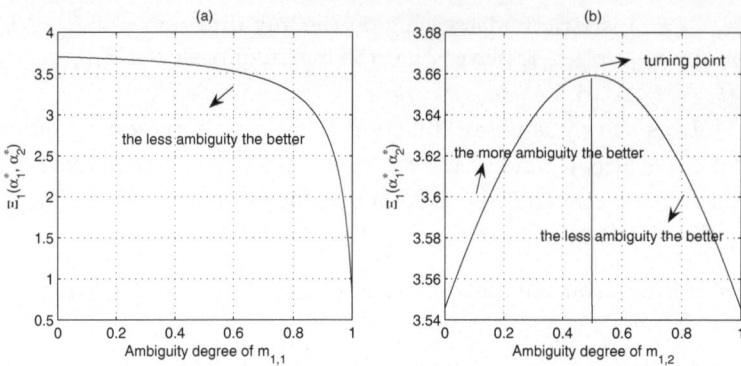

Fig. 1. Ambiguity degree and Sum of Interval

The concept of equilibrium is one of the most important concepts in game theory. Since Theorem 2 and its corollary hold for any mixed-strategy profile, they hold also for the ambiguous equilibrium profile of mixed strategy particularly.

Now we return to that selling cell-phone example. For mass function $m_{1,1}$, let $m_{1,1}(\{b_{1,1}\}) = m_{1,1}(\{s_4\}) = \xi$, where ξ be a variable (by formula (1), the ambiguity degree of function $m_{1,1}$, $\delta_{m_{1,1}} = 1 - \xi$), and other focused masses remain as the forenamed. Then similarly we can obtain the ambiguous equilibrium of mixed strategy α^* and $\Xi_1(\alpha^*)$. The latter is a function of variable ξ. Noting $u_1(s_i) = i$, $y = \min\{u_1(s_1), \ldots, u_1(s_4)\} = 1$, and $Y = \max\{u_1(s_1), \ldots, u_1(s_4)\} = 4$, and thus we have $\frac{Y+y}{2} = 2.5$. So, $u_1(b_{1,1}) = u_1(s_4) = 4 > \frac{Y+y}{2}$, by Corollary 1, retailer 1 has the maximum value of Ξ_1 at point $\xi = 1$ $(\delta_{m_{1,1}} = 0)$. Fig. 1(a) shows that relation between the ambiguity degree of $m_{1,1}$ and $\Xi_1(\alpha^*)$. Again, let $m_{1,2}(\{b_{1,2}\}) = m_{1,1}(\{s_1\}) = \xi'$, where ξ' is a variable, then $u_1(b_{1,2}) = u_1(s_1) < \frac{Y+y}{2}$. By Corollary 1, retailer 1 has the maximum value of Ξ_1 at point $\xi' = \frac{2u_1(b_{1,2})+Y-3y}{2(Y-y)} = \frac{2\times1+4-3\times1}{2(4-1)} = 0.5$ (by formula (1), $\delta_{m_{1,2}} = 0.5$). Fig. 1(b) shows that relation between the ambiguity degree of $m_{1,2}$ and $\Xi_1(\alpha^*)$. The calculation and Fig. 1 illustrate under which condition the smaller degree of ambiguity the better for a player, and under which condition it is *not*.

5   Related Work

Harsanyi [8] is the first person who studied games played under uncertainty. He defined Bayesian games, which are played by different types of players with a probability distribution over the type set. Using expected utility method, a Bayesian game can be solved by the idea of Nash equilibrium. Clearly, it assumes that precise probabilities are available and a strategy taking is accurate. However, in real world, it is not always the case [11,21,22]. This problem does not exist in our model.

To handle uncertainty of strategy taking in games, the concepts of trembling hand perfect equilibrium [20] and proper equilibrium [16] are also introduced. Unfortunately, these two concepts also assume the probability of taking each single strategy can be accurately estimated. And the main concern of the two concepts is the probability of strategy mistaking. This is not our concern. Ours is the uncertainty about the consequences of strategies. A stochastic game [15] is a dynamic game with probabilistic transitions, which also assumes the probabilities of the moves to a new random state are precise. Similarly, in [6], the uncertainty on the consequences of strategy is dealt with. However, these are just precise probabilities of each single consequence, and no ambiguity is involved like we did in this paper.

Currently, fuzzy games are analysed [2,10,12,13]. In these games, the fuzziness is mainly concerned with fuzzy payoffs. However, its meaning is different from that of ambiguity. In fact, for each possibility of a fuzzy payoff, it is assigned an accurate value in $[0, 1]$, indicating how possible it is in the fuzzy payoff set. While the meaning of ambiguity is that we are uncertain about the probability of each possibility, but we know probabilities of some subsets of possibilities [22]. So, fuzzy games cannot deal with the ambiguity that we did in this paper.

Choquet expected utility theory is another kind of a non-expected utility theory. In [1,9,19], the expected payoff of a strategy is calculated by the Choquet expected utility theory, and some solution concepts of games are discussed. More recently, Halpern [7] studied strategic games with a new decision rule of iterated regret minimization to reflect how people actually play games with regret attitude. However, these two kinds of work still assume that the consequences in a game are sure, but we relax the assumption.

6   Conclusion

This paper provides a model of static games played by players with ambiguous beliefs about consequences of their strategies. To solve this kind of games, we introduce a new solution concept. Moreover, we reveal how ambiguity degrees of players' belief about consequences impact the outcomes of a game. We find a turning point that the smaller or bigger degree of ambiguity the better for a player. In the future, it is interesting to extend our theory to extensive games.

Acknowledgements. This paper is supported by National Fund of Philosophy and Social Science (No. 11BZX060), Office of Philosophy and Social Science of Guangdong Province of China (No. 08YC-02), Fundamental Research Funds for the Central Universities in China, Bairen plan of Sun Yat-sen University, National Natural Science Foundation of China (No. 61173019), and major projects of the Ministry of Education (No. 10JZD0006).

References

1. Bade, S.: Electoral Competition with Uncertainty Averse Parties. Games and Economic Behavior 72(1), 12–29 (2011)
2. Clemente, M., Fernandez, F.R., Puerto, J.: Pareto-Optimal Security Strategies in Matrix Games with Fuzzy Payoffs. Fuzzy Sets and Systems 176(1), 36–45 (2011)

3. Dubois, D., Prade, H.: A Note on Measures of Specificity for Fuzzy Sets. International Journal of General Systems 10(4), 279–283 (1985)
4. Ellsberg, D.: Risk, Ambiguous, and the Savage Axioms. Quarterly Journal of Economics 75(4), 643–669 (1961)
5. Gintis, H.: The Bounds of Reason: Game Theory and the Unification of the Behavioral Sciences. Princeton University Press, Princeton (2009)
6. Gurnani, H., Shi, M.: A Bargaining Model for a First-Time Interaction under Asymmetric Beliefs of Supply Reliability. Management Science 56(2), 865–880 (2006)
7. Halpern, J.Y., Pass, R.: Iterated Regret Minimization: A New Solution Concept. Games and Economic Behavior 74(1), 184–207 (2012)
8. Harsanyi, J.C.: Games with Incomplete Information Played by "Bayesian" Players, Part I. The Basic Model. Management Science 3(14), 159–182 (1967)
9. Kozhan, R.: Non-Additive Anonymous Games. International Journal of Game Theory 40(2), 215–230 (2011)
10. Larbani, M.: Solving Bimatrix Games with Fuzzy Payoffs by Introducing Nature as a Third Player. Fuzzy Sets and Systems 160(5), 657–666 (2009)
11. Levi, I.: Why Indeterminate Probability Is Rational. Journal of Applied Logic 7(4), 364–376 (2009)
12. Li, C., Zhang, Q.: Nash Equilibrium for Fuzzy Non-Cooperative Games. Fuzzy Sets and Systems 176(1), 46–55 (2011)
13. Mallozzi, L., Sclazo, V., Tijs, S.: Fuzzy Interval Cooperative Games. Fuzzy Sets and Systems 165(1), 98–105 (2011)
14. Ma, W., Xiong, W., Luo, X.: A D-S Theory Based AHP Decision Making Approach with Ambiguous Evaluations of Multiple Criteria. In: Anthony, P., Ishizuka, M., Lukose, D. (eds.) PRICAI 2012. LNCS, vol. 7458, pp. 297–311. Springer, Heidelberg (2012)
15. Mertens, J.F., Neyman, A.: Stochastic Games. International Journal of Game Theory 10(2), 53–66 (1981)
16. Myerson, R.B.: Refinements of the Nash Equilibrium Concept. International Journal of Game Theory 15(2), 133–154 (1978)
17. Nash, J.: Non-Cooperative Games. The Annals of Mathematics 54(2), 286–295 (1951)
18. Rahwan, T., Michalak, T., Wooldridge, M., Jennings, N.R.: Anytime Coalition Structure Generation in Multi-Agent Systems with Positive or Negative Externalities. Artificial Intelligence 186, 95–122 (2012)
19. Rothe, J.: Uncertainty Aversion and Equilibrium in Normal Form Games (2010), http://eprints.lse.ac.uk/37542/1/Uncertainty_aversion_and_equilibrium_in_normal_form_games(lsero).pdf
20. Selten, R.: A Reexamination of the Perfectness Concept for Equilibrium Points in Extensive Games. International Journal of Game Theory 4(1), 25–55 (1975)
21. Shafer, G.: A Mathematical Theory of Evidence. Princeton University Press, Princeton (1976)
22. Snow, A.: Amgibuity and the Value of Information. Journal of Risk and Uncertainty 40(2), 133–145 (2010)
23. Strat, T.M.: Decision Analysis Using Belief Functions. International Journal of Approximate Reasoning 4(5-6), 391–418 (1990)
24. Xiong, W., Luo, X., Ma, W.: An Expected Utility Interval Theory for Decision-Making under Uncertainty of Ambiguity: To Avoid Ambiguity and Minimise Regret. Fuzzy Sets and Systems. Technique Report, Institute of Logic and Cognition, Sun Yatsen Univerisity (submitted 2012)
25. Zorich, V.A.: Mathematical Analysis I. Springer, Heidelberg (2004)

Query Expansion Powered
by Wikipedia Hyperlinks

Carson Bruce, Xiaoying Gao, Peter Andreae, and Shahida Jabeen

School of Engineering and Computer Science
Victoria University of Wellington
PO Box 600, Wellington, New Zealand
{brucecars,Xiaoying.Gao,Peter.Andreae,shahidarao}@ecs.vuw.ac.nz
http://www.victoria.ac.nz/

Abstract. This research introduces a new query expansion method that uses Wikipedia and its hyperlink structure to find related terms for reformulating a query. Queries are first understood better by splitting into query aspects. Further understanding is gained through measuring how well each aspect is represented in the original search results. Poorly represented aspects are found to be an excellent source of query improvement. Our main contribution is the way of using Wikipedia to identify aspects and underrepresented aspects, and to weight the expansion terms. Results have shown that our approach improves the original query and search results, and outperforms two existing query expansion methods.

1   Introduction

Search engines enable us to sift through billions of web pages allowing us to find required information over a manageable list of documents ordered by their relevance to the query. Translation from a search goal to a search query is a difficult task for the user, requiring a specialized understanding of the search engine's mechanism coupled with a strong linguistic proficiency to best express the search goal. Search engines treat a query as a character string to be compared with character strings in the searched document set. This interpretation of a query is limited in light of the original information need of the user, resulting in a semantic gap between the search query and the search goal. Query Expansion (QE) is a solution that addresses this problem. The idea is to reformulate a query by adding new terms to the query so that more relevant documents can be retrieved.

Wikipedia has become the largest and most accessed web-based encyclopedia with 19.8 million articles (3.7 million in the English Wikipedia). Each article contains information relevant to a focused concept. Within each article are hyperlinks, 60 million of them in total, referencing other article concepts to support its own contents. Through these hyperlinks, each Wikipedia article is heavily linked with other articles, resulting in a huge hyperlink structure. These hyperlinks contain useful information in the form of anchor text – the terms or phrases in the article to which hyperlinks are attached. These features make Wikipedia a

M. Thielscher and D. Zhang (Eds.): AI 2012, LNCS 7691, pp. 421–432, 2012.

promising lexical resource for the problem of query expansion. The main focus of our research is to use Wikipedia as a knowledge source for supporting query interpretation and reformulation.

Section 2 of the paper discusses related research on query expansion. Section 3 describes our proposed query expansion approach. Section 4 explains our method of evaluation along with the results and discussion and section 5 summarizes the outcomes of this research, possible limitations and the future work directions.

2   Related Work

Web users that have used a search engine are likely to have been exposed to some form of query expansion system operating at the back end or providing visible suggestions for users to reformulate their queries manually. There is a large set of query expansion solutions summarized through multiple information retrieval surveys [2, 11, 18].

2.1   WordNet and Wikipedia Based Query Expansion

Many query expansion systems [10, 9, 1, 19] utilize WordNet [8], a lexical database for the English language, to find query expansion terms. WordNet resembles a thesaurus, classifying words into sets of cognitive synonyms. This classification can be used to find the synonyms of terms within a query. By using these synonyms to reformulate a query has shown to be effective to improve recall, but sometimes hurt precision.

The works of [15, 12, 16, 22, 1, 9, 19, 10] focus on using Wikipedia as its source for finding and weighing terms. This has values over WordNet and other web source as the Wikipedia source is large, dynamic, clean, objective, and is revolved around articles focused upon single concepts. A single article provides a valuable source of terms so long as the concept expressed in the article holds relevance to the sense of the query. These works concluded that a key to success is to use Wikipedia as a source for selecting articles most closely related to the query.

Koru [15], a knowledge-based web search engine, uses Wikipedia Link based Measure [13] for query expansion. Wikipedia Link-based Measure is a method of measuring semantic relatedness between two words. Suppose each word is linked to a Wikipedia article, it uses the hyperlinks shared between the two Wikipedia articles to find the semantic similarity between the two terms, as shown by the formula below:

$$sr(a,b) = \frac{log(\max(|A|,|B|)) - log(|A \cap B|)}{log(|W|) - log(\min(|A|,|B|))} \tag{1}$$

In the above equation, A and B are the set of articles that link to articles a and b, and W is the entire Wikipedia. Koru's search was based on an interactive query expansion system which identified related Wikipedia topics that users could select after finishing their queries. These selected topics mapped to article concepts are used to identify candidate terms for the expansion. This interactive application is valuable in that it allows direct feedback from the user to be used to disambiguate the query often seen as providing an optimal query expansion solution [18]. Limitations come in the behavior of the users, very rarely taking the effort to provide relevance feedback to the system, preferring to simply reformulate their own queries alone [21, 3].

Our research is a Wikipedia-based approach and we also use Wikipedia Link based Measure [13] in our system. Our system is unique in that it is based on an idea of identifying underrepresented aspect of a query for query extension, which is introduced in our previous research on AbraQ [17, 7]. The rest of this section details AbraQ.

2.2   Aspect-Based Query Expansion: AbraQ

AbraQ [17, 7], is a query expansion system using a unique step named query aspect identification in their solution. This step divides a query into various term combinations that represent individual concepts contained. These combinations are termed Query Aspects. For example, a query "black bear attacks" has two aspects: "black bear" and "attacks". This step creates additional meta-data, providing a greater source of information for the expansion system to understand the query.

The AbraQ system can be divided into three distinct stages. First, the query is split into aspects based on global document analysis. This is done in two steps: subsequences of the query are executed as queries to retrieve their hit counts (total respective document number); the count of the focused aspect is measured relative to the counts of the individual terms of the aspect and the counts of the possible permutations of the aspect.

With the aspects defined, AbraQ looks to identify how well the aspects are represented in the original search results so it is able to identify the most underrepresented aspect. Identifying the underrepresented aspects is done by building and comparing vocabulary models for each of the aspects and for the entire query. The vocabulary is generated from the initial results retrieved by the aspects (for aspect vocabulary) and query (for query vocabulary), counting the frequencies of the terms appearing in the documents. A strong similarity between the query vocabulary and a single aspects vocabulary suggests that the aspect is already well represented in the search results. The focus of the second phase is to find out the biggest difference in vocabulary models for identifying the most underrepresented aspect of the query.

The final step of the AbraQ method is the term selection for query refinement. The vocabulary model of the underrepresented aspect is used as a source of terms to extend the original query. The new query is then re-evaluated to see if the aspect representation is improved. The goal of this step is to generate a query whose aspects are all equally represented.

The AbraQ system uses web documents retrieved through web search engines as its source for aspect identification, vocabulary building, and term weighting functions. This has its limitations as the document results can be noisy, populated with messy spam and advertising advocating individual companies. This research chose to use Wikipedia as a better alternative.

3   Query Expansion Method

This section will first detail our core method (Aspect Representation), and then outline its three variations (Relatedness, TFIDF, Combined).

3.1   Core Method: Aspect Representation

Aspect Representation is our core method further divided into four major steps. Figure 1. explains these four steps along with the supporting measurements used in each of them.

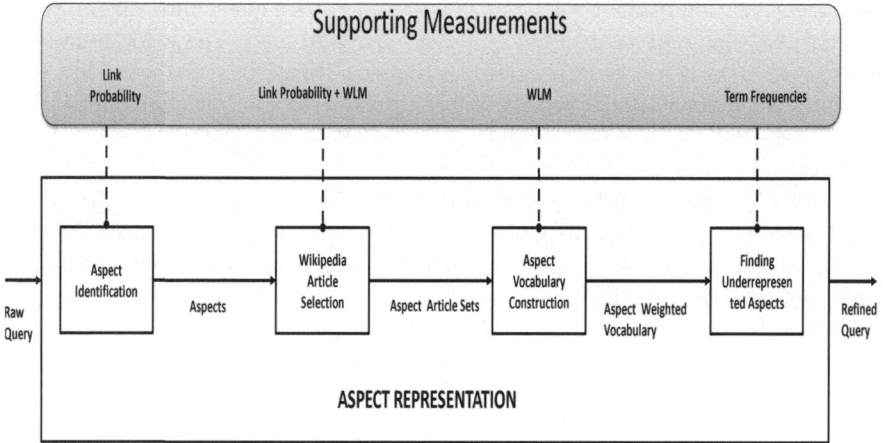

Fig. 1. Overview of Aspect Representation method along with the supporting measurements

An example of the whole QE process taking raw query "Discovery Channel Store" as input and generating reformulated query "Discovery Channel Store History" is shown in the Table 1.

Table 1. Process overview with an example query

Step	Output
1. Query	**"Discovery Channel Store"**
2. Aspect Identification	"Discovery Channel" + "Store"
3. Wikipedia Article Selection	["Discovery Channel", "Store"]
4. Aspect Vocabulary Construction	"history(Discovery Channel)", "shops(Store)"
5. Finding Underrepresented Aspects	0.4(Discovery Channel), 0.6(Store)
6. Query Expansion	**"Discovery Channel Store History"**

Step 1: Aspect Identification. An aspect is a topic or concept which is a term or phrase appearing in the query that preserves the original ordering. Aspect Identification is the initial stage of our method, taking the original query as its input to give a set of query aspects. This added information helps support all subsequent stages of the system aiming to put boundaries between the single concepts that may exist in a multi-concept query. A query term can be used in more than one aspect. Identifying aspects within the query allows us to better source articles for our expansion terms than trying to source articles from the whole query alone.

We identify aspects based on their Link Probability [14] weighting. Link Probability is a proved feature for measuring 'keyphraseness'. It estimates the probability of a term to be selected as a hyperlink in a new document by counting the number of documents where the term was already selected as a hyperlink divided by the total number of documents where the term appeared. This probability can be interpreted as, the more often a term is selected as a hyperlink among its total number of occurrences, the more likely it will be selected again. We first identify each possible aspect of our query and list them in order of link probability weight. From this list we finalize a set of query aspects by following a set of selection rules:

- Aspects are selected from highest value through to the lowest.
- An aspect is ignored if it is a subset of an already selected aspect.
- No aspects with a weighting of 0 should be added unless they contain terms that are yet to be covered by the selected aspects.
- Aspect Identification is complete when each term of the query has been covered by an aspect.

Step 2: Wikipedia Article Selection. This phase creates a single set of Wikipedia articles with close connection to our query and its aspects defined by the previous stage. This article set is used as a source for extracting terms for query reformulation and building aspect vocabularies used in the following stage. Wikipedia structure continues to help us through this stage with each aspect likely to map to a single Wikipedia article. For each aspect we aim to add at least one article to our set. Each aspect is disambiguated individually using Link Probability measure, giving a list of possible articles and their weights of disambiguation confidence. We introduce a cut-off threshold to our selection criteria relative to the highest confidence appearing over all the query aspects. All articles that have a confidence greater than half of the maximum measure are included in our article set.

We also utilize the ability to disambiguate aspects in pairs through the Wikipedia Link Based measure [13] providing added context for better disambiguation relative to the other query aspects. The same threshold mechanics are applied to the Wikipedia Link based measurement and its disambiguation confidences.

Step 3: Aspect Vocabulary Construction. This stage aims to build a weighted vocabulary for each aspect using the article set produced during the previous stage. All terms appearing in the selected articles are vocabulary candidates weighted by their relation to their corresponding aspects. For each aspect, a vocabulary is produced by adding to it each candidate term from the article set along with the score based on Wikipedia Link Based Measure [13]. This produces a weighted list of terms, named an aspects vocabulary, sorted by their semantic relation to the aspect.

Step 4: Finding Underrepresented Aspects. The final step is to select the best expansion term by supporting the least represented aspect of the query. We build the vocabulary of the entire query by counting term frequencies of all terms in the first 10 documents of the initial Bing search results. We select first 50 highest weighted terms and normalize them so the weights of each term add to give 1. Then the vocabulary of each aspect is compared with the query vocabulary. Each aspect is given a score by multiplying the terms weightings in the aspect vocabulary by their frequency weighting in the query vocabulary. The aspect that produces the lowest score is determined to be the least represented with its highly weighted terms in this aspect's vocabulary assigned as the final output for query expansion.

3.2   Variations to Core Method

The following three methods are devised to deviate in some way from the core method for performance comparison. The three methods share the same Aspect Identification step (Step 1) and Wikipedia Article Selection step (Step 2) with the Core, but their step 3 is changed and they don't have step 4. Their Aspect Vocabulary Construction step (Step 3) changes its priorities from creating a vocabulary for each of the aspects to creating a complete vocabulary for the entire query that provides an output of weighted terms to conclude the query expansion method. In other words, they only build the query vocabulary and weight the terms in the vocabulary for output. The difference between the three methods is the way they weight the terms in the vocabulary.

Relatedness. This method differs the least from the core method. The query vocabulary is built by taking each term existing in the article selection and weighting it equally against all the query aspects. The weighting measure is found by taking the dot product of the terms semantic relation to each of the aspects using the Wikipedia Link Based Measure (WLM) [13], as shown below,

$$w(t) = \prod_{x=1}^{n}(WLM(t, A_x)) \tag{2}$$

where n represents the number of query aspects and WLM is the way of assigning scores to a term based on its relatedness to the corresponding aspect.

TF.IDF This method uses the TF.IDF weighting to build a vocabulary that represents the entire query. Term frequencies are taken from the Wikipedia Article Selection step (Step 2) with term document occurrences based upon the total collection of Wikipedia articles. The formula used to calculate TF.IDF weighting is given by: The inverse documents frequency is used to measure the general importance of a term to the entire documents collection.

Combined. Combined method involves intersecting our Relatedness and TF.IDF methods where vocabulary construction is determined by terms Relatedness (WLM) and TF.IDF weightings as shown below.

$$combined(t) = w(t) \times tfidf(t) \tag{3}$$

4   Evaluation

For evaluation, we compared the performance of our query expansion core method with that of alternate query expansion methods. Each system processed a set of 150 queries producing a reformulated query. This query is then searched over a web collection to retrieve a ranked set of documents. The retrieval lists for each query are compared with a set of relevance judgments allowing us to calculate evaluation measures. Averages of system queries give the grounds for us to compare the query expansion methods and validate our own.

4.1   Test Data

Three main elements for the performance evaluation of our query expansion method are: the set of queries, a static web document collection and the set of relevance judgment. We use all the 150 testing queries from 2009, 2010, and 2011 TREC Web Track [4, 5, 6], each containing a brief topic and subtopics description. Queries from the 2011 TREC Web Track were aimed to be harder than the previous year's queries, providing our evaluation with a range of query difficulties. The ClueWeb09 dataset at http://www.lemurproject.org/clueweb09.php/ is our static web collection containing over 1 billion web pages.

Relevance judgments were taken from the TREC Web Track workshop, consisting of manually labeled document set for each query by a panel of experts from their respective years. Judgments were based on the topics of the query. Indri search engine [20] is used to retrieve the documents.

4.2   Measurements

Traditional measures such as Precision and Recall are not suitable for our task. For example, an extended query which increases the first relevant judgement from rank 5 to rank 1, does not change precision or recall, but is understood to be an improvement of retrieval. We develop our own evaluating criteria which consider the ranking/index of each retrieved document.

The documents retrieved by each query expansion method for each query are classified under one of three categories: Relevant, Non-Relevant, or Non-Judged.

Relevant documents indicate that the retrieval fits the description of the queries topic or subtopic, with Non-Relevant documents straying from the query sense. Non-Judged documents are documents that have neither label nor part of the judgments of the Web Track workshops. We can not ignore these Non-Judged documents because they change the ranking of other relevant or non-relevant documents. It is too harsh to treat them as Non-relevant because that is not true. So we value these Non-Judged documents higher than Non-Relevant documents and give them a weighting based upon the fraction of relevant judgments to total judgments existing for that query.

We created two metrics to evaluate our systems, the first describes the performance of a query (original query or an extended query using a single system) and the second describes the performance of an extended query using a single system relative to the performance of the original query. Results will focus on the second metric where we are able to compare the improvements between systems. The first single query measurement is scored with a maximum value of 5050, evaluating the first 100 documents retrieved. Each document is scored based on its index in the retrieval and its label. A documents index score begins at a value of 100 for the first document down to a value of 1 for the hundredth document. This index score is multiplied by its label score to give the document score as shown below. Label scores range in values from 0 to 1 with Relevant documents getting a score of 1 and Non-Relevant documents a score of 0. The Non-Judged documents get a label score relative to the ratio of total relevant to total judgments that exist for the query. This measurement combines a sense of precision and recall measurements. Adding all the document scores of a query together gives the system its query score.

$$queryScore(|D|) = \sum_{idx=0}^{99} (100 - idx) \times labelScore(d_{idx})$$

The second metric presents the performance of the target system relative to the performance of the unaltered query. For each system we select query pairs with the original query and its extended query and both queries have to be meaningful. Meaningfulness is enforced by a threshold to include the query based on the number of Non-Judged document labels of a query. For a query to be included its retrieved document set is required to have at least 25 of the first 50 documents to have a Relevant or Non-Relevant judgment. Using the meaningful query pairs, we can define the performance of an entire system being the average ratio of change of the system relative to the original queries, defined as follows.

$$relativePerformance(extended|Q|, original|Q|) =$$
$$\frac{1}{n} \sum_{x=0}^{n} 100 \times \frac{2 \times queryScore(extended[Q_x])}{queryScore(original[Q_x]) + queryScore(extended[Q_x])} - 1$$

4.3   Results and Discussion

This section presents the comparison results of our four methods introduced in this paper and two exiting solutions based on previous research in query expansion. The two alternative solutions are outlined as follows:

Wikipedia Local TF.IDF. Uses the default Wikipedia search interface to retrieve a list of 10 articles to build a query vocabulary. Candidate terms come from the contents of the articles using a TF.IDF measurement to weight them, selecting the highest weighted terms for expansion.

Bing Local TF.IDF. Uses the Bing web search to retrieve a list of 10 documents to build a query vocabulary. Candidate terms come from the contents of the documents using a TF.IDF measurement to weight them, selecting the highest weighted terms for expansion.

Because AbraQ doesn't handle single aspect queries, we are unable to compare the performance of our system with it.

Table 2. Number of queries tested per system

System	Number of Querys evaluated		
	1 Term	2 Terms	5 Terms
Aspect Representation	34	26	16
Combined	31	23	19
TF.IDF	29	27	13
Relatedness	33	23	19
Web Local TF.IDF	43	33	27
Wikipedia Local TF.IDF	33	30	25

We computed relative performance metric over all query expansion solutions posed with the 150 queries from TREC 2009, 2010, and 2011. Each of the six systems, four introduced in this paper and two comparison solutions emulating previous work, is measured through three different sizes of expansion terms. The three sizes are a single term, two terms, and five terms resulting in a total of 18 systems. Table 2 shows the number of queries tested with each expansion size. They are grouped by the number of terms added by the method. With our relative performance metric resulting in varying sizes of query test sets, the average number of queries tested for each system was 26.9 with a maximum of 43 and a minimum of 13, as shown in Table 2.

The following three figures show the comparison results. The y-axis gives the values of our performance metric for each of the methods of the x-axis. Results across the single term expansion, as shown in Figure 2, are in a similar range with the highest performance coming from the Aspect Representation method at 8.6% and the lowest from the Web TF.IDF method at 5.4%.

Increasing the number of terms from one to two reveals a reduced performance to all methods except two, the Combined and Web TF.IDF methods, indicated by Figure 3. The performance of the Combined method at 11.3% comes close to doubling the next method of Wikipedia TF.IDF at 6.8%. This is unexpected as the Combined method is basically a concatenation of the TF.IDF and Relatedness methods which are the two lowest performing.

The general reduction in performance when expanding a query with two terms, contrasted with the Combined methods best performance coming from the two

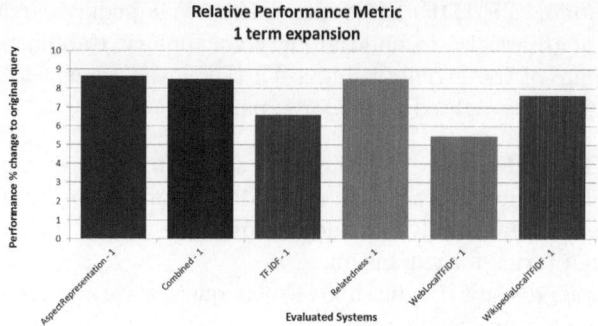

Fig. 2. Performance comparison of six QE methods on one term query expansion

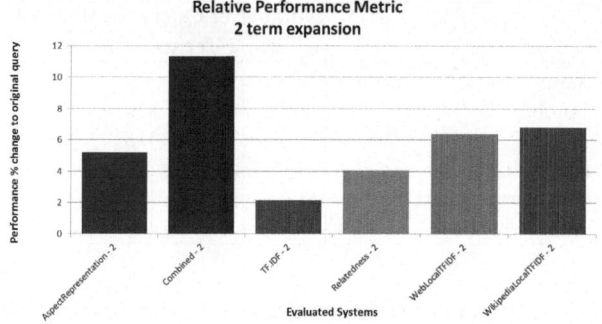

Fig. 3. Performance comparison of six QE methods on two term query expansion

term expansion, highlights the influence of the expansion term quantities. Analysis of a few method expansions shows growing the number of terms steers the retrieval to either provide more matches or produce one of two forms of drifting. The first kind of drift involves the change of topic to something completely detached from the original sense. The second form of drift involves the query sense narrowing too finely on a subset of the query sense. With a lower number of query terms present, their weighting effect on the query is greater, as more are added, their presence reduces. This, coupled with the two forms of drifting, could account for the inconsistent results occurring through the two term expansion evaluation. Our core method could have utilised a dynamic number of expansion terms by re-evaluating the representations of aspects through alternate numbers of expansion terms to search for an optimal number of terms.

Extending the number of terms to 5, in figure 4, shows the largest performance jumps. Aspect Representation at 5 terms performs better than all other methods at 23.6%. The Relatedness method is similar to the Aspect Representation method and trails closely at 21.7%. The third performer of the 5 term methods is the Web TF.IDF method with a strong performance of 17.7% doubling the fourth equal methods of Combined and Wikipedia TF.IDF at 8.3%.

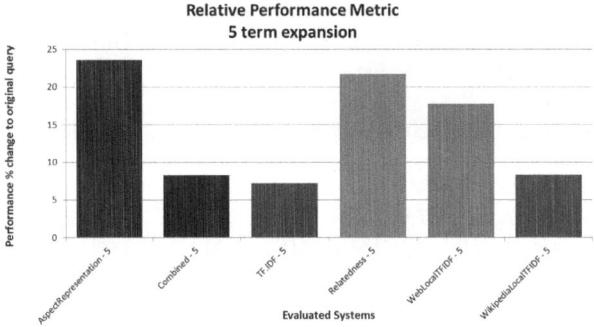

Fig. 4. Performance comparison of six QE methods on five term query expansion

5 Conclusion

This paper presented a query expansion system with Wikipedia as the source
for finding related terms. Our system is tested on a large dataset and all four
methods show performance improvements. The experiments show that the Aspect Presentation method outperforms other methods. When the aspects of a
query are identified well, the vocabularies produced by our Aspect Representation method provide strong candidate terms for a query expansion system.

The limitations of Wikipedia as a sole knowledge base have become apparent
through this research. Wikipedia's ability to identify query aspects is powerful
because of the close similarities between Wikipedia articles and query aspects
although its encyclopedic style is not broad enough to platform the diversity of
web search goals. Future work would focus on complementing Wikipedia with
alternative sources and forming methods to evaluate each source's performance
relative to the query so to avoid the limitations of individual sources.

References

[1] Bernhard, D.: Query expansion based on pseudo relevance feedback from definition
    clusters. In: Proceedings of the 23rd International Conference on Computational
    Linguistics: Posters, COLING 2010, pp. 54–62. Association for Computational
    Linguistics, Stroudsburg (2010)
[2] Bhogal, J., Macfarlane, A., Smith, P.: A review of ontology based query expansion.
    Inf. Process. Manage. 43, 866–886 (2007)
[3] Brenes, D.J., Gayo-Avello, D.: Stratified analysis of aol query log. Inf. Sci. 179,
    1844–1858 (2009)
[4] Clarke, C.L., Craswell, N., Soboroff, I.: Overview of the trec 2009 web track (2010)
[5] Clarke, C.L., Craswell, N., Soboroff, I., Cormack, G.V.: Overview of the trec 2010
    web track (2011)
[6] Clarke, C.L., Craswell, N., Soboroff, I., Voorhees, E.M.: Overview of the trec 2011
    web track (2012)

[7] Crabtree, D.W., Andreae, P., Gao, X.: Exploiting underrepresented query aspects for automatic query expansion. In: Proceedings of the 13th ACM SIGKDD International Conference on Knowledge Discovery and Data Mining, KDD 2007, pp. 191–200. ACM, New York (2007)

[8] Fellbaum, C. (ed.): WordNet An Electronic Lexical Database. The MIT Press, Cambridge (1998)

[9] Jiang, X.: Query expansion based on a semantic graph model. In: Proceedings of the 34th International ACM SIGIR Conference on Research and Development in Information, SIGIR 2011, pp. 1315–1316. ACM, New York (2011)

[10] Klyuev, V., Haralambous, Y.: Query expansion: Term selection using the ewc semantic relatedness measure. CoRR, abs/1108.4052 (2011) (informal publication)

[11] Manning, C., Raghavan, P., Schütze, H.: Introduction to information retrieval. Cambridge University Press (2008)

[12] Meij, E., de Rijke, M.: Supervised query modeling using wikipedia. In: Proceeding of the 33rd International ACM SIGIR conference on Research and Development in Information Retrieval, SIGIR 2010, pp. 875–876. ACM, New York (2010)

[13] Milne, D., Witten, I.H.: An effective, low-cost measure of semantic relatedness obtained from wikipedia links. In: Proceedings of AAAI 2008 (2008)

[14] Milne, D., Witten, I.H.: Learning to link with wikipedia. In: Proceeding of the 17th ACM Conference on Information and Knowledge Management, CIKM 2008, pp. 509–518. ACM, New York (2008)

[15] Milne, D.N., Witten, I.H., Nichols, D.M.: A knowledge-based search engine powered by wikipedia. In: Proceedings of the Sixteenth ACM Conference on Conference on Information and Knowledge Management, CIKM 2007, pp. 445–454. ACM, New York (2007)

[16] Nguyen, D., Callan, J.: Combination of evidence for effective web search. In: The Nineteenth Text REtrieval Conference Proceedings TREC 2010 (2010)

[17] Robertson, G., Gao, X.: Improving abraq: An automatic query expansion algorithm. In: Proceedings of the 2010 IEEE/WIC/ACM International Conference on Web Intelligence and Intelligent Agent Technology, WI-IAT 2010, vol. 1, pp. 653–656. IEEE Computer Society, Washington, DC (2010)

[18] Ruthven, I., Lalmas, M.: A survey on the use of relevance feedback for information access systems. Knowl. Eng. Rev. 18, 95–145 (2003)

[19] Santamaría, C., Gonzalo, J., Artiles, J.: Wikipedia as sense inventory to improve diversity in web search results. In: Proceedings of the 48th Annual Meeting of the Association for Computational Linguistics, ACL 2010, pp. 1357–1366. Association for Computational Linguistics, Stroudsburg (2010)

[20] Strohman, T., Metzler, D., Turtle, H., Croft, W.B.: Indri: a language-model based search engine for complex queries. In: Proceedings of the International Conference on Intelligent Analysis, Technical report (2005)

[21] White, R.W., Marchionini, G.: Examining the effectiveness of real-time query expansion. Inf. Process. Manage. 43, 685–704 (2007)

[22] Xu, Y., Jones, G.J., Wang, B.: Query dependent pseudo-relevance feedback based on wikipedia. In: Proceedings of the 32nd International ACM SIGIR Conference on Research and Development in Information Retrieval, SIGIR 2009, pp. 59–66. ACM, New York (2009)

Constrained Grouped Sparsity

Yi Guo[1,*], Junbin Gao[2], and Xia Hong[3]

[1] CSIRO Mathematics and Information Sciences
North Ryde, NSW 1670, Australia
yi.guo@csiro.au
[2] School of Computing and Mathematics,
Charles Sturt University, Bathurst, NSW 2795, Australia
jbgao@csu.edu.au
[3] School of Systems Engineering, University of Reading, Reading, RG6 6AY,UK
x.hong@reading.ac.uk

Abstract. In this paper, we propose an algorithm encouraging group sparsity under some convex constraint. It stems from some applications where the regression coefficients are subject to constraints, for example nonnegativity and the explanatory variables are not suitable to be orthogonalized within groups. It takes the form of the group LASSO based on linear regression model where a L1/L2 norm is imposed on group coefficients to achieve group sparsity. It differs from the original group LASSO in the following ways. First, the regression coefficients must obey some convex constraints. Second, there is no requirement for orthogonality of the variables within individual groups. For these reasons, the simple blockwise coordinate descent for all group coefficients is no longer applicable and a special treatment for the constraint is necessary. The algorithm we proposed in this paper is an alternating direction method, and both exact and inexact solutions are provided. The inexact version simplifies the computation while retaining practical convergence. As an approximation to group L0, it can be applied to data analysis where group fitting is essential and the coefficients are constrained. It may serve as a screening procedure to reduce the number of the groups when the number of total groups is prohibitively high.

1 Introduction

In this paper, we consider the variable selection problem for the following linear regression model

$$\mathbf{y} = \sum_{i=1}^{M} \mathbf{x}_i \beta_i + \boldsymbol{\epsilon} \tag{1}$$

where $\mathbf{y} \in \mathbb{R}^D$ is the dependent variable, $\mathbf{x}_i \in \mathbb{R}^D$ are the explanatory variables (the ith column from the full explanatory matrix $\mathbf{X}$), $\beta_i \in \mathbb{R}$ are corresponding coefficients, and $\boldsymbol{\epsilon}$ is an error term. The variable selection problem in this setting

---

* The author to whom all the correspondences should be addressed.

M. Thielscher and D. Zhang (Eds.): AI 2012, LNCS 7691, pp. 433–444, 2012.

means to choose M from N total explanatory variables for (1) to achieve some optimum. For a set of indices $\mathcal{A} = \{a_1, \ldots, a_M\}$, let $X_{\mathcal{A}} = [\mathbf{x}_{a_1}, \ldots, \mathbf{x}_{a_M}]$ be the $D \times M$ submatrix of $\mathbf{X}$ and $\boldsymbol{\beta}_{\mathcal{A}} = [\beta_{a_1}, \ldots, \beta_{a_M}]^T$ the corresponding subvector of $\boldsymbol{\beta}$ ($\boldsymbol{\beta} = [\beta_1, \ldots, \beta_N]^T$). The problem is usually formulated as the following least squares problem

$$\min_{\mathcal{A}, \boldsymbol{\beta}_{\mathcal{A}}} ||\mathbf{y} - \mathbf{X}_{\mathcal{A}} \boldsymbol{\beta}_{\mathcal{A}}||_2^2 \tag{2}$$

$$\text{s.t. } |\mathcal{A}| = M$$

so that the optimum is described by the least residuals sum of squares (RSS). If M is unknown, which is usually the case, there is a further problem of model selection.

In some real world applications such as spectroscopy, it is often the case that the variables have some group structure. For example, in the unmixing problem [1] for mineral composition analysis, variables (typical mineral spectra) having very high correlations are often from the same group. It is desirable to fit those groups instead of individual variables, i.e. in the regression model, the variables in a group either stay or leave altogether. Formally, we rewrite the model as follows

$$\mathbf{y} = \sum_{g=1}^{M} \sum_{i=1}^{N_g} \mathbf{x}_{g_i} \beta_{g_i} + \boldsymbol{\epsilon}, \tag{3}$$

where N_g is the number of variables in group g. Accordingly the group wise least square regression becomes

$$\min_{\beta_{g_i}} ||\mathbf{y} - \sum_{g=1}^{M} \sum_{i=1}^{N_g} \mathbf{x}_{g_i} \beta_{g_i}||_2^2, \tag{4}$$

and subset selection takes the same form of (2) but each element in $\mathcal{A}$ is now a set, i.e. $a_g = \{a_{g_1}, \ldots, a_{g_{N_g}}\}$ corresponding to indices of variables in group g. In other words, the subset selection is performed in a group fashion, that is to select M out of total G groups that minimizes the RSS in (4).

Subset selection is a combinatorial optimization problem in essence and hence has NP complexity. There are quite a few of methods trying to solve (2) heuristically [2,3,4]. Full subset selection [5], a fast exhaustive search based on QR decomposition and branch-and-bound techniques, guarantees the best subset of given size, i.e. M, is found. Its extension, called grouped subset selection (GSS) [6], finds M groups minimising RSS in (4). However it only works for moderate size problems, e.g. less than 200 groups with half a dozen variables in each group on average in a space with several hundred dimensions depending on the computer system.

2   Sparse Models for Variable Selection

To solve the variable selection efficiently, there is a recent trend of using sparse approximation to solve this problem which has attracted attention in statistics, machine learning and other disciplines. The earliest work is from [7] called the LASSO. By adding an L1 constraint on the coefficients to (2), the original combinatorial optimization problem is converted to a convex optimization problem as follows

$$\min_{\beta_i} ||\mathbf{y} - \sum_{i=1}^{N} \mathbf{x}_i \beta_i||_2^2 \tag{5}$$

$$\text{s.t.} \sum_{i=1}^{N} |\beta_i| < t. \tag{6}$$

Note that in the LASSO, it fits all explanatory variables in the model but forces some of their coefficients to be zero to implement subset selection. The parameter t is the handle for controlling how many variables are actually included in the model. It is normally reformulated as L1 regularization in practice

$$\min_{\beta_i} ||\mathbf{y} - \sum_{i=1}^{N} \mathbf{x}_i \beta_i||_2^2 + \lambda \sum_{i=1}^{N} |\beta_i|, \tag{7}$$

where λ has the same function as t in (5). The LASSO has several advantages. Firstly, it is a convex optimization problem and hence has a global minimum which can be found by efficient algorithms such as coordinate descent [8], and iterative shrinkage-thresholding [9]. The entire regularization path [10] can also be found by various algorithms such as LARS [11], and GPS [12]. Secondly, it is easy to group variables under this framework. For example, the group LASSO [13] has the group selection property by applying the L1/L2 norm to the group coefficients. The optimization is almost the same as that for the LASSO under certain conditions. Coordinate descent type of search e.g blockwise coordinate descent [14] is still applicable in this case with some limitation. It can also be extended to the online learning setting [15] for a continuously growing training data set.

The group LASSO [13] minimizes the following objective function

$$\min. \frac{1}{2}||\mathbf{y} - \sum_{g=1}^{G} \mathbf{X}_g \boldsymbol{\beta}_g||_2^2 + \lambda \sum_{g=1}^{G} \sqrt{N_g}||\boldsymbol{\beta}_g||_2 \tag{8}$$

where $\mathbf{X}_g$ is the submatrix of group g and $\boldsymbol{\beta}_g$ is the vector of corresponding coefficients. It resembles the normal LASSO in Eq. (7) by using a sparse penalty to implement group selection. It differs in replacing the L1 norm with the L2 norm on the group coefficients to impose group sparsity.

There are two limitations in the original group LASSO implementation. First, the regression coefficients are supposed to be free, i.e. no constraints on them. Second, it is required that the variables within individual group are orthornomal, i.e. $\mathbf{X}_g^T \mathbf{X}_g = \mathbf{I}$ and $\mathbf{I}$ is the identity matrix of compatible size. Under these assumptions, the blockwise coordinate descent for all group coefficients is applicable and conveniently derived from the subgradient of $\boldsymbol{\beta}_g$ which is separable.

However, the assumptions do not always hold. The physics in some real world applications require some constraints such as nonnegativity. Furthermore, it is more appropriate to maintain the original form of the group variables than to orthogonalise them.

To tackle these problems, we propose a fast algorithm in this paper based on the alternating direction multiplier method. Both exact and inexact solutions are provided. The inexact solution simplifies the computation while retaining convergence in practice. As an approximation to the group L0 (GSS), it can be applied to data analysis where group fitting is essential and the coefficients are constrained. It has the potential to be employed as a screening tool to eliminate redundant groups so that GSS can work on a reduced problem to find the optimal solution.

The next section introduces the constrained group LASSO algorithms. It is followed by a section which compares the constrained group LASSO and GSS using spectral unmixing in the setting of multiple PC regression. We summarize the paper in the last section.

3   The Constrained Group LASSO Algorithm

As mentioned earlier, in some applications, it is desirable to constrain the regression coefficients, e.g. nonnegativity. Also it has some fixed variables which must be in the model. For example, a vector of all 1 can be used to model the intercept. More generally, fixed variables are used to model the common features of all data, for instance, the background in spectroscopy. So it takes the following form

$$\text{min. } \frac{1}{2}\|\mathbf{y} - \mathbf{B}\boldsymbol{\alpha} - \sum_{g=1}^{G} \mathbf{X}_g\boldsymbol{\beta}_g\|_2^2 + \lambda \sum_{g=1}^{G} \sqrt{N_g}\|\boldsymbol{\beta}_g\|_2 \tag{9}$$

$$\text{s.t. } \{\boldsymbol{\alpha}, \boldsymbol{\beta}\} \in \mathcal{C}$$

where $\mathbf{B} = [\mathbf{b}_1, \ldots, \mathbf{b}_{N_b}]$ is the matrix of given fixed variables, $\boldsymbol{\alpha} = [\alpha_1, \ldots, \alpha_{N_b}]^T$ is the vector of corresponding weights, $\boldsymbol{\beta} = [\boldsymbol{\beta}_1^T, \ldots, \boldsymbol{\beta}_G^T]^T$, and $\mathcal{C}$ is some convex set. For example, for the nonnegativity constraint, it is $\boldsymbol{\beta}_g \geq 0$. We call this constrained group LASSO, or CGL for short. Note that requiring $\mathcal{C}$ to be a convex set is to make the whole optimization problem convex. If $\mathcal{C}$ is not a convex set, we must seek nonconvex optimization.

The algorithm in [13] does not handle constraints such as the one in (9). Moreover, it requires the variables in one group to be orthonormal as mentioned before. To handle the convex constraint, we introduce an indicator function attached to the objective function. We put a coordinate descent for coefficients within a group to drop the orthonormal condition which is similar to the work in [16].

We write $\boldsymbol{\theta} = \{\boldsymbol{\alpha}, \boldsymbol{\beta}\}$ the set of all the regression coefficients, and

$$f(\boldsymbol{\theta}) = \frac{1}{2}\|\mathbf{y} - \mathbf{B}\boldsymbol{\alpha} - \sum_{g=1}^{G} \mathbf{X}_g\boldsymbol{\beta}_g\|_2^2 + \lambda \sum_{g=1}^{G} \sqrt{N_g}\|\boldsymbol{\beta}_g\|_2$$

to avoid cluttered notation. We minimize the following equivalent target

$$\min_{\boldsymbol{\theta},\mathbf{z}} . \; f(\boldsymbol{\theta}) + \mathcal{I}(\mathbf{z}) \qquad (10)$$

$$\text{s.t. } \mathbf{z} = \boldsymbol{\theta}$$

where $\mathcal{I}(\mathbf{x})$ is an indicator function associated with the convex set $\mathcal{C}$ corresponding to the constraint. It returns 1 if $\mathbf{x} \in \mathcal{C}$ and 0 otherwise. Douglas-Rachford splitting with the promixal operator of (10) gives us the so-called alternating direction multiplier method (ADMM) [17] with a feasible set projection. It is equivalent to minimizing the following

$$\min_{\boldsymbol{\theta},\mathbf{z}} . \; f(\boldsymbol{\theta}) + \mathcal{I}(\mathbf{z}) + \mathbf{a}^T(\mathbf{z} - \boldsymbol{\theta}) + \frac{\rho}{2}||\mathbf{z} - \boldsymbol{\theta}||_2^2$$

where $\mathbf{a}$ is the dual variable from the equality condition in (10) and $\frac{\rho}{2}||\mathbf{z} - \boldsymbol{\theta}||_2^2$ is from the augmented Lagrange multiplier method for better stability. It can be shown that this is equivalent to minimizing the final scaled dual variable form

$$\min_{\boldsymbol{\theta},\mathbf{z},\mathbf{u}} . \; f(\boldsymbol{\theta}) + \mathcal{I}(\mathbf{z}) + \frac{\rho}{2}||\mathbf{z} - \boldsymbol{\theta} + \mathbf{u}||_2^2$$

where $\mathbf{u}$ is the scaled dual variable $\mathbf{a}$ absorbed inside of the quadratic form. We alternatively optimize $\boldsymbol{\theta}$, $\mathbf{z}$, $\mathbf{u}$ with other parameters fixed until the objective function converges. The detailed algorithm is shown in Table 1 and Table 2

Table 1. Constrained Grouped LASSO algorithm. $P_{\mathcal{C}}(\mathbf{x})$ is the Euclidean projection of $\mathbf{x}$ on to the convex set $\mathcal{C}$. For a nonnegativity constraint, it is as simple as setting $\beta_{g_i} = \frac{1+\text{sign}(\beta_{g_i})}{2}\beta_{g_i}$ meaning if β_{g_i} is negative then set it to be zero and just leave it otherwise.

---

*Constrained grouped **LASSO** for* (9) *- exact solution*

Input: $\mathbf{y}$, $\mathbf{X}$, $\mathbf{B}$, λ and group information
Output: $\boldsymbol{\alpha}$, $\boldsymbol{\beta}$ (regression coefficients)

$\{\boldsymbol{\alpha}^0, \boldsymbol{\beta}^0\} = \arg\min_{\boldsymbol{\alpha},\boldsymbol{\beta}} \frac{1}{2}||\mathbf{y} - \mathbf{B}\boldsymbol{\alpha} - \sum_{g=1}^G \mathbf{X}_g\boldsymbol{\beta}_g||_2^2$
$\mathbf{z}^0 = \mathbf{u}^0 = \boldsymbol{\beta}^0, \; k = 0.$
Loop if convergence is not reached
  1. $\boldsymbol{\theta}^{k+1} = \arg\min_{\boldsymbol{\theta}} f(\boldsymbol{\theta}) + \frac{\rho}{2}||\boldsymbol{\theta} - \mathbf{z}^k + \mathbf{u}^k||_2^2$
  2. $\mathbf{z}^{k+1} = P_{\mathcal{C}}(\boldsymbol{\theta}^{k+1} + \mathbf{u}^k)$
  3. $\mathbf{u}^{k+1} = \mathbf{u}^k + \boldsymbol{\theta}^{k+1} - \mathbf{z}^{k+1}$
  4. $k = k + 1$
End loop

In Tables 1 and 2, the skeleton of the algorithm is the alternating direction method. ρ is the augmented Lagrange multiplier which is typically set to 1. It is possible to apply some penalty rules for ρ to accelerate the computation [18].

Table 2. Block coordinate descent for solving step 1 in Table 1. $\mathbf{z}_g$ and $\mathbf{u}_g$ are subvectors of $\mathbf{z}$ and $\mathbf{u}$ corresponding to $\boldsymbol{\beta}_g$. See the text about Line 6 for details.

Solve step 1 in Table 1 - **Block coordinate descent**

Input: $\mathbf{y}$, $\mathbf{X}$, $\mathbf{B}$, λ and group information
Output: $\boldsymbol{\beta}$, $\boldsymbol{\alpha}$ (regression coefficients)

Loop until $\boldsymbol{\beta}$ and $\boldsymbol{\alpha}$ converge
1. For $g = 1$ to G
2.   if $||\frac{\mathbf{X}_g^T \mathbf{r} + \rho(\mathbf{z}_g^k - \mathbf{u}_g^k)}{\lambda\sqrt{N_g}}||_2 \leq 1$ then $\boldsymbol{\beta}_g^{k+1} = 0$ ($\mathbf{r} = \mathbf{y} - \sum_{s \neq g} \mathbf{X}_s \boldsymbol{\beta}_s^k - \mathbf{B}\boldsymbol{\alpha}^k$)
3.   else
4.   loop until $\boldsymbol{\beta}_g$ converge (coordinate descent within $\boldsymbol{\beta}_g$)
5.   For $i = 1$ to N_g
6. $\beta_{g_i}^{k+1} = \arg\min_{\beta_{g_i}} \frac{1}{2}||\mathbf{r} - \mathbf{X}_g\boldsymbol{\beta}_g||_2^2 + \lambda\sqrt{N_g}||\boldsymbol{\beta}_g||_2 + \frac{\rho}{2}||\boldsymbol{\beta}_g - \mathbf{z}_g^k + \mathbf{u}_g^k||_2^2$
7.   End for
8.   end loop
9. End for
10. $\boldsymbol{\alpha}^{k+1} = \mathbf{VD}^{-1}\mathbf{U}^T(\mathbf{y} - \mathbf{X}\boldsymbol{\beta})$ and ($\mathbf{B} = \mathbf{UDV}^T$)
End loop

Line 1 of Table 1 is implemented by block coordinate descent, as detailed in Table 2. Line 2 in Table 2 is group wise soft thresholding resembling the soft threshold operator in [19]. It sets the coefficients of a whole group to 0 if the 2-norm of the rescaled biased correlation between group variables and residuals from fitting other groups is less than 1. It comes from the fact that the subgradient of $||\boldsymbol{\beta}_g||_2$ is $||\boldsymbol{\beta}_g||_2 \leq 1$ when $\boldsymbol{\beta}_g = 0$. When $\boldsymbol{\beta}_g \neq 0$, we have to estimate each individual coefficient in $\boldsymbol{\beta}_g$ because $\mathbf{X}_g$ is not necessarily assumed to be orthonormal. It is another coordinate descent process (Line 4 to Line 8 in Table 2) and each element in $\boldsymbol{\beta}_g$ is searched by a one dimensional optimization, i.e.

$$\beta_{g_i}^{k+1} = \arg\min_{\beta_{g_i}} \frac{1}{2}||\mathbf{r} - \mathbf{X}_g\boldsymbol{\beta}_g||_2^2 + \lambda\sqrt{N_g}||\boldsymbol{\beta}_g||_2 + \frac{\rho}{2}||\boldsymbol{\beta}_g - \mathbf{z}_g^k + \mathbf{u}_g^k||_2^2$$

with some abuse of notation. We minimize β_{g_i} with other elements in $\boldsymbol{\beta}_g$ fixed and the new version of β_{g_i} will be used to estimate the next ones immediately after it becomes available. So once we have $\beta_{g_1}^{k+1}$ which is estimated by using $\beta_{g_j}^k$ for $j \neq 1$, we use it to optimize the next element in $\boldsymbol{\beta}_g$, that is $\beta_{g_2}^{k+1}$ and so on. After we obtain a new $\boldsymbol{\beta}$, we update $\boldsymbol{\alpha}$. Note that in Table 2 Line 10, we use SVD which is a numerically stable solution of $(\mathbf{B}^T\mathbf{B})^{-1}\mathbf{B}(\mathbf{y} - \mathbf{X}\boldsymbol{\beta})$. What follows is the update of $\mathbf{z}$ by feasible set projection and then an update of $\mathbf{u}$. Updating $\mathbf{z}$ is by Euclidean projection of the estimated coefficients to the feasible set $\mathcal{C}$ which is derived from the proximal operator on the indicator function $\mathcal{I}(\mathbf{x})$. This originates from optimizing $\mathbf{z}$ while fixing other variables.

The algorithm converges very quickly typically. The stopping criterion could be the difference between adjacent updates of the objective function being less than a threshold. Note that for $\lambda = 0$ or some values close to 0, we can simply obtain β by normal least squares replacing Line 1 to Line 9 in Table 2. This algorithm can certainly handle various constraints as long as they are convex. What we need to do is to use a suitable feasible set projection P_C in Table 1 Line 2.

A very interesting observation inspired by the work in [20] is that the solution of β^{k+1} and α^{k+1} in Table 1 Line 1 implemented in Table 2 does not need to be exact. The algorithm in Table 2 is dedicated to finding the exact minimum subject to a small tolerance for numerical implementation. There are two loops there to drive the solution towards the descent direction, one for α and β and the other for β_g in Table 2 Line 4-8. It turns out that both of these loops can be skipped. The result is that the algorithm still converges but more quickly. The revised algorithm is shown in Table 3 which we call the inexact solution for constrained group LASSO.

Table 3. Inexact algorithm for constrained grouped LASSO

---

*Constrained grouped **LASSO** for* (9) - *inexact solution*

Input: $\mathbf{y}$, $\mathbf{X}$, $\mathbf{B}$, λ and group information
Output: α, β (regression coefficients)

$\{\alpha^0, \beta^0\} = \arg\min_\theta \frac{1}{2}\|\mathbf{y} - \mathbf{B}\alpha - \sum_{g=1}^{G}\mathbf{X}_g\beta_g\|_2^2$
$\mathbf{z}^0 = \mathbf{u}^0 = \beta^0$, $k = 0$.
Loop until α and β converge
1. For $g = 1$ to G
2.   if $\|\frac{\mathbf{X}_g^T\mathbf{r}+\rho(\mathbf{z}_g^k-\mathbf{u}_g^k)}{\lambda\sqrt{N_g}}\|_2 \leq 1$ then $\beta_g^{k+1} = 0$ ($\mathbf{r} = \mathbf{y} - \sum_{s\neq g}\mathbf{X}_s\beta_s^k - \mathbf{B}\alpha^k$)
3.   else
4.   For $i = 1$ to N_g
5. $\beta_{g_i}^{k+1} = \arg\min_{\beta_{g_i}} \frac{1}{2}\|\mathbf{r} - \mathbf{X}_g\beta_g\|_2^2 + \lambda\sqrt{N_g}\|\beta_g\|_2 + \frac{\rho}{2}\|\beta_g - \mathbf{z}_g^k + \mathbf{u}_g^k\|_2^2$
6.   End for
7. End for
8. $\alpha^{k+1} = \mathbf{V}\mathbf{D}^{-1}\mathbf{U}^T(\mathbf{y} - \mathbf{X}\beta^{k+1})$ and ($\mathbf{B} = \mathbf{U}\mathbf{D}\mathbf{V}^T$)
9. $\mathbf{z}^{k+1} = P_C(\beta^{k+1} + \mathbf{u}^k)$
10. $\mathbf{u}^{k+1} = \mathbf{u}^k + \beta^{k+1} - \mathbf{z}^{k+1}$
11. $k = k + 1$
End loop

As we can see from Table 3, there is only one iteration for β^{k+1} and α^{k+1} and the same for β_g^{k+1}. This inexact solution saves several iterations required in the original algorithm. It updates the introduced variable $\mathbf{z}$ and scaled dual variable $\mathbf{u}$ more frequently than the original version does, which ensures that the algorithm is heading towards the right direction and hence convergence. It makes sense because both the exact and inexact solutions of β^{k+1} and α^{k+1} are only suboptimum along the optimization path. Since they both guarantee to find the optimum, the faster algorithm is preferable in practice.

4   Experimental Results

4.1   Simulation

We performed a simulation to test CGL to see how well it can approach the correct group sparsity. The baseline is provided by GSS. We simply sampled 60 groups of various randomly chosen sizes from 1 to 4 from a standard normal distribution $\mathcal{N}(0, \mathbf{I})$. $\mathbf{y}$ is generated by adding randomly chosen groups with positive weights sampled from a uniform distribution on $[0, 1]$. We added Gaussian noise from $\mathcal{N}(0, \sigma \mathbf{I})$ to $\mathbf{y}$ and varied σ to see the influence of this particular noise. We ran this simulation 1000 times for each value of σ to collect the correct rate. In the noise free case ($\sigma = 0$), CGL performed very well with 97.7% correct rate. CGL has some noise resistance as shown in Table 4 as its correct rate isstable when $\sigma < 0.01$. When the noise level increases, the correct rates of both CGL and GSS degenerate. Interestingly, when $\sigma = 1$, it turns out that CGL is even better than GSS. In this case, $\mathbf{y}$ is almost overwhelmed by noise. Since GSS is RSS driven exhaustive search, it is guaranteed to find the groups with minimum RSS, which is 0 in this simulation. However, when the noise level is high, it deviates from the truth. On the other hand, CGL needs to balance RSS and regularization which provides CGL some robustness.

Table 4. Simulation on CGL and GSS. When $\sigma = 0$, it is noise free

σ	0	0.0001	0.001	0.01	0.1	1
CGL	97.7%	97.2%	97.2%	97.5%	94.5%	61.1%
GSS	100.0%	100.0%	100.0%	100.0%	95.5%	55.8%

4.2   Experiments on Spectral Unmixing

The Data and Model. We applied the fast constrained group LASSO algorithm to a spectral unmixing problem with a reference library [21,22] which is a typical subset selection problem based on linear regression model. Grouped level fitting is of important interest. It can be used in two ways. First is to fit a group of variables (typical spectra of materials) as a bundle since the materials in the group are similar and highly correlated. Second is to apply multiple principal components regression where a group is a bunch of PC's extracted from training samples of some material. Please refer to [23] for details.

We started with a library with 493 spectra from 60 classes. We used the following rules to determine how many PC's were used for each class: a. at least 95% of the variation should be explained by the PC's used; b. If the first PC explains at least 95% of the variation and the first two PC's explain at least 98%

of the variation, then the second PC should be included; c. The total number of PC's for a class should be no more than 2. The purpose of these rules is to include PC's conservatively. We only model a class with two PC's when it is necessary in terms of capturing enough variation. Note that the rules are not optimized yet. We will optimize the number of PC's chosen for each class in our future work. There are 7 fixed variables which must be fitted in the model. So the multiple PC regression model is similar to (3) as

$$\mathbf{y} = \sum_{i=1}^{N_b} \mathbf{b}_i \alpha_i + \sum_{g=1}^{M} \sum_{i=1}^{N_g} \mathbf{x}_{g_i} \beta_{g_i} + \boldsymbol{\epsilon} \tag{11}$$

and in this case each group is one or two principal components associated with a class. The task is to find M out of a total of G groups that best fit the above model regarding the overall error described by RSS. Because the first PC is associated with a particular material and therefore its weight has physical meaning, it is natural that the weights for *all first PC's* should be non-negative. So in our experiment the optimization problem becomes

$$\min_{\mathcal{S}, \boldsymbol{\alpha}, \boldsymbol{\beta}_g} \frac{1}{2} \|\mathbf{y} - \mathbf{B}\alpha - \sum_{g \in \mathcal{S}} \mathbf{X}_g \boldsymbol{\beta}_g\|_2^2 \tag{12}$$

$$\text{s.t. } \beta_{g_1} \geq 0, |\mathcal{S}| = M.$$

The test data are from 4 fully characterized evaluation data sets [22]. So we have ground truth for each sample in these data sets to evaluate different methods. The ground truth tells us how many groups are in a certain sample and what they are, but no proportions are given, which is less important than getting the groups correct. This also frees us from model selection. Knowing M for each test sample, we can focus on the group selection which will make the comparison more informative.

The Results. The method we compared with is GSS. We used bisection to choose a suitable λ which retains only M groups in each case for CGL. Note that it is also possible to use variable (group) screening procedures such as the sequential strong rules in [24]. However, it is necessary to work out the right form of the rules in the circumstances with constrained variables.

We applied two methods to the evaluation data sets. Sine GSS is exhaustive search which guarantees finding the solution of M groups with minimum RSS and CGL is only an approximation, we should expect that CGL's performance to be bounded by GSS. However, the ground truth is not always the combination of groups with minimum RSS because the mixing process is not fully understood and/or not perfectly modeled.

We summarise the number of incorrectly unmixed samples in Table 5. CGL has comparable performance with GSS on one data sets but is significantly worse on the other three. It is not surprising that GSS outperforms CGL in general because CGL is a convex relaxation of the cardinality minimization or L0 norm

Table 5. Comparison of CGL and GSS on four evaluation data sets

Data set Names.	No. of Samples	Method	No. (%) Incorrect
Dobbyn1	88	GSS	37 (42.0%)
		CGL	65 (77.3%)
GL14	88	GSS	34 (38.6%)
		CGL	44 (50%)
Sasha	81	GSS	15 (18.5%)
		CGL	36 (44.4%)
BEU162	82	GSS	25 (30.5%)
		CGL	24 (29.3%)

in group fashion. Nevertheless, the combinations with the lowest RSS may not be the right answers to the samples for noise or model inadequacy. CGL is slightly better than GSS on the BEU162 data set. This suggests that the noise level may be a bit high for this data set on which a more robust method is preferable.

An advantage of CGL is that it is much faster than GSS given a suitable λ. Based on the comparison in Table 5, CGL may be a fast approximation to give a crude interpretation to the data. It is very useful in the cases where there are too many groups such that GSS is no longer applicable. Furthermore, it is possible that we use CGL as a screening tool to remove groups that can never get into the model [22].

Figure 1 shows the fitting of GSS and CGL for sample No. 53 in the Dobbyn1 data set which is a mixture of Kaolinites, and Gypsum. GSS correctly identified all materials while CGL substituted Gypsum by White Micas. Both fitted curves follow the main features of the original spectrum largely. GSS captured the doublet at 1900nm reasonably well while CGL missed it because of the incorrect substitution of White Micas for Gypsum. As we can see that the visual fits of these two methods are very similar. This reveals that CGL approximates the optimum to some extent. There are quite a lot of cases like this in this

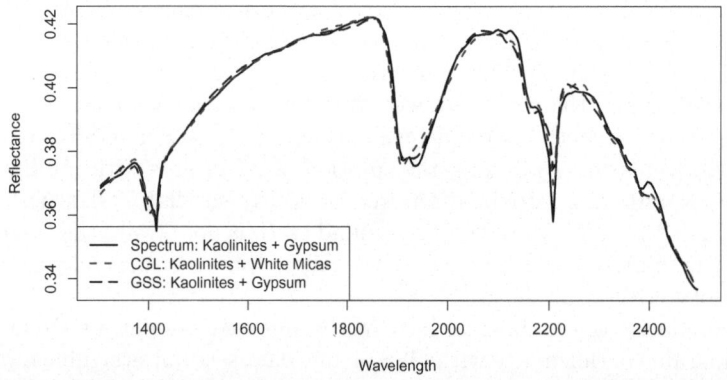

Fig. 1. The fitting of GSS and CGL for sample No. 53 in Dobbyn1 data set

experiment where CGL missed subtle features such as the little doublet which is a compromise between RSS and regularisation.

5 Discussion

As a convex approximation to GSS, constrained group LASSO uses L1/L2 norm $\sum_{g=1}^{G} \sqrt{N_g} \|\beta_g\|_2$ to encourage group sparsity under some convex constraints on regression coefficients. We have proposed the constrained group LASSO (CGL) algorithm in the form of (9) for some real world applications e.g. spectral unmixing. CGL does not require the variables within a group to be orthonormal which simplifies the problem in some applications. The algorithm converges very quickly. The inexact algorithm is even faster while maintaining the same convergence.

Although CGL is only an approximation to the optimum and therefore its performance is inferior to GSS in this sense, an attractive advantage of CGL is that it is much faster than GSS. As an exhaustive search algorithm in essence, GSS is not suitable for large scale problems where CGL is applicable. Another promising method for problems with thousands of groups/variables is to screen groups/variables [25,24] to about 100 or less and then apply GSS to find the accurate solution. CGL, smoothed L0 [26] and some other approximation methods may be good candidates.

References

1. Berman, M., Bischof, L., Lagerstron, R., Guo, Y., Huntington, J., Mason, P.: An unmixing algorithm based on a large library of shortwave infrared spectra. Technical Report EP117468, CMIS (2011)
2. Khana, J.A., Aelstb, S.V., Zamara, R.H.: Building a robust linear model with forward selection and stepwise procedures. Computational Statistics And Data Analysis 52, 239–248 (2007)
3. Hofmann, M., Gatu, C., Kontoghiorghes, E.J.: Efficient algorithms for computing the best subset regression models for large-scale problems. Computational Statistics and Data Analysis 52(1), 16–29 (2007)
4. Cho, S.J., Hermsmeier, M.A.: Genetic algorithm guided selection: Variables selection and subset selection. Journal of Chemical Information and Computer Sciences, 927–936 (2002)
5. Miller, A.: Subset Selection in Regression, 2nd edn. Monographs on Statistics and Applied Probability, vol. 95. Chapman & Hall/CRC (2002)
6. Guo, Y., Berman, M., Gao, J.: Grouped subset selection for least squares regression (in preparation, 2012)
7. Tibshirani, R.: Regression shrinkage and selection via the Lasso. Journal of Royoal Statistical Society 58(1), 267–288 (1996)
8. Friedman, J.H., Hastie, T., Tibshirani, R.: Regularization paths for generalized linear models via coordinate descent. Journal of Statistical Software 33(1), 1–22 (2010)
9. Beck, A., Teboulle, M.: A fast iterative shrinkage-thresholding algorithm for linear inverse problems. SIAM Journal on Imaging Sciences 2(1), 183–202 (2009)

10. Hastie, T., Rosset, S., Tibshirani, R., Zhu, J.: The entire regularization path for the support vector machine. Journal of Machine Learning Research 5, 1391–1415 (2004)
11. Efron, B., Hastie, T., Johnstone, I., Tibshirani, R.: Least angle regression. Annals of Statistics 32, 407–499 (2004)
12. Friedman, J.: Fast sparse regression and classification. In: The 23rd International Workshop on Statistical Modelling, pp. 27–57 (2008)
13. Yuan, M., Lin, Y.: Model selection and estimation in regression with grouped variables. Journal of the Royal Statistical Society: Series B (Statistical Methodology) 68(1), 49–67 (2006)
14. Liu, H., Palatucci, M., Zhang, J.: Blockwise coordinate descent procedures for the multi-task lasso, with applications to neural semantic basis discovery. In: The Proceedings of 26th International Conference of Machine Learning (2009)
15. Yang, H., Xu, Z., King, I., Lyu, M.R.: Online learning for group lasso. In: The Proceedings of 27th International Conference of Machine Learning (2010)
16. Friedman, J., Hastie, T., Tibshirani, R.: A note on the group lasso and a sparse group lasso. Technical report, Standford University (2010)
17. Boyd, S., Vandenberghe, L.: Convex Optimization. Cambridge University Press (2004)
18. Lin, Z., Liu, R., Su, Z.: Linearized alternating direction method with adaptive penalty for low rank representation. In: NIPS (2011)
19. Beck, A., Teboulle, M.: A fast iterative shrinkage-thresholding algorithm for linear inverse problems. SIAM Journal of Imaging Sciences 2(1), 183–202 (2009)
20. Lin, Z., Chen, M., Ma, Y.: The augmented lagrange multiplier method for exact recovery of corrupted low-rank matrices. Technical Report UILU-ENG-09-2215, University of Illinois at Urbana-Champaign (2009)
21. Berman, M., Bischof, L., Huntington, J.: Algorithms and software for the automated identification of minerals using field spectra or hyperspectral imagery. In: Thirteenth International Conference on Applied Geologic Remote Sensing (1999)
22. Guo, Y., Berman, M.: A comparison between subset selection and L1 regularisation with an application in spectroscopy. Chemometrics and Intelligent Laboratory Systems (to appear)
23. Guo, Y., Berman, M.: An investigation of some regularization approaches to the unmixing of mineral reflectance spectra. Technical Report CMIS 09/119, CMIS (2010)
24. Tibshirani, R., Bien, J., Friedman, J., Hastie, T., Simon, N., Taylor, J., Tibshirani, R.J.: Strong rules for discarding predictors in lasso-type problems. Journal of the Royal Statistical Society, Series B 74, 245–266 (2012)
25. Fan, J., Lv, J.: Sure independence screening for ultrahigh dimensional feature space. Journal of the Royal Statistical Society: Series B (Statistical Methodology) 70, 849–911 (2008)
26. Mohimani, H., Babaie-Zadeh, M., Jutten, C.: A fast approach for overcomplete sparse decomposition based on smoothed l0 norm. IEEE Transactions on Signal Processing 57(1), 289–301 (2009)

Reverse Active Learning for Optimising Information Extraction Training Production

Dung Nguyen and Jon Patrick

School of IT, University of Sydney
1 Cleveland, Sydney 2006, NSW, Australia
{nguyend,jonpat}@it.usyd.edu.com

Abstract. When processing a noisy corpus such as clinical texts, the corpus usually contains a large number of misspelt words, abbreviations and acronyms while many ambiguous and irregular language usages can also be found in training data needed for supervised learning. These are two frequent kinds of noise that can affect the overall performance of machine learning process. The first noise is usually filtered by the proof reading process. This paper proposes an algorithm to deal with noisy training data problem, for a method we call reverse active learning to improve performance of supervised machine learning on clinical corpora. The effects of reverse active learning are shown to produce results on the i2b2 clinical corpus that are state-of-the-art of supervised learning method and offer a means of improving all processing strategies in clinical language processing.

Keywords: Active Learning, Clinical, Information extraction.

1 Introduction

1.1 Learning from Noisy Gold-Standard

Clinical notes contain valuable information about a patient's health status, however, retrieving information from them is challenging. The popular challenge to supervised machine learning approaches in clinical domain is the level of noise that arises in training data, even if tagging is created by human experts, they may not always be reliable because some instances are implicitly difficult for annotators and them becoming distracted or fatigued over time, introduces variability in the quality of their annotations [1].

The process of removing noisy training data is conventionally known as data selection and data reduction for machine learning [2,3]. The work nearest to our problem with noisy training data is estimating the quality of annotators and then only querying the more reliable annotators in subsequent iterations of active learning (AL) [4]. However, this method only works with an online annotation process and does not analyse the performance of annotators over time. Furthermore, in the case where the gold-standard instances are available but they do not contain any information about the authors, the method of

M. Thielscher and D. Zhang (Eds.): AI 2012, LNCS 7691, pp. 445–456, 2012.
© Springer-Verlag Berlin Heidelberg 2012

estimating the performance of annotators is not applicable. Other similar idea come from the Corrective Active Learning which try to clean up the noisy labeled data through human interaction [5]. But using human resources is always costly and this method is only practical when the correctors have intensive knowledge and familiar with the training data. This is not the case when training data usually come from different sources and organizations. Our filtering methods for classification task does not require any human involvement and will work for any source of noisy training data without information about annotators.

1.2 Active Learning

Active learning (AL) is a subfield of machine learning where the learner is allowed to query the most informative instances to retrain the model instead of making a random selection. Based on this approach, with the same number of sample selections, the performance of active learners dominates random learners in most cases. There are three main scenarios for AL: (i) membership query synthesis, (ii) stream-based selective sampling, and (iii) pool-based sampling [1].

All AL scenarios involve evaluating the informativeness of unlabelled instances. There are several strategies to estimate the value of information for each instance. The simplest and most popular strategy is uncertainty sampling which selects the instances that it is least certain to label [6]. Some variations to this query framework used margin and entropy as uncertainty measures [7,8]. Query-by-committee method maintains a list of models trained on the same labelled data but with competing hypotheses and query the instance with lowest agreement [9,10]. The important research question in AL is when to stop querying. Several stopping criteria have been introduced and are based on measures of stability or self-confidence within the learner [11,12].

1.3 The Active Learning's Sampling Bias Problem

A well-known problem with many AL algorithms, especially at the early steps of learning is that they are prone to generate a biased training set rather than be representative of the true underlying data distribution. This is due to the limitations in model initialization and the selection strategy. Many algorithms just randomly select a few instances to train the first model which is usually not a good starting point for the real data distribution. Experiments with various text data sets have shown that an active learner starting from a better initial training set such as clustered-based sampling has better uncertainty estimation than one starting from a randomly generated initial training set [13].

The selection strategies which focus on individual instances (Uncertainty sampling or Query-by-Committee) have a high chance of querying the outliers in the data. To overcome this problem, some algorithms such as Density-Weighted Methods and Balance Exploration and Exploitation are designed based on the main idea that informative instances should not only be those which are uncertain, but also those which are "representative" of the underlying distribution [8]. Expected model change approach has higher priority for instances that will impact the greatest change to the current model [8]. By focusing on the entire input space rather than individual instances, expected error reduction and variance reduction AL try to minimise the estimated future error and output variance of the model respectively [14]. However, all of these methods are just the approximations of the data distribution over each AL iteration and these approximations are only close to the real distribution when we have enough "representative" in the training set. Before reaching that state, the model is still an approximation and easy to query some outliers.

In our new approach of applying AL in reverse order, the model initialization and sampling bias problems is no longer need to be considered during the AL querying process and the model is guaranteed to be the best representation of underlying data rather than just the approximation. The detailed explanation is given in section 5.

1.4   Contributions

In this paper, we introduce one new practical consideration of AL that we call Reverse Active Learning (RAL), that is, the use of AL evaluation methods to remove the less informative instances and inconsistencies in the available training data to improve the best performance of supervised machine learning. The quality of the gold-standard and individual instances are evaluated by the system regardless of who annotated them. This approach is time efficient to normal AL especially when we need to select the large amount of training data to guarantee a better performance. More importantly, RAL can overcome the main obstacles in traditional AL: model initialization and biased training subset. These advantages of RAL are discussed in section 5 of this paper.

In much AL research, the experiments are set up by a set of training instances and a test set used to evaluate the performance achieved. The savings estimation are commonly computed as the percentage of the training instances selected during AL to achieve the same performance compared to using all the available training instances, or, as the difference in performance between AL and random selection for a given amount of annotation. This however implies that all the candidate training instances are annotated in advance. The more practical experiment when the annotations are available is how to select the best subset of the training data to build the model.

The traditional AL approach is based on using a small set of training data to build the initial model, and then using the model to query the most informative unlabelled instances to get their labels then retrain the current model. The central idea of RAL is to make use of available training data to generate better performance by removing less informative or inconsistent instances. The noisier the gold-standard is the better improvement the RAL can achieve.

2   Materials and Methods

Figure 1 shows the system architecture. The processing pipeline is described by an Experiment Descriptive Language (EDL) and executed by the Experiment

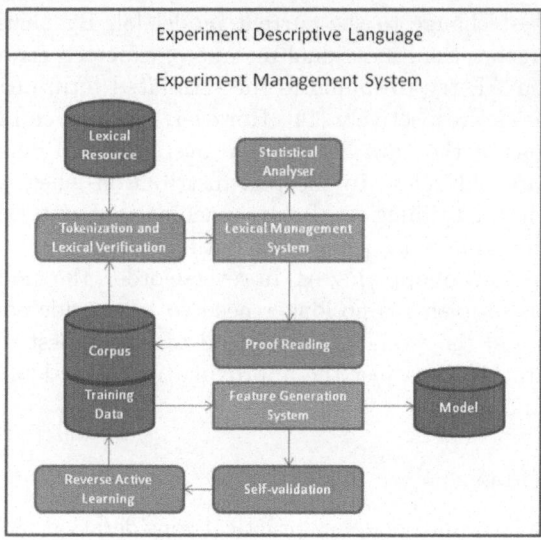

Fig. 1. System Architecture

Management System (EMS). The EMS ensures that a series of experiments and results are described, executed and compared in an expeditious and reusable way. An experiment is the execution of modules in a certain order. Experiment management is primarily the storage of an experiment in a deterministically reproducible form, as well as the storage of results associated with an experiment. A series of experiments need to be executed to compare the results. Instead of manually running the same modules on the original and refined corpora with different tags then comparing the results, using the EMS makes this process automatic and efficient. Using the EDL to describe an experiment allows a flexible execution order of modules within the same program as well as across multiple programs.

The Lexicon Management System (LMS) supports automated and manual resolution of unknown tokens. The LMS is a system developed to store the accumulated lexical knowledge and contains categorizations of spelling errors, abbreviations, acronyms and a variety of non-word tokens. It also has a web interface that supports rapid manual correction of unknown words with a high accuracy clinical spelling suggestor plus the addition of grammatical information and the categorization of such words into gazetteers [15]. The method of the clinical spelling suggestor is based on combining heuristic-based suggestion generation and ranking algorithms based on word frequencies and trigram probabilities. This approach achieved high accuracies on test data sets with over 93.5%.

The proof reading process can be applied directly or indirectly to improve performance of the text extraction system. Firstly, for the available annotation tools, the proof correcting process is applied directly to the corpus with the expectation of finding more concepts from misspelling corrections, abbreviations and acronym expansions. However, during supervised learning experiments, this transformation should not be made in the original corpus because it would affect the offsets of tokens which in turn will lead to retrieval of incorrect annotations. Consequently, these corrections can be used indirectly as features which will support the model in learning the correct form of misspelt words ("medicla" and "medcial" refer to the same word "medical") and variations of abbreviations ("amnt" and "amt" are both "amount"), and multiple acronyms of the same term ("ABG", "ABGs" are both "arterial blood gases").

The automated proof reading process is applied to clean the noisy corpus while RAL is used for removing less informative or inconsistencies in gold-standard training data. Traditional supervised learning generates the model based on training data with the best feature set. The popular methods to achieve the best feature set is by running experiments with n-fold cross-validation on training data with different feature sets and select the model with highest performance. In our method, active de-sampling is applied after the best feature sets are selected to refine the gold-standard and improve the best performance on the current training data. Two different refining strategies for two popular annotation tasks are developed and evaluated; these are self-validation for Named-entity Recognition (NER) and RAL for relationship classification.

3   Methods

3.1   Named-Entity Recognition Self Validation

Conditional Random Fields (CRFs) have been used to recognize clinical entities [16]. In clinical NER, the gold standard was created by manual annotation, which usually contains minor errors and inconsistencies. The self-validation (or reflexive validation) process can estimate the level of these inconsistencies in training data and extract them for further analysis and correction. The gold standard can be corrected for inconsistencies between annotations by using this process, which we also denote as "100% train and test". This involves using 100% of the training set to build a model and then testing on the same set. As theoretically all data items used for training should be correctly identifiable by the model, any errors represent either inconsistencies in annotations or weaknesses in the computational linguistic processing. The former faults identify training items that are rejected, and the latter faults identify where to concentrate efforts to improve the preprocessing system. The self-validation is an automated process to identify inconsistent candidates and these candidates are then reviewed by human to remove noise that come from the training data.

3.2   Text and Relationship Classification

The base learner used in AL for text classification is a support vector machine (SVM) [17]. We have developed the AL framework for clinical data on top of the

---
Algorithm 1. Algorithm MCAL

Input

- A pool $U = \{u_1, u_2, \dots u_n\}$.
- randomly selected training set L (at least one instance for each of m classes).
- number of query q for each iteration.

For each class c in m classes:

1. Init:
   - Set class value of c in L as 1 (positive).
   - Set all other classes in L as -1 (negative).
   - Using L to train the model M.
2. For t = 1, 2 ... q
   - Get label v for the most informative instance u_i from U.
   - If u_i not in S: add u_i to S with value v.
   - If v == c: Add instance u_i to L with value of 1.
     Else: Add instance u_i to L with value of -1.
   - Retrain model with L.
   - Remove u_i from U.

Return: Selected instances list S.

---

choice of the online AL algorithm (COMB) which contains 4 AL algorithms (Simple, Self confident, KFF and Balanced EE) [18]. Two enhancements of COMB have been implemented: (i) multi-class AL from COMB's AL binary classifier, (ii) Reverse Active Learning (RAL).

The "one versus the rest" method to build multi-class classifier (MCAL) is applied and can be executed in a parallel environment. The main purpose of AL is to select the most informative instances to train the model. In our method, by obtaining the union of selected instances over binary active learners, the best training set for multi-class text classification are generated so that the available multi-class SVMs tool such as libsvm can be used to build the final model [19]. This process is simpler than normal binary SVM AL combinations which usually require an additional probabilistic comparison step to resolve inconsistencies between different predictions on the same instance. The pseudo code for multi-class AL is illustrated in algorithm 1.

The m-class initial training data must have at least one instance for each class. Because the selection step for each class is independent, this process can be executed concurrently so that the nary AL will have similar running time to binary AL. The pseudo code for the RAL is presented in algorithm 2. The RAL algorithm follows similar steps in AL but shows modifications in the initial configuration and output selection strategy. The RAL starts with a large training data and outputs the list of instances that should be removed to achieve a better gold-standard to train the model.

Algorithm 2. Algorithm Reverse Active Learning

Input

- m-class full training set L = x_1, x_2, ... x_n.
- number of query q for each iteration.

Init

- Build index on L to store original class value.

For each class c in m classes:

1. Init:
   - Set class value of class c in L as 1 (positive).
   - Set all other classes in L as -1 (negative).
   - Using L to train the model M.
2. For t = 1, 2 ... q.
   - Get the least informative instance x_i from L.
   - Remove instance x_i from L.
   - If value(x_i) == 1: original_class_value = c.
      Else: original_class_value = get_original_class(x_i).
   - If x_i not in S: add x_i to S with original_class_value.
   - Retrain model with L.

Return: Removed instances list S.

4   Results

4.1   Clinical Concept Recognition

The experiments in this section were conducted to attempt the Clinical Concept Recognition task in the i2b2 2010 challenge on Clinical Information Extraction and CRF++ toolkit[1] was used to build the NER model [20]. During the training experiment, the best feature sets were selected after many cycles of n-fold cross validation. This section focuses on evaluate the effect of Self-validation process for refining the training data in order to boost up performance of supervised NER even when the best feature sets were decided.

With a self-validation process, approximately 150 errors in the training data were recognized and manually corrected. The three most frequent error types in concept annotation were: (1) missing modifier (any, some) within the noun phrase; (2) including punctuation at the end of concepts (full stop, comma, and hyphen); (3) missing annotation (false negative). When the model is trained with both correct and incorrect examples on some concepts, the probability of identifying the correct instances is definitely reduced and this might lead to series of wrong annotations on these concepts. Thus, automated detection and manual correction of errors in the training data contributed to improve the consistency and overall performance of the current model.

---

[1] CRF++. Yet another CRF toolkit. Software. Http://crfpp.sourceforge.net

Proof reading and self-validation of the gold-standard brought approximately 1.5% improvement to the overall F-score of concept annotation supervised learning. This contribution was significant to make our result attain the state of the art of supervised learning method at i2b2 2010 challenge which was evaluated and reported by the organizers. Because the training and testing data come from the same source of corpora and annotators, the same kind of noise on testing data is unavoidable. Based on this assumption, we executed the same process on released testing data and over 200 similar errors were discovered. After correcting all of these errors for a better testing set, our system performance increased another 0.5%. Overall, the improvement of RAL for NER is approximately 2.0% as recorded in Table 1.

Table 1. System performance before and after Self-validation process

CONCEPT	TP	FP	FN	P	R	F
Problem	14423	2896	4127	83.28%	77.75%	80.42%
	14486	2752	3664	84.40%	80.25%	82.27%
Test	9945	1629	2954	85.93%	77.10%	81.27%
	10233	1504	2666	87.19%	79.33%	83.07%
Treatment	10134	1877	3426	84.37%	74.73%	79.26%
	10542	1722	3018	85.96%	77.74%	81.64%
OVERALL	34502	6402	10507	84.35%	76.66%	80.32%
	35661	5978	9348	85.64%	79.23%	82.31%

4.2   Text Classification

A multi-class AL algorithm was tested on the i2b2 2010 9-class relationship classification test data (no-relation is treated as one class). The simple Libsvm classifier is built mainly based on local context features (bag of words) and semantic features (concept and assertion type from the ground truth) supplied by the organizer. With these minimal and simple features, the classifier achieved an F-score of 68.86% test accuracy by using all 16475 instances of the training data (including no-relation instances). After adding proof reading as features, the result increased to 70.02% which was reported as equal second performance for relationship classification task at the challenge.

For a large-scale classification problem with many thousands instances and features as in i2b2 relationship classification task, linear kernel is usually a promising learning technique for this data [21]. Because of this assumption, further experiments are taken with the use of Liblinear as a base classifier rather than Libsvm with non-linear kernels [22]. Liblinear is an open source library for large-scale linear classification with ease of solvers and parameters selection. The use of Liblinear classifier improved the F-score by 1.5%. Three of the 4 AL algorithms that have high performance on the i2b2 clinical data set are Simple, Self confidence and Balance EE while the KFF algorithm returns a significantly lower result. Table 2 shows the comparisons of the AL algorithms with a maximum of 500 queries for each class. The combined training data is a union of all

Table 2. Performance of multi-class AL

Method	Training size(AL instances)	Training percent	F-Score
Simple	2076	12.60%	66.25%
Self-confidence	1900	11.53%	64.58%
Balance EE	2069	12.56%	65.76%
Combined	4361	26.47%	68.03%

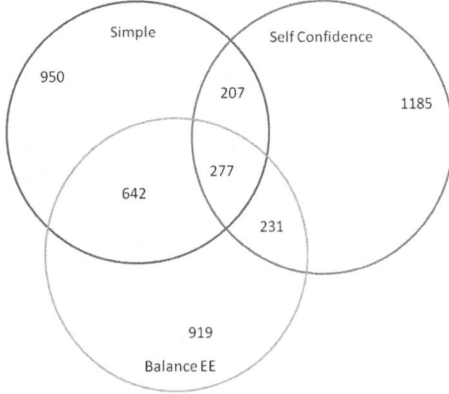

Fig. 2. The distribution of selected instances over 3 AL algorithms: Simple, Self Confidence and Balance EE

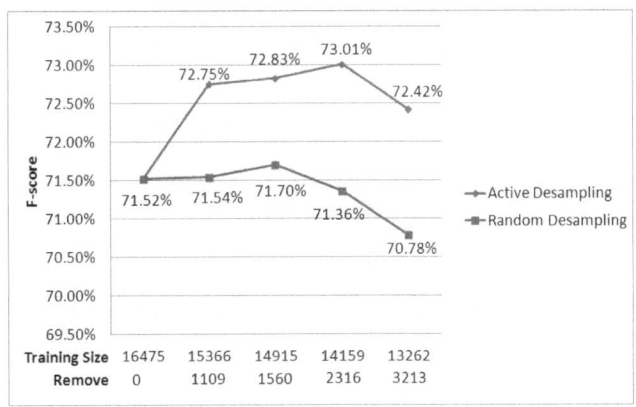

Fig. 3. Active desampling and random desampling on test data

instances selected by three AL algorithms. The overlapping selected instances between the 3 algorithms are shown in Figure 2 where Simple and Balance EE show the greatest overlap in selected instances.

RAL applied with the Simple method can improve the best result on supervised learning (1.5%) by removing over 1500 less informative instances. The final result after using Liblinear and applied RAL is comparable to the current state of the art of the dataset who also using Liblinear as base classifier. Furthermore, the i2B2 challenge papers have been studied and there is no AL approach for relationship classification used in any of the top submitted processing systems. Figure 3 shows that the F-scores of active desampling dominates random desampling with the same number of removed instances.

5   Discussion

Our methods of applying RAL can improve the supervised learning performance from 1.5% to 2% on two popular clinical information extraction tasks: clinical NER and relationship classification. These improvement may not be significant in general, but these are the additional improvements to the best performance of the available training data. In supervised learning, experiments are set up in order to select the best feature sets to build the model. The closer a model is to the best possible performance, the harder (or smaller) is the improvement that can be made. In our experience, after the best feature sets are determined for the available training data, the contribution of 1.5% to 2% is remarkable. Furthermore, the improvement of one percent and above was considered as statistical difference in the i2b2 challenge's ranking system [20].

From the experiment's results, with equivalent number of selected instances during AL processes (approximately 2000 instances), the performance of RAL is at least 4.84% higher than any single AL setting and 3% higher than the union of all three popular AL methods with double selected instances (table 2). The most important aspect is RAL can produce a better result than using all available training data right at the very first removing instances as seen in Figure 3. In order to normal AL to achieve the same performance with this clinical dataset, the number of data evaluation and selection process might be up to 14,000 cycles which will take much more time to complete.

For the relationship classification, our classifier is only based on very simple, easy implemented feature sets and mainly using resources supplied by the organizer while the winner used a wide range of complicated features from external syntactic (chunking and parsing) tools; medical ontology and Wikipedia knowledge [23]. Without using any external and huge resources as features, our classifiers is more practical to be installed and evaluated in real clinical environment.

RAL starts with a full training set which is best in initial model representation and informativeness for instance evaluation. Then the model sequentially removes small portions of less useful instances which causes minor impact on the data distribution. Consequently, the initial model building and training bias are no longer considered as obstacle to RAL. In this situation, complicated algorithms to deal with these problems are also no longer needed. The original and "Simple" AL method based on Uncertainty estimation is a reasonable choice in the RAL setting. As shown in the result, with a noisy gold standard such as in clinical domain, application of RAL is preferred to normal AL because the simple RAL can generate better results than supervised learning right from the first steps of removal.

6   Conclusions

In this study, a general system architecture for refining the training data is developed and evaluated. RAL is used as a final step to improve the quality of training data after the best feature sets are decided. Our work focuses on the clinical domain which suffers from a high level of noise in both the corpus and training data. However, our method and system architecture are easy to adapt to any domain with modification of resources and feature sets for supervised learning.

We also introduce and illustrate a simple combination of binary active learners into multi-class AL as well as the application of AL in reverse order to improve the best performance of supervised learning. To sum up, we recommend the use of proof reading and RAL in supervised learning for a noisy domain such as clinical natural language processing. RAL is not only simple and suitable but also can generate better performance and is less prone to biased training problem.

References

1. Settles, B.: Active learning literature survey. Computer Sciences Technical Report 1648, University of Wisconsin-Madison (2010)
2. Blum, A.L., Langley, P.: Selection of relevant features and examples in machine learning. J. Artif. Intell. 97(1-2), 245–271 (1997)
3. Fung, G., Mangasarian, O.L.: Data selection for support vector machine classifiers. In: Proceedings of the Sixth ACM SIGKDD International Conference on Knowledge Discovery and Data Mining, KDD 2000, pp. 64–70. ACM, New York (2000)
4. Donmez, P., Carbonell, J.G., Schneider, J.: Efficiently learning the accuracy of labeling sources for selective sampling. In: Proceedings of the 15th ACM SIGKDD International Conference on Knowledge Discovery and Data Mining, KDD 2009, pp. 259–268. ACM, New York (2009)
5. Nallapati, R., Surdeanu, M., Manning, C.: Corrective learning: Learning from noisy data through human interaction. In: IJCAI Workshop on Intelligence and Interaction (2009)
6. Lewis, D., Gale, W.: Training text classifiers by uncertainty sampling. In: Proceedings of ACM-SIGIR Conference on Information Retrieval, pp. 3–12 (1994)
7. Scheffer, T., Decomain, C., Wrobel, S.: Active Hidden Markov Models for Information Extraction. In: Hoffmann, F., Adams, N., Fisher, D., Guimarães, G., Hand, D.J. (eds.) IDA 2001. LNCS, vol. 2189, pp. 309–318. Springer, Heidelberg (2001)
8. Settles, B., Craven, M.: An analysis of active learning strategies for sequence labeling tasks. In: Proceedings of the Conference on Empirical Methods in Natural Language Processing, EMNLP 2008, pp. 1070–1079. Association for Computational Linguistics, Stroudsburg (2008)
9. Seung, H.S., Opper, M., Sompolinsky, H.: Query by committee. In: Proceedings of the Fifth Annual Workshop on Computational Learning Theory, COLT 1992, pp. 287–294. ACM, New York (1992)
10. McCallum, A., Nigam, K.: Employing em and pool-based active learning for text classification. In: Proceedings of the Fifteenth International Conference on Machine Learning, ICML 1998, pp. 350–358. Morgan Kaufmann Publishers Inc., San Francisco (1998)

11. Vlachos, A.: A stopping criterion for active learning. Computer Speech and Language 22(3), 295–312 (2008)
12. Olsson, F., Tomanek, K.: An intrinsic stopping criterion for committee-based active learning. In: Proceedings of the Thirteenth Conference on Computational Natural Language Learning, CoNLL 2009, pp. 138–146. Association for Computational Linguistics, Stroudsburg (2009)
13. Kang, J., Ryu, K., Kwon, H.C.: Using Cluster-Based Sampling to Select Initial Training Set for Active Learning in Text Classification. In: Dai, H., Srikant, R., Zhang, C. (eds.) PAKDD 2004. LNCS (LNAI), vol. 3056, pp. 384–388. Springer, Heidelberg (2004)
14. Roy, N., McCallum, A.: Toward optimal active learning through sampling estimation of error reduction. In: Proceedings of the Eighteenth International Conference on Machine Learning, ICML 2001, pp. 441–448. Morgan Kaufmann Publishers Inc., San Francisco (2001)
15. Patrick, J., Sabbagh, M., Jain, S., Zheng, H.: Spelling correction in clinical notes with emphasis on first suggestion accuracy. In: 2nd Workshop on Building and Evaluating Resources for Biomedical Text Mining, pp. 2–8 (2010)
16. Lafferty, J., Pereira, F.: Conditional random fields: Probabilistic models for segmenting and labeling sequence data (2001)
17. Cristianini, N., Shawe-Taylor, J.: An introduction to support Vector Machines: and other kernel-based learning methods. Cambridge Univ. Pr. (2000)
18. Baram, Y., El-Yaniv, R., Luz, K.: Online choice of active learning algorithms. Journal of Machine Learning Research 5, 255–291 (2004)
19. Chang, C.C., Lin, C.J.: LIBSVM: A library for support vector machines. ACM Transactions on Intelligent Systems and Technology 2, 27:1–27:27 (2011), Software http://www.csie.ntu.edu.tw/
20. Uzuner, O., South, B.R., Shen, S., DuVall, S.L.: 2010 i2b2/va challenge on concepts, assertions, and relations in clinical text. J. Am. Med. Inform. Assoc. 18(5), 552–556 (2011)
21. Chih-Wei Hsu, C.C.C., Lin, C.J.: A practical guide to support vector classification. Technical report (2003-2010)
22. Fan, R.E., Chang, K.W., Hsieh, C.J., Wang, X.R., Lin, C.J.: Liblinear: A library for large linear classification. J. Mach. Learn. Res. 9, 1871–1874 (2008)
23. Rink, B., Harabagiu, S., Roberts, K.: Automatic extraction of relations between medical concepts in clinical texts. J. Am. Med. Inform. Assoc. 18(5), 594–600 (2011)

Adopting Relevance Feature
to Learn Personalized Ontologies

Yan Shen, Yuefeng Li, and Yue Xu

Electrical Engineering, Computer Science, Science and Engineering Faculty,
Queensland University of Technology, Australia
{y12.shen,y2.li,yue.xu}@qut.edu.au

Abstract. Relevance feature and ontology are two core components to learn personalized ontologies for concept-based retrievals. However, how to associate user native information with common knowledge is an urgent issue. This paper proposes a sound solution by matching relevance feature mined from local instances with concepts existing in a global knowledge base. The matched concepts and their relations are used to learn personalized ontologies. The proposed method is evaluated elaborately by comparing it against three benchmark models. The evaluation demonstrates the matching is successful by achieving remarkable improvements in information filtering measurements.

Keywords: Relevance Feature, Specificity Term, Ontology, Local Instance, Global Knowledge Base, Concept Matching.

1 Introduction

Information overload is continuously a hard problem for Information Retrieval (IR). Current retrieval methods acquire a precise query upfront to express search intents, which is fairly difficult for any user who has no background knowledge or past experience. Relevance Feature (RF) has been alternatively taken into account to indicate user needs in data mining methods [1] [2]. Generally, it comprises of patterns, terms and their weights while the weights are used to measure relevance. The feature extractions are mainly based on two aspects: 1) relevance feedback, where a user judges the results from previous retrieval and tells the system which documents are relevant or not [3]; and 2) pattern mining, which is an efficient technique against previous retrievals to filter out noisy by studying frequent, closed, and closed sequential patterns. Note that the extracted features are useful to point out user preferences.

Ontology-based technique has been recognized as a critical part of advanced search over last decade. It assists to refine search intents within specific domains and access new knowledge by tracking semantic relations. Recently, some researchers [4] have attempted to build ontological user profiles according to discovered user background knowledge. Some of the knowledge is integrated by both global and local analyses [5]. The global employs a global knowledge base (ontologies, thesauruses, or online knowledge bases) that mirrors the content of the

M. Thielscher and D. Zhang (Eds.): AI 2012, LNCS 7691, pp. 457–468, 2012.

world wide web for common knowledge representation, whereas the local investigates native information or observes user behaviours from local instances [6]. A same motivation is to produce personalized ontologies so as to better understand user needs by concepts.

A key challenge here is how to accurately match local information and global knowledge. The basic idea of existing method [6] is to use a conditional probability to determine relevant concepts for describing a theme of local instances. However, this technique usually obtains a low performance because of the mismatch problem [4]. Mismatch means some relevant specific concepts have been omitted. The problem of mismatch occurs when the popular features (useful or high frequent features) match many relevant but general concepts (usually appear in the top of the ontology); but do not match some relevant specific concepts (usually appear at the bottom of the ontology). This paper presents an alternative method to address the mismatch problem. The solution aims to learn personalized ontologies for user knowledge understanding. A pattern mining method is developed to discover RF from local instances automatically. All extracted terms in the RF are classified into three groups: Positive specific (SPE), General, and Negative specific respectively. Library of Congress Subject Headings (LCSH) is learned as a global knowledge base. The SPE terms are selected to match subject headings in the LCSH. The attempt-to-proposed approach is evaluated by comparing against three benchmark models with a standard Reuters Corpus Volume 1 (RCV1) testing set. The experimental results show the proposed matching is successful and achieve significant improvements in information filtering measurements. This research contributes to ontological user profiling and knowledge engineering. The related outputs are critical when systems expect to return proper search results and provide personalized services.

The rest of the paper is organized as below. Section 2, significant related work is involved; Section 3 outlines an overview of proposed approach, and requisite definitions are provided; Section 4 describes the extraction of RF; Section 5 introduces concept matching method; Section 6 shows conducted experiments and results; The paper is concluded by Section 7.

2   Related Work

2.1   Relevance Feature Extraction

Feature extraction is a fundamental stage for the majority of IR models. One of the most popular methods is TF*IDF. It uses keywords as elements in the vector of the feature space. The bag of words can be obtained by diverse term weighting approaches. However, these approaches struggle against the problem of selecting appropriate number of features among an enormous set of terms to guarantee the retrieval efficiency [7], or said over-fitting. In addition, the corresponding approaches are restricted on term statistics in the entire collection, but do not take relevance information (e.g. user feedback) into account. As an extension of term-based methods, pattern mining techniques are investigated by data mining communities for many years. These techniques extract useful patterns from large data collections instead of terms. Some studies categorize patterns into frequent, closed, and closed sequential. Simultaneously, they measure the specificity of pattens explicitly according to relevance feedback from human beings. Pattern taxonomy model (PTM) was first introduced by Wu et al. [1]. It improves search performance by using both frequent and closed patterns. Later on, it has been further researched by [2] to develop a two-stage model for irrelevant information filtering. Li et al. [3] build the Relevance Feature Discovery (RFD) model by mining patterns from positive and negative documents respectively. The related output shows potentials for enhancing information filtering and user profiling.

2.2 Ontology-Based Techniques

Since ontology-based techniques can bring more discriminative and arguably capabilities by carrying "semantics", people commenced to build user profiles by accessing common knowledge. Li and Zhong [8] develop a term-based ontology leaning method to automatically discover ontologies from data sets in order to understand user information needs by concepts. Gauch et al. [9] use ontology references based on the categorization of online portals and propose to learn personalized ontologies for users. Developed by King et al. [4], IntelliOnto is built based on the Dewey Decimal Classification (DDC) system and attempt to describe the background knowledge. Sieg et al. [5] utilize ontological user profile on the basis of the user's interaction with a concept hierarchy which aims to extract the domain knowledge. More recently, Tao et al. [6] propose an ontology-based knowledge retrieval framework, namely ONTO model, to capture user information needs by analyzing general knowledge and local instance repository. However, they disregard the work of matching and assume the local information can be ideally referred to the proper concepts in a global knowledge base.

Of all related work, the process in [6] seems the most similar to ours but two differences are: 1) our study adopts relevance feedback as user information needs rather than asking users to specify their needs manually, and 2) provides a sound solution to cope with local information and global knowledge mismatch.

3   Design and Definitions

Figure 1 illustrates a design of the proposed approach. Local instances as input consist of two parts: relevance feedback and a set of training documents. The relevance feedback is initialized as positive and negative. The positive indicates the document is relevant to user interests, whereas the negative is irrelevant. By applying the following method discussed in subsection 4.1, the extracted relevance features can be categorized into three groups: SPE, General, and Negative. Here, the approach only selects terms in the SPE group as candidates because they contain more topic-related interests rather than other groups [3]. LCSH, which is a thesaurus of subject headings, is chosen to be the global knowledge representation. Each subject heading denotes a concept among the knowledge base. The concept is a short phase where contains one or couple of terms. We match

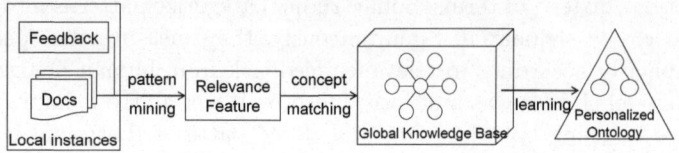

Fig. 1. Overview for the Entire Approach

the SPE terms to the subject headings, and personalized ontologies learning will eventually take advantage of the matched concepts and their original relations in the LCSH.

3.1   Definitions about Patterns and Closed Patterns

Relevance feature discovery is to find useful features, including patterns, terms and their weights, in a training set D, which consists of a set of positive documents, D^+, and a set of negative documents, D^-. In this paper, we assume that all documents are split into paragraphs. So a given document d yields a set of paragraphs $PS(d)$.

Let $T = \{t_1, t_2, \ldots, t_m\}$ be a set of terms which are extracted from D^+. Given a *termset* X, a set of terms, in document d, $coverset(X) = \{dp | dp \in PS(d), X \subseteq dp\}$. Its *absolute support*

$$sup_a(X) = |coverset(X)|;$$

and its *relative support*

$$sup_r(X) = \frac{|coverset(X)|}{|PS(d)|}.$$

A termset X is called *frequent pattern* if its sup_a (or sup_r) $\geq min\_sup$, a minimum support. Given a set of paragraphs $Y \subseteq PS(d)$, we can define its *termset*, which satisfies

$$termset(Y) = \{t | \forall dp \in Y \Rightarrow t \in dp\}.$$

Let $Cls(X) = termset(coverset(X))$ be the closure of X. We call X *closed* if and only if $X = Cls(X)$. Let X be a closed pattern. We have

$$sup_a(X_1) < sup_a(X) \tag{1}$$

for all pattern $X_1 \supset X$.

Closed Sequential Patterns. A sequential pattern $s = <t_1, \ldots, t_r> \ (t_i \in T)$ is an ordered list of terms. A sequence $s_1 = <x_1, \ldots, x_i>$ is a sub-sequence of another sequence $s_2 = <y_1, \ldots, y_j>$, denoted by $s_1 \sqsubseteq s_2$, iff $\exists j_1, \ldots, j_i$ such that $1 \leq j_1 < j_2 \ldots < j_i \leq j$ and $x_1 = y_{j_1}, x_2 = y_{j_2}, \ldots, x_i = y_{j_i}$. Given $s_1 \sqsubseteq s_2$, we usually say s_1 is a sub-pattern of s_2, and s_2 is a super-pattern of s_1. In the following, we refer to sequential patterns as patterns.

Given a sequential pattern X in document d, $coverset(X)$ is still used to denote the covering set of X, which includes all paragraphs $ps \in PS(d)$ such that $X \sqsubseteq ps$, i.e., $coverset(X) = \{ps|ps \in PS(d), X \sqsubseteq ps\}$. Its *absolute support* and *relative support* are defined as the same as for the normal patterns.

A sequential pattern X is called a *frequent pattern* if its relative support $\geq$ *min_sup*, a minimum support. The property of closed patterns (see Eq. (1)) can be used to define closed sequential patterns. A frequent sequential pattern X is called *closed* if not $\exists$ any super-pattern X_1 of X such that $sup_a(X_1) = sup_a(X)$.

3.2   Global Knowledge Base: LCSH

Global knowledge is the common-sense knowledge acquired by people based on their experience and education. LCSH is an ideal global knowledge representation because of a rich vocabulary is used to cover all subject areas. In the LCSH, subject headings are basic elements to convey knowledge in the format of concept, they have three main types of references: *Broader Term* (BT), *Narrower Term* (NT) and *Related Term* (RT). Related definitions are clarified as follows. Definition of Subject headings: Let C denote a set of subject headings in LCSH, a subject $s \in C$ is formalized as a pair $(label, reference)$, where

- *label* is the heading of s in LCSH thesaurus;
- *reference* is a statement regarding all references that the subject c has.

The LCSH world knowledge base can be formalized as:
Definition of World Knowledge Base: A world knowledge base ontology is a directed acyclic graph structure defined as a pair $\Theta := (C, R)$, consisting of

- C is a set of subjects in LCSH $C = \{s_1, s_2, ..., s_n\}$;
- R is the semantic relations $R = \{ref_1, ref_2, ..., ref_n\}$ existing among the subjects in C.

4   Relevance Feature Acquisition

In general, the concept of relevance is subjective. People can easily determine the relevance of a topic (or document) in specificity or generality. However, it is hard to use these concepts for interpreting relevance features in text documents. This section first discusses how to use the concepts for understanding the different roles of the low-level feature terms for answering what users want. We also present the ideas for accurately weighting terms based on their specificity and distributions in the discovered higher level features. Finally, we describe algorithms for both the discovery of higher level features and the revision of weights of low-level terms.

4.1   Specificity of Low-Level Features

A term's specificity describes the extent of the term to which the topic focuses on what users want. It is very difficult to measure the specificity of terms because a term's specificity depends on users' perspectives for their information needs [6]. The paper discusses how terms are grouped into three groups (SPE, general, and negative specific terms) based on their appearances in a training set. Given a term $t \in T$, its *coverage*$^+$ is the set of positive documents that contain t, and its *coverage*$^-$ is the set of negative documents that contain t. We assume that terms frequently used in both positive documents and negative documents are general terms. Therefore, we want to classify terms that are more frequently used in the positive documents into the positive specific category; and the terms that are more frequently used in the negative documents into the negative specific category. Based on the above analysis, we define the *specificity* of a given term t in the training set $D = D^+ \cup D^-$ as follows:

$$spe(t) = \frac{|coverage^+(t)| - |coverage^-(t)|}{n}$$

where $coverage^+(t) = \{d \in D^+ | t \in d\}$, $coverage^-(t) = \{d \in D^- | t \in d\}$, and $n = |D^+|$. $spe(t) > 0$ means that term t is used more frequently in positive documents than in negative documents. We present the following classification rules for determining the general terms G, the SPE terms T^+, and the negative specific terms T^-:

$$G = \{t \in T | \theta_1 \leq spe(t) \leq \theta_2\},$$

$$T^+ = \{t \in T | spe(t) > \theta_2\}, \ and$$

$$T^- = \{t \in T | spe(t) < \theta_1\}.$$

where θ_2 is an experimental coefficient, the maximum bound of the specificity for the general terms, and θ_1 is also an experimental coefficient, the minimum bound of the specificity for the general terms. We assume that $\theta_2 > 0$ and $\theta_2 \geq \theta_1$. It is easy to verify that $G \cap T^+ \cap T^- = \emptyset$. Therefore, $\{G, T^+, T^-\}$ is a partition of all terms. To describe relevance features for a given topic, we believe that specific terms are very useful for the topic in order to distinguish it from other topics.

4.2   Term Weighting

In Pattern Taxonomy Model (PTM), relevance features are discovered from a set of positive documents. To improve the efficiency of the PTM, an algorithm, $SPMining(D^+, min\_sup)$ [10], was proposed (also used in [1]) to find closed sequential patterns for all documents $\in D^+$, which used the well-known *Apriori* property in order to reduce the searching space. For all positive documents $d_i \in D^+$, the *SPMining* algorithm can discover all closed sequential patterns, SP_i, based on a given min_sup. (We omit this algorithm to save space.)

Let $SP_1, SP_2, ..., SP_n$ be the sets of discovered closed sequential patterns for all documents $d_i \in D^+ (i = 1, \cdots, n)$, where $n = |D^+|$. For a given term t, its support (or called *weight*) in discovered patterns can be described as follows:

$$support(t, D^+) = \sum_{i=1}^{n} \frac{|\{p | p \in SP_i, t \in p\}|}{\sum_{p \in SP_i} |p|} \tag{2}$$

where $|p|$ is the number of terms in p. After the supports of terms have been computed from the training set, the following rank will be assigned to every incoming document d to decide its relevance:

$$rank(d) = \sum_{t \in T} weight(t)\tau(t, d) \qquad (3)$$

where $weight(t) = support(t, D^+)$; and $\tau(t, d) = 1$ if $t \in d$; otherwise $\tau(t, d) = 0$.

Because of many noises in the discovered patterns (an inherent disadvantage of data mining), the evaluated supports are not accurate enough. To improve the effectiveness of PTM, we use negative documents in the training set in order to remove the noises. If a document's rank (see Eq. (3)) is less than or equals to zero, this document is clearly negative to the system. If a negative document has a high rank, the document is called an offender [8] because it forces the system to make a mistake. The offenders are normally defined as the top-K negative documents in a ranked set of negative documents, D^-. The basic hypothesis is that the relevance features should be mainly discovered from the positive documents. Therefore, in our experiments, we set $K = \frac{n}{2}$, the half of the number of positive documents.

Once we select the top-K negative documents, the set of negative document D^- will be reduced to include only K offenders (negative documents). The next step is to classify terms into three categories, G, T^+, and T^-, based on D^+ and the updated D^-. We can easily verify that the experimental coefficients θ_1 and θ_2 satisfy the following properties if $K = \frac{n}{2}$:

$$0 \leq \theta_2 \leq 1, \quad \text{and} \quad -\frac{1}{2} \leq \theta_1 \leq \theta_2.$$

Here, we show the basic process of revising discovered features in a training set. This process can help readers to understand the proposed strategies for revising weights of low-level terms in different categories. Formally, let DP^+ be the union of all discovered closed sequential patterns in D^+, DP^- be the union of all discovered closed sequential patterns in D^- and T be the set of terms that appear in DP^+ or DP^-, where a closed sequential pattern of D^+ (or D^-) is called a *positive pattern* (or *negative pattern*).

It is obviously that $\exists d \in D^+$ such that $t \in d$ for all $t \in T^+$ since $spe(t) > \theta_2 \geq 0$ for all $t \in T^+$. Therefore, for each $t \in T^+$, it can obtain an initial weight by the deploying method on D^+ (using the higher level features, see Eq. (2)).

For the term in $(T^- \cup G)$, there are two cases. If $\exists d \in D^+$ such that $t \in d$, t will get its initial weight by using the deploying method on D^+; otherwise it will get a negative weight by using the deploying methods on D^-.

The initial weights of terms finally are revised according to the following principles: increment the weights of the SPE terms, decline the weights of the negative specific terms, and do not update the weights of the general terms. The details are described as follows:

$$weight(t) = \begin{cases} w(t) + w(t) \times spe(t), & \text{if } t \in T^+ \\ w(t), & \text{if } t \in G \\ w(t) - |w(t) \times spe(t)|, & \text{if } t \in T^- \end{cases} \qquad (4)$$

where w is the initial weight(or the support in Eq. (2)).

5   Concept Matching Method

The matching occurs between terms mined from previous sections and subjects appearing $s \in C$ in LCSH. Note that the mined terms are distinguished into three groups and their values can be calculated by the weight function in Eq. (4). In this method, we use only terms in the first scenario where $t \in T^+$ for matching the concepts among the LCSH. The SPE terms are sufficient and indispensable to represent user desired information according to our prior testing. The matching method is divided into several steps below:

1) To gather the importance of terms in T^+, we first sort them based on weight values from Eq. (4). The action aims to identify the significant terms from text mining perspective and highlight them.

2) The second step consists of two phases. At phase one, we get the top 25% terms in T^+ based on their values. They are considered as the core portion of local information. Consequently, four most relevant subjects $s \in C$ are referred to each of the top 25% terms. Phase two, the relevance of subjects is computed by $rel(s) = |T^+ \cap s|/|s|$, where $|T^+ \cap s|$ denotes the number of overlapped terms between T^+ and subject s, $|s|$ stands for the total number of terms in the subject s. According to the rel values, four subjects can be confirmed. The idea of choosing 25% and 4 parameters is supported by empirical experiments. The matching performance can be impacted while modifying these parameters. A comparison of using other parameters will be shown in evaluation.

Algorithm 1. Concept Matching Algorithm

Input:
    A set of SPE terms T^+; $weight(t)$ from Eq. (4); a set of LCSH subjects C.

Output:
    A set of matched concepts SC.

1: Let $SC = \emptyset$;
2: Sort T^+ using $weight(t)$ as descendant order;
3: Let $K = |T^+|/4$, Let T_1^+ be the top-K terms in T^+;
4: for each $t \in T_1^+$ {
5:       Let $s_1 = s_2 = s_3 = s_4 = t$;
6:       Let $c(t) = \{s \in C | t \in s\}$;
7:       Select the top-4 relevant concepts in $c(t)$ using $rel(s)$, and let s_1, s_2, s_3, s_4 be
        the subjects; //if $|c(t)| < 4$, t will be the default value of s_i because of step 5
8:       Let $SC = SC \cup \{s_1, s_2, s_3, s_4\}$ }
9: for each $t \in (T^+ - T_1^+)$ {
10:     Let $s_1 = t$, $rel(s_1) = 0$;
11:     for each $(s \in C \& t \in s)$
12:         if $\frac{|s \cap T^+|}{|s|} > rel(s_1)$ then
13:            Let $s_1 = s$, $rel(s_1) = \frac{|s \cap T^+|}{|s|}$;
14:     Let $SC = SC \cup \{s_1\}$ }

---

3) This step is for the rest of terms (75%) in T^+. To find out accurate subject for each of these terms, we select the most relevant one based on rel value instead of four.

4) A set of specified concepts and their references existing in the LCSH can be obtained to form a personalized ontology. By taking advantage of the ontology, a scope of user background knowledge can be defined, and search systems can offer tailoring results after understanding precise user preferences.

In most cases, a term $t \in T^+$ can successfully find a subject or a set of subjects $s = \{s|s \in C\}$ in the LCSH. It is a hard issue when a term cannot match concepts in the global knowledge base. For example, "dutroux" is not a valid word/term in vocabulary but appears frequently in the training documents. It should be important to describe user needs. However, no subject can be matched by the proposed method. To overcome this issue, we count the term itself as a subject directly as if $c(t) = \{s \in C|t \in s\} = \emptyset$.

Algorithm 1 illustrates an entire process for our concept matching method, which facilitates to repeat and optimize the work. Note that the output is a set of specific concepts SC, the process can be also understand as a transition of informative descriptor and conceptional descriptor. These acquired concepts and their semantic relations in LCSH are used to construct personalized ontologies.

6 Evaluation

The hypothesis in this paper is that the SPE terms extracted from RF contain user focusing needs. By adopting the RF for ontology matching, gathered concepts should be helpful to improve search effectiveness. Related experiments were conducted to support this hypothesis. This section states data collections, baseline models, information filtering measurements, and results.

6.1 Data Collections

A LCSH database was selected to build the world knowledge base. Its size is 719 mega bytes stored in Microsoft Office Access. Initially, 491,250 subject headings and their internal references between the headings were extracted.

RCV1 corpus consists of all and only English language stories produced by Reuter's journalists between August 20, 1996, and August 19, 1997, a total of 806,791 documents that cover very large topics and information. TREC (2002) has developed and provided 50 assessor topics [11] for the filtering track, aiming at building a robust filtering system. The relevance judgements on RCV1 have also been made by the assessors. The assessor topics are more reliable than any artificially constructed topics [12]. For each topic, some documents in RCV1 are divided into a training set and a testing set. According to Buckley and others [13], first 50 topics are stable and enough for high quality experiments. This research uses RCV1 and the first 50 assessor topics to evaluate the proposed model. Documents in RCV1 are marked in XML. To avoid bias in experiments, all the documents have been preprocessed by stemming and stop-words removal.

6.2 Baseline Models and Measurements

For evaluation, we employed three baseline models: 1) PTM, is the up-to-date pattern mining based model. It discovers sequential closed patterns from positive documents, deploys discovered patterns on their terms using Eq. (2) and ranks documents using Eq. (3). For the pattern-based models, we rank a document based on the total relative supports of discovered patterns that appear in the document. We also set $min\_sup = 0.2$ (relative support) for PTM; 2) TF*IDF, is a term-based model for comparison with new retrieval models. For each topic, we sorted terms in the positive documents according to original TF*IDF values and chose first 150 terms; 3) ONTO, is a ontology-based model developed by Tao et al. in 2011 [6]. The idea of the model is to use a similarity to determine relevant concepts c for describing the themes of the local instances, $P(c|F) = P(c \cap F)/P(F)$, where F is a set of features discovered in the local instances. The comparison is worth to indicate our discovered concepts are more specific for user requisitions. The proposed model named POM is estimated by five state-of-the art IR measuring metrics, including top 20 precision based on the relevance judgement in RCV1 ($top@20$), the precision averages at 11 standard recall levels ($11 - points$), the *Mean Average Precision* (MAP), the F_1-*measure* (F_1), and the *breakeven point* (b/p).

Table 1. Comparison Results for Different Parameter Settings. (Refer to Section 5, the table shows the reason to predefine parameters as top 25% terms with 4 subjects and 1 for the rest. A number of combination settings like 50% 33%, and 25% with different numbers of subject have been tested but omitted here for space.)

#subjects	%	top@20	MAP	F_1	b/p
	50	0.43	0.3967	0.4103	0.3880
4	33	0.42	0.3941	0.4084	0.3855
	25	**0.46**	**0.4124**	**0.4195**	**0.4042**
	50	0.44	0.4029	0.4141	0.3968
3	33	0.44	0.4008	0.4125	0.4001
	25	0.45	0.4053	0.4157	0.3971
2			......		

6.3   Experiment Design and Results

To prove that our matched concepts can truly contain user information needs, all terms in the concepts are deployed to revise a new weight as follows:

$$weight(t, \Theta) = \sum_{t \in s, s \in SC} rel(s)/|s|$$

For the POM, we use the revised weights computed by Eq. (3) to rank documents for each topic in the RCV1 testing set. For the baseline models, we apply features extracted by their methods, and then keep their original term weight pairs to implement our matching process. After that, the matched concepts are collected and deployed by the same formula upon. To indicate the influences affected, *the percentage change in performance* is used to compute the difference, which is formulated as:

$$\%chg = \frac{Result_{POM} - Result_{baseline}}{Result_{baseline}} \times 100$$

The lager %*chg* is, the more significant improvement it achieves.

As shown in Table 2, POM achieves excellent performance with 16.12% (max 25.13% and min 9.7%) in percentage change on average for all four measures. Another big different is the number of extracted terms by different techniques. There are 23.12 SPE terms in average, which is approximately 7 times less than the number of terms extracted by TF*IDF (147.32) and PTM (154.82). This demonstrates that SPE terms are quantitatively enough to summarize all user needs with a few number of words. The matched concepts should capture all concrete user knowledge. Fig. 2 shows the 11 − *points* comparison where the POM model distinctly outperforms than others.

Table 2. Comparison Results for All Models in First 50 Topics

	#*terms*	*top*@20	MAP	F_1	b/p
POM	**23.12**	**0.46**	**0.4124**	**0.4195**	**0.4042**
TF*IDF	147.32	0.391	0.35	0.378	0.3536
PTM	154.82	0.382	0.3649	0.3915	0.3652
ONTO	75.96	0.335	0.3403	0.3787	0.3355
%*cha*		**+25.13%**	**+17.3%**	**+9.7%**	**+15.16%**

In sum, to address the problem local instances and global knowledge mismatch, the proposed solution has been demonstrated successfully based on the evaluation. The substantial results indicate our method can effectively discover desired concepts to represent user specific needs by adopting RF. The dramatical improvements are significant after comparing with three classic baseline models.

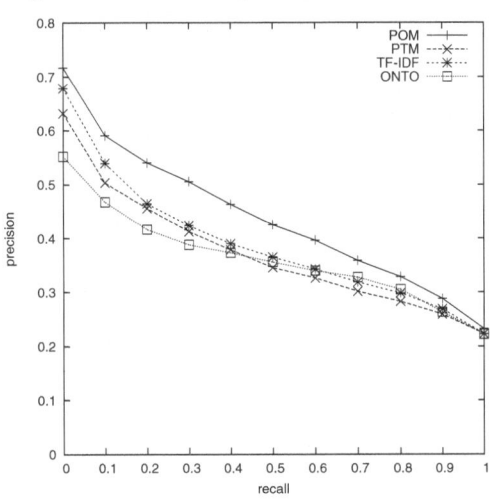

Fig. 2. 11 Points Result in First 50 Topics

7   Conclusion

This paper proposes a systematic method to build personalized ontologies by adopting relevance feature. The user orientated feature is used to represent user information need and match concepts appearing in global knowledge base. It is an effective solution to solve the problem of local informative references and common knowledge mismatch. In evaluation, the standard topics and a huge testbed were employed for scientific experiments. The substantial results prove that the proposed model is reliable after comparing with baseline models.

In future, we plan to investigate the usage of learned ontologies by utilizing abundant semantic relations among concepts. Note that ontologies play an important role as a backbone to facilitate accessing information in knowledge management systems. The present work aims to define user wants in terms of extensive concepts in world knowledge. Besides, we are also interested in weight revising methods for performance enhancement. The investigation will extend the applicability for the majority of existing Web documents, and maximum the contribution of the present work.

References

1. Wu, S., Li, Y., Xu, Y.: Deploying approaches for pattern refinement in text mining. In: Proceedings of the 6th IEEE Conference on Data Mining (ICDM 2006), pp. 1157–1161 (2006)
2. Li, Y., Zhou, X., Bruza, P., Xu, Y., Lau, R.: A two-stage text mining model for information filtering. In: Proceedings of the 17th ACM Conference on Information and Knowledge Management (CIKM 2008), pp. 1023–1032 (2008)
3. Li, Y., Algarni, A., Zhong, N.: Mining positive and negative patterns for relevance feature discovery. In: Proceedings of the 16th ACM SIGKDD Conference on Knowledge discovery and Data mining (KDD 2010), pp. 753–762 (2010)
4. King, J., Li, Y., Tao, X., Nayak, R.: Mining world knowledge for analysis of search engine content. Web Intelligence and Agent Systems 5(3), 233–253 (2007)
5. Sieg, A., Mobasher, B., Burke, R.: Web search personalization with ontological user profiles. In: Proceedings of the 16th ACM Conference on Information and Knowledge Management (CIKM 2007), pp. 525–534 (2007)
6. Tao, X., Li, Y., Zhong, N.: A personalized ontology model for web information gathering. IEEE Transactions on Knowledge and Data Engineering 23(4), 496–511 (2011)
7. Zhong, N., Li, Y., Wu, S.: Effective pattern discovery for text mining. IEEE Transactions on Knowledge and Data Engineering 24(1), 30–44 (2012)
8. Li, Y., Zhong, N.: Mining ontology for automatically acquiring web user information needs. IEEE Transactions on Knowledge and Data Engineering 18(4), 554–568 (2006)
9. Gauch, S., Chaffee, J., Pretschner, A.: Ontology-based personalized search and browsing. Web Intelligence and Agent Systems 1(3), 219–234 (2003)
10. Wu, S., Li, Y., Xu, Y., Pham, B., Chen, P.: Automatic pattern-taxonomy extraction for web mining. In: Proceedings of IEEE/WIC/ACM International Conference on Web Intelligence (WI 2004), pp. 242–248 (2004)
11. Robertson, S., Soboroff, I.: The trec 2002 filtering track report. In: Proceedings of the 10th Text REtrieval Conference (TREC 2001), pp. 26–37 (2002)
12. Soboroff, I., Robertson, S.: Building a filtering test collection for trec 2002. In: Proceedings of the 26th ACM SIGIR Conference on Research and Development in Informaion Retrieval (SIGIR 2003), pp. 243–250 (2003)
13. Buckley, C., Voorhees, E.: Evaluating evaluation measure stability. In: Proceedings of the 23rd ACM SIGIR Conference on Research and Development in Information Retrieval (SIGIR 2000), pp. 33–40 (2000)

Towards Domain Independent Why Text Segment Classification Based on Bag of Function Words

Katsuyuki Tanaka, Tetsuya Takiguchi, and Yasuo Ariki

Kobe University
1-1 Rokkodai, Nada, Kobe 657-8501, Japan
katsutanaka@puppy.kobe-u.ac.jp,{takigu,ariki}@kobe-u.ac.jp

Abstract. Increased attention has been focused on question answering (QA) technology as next generation search since it improves the usability of information acquisition from web. However, not much research has been conducted on "non-factoid-QA", especially on *Why Question Answering (Why-QA)*. In this paper, we introduce a machine learning approach to automatically construct a classifier with function words as features to perform *Why Text Segments Classification* (*WTS* classification) by using SVM. It is a process of detecting text segments describing *"reasons-causes"* and is a subtask of *Why-QA* mainly related to an answer extraction part. We argue that function words are a strong discriminator for *WTS* classification. Furthermore, since function words appear in almost all text segments regardless of the domain of the topic, it also enables construction of a domain independent classifier. The experimental results showed significant improvement over state-of-the-art results in terms of accuracy of *WTS* classification as well as domain independent capability.

Keywords: Non-Factoid QA, Classification, Machine Learning.

1   Introduction

The recent progression of internet technology has increased with the number of internet users. Trends such as the development of online knowledge bases like Wikipedia and community portal sites such as Yahoo!Answers have emerged, and the diversity of information now available on the internet has increased. That has lead to the dramatic growth of information availability on the internet, and as such it has become increasingly difficult for users to acquire the information that they really need. It requires changes to the way of obtaining information, from simple knowledge acquisition to complicated or deeper knowledge acquisition.

Increased attention has been focused on the question answering (QA) technology as next generation search. This is because QA systems return a list of exact answers as search results while most of the commercial information retrievers, such as Google, return a list of documents. Returning the list of exact answers reduces the labour intensive filtering process to obtain information since it does not need to look into each document to find chunks of information from the lists of retrieved documents, which are often very large.

M. Thielscher and D. Zhang (Eds.): AI 2012, LNCS 7691, pp. 469–480, 2012.
© Springer-Verlag Berlin Heidelberg 2012

A significant amount of literature on QA has reported on "factoid-QA", which deals with a question asking for a fact that can be answered by few words (*what is the height of Mt. Everest?*), and achieved high performance in terms of the answer acquisition [3, 8, 9]. However, not much research has been conducted on "non-factoid-QA", which requires more complicated question answering mechanisms to obtain the answers (*what is non-factoid question answering?* or *why is the sky blue?*). Especially *Why Question Answering (Why-QA)* is not a very active area of research on non-factoid-QA field. *Why-QA* is a process of finding answers describing "*reasons-causes*" (*why-answer*) for a question asking the "*reasons-causes*" for some facts (*why-question*). The main obstacles of under-developed *Why-QA* techniques are that it becomes increasingly difficult to obtain *why-answers* since it requires deeper understanding of text content than that of factoid-QA.

Among the several recent works explored on *Why-QA* methods, the most popular method is a rule based method (*RB* method) [6, 16, 18]. *RB* method detects *why-answer* by referring to a manually predefined list of keyword cues or patterns based on "*reasons-causes*" characteristics, which are called 'rule dictionary'. However, the rule dictionary construction is laborious and the performance of *RB* method is not very stable in terms of *why-answer* extraction accuracy.

As a subtask of *Why-QA*, Tanaka [4] developed a machine learning approach to detect a group of sentences, a text segments (*TS*), describing "*reasons-causes*" based on "bag-of-words (*BOW*)" representation. Even though *BOW* effective representation of text to deal with topic classification, since the vocabulary size of nouns is very large and they carry domain dependent information, they increase the computation of building a classifier while decreasing the domain independency of the classifier. Moreover, most of the nouns are not effective discriminators to detect *TS* describing "*reasons-causes*" hence *BOW* may not be an optimal representation to apply in such a task.

The objective of our research is to introduce the methodology of automatically building a highly discriminative classifier to detect *TS* indicating "*reasons-causes*" regardless of the domain of *TS*. The classifier is constructed by making use of function words, which are usually ignored by most of the *BOW* based information retrieval research, as bases of feature space for machine learning. We call such *TS* describing "*reasons-causes*" as "*Why Text Segment (WTS)*" and *TS* that is not *WTS* as "*NotWhy Text Segment (NWTS)*". We define the process of detecting *WTS* as *WTS* classification and the classifier to perform such a classification as *WTS* classifier. *WTS* classification is a subtask of *Why-QA* mainly related to Answer Extraction part of QA system. Here, *TS* could be some answers on an online forum or community portal or chunks of sentences extracted from any web page. Domain means a group of words or terms share the same concept such as sports, science, finance, and so forth.

As an example of *WTS* classification, consider the following three *TS* extracted from Wikipedia[1] and one of its reference links[2] related to the topic of the sky. It is clear that 1 is an explanation of "sky" while 2 and 3 state the reason why the sky is blue or yellow (red).

---

[1] http://en.wikipedia.org/wiki/Sky
[2] http://math.ucr.edu/home/baez/physics/General/BlueSky/blue_sky.html

1. "The sky is the part of the atmosphere or of outer space visible from the surface of any astronomical object."
2. "The light from the sky is a result of the scattering of sunlight, which results in a light blue colour perceived by the human eye. On a sunny day Rayleigh Scattering gives the sky a blue gradient - dark in the zenith, light near the horizon."
3. "When the air is clear the sunset will appear yellow, because the light from the sun has passed a long distance through air and some of the blue light has been scattered away. If the air is polluted with small particles, natural or otherwise, the sunset will be more red.

Applying *WTS* classification on these *TS* means to classify 2 and 3 as *WTS* and 1 as *NWTS*.

Like *BOW*, we call bag representation of function words *"bag-of-function-words (BOFW)"*, therefore, we refer to our proposed method as *BOFW* method. In this paper, *WTS* classification is considered as a binary classification into binary classes, *WTS* and *NWTS* as binary classes and we use SVM [15] to build the classifier.

Our research is similar to existing literature [5, 13, 14] in terms of utilizing function words, but our approach differs in the way of utilizing the function words. Our method only uses morpheme based function word as a unit for a machine learning feature whereas [5] use structured clause with function words as a feature and [13], [14] use more than function words. Moreover, we propose machine learning frame work as classification to discriminate *WTS* rather than ranker learning to re-rank *TS* according to *WTS* [5]. The proposed *BOFW* method does not require laboriously labelled training data [5], or deep language analyses [21] to choose features.

Even though *BOFW* provides limited contribution in terms of topic classification (*BOW* is more useful for topic classification), the focus of this research is not about classification based on topic, but it is classification of *WTS*. Consequently, the essence of the proposed *BOFW* methodology is that despite its simplicity, it provides a strong discriminative power for *WTS* classification regardless of domain of *TS*. Hence it could provide a simple yet effective way of boosting the performance of QA system to build finer *Why-QA* technology. Moreover, even though this research is conducted on Japanese, it is adaptable to different languages by simply changing the *BOFW* definitions as we have proved in [11]. In this paper, we describe the details of *BOFW* methods and its set up in Japanese. In addition we discuss the domain independent issues of *WTS* classification based on *BOFW* method which has not stated in [11]. In summary, the main contributions of this paper are as follows:

- **Classification performance issue:** We experimentally show that *BOFW* method boosts the performance of *WTS* classification, yielding performance of prior works.
- **Domain independent issue:** *WTS* classifier with *BOFW* method provides stable classification performance regardless of the domain of *TS* than any prior works.

The rest of this paper is organised as follows. Section 2 describes the related work done on *Why-QA*. Section 3 states our proposed *BOFW* approaches to construct *WTS* classifier. Finally, Section 4 discusses the experiment.

2   Related Work

Shibusawa [16] proposed a method to extract the location of a sentence with *"reasons-causes"* as *why-answer* with respect to the contiguous "fact sentence", which defines a sentence including all keywords on a question. Shibusawa defines four possible locations of the *why-answer*, 1) pre Case, 2) and 3) post Case, and 4) within Case regard with the "fact sentence". A location of *why-answer* is determined by appearance patterns of rules with respect to "fact sentence" by refering to manually constructed rule dictionary. Rule dictionary contains the list of rules such as the reason keywords ("kara", "karakoso", etc) and reference terms (such as "ikano", "tsugi", etc). This is a typical *RB* method as it defines such rules manually from manually extracted terms which characterises *"reasons-causes"*. The problem with a *RB* method is that it is a very troublesome and labour-intensive task to produce a rule dictionary. Besides, it may not be possible to find all rules to define *"reasons-causes"* characteristics. Hence the lack of rule coverage causes an inaccuracy of *why-answers* detection from corpus.

Instead of building a rule dictionary manually, Higashinaka and Isozaki [5] proposed automatic rule extraction methods to overcome the rule coverage problem in *RB* method by exploiting Japanese EDR dictionary. EDR dictionary is a collection of Japanese sentences, in which terms or phrases are labelled with its semantic role to represent semantic relations. Labelling is maintained by linguists manually. Higashinaka extracted sentences labelled with "reason" from EDR and decomposed all the sentences into clauses. Then, all content words in each clause were replaced by "*" to form a clause structured with function words (we call it a "structured clause with function words"). Higashinaka then trained SVM ranker based on these structured clauses with function words as well as manually extracted *"reasons-causes"* terms. They considered the *Why-QA* as ranking problem to boost *WTS* in higher ranking. Although the EDR approach may be able to construct why-type rules efficiently, the accessibility of such a commercial dictionary is not easy and costly. Besides, this method requires training dataset labelled with ranking according with *WTS*, which is not easy to obtain.

Intensive studies on *Why-QA* have been undertaken by Verberne [19, 20, 21]. Verberne [21] regarded *Why-QA* as re-ranking of *TS* retrieved by Wumps Search Engine. Verberne carried out deep natural language analysis on English sentence structure and utilised syntactically analysed information of *TS* to re-rank in the order of *WTS*. However, since it requires heavy language analysis and deep natural language processing skill, it is not easily adaptable to different languages.

Tanaka [4] proposed a machine learning [1, 2] method based on *BOW* to perform *WTS* classification. However, this method has a domain dependency problem on the produced classifier. This is because *BOW* representations of *TS* include noun information, and nouns are very domain specific information. Therefore, trained classifier has a bias towards the training data and it is not suitable for a domain independent classification. It also requires a re-collecting of training data and re-training to build classifier for different task and it is a troublesome for a large data set.

Brill [17] proposed a statistical translation technique to answer various types of non-factoid questions. Brill produced language model based on large sets of parallel corpus. However, the performance of the model is highly dependent on the quality of the word translation probabilities. It requires a large amount of semantically similar yet lexically different data for training the model to capture better correlations of words and such corpus is not easily available. Moreover, most of non-factoid type QA research is not specialised in *Why-QA* [14, 17] and some of them suffer from accuracy of the results on *Why-QA*. This may be due to the adaptation of factoid-QA framework into non-factoid-QA even though the representation of answers is different between factoid-QA and non-factoid-QA.

3   Domain Independent Why Text Segment Classifier Based on Bag of Function Words

In order to build *WTS* classifier with SVM, it is necessary to collect labelled data, define representations of *TS*, choose appropriate bases for features space, and build the classifier by learning patterns from training data. These are important processes not only to construct a classifier with good performance, but also to decide the task of classification. In this paper, we introduce the method of domain independent *WTS* classifier construction by clarifying these points.

In this paper, the task is clearly *WTS* classification that discriminates *WTS* or *NWTS* of *TS* input. We consider *WTS* classification as binary classification problem with *WTS/NWTS* as its classes. We used Yahoo!Answer to automatically collect and label datasets for training and testing. We trained *WTS* classifiers with SVM with function words as features. Figure1 describes the overview of *BOFW* method.

3.1   Collecting Data

Manual data labelling [4, 5, 16] is laborious and causes a problem of collecting large number of data. To overcome such shortcomings, we introduce the automatic as well as systematic way of collecting and labelling of data using Yahoo!Answer (known as Yahoo!Chiebukuro[3] in Japanese). To retain the quality and reliability of answers, we only used answers from best-answer-corpus and we used each answer as *TS*. The processes of collecting *TS* from Yahoo!Answer corpus are as follows.

Firstly, *why-questions* were collected from question-corpus. We defined *why-questions* as the questions containing keywords with typical question style of seeking for *why-answers*. We choose "naze (why...)", "doushite (why...)" and "no riyuu ha nani (what is the reason...)" as such keywords. Subsequently, we collected an answer paired with each *why-question* as *why-answer* from best-answer-corpus. The group of collected *why-answers* is called *WTS* dataset.

Similarly, we defined questions with keywords, such as "no houhou ha nani (what is the methods of....)" and "no chigai ha (what is the difference between...)", which

---

[3] http://chiebukuro.yahoo.co.jp/

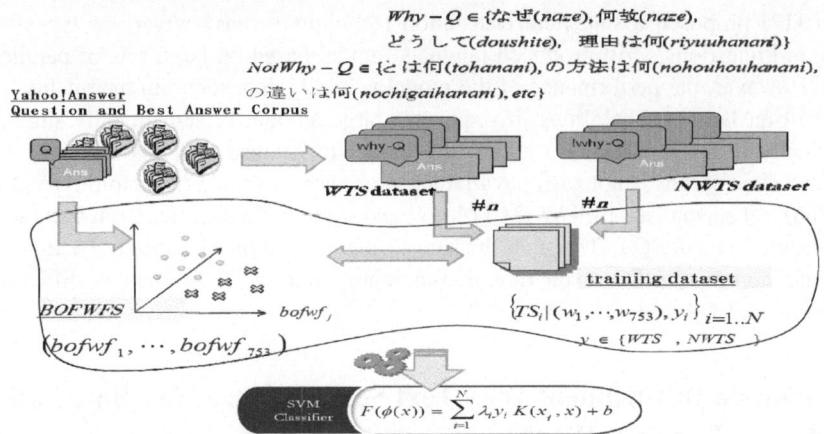

Fig. 1. Overview of *BOFW* method

are not typical question styles of seeking for *why-answers* as *notwhy-questions*. The answers paired with the *notwhy-questions* were collected as *notwhy-answers* and they are called *NWTS* dataset.

Training datasets for machine learning and test datasets for evaluation are produced by randomly selected *n TS* from *WTS* and *NWTS* datasets with no overlapping.

3.2   Bag of Function Words Method

We propose the methodology to build domain independent *WTS* classifier. A domain independent means that *WTS* classifier has the capacity of recognising any incoming *TS* regardless of its domain. In order to do so, it is important to design features representing *TS* as well as the bases of feature space properly so that it is possible for learners to capture patterns of training data to produce accurate *WTS* classifier. We leverage function words to achieve our goal.

In this paper, we define a morpheme of a function word with its part of speech as a *function-word-feature (fw-feature)*, extracting such features from *TS* is called *fw-feature extraction*. In this paper, we define the process of the feature extraction as a breaking *TS* into some form of units and a unit as a feature. Furthermore, we define a group of unique units as a bag and a bag representation of such *fw-feature* is called *BOFW*. It is clear that a unique representation of *fw-feature* is *BOFW* hence we call such features as *BOFW-feature*. All the *fw-feature* extractions were conducted by using morphological analysis tool ChaSen [12] in this paper. If a unit is a *word-feature* = "any word with a part of speech" then the group of unique *word-features* is a well knowledge *BOW* representation. Figure2 lists the type of part of speech used for *BOFW* together with an example of *fw-features extraction* and in the form of *BOFW* from the sentence "tesuto na node, gakkou ni i tta. (I went to school because there is test.)".

Clearly, we use *BOFW-features* as bases of machine learning feature space. In a machine learning scheme, the choice of bases are important for a learner to capture

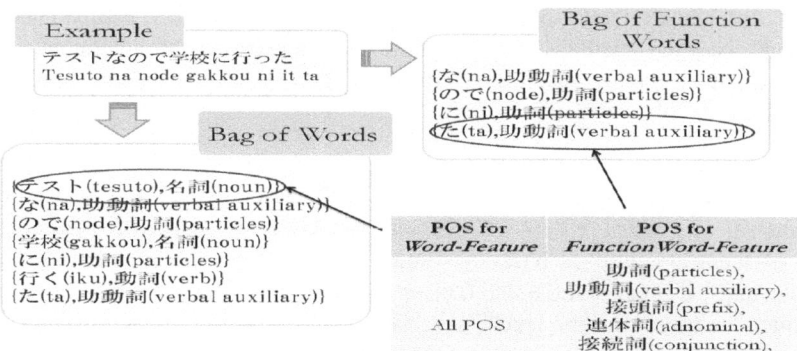

Fig. 2. Example of *function-word-features, BOFW-features, word-features*, and *BOW-features*

appropriate patterns to build an accurate classifier. We constructed such feature space by *BOFW-features* extracted from all answers in best-answer-corpus on Yaoo!Answer. We collected 753 *BOFW-features* as bases $\{bofwf_j \in \mathcal{R}^{753}\}$. We randomly collected n *WTS* and *NWTS* from *WTS* dataset and *NWTS* dataset respectively, and for each drawn *TS*, we created a 753 dimensional vector with a weight w_j as an element of $bofwf_j$. In this paper, we used *tf-idf* to calculate a weight w_j for $bofwf_j$. The calculations of *tf-idf* were made based on the frequency of $bofwf_j$ in best-answer-corpus as well as its document frequency (precisely, *TS* frequency). We used $N=2n$ vector quantised *TS* as training dataset $\{TS_i \mid tf\text{-}idf_i$, $y_i\}_{i=1..N}$ with $tf\text{-}idf \in \mathcal{R}^{753}$, $y \in$ (*WTS*, *NWTS*). Figure.1 describes these processes. The intention of this weighting scheme is to normalise terms in *TS* so that all *TS* have same weighting scheme because the length of *TS* may varies.

The rationale behind the *BOFW* method to construct *WTS classifier* is that 1) It is an effective discriminator to perform *WTS* classification and 2) because the function words appear almost in all text so that it is possible to construct domain independent *WTS classifier*.

4   Experiments

In this paper, the main purpose of our research is to carry out experiments on *WTS* classification and its evaluation. It is clear that filtering process for *WTS* detection is an important part of *Why-QA* process. The extracting the actual position of the answer and fully functional implementations of *Why-QA* are beyond our scope therefore they are left as our future works.

4.1   Experimental Setup

As an evaluation, we compare the performance of *WTS* classifier produced by *BOFW* method with 5 different baselines: *RB* method [16], *EDR+RB* and *EDR* methods based on [5] and *BOW* and *BOW-BOFW* methods based on [4]. It is difficult to reconstruct all the baselines since some of them require more than simply labelled data

[5, 16], different evaluation method [5], or different experimental setup. Therefore, we adapt baseline methods into machine learning classification framework by defining features mainly based on their rule dictionary so that we can conduct the evaluation smoothly and fairly.

Baseline.1 (*RB method*) : Among the rules in rule dictionary on Table.1 of [16], we defined each rule under "reference terms with reason-cause" and "reason-cause terms" as *rule-based-feature (RB-feature)*. We collected 83 such *RB-features* and all of them are used as bases of feature space. *RB-feature* is a binary feature indicating 1 if it exists in *TS* and 0 otherwise and. *RB-features* are typical terms indicate *"reasons-causes"* such as "dakara (because)", "riyuu (reason)" and "genninn (cause)" etc.

Baseline.2 (*EDR+RB method*) : In [5], 399 features (f1-f399) are used to as bases of feature space to train a SVM ranker. Among the features defined in [5], f1-f394 are rules, indicating *"reasons-causes"*, extracted from EDR, f395 is a feature with a list of manually extracted rules, f396-f398 are related to topic information, and f399 is related to question. We defined features for baseline.2 method as combination of automatically and manually extracted rules indicating *"reasons-causes"*. Since features f396-f398 and f399 are not directly related to our scope of *WTS* classification they were discarded. By referring to the method of rules extraction [5], we collected sentences labelled with "reason" from EDR, and they were transformed into a structured clause with function words as it is described in Section 2. We obtained 593 most frequently occurred such structure as *EDR-features*. Element of *EDR-features* are binary indicating the existence of the attributes in *TS* as 0/1. As for manual rules for f395, we used *RB-features* from baseline.1. We defined a binary feature representing the existence of any rules matched with *RB-features* in *TS* by 0/1. The bases of feature space for *EDR+RB* method, therefore, is 594 dimensional features with 593 binary *EDR-features* and 1 binary feature with a list of *RB-features*.

Baseline.3 (*EDR method*) : This baseline only use 593 *EDR-features* stated above.

Baseline.4 (*BOW method*) : By following the experimental setup of [4], we extracted words from all *TS* in training dataset and use *BOW* as bases of feature space. As for an element of *BOW-feature*, we obtained *tf-idf* according with the *BOW-feature's* term frequencies and *TS* frequencies.

Baseline.5 (*BOW-BOFW method*) : This feature space is formed by subtracting *BOFW-features* from *BOW-features* in *BOW* method.

We conducted two experiments to evaluate the effectiveness of *BOFW* method. The first experiment shows the effectiveness of on *BOFW* method in term of comparative accuracy of *WTS* classification against baselines. The purpose of the second experiment is to evaluate domain independent classification ability of *WTS* classifier constructed by *BOFW* method. All evaluations were done by comparing F-Score and the rate of correctly classified *TS* of proposed method and baselines. We used SMO [10], provided in data mining software Weka [7], with the first order of polynomial kernel $(K(x_i,x_j)=(x^Tx+1))$ to train five *WTS classifiers*. We also performed paired-t-test to show the statistical significance of the experimental results.

4.2   Effectiveness on *WTS* Classification Accuracy

To train *WTS* classifier, we produced five datasets for each containing randomly selected 5000 *WTS* and *NWTS* from *WTS* and *NWTS* datasets collected in 3.1 respectively (they are called $D_{10k.[1..5]}$). To record F-Score and classification accuracy, we used one dataset of $D_{10k.[1..5]}$ to train *WTS* classifier and others as test dataset. We repeated this process 5 times and take the macro-averages of F-score and the rate of correctly classified *TS* for each method. Table1 shows the results of evaluations. A value of inside the bracket on each baseline shows the difference of *BOFW* method and baseline method.

It was found that it is possible to construct *WTS* classifier with F-Score=0.661 with 63.25% of *WTS* classification accuracy by using *BOFW* method. The results show that the performance of *WTS* classifier produced by *BOFW* method outperforms baseline methods (*RB, EDR+RB, EDR, BOW*) by 4.5%~16.3% on F-Score and 1.8%~5.3% on classification accuracy.

To check the statistical significance of the results, we performed paired-t-test on both F-Scores and classification accuracies. All results on paired-t-test against baselines showed significant difference of the results at the level of 0.01.

One of the reasons why the results of the *BOFW* method outweigh baseline methods is that *BOFW-features* work more effectively to form hyper-plane that separates *WTS* and *NWTS* class on SVM learning process. This can be explained by comparing the results of *BOFW* method, *BOW* method, and *BOW-BOFW* method.

As it is stated in 4.2, *BOW* method construct the classifier with both content words and function words, while *BOW-BOFW* method only use content words. Now the results on *BOW* method and *BOW-BOFW* method showed that it is possible to perform *WTS* classification with F-Score=0.617 with 60.20% of classification accuracy and F-Score=0.56 with 57.95% classification accuracy respectively. Clearly, the performance of *WTS* classification dropped significantly by discarding *BOFW-features* from *BOW-features*. This indicates the *BOFW-features* provide a significant contribution in order to form an effective decision boundary to distinguish *WTS* and *NWTS* classes. This also can be supported by the results of *BOFW* method, only using *BOFW-features* provides higher discriminative *WTS* classifier than *BOW* method and *BOW-BOFW* method.

Table 1. Average F-Score and Correctly Classified Rate of *WTS* classifiers using $D_{10k.[1..5]}$

	BOFW	*RB*	*EDR+RB*	*EDR*	*BOW*	*BOW-BOFW*
F-Score	0.661	0.499 (-0.163)*	0.605 (-0.056)*	0.584 (-0.077)*	0.617 (-0.045)*	0.596 (-0.065)*
Correct Classified	63.25	60.57 (-2.68)*	61.43 (-1.82)*	59.11 (-4.14)*	60.20 (-3.05)*	57.95 (-5.30)*

*paired-t test with significance at a level of 0.01.

4.3   Capability of *BOFW* Method as Domain Independent *WTS* Classification

Yahoo!Answer provides various topics in answers and it can be considered as open domain corpus. Therefore, from the experimental results in 4.2, it is possible to say that *BOFW* method is capable of classifying any *TS* regardless of its domain. We conducted further experiment to test the effectiveness of the proposed method as a domain independent classifier. Evaluation of this experiment is conducted by creating *WTS* classifier with training dataset containing only one domain and test the classifier by test dataset not containing the domain. Since Yahoo!Answer provides various categories sharing the same topic, we define a category as a domain and created datasets with/without domain as follow.

First, we extracted *WTS* and *NWTS* only belonging to one category to form a dataset D_{cat} and *TS* not belonging to the category to form a dataset D_{nocat}. In order to obtain enough data, we only used categories provides more than 3000 *WTS* and *NWTS* on *WTS* datasets and *NWTS* datasets to create D_{cat}. There were 4 such categories. From D_{nocat} we randomly selected 5000 *WTS* and *NWTS* each and created 5 datasets $D_{nocat[1..5]}$. In effect, we have 4pairs of D_{cat} and $D_{nocat[1..5]}$.

Evaluation method is the same as 4.2, we compared the performance of *WTS* classifier by comparing F-Score and classification accuracy of *BOFW* method with baselines. F-Score and classification accuracy were recorded by testing each $D_{nocat[1..5]}$ on *WTS* classifier build by D_{cat} as training dataset. Similarly, we recorded F-Score and classification accuracy of 5 *WTS* classifier trained by $D_{nocat.[1..5]}$ tested by D_{cat}. Table2 shows F-Score and classification accuracy macro-average of evaluation results of 4 categories (4 D_{cat} x $D_{nocat.[1..5]}$ = 20 results per each evaluation) and its total average.

Table 2. Average F-Score and Correctly Classified Rate Experimental Results of *WTS* classifiers using D_{cat} and $D_{nocat.[1..5]}$

	BOFW	*RB*	*EDR+RB*	*EDR*	*BOW*	*BOW-BOFW*
	D_{cat} classifier vs $D_{nocat.[1..5]}$ test datasets					
F-Score	0.636	0.487 (-0.149)[*]	0.568 (-0.068)[*]	0.567 (-0.069)[*]	0.591 (-0.045)[*]	0.563 (-0.072)[*]
Correctly Classified	61.99	60.20 (-1.79)[*]	59.09 (-2.90)[*]	57.60 (-4.38)[*]	58.41 (-3.58)[*]	55.34 (-6.65)[*]
	$D_{nocat.[1..5]}$ classifiers vs D_{cat} test dataset					
F-Score	0.626	0.475 (-0.151)[*]	0.574 (-0.053)[*]	0.562 (-0.063)[*]	0.577 (-0.048)[*]	0.555 (-0.070)[*]
Correctly Classified	61.01	58.11 (-2.90)[*]	59.07 (-1.94)[**]	58.15 (-2.86)[*]	58.38 (-2.63)[*]	56.17 (-4.84)[*]
	Average Results					
F-Score	0.632	0.481[*]	0.571[*]	0.565[*]	0.585[*]	0.632
Correctly Classified	61.50	59.16[*]	59.08[*]	57.88[*]	58.40[*]	61.50

*, ** paired-t test with significance at a level of 0.01 and 0.005.

The results shows that proposed method performed *WTS* classification with average F-Score=0.632 and average classification accuracy=61.50%, it was found *BOFW* method outperformed all baselines methods.

A pair-t-test showed that the results of *BOFW* method significantly differed at the level of 0.05 on the classification accuracy of *ERD+RB* method ($D_{nocat.[1..5]}$ *classifiers* vs D_{cat} *test dataset*) and the rest at the level of 0.01.

5   Conclusions

In this paper, we proposed new methodologies to construct domain independent *WTS* classifiers based on function words as features. Experimental results showed that the proposed method provides higher *WTS* classification capability than previous methods. The proposed method also provides a simple way to build the *WTS* classifier hence it reduces the labour required for manually defining a rule dictionary. It also showed that the *BOFW* method provides the more stable *WTS* classification performance regardless of the domain of training dataset and test dataset. Consequently, we accomplished our aim to introduce a simple yet effective way to build a domain independent *WTS* classifier to perform accurate *WTS* classification.

In the future, we are interested in building a non-factoid based QA system by extending the *BOFW* method to develop automated non-factoid *TS* classification of answers describing *"definition"* and *"method"*. We believe that these technologies greatly contribute to developing next generation searching techniques which will improve the information retrieval on the web.

Acknowledgements. This research is supported by Yahoo!Answer. We would like to show our gratitude to NII and Yahoo! for providing QA data.

References

1. Freund, Y., Schapire, R.E.: Experiments with a new boosting algorithm. Machine Learning, 148–156 (1996)
2. Friedman, J.H., Hastie, T., Tibshirani, R.: Additive logistic regression: A statistical view of boosting. Technical Report, Stanford University (1998)
3. Radev, D., Fan, W., Qi, H., Wu, H., Grewal, A.: Probabilistic question answering on the web. In: WWW, pp. 408–419 (2002)
4. Tanaka, K., Takiguchi, T., Ariki, Y.: Automatic Why Text Segment Classification and Answer Extraction by Machine Learning. IPSJ Journal 49(6), 57–64 (2008) (Japanese)
5. Higashinaka, R., Isozaki, H.: Automatically Acquiring Causal Expression Patterns from Relation-annotated Corpora to Improve Question Answering for why-Questions. TALIP 7, 1–29 (2008)
6. Yin, L.A.: Two-Stage Approach to Retrieving Answers for How-To Questions. In: EACL 2006, pp. 63–70 (2006)
7. Witten, I.H., Frank, E.: Data Mining: Practical machine learning tools and techniques, 2nd edn. Morgan Kaufmann, San Francisco (2005)

8. Kwok, C.C.T., Etzioni, O., Weld, D.S.: Scaling Question and Answering to the Web. In: WWW, pp. 150–161 (2002)
9. Lin, J., Katz, B.: Question answering from the web using knowledge annotation and knowledge mining techniques. In: CIKM, pp. 116–123 (2003)
10. Platt, J.C.: Fast Training of Support Vector Machines using Sequential Minimal Optimization, pp. 185–208. MIT Press (1999)
11. Nagy, I., Tanaka, K., Ariki, Y.: Why Text Segment Classification Based on Part of Speech Feature Selection. In: Pfahringer, B., Holmes, G., Hoffmann, A. (eds.) DS 2010. LNCS, vol. 6332, pp. 87–101. Springer, Heidelberg (2010)
12. Matsumoto, Y.: Morphological Analysis System Chasen. IPSJ 41(11), 1208–1214 (2000) (Japanese)
13. Mizuno, J., Akiba, T., Fujii, A., Itou, K.: Non-factoid Question Answering Experiments at NTCIR-6: Towards Answer Type Detection for Realworld Questions. In: The Sixth NTCIR Workshop, pp. 487–492 (2007)
14. Ishioroshi, M., Sato, M., Mori, T.: Answering Any Class of Japanese Non-factoid Question by Using the Web and Example Q&A Pairs from a Social Q&A Website. In: WAIIT, pp. 59–65 (2008)
15. Cortes, C., Vapnik, V.: Support Vector Networks. Mach. Learn. 20(3), 273–297 (1995)
16. Shibusawa, U., Hayashi, T., Onai, R.: Development and Evaluation of a System for Extracting Answers of a "Why" Type Question from the WEB. IPSJ Journal 48(3), 1512–1523 (2007) (Japanese)
17. Soricut, R., Brill, E.: Automatic Question Answering: Beyond the Factoid. In: HLT/NAACL, pp. 54–64 (2004)
18. Srihari, R., Li, W.: Information Extraction Supported Question Answering. In: TREC, pp. 185–196 (1999)
19. Verberne, S., Boves, L., Oostdijk, N., Coppen, P.A.J.M.: What is not in the Bag of Words for Why-QA? Comput. Linguist. 36(2), 229–245 (2010)
20. Verberne, S., Boves, L., Oostdijk, N.H.J., Coppen, P.A.J.M.: Evaluating Discourse-based Extraction for Why-Question Answering. In: SIGIR, pp. 735–737 (2007)
21. Verberne, S., Boves, L., Oostdijk, N., Coppen, P.: Using Syntactic Information for Improving Why-Question Answering. In: COLING, pp. 953–960 (2008)

A Delayed Splitting Bottom-Up Procedure for Model Generation

Kiyoshi Akama[1] and Ekawit Nantajeewarawat[2]

[1] Information Initiative Center, Hokkaido University, Hokkaido, Japan
akama@iic.hokudai.ac.jp
[2] Computer Science Program, Sirindhorn International Institute of Technology
Thammasat University, Pathumthani, Thailand
ekawit@siit.tu.ac.th

Abstract. Meaning-preserving Skolemization is essential for development of a correct and efficient method of solving query-answering problems. It requires global existential quantifications of function variables, which in turn require an extended space of logical formulas. This paper proposes a bottom-up procedure for computing a set of models that sufficiently represents the set of all models of a given clause set in the extended formula space. Instantiations of function variables often result in generation of infinitely many models. To overcome the difficulty, a model-making pattern is introduced for representing a possibly infinite number of models, and such a pattern is split as late as possible. The proposed procedure provides a method for solving query-answering problems that include unrestricted use of universal and existential quantifications.

Keywords: Query-answering problems, automated reasoning, bottom-up computation, meaning-preserving Skolemization.

1 Introduction

A *query-answering problem* (*QA problem*) [6,8] is a pair $\langle K, a \rangle$, where K is a logical formula, representing background knowledge, and a is an atomic formula (atom), representing a query. The answer to a QA problem $\langle K, a \rangle$ is the set of all ground instances of a that are logical consequences of K. According to the types of background knowledge, QA problems can be classified into several subclasses, e.g., QA problems on definite clauses, where background knowledge is a set of definite clauses, QA problems on description logics (DLs), where background knowledge is a conjunction of axioms and assertions in DLs. QA problems on definite clauses have been extensively discussed in logic programming [4]. QA problems on DLs have been discussed in [8]. Answering queries in deductive databases [5] can be regarded as solving QA problems on a restricted form of definite clauses.

Given a set K of definite clauses, since K has a unique minimal model, the answer set of a QA problem $\langle K, a \rangle$ becomes the intersection of the minimal model of K and $rep(a)$, where $rep(a)$ is the set of all ground instances of a. When K

M. Thielscher and D. Zhang (Eds.): AI 2012, LNCS 7691, pp. 481–492, 2012.
© Springer-Verlag Berlin Heidelberg 2012

is an arbitrary first-order formula, determining the answer set of a QA problem $\langle K, a \rangle$ is more complicated since K possibly has multiple minimal models, none of which is included by the others.

We aim at dealing with QA problems on full first-order logic, where background knowledge can be any arbitrary first-order formula, without any restriction on its form. Let $\langle K, a \rangle$ be a QA problem in this class. The answer to $\langle K, a \rangle$ can be equivalently formulated as $(\bigcap Models(K)) \cap rep(a)$, where $\bigcap Models(K)$ is the intersection of all models of K. We adopt the following three computation phases for computing the answer to $\langle K, a \rangle$: (i) convert K into a set Cs of clauses using Skolemization, (ii) use bottom-up computation to construct a set of models that sufficiently represents the set of all models of Cs, and (iii) find the intersection of the obtained models and $rep(a)$. The following fundamental issues need to be addressed:

1. How to preserve the meaning of a logical formula in a Skolemization process? Conventional Skolemization does not preserve the meaning of a formula [2]. In order to obtain meaning-preserving Skolemization, an extended formula space that allows existential quantifications of function variables is required.
2. How to compute models of an extended clause set? A clause set in the extended space contains existentially quantified global function variables. How to compute models of such an extended clause set has not been discussed in the literature.

A solution to the first problem has been provided by our recent work [1], in which a theory for extending a space of logical formulas by incorporation of function variables was developed and how meaning-preserving Skolemization could be achieved in the obtained extended space was shown. A procedure for converting a logical formula into a set of extended clauses on the extended space was also given in [1].

This paper addresses the second problem. A set of extended clauses may contain occurrences of function variables, which can be instantiated into infinitely many functions. Instantiations of function variables therefore often result in infinitely many models. Instead of generating models themselves, patterns of model construction, called *model-making patterns*, are generated. A model-making pattern is represented by a set of atoms with parameters. In bottom-up model generation, some model-making patterns may need to be split. To reduce the number of model-making patterns to be considered, a pattern is split only when necessary. A procedure for bottom-up generation of models based on such delayed pattern splitting is proposed in this paper.

To begin with, Section 2 explains the basic idea of meaning-preserving Skolemization and introduces the extended clause space. Section 3 presents our delayed splitting bottom-up procedure for model generation. Section 4 illustrates how the procedure works. Section 5 describes fundamental differences between this work and existing approaches. Section 6 provides concluding remarks.

2 Meaning-Preserving Skolemization on an Extended Clause Space

2.1 Need for Meaning-Preserving Skolemization

To solve a QA problem $\langle K, a \rangle$ on first-order logic, the first-order formula K is usually converted into a conjunctive normal form. The conversion involves removal of existential quantifications by Skolemization, i.e., by replacement of an existentially quantified variable with a Skolem term determined by a relevant part of a formula prenex. Classical Skolemization, however, does not preserve the logical meaning of a formula—the formula resulting from Skolemization is not necessarily equivalent to the original one [2].

In [1], we developed a theory for extending the space of first-order logical formulas and showed how meaning-preserving Skolemization can be achieved in the obtained extended space. The basic idea of meaning-preserving Skolemization is to use existentially quantified function variables instead of usual Skolem functions. Function variables and extended conjunctive normal forms are introduced below.

2.2 Function Constants, Function Variables and *func*-Atoms

A usual function symbol in first-order logic denotes an unevaluated function; it is used for constructing a syntactically new term from existing terms (possibly recursively) without evaluating those existing terms. A different class of functions is used in the extended space. A function in this class is an actual mathematical function; it takes ground terms as input, and associates with them an output ground term. The input ground terms are evaluated for determining the output. We called a function in this class a *function constant*. Variables of a new type, called *function variables*, are introduced; each of them can be instantiated into a function constant or a function variable, but not into a usual term.

In order to clearly separate function constants and function variables from usual function symbols and usual terms, a new built-in predicate *func* is introduced. Given any n-ary function constant or n-ary function variable $\bar{f}$, an expression

$$func(\bar{f}, t_1, \ldots, t_n, t_{n+1}),$$

where the t_i are usual terms, is considered as an atom of a new type, called a *func-atom*. When $\bar{f}$ is a function constant and the t_i are all ground, the truth value of this atom is evaluated as follows: it is true iff $\bar{f}(t_1, \ldots, t_n) = t_{n+1}$.

2.3 An Extended Clause Space

A procedure for converting a first-order logical formula into an equivalent formula in an extended conjunctive normal form, called an existentially quantified conjunctive normal form (ECNF), is given in [1]. To define an ECNF, an extended clause is introduced.

Extended Clauses. An *extended clause* C is an extended formula of the form

$$\forall v_1, \ldots, \forall v_m : (a_1 \vee \cdots \vee a_n \vee \neg b_1 \vee \cdots \vee \neg b_p \vee \neg \mathbf{f}_1 \vee \cdots \vee \neg \mathbf{f}_q),$$

where $v_1, \ldots, v_m$ are usual variables, each of $a_1, \ldots, a_n, b_1, \ldots, b_p$ is a usual atom or a constraint atom, and $\mathbf{f}_1, \ldots, \mathbf{f}_q$ are *func*-atoms. It is often written simply as

$$a_1, \ldots, a_n \leftarrow b_1, \ldots, b_p, \mathbf{f}_1, \ldots, \mathbf{f}_q.$$

The sets $\{a_1, \ldots, a_n\}$ and $\{b_1, \ldots, b_p, \mathbf{f}_1, \ldots, \mathbf{f}_q\}$ are called the *left-hand side* and the *right-hand side*, respectively, of the extended clause C, denoted by $lhs(C)$ and $rhs(C)$, respectively. When $n = 0$, C is called a *negative extended clause*. When $n = 1$, C is called an *extended definite clause*, the only atom in $lhs(C)$ is called the *head* of C, denoted by $head(C)$, and the set $rhs(C)$ is also called the *body* of C, denoted by $body(C)$. When $n > 1$, C is called a *multi-head extended clause*. All usual variables in an extended clause are universally quantified and their scope is restricted to the clause itself. When no confusion is caused, an extended clause, a negative extended clause, an extended definite clause and a multi-head extended clause will also be called a *clause*, a *negative clause*, a *definite clause* and a *multi-head clause*, respectively.

Existentially Quantified Conjunctive Normal Forms. A formula in an *existentially quantified conjunctive normal form* (*ECNF*) is an extended formula of the form

$$\exists v_{h1}, \ldots, \exists v_{hm} : (C_1 \wedge \cdots \wedge C_n),$$

where $v_{h1}, \ldots, v_{hm}$ are function variables and $C_1, \ldots, C_n$ are extended clauses. It is often identified with the set $\{C_1, \ldots, C_n\}$, with implicit existential quantifications of function variables and implicit clause conjunction. Each function variable occurring in such a clause set is existentially quantified and its scope covers all clauses in the set.

An Extended Clause Space and QA Problems Thereon. The set of all ECNFs is referred to as the *extended clause space* (*ECLS*$_{\mathrm{F}}$). By the above identification of an ECNF with a clause set, we often regard an element of ECLS$_{\mathrm{F}}$ as a set of (extended) clauses. Given a QA problem $\langle K, a \rangle$ on first-order logic, the first-order formula K is converted by meaning-preserving Skolemization [1] into a clause set Cs in the ECLS$_{\mathrm{F}}$ space. A QA problem $\langle Cs, a \rangle$ such that Cs is a clause set in ECLS$_{\mathrm{F}}$ and a is a usual atom is called a *QA problem on ECLS*$_{\mathrm{F}}$.

3   A Bottom-Up Procedure for Model Generation

After introducing the notions of parameterized terms and parameterized atoms (Section 3.1), how to split a pattern of ground atom sets by parameter splitting is described (Section 3.2). Solving equalities and inequalities with occurrences of parameterized terms is presented (Section 3.3). It is followed by a one-step bottom-up inference procedure (Section 3.4), which is used in our main procedure for model generation (Section 3.5).

3.1   Parameterized Terms and Parameterized Atoms

A parameter ρ takes the form $p : except(E)$, where p is a marker and E is a set of ground usual terms. It represents any arbitrary ground usual term that does not belong to E. When $E = \emptyset$, it represents any arbitrary ground usual term and the expression $p : except(E)$ is also written simply as p.

A *parameterized term* (for short, *P-term*) is defined as follows: (i) constants, usual variables, and parameters are P-terms, and (ii) if f is an m-ary function symbol and $t_1, \ldots, t_m$ are P-terms, then $f(t_1, \ldots, t_m)$ is a P-term. A *ground P-term* is a P-term with no occurrence of any usual variable. A *parameterized atom* (for short, *P-atom*) is an expression of the form $p(t_1, \ldots, t_n)$, where p is an n-ary predicate symbol and $t_1, \ldots, t_n$ are P-terms. It is called a *ground P-atom* when $t_1, \ldots, t_n$ are ground P-terms. Let $\mathcal{G}_\mathrm{P}$ denote the set of all ground P-atoms and $pow(\mathcal{G}_\mathrm{P})$ the power set of $\mathcal{G}_\mathrm{P}$.

3.2   Splitting Ground P-Atom Sets by Parameter Splitting

Assume that ρ is a parameter $p : except(E)$ and t is a ground term such that $t \notin E$. A set of ground P-terms with occurrence of ρ may be split by splitting the parameter ρ into two cases: (i) the case when ρ represents t, and (ii) the case when it represents a usual ground term that does not belong to $E \cup \{t\}$.

Given $M \subseteq pow(\mathcal{G}_\mathrm{P})$, a parameter $\rho = p : except(E)$, and a ground term $t \notin E$, $\mathrm{SPLIT}(M, \rho, t)$ is defined as the subset of $pow(\mathcal{G}_\mathrm{P})$ obtained from M by splitting ρ with respect to t as follows:

1. Let $M_\rho = \{m \mid (m \in M) \; \& \; (\rho \text{ occurs in } m)\}$.
2. Let ρ_{new} be a new parameter $p_{\mathrm{new}} : except(E \cup \{t\})$, where p_{new} is a new marker.
3. Let $\sigma = \{\rho/t\}$ and $\sigma' = \{\rho/\rho_{\mathrm{new}}\}$.
4. Let $\mathrm{SPLIT}(M, \rho, t) = (M - M_\rho) \cup M_\rho\sigma \cup M_\rho\sigma'$.

3.3   Solving Equalities and Inequalities

Let Es be a set of equalities and inequalities, with occurrences of P-terms. $\mathrm{SOLVE}(Es)$ is defined by

$$\mathrm{SOLVE}(Es) = \mathrm{SOLVE}(\emptyset, Es),$$

where for any set S of bindings and any set $\hat{Es}$ of equalities and inequalities, $\mathrm{SOLVE}(S, \hat{Es})$ is defined as follows:

1. If $\hat{Es} = \emptyset$, then $\mathrm{SOLVE}(S, \hat{Es}) = S$.
2. Assume that f and g are function symbols and $t_1, \ldots, t_m, t'_1, \ldots, t_n$ are P-terms.
   (a) If $\hat{Es} = \{(f(t_1, \ldots, t_m) = g(t'_1, \ldots, t'_n))\} \cup \tilde{Es}$, then:
      i. If $f = g$ and $m = n$, then

$$\mathrm{SOLVE}(S, \hat{Es}) = \mathrm{SOLVE}(S, \{(t_1 = t'_1), \ldots, (t_m = t'_m)\} \cup \tilde{Es}).$$

    ii. If $f \neq g$ or $m \neq n$, then $\text{SOLVE}(S, \hat{E}s) = \langle \text{FAIL} \rangle$.

(b) If $\hat{E}s = \{(f(t_1, \ldots, t_m) \neq g(t'_1, \ldots, t'_n))\} \cup \tilde{E}s$, then:

    i. If $f = g$ and $m = n$, then

$$\text{SOLVE}(S, \hat{E}s) = \text{SOLVE}(S, \{(t_i \neq t'_i)\} \cup \tilde{E}s),$$

    where i is a selected index in $\{1, \ldots, m\}$.

    ii. If $f \neq g$ or $m \neq n$, then $\text{SOLVE}(S, \hat{E}s) = \text{SOLVE}(S, \tilde{E}s)$.

3. If $\hat{E}s = \{(t_1 = t_2)\} \cup \tilde{E}s$, where t_1, t_2 are usual terms, then:

  (a) If t_1 and t_2 are unifiable, then $\text{SOLVE}(S, \hat{E}s) = \text{SOLVE}(S \cup \sigma, \tilde{E}s\sigma)$, where σ is the most general unifier of t_1 and t_2.

  (b) If they are not unifiable, then $\text{SOLVE}(S, \hat{E}s) = \langle \text{FAIL} \rangle$.

4. If $\hat{E}s = \{(t_1 \neq t_2)\} \cup \tilde{E}s$, where t_1, t_2 are usual terms, then:

  (a) If t_1 and t_2 are not unifiable, then $\text{SOLVE}(S, \hat{E}s) = \text{SOLVE}(S, \tilde{E}s)$.

  (b) If t_1 and t_2 are equal, then $\text{SOLVE}(S, \hat{E}s) = \langle \text{FAIL} \rangle$.

  (c) If t_1 and t_2 are not equal but they are unifiable, then $\text{SOLVE}(S, \hat{E}s) = \langle \text{OUTRANGE} \rangle$.

5. If ρ is a parameter $p : except(E)$ and $\hat{E}s = \{(\rho = \hat{t})\} \cup \tilde{E}s$, then:

  (a) If $\hat{t}$ is the parameter ρ itself, then $\text{SOLVE}(S, \hat{E}s) = \text{SOLVE}(S, \tilde{E}s)$.

  (b) If $\hat{t}$ is a usual variable v, then $\text{SOLVE}(S, \hat{E}s) = \text{SOLVE}(S \cup \{v/\rho\}, \tilde{E}s\{v/\rho\})$.

  (c) If $\hat{t}$ is a ground term in E, then $\text{SOLVE}(S, \hat{E}s) = \langle \text{FAIL} \rangle$.

  (d) If $\hat{t}$ is a ground term and $\hat{t} \notin E$, then $\text{SOLVE}(S, \hat{E}s) = \langle \text{SPLITREQ}, \rho, t \rangle$.

  (e) Otherwise $\text{SOLVE}(S, \hat{E}s) = \langle \text{OUTRANGE} \rangle$.

6. If ρ is a parameter $p : except(E)$ and $\hat{E}s = \{(\rho \neq \hat{t})\} \cup \tilde{E}s$, then:

  (a) If $\hat{t}$ is a ground term in E, then $\text{SOLVE}(S, \hat{E}s) = \text{SOLVE}(S, \tilde{E}s)$.

  (b) If $\hat{t}$ is a ground term and $\hat{t} \notin E$, then $\text{SOLVE}(S, \hat{E}s) = \langle \text{SPLITREQ}, \rho, t \rangle$.

  (c) Otherwise $\text{SOLVE}(S, \hat{E}s) = \langle \text{OUTRANGE} \rangle$.

Note that $\text{SOLVE}(S, \hat{E}s)$ is not uniquely determined, owing to nondeterministic selection of the index i in Case 2(b)i.

3.4   A One-Step Bottom-Up Inference Procedure

Next, a one-step bottom-up inference procedure is presented. It takes a subset M of $pow(\mathcal{G}_P)$ as input, and nondeterministically outputs one of the following results: (i) a set M' of ground atom sets with parameters, (ii) $\langle \text{NOCHANGE} \rangle$, (iii) $\langle \text{OUTRANGE} \rangle$. The procedure works as follows:

1. Select $m \in M$.
2. Select a clause C in Cs.
3. Let A be the set of all usual atoms in $rhs(C)$. Assuming that $A = \{a_1, \ldots, a_n\}$, where $n \geq 0$, perform the following steps:

  (a) Select $A' = \{a'_1, \ldots, a'_n\} \subseteq m$.

(b) Let EQ be the set of equalities and inequalities constructed from all eq-atoms and neq-atoms in $rhs(C)$.

(c) Let $U = \text{SOLVE}(\{(a_1 = a_1'), \ldots, (a_n = a_n')\} \cup EQ)$. Then:

   i. If U is a substitution, then let $\theta = U$.

   ii. If $U = \langle \text{SPLITREQ}, \rho, t \rangle$, then let $M' = \text{SPLIT}(M, \rho, t)$ and stop with the output M'.

   iii. If $U = \langle \text{FAIL} \rangle$, then stop with the output $\langle \text{NOCHANGE} \rangle$.

   iv. If $U = \langle \text{OUTRANGE} \rangle$, then stop with the output $\langle \text{OUTRANGE} \rangle$.

4. Let F be the set of all func-atoms in $rhs(C)$.

5. While $F \neq \emptyset$, perform the following steps:

(a) Select a func-atom $\mathbf{f} = func(f, t_1, \ldots, t_n, t_{n+1}) \in F$, where $n \geq 0$, such that $t_1\theta, \ldots, t_n\theta$ are ground terms. If there is no such func-atom in F, then stop with the output $\langle \text{OUTRANGE} \rangle$.

(b) Select a func-atom $f(t_1\theta, \ldots, t_n\theta, t') \in m$. If there is no such func-atom in m, then let

$$M' = (M - \{m\}) \cup \{m \cup \{f(t_1\theta, \ldots, t_n\theta, \rho_{\text{new}})\}\},$$

where ρ_{new} is a new parameter $p_{\text{new}} : except(\emptyset)$ with a new marker p_{new}, and stop with the output M'.

(c) Let $U = \text{SOLVE}(\{(t_{n+1}\theta = t')\})$. Then:

   i. If U is a substitution σ, then let $\theta' = \theta \circ \sigma$.

   ii. If $U = \langle \text{SPLITREQ}, \rho, t \rangle$, then let $M' = \text{SPLIT}(M, \rho, t)$ and stop with the output M'.

   iii. If $U = \langle \text{FAIL} \rangle$, then stop with the output $\langle \text{NOCHANGE} \rangle$.

   iv. If $U = \langle \text{OUTRANGE} \rangle$, then stop with the output $\langle \text{OUTRANGE} \rangle$.

(d) Remove $\mathbf{f}$ from F.

6. If $lhs(C\theta') \cap m \neq \emptyset$, then stop with the output $\langle \text{NOCHANGE} \rangle$.

7. Assume that $lhs(C\theta') = \{b_1, \ldots, b_{n'}\}$, where $n' \geq 0$. Then let

$$M' = (M - \{m\}) \cup \{m \cup \{b_1\}\} \cup \cdots \cup \{m \cup \{b_{n'}\}\}$$

and stop with the output M'.

3.5 A Delayed Splitting Bottom-Up Procedure

For any given subset M of $pow(\mathcal{G}_P)$, let $\text{POSS}(M)$ and $\text{DONE}(M)$ be defined as follows: (i) $\text{POSS}(M)$ is the set of all sets M' of ground atom sets with parameters possibly obtained when applying the above procedure to the input M; (ii) $\text{DONE}(M) = \langle \text{SUCC} \rangle$ if $\langle \text{NOCHANGE} \rangle$ is the only possible output when applying the above procedure to the input M. Given a clause set Cs in ECLS_F, models of Cs, represented by a subset M of $pow(\mathcal{G}_P)$, are generated using a delayed splitting bottom-up procedure described below.

1. Initially, let $M = \{m_0\}$, where $m_0 = \emptyset$.

2. While $\text{POSS}(M) \neq \emptyset$, perform the following two steps:
   (a) Select $M' \in \text{POSS}(M)$.
   (b) $M := M'$.
3. If $\text{DONE}(M) = \langle \text{SUCC} \rangle$, then stop with M being the output, otherwise stop with a failure.

Now let $\langle Cs, a \rangle$ be a given QA problem on ECLS$_F$. To compute the answer to $\langle Cs, a \rangle$, we first compute a subset M of $pow(\mathcal{G}_P)$ using the delayed splitting bottom-up procedure above. Then the computed answer to $\langle Cs, a \rangle$ is the set $(\bigcap M) \cap rep(a)$. Note that although P-atoms may occur in the set M obtained from the delayed splitting bottom-up procedure, they do not belong to $rep(a)$ and therefore do not occur in the computed answer.

4   Examples

Three examples illustrating application of the presented bottom-up procedure are given below. It is assumed that a usual variable as well as a function variable begins with an asterisk.

Example 1. Let Cs consist of the following five clauses, where $*h$ is a 0-ary function variable and *neq* stands for "not equal":

$C_1:$ $q(*x) \leftarrow r(*x)$ $C_2:$ $r(*x) \leftarrow func(*h, *x)$
$C_3:$ $s(*x) \leftarrow func(*h, *x)$ $C_4:$ $\leftarrow s(*x), neq(*x, A), neq(*x, B)$
$C_5:$ $\leftarrow s(B)$

Assume that q-, r-, and s-atoms are usual atoms and *neq*-atoms are constraint atoms. Consider a QA problem $prb_1 = \langle Cs, q(*x) \rangle$. Let $M_0 = \{m_0\}$, where $m_0 = \emptyset$. The one-step inference procedure in Section 3.4 is applied successively with M_0 being the first input as follows:

1. M_0 is input to the procedure. The set m_0 is selected at Step 1. Suppose that C_3 is selected at Step 2. At Step 3, $\text{SOLVE}(\emptyset)$ is called and it returns the identity substitution. At Step 5b, the procedure constructs $m_1 = m_0 \cup \{*h(p_1)\} = \{*h(p_1)\}$, where p_1 is a parameter marker, and outputs $M_1 = \{m_1\}$.
2. M_1 is input to the procedure. The set m_1 is selected at Step 1. Suppose that C_3 is selected at Step 2. At Step 5c, $\text{SOLVE}(\{(*x = p_1)\})$ is called, with the output substitution being $\sigma = \{*x/p_1\}$. At Step 7, the procedure constructs $m_2 = m_1 \cup \{s(*x)\sigma\} = \{*h(p_1), s(p_1)\}$ and outputs $M_2 = \{m_2\}$.
3. M_2 is input to the procedure. The set m_2 is selected at Step 1. Suppose that C_4 is selected at Step 2. At Step 3, $\text{SOLVE}(\{(*x = p_1), (*x \neq A), (*x \neq B)\})$ is called and it returns $\langle \text{SPLITREQ}, p_1, A \rangle$; accordingly, m_2 is split into
   - $m_3 = \{*h(A), s(A)\}$, and
   - $m_4 = \{*h(p_2 : except(\{A\})), s(p_2 : except(\{A\}))\}$,
   where p_2 is a new marker. The procedure outputs $M_3 = \{m_3, m_4\}$.

4. M_3 is input to the procedure. Suppose that m_4 is selected at Step 1 and C_4 is selected at Step 2. At Step 3, SOLVE($\{(*x = p_2 : except(\{A\})), (*x \neq A), (*x \neq B)\}$) is called, with $\langle$SPLITREQ, $p_2 : except(\{A\}), B\rangle$ being returned. So m_4 is split into
   - $m_5 = \{*h(B), s(B)\}$, and
   - $m_6 = \{*h(p_3 : except(\{A, B\})), s(p_3 : except(\{A, B\}))\}$,
   where p_3 is a new marker, and the procedure outputs $M_4 = \{m_3, m_5, m_6\}$.
5. M_4 is input to the procedure. Suppose that m_6 is selected at Step 1 and C_4 is selected at Step 2. At Step 3, SOLVE($\{(*x = p_3 : except(\{A, B\})), (*x \neq A), (*x \neq B)\}$) is called and it returns the identity substitution (since the possibility of splitting the parameter $p_3 : except(\{A, B\})$ is excluded by the inequalities $(*x \neq A)$ and $(*x \neq B)$). At Step 7, since C_4 is a negative clause, m_6 is removed from M_4 and the procedure outputs $M_5 = \{m_3, m_5\}$.
6. M_5 is input to the procedure. Suppose that m_5 is selected at Step 1 and C_5 is selected at Step 2. At Step 3, SOLVE($\{(B = B)\}$) is called and it returns the identity substitution. At Step 7, since C_5 is a negative clause, m_5 is removed from M_5 and the procedure outputs $M_6 = \{m_3\}$.
7. M_6 is input to the procedure. The set m_3 is selected at Step 1. Suppose that C_2 is selected at Step 2. At Step 3, SOLVE($\emptyset$) is called and it returns the identity substitution. At Step 5c, SOLVE($\{(*x = A)\}$) is called and it returns the substitution $\sigma = \{*x/A\}$. At Step 7, the procedure constructs $m_7 = m_3 \cup \{r(*x)\sigma\} = \{*h(A), s(A), r(A)\}$ and outputs $M_7 = \{m_7\}$.
8. M_7 is input to the procedure. The set m_7 is selected at Step 1. Suppose that C_1 is selected at Step 2. At Step 3, SOLVE($\{(*x = A)\}$) is called and it returns the substitution $\theta = \{*x/A\}$. At Step 7, the procedure constructs $m_8 = m_7 \cup \{q(*x)\theta\} = \{*h(A), s(A), r(A), q(A)\}$ and outputs $M_8 = \{m_8\}$.

Since POSS(M_8) $= \emptyset$ and DONE(M_8) $= \langle$SUCC$\rangle$, the main algorithm stops with M_8 being the output. The answer to prb_1 is $(\bigcap M_8) \cap rep(q(*x)) = \{q(A)\}$.   □

Example 2. Consider a QA problem $prb_2 = \langle Cs, q(*x)\rangle$, where Cs consists of the following four clauses, assuming that $*h$ is a 0-ary function variable:

$C_1 : \quad q(*x), r(*x) \leftarrow s(*x), func(*h, *x) \qquad C_2 : \quad s(1) \leftarrow$
$C_3 : \quad s(2) \leftarrow \qquad\qquad\qquad\qquad\qquad\quad C_4 : \quad \leftarrow q(1)$

Note that C_1 is a multi-head clause. Again assume that q-, r-, and s-atoms are usual atoms. Let $M_0 = \{m_0\}$, where $m_0 = \emptyset$. The one-step bottom-up inference procedure is applied successively with M_0 being the first input as follows:

1. M_0 is input to the procedure. Suppose that C_2 is selected. The procedure constructs $m_1 = m_0 \cup \{s(1)\} = \{s(1)\}$ and outputs $M_1 = \{m_1\}$.
2. M_1 is input to the procedure. Suppose that C_3 is selected. The procedure constructs $m_2 = m_1 \cup \{s(2)\} = \{s(1), s(2)\}$ and outputs $M_2 = \{m_2\}$.
3. M_2 is input to the procedure. Suppose that C_1 is selected. At Step 3, supposing that $s(1)$ is selected, SOLVE($\{(*x = 1)\}$) is called and it returns the substitution $\{*x/1\}$. At Step 5b, the procedure constructs $m_3 = m_2 \cup \{*h(p_1)\} = \{s(1), s(2), *h(p_1)\}$, where p_1 is a parameter marker, and outputs $M_3 = \{m_3\}$.

4. M_3 is input to the procedure. Suppose that C_1 is selected. At Step 3, supposing that $s(1)$ is selected, $\text{SOLVE}(\{(*x = 1)\})$ is called and it returns the substitution $\{*x/1\}$. At Step 5c, $\text{SOLVE}(\{(1 = p_1)\})$ is called and it returns $\langle \text{SPLITREQ}, p_1, 1 \rangle$. As a result, m_3 is split into
   - $m_4 = \{s(1), s(2), *h(1)\}$, and
   - $m_5 = \{s(1), s(2), *h(p_2 : except(\{1\}))\}$,
   where p_2 is a new marker. The procedure outputs $M_4 = \{m_4, m_5\}$.
5. M_4 is input to the procedure. Suppose that m_4 and C_1 are selected. At Step 3, supposing that $s(1)$ is selected, $\text{SOLVE}(\{(*x = 1)\})$ is called and it returns the substitution $\{*x/1\}$. At Step 5c, $\text{SOLVE}(\{(1 = 1)\})$ is called and it returns the identity substitution. At Step 7, the procedure construct
   - $m_6 = m_4 \cup \{q(1)\} = \{s(1), s(2), *h(1), q(1)\}$, and
   - $m_7 = m_4 \cup \{r(1)\} = \{s(1), s(2), *h(1), r(1)\}$,
   and outputs $M_5 = \{m_6, m_7, m_5\}$.
6. M_5 is input to the procedure. Suppose that m_6 and C_4 are selected. Since C_4 is a negative clause, m_6 is removed at Step 7. The procedure outputs $M_6 = \{m_7, m_5\}$.
7. M_6 is input to the procedure. Suppose that m_5 and C_1 are selected. At Step 3, supposing that $s(2)$ is selected, $\text{SOLVE}(\{(*x = 2)\})$ is called and it returns the substitution $\{*x/2\}$. At Step 5c, $\text{SOLVE}(\{(2 = p_2 : except(\{1\}))\})$ is called and it returns $\langle \text{SPLITREQ}, p_2 : except(\{1\}), 2 \rangle$. Then m_5 is split into
   - $m_8 = \{s(1), s(2), *h(2)\}$, and
   - $m_9 = \{s(1), s(2), *h(p_3 : except(\{1, 2\}))\}$,
   where p_3 is a new marker. The procedure outputs $M_7 = \{m_7, m_8, m_9\}$.
8. M_7 is input to the procedure. Suppose that m_8 and C_1 are selected. At Step 3, supposing that $s(2)$ is selected, $\text{SOLVE}(\{(*x = 2)\})$ is called and it returns the substitution $\{*x/2\}$. At Step 5c, $\text{SOLVE}(\{(2 = 2)\})$ is called and it returns the identity substitution. At Step 7, the procedure construct
   - $m_{10} = m_8 \cup \{q(2)\} = \{s(1), s(2), *h(2), q(2)\}$, and
   - $m_{11} = m_8 \cup \{r(2)\} = \{s(1), s(2), *h(2), r(2)\}$,
   and outputs $M_8 = \{m_7, m_{10}, m_{11}, m_9\}$.

Since $\text{POSS}(M_8) = \emptyset$ and $\text{DONE}(M_8) = \langle \text{SUCC} \rangle$, the main algorithm stops with the output M_8. The answer to prb_2 is $(\bigcap M_8) \cap rep(q(*x)) = \emptyset$. $\quad\square$

Example 3. Next, consider the "Tax-cut" problem discussed in [6]. This problem is to find all persons who can have discounted tax, with the knowledge consisting of the following statements: (i) Any person who has two children or more can get discounted tax. (ii) Men and women are not the same. (iii) A person's mother is always a woman. (iv) Peter has a child, who is someone's mother. (v) Peter has a child named Paul. (vi) Paul is a man. These six statements are represented by the following extended clauses:

C_1: $TaxCut(*x) \leftarrow hasChild(*x, *y), hasChild(*x, *z), notSame(*y, *z)$
C_2: $notSame(*x, *y) \leftarrow Man(*x), Woman(*y)$
C_3: $\leftarrow notSame(*x, *x)$
C_4: $Woman(*x) \leftarrow motherOf(*x, *y)$

C_5: $hasChild(Peter, *x) \leftarrow func(*h_1, *x)$

C_6: $motherOf(*x, *y) \leftarrow func(*h_1, *x), func(*h_2, *y)$

C_7: $hasChild(Peter, Paul) \leftarrow$

C_8: $Man(Paul) \leftarrow$

The clauses C_5 and C_6 together represent the fourth statement (i.e., "Peter has a child, who is someone's mother"), where $*h_1$ and $*h_2$ are 0-ary function variables. The "Tax-cut" problem is then formulated as a QA problem $prb_3 = \langle Cs, TaxCut(*x) \rangle$, where Cs consists of the clauses C_1–C_8 above.

Let $M_0 = \{m_0\}$, where $m_0 = \emptyset$. Taking M_0 as the first input, the one-step inference procedure is applied successively as follows:

1. In the first two application of the procedure, suppose that C_6 is selected. The obtained output is $M_1 = \{m_1\}$, where $m_1 = \{*h_1(p_1), *h_2(p_2)\}$ and p_1 and p_2 are parameter markers.
2. In the next six application of the procedure, suppose that the clauses C_5, C_6, C_7, C_8, C_4, and C_2 are selected successively. The obtained output is $M_2 = \{m_2\}$, where $m_2 = \{hasChild(Peter, p_1), motherOf(p_1, p_2), hasChild(Peter, Paul), Man(Paul), Woman(p_1), notSame(Paul, p_1)\}$.
3. M_2 is input to the procedure. Suppose that C_3 is selected. At Step 3, $\text{SOLVE}(\{(*x = Paul), (*x = p_1)\})$ is called and it returns $\langle \text{SPLITREQ}, p_1, Paul \rangle$. Accordingly, m_2 is split into
   - $m_3 = m_2\sigma$, where $\sigma = \{p_1/Paul\}$, and
   - $m_4 = m_2\sigma'$, where $\sigma' = \{p_1/p_3 : except(\{Paul\})\}$ and p_3 is a new marker.
   The procedure outputs $M_3 = \{m_3, m_4\}$.
4. M_3 is input to the procedure. Suppose that m_3 and C_3 are selected. At Step 3, $\text{SOLVE}(\{(*x = Paul)\})$ is called and it returns the substitution $\{*x/Paul\}$. Since C_3 is a negative clause, m_3 is removed at Step 7. The procedure outputs $M_4 = \{m_4\}$.
5. M_4 is input to the procedure. Suppose that C_1 is selected. The procedure outputs $M_5 = \{m_5\}$, where $m_5 = m_4 \cup \{TaxCut(Peter)\}$.

Now $\text{POSS}(M_5) = \emptyset$ and $\text{DONE}(M_5) = \langle \text{SUCC} \rangle$. The main algorithm then stops with the output M_5. The answer to the "Tax-cut" problem is thus $(\bigcap M_5) \cap rep(TaxCut(*x)) = \{TaxCut(Peter)\}$.   □

5   Fundamental Differences from Existing Approaches

This work differs from existing approaches for model generation, e.g., [3,7], and those for solving QA problems, e.g., [4,6,8], in the following main points:

1. *Use of meaning-preserving Skolemization:* Existing theories do not use meaning-preserving Skolemization. They use usual Skolemization, which does not preserve the meaning of a logical formula [2]. A model of a given formula is not necessarily a model of the formula obtained from it by usual Skolemization. Without meaning-preserving Skolemization, the range of possible processing methods is restricted, making it difficult to devise an effective solution for dealing with QA problems.

2. *Bottom-up computation with existentially quantified function variables:* Since usual Skolemization results in clauses with usual terms, previously existing theories do not use function variables. Resolution is used for usual proof methods [2,4], which deal with usual clauses without function variables. The use of function variables presents a new challenge to bottom-up computation. A fundamental distinction between our proposed algorithm and usual bottom-up proof methods is that our algorithm deals with instantiations of function variables whose scope covers an entire clause set, while the usual methods consider only instantiations of usual variables within an individual clause.

3. *Use of model-making patterns:* Instantiations of a function variable yield infinitely many potential model-generation cases to be considered, making it impossible to examine all cases individually. Model-making patterns classify an infinite number of model-generation cases, allowing one to handle all those cases using finite representation.

6   Concluding Remarks

This paper has proposed a bottom-up model-generation procedure in the extended space with function variables. To solve infiniteness caused by the instantiation of function variables, model-making patterns are used for model representation. Such patterns classify an infinite number of model-generation cases, making it possible to examine all those cases using finite representation. To reduce the number of model-making patterns to be considered, a pattern is split only when needed. The work provides a basis for construction of QA-problem solvers.

References

1. Akama, K., Nantajeewarawat, E.: Meaning-Preserving Skolemization. In: 2011 International Conference on Knowledge Engineering and Ontology Development, Paris, France, pp. 322–327 (2011)
2. Chang, C.-L., Lee, R.C.-T.: Symbolic Logic and Mechanical Theorem Proving. Academic Press (1973)
3. Hasegawa, R., Fujita, H., Koshimura, M.: MGTP: A Model Generation Theorem Prover—Its Advanced Features and Applications. In: Galmiche, D. (ed.) TABLEAUX 1997. LNCS, vol. 1227, pp. 1–15. Springer, Heidelberg (1997)
4. Lloyd, J.W.: Foundations of Logic Programming, 2nd edn. Springer (1987)
5. Minker, J.: Foundations of Deductive Databases and Logic Programming. Morgan Kaufmann Publishers (1988)
6. Motik, B., Sattler, U., Studer, R.: Query Answering for OWL-DL with Rules. Journal of Web Semantics 3, 41–60 (2005)
7. Schütz, H., Geisler, T.: Efficient Model Generation Through Compilation. In: McRobbie, M.A., Slaney, J.K. (eds.) CADE 1996. LNCS, vol. 1104, pp. 433–447. Springer, Heidelberg (1996)
8. Tessaris, S.: Questions and Answers: Reasoning and Querying in Description Logic. PhD Thesis, Department of Computer Science, The University of Manchester, UK (2001)

A Goal-Oriented Algorithm for Unification in $\mathcal{ELH}_{R^+}$ w.r.t. Cycle-Restricted Ontologies*

Franz Baader, Stefan Borgwardt, and Barbara Morawska

Theoretical Computer Science, TU Dresden, Germany
{baader,stefborg,morawska}@tcs.inf.tu-dresden.de

Abstract. Unification in Description Logics (DLs) has been proposed as an inference service that can, for example, be used to detect redundancies in ontologies. For the DL $\mathcal{EL}$, which is used to define several large biomedical ontologies, unification is NP-complete. A goal-oriented NP unification algorithm for $\mathcal{EL}$ that uses nondeterministic rules to transform a given unification problem into solved form has recently been presented. In this paper, we extend this goal-oriented algorithm in two directions: on the one hand, we add general concept inclusion axioms (GCIs), and on the other hand, we add role hierarchies ($\mathcal{H}$) and transitive roles (R^+). For the algorithm to be complete, however, the ontology consisting of the GCIs and role axioms needs to satisfy a certain cycle restriction.

1 Introduction

The DL $\mathcal{EL}$, which offers the constructors conjunction ($\sqcap$), existential restriction ($\exists r.C$), and the top concept ($\top$), has recently drawn considerable attention since, on the one hand, important inference problems such as the subsumption problem are polynomial in $\mathcal{EL}$, even in the presence of general concept inclusions (GCIs) [12]. On the other hand, though quite inexpressive, $\mathcal{EL}$ can be used to define biomedical ontologies, such as the large medical ontology SNOMED CT.[1] A tractable extension of $\mathcal{EL}$ [7], which includes role hierarchy and transitivity axioms, is the basis of the OWL 2 EL profile of the new Web Ontology Language OWL 2.[2]

Unification in DLs has been proposed in [11] as a novel inference service that can, for instance, be used to detect redundancies in ontologies. For example, assume that one developer of a medical ontology defines the concept of a *patient with severe injury of the frontal lobe* as

$$\exists \mathsf{finding}.(\mathsf{Frontal\_lobe\_injury} \sqcap \exists \mathsf{severity}.\mathsf{Severe}), \tag{1}$$

whereas another one represents it as

$$\exists \mathsf{finding}.(\mathsf{Severe\_injury} \sqcap \exists \mathsf{finding\_site}.\exists \mathsf{part\_of}.\mathsf{Frontal\_lobe}). \tag{2}$$

---

* Supported by DFG under grant BA 1122/14-1.
[1] see http://www.ihtsdo.org/snomed-ct/
[2] See http://www.w3.org/TR/owl2-profiles/

M. Thielscher and D. Zhang (Eds.): AI 2012, LNCS 7691, pp. 493–504, 2012.
© Springer-Verlag Berlin Heidelberg 2012

These two concept descriptions are not equivalent, but they are nevertheless meant to represent the same concept. They can obviously be made equivalent by treating the concept names Frontal_lobe_injury and Severe_injury as variables, and substituting the first one by Injury ⊓ ∃finding_site.∃part_of.Frontal_lobe and the second one by Injury ⊓ ∃severity.Severe. In this case, we say that the descriptions are unifiable, and call the substitution that makes them equivalent a *unifier*.

Our interest in unification w.r.t. GCIs, role hierarchies, and transitive roles stems from the fact that these features are important for expressing medical knowledge. For example, assume that the developers use the descriptions (3) and (4) instead of (1) and (2):

$$\exists\mathsf{finding}.\exists\mathsf{finding\_site}.\exists\mathsf{part\_of}.\mathsf{Brain} \sqcap$$
$$\exists\mathsf{finding}.(\mathsf{Frontal\_lobe\_injury} \sqcap \exists\mathsf{severity}.\mathsf{Severe}) \qquad (3)$$

$$\exists\mathsf{status}.\mathsf{Emergency} \sqcap$$
$$\exists\mathsf{finding}.(\mathsf{Severe\_injury} \sqcap \exists\mathsf{finding\_site}.\exists\mathsf{part\_of}.\mathsf{Frontal\_lobe}) \qquad (4)$$

The descriptions (3) and (4) are not unifiable without additional background knowledge, but they are unifiable, with the same unifier as above, if the GCIs

$$\exists\mathsf{finding}.\exists\mathsf{severity}.\mathsf{Severe} \sqsubseteq \exists\mathsf{status}.\mathsf{Emergency},$$
$$\mathsf{Frontal\_lobe} \sqsubseteq \exists\mathsf{proper\_part\_of}.\mathsf{Brain}$$

are present in a background ontology and this ontology additionally states that part_of is transitive and proper_part_of is a subrole of part_of.

In [8], we were able to show that unification in the DL $\mathcal{EL}$ (without GCIs and role axioms) is NP-complete. In addition to a brute-force "guess and then test" NP-algorithm [8], we have developed a goal-oriented unification algorithm for $\mathcal{EL}$, in which nondeterministic decisions are only made if they are triggered by "unsolved parts" of the unification problem [10], and an algorithm that is based on a reduction to satisfiability in propositional logic (SAT) [9], which enables the use of highly-optimized SAT solvers [14]. Whereas both approaches are clearly better than the brute-force algorithm, none of them is uniformly better than the other. First experiments with our system UEL [1] show that the SAT translation is usually faster in deciding unifiability, but it needs more space than the goal-oriented algorithm and it produces more uninteresting and large unifiers. In fact, the SAT translation generates all so-called local unifiers, whereas the goal-oriented algorithm produces all so-called minimal unifiers, though it may also produce some non-minimal ones. The set of minimal unifiers is a subset of the set of local unifiers, and in our experiments the minimal unifiers usually made more sense in the application.

In [10] it was shown that the approaches for unification of $\mathcal{EL}$-concept descriptions (without any background ontology) mentioned above can easily be extended to the case of a so-called acyclic TBox (a simple form of GCIs, which basically introduce abbreviations for concept descriptions) as background ontology without really changing the algorithms or increasing their complexity.

For more general GCIs, such a simple solution is no longer possible. In [2], we extended the brute-force "guess and then test" NP-algorithm from [8] to the case of GCIs, which required the development of a new characterization of subsumption w.r.t. GCIs in $\mathcal{EL}$. Unfortunately, the algorithm is complete only for general TBoxes (i.e., finite sets of GCIs) that satisfy a certain restriction on cycles, which, however, does not prevent all cycles. For example, the cyclic GCI $\exists$child.Human $\sqsubseteq$ Human satisfies this restriction, whereas the cyclic GCI Human $\sqsubseteq$ $\exists$parent.Human does not. In [5] we provide a more practical unification algorithm that is based on a translation into SAT, and can also deal with role hierarchies and transitive roles, but still needs the ontology (now consisting of GCIs and role axioms) to be cycle-restricted. In the presence of role hierarchies ($\mathcal{H}$) and transitive roles (R^+), we use the name $\mathcal{ELH}_{R^+}$ rather than $\mathcal{EL}$ for the logic.

Motivated by our experience that, for the case of $\mathcal{EL}$ without background ontology, the goal-oriented algorithm sometimes behaves better than the one based on a translation into SAT, we introduce in this paper a goal-oriented algorithm for unification in $\mathcal{ELH}_{R^+}$ w.r.t. cycle-restricted ontologies.[3] Full proofs of the presented results can be found in [3].

2   The Description Logics $\mathcal{EL}$ and $\mathcal{ELH}_{R^+}$

The expressiveness of a DL is determined both by the formalism for describing concepts (the concept description language) and the terminological formalism, which can be used to state additional constraints on the interpretation of concepts and roles in a so-called ontology.

The *concept description language* considered in this paper is called $\mathcal{EL}$. Starting with a finite set N_C of *concept names* and a finite set N_R of *role names*, $\mathcal{EL}$-concept descriptions are built from concept names using the constructors *conjunction* ($C \sqcap D$), *existential restriction* ($\exists r.C$ for every $r \in N_R$), and *top* ($\top$). Since in this paper we only consider $\mathcal{EL}$-concept descriptions, we will sometimes dispense with the prefix $\mathcal{EL}$.

On the *semantic side*, concept descriptions are interpreted as sets. To be more precise, an *interpretation* $\mathcal{I} = (\Delta^{\mathcal{I}}, \cdot^{\mathcal{I}})$ consists of a non-empty domain $\Delta^{\mathcal{I}}$ and an interpretation function $\cdot^{\mathcal{I}}$ that maps concept names to subsets of $\Delta^{\mathcal{I}}$ and role names to binary relations over $\Delta^{\mathcal{I}}$. This function is inductively extended to concept descriptions as follows:

$$\top^{\mathcal{I}} := \Delta^{\mathcal{I}}, \quad (C \sqcap D)^{\mathcal{I}} := C^{\mathcal{I}} \cap D^{\mathcal{I}}, \quad (\exists r.C)^{\mathcal{I}} := \{x \mid \exists y : (x,y) \in r^{\mathcal{I}} \wedge y \in C^{\mathcal{I}}\}$$

A *general concept inclusion axiom (GCI)* is of the form $C \sqsubseteq D$ for concept descriptions C, D, a *role hierarchy axiom* is of the form $r \sqsubseteq s$ for role names

---

[3] A previous version of this paper, which considers unification in $\mathcal{EL}$ w.r.t. cycle-restricted ontologies, but without role hierarchies and transitive roles, has been presented in 2012 at the Description Logic workshop (see [4]).

r, s, and a *transitivity axiom* is of the form $r \circ r \sqsubseteq r$ for a role name r. An interpretation $\mathcal{I}$ *satisfies* such an axiom $C \sqsubseteq D$, $r \sqsubseteq s$, $r \circ r \sqsubseteq r$, respectively, iff

$$C^{\mathcal{I}} \subseteq D^{\mathcal{I}}, \quad r^{\mathcal{I}} \subseteq s^{\mathcal{I}}, \quad \text{and} \quad r^{\mathcal{I}} \circ r^{\mathcal{I}} \subseteq r^{\mathcal{I}},$$

where $\circ$ stands for composition of binary relations. An $\mathcal{ELH}_{R^+}$-*ontology* is a finite set of such axioms. It is an $\mathcal{EL}$-*ontology* if it contains only GCIs. An interpretation is a *model* of an ontology if it satisfies all its axioms.

A concept description C is *subsumed* by a concept description D w.r.t. an ontology $\mathcal{O}$ (written $C \sqsubseteq_{\mathcal{O}} D$) if every model of $\mathcal{O}$ satisfies the GCI $C \sqsubseteq D$. We say that C is *equivalent* to D w.r.t. $\mathcal{O}$ ($C \equiv_{\mathcal{O}} D$) if $C \sqsubseteq_{\mathcal{O}} D$ and $D \sqsubseteq_{\mathcal{O}} C$. If $\mathcal{O}$ is empty, we also write $C \sqsubseteq D$ and $C \equiv D$ instead of $C \sqsubseteq_{\mathcal{O}} D$ and $C \equiv_{\mathcal{O}} D$, respectively. As shown in [12,7], subsumption w.r.t. $\mathcal{ELH}_{R^+}$-ontologies (and thus also w.r.t. $\mathcal{EL}$-ontologies) is decidable in polynomial time.

Since conjunction is interpreted as intersection, the concept descriptions $(C \sqcap D) \sqcap E$ and $C \sqcap (D \sqcap E)$ are always equivalent. Thus, we dispense with parentheses and write nested conjunctions in flat form $C_1 \sqcap \cdots \sqcap C_n$. Nested existential restrictions $\exists r_1.\exists r_2.\ldots.\exists r_n.C$ will sometimes also be written as $\exists r_1 r_2 \ldots r_n.C$, where $r_1 r_2 \ldots r_n$ is viewed as a word over the alphabet of role names, i.e. an element of N_R^*.

The *role hierarchy* induced by $\mathcal{O}$ is a binary relation $\trianglelefteq_{\mathcal{O}}$ on N_R, which is defined as the reflexive-transitive closure of the relation $\{(r, s) \mid r \sqsubseteq s \in \mathcal{O}\}$. Using elementary reachability algorithms, the role hierarchy can be computed in polynomial time in the size of $\mathcal{O}$. It is easy to see that $r \trianglelefteq_{\mathcal{O}} s$ implies that $r^{\mathcal{I}} \subseteq s^{\mathcal{I}}$ for all models $\mathcal{I}$ of $\mathcal{O}$. Given an $\mathcal{ELH}_{R^+}$-ontology $\mathcal{O}$, we call the role t *transitive w.r.t.* $\mathcal{O}$ if $\mathcal{O}$ contains the axiom $t \circ t \sqsubseteq t$. If $\mathcal{O}$ is clear from the context, we often omit the suffix "w.r.t. $\mathcal{O}$" and call t a *transitive role*.

An $\mathcal{EL}$-concept description is an *atom* if it is an existential restriction or a concept name. The atoms of an $\mathcal{EL}$-concept description C are the subdescriptions of C that are atoms, and the top-level atoms of C are the atoms occurring in the top-level conjunction of C. Obviously, any $\mathcal{EL}$-concept description is the conjunction of its top-level atoms, where the empty conjunction corresponds to $\top$. The atoms of an $\mathcal{ELH}_{R^+}$-ontology $\mathcal{O}$ are the atoms of all the concept descriptions occurring in GCIs of $\mathcal{O}$.

We say that a subsumption between two atoms is *structural* if their top-level structure is compatible. To be more precise, following [5] we define structural subsumption between atoms as follows: the atom C is *structurally subsumed* by the atom D w.r.t. $\mathcal{O}$ ($C \sqsubseteq_{\mathcal{O}}^s D$) iff one of the following holds:

1. $C = D$ is a concept name,
2. $C = \exists r.C'$, $D = \exists s.D'$, $r \trianglelefteq_{\mathcal{O}} s$, and $C' \sqsubseteq_{\mathcal{O}} D'$.
3. $C = \exists r.C'$, $D = \exists s.D'$, and $C' \sqsubseteq_{\mathcal{O}} \exists t.D'$ for a transitive role t such that $r \trianglelefteq_{\mathcal{O}} t \trianglelefteq_{\mathcal{O}} s$.

It is easy to see that subsumption w.r.t. $\emptyset$ between two atoms implies structural subsumption w.r.t. $\mathcal{O}$, which in turn implies subsumption w.r.t. $\mathcal{O}$. The unification algorithm presented below crucially depends on the following characterization of subsumption:

Lemma 1. *Let $\mathcal{O}$ be an $\mathcal{ELH}_{R^+}$-ontology and $C_1, \ldots, C_n, D_1, \ldots, D_m$ be atoms. Then $C_1 \sqcap \cdots \sqcap C_n \sqsubseteq_{\mathcal{O}} D_1 \sqcap \cdots \sqcap D_m$ iff for every $j \in \{1, \ldots, m\}$*

1. *there is an index $i \in \{1, \ldots, n\}$ such that $C_i \sqsubseteq_{\mathcal{O}}^s D_j$ or*
2. *there are atoms $A_1, \ldots, A_k, B$ of $\mathcal{O}$ $(k \geq 0)$ such that*
   (a) $A_1 \sqcap \cdots \sqcap A_k \sqsubseteq_{\mathcal{O}} B$,
   (b) for every $\eta \in \{1, \ldots, k\}$ there is $i \in \{1, \ldots, n\}$ with $C_i \sqsubseteq_{\mathcal{O}}^s A_\eta$, and
   (c) $B \sqsubseteq_{\mathcal{O}}^s D_j$.

Our proof of this lemma in [3] is based on a Gentzen-style proof calculus for subsumption w.r.t. $\mathcal{ELH}_{R^+}$-ontologies, which is similar to the one developed in [15] for subsumption w.r.t. $\mathcal{EL}$-ontologies. Although this characterization looks identical to the one given in [2] for the case of $\mathcal{EL}$-ontologies it differs from that characterization in that it uses a more general notion of structural subsumption. Also note that the characterization of subsumption w.r.t. $\mathcal{ELH}_{R^+}$-ontologies employed in [5] to show correctness of the the SAT translation is different from the one given above, and it is proved using a rewriting approach rather than a Gentzen-style proof calculus.

As mentioned in the introduction, our unification algorithm is complete only for $\mathcal{ELH}_{R^+}$-ontologies that satisfy a certain restriction on cycles.

Definition 2. *The $\mathcal{ELH}_{R^+}$-ontology $\mathcal{O}$ is called* cycle-restricted *iff there is no nonempty word $w \in N_R^+$ and $\mathcal{EL}$-concept description C such that $C \sqsubseteq_{\mathcal{O}} \exists w.C$.*

In [5] we show that a given $\mathcal{ELH}_{R^+}$-ontology can be tested for cycle-restrictedness in polynomial time. The main idea is that it is sufficient to consider the cases where C is a concept name or $\top$.

3   Unification in $\mathcal{ELH}_{R^+}$

We partition the set N_C into a set N_v of concept variables (which may be replaced by substitutions) and a set N_c of concept constants (which must not be replaced by substitutions). A *substitution* σ maps every concept variable to an $\mathcal{EL}$-concept description. It is extended to concept descriptions in the usual way:

- $\sigma(A) := A$ for all $A \in N_c \cup \{\top\}$,
- $\sigma(C \sqcap D) := \sigma(C) \sqcap \sigma(D)$ and $\sigma(\exists r.C) := \exists r.\sigma(C)$.

An $\mathcal{EL}$-concept description C is *ground* if it does not contain variables. Obviously, a ground concept description is not modified by applying a substitution. An $\mathcal{ELH}_{R^+}$-ontology is *ground* if it does not contain variables.

Definition 3. *Let $\mathcal{O}$ be an $\mathcal{ELH}_{R^+}$-ontology that is ground. An $\mathcal{ELH}_{R^+}$-unification problem w.r.t. $\mathcal{O}$ is a finite set $\Gamma = \{C_1 \sqsubseteq^? D_1, \ldots, C_n \sqsubseteq^? D_n\}$ of subsumptions between $\mathcal{EL}$-concept descriptions. A substitution σ is a* unifier *of Γ w.r.t. $\mathcal{O}$ if σ solves all the subsumptions in Γ, i.e. if $\sigma(C_1) \sqsubseteq_{\mathcal{O}} \sigma(D_1), \ldots, \sigma(C_n) \sqsubseteq_{\mathcal{O}} \sigma(D_n)$. We say that Γ is* unifiable *w.r.t. $\mathcal{O}$ if it has a unifier.*

Note that some of the previous papers on unification in DLs use equivalences $C \equiv^? D$ instead of subsumptions $C \sqsubseteq^? D$. This difference is, however, irrelevant since $C \equiv^? D$ can be seen as a shorthand for the two subsumptions $C \sqsubseteq^? D$ and $D \sqsubseteq^? C$, and $C \sqsubseteq^? D$ has the same unifiers as $C \sqcap D \equiv^? C$. Also note that we have restricted the background ontology $\mathcal{O}$ to be ground. This is not without loss of generality. If $\mathcal{O}$ contained variables, then we would need to apply the substitution also to its GCIs, and instead of requiring $\sigma(C_i) \sqsubseteq_{\mathcal{O}} \sigma(D_i)$ we would thus need to require $\sigma(C_i) \sqsubseteq_{\sigma(\mathcal{O})} \sigma(D_i)$, which would change the nature of the problem considerably (see [6] for a more detailed discussion).

Preprocessing. To simplify the description of the algorithm, it is convenient to first normalize the ontology and the unification problem appropriately. An atom is called *flat* if it is a concept name or an existential restriction of the form $\exists r.A$ for a concept name A. The $\mathcal{ELH}_{R+}$-ontology $\mathcal{O}$ is called *flat* if it contains only GCIs of the form $A \sqcap B \sqsubseteq C$, where A, B are flat atoms or $\top$ and C is a flat atom. The unification problem Γ is called *flat* if it contains only flat subsumptions of the form $C_1 \sqcap \cdots \sqcap C_n \sqsubseteq^? D$, where $n \geq 0$ and $C_1, \ldots, C_n, D$ are flat atoms.[4] Let Γ be a unification problem and $\mathcal{O}$ an $\mathcal{ELH}_{R+}$-ontology. By introducing auxiliary variables and concept names, respectively, Γ and $\mathcal{O}$ can be transformed in polynomial time into a flat unification problem Γ' and a flat $\mathcal{ELH}_{R+}$-ontology $\mathcal{O}'$ such that the unifiability status remains unchanged, i.e., Γ has a unifier w.r.t. $\mathcal{O}$ iff Γ' has a unifier w.r.t. $\mathcal{O}'$. In addition, if $\mathcal{O}$ was cycle-restricted, then so is $\mathcal{O}'$ (see [6] for details). Thus, we can assume without loss of generality that the input unification problem and ontology are flat.

Local Unifiers. The main idea underlying the "in NP" results in [8,2] is to show that any unification problem that is unifiable has a so-called local unifier.

We denote by At the set of atoms occurring as subdescriptions in subsumptions in Γ or axioms in $\mathcal{O}$ and define

$$\text{At}_{\text{tr}} := \text{At} \cup \{\exists t.D' \mid \exists s.D' \in \text{At},\ t \trianglelefteq_{\mathcal{O}} s,\ t \text{ transitive}\}.$$

Furthermore, we define the set of *non-variable atoms* by $\text{At}_{\text{nv}} := \text{At}_{\text{tr}} \setminus N_v$. Though the elements of At_{nv} cannot be variables, they may contain variables if they are of the form $\exists r.X$ for some role r and a variable X.

We call a function S that associates every variable $X \in N_v$ with a set $S_X \subseteq \text{At}_{\text{nv}}$ an *assignment*. Such an assignment induces the following relation $>_S$ on N_v: $>_S$ is the transitive closure of

$$\{(X, Y) \in N_v \times N_v \mid Y \text{ occurs in an element of } S_X\}.$$

We call the assignment S *acyclic* if $>_S$ is irreflexive (and thus a strict partial order). Any acyclic assignment S induces a unique substitution σ_S, which can be defined by induction along $>_S$:

---

[4] If $n = 0$, then we have an empty conjunction on the left-hand side, which as usual stands for $\top$.

- If $X \in N_v$ is minimal w.r.t. $>_S$, then we define $\sigma_S(X) := \bigsqcap_{D \in S_X} D$.
- Assume that $\sigma(Y)$ is already defined for all Y such that $X >_S Y$. Then we define $\sigma_S(X) := \bigsqcap_{D \in S_X} \sigma_S(D)$.

We call a substitution σ *local* if it is of this form, i.e., if there is an acyclic assignment S such that $\sigma = \sigma_S$. If the unifier σ of Γ w.r.t. $\mathcal{O}$ is a local substitution, then we call it a *local unifier* of Γ w.r.t. $\mathcal{O}$.

The main technical result shown in [2] is that any unifiable $\mathcal{EL}$-unification problem w.r.t. a cycle-restricted ontology has a local unifier. This yields the following brute-force unification algorithm for $\mathcal{EL}$ w.r.t. cycle-restricted ontologies: first guess an acyclic assignment S, and then check whether the induced local substitution σ_S solves Γ. As shown in [2], this algorithm runs in nondeterministic polynomial time. NP-hardness follows from the fact that already unification in $\mathcal{EL}$ w.r.t. the empty ontology is NP-hard [8]. In [2] it is also shown why cycle-restrictedness is needed: there is a non-cycle-restricted $\mathcal{EL}$-ontology $\mathcal{O}$ and an $\mathcal{EL}$-unification problem Γ such that Γ has a unifier w.r.t. $\mathcal{O}$, but it does not have a local unifier.

4 A Goal-Oriented Unification Algorithm

The brute-force algorithm is not practical since it blindly guesses an acyclic assignment and only afterwards checks whether the guessed assignment induces a unifier. We now introduce a more goal-oriented unification algorithm, in which nondeterministic decisions are only made if they are triggered by "unsolved parts" of the unification problem. In addition, failure due to wrong guesses can be detected early. Any non-failing run of the algorithm produces a unifier, i.e., there is no need for checking whether the assignment computed by this run really induces a unifier. This goal-oriented algorithm generalizes the algorithm for unification in $\mathcal{EL}$ (without background ontology) introduced in [10], though the rules look quite different because in the present paper we consider unification problems that consist of subsumptions whereas in [10] we considered equivalences. We assume without loss of generality that the cycle-restricted $\mathcal{ELH}_{R^+}$-ontology $\mathcal{O}$ and the unification problem Γ_0 are flat. Given $\mathcal{O}$ and Γ_0, the sets At, $\mathrm{At_{tr}}$, and $\mathrm{At_{nv}}$ are defined as above. Starting with Γ_0, the algorithm maintains a current unification problem Γ and a current acyclic assignment S, which initially assigns the empty set to all variables. In addition, for each subsumption in Γ it maintains the information on whether it is *solved* or not. Initially, all subsumptions are unsolved, except those with a variable on the right-hand side. Rules are applied only to unsolved subsumptions. A (non-failing) rule application does the following:

- it solves exactly one unsolved subsumption,
- it may extend the current assignment S, and
- it may introduce new flat subsumptions built from elements of $\mathrm{At_{tr}}$.

Each rule application that extends S_X additionally *expands* Γ w.r.t. X as follows: every subsumption $\mathfrak{s} \in \Gamma$ of the form $C_1 \sqcap \cdots \sqcap C_n \sqsubseteq^? X$ is *expanded* by adding the subsumption $C_1 \sqcap \cdots \sqcap C_n \sqsubseteq^? A$ to Γ for every $A \in S_X$.

Eager Ground Solving:

> **Condition:** This rule applies to $\mathfrak{s} = C_1 \sqcap \cdots \sqcap C_n \sqsubseteq^? D$ if it is ground.
> **Action:** If $C_1 \sqcap \cdots \sqcap C_n \sqsubseteq_{\mathcal{O}} D$ does not hold, the rule application fails. Otherwise, $\mathfrak{s}$ is marked as *solved*.

Eager Solving:

> **Condition:** This rule applies to $\mathfrak{s} = C_1 \sqcap \cdots \sqcap C_n \sqsubseteq^? D$ if either
> - there is $i \in \{1, \ldots, n\}$ such that $C_i = D$ or $C_i = X \in N_v$ and $D \in S_X$, or
> - D is ground and $\sqcap \mathcal{G} \sqsubseteq_{\mathcal{O}} D$ holds, where $\mathcal{G}$ is the set of all ground atoms in $\{C_1, \ldots, C_n\} \cup \bigcup_{X \in \{C_1, \ldots, C_n\} \cap N_v} S_X$.
> **Action:** Its application marks $\mathfrak{s}$ as *solved*.

Eager Extension:

> **Condition:** This rule applies to $\mathfrak{s} = C_1 \sqcap \cdots \sqcap C_n \sqsubseteq^? D$ if there is $i \in \{1, \ldots, n\}$ with $C_i = X \in N_v$ and $\{C_1, \ldots, C_n\} \setminus \{X\} \subseteq S_X$.
> **Action:** Its application adds D to S_X. If this makes S cyclic, the rule application fails. Otherwise, Γ is expanded w.r.t. X and $\mathfrak{s}$ is marked as *solved*.

Fig. 1. The eager rules of the unification algorithm

Subsumptions are only added if they are not already present in Γ. If a new subsumption is added to Γ, either by a rule application or by expansion of Γ, then it is initially designated unsolved, except if it has a variable on the right-hand side. Once a subsumption is in Γ, it will not be removed. Likewise, if a subsumption in Γ is marked as solved, then it will not become unsolved later.

If a subsumption is marked as solved, this does not mean that it is already solved by the substitution induced by the current assignment. It may be the case that the task of satisfying the subsumption was deferred to solving other subsumptions which are "smaller" than the given subsumption in a well-defined sense. The task of solving a subsumption whose right-hand side is a variable is deferred to solving the subsumptions introduced by expansion.

The rules of the algorithm consist of the three *eager* rules Eager Ground Solving, Eager Solving, and Eager Extension (see Figure 1), and several *nondeterministic* rules (see Figures 2 and 3). Eager rules are applied with higher priority than nondeterministic rules. Among the eager rules, Eager Ground Solving has the highest priority, then comes Eager Solving, and then Eager Extension.

Algorithm 4. Let Γ_0 be a flat $\mathcal{EL}$-unification problem. We set $\Gamma := \Gamma_0$ and $S_X := \emptyset$ for all $X \in N_v$. While Γ contains an unsolved subsumption, apply the steps (1), (2), and (3).

(1) **Eager rule application:** If some eager rules apply to an unsolved subsumption $\mathfrak{s}$ in Γ, apply one of highest priority. If the rule application fails, then return "not unifiable".

(2) **Nondeterministic rule application:** If no eager rule is applicable, let $\mathfrak{s}$ be an unsolved subsumption in Γ. If one of the nondeterministic rules applies to $\mathfrak{s}$, nondeterministically choose one of these rules and apply it. If none of these rules apply to $\mathfrak{s}$ or the rule application fails, then return "not unifiable".

Decomposition 1:

> **Condition:** This rule applies to $\mathfrak{s} = C_1 \sqcap \cdots \sqcap C_n \sqsubseteq^? \exists s.D'$ if there is an index $i \in \{1, \ldots, n\}$ with $C_i = \exists r.C'$ and $r \trianglelefteq_{\mathcal{O}} s$.
> **Action:** Its application chooses such an index i, adds the subsumption $C' \sqsubseteq^? D'$ to Γ, expands it w.r.t. D' if D' is a variable, and marks $\mathfrak{s}$ as *solved*.

Decomposition 2:

> **Condition:** This rule applies to $\mathfrak{s} = C_1 \sqcap \cdots \sqcap C_n \sqsubseteq^? \exists s.D'$ if there is an index $i \in \{1, \ldots, n\}$ and a transitive role t with $C_i = \exists r.C'$ and $r \trianglelefteq_{\mathcal{O}} t \trianglelefteq_{\mathcal{O}} s$.
> **Action:** Its application chooses such an index i, adds the subsumption $C' \sqsubseteq^? \exists t.D'$ to Γ and marks $\mathfrak{s}$ as *solved*.

Extension:

> **Condition:** This rule applies to $\mathfrak{s} = C_1 \sqcap \cdots \sqcap C_n \sqsubseteq^? D$ if there is an index $i \in \{1, \ldots, n\}$ with $C_i \in N_v$.
> **Action:** Its application chooses such an i and adds D to S_{C_i}. If this makes S cyclic, the rule application fails. Otherwise, Γ is expanded w.r.t. C_i and $\mathfrak{s}$ is marked as *solved*.

Fig. 2. The nondeterministic rules *Decomposition 1 and 2* and *Extension*

(3) **Eager application of Decomposition:** If in the previous step one of the rules *Mutation 2 or 3* was applied, do the following for all subsumptions $\mathfrak{s}'$ added to Γ by this rule application: If one of the rules *Decomposition 1 or 2* applies to $\mathfrak{s}'$, nondeterministically choose one of the applicable decomposition rules and apply it to $\mathfrak{s}'$.[5]

Once all subsumptions are solved, return the substitution σ induced by the current assignment.

In step (2), the choice which unsolved subsumption to consider next is don't care nondeterministic. However, choosing which rule to apply to the chosen subsumption is don't know nondeterministic. Additionally, the application of nondeterministic rules requires don't know nondeterministic guessing.

The *eager rules* are mainly there for optimization purposes, i.e., to avoid nondeterministic choices if a deterministic decision can be made. For example, a ground subsumption, as considered in the *Eager Ground Solving* rule, either follows from the ontology, in which case any substitution solves it, or it does not, in which case it does not have a solution. This condition can be checked in polynomial time using the polynomial time subsumption algorithm for $\mathcal{ELH}_{R^+}$ [7]. In the case considered in the *Eager Solving* rule, the substitution induced by the current assignment obviously already solves the subsumption. The *Eager Extension* rule solves a subsumption that contains only a variable X and some elements of S_X on the left-hand side. The rule is motivated by the following observation: for any assignment S' extending the current assignment, the induced

---

[5] Note that *Decomposition 1* always applies to the new subsumptions. Whether *Decomposition 2* is also applicable depends on the existence of an appropriate transitive role t.

Mutation 1:

> **Condition:** This rule applies to $\mathfrak{s} = C_1 \sqcap \cdots \sqcap C_n \sqsubseteq^? D$ if $n > 1$ and there are atoms $A_1, \ldots, A_k, B$ of $\mathcal{O}$ such that $A_1 \sqcap \cdots \sqcap A_k \sqsubseteq_{\mathcal{O}} B$ holds.
> **Action:** Its application chooses such atoms, marks $\mathfrak{s}$ as *solved*, and generates the following subsumptions:
>
> - it chooses for each $\eta \in \{1, \ldots, k\}$ an $i \in \{1, \ldots, n\}$ and adds the subsumption $C_i \sqsubseteq^? A_\eta$ to Γ,
> - it adds the subsumption $B \sqsubseteq^? D$ to Γ.

Mutation 2:

> **Condition:** This rule applies to $\mathfrak{s} = \exists r.X \sqsubseteq^? D$ if X is a variable, D is ground, and there are atoms $\exists r_1.A_1, \ldots, \exists r_k.A_k$ of $\mathcal{O}$ such that $r \trianglelefteq_{\mathcal{O}} r_1, \ldots, r \trianglelefteq_{\mathcal{O}} r_k$, and $\exists r_1.A_1 \sqcap \cdots \sqcap \exists r_k.A_k \sqsubseteq_{\mathcal{O}} D$ hold.
> **Action:** Its application chooses such atoms, adds the subsumptions $\exists r.X \sqsubseteq^? \exists r_1.A_1, \ldots, \exists r.X \sqsubseteq^? \exists r_k.A_k$ to Γ, and marks $\mathfrak{s}$ as *solved*.

Mutation 3:

> **Condition:** This rule applies to $\mathfrak{s} = \exists r.X \sqsubseteq^? \exists s.Y$ if X and Y are variables, and there are atoms $\exists r_1.A_1, \ldots, \exists r_k.A_k, \exists u.B$ of $\mathcal{O}$ such that $r \trianglelefteq_{\mathcal{O}} r_1, \ldots, r \trianglelefteq_{\mathcal{O}} r_k$, $u \trianglelefteq_{\mathcal{O}} s$, and $\exists r_1.A_1 \sqcap \cdots \sqcap \exists r_k.A_k \sqsubseteq_{\mathcal{O}} \exists u.B$ hold.
> **Action:** Its application chooses such atoms, adds the subsumptions $\exists r.X \sqsubseteq^? \exists r_1.A_1, \ldots, \exists r.X \sqsubseteq^? \exists r_k.A_k, \exists u.B \sqsubseteq^? \exists s.Y$ to Γ, and marks $\mathfrak{s}$ as *solved*.

Mutation 4:

> **Condition:** This rule applies to $\mathfrak{s} = C \sqsubseteq^? \exists s.Y$ if C is a ground atom or $\top$, Y is a variable, and there is an atom $\exists u.B$ of $\mathcal{O}$ such that either
>
> - $C \sqsubseteq_{\mathcal{O}} \exists u.B$ and $u \trianglelefteq_{\mathcal{O}} s$, or
> - $C \sqsubseteq_{\mathcal{O}} \exists t.B$ for a transitive role t with $u \trianglelefteq_{\mathcal{O}} t \trianglelefteq_{\mathcal{O}} s$.
>
> **Action:** Its application chooses such an atom, adds the subsumption $B \sqsubseteq^? Y$ to Γ, and marks $\mathfrak{s}$ as *solved*.

Fig. 3. The nondeterministic *Mutation* rules of the unification algorithm

substitution σ' satisfies $\sigma'(X) \equiv \sigma'(C_1) \sqcap \ldots \sqcap \sigma'(C_n)$. Thus, if S'_X contains D, then $\sigma'(X) \sqsubseteq_{\mathcal{O}} \sigma'(D)$, and σ' solves the subsumption. Conversely, if σ' solves the subsumption, then $\sigma'(X) \sqsubseteq_{\mathcal{O}} \sigma'(D)$, and thus adding D to S'_X yields an equivalent induced substitution.

The *nondeterministic rules* only come into play if no eager rules can be applied. In order to solve an unsolved subsumption $\mathfrak{s} = C_1 \sqcap \cdots \sqcap C_n \sqsubseteq^? D$, we consider the two conditions of Lemma 1. Regarding the first condition, which is addressed by the rules *Decomposition 1 and 2* and *Extension*, assume that γ is induced by an acyclic assignment S. To satisfy the first condition of the lemma with γ, the atom $\gamma(D)$ must structurally subsume a top-level atom in $\gamma(C_1) \sqcap \cdots \sqcap \gamma(C_n)$. This atom can either be of the form $\gamma(C_i)$ for an atom C_i, or it can be of the form $\gamma(C)$ for an atom $C \in S_{C_i}$ and a variable C_i. In the second case, the atom C can either already be in S_{C_i} or it can be put into S_{C_i} by an application of the Extension rule. The two versions of *Decomposition* correspond to the cases (2) and (3) in the definition of structural subsumption.

The *Mutation rules* cover the second condition in Lemma 1. For example, let us analyze how *Mutation 1* ensures that all the requirements of this condition are satisfied. The rule guesses atoms $A_1, \ldots, A_k, B$ such that $A_1 \sqcap \cdots \sqcap A_k \sqsubseteq_{\mathcal{O}} B$ holds. This can be checked using the polynomial-time subsumption algorithm for $\mathcal{ELH}_{R^+}$. Whenever the second condition of Lemma 1 requires a structural subsumption $\gamma(E) \sqsubseteq_{\mathcal{O}}^s \gamma(F)$ to hold for a (hypothetical) unifier γ of Γ, the rule creates the new subsumption $E \sqsubseteq^? F$, which has to be solved later on. This way, the rule ensures that the substitution built by the algorithm actually satisfies the conditions of the lemma. The *other mutation rules* follow the same idea, but they consider cases where only a single atom occurs on the left-hand side of the subsumption to be solved. The reason for considering these cases separately is that in the proof of soundness we need the newly introduced subsumptions to be "smaller" than the subsumption that triggered their introduction. For *Mutation 1* this is the case due to the smaller left-hand side (only one atom), whereas for the other mutation rules this is not so clear. Actually, for *Mutation 2 and 3*, the new subsumptions turn out to be smaller only after *Decomposition* is applied to them. *Mutation 4* implicitly applies a form of decomposition.

Due to the space restrictions, we cannot give more details on how to prove that the algorithm is correct. Complete proofs of soundness, completeness and termination can be found in [3].

Theorem 5. *Algorithm 4 is an NP-decision procedure for testing solvability of $\mathcal{ELH}_{R^+}$-unification problems w.r.t. cycle-restricted ontologies.*

5   Conclusions

Above, we have presented a goal-oriented NP-algorithm for unification in $\mathcal{ELH}_{R^+}$ w.r.t. cycle-restricted ontologies. In [5], we have developed a reduction of this problem to SAT, which is based on a characterization of subsumption different from the one in Lemma 1. Though clearly better than the brute-force algorithm introduced in [2], both algorithms suffer from a high degree of nondeterminism due to having to guess true subsumptions between concepts built from atoms of the background cycle-restricted ontology. We must find optimizations to tackle this problem before an implementation becomes feasible.

On the theoretical side, the main topic for future research is to consider unification w.r.t. unrestricted $\mathcal{ELH}_{R^+}$-ontologies. In order to generalize the brute-force algorithm in this direction, we need to find a more general notion of locality. Starting with the goal-oriented algorithm, one idea could be not to fail when a cyclic assignment is generated, but rather to add rules that can break such cycles, similar to what is done in procedures for general E-unification [16].

Another idea could be to use just the rules of our goal-oriented algorithm, and not fail when a cyclic assignment S is generated. Our conjecture is that then the background ontology $\mathcal{O}$ together with the cyclic TBox $\mathcal{T}_S := \{X \equiv \sqcap_{C \in S_X} C \mid X \in N_v\}$ induced by S satisfies $C \sqsubseteq_{\mathcal{O} \cup \mathcal{T}_S} D$ for all subsumptions $C \sqsubseteq^? D$ in Γ_0 if an appropriate hybrid semantics [13] for the combined ontology $\mathcal{O} \cup \mathcal{T}_S$ is used.

All the results on unification in Description Logics mentioned in this paper are restricted to relatively inexpressive logics that do not support all Boolean operators. If we close $\mathcal{EL}$ under negation, then we obtain the DL $\mathcal{ALC}$, which corresponds to the modal logic K [17]. Whether unification in K is decidable is a long-standing open problem. It is only known that relatively minor extensions of K have an undecidable unification problem [18].

References

1. Baader, F., Borgwardt, S., Mendez, J., Morawska, B.: UEL: Unification solver for $\mathcal{EL}$. In: Proc. DL 2012. CEUR Workshop Proceedings, vol. 846 (2012)
2. Baader, F., Borgwardt, S., Morawska, B.: Extending unification in $\mathcal{EL}$ towards general TBoxes. In: Proc. KR 2012, pp. 568–572. AAAI Press (2012) (short paper)
3. Baader, F., Borgwardt, S., Morawska, B.: A goal-oriented algorithm for unification in $\mathcal{ELH}_{R^+}$ w.r.t. cycle-restricted ontologies. LTCS-Report 12-05, TU Dresden, Germany (2012), http://lat.inf.tu-dresden.de/research/reports.html
4. Baader, F., Borgwardt, S., Morawska, B.: A goal-oriented algorithm for unification in $\mathcal{EL}$ w.r.t. cycle-restricted TBoxes. In: Proc. DL 2012. CEUR Workshop Proceedings, vol. 846 (2012)
5. Baader, F., Borgwardt, S., Morawska, B.: SAT Encoding of Unification in $\mathcal{ELH}_{R^+}$ w.r.t. Cycle-Restricted Ontologies. In: Gramlich, B., Miller, D., Sattler, U. (eds.) IJCAR 2012. LNCS, vol. 7364, pp. 30–44. Springer, Heidelberg (2012)
6. Baader, F., Borgwardt, S., Morawska, B.: SAT encoding of unification in $\mathcal{ELH}_{R^+}$ w.r.t. cycle-restricted ontologies. LTCS-Report 12-02, TU Dresden, Germany (2012), http://lat.inf.tu-dresden.de/research/reports.html
7. Baader, F., Brandt, S., Lutz, C.: Pushing the $\mathcal{EL}$ envelope. In: Proc. IJCAI 2005, pp. 364–369. Morgan Kaufmann (2005)
8. Baader, F., Morawska, B.: Unification in the Description Logic $\mathcal{EL}$. In: Treinen, R. (ed.) RTA 2009. LNCS, vol. 5595, pp. 350–364. Springer, Heidelberg (2009)
9. Baader, F., Morawska, B.: SAT Encoding of Unification in $\mathcal{EL}$. In: Fermüller, C.G., Voronkov, A. (eds.) LPAR-17. LNCS, vol. 6397, pp. 97–111. Springer, Heidelberg (2010)
10. Baader, F., Morawska, B.: Unification in the description logic $\mathcal{EL}$. Log. Meth. Comput. Sci. 6(3) (2010)
11. Baader, F., Narendran, P.: Unification of concept terms in description logics. J. Symb. Comput. 31(3), 277–305 (2001)
12. Brandt, S.: Polynomial time reasoning in a description logic with existential restrictions, GCI axioms, and—what else? In: Proc. ECAI 2004, pp. 298–302 (2004)
13. Brandt, S., Model, J.: Subsumption in $\mathcal{EL}$ w.r.t. hybrid TBoxes. In: Furbach, U. (ed.) KI 2005. LNCS (LNAI), vol. 3698, pp. 34–48. Springer, Heidelberg (2005)
14. Gomes, C.P., Kautz, H., Sabharwal, A., Selman, B.: Satisfiability solvers. In: Handbook of Knowledge Representation, pp. 89–134. Elsevier (2008)
15. Hofmann, M.: Proof-theoretic approach to description-logic. In: Proc. LICS 2005. pp. 229–237. IEEE Press (2005)
16. Morawska, B.: General E-unification with eager variable elimination and a nice cycle rule. J. Autom. Reasoning 39(1), 77–106 (2007)
17. Schild, K.: A correspondence theory for terminological logics: Preliminary report. In: Proc. IJCAI 1991, pp. 466–471 (1991)
18. Wolter, F., Zakharyaschev, M.: Undecidability of the unification and admissibility problems for modal and description logics. ACM Trans. Comput. Log. 9(4) (2008)

Normal Modal Preferential Consequence

Katarina Britz, Thomas Meyer, and Ivan Varzinczak

Centre for Artificial Intelligence Research
CSIR Meraka Institute and UKZN, South Africa
{arina.britz,tommie.meyer,ivan.varzinczak}@meraka.org.za

Abstract. One of the most successful approaches to the formalization of commonsense reasoning is the work by Lehmann and colleagues, known as the KLM approach, in which defeasible consequence relations with a preferential semantics are studied. In spite of its success, KLM is limited to propositional logic. In recent work we provided the semantic foundation for extending defeasible consequence relations to modal logics and description logics. In this paper we continue that line of investigation by going beyond the basic (propositional) KLM postulates, thereby making use of the additional expressivity provided by modal logic. In particular, we show that the additional constraints we impose on the preferential semantics ensure that the rule of necessitation holds for the corresponding consequence relations, as one would expect it to. We present a representation result for this tightened framework, and investigate appropriate notions of entailment in this context — normal entailment, and a rational version thereof.

Keywords: Non-monotonic reasoning, preferential consequence, modal logic.

1 Introduction and Motivation

The formalization of commonsense reasoning, as usually studied in the AI tradition, depends crucially on the eschewal of the monotonicity property of classical logic, or, at the very least, on a careful neutralization thereof. This issue has been dealt with in a variety of ways in the non-monotonic literature. One particular approach that has been quite successful is the one by Lehmann and colleagues. In their seminal papers [12,14], the authors consolidated what became known as the *KLM approach*, in which (propositional) defeasible consequence relations $\mid\!\sim$ with a preferential semantics are studied. In this setting, $\alpha \mid\!\sim \beta$ is given the meaning that "all normal (i.e., most preferred) α-worlds are β-worlds", leaving it open for α-worlds that are exceptional (or less preferred) not to satisfy β. The theory that has been developed around this notion allows us to cope with exceptionality when performing reasoning. Besides its simplicity and elegance, the type of consequence relations studied by Lehmann and colleagues has also played an important role in the formalization of commonsense reasoning in providing the foundation for the important notion of rational closure [14].

Notwithstanding its fruitfulness, the KLM approach is limited to *propositional* logic and so it remained until recently despite some attempts to recast it

M. Thielscher and D. Zhang (Eds.): AI 2012, LNCS 7691, pp. 505–516, 2012.
© Springer-Verlag Berlin Heidelberg 2012

in more expressive formalisms [5,9,11,13,15,16]. Indeed, many scenarios that are
interesting from the standpoint of modern AI cannot be satisfactorily formalized in a propositional language. Extensions of the KLM approach have therefore
been driven by either extending the syntax [9,11,16] or the underlying preferential semantics [5,13] to logics with more expressivity. A unifying semantics,
with a corresponding representation result, was nevertheless still missing until
a recent work by the present authors [6,7] provided the semantic foundation for
extending defeasible consequence relations to modal logics [2] and description
logics (DLs) [1]. In the referred papers we lifted the notion of rational closure
as defined by Lehmann and Magidor in the propositional case [14] to modal and
description logics, thereby providing a preliminary account of this construction
in logics with more structure than the propositional one.

It turns out that the aforementioned approach, although counting as a true
extension of the KLM framework to non-propositional languages, is still limited
in the sense that it does not make use of the additional expressivity of e.g. modal
languages. To make this more precise, one can state defeasible statements of the
form $\alpha \mathrel{|\!\sim} \beta$, where α and β now can be *any* modal sentence; however the syn-
tactic characterization of defeasible consequence (i.e., the set of Gentzen-style
properties specifying the expected behavior of $\mathrel{|\!\sim}$) is confined to the original
Boolean postulates proposed by Kraus et al. In other words, the additional expressivity of modal logic is not reflected in terms of new properties, which means
that modal sentences are basically opaque to the postulates. Moreover, despite
the underlying modal formalism, some inference rules that are seen as important
in a modal context such as the necessitation rule behave in an unexpected way.

In this paper we analyze these issues and address them by proposing additional
properties that a truly modal-based defeasible consequence relation $\mathrel{|\!\sim}$ ought to
satisfy. In particular, we study what semantic constraints should be added to
the original preferential semantics for the new properties to hold.

The remainder of the present paper is organized as follows: After some logical preliminaries (Section 2), we recap our preferential semantics for defeasible
modal logic (Section 3). We then motivate the need for KLM-style properties
reflecting the additional expressivity of modal languages (Section 4). In particular, we define appropriate semantic constraints warranting the new postulates
and establish the corresponding representation result. In Section 5 we define
entailment from defeasible knowledge bases and motivate the need to move beyond rational closure. We conclude with a summary of our contributions and
directions for future research.

2   Modal Logic

We work in a (finite) set of *atomic propositions* $\mathcal{P}$, using the logical connectives
$\wedge$ (conjunction), $\neg$ (negation), and a set of modal operators $\Box_i$, $1 \leq i \leq n$.
Propositions are denoted by $p, q, \ldots$, and formulas by $\alpha, \beta, \ldots$, built up in the
usual way according to the rule: $\alpha \ ::= p \mid \neg\alpha \mid \alpha \wedge \alpha \mid \Box_i\alpha$. All the other
truth functional connectives ($\vee, \rightarrow, \leftrightarrow, \ldots$) are defined in terms of $\neg$ and $\wedge$ in

the usual way. Given $\Box_i$, with $\Diamond_i$ we denote its *dual* operator, i.e., for any α, $\Diamond_i \alpha \equiv_{\text{def}} \neg\Box_i \neg\alpha$. We use $\top$ as an abbreviation for $p \vee \neg p$ and $\bot$ for $p \wedge \neg p$, for some $p \in \mathcal{P}$. With $\mathcal{L}$ we denote the set of all formulas of the modal language.

As for the semantics, we assume the standard possible-worlds one:

Definition 1. *A Kripke model is a tuple $\mathcal{M} = \langle W, R, V \rangle$ where W is a set of possible worlds, $R = \langle R_1, \ldots, R_n \rangle$, where each $R_i \subseteq W \times W$ is an accessibility relation on W, $1 \leq i \leq n$, and $V \colon W \times \mathcal{P} \longrightarrow \{0, 1\}$ is a valuation function.*

Figure 1 depicts two examples of Kripke models for $\mathcal{P} = \{p, q\}$.

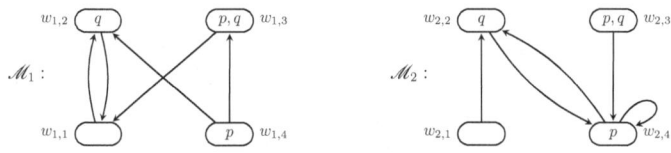

Fig. 1. Examples of Kripke models

Sometimes it is convenient to talk about possible worlds in the context of their respective Kripke models. Given $\mathcal{M} = \langle W, R, V \rangle$ and $w \in W$, a pair $(\mathcal{M}, w)$ is a *pointed Kripke model*. Pointed Kripke models are not to be viewed as objects, as variables are commonly regarded in first-order contexts. A set of pointed Kripke models describes the *intention* of a modal statement — cf. Definition 2 below.

Formulas of our modal language are true or false relative to a possible world in a Kripke model. This is formalized by the following truth conditions:

Definition 2. *Given $\mathcal{M} = \langle W, R, V \rangle$ and $w \in W$:*

- $\mathcal{M}, w \Vdash p$ *if and only if $V(w, p) = 1$;*
- $\mathcal{M}, w \Vdash \neg\alpha$ *if and only if $\mathcal{M}, w \not\Vdash \alpha$;*
- $\mathcal{M}, w \Vdash \alpha \wedge \beta$ *if and only if $\mathcal{M}, w \Vdash \alpha$ and $\mathcal{M}, w \Vdash \beta$;*
- $\mathcal{M}, w \Vdash \Box_i \alpha$ *if and only if $\mathcal{M}, w' \Vdash \alpha$ for all w' such that $(w, w') \in R_i$.*

Given $\alpha \in \mathcal{L}$ and $\mathcal{M} = \langle W, R, V \rangle$, $\mathcal{M}$ *satisfies* α if there is $w \in W$ such that $\mathcal{M}, w \Vdash \alpha$. We say that α is *true* in $\mathcal{M}$ (alias $\mathcal{M}$ is a *model* of α) if $\mathcal{M}, w \Vdash \alpha$ for every $w \in W$. For a given system of modal logic, we say that α is *valid* (denoted $\models \alpha$) if α is true in every model of the underlying system. Here we shall assume the system of normal modal logic K, of which all the other normal modal logics are extensions. Semantically, K is characterized by the class of all Kripke models (Definition 1). We say that α *locally entails* β in the system K (denoted $\alpha \models \beta$) if for every model $\mathcal{M}$ and every w in $\mathcal{M}$, $\mathcal{M}, w \Vdash \alpha$ implies $\mathcal{M}, w, \Vdash \beta$.

Syntactically, K corresponds to the smallest set of sentences containing all propositional tautologies, all instances of the axiom schema $K : \Box_i(\alpha \to \beta) \to (\Box_i \alpha \to \Box_i \beta)$, $1 \leq i \leq n$, and closed under the *rule of necessitation* below:

$$(\text{RN}) \quad \frac{\alpha}{\Box_i \alpha} \tag{1}$$

The following are derived rules in the system K:

$$\text{(RK)}\ \frac{\alpha_1 \wedge \ldots \wedge \alpha_k \rightarrow \beta}{\Box_i \alpha_1 \wedge \ldots \wedge \Box_i \alpha_k \rightarrow \Box_i \beta} \qquad \text{(Mon)}\ \frac{\alpha \rightarrow \beta}{\Box_i \alpha \rightarrow \Box_i \beta} \qquad \text{(Cgr)}\ \frac{\alpha \leftrightarrow \beta}{\Box_i \alpha \leftrightarrow \Box_i \beta}$$

Given a system of modal logic, from a knowledge representation perspective it is convenient to be able to work within a class of models $\mathcal{M}$ of the corresponding system, representing e.g. some background knowledge of relevance for a given application domain.

3   Modal Defeasible Consequence

A modal defeasible consequence relation $\mathrel|\!\sim$ is defined as a binary relation on formulas of our underlying modal logic, i.e., $\mathrel|\!\sim\ \subseteq \mathcal{L} \times \mathcal{L}$. We say that $\mathrel|\!\sim$ is a *preferential* consequence relation [6] if it satisfies the following set of properties (alias postulates or Gentzen-style rules, as they are sometimes referred to):

$$\text{(Ref)}\ \alpha \mathrel|\!\sim \alpha \qquad \text{(LLE)}\ \frac{\models \alpha \leftrightarrow \beta,\ \ \alpha \mathrel|\!\sim \gamma}{\beta \mathrel|\!\sim \gamma} \qquad \text{(And)}\ \frac{\alpha \mathrel|\!\sim \beta,\ \ \alpha \mathrel|\!\sim \gamma}{\alpha \mathrel|\!\sim \beta \wedge \gamma}$$

$$\text{(Or)}\ \frac{\alpha \mathrel|\!\sim \gamma,\ \ \beta \mathrel|\!\sim \gamma}{\alpha \vee \beta \mathrel|\!\sim \gamma} \qquad \text{(RW)}\ \frac{\alpha \mathrel|\!\sim \beta,\ \ \models \beta \rightarrow \gamma}{\alpha \mathrel|\!\sim \gamma} \qquad \text{(CM)}\ \frac{\alpha \mathrel|\!\sim \beta,\ \ \alpha \mathrel|\!\sim \gamma}{\alpha \wedge \beta \mathrel|\!\sim \gamma}$$

The semantics of preferential consequence relations is in terms of *modal preferential models*; these are partially ordered structures with states labeled by pointed Kripke models (cf. Section 2):

Definition 3. *Let $\mathcal{M}$ be a class of Kripke models.* $\mathscr{U}_{\mathcal{M}} := \{(\mathcal{M}, w) \mid \mathcal{M} = \langle W, R, V \rangle \in \mathcal{M} \text{ and } w \in W\}.$

Let S be a set and $\prec\ \subseteq S \times S$ be a strict partial order on S, i.e., $\prec$ is *irreflexive* and *transitive*. Given $S' \subseteq S$, we say that $s \in S'$ is *minimal* in S' if there is no $s' \in S'$ such that $s' \prec s$. With $\min_{\prec} S'$ we denote the minimal elements of $S' \subseteq S$. We say that $S' \subseteq S$ is *smooth* [12] if for every $s \in S'$ either s is minimal in S' or there is $s' \in S'$ such that s' is minimal in S' and $s' \prec s$.

Definition 4 (Preferential Model). *A preferential model is a tuple $\mathscr{P} = \langle S, \ell, \prec \rangle$ where S is a set of states; $\ell : S \longrightarrow \mathscr{U}_{\mathcal{M}}$ is a labeling function; $\prec \subseteq S \times S$ is a strict partial order on S satisfying the smoothness condition.*[1]

Given a preferential model $\mathscr{P} = \langle S, \ell, \prec \rangle$ and $\alpha \in \mathcal{L}$, with $[\![\alpha]\!]$ we denote the set of states satisfying α (α-*states* for short) according to the following definition:

Definition 5. *Let $\mathscr{P} = \langle S, \ell, \prec \rangle$ and let $\alpha \in \mathcal{L}$. Then $[\![\alpha]\!] := \{s \in S \mid \ell(s) \Vdash \alpha\}$.*

States lower down in the order are *more preferred* (or *more normal*) than those higher up. As an example, let $\mathcal{M}$ be the class of K-models depicted in Figure 1. Then $\mathscr{U}_{\mathcal{M}} = \{(\mathcal{M}_i, w_{i,j}) \mid i = 1, 2 \text{ and } 1 \le j \le 4\}$. Figure 2 below

---

[1] That is, for every $\alpha \in \mathcal{L}$, the set $[\![\alpha]\!]$ (cf. Definition 5) is smooth.

depicts the preferential model $\mathscr{P} = \langle S, \ell, \prec \rangle$ where $S = \{s_i \mid 1 \leq i \leq 8\}$, ℓ is such that $\ell(s_1) = (\mathscr{M}_1, w_{1,1})$, $\ell(s_2) = (\mathscr{M}_2, w_{2,1})$, $\ell(s_3) = (\mathscr{M}_1, w_{1,2})$, $\ell(s_4) = (\mathscr{M}_1, w_{1,3})$, $\ell(s_5) = (\mathscr{M}_2, w_{2,3})$, $\ell(s_6) = (\mathscr{M}_2, w_{2,2})$, $\ell(s_7) = (\mathscr{M}_1, w_{1,4})$, and $\ell(s_8) = (\mathscr{M}_2, w_{2,4})$, and $\prec$ is the transitive closure of $\{(s_1, s_3), (s_2, s_3), (s_3, s_4), (s_3, s_5), (s_4, s_6), (s_5, s_6), (s_6, s_7), (s_6, s_8)\}$.

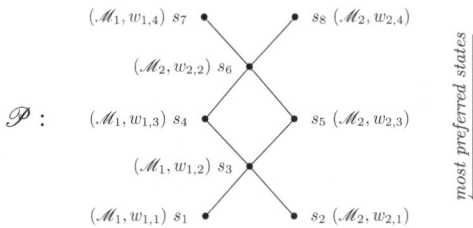

Fig. 2. A preferential model for $\mathcal{M} = \{\mathscr{M}_1, \mathscr{M}_2\}$, with $\mathscr{M}_1$ and $\mathscr{M}_2$ as in Figure 1

Given $\mathscr{P} = \langle S, \ell, \prec \rangle$ and $\alpha \in \mathcal{L}$, α is *satisfiable* in $\mathscr{P}$ if $[\![\alpha]\!] \neq \emptyset$, otherwise α is *unsatisfiable* in $\mathscr{P}$. We say that α is *true* in $\mathscr{P}$ (denoted $\mathscr{P} \Vdash \alpha$) if $[\![\alpha]\!] = S$.

From the definition of a preferential model one can see that a class $\mathcal{M}$ of Kripke models determines a class of preferential models. We denote the class of preferential models based on $\mathcal{M}$ with $\mathcal{M}^{\mathscr{P}}$. We say that α is *valid* in $\mathcal{M}^{\mathscr{P}}$ if α is true in every preferential model $\mathscr{P}$ of $\mathcal{M}^{\mathscr{P}}$, i.e., $\mathscr{P} \Vdash \alpha$ for every $\mathscr{P} \in \mathcal{M}^{\mathscr{P}}$.

Given $\mathscr{P} = \langle S, \ell, \prec \rangle$, the defeasible statement $\alpha \mathrel{|\!\sim}_{\mathscr{P}} \beta$ holds in $\mathscr{P}$ if and only if $\min_{\prec} [\![\alpha]\!] \subseteq [\![\beta]\!]$, i.e., every $\prec$-minimal α-state is a β-state. As an example, in the model $\mathscr{P}$ of Figure 2, we have $\neg q \mathrel{|\!\sim}_{\mathscr{P}} \Box \neg p$ and also $q \mathrel{|\!\sim}_{\mathscr{P}} \Diamond(\neg p \wedge \neg q)$.

The representation theorem for preferential consequence relations then states:

Theorem 1 (Britz et al. [6]). *A modal defeasible consequence relation is a preferential consequence relation if and only if it is defined by some preferential model, i.e., $\mathrel{|\!\sim}$ is preferential if and only if there exists $\mathscr{P}$ such that $\mathrel{|\!\sim} = \mathrel{|\!\sim}_{\mathscr{P}}$.*

If, in addition to the preferential properties, the defeasible consequence relation $\mathrel{|\!\sim}$ also satisfies the following Rational Monotonicity property [14], it is said to be a *rational* consequence relation:

$$(\text{RM}) \quad \frac{\alpha \mathrel{|\!\sim} \beta, \quad \alpha \mathrel{|\!\not\sim} \neg \gamma}{\alpha \wedge \gamma \mathrel{|\!\sim} \beta}$$

The semantics of rational consequence relations is in terms of *ranked* models, i.e., preferential models in which the preference order is *modular*.

Definition 6 (Modular Order). *Given a set S, $\prec \subseteq S \times S$ is modular if and only if there is a ranking function $rk : S \longrightarrow \mathbb{N}$ such that for every $s, s' \in S$, $s \prec s'$ if and only if $rk(s) < rk(s')$.*

Definition 7 (Ranked Model). *A ranked model* $\mathscr{R} = \langle S, \ell, \prec \rangle$ *is a preferential model such that* $\prec$ *is modular.*

The preferential model in Figure 2 is also an example of a ranked model.

Theorem 2 (Britz et al. [6]). *A modal defeasible consequence relation is a rational consequence relation if and only if it is defined by some ranked model, i.e.,* $\vdash$ *is rational if and only if there exists* $\mathscr{R}$ *such that* $\vdash = \vdash_{\mathscr{R}}$.

4   Beyond the KLM Postulates

Britz et al.'s constructions and representation results are with respect to the same set of properties used to characterize propositional rational consequence. This has the advantage that methods employed in a propositional non-monotonic setting translate seamlessly to a modal context. This includes reasoning tasks such as computing the rational closure of defeasible knowledge bases [6,7]. In that respect, the definitions in Section 3 provide a good starting point for investigating more elaborated versions of modal rational consequence. Here we are interested in doing precisely this and we start by making an important observation:

Proposition 1. *Let* $\alpha \in \mathcal{L}$ *and let* $\mathcal{M}$ *be a class of Kripke models. Then* α *is valid in* $\mathcal{M}$ *if and only if* α *is valid in* $\mathcal{M}^{\mathscr{P}}$.

That is, all the validities of the underlying system of modal logic (or of the specific class of models we are working with) remain valid with respect to our preferential semantics. An immediate consequence of this is the following result:

Corollary 1. *All inference rules of the underlying modal logic are sound with respect to the preferential semantics.*

It is easy to see why: given a rule ρ which is sound in the respective system of modal logic and of which the premise α is preferentially valid, from Proposition 1 follows that α is (modally) valid, from which follows the validity of ρ's consequent β, which, by Proposition 1 again, must be preferentially valid.

In spite of preserving all modal validities and rules of inference, the current preferential semantics gives rise to a rather odd phenomenon: Contrary to the classical possible worlds semantics, in the preferential semantics some inference rules need not be satisfied by *individual* (preferential or ranked) models. To make this more precise, one can devise models in which the rule of necessitation (RN) does *not* hold. Indeed, the current preferential semantics is too liberal in the sense that it allows for legitimate models in which α is true (i.e., $[\![\alpha]\!] = S$) but in which $\square_i \alpha$ fails to hold (i.e., $[\![\square_i \alpha]\!] \neq S$), for some $1 \leq i \leq n$. To witness, let $\mathcal{M}_1$ be as in Figure 1, and let $S = \{s_1\}$, $\ell(s_1) = (\mathcal{M}_1, w_{1,4})$, and $\prec = \emptyset$. It is easy to check that $\mathscr{P} = \langle S, \ell, \prec \rangle$ is a preferential model and that $\mathscr{P} \Vdash p$ but $\mathscr{P} \not\Vdash \square p$. Hence the preferential semantics for modal consequence is not, strictly speaking, truly normal in the modal sense.

It should not be that hard to see that this is not an inoffensive feature: In a given $\mathscr{P}$ one is told that every state is an α-state, but at the same time it is possible to refer to a $\neg\alpha$-world that is part of the structure of $\mathscr{P}$. It sounds as though $\mathscr{P}$ is not particularly accurate in the knowledge it conveys. The consequences of this become apparent when considering specific application domains. For instance, in an action context, this could mean that there is a possible execution of tossing a coin having as outcome "not-heads and not-tails", even though there is no configuration of states other than "heads or tails".

With a similar argument we can also show that the rule of congruence (Cgr) in general is not satisfied 'locally', i.e., in an arbitrary model: Let $\mathscr{M}_1$ be as in Figure 1, and let $S = \{s_1\}$, $\ell(s_1) = (\mathscr{M}_1, w_{1,1})$, and $\prec = \emptyset$. Then $\mathscr{P} = \langle S, \ell, \prec \rangle$ is a preferential model and $\mathscr{P} \Vdash \neg p \leftrightarrow \neg q$ but $\mathscr{P} \not\Vdash \Box\neg p \leftrightarrow \Box\neg q$. (That this is not particularly desirable should not be that hard to see.) The same counter-example applies to Rules RK and Mon.

Surely all of this has to do with the extra richness of modal structures when compared to the propositional ones, but also, as alluded to above, to the rather liberal character of our original preferential semantics and its interplay with the corresponding syntactic characterization.

The obvious direction to follow in tackling the above issues is through the requirement of additional restrictions in the semantics with appropriate postulates characterizing them. Indeed, the rationality properties from Section 3 seem too weak in a modal context, as they do not really make use of the full expressiveness of modal logic. Without properties referring directly to the extra operator $\Box$, modal formulas are treated in a completely opaque way by the remaining Boolean postulates. Hence we shall investigate extra KLM-style properties that do make use of the non-Boolean connectives of the underlying language.

The requirement that every preferential model also satisfy the rule of necessitation provides us with insights towards our stated aim. In what follows we shall have a closer look at it.

Proposition 2. *Let $\alpha \in \mathcal{L}$ and $\mathscr{P}$ be a preferential model. Then $\mathscr{P} \Vdash \alpha$ if and only if $\neg\alpha \mathrel{\vert\!\sim}_{\mathscr{P}} \bot$ holds in $\mathscr{P}$.*

'Local' (i.e., model-wise) satisfaction of the rule of necessitation amounts to having $\Box\alpha$ true in a model whenever α is true in the same model. That is to say, RN holds in $\mathscr{P}$ if $\mathscr{P} \Vdash \alpha$ implies $\mathscr{P} \Vdash \Box_i\alpha$, for every $1 \le i \le n$. Given this and Proposition 2, we obtain the following KLM-style version of RN:

$$\text{(Norm)} \quad \frac{\alpha \mathrel{\vert\!\sim} \bot}{\Diamond_i\alpha \mathrel{\vert\!\sim} \bot}, \text{ for } 1 \le i \le n \tag{2}$$

We call Property (2) *Normality*, as it is the KLM version of a fundamental property of normal modal logics, namely the rule of necessitation. Intuitively it says that what is inconsistent should not be possible.

The result in Proposition 2 also allows us to derive a KLM-style version of the rule of congruence. Cgr holds in $\mathscr{P}$ if $\mathscr{P} \Vdash \alpha \leftrightarrow \beta$ implies $\mathscr{P} \Vdash \Box_i\alpha \leftrightarrow \Box_i\beta$, for every $1 \le i \le n$, that is, if the following rule holds in $\mathscr{P}$:

$$\text{(Equiv)} \quad \frac{\neg(\alpha \leftrightarrow \beta) \mathrel{\vert\!\sim} \bot}{\neg(\Box_i\alpha \leftrightarrow \Box_i\beta) \mathrel{\vert\!\sim} \bot}, \text{ for } 1 \le i \le n \tag{3}$$

With an analogous argument one can derive the following properties ensuring, respectively, Mon and RK:

$$(\text{Imp}) \quad \frac{\neg(\alpha \rightarrow \beta) \mathrel{\big|\!\sim} \bot}{\neg(\Box_i \alpha \rightarrow \Box_i \beta) \mathrel{\big|\!\sim} \bot}, \text{ for } 1 \leq i \leq n \tag{4}$$

$$(\text{RK}^{\mathrel{\mid\!\sim}}) \quad \frac{\neg(\alpha_1 \wedge \ldots \wedge \alpha_k \rightarrow \beta) \mathrel{\big|\!\sim} \bot}{\neg(\Box_i \alpha_1 \wedge \ldots \wedge \Box_i \alpha_k \rightarrow \Box_i \beta) \mathrel{\big|\!\sim} \bot}, \text{ for } 1 \leq i \leq n \tag{5}$$

Being derived from inference rules that hold in every system of classical normal modal logics, the postulates in (2)–(5) stand as reasonable properties to have in modal preferential reasoning. As we have seen, *none* of them hold in the standard preferential semantics.

New postulates are usually captured in the semantics by means of additional restrictions on the preferential models. For instance, in the evolution from preferential consequence relations to rational ones, the rational monotonicity property became warranted by requiring the partial order $\prec$ to be a modular ordering [14]. As we shall see, it turns out that one can also force extra properties (as the ones we stated above) by imposing additional restrictions on the set of *states* and on the *labeling* function, a route that seems not to have been explored so far.

Looking back at the counter-examples to local satisfaction of the inference rules, a common pattern emerges: a given rule is violated because of a pointed Kripke model acting "behind the curtain", i.e., a pointed model labeling no state whatsoever but which (implicitly) still interferes with states that are labeled with pointed models it relates to. We call these pointed models occurring implicitly in a preferential model *spurious models*.[2]

We claim that a modal preferential semantics should not allow for spurious models. The set of states and the labeling function must be disciplined in such a way as to prevent a pointed model from determining the truth of formulas without being itself associated with any state. We make this more precise now.

Definition 8 (Non-Spuriousness). *A pair (S, ℓ) is non-spurious if and only if, for all $s \in S$ with $\ell(s) = (\mathcal{M}, w)$ for some $\mathcal{M} = \langle W, R, V \rangle$, and for all $w' \in W$ such that $(w, w') \in R_i$ for some i, there exists $s' \in S$ with $\ell(s') = (\mathcal{M}, w')$.*

The non-spuriousness condition requires that whenever a possible world can be referred to indirectly, then it is indeed a world that can be accessed directly.

Definition 9 (Non-Spurious Model). *A non-spurious model $\mathcal{N} = \langle S, \ell, \prec \rangle$ is a preferential model such that (S, ℓ) is non-spurious.*

Given a non-spurious model $\mathcal{N} = \langle S, \ell, \prec \rangle$ and a formula $\alpha \in \mathcal{L}$, as before with $\llbracket \alpha \rrbracket$ we denote the set of elements of S satisfying α (cf. Definition 5). The model depicted in Figure 2 is also an example of a non-spurious (ranked) model.

The definition of non-spurious model puts us in a position to state the first of the results leading us to the realization of our stated aims:

---

[2] Note that requiring the labeling function to be surjective would be too strong as it would require the cardinality of S to be at least that of $\mathcal{U}_{\mathcal{M}}$.

Lemma 1 (Soundness). *Let $\mathcal{N} = \langle S, \ell, \prec \rangle$ be a non-spurious model and let $\vdash_{\mathcal{N}}$ be the defeasible consequence relation it defines. Then $\vdash_{\mathcal{N}}$ satisfies the preferential properties (Ref), (LLE), (And), (Or), (RW) and (CM), as well as the properties (Norm), (Equiv), (Imp) and $(RK^{\vdash})$. If $\mathcal{N}$ is moreover a ranked model, then $\vdash_{\mathcal{N}}$ also satisfies (RM).*

Before we address completeness, it is worth making an observation:

Proposition 3. *Let $\vdash$ be a preferential consequence relation. If $\vdash$ satisfies (Norm), then it satisfies (Equiv), (Imp) and $(RK^{\vdash})$.*

The proof of Proposition 3 relies on Propositions 1 and 2 and on the fact that Rules RK, Mon and Cgr can be derived from RN and the modal validities in the classical case. From the result above we conclude that it is enough to restrict our attention to those consequence relations satisfying (Norm).

Definition 10 (Normal Consequence). *A modal consequence relation $\vdash$ is a normal consequence relation if it satisfies all the preferential properties from Section 3 together with (Norm).*

Lemma 2 (Completeness). *Let $\vdash \subseteq \mathcal{L} \times \mathcal{L}$ be a normal consequence relation. Then there exists a non-spurious ranked model $\mathcal{N}$ such that $\vdash_{\mathcal{N}} = \vdash$.*

We are now ready to state one of the main results of the present paper:

Theorem 3. *A defeasible consequence relation is a normal consequence relation if and only if it is defined by some non-spurious model.*

If $\vdash$ is a normal consequence relation also satisfying RM, we call $\vdash$ a *rational normal* consequence relation. This leads us to our second representation result:

Theorem 4. *A defeasible consequence relation is a rational normal consequence relation if and only if it is defined by some non-spurious ranked model.*

5   Normal Entailment

So far we have assessed $\vdash$ from the perspective of consequence relations. Following Lehmann and Magidor [14], one can also view $\vdash$ as a connective in an enriched modal language, which allows us to write down defeasible statements (or 'conditionals', as they are also referred to). Given a set of defeasible statements of the form $\alpha \vdash \beta$, from a knowledge representation and reasoning perspective it becomes important to address the question of what it means for a defeasible statement to be *entailed* by others [14].

A *defeasible knowledge base* $\mathcal{K}^{\vdash}$ is a finite set of statements $\alpha \vdash \beta$, where $\alpha, \beta \in \mathcal{L}$ [6]. Given a non-spurious model $\mathcal{N}$, we extend the notion of satisfaction to knowledge bases in the obvious way: $\mathcal{N} \Vdash \mathcal{K}^{\vdash}$ if $\alpha \vdash_{\mathcal{N}} \beta$ for every $\alpha \vdash \beta \in \mathcal{K}^{\vdash}$. This leads us to an obvious definition of entailment:

Definition 11 (Normal Entailment). *$\mathcal{K}^{\vdash}$ normally entails $\alpha \vdash \beta$ if and only if for every non-spurious model $\mathcal{N}$, if $\mathcal{N} \Vdash \mathcal{K}^{\vdash}$, then $\alpha \vdash_{\mathcal{N}} \beta$.*

On a related note, the *normal* closure of $\mathcal{K}^{\vdash}$ is defined as the intersection of all the normal consequence relations containing $\mathcal{K}^{\vdash}$.

Theorem 5. *Let $\mathcal{K}^{\vdash}$ be a defeasible knowledge base. Then (i) the set of all sentences normally entailed by $\mathcal{K}^{\vdash}$ is a Tarskian consequence relation; (ii) it is a normal consequence relation; (iii) it coincides with the normal closure of $\mathcal{K}^{\vdash}$.*

In the context of normal consequence, normal entailment is therefore the appropriate notion of entailment for defeasible knowledge bases. However, if we shift our focus to the class of *rational normal* consequence relations, the obvious definition of rational normal entailment does not provide a desirable result.

Definition 12 (Rational Normal Entailment). *$\mathcal{K}^{\vdash}$ rationally normally entails $\alpha \mathrel{\vdash} \beta$ if and only if for every non-spurious ranked model $\mathcal{N}$, if $\mathcal{N} \Vdash \mathcal{K}^{\vdash}$, then $\alpha \mathrel{\vdash}_{\mathcal{N}} \beta$.*

Theorem 6. *Given a defeasible knowledge base $\mathcal{K}^{\vdash}$, the set of defeasible statements rationally normally entailed by $\mathcal{K}^{\vdash}$ is exactly the normal closure of $\mathcal{K}^{\vdash}$.*

So from Theorem 6 it follows that rational normal entailment generates a consequence relation that is normal, but is not always rational. This is similar to a result obtained for rational consequence relations [6]. The following proposal to define and construct a viable notion of rational normal closure is analogous to that proposed by Britz et al. [6] which, in turn, is based on the proposal by Lehmann and Magidor [14].

Definition 13. *Let $\mathcal{K}^{\vdash}$ be a defeasible knowledge base. The preference order $\ll$ generated by $\mathcal{K}^{\vdash}$ is a binary relation on the set of rational normal consequence relations containing $\mathcal{K}^{\vdash}$, defined as follows: $\mathrel{\vdash}_0$ is preferable to $\mathrel{\vdash}_1$ (written $\mathrel{\vdash}_0 \ll \mathrel{\vdash}_1$) if and only if*

- *there is an $\alpha \mathrel{\vdash} \beta \in \mathrel{\vdash}_1 \setminus \mathrel{\vdash}_0$ such that for all γ such that $\gamma \vee \alpha \mathrel{\vdash}_0 \neg\alpha$ and for all δ such that $\gamma \mathrel{\vdash}_0 \delta$, we also have $\gamma \mathrel{\vdash}_1 \delta$, and*
- *for every $\gamma, \delta \in \mathcal{L}$, if $\gamma \mathrel{\vdash} \delta$ is in $\mathrel{\vdash}_0 \setminus \mathrel{\vdash}_1$, then there is an assertion $\rho \mathrel{\vdash} \nu$ in $\mathrel{\vdash}_1 \setminus \mathrel{\vdash}_0$ such that $\rho \vee \gamma \mathrel{\vdash}_1 \neg\gamma$.*

The idea is to define rational normal closure as the most preferred (with respect to $\ll$) of all the rational normal consequence relations containing $\mathcal{K}^{\vdash}$.

Definition 14. *Let $\mathcal{K}^{\vdash}$ be a defeasible knowledge base, let $\mathcal{K}^R$ be the class of rational normal consequence relations containing $\mathcal{K}^{\vdash}$, and let $\ll$ be the preference ordering on $\mathcal{K}^R$ generated by $\mathcal{K}^{\vdash}$. If $\ll$ has a (unique) minimum element $\mathrel{\vdash}$, then the rational normal closure of $\mathcal{K}^{\vdash}$ is defined as $\mathrel{\vdash}$.*

In order to provide the conditions for the existence of rational normal closure, we first need to define a *ranking* of formulas with respect to $\mathcal{K}^{\vdash}$ which, in turn, is based on a notion of *exceptionality*. A formula α is said to be *exceptional* for a defeasible knowledge base $\mathcal{K}^{\vdash}$ if and only if $\mathcal{K}^{\vdash}$ *normally* entails $\top \mathrel{\vdash} \neg\alpha$. A defeasible statement $\alpha \mathrel{\vdash} \beta$ is exceptional for $\mathcal{K}^{\vdash}$ if and only if its antecedent α is exceptional for $\mathcal{K}^{\vdash}$.

Let $E(\mathcal{K}^{\vdash})$ denote the subset of $\mathcal{K}^{\vdash}$ containing statements that are exceptional for $\mathcal{K}^{\vdash}$. We define a non-increasing sequence of subsets of $\mathcal{K}^{\vdash}$ as follows: $\mathcal{E}_0 = \mathcal{K}^{\vdash}$, and for $i > 0$, $\mathcal{E}_i = E(\mathcal{E}_{i-1})$. Clearly there is a smallest integer k such that for all $j \geq k$, $\mathcal{E}_j = \mathcal{E}_{j+1}$. From this we define the *rank* of a formula with respect to $\mathcal{K}^{\vdash}$ as follows:[3] $r_{\mathcal{K}^{\vdash}}(\alpha)$ is the smallest integer i such that α is not exceptional for $\mathcal{E}_i$. If α is exceptional for $\mathcal{E}_k$ (and therefore exceptional for all $\mathcal{E}$s), then α does not have a rank (denoted as $r_{\mathcal{K}^{\vdash}}(\alpha) = \infty$). Intuitively, the higher the rank of a formula, the more exceptional it is with respect to $\mathcal{K}^{\vdash}$.

Theorem 7. *Let $\mathcal{K}^{\vdash}$ be a defeasible knowledge base. The rational normal closure of $\mathcal{K}^{\vdash}$ exists and is the set $\mathcal{R}^{\vdash}$ of defeasible statements $\alpha \mathrel{\vdash} \beta$ such that either $r_{\mathcal{K}^{\vdash}}(\alpha) < r_{\mathcal{K}^{\vdash}}(\alpha \wedge \neg \beta)$, or $r_{\mathcal{K}^{\vdash}}(\alpha) = \infty$ (in which case $r_{\mathcal{K}^{\vdash}}(\alpha \wedge \neg \beta) = \infty$).*

We conclude this section by observing that exceptionality checking for normal entailment *cannot* be reduced to (local) classical entailment, as is the case for preferential entailment. More precisely, given a defeasible knowledge base $\mathcal{K}^{\vdash}$, let $\mathcal{K}^{\rightarrow}$ be its classical counterpart in which every defeasible statement of the form $\gamma \mathrel{\vdash} \delta$ in $\mathcal{K}^{\vdash}$ is replaced by $\gamma \rightarrow \delta$. It can be shown that $\mathcal{K}^{\vdash}$ preferentially entails $\neg \alpha$ if and only if $\neg \alpha$ is (locally) entailed by $\mathcal{K}^{\rightarrow}$ [6]. And while it is easy to show that $\neg \alpha$ being (locally) entailed by $\mathcal{K}^{\rightarrow}$ implies that $\mathcal{K}^{\vdash}$ normally entails $\neg \alpha$ (i.e., α is exceptional for $\mathcal{K}^{\vdash}$), it is just as easy to construct a counterexample which shows that the converse does not always hold.

On the one hand the result above is a negative one as it rules out a reduction to classical entailment for computing rational normal closure. On the other hand it is of theoretical importance since it is a concrete indication that normal rational consequence is a *true* extension of propositional defeasible consequence.

6   Concluding Remarks

Recapitulating the main contributions of this paper, they can be summarized as follows: (*i*) We have provided concrete evidence that the move from propositional to modal-based defeasible consequence relations bring about gaps that the original KLM postulates are not able to cope with; (*ii*) We have tightened our preferential semantics for modal logic by motivating and defining additional constraints on preferential models; (*iii*) We have motivated extra KLM-style postulates that do make use of the additional expressiveness of modal logic; (*iv*) We have proved new representation theorems establishing the link between the semantic constraints and the new set of postulates, and (*v*) We have extended the notion of rational closure for the case of normal consequence relations.

Crocco and Lamarre [10] as well as Boutilier [4] have also investigated defeasible consequence in a modal context. In particular, Boutilier showed that (propositional) nonmonotonic consequence can be embedded in conditional logics via a binary modality $\Rightarrow$. The links between our richer framework and the conditional $\Rightarrow$ remain to be explored in more detail, though.

---

[3] Observe that our terminology differs from that of Britz et al. [6], but is consistent with that of Lehmann and Magidor [14].

Our representation result paves the way for both the investigation into further modal properties and the definition of effective decision procedures for modal preferential reasoning. Another avenue for future research is the integration of the refined approach here presented with notions of *typicality* [3] and *defeasible modalities* [8], thereby establishing the foundation of a general framework for modal defeasible reasoning.

Acknowledgements. This work is based upon research supported by the National Research Foundation. Any opinion, findings and conclusions or recommendations expressed in this material are those of the author(s) and therefore the NRF do not accept any liability in regard thereto. This work was partially funded by Project number 247601, Net2: Network for Enabling Networked Knowledge, from the FP7-PEOPLE-2009-IRSES call.

References

1. Baader, F., Calvanese, D., McGuinness, D., Nardi, D., Patel-Schneider, P. (eds.): The Description Logic Handbooks. Cambridge University Press (2007)
2. Blackburn, P., van Benthem, J., Wolter, F.: Handbook of Modal Logic. Elsevier, North-Holland (2006)
3. Booth, R., Meyer, T., Varzinczak, I.: PTL: A Propositional Typicality Logic. In: del Cerro, L.F., Herzig, A., Mengin, J. (eds.) JELIA 2012. LNCS, vol. 7519, pp. 107–119. Springer, Heidelberg (2012)
4. Boutilier, C.: Conditional logics of normality: A modal approach. Artificial Intelligence 68(1), 87–154 (1994)
5. Britz, K., Heidema, J., Meyer, T.: Semantic preferential subsumption. In: Proc. of KR, pp. 476–484 (2008)
6. Britz, K., Meyer, T., Varzinczak, I.: Preferential reasoning for modal logics. Electronic Notes in Theoretical Computer Science 278, 55–69 (2011)
7. Britz, K., Meyer, T., Varzinczak, I.: Semantic foundation for preferential description logics. In: Proc. of Australasian AI Conference, pp. 491–500 (2011)
8. Britz, K., Varzinczak, I.: Defeasible modes of inference: A preferential perspective. In: 14th International Workshop on Nonmonotonic Reasoning, NMR (2012)
9. Casini, G., Straccia, U.: Rational Closure for Defeasible Description Logics. In: Janhunen, T., Niemelä, I. (eds.) JELIA 2010. LNCS, vol. 6341, pp. 77–90. Springer, Heidelberg (2010)
10. Crocco, G., Lamarre, P.: On the connections between nonmonotonic inference systems and conditional logics. In: Proc. of KR, pp. 565–571 (1992)
11. Giordano, L., Olivetti, N., Gliozzi, V., Pozzato, G.: $\mathcal{ALC} + T$: a preferential extension of description logics. Fundamenta Informaticae 96(3), 341–372 (2009)
12. Kraus, S., Lehmann, D., Magidor, M.: Nonmonotonic reasoning, preferential models and cumulative logics. Artificial Intelligence 44, 167–207 (1990)
13. Lehmann, D., Magidor, M.: Preferential logics: The predicate calculus case. In: Proc. of TARK, pp. 57–72 (1990)
14. Lehmann, D., Magidor, M.: What does a conditional knowledge base entail? Artificial Intelligence 55, 1–60 (1992)
15. Moodley, K., Meyer, T., Varzinczak, I.: A Protégé plug-in for defeasible reasoning. In: 25th International Workshop on Description Logics (2012)
16. Quantz, J.: A preference semantics for defaults in terminological logics. In: Proc. of KR, pp. 294–305 (1992)

Trust in Context

Abhaya C. Nayak

Department of Computing
Macquarie University
Sydney, Australia 2109
Abhaya.Nayak@mq.edu.au

Abstract. This paper examines how Spohn's *Ordinal Conditional Functions*, which are used to model belief dynamics, when appropriately adapted and interpreted, can fruitfully model the dynamics of trust. In this framework, trust is defined in terms of lack of trust (trust deficit) which is taken to be a primitive notion. It explores the notion of context sensitive trust, i.e., how in different domains of human interaction, one agent might trust another agent in varying degrees, and suggests the dynamics of such trust.

> *One can judge a man by the company he keeps.*
> Euripides (480 – 406 A.D.)

1 Introduction

The concept of trust is playing an increasingly important role in different fields related to information technology [13], such as multi agent systems [21], communication networks [15], and social networks [9]. Given the similarity between *trust* and *belief*, as betrayed by the words used in many languages to denote them, such as in Hebrew (*emun/emunah*), Latin (*credo*) and Sanskrit (*bishwas*), one would expect that the approaches adopted to model beliefs can be easily adapted to represent trust and reason with it. In fact, some existing approaches have already done it. In some accounts, this acknowledgement is only implicit. For instance, Yu and Singh [23] employ a Dempster-Shafer *belief functions* [17] with respect to every agent *a* telling to what extent *a* is to be trusted, and to what extent distrusted, and use Dempster Rules of combination to process recommendations about an agent. Similarly Colin Tan's approach to trust computation [20] also uses belief functions. In some other approaches, such as Demolombe's account of graded trust [4], the connection between belief and trust is made quite explicit.

Both belief and trust are mental attitudes; nonetheless there is a crucial difference. Belief is a propositional attitude, but trust is not. In the sentence *John believes X*, the place holder *X* is more likely than not to be a proposition, as in, "John believes *that dragons breath fire*". On the other hand, in the sentence *John trusts Y*, the place holder *Y* is more likely than not to be a person (or agent), as in "John trusts Betty but not Adam" which says something akin to: *John trusts (can count on) what Betty will do, but not on what Adam will.* Hence, while as an attitude, belief is propositional, trust is *actional*. Thus a thorough investigation into the foundation of trust must take into account not only the agents, but also their ability to perform different actions, their

M. Thielscher and D. Zhang (Eds.): AI 2012, LNCS 7691, pp. 517–529, 2012.
© Springer-Verlag Berlin Heidelberg 2012

intention behind performing (or not performing) some action, as well as the relevant *speech acts* [14]. Literature in the area [3, 8, 18] indicates support for such a view point.

In an earlier work [11] I proposed an alternative framework for reasoning about trust, inspired by Wolfgang Spohn's account of *ordinal conditional functions* [19] that is used to model belief dynamics. In this work, invoking political realism, I took *distrust* or *trust deficit* to be a more basic notion, and defined trust via distrust, and proposed how the statics and dynamics of trust can be represented. The notion of trust in this account is also *graded trust* as in Demolombe's account [4]; however it is also *unqualified trust*. It is as if, if I were to trust John more than I trust Jack, I must trust John more in every context. It is possible that John is better at writing programs and Jack at proof reading; so depending upon the context I might trust Jack more than John, or the other way around. Hence, the notion of trust must not only be graded, but also be contextualised. The basic sentences in the language of trust would have the form somewhat along the line: *(agent) A trusts (agent) B in the context (of carrying out the task) C to the degree D*. Ungraded trust as well as unqualified (bare) trust should be reducible to such fine-grained trust. The aim of this paper is to develop the semantic framework for such an account. For the sake of simplicity, the framework does not take into account the intentions and plans of agents, and the proposal is primarily semantic. Since the framework for trust being developed is very new, not much can be assumed as background knowledge. Hence I will need to introduce a relatively large number of concepts.

In the section *Bare Trust* we summarise and expand upon the account of the statics of trust developed in [11]. This accounts for graded, but unqualified trust. In the next section, *Trust Contextualized*, we examine a qualified notion of trust. The account of how the trustworthiness of different agents are updated is developed in the section *Trust Dynamics*. In the final section we conclude with a brief outline of some related issues that we will take up in our future work.

2   Bare Trust

In a Hobbesian state of nature, there is "continuall feare, and danger of violent death; And the life of man, solitary, poore, nasty, brutish, and short" [7]. If we assume that trust and cooperation must emerge out of human behaviour in such a state of nature [2], then it is not trust but rather its deficit, *distrust* that should be taken to be a more basic concept, and trust be defined in terms of it. However, trust is more than just the absence of distrust. We define trust in terms of suspicion in the following manner:

Definition 1. *An agent a trusts b iff a distrusts (suspicious of) the "enemies" of b.*

This definition of trust via suspicion or distrust raises two immediate questions.

1. *Why should an agent a's trust in b depend on a's attitude towards the enemies of b at all? After all it is conceivable that a distrusts (or, for that matter trusts) both b and the enemies of b!*[1] In response, we note that there is no mathematical compulsion to define *a*'s trust in *b* in terms of *a*'s attitude towards the enemies of *b*. However, as the Euripidean saying (quoted on the title page) implies, a person's

---

[1] I am thankful to Professor David Makinson for raising this issue in a private communication.

character may be judged based on the character of their friends. By the same token, a person's character may also be judged based on the character of their enemies. As we would see later, we are advocating that a's assessment of both the enemies as well as friends of b should be taken into account in order to judge a's trust in b. The scene of a (dis-)trusting both b and the enemies of b is a special case; and in our model it will correspond to the situation where a suspends making any "trust judgment" on b.

2. *What will happen if the agent b does not have any enemy at all? Would it then mean that a cannot trust b?* This is a special case, and it is not really that important how we deal with it. We can avoid the problem by assuming that avery agent has at least one enemy. It is a fair assumption since (a) in general, by eliminating enemies, an agent creates more enemies, and (b) success of an agent creates envy and enemity.

Accordingly, we make the following two assumptions, while Definition 2 provides an operational (but very informal) definition of suspicion.

Assumption 1. *Every agent a has at least one enemy b.*

Assumption 2. *No agent is paranoid; i.e., for every agent a there is an agent b (different from a) such that a is not suspicious of b.*

Definition 2. *An agent a is suspicious of b just in case a expects to be surprised or disappointed by b's behaviour at some point.*

Agent a is suspicious of b just in case a expects that b may disappoint a at any moment. Thus a's trust in b is reducible to b's potential for disappointing/surprising a. In this context Shackle's concept of *degree of potential surprise* [16] that is similar to Wolfgang Spohn's notion of *ordinal conditional functions* [19] is very pertinent, considering its role in the development of the *logic of belief change* [1,5,12]. The framework developed below is inspired by Spohn's account of belief change.

We will assume a pre-theoretic notion of *agent*. Let $\mathscr{A}^{+} = \{a_0, a_1, \ldots, a_n\}$ be the set of all agents. We use a with possible decoration to denote individual agents. Presumably, members of $\mathscr{A}^{+}$ observe each other's behaviour, manipulate them, trust them, distrust them, and what have you. We are not going to deal with most of those issues. We will, instead, assume a contextually fixed, prominent member, say a_0, and develop an account of how the trust of a_0 in *other members* of $\mathscr{A}^{+}$, namely $\mathscr{A} = \{a_1, \ldots, a_n\}$, is defined and maintained. So although a_0 is a member of the agent-system, and is subject to all the systemic constraints that other members of are subject to, and members of $\mathscr{A}$ trust/distrust a_0 just as a_0 does to them, we will abstract away most of those things. In particular, we will assume that a_0 has the ability to distinguish itself from the rest of $\mathscr{A}^{+}$, and primarily deals with the members of $\mathscr{A}$ in its "model of the world".

Suspicion Directed Toward an Individual

We assume that a_0 has views as to which members of $\mathscr{A}$ are friends (resp. foes) of which members. Hence, a_0 assigns to each member a_i of $\mathscr{A}$ a set of members of $\mathscr{A}$ that it considers are friends of a_i, and another set of members that it considers are foes of a_i. Hence we assume two unary functions: $friends_{a_0}(\cdot)$ and $foes_{a_0}(\cdot)$ as defined below. Since the agent a_0 is contextually fixed, we will drop the subscripts for readability.

Definition 3

1. *The function friends* : $\mathscr{A} \longrightarrow 2^{\mathscr{A}}$ *maps an agent* $a \in \mathscr{A}$ *to the set of agents friends(a) that are considered (by a_0) to be a's friends.*
2. *The function foes* : $\mathscr{A} \longrightarrow 2^{\mathscr{A}}$ *maps an agent* $a \in \mathscr{A}$ *to the set of agents foes(a) that are considered (by a_0) to be a's enemies.*
3. *The sets friends(a) and foes(a) are mutually disjoint for every agent* $a \in \mathscr{A}$.

We leave open many issues including where a_0 obtains these two functions from, and whether, the *Friend* and *Foe* relations corresponding to the $friends(\cdot)$ and $foes(\cdot)$ functions are reflexive, symmetric or transitive. We can graphically illustrate who is whose friend (or enemy) by drawing different types of arrows. In Fig. 1 below, we take $\mathscr{A}$ to be composed of agents $a_1 \ldots a_{10}$. We identify the sets $friends(a_1) = \{a_4, a_9\}$ and $foes(a_1) = \{a_7, a_{10}\}$ by drawing appropriate solid and broken arrows respectively. The friends and enemies of other agents are not being shown to avoid clutter.

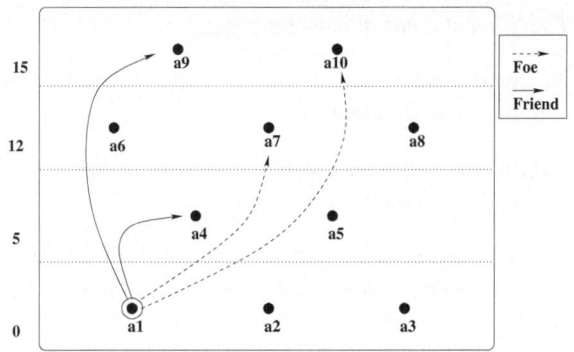

Fig. 1. The trustworthiness of agent a_1 is 12 since its suspicion index is 0 and the least degree of suspicion directed toward its foes is 12

Apart from keeping information as to who is whose friend or enemy, agent a_0 also has its opinion on who is likely to disappoint it how much. We do this by assigning another function $susp_{a_0}(\cdot)$ to it, which, for each agent a in $\mathscr{A}$, gives a non-negative integer indicating a's degree of suspicion (trust deficit, or potential disappointment). As before, we will drop the subscript a_0 for readability.

Definition 4. *The suspicion function susp* : $\mathscr{A} \longrightarrow \mathscr{N}$ *maps an agent* $a \in \mathscr{A}$ *to a non-negative integer susp(a) which indicates how disappointing a could be.*

If $susp(a)$ is 0, it indicates that the agent a_0 is not suspicious of a at all. On the other hand, an inequality such as $susp(a_i) < susp(a_j)$ would indicate that the agent a_0 is more suspicious of a_j than of a_i. For all practical purpose, these values are ordinal numbers, and we use them by and large for comparison. It immediately follows from Assumption 2 that agent a_0 is not paranoid if and only if $susp(a) = 0$ for some agent $a \in \mathscr{A}$. Accordingly, in Fig. 1, there are some agents (namely, a_1, a_2, and a_3) that are assigned the degree of potential suspicion 0. In fact, Assumption 2 leads to a more general constraint on the functions $susp(\cdot)$ as follows:

Observation 1. *In presence of Assumption 2, given an arbitrary agent a_i, there exists some agent $a_j \in \mathscr{A}^+ \setminus \{a_i\}$ such that $susp_{a_i}(a_j) = 0$.*

This observation states that since the agents we are dealing with are not paranoid, each of them places the minimum possible degree of distrust, 0, on at least one agent.

Suspicion Directed Toward a Group

Suspicion is often directed toward a group of individuals. For instance, during an election, one might have strong suspicion against a particular interest groups. In principle, any subset $\mathscr{A}' \subseteq \mathscr{A}$ could constitute an interest group; and hence we should be able to discuss the degree to which a_0 suspects $\mathscr{A}'$. In general, a group of individuals will have an underlying power structure which will play a crucial role in determining an individual's attitude towards it. If the group leader is not trustworthy, individuals will have little trust in the group itself. However, we do not assume any power structure for the groups. In absence of such a structure it is not quite clear how suspicion directed towards a group can be reduced to suspicion directed towards its members. Analogous to the *weakest link principle*, we postulate that *a group is only as bad as its least bad member*, implying that no better person could have survived as a member of the group.[2] Accordingly we generalize the definition of the function $susp(\cdot)$ as follows:

Definition 5. $susp(\mathscr{A}') = min_{a \in \mathscr{A}'} susp(a)$ *for any group of agents* $\mathscr{A}' \subseteq \mathscr{A}$.

Note that this general definition of $susp(\cdot)$ gracefully deals with the special case when $\mathscr{A}'$ is a singleton set in that $susp(\{a\}) = susp(a)$ for any $a \in \mathscr{A}$. Going back to Fig. 1, of particular interest would be the calculation of the degree to which agent a_0 would be suspicious of the friends of a_1 and of the enemies of a_1, that is, calculation of the values of $susp(friends(a_1))$ and of $susp(foes(a_1))$. Note that in this figure the set $\mathscr{A}$ is partitioned into equivalence classes modulo the *susp*-rank of its members, and the ranks (0, 5, 12 and 15) of different agents are indicated on the left. It is easily verified that these two values are respectively 5 and 12.

From Suspicion to Trust

As noted earlier as a rationale behind Definition 1, trust is more than simply the lack of suspicion or distrust. In order that agent a_0 positively trust some agent a, it is a necessary condition that a_0 bears no suspicion toward a; but that does not constitute a sufficient condition. Although I have no reason to be suspicious of a perfect stranger, I have no reason to trust them either. We can now offer a more formal definition of trust. As before, the reference to the agent a_0 is being dropped for readability.

Definition 6

1. *An agent a is trusted (by a_0) if and only if both $susp(a) = 0$ and $susp(foes(a)) > 0$ for all $a \in \mathscr{A}$.*
2. *Given an agent $a \in \mathscr{A}$ trusted by a_0, the degree of trust that a_0 places on a is given by $trust(a) = susp(foes(a))$.*

---

[2] Indeed, as an image building exercise, often "bad" groups enrol "good" individuals, intending to mislead others. This deceit works precisely because there is a presumption that the group could not be worse then its least bad member.

Thus, going back to Fig. 1, the degree of trust that a_0 places on the agent a_1 is 12 since $susp(a_1) = 0$ and $susp(foes(a_1)) = susp(\{a_7, a_{10}\}) = 12$. On the other hand, since $susp(a_5) = 5$, it follows that a_0 does not trust a_5 at all. In fact, a_0 distrusts (is suspicious of) a_5 to the degree 5.

Now we are in a position to define *trust in a group*. Trusting a set of agents $\mathscr{A}'$ entails trusting every member of that group. The degree of that trust is the minimal trust earned by members of that group in the relevant manner.[3]

Definition 7

1. Given any $\mathscr{A}' \subseteq \mathscr{A}$, agent a_0 trusts $\mathscr{A}'$ if and only if a_0 trusts every agent $a \in \mathscr{A}'$.
2. Given that agent a_0 trusts some $\mathscr{A}' \subseteq \mathscr{A}$, the degree of trust that a_0 places on $\mathscr{A}'$ is given by $trust(\mathscr{A}') = min_{a \in \mathscr{A}'} trust(a)$.

Referring back to Fig. 1, we easily verify that $trust(\{a_1, a_5, a_6\})$ is undefined since the agents a_5 and a_6 are not trusted. On the other hand, $trust(\{a_1, a_2, a_3\})$ cannot be evaluated at this point since the values of $foes(a_2)$ and $foes(a_3)$ are not available.

3 Trust Contextualised

The account we provided of trust above pretends that trust is not context-sensitive. However, trust is an actional attitude – it is sensitive to the action at hand, and perhaps to other contextual factors. We will assume that there are certain things called *contexts*, and actions are part of the relevant contexts. We will not investigate into the inner mechanism of contexts, but assume that a context encodes such information as the relevant action, and the agent's plan, ability, and intention. Our purpose here is simply to generalize the account of bare trust presented earlier in order that contexts can be incorporated into the accounts of trust. Accordingly, we assume that there is a fixed set of contexts, $\mathscr{C}$, and we denote the member contexts by c with possible decorations.

From the Section *Bare Trust* it is clear that the two central notions used here are the functions $friends(\cdot)$ vs. $foes(\cdot)$ on the one hand and the function $susp(\cdot)$ on the other. The concept of trust is defined in terms of them. We will need to consider which of these primary notions need to be parametrized by a context argument.

Let us first examine if the functions $friends(\cdot)$ and $foes(\cdot)$ should be contextualised. We note that the words "friend" and "foe" as used here are convenient labels standing for similar clusters of properties as the concepts *friend* and *enemy*. In a certain sense, one might take the concept *friends* to denote a cohort group; thus, for instance, the set of agents that a hangs around with in a fishing trip could be very different from the set of agents it accompanies in a shopping expedition. We can similarly argue that one's set of *enemies* can change from context to context. Note that letting these functions accept the context as a parameter will not force us to change the output of the functions as the context changes. Accordingly we introduce two corresponding functions as follows:

---

[3] It is not always correct. I might trust a company because its CEO is my trusted friend, even if I don't trust many employees of this company. But such power relations cannot be captured in our framework without adding further structure to it.

Definition 8

1. *The function $friends_{con} : \mathscr{A} \times \mathscr{C} \longrightarrow 2^{\mathscr{A}}$ maps an agent $a \in \mathscr{A}$ in a context $c \in \mathscr{C}$ to the set $friends_{con}(a,c)$ considered by a_0 to be a's friends in the context c.*
2. *The function $foes_{con} : \mathscr{A} \times \mathscr{C} \longrightarrow 2^{\mathscr{A}}$ maps an agent $a \in \mathscr{A}$ in a context $c \in \mathscr{C}$ to the set $foes_{con}(a,c)$ considered by a_0 to be a's enemies in the context c.*

It is very natural to assume that distrust is context sensitive. Accordingly:

Definition 9. *The function $susp_{con} : \mathscr{A} \times \mathscr{C} \longrightarrow \mathscr{N}$ maps $a \in \mathscr{A}$ in $c \in \mathscr{C}$ to a non-negative integer $susp_{con}(a,c)$ telling how disappointing a could be to a_0 in that context.*

Definition 10. *$susp_{con}(\mathscr{A}',c) = min_{a \in \mathscr{A}'} susp_{con}(a,c)$ for any group of agents $\mathscr{A}' \subseteq \mathscr{A}$ and context $c \in \mathscr{C}$.*

We again refer to the figure Fig. 1 which can be taken to illustrate the the notion of suspicion or distrust in a given context c. Finally, we contextualize the notions of trust (directed towards an individual as well as at a group) in the obvious fashion.

Definition 11

1. *An agent a is trusted (by a_0) in context c if and only if both $susp_{con}(a,c) = 0$ and $susp_{con}(foes_{con}(a,c)) > 0$ for all $a \in \mathscr{A}$.*
2. *Given an agent $a \in \mathscr{A}$ trusted by a_0, the degree of trust that a_0 places on a in c is given by $trust_{con}(a,c) = susp_{con}(foes_{con}(a,c))$.*

Definition 12

1. *Given any $\mathscr{A}' \subseteq \mathscr{A}$ and context $c \in \mathscr{C}$, agent a_0 trusts $\mathscr{A}'$ in context c if and only if a_0 trusts every agent $a \in \mathscr{A}'$ in context c.*
2. *Given that agent a_0 trusts some $\mathscr{A}' \subseteq \mathscr{A}$ in context c, the degree of trust that a_0 places on $\mathscr{A}'$ in c is given by $trust_{con}(\mathscr{A}',c) = min_{a \in \mathscr{A}'} trust_{con}(a,c)$.*

Thus we see that the concept of bare trust is naturally generalised to a more notion of trust that is context sensitive, and hence is a more appropriate model of trust.

4 The Dynamics of Trust

In the section *Bare Trust* we outlined the basic framework to describe a *trust state* that is in equilibrium. In the subsequent section *Trust Contextualised* we generalised this framework to reflect that trust is a context-sensitive notion. Apart from context, trust also changes over time subject to an agent making new observations, receiving new information, and even receiving recommendations from others. For instance, if agent a_0 were to receive a recommendation from a reputable source that a_5 is very trustworthy, a_0's evaluation of the trustworthiness of a_5 will change. How this change is effected – the *dynamics of trust* – is the topic of this section. Without any loss of generality, we take it to be the study of how the function $susp(\cdot)$ [resp. $susp_{con}(\cdot)$] changes in response to relevant triggers. We will restrict the discussion of trust dynamics to how $susp(\cdot)$ responds to received recommendations of the appropriate sort.

Let us first note that *who* makes the recommendation makes a difference. If the recommendation comes from someone that a_0 considers to be completely unreliable, a_0 is likely to ignore the recommendation. On the other hand, if the recommendation comes from someone whose judgment a_0 trusts, then it will take up the recommendation seriously and "update" its trust values in different agents. There are other relevant factors as well. If the recommendation regarding a_j comes from a_i, and a_0 "knows" that a_j is a friend of a_i, then chances are a_0 would take the recommendation not as seriously as it normally would; it might in fact "discount" the recommendation to some extent. On the other hand, if a_j is believed to be an enemy of a_i, then it would have the opposite effect. The framework developed here can deal with these variations in a judicious manner. In this paper we will make many simplifying assumptions. In particular, we will assume that the agent a_0 considers the recommendation received to be practically infallible, the recommending agent has no (relevant) conflict of interest, and means what she says – in other words, no special *speech acts* [14] and *conversational implicature* [6] are being employed. We will first recapitulate the account of (bare) trust dynamics proposed in [11], and then outline a more general dynamics for contextual trust.

4.1   Bare Trust Dynamics

In this section we discuss how bare trust, represented in terms of the un-contextualised functions $susp(\cdot)$, $foes(\cdots)$, etc., gets updated in light of received recommendations. Let us assume that agent a_0 has received a recommendation from an infallible source to trust agent a_5 to degree 3. This recommendation has the general form *new_trust(agent a, value x)*. In response, agent a_0 will update its function $susp(\cdot)$ to, say, $susp'(\cdot) = susp(\cdot \mid \langle a,x \rangle)$ such that when the trust value of agent a is computed modulo $susp'(\cdot)$, we will get the result x. Borrowing terminology from probability theory, we will term $susp(\cdot)$ to be the *prior suspicion function* of the agent a_0, and $susp'(\cdot) = susp(\cdot \mid \langle a,x \rangle)$ to be its *posterior suspicion function*. When no confusion is imminent, we will represent the posterior $susp'(\cdot) = susp(\cdot \mid \langle a,x \rangle)$ simply as $susp_{\langle a,x \rangle}(\cdot)$.

Definition 13

1. A trust recommendation *is denoted by a pair* $\langle a,x \rangle$ *where* $a \in \mathscr{A}$ *is an agent, and* $x \in \mathscr{N}$ *is the recommended trust-value of a.*
2. $susp(\cdot \mid \langle a,x \rangle)$ *represents the "posterior suspicion function", also denoted* $susp_{\langle a,x \rangle}(\cdot)$, *after the prior* $susp(\cdot)$ *has been updated in light of the trust recommendation* $\langle a,x \rangle$.

Since the recommendation is accepted as is, the posterior suspicion function $susp_{\langle a,x \rangle}(\cdot)$ should be so constructed that the trust value for the agent a generated from it as per Definition 6 should be x. This naturally leads to the following two constraints:

Assumption 3

1. $susp_{\langle a,x \rangle}(a) = 0$
2. $susp_{\langle a,x \rangle}(foes(a)) = x$

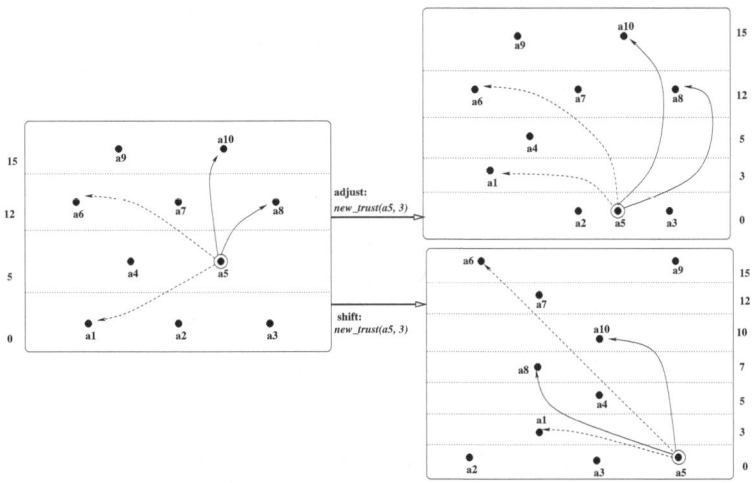

Fig. 2. Agent a_5 who was distrusted to degree 5, is now trusted to degree 3

Let us consider the prior suspicion function $susp(\cdot)$ represented by the left rectangle in Fig. 2. The agent a_0 distrusts a_5 to degree 5; the friends of a_5 are two, namely a_8 and a_{10}; and a_5 also has two enemies: a_1 and a_6. Suppose also that the agent a_0 receives a recommendation $\langle a_5, 3 \rangle$ that it must accept at face value. Given Assumption 3, it then follows that $susp_{\langle a_5,3 \rangle}(a_5) = 0$, and $susp_{\langle a_5,3 \rangle}(\{a_1, a_6\}) = 3$. This raises three questions.

1. Clearly the posterior suspicion function $susp'(\cdot) = susp_{\langle a_5,3 \rangle}(\cdot)$ will assign a_5 the value 0. What would it do to the friends of a_5? For instance, should $susp(a_8)$ be left untouched in this updating process? If not, what would be the correct value?
2. Since $susp_{\langle a_5,3 \rangle}(\{a_1, a_6\}) = 3$, the minimum of the values assigned by $susp_{\langle a_5,3 \rangle}(\cdot)$ to a_1 and a_6 is 3. But which of them should receive this minimum value?
3. As in the case (1) above, given that in this trust updating process, the $susp(\cdot)$ value of a_1 is changed from 0 to 3, should that of a_6 be left unchanged?

Each of these issues admits multiple, even bizarre solutions such as:

Proposal 1. *For all $a' \in \mathscr{A}$,*

$$susp_{\langle a_5,3 \rangle}(a') = \begin{cases} 0 & \text{if either } a' = a_5 \text{ or } a' \in friends(a_5) \\ 3 & \text{otherwise} \end{cases}$$

In order to block such solutions, we propose *trust adjustment* and *trust shift*, two proposals that are inspired by work in iterated belief revision [10, 22].

Trust Adjustment. This approach strictly follows the *principle of minimal repair*. We may assume that agent a_0's function $susp(\cdot)$ summarizes a lot of valuable, historical information. that should not be lost without very good reason. However, Proposal 1 will obliterate such distinction, even when the trust recommendation, $\langle a_5, 3 \rangle$ has nothing to do, directly or indirectly, either with a_2 or with a_9. It is guilty of *over repair*. We should not rectify the $susp(\cdot)$ function more than necessary. The changes that are *really necessary* are explicitly identified in Assumption 3. If we follow this recipe, then, in the context of Fig.2, the following modification in $susp(\cdot)$ would appear to be appropriate:

Proposal 2. *For all $a' \in \mathscr{A}$,*

$$susp_{\langle a_5,3 \rangle}(a') = \begin{cases} 0 & \text{if } a' = a_5 \\ 3 & \text{if } a' \text{ is susp-minimalin } foes(a_5) \\ susp(a') & \text{otherwise.} \end{cases}$$

According to this proposal, the $susp$-value of a_5 will be reduced to 0, and that of a_1 will be increased to 3. The $susp$-value of every other agent in $\mathscr{A}$ will be left as is, ensuring that the a_5 will be trusted to degree 3 with minimal repair to the function $susp(\cdot)$. However, in general this approach will not work. In particular, suppose that the agent a_5 had one more enemy, say a_4 with $susp(a_4) = 2$. In such a case, after $susp(\cdot)$ was updated to $susp_{\langle a_5,3 \rangle}(\cdot)$ in response to the received trust-recommendation $\langle a_5,3 \rangle$ following the procedure specified in Proposal 2, the agent will be trusted to the degree 2 instead of the desired degree 3. Hence a slight correction in Proposal 2 is due:

Definition 14 (Trust Adjustment). *Let $a, a' \in \mathscr{A}$ and $x \in \mathscr{N}$. The updated suspicion function is given by:*

$$susp_{\langle a,x \rangle}^{adjust}(a') = \begin{cases} 0 & \text{if } a = a' \\ x & \text{if both } a' \in foes(a), \text{ and } susp(a') < x \\ susp(a') & \text{otherwise.} \end{cases}$$

The figure Fig. 2 (top-right) graphically illustrates how the $susp$-values of different agents get adjusted in this process.

Trust Shift. Although *trust adjustment* satisfies both Assumption 3, and the principle of minimal repair, the way it distorts the relationship between different friends (or enemies) of the agent a is debatable. Consider again Fig. 2. All the three friends, a_5, a_8 and a_{10} were distrusted to various degrees, ranging from 5 to 15. A recommendation was received that the agent a_5 is fairly trust worthy, and should be trusted to degree 3, and a_0 accordingly trusted a_5. It is only rational to expect that agent a_0 would now distrust a_8 and a_{10} less than it did before. But that does not happen. Similarly, this recommendation "taints" a_5's enemy a_1, who was not distrusted before. However, there is no corresponding loss of trust in a_6, the other enemy of a_5. It will be more appropriate to shift *en bloc* the suspicion values of a_5's friends (or enemies), up or down as the case may be, by the same magnitude. This is captured as follows:

Proposal 3. *For all $a' \in \mathscr{A}$,*

$$susp_{\langle a_5,3 \rangle}(a') = \begin{cases} 0 & \text{if } a' = a_5 \\ max(0,(susp(a') - 5)) & \text{if } a' \in friends(a_5) \\ susp(a') + 3 & \text{if } a' \in foes(a_5) \\ susp(a') & \text{otherwise.} \end{cases}$$

The result of such uniform shift is illustrated in the figure Fig.2 (bottom-right). It is easily verified that the relative *trust deficit* between different friends (or enemies) of a_5 is not affected in this process. Definition 15 generalises this proposal.

Definition 15 (Trust Shift). *Let a, $a' \in \mathscr{A}$, $x \in \mathcal{N}$, and y denote $susp(foes(a))$. Then, the new (updated) suspicion function is given by:*

$$susp^{shift}_{\langle a,x \rangle}(a') = \begin{cases} 0 & \text{if } a = a' \\ max(0, (susp(a') - susp(a))) & \text{if } a' \in friends(a) \\ susp(a') - y + x & \text{if both } a' \in foes(a) \text{ and } x \neq y \\ susp(a') & \text{otherwise.} \end{cases}$$

The first clause in this definition ensures that a is not distrusted. This reduces the *susp*-value of a by $susp(a)$; and that is the magnitude by which we would like to reduce the *susp*-value of all its friends. This is done in the second clause, with the proviso that the revised *susp*-value has a floor value of 0. The more interesting case is captured by the third clause. Note that y, defined as $susp(foes(a))$, is really, as per Definition 5, the minimal *susp*-value associated with any enemy of a. Since a' is an enemy of a, it follows that y will never exceed $susp(a')$, and hence $susp(a') - y + x$ will always be non-negative, and the *susp*-value of all enemies of a will be uniformly shifted by the same magnitude $|x - y|$, as desired. The last clause effectly says that agents that are neither friends nor enemies of a are not affected.

4.2 Dynamics of Contextual Trust

Since trust is an actional attitude, one's trust towards a person could fluctuate depending on the action being considered to be carried out. While in the section *Bare Trust* we ignored this aspect of trust, in the section *Trust Contextualised* we sensitized our notion of trust by introducing *context* as an extra parameter to the relevant functions, $friends_{con}$, $foes_{con}$ and $susp_{con}$ being the primary ones. In the current section, *The Dynamics of Trust*, so far we have looked at the dynamics of bare trust. We now consider the dynamics of trust that is sensitive to context.

We assume that the current trust state of the agent a_0 is given by a function $susp_{con}(\cdot)$ that accepts two parameters, namely, an agent a and a context c, and returns a suspicion value. Since the recommendation of the form $new\_trust(agent\ a, value\ x)$ does not tell in which context the recommendation is being made, the only reasonable thing the agent a_0 can do with it is to discard it altogether, or to revise all the trust values it has for a. The first option wastes a recommendation, the second results in serious loss of information.Hence it is appropriate to assume that that the recommendation will have the general form $new\_trust(agent\ a, value\ x, context\ c)$. The intended reading is that agent a_0's trust in a should be left unchanged in all contexts except c where the new trust value should be x. Accordingly, we generalise Definitions 14 and 15.

Definition 16 (Contextual Trust Adjustment). *Let a, $a' \in \mathscr{A}$, $x \in \mathcal{N}$, and $c \in \mathscr{C}$. Let the (contexualized) trust state of an agent a_0 be given by the suspicion function $susp_{con}(\cdot)$. Then, the revised suspicion function is given by:*

$$susp_{con}{}_{\langle a,x,c\rangle}^{adjust}(a') = \begin{cases} susp_{con}(a',c') & \text{if } c \neq c' \\ \quad \textbf{ELSE } \textit{(i.e. if } c = c') \\ 0 & \text{if } a = a' \\ x & \text{if both } a' \in foes_{con}(a,c), \\ & \text{and } susp_{con}(a',c) < x \\ susp_{con}(a',c) & \textit{otherwise.} \end{cases}$$

It is easily verified that the Definition 16 leaves the trust state unchanged when the input context is different from the context in which the agent a is being "assessed", and in the relevant context c it changes as does bare trust adjustment defined by Definition 14.

Definition 17 (Contextual Trust Shift). *Let* a, $a' \in \mathscr{A}$, $x \in \mathscr{N}$, *and and* $c \in \mathscr{C}$. *Let the (contextualized) trust state of an agent* a_0 *be given by the suspicion function* $susp_{con}(\cdot)$. *Also, let* y *denote* $susp_{con}(foes_{con}(a))$. *Then, the revised suspicion function is given by:*

$$susp_{con}{}_{\langle a,x,c\rangle}^{shift}(a') = \begin{cases} susp_{con}(a',c') & \text{if } c \neq c' \\ \quad \textbf{ELSE } \textit{(i.e. if } c = c') \\ 0 & \text{if } a = a' \\ max(0,(susp_{con}(a',c)- & \\ \qquad susp_{con}(a,c))) & \text{if } a' \in friends_{con}(a,c) \\ susp_{con}(a',c) - y + x & \text{if both } a' \in foes_{con}(a,c) \text{ and } x \neq y \\ susp_{con}(a',c) & \textit{otherwise.} \end{cases}$$

As in the case of the Definition 16, the trust state is left unchanged when the input context is different from the context in which the agent a is being "assessed", otherwise it behaves like bare trust shift defined by Definition 15.

We end this section making an important but obvious point, that the definitions of trust adjustment and trust shift, be it for the bare version (Definitions 14 and 15) or the contextualised version (Definitions 16 and 17), indeed define how the appropriate *susp* functions change, and the change in the corresponding *trust* functions, defined in terms of the *susp* functions, is made is only implicitly defined.

5   Discussion and Future Work

In this paper we developed a simple framework for representing the statics of trust – both bare and contextualized – and provided two reasonable mechanisms for managing its dynamics. There are many issues that we will address in future work:

1. We intend to re-interpret less informative recommendations such as *"trust a"* as: $\langle a, susp(foes(a)) \rangle$ (or as $\langle a, susp_{con}(foes(a)), c \rangle$), and investigate its consequences.
2. This framework can be enhanced to deal with recommendations about a group, or originating from a group.
3. The current trust-value (*reputation*) of the recommender is not taken into account while processing a reputation. This can be used to further fine-tune this framework.

4. Apart from the dynamics of the suspicion functions, we also need to investigate the dynamics of friendship and enmity (the functions *friends* and *foes*)
5. The account we provided is semantic. We need to devise an appropriate language of trust, and syntactically characterise the trust shift and trust adjustment operations.
6. Finally, it will be important to examine how it fares against existing relevant approaches such as [8], and how it can be practically validated.

References

1. Alchourrón, C.E., Gärdenfors, P., Makinson, D.: On the logic of theory change: Partial meet contraction and revision functions. Journal of Symbolic Logic 50, 510–530 (1985)
2. Axelrod, R.M.: Evolution of Cooperation. Basic Books (1984)
3. Castelfranchi, C., Tan, Y.H. (eds.): Trust and Deception in Virtual Societies. Springer (2001)
4. Demolombe, R.: Graded trust. In: AAMAS Trust, pp. 1–12 (2009)
5. Gärdenfors, P.: Knowledge in Flux: Modeling the Dynamics of Epistemic States. Bradford Books, MIT Press, Cambridge, Massachusetts (1988)
6. Grice, H.P.: Utterer's meaning and intentions. Philosophical Review 78, 147–177 (1969)
7. Hobbes, T.: Leviathan or the Matter, Forme, & Power of a Common-Wealth Ecclesiastical and Civill (Gutenberg EBook #3207). The Green Dragon in St. Paul's Churchyard (1651)
8. Jones, A.J.I.: On the concept of trust. Decision Support Systems 33(3), 225–232 (2002)
9. Jøsang, A., Hayward, R., Pope, S.: Trust network analysis with subjective logic. In: Proc. of the 29th Australasian Comp. Sc. Conf., ACSC 2006, vol. 48, pp. 85–94 (2006)
10. Nayak, A.C.: Iterated belief change based on epistemic entrenchment. Erkenntnis 41, 353–390 (1994)
11. Nayak, A.C.: The deficit and dynamics of trust. In: EUC, pp. 517–522. IEEE (2010)
12. Nayak, A.C., Pagnucco, M., Peppas, P.: Dynamic belief revision operators. Artif. Intell. 146(2), 193–228 (2003)
13. Sabater, J., Sierra, C.: Review on computational trust and reputation models. Artif. Intell. Rev. 24(1), 33–60 (2005)
14. Searle, J.: Speech Acts: An Essay in the Philosophy of Language. Cambridge University Press (1969)
15. Sen, J.: A Distributed Trust and Reputation Framework for Mobile Ad Hoc Networks. In: Meghanathan, N., Boumerdassi, S., Chaki, N., Nagamalai, D. (eds.) CNSA 2010. CCIS, vol. 89, pp. 538–547. Springer, Heidelberg (2010)
16. Shackle, G.L.S.: The logic of surprise. Econometrica New Series 149(78), 112–117 (1953)
17. Shafer, G.: A Mathematical Theory of Evidence. Princeton University Press (1976)
18. Singh, M.P.: Trust as dependence: a logical approach. In: Sonenberg, L., Stone, P., Tumer, K., Yolum, P. (eds.) AAMAS, pp. 863–870. IFAAMAS (2011)
19. Spohn, W.: Ordinal conditional functions: A dynamic theory of epistemic states. In: Harper, W.L., Skryms, B. (eds.) Causation in Decision, Belief Change, and Statistics, II, pp. 105–134. Kluwer Academic Publishers (1988)
20. Tan, C.K.Y.: A belief augmented frame computational trust model. In: Russell, I., Markov, Z. (eds.) FLAIRS Conference, pp. 647–652. AAAI Press (2005)
21. Wang, Y., Singh, M.P.: Formal trust model for multiagent systems. In: Veloso, M.M. (ed.) IJCAI, pp. 1551–1556 (2007)
22. Williams, M.A.: Transmutations of knowledge systems. In: Doyle, J., et al. (eds.) KR, pp. 619–629. Morgan Kaufmann (1994)
23. Yu, B., Singh, M.P.: Distributed reputation management for electronic commerce. Computational Intelligence 18(4), 535–549 (2002)

Complex Analogies:
Remarks on the Complexity of HDTP

Robert Robere[1] and Tarek Richard Besold[2]

[1] University of Toronto
robere@cs.toronto.edu
[2] Institute of Cognitive Science, University of Osnabrück
tbesold@uos.de

Abstract. After an introduction to Heuristic-Driven Theory Projection (HDTP) as framework for computational analogy-making, and a compact primer on parametrized complexity theory, we provide a complexity analysis of the key mechanisms underlying HDTP, together with a short discussion of and reflection on the obtained results. Amongst others, we show that restricted higher-order anti-unification as currently used in HDTP is $W[1]$-hard (and thus NP-hard) already for quite simple cases. Also, we obtain $W[2]$-hardness, and NP-completeness, for the original mechanism used for reducing second-order to first-order anti-unifications in the basic version of the HDTP system.

1 Introduction and Preliminaries

During the course of a day, we use different kinds of reasoning processes: We solve puzzles, play instruments, or discuss problems. Often we will find ourselves in situations in which we apply our knowledge of a familiar situation to the structurally similar novel one. Today it is undoubted that one of the basic elements of human cognition is the ability to see two a priori distinct domains as similar based on their shared relational structure (i.e., analogy-making). Key abilities within everyday life, such as communication, social interaction, tool use and the handling of previously unseen situations crucially rely on the use of analogy-based strategies and procedures. Relational matching, one of the key mechanisms underlying analogy-making, is also the basis of perception, language, learning, memory and thinking, i.e., the constituent elements of most conceptions of cognition [1].

Since the advent of computer systems, researchers in cognitive science and artificial intelligence have been trying to create computational models of analogy-making. This line of work has resulted in several different frameworks for computational analogical reasoning, starting with Reitman's ARGUS [2] and Evan's ANALOGY engine [3] and featuring systems as prominent as Hofstadter's Copycat [4] or the famous Structure-Mapping Engine (SME) [5] and MAC/FAC [6]. Whilst the latter two systems implement a version of Gentner's Structure-Mapping Theory (SMT) [7], more recently a different, generalization-based approach has been proposed: Heuristic-Driven Theory Projection (HDTP) [8,9]. Since its presentation, HDTP has continuously been refined and applied to different scenarios and domains, most prominently to mathematical reasoning [10] and conceptual blending in mathematics [11]. Still, except for a few accidental

M. Thielscher and D. Zhang (Eds.): AI 2012, LNCS 7691, pp. 530–542, 2012.
© Springer-Verlag Berlin Heidelberg 2012

observations, this far no formal analysis of the computational complexity of HDTP on a systematic basis has been provided. In this paper, we present several results concerning the computational complexity of HDTP and the corresponding anti-unification formalism for analogy-making.

The paper is structured as follows: Sect. 1.1 presents a short introduction to the Heuristic-Driven Theory Projection framework, followed by necessary preliminaries of parametrized complexity theory in Sect. 1.2. Then, Sect. 2 initially gives the definitions on the basic mechanisms of anti-unification, before Sect. 2.1 provides a complexity analysis of several forms of restricted higher-order anti-unification as applied in HDTP. Sect. 3 contains a complexity analysis of the use of equational theories in HDTP to simplify higher-order anti-unifications. Sect. 4 offers an interpretation of and reflection on the given complexity results, and Sect. 5 concludes the paper.

1.1 HDTP: Heuristic-Driven Theory Projection

The Heuristic-Driven Theory Projection (HDTP) framework [8] has been conceived as a mathematically sound framework for analogy-making. HDTP has been created for computing analogical relations and inferences for domains which are given in form of a many-sorted first-order logic representation [11]. Source and target of the analogy-making process are defined in terms of axiomatisations, i.e., given by a finite set of formulae. From there, HDTP tries to align pairs of formulae from the two domains by means of anti-unification (as firstly studied by Plotkin [12,13]): Anti-unification tries to solve the problem of generalizing terms in a meaningful way, yielding for each term an anti-instance, in which distinct subterms have been replaced by variables (which in turn would allow for a retrieval of the original terms by a substitution of the variables by appropriate subterms).[1] In it's present form, HDTP extends Plotkin's classical first-order anti-unification to a restricted form of higher-order anti-unification, as mere first-order structures have shown to be too weak for the purpose of analogy-making [9].

Restricted higher-order anti-unification as presently used in HDTP was introduced in [14]. In order to restrain generalizations from becoming arbitrarily complex, a new notion of substitution is introduced. Classical first-order terms are extended by the introduction of variables which may take arguments (where classical first-order variables correspond to variables with arity 0), making a term either a first-order or a higher-order term. Then, anti-unification can be applied analogously to the original first-order case, yielding a generalization subsuming the specific terms. As already indicated by the naming, the class of substitutions which are applicable in HDTP is restricted to (compositions of) the following four cases: renamings, fixations, argument insertions, and permutations (cf. Sect. 2.1). Unfortunately, in the higher-order case, the least general generalization loses its uniqueness. Therefore, the current implementation of HDTP ranks generalizations according to a complexity measure on generalizations and chooses the least complex generalizations as preferred ones [9,15].

From a practical point of view, it is also necessary to anti-unify not only terms, but formulae. Therefore, HDTP extends the notion of generalization also to formulae

---

[1] In [12], Plotkin demonstrated that for a proper definition of generalization, for a given pair of terms there always is a generalization, and that there is exactly one least general generalization (up to renaming of variables).

by basically treating formulae in clause form and terms alike (as positive literals are structurally equal to function expressions, and complex clauses in normal form may be treated component wise). Furthermore, analogies do in general not only rely on an isolated pair of formulae from source and target, but on two sets of formulae. Here, heuristics are applied when iteratively selecting pairs of formulae to be generalized: Coherent mappings outmatch incoherent ones, i.e., mappings in which substitutions can be reused are preferred over isolated substitutions, as they are assumed to be better suited to induce the analogical relation. Once obtained, the generalized theory and the substitutions specify the analogical relation, and formulae of the source for which no correspondence in the target domain can be found may be transferred, constituting a process of analogical transfer between the domains.

The HDTP framework has successfully been tested in different application scenarios, and its use in several others has been proposed and theoretically grounded. [10] shows a way how HDTP can be applied to model analogical reasoning in mathematics by a case study on the inductive analogy-making process involved in establishing the fundamental concepts of arithmetic, [11] applies HDTP to conceptual blending in the mathematics domain by providing an account of a process by which different conceptualizations of number can be blended together to form new conceptualizations via recognition of common features, and judicious combination of distinctive ones. In [16], HDTP has been used in the context of solving geometric analogies. On the more theoretical side, [17] considers how the framework could fruitfully be applied to modeling human decision-making and rational behaviour, [18] elaborates on how to expand HDTP into a domain-independent framework for conceptual blending, and [19] provides considerations on the applicability of HDTP in a computational creativity context.

1.2   (Parameterized) Complexity Theory Preliminaries

As usual, P denotes the class of decision problems solvable in deterministic polynomial time, and NP denotes the class of decision problems solvable in non-deterministic polynomial time. We assume familiarity with the basic concepts of the theory of NP-completeness: NP-hardness, polynomial-time reductions, etc.

We briefly describe the basics of parameterized complexity theory. An instance of a *parameterized* decision problem $\mathcal{P}$ is a tuple (x,k), where $x \in \{0,1\}^*$ is a string describing the problem and $k \in \mathbb{Z}$, which is called the *parameter* of the problem (codifying other aspects of the problem besides n). We say a parameterized decision problem $\mathcal{P}$ is *fixed parameter tractable*, written $\mathcal{P} \in$ FPT, if it is solvable in time bounded by $f(k) \cdot |x|^{O(1)}$, where $f(k)$ is some computable function of the parameters and $|x|^{O(1)}$ denotes a polynomial of the length of the input. As suggested by notation, we let FPT denote the class of all fixed parameter tractable problems.

Given two parameterized problems $\mathcal{P}, Q$, a *parameterized reduction* is a function ϕ from $\mathcal{P}$ to Q such that the following holds, for an instance $(x,k) \in \mathcal{P}$:

1. $\phi(x)$ is computable in time $f(k) \cdot |x|^{O(1)}$, where f is a computable function of the parameter,
2. $x \in P$ iff $\phi(x) \in Q$, and
3. If k' is the parameter of $\phi(x)$, then $k' = g(k)$ for some function g.

Let the *weft* of a boolean circuit (containing only NOT gates, small AND and OR gates of fan-in ≤ 2 and large AND or OR gates of arbitrary finite fan-in) be the maximum number of large gates on any path from an input to the output, and let the *depth* be the maximum number of all gates on a path. Let $C[t,d]$ be the set of all circuits of weft at most t and depth at most d. Finally, define the *(Hamming) weight* of an assignment of truth values to the input variables of the circuit as the number of variables set to 1.

Problem 1. Weighted Circuit Satisfiability$[t,d]$
Input: A circuit C of depth d and weft t, a natural $k \in \mathbb{N}$.
Problem: Is there a satisfying assignment to C with weight k?

We say a parameterized problem $\mathcal{P}$ is in $W[i]$ if it is reducible by a parameterized reduction to Weighted Circuit Satisfiability$[i,d]$ for some constant d, and is $W[i]$-hard if every problem in $W[i]$ is reducible to $\mathcal{P}$ under a parameterized reduction. The assumption that $W[1] \neq \mathsf{FPT}$ can be seen as analogous to the assumption that $\mathsf{P} \neq \mathsf{NP}$ in classical complexity, although it is indeed conjectured that $W[i] \subset W[j]$ for any $i < j$. For a more in-depth introduction to parameterized complexity, see for instance [20,21].

2   Anti-unification: Initial Considerations

We begin our considerations on the complexity of anti-unification with some requisite definitions. HDTP uses many-sorted term algebras to define the input conceptual domains. A term algebra requires two ingredients: a *signature* and a set of *variables*.

Definition 1. *A many-sorted signature* $\Sigma = \langle Sort, Func \rangle$ *is a tuple containing a finite set Sort of* sorts, *and a finite set Func of* function symbols. *An n-ary function symbol* $f \in Func$ *is specified by* $f : s_1 \times s_2 \times \cdots \times s_n \to s$, *where* $s, s_1, \ldots, s_n \in Sort$. *We will consider function symbols of any non-negative arity, and we will use 0-ary function symbols to represent* constants.

Definition 2. *Let* $\Sigma = \langle Sort, Func \rangle$ *be a many-sorted signature, and let* $\mathcal{V} = \{x_1 : s_1, x_2 : s_2, \ldots\}$ *be an infinite set of sorted variables, where the sorts are chosen from Sort. Associated with each variable* $x_i : s_i$ *is an* arity, *analogous to the arity of function symbols above. For any* $i \geq 0$, *we let* $\mathcal{V}_i$ *be the variables of arity i. The set* $Term(\Sigma, \mathcal{V})$ *and the function* sort : $Term(\Sigma, \mathcal{V}) \to Sort$ *are defined inductively as follows:*

1. *If* $x : s \in \mathcal{V}$, *then* $x \in Term(\Sigma, \mathcal{V})$ *and* $sort(x) = s$.
2. *If* $f : s_1 \times s_2 \times \cdots \times s_n \to s$ *is a function symbol in* Σ, *and* $t_1, \ldots, t_n \in Term(\Sigma, \mathcal{V})$ *with* $sort(t_i) = s_i$ *for each i, then* $f(t_1, \ldots, t_n) \in Term(\Sigma, \mathcal{V})$ *with* $sort(f(t_1, \ldots, t_n)) = s$.

We refer to the structure $\langle Term(\Sigma, \mathcal{V}), sort \rangle$ *as a* term algebra, *often suppressing sort. If* $t \in Term(\Sigma, \mathcal{V})$ *then we define* $|t|$ *to be the number of variables appearing in t.*

From here on out, we will fix a term algebra $Term(\Sigma, \mathcal{V})$. In the next sections we will be considering several different forms of restricted higher-order anti-unification. First we introduce the *term substitutions* and *generalizations* allowed in first-order anti-unification.

Definition 3. *A* term substitution *is a partial function* $\sigma : \mathcal{V}_0 \to Term(\Sigma, \mathcal{V})$ *mapping 0-ary variables to terms. An application of a term substitution σ on a term is defined inductively by:*

1. $apply(x, \sigma) = \begin{cases} t & x \to t \in \sigma \\ x & otherwise. \end{cases}$

2. $apply(f(t_1, \ldots, t_n), \sigma) = f(apply(t_1, \sigma), \ldots, apply(t_n, \sigma))$.

Given two terms t, t' and a substitution σ such that $apply(t, \sigma) = t'$, then we call t' an instance *of t and t an* anti-instance *of t'. We will often shorten $apply(t, \sigma) = t'$ to $t \overset{\sigma}{\to} t'$, or $t \to t'$ if the substitution is clear from context.*

Let f, g be terms from a term algebra $Term(\Sigma, \mathcal{V})$. A generalization *of f and g is a triple $\langle h, \sigma, \tau \rangle$ where $h \in Term(\Sigma, \mathcal{V})$ and σ, τ are substitutions such that $h \overset{\sigma}{\to} f$ and $h \overset{\tau}{\to} g$. The generalization $\langle h, \sigma, \tau \rangle$ is called the* least general generalization *(lgg) if for any generalization $\langle h', \sigma', \tau' \rangle$ of f, g, there exists a substitution ϕ such that $h' \overset{\phi}{\to} h$.*

As mentioned earlier, the lgg is *unique* when considering only term substitutions. We can thus state the first-order anti-unification problem as follows:

Problem 2. First Order Anti-Unification
Input: Two terms f, g from a term algebra $Term(\Sigma, \mathcal{V})$
Problem: Find the least general generalization $\langle h, \sigma, \tau \rangle$ of f and g.

While this simple anti-unification problem has many efficient algorithms (see, for example, [12,22]), we will recall one algorithm which will form the basis of an efficient method for one of the forms of restricted higher-order anti-unification we consider. The algorithm will not operate on the terms themselves, per say, but rather rooted trees which can be naturally associated with each term.

Definition 4. *Let f be a term in $Term(\Sigma, \mathcal{V})$. The* tree form *of f, denoted T_f, is a rooted labelled tree defined inductively as follows.*

If f is a 0-ary (constant) term, then T_f consists of a single node r, labelled with $(f, 0)$. If f is an n-ary term, denote it as $f(t_1, \ldots, t_n)$. Then the root of T_f is a node r, labelled with (f, n), which has n ordered children $c_1, \ldots, c_n$. The child c_i is the root of T_{t_i}, the tree form of the term t_i.

Algorithm 1. FO-AntiUnify. **Input**: The tree forms T_f, T_g of two terms f, g with respective roots r_f, r_g. **Output**: An anti-unifier h of f and g, with two substitutions σ, τ.

Let (f, n) be the label of r_f and (g, m) be the label of r_g.
if f or g is a 0-ary term or $n \neq m$ **then return** $h = X, \sigma = \{X \mapsto f\}, \tau = \{X \mapsto g\}$
end if
Let h be the empty term, and σ, τ be empty substitutions.
Let $a_1, \ldots, a_n$ be the children of r_f, and $b_1, \ldots, b_n$ be the children of r_g.
for $i = 1, \ldots n$ **do** $\langle y, \alpha, \beta \rangle$ = FO-AntiUnify(a_i, b_i); Merge $\langle y, \alpha, \beta \rangle$ with $\langle h, \sigma, \tau \rangle$.
end for; return $\langle h, \sigma, \tau \rangle$.

This algorithm performs a depth-first search of the two input trees, replacing subtrees with variables if they do not match structurally. It plainly runs in time linear in the size of the two input terms. We will return to this algorithm shortly, as it also efficiently solves a slightly more general anti-unification problem.

2.1 Restricted Higher-Order Anti-unification

In [14], a restricted form of higher-order anti-unification was presented for use in HDTP, defined as any composition of a certain set of unit substitutions.

Definition 5. *The following are the types of unit substitutions allowed in restricted higher-order anti-unification.*

1. *A renaming* $\rho(F, F')$ *replaces a variable* $F \in \mathcal{V}_n$ *with another variable* $F' \in \mathcal{V}_n$:
   $$F(t_1, \ldots, t_n) \xrightarrow{\rho(F, F')} F'(t_1, \ldots, t_n).$$
2. *A fixation* $\phi(F, f)$ *replaces a variable* $F \in \mathcal{V}_n$ *with a function symbol* $f \in C_n$:
   $$F(t_1, \ldots, t_n) \xrightarrow{\phi(F, f)} f(t_1, \ldots, t_n).$$
3. *An argument insertion* $\iota(F, F', V, i)$ *is defined as follows, where* $F \in \mathcal{V}_n, F' \in \mathcal{V}_{n-k+1}, V \in \mathcal{V}_k, i \in [n]$:
   $$F(t_1, \ldots, t_n) \xrightarrow{\iota(F, F', V, i)} F'(t_1, \ldots, t_{i-1}, V(t_i, \ldots, t_{i+k}), t_{i+k+1}, \ldots, t_n).$$
   It "wraps" k of the subterms in a term using a k-ary variable, or can be used to insert a 0-ary variable.
4. *A permutation* $\pi(F, \tau)$ *rearranges the arguments of a term, with* $F \in \mathcal{V}_n$, $\tau : [n] \to [n]$ *a bijection:*
   $$F(t_1, \ldots, t_n) \xrightarrow{\pi(F, \tau)} F(t_{\pi(1)}, \ldots, t_{\pi(n)}).$$

A restricted substitution *is a substitution which results from the composition of any sequence of unit substitutions.*

Clearly, restricted substitutions are strictly more general than term substitutions. By considering different combinations of restricted substitutions we can define several different forms of higher-order anti-unification. Unfortunately, the lgg is no longer necessarily unique [14], and so we will instead consider decision version of the problems parameterized by the number of substitutions, variables, and types of variables used.

Problem 3. F Anti-Unification
Input: Two terms f, g, and a natural $k \in \mathbb{N}$
Problem: Is there an anti-unifier h, containing at least k variables, using only renamings and fixations?

Problem 4. FP Anti-Unification
Input: Two terms f, g, and naturals $l, m, p \in \mathbb{N}$.
Problem: Is there an anti-unifier h, containing at least l 0-ary variables and at least m higher arity variables, and two substitutions σ, τ using only renamings, fixations, and at most p permutations such that $h \xrightarrow{\sigma} f$ and $h \xrightarrow{\tau} g$?

Problem 5. FPA Anti-Unification

Input: Two terms f, g and naturals $l, m, p, a \in \mathbb{N}$.

Problem: Is there an anti-unifier h, containing at least l 0-ary variables, at least m higher arity variables, and two substitutions σ, τ using renamings, fixations, at most p permutations, and at most a argument insertions such that $h \xrightarrow{\sigma} f$ and $h \xrightarrow{\tau} g$?

We summarize our (parameterized) complexity-theoretic results of higher-order anti-unification in the following theorem, which will be our next focus.

Theorem 1

1. *F Anti-Unification is solvable in polynomial time.*
2. *FP Anti-Unification is NP-complete and W[1]-hard w.r.t. parameter set $\{h, p\}$.*
3. *Let r be the maximum arity and s be the maximum number of subterms of the input terms. Then FP Anti-Unification is in FPT w.r.t. parameter set $\{r, p\}$.*
4. *FPA Anti-Unification is NP-complete and W[1]-hard w.r.t. parameter set $\{m, p, a\}$.*

F Anti-Unification. The F Anti-Unification problem can easily be seen to be solvable in linear time by a simple modification of Algorithm 1. When we consider the roots of two subtrees labelled with f, g, if the arities of the terms (i.e. the number of children) match (say, they are both n) we can add a new fixation using an n-ary variable. Moreover, up to renaming, this implies that when considering the F Anti-Unification problem the least general generalization is unique, just like First-Order Anti-Unification.

FP Anti-Unification

Theorem 2. *FP Anti-Unification is W[1]-hard w.r.t. parameter set $\{h, p\}$, and NP-complete.*

Proof. FP Anti-Unification is clearly in NP, by just non-deterministically guessing a generalization $\langle h, \sigma, \tau \rangle$ and applying the substitutions σ and τ to h. We will show W[1]-hardness and NP-completeness by reduction from the well-known W[1]-hard problem k-Clique.

Problem 6. Clique

Input: A graph G and a natural $k \in \mathbb{N}$

Problem: Does G contain a clique, that is a complete induced subgraph, of size k?

The theorem follows by the well-known reduction between Subgraph Isomorphism and Clique. Let G, k be an instance of Clique, and let $E = \{e_i = (u_i, v_i)\}_{i=1}^{e}$ be the set of edges in G. Set $n = k(k+1)/2$, the number of edges in a k-clique. Define the term g using G as follows. We will begin with an e-ary term gr, which contains terms $e_i(u_i, v_i)$, one for each edge in E.

We define f in the same way using K_k, the complete graph on k vertices. That is we start with the term gr, which contains a term $a_i(b_i, c_i)$ for each edge (b_i, c_i) in K_k. However, we will pad f using $m - n$ ternary terms $t_i(x_i, y_i, z_i)$, with unique symbols used for each term. Therefore, both terms will look like so:

$$g = gr(e_1(u_1, v_1), \ldots, e_e(u_e, v_e))$$

$$f = gr(a_1(b_1, c_1), \ldots, a_n(b_n, c_n), t_1(x_1, y_1, z_1), \ldots, t_{e-n}(x_{e-n}, y_{e-n}, z_{e-n}))$$

Set $l = e - n + k, m = k, p = 1$.

Suppose that G contains a k-clique, denote $P \subseteq G$. Then clearly there exists an isomorphism ϕ from K_k to P, and so there exists a bijection between the edges of P and K_k. Using a single permutation, if necessary, move the edges in the terms f, g to occupy the first k arguments of gr, lining up the edges that are in correspondence under ϕ. We define the anti-unifier h of f and g like so:

$$h = gr(E_1(U_1, V_1), \dots, E_n(U_N, V_N), X_1, \dots, X_{m-n}),$$

using k 0-ary variables (corresponding to the *vertices*) for the terms inside the E_i variables, and using the E_i variables (corresponding to the *edges*), and define the fixation substitutions accordingly. Finally, use $n - k$ 0-ary variables to anti-unify the ternary terms at the end of f with the edges of g not occurring in the clique.

The reverse direction is simple, but technically tedious. One simply has to show that the term h described above is the only anti-unifier of f and g satisfying the values of the parameters (up to a renaming of the variables and a permutation of the subterms of gr). Once this is shown, it is simple to pull out a k-Clique in G, using the corresponding edge terms $E_i(U_i, V_i)$ occurring in the anti-unifier.

It seems that determining how to use permutations to order the subterms of f and g to maximize structural similarity is a quite difficult problem since even allowing *single* permutation implies computational hardness. On the tractability side, we can get a simple FPT result from restricting the arity and number of subterms of f and g.

Proposition 1. *FP Anti-Unification is in* FPT *w.r.t. parameter set* $\{s, p, r\}$, *where r is maximum arity and s is the maximum number of subterms of the input terms.*

Proof. Clearly, there are at most $\binom{s}{p}$ ways to apply permutations in any FP Anti Unification of f and g, and there will be at most $r!$ ways to apply each permutation. Running the algorithm for F Anti-Unification on each possible set of subterms gives an algorithm which runs in time at most $O(\binom{s}{p} r! \cdot n)$, where n is the number of symbols in the input.

FPA Anti-Unification We can get a parameterized hardness result for FPA Anti-Unification as a corollary of the above proof.

Theorem 3. *FPA Higher-Order Anti-Unification is* W[1]-*hard with respect to parameter set* $\{m, p, a\}$, *and* NP-*complete.*

Proof. This result follows from the reduction above, where we can additionally set $a = 0$.

3 Equational Theories and HDTP

HDTP uses equational theories, which are conjunctions of first-order formulae with equality over a term algebra, to describe the input analogical domains. In certain cases, we can reduce a higher-order anti-unification to a first-order anti-unification by introducing new terms constructed from the terms in input theories. In this section we will show that finding such an expansion of the input theories is computationally intractable. We begin with some definitions.

Definition 6. *Let $Term(\Sigma, \mathcal{V})$ be a term algebra. An equational theory E is a conjunction of statements of the form $t_1 = t_2$, where t_1, t_2 are first order formulae over terms from $Term(\Sigma, \mathcal{V})$. Given an equational theory E and an equation $t_1 = t_2$, we say that E implies $t_1 = t_2$, written $E \vdash t_1 = t_2$, if $t_1 = t_2$ can be proven from the input formulae, using any complete and sound proof system.*

Given a term t we denote the set of all subterms of t as $st(t)$ and the set of variables in t as $var(t)$.

Definition 7. *Let X be a set of terms. A set $\{t_1, \ldots, t_n\} \subseteq X$ is called* admissible relative to X *if $\bigcup_{i=1}^{n} var(t_i) = \bigcup_{t \in X} var(t)$.*

We can simplify some higher-order anti-unifications to first-order anti-unifications by introducing subterms built from the admissible sequences from the terms (for a description of how this reduces higher-order anti-unifications to first-order, see [8]).

Definition 8. *Let $Term(\Sigma, \mathcal{V})$ be a term algebra, let E be an equational theory defined w.r.t. this algebra, and let $f(t_1, \ldots, t_n) \in Term(\Sigma, \mathcal{V})$ be a term. An* expansion *of Σ and E relative to $f(t_1, \ldots, t_n)$ is constructed as follows: for each admissible sequence $\{u_1, \ldots, u_k\}$ relative to $st(f(t_1, \ldots, t_n))$, a new function symbol h and an equation $h(u_1, \ldots, u_k) = f(t_1, \ldots, t_n)$ are added to Σ and E, respectively.*

As shown in [8], the expanded equational theory can be used to reduce a selected class of higher-order anti-unifications to first-order anti-unifications. Now, confronted with the computational hardness results from Sect. 2.1, a naive attempt at dealing with the high complexity of higher-order anti-unification might be based on this seemingly simpler approach. Unfortunately, intuition here goes astray, and finding an admissible subset is actually quite a difficult problem by itself.

Problem 7. Function Admissible-Sequence
Input: A term $f(t_1, t_2, \ldots, t_n) \in Term(\Sigma, \mathcal{V})$, a natural $k < |st(f(t_1, t_2, \ldots, t_n))|$
Problem: Is there a set $X \subseteq st(f(t_1, t_2, \ldots, t_n))$ such that $|X| \leq k$ and X is admissible relative to $st(f(t_1, t_2, \ldots, t_n))$?

Theorem 4. *Function Admissible-Sequence is $\mathsf{W}[2]$-Hard (and NP-Complete) w.r.t. parameter k.*

Proof. Function Admissible Sequence is clearly in NP, by guessing a set $X \subseteq st(f(t_1, t_2, \ldots, t_n))$, and checking in polynomial time if $\bigcup_{i=1}^{n} var(t_i') = \bigcup_{x \in X} var(f(t_1, t_2, \ldots, t_n))$. We will perform a reduction from the $\mathsf{W}[2]$-Hard problem Set Cover [23]:

Problem 8. Set Cover
Input: A finite family of sets $S = \{S_1, \ldots, S_n\}$, a natural $k \in \mathbb{N}$.
Problem: Is there a subset $R \subseteq S$ with $|R| \leq k$ whose union is all elements in the union of S?

Let $S = \{S_1, \ldots, S_n\}$, be a family of sets and k' be a natural. Then it's straightforward to create a term $f(t_1, \ldots, t_n)$, where each subterm t_i is a $|S_i|$-ary term containing the elements of S_i as 0-ary terms. Finish by setting $k = k'$ in the definition of Function Admissible Sequence. In any solution of Set Cover or Function Admissible Sequence, the sets R and X are in direct correspondence with each other.

4 Interpretation of the Results

We want to provide some thoughts on the impact and the consequences of the complexity results from the previous sections, putting the obtained insights into a (cognitive) AI context. Presented with the complexity theoretic results, a critic may wonder why these results even matter for HDTP, for which undecidability follows quite straightforwardly from the undecidability of first-order logic. However it is important to note that HDTP is naturally split into two mechanisms: one which performs analogical matching of input theories, and one which performs re-representation of the input theories by deduction in first-order logic. It is the re-representational mechanism which is undecidable, where our above results apply solely to the analogical matching mechanism.

We focus on two results directly affecting HDTP. The $W[2]$-hardness of the function admissible-sequence problem (cf. Theorem 4) deserves special attention, as this clearly shows that problems can already arise when only treating with reductions from higher-order to first-order anti-unification. Here it should be kept in mind that this was HDTP's original mechanism for anti-unification, and thus was frequently used on a basic level when, in order to reduce a higher-order anti-unification to a first order anti-unification, expanding the theory by including first-order projections of any higher-order terms. The result showing that FP higher-order anti-unification is $W[1]$-hard (cf. Theorem 2) gives a hint at the difficulty introduced by the operations admissible within the restricted higher-order anti-unification on the complexity of the analogy-making process. Indeed, the only way that FP anti-unification can restructure the order of the terms is by argument permutations, and our results show that even allowing a *single* permutation is enough to imply computational hardness. If we contrast this result against the polynomial-time algorithm for F anti-unification, we have evidence that even a slight ability to restructure the input terms makes higher-order anti-unification a difficult problem to solve.

We now want to also present some remarks from a more integrated perspective. Mostly originating from within cognitive science, the recognition that human minds or brains are finite systems with limited resources for computation has led some researchers to advance the thesis that human cognitive capacities are constrained by computational tractability. This *Tractable Cognition Thesis* [24], if true, amongst others can serve researchers by limiting and narrowing down the space of computational-level theories of cognition. But this thesis can also have ramifications for work in AI, namely for the branch following the original artificial general intelligence (AGI) tradition in trying to create a system with human-like intelligence capacities. Adapting the *Tractable Cognition Thesis* to the new setting, converting it into a *Tractable AGI Thesis*, it seems recommendable to demand for computer models of artificial general intelligence to also be of the tractable type (i.e. polynomially-solvable) – as also all of the currently available computing systems are ultimately finite systems with limited resources, in this respect being very similar to the aforementioned human minds or brains.

Taking this stance, and additionally assuming that $P \neq NP$ (and $FPT \neq W[1]$) holds, the classical and parameterized hardness results presented in this paper cast a shadow on the suitability of the HDTP framework in its present state as basis for a general model for high-level cognitive capacities or a general cognitive architecture. Still, it should be noticed that the mere fact that HDTP in its present state is basically intractable does not mean that future versions cannot be made tractable: One of the main questions for future theoretical research in relation to HDTP will have to address the question of how HDTP's version of computing generalizations via restricted higher-order anti-unification can be further constrained in a meaningful way as to obtain maximal expressivity and applicability whilst still staying within the domain of polynomial solvability. Also, more parametrized analysis will be needed, showing which are the factors that really impact complexity, and which are aspects of a problem that are not really harmful. Secondly, even when being intractable, HDTP can still be put to good use, serving as a testbed for possible uses of analogy-making engines. Coming back to the AGI setting, although it might not be held likely that an intractable system will grow into a general architecture providing artificial intelligence at a human level, it can still be used for exploring the possibilities and limitations of theories and paradigms incorporating analogy as a cognitive function (as, e.g., in the context of the already mentioned cognitive capacities conceptual blending, creativity, and rationality), and thus finally also contribute on a theoretical level to the development of a generally intelligent system. Even though HDTP in its current form might not scale to applications to real-world problems under real-world constraints, when relaxing these constraints the system might still fruitfully be applied to proof-of-concept scenarios.

5   Conclusion and Future Work

In this paper, after a compact introduction to the overall Heuristic-Driven Theory Projection framework for computational analogy-making, we provided a complexity analysis of the key mechanisms underlying HDTP, together with a short reflection on the obtained results. The obtained classical and parameterized complexity results do not affect the overall usefulness and functionality of HDTP as a computational tool for implementing an analogy-making mechanism, but currently do set limits to HDTP's status as a cognitive system: Although analogy-making as cognitive capacity can be modelled, tractability of the system can in general not be assumed.

With respect to future work, the main task is in searching for possibilities to reduce the complexity whilst still maintaining the functionality of HDTP. Besides further investigations into the complexity-relevant parameters within the setting, we see three possible lines of work. First, a study of the true power of argument insertion from a complexity theoretic perspective. Using argument insertion in it's full generality, one can build any term incrementally by a sequence of argument insertions and fixations, which implies that it could be a source of much additional complexity. Next, a study searching possible restrictions on the representation language underlying HDTP, so as to limit complexity whilst still staying as expressive as possible (i.e. taking a step back from first-order logic into a less expressive but still suitable formalism). Finally, and perhaps most importantly, a direct address to the undecidability of the re-representational mechanism of the basic HDTP problem.

References

1. Schwering, A., Kühnberger, K.U., Kokinov, B.: Analogies: Integrating multiple cognitive abilities - guest editorial. Journal of Cognitive Systems Research 10 (2009)
2. Reitman, W.R., Grove, R.B., Shoup, R.G.: Argus: An information-processing model of thinking. Behavioral Science 9, 270–281 (1964)
3. Evans, T.G.: A heuristic program to solve geometric-analogy problems. In: Proceedings of the Spring Joint Computer Conference, AFIPS 1964, April 21-23, pp. 327–338. ACM, New York (Spring 1964)
4. Hofstadter, D., Mitchell, M.: The Copycat project: a model of mental fluidity and analogy-making. In: Advances in Connectionist and Neural Computation Theory. Analogical Connections, vol. 2, pp. 31–112. Ablex, New York (1994)
5. Falkenhainer, B., Forbus, K.D., Gentner, D.: The structure-mapping engine: Algorithm and examples. Artificial Intelligence 41, 1–63 (1989)
6. Gentner, D., Forbus, K.D.: MAC/FAC: A Model of Similarity-based Retrieval. Cognitive Science 19, 141–205 (1991)
7. Gentner, D.: Structure-mapping: A theoretical framework for analogy. Cognitive Science 7, 155–170 (1983)
8. Gust, H., Kühnberger, K.U., Schmid, U.: Metaphors and Heuristic–Driven Theory Projection (HDTP). Theoretical Computer Science 354, 98–117 (2006)
9. Schwering, A., Krumnack, U., Kühnberger, K.U., Gust, H.: Syntactic principles of Heuristic-Driven Theory Projection. Journal of Cognitive Systems Research 10(3), 251–269 (2009)
10. Guhe, M., Pease, A., Smaill, A., Schmidt, M., Gust, H., Kühnberger, K.U., Krumnack, U.: Mathematical reasoning with higher-order anti-unifcation. In: Proceedings of the 32st Annual Conference of the Cognitive Science Society, pp. 1992–1997 (2010)
11. Guhe, M., Pease, A., Smaill, A., Martinez, M., Schmidt, M., Gust, H., Kühnberger, K.U., Krumnack, U.: A computational account of conceptual blending in basic mathematics. A computational account of conceptual blending in basic mathematics. Journal of Cognitive Systems Research 12(3), 249–265 (2011)
12. Plotkin, G.D.: A note on inductive generalization. Machine Intelligence 5, 153–163 (1970)
13. Plotkin, G.D.: A further note in inductive generalization. Machine Intelligence 6, 101–124 (1971)
14. Krumnack, U., Schwering, A., Gust, H., Kühnberger, K.: Restricted Higher-Order Anti-Unification for Analogy Making. In: Orgun, M.A., Thornton, J. (eds.) AI 2007. LNCS (LNAI), vol. 4830, pp. 273–282. Springer, Heidelberg (2007)
15. Schmidt, M., Gust, H., Kühnberger, K.U., Krumnack, U.: Refinements of restricted higher-order anit-unification for heuristic-driven theory projection. In: Proceedings 34th Annual German Conference on Artificial Intelligence, Springer (2011)
16. Schwering, A., Gust, H., Kühnberger, K.U.: Solving geometric analogies with the analogy model hdtp. In: Taaten, N.A., van Rijn, H. (eds.) Proceedings of the 31st Annual Meeting of the Cognitive Science Society, pp. 1780–1785. Cognitive Science Society, Austin (2009)
17. Besold, T.R., Gust, H., Krumnack, U., Abdel-Fattah, A., Schmidt, M., Kühnberger, K.U.: An argument for an analogical perspective on rationality & decision-making. In: van Eijck, J., Verbrugge, R. (eds.) Proceedings of the Workshop on Reasoning About Other Minds: Logical and Cognitive Perspectives (RAOM 2011). CEUR Workshop Proceedings, Groningen, The Netherlands, vol. 751, pp. 20–31 (2011) CEUR-WS.org
18. Martinez, M., Besold, T.R., Abdel-Fattah, A., Kühnberger, K.U., Gust, H., Schmidt, M., Krumnack, U.: Towards a Domain-Independent Computational Framework for Theory Blending. In: AAAI Technical Report of the AAAI Fall 2011 Symposium on Advances in Cognitive Systems, pp. 210–217 (2011)

19. Martinez, M., Besold, T.R., Abdel-Fattah, A., Gust, H., Schmidt, M., Krumnack, U., Kühnberger, K.U.: Theory Blending as a Framework for Creativity in Systems for General Intelligence. In: Wang, P., Goertzel, B. (eds.) Theoretical Foundations of AGI. Atlantis Press (in press, 2012)
20. Jörg Flum, M.G.: Parameterized Complexity Theory. Springer (2006)
21. Downey, R.G., Fellows, M.R.: Parameterized Complexity. Springer (1999)
22. Kuper, G.M., McAloon, K.W., Palem, K.V., Perry, K.J.: Efficient parallel algorithms for anti-unification and relative complement (1988)
23. Cesati, M.: Compendium of parameterized problems, http://www.sprg.uniroma2.it/home/cesati/research/compendium/
24. van Rooij, I.: The tractable cognition thesis. Cognitive Science 32, 939–984 (2008)

A General Representation and Approximate Inference Algorithm for Sensing Actions

Hanne Vlaeminck[1,*], Joost Vennekens[1,2], and Marc Denecker[1]

[1] Department of Computer Science, KU Leuven
[2] Campus De Nayer, Lessius Mechelen, Sint-Katelijne-Waver

Abstract. Sensing actions, which allow an agent to increase its knowledge about the environment, are problematic for traditional planning languages. In this paper we propose a very general framework for representing both changes to the real world and to the knowledge of an agent, based on a first order linear time calculus. Our framework is more general than most existing approaches, because our semantics explicitly represents, for each point in time, not only the agent's knowledge about that timepoint, but also about the past and the future. By applying a general approximation method for classical logic to this framework, we obtain an efficient and sound but incomplete reasoning method.

1 Introduction

Classical planning assumes that agents have complete information about the world. A more realistic assumption, however, is that they only partially know their environment, and must use *sensing actions* to gain additional knowledge. Several approaches exist that formalize such reasoning [9,12,14,7,13,4,5]. One thing that is lacking from these approaches, however, is that their semantics do not (explicitly) model that, at every point in time, an agent can also have knowledge about both the past and the future, and not just about the current time point itself. For example, an agent might initially already know that he will *never* be able to do a certain action and that he therefore will not be able to reach a certain state. Conversely, by observing the effects of one of its past actions, the agent might learn that some property held at the time of this action, even if it currently no longer does. In this paper, we propose a more general semantic framework, based on a linear time calculus, which supports this.

The aforementioned approaches, as well as ours, all use a Kripke-style representation of the agent's knowledge. While this is semantically the right way of doing it, it is also computationally quite challenging. Therefore, several other approaches use more limited representations of knowledge with better computational properties [1,8,10,15]. Ideally, it would be possible to view such an approach as an incomplete approximation, in some sense, of a semantically correct approach. However, proving such a connection is often non-trivial [11]. An interesting property of our framework is that it allows us to apply a general approximation method for first-order logic (FO) [17] to obtain an incomplete method

---

* Hanne Vlaeminck is supported by IWT-Vlaanderen.

M. Thielscher and D. Zhang (Eds.): AI 2012, LNCS 7691, pp. 543–554, 2012.

for solving the projection problem in polynomial time. The soundness of this method follows immediately from the fact that this approximation is sound for FO in general. Even though the method is incomplete, it is able to reach conclusions about properties that must have held at an earlier point in time, even if they no longer hold now. This is something that other incomplete reasoning methods either cannot do [15,8,1], or can only do in an ad-hoc way [10].

2   Preliminaries

We assume familiarity with first order logic (FO). For simplicity, we consider only relational vocabularies (no function symbols of arity > 0). As usual, an *interpretation* S for a vocabulary Σ consists of a non-empty domain D, a mapping from each constant symbol c to a domain element $d \in D$, and a mapping from each predicate symbol P/n to a relation $R \subseteq D^n$.

Definition 1. *A* Linear Time Calculus vocabulary Σ_{ltc} *consists of*

- *a set of types, including a type* $Time$,
- *for every type* S, *a set of constants* Σ_S *of type* S,
- *a set* Σ_{stat} *of* static *predicate symbols without an argument of type* $Time$,
- *a set* Σ_{dyn} *of* dynamic *predicate symbols that have exactly one temporal argument;* Σ_{dyn} *is divided into a set* Σ_{act} *of actions and* Σ_{flu} *of fluents,*
- *a set* Σ_{init} *containing for every predicate* $P/n \in \Sigma_{flu}$ *a predicate* $Init\_P/n$–1 *having only the non-temporal arguments of* P.

Throughout this paper, we assume that every type S apart from $Time$ has only a finite number of constants and restrict attention to Herbrand interpretations of S, i.e., each constant is interpreted by itself. We will fix the interpretation of $Time$ to the natural numbers $\mathbb{N}$, and use constants $0, 1, \ldots$, the arithmetic functions $+$, and the comparison operator $\leq$, also all fixed to their usual interpretation in $\mathbb{N}$.

This paper uses the logic FO(ID) [3], an extension of FO with a construct to represent common forms of inductive definitions, such as monotone induction and induction over a well-founded order. Such a definition is represented by a set of logic programming-style rules of the form $P(\bar{t}) \leftarrow \varphi$, with φ an FO formula. The semantics of such a definition is given by a parametrized version of the well-founded semantics for logic programs, which construct an interpretation for the defined predicates (those that appear in the head of a rule) given an input interpretation for the open predicates (those that do not), by applying the rules in appropriate way. Due to space restrictions, we refer to [3] for details.

To represent a dynamic domain, one of the central problems is to define the values of the fluents at different points in time, in terms of their initial values and the actions that happen. The inductive definition construct of FO(ID) allows this to be done in a natural and elegant way [2].

Example 1. An agent has a glass, which can be clean or not. A glass can be used for drinking, which makes the glass dirty, and it can be cleaned by wiping it. The agent's room has a light, which can be switched on and off.

This domain can be represented in FO(ID) by the following inductive definition Δ_{flu}, which defines fluents $Clean(t)$ and $Light(t)$ in terms of their initial values $Init\_Clean$ and $Init\_Light$, and of the actions $Wipe(t), Drink(t)$ and $Switch(t)$.

$$\Delta_{flu} = \left\{ \begin{array}{ll} Clean(t+1) \leftarrow (Clean(t) \wedge \neg Drink(t)) \vee Wipe(t). \\ Clean(0) \quad \leftarrow Init\_Clean. \\ Light(t+1) \leftarrow (\neg Switch(t) \wedge Light(t)) \vee (Switch(t) \wedge \neg Light(t)). \\ Light(0) \quad \leftarrow Init\_Light. \end{array} \right\}.$$

3 Representing Knowledge and Sensing Actions

When an agent operates in a partially known environment, its actions will be constrained by its knowledge of the world. At the same time, its knowledge may also evolve through sensing actions. Let us extend Example 1 as follows.

Example 2. The agent may only drink if it *knows* the glass to be clean. If the light is on, then the sensing action of *inspecting* the glass will reveal if it is clean.

To handle such examples, we introduce two new language constructs. The first is a dynamic modal operator $K(\cdot, t)$ that refers to the agent's knowledge at time t.

Definition 2. *For a LTC signature Σ_{ltc}, a modal atom is an expression of the form $K(\varphi[\bar{x}], t)$, where $\varphi[\bar{x}]$ is a formula in Σ_{ltc} and $t \in \mathbb{N}$. We define $\mathcal{L}_K$ as the language that extends FO by allowing both atoms and modal atoms as base cases and closing under the usual operators $\wedge, \vee, \neg, \forall, \exists$. An $\mathcal{L}_K$-formula is called* objective *if no modal operator $K(\cdot, t)$ occurs in it and* subjective *if every atom occurs in the scope of such a modal operator.*

We will use formulas of $\mathcal{L}_K$ to express that an agent may perform certain actions only if it knows that its preconditions are satisfied.

Definition 3. *For a LTC vocabulary Σ_{ltc}, a knowledge precondition is a formula $\forall \bar{x}t \, (A(\bar{x}, t) \Rightarrow \varphi)$, where A is an action and φ a subjective $\mathcal{L}_K$-formula.*

The precondition that an agent may drink from a glass only if he knows that it is clean can now be expressed by the $\mathcal{L}_K$-formula $\forall t \, Drink(t) \Rightarrow K(Clean(t), t)$. Note that the formula φ in a modal atom $K(\varphi, t)$ may contain its own temporal argument, not necessary equal to t. For example, if the agent only wants to drink from a glass that has never been used before, this can be expressed as: $\forall t \, Drink(t) \Rightarrow K(\forall t' \, (t' < t \Rightarrow \neg Drink(t')), t)$. This is more general than most existing approaches, in which it is typically not even syntactically possible to refer to the knowledge in one situation about another situation.

These knowledge preconditions will actually be the only place in which we allow the modal operators $K(\cdot, t)$. On the one hand, this is motivated by the fact that the agent has no direct access to the real world, i.e., it can use only its own knowledge to decide upon its actions. On the other hand, the agent also only affects the state of the world through its actions: the real world does not respond to what the agent *knows* but only to what it *does*. For instance, if the agent enters the correct code into a safe, this will open regardless of whether the agent actually knew the code or was just guessing.

To represent the effects of sensing actions, we introduce the following construct.

Definition 4. *For a LTC signature Σ_{ltc}, a sensing definition is of the form:*

$$A(\bar{x}, t) \textbf{ senses } \xi[\bar{x}, \bar{y}, t+1] \textbf{ if } \gamma[\bar{x}, \bar{y}, t+1], \tag{1}$$

where $A \in \Sigma_{act}$, and both $\xi[\bar{x}, \bar{y}, t+1]$ and $\gamma[\bar{x}, \bar{y}, t+1]$ are FO formulas in which $t + 1$ is the only term of type Time. The action A is called a sensing action. *When $\gamma = \mathbf{t}$, the sensing action is called* unconditional.

Note that a sensing action performed at time t yields information about the state of the world at the next timepoint $t + 1$. For our running example, the *Inspect* action is described by the following sensing definition.

$$Inspect(t) \textbf{ senses } Clean(t+1) \textbf{ if } Light(t+1). \tag{2}$$

Putting this all together, we now arrive at the following.

Definition 5. *Let Σ_{ltc} be an LTC vocabulary. An $LTC_{K,S}$ theory consist of*

- *a inductive definition Δ_{flu} of the fluents,*
- *a constraint theory T_{constr} of FO formulas over $\Sigma_{act} \cup \Sigma_{stat}$ in which the action predicates appear only negatively,*
- *an FO theory T_{init} over Σ_{init} about the initial state of the fluents,*
- *a precondition theory T_{prec}, consisting of knowledge preconditions*
- *a set of sensing definitions, denoted by T_{sense} .*

The purpose of the theory T_{constr} is to express constraints on the occurrences of actions. However, we only allow to specify that actions cannot occur in certain circumstances, and not that they must sometimes occur. This will make it easier to define the semantics. The theory T_{init} specifies *all that is known* about the initial situation. In our running example, we take T_{init} to be empty, meaning that the agent knows *nothing* about the initial situation. Our Δ_{flu} is as in Example 1, T_{constr} is also empty, T_{prec} consists of the single formula $\forall t\, Drink(t) \Rightarrow K(Clean(t), t)$ and T_{sense} contains expression (2).

3.1   Semantics

Our semantics needs to consider both the real world I and the agent's knowledge about I. To represent this knowledge, we use a set of interpretations $\mathcal{K}$, which we refer to as *possible worlds*. Since each possible world $K \in \mathcal{K}$ interprets the entire vocabulary, it specifies the value of all actions and fluents at *each* point in time.

Definition 6. *A knowledge structure $\mathcal{S}$ is a pair $(I, \mathcal{K})$ of an interpretation I and a set of interpretations $\mathcal{K}$, such that all these interpretations have the same vocabulary (and therefore also the same domain).*

Because we only care about knowledge, and not beliefs that might be false, we often require that knowledge structures be *consistent*, in the sense that $I \in \mathcal{K}$.

We first focus on the semantics of the sensing definitions. The purpose of these is to allow the agent to increase its knowledge. For a set Ψ of sentences, we denote by $\mathcal{K} \circ \Psi$ the set of all $J \in \mathcal{K}$ for which $J \models \Psi$. The smaller set of possible worlds $\mathcal{K} \circ \Psi$ now describes the agent's knowledge after it has learned Ψ in a situation where it already knew $\mathcal{K}$. We will now define a set of formulas Ψ that captures precisely what the agent learns from a sensing action. Without loss of generality, we assume that the theory T contains at most one sensing definition for each action $A \in \Sigma_{act}$. If the unique sensing definition for $A(\bar{x}, t)$ is of form (1), then we denote the formula ξ as ξ_A and the formula γ as γ_A.

Definition 7. *Given an interpretation I, a sensing action $A(\bar{x}, t)$ and a time point $i \in \mathbb{N}$, the* scope *of $A(\bar{x}, i)$ in I is defined as the set of all tuples $(\bar{d}, \bar{e})$ of constants such that $I \models \gamma_A[\bar{d}, \bar{e}, i + 1]$.*

For the sensing action $Inspect(t)$ in our running example, a timepoint i and an interpretation I, the scope is either the empty tuple $\{()\}$ (i.e., "true") $I \models Light(i)$ or the empty set $\emptyset$ (i.e., "false") if $I \not\models Light(i)$.

Definition 8. *For a sensing action $A(\bar{x}, t)$, an interpretation I, a tuple $\bar{d}$ of constants, and a time point i, the* effect *of $A(\bar{d}, i)$ given I is denoted as $Eff_I(A(\bar{d}, i))$ and defined as the set of all formulas $\varphi[\bar{d}, \bar{e}, i + 1]$ such that φ is either ξ_A or $\neg \xi_A$, the tuple $(\bar{d}, \bar{e})$ is in the scope of $A(\bar{x}, i)$, and $I \models \varphi[\bar{d}, \bar{e}, i + 1]$.*

Intuitively, the set $Eff_I(A(\bar{d}, i))$ contains all ground formulas that the agent learns by performing the sensing action $A(\bar{d}, i)$ in the real world I. To illustrate with our running example, consider an interpretation I such that $Light^I = \mathbb{N}$, $Clean^I = \{\}$ and $Inspect^I = \{0\}$. Then $Eff_I(Inspect(0)) = \{\neg Clean(1)\}$.

In addition to the results of its sensing actions, the agent also has a second source of information, namely, it will also know its own actions at each timepoint. Thus, in total, the agent gains the following information at timepoint i.

Definition 9. *For a time point $i \geq 0$ and an interpretation I, the* action information *at i, denoted $Act_I(i)$, is defined as the set of all literals $L(\bar{d}, i)$ such that $I \models L(\bar{d}, i)$ and $L(\bar{d}, i)$ is either $A(\bar{d}, i)$ or $\neg A(\bar{d}, i)$ with $A \in \Sigma_{act}$. The ith* update *of I, denoted $Upd_I(i)$, is defined as the union of $Act_I(i)$ and all sets $Eff_I(A(\bar{d}, i))$ for which $I \models A(\bar{d}, i)$ and $A(\bar{x}, t)$ is a sensing action.*

Note that this definition assumes that an agent knows its actions and its effects the next timepoint after performing them. For our running example, we have that $Upd_I(0) = \{\neg Wipe(0), \neg Switch(0), Inspect(0), \neg Clean(1)\}$, and $Upd_I(1) = \{\neg Wipe(1), \neg Switch(1), \neg Inspect(1)\}$. We now arrive at the following update operation.

Definition 10. *For a knowledge structure $\mathcal{S} = (I, \mathcal{K})$, the i-*update *of $\mathcal{S}$, denoted by $\mathcal{S} \circ i$, is defined as $(I, \mathcal{K} \circ Upd_I(i))$.*

After performing such an update, the agent's new knowledge $\mathcal{K} \circ Upd_I(i)$ will contain all the information that was obtained as a direct result of its sensing actions at time $i - 1$. However, by *reflecting* on the difference between $\mathcal{K}$ and $\mathcal{K} \circ Upd_I(i)$, the agent may be able to deduce more information. For instance, if in our running example an *Inspect* action fails to produce knowledge about whether the glass is clean, the agent could deduce that the light must be switched off. So, in addition to ruling out all worlds $J \not\models Upd_I(i)$, the agent could also rule out all worlds $J \in \mathcal{K}$ in which the knowledge contained in $\mathcal{K} \circ Upd_J(i)$ would not have been the same as the knowledge $\mathcal{K} \circ Upd_I(i)$ that the agent actually gained in the real world. Let us define that two knowledge structures $\mathcal{S} = (I, \mathcal{K})$ and $\mathcal{S}' = (I', \mathcal{K}')$ are *epistemically equal*, denoted $\mathcal{S} =_k \mathcal{S}'$, if $\mathcal{K} = \mathcal{K}'$. We now define a *second-order* update operator $(I, \mathcal{K}) \circ^2 i$ as follows.

Definition 11. *For a knowledge structure* $\mathcal{S} = (I, \mathcal{K})$, *if* $\mathcal{S} \circ i = (I, \mathcal{K}')$, *then* $(I, \mathcal{K}) \circ^2 i$ *is defined as* $(I, \mathcal{K}'')$ *with* $\mathcal{K}'' = \{J \in \mathcal{K}' \mid (I, \mathcal{K}) \circ i =_k (J, \mathcal{K}) \circ i\}$.

Based on this principle, we can define an infinite sequence $(\circ^n)_{n \in \mathbb{N}}$ of ever more introspective update operators.

Definition 12. *For a knowledge structure* $\mathcal{S} = (I, \mathcal{K})$, *if* $\mathcal{S} \circ^n i = (I, \mathcal{K}_n)$, *then* $(I, \mathcal{K}) \circ^{n+1} i = (I, \mathcal{K}_{n+1})$ *with* $\mathcal{K}_{n+1} = \{J \in \mathcal{K}_n \mid (I, \mathcal{K}) \circ^n i =_k (J, \mathcal{K}) \circ^n i\}$. *We define* • *as the limit of this sequence, i.e.,* $\mathcal{S} \bullet i = \bigcap_{n \in \mathbb{N}} \mathcal{S} \circ^n i$.

The limit • is a strong operator, which allows the agent to reason about its knowledge of its knowledge of its knowledge of ... of its knowledge of the world. Luckily, however, it is never necessary to go more than two levels deep.

Proposition 1. *For any set of sensing definitions,* • $= \circ^2$. *Moreover, if all of the sensing actions are* unconditional, *then even* • $= \circ$.

This operator • now allows us to define how the agent's knowledge will evolve over time, starting from an initial knowledge structure $\mathcal{S}_0 = (I, \mathcal{K})$.

Definition 13. *A knowledge line* $\mathbb{K}$ *is a function that maps each time point* $i \in \mathbb{N}$ *to a set* $\mathbb{K}(i)$ *of possible worlds. For an initial knowledge structure* $\mathcal{S}_0 = (I, \mathcal{K})$, *we construct the sequence* $(\mathcal{S}_i)_{i \geq 0}$ *such that* $\mathcal{S}_{i+1} = \mathcal{S}_i \bullet i$. *By* $\overline{\mathcal{S}_0}$, *we denote the associated knowledge line* $\mathbb{K}$, *i.e., for each* i, $\mathbb{K}(i)$ *is such that* $\mathcal{S}_i = (I, \mathbb{K}(i))$.

If $\mathcal{K}$ represents the agent's initial knowledge (note again that $\mathcal{K}$ may contain knowledge about *any* point in time), then a knowledge line $\overline{(I, \mathcal{K})}$ represents how this knowledge evolves over time according to the real world I. A *knowledge line structure* is now a pair $(I, \mathbb{K})$ of an interpretation I and a knowledge line $\mathbb{K}$. Since $I \models Upd_I(i), \forall i$, we have that for a consistent knowledge structure $(I, \mathcal{K})$, for each i, $I \in \mathbb{K}(i)$, where $\mathbb{K} = \overline{(I, \mathcal{K})}$. It is now straightforward to evaluate formulas of $\mathcal{L}_K$ in a knowledge line structure $(I, \mathbb{K})$.

Definition 14. *For a formula* φ *of* $\mathcal{L}_K$, *a knowledge line structure* $(I, \mathbb{K})$ *and a variable assignment* θ, *we inductively define the relation* $(I, \mathbb{K}), \theta \models \varphi$ *as follows:*

- *For an atom* $P(\bar{t})$, *we define* $(I, \mathbb{K}), \theta \models P(\bar{t})$ *iff* $I, \theta \models P(\bar{t})$;

- For $K(\varphi, t)$, we define $(I, \mathbb{K}), \theta \models K(\varphi, t)$ iff for each $J \in \mathbb{K}(t)$, $J, \theta \models \varphi$;
- The cases for $\neg, \wedge, \vee, \forall, \exists$ are defined as usual.

For sentences, the variable assignment θ is irrelevant and we omit it from notation.

This evaluation is a multi-modal extension of the standard Kripke evaluation, since each $K(\cdot, t)$ is evaluated w.r.t. the set $\mathbb{K}(t)$ of possible worlds. We now have the following obvious way of defining the semantics of a $LTC_{K,S}$ theory T.

Definition 15. *A knowledge structure $\mathcal{S} = (I, \mathcal{K})$ is a* weak model *of T if $(I, \mathcal{K})$ is consistent, and for each $J \in \mathcal{K}$, it holds that $(J, \overline{\mathcal{S}}) \models T$.*

Every possible world in $\mathcal{K}$ represents a world such that with $\mathcal{K}$ as initial knowledge, the theory (that is, both non-epistemic and epistemic constraints) are satisfied. Note that this definition of weak model is completely symmetric in the sense that each $J \in \mathcal{K}$ is just as plausible for the agent, i.e., if $(I, \mathcal{K})$ is a weak model of T, then $(J, \mathcal{K})$ is a *weak model* for each $J \in \mathcal{K}$.

A limitation of weak models is that they do not restrict the agent's knowledge about the initial situation: the agent must know *at least* the theory T_{init}, but is not prevented from arbitrarily knowing more. In our running example, the theory T_{init} is empty, so the agent cannot know whether the light is initially on or off (or, to be more precise, the agent *initially* does not know this, even though it is possible that later sensing actions will reveal that the light was actually on or off all along). Our theory now indeed correctly has a weak model $(I, \mathcal{K})$ in which $\mathcal{K}$ is simply the set of all possible interpretations in which $Inspect(0)$ holds. However, there is also a weak model $(I, \mathcal{K}')$ where $\mathcal{K}'$ contains only interpretations J in which the light is always on, even though the agent should not know this.

As a final step, our semantics will therefore select precisely those weak models in which the agent knows *only* what it should, and nothing more. The agent's initial knowledge about the initial situation should consist of all models of T_{init}. Of course, the agent initially also has knowledge about the future timepoint 1. This should consist of all that is possible given the agent's initial knowledge about timepoint 0 and the theories Δ_{flu}, T_{constr} and T_{prec}. And so on for the initial knowledge about the next timepoints $i \geq 2$. To define our semantics properly, we first define when two sets of possible worlds contain the same knowledge about the time points up to some $i \in \mathbb{N}$.

Definition 16. *We write $I \overset{f}{\sim}_i J$ if I and J coincide on the static predicates (i.e., for each static predicate P, $P^I = P^J$) and on the fluents for all $t \leq i$ (i.e., for each fluent predicate P and each correctly typed tuple $\bar{d}$ whose temporal argument t is such that $t \leq i$, it holds that $\bar{d} \in P^I$ iff $\bar{d} \in P^J$). Similarly, we write $I \overset{a}{\sim} J$ if I and J coincide on the static predicates and on the actions for all $t \leq i$. Given two possible world sets $\mathcal{K}_1$ and $\mathcal{K}_2$, we write $\mathcal{K}_1 \sim_i \mathcal{K}_2$ iff for each $I \in \mathcal{K}_1$ there is a $J \in \mathcal{K}_2$ such that $I \overset{f}{\sim}_i J$ and $I \overset{a}{\sim}_{i-1}$, and vice versa.*

We now define a sequence of ever smaller possible world sets, in which we gradually eliminate the weak models in which the agent has unwarranted knowledge.

Definition 17. *We define a sequence* $(\mathcal{K}_i)_{i \geq 0}$ *as follows:*

- $\mathcal{K}_0 = \{I \mid \exists \mathcal{K} \text{ such that } (I, \mathcal{K}) \text{ is a weak model.}\}$
- $\mathcal{K}_{i+1} = \{I \mid \exists \mathcal{K} \sim_i \mathcal{K}_i \text{ such that } (I, \mathcal{K}) \text{ is a weak model.}\}$

The limit of this sequence can now be used for the agent's initial knowledge.

Proposition 2. *For a theory* T, *the sequence* $(\mathcal{K}_i)_{i \geq 0}$ *defined above is descending, and thus has a limit, which we will denote by* $\mathcal{K}_\infty$. *Given an interpretation* I, *if the knowledge structure* $(I, \mathcal{K}_\infty)$ *is consistent, then it is a weak model.*

This now leads to the following definition of our semantics.

Definition 18. *A weak model* $(I, \mathcal{K})$ *is a* model *of* T *if* $\mathcal{K}$ *is the limit of the sequence* $(\mathcal{K}_i)_{i \geq 0}$ *(as defined in Definition 17).*

The question that remains now is whether models of a theory T indeed know nothing more about time 0 then specified by T_{init}. First let us look at the simple case where T_{prec} is empty. A weak model $(I, \mathcal{K})$ is a model iff $\mathcal{K} = \{J \mid J \models \Delta_{fu} \wedge T_{constr} \wedge T_{init}\}$. It is clear that this $\mathcal{K}$ indeed has minimal knowledge about $t = 0$. In its full generality, $LTC_{K,S}$ allows some unintuitive constraints to be expressed, such as stating that an agent's current action depends on its future knowledge. It turns out that such theories can lead to models that not always have minimal knowledge. We therefore restrict attention to a more sensible fragment, in which the agent's current actions depend only on its current knowledge about current or past events.

Definition 19. *An* $LTC_{K,S}$ *theory* T *is called a* basic action theory *if all of its knowledge preconditions are of the form* $\forall \bar{x} t \, A(\bar{x}, t) \Rightarrow K(\varphi[\bar{x}, t'], t)$, *where* $t' \leq t$.

It is possible to define a concept of 'minimal initial knowledge', that formalizes our informal description on the previous page. Because of space constraints we refrain from giving it here, but it turns out that with this formal definition, one can prove that basic action theories indeed have minimal initial knowledge.

4 An Approximative Algorithm for the Projection Problem

A basic reasoning problem in temporal systems is the *projection problem*: given an action theory that formalizes the temporal domain, determine whether a formula holds after a sequence of actions is performed. In the context of incomplete information, we typically want to know whether the agent *knows* that a certain formula holds, since this will allow us to determine whether the preconditions to its actions are satisfied as well as whether it knows that it has reached its goal. Up to timepoint i, the information that the agent has so far learned about the real world I is precisely $Upd_I^<(i) = \bigcup_{j<i} Upd_I(j)$. We write $I \sim_i J$ to say that J coincides with I on these formulas $Upd_I^<(i)$, i.e., for each $\varphi \in Upd_I^<(i)$, $I \models \varphi$ iff $J \models \varphi$. The projection problem can now be defined as follows.

Definition 20. *Given a* $LTC_{K,S}$ *theory* T, *an interpretation* I, *a timepoint* i *and a formula* φ, *the* projection problem *is the problem of deciding whether for all models* $(J, \mathcal{K})$ *of* T *such that* $J \sim_i I$, *it holds that* $(J, \mathcal{K}) \models K(\varphi, i)$.

Typically, this problem is only of interest for interpretations I in which the agent does not perform impossible actions (i.e., there exists some $\mathcal{K}$ such that $(I, \mathcal{K}) \models T$), so we will assume this is the case. We can therefore forget about the knowledge preconditions. Once we know the information that the agent has sensed, as it is recorded in $Upd_I^{\leq}(i)$, also the sensing definitions become irrelevant. Our method will therefore only look at the following theory.

Definition 21. *For an* $\mathcal{L}_{K,S}$ *theory* T, *an interpretation* I *such that* $(I, \mathcal{K}) \models T$ *for some* $\mathcal{K}$, *and a timepoint* i, *let* $T_{proj}^{I,i}$ *be the theory* $\{\Delta_{flu}, T_{init}, T_{constr}, Upd_I^{\leq}(i)\}$.

As the following proposition shows, we can use the set of all models of $T_{proj}^{I,i}$ as a sound approximation of the agent's real knowledge at timepoint i.

Proposition 3. *Given a model* $(I, \mathcal{K})$ *of a basic action theory* T, *let* $\mathcal{M}$ *be the set of all models (in the classical FO sense) of* $T_{proj}^{I,i}$. *Then* $\mathcal{M}$ *is a superset of the agent's knowledge at time* i *according to* $\mathbb{K} = \overline{(I, \mathcal{K})}$, *i.e.,* $\mathcal{M} \supseteq \mathbb{K}(i)$.

The theory $T_{proj}^{I,i}$ incorporates the knowledge that the agent has gained through his sensing actions by simply including $Upd_I^{\leq}(i)$. However, knowledge that the agent might gain through introspection is therefore not taken into account. In other words, this theory represents the $\circ$ operator instead of $\bullet$, and this is what accounts for its possible incompleteness. As shown earlier, however, these two operators are identical for theories containing only unconditional sensing actions.

Proposition 4. *Given a basic action theory* T *that contains only unconditional sensing actions, let* $(I, \mathcal{K})$ *be a model of* T *and* $\mathcal{M}$ *the set of all models of* $T_{proj}^{I,i}$. *Then* $\mathcal{M}$ *and* $\mathbb{K}(i)$ *have the same knowledge about all timepoints* $j \leq i$, *i.e., for each formula* $\varphi[j]$ *with* $j \leq i$, *we have:* $\forall J \in \mathcal{M}, J \models \varphi[j]$ *iff* $\forall J \in \mathbb{K}(i), J \models \varphi[j]$.

Finding out whether a formula holds in all models of a first order theory is co-NP complete. Since applications such as planning need to solve the projection problem as an atomic step, a direct application of the above proposition would be infeasible in practice. However, it is possible to efficiently approximate the set of all models of a theory. We will use here a general approximation method for FO(ID), that efficiently allows us to detect that a formula holds in all models of a theory [17,16]. While we lack space to recall this method in detail, the essence is as follows. An FO(ID) theory T over a vocabulary Σ is syntactically transformed into an inductive definition $Approx(T)$ over a new vocabulary that contains, for every predicate $P/n \in \Sigma$, two predicates P^{ct}/n and P^{cf}/n that represent whether P is certainly true (i.e., true in all models of T) or certainly false (i.e., false in all models of T). The definition $Appox(T)$ has the property that if $Approx(T) \models P^{ct}(\bar{d})$, then $T \models P(\bar{d})$ (see [16], proposition 5.4) and similar for P^{cf}. In addition, $Approx(T)$ also defines a number of predicates A_{φ}^{ct} and A_{φ}^{cf} that tell us whether certain non-atomic formulas φ (or their negations, respectively) are entailed by T. In a finite domain, the model of an inductive definition can be computed in *polynomial time*. Since we only need natural numbers up to i to solve the projection problem, $Approx(T_{proj}^{I,i})$ therefore offers a polynomial time approximate solution to the projection problem.

Example 3. We have a gun that can be loaded or not, and a turkey, which can be alive or dead. Shooting kills the turkey if the gun was loaded, and also unloads the gun. Finally, the agent can inspect the turkey to see whether it is dead.

$$\Delta_{flu} = \begin{cases} Alive(t+1) & \leftarrow Alive(t) \wedge \neg(Shoot(t) \wedge Loaded(t)). \\ Alive(0) & \leftarrow Init\_Alive. \\ Loaded(t+1) \leftarrow Loaded(t) \wedge Shoot(t). \\ Loaded(0) & \leftarrow Init\_Loaded. \end{cases}$$

$$T_{sense} = \{CheckAlive(t) \textbf{ senses } Alive(t+1) \textbf{ if } \textbf{t}.\}$$
$$T_{init} = \{Init\_Alive.\}$$

If, after shooting a turkey that was known to be alive, the agent discovers that the turkey is dead, it should be able to conclude that the gun was previously loaded, even though it also knows that it is currently no longer loaded. We consider the real world I in which $Shoot^I = \{0\}$, $CheckAlive^I = \{1\}$, $Alive^I = \{0\}$, $Loaded^I = \{0\}$, $Init\_Alive^I = \textbf{t}$ and $Init\_Loaded^I = \textbf{t}$. Let us define $\psi_1 = Alive(t)$, $\psi_2 = \neg Shoot(t) \vee \neg Loaded(t)$, $\varphi = \psi_1 \wedge \psi_2$. The definition $Approx(T_{proj}^{I,3})$ now contains, among others, the following rules.

$$\begin{cases} Alive^{ct}(t+1) \leftarrow A_\varphi^{ct}(t). \\ A_\varphi^{cf}(t) & \leftarrow Alive^{cf}(t+1). \\ A_{\psi_2}^{ct}(t) & \leftarrow Shoot^{cf}(t) \vee Loaded^{cf}(t). \\ A_{\psi_2}^{cf}(t) & \leftarrow A_\varphi^{cf}(t) \wedge Alive^{ct}(t). \\ Alive^{cf}(t) & \leftarrow A_\varphi^{cf}(t) \wedge A_{\psi_2}^{ct}(t). \\ Loaded^{ct}(t) & \leftarrow A_{\psi_2}^{cf}(t). \\ \quad \cdots \\ Init\_Alive^{ct} & \leftarrow \\ Shoot^{ct}(t) & \leftarrow t = 0. \\ Shoot^{cf}(t) & \leftarrow t = 1 \vee t = 2. \\ Alive^{cf}(t) & \leftarrow t = 2. \end{cases}$$

This definition is able to derive that, because the turkey is certainly not alive at 2, the conjunction $\varphi(1)$ cannot hold. Since there is no *Shoot* at timepoint 1, the second disjunct $\psi_2(1)$ is certainly true and so the first disjunct $Alive(1)$ must be false. Again, this means that the disjunction $\varphi(0)$ must be false. Now, it is the first disjunct $Alive(0)$ that is certainly true, since $Init\_Alive$ is true. Hence, the second disjunct $\psi_2(1)$ cannot hold. Since $\psi_2(1)$ is itself again a disjunction, neither of its disjuncts hold, and one of these is $\neg Loaded(0)$. Therefore, this approximation is indeed able to reason backwards in time to conclude that initially the gun must have been loaded. Moreover, it will also be able to conclude that, because of the $Shoot(0)$ action, $Loaded(1)$ and $Loaded(2)$ no longer hold.

5   Discussion and Related Work

Knowledge and sensing actions were first investigated in [9], and combined with a solution for the frame problem in [12]. Since then many other approaches have been developed. A large number of these cannot handle the *postdiction* reasoning of Example 3, i.e., they cannot draw the conclusion that at time point 2 the agent knows that the gun was initially loaded, but not anymore. To handle such examples, it must be possible to trace back the current objective state of the world to the state from which it originated. This is not possible in the approaches to sensing that were developed in the context of the action language $\mathcal{A}$ [13,15], since they only allow forward reasoning. An interesting feature of this approach, however, is that they also develop an approximation method, which transforms an $\mathcal{A}$ specification into an answer set program. This method has a very similar flavour to ours, and also to that of [8], which defines a three-valued progression operator. Again, since only progression is considered, postdiction is not possible here. The approach of [5] uses epistemic logic and has both progression and regression operations. However, the regression operator cannot take into account current knowledge about previous points in time, and therefore this semantics is also unable to handle our Example 3.

Some approaches do have the necessary semantic machinery in place, but simply lack the syntax to refer to knowledge about past or future events. This is the case for several approaches based on situation calculus or similar formalisms [12,14,7], where the structure of the situation terms tracks the history of each state. While it would therefore be less problematic to extend these formalisms to handle postdiction, this has, as far as we know, not yet been done. The same can be said about the dynamic epistemic logic of [4].

Rather than extend an existing approach, however, we have chosen to develop a new framework. The main motivation for this was to be able to apply the approximation method of Section 3.1 to obtain an efficient but incomplete solution to the projection problem. The approaches of [1,10] try to achieve the same goal by abandoning a Kripke-style semantics in favour of a a more limited concept of knowledge. This is done by introducing, for every original fluent F, a new "knowledge fluent" K_F. The way in which such a K_F changes over time is then explicitly modeled by separate update axioms. The approach of [10] is also able to handle knowledge about past or future events, and do postdiction reasoning. However, this is done in an algorithmic way, through a syntactical analysis of the specification. A disadvantage of these approaches in general is that it takes a substantial amount of work to prove a semantic connection between the knowledge fluents and the actual knowledge of that fluent [11]. The semantics of our approach allowed us to apply a general approximation method for FO, which means that soundness follows almost immediately.

Finally, [6] focuses mainly on belief change due to actions and observations where the agents may have erroneous beliefs. This is more general than our setting, since we assume that the agent's beliefs are always correct. As we do, they also allow beliefs about previous timepoints to change as a result of later (sensing) actions. However, their work does not focus on the knowledge representation side, assuming a given transition system instead of a logical representation.

In summary, this paper introduces a general framework for representing sensing actions, knowledge preconditions, conditional action effects, and knowledge about the past or the future. We also present a polynomial, sound but incomplete inference method for solving the projection problem, that we obtain directly by making use of a general approximation method for FO(ID). Even though this is an incomplete method, it still is capable to reach conclusions about properties that must have held at an earlier point in time, which is something that typical progression based reasoning methods cannot do.

References

1. Demolombe, R., del Pilar Pozos Parra, M.: A Simple and Tractable Extension of Situation Calculus to Epistemic Logic. In: Ohsuga, S., Raś, Z.W. (eds.) ISMIS 2000. LNCS (LNAI), vol. 1932, pp. 515–524. Springer, Heidelberg (2000)
2. Denecker, M., Ternovska, E.: Inductive situation calculus. Artificial Intelligence 171(5-6), 332–360 (2007)
3. Denecker, M., Ternovska, E.: A logic of nonmonotone inductive definitions. ACM Transactions on Computational Logic (TOCL) 9(2), Article 14 (2008)
4. van Ditmarsch, H., van der Hoek, W., Kooi, B.: Dynamic Epistemic Logic, 1st edn. Springer (2007) (incorporated)
5. Herzig, A., Lang, J., Marquis, P.: Action representation and partially observable planning using epistemic logic. In: IJCAI, pp. 1067–1072 (2003)
6. Hunter, A., Delgrande, J.P.: Iterated belief change due to actions and observations. J. Artif. Intell. Res (JAIR) 40, 269–304 (2011)
7. Lakemeyer, G., Levesque, H.J.: AoI: A logic of acting, sensing, knowing, and only knowing. In: KR, pp. 316–329 (1998)
8. Liu, Y., Levesque, H.: Tractable reasoning with incomplete first-order knowledge in dynamic systems with context-dependent actions. In: IJCAI, pp. 522–527 (2005)
9. Moore, R.C.: A Formal Theory of Knowledge and Action. In: Formal Theories of the Commonsense World, pp. 319–358 (1985)
10. Petrick, R.P.A., Bacchus, F.: Extending the knowledge-based approach to planning with incomplete information and sensing. In: ICAPS, pp. 2–11 (2004)
11. Petrick, R.P.A., Levesque, H.J.: Knowledge equivalence in combined action theories. In: KR, pp. 303–314 (2002)
12. Scherl, R.B., Levesque, H.J.: Knowledge, action, and the frame problem. Artificial Intelligence 144, 1–39 (2003)
13. Son, T.C., Baral, C.: Formalizing sensing actions a transition function based approach. Artif. Intell. 125(1-2), 19–91 (2001)
14. Thielscher, M.: Representing the knowledge of a robot. In: KR, pp. 109–120 (2000)
15. Tu, P.H., Son, T.C., Baral, C.: Reasoning and planning with sensing actions, incomplete information, and static causal laws using answer set programming. TPLP 7(4), 377–450 (2007)
16. Vlaeminck, H., Vennekens, J., Denecker, M., Bruynooghe, M.: An approximate inference method for solving ∃∀SO satisfiability problems. Technical Report (2012)
17. Wittocx, J., Denecker, M., Bruynooghe, M.: Constraint propagation for extended first-order logic. CoRR, abs/1008.2121 (2010)

Systematicity, Accessibility, and Universal Properties

William H. Wilson[1] and Steven Phillips[2]

[1] School of Computer Science and Engineering
The University of New South Wales
billw@cse.unsw.edu.au
[2] Mathematical Neuroinformatics Group
Human Technology Research Institute
National Institute of Advanced Industrial Science and Technology (AIST)
Tsukuba, Ibaraki, Japan
steve@ni.aist.go.jp

Abstract. Human cognition is a mixture of the systematic and the non-systematic. One thing we can do systematically can be described as follows. If we know about multiplication, and the facts of basic multiplication, and we know conceptually what division is, then we can utilise the facts of multiplication that we know in order to solve division problems that correspond to those facts. For example, once children know that $4 \times 7 = 28$, and once they understand about division, they can work out that $28/4 = 7$. Aizawa has defined standards for what counts as an explanation of systematicity. In this paper, in accordance with Aizawa's framework, we apply concepts from category theory to this problem, and resolve it by identifying the unique natural transformation that underpins this example of systematicity, and others in the same class.

1 Introduction

Systematicity is a property of cognitive systems whereby the capacity for certain cognitive abilities implies that capacity for certain other cognitive abilities. In their seminal paper [1], Fodor and Pylyshyn introduced systematicity to cognitive science/artificial intelligence as something that needed to be explained to have a theory of cognition. As the title of their article suggests, the authors emphasised the problem that systematicity poses for connectionism, in particular. So what is systematicity? The usual way of describing it is by example: if a person has the capacity to infer John as the lover from the statement *John loves Mary* then they will also have the capacity to infer Mary as the lover from the statement *Mary loves John*, and conversely. There are many other examples. This type of phenomenon is termed systematicity.

Naturally, connectionists responded to the explanatory challenge raised by [1], an early and prominent instance being [2]. Systematicity grew into an industry, initially focusing on whether connectionist architectures could be devised that met the systematicity requirements posed by Fodor and Pylyshyn. Yet, despite

M. Thielscher and D. Zhang (Eds.): AI 2012, LNCS 7691, pp. 555–566, 2012.

numerous attempts at addressing the systematicity problem in a way that did not simply implement a classical theory, no consensus was reached on a explanation (see [5]). Perhaps most interestingly, although connectionism has generally failed to provide an explanation for systematicity, so too has the classical approach (again, see [5]).

1.1   Characterising Systematicity

Before exploring the reasons why connectionism (and classicism) have not provided a complete explanation for systematicity, we give more detail how systematicity can be characterised. McLaughlin [3] noted that although there had been no clear, non-circular definition (as classes of examples) of systematicity, one can nonetheless provide useful schemas characterising instances of systematicity. McLaughlin provided five such schemas, all of which are of the form: *Ceteris paribus, a cognizer is able to mentally represent that P if and only if the cognizer is able to mentally represent that $\tau(P)$, where τ is some transformation of propositions P.* In McLaughlin's first collection of systematic schemata (which he calls SG1), P is aRb, where R is a relational predicate, and $\tau(P)$ is bRa. McLaughlin's SG1 takes in the *John loves Mary* example.

One could go a little further with McLaughlin [3], as in [4], and formulate a characterisation of systematicity: *in general, an instance of systematicity is when a cognizer has cognitive capacity c_1 if and only if the cognizer has cognitive capacity c_2.* In such a case, c_1 and c_2 are systematically related. This characterisation admits another type of systematicity, which we address in this paper.

1.2   Explaining Systematicity: Are Classical Systems Systematic?

The essential aspect of the systematicity problem is to provide an account whereby systematicity entails as a necessary, not just possible consequence of the assumptions and principles of the theory. So, although it is possible to devise a connectionist network that can represent John loves Mary if and only if it can represent Mary loves John, it is also possible to devise a connectionist network that can represent John loves Mary without being able to represent Mary loves John. So, without some principled reason for preferring the systematic over the non-systematic network, connectionism fails to *explain* systematicity [1].

Importantly, the classical explanation for systematicity also falls short in the same way, as analysed by Aizawa in great detail [5]. The ins and outs of his analysis are lengthy, but perhaps it can be summarised as follows. Aizawa argued that classicism failed to fully explain systematicity, because it is possible to design classical systems that will, for example, generate (or make inferences about) *John loves Mary* without being able to generate/infer about *Mary loves John.* Thus, context-free grammars, viewed as a way of producing sentences with compositional structure are normally chosen with grammar rules that support compositionality: $S \rightarrow Person\ loves\ Person$ and $Person \rightarrow John|Mary$ generate both *John loves Mary* and *Mary loves John,* and so on [6]. However, this does involve choices. If we had chosen $S \rightarrow Person1\ loves\ Person2,\ Person1 \rightarrow John|Mary$

and *Person2* → *Mary* then *Mary loves John* is no longer generated. Arguing along these lines, Aizawa inferred that systematicity is not a necessary property of classical systems, either. He characterised the problem by noting that the choice of grammar rules is *ad hoc*—the classical AI approach does not provide a *principled* way to choose between the alternative grammar rule sets. One rule set "works" and one doesn't, but that is not principle, it's model-fitting.

So now we are facing a problem: neither connectionism nor classicism provides a complete explanation for systematicity. Note that dynamic systems and Bayesian approaches suffer the same shortcoming. Like connectionism and classicism, dynamic systems and Bayesian models could be devised with the systematicity property, but equally dynamic systems and Bayesian models can also be devised without the systematicity property. What is required is an explanation that produces only the systematic models, and none has been forthcoming classicists, connectionists, Bayesian or dynamic systems modellers.

1.3   A Category Theory Explanation: Synopsis

In the face of this problem, we turned to an alternative approach that uses a branch of mathematics called Category Theory to explain systematicity without the need to introduce additional assumptions [6,16,4]. In Section 2, we provide some formal background to our category theory explanation; here, we summarise the general form of our explanation, as we will use it later in explaining yet another type of systematicity.

Category theory provides a formal notion of a *universal construction*: a construction that is a component of all constructions within the context of interest. For example, suppose we need a construction for representing *John loves Mary*, and inferring John as the lover. Connectionist and classical frameworks provide many constructions for this purpose. The problem with these methods is that there is no guarantee that the method for representing *John loves Mary* is the same as that for *Mary loves John*. A universal construction (in this case a *categorical product*), by contrast, means that there is exactly one way each instance is constructed, i.e., via that universal construction. Thus, all capacities within a systematically related group are connected via that arrow in a unique way.

We used the notion of universal construction to account for systematicity with regard to the capacity to represent and infer from relationally and recursively definable capacities [6,16,4]. In this paper, we sketch how our explanation also extends to another form of systematicity, called *accessibility* (introduced next), in terms of universal constructions. For reasons of space, we omit some background category theory relating to systematicity, (see [6,16,4]).

1.4   Accessibility

First, we characterise *accessibility*. When a child learns multiplication of small natural numbers, they (eventually) learn a largish set of facts like $9 \times 7 = 63$. Just as with the pizza example (above), not only can they make the required inference given $9 \times 7 = \square$ (i.e., fill in the empty square), but they can also make related inferences given $\square \times 7 = 63$, $9 \times \square = 63$, and $9 \square 7 = 63$.

Once they are familiar with the concept of division of natural numbers, children can access these facts without further memorisation in order to do division of natural numbers, at least where the quotient is again a whole number: $63/7 = 9$ and $63/9 = 7$. Again, we are accessing the data via multiple routes.

We originally termed this phenomenon *omni-directional access*, but later adopted the less cumbersome term *accessibility* to refer to the same phenomenon. A fuller description of this cognitive phenomenon can be found in [7].

It is easy to see that accessibility is an instance of systematicity, in the broad sense defined by McLaughlin [3] and outlined above. We are saying, for example, that, given an suitable set of facts, one can answer questions like *Who ate a pizza?* if and only if they can answer questions like *What did Fred eat?* This fits the template definition of systematicity: i.e. when a cognizer has cognitive capacity c_1 if and only if the cognizer has cognitive capacity c_2.

Our aim in this paper is to outline a theory of accessibility that meets the requirements of systematicity. In Section 2, we give category theory background for our explanation of accessibility, which follows in Section 3. Our explanation has general implications for supposedly alternative notions of (connectionist) compositionality, presented in Section 4. Discussion is provided in Section 5.

2   Category Theory and Universality

In this section we will introduce enough category theory to provide a mathematical framework for our theory of accessibility and to allow us to demonstrate systematicity for this theory.

Category theory is a branch, or maybe an arch, of mathematics that deals with structure. It has previously been applied in a number of areas of computer science, though more scantily in cognitive science. In computer science, it is conspicuous in the design of aspects of modern functional programming languages, e.g. [8], but it has long been known in connection with automata theory e.g, [9], and it is relevant in standard and non-standard logics [10]. In cognitive science, while some of the fundamental ideas had been mentioned in the cognitive psychology literature as early as 1963 [11], the first detailed application of categorical ideas (commutative diagrams) appears to have been [12].

2.1   Categories: States and Transitions

Category theory in mathematics deals with common structures. It has been applied in theoretical physics (string theory) and in functional programming. From a computational perspective, a cognitive system is often regarded as a collection of cognitive states together with cognitive processes realising transitions between those states. In category theory, formal constructions reside in a *category* of some description, which consists of a collection of *objects* and a collection of *maps* between objects obeying certain rules. To help ground category theory concepts for the purposes of explaining systematicity, we will often interpret objects as sets of states and arrows as functions mapping states to states.

Definitions of basic category theory are available in a range of introductory texts on the subject, e.g. [13,14,15], but are recalled here for convenience.

Definition. A category **C** consists of a set of *objects* and a set of *arrows*, with the following properties: (i) every arrow f is associated with two objects, its *domain*, say a, and *codomain*, say b. This is usually written as $f : a \to b$; (ii) Given two arrows $f : a \to b$ and $g : b \to c$, where the codomain of f is the domain of g, we can form the composition $g \circ f : a \to c$; (iii) This composition is associative: if $f : a \to b$, $g : b \to c$, and $h : c \to d$ are composable arrows, then $h \circ (g \circ f) = (h \circ g) \circ f$. (iv) For every object $a \in \mathbf{C}$ there is an *identity* arrow 1_a. For identity arrows 1_a and 1_b and any arrow $f : a \to b$, $1_b \circ f = f = f \circ 1_a$.

Examples. 1. **Set**, the category of sets and functions: composition is composition of functions and identity arrows are identity functions from a set to itself.

2. **Vect**, the category of vector spaces and linear mappings: composition is composition of linear mappings and identity arrows are identity linear mappings from a vector space to itself.

3. A partially ordered set $(P, \leq)$ is a category, with objects the elements of the set P. Each relation $p \leq q$ is a unique arrow between p, q. Since $p \leq p$, there are identity arrows. Since $\leq$ is transitive, composition is defined.

4. **Poset**, the collection of partially ordered sets, is a category, with posets as objects and order-preserving maps as arrows.

5. A monoid M (that is, a set closed under an associative binary operation and possessing an identity element) is a category. There is a single object, and the arrows are the members of the monoid. The identity element is the identity arrow. (A familiar monoid is the set of all strings over an alphabet A.)

6. **Mon**, the collection of monoids, is a category, with monoids as objects and monoid homomorphisms as arrows.

Arrows are also often referred to as *maps* or *morphisms* (from *homomorphism*), typically in categories like **Set**, **Vect**, **Poset** and **Mon** where they are realised as functions between (structured) sets.

An arrow $f : a \to b$ is called an *isomorphism* if there is an arrow $g : b \to a$ such that $f \circ g = 1_b$ and $g \circ f = 1_a$.

2.2 Functors and Natural Transformations: Natural Constructions

If we regard categories as cognitive (sub)systems, then we can regard functors as relations between cognitive systems, possibly constructing cognitive processes from the components of other systems, and natural transformations as relations between such constructions. Functors preserve structure from one category to another, suggesting that they are important for an explanation of systematicity over structurally-related cognitive capacities. Natural transformations are important because they provide a formal basis for distinguishing constructions that are "natural" in a principled (rather than some arbitrary informal) way, suggesting that they are important for meeting Aizawa's explanatory standard.

Definition. If $\mathbf{C}$ and $\mathbf{D}$ are categories, then a *functor* $F : \mathbf{C} \to \mathbf{D}$ maps objects of a, b of $\mathbf{C}$ to objects Fa, Fb of $\mathbf{D}$ and also maps arrows $f : a \to b$ of $\mathbf{C}$ to arrows $Ff : fa \to Fb$ of $\mathbf{D}$, in a way preserves identity arrows and respects composition of arrows: that is (i) for $c \in \mathbf{C}, F1_c = 1_{Fc}$ and (ii) given $f : a \to b$, $g : b \to c$, $F(g \circ f) = Fg \circ Ff$.

Examples. One functor from **Vect** to **Set** is the forgetful functor that maps the vector space to its underlying set, and linear maps to functions. A functor from **Set** to **Vect** is the free vector space functor which maps a set to a vector space with the members of that set as the basis, and maps a function between sets to a linear map that maps the basis vectors as indicated by the function. We'll have more relevant examples of functors later.

The functors from $\mathbf{C} \to \mathbf{D}$ actually form the objects of a category. The arrows of this category are called *natural transformations*.

Definition. Given two functors $F, G : \mathbf{C} \to \mathbf{D}$, a *natural transformation* $\eta : F \to G$ is a collection of arrows ("components") in $\mathbf{D}$: one for every object $c \in \mathbf{C}$: $\eta_c : Fc \to Gc$ such that for every arrow $f : c_1 \to c_2$ in $\mathbf{C}$, $Gf \circ \eta_{c_1} = \eta_{c_2} \circ Ff$. This is summarised in a *commutative diagram*, in which compositions of arrows indicated by paths with the same start point and same end point are equal:

$$\begin{array}{ccc} Fc_1 & \xrightarrow{\eta_{c_1}} & Gc_1 \\ {\scriptstyle Ff}\downarrow & & \downarrow{\scriptstyle Gf} \\ Fc_2 & \xrightarrow[\eta_{c_2}]{} & Gc_2 \end{array} \qquad (1)$$

Since natural transformations are to be arrows, they must be composable: if $\eta : F \to G$ and $\mu : G \to H$ are natural transformations, then $\mu \circ \eta : F \to H$ has components $(\mu \circ \eta)_c : Fc \to Hc$ for each $c \in C$. The identity natural transformation $1_F : F \to F$ has components $1_c : Fc \to Fc$.

Hopefully, we've made it fairly clear why natural transformations are reasonable as morphisms of functors. Examples of natural transformations can be found in [13,14,15], and also in [6] (list reversal example) and [16] (in attached Text S2: clock example). This is addressed further in Section 4.

2.3   Universal Constructions

The final concept we need, which is central to our explanation of systematicity, is *universal construction*. A universal construction is a construction that captures an essential property shared by all instances in the category (system) of interest. In terms of cognitive processes, a universal construction is a process common to all processes, suggesting how systematically-related capacities are intrinsically connected. Moreover, all processes are composed of the universal process in a unique way, so no further assumptions are needed to guarantee systematicity, meeting Aizawa's explanatory standard.

The most general definition of universal properties is not very transparent, and goes beyond our current needs; it can be found in [13,16,4]. Here we shall describe the universality property of the more-familiar Cartesian products (and of categorical products in general). A Cartesian product is an instance of the more general categorical product, which we employed to explain systematicity with regard to particular relations (e.g., John loves Mary) in [6]. Here, we show how this construct is used to explain systematic connections between relations such as multiplication and division.

Definition. cf. [13,18]. A *product* of two objects a, b in a category $\mathbf{C}$ is a triple $\langle p, \pi_1, \pi_2 \rangle$ where $\pi_1 : p \to a$ and $\pi_2 : p \to b$, such that for any triple $\langle r, \rho_1, \rho_2 \rangle$ with $\rho_1 : r \to a$ and $\rho_2 : r \to b$, there is a unique arrow $u : r \to p$ such that $\pi_1 \circ u = \rho_1$ and $\pi_2 \circ u = \rho_2$. ρ_1, ρ_1 are called *projections* onto the factors a, b.

A categorical product is an instance of a universal construction, which we will use later to address accessibility. In the category **Set**, the Cartesian product $a \times b$ of two sets a, b has this property, with π_1 and π_2 being the projections $\pi_1(x, y) = x$ and $\pi_2(x, y) = y$. The product object, in any category, is often written as $a \times b$, rather than p. With this convention, the product condition is that there is a *unique* arrow u such that the following diagram commutes:

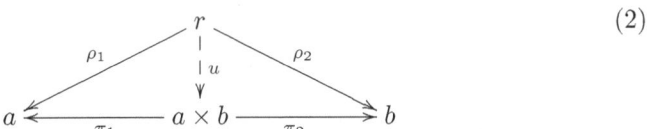

$$(2)$$

It is easy to check that if $\langle r, \rho_1, \rho_2 \rangle$ is also a product, then u is the unique isomorphism between r and $a \times b$ (that makes the diagram commute)—that is, products are unique up to a unique isomorphism. This uniqueness property is a feature of all universal constructions.

The Cartesian product of two categories can easily be checked to be a category, and we will use such constructions later in this paper.

3 A Uniqueness Property for Multiplication-Division

In order to meet Aizawa's requirement, we need to show why there is a unique correspondence multiplication and division. In fact, multiplication and division of natural numbers can be viewed as relations - for example, $(8, 3, 24)$ belongs to the multiplication relation because $8 \times 3 = 24$. If $F_1 = \{1, 2, 3, 4, 5, 6, 7, 8, 9\} = F_2$ are the sets of factors for multiplication of digits, and $P = \{a \times b | a \in F_1, b \in F_2\}$ is the set of products of digits, then the multiplication relation is a subset of the product $F_1 \times F_2 \times P$, and similarly the division relation (for the sets of numbers) is a subset of the product $P \times F_1 \times F_2$. The correspondence between these products is the function $\tau : F_1 \times F_1 \times P \to P \times F_1 \times F_2 : (f_1, f_2, p) \mapsto (p, f_1, f_2)$ (the notation $\mapsto$ (maps to) is a way that is sometimes convenient for expressing the action of a function: $h : x \mapsto y$ means $h(x) = y$. Our aim is to show that this function is natural and unique.

We'll do this in a more general setting, so that our argument can be applied to this transformation of other ternary relations. Given sets (or objects in any category with products) A, B, and C, we can form their product $A \times B \times C$. Technically, this product will, by a slight elaboration of the definition of product above, be a quadruple $\langle A \times B \times C, \pi_1, \pi_2, \pi_3 \rangle$, where $\pi_1 : A \times B \times C \to A : (a, b, c) \mapsto a$ is the projection onto A, and similarly π_2, π_3 are the projections onto B, C. This triple product has a uniqueness property like that of the product of two objects: given another such quadruple $\langle R, \rho_1, \rho_2, \rho_3 \rangle$, there is a unique arrow $u : R \to A \times B \times C$ such that $\pi_1 \circ u = \rho_1$, $\pi_2 \circ u = \rho_2$ and $\pi_3 \circ u = \rho_3$.

We shall use a construction analogous to one in [15]: we can also form the product $(C \times A \times B, \sigma_1, \sigma_2, \sigma_3)$, where $\sigma_1, \sigma_2, \sigma_3$ are respectively the projections onto C, A, and B. Since $C \times A \times B$ is a product of A, B, and C, there is a unique map $v : A \times B \times C \to C \times A \times B$ such that $\sigma_2 \circ v = \pi_1, \sigma_3 \circ v = \pi_2$ and $\sigma_1 \circ v = \pi_3$. Note the cross-over of subscripts. In the same way, since $A \times B \times C$ is also a product of A, B, and C, there is a unique map $w : C \times A \times B \to A \times B \times C$ such that $\pi_3 \circ w = \sigma_1, \pi_1 \circ w = \sigma_2$ and $\pi_2 \circ w = \sigma_3$.

Since $\sigma_1 \circ v = \pi_3$ and $\pi_3 \circ w = \sigma_1, \sigma_1 \circ v \circ w = \sigma_1$ and similarly $\sigma_2 \circ v \circ w = \sigma_2$ and $\sigma_3 \circ v \circ w = \sigma_3$, so by the uniqueness property of $C \times A \times B$, $v \circ w = 1_{C \times A \times B}$. A similar argument shows that $w \circ v = 1_{A \times B \times C}$. Thus u is an isomorphism, and so it is the unique isomorphism $A \times B \times C \to C \times A \times B$ satisfying $\pi_3 \circ w = \sigma_1, \pi_1 \circ w = \sigma_2$ and $\pi_2 \circ w = \sigma_3$.

Thus there is a unique correspondence between the two products. In fact, this correspondence is natural in A, B, and C as well. To see this, we have to set up functors and a natural transformation between them. If $\mathbf{C}$ is the category, then the two functors are $\times : \mathbf{C} \times \mathbf{C} \times \mathbf{C} \to \mathbf{C} : (A, B, C) \mapsto A \times B \times C$ and $\hat{\times} : \mathbf{C} \times \mathbf{C} \times \mathbf{C} \to \mathbf{C} : (A, B, C) \mapsto C \times A \times B$. The transformation $\tau : \times \dot{\to} \hat{\times}$ that we are going to show is natural, has components $\tau_{A,B,C} : \times(A, B, C) \to \hat{\times}(A, B, C)$, i.e. $\tau_{A,B,C} : A \times B \times C \to C \times A \times B$. These components are of course chosen to be the map that we have just shown is a unique isomorphism for each A, B, and C. In a category where objects have elements, these components are given by $\tau_{A,B,C}(a, b, c) = (c, a, b)$. To prove naturality, we need to show that for arrows $\alpha : A \to A_1$, $\beta : B \to B_1$, and $\gamma : C \to C_1$, the following diagram commutes:

$$
\begin{array}{ccc}
A \times B \times C & \xrightarrow{\ \tau_{A,B,C}\ } & C \times A \times B \\
{\scriptstyle \alpha \times \beta \times \gamma}\big\downarrow & & \big\downarrow{\scriptstyle \gamma \times \alpha \times \beta} \\
A_1 \times B_1 \times C_1 & \xrightarrow[\ \tau_{A_1,B_1,C_1}\ ]{} & C_1 \times A_1 \times B_1
\end{array}
\qquad (3)
$$

In a category where objects have elements, we assume $a \in A, b \in B, c \in C$:

$$
\begin{aligned}
(\gamma \times \alpha \times \beta) \circ \tau_{A,B,C}(a,b,c) &= \gamma \times \alpha \times \beta(c,a,b) \\
&= (\gamma(c), \alpha(a), \beta(b)) \\
&= \tau_{A_1,B_1,C_1}(\alpha(a), \beta(b), \gamma(c)) \\
&= \tau_{A_1,B_1,C_1} \circ (\alpha \times \beta \times \gamma)(a,b,c)
\end{aligned}
$$

That is, $(\gamma \times \alpha \times \beta) \circ \tau_{A,B,C} = \tau_{A_1,B_1,C_1} \circ (\alpha \times \beta \times \gamma)$, so the diagram commutes, and τ is natural in A, B, and C. Thus we have shown:

Proposition. The map $\tau_{A,B,C} : A \times B \times C \to C \times A \times B$ is a unique isomorphism natural in A, B, and C. It is unique with respect to the product structures of its domain and codomain.

A Cartesian product of two sets consists of *all* pairwise combinations of elements the two sets. Thus multiplication (as a relation) is not a whole Cartesian product: e.g. $1 \times 2 \neq 3$, but triple $(1,2,3) \in A \times B \times C$. Restriction to a subset of the Cartesian product is achieved by using a *pullback* (or *constrained product*), where additional morphisms restrict the construction to a subset of the Cartesian product. Pullbacks are a further instance of a universal construction, and their role in explaining systematicity parallels that of products. For reasons of space, we omit the details here. A detailed explanation of pullbacks, pullback functors and their roles in explaining (quasi-)systematicity, where some but not all possible combinations of constituents are systematically related, is in [16].

4   Natural Constructions

The argument against the classical explanation for systematicity is that it relies on stipulating specific modes of classical compositionality (i.e., grammars), since not all modes account for systematicity [5]. The general retort is to appeal to "canonical" constructions. But classicism has no principle that dictates such constructions, whatever they may be [5]. In this section, we show how the category theory notion of a natural transformation provides this principle, and how constructions that are not natural transformations do not support systematicity.

Some constructions seem more intuitively "natural" than others. To illustrate, suppose we have pairs of ordered blocks. A "natural" construction is to compose a representation of each pair of blocks from symbols representing each block, such that the first symbol in the representation of the pair corresponds to the first block and the second symbol corresponds to the second block. For example, the composition ab represents the pair of blocks (a,b). An alternative construction is to compose a representation of each pair as a number constructed from numbers representing each block. *Godel numbering* is one possibility, proposed as an alternative non-classical form of compositionality [17]. For example, $2^n 3^m$ represents the pair (n, m). Given that the numbers representing pairs of blocks are composed from prime powers (where each unique exponent n, m, corresponds to a unique block, and the prime numbers 2, 3, correspond to the first and second positions in the pair), we know from the *fundamental theorem of arithmetic* that the numbers corresponding to the individual blocks are recoverable by a prime decomposition procedure. Although both constructions are isomorphisms, there is a sense in which the second construction is less "natural" than the first. A Godel numbering scheme provides a unique way of getting from the object represented (such as the pair (n, m)) to the representation $(2^n 3^m)$.

To illustrate, consider an instance of Diagram 1, involving Godel numbers:

$$
\begin{array}{ccc}
A \times B & \xrightarrow{g_{A,B}} & G(A \times B) \\
\downarrow{\scriptstyle 1_A \times i} & & \downarrow{\scriptstyle G(1_A \times i)} \\
A \times B' & \xrightarrow[g_{A,B'}]{} & G(A \times B')
\end{array} \tag{4}
$$

where F (in Diagram 1) is instantiated as the functor $\mathbf{Set} \times \mathbf{Set} \to \mathbf{Set}$ that maps pairs of sets (A, B) to $A \times B$ and pairs of arrows (functions in this case) $p : A \to A'$ and $q : B \to B'$ to $p \times q : A \times B \to A' \times B'$, where $(p \times q)(a, b) = (p(a), q(b))$. In our case, $B \subset B'$, and we have the inclusion map $i : B \to B' : b \mapsto b$, and in the vertical arrows in Diagram 4, $(1_A, i)$ is mapped to $1_A \times i : A \times B \to A \times B'$.

The functor $G : \mathbf{Set} \times \mathbf{Set} \to \mathbf{Set}$ is a "change of basis" functor whereby maps between sets of elements become maps between sets of corresponding Godel numbers, where each unique element has a unique Godel number. For example, suppose A and B are sets of people's names (e.g., *John* and *Mary*), so that $A \times B$ is a Cartesian product that includes pairs of names, e.g., $(John, Mary)$. Each name is assigned a unique number j, e.g., *John* is 1, *Mary* is 2, and so on. Functor G constructs a set of Godel numbers for each argument set by using the number assigned to each name (j) as the exponent to a prime number assigned to each tuple position: e.g., the first tuple position is 2, the second is 3, the third is 5, and so on. Thus, the pair $(a_j, b_k) \in A \times B$ is assigned the unique Godel number $2^j 3^k$, from which j and k are recoverable by prime number decomposition. As each element is assigned a unique Godel number, the action of functor G on arrows is essentially a change of basis. So identities and compositions are preserved.

Transformation g is a family of maps, one for each set, sending each element $(a, b) \in A \times B$ to a corresponding Godel number. The critical point here is that each map in g is only locally-consistent: i.e., as already noted, we are guaranteed to have a bijection $g_{A,B} : A \times B \to G(A \times B)$, but this bijection is generally not unique. Another map $g_{A,B'} : A \times B' \to G(A \times B')$, where $B' \supset B$, is also a bijection, yet together they do not necessarily make Diagram 4 commute (i.e., they do not necessarily constitute a natural transformation).

To see why, suppose we have sets $A = \{John\}$, and $B = \{Mary\}$, so that $g_{A \times B} : (John, Mary) \mapsto 2^1 3^2 = 18$. Now, we introduce a new name *Akiko*, which is an element of the set $B' = B \cup \{Akiko\}$, which is assigned 3 for the purpose of constructing Godel numbers via G. Suppose, however, that g assigns elements to the available indices (j) based on local information only (e.g., within-set lexical order, not the globally assigned index used by G). In this

case, we have for map $g_{A,B'}$, $Akiko < John < Mary$, where $Akiko$ is assigned
1, and $John$ and $Mary$ are assigned 2 and 3 respectively. Although this locally
defined ordering scheme affords the needed bijections, these bijections are not
consistent across objects. We have the mapping $g_{A,B'} : (John, Akiko) \mapsto 2^2 3^1 =$
$24, (John, Mary) \mapsto 2^2 3^3 = 108$. However, Diagram 4 does not commute for i,
since $G(i) \circ g_{A,B}(John, Mary) = G(i)(6) = 18 \neq 108 = g_{A,B'}(John, Mary) =$
$g_{A \times B'} \circ i(John, Mary)$.

We can, of course, modify the Godel numbering scheme above to make Diagram 4 commute by reordering the new element $Akiko$: e.g., assign the order
$John < Mary < Akiko$ to set B'. To do so, however, requires prior knowledge
of all possible elements in all possible sets, which the cognitive system cannot
have in general. Or, conversely, upon knowing the existence of a new element,
the cognitive system must update all construction schemes involving the new element, clearly violating the systematicity requirement: i.e., prior to the update
the cognitive system is in a state whereby it has the capacity for some but all
related instances. Hence, such a scheme fails to explain systematicity.

Characteristically, natural constructions make no reference to an object's contents; constructions that are not natural do. Also, the specific assignment of elements to (in this case) numbers is arbitrary: while the Godel numbering scheme
maps items uniquely, we could easily provide an alternative mapping, such as
the function $(j, k) \mapsto 5^j 7^k$, thus the mapping is *ad hoc*.

5   Discussion and Conclusions

Our argument in section 3 was expressed in terms of (Cartesian) products, because they are somewhat familiar and have the needed universal mapping property. As already noted, though, where the relations in question involve a subset of
the Cartesian product, a pullback can be employed and the explanation parallels
the explanation using products. In some cases, however, the form of accessibility
in question is not a function. For example, in the presence of other facts such as
John ate ice-cream, the link from person to what they ate is no longer a function,
in the usual sense, since John is now associated with both pizza and ice-cream.
One possible way of addressing such cases is to consider another kind a universal
construction, called an *adjunction* (see [6,16]), that connects the category **Set**
of sets with functions as arrows, and the category **Rel** of sets with *relations* as
arrows.

Accessibility is a property of human cognition that we believe is important
in itself, but also in distinguishing between the capabilities of different theories
and classes of cognitive models. It may also be important to bear in mind when
designing human-computer interfaces as well as intelligent tutoring systems, etc.
Systematicity is interesting as a frequent property of cognitive systems and models, and also as a desirable property for AI applications. We have shown in this
paper that accessibility can be analysed in terms of systematicity by means of a
simple construction that is natural and universal in the category-theoretic sense
of these terms. This provides guidelines for determining, for a given model, in

principle, whether it meets the standard of systematicity of accessibility. Not all cognitive models will specifically draw on accessibility, but those that do should benefit from our contribution.

Systematicity (hence accessibility) is important for AI and cognitive science: the advantage of a systematicity property is that one gets a *collection* of intelligent capacities for free once one has a universal construction. Naturality provides a general, formal category-theory-based notion of content independence in cognitive science and artificial intelligence, where mental capacity extends to a variety of situations that have a common form, despite their specific differences.

References

1. Fodor, J., Pylyshyn, Z.: Connectionism and cognitive architecture: A critical analysis. Cognition 28, 3–71 (1988)
2. Smolensky, P.: The constituent structure of mental states: A reply to Fodor and Pylyshyn. The Southern Journal of Philosophy 26(suppl.), 137–161 (1987)
3. McLaughlin, B.: Systematicity redux. Synthese 170, 251–274 (2009)
4. Phillips, S., Wilson, W.H.: Categorial compositionality III: F-(co)algebras and the systematicity of recursive capacities in human cognition. PLoS One 7(4), e35028 (2012)
5. Aizawa, K.: The systematicity arguments. Kluwer Academic, New York (2003)
6. Phillips, S., Wilson, W.H.: Categorial compositionality: A category theory explanation for the systematicity of human cognition. PLoS Computational Biology 6(7), e1000858 (2010)
7. Halford, G.S., Wilson, W.H., Phillips, S.: Processing capacity defined by relational complexity: Implications for comparative, developmental and cognitive psychology. Behavioral and Brain Sciences 21(6), 803–831 (1998)
8. Bird, R., de Moor, O.: Algebra of programming. Prentice-Hall (1997)
9. Arbib, M.A., Manes, E.G.: Arrows, structures, functors: the categorical imperative. Academic Press, New York (1975)
10. Goldblatt, R.: Topoi: the categorical analysis of logic, revised edn. Dover, New York (2006); Original ed. Elsevier (1984)
11. Suppes, P., Zinnes, J.L.: Basic measurement theory. In: Luce, R.D. (ed.) Handbook of Mathematical Psychology, pp. 1–76. Wiley (1963)
12. Halford, G.S., Wilson, W.H.: A category theory approach to cognitive development. Cognitive Psychology 12, 356–411 (1980)
13. Mac Lane, S.: Categories for the working mathematician, 2nd edn. Springer, New York (2000)
14. Barr, M., Wells, C.: Category theory for computing science, 1st edn. Prentice Hall, New York (1990)
15. Awodey, S.: Category theory, 2nd edn. Oxford University Press (2010)
16. Phillips, S., Wilson, W.H.: Categorial Compositionality II: Universal Constructions and a General Theory of (Quasi-) Systematicity in Human Cognition. PLoS Computational Biology 7(8), e1002102 (2011)
17. van Gelder, T.: Compositionality: A connectionist variation on a classical theme. Cognitive Science 14, 355–384 (1990)
18. Phillips, S., Wilson, W.H., Halford, G.S.: What do Transitive Inference and Class Inclusion have in common? Categorical (co)products and cognitive development. PLoS Computational Biology 5(12), e1000599 (2009)

RDL: Enhancing Description Logic with Rules

Yi Zhou and Yan Zhang

Artificial Intelligence Research Group
School of Computing, Engineering and Mathematics
University of Western Sydney, Australia

Abstract. In this paper, we propose Rule Description Logic (RDL) for enhancing Description Logic (DL) with nonmonotonic recursive rules, like those in Answer Set Programming (ASP). We define the world view semantics for RDL and show that it is faithful with respect to both DL and ASP. More importantly, we show that the full language of RDL is decidable.

1 Introduction

In the last two decades, the integration of Description Logics (DL) and nonmonotonic formalisms and/or rule-based formalisms has been one of the major challenging tasks in the area of knowledge representation [1–11]. Recently, research on this topic has become even more attractive due to the success of applying description logics to Semantic Web [12] and the urgent task in it of adding rules onto the ontology layer.

Meanwhile, Answer Set Programming (ASP) has emerged as a promising paradigm for nonmonotonic rule-based reasoning due to its declarative semantics and computational advantages [13–15]. In fact, ASP is exactly a representative approach that combines nonmonotonic reasoning and recursive rule-based reasoning in a simple and natural way.

Under this backdrop, we consider the task of enhancing Description Logics with nonmonotonic recursive rules, like those in Answer Set Programming. By nonmonotonic, we mean, syntactically, the negation-as-failure operator might be used in rules, and semantically, some consequences might not be preserved when adding new knowledge. By recursive, we mean iterative reasoning procedure will be applied on rules.

As argued in [7], work in this aspect should satisfy the following criteria:

- *Faithfulness.* The integration of DL and ASP should preserve the semantics of both formalisms.
- *Tightness.* Both the DL and the ASP component should be able to contribute to the consequences of the other.
- *Flexibility.* The integration should be flexible to the Closed/Open World Assumption.
- *Decidability.* The integration should be decidable.

In addition, we believe that a *direct* semantics is essential for the integration (of DL and ASP) in order to capture its underlying intuitions.

M. Thielscher and D. Zhang (Eds.): AI 2012, LNCS 7691, pp. 567–578, 2012.

Although it looks natural, these criteria are hard to be achieved at the same time. As far as we know, none of the existing work satisfies all the above criteria. For instance, some of them are not tight as one component is building upon another. More importantly, many of the existing approaches are not decidable for their full language. Usually, a strong syntactic condition called safety needs to be assumed in order to obtain decidability. This, indeed, loses the most favorable feature of Description Logic.

In this paper, we propose a novel formalism, called Rule Description Logic (RDL for short), whose syntax is extended from description logic with the rules of the form

$$C_0 \leftarrow C_1, \ldots, C_m, \text{not } C_{m+1}, \ldots, \text{not } C_n,$$

where $0 \leq m \leq n$, and all $C_i (0 \leq i \leq n)$ are $\bot$ or concepts in description logic. We define a world view semantics for RDL based on a fixed-point definition, similar to Reiter's default logic [16]. Roughly speaking, a world view of an RDL rule base is a collection of interpretations, representing a possible set of models that an agent believes by the given rule base.

We show that RDL satisfies all the criteria mentioned previously. We prove that the world view semantics is faithful in the sense that restricting an RDL rule base to a knowledge base in DL (a logic program in ASP), the world views of the rule base coincide with the models of the knowledge base (the answer sets of the program, resp.). More importantly, we prove the bounded model property for RDL. As a consequence, the full language of RDL (i.e., no further syntactic restriction required) is decidable.

The rest of the paper is organized as follows. The following section briefly introduces the basic description logic $\mathcal{ALC}$. Next, section 3 presents the syntax as well as the semantics of RDL and addresses some basic related issues. Section 4 proves that RDL is faithful with respect to both DL and ASP, while section 5 proves that RDL is decidable. Then, section 6 discusses some related works. Finally, section 7 concludes the paper with some remarks.

2   The Description Logic $\mathcal{ALC}$

In this paper, we focus on the basic description logic $\mathcal{ALC}$, which includes and only includes the basic concept constructors of conjunction, disjunction, negation and existential and universal quantifications [17]. The syntax of $\mathcal{ALC}$ is defined over a set $\mathrm{N_C}$ of *concept names*, a set $\mathrm{N_R}$ of *role names*, a set $\mathrm{N_I}$ of *individual names* and the connectives $\top$ (tautology), $\bot$ (falsity), $\neg$ (negation), $\sqcap$ (conjunction), $\sqcup$ (disjunction), $\exists$ (existential quantification) and $\forall$ (universal quantification). In $\mathcal{ALC}$, concepts are defined recursively as follows:

$$\top \mid \bot \mid A \mid \neg C \mid C \sqcap D \mid C \sqcup D \mid \forall R.C \mid \exists R.C,$$

where $A \in \mathrm{N_C}$ and $R \in \mathrm{N_R}$.

The semantics of $\mathcal{ALC}$ is defined in terms of an *interpretation* $\mathcal{I} = (\Delta^{\mathcal{I}}, \cdot^{\mathcal{I}})$, where $\Delta^{\mathcal{I}}$ is the *domain* that contains a non-empty set of elements, and $\cdot^{\mathcal{I}}$ is the *interpretation function* that maps each concept name $A \in \mathrm{N_C}$ to a subset $A^{\mathcal{I}}$ of $\Delta^{\mathcal{I}}$, each role name $R \in \mathrm{N_R}$ to a binary relation $R^{\mathcal{I}}$ on $\Delta^{\mathcal{I}}$, and each individual name $a \in \mathrm{N_I}$ to an element $a^{\mathcal{I}}$ in $\Delta^{\mathcal{I}}$. The interpretation function is extended to all concepts recursively as follows:

- $\top^{\mathcal{I}} = \Delta^{\mathcal{I}}$.
- $\bot^{\mathcal{I}} = \emptyset$.
- $(\neg C)^{\mathcal{I}} = \Delta^{\mathcal{I}} \setminus C^{\mathcal{I}}$.
- $(C \sqcap D)^{\mathcal{I}} = C^{\mathcal{I}} \cap D^{\mathcal{I}}$.
- $(C \sqcup D)^{\mathcal{I}} = C^{\mathcal{I}} \cup D^{\mathcal{I}}$.
- $(\forall R.C)^{\mathcal{I}} = \{a \in \Delta^{\mathcal{I}} \mid \forall b. \text{ if } (a, b) \in R^{\mathcal{I}}, \text{ then } b \in C^{\mathcal{I}}\}$.
- $(\exists R.C)^{\mathcal{I}} = \{a \in \Delta^{\mathcal{I}} \mid \exists b.(a, b) \in R^{\mathcal{I}} \text{ and } b \in C^{\mathcal{I}}\}$.

We say that an interpretation $\mathcal{I}$ *satisfies* a concept C, or $\mathcal{I}$ is a *model* of C, iff $C^{\mathcal{I}} \neq \emptyset$.

A *TBox* is a finite set of *general concept implications* of the form $C \sqsubseteq D$, where C and D are concepts. In addition, we write $C \equiv D$ as a shorthand of $C \sqsubseteq D$ and $D \sqsubseteq C$. An *ABox* is a finite set of *concept assertions* of the form $C(a)$ and *role assertions* of the form $R(a, b)$, where a and b are individual names, R is a role name and C is a concept. A *(DL) knowledge base (KB)* is a pair $(\mathcal{T}, \mathcal{A})$, where $\mathcal{T}$ is a TBox and $\mathcal{A}$ is an ABox.

An interpretation $\mathcal{I}$ *satisfies* a general concept implication $C \sqsubseteq D$ if $C^{\mathcal{I}} \subseteq D^{\mathcal{I}}$; $\mathcal{I}$ *satisfies* a concept assertion $C(a)$ if $a \in C^{\mathcal{I}}$; $\mathcal{I}$ *satisfies* a role assertion $R(a, b)$ if $(a, b) \in R^{\mathcal{I}}$. Then, $\mathcal{I}$ *satisfies*, or $\mathcal{I}$ is a *model* of, a TBox $\mathcal{T}$ if it satisfies all general concept implications in $\mathcal{T}$, an ABox $\mathcal{A}$ if it satisfies all (concept and role) assertions in $\mathcal{A}$ and a DL knowledge base $(\mathcal{T}, \mathcal{A})$ if it satisfies both $\mathcal{T}$ and $\mathcal{A}$.

3 RDL: Syntax and Semantics

This section presents the syntax as well as the semantics of RDL, which can be regarded as an integration of Description Logic and Answer Set Programming. However, although Description Logic (i.e. $\mathcal{ALC}$) is fully embraced, RDL only contains a fragment of Answer Set Programming. Nevertheless, as we will argue later, this fragment is indeed adequate for the task of enhancing DL with rules.

The syntax of RDL is extended from $\mathcal{ALC}$ by adding rules of the form

$$C_0 \leftarrow C_1, \ldots, C_m, \text{not } C_{m+1}, \ldots, \text{not } C_n, \tag{1}$$

where $0 \leq m \leq n$, and $C_i (0 \leq i \leq n)$ is a concept or $\bot$. Roughly speaking, this represents a nonmonotonic recursive rule that applies on all individuals.

An *RBox*[1] is a finite set of rules of form (1). An *(RDL) rule base (RB)* is a triple $(\mathcal{R}, \mathcal{T}, \mathcal{A})$, where $\mathcal{R}$ is an RBox and $(\mathcal{T}, \mathcal{A})$ is a standard DL knowledge base. In particular, a knowledge base can be considered as a rule base with empty RBox.

The semantics of RDL is defined in terms of collections of interpretations instead of interpretations by fixing a domain and the interpretations on individuals. Let Δ be a non-empty set of elements, called a *domain*. A *collection of interpretations* on Δ (*collection* for short if clear from the context) is a non-empty set of interpretations that share the same domain Δ and map each individual $a \in \mathtt{N_I}$ to the same element in Δ. In other words, each collection $\mathcal{W}$ is associated with a domain Δ and a mapping M from all individuals to elements in Δ, which are recognized by all interpretations in the

---

[1] Although this term appeared elsewhere in the literature, we use it in RDL for convenience. The syntactic and semantic meanings are different from other approaches.

collection. For convenience, we use $\Delta^{\mathcal{W}}$ to denote the domain and $M^{\mathcal{W}}$ to denote the *individual mapping*.

Let $\Gamma = (\mathcal{R}, \mathcal{T}, \mathcal{A})$ be a rule base and $\mathcal{W}$ a collection. We define an operator $\Gamma(\mathcal{W})$ by the maximal collection (in the sense of set inclusion) satisfying the following conditions.

1. $\Gamma(\mathcal{W})$ has the same domain and the same individual mapping as $\mathcal{W}$.
2. Every interpretation in $\Gamma(\mathcal{W})$ is a model of the knowledge base $(\mathcal{T}, \mathcal{A})$.
3. For each rule r in R of the form (1) and each d in $\Delta^{\mathcal{W}}$, if
   (a) for all $i(1 \leq i \leq m)$, and all $\mathcal{I} \in \Gamma(\mathcal{W})$, $d \in C_i^{\mathcal{I}}$ and
   (b) for all $j, (m + 1 \leq j \leq n)$, there exists $\mathcal{J} \in \mathcal{W}$ such that $d \notin C_j^{\mathcal{J}}$,
   then $d \in C_0^{\mathcal{I}}$ for all $\mathcal{I} \in \Gamma(\mathcal{W})$.

We say that a collection $\mathcal{W}$ is a *world view*[2] of a rule base Γ iff $\mathcal{W}$ is a fixed point of the operator Γ, i.e. $\Gamma(\mathcal{W}) = \mathcal{W}$. In this case, we say that $\mathcal{W}$ is a world view of Γ with respect to $\Delta^{\mathcal{W}}$ and $M^{\mathcal{W}}$.

The world view semantics for RDL follows some basic ideas of the well-known semantics for default logic [16]. First of all, both semantics define an operator Γ, and take the fixed point of Γ into account. Secondly, all the (nonmonotonic recursive) rules need to be satisfied by fixing their negation-as-failure part with the original candidate. However, in Reiter's semantics [16], Γ is defined on propositional deductive closures, while in the world view semantics, it is defined on collections of interpretations.

Similar to ASP, a rule base may have zero, one or more world views. Intuitively, each world view represents an agent's view of all the possible models by given the rule base. A world view of a rule base may consist of a single or multiple interpretations. Each interpretation represents a possible world that the agent believes in this view.

Example 1. (Originated from [2]) Consider the following example of reasoning about exceptions: "Usually, mammals live on lands. However, whales are mammals but not living on lands." Formalized in RDL, this can be represented as

$$\exists live.Land \leftarrow Mammal, \text{not} \neg \exists live.Land, \tag{2}$$

$$Whale \sqsubseteq Mammal \sqcap \neg \exists live.Land, \tag{3}$$

where (2) forms the RBox, and (3) forms the TBox of this rule base.

Suppose that the ABox is

$$\{Mammal(snoopy)\}. \tag{4}$$

Fix a domain $\Delta = \{d_1\}$ and an individual mapping M such that $M(snoopy) = d_1$. Then, the rule base $\Gamma_1 = \{(2), (3), (4)\}$ has the following world view with respect to Δ and M:

$$\mathcal{W}_1 = \{\{Mammal(d_1), Land(d_1), live(d_1, d_1)\}\}.[3]$$

---

[2] This term is borrowed from [18].

[3] Note that $Mammal(d_1)$ and $Land(d_1)$ appear at the same time since there is no common-sense restriction in the rule base that these two concepts are disjoint.

To verify this, firstly it is obvious that the interpretation in $\mathcal{W}_1$ satisfies the knowledge base $\{(3),(4)\}$. Secondly, $\mathcal{W}_1$ itself satisfies condition 3 in the definition of the operator Γ. Hence, $\mathcal{W}_1 \subseteq \Gamma(\mathcal{W}_1)$. To show $\mathcal{W}_1 = \Gamma(\mathcal{W}_1)$, it suffices to prove that for any $\mathcal{W}_1'$ such that $\mathcal{W}_1 \subset \mathcal{W}_1'$, if all the interpretations in it satisfy the knowledge base $\{(3),(4)\}$, then it does not satisfy condition 3. This is indeed the case since $\exists live.Land(d_1)$ must hold according to condition 3.

It can be checked that $\mathcal{W}_1$ is the unique world view of Γ_1 w.r.t Δ and M. For instance, consider the collection

$$\{\{Whale(d_1), Mammal(d_1)\}\}.$$

Although the interpretation in this collection satisfies the TBox, and itself satisfies condition 1-3 of the operator Γ, it is not a maximal one since

$$\{\{Whale(d_1), Mammal(d_1)\},$$
$$\{Whale(d_1), Mammal(d_1), Land(d_1)\}\}$$

also satisfies conditions 1-3 of the operator Γ.

Now, suppose that the ABox is

$$\{Whale(mobydick)\}. \tag{5}$$

Fix a domain $\Delta' = \{d_2\}$ and an individual mapping M' such that $M'(mobydick) = d_2$. It can be checked that the unique extension of $\{(2),(3),(5)\}$ with respect to Δ' and M' is

$$\{\{Whale(d_2), Mammal(d_2), Land(d_2)\},$$
$$\{Whale(d_2), Mammal(d_2)\},$$
$$\{Whale(d_2), Mammal(d_2), live(d_2, d_2)\}\}.$$

Semantically, a major difference between Description Logic (DL) and Rule Description Logic (RDL) is that the semantics for former is defined in terms of interpretations, while the semantics for the latter is defined in terms of collections (of interpretations). It is necessary to consider collections instead of interpretations for RDL. Consider a simple rule base Γ, whose RBox consists of the following two rules:

$$A_1 \sqcup A_2 \leftarrow \mathsf{not}\ B$$
$$B \leftarrow \mathsf{not}\ A_1 \sqcup A_2.$$

Given a domain $\Delta = \{d\}$, Γ has two world views with respect to Δ:

$$\{\{A_1(d)\}, \{A_2(d)\}, \{A_1(d), A_2(d)\}\},$$
$$\{\{B(d)\}\},$$

where the first world view contains three interpretations and the second one contains only a unique interpretation. One can observe that the relationship between $\{A_1(d)\}$

and $\{A_2(d)\}$ is different from the relationship between $\{A_1(d)\}$ and $\{B(d)\}$. To conclude, $\{A_1(d)\}$ and $\{A_2(d)\}$ are complementary in the sense that these two interpretations complement each other according to the rule base, while $\{A_1(d)\}$ and $\{B(d)\}$ are contradictory in the sense that one contradicts to another according to the rule base.

The reason why collections are needed instead of interpretations can also be evidenced from propositional default logic [16], which can be regarded as a natural combination of classical logic and answer set programming in the propositional case. Notice that the extensions in default logic are propositional theories, which indeed correspond to a collection of propositional interpretations (assignments) but not merely interpretations (assignments). Lifting this idea for integrating DL and ASP, it is natural to consider world views in our task as collections rather than interpretations.

4 RDL vs DL/ASP

Since RDL claims to be an approach to enhance Description Logics with rules in Answer Set Programming, it is important to investigate the relationship between RDL and DL as well as the relationship between RDL and ASP. One important measure is so-called faithfulness [7]. That is, when restricting the syntax of RDL with DL (ASP resp.), does the semantics of RDL coincide with the semantics of DL (ASP resp.)? Another measure is expressiveness, i.e., does RDL have the full expressive power of DL (ASP resp.)?

This section answers the first question positively. We show that RDL is indeed faithful with respect to both DL and ASP. For the second question, it can be observed that RDL embraces the full expressive power of DL, but only contains a conservative fragment of ASP.

The relationship between RDL and DL is illustrated by the following theorem.

Theorem 1 (RDL vs DL). *Let Γ be a rule base with empty RBox, i.e. $\Gamma = (\mathcal{R}, \mathcal{T}, \mathcal{A})$, where $\mathcal{R} = \emptyset$. Let Δ be a domain and M an individual mapping on Δ. Then, Γ has a unique world view with respect to Δ and M, which is the collection of all models of the knowledge base $(\mathcal{T}, \mathcal{A})$ sharing the domain Δ and the individual mapping M.*

Theorem 1 shows that, fixing a domain and an individual mapping, the unique world view of a knowledge base contains and only contains all models of it. Hence, RDL is faithful with respect to DL. On the other hand, from Theorem 1, it can be observed that RDL embraces the full expressive power of DL in the sense that, given any knowledge base, its models (under the context of DL) are exactly captured by its unique world view (under the context of RDL).

To compare RDL and ASP,[4] we need to figure out the syntactic intersection of these two approaches. A simple idea is to eliminate all the compositional connectives $\neg$, $\sqcap$, $\sqcup$, $\exists$ and $\forall$ and to eliminate TBox in RDL. In fact, this fragment of RDL only allows atomic concepts; it allows neither roles nor compounded concepts. Moreover, TBox assertions are forbidden. This fragment can be straightforwardly transformed to a fragment of first-order ASP, which only allows unary predicates and rules of the following form.

---

[4] In this paper, we consider the recent generalization of the first-order answer set semantics [14, 15], which is defined over arbitrary structures rather than the Herbrand structure [13].

$$A_0(x) \leftarrow A_1(x), \ldots, A_m(x), \text{not } A_{m+1}(x), \ldots, \text{not } A_n(x), \tag{6}$$

where $0 \leq m \leq n$, x is a variable and $A_i(0 \leq i \leq n)$ is a unary predicate or $\bot$. This fragment of ASP is indeed a very small fragment of ASP since it only allows unary predicates and all atoms in a rule must share the same variable.

Theorem 2 (RDL vs. ASP). *Let Γ be a rule base that only allows atomic concepts and has no TBox. Let Π^Γ be the answer set program obtained from Γ by translating each rule r in Γ of form (1) to a rule of form (6). Then, every world view of Π has and only has a unique interpretation, which is an answer set of Π^Γ. Conversely, an answer set of Π^Γ itself composes a world view of Γ.*

Theorem 2 shows that, by restricting to the common syntax of RDL and ASP, the world views (under the context of RDL) exactly correspond to the answer sets (under the context of ASP) in the sense that every world view contains and only contains a unique interpretation, which corresponds to an answer set. Hence, RDL is faithful with respect to ASP.

It can be observed that RDL does not fully embrace the expressive power of ASP. A simple observation is that roles (i.e. binary predicates) cannot be minimized in RDL, i.e., the head of all rules cannot be roles. Also, RDL does not allow predicates with arity more than 2.

However, we argue that rules of the form (1) in RDL are adequate enough from a Description Logic point of view. This is due to the fact that DLs only allow assertions like $C \sqsubseteq D$ in TBox. More expressive forms of assertions, e.g. $R_1 \sqsubseteq R_2$, are not allowed in DLs either. In fact, syntactically, the rule form in RDL (i.e. form (1)) is very similar to a general concept implication in standard DL, except that the negation-as-failure operator is introduced. Nevertheless, their semantically meanings are essentially different.

Also, it can be observed from Theorems 1 and 2 that, semantically, the DL and the ASP components are actually corresponding to two dimensions of RDL. More precisely, the DL component is corresponding to the interrelationships among interpretations in a particular world view, while the ASP component is corresponding to the interrelationships among different world views.

5   Decidability of RDL

Different from standard DLs, there are more typical decision problems in RDL as models are generalized to world views. For instance, the problem of checking whether a concept is satisfiable by all interpretations in some world views of an RDL rule base is different from the problem of checking whether it is satisfiable by some interpretations in all world views.

The decidability of all kinds of decision problems follows from the bounded model property of RDL.

Theorem 3 (Bounded model property). *If a rule base has a world view, then it has a world view whose domain size is bounded.*

Proof. In particular, we show that there is a world view whose domain size is less than $O(2^{2^n})$, where n is the length of the rule base. As the full proof is rather tedious, here we only outline the basic ideas due to a space limit.

We can assume that the individual set is empty and all the rules in RBox only contain atomic concepts. Suppose that $\Gamma = (\mathcal{R}, \mathcal{T}, \emptyset)$, where $\mathcal{R}$ only contains atomic concepts. Let $cl(\Gamma)$ be the smallest set of concepts that contains all sub-concepts occurring in Γ, and is closed under single negation. Given a subset $S \subseteq cl(\Gamma)$, we use i_S to denote the index of S, and Ind to denote the set of all indices (with respect to Γ).

Suppose that $\mathcal{I}$ is an interpretation whose domain is Δ. Construct a mapping $f_\mathcal{I}$ from Δ to Ind (with respect to $\mathcal{I}$) such that for all $d \in \Delta$, $f_\mathcal{I}(d) = i_S$, where $S = \{C \mid C \in cl(\Gamma), d \in C^\mathcal{I}\}$. By $f(\mathcal{I})$, we denote the set of indices mapped from all elements in Δ, i.e., $f(\mathcal{I}) = \{f_\mathcal{I}(d) \mid d \in \Delta\}$.

Let $\mathcal{W}$ be a collection with the domain Δ. Let F be a set of indices and i an index. By $\mathcal{P}(\mathcal{W})$, we denote the set $\{(F, i) \mid \exists \mathcal{I} \in \mathcal{W}, d \in \Delta$ such that $f(\mathcal{I}) = F$ and $f_\mathcal{I}(d) = i\}$. Then, $\mathcal{P}(\mathcal{W})$ is a finite set of pairs of the form (F, i). By $Ind(\mathcal{W})$, we denote the power set of $\mathcal{P}(\mathcal{W})$. We construct a mapping f (with respect to $\mathcal{W}$) from Δ to $Ind(\mathcal{W})$ that for all $d \in \Delta$, $f(d) = \{(F, i) \mid \mathcal{I} \in \mathcal{W}, f(\mathcal{I}) = F, f_\mathcal{I}(d) = i\}$.

Let $\Delta' = \{f(d) \mid d \in \Delta\}$. Clearly, for every $d' \in \Delta'$, there exists $d \in \Delta$ such that $f(d) = d'$. Given an interpretation $\mathcal{I} \in \mathcal{W}$, construct a new interpretation $\mathcal{I}'$ (with respect to $\mathcal{W}$) as follows:

- the domain of $\mathcal{I}'$ is Δ';
- for each atomic concept A and each $d \in \Delta$, if $d \in A^\mathcal{I}$, then $f(d) \in A^{\mathcal{I}'}$;
- for each atomic role R and each two $d_1, d_2 \in \Delta$, if $(d_1, d_2) \in R^\mathcal{I}$, then $(f(d_1), f(d_2)) \in R^{\mathcal{I}'}$.

By induction on the structure of C, it can be proved that:

Claim. For any $d \in \Delta, \mathcal{I} \in \mathcal{W}$ and $C \in cl(\Gamma)$, $d \in C^\mathcal{I}$ iff $f(d) \in C^{\mathcal{I}'}$.

Now suppose that a collection $\mathcal{W}$ is a world view of Γ. Then, we show that the collection $\mathcal{W}' = \{\mathcal{I}' \mid \mathcal{I} \in \mathcal{W}\}$ is a world view of Γ as well. Firstly, $\mathcal{W}' \subseteq \Gamma(\mathcal{W}')$ since $\mathcal{W}'$ itself satisfies conditions 1-3 in the definition of the operator Γ according to Claim 1.

Hence, $\Gamma(\mathcal{W}') = \mathcal{W}'$. Otherwise, $\mathcal{W}' \subset \Gamma(\mathcal{W}')$. Suppose that $\mathcal{J}'$ is in $\Gamma(\mathcal{W}')$ but not in $\mathcal{W}'$. We construct a new interpretation $\mathcal{J}$ as follows:

- the domain of $\mathcal{J}$ is Δ,
- for each atomic concept A and each $d \in \Delta$, if $f(d) \in A^{\mathcal{J}'}$, then $d \in A^\mathcal{J}$.
- for each atomic role R and each pair $(d_1, d_2) \in \Delta \times \Delta$, if $(f(d_1), f(d_2)) \in R^{\mathcal{J}'}$, then $(d_1, d_2) \in R^\mathcal{J}$.

Again, by induction, it can be proved that:

Claim. For any $d \in \Delta, \mathcal{J} \in \mathcal{W}^* \setminus \mathcal{W}$ and $C \in cl(\Gamma)$, $d \in C^\mathcal{J}$ iff $f(d) \in C^{\mathcal{J}'}$.

Let $\mathcal{W}^* = \mathcal{W} \cup \{\mathcal{J} \mid \mathcal{J}' \in \Gamma(\mathcal{W}') \setminus \mathcal{W}'\}$. Then, $\mathcal{W} \subset \mathcal{W}^*$. Clearly, $\mathcal{W}^*$ satisfies conditions 1-2 in the definition of the operator Γ with respect to $\mathcal{W}$. We now show that it satisfies condition 3 as well. Let $d \in \Delta$ and r a rule in Γ of form (1). Suppose that $d \in C_i^\mathcal{I}$ for all $i (1 \le i \le m)$ and all $\mathcal{I} \in \mathcal{W}^*$, and $d \notin C_j^\mathcal{J}$ for all $j (m + 1 \le j \le n)$

and all $\mathcal{J} \in \mathcal{W}$. Then, by Claims 1 and 2, $f(d) \in C_i^{\mathcal{I}'}$ for all $i(1 \leq i \leq m)$ and all $\mathcal{I}' \in \Gamma(\mathcal{W}')$, and $d \notin C_j^{\mathcal{J}'}$ for all $j(m + 1 \leq j \leq n)$ and all $\mathcal{J}' \in \mathcal{W}'$. Hence, $f(d) \in C_0^{\mathcal{I}'}$ for all $\mathcal{I}' \in \Gamma(\mathcal{W}')$. Again, by Claims 1 and 2, $d \in C_0^{\mathcal{I}}$ for all $\mathcal{I} \in \mathcal{W}^*$. This shows that $\mathcal{W}^* \subseteq \Gamma(\mathcal{W})$. Therefore, $\mathcal{W} \subset \mathcal{W}^* \subseteq \Gamma(\mathcal{W})$, a contradiction.

We end up this proof by noticing that Δ' is bounded since the sizes of $cl(\Gamma)$, $P(\mathcal{W})$ and $Ind(\mathcal{W})$ are no more than $O(n)$, $O(2^n)$ and $O(2^{2^n})$, respectively.

As a consequence, the decidability of the existence checking problem follows directly from Theorem 3.

Corollary 1. *Checking whether a rule base has a world view is decidable.*

6   Discussions and Related Work

Discussions. The criteria mentioned in the introduction section are regarded to be important for the task of integrating DL and ASP. RDL indeed satisfies all these criteria. First of all, the world view semantics for RDL is a direct semantics, which is very similar to Reiter's semantics for default logic. Also, RDL is highly tight since concepts (predicates) in the DL component and those in the ASP component are not distinguished. Thirdly, RDL is faithful with respect to both DL and ASP, as shown in Section 4. Also, as proved in Section 5, the full language of RDL is decidable.

Finally, it can be observed that RDL is flexible to the Closed/Open World Assumption. The world view semantics for RDL does not force the Closed World Assumption. For instance, only from the rule base with a single concept assertion $Person(Mike)$, one cannot derive that $Mike$ is innocent. For employing Closed world Assumption for a particular concept C, one can simply add a rule $C \leftarrow$ not $\neg C$ to the RBox. For instance, together with the Closed World Assumption on the concept $Innocent$ (i.e. $Innocent \leftarrow$ not $\neg Innocent$), from the concept assertion $Person(Mike)$, one can actually derive that $Mike$ is innocent since the unique world view (w.r.t. a domain d and an individual mapping from $Mike$ to d) of the rule base is $\{Person(d), Innocent(d)\}$.

Related Work. As mentioned in the introduction section, the tasks of enhancing description logics with nonmonotonic formalisms and/or with rules have attracted many attentions in the literature. In this section, we briefly review some of the related work. Due to a space limit, we are not able to discuss all in very detail, and we leave this task to our full version.

Perhaps the closest work to RDL is other approaches of integrating DL and ASP. As far as we are concerned, there are five representative approaches in this category, the tight hybrid approach DL+log [8], the loose hybrid approach DL-programs [9], the embedding approach to MKNF$^+$ [7], the embedding approach to QEL [10], and the grounding approach disjunctive DL-programs [11].

Rosati [8] proposed a hybrid approach, called DL+log, which is extended from DL by adding disjunctive rules of the following form

$$p_1; \ldots; p_n \leftarrow p_{n+1}, \ldots, p_m, \text{not } p_{m+1}, \ldots, \text{not } p_l,$$

where $p_i(1 \leq i \leq l)$ is a first-order atom. Predicates in DL+log are distinguished by DL-predicates and non-DL-predicates, and the former cannot occur in the scope of not .

DL+log is a tight and faithful integration. However, it is not flexible since the Closed World Assumption cannot be applied on DL-predicates. In addition, the full language of DL+log is not decidable. In order to achieve decidability, a notion called weak-safety, similar to safety, is required.

Different from the above, Eiter et al. [9] proposed another hybrid approach, called dl-programs. The key idea is to allow the query results of DL knowledge bases as so-called *dl-atoms* in the bodies of a standard rule in ASP. The semantics is then defined based on grounding on the Herbrand base. This approach is faithful, flexible and decidable. However, it is not tight since the ASP component is building upon the DL component. This approach is significantly different from RDL. Firstly, RDL does not distinguish DL predicates and ASP predicates, which are indeed highly interactive in RDL. Secondly, the semantics of RDL is defined not only on Herbrand structures but, in general, on arbitrary ones. Last but not least, the elements in an RDL rule are regular concepts in DL but not atoms/literals.

An alternative direction of combing DLs and ASP is to define a "indirect" semantics of the integration by embedding it into another host language. One predominant work in this category is to use MKNF^+ as the host langauge [7]. The rules are of the form

$$Kh_1 \vee \ldots \vee Kh_l \leftarrow Kb_1, \ldots, Kb_m, \text{not } b_{m+1}, \ldots, \text{not } b_n,$$

where all h_i, b_j are first-order atoms. The semantics is defined via an embedding to the logic of MKNF [19]. As shown in [7], this approach is faithful, tight and flexible. However, its full language is not decidable. Again, a similar notion of safety is required to obtain decidability.

Another embedding approach is to use Quantified Equilibrium Logic (QEL) as the host language [10], which is demonstrated to be powerful enough to capture some other integrations, such as DL+log [8]. However, more detailed analysis, e.g. the decidability issue, are missing.

Lukasiewicz [11] proposed an alternative approach, called disjunctive dl-programs, by grounding on finite domains. However, as pointed out in [7], although this approach is faithful *w.r.t.* ASP, it seems not faithful *w.r.t.* the standard semantics of DL, and it seems only capable of reasoning about positive atoms. Moreover, the grounding-based semantics is defined only over Herbrand structures rather than arbitrary ones.

To conclude, comparing RDL with the above approaches for enhancing DLs with rules in ASP, there are several major issues worthy to be highlighted. Syntactically, RDL uses concepts instead of atoms/literals in the rules. Semantically, RDL employs collections instead of interpretations. Most importantly, the full language of RDL is decidable, and no strong syntactic restrictions (e.g. safety) are forced. To sum up, RDL satisfies all the desirable criteria as listed in the introduction section.

7   Conclusion

In this paper, we introduced a novel formalism, called Rule Description Logic (RDL), to enhance Description Logic with nonmonotonic recursive rules in Answer Set

Programming. RDL embraces the full expressive power of DL as well as a conservative but powerful fragment of ASP. We showed that RDL is faithful *w.r.t.* both DL and ASP (see Theorems 1 and 2). Moreover, we proved the bounded model property of RDL (see Theorem 3), which indicates that RDL, not only its subclasses but its full language, preserves the most important feature of Description Logic - decidability. To the best of our knowledge, RDL is the first approach that meets all the criteria mentioned in the introduction section for the promising task of integrating DLs and ASP.

This work is only a first step. For future work, one task is to consider alternative Description Logics, such as $\mathcal{SHIQ}$ and DL-lite. Another task worth pursuing is to further extend the syntax as well as the semantics of RDL, e.g. to disjunctive rules. Certainly, it is also important to work out the exact upper/lower bounds of the related decision problems in RDL. Last but not least, the implementation task of RDL is crucial for its applications.

References

1. Baader, F., Hollunder, B.: Embedding defaults into terminological knowledge representation formalisms. Journal of Automated Reasoning 14(1), 149–180 (1995)
2. Bonatti, P.A., Lutz, C., Wolter, F.: The complexity of circumscription in DLs. Journal of Artifical Intelligence Research 35, 717–773 (2009)
3. de Bruijn, J., Eiter, T., Polleres, A., Tompits, H.: Embedding non-ground logic programs into autoepistemic logic for knowledge-base combination. In: IJCAI, pp. 304–309 (2007)
4. Horrocks, I., Patel-Schneider, P.F., Bechhofer, S., Tsarkov, D.: OWL rules: A proposal and prototype implementation. Journal of Web Semantics 3(1), 23–40 (2005)
5. Grosof, B.N., Horrocks, I., Volz, R., Decker, S.: Description logic programs: combining logic programs with description logic. In: WWW, pp. 48–57 (2003)
6. Donini, F.M., Lenzerini, M., Nardi, D., Schaerf, A.: AL-log: Integrating datalog and description logics. Journal of Intelligent Information Systems 10(3), 227–252 (1998)
7. Motik, B., Rosati, R.: Reconciling description logics and rules. Journal of the ACM 57(5) (2010)
8. Rosati, R.: DL+log: Tight integration of description logics and disjunctive datalog. In: KR, pp. 68–78 (2006)
9. Eiter, T., Ianni, G., Lukasiewicz, T., Schindlauer, R., Tompits, H.: Combining answer set programming with description logics for the semantic web. Artifial Intelligence 172(12-13), 1495–1539 (2008)
10. de Bruijn, J., Pearce, D., Polleres, A., Valverde, A.: Quantified Equilibrium Logic and Hybrid Rules. In: Marchiori, M., Pan, J.Z., de Marie, C.S. (eds.) RR 2007. LNCS, vol. 4524, pp. 58–72. Springer, Heidelberg (2007)
11. Lukasiewicz, T.: A novel combination of answer set programming with description logics for the semantic web. IEEE Transactions on Knowledge and Data Engineering 22(11), 1577–1592 (2010)
12. Horrocks, I., Patel-Schneider, P.F., van Harmelen, F.: From SHIQ and RDF to OWL: the making of a web ontology language. J. Web Sem. 1(1), 7–26 (2003)
13. Gelfond, M., Lifschitz, V.: The stable model semantics for logic programming. In: ICLP 1988, pp. 1070–1080 (1988)
14. Lin, F., Zhou, Y.: From answer set logic programming to circumscription via logic of GK. Artifial Intelligence 175(1), 264–277 (2011)

15. Ferraris, P., Lee, J., Lifschitz, V.: Stable models and circumscription. Artifial Intelligence 175(1), 236–263 (2011)
16. Reiter, R.: A logic for default reasoning. Artifial Intelligence 13(1-2), 81–132 (1980)
17. Baader, F., Calvanese, D., McGuinness, D.L., Nardi, D., Patel-Schneider, P.F. (eds.): The Description Logic Handbook: Theory, Implementation, and Applications. Cambridge University Press (2003)
18. Gelfond, M.: Logic programming and reasoning with incomplete information. Annals of Maththematics and Artifial Intelligence 12(1-2), 89–116 (1994)
19. Lifschitz, V.: Minimal belief and negation as failure. Artifial Intelligence 70(1-2), 53–72 (1994)

Approximate Document Outlier Detection
Using Random Spectral Projection

Mazin Aouf and Laurence A.F. Park

School of Computing, Engineering and Mathematics,
University of Western Sydney, Australia
{mazin,lapark}@scem.uws.edu.au

Abstract. Outlier detection is an important process for text document
collections, but as the collection grows, the detection process becomes a
computationally expensive task. Random projection has shown to provide a good fast approximation of sparse data, such as document vectors,
for outlier detection. The random samples of Fourier and cosine spectrum
have shown to provide good approximations of sparse data when performing document clustering. In this article, we investigate the utility of using
these random Fourier and cosine spectral projections for document outlier detection. We show that random samples of the Fourier spectrum for
outlier detection provides better accuracy and requires less storage when
compared with random projection. We also show that random samples
of the cosine spectrum for outlier detection provides similar accuracy
and computational time when compared with random projection, but
requires much less storage.

1 Introduction

To perform outlier detection is to examine a data set for items that are dissimilar
to the majority of the set. Outlier detection has been used for tasks such as
computer network intrusion detection, medical fraud detection and credit card
fraud detection, and novelty detection. It is also useful in finding clusters in
highly imbalanced data sets.

The use of computers to automate tasks and communicate through the Internet, has led to the generation and storage of large amounts of information
that must be processed for each outlier detection task. Therefore, we must be
able to efficiently and effectively perform outlier detection on a large scale. Most
recorded human interaction is in the form of free text (e.g. email, wikis, blogs,
social network posts), therefore identifying outliers in large text document collections is a relevant problem that is useful for finding interesting items or suspicious
documents that do not belong.

The definition of outlier detection implies that the data must be thoroughly
examined to find the small set of outliers. Therefore, outlier detection is a computationally expensive task. It has been recently shown [1] that random projection
can be used to project sparse data sets, such as text documents, into a lower
dimensional space and approximately preserve the distances between all of the
data objects. It has also been shown [2] that random samples of the Fourier
and cosine spectrum provide us with a good lower dimensional approximation

M. Thielscher and D. Zhang (Eds.): AI 2012, LNCS 7691, pp. 579–590, 2012.

of sparse data sets for effectively and efficiently identifying clusters. In this article, we will investigate the utility (in terms of accuracy, efficiency and storage required) of these random spectral projections for outlier detection on large text document collections.

The contributions of this article are:

- A description of random spectral projection using the Fourier and cosine transforms (Section 3).
- A comparison of the speed and accuracy of random spectral projection and random projection for outlier detection (Section 4.4).
- An examination of the storage, speed and accuracy of random spectral projection and random projection when performing outlier detection on a large document set (Section 4.6).

The article will proceed as follows: Section 2 describes the current methods used for text document outlier detection. Section 3 describes the theory behind compressive sampling and shows how we will apply this to outlier detection. Section 4 contains the experimental method, results and discussion.

2   Text Document Outlier Detection

In this section we will examine how to perform outlier detection on a collection of text documents. Text document sets exist in high dimensional spaces, therefore, we require a simple method for detecting outliers. We first present the outlier detection method that we will be using and then describe how we will compute the similarity of each document during the outlier detection process.

2.1   Outlier Detection

An outlier is an element of a set that has different qualities in some respect to the majority of the set. Identifying an outlier may be subjective and therefore requires a clear definition in order for detection to take place. In this article, we are focusing on text documents, so an outlier document is one that is written on a different topic to the majority of the document collection. We will be representing each text document as a vector in a high dimensional space, implying that we need an efficient and effective outlier detection method that can be used on high dimensional vector spaces.

A simple outlier detection method examines the similarity of each document to its neighbours [3]. If a document is similar to many documents then it is considered an inlier, if a document is similar to only a few other documents, then it may be an outlier. This simple distance based outlier detection method has order $O(TN^2)$ where N is the number of documents in the collection and T is the dimensionality of the document space. The computational complexity comes from us having to compute the distance of each document from a given document to obtain its outlier likelihood score. An advancement on the distance based method is to also examine the density of the document distributions. If a region in the vector space is densely populated, while another is more spread out, the simple method may wrongly detect a document in the latter region of the vector space as an outlier. Local Outlier Factor (LOF) [4] is an outlier detection method that examines the local data distribution, and computes the outlier likelihood score based on the density around the point. Unfortunately the LOF method requires us to store the identity of each of document's k neighbours and the distances to these neighbours. The computation of the LOF scores requires a scan of the complete set of document vectors to compute the neighbours, having order $O(TN^2)$, then a scan of each point's neighbours to compute the document density, having order $O(Nk)$, and a final scan of the density scores and neighbours, also having order $O(Nk)$, where k is the number of neighbours chosen.

We are not investigating the accuracy of the outlier detection method itself, but we are interested in how the choice of random projection type affects the accuracy of the outlier detection. To simplify our experiments so that they focus on the effect of the projection, we will use simple distance based outlier detection.

2.2   Comparing Documents

A text document is a sequence of terms, where the terms describe the content of the document. Each document can be represented as a vector in a vector space, where the vector space has one dimension for each unique term in the document collection. Within this T dimensional space (where T is the number of unique terms in the collection), we can construct a document vector by using the frequency of each term in a document as the corresponding value of each element in the document vector. Doing this, we have:

$$\boldsymbol{d} = \begin{bmatrix} f_{d,t_0} & f_{d,t_1} & \cdots & f_{d,t_{T-1}} \end{bmatrix}$$

where f_{d,t_j} is the frequency of term t_j in document d. There has been many similarity functions developed to compare document vectors to queries for information retrieval (vector space methods [5], probabilistic methods [6], language models [7]), but when comparing documents to documents, it has been found that the TF-IDF weighting with cosine similarity is the most appropriate [8]. The TF-IDF weighting we use in this article is of the form:

$$w_{d,t} = w(f_{d,t}) = \log\left(\frac{N}{f_t} + 1\right) f_{d,t}$$

where $w_{d,t}$ is the weight of term t in document d, f_t is the number of documents term t appears in, and N is the number of documents in the collection. We can see that if the term t is common, meaning that f_t is large, then $\frac{N}{f_t}$ will be close to 1 and $\log\left(\frac{N}{f_t} + 1\right)$ will be close to $\log(2) = 0.6931$. If term t is rare, meaning that f_t is small, then $\frac{N}{f_t}$ will be close to N and $\log\left(\frac{N}{f_t} + 1\right)$ will be close to $\log(N + 1)$. Therefore, the TF-IDF weighting gives less weight to common terms and more weight to rare terms that define the document. The weighted document vector is given as:

$$\boldsymbol{\delta} = \begin{bmatrix} w_{d,t_0} & w_{d,t_1} & \cdots & w_{d,t_{T-1}} \end{bmatrix}$$

The document similarity function is given as:

$$S(d_i, d_j) = \frac{\delta_i \cdot \delta_j}{\|\delta_i\| \|\delta_j\|}$$

where δ_i is the ith weighted document vector, the inner product $\delta_i \cdot \delta_j = \sum_{k=i}^{T} w_{d_i,t_k} w_{d_j,t_k}$ and the vector norm $\|\delta_i\|$ is $\sqrt{\delta_i \cdot \delta_i}$. We can see that this document similarity function measures the cosine of the angle between the weighted document vectors. If both vectors are the same, the similarity is 1; as the documents become more different, the similarity approaches 0. Note that also the denominator of the similarity function normalises the document lengths, meaning that the weight of a word in a long document will be less than the weight of the same word in a smaller document.

2.3   Random Projection

Outlier detection is dependent on the vector space dimensionality. As the dimensionality of the space increases, so does the time required to compute the outliers. Methods of dimension reduction (such as PCA, NMF and PLSA [9,10,11]) can be used to map the vector space into a smaller space, where each vector in the smaller space is an approximation of the vectors in the original space. Unfortunately, these methods are computationally expensive and therefore many not be feasible for high dimensional spaces. In this section we will examine a simple method that has been used for dimension reduction as a preprocessing step for outlier detection.

Random projection is the act of projecting a vector space to a lower dimensional space using a randomly generated mapping. It has been shown [1] that a random projection of sparse data that approximately preserves the similarity between vectors can computed using the mapping where each element is sampled from a random variable X having the distribution:

x	-1	0	1
$P(X = x)$	1/6	2/3	1/6

To map the document vector space from a T dimensional space to an S dimensional space, we generate an $S \times T$ matrix P_R containing values randomly sampled from X. We can then project the weighted document matrix D (containing the weighted document vectors as its columns) using:

$$D_R = P_R D$$

where D_R is an $S \times N$ matrix containing the projected document vectors as columns.

3   Random Spectral Projection

Compressive sampling [12,13] is a sampling and reconstruction theory that has popularity in the image processing field [14] but has found its way into machine learning [2]. The idea is that if we are able to represent our data in a sparse vector space though the linear transformation Ψ^{-1}, then we are able to spread the information in our data set throughout the dimensions of the vector space using an linear transformation Φ that is maximally incoherent to Ψ. Using this knowledge, we are able to sample at a rate less than given by the Nyquist theorem and still be able to perfectly reconstruct the original signal from the sample. In our case, we have:

$$\boldsymbol{x} = \min \|z\|_1, \text{ s.t. } \boldsymbol{\xi} = \Phi\Psi\boldsymbol{z}$$

where $\boldsymbol{d} = \Psi\boldsymbol{x}$ is our document vector, $\boldsymbol{x}$ is sparse, Φ is the sampling function, $\boldsymbol{\xi}$ is the sample of $\boldsymbol{d}$, and $\|\cdot\|_1$ is the l_1 norm. The coherence of a pair of basis vectors is a measure of how similar they are. Coherence is given as:

$$\mu(\Phi, \Psi) = \sqrt{N} \max_{1 \leq i,j \leq N} |\langle \boldsymbol{\phi}_i, \boldsymbol{\psi}_j \rangle|$$

where $\boldsymbol{\phi}_i$ and $\boldsymbol{\psi}_j$ are basis vectors of the linear functions Φ and Ψ respectively, and $\mu(\Phi, \Psi) \in [1, \sqrt{N}]$. Therefore if two isometric transformations are maximally incoherent, $\mu(\Phi, \Psi) = 1$.

For outlier detection, we do not need to reconstruct the document vectors, but we do require a method of projecting most of the information in the document collection into a smaller vector space. By performing the projection, we are able to reduce the computation time required, and by preserving most of the data, we will be able to maintain the accuracy of the outlier detection method.

In this article, our data consists of document vectors, which are sparse, therefore, the transformation Ψ^{-1} required to map our document vectors to a sparse set of vectors is simply the identity matrix; we choose $\Psi = I$. Our choice of Φ must be maximally incoherent to $\Psi = I$, therefore, we use $\Phi = \Sigma P_{\mathrm{DFT}}$, where P_{DFT} is the discrete Fourier transform projection, and the matrix Σ selects a sample of s rows from P_{DFT}.

In this section, we will examine the discrete Fourier transform and the discrete cosine transform (a real approximation to the discrete Fourier transform) and how sampling is performed.

3.1 Discrete Fourier Transform

The Discrete Fourier Transform (DFT) is an isometric transformation that decomposes a vector into its various frequency components. The DFT used in this article has the form:

$$W_{d,f} = \sum_{t=0}^{T-1} w_{d,t} \exp\left(\frac{-2i\pi ft}{T}\right)$$

where $i = \sqrt{-1}$ and $W_{d,f}$ is the fth Fourier coefficient of document d. The DFT can also be given as a matrix multiplication:

$$D_{\mathrm{DFT}} = P_{\mathrm{DFT}} D$$

where P_{DFT} contains the elements $\exp\left(-2i\pi ft/T\right)$ and D is the matrix containing the set of weighted document vectors as columns. To sample from the transformed vector, we randomly take s coefficients of the DFT. This can be accomplished by randomly selecting s rows of P_{DFT} and the applying the transformation. The sample vectors (the columns of D_{DFT}) now become our representation of the document d to compute outliers from.

The sample vector contains complex elements, therefore we must ensure that the document similarity function $S(d_i, d_j)$ is modified to reflect this. We must ensure that the we take the complex conjugate of one of the document vectors being compared (for use in the inner product), and that we take the real portion of the inner product.

3.2   Discrete Cosine Transform

Use of the Fourier transform requires us to work in the complex domain, in which tools may not be readily available to many readers. Therefore, we will also examine the discrete cosine transform (DCT), which is a close approximation to the DFT, but its coefficients are real. The DCT used in this article has the form:

$$W_{d,c} = \begin{cases} \frac{1}{\sqrt{T}} \sum_{t=0}^{T-1} w_{d,t} \cos\left[\left(t + \frac{1}{2}\right) \frac{c\pi}{T}\right] & \text{if } c = 0 \\ \sqrt{\frac{2}{T}} \sum_{t=0}^{T-1} w_{d,t} \cos\left[\left(t + \frac{1}{2}\right) \frac{c\pi}{T}\right] & \text{if } c \neq 0 \end{cases}$$

where $W_{d,c}$ is the cth cosine coefficient, The DCT can be represented as a matrix multiplication, in the same fashion as the DFT. We also randomly sample s coefficients from the DCT spectrum to use as our document vector representation in the s dimensional space.

4   Experiments

We will now compare the effects, in terms of accuracy, time and storage required, for outlier detection when using random projection and the DFT and DCT random projections.

4.1   Experimental Environment

Our initial experimental environment consisted of a document set with ten artificially inserted documents from another document collection. For this we used two document sets from the SMART collection[1]. The first document set we used contained all documents from the CRAN document set (aerodynamics documents) and the first ten documents from the MED document set (medical abstracts), giving us 1408 documents and 4589 unique terms. We called this document set CRAN+10MED. The second document set we used contained all of the documents from the CISI document set (information science abstracts) and the first ten documents from the CRAN document set, giving us 1470 documents containing 5676 unique terms. We called this collection CISI+10CRAN. Note that each of the documents sets were parsed and converted into matrices using the textIR indexing software[2]. This software removes a predefined set of stopwords and performs stemming using the Lovins stemmer.

---

[1] Available from: ftp://ftp.cs.cornell.edu/pub/smart
[2] Available from: http://staff.scm.uws.edu.au/~lapark/textIR/

4.2   Evaluation

Rather than examine the number of outliers predicted correctly, we instead examined the likelihood of a document being an outlier, allowing us to obtain a finer scale for accuracy measurement. Our experiments involved ranking all points in terms of their distance based outlier likelihood score. The ranked lists were then examined and the ranks of the true outliers were found. A method that provides all of the outliers higher in the ranked list is evaluated as being more accurate than a method where the outliers are found in the lower ranks of the ranked list.

To evaluate each outlier detection method's outlier ranked list, we used Average Precision. Average precision uses r, the rank of each true outlier in the outlier ranked list, where r_i is the rank of the ith outlier provided by the method under evaluation, and r_i is ordered from highest rank to lowest rank. For example, if $r_3 = 10$, it means that the outlier detection method ranked an outlier as the 10th most likely outlier, and two other outliers were ranked somewhere from rank 1 to 9. Average precision is defined as:

$$\mathrm{AP}(r) = \frac{1}{O} \sum_{i=1}^{O} \frac{i}{r_i}$$

where O is the number of outliers. If there were three outliers and an outlier detection method ranked the outliers in positions $r = \{1, 3, 6\}$, the Average Precision would be $(1/1 + 2/3 + 3/6)/3 = 0.72$. We can see that if all of the outliers were ranked above all non-outliers, the Average Precision would be 1.

4.3   Procedure

The outlier likelihood score computation requires the parameter k (the number of neighbours to consider). We computed outlier likelihood scores using neighbour distance of $k = 10, 20, 50, 100, 200$ and 500. Each of the sampling methods requires the parameter s (the number of coefficients to sample). We computed outlier likelihood scores using sample sizes $s = 32, 64, 128, 256, 512, 1024$ and 2048. Each trial of the experiment involves random sampling, therefore we repeated each trial ten times to take into account the variability. The mean speed and average precision of the ten trials is reported as the expected value.

4.4   Results

Analysis of the results showed us that similar trends were displayed for each value of k, therefore we will only present the results for $k = 100$ but use the entire set of results in later significance tests. Figures 1 and 2 present the mean AP versus computation time plots for the CISI+10CRAN and CRAN+10MED document sets respectively. It should be noted that the plots show that as s increases, so does the computation time. For the majority of the cases, we see that the mean AP increases as s increases. The Raw result, is the AP obtained when no projection is used. If we examine the vertical alignment of each of the plots, we see that the RP and DCTP times closely match, meaning that for a

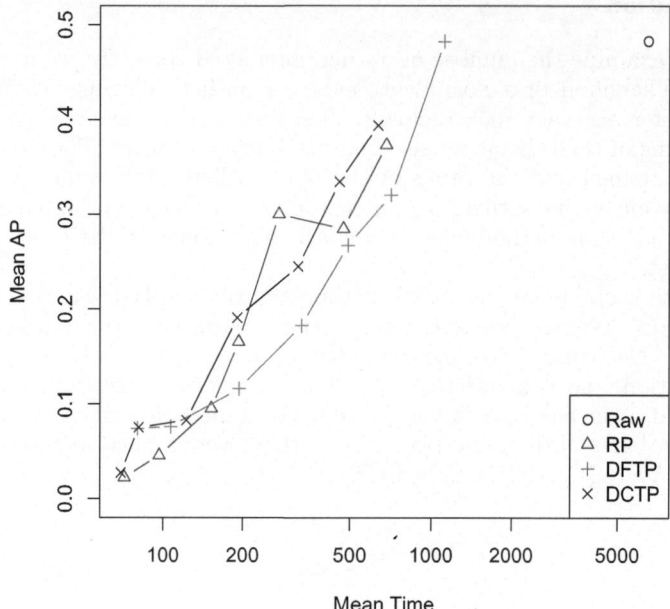

Fig. 1. The mean AP and computation time for outlier detection in the original space (Raw), and for random projection (RP), DFT projection (DFTP), and DCT projection (DCTP) for $k = 100$ on the CISI+10CRAN data set. The results for each projection method have been recorded for projections into 32, 64, 128, 256, 512, 1024 and 2048 dimensions. Note that the time axis is presented in a log scale.

given s, we expect them to complete in the same time. If we examine the times for each DFTP point, we see that they almost match the times of the RP and DCTP methods for the previous s values. Therefore the DFTP method is slower than the DCT and RP; this is likely to be due to the DFTP method producing complex values.

We can compare the mean AP for a given s by examining the horizontal alignment of the points, It can be seen that the DCTP mean AP is greater than RP for Figure 1, but less for Figure 2. We can also see that the mean AP of DFTP for a given s is greater than RP for both plots.

4.5   Significance of Results

We have generated 10 results for each s,k pair for each method. To test the hypothesis that the DFT and DCT spectral random projection provides a greater mean AP for a given s,k pair when compared to random projection, we used bootstrap sampling to generate the distribution of the increase in the mean AP of the DFTP and DCTP outlier detection over RP outlier detection. We can test for a significant increase in mean AP for each of the methods, using the bootstrap distribution. The resulting distributions were approximately Normal for each method on each document set. We obtain p values of 0.060 and 0.0001

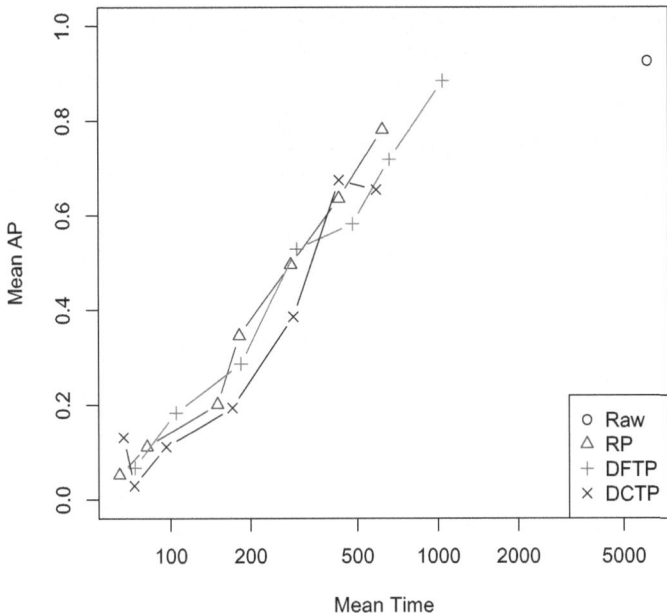

Fig. 2. The mean AP and computation time for outlier detection in the original space (Raw), and for random projection (RP), DFT projection (DFTP), and DCT projection (DCTP) for $k = 100$ on the CRAN+10MED data set. The results for each projection method have been recorded for projections into 32, 64, 128, 256, 512, 1024 and 2048 dimensions. Note that the time axis is presented in a log scale.

for the DFT projection on the CISI+10CRAN and CRAN+10MED collections respectively. This shows that the DFT random spectral projection provides a significant increase in mean AP over random projection. For DCT projection, we obtained p values of 0.398 and 0.995 on the CISI+10CRAN and CRAN+10MED collections respectively. This implies that we have no evidence of the DCT projection providing a significant increase in mean AP over random projection.

From these results, we can see that using DFTP produced more accurate results than when using RP for both document sets. But we must ask what caused the change in accuracy of the DCTP method across document sets? If we examine the Raw scores for each document set, we see 0.48 for the CISI+10CRAN set and 0.92 for the CRAN+10MED set, meaning that the outliers had more separation in the CRAN+10MED set, but were harder to find in the CISI+10CRAN set. From this, we can make the hypothesis that the separation of the RP and DCTP methods grow as the difficulty in detecting the outliers increases. Testing this hypothesis will be left for future work.

4.6   Large Document Collection

To examine the benefit of using the DFTP and DCTP methods on large documents sets, we combined the 56920 articles from the TREC[3] Disk 2 Ziff

---

[3] http://trec.nist.gov/

Publishing collection (computing articles) and the first 10 newspaper articles from the TREC Disk 2 Financial Review collection (finance articles). This formed a document collection with 56930 documents and 82295 unique terms; we call this document set ZIFF+10FR. Using a sparse matrix format, we were able to store the term frequency matrix in 83.93 megabytes.

We then ran the outlier detection method on the weighted term frequency matrix, and on random projections of the matrix using RP, DFTP and DCTP. Each method projected the matrix to $s = 512$ sample features and we computed the $k = 5$, 10, 20, 50, 100, 200 and 500 neighbour distances. The memory consumption and timing results are presented in Table 1, while the accuracy results are in Table 2.

We can see that even though the random projection and both spectral random projections required more storage than the sparse raw data, the computation time for the projected data was much faster, allowing us to obtain results. DCTP required the least storage and computation time, while RP required the most storage (due to it needing storage for its projection matrix), and DFTP required the most time (due to it using complex numbers). The accuracy results show us that the outlier detection task was difficult (shown by the low AP scores). We can see that for each k the DFTP AP is the greatest (for some values of k it is

Table 1. The memory used for the projection function (Function) and the projected matrix (Projection), and the time taken to perform the projection (Projection) and compute the outliers (Outlier) when using no projection (Raw), random projection (RP), DCT projection (DCTP), and DFT projection (DFTP) on the ZIFF+10FR document collection. Note that the Raw completion time of 3.4 years was extrapolated.

Method	Memory		Time	
	Function	Projection	Projection	Outlier
Raw	NA	NA	NA	3.4 years
RP	321.4 MiB	222.3 MiB	16.6 sec	2.6 days
DCTP	NA	222.3 MiB	38.2 min	2.4 days
DFTP	NA	444.7 MiB	38.6 min	4.4 days

Table 2. Accuracy results for outlier detection on each projection method using the ZIFF+10FR document collection. The average precision (AP) for $k = 5$, 10, 20, 50, 100, 200 and 500 is shown.

Method	AP						
	5	10	20	50	100	200	500
RP	0.0001	0.0016	0.0029	0.0027	0.0022	0.0017	0.0011
DCTP	0.0001	0.0016	0.0036	0.0034	0.0025	0.0019	0.0013
DFTP	0.0001	0.0021	0.0107	0.0209	0.0303	0.0290	0.0196

at least 10 times greater than the RP and DCTP AP). We can also see that the DCTP AP is either greater than or equal to the RP AP.

4.7 Discussion

This work shows the potential of the DFT and DCT projections when compared to random projection, but is only one component in high dimensional outlier detection. There have been other methods proposed in the literature to increase the speed of distance based outlier detection, but they were not used in this analysis. We kept this analysis as simple as possible, to examine the effect of the sample projection only.

The findings from this work can be combined with existing methods of approximation to increase speed. For example, neighbour distances can be computed on a random sample of documents rather than the whole set [15]. This approximation can also be applied to increase the speed of a DFT or DCT projection. LOF [4] can be used in place of the distance based outlier detection method. Methods of increasing the speed of distance based outlier detection method are given in [3]. These may be directly applied to the projected document space to further reduce the computation time of the DFTP and DCTP methods.

Rather than using random projection to compute the distances, it can be used to select a candidate set of neighbours [16]. The distances to all candidates may then be computed in the original space. The analysis in this article has shown that the DCT or DFT can also be used in place of random projection in this case.

5   Conclusion

Outlier detection is an important process that allows us to automatically identify objects that are different from the majority of the data. When examining text, we can use outlier detection to identify documents that are interesting or out of place. Random projection is used in outlier detection to obtain a lower dimensional approximation of the data, in order to speed up the detection process.

In this article, we presented the concept of spectral random projection, using the discrete Fourier transform (DFT) and the discrete cosine transform (DCT), and we examined its utility for outlier detection on a text document collection.

We showed that using the DFT projection provides significantly greater accuracy than when using random projection and requires less storage, but requires additional time. We also showed that the DCT projection provides similar accuracy and computation time as random projection, but it requires much less storage (60% less for the large document set).

References

1. Deegalla, S., Bostrom, H.: Reducing high-dimensional data by principal component analysis vs. random projection for nearest neighbor classification. In: Proceedings of the 5th International Conference on Machine Learning and Applications, ICMLA 2006, pp. 245–250. IEEE Computer Society, Washington, DC (2006)

2. Park, L.A.F.: Fast Approximate Text Document Clustering Using Compressive Sampling. In: Gunopulos, D., Hofmann, T., Malerba, D., Vazirgiannis, M. (eds.) ECML PKDD 2011, Part II. LNCS, vol. 6912, pp. 565–580. Springer, Heidelberg (2011)

3. Knorr, E.M., Ng, R.T., Tucakov, V.: Distance-based outliers: algorithms and applications. The VLDB Journal 8(3-4), 237–253 (2000)

4. Breunig, M.M., Kriegel, H.P., Ng, R.T., Sander, J.: Lof: identifying density-based local outliers. In: Proceedings of the 2000 ACM SIGMOD International Conference on Management of Data, SIGMOD 2000, pp. 93–104. ACM, New York (2000)

5. Zobel, J., Moffat, A.: Exploring the similarity space. ACM SIGIR Forum 32(1), 18–34 (1998)

6. Jones, K.S., Walker, S., Robertson, S.E.: A probabilistic model of information retrieval: development and comparative experiments, part 2. Information Processing and Management 36(6), 809–840 (2000)

7. Song, F., Croft, W.B.: A general language model for information retrieval. In: CIKM 1999: Proceedings of the Eighth International Conference on Information and knowledge Management, pp. 316–321. ACM Press (1999)

8. Park, L.A.F., Leckie, C.A., Ramamohanarao, K., Bezdek, J.C.: Adapting Spectral Co-clustering to Documents and Terms Using Latent Semantic Analysis. In: Nicholson, A., Li, X. (eds.) AI 2009. LNCS, vol. 5866, pp. 301–311. Springer, Heidelberg (2009)

9. Ding, C., He, X., Simon, H.D.: On the equivalence of nonnegative matrix factorization and spectral clustering. In: Proc. SIAM Int'l Conf. Data Mining (SDM 2005), pp. 606–610 (April 2005)

10. Park, L.A.F., Ramamohanarao, K.: An analysis of latent semantic term self-correlation. ACM Transactions on Information Systems 27(2), 1–35 (2009)

11. Park, L.A.F., Ramamohanarao, K.: Efficient storage and retrieval of probabilistic latent semantic information for information retrieval. The International Journal on Very Large Data Bases 18(1), 141–156 (2009)

12. Candes, E., Wakin, M.: An introduction to compressive sampling. IEEE Signal Processing Magazine 25(2), 21–30 (2008)

13. Candes, E.J.: Compressive sampling. In: Proceedings of the International Congress of Mathematicians. European Mathematical Society, Madrid (2006)

14. Goyal, V., Fletcher, A., Rangan, S.: Compressive sampling and lossy compression. IEEE Signal Processing Magazine 25(2), 48–56 (2008)

15. Wu, M., Jermaine, C.: Outlier detection by sampling with accuracy guarantees. In: Proceedings of the 12th ACM SIGKDD International Conference on Knowledge Discovery and Data Mining, KDD 2006, pp. 767–772. ACM, New York (2006)

16. de Vries, T., Chawla, S., Houle, M.: Density-preserving projections for large-scale local anomaly detection. Knowledge and Information Systems 32, 25–52 (2012), doi:10.1007/s10115-011-0430-4

Exploration / Exploitation Trade-Off
in Mobile Context-Aware Recommender Systems

Djallel Bouneffouf, Amel Bouzeghoub, and Alda Lopes Gançarski

Department of Computer Science, Télécom SudParis, UMR CNRS Samovar,
91011 Evry Cedex, France
{Djallel.Bouneffouf,Amel.Bouzeghoub,
Alda.Gancarski}@it-sudparis.eu

Abstract. The contextual bandit problem has been studied in the recommender system community, but without paying much attention to the contextual aspect of the recommendation. We introduce in this paper an algorithm that tackles this problem by modeling the Mobile Context-Aware Recommender Systems (MCRS) as a contextual bandit algorithm and it is based on dynamic exploration/exploitation. Within a deliberately designed offline simulation framework, we conduct extensive evaluations with real online event log data. The experimental results and detailed analysis demonstrate that our algorithm outperforms surveyed algorithms.

Keywords: recommender system, machine learning, exploration/exploitation dilemma, artificial intelligence.

1   Introduction

A considerable amount of research has been done in recommending interesting content for mobile users. Earlier techniques in Mobile Context-Aware Recommender Systems (MCRS) [3, 6, 12, 5, 22] are based solely on the computational behavior of the user to model his interests regarding his surrounding environment like location, time and near people (the user's situation).

The main limitation of such approaches is that they do not take into account the dynamicity of the user's content. This gives rise to another category of recommendation techniques that try to tackle this limitation by using collaborative, content-based or hybrid filtering techniques.

Collaborative filtering, by finding similarities through the users' history, gives an interesting recommendation only if the overlap between users' history is high and the user's content is static[18]. Content-based filtering, identify new documents which match with an existing user's profile, however, the recommended documents are always similar to the documents previously selected by the user [15].

Hybrid approaches have been developed by combining the two latest techniques; so that, the inability of collaborative filtering to recommend new documents is reduced by combining it with content-based filtering [13]. However, the user's content

M. Thielscher and D. Zhang (Eds.): AI 2012, LNCS 7691, pp. 591–601, 2012.
© Springer-Verlag Berlin Heidelberg 2012

in mobile undergoes frequent changes. These issues make content-based and collaborative filtering approaches difficult to apply [8].

The bandit algorithm is a well-known solution that has the advantage of following
the evolution of the user's content and addresses this problem as a need for balancing
exploration/exploitation (exr/exp) tradeoff.

One classical solution to the multi-armed bandit problem is the ε-greedy strategy
[9]. With the probability 1-ε, this algorithm chooses the best documents based on
current knowledge; and with the probability ε, it uniformly chooses any other documents uniformly.

The ε parameter controls essentially the exp/exr tradeoff between exploitation and
exploration. One drawback of this algorithm is that it is difficult to decide the optimal
value in advance. Instead, we extend the ε-greedy strategy with an update of the ε
value by doing an exr/exp-tradeoff using a finite set of ε candidates.

The rest of the paper is organized as follows. Section 2 gives the key notions used
throughout this paper. Section 3 reviews some related works. Section 4 presents our
MCRS model and Section 5 describes the algorithms involved in the proposed approach. The experimental evaluation is illustrated in Section 6. The last section
concludes the paper and points out possible directions for future work.

2   Key Notions

In this section, we sketch briefly the key notions that will be of use in the remainder
of this paper.

2.1   The User's Model

The user's model is structured as a case based, which is composed of a set of situations with their corresponding user's preferences, denoted $U = \{(S^i; UP^i)\}$, where S^i is
the user's situation and UP^i its corresponding user's preferences.

2.2   The User's Preferences

The user's preferences are deduced during the user's navigation activities. A navigation activity expresses the following sequence of events:

- The user's logs in the system and navigates across documents to get the desired
  information;
- The user expresses his preferences on the visited documents.

We assume that the preference is the information that we extract from the user's system interaction, for example the number of clicks on the visited documents or the time
spent on a document.

Let UP be the preferences submitted by a specific user in the system at a given situation. Each document in UP is represented as a single vector $d=(c_1,...,c_n)$, where c_i
$(i=1, .., n)$ is the value of a component characterizing the preferences of d. We

consider the following components: the total number of clicks on d, the total time spent reading d and the number of times d was recommended.

2.3   Context

A user's context C is a multi-ontology representation where each ontology corresponds to a context dimension $C=(O_{Location}, O_{Time}, O_{Social})$.

Each dimension models and manages a context information type. We focus on these three dimensions since they cover all needed information. These ontologies are described in [6] and are not developed in this paper.

2.4   Situation

A situation is an instantiation of the user's context. We consider a situation as a triple $S = (O_{Location}.x_i, O_{Time}.x_j, O_{Social}.x_k)$ where x_i, x_j and x_k are ontology concepts or instances. Suppose the following data are sensed from the user's mobile phone: the GPS shows the latitude and longitude of a point "48.8925349, 2.2367939"; the local time is "Mon Oct 3 12:10:00 2011" and the calendar states "meeting with Paul Gerard". The corresponding situation is:
$S=(O_{Location}.$"48.89, 2.23"$, O_{Time}.$"Mon_Oct_3_12:10:00_2011"$, O_{Social}.$ "Paul_Gerard").

To build a more abstracted situation, we interpret the user's behavior from this low-level multimodal sensor data using ontologies reasoning means. For example, from S, we obtain the following situation:
$MeetingAtRestaurant=(O_{Location}.Restaurant, O_{Time}.Work\_day, O_{Social}.Financial\_client).$

For simplification reasons, we adopt in the rest of the paper the following notation: $S = (x_i, x_j, x_k)$. The previous example situation became thus:
$MeetingAtRestaurant=(Restaurant, Work\_day, Financial\_client).$

Among the set of captured situations, some of them are characterized as high-level critical situations.

3   Related Work

We refer, in the following, recent recommendation techniques that tackle both making dynamic exr/exp (bandit algorithm) and considering the user's situation in recommendation.

3.1   Bandit Algorithms Overview (ε-greedy)

The (exr/exp) tradeoff was firstly studied in reinforcement learning in 1980's, and later flourished in other fields of machine learning [16, 19]. Very frequently used in reinforcement learning to study the (exr/exp) tradeoff, the multi-armed bandit problem was originally described by Robbins [16].

The ε-greedy is the one of the most used strategy to solve the bandit problem and was first described in [20]. The ε-greedy strategy choose a random document with epsilon-frequency (ε), and choose otherwise the document with the highest estimated mean, the estimation is based on the rewards observed thus far. ε must be in the open interval [0, 1] and its choice is left to the user.

The first variant of the ε-greedy strategy is what [9, 2] refer to as the ε-beginning strategy. This strategy makes exploration all at once at the beginning. For a given number $I \in N$ of iterations, the documents are randomly pulled during the εI first iterations. During the remaining $(1-\varepsilon)I$ iterations, the document of highest estimated mean is pulled.

Another variant of the ε-greedy strategy is what Cesa-Bianchi and Fisher [2] call the ε-decreasing strategy. In this strategy, the document with the highest estimated mean is always pulled except when a random document is pulled instead with an ε_i frequency, where n is the index of the current round. The value of the decreasing ε_i is given by $\varepsilon_i = \{\varepsilon_0 / i\}$ where $\varepsilon_0 \in]0, 1]$.

Besides ε-decreasing, four other strategies are presented in [14]. Those strategies are not described here because the experiments done by [14] seem to show that, with carefully chosen parameters, ε-decreasing is always as good as the other strategies.

Compared to the standard multi-armed bandit problem with a fixed set of possible actions, in MCRS, old documents may expire and new documents may frequently emerge. Therefore it may not be desirable to perform the exploration all at once at the beginning as in [9] or to decrease monotonically the effort on exploration as the decreasing strategy in [2].

Few research works are dedicated to study the contextual bandit problem on Recommender System, where they consider user's behavior as the context of the bandit problem.

In [10], authors extend the ε-greedy strategy by updating the exploration value ε dynamically. At each iteration, they run a sampling procedure to select a new ε from a finite set of candidates. The probabilities associated to the candidates are uniformly initialized and updated with the Exponentiated Gradient (EG) [10]. This updating rule increases the probability of a candidate ε if it leads to a user's click. Compared to both ε-beginning and decreasing strategy, this technique improves the results.

In [21], authors model the recommendation as a contextual bandit problem. They propose an approach in which a learning algorithm selects sequentially documents to serve users based on contextual information about the users and the documents. To maximize the total number of user's clicks, this work proposes the LINUCB algorithm that is computationally efficient.

The authors in [2, 4, 9, 14, 21] describe a smart way to balance exploration and exploitation. However, none of them consider the user's situation during the recommendation.

3.2   Managing the User's Situation

Few research works are dedicated to manage the user's situation on recommendation. In [7, 17] the authors propose a method which consists of building a dynamic user's profile based on time and user's experience. The user's preferences in the user's profile are weighted according to the situation (time, location) and the user's behavior.

To model the evolution on the user's preferences according to his temporal situation in different periods, (like workday or vacations), the weighted association for the concepts in the user's profile is established for every new experience of the user. The user's activity combined with the user's profile are used together to filter and recommend relevant content.

Another work [12] describes a MCRS operating on three dimensions of context that complement each other to get highly targeted. First, the MCRS analyzes information such as clients' address books to estimate the level of social affinity among the users. Second, it combines social affinity with the spatiotemporal dimensions and the user's history in order to improve the quality of the recommendations.

In [3], the authors present a technique to perform user-based collaborative filtering. Each user's mobile device stores all explicit ratings made by its owner as well as ratings received from other users. Only users in spatiotemporal proximity are able to exchange ratings and they show how this provides a natural filtering based on social contexts.

Each work cited above tries to recommend interesting information to users on contextual situation; however they do not consider the evolution of the user's content. As shown above, none of the mentioned works tackles both problems of exr/exp dynamicity and user's situation consideration in the exr/exp strategy. This is precisely what we intend to do with our approach.

We propose for exr/exp-tradeoff a calibration, which consists in updating the value of ε dynamically. At each iteration, we run the ε-decreasing algorithm to select a new ε from a finite set of candidates. The weight associated to the candidates increases if it leads to a user click.

4   MCRS Model

In our recommender system, the recommendation of documents is modeled as a contextual bandit problem including the user's situation information. Formally, a bandit algorithm proceeds in discrete trials $t = 1...T$. For each trial t, the algorithm performs the following tasks:

4.1   Task 1

Let S^t be the current user's situation, and PS the set of past situations. The system compares S^t with the situations in PS in order to choose the most similar S^p using the following semantic similarity metric:

$$S^p = \underset{s^c \in PS}{\arg\max}\left(\sum_j \alpha_j \cdot sim_j\left(x_j^t, x_j^c\right)\right) \tag{1}$$

In Eq.1, sim_j is the similarity metric related to dimension j between two concepts x^t and x^c and α_j the weight associated to dimension j. This similarity depends on how closely x^t and x^c are related in the corresponding ontology (location, time or social). We use the same similarity measure as [24] defined by Eq. 2:

$$sim_j\left(x_j^t, x_j^c\right) = 2 * \frac{deph(LCS)}{(deph(x_j^c) + deph(x_j^t))} \tag{2}$$

In Eq. 2, LCS is the Least Common Subsumer of x_j^t and x_j^c, and $deph$ is the number of nodes in the path from the node to the ontology root.

4.2   Task 2

Let D be the document collection and $D_p \in D$ the set of documents recommended in situation S^p. After retrieving S^p, the system observes the user's behavior when reading each document $d_t \in D_p$. Based on observed rewards, the algorithm chooses the document d_p with the greater reward r_{t_i}.

4.3   Task 3

The algorithm improves its arm-selection strategy with the new observation: in situation S^t, document d_p obtained a reward r_t.

In the field of document recommendation, when a document is presented to the user and this one selects it by a click, a reward of 1 is incurred; otherwise, the reward is 0. With this definition of reward, the expected reward of a document is precisely its Click Through Rate (CTR). The CTR is the average number of clicks on a recommended document, computed dividing the total number of clicks on it by the number of times it was recommended.

5   Exploration/Exploitation Tradeoff

In this section, we firstly present the *ε-greedy* algorithm (sub-section 5.1) and our proposed exr/exp-tradeoff algorithm named *decreasing-ε-greedy* (sub-section 5.2).

5.1   The ε-Greedy() Algorithm

The ε-greedy strategy is sketched in Algorithm 1. For a given user's situation, the algorithm recommends a predefined number of documents, specified by parameter N. In this algorithm, $UP=\{d_1,...,d_P\}$ is the set of documents corresponding to the current user's preferences; $D=\{d_1,....,d_N\}$ is the set of documents to recommend; getCTR (Alg. 1) is the function which estimates the CTR of a given document; Random (Alg. 1) is the function returning a random element from a given set; q is a random value uniformly distributed over [0, 1] which defines the exploration/exploitation tradeoff; ε is the probability of recommending a random exploratory document.

```
Algorithm 1 The ε-greedy algorithm
Input: ε, UP, D = ∅, N
Output:  D
For i = 1 to i = N do
q = Random({0,1})
        ⎧ argmax_UP(getCTR(d))  if  q > ε
dᵢ =   ⎨
        ⎩ Random(UP)            otherwise
          D = D ∪ dᵢ
Endfor
```

5.2   The Decreasing-ε-Greedy

To improve exploitation of the *ε-greedy* algorithm, we propose to extend it with setting out the optimal trade-off value *ε*. We iteratively update it by the method *(decreasing-ε-greedy* (Alg.2).

First we assume that we have a finite number of candidate values for ε, denoted by $H\varepsilon = (\varepsilon_1, \ldots, \varepsilon_T)$. Our goal is to select the optimal ε from $H\varepsilon$.

To this end, we apply the ε-*decreasing* strategy to propose an ε_i, and then we use a set of weights $w = (w_1, \ldots, w_T)$ to keep track of the feedback of each ε_i, w_i is increased if we receive a number of clicks l_i from the user when we use ε_i.

```
Algorithm 2 decreasing-ε-greedy ()
Input: Hε, N, Sᵗ, UP, n
Output: D
εε = Ø, τ= 0, w  = 1, i = 1,…,T
                i
For t = 1 to n do
     τ = 0.01* t
     q = Random ([0,1])
        ⎰ argmax   (w )                if q ≤ τ
        ⎰        (i)  i
ε  =  ⎰
 i      ⎰
        ⎱ Random(Hε-εε)                otherwise
D = ε-greedy(ε , UP, D = Ø, N);
              i
Receive a click feedback l  from the user
                          i
w  = w   l ;  εε = εε U ε ;
 i    i+  i              i
Endfor
```

In Alg. 2. $\varepsilon\varepsilon$ is the set of ε that have been previously selected, n is the number of iteration of the learning algorithm, i is the identifier of ε and τ is the probability of proposing the $argmax_i (w_i)$, this parameter starts at low value and iteratively increases until the end of the learning ($\tau = 1$).

6   Experimental Evaluation

In order to evaluate empirically the performance of our approach, and in the absence of a standard evaluation framework, we propose an evaluation framework based on a diary set of study entries. The main objectives of the experimental evaluation are: to evaluate the performance of the proposed algorithms (Alg. 2).

In the following, we describe our experimental datasets and then present and discuss the obtained results.

6.1   Evaluation Framework

We have conducted a diary study with the collaboration of the French software company Nomalys[1]. This company provides a history application, which records the time, current location, social and navigation information of its users during their application use.

The diary study has taken 18 months and has generated 178 369 diary situation entries. Each diary situation entry represents the capture, of contextual time, location

---

[1] Nomalys is a company that provides a graphical application on Smartphones allowing users to access their company's data.

and social information. For each entry, the captured data are replaced with more abstracted information using time, spatial and social ontologies.

From the diary study, we have obtained a total of 2 759 283 entries concerning the user's navigation, expressed with an average of 15.47 entries per situation.

6.2   Experimental Results

In our experiments, we firstly have collected the 3000 situations with an occurrence greater than 100 to be statistically meaningful. Then, we have sampled 10000 documents that have been shown on any of these situations.

The testing step consists of evaluating the algorithms for each testing situation using the average CTR. The average CTR for a particular iteration is the ratio between the total number of clicks and the total number of displays. Then, we calculate the average CTR every 1000 iterations.

We have run the simulation until the number of iterations reaches 10000 and the number of documents (n) returned by the recommender system for each situation is 10.

In the first experiment, we have evaluated the two exr/exp algorithms described in section 5. In addition to a pure exploitation baseline, we have compared our algorithms (decreasing-ε-greedy) to the algorithms described in section 3: ε-greedy; ε-beginning, ε-decreasing and EG. In Fig. 1, the horizontal axis is the number of iterations and the vertical axis is the performance metric.

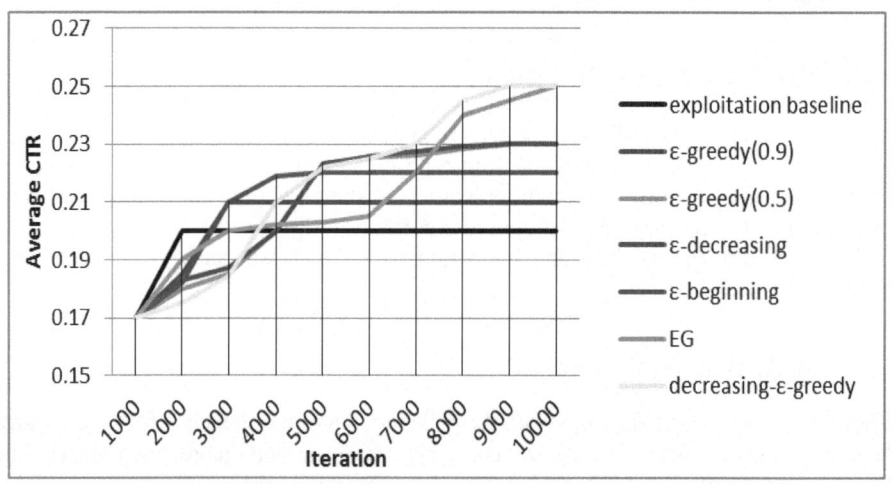

Fig. 1. Average CTR for different exr/exp algorithms

We have parametered the different algorithms as follows: For the *ε-greedy* algorithm, we experiment with two parameter values: 0.5 and 0.9. The *ε-decreasing, EG, decreasing-ε-greedy* share the same set of candidates $\{\varepsilon_i = 1\text{-}0.01 * i,\ i = 1,...,100\}$.

The *ε-decreasing* starts with the largest value and reduces it by 0.01 every 100 iterations until ε reaches the smallest value.

Overall exr/exp algorithms have better performance than the baseline. However, for the first 2000 iterations, with pure exploitation the exploitation baseline achieves a faster increase convergence. But in the long run, all exr/exp algorithms improve the average CTR at convergence.

We have several interesting observations regarding the behaviors of the different exr/exp algorithms. The *EG* algorithm has a similar convergence threshold than *decreasing-ε-greedy*.

The *decreasing-ε-greedy* method effectively learns the optimal ε and its convergence rate is close to the best setting. But for *EG* algorithm, it is only after the 6000 iterations that, the algorithm begins to show its advantage. For the *ε-decreasing* algorithm, the converged CTR increases as ε decreases.

Even after convergence, the *0.9-greedy* and *0.5-greedy* algorithms still give respectively 90% and 50% of the opportunities to documents with low average CTR, which decreases significantly their average CTR.

While the *ε-decreasing* algorithm converges to a higher CTR, its overall performance is not as good as *0.5-greedy*. Its CTR drops a lot at the early stage because of more exploration but does not converge faster.

The *decreasing-ε-greedy* algorithm has the best convergence rate, and increases CTR by a factor of 1.5 over the baseline and outperforms over all other exr/exp algorithms. The improvement comes from a dynamic tradeoff between exr/exp, controlled by reinforcement learning (ε-decreasing).

6.3   Size of Data

To compare the algorithms when data is sparse in our experiments, we reduce data sizes of 30%, 20%, 10%, 5%, and 1%, respectively. To better visualize the comparison results, figure 2 shows algorithms' average CTR graphs with the previous referred data sparseness levels.

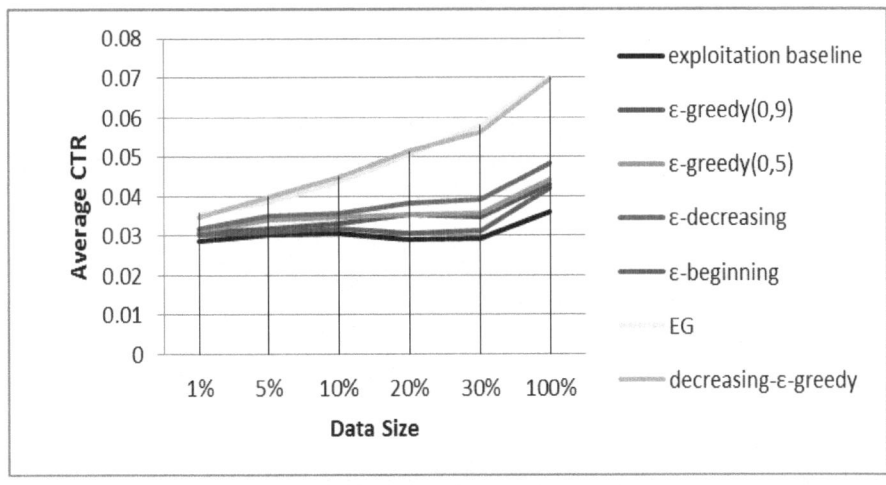

Fig. 2. Average CTR for different data size

Our main observation is that, Although very different from the EG algorithms, the Decreasing-ε-greedy tends to very similar results.

Except for exploitation baseline the ε-beginning seems to have a rather poor performance, its results are worse than any other strategy independently of the chosen parameters. The reason probably lies in the fact that the ε-beginning makes the exploration only at the beginning.

7   Conclusion

In this paper, we study the exploitation and exploration in mobile context-aware recommender systems and propose a novel approach that balances adaptively exr/exp.

We have evaluated our approach according to the proposed evaluation protocol and show that it is effective. In order to evaluate the performance of the proposed algorithm, we compare it with other standard exr/exp strategies.

The experimental results demonstrate that our algorithm performs better on CTR in various configurations. In the future, we plan to evaluate the scalability of the algorithm on-board a mobile device.

References

1. Alexandre, S., Moira Norrie, C., Grossniklaus, M., Signer, B.: Spatio-Temporal Proximity as a Basis for Collaborative Filtering in Mobile Environments. In: CAiSE (2006)
2. Auer, P., Cesa-Bianchi, N., Fischer, P.: Finite Time Analysis of the Multiarmed Bandit Problem. Machine Learning 47, 235–256 (2002)
3. Bader, R., Neufeld, E., Woerndl, W., Prinz, V.: Context-aware POI recommendations in an automotive scenario using multi-criteria decision making methods. In: Proceedings of the 2011 Workshop on Context-awareness in Retrieval and Recommendation, USA, pp. 23–30 (2011)
4. Baltrunas, L., Ludwig, B., Peer, S., Ricci, F.: Context relevance assessment and exploitation in mobile recommender systems. Personal and Ubiquitous Computing 16(5) (2011)
5. Bellotti, V., Begole, B., Chi, E.H., Ducheneaut, N., Fang, J., Isaacs, E.: Activity-Based Serendipitous Recommendations. In: Proceedings on the Move, pp. 1157–1166. ACM, USA (2008)
6. Bouneffouf, D., Bouzeghoub, A., Gançarski, A.L.: Following the User's Interests in Mobile Context-Aware recommender systems. In: AINA Workshops, pp. 657–662. IEEE Computer Society, USA (2012)
7. Adomavicius, G., Mobasher, B., Ricci, F., Tuzhilin, A.: Context-Aware Recommender Systems. AI Magazine 32(3), 67–80 (2011)
8. Chu, W., Park, S.: Personalized recommendation on dynamic content using predictive bilinear models. In: Proc. of World Wide Web, pp. 691–700. ACM, Spain (2009)
9. Even-Dar, E., Mannor, S., Mansour, Y.: PAC Bounds for Multi-armed Bandit and Markov Decision Processes. In: Kivinen, J., Sloan, R.H. (eds.) COLT 2002. LNCS (LNAI), vol. 2375, pp. 255–270. Springer, Heidelberg (2002)
10. Kivinen, J., Manfred, K.W.: Exponentiated gradient versus gradient descent for linear predictors. In: Information and Computation, vol. 132, pp. 132–163. Academic Press, USA (1997)

11. Langford, J., Zhang, T.: The epoch-greedy algorithm for contextual multi-armed bandits. In: Advances in Neural Information Processing Systems, vol. 20, pp. 1096–1103. Curran Associates, Canada (2008)
12. Lakshmish, R., Deepak, P., Ramana, P., Kutila, G., Garg, D., Karthik, V., Shivkumar, K.: A Mobile context-aware, Social Recommender System for Low-End Mobile Device. In: Mobile Data Management: Systems, Services and Middleware CAESAR, pp. 338–347. IEEE Computer Society, USA (2009)
13. Lihong, L., Wei, C., Langford, J., Schapire, E.: A Contextual-Bandit Approach to Personalized News Document Recommendation. CoRR, Presented at the Nineteenth International Conference on World Wide Web, Raleigh, pp. 661–670. ACM, USA (2010)
14. Mannor, S., Tsitsiklis, J.: The Sample Complexity of Exploration in the Multi-Armed Bandit Problem. Computational Learning Theory 5, 623–648 (2004)
15. Mladenic, D.: Text-learning and related intelligent agents: A survey. IEEE Intelligent Agents 14, 44–54 (1999)
16. Robbins, H.: Some aspects of the sequential design of experiments. Bulletin of the American Mathematical Society (1952)
17. Samaras, G., Panayiotou, C.: Personalized portals for the wireless user based on mobile agents. In: Proc. 2nd Int'l Workshop on Mobile Commerce, pp. 70–74. ACM, USA (2002)
18. Schafer, J.B., Konstan, J.: Riedi. J.: Recommender systems in e-commerce. In: Proc. of the 1st ACM Conf. on Electronic Commerce, pp. 158–166. ACM, USA (1999)
19. Sutton, R., Barto, A.: Reinforcement Learning: An Introduction. MIT Press (1998)
20. Watkins, C.J.: Learning from Delayed Rewards. Ph.D. thesis. Cambridge University (1989)
21. Wei, L., Wang, X., Zhang, R., Cui, Y., Mao, J., Jin, R.: Exploitation and Exploration in a Performance based Contextual Advertising System. In: KDD, pp. 133–138. ACM, USA (2010)
22. Woerndl, W., Schulze, F.: Capturing, Analyzing and Utilizing Context-Based Information About User Activities on Smartphones. In: Activity Context Representation Techniques and Languages: Papers from the 2011 AAAI Workshop (2011)
23. Wu, Z., Palmer, M.: Verb Semantics and Lexical Selection. In: Proceedings of the 32nd Annual Meeting of the Association for Computational Linguistics, pp. 133–138 (1994)

Simultaneous Interval Regression
for K-Nearest Neighbor

Mohammad Ghasemi Hamed[1,2], Mathieu Serrurier[1], and Nicolas Durand[1,2]

[1] IRIT - Université Paul Sabatier
118 route de Narbonne 31062, Toulouse Cedex 9, France
[2] ENAC/MAIAA - 7 Avenue Edouard Belin 31055 Toulouse, France

Abstract. In some regression problems, it may be more reasonable to
predict intervals rather than precise values. We are interested in finding
intervals which simultaneously for all input instances $x \in \mathcal{X}$ contain a β
proportion of the response values. We name this problem simultaneous
interval regression. This is similar to simultaneous tolerance intervals for
regression with a high confidence level $\gamma \approx 1$ and several authors have
already treated this problem for linear regression. Such intervals could
be seen as a form of confidence envelop for the prediction variable given
any value of predictor variables in their domain. Tolerance intervals and
simultaneous tolerance intervals have not yet been treated for the K-
nearest neighbor (KNN) regression method. The goal of this paper is
to consider the simultaneous interval regression problem for KNN and
this is done without the homoscedasticity assumption. In this scope, we
propose a new interval regression method based on KNN which takes
advantage of tolerance intervals in order to choose, for each instance,
the value of the hyper-parameter K which will be a good trade-off between the precision and the uncertainty due to the limited sample size
of the neighborhood around each instance. In the experiment part, our
proposed interval construction method is compared with a more conventional interval approximation method on six benchmark regression data
sets.

1 Introduction

When dealing with regression problems, it may be risky to predict a point which
may be illusionary precise. Due to the existence of learning biases, especially
the limited amount of available data and the necessarily incomplete language
used for describing them, the obtained model does not describe exactly the
true unknown model. In situations with lack of sufficient observations to obtain
precise results or when the considered model is too complex, one may rather want
to find intervals which are the most likely to contain a desired proportion of the
population of the response values. Such intervals are mostly used in application
demanding a high level of confidence, like aircraft trajectory prediction, security
systems. The most common approach to estimate these prediction intervals is to
use statistical inference to calculate confidence intervals on the error's variable.

M. Thielscher and D. Zhang (Eds.): AI 2012, LNCS 7691, pp. 602–613, 2012.

However, this corresponds to a confidence interval about the error and not about the real prediction value. Another disadvantage of this approach is to assume that the prediction interval sizes are constant and so independent of the considered instance.

It is known that taking a quantile of an estimated distribution using a sample set having a limited number of instance is not a statistically approved way to infer an interval that must contain a desired proportion of the true unknown distribution that might have generated this sample set. This is because the estimation procedure did not take into account the uncertainty related due to the limited sample size used for estimating the distribution. In statistics, there are already many ways to build confidence intervals around a prediction variable like prediction intervals, tolerance intervals, confidence intervals of quantiles and simultaneous confidence intervals of quantiles, etc. and each of them has its own properties. In this work, we are interested in intervals which have similar properties to the simultaneous tolerance intervals for regression. Simultaneous interval regression, introduced in this paper, could be seen as a form of confidence envelop for the real value of the prediction variable Y given any value of predictor variables in their domain $x \in \mathcal{X}$. This concept is similar to simultaneous tolerance interval for regression with an high confidence level $\gamma \approx 1$. This type of approach is different to quantile regression introduced by Koenker and Bassett (1978) [8] in which conditional quantile of the response variable Y given the predictor values $X = x$ is calculated. Quantile regression is much more flexible than least square regression when dealing with heterogeneous conditional distributions, because it makes no distributional assumption about the error term in the model and just provide a conditional distribution of the prediction given the predictor values [9]. Quantile regression focus on the direct estimation of regression quantile and ignores the uncertainty related to the limited number of observations. Some authors have already treated the problem of confidence intervals for regression quantiles [7,2,6], however they always focus to find confidence interval on the regression parameters and not on the prediction variable. One might think to use the confidence interval on the regression parameters in quantile regression to derive intervals on the conditional quantile. However, The major difference of these derived confidence intervals with tolerance intervals in least square regression is that they are not two-sided, but just a one-sided confidence interval on the prediction variable. Another fundamental difference with simultaneous tolerance interval in least square regression is that they are confidence intervals of regression quantiles given $X = x$ and not simultaneous on the entire domain of independent variables.

Simultaneous tolerance intervals have already been treated by several authors [11,19,12] for linear regression. These works are based on three assumptions. First, the error follows a normal distribution. Second, the mean is linear with respect to the input variable. Finally, the standard deviation around the mean is constant and independent with respect to the input variables (homoscedasticity assumption). This paper tries to overcome the last two limitations by using tolerance interval and a non parametric regression method, however we still assume that the error distribution is normal. Thus, we define simultaneous interval regression for K-nearest neighbor. In simultaneous interval regression for KNN, the local tolerance interval is used in order to find the value of the parameter K that has the better trade-off between the precision and the uncertainty. Given a dataset and a desired proportion of response value β, the goal is to find the optimal combination of hyper-parameters (MIN_K, MAX_K and γ), for which the simultaneous condition on the obtained intervals of the underlying data set is satisfied. The interval construction approach is proposed for KNN in general. This method exploits the local density of the neighborhood to find the most appropriate intervals to contain the desired proportion of response values, so the proposed interval construction method may be more effective with heterogeneous data set with heteroscedastic error.

This paper is organized as follows: section 2 is a brief introduction of tolerance interval and simultaneous tolerance interval for least square regression. Section 3 is devoted to the description of our approach with KNN and in the last section, we apply our method on six benchmark regression databases.

2   Tolerance Interval and Least Square Regression

2.1   Tolerance Interval

Let $X_1, \cdots, X_n$ denote a random sample from a continuous probability distribution and let $\mathbb{X} = (X_1, \cdots, X_n)$. A tolerance interval is an interval which guarantees with a specified confidence level γ, to contain a specified proportion β of the population. The $I_{\gamma,\beta}^T$ sign, is used to refer to a β-content γ-coverage tolerance interval [1]. Then, we have:

$$\forall \beta \in (0,1), \; P_{\mathbb{X}}(P(X \in I_{\gamma,\beta}^T | \mathbb{X}) \geq \beta) = \gamma \tag{1}$$

By making the assumption that our sample set comes from a univariate normal distribution, then the lower and the upper bound of the tolerance interval $I_{\gamma,\beta}^T = [X_l, X_u]$ for a sample of size n is obtained as follows :

$$X_l = \hat{\theta} - \mathbf{k}\hat{\sigma}, \; X_u = \hat{\theta} + \mathbf{k}\hat{\sigma} \tag{2}$$

$$\mathbf{k} = \sqrt{\frac{(n-1)(1+\frac{1}{n})Z_{1-\frac{1-\beta}{2}}^2}{\chi_{1-\gamma,n-1}^2}} \tag{3}$$

where $\hat{\theta}$ is the sample mean of the distribution, $\hat{\sigma}$ its sample standard deviation, $\chi_{1-\gamma,n-1}^2$ represents the $1 - \gamma$ quantile of the chi-square distribution with $n - 1$ degree of freedom and $Z_{1-\frac{1-\beta}{2}}^2$ is the squared of $(1 - \frac{1-\beta}{2})$ quantile value of the standard normal distribution [5]. For more details on tolerance intervals see [1].

Regression is the process of creating an approximating function that looks for capturing relevant patterns in the data. In a classical fixed design regression problem (parametric or nonparametric), there are m pairs $(x_i, y(x_i))$ of observation where x_i is a vector of input variables and $y(x_i)$ is the observed value of the response variable. It is usually supposed that the mean of the random variable $Y(x_i)$ follows an unknown function f^* with a random error term ε_i defined as:

$$Y(x_i) = f^*(x_i) + \varepsilon_i, \ where \ E(\varepsilon_i) = 0. \tag{4}$$

Thus, the goal of regression is to learn from data a function f that is as close as possible to the unknown function f^*. In least square regression, it results to find the function that minimize the mean square of the error (MSE), i.e. find f that minimize :

$$MSE(f) = \frac{1}{m} \sum_{1}^{m} (y(x_i) - f(x_i))^2 \tag{5}$$

In the following, we will always assume that the error follows a normal distribution. A conventional approach employed by some practitioners is to assume that f is a non-biased estimator of f^* with $Var(\varepsilon_i) = \sigma^2$ being constant which means that it does not depends of the input vector (homoscedasticity assumption), and to use the MSE of the found f as an estimation of σ^2 (i.e. $MSE(f) = \hat{\sigma}^2$). Thus the conventional approach assumes that the error distribution normal and homoscedastic. In this approach inter-quantiles of the estimated normal distribution are used, as an approximate solution to find intervals that contain a chosen proportion of the underlying distribution for a given value of dependent variables or intervals that contain a chosen amount of underlying distribution for all the possible values of dependent variables, (respectively similar to tolerance intervals and simultaneous tolerance intervals). For instance, the 0.95 inter-quantile $[f(x) - 1.96\hat{\sigma}, f(x) + 1.96\hat{\sigma}]$ is often used as an interval that will contain 95% of the distribution of $Y(x)$ (i. e. as a regression tolerance interval). As shown by Wallis [17], this statement is not true since $\hat{\sigma}$ and $f(x)$ are only estimations of the true standard deviation σ and the true mean function f^*. These estimations are usually made on a finite sample and are then pervaded with uncertainty. Thus, tolerance intervals for least square regression have been introduced in order to take into account this uncertainty. These intervals are described formally by (6). We name such intervals, β-content γ-coverage regression tolerance intervals and they are represented by $I(x)_{\gamma,\beta}^T$.

$$\forall x, \ P\left(\int_{L_{\beta,\gamma}(x)}^{U_{\beta,\gamma}(x)} p_x(t)dt \geq \beta \right) \geq \gamma \ where \ Y(x) = f^*(x) + \varepsilon_i \tag{6}$$

Where $p_x(t)$ represents the the probability density function of $Y(x)$ for an specified value of predictor variable x. It is important to observe that tolerance intervals in regression are defined separately for each input vector x. Therefore, for two different input vectors x_1 and x_2, $I(x_1)_{\gamma,\beta}^T$ and $I(x_2)_{\gamma,\beta}^T$ are different and the event of $Y(x_1) \in I(x_1)_{\gamma,\beta}^T$ is independent of $Y(x_2) \in I(x_2)_{\gamma,\beta}^T$.

2.2 Difference between Tolerance and Prediction Intervals

One might think to use prediction intervals instead of tolerance intervals. Note that in terms of prediction, tolerance intervals are not the same as prediction intervals. For a given x, tolerance intervals contain at least $100\beta\%$ of the population of $Y(x)$, however a β prediction interval contains in mean $100\beta\%$ of the distribution of $Y(x)$. In other words, the expected percentage of the population of $Y(x)$ contained in its β prediction interval $I(x)_\beta^{Pred}$ is β. This is stated formally as follows:

$$\forall x, E(P(Y(x) \in I(x)_\beta^{Pred})) = \beta \ where \ Y(x) = f^*(x) + \varepsilon_i \qquad (7)$$

For a detailed discussion about the differences between prediction and tolerance intervals, the reader can find more in [4].

2.3 Simultaneous Tolerance Intervals for Least Square Regression

As seen above, tolerance intervals for least square regression are point-wise intervals which are obtained separately for each vector of x. Lieberman and Miller [11] extended the Wallis [17] idea to the simultaneous case. Simultaneous tolerance intervals are constructed so that with confidence level γ, simultaneously for all possible values of input vector x, at least β proportion of the whole population of the response variable Y is contained in the obtained intervals. In fact simultaneous tolerance interval for least square regression $[LS_{\beta,\gamma}(x), US_{\beta,\gamma}(x)]$ create an envelope around the entire mean regression function $f(\cdot)$ such that for all $x \in \mathcal{X}$, the probability that $Y(x)$ is contained in $[LS_{\beta,\gamma}(x), US_{\beta,\gamma}(x)]$ is simultaneously β, and this coverage is guaranteed with a confidence level γ. We name such intervals, β-content γ-coverage simultaneous regression tolerance intervals, we represent them by $I(x)_{\gamma,\beta}^{TS}$ and they are described formally by Equation (8), where $p_x(t)$ represents the the probability density function of $Y(x)$ for an specified value of predictor variable x.

$$P\left(\min_{x \in \mathcal{X}} \left(\int_{LS_{\beta,\gamma}(x)}^{US_{\beta,\gamma}(x)} p_x(t)dt\right) \geq \beta\right) \geq \gamma \ where \ Y(x) = f^*(x) + \varepsilon_i \qquad (8)$$

These intervals have been studied for the linear regression by several authors [11,19,12]. For an introduction to the subject, the reader can see Lieberman and Miller [11]. They explained the problem in details and presented four different methods to construct such intervals for linear regression. For more information about simultaneous inference, see [1,13].

3 Simultaneous Interval Regression for K-Nearest Neighbor (KNN)

3.1 K-Nearest Neighbor (KNN)

Non-parametric regression is a type of regression analysis in which the response value is not a predefined function of the predictor variables and vector of parameter θ which must be estimated form data. In contrary to parametric regression, which is based on the construction on a model based on a training set, the prediction for a vector x is made by a local estimation inside the training set. The motivation of non-parametric methods is their utility when dealing with too complex models or when having non-linear or linear with heteroscedastic data. Therefore, in such situations, exploiting the neighborhood of the input data to estimate the local distribution of response value may be justified. KNN uses the distribution of response values in the neighborhood of the input vector x to find its unknown response value. In this work, we assume that the local distributions are normal, and we will use tolerance intervals of normal distribution to obtain the required intervals. This section, makes also the general assumptions of fixed regression design described in the previous section. With KNN, which are linear smoothers, the estimated function for the input vector x, $f(x)$ will be defined as:

$$f(x) = \sum_{i=1}^{n} l_i y(x_i). \tag{9}$$

where l_i, is the weight associated to the observation $y(x_i)$. The computation of these weights, requires an unknown hyper-parameter named as the bandwidth. The bandwidth is the size of the neighborhood (K) around the considered input vector which is used to compute these weights. Then, KNN which is a kernel smoother is defined as follows :

$$f(x) = \frac{\sum_{i=1}^{n} Ker_b(d(x, x_i))y(x_i)}{\sum_{i=1}^{n} Ker_b(d(x, x_i))} \tag{10}$$

where

$$Ker_b(u) = \frac{1}{b} Ker(\frac{u}{b}),$$

$Ker(\cdot)$ is an a kernel function, $d(\cdot)$ is a distance function and b is the distance between the input vector x and its furthest K-nearest neighbor. In fact KNN is a specialized form of Nadaraya-Watson (NW) [14,18] kernel estimator in which the bandwidth b is not constant and depends on the distance between input vector x and its furthest K-nearest neighbor. Usually, The size of the neighborhood, K, has to be fixed before the learning phase and it will be constant for all the input vectors. In the following, the neighborhood of x is denoted as :

$$Kset_x = \{(x_i, y(x_i)), d(x, x_i) \leq b\}.$$

Some of the common kernel functions are defined as belows [10] where $I(\cdot)$ is the indicator function:

Tricube: $K(u) = \frac{70}{81}(1 - |u|^3)^3 \, I(|u| \leq 1)$,

Gaussian : $K(u) = \frac{1}{\sqrt{2\pi}} e^{-\frac{1}{2}u^2}, I(|u| \leq 1)$,

Epanechnikov: $K(u) = \frac{3}{4}(1 - u^2) \, I(|u| \leq 1)$,

Uniform: $K(u) = \frac{1}{2} I(|u| \leq 1)$.

3.2 KNN Simultaneous Interval Regression

Our goal is to find intervals which contain simultaneously a proportion of the response values for all input instances $x \in \mathcal{X}$. We name the problem stated just above as simultaneous interval regression. This is similar to consider simultaneous tolerance interval for regression with a high confidence level $\gamma \approx 1$. The goal of this paper is to consider the simultaneous interval regression problem for KNN. The interval construction approach is proposed for KNN in general. This method exploits the local density of the neighborhood to find the most appropriate intervals to contain the desired proportion of response values, so the proposed interval construction method may be more effective with heterogeneous data set with heteroscedastic error. Note that, tolerance and simultaneous tolerance intervals have not yet been treated for non-parametric methods. Thus, given an input vector x, K, β, and γ, the tolerance interval for the response variable is computed by using Equation (2) with

$$\hat{\theta} = f(x), n = K$$

and

$$\sigma = (K-1)^{-1} \sum_{y(x_i) \in Kset_x} (y(x_i) - \bar{y})^2, \; where \; \bar{y} = K^{-1} \sum_{y(x_i) \in Kset_x} y(x_i).$$

Note that, in contrary to the sample mean, the sample standard deviation does not take into account the distance between the considered input vector and its neighbors. Indeed, if the weights l_i was embedded in the computation of σ, K would overestimate the amount of information used for the estimation of the standard derivation.

As pointed out previously, it is common to fix K and use a general KNN estimator. These settings are denoted as "KNN regression with fixed K". The fixed K idea in KNN regression comes from the assumption which suppose that the data are homogeneously distributed in the feature space. In this section tolerance intervals are used to find the "best" K for each input vector x. Let the sample set containing the response values of the K-nearest neighbors of x be $Kset_x$. For a fixed value of β, and for each input vector x, the computation begins by an initial value of K, then the β-content γ-coverage normal tolerance interval of $Kset_x$ is calculated. This process is repeated for the same input vector x but different values of $K, MIN_K \leq K \leq MAX_K$. Finally, for a given x, the interval having the smallest size between other tolerance intervals resulted by different $Kset_x$ for $MIN_K \leq K \leq MAX_K$ is chosen as the desired interval.

This leads us to choose the interval that has the best trade-off between the precision and the uncertainty to contain the response value. Indeed, when K decreases the neighborhood considered is more faithful but it increases the uncertainty of the estimation. On the contrary, when K increases, the neighborhood becomes less faithful but the size of the tolerance intervals decreases. In fact the mentioned intervals take into account the number of instances in the neighborhood, and their size reflects also the neighborhood's density . Thus, choosing the

K that minimizes a fixed β-content γ-coverage normal tolerance ensures to have the best trade off between the faithfulness of the neighborhood and the uncertainty of the prediction due to the sample size. This is summarized in Algorithm 1. For the case of the computational complexity, the computation process of KNN simultaneous interval regression is $(MAX_K - MIN_K)$ times higher than the complexity of KNN regression with fixed K. Because from the beginning to the $Kset_x$ finding step, everything remains the same for both of the regression methods, then in the interval calculation phase, KNN regression with fixed K computes just one interval and instead our method computes MAX_K ones. For more detail on the complexity of KNN see [15].

Algorithm 1. Simultaneous interval regression with KNN

1: **for all** $x \in testSet$ **do**
2:    $IntervalSize_{min} \leftarrow Inf$
3:    **for all** $i \in MIN_K, \ldots, MAX_K$ **do**
4:       $Kset_x \leftarrow$ response value of the K nearest instances to x
5:       $Interval \leftarrow \beta$-content γ-coverage normal tolerance interval of $Kset_x$
6:       **if** $size(Interval) \leq IntervalSize_{min}$ **then**
7:          $K \leftarrow i$
8:          $foundInterval \leftarrow Interval$
9:          $IntervalSize_{min} \leftarrow size(Interval)$
10:      **end if**
11:    **end for**
12:    $Interval_x \leftarrow foundInterval$
13: **end for**

3.3   Tunning MIN_K, MAX_K and γ

MIN_K and MAX_K are global limits that stop the search if the best K value is not before . This may occur when in some part of the data set, the local density of the response variable is relatively high. In practice, it is known that this kind of local density is not always a sign of similarity, therefore these two bounds serve to restrict the search process in a region where it is most likely to contain the best neighborhood of x. MIN_K ,MAX_K and γ are algorithms hyper-parameter and they can be found by evaluating the effectiveness of the algorithm on the training set.

Our goal is to find an envelop that gives β proportion of all the predictions. In this scope β is chosen with respect to the user expectation. Given a KNN function f and a validation set that contains m pairs $(x_i, y(x_i))$ the proportion of data inside the tolerance envelope is computed by the MIP function (Mean Inclusion Percentage) :

$$MIP = \frac{\sum I(y(x_i) \in I_{f(x)}^T)}{m} \tag{11}$$

where I is the indicator function and $I_{f(x)}^T$ is the interval found by the algorithm above. The process of finding the optimal value of γ is more tricky. Indeed,

The choice of a good value γ is crucial in order to have simultaneous tolerance intervals that guarantee the expected value of MIP (i.e. $MIP \geq \beta$). High values of γ will guarantee that $MIP \geq \beta$ but the computed intervals can become very large. Thus,we experimentally search for the smallest value of γ that makes $MIP \geq \beta$. Note that, with this approach, the value of γ can be much lower that β and this may happen when the local density of the response values is quite dense.

4   Experiments

4.1   The Experiment's Approach

We compare the effectiveness of our methods based on tolerance intervals with the conventional interval construction approach described in section 2.1 (represented by "Conv.") for a given β proportion of the response values . Thus, the conventional approach is the computation of inter-quantile of population based on the classical KNN algorithm with a fixed K. The goal is to find simultaneous β-content regression intervals where $\beta = 0.9, 0.95$ and 0.99. The motivation of this choice of β is that these inter-quantiles are the most used ones in machine-learning and statistical hypothesis-testing. Another reason justifying our choice is that they are harder to approximate.

When considering the simultaneous interval regression, it is expected for the fraction of prediction values inside the envelope, for each of the 10 models in cross validation, to be greater or equal to β. For example, for $\beta = 0.95$ in a 10-fold cross validation, it is expected for each of the 10 built model to have a Mean Inclusion Percentage (MIP) greater or equal to 0.95 ($MIP \geq \beta$). In our experiments part, we are interested to compare the obtained intervals by the mentioned methods regardless to any variable selection or outliers detection preprocessing. The mentioned results are the mean inclusion percentages and the Mean of Interval Size (MIS) in each of the 10-fold in the cross validation scheme. The MIP (see Equation (11)) and MIS over all the 10-fold cross validation is also contained in the results.

In a first attempt, data set is divided into two parts of $\frac{2}{3}n$ and $\frac{1}{3}n$, where n represents the data set size. The part containing $\frac{2}{3}$ of instances are used to tune the hyper-parameters. The hyper-parameters are MIN_K, MAX_K and γ for our proposed interval regression method and just K value for the Fixed KNN (denoted as Conv.). For the classical KNN, the fixed K maximizing the Root Mean Squared Error (RMSE) of response variable is chosen. For our proposed method, the hyper-parameters having the smallest MIS and also satisfying the simultaneous β-inclusion constraint (see Section 3.3) are selected. Finally, all of the instances will serve to validate the results using a 10-cross validation scheme.

4.2   Results

For this purpose the following six well known regression data sets are used : "Auto MPG" (Auto) [3] , "Concrete Compressive Strength" (Concrete) [3],

Table 1. Comparing the interval construction approachs proposed to perform simultaneous interval regression for KNN

Dataset	Algo.	90%		95%		99%	
		Min(MFIP)	$\overline{MIS}$ (σ_{is})	Min(MFIP)	$\overline{MIS}$ (σ_{is})	Min(MFIP)	$\overline{MIS}$ (σ_{is})
Parkinson1 (n=5875, p=25)	Conv.	94.54 *	6.62	94.55	7.88	95.4	10.36
	Var. K	90.98 *	5.01 (6.92)	**95.23 ***	6.38 (8.75)	**99.14 ***	11.19 (14.47)
	Hyper. params.	$(MIN_K, MAX_K, \gamma) =$ $(5, 40, 0.25)$		$(MIN_K, MAX_K, \gamma) =$ $(5, 40, 0.35)$		$(MIN_K, MAX_K, \gamma) = (5, 40, 0.8)$	
Parkinson2 (n=5875, p=25)	Conv.	94.04 *	4.73	94.55	5.64	95.57	7.41
	Var. K	92.34 *	3.97 (5.37)	**95.23 ***	5.06 (6.77)	**99.14 ***	9.37 (11.85)
	Hyper. params.	$(MIN_K, MAX_K, \gamma) =$ $(5, 25, 0.3)$		$(MIN_K, MAX_K, \gamma) =$ $(5, 25, 0.4)$		$(MIN_K, MAX_K, \gamma) = (5, 25, 0.87)$	
Wine (n=4898, p=12)	Conv.	78.93	1.84	90.59	2.19	93.46	2.88
	Var. K	**90.2 ***	2.5 (0.55)	**95.71 ***	3.51 (1.48)	98.77	5.04 (1.05)
	Hyper. params.	$(MIN_K, MAX_K, \gamma) =$ $(20, 50, 0.9)$		$(MIN_K, MAX_K, \gamma) =$ $(5, 25, 0.99)$		$(MIN_K, MAX_K, \gamma) = (20, 50, 0.999)$	
Concrete (n=1030, p=9)	Conv.	80.58	25.58	86.4	30.48	94.17	40.05
	Var. K	**91.26 ***	33.29 (11.86)	**95.14 ***	41.91 (14.8)	**99.02 ***	80.72 (26.47)
	Hyper. params.	$(MIN_K, MAX_K, \gamma) =$ $(10, 25, 0.6)$		$(MIN_K, MAX_K, \gamma) =$ $(10, 25, 0.7)$		$(MIN_K, MAX_K, \gamma) = (10, 25, 0.99)$	
Auto (n=398, p=8)	Conv.	87.17	9.96	90	11.87	94.87	15.6
	Var. K	**94.87 ***	12.57 (6.48)	**95 ***	14.98 (7.72)	97.43	23.54 (11.98)
	Hyper. params.	$(MIN_K, MAX_K, \gamma) =$ $(7, 20, 0.95)$		$(MIN_K, MAX_K, \gamma) =$ $(7, 20, 0.95)$		$(MIN_K, MAX_K, \gamma) = (7, 20, 0.99)$	
Housing (n=506, p=14)	Conv.	84.31	14.23	90.19	16.96	94	22.29
	Var. K	**92.15 ***	22.9 (13.09)	**96 ***	27.28 (15.6)	98	43.45 (24.44)
	Hyper. params.	$(MIN_K, MAX_K, \gamma) =$ $(10, 20, 0.99)$		$(MIN_K, MAX_K, \gamma) =$ $(10, 20, 0.99)$		$(MIN_K, MAX_K, \gamma) = (10, 20, 0.999)$	
Slump (n=103, p=10)	Conv.	80	12.73	80	15.16	80	19.93
	Var. K	**90 ***	29.58 (9.83)	90	35.25 (11.71)	**100 ***	46.32 (15.4)
	Hyper. params.	$(MIN_K, MAX_K, \gamma) =$ $(5, 15, 0.99)$		$(MIN_K, MAX_K, \gamma) =$ $(5, 15, 0.99)$		$(MIN_K, MAX_K, \gamma) = (5, 15, 0.99)$	

"Concrete Slump Test" [3] (Slump), "Housing" [3], "Wine Quality" [3] (Wine) (the red wine) and "Parkinsons Telemonitoring" [16]. "Parkinsons Telemonitoring" data set contains two regression variable named as "motor_UPDRS" and "total_UPDRS", so we consider it as two distinct datasets named respectively as "Parkinson1" (containing "total_UPDRS" values without "motor_UPDRS") and "Parkinson2" (containing "motor_UPDRS" values without "total_UPDRS").

Table 1 summarizes the application of the algorithm 1 ("Var. K") and the conventional interval construction approach combined with KNN ("Conv.") to the seven datasets seen above. For each 10-fold cross validation scheme, the following quality measures are computed:

- MFIP: Mean Fold Inclusion Percentage (value of the MIP for one fold). It must be greater or equal to the desired β for each of the 10 models build in the cross validation phase.

- Min(MFIP): minimum value of MFIP between all the 10 models. If we have $min(MFIP) < \beta$, that represents the failures of the approach to cover the required β proportion of the response values .

The column MIS is the Mean of Interval Size for all the 10 models and σ_{is} is the standard deviation of the interval size over the whole dataset. Note that σ_{is} is not defined for the conventional method because its interval size is constant over the entire data set. The star * sign appears when Min(MFIP) satisfies the requirement (i.e. $Min(MFIP) \geq \beta$). When only one of the two compared methods satisfies this requirement, the result is put in bold.

For $\beta = 0.9$ $\beta = 0.95$ and for the data sets Parkinson1 and Parkinson2 in table 1, we can see that our method gives smaller intervals than the Conv. approach. However in contrary to the Conv. approach, the mentioned intervals contain the required β proportion of the response values. It is usually, a difficult task to satisfy the requirement for $\beta = 0.99$ and it becomes even harder for small data sets. Because each fold contains $\frac{n}{10}$ of total instances, so one percent is equals to $\frac{n}{1000}$. It means that the constructed intervals must miss at max $\frac{n}{1000}$ of total instances and this is a quite hard task for small and even medium data sets. But we can see that our method satisfies this condition for half of datasets and the mean of inferred intervals has not a big size compared to the required constraint. It is also interesting to note that our proposed method performs better in general for bigger datasets. This is because, our method is based on the local density of the data.

5   Conclusion

In this work, we have defined the idea of simultaneous interval regression for K-Nearest Neighbor (KNN). In simultaneous interval regression, the goal is to find intervals which simultaneously contain a required proportion of the response values for all input instances. We have introduced one approach to build such intervals which can be applied to KNN. Since tolerance intervals take into account the neighborhood size, it allows us to automatically find the best value of K for each example rather than using a fixed K for all the test set. This can be useful in presence of heterogeneous data. In the experiments part, the introduced methods and its conventional versions are applied on six different regression data sets. The results show that our approach performs very well on dense datasets. In the case of dataset with small sample sizes compared to their number of variables, our method is less reliable, but it is still better than the conventional interval construction method in KNN.

Predicting simultaneous confidence intervals may be useful when we are interested in the combination of predictions. For instance, in the wine database, the computation of simultaneous interval ensures that for a set of "m" bottles, "$m * \beta$" of the bottles will have simultaneously their score in their predicted interval. This can become more important in safety and security applications. As another example, let us take the aircraft trajectory prediction using a regression model. A warning occurs when the prediction intervals of two or more aircraft overlap. In this case, intervals found using simultaneous interval regression guarantee the safety measure of the collision detection approach.

As future work, we will focus on different non-parametric estimators such as Locally Weighed Scatter-plot Smoothing as well as regression cases where the error's distribution are not normal.

References

1. Statistical Tolerance Regions: Theory, Applications, and Computation. Wiley (2009)
2. Boos, D.D.: A new method for constructing approximate confidence intervals from m estimates. J. Amer. Statistical Assoc. 75(369), 142–145 (1980)
3. Frank, A., Asuncion, A.: UCI machine learning repository (2010)
4. Hahn, G.J., Meeker, W.Q.: Statistical Intervals: A Guide for Practitioners. John Wiley and Sons (1991)
5. Howe, W.G.: Two-sided tolerance limits for normal populations, some improvements. J. Amer. Statistical Assoc. 64(326), 610–620 (1969)
6. Kocherginsky, M., He, X., Mu, Y.: Practical confidence intervals for regression quantiles. J. Comp. and Graph. Stat. 14(1), 41–55 (2005)
7. Koenker, R.: Confidence intervals for regression quantiles. In: Proc. of 5th Symp. Asymp. Stat. (1994)
8. Koenker, R., Bassett, G.: Regression quantiles. Econometrica 46(1), 33–50 (1978)
9. Koenker, R., Hallock, K.: Quantile Regression: An Introduction. J. Economic Perspectives 15(4), 43–56 (2001)
10. Li, Q., Racine, J.S.: Nonparametric econometrics: theory and practice. Princeton University Press (2007)
11. Lieberman, G.J., Miller Jr., R.G.: Simultaneous tolerance intervals in regression. Biometrika 50(1/2), 155–168 (1963)
12. Mee, R.W., Eberhardt, K.R., Reeve, C.P.: Calibration and simultaneous tolerance intervals for regression. Technometrics 33(2), 211–219 (1991)
13. Miller, R.G.: Simultaneous Statistical Inference. Springer, New York (1991)
14. Nadaraya, E.A.: On estimating regression. Theory of Probability and its Applications 9, 141–142 (1964)
15. Silverman, B.W.: Density estimation for statistics and data analysis. Chapman and Hall, London (1986)
16. Tsanas, A., Little, M.A., McSharry, P.E., Ramig, L.O.: Accurate telemonitoring of parkinson's disease progression by non-invasive speech tests (2009)
17. Wallis, W.A.: Tolerance intervals for linear regression. In: Proc. Second Berkeley Symp. on Math. Statist. and Prob., pp. 43–51. Univ. of Calif. Press (1951)
18. Watson, G.S.: Smooth regression analysis. Sankhyā Ser. 26, 359–372 (1964)
19. Wilson, A.L.: An approach to simultaneous tolerance intervals in regression. Ann. of Math. Stat. 38(5), 1536–1540 (1967)

Kernel-Tree: Mining Frequent Patterns in a Data Stream Based on Forecast Support

David Tse Jung Huang[1], Yun Sing Koh[1], Gillian Dobbie[1], and Russel Pears[2]

[1] Department of Computer Science, University of Auckland, New Zealand
dhua035@aucklanduni.ac.nz, {ykoh,gill}@cs.auckland.ac.nz
[2] School of Computing and Mathematical Sciences, AUT University, New Zealand
rpears@aut.ac.nz

Abstract. Although frequent pattern mining techniques have been extensively studied, the extension of their application onto data streams has been challenging. Due to data streams being continuous and unbounded, an efficient algorithm that avoids multiple scans of data is needed. In this paper we propose Kernel-Tree (KerTree), a single pass tree structured technique that mines frequent patterns in a data stream based on forecasting the support of current items in the future state. Unlike previous techniques that build a tree based on the support of items in the previous block, KerTree performs an estimation of item support in the next block and builds the tree based on the estimation. By building the tree on an estimated future state, KerTree effectively reduces the need to restructure for every block and thus results in a better performance and mines the complete set of frequent patterns from the stream while maintaining a compact structure.

Keywords: Data Streams, Kernel Regression, Frequent Pattern Mining.

1 Introduction

The introduction of FP-Tree by Han et al. [1] directed focus in frequent pattern mining from the traditional Apriori-like candidate generation-and-test approach to tree structured approaches. Most of the tree-based frequent pattern mining techniques are designed to work in static databases which only provides snapshots in time of the patterns found. As the generation of data streams increases, the ability to derive useful information in an efficient manner becomes more necessary.

Ever since its inception, data stream mining has remained one of the challenging problems in data mining. This is mainly due to the nature of data streams being continuous and unbounded in data flow as opposed to traditional databases where data is static and stable. Examples of situations where streams of data can be generated range from online retail such as auctions, book stores, telecommunications calling data to credit card transactions and weather/climate data. Because these data arrive at a fast rate and in a continuous manner, traditional techniques designed for databases which perform multiple scans on the data are

M. Thielscher and D. Zhang (Eds.): AI 2012, LNCS 7691, pp. 614–625, 2012.

not suitable for mining these streams of data. The other issue is with memory usage during mining of such unbounded data. The capability of any technique that mines a stream is bounded by the memory space (buffer) available for storing the most recent transactions in order to update item support. If the data stream miner cannot process the data fast enough, the buffer will eventually be filled and data from the stream will inevitably be lost. This restriction requires that the mining of data streams be single pass and as fast as possible.

Techniques that mine data streams based on a tree structure have been studied recently. An example is CPS-Tree [2], which builds its tree based on the frequency-descending order of items from the previous block and thus maintains a compact tree and is an ideal single scan approach. A disadvantage of CPS-Tree is that it assumes that the state of the data stream in the next block is the same as the current block and that there is minimal to no concept drift in item support. In this paper we propose an approach called KerTree where we implement a concept drift detection mechanism to signal when item support changes from one block to the next and present an inexpensive but accurate extrapolation function that is capable of estimating item support in the future states of the data stream. An accurate assessment of the next state has a flow-on effect on subsequent states, minimizing the changes required to the tree, thus improving the overall tree maintenance time.

The key contribution of this paper is a tree structure mining technique called the KerTree that finds the complete set of frequent patterns in a data stream using a sliding window. Specifically in our approach, we use an extrapolation function to estimate the state (support) of items in a future block; thus, our extrapolation function allows us to compensate for the concept change (i.e. shifts in the pattern of support amongst items) in incoming transactions while keeping a compact tree structure.

The paper is organized as follows. In Section 2 we discuss related work. Section 3 presents the preliminaries and the detail of our proposed algorithm. Our experimentation and evaluation of KerTree and comparison with CPS-Tree is presented in Section 4. Finally in Section 5 we conclude our work and discuss future directions.

2 Related Work

In this section, we discuss some previous work that is relevant to our work. FP-Tree [1] is a widely known frequent pattern mining technique that uses a tree structure. Prior to FP-Tree, most approaches adopt an Apriori-like candidate generation-and-test approach which is usually costly and less efficient. FP-Tree is efficient at finding the complete set of frequent patterns in a database, but its multi-pass approach is unfavorable and considered too memory intensive to be used in a data stream environment.

To resolve this, Giannella et al. [3] proposed a technique called FP-Stream which adapts the FP-Tree for mining data streams. The major disadvantage of the FP-Stream approach is that it finds an approximate set of frequent patterns instead of the complete set of frequent patterns.

A tree structure that is developed by Leung et al. [4] called DSTree is a technique that finds the complete set of frequent patterns in a data stream. This particular structure is adapted from CanTree [5] which is a technique that is designed for incremental mining. DSTree, like CanTree, builds its tree structure based on a canonical-ordering of items that is determined by the user prior to the mining process or at runtime during mining.

Tanbeer et al. [2] proposed a tree structure called CPS-Tree that builds a compact tree and mines the complete set of frequent patterns. CPS-Tree has a frequency descending structure that captures data from the dataset and dynamically restructures itself. The tree construction of the CPS-Tree has two phases: insertion phase and restructure phase. In the insertion phase, the items in the currently processed transaction are inserted into the tree based on the current sorted order of the item list and the frequency counts of the items are updated. During the restructure phase, the item list is sorted based on frequency descending order and the tree is reorganized based on the newly sorted item list. The two phases are executed consecutively. CPS-Tree works under the assumption that drift within the stream remains fairly constant, an assumption which is not always true in practice. The relaxation of this assumption requires both a drift detection mechanism as well as an estimation mechanism which our proposed approach implements.

Koh et al. [6] proposed the Extrap-Tree, which builds the prefix tree based on a forecast support, like that of KerTree. However, Extrap-Tree uses a landmark model where linear interpolation is used as the estimation mechanism. In a landmark model, the support of items increases monotonically with time, making linear interpolation the suitable estimation function whereas the KerTree introduced in this paper assumes a sliding window approach where the support of items can both increase and decrease with time.

3   Kernel-Tree (KerTree)

In this section we will first give the general framework of KerTree then later in the section we will detail each of the steps taken to construct KerTree for mining frequent patterns.

3.1   Preliminaries

In this section we provide definitions of key terms that explain the concepts of frequent pattern mining in a data stream. A transaction data stream S can be formally defined as an infinite sequence of transactions, $S = [t_1, t_2, t_3, \ldots, t_m]$, where t_i is the ith transaction in the data stream and $i \in [1, m]$. A window W is a set of all transactions between the ith and jth (where $j > i$) transactions and the size of W is $|W|$ calculated by $j - i$. The frequency of an itemset X denoted as $count_W(X)$ in a window W, is the number of transactions in W that contain X. The support of X in W, denoted as $supp_W(X)$, is defined as

$\frac{count_W(X)}{|W|}$, where $|W|$ is the size of the window W. X is a frequent itemset in W if $supp_W(X) \geq minsup$ where $minsup$ is the minimum support threshold.

Given a transaction data stream and a $minsup$, the problem of frequent itemset mining over a window W in the transaction data stream S, is to find the set of all itemsets whose support is greater than $minsup$. A block B is a set of transactions with the size of $|B|$. A data stream is consisted of a continuous sequence of blocks, $S = [B_1, B_2, \ldots)$.

3.2   Framework and Overview of KerTree

KerTree, like many other tree structured pattern mining techniques, goes through two phases: construction phase and mining phase. During the construction phase, a tree is storing the items in the transactions is built. The mining phase follows the construction phase where FP-Growth proposed in the FP-Tree [1] is used to mine the tree for frequent itemsets. FP-Growth is also used in some previous work [5,2,7,6].

The construction of KerTree consists of several steps. First, an initial tree is built as transactions are read from the stream. At the end of each block, KerTree uses a delay condition to determine whether the initial tree built requires re-structuring. If re-structuring is deemed unnecessary, all following construction steps are skipped and KerTree goes into mining phase. If re-structuring is deemed necessary, KerTree continues with the construction phase by determining whether there is drift in the support of items from the previous block to the current block. Then, the ordering of items in the tree is adjusted based on the results using kernel regression. Lastly, the tree is re-structured based on the adjusted ordering.

Figure 1 is an example of KerTree showing the construction of the tree in the first block. Shown in Figure 1 (a) is the result of the inital tree built at the end of the block. Because this is an example of the first block, items are initially ordered in the canonical ordering (alphabetical). For all blocks after the first, the initial tree is built using the forecast ordering of items from the previous block. This ordering is determined using kernel regression. Using kernel regression as the extrapolation function to forecast item supports in the future is also one of the major contributions of this paper. The actual technique on how we perform kernel regression is detailed in Section 3.3. For the first block of the stream, we always deem the tree needing re-structuring. After the first block, whether we decide to re-structure and continue with construction is determined by the delay condition presented in Section 3.4. If re-structuring is needed, KerTree first uses a dirft detection mechanism to detect changes in item supports. The details of this mechanism is presented in Section 3.5. After determining drift and forecasting item supports using kernel regression, we continue with re-structuring the tree based on the forecast order and the resulting tree is shown in Figure 1 (b). Notice that the re-structured tree is more compact (fewer nodes). When the second block of transactions come in, the tree will be updated and built according to the forecast order determined in block one. At the end of block two, KerTree will then go through the same procedures as presented above.

Transactions for the first block

tid	transactions	tid	transactions
1	a d e g i	6	d e i
2	a d e h i	7	c d e h
3	b c d e i	8	d e f i
4	b d e f	9	d e i
5	c d e g i	10	c d e f

Canonical Order	Forecast Order
a	d
b	e
c	i
d	a
e	c
f	g
g	b
h	h
i	f

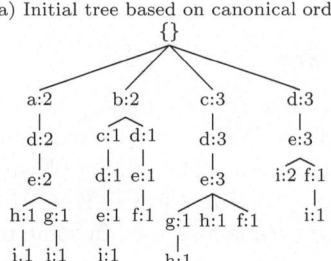

(a) Initial tree based on canonical order

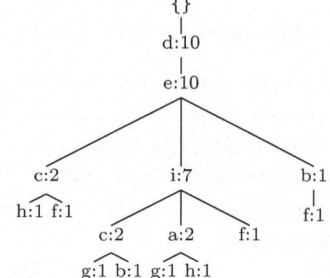

(b) Reorganization based on forecast order

Fig. 1. Example of KerTree

3.3 Kernel Regression

Kernel regression is a non-parametric regression technique. Unlike linear regression or polynomial regression, the underlying distribution to estimate the kernel function is not assumed.

The problem is: given a set of data points (t, y_t) where t indicates a time point in the stream and y_t the support of a given item, we find a regression function that best fits the given data. Given the best fit function, we can determine the estimated support $\hat{y}_{t+1}$ at time $t+1$. The set of data points (t, y_t) used in KerTree is obtained through tracking the support of items in the current block at various points. The amount of points tracked is user defined and can be increased to improve estimating accuracy (but reducing efficiency). The points are assigned in a manner where the distance from one point to the next is uniform. For example, given a block B of 10 transactions with 5 points defined, the support of an item would be tracked at transactions 2, 4, 6, 8, and 10. Generally about five to ten points is enough to provide the regression technique with sufficient data for an accurate estimation.

In kernel regression, a weight function called a kernel is first associated at each time point, t. The kernel then estimates the probability of point x occurring based on the weight function of the kernel (ie. Radial Basis Kernel estimates the probability using a Gaussian function). Apart from the probability calculated at each kernel, a weight is also assigned to each kernel. In our implementation we used the KRLS algorithm [8] to calculate the optimal weight vector α. The optimal weight vector is obtained through minimizing the sum of the squared errors calculated as the difference between the estimated and actual support values. The estimated value $\hat{y}_{t+1}$ at the $(t+1)^{th}$ observation is given by:

$$\hat{y}_{t+1} = \frac{\sum\limits_{j \in s} w_j y_j}{\sum\limits_{j \in s} y_j}$$

where s is the set of data points or kernels; w_j is the kernel weight of the jth kernel data point . Each $\hat{y}_j$ is fitted by the Polynomial kernel function of degree 2: $(z \cdot y_j + 1)^2$, where z takes values in the range $[0, 1, 2, ..., (\frac{s}{dX} + 1)]$; dy is the sampling rate for each observation y_j in the current block t.

Thus in KerTree, by calculating the estimated support for each item at a future block, we can generate a forecast order of items at which the tree in the next block can be built from.

3.4 Delay Condition

The reason that sometimes restructuring of the tree could be delayed at some blocks is because we are constructing the tree based on forecast support of items from the previous block; therefore, if the prediction is accurate, the initial tree built would already have been representative of the state of items in the current block and is usually a compact tree. However, even though our proposed kernel regression extrapolation function is capable of predicting the support of items in the near future, the estimation function will eventually lose its predicting strength as time progresses and a tree reorganization will be inevitable at some stage. We deem whether reorganization of the tree is necessary based on a tree growth threshold (γ). The growth threshold is measured using the number of nodes in the tree at the previous block and comparing it with the number of nodes in the tree at the current block. We then calculate the percentage of increased nodes which we call percentage of growth. If the percentage of growth is less than γ, then we delay reorganization at the current block and skip drift detection and extrapolation in the rest of the construction phase.

3.5 Drift Detection

After deciding to re-structure the tree based on growth threshold γ, we go into drift detection where we determine whether a drift in the support of items is present or absent. We then use the extrapolation function (kernel regression) to forecast the support of items if a drift is deemed present. A drift is a change in the support of an item from the previous block to the current block. For example, if item X is seen with a support of 0.8 in the previous block and 0.2 in the current, then we say that there is a drift. We use the drift detection mechanism proposed in Extrap-Tree called the Hoeffding Bound [9] in KerTree.

In order to determine whether there is a concept drift in the support of items from the previous block to the current block, we utilize the change in support of an item from the previous block to the current block given by:

$$\Delta supp(X) = supp_{B_{n-1}}(X) - supp_{B_n}(X) \tag{1}$$

We use the Hoeffding Bound to determine whether a drift is present. The Hoeffding bound states that, with probability $1 - \delta$, the true mean of a random variable r is at least $\bar{r} - \epsilon$ when the mean is estimated over t samples, where

$$\epsilon = \sqrt{\frac{R^2 \ln(1/\delta)}{2t}}$$

R is the range of r. In our case the variable r is denoted by $|\Delta supp(X)|$, which has a range value R of 1, and the number of samples $t = |B|$, the block size. There are two possible scenarios that we need to consider when using $|\Delta supp(X)|$ to determine drift. In the first scenario, we assume that there is no concept drift when $|\Delta supp(X)| \leq \epsilon$ and the previously forecasted support holds the same and we do not need to re-calculate the support of item X using kernel regression. In the second scenrio, we assume that concept drift is present when $|\Delta supp_{B_n}(X)| > \epsilon$ and we need to re-calculate and forecast the support of item X.

To obtain $supp_{B_{n+1}}^{extrap}(X)$ when concept drift is assumed present, we use kernel regression to estimate and extrapolate item support at the next block as specified earlier in Section 3.3.

4   Experimental Results

We have conducted various experiments on both real-world and synthetic datasets to test the efficiency and efficacy of our proposed technique. The algorithms are all coded in Microsoft Visual C++ and run on a Intel Core i5-2400 CPU @ 3.10 GHz with 4GB of RAM running Windows 7 x64. In all experiments, runtime excludes I/O costs.

4.1   Synthetic Data Generator

In order to evaluate the performance of KerTree with relation to the effects of concept drift, we modified the IBM synthetic data generator to inject drift patterns into the generated datasets based on known polynomial equations shown in Table 1. These equations allow us to model and control different item distributions and produce different datasets of varying characteristics. The stream is based on a Gaussian distribution with the polynomial equations giving the probability at which we introduce or remove itemsets. The generator produces large and small itemsets with the items in the large set having higher support than those in the small set. We select x random points at which we introduce or remove large itemsets. Through introducing and removing these itemsets at these points, we are able to simulate drifts in patterns in the dataset. The introduction of large itemsets at a drift point corresponds to the simulation of emerging frequent patterns in the dataset whereas the removal of large itemsets corresponds to the simulation of disappearing patterns in the dataset.

The eight synthetic datasets generated in our experiments used the same parameters where the average transaction length was 10, the number of frequent

Table 1. Kernel equations

Dataset	Equation	Dataset	Equation
Synthetic 1	x^2	Synthetic 5	$-4x^3 - 3x^2 + 5x - 10$
Synthetic 2	$3x^2 - 4x + 10$	Synthetic 6	$-3x^2 + x$
Synthetic 3	$-2x^2 + 10x - 4$	Synthetic 7	$4x^3 - 4x + 4$
Synthetic 4	$3x^3 + 4x^2 - x + 1$	Synthetic 8	$3x^2 - 4x - 10$

items was 100, the average length of a large item was 4, the number of drift points is 50,000 and the number of transactions was 1 million using 1000 unique items.

4.2 Experimentation on Synthetic Data

In this section we present our experimentation and evaluation on the eight synthetic datasets. We evaluate our approach against CPS-Tree based on the following features: (1) Overall execution time, (2) Average number of nodes in tree, and (3) Correlation of the extrapolated support vs. the actual support. In the first evaluation, we primarily look at the performance of KerTree against the CPS-Tree through comparing the execution time. In the second evaluation, we aim at comparing the compactness of the trees built between KerTree and the CPS-Tree by looking at the average number of nodes in the trees built by the two techniques. In the third evaluation, we particularly wanted to look at the accuracy of our kernel extrapolation function through the correlation measure of the extrapolated support vs the actual observed support.

For all the synthetic dataset experiments we used varying block sizes of 50K, 100K, 150K and 200K, minsup of 0.1, tree growth threshold (γ) of 0.01, Hoeffding bound (δ) of 0.001, and a polynomial kernel of degree 2. Table 2 reports the comparison based on execution time. For ease of comparison, we have included the relative time measure of KerTree vs. CPS-Tree, which is calculated as follows:

$$\text{Relative Time (Rel. Time)} = \frac{\text{Time taken by KerTree}}{\text{Time taken by CPS-Tree}}$$

Table 2. Comparison based on Execution Time

Dataset	50K			100K			150K			200K		
	Ker-Tree	CPS-Tree	Rel. Time	Ker-Tree	CPS-Tree	Rel. Time	Ker-Tree	CPS-Tree	Rel. Time	Ker-Tree	CPS-Tree	Rel. Time
Synthetic 1	14.57	18.24	0.8	13.73	17.16	0.8	13.45	16.07	0.84	13.43	15.94	0.84
Synthetic 2	13.67	16.88	0.81	13.26	15.79	0.84	13.2	15.01	0.88	13.04	14.96	0.87
Synthetic 3	13.85	16.77	0.83	13.48	15.79	0.85	12.93	14.96	0.86	12.87	14.87	0.87
Synthetic 4	13.85	17.32	0.8	13.31	16.47	0.81	13.14	15.51	0.85	13.1	15.69	0.83
Synthetic 5	14.87	17.32	0.86	13.67	16.33	0.84	13.57	15.59	0.87	13.67	15.69	0.87
Synthetic 6	14.24	16.6	0.86	13.21	15.76	0.84	12.84	14.91	0.86	12.92	14.99	0.86
Synthetic 7	13.56	16.65	0.81	13.37	15.68	0.85	12.82	14.79	0.87	12.82	14.79	0.87
Synthetic 8	14.42	17.3	0.83	13.71	16.43	0.83	13.78	15.8	0.87	13.68	15.51	0.88

Looking at Table 2 we can see that KerTree is about 12%-20% faster for all experiments against CPS-Tree. This is shown in Figure 2 where the execution time for KerTree is plotted against the execution time of CPS-Tree to show a comparison. The reduction in execution time is due to the ability of KerTree to delay the reorganization phase in a majority of the blocks by accurately predicting the future support of items.

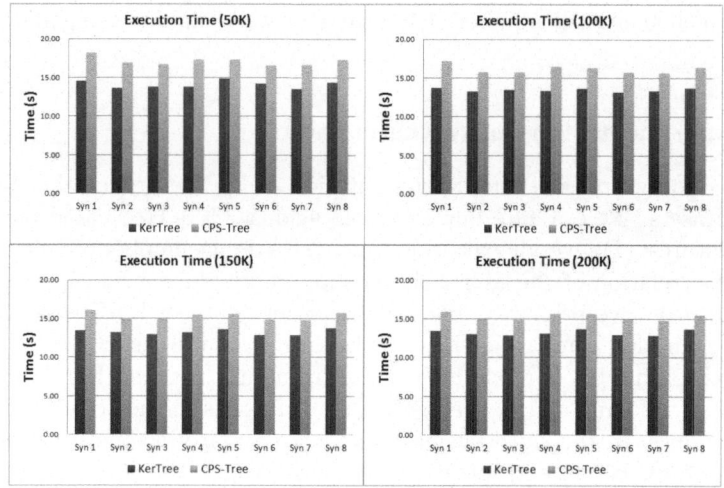

Fig. 2. Execution Time

For the comparison based on the average number of nodes in tree, we calculate the percentage variance of the trees constructed by KerTree and CPS-Tree. We observed that the percentage variance ranges from 0.001% to 0.261%. This shows that the two techniques end up with tree structures that are similar in the number of nodes and therefore similar in compactness.

Table 3 shows the comparison of KerTree against the CPS-Tree based on the number of nodes in the tree constructed for each block for synthetic dataset 6. The table also presents whether our KerTree delays reorganization and the correlation associated with the actual and forecasted support of items in the block. We can see that our technique is capable of delaying a majority of the reorganization phase which contributes to the faster execution time. The correlation of the forecasted supports and actual supports of items observed ranges from 0.9995 to 0.9997 which signifies that the predictions based on our kernel regression extrapolation is accurate at predicting item supports in future blocks. Note that the first block has no associated correlation value because the item support in the first block is not extrapolated prior to that and the tree is constructed based on canonical ordering.

Table 3. Number of Nodes from Synthetic Dataset 6

Window	KerTree		CPS-Tree	Correlation
	After Reorganization	Current Nodes in Tree	After Reorganization	
50000	80301		80358	-
100000	Delayed	78196	77790	0.9997
150000	Delayed	77146	77054	0.9996
200000	78607		78527	0.9995
250000	Delayed	77713	77593	0.9997
300000	Delayed	77886	77894	0.9996
350000	Delayed	77663	77366	0.9996
400000	Delayed	77385	77358	0.9996
450000	Delayed	78073	78100	0.9996
500000	Delayed	77400	77450	0.9995
550000	Delayed	76736	76798	0.9996
600000	78436		78254	0.9995
650000	Delayed	77797	77491	0.9997
700000	Delayed	78315	77909	0.9996
750000	Delayed	77858	77831	0.9996
800000	Delayed	77024	77093	0.9996
850000	78305		78214	0.9995
900000	Delayed	77834	77732	0.9997
950000	Delayed	77867	77462	0.9996
1000000	Delayed	77667	77585	0.9995

4.3 Experimentation on Real World Data

This section presents the results of comparing our KerTree to CPS-Tree on real world datasets from the FIMI repository (http://fimi.ua.ac.be/) and UCI repository (http://archive.ics.uci.edu/ml/). Table 4 shows the results based on execution time and relative time and Table 5 and Table 6 shows the number of nodes in the tree at each block and the correlation of forecasted supports and actual supports of items.

The table also identifies blocks at which KerTree decides to delay the reorganization phase. The results produced by these datasets follow the same trend as the results produced by the synthetic datasets. Both KerTree and CPS-Tree produce a similar number of nodes, whereas the total time taken by KerTree remains lower than that of CPS-Tree. A graph representation of the execution time for the real world datasets is shown in Figure 3.

From Table 5 and Table 6 we can see that for real world datasets, the correlation values we observed are still very promising with lowest in BMS-POS being 0.9634 and Kosarak being 0.9941. This signifies that our kernel regression estimation function is capable of predicting item supports in these real-world datasets.

Table 4. Results based on Real-World Dataset

Dataset	Block Size	KerTree		CPS-Tree		
		Avg. Nodes	Time(s)	Avg. Nodes	Time(s)	Rel. Time
BMS-POS	25K	177575	6.63	177247	8.00	0.83
Kosarak	25K	271999	26.57	271667	29.47	0.90
Poker-hand-testing	25K	241894	15.04	242045	22.07	0.68
T10I4D100K	10K	79536	2.20	79501	2.76	0.80
T40I10D100K	10K	365386	7.41	365380	9.92	0.75

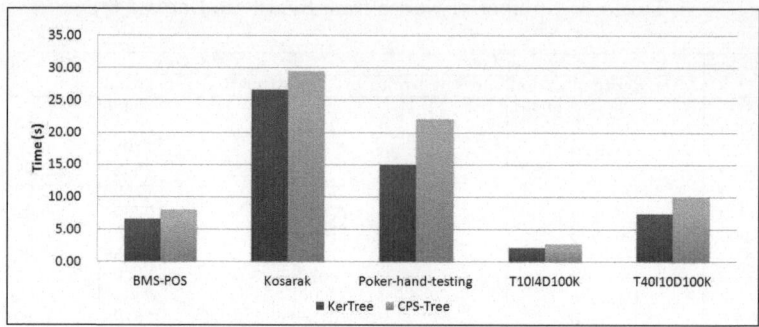

Fig. 3. Real World Dataset Execution Time

Table 5. Number of Nodes from BMS-POS

Window	KerTree		CPS-Tree	Correlation
	After Reorganization	Current Nodes in Tree	After Reorganization	
50000	206419		206440	-
100000	Delayed	187126	186689	0.9978
150000	Delayed	178284	178091	0.9936
200000	Delayed	171222	171095	0.9943
250000	Delayed	139596	138964	0.9939
300000	Delayed	129738	129128	0.9766
350000	Delayed	119447	118496	0.9820
400000	199553		199488	0.9634
450000	224030		223989	0.9971
500000	Delayed	220338	220085	0.9969

Table 6. Number of Nodes from Kosarak

Window	KerTree		CPS-Tree	Correlation
	After Reorganization	Current Nodes in Tree	After Reorganization	
50000	268589		268456	-
100000	272690		272580	0.9949
150000	Delayed	269602	269421	0.9946
200000	274966		274818	0.9946
250000	282401		282285	0.9946
300000	Delayed	280351	280242	0.9942
350000	Delayed	278955	278740	0.9942
400000	Delayed	278764	278681	0.9945
450000	Delayed	280405	280317	0.9943
500000	Delayed	266822	266717	0.9941
550000	272464		272283	0.9945
600000	Delayed	269292	269216	0.9944
650000	274358		274216	0.9945
700000	Delayed	276249	276100	0.9944
750000	Delayed	276956	276827	0.9944
800000	282049		281936	0.9943
850000	Delayed	269211	269169	0.9942
900000	Delayed	270788	270657	0.9945
950000	275478		275392	0.9945
1000000	Delayed	215350	215253	0.9941

5   Conclusions and Future Work

In this paper we have proposed the Kernel-Tree algorithm that mines frequent patterns from a data stream based on forecast support of items. From the results of our experiments we have shown that kernel regression is a suitable technique that is capable of accurately predicting item supports in a data stream at a future time. Because KerTree can preemptively build trees based on a predicted future state, the need to restructure the tree is largely reduced resulting in a faster run-time. KerTree also maintains a similar level of tree compactness as the CPS-Tree while capable of achieving a faster overall run-time. Our future work includes testing the effectiveness of kernel regression using different types of kernels (weight functions) and also looking at cost functions.

References

1. Han, J., Pei, J., Yin, Y.: Mining frequent patterns without candidate generation. SIGMOD Rec. 29, 1–12 (2000)
2. Tanbeer, S.K., Ahmed, C.F., Jeong, B.S., Lee, Y.K.: Efficient frequent pattern mining over data streams. In: Proceedings of the 17th ACM Conference on Information and Knowledge Management, CIKM 2008, pp. 1447–1448. ACM, NY (2008)
3. Giannella, C., Han, J., Pei, J., Yan, X., Yu, P.S.: Mining frequent patterns in data streams at multiple time granularities (2002)
4. Leung, C.K.S., Khan, Q.I.: DSTree: A tree structure for the mining of frequent sets from data streams. In: Sixth International Conference on Data Mining, ICDM 2006, pp. 928–932 (December 2006)
5. Leung, C.K.S., Khan, Q.I., Li, Z., Hoque, T.: CanTree: a canonical-order tree for incremental frequent-pattern mining. Knowl. Inf. Syst. 11, 287–311 (2007)
6. Koh, Y.S., Pears, R., Dobbie, G.: Extrapolation Prefix Tree for Data Stream Mining Using a Landmark Model. In: Cuzzocrea, A., Dayal, U. (eds.) DaWaK 2012. LNCS, vol. 7448, pp. 340–351. Springer, Heidelberg (2012)
7. Koh, Y.S., Dobbie, G.: SPO-Tree: Efficient Single Pass Ordered Incremental Pattern Mining. In: Cuzzocrea, A., Dayal, U. (eds.) DaWaK 2011. LNCS, vol. 6862, pp. 265–276. Springer, Heidelberg (2011)
8. Engel, Y., Mannor, S., Meir, R.: The kernel recursive least-squares algorithm. IEEE Transactions on Signal Processing 52(8), 2275–2285 (2004)
9. Hoeffding, W.: Probability inequalities for sums of bounded random variables. Journal of the American Statistical Association 58(301), 13–30 (1963)

An Empirical Comparison of Two Common Multiobjective Reinforcement Learning Algorithms

Rustam Issabekov and Peter Vamplew

School of Science, Information Technology and Engineering,
University of Ballarat, Ballarat VIC 3353, Australia
rus.issabekov@gmail.com,
p.vamplew@ballarat.edu.au

Abstract. In this paper we provide empirical data of the performance of the two most commonly used multiobjective reinforcement learning algorithms against a set of benchmarks. First, we describe a methodology that was used in this paper. Then, we carefully describe the details and properties of the proposed problems and how those properties influence the behavior of tested algorithms. We also introduce a testing framework that will significantly improve future empirical comparisons of multiobjective reinforcement learning algorithms. We hope this testing environment eventually becomes a central repository of test problems and algorithms The empirical results clearly identify features of the test problems which impact on the performance of each algorithm, demonstrating the utility of empirical testing of algorithms on problems with known characteristics.

1 Introduction

Reinforcement learning (RL) has primarily been limited in its applicability to solving only single objective problems. However, many industrial and scientific problems are inherently complex and cannot be expressed in terms of just a single objective. This has motivated a spike in multiobjective optimization research which in turn gave birth to multiobjective reinforcement learning (MORL). MORL combines advances in multiobjective optimization and techniques from reinforcement learning, thus extending RL techniques into the realms of multiobjective problems. A number of MORL algorithms were proposed in [1, 3, 5, and 6].

However, as was outlined in [8] currently there is a need for empirical comparison of these proposed algorithms to provide detailed guidance about each algorithm's strengths and weaknesses. [8] motivated this need of guidance with the following arguments:

- Most of the proposed algorithms were tested in isolation, with only a small number of tested problems. This leads to the uncertainty about algorithm's performance under a variety of problems with different natures.
- Different testing methodologies and test problems have been used in different papers. This leads to the inability to perform direct comparison of algorithms.

M. Thielscher and D. Zhang (Eds.): AI 2012, LNCS 7691, pp. 626–636, 2012.
© Springer-Verlag Berlin Heidelberg 2012

This paper will provide an empirical comparison of two of the most commonly used ways to provide preferences over objectives. One way, called weighted scalarization (WS), assigns weight to each objective and forms a scalar reward based on weighted sum of individual objectives. The WS essentially turns the problem into a single objective RL task. This approach was used in [2,6]. Another way, called threshold lexicographic ordering (TLO), assigns thresholds to objectives, i.e. minimum acceptable value reward. This approach was used in [3,4].

2   Testing Framework

The introduction section showed why we are motivated to provide much needed guidance based on empirical analysis. This section will briefly explain why it was difficult to provide such guidance before.

One of the features of the reinforcement learning process is the dynamic nature of the test problem – it is a multistep decision making process, where the next state and reward depend on the currently applied action. This dynamic nature implies an interaction of the test problem and an action provider (learning algorithm). So rather than being able to use common test datasets as in other research fields such as supervised learning, RL researchers must rely on implementations of dynamic test environments. Issues then arise in terms of ensuring consistency between different implementations of the same test, and ensuring compatibility between the interfaces used for test and the varying implementations of learning algorithms created by different researchers.

In single objective reinforcement learning these issues were tackled in [7], with their software called RL-Glue. RL-Glue consists of standard application programming interfaces for problems, learning algorithms, experiments and server software that connects all them together. RL-Glue lays a solid foundation for empirical analysis in reinforcement learning. RL-Glue is very good and very useful software but is restricted to single objective reinforcement learning. In this paper we present a modified version of RL-Glue (which we call MORL-Glue) that was extended to cope with multiple number of objectives. First application programming interfaces were changed, and then server software and Java codec were altered to reflect changes in those programming interfaces.

To support the evaluation methodology proposed in [8] we also integrated hypervolume calculation code into the framework. Currently the leading algorithm for calculation of hypervolume is the one provided by the Walking Fish Group from the University of Western Australia [9]. Walking Fish Group distributes their algorithm as program written in C language. As MORL-Glue is implemented in the Java programming language, as part of its development we have ported their algorithm to Java. The MORL-Glue server's source code is available through SVN repository at http://subversion.assembla.com/svn/mo-rl-glue/. All the benchmarks and the algorithms that were used in this paper along with compiled Java code are available through SVN repository at https://subversion.assembla.com/svn/rl-glue-plugins/. Use phrase "mo-rl-glue" without quotes as a username and password, if required.

3   Methodology

Because we deal with multiple numbers of objectives we need to define the notion of dominant policy. We use the notion of Pareto dominance, which allows us to compare a pair of policies when a number of objectives is greater than one. According to the Pareto dominance, a policy A strongly dominates a policy B if it is superior on all objectives. If the policy A is equal to the policy B on at least one objective and superior on all other objectives then we say that the policy A weakly dominates the policy B. We say that the policy A is not comparable to the policy B if they dominate each other on at least one objective.

In this paper the hypervolume indicator [11] is used to measure the quality of a Pareto front approximation produced by a learning algorithm. Given a frontal set and a reference point (which is dominated by all members of the frontal set) we can calculate the hypervolume of the objective space region which is formed by the frontal set and the reference point, as shown in Figure 1. Each black dot on the figure represents a single non-dominated solution and all black dots represent an approximation to the Pareto front. Reference point is represented as a red dot. The hypervolume is the area of the shaded region, bounded by the black dots and the red dot. Improvement in any of the main characteristics of a Pareto front (accuracy, extent, diversity) translates into a higher value of the hypervolume. The meaningful interpretation of an experiment's results requires a consistency of a reference point between those experiments.

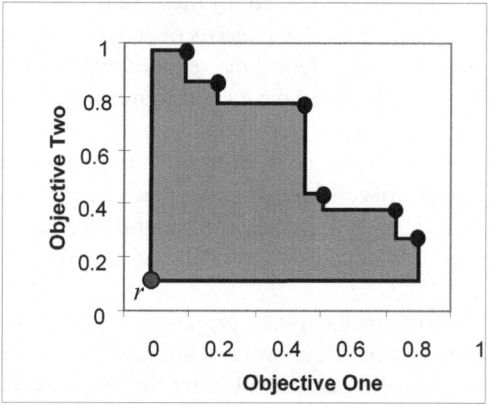

Fig. 1. An example hypervolume: The shaded area, bounded by the prevailing front(black dots) and the reference point r (red dot), represents the region from which the hypervolume is derived

Our goal is to measure the hypervolume of the Pareto front produced by given algorithms: Weighted Scalarization(WS) and Threshold Lexicographic ordering(TLO), on a variety of problems. Both of these algorithms, given a weight for each objective or a threshold for the first n-1 objectives, will converge to a single point in an objective space. Thus any given run of the algorithm will produce only one member of the Pareto front. To overcome this limitation the following approach was used.

3.1   Weighted Scalarization

It is well known that using the WS algorithm we can point the algorithm to a specific part of the objective space by favoring one objective over another. Thus we can target points in all regions of the objective space by gradually changing weights on all objectives. This method leads to a set of policies found using different weight combinations - each of them is only a member of the Pareto front, but all of them together approximate the Pareto front.

To summarize, first we prepare a set of weight combinations that will target points all over objective space, then we run WS algorithm on each weight combination in that set and observe a point to which algorithm converged. Eventually we will have a set of optimal points, which will be a suitable approximation of the Pareto front. The following pseudo code describes an action selection mechanism for the WS algorithm.

```
bestAction = argmax_a getWeightedSum(state, a)
```

We assume that information about number of objectives, weights assigned to these objectives and value function for each objective is provided in `getWeighted-Sum()` function. For each action we calculate a weighted sum and we pick an action with maximum value of the weighted sum. In this paper we use Q-learning version of the WS algorithm across all tested problems.

3.2   Threshold Lexicographic Ordering

TLO, due to its nature, requires some knowledge about the problem under consideration. Namely, thresholds should be provided for the first n-1 objectives, which clearly require some prior knowledge of the range of values expected for each objective. One way to obtain the required knowledge is to observe the results produced by the WS algorithm. The WS produced approximation to the Pareto front and by observing the actual points from that approximated front we can identify the region of objective space in which all points fell. Thus we can find min and max value for first n-1 objectives. Then we can use that information to tell TLO to look in the specific objective space region. Effectively we bound first n-1 objectives and leave the last objective unbound to see whether TLO can produce better results than WS. The following pseudo code sketches an action selection mechanism for the TLO algorithm.

```
chooseGreedyAction(state) {
  actions = { all available actions };
  bestActions = { };
  for(int i = 1; i <= numOfObjectives ; i++) {
    if( i < numOfObjectives  ) {
      bestActions=getAboveThreshold(state,i,actions);
      if(bestActions is empty) {
        bestActions = getMaximum(state,actions,i);
        break;
      } else {
```

```
            actions = bestActions;
          }
       } else {
          bestActions = getMaximum(state,actions,i);
       }
    }
    return bestActions;
}
```

We assume that an array of thresholds is provided and is accessible in the getAbo-veOrEqualThreshold() function. Also we assume that the first n-1 objectives are to be thresholded and the last objective is to be maximized. As we run through the first n-1 objectives we leave only the actions that are in compliance with provided thresholds and when we reach our final objective we just pick a greedy action. In this paper we use Q-learning version of the TLO algorithm across all tested problems.

3.3 Hypervolume Sampling

To better understand the behavior of a learning algorithm we measure the hypervolume not only after convergence but also periodically during the exploration phase. To make that hypvervolume sample we turn off exploration and make one run through the environment picking only greedy actions in every state, after that we turn back exploration and proceed normally.

This intermediate sampling allows us to understand a lifetime performance of a learning algorithm and compare it with other algorithms. This can be important if we are interested in good performance from the start of the problem.

4   Benchmarks

As was mentioned in first two chapters of this paper MORL-Glue facilitates the creation of a central repository of test problems. This central repository should have a wide variety of test problems each of which subjects a learning algorithm to a particular property which is found in real life problems. All these properties should be well documented to facilitate exchange of the test problems.

An example of such property is the type of rewards being used in a test problem. There are two types of rewards: extrinsic and intrinsic [10]. Intrinsic rewards are non-zero most of the time (like time penalty applied every time step), extrinsic rewards are non-zero only at special moments (like reaching a goal state). This is an important property as the algorithms may behave differently depending on the type of rewards. Another important property is the shape of the Pareto front. Research in multiobjective optimization has shown that frontal properties such as the presence of concave regions, discontinuities or uneven distribution of frontal points can significantly affect the performance of some algorithms.

In this paper we will examine three benchmarks that were presented in [8]. Further details of these benchmarks are available at http://uob-community.ballarat.edu.au/~pvamplew/MORL.html

4.1   Deep Sea Treasure

Deep Sea Treasure is a two-dimensional environment. The environment represents an undersea world with multiple numbers of treasure locations with varying values. The agent controls a submarine, four actions are available: left, right, up, down. The agent faces two objectives: maximizing found treasure value and minimizing time penalty.

Deep Sea Treasure is an interesting problem because of the fact that one of the objectives, treasure, is extrinsic and the second one, time, is intrinsic. In addition the Pareto front for this problem is globally concave. This structure of rewards is really suitable for showcasing advantages of TLO algorithm over WS.

Table 1 shows the results of WS and TLO runs on the Deep Sea Treasure. As was expected the WS algorithm was not able to find concave Pareto front members. Contrary to the WS, the TLO algorithm was able to locate concave Pareto front members. So the TLO was able to find extreme members of the Pareto front as well as intermediate, this leads to higher hypervolume values.

Table 1. TLO and WS algorithms tested on Deap Sea Treasure. Reference point is (0,-20). Epsilon is 0.17, alpha is 0.9, gamma is 1.0. Step limit is 200 per episode.

	10k	**20k**	**30k**	**40k**	**50k**
WS	388	292	462	288	142
TLO	460	510	510	510	510

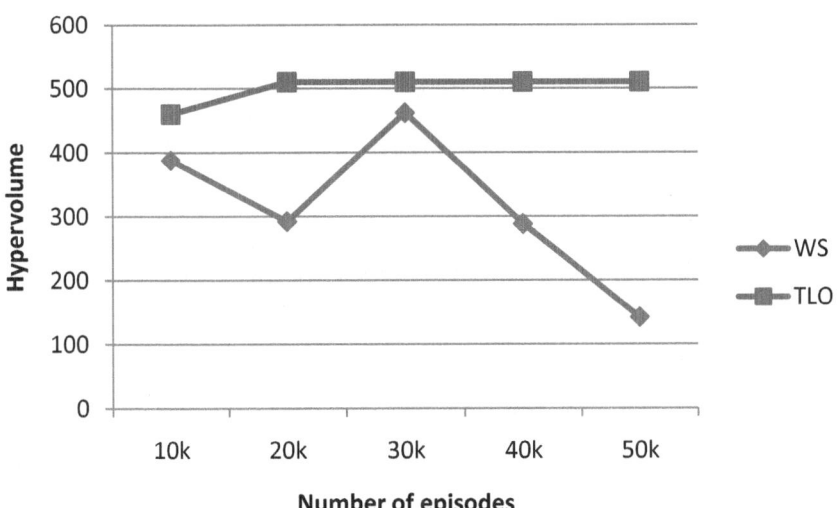

Fig. 2. WS vs TLO tested on Deep Sea Treasure. Reference point is (0;-20). Epsilon is 0.17, alpha is 0.9, gamma is 1.0.

Figure 2 summarizes the difference in performance between the TLO and the WS. The WS line on the graph is erratic due to the fact that between 10k and 40k episodes the WS algorithm was able to temporarily find concave members of the Pareto front but these members are merely a milestone and the algorithm has not yet converged. As the state-action values converge to their true values, the weighted sum approach to action selection is unable to produce any policies other than those corresponding to the extremes of the front.

4.2   MO-PuddleWorld

MO-PuddleWorld is a two-dimensional environment with puddles located at different places. The agent starts at a random location and must reach a goal state at the top-right corner. A time penalty is applied at every state except the goal state and another penalty is applied when the agent steps into the puddles.

The reward structure for MO-PuddleWorld has one intrinsic reward, namely the time penalty, which is -1 on all steps except goal state, when penalty is 0. The second reward, namely puddle penalty, is extrinsic. The MO-PuddleWorld test problem represents a state as a combination of two continuous variables: x position and y position. A 20 by 20 discretization was used in case of both the TLO and the WS algorithms. Tables 2 and 3 provide details of WS and TLO algorithms ran from 5 different starting positions. Fixed positions were used to remove the effects of noise due to random starting positions.

The results of the two algorithms are very similar. This can be explained by the nature of the problem itself. In the deep sea treasure problem the shape of the Pareto front provides a number of concave solutions and the TLO algorithm can converge to any point in that front, which increases the hypervolume. Contrary, the MO-PuddleWorld's Pareto front from most of the starting points is primarily convex in shape, and when concave solutions are available, a number of those solutions is very small and they contribute only slightly to the overall hypervolume attainable. So the TLO algorithm never receives a chance to showcase its benefits over the WS algorithm.

Table 2. WS algorithm tested on MO-PuddleWorld problem with 5 different starting positions. Reference point is (-100,-100). Epsion is 0.15, alpha is 0.9, gamma is 1.0. Step limit is 100 steps per episode.

	(0.25;0.6)	(0.35;0.55)	(0.3;0.55)	(0.3;0.7)	(0.2;0.7)
0	1084	988	99	99	99
500	7998	8084	7984	8287	8087
1000	7998	8084	7998	8297	8098

Table 3. TLO algorithm tested on MO-PuddleWorld problem with 5 different starting positions. Reference point is (-100,-100). Epsion is 0.15, alpha is 0.9, gamma is 1.0. Step limit is 100 steps per episode.

	(0.25;0.6)	**(0.35;0.55)**	**(0.3;0.55)**	**(0.3;0.7)**	**(0.2;0.7)**
0	99	100	99	99	99
500	7984	8083	7984	8287	8087
1000	7984	8083	7984	8287	8087

4.3   MO-MountainCar

Mountain car is a well known reinforcement learning benchmark. Original version of the benchmark is single objective. To create the MO-MountainCar test the reward structure was modified from one objective to three.

The reward structure for mountain car problem consists of 3 intrinsic rewards. The first is a penalty of -1 applied each time step, the second is a penalty of -1 applied at every backward acceleration and the third one is a penalty of -1 applied at every forward acceleration. The MO-MountainCar test problem represents a state as a combination of two continuous variables: a position and a velocity. A 170(position) by 140(velocity) discretization was used in case of both the TLO and the WS algorithms.

Table 4. WS algorithm results on MO-MountainCar problem over 5 runs. Starting position is always fixed and is -0.5. Reference point is (-300;-300;-300). Epsilon is 0.0, alpha is 0.9, gamma is 1.0.

	5k	**15k**	**25k**	**35k**	**40k**
1	6,065,247	11,819,348	15,175,815	15,322,349	15,322,597
2	5,357,800	10,926,832	15,137,425	15,417,314	15,416,766
3	5,785,239	11,629,691	14,865,468	15,302,728	15,303,667
4	6,786,636	10,713,965	15,068,736	15,442,287	15,443,135
5	7,870,923	10,963,501	14,941,997	15,270,617	15,326,463
AVG	**6,373,169**	**11,210,667**	**15,037,888**	**15,351,059**	**15,362,525**

Tables 4 and 5 show results of the WS and the TLO algorithms. As you can see the WS algorithm outperformed the TLO algorithm. This can be explained by the intrinsic rewards. The linear combination of objectives used to perform action-selection in the WS algorithm is compatible with both intrinsic and extrinsic rewards. However TLO's non-linear action selection mechanism performs poorly when thresholding is applied to intrinsic rewards, as it fails to account for the rewards already received earlier in the episode. Thus TLO was heavily impacted by the intrinsic rewards, which resulted in poor figures of hypervolume. This observation is compatible with the preliminary results reported in [8], who noted TLO performs poorly on the Deep Sea Treasure task if the ordering of the objectives is changed such that the intrinsic reward is being thresholded.

Table 5. TLO algorithm results on MO-MountainCar problem over 5 runs. Starting position is always fixed and is -0.5. Reference point is (-300;-300;-300). Epsilon is 0.0, alpha is 0.9, gamma is 1.0.

	5k	**25k**	**40k**	**55k**	**65k**
1	85,349	9,315,462	11,798,739	11,925,448	11,942,691
2	85,591	9,970,806	12,590,952	12,883,731	12,879,446
3	85,528	8,483,264	12,282,405	12,386,070	12,465,344
4	85,460	10,951,818	12,525,832	12,549,660	12,549,715
5	87,309	9,206,131	12,509,929	12,617,007	12,623,177
AVG	**85,847**	**9,585,496**	**12,341,571**	**12,472,383**	**12,492,074**

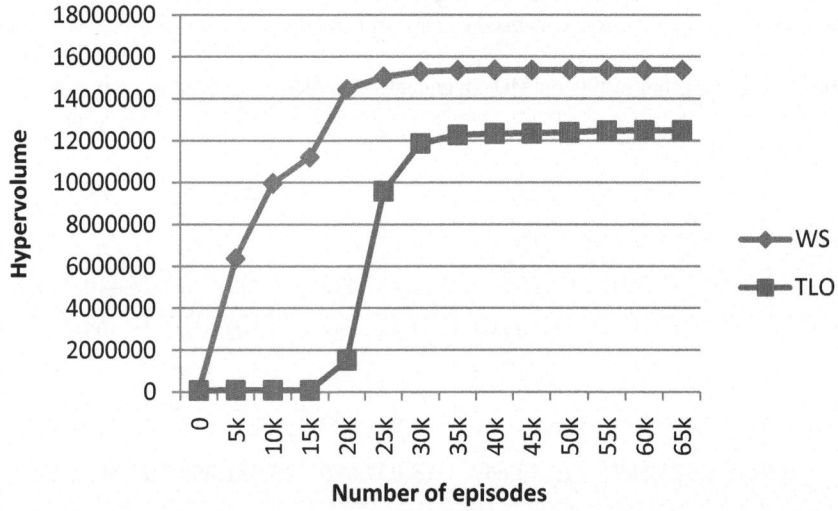

Fig. 3. WS vs TLO hypervolume growth on MO-MountainCar problem. Starting position is always fixed and is -0.5. Reference point is (-300;-300;-300). Epsilon is 0.0, alpha is 0.9, gamma is 1.0.

5   Conclusion and Future Work

Three different problems were presented. Deep Sea Treasure and MO-PuddleWorld has similar reward structure. In that one of the objectives is extrinsic and the other one is intrinsic. Meanwhile the MO-MountainCar has all of its objectives being intrinsic.

Deep Sea Treasure has a number of concavities in Pareto front. The TLO algorithm clearly benefited from its ability to locate those concavities. The WS algorithm doesn't have this ability and this leads to a situation where the WS algorithm was dominated by the TLO algorithm. The MO-PuddleWorld's reward structure is similar to the one of Deep Sea Treasure but this doesn't lead to similar dominance. This can be explained by the nature of the MO-PuddleWorld problem. The MO-PuddleWorld's Pareto front from any starting position has concavities, but the number of those concavities is not comparable to Deep Sea Treasure and for some starting positions there are no concavities at all. This lead to a situation where the TLO algorithm was not able to benefit from its main strength and showed similar results as the WS algorithm. The MO-MountainCar benchmark highlighted the dominance of the WS algorithm over the TLO in problems with intrinsic rewards.

In summary this paper demonstrates the importance of empirical studies on benchmark problems with known characteristics in establishing the conditions under which different MORL algorithms will work effectively. Clearly the TLO algorithm can only be used reliably on problems with no more than one intrinsic reward. However where the reward structure of an environment does meet this criteria, TLO is likely to outperform WS due to its capacity to discover policies which lie in concave regions of the Pareto front which cannot be found by the WS algorithm. In the future we will expand upon these results by extending the number and range of benchmarks to include other important characteristics such as larger numbers of objectives, partial-observability and non-episodic environments. We will also extend the number of MORL algorithms included in the comparison, to provide the first comprehensive comparison of a wide assortment of MORL methods.

References

1. Barrett, L., Narayanan, S.: Learning all optimal policies with multiple criteria. In: Proceedings of the International Conference on Machine Learning (2008)
2. Castelletti, A., Corani, G., Rizzolli, A., Soncinie-Sessa, R., Weber, E.: Reinforcement learning in the operational management of a water system. In: IFAC Workshop on Modeling and Control in Environmental Issues, pp. 325–330. Keio University, Yokohama (2002)
3. Gabor, Z., Kalmar, Z., Szepesvari, C.: Multi-criteria reinforcement learning. In: The Proceedings of the 15th International Conference on Machine Learning, pp. 197–205 (1998)
4. Geibel, P.: Reinforcement Learning for MDPs with Constraints. In: Fürnkranz, J., Scheffer, T., Spiliopoulou, M. (eds.) ECML 2006. LNCS (LNAI), vol. 4212, pp. 646–653. Springer, Heidelberg (2006)
5. Mannor, S., Shimkin, N.: The steering approach for multi-criteria reinforcement learning. In: Neural Information Processing Systems, Vancouver, Canada, pp. 1563–1570 (2001)

6. Natarajan, S., Tadepalli, P.: Dynamic preferences in multi-criteria reinforcement learning. In: The Proceedings of the International Conference on Machine Learning, Bonn, Germany, pp. 601–608 (2005)
7. Tanner, B., White, A.: RL-Glue: Language-Independent Software for Reinforcement-Learning Experiments. Journal of Machine Learning Research 10, 2133–2136 (2009)
8. Vamplew, P., Dazeley, R., Berry, A., Issabekov, R., Dekker, E.: Empirical Evaluation Methods for Multiobjective Reinforcement Learning Algorithms. Machine Learning, Special Issue on Empirical Evaluation of Reinforcement Learning 84(1-2), 51–80 (2011)
9. While, L., Bradstreet, L., Barone, L.: A Fast Way of Calculating Exact Hypervolumes. IEEE Transactions on Evolutionary Computation (2010)
10. Uchibe, E., Doya, K.: Finding intrinsic rewards by embodied evolution and constrained reinforcement learning. Neural Networks 21(10), 1447–1455 (2008)
11. Zitzler, E.: Evolutionary Algorithms for Multiobjective Optimization: Methods and Applications. PhD thesis, Swiss Federal Institute of Technology (ETH), Zurich, Switzerland (November 1999)

A Comparative Study of Sampling Methods and Algorithms for Imbalanced Time Series Classification

Guohua Liang and Chengqi Zhang

The Centre for Quantum Computation & Intelligent Systems, FEIT,
University of Technology Sydney NSW 2007 Australia
{Guohua.Liang,Chengqi.Zhang}@uts.edu.au
http://www.qcis.uts.edu.au/index.html

Abstract. Mining time series data and imbalanced data are two of ten challenging problems in data mining research. Imbalanced time series classification (ITSC) involves these two challenging problems, which take place in many real world applications. In the existing research, the structure-preserving over-sampling (SOP) method has been proposed for solving the ITSC problems. It is claimed by its authors to achieve better performance than other over-sampling and state-of-the-art methods in time series classification (TSC). However, it is unclear whether an under-sampling method with various learning algorithms is more effective than over-sampling methods, e.g., SPO for ITSC, because research has shown that under-sampling methods are more effective and efficient than over-sampling methods. We propose a comparative study between an under-sampling method with various learning algorithms and over-sampling methods, e.g. SPO. Statistical tests, the Friedman test and post-hoc test are applied to determine whether there is a statistically significant difference between methods. The experimental results demonstrate that the under-sampling technique with KNN is the most effective method and can achieve results that are superior to the existing complicated SPO method for ITSC.

Keywords: Imbalanced Time Series Classification, Supervised Learning Algorithms, Under-sampling, Over-sampling

1 Introduction

The problems of mining time series data and imbalanced data are two of ten challenging problems in data mining research [1], which have captured the interest and attention of the data mining and machine learning communities for almost two decades. Imbalanced time series classification (ITSC) involving these two problems can be widely observed in many real-world applications in various domains.

ITSC refers to training examples of time series classification (TSC) which are unevenly distributed with unequal cost among classes [2]. ITSC involves many real world applications, such as ECG beats classification [3, 4]. The various challenges, i.e., high dimensionality, large scale, uneven distribution with different

M. Thielscher and D. Zhang (Eds.): AI 2012, LNCS 7691, pp. 637–648, 2012.
© Springer-Verlag Berlin Heidelberg 2012

costs for mis-classification errors between different classes, and the nature of numerical attributes considered as a whole instead of individual numerical attributes, such as the sequence of attributes carrying information with a special connection between them [5], mean that many supervised learning algorithms are not effective for ITSC [2]. Many techniques have been proposed for TSC, such as one-nearest-neighbor (1NN) with Dynamic Time Warping (DTW) [6] because the distance measure has proven "exceptionally difficult to beat" [7], but the drawback is that the computational cost is too high [7, 8].

Research into imbalanced data has attracted growing attention in several communities, particularly two major workshops on Learning from Imbalanced Data Sets, AAAI'00 [9] and ICML'03 [10], and a special issue in ACM SIGKDD Explorations'04 [11]. Imbalanced class distribution refers to the numbers of training instances and/or the costs of mis-classification errors are unevenly distributed among different classes [12]. Most traditional supervised learning algorithms have drawbacks with regard to highly imbalanced class distribution. In addition, the overall accuracy/misclassification error rate is an ineffective evaluation metric for imbalanced class distribution data, because it cannot represent the accuracy of minority class, which is the users interested class [2, 12–16]. Many researchers have attempted a number of ways to improve the performance of the prediction model for the imbalanced class distribution problem, at data level, algorithm level, in cost-sensitive learning and ensemble learning. Re-sampling techniques have been the most commonly used techniques to solve imbalanced classification problems at data level, from the simple random under-sampling and over-sampling methods to advanced sampling techniques such as SMOTE [17], SMOTEBoost [18], and Borderline SMOTE [19]. The main advantage of under-sampling methods is that they significantly reduce the computational cost of training a classification model, because only a proportion of majority class instances are selected to train a classification model. Previous works comparing under-sampling and over-sampling methods with Decision Tree learner C4.5 indicate that under-sampling is more effective than over-sampling [20–22].

In the existing research, a structure-preserving over-sampling (SPO) method with support vector machines (SVM) has been proposed for solving the ITSC problem. Its authors claim that it achieves better performance than other over-sampling methods and state-of-the-art methods in TSC [23]. However, the authors have not compared it with under-sampling methods for ITSC; their claim is based on a comparison of the average values of two evaluation metrics, $F - value$ and Geometric mean $(G - mean)$, without statistical analysis to support their conclusion. In addition, evaluating the performance of multiple methods over multiple data-sets to draw valid conclusions is a challenging issue in analyzing experimental results in data mining research.

Our previous work proposed an under-sampling technique integrated with SVM; we observed that our previous proposed method is more efficient than other more complicated approaches, such as SPO with SVM for ITSC [2]. However, it is unclear whether the under-sampling method with various supervised learning algorithms is more effective than over-sampling methods, SPO, and the under-sampling technique integrated with SVM for ITSC.

These issues have motivated us to conduct a comparative evaluation of the performance of over-sampling methods (e.g., the complex SPO [23]) and under-sampling with different supervised learning algorithms for ITSC. Statistical tests are adopted to validate our conclusions; moreover, it provides a correction of the claim for the SPO method by using statistical analysis. As the overall accuracy/mis-classification error rate is ineffective for imbalanced classification, this work adopts two evaluation metrics: $F - value$ and $G - mean$. The experimental results demonstrate that the under-sampling technique with KNN is the most effective method and can achieve results that are superior to the existing complicated SPO method for ITSC.

The paper is organized as follows. Section 2 presents an outline of the designed framework. Section 3 presents the evaluation metrics. Sections 4 and 5 provide the experimental setting and experimental analysis. Section 6 concludes this work.

2   Designed Framework

Fig. 1 presents the designed framework. The comparative study is evaluated as follows:

1. For each imbalanced binary class data-set, the random under-sampling method is used to alter the levels of class distribution:
   - Firstly, all the positive examples are distributed equally to a set of five subsets.
   - Secondly, negative examples are randomly allocated to each subset according to the ratio of positive and negative examples (positive:negative) as follows: (30%:70%), (40%:60%), (50%:50%), (60%:40%), and (70%:30%).

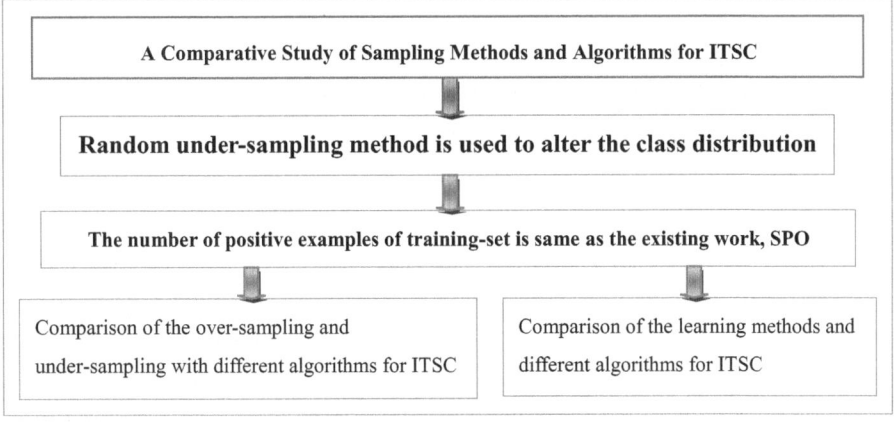

Fig. 1. Designed framework

As a result, each original imbalanced data-set is altered to become five subsets with the same number of positive examples and five different ratios of negative examples.

2. The number of positive and negative examples in the altered data-sets in Table 2, which are the same as those in the data-sets of the existing work [23], are used for the evaluation of the performance of each learning algorithm on each subset, based on two evaluation metrics, $F-value$ and $G-mean$. As a result, each learning algorithm has the outputs of five pairs of $F-value$ and $G-mean$ on each original data-set. Only the output pair with the maximum $G-mean$ is selected for reporting.

3. A comparison is made of the performance of the over-sampling methods, SPO, and under-sampling method with five learning algorithms.

4. A comparison is made of the performance of the state-of-the-art learning methods, SPO, and under-sampling with five learning algorithms.

5. Statistical tests, the Friedman test and post-hoc Nemenyi test are applied to determine whether there is a statistically significant difference between methods.

3   Evaluation Metrics

The estimated misclassification error rate/overall accuracy is commonly used as an evaluation metric to assess the performance of a learning algorithm, but it is an ineffective evaluation metric for the imbalanced classification task. This is especially true for ITSC, because it cannot present a true prediction for the minority class, which normally has a higher misclassification error cost than the majority class. Therefore, we have adopted two evaluation metrics for this study as follows: $F-value$ and $G-mean$.

Table 1 presents a confusion matrix, which is used to evaluate the performance of machine learning algorithms; the columns represent the predicted class, and the rows represent the actual class. In the confusion matrix, True Positives (TP) and True Negatives (TN) denote the number of examples correctly classified as positive and negative, respectively. False Positives (FP) and False Negatives (FN) denote the number of misclassified negative examples and positive examples, respectively.

True Positive Rate (TPR) and True Negative Rate (TNR) refer to the proportion of the positive samples and negative samples that have been correctly classified as a positive class and negative class, respectively.

Table 1. Confusion matrix for a binary classification problem

	Predicted Positives	Predicted Negatives
Actual Positives (P)	True Positive (TP)	False Negative (FN)
Actual Negatives (N)	False Positive(FP)	True Negative (TN)

$F - value$ is integrated from both recall and precision into a single number, and represents a harmonic mean between recall and precision [24]. As a result, it is closed to one of the smaller number of two (recall and precision). This measure is concerned with the performance of the positive class, so a high F-value indicates that high results in both precision and recall are achieved. On the other hand, the $G - mean$ measure considers the performance of a learning algorithm between two classes to monitor TPR and TNR. The formulas of the evaluation metrics are as follows:

$$TPR = \frac{TP}{TP + FN} \tag{1}$$

$$TNR = \frac{TN}{TN + FP} \tag{2}$$

$$recall = \frac{TP}{TP + FN} \tag{3}$$

$$precision = \frac{TP}{TP + FP} \tag{4}$$

$$F - value = \frac{2 recall * precision}{recall + precision} \tag{5}$$

$$G - mean = \sqrt{TPR * TNR} \tag{6}$$

4   Experimental Setup

This section includes data-set characteristics and the selection of the five learning algorithms. Java platform is used to implement the under-sampling technique to alter the ratio between the positive samples and negative samples. SPSS software is used for the calculation of the Friedman test.

4.1   Data-Sets

Table 2 displays a summary of the characteristics of the five time series data-sets from the public UCR time series repository [25], which were used as the benchmark data-sets of SPO [23]. The first column indicates the index and name of each data-set; the second column presents the data information of the original data-sets, and the altered data-sets (with the number of positive, negative examples, and the ratio between the positive and negative classes), which has the same setting as the existing work [23]; and the last column indicates the class information of the original and the altered data-sets. We also alter three out of five data-sets from multi-class change to binary-class, as follows. For the Adiac data-set, the second class with 23 samples is considered as a positive class, and the remaining samples are considered as a negative class. For FaceAll and S-Leaf data-sets, the first class is considered as the positive class with 112 and 75 samples, respectively.

Table 2. Time series data-sets

Data-sets		Data Information					Class Information	
Index	Name	TS Length	Instances $(P^+\&N^-)$	P^+	N^-	Ratio P^+/N^-	Previous Class	Altered class
1	Adiac	176	781	23	758	0.0303	37	2
2	S-Leaf	128	1125	75	1050	0.0714	15	2
3	Wafer	152	7164	762	6402	0.0119	2	2
4	FaceAll	131	2250	112	2138	0.0524	14	2
5	Yoga	426	3300	1530	1770	0.8644	2	2

4.2   Selection of Learning Algorithms

Five learning algorithms are selected from WEKA [26] for this study: Sequential Minimal Optimization (SMO) of SVM, Decision Tree (J48), Random Tree (RTree), KNN, and Multi-layer Proceptron (MLP).

5   Experimental Results Analysis

This section contains two subsections: 5.1 comparison of the performance of over-sampling methods, SPO, and the under-sampling method with different learning algorithms on ITSC; and 5.2 comparison of the performance of other learning methods, SPO, and under-sampling methods with different algorithms for ITSC.

Demar [27] suggests that it is inappropriate to validate the conclusions by using the averaged results over multiple data-sets when the performances of multi-methods are compared. The main reason is that the averages are susceptible to outliers. For example, the KNN algorithm with the under-sampling method has an excellent $F-value$ performance (0.999 on one data-set, wafer) to compensate for other bad $F-value$ performances. It is preferable for the classifiers to perform well on as many problems as possible, which is why it is inappropriate to draw conclusions by averaging the results over multiple data-sets. Previous authors [23] have based their conclusions on the averaged results of the $F-value$ and $G-mean$; thus, their conclusions cannot be validated. This work therefore utilizes statistical tests, the Friedman test and post-hoc Nemenyi test to compare the performance of the multiple learning methods on multiple data-sets, as suggested by [27].

5.1   Comparison of the Performance of Over-Sampling Methods and Different Learning Algorithms with the Under-Sampling Method

Table 3 presents a comparison of the performance of over-sampling methods and five learning algorithms with the under-sampling method based on the $F-value$ and $G-mean$ metrics. The experimental results indicate that KNN with the under-sampling method achieves better performance with $F-value$ than all

Table 3. Comparison of the performance of over-sampling and under-sampling methods with different learning algorithms based on the evaluation metrics $F-value$ and $G-mean$

Metrics	Data-set	Results from Previous Research [23]						Results from This Work				
		Over-sampling Methods						Under-sampling				
	Name	REP	SMO	BoS	ADA	DB	SPO	SVM	J48	RTree	KNN	MLP
$F-value$	Adiac	0.375	0.783	0.783	0.783	0.136	0.963	0.967	0.883	0.903	0.918	0.947
	S-Leaf	0.761	0.764	0.764	0.759	0.796	0.796	0.841	0.820	0.849	0.836	0.786
	Wafer	0.962	0.968	0.968	0.967	0.977	0.982	0.891	0.929	0.956	0.999	0.933
	FaceAll	0.935	0.935	0.935	0.935	0.890	0.936	0.957	0.876	0.863	0.909	0.919
	Yoga	0.710	0.729	0.721	0.727	0.689	0.702	0.744	0.771	0.811	0.807	0.780
	AverageValue	0.740	0.836	0.834	0.834	0.698	0.876	0.880	0.856	0.876	0.894	0.873
	AverageRank	8.3	6.3	6.7	7.1	7.9	4.3	4	6.8	5.2	3.6	5.8
$G-mean$	Adiac	0.480	0.831	0.831	0.831	0.748	0.999	0.957	0.910	0.920	0.958	0.975
	S-Leaf	0.800	0.861	0.861	0.849	0.898	0.898	0.902	0.809	0.812	0.887	0.856
	Wafer	0.965	0.969	0.970	0.970	0.980	0.984	0.903	0.907	0.956	0.998	0.937
	FaceAll	0.950	0.950	0.950	0.950	0.948	0.957	0.966	0.870	0.860	0.929	0.925
	Yoga	0.741	**0.756**	0.750	0.755	0.724	0.735	0.630	0.807	0.803	0.808	0.774
	AverageValue	0.787	**0.783**	0.872	0.871	0.860	0.915	0.872	0.861	0.870	0.916	0.893
	AverageRank	8.3	5.8	5.9	6.2	6.5	3.3	5.6	7.6	7.2	3.4	6.2

over-sampling methods and other learning algorithms with the under-sampling method on average value and average rank of $F-value$; while KNN achieves 0.894 and 3.6, respectively, which is better than all over-sampling methods and all learning algorithms with the under-sampling method.

On average value and average rank of the $G-mean$ metric, however, the SPO over-sampling method achieves 0.915 and 3.3, respectively, which is the best among all the over-sampling and under-sampling methods on average rank of the $G-mean$ metric, whereas KNN with the under-sampling method achieves 0.916 and 3.4, respectively, which is the best among all algorithms with the under-sampling method and all over-sampling methods on average of the $G-mean$ metric. The results highlighted in red indicate the correction of the previous work [23].

Figs 2 and 3 present a comparison of over-sampling and under-sampling methods with the Nemenyi test, where the x-axis indicates the ranking order of the sampling methods; the y-axis indicates the average rank of the $F-value$ and $G-mean$ performance, respectively, and the vertical bars indicate the "Critical Difference". Groups of sampling methods that are not significantly different at a 95% confidence interval are indicated when the vertical bars overlap. The results indicate that there is no statistically significant difference between the over-sampling method and the under-sampling method, based on both $F-value$ and $G-mean$ metrics, even though KNN and SPO show better average rank in $F-value$ and $G-mean$, respectively.

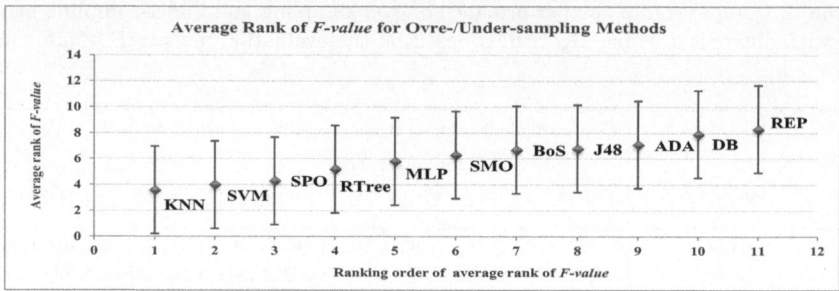

Fig. 2. Comparison of average rank of the $F - value$ with the Nemenyi test for the over-sampling and under-sampling methods, where the x-axis indicates the ranking order of all the sampling methods and learning algorithms, the y-axis indicates the average rank of the $F - value$, and the vertical bars indicate the "Critical Difference"

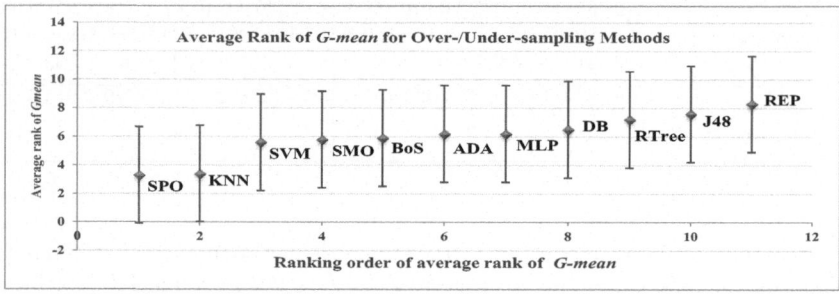

Fig. 3. Comparison of average rank of the $G - mean$ with the Nemenyi test for all the over-sampling and under-sampling methods, where the x-axis indicates the ranking order of all the sampling methods and learning algorithms, the y-axis indicates the average rank of the $G - mean$, and the vertical bars indicate the "Critical Difference"

Comparing SPO, KNN, and the other over-sampling and under-sampling methods, the complex over-sampling method SPO, and simple under-sampling method KNN are not statistically significantly better than any over-sampling methods and learning algorithms with the under-sampling method based on both $F - value$ and $G - mean$. Therefore, the statistical tests demonstrate that there is no statistically significant difference between SPO, KNN and the other over-sampling methods and learning algorithms with under-sampling, even though SPO and KNN have the best average rank in $G - mean$ or $F - value$.

5.2   Comparison of the Performance Learning Methods, Over-Sampling SPO, and Under-Sampling Method with Five Learning Algorithms

Table 4 presents a comparison of the performance of learning methods (results from previous research [23]) and five learning algorithms using the

Table 4. Comparison of the performance of learning methods from previous research [23] and five learning algorithms using the under-sampling method from this work based on evaluation metrics: $F - value$ and $G - mean$

Metrics	Data-set	Results from Previous Research [23]					Results from This Work				
		Learning Methods					Under-sampling				
	Name	Easy	Bal.	1NN	1NN_DW	SPO	SVM	J48	RTree	KNN	MLP
$F - value$	Adiac	0.534	0.348	0.800	0.917	0.963	0.967	0.883	0.903	0.918	0.947
	S-Leaf	0.521	0.578	0.716	0.429	0.796	0.841	0.820	0.849	0.836	0.786
	Wafer	0.795	0.954	0.949	0.857	0.982	0.891	0.929	0.956	0.999	0.933
	FaceAll	0.741	0.625	0.802	0.959	0.936	0.957	0.876	0.863	0.909	0.919
	Yoga	0.356	0.689	0.652	0.710	0.702	0.744	0.771	0.811	0.807	0.780
	AverageValue	0.589	0.639	0.784	0.774	0.876	0.880	0.856	0.876	0.894	0.873
	AverageRank	9.4	8	7.4	6.2	3.8	3.6	5.6	3.6	3	4.4
$G - mean$	Adiac	0.782	0.897	0.875	0.920	0.999	0.957	0.910	0.920	0.958	0.975
	S-Leaf	0.721	0.898	0.798	0.572	0.898	0.902	0.809	0.812	0.887	0.856
	Wafer	0.817	0.970	0.953	0.870	0.984	0.903	0.907	0.956	0.998	0.937
	FaceAll	0.792	0.918	0.983	0.985	0.957	0.966	0.870	0.860	0.929	0.925
	Yoga	0.464	0.688	0.695	0.741	0.735	0.630	0.807	0.803	0.808	0.774
	AverageValue	0.713	0.874	0.861	0.818	0.915	0.872	0.861	0.870	0.916	0.893
	AverageRank	9.8	5.5	6.2	6.1	2.7	6.1	6.2	5.5	2.4	4.5

under-sampling method (results from this work) based on $F - value$ and $G - mean$ evaluation metrics. The experimental results indicate that KNN using the under-sampling method achieves better performance of $F - value$ and $G - mean$ than the remaining learning methods and learning algorithms using the under-sampling method on average value and average rank of $F - value$ and $G - mean$. For $F - value$ and $G - mean$ metrics, KNN achieves an average value of 0.894 and 0.916, and an average rank of 3.0 and 2.4, respectively, which is the best among all the remaining learning methods and learning algorithms using the under-sampling method. The results highlighted in red indicate the correction of the previous work [23].

Figs 4 and 5 present a comparison of learning methods (results from previous research) and five learning algorithms using the under-sampling method with the Nemenyi test, where the x-axis indicates the ranking order of the learning methods and learning algorithms; the y-axis indicates the average rank of $F - value$ and $G - mean$ performance, respectively, and the vertical bars indicate the "Critical Difference". Groups of learning methods and learning algorithms that are not significantly different at a 95% confidence interval are indicated when the vertical bars overlap. The statistical test results demonstrate that over-sampling SPO and under-sampling KNN are statistically significantly better than the learning method, Easy; however, there is no statistically significant difference between over-sampling SPO, under-sampling KNN, and the remaining learning methods and algorithms based on the average rank of both the $F - value$ and $G - mean$ metrics.

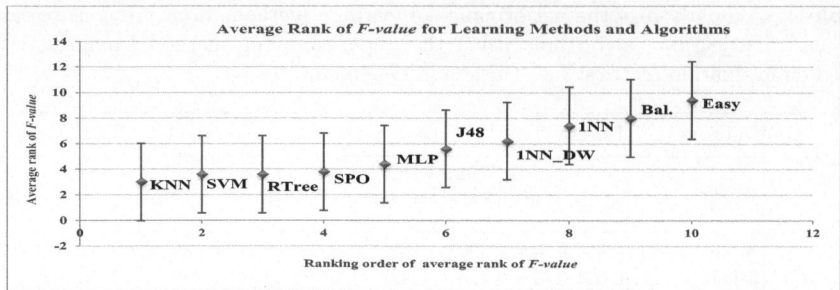

Fig. 4. Comparison of average rank of the $F - value$ metric with the Nemenyi test for the learning methods and five learning algorithms using the under-sampling method, where the x-axis indicates the ranking order of all the learning methods and learning algorithms, the y-axis indicates the average rank of $F - value$, and the vertical bars indicate the "Critical Difference"

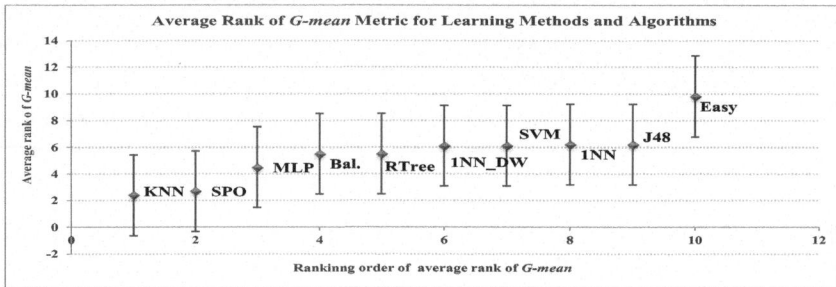

Fig. 5. Comparison of average rank of the $G - mean$ metric with the Nemenyi test for the learning methods and five learning algorithms using the under-sampling method, where the x-axis indicates the ranking order of all the learning methods and learning algorithms, the y-axis indicates the average rank of $G - mean$, and the vertical bars indicate the "Critical Difference"

6   Conclusion

This study empirically evaluates the performance of complex over-sampling SPO and simple under-sampling with five learning algorithms for ITSC, based on two evaluation metrics, $F - value$ and $G - mean$. The existing over-sampling techniques generate more synthetic samples to balance training sets to improve prediction models, while the under-sampling method selects a part of negative samples for training. The drawback of the over-sampling method is that it is considered to increase computational cost in training classifiers. The advantages of the under-sampling method is that it is considered to be faster and to have less computational cost than the over-sampling method for training the prediction model. These issues have motivated us to investigate whether different learning algorithms combining a random under-sampling method with different ratios between positive samples and negative samples in the training set outperform the complex over-sampling SPO. The experimental results indicate that simple under-sampling KNN achieves better results on average for both evaluation metrics $F - value$ and $G - mean$, and achieves better results in average rank for the $G - mean$ metric. However, when we apply statistical tests to analyze the results, we find that there is no statistically significant difference between the complex over-sampling SPO and the simple under-sampling KNN; the over-sampling SPO and under-sampling KNN are statistically significantly better than the learning method, Easy; and there is no statistically significant difference between the remaining learning methods and algorithms for ITSC. Therefore, the experimental results demonstrate that the simple under-sampling KNN can achieve results that compare favorably with the existing complicated SPO method for ITSC.

References

1. Yang, Q., Wu, X.: 10 challenging problems in data mining research. International Journal of Information Technology & Decision Making 5(4), 597–604 (2006)
2. Liang, G., Zhang, C.: An efficient and simple under-sampling technique for imbalanced time series classification. In: CIKM 2012 (in press, 2012)
3. Acır, N.: Classification of ECG beats by using a fast least square support vector machines with a dynamic programming feature selection algorithm. Neural Computing & Applications 14(4), 299–309 (2005)
4. Übeyli, E.: ECG beats classification using multiclass support vector machines with error correcting output codes. Digital Signal Processing 17(3), 675–684 (2007)
5. Hidasi, B., Gáspár-Papanek, C.: ShiftTree: An Interpretable Model-Based Approach for Time Series Classification. In: Gunopulos, D., Hofmann, T., Malerba, D., Vazirgiannis, M. (eds.) ECML PKDD 2011, Part II. LNCS, vol. 6912, pp. 48–64. Springer, Heidelberg (2011)
6. Sakoe, H., Chiba, S.: Dynamic programming algorithm optimization for spoken word recognition. IEEE Transactions on Acoustics, Speech and Signal Processing 26(1), 43–49 (1978)
7. Xi, X., Keogh, E., Shelton, C., Wei, L., Ratanamahatana, C.: Fast time series classification using numerosity reduction. In: Proceedings of 23rd International Conference in Machine Learning, ICML 2006, pp. 1033–1040 (2006)
8. Buza, K., Nanopoulos, A., Schmidt-Thieme, L.: INSIGHT: Efficient and Effective Instance Selection for Time-Series Classification. In: Huang, J.Z., Cao, L., Srivastava, J. (eds.) PAKDD 2011, Part II. LNCS, vol. 6635, pp. 149–160. Springer, Heidelberg (2011)
9. Japkowicz, N., et al.: Learning from imbalanced data sets: A comparison of various strategies. In: AAAI Workshop on Learning from Imbalanced Data Sets, vol. 68 (2000)
10. Chawla, N., Japkowicz, N., Kolcz, A.: Proceedings of the ICML 2003 Workshop on Learning from Imbalanced Data Sets (2003)
11. Chawla, N., Japkowicz, N., Kotcz, A.: Editorial: Special issue on learning from imbalanced data sets. ACM SIGKDD Explorations Newsletter 6(1), 1–6 (2004)
12. Liang, G., Zhu, X., Zhang, C.: The effect of varying levels of class distribution on bagging with different algorithms: An empirical study. International Journal of Machine Learning and Cybernetics (in press, 2012)

13. Liang, G.: An investigation of sensitivity on bagging predictors: An empirical approach. In: 26th AAAI Conference on Artificial Intelligence, pp. 2439–2440 (2012)
14. Liang, G., Zhang, C.: An Empirical Evaluation of Bagging with Different Algorithms on Imbalanced Data. In: Tang, J., King, I., Chen, L., Wang, J. (eds.) ADMA 2011, Part I. LNCS, vol. 7120, pp. 339–352. Springer, Heidelberg (2011)
15. Liang, G., Zhang, C.: Empirical study of bagging predictors on medical data. In: 9th Australian Data Mining Conference, AusDM 2011, pp. 31–40 (2011)
16. Liang, G., Zhu, X., Zhang, C.: An Empirical Study of Bagging Predictors for Imbalanced Data with Different Levels of Class Distribution. In: Wang, D., Reynolds, M. (eds.) AI 2011. LNCS, vol. 7106, pp. 213–222. Springer, Heidelberg (2011)
17. Chawla, N., Bowyer, K., Hall, L., Kegelmeyer, W.: SMOTE: Synthetic minority over-sampling technique. Journal of Artificial Intelligence Research 16(1), 321–357 (2002)
18. Chawla, N., Lazarevic, A., Hall, L., Bowyer, K.: SMOTEBoost: Improving Prediction of the Minority Class in Boosting. In: Lavrač, N., Gamberger, D., Todorovski, L., Blockeel, H. (eds.) PKDD 2003. LNCS (LNAI), vol. 2838, pp. 107–119. Springer, Heidelberg (2003)
19. Han, H., Wang, W., Mao, B.: Borderline-SMOTE: A New Over-Sampling Method in Imbalanced Data Sets Learning. In: Huang, D.-S., Zhang, X.-P., Huang, G.-B. (eds.) ICIC 2005. LNCS, vol. 3644, pp. 878–887. Springer, Heidelberg (2005)
20. Drummond, C., Holte, R., et al.: C4.5, class imbalance, and cost sensitivity: Why under-sampling beats over-sampling. In: Proceedings of the ICML 2003 Workshop on Learning from Imbalanced Datasets II (2003)
21. Liu, X., Wu, J., Zhou, Z.: Exploratory undersampling for class-imbalance learning. IEEE Transactions on Systems, Man, and Cybernetics, Part B: Cybernetics 39(2), 539–550 (2009)
22. Ling, C., Li, C.: Data mining for direct marketing: Problems and solutions. In: Proceedings of the Fourth International Conference on Knowledge Discovery and Data Mining, pp. 73–79 (1998)
23. Cao, H., Li, X., Woon, Y., Ng, S.: SPO: Structure preserving oversampling for imbalanced time series classification. In: : Proceedings of the IEEE 11th International Conference on Data Mining, ICDM 2011, pp. 1008–1013 (2011)
24. Tan, P., Steinbach, M., Kumar, V., et al.: Introduction to data mining. Pearson, Addison Wesley (2006)
25. Keogh, E., Zhu, Q., Hu, B., Hao, Y., Xi, X., Wei, L., Ratanamahatana, C.A.: *UCR* Repository of time series classification/clustering homepage, http://www.cs.ucr.edu/~eamonn/time_series_data/ (2011)
26. Witten, I., Frank, E.: Data Mining: Practical Machine Learning Tool and Techniques. Morgan Kaufmann (2005)
27. Demšar, J.: Statistical comparisons of classifiers over multiple data sets. Journal of Machine Learning Research 7, 1–30 (2006)

An Efficient Adversarial Learning Strategy for Constructing Robust Classification Boundaries*

Wei Liu[1,**], Sanjay Chawla[2], James Bailey[1],
Christopher Leckie[1], and Kotagiri Ramamohanarao[1]

[1] Dept of Computing and Information Systems, The University of Melbourne
wei.liu@unimelb.edu.au
[2] School of Information Technologies, The University of Sydney

Abstract. Traditional classification methods assume that the training and the test data arise from the same underlying distribution. However in some adversarial settings, the test set can be deliberately constructed in order to increase the error rates of a classifier. A prominent example is email spam where words are transformed to avoid word-based features embedded in a spam filter. Recent research has modeled interactions between a data miner and an adversary as a sequential Stackelberg game, and solved its Nash equilibrium to build classifiers that are more robust to subsequent manipulations on training data sets. However in this paper we argue that the *iterative* algorithm used in the Stackelberg game, which solves an optimization problem at each step of play, is sufficient but not necessary for achieving Nash equilibria in classification problems. Instead, we propose a method that transforms singular vectors of a training data matrix to simulate manipulations by an adversary, and from that perspective a Nash equilibrium can be obtained by solving a novel optimization problem only *once*. We show that compared with the *iterative* algorithm used in recent literature, our *one-step* game significantly reduces computing time while still being able to produce good Nash equilibria results.

1 Introduction

Conventional supervised learning algorithms build classification models by learning relationships between independent variables (features) and dependent variables (classes) from given input data. Typically, the often unstated underlying assumption is that the relationship between the features and the class remain unchanged over time. However in many real world applications, such as email spam detection systems, there often exist adversaries who are continuously modifying the underlying relationships in order to avoid detection by the classifier. Therefore, in order to minimize the effects of the adversaries, data miners should not only learn from data in the past, but also from potential data manipulations

---

* This research was partially funded by Australia Research Council Discovery Grants (DP110102621 and DP0881537).
** Corresponding author.

that adversaries are likely to make in future. As a result, the problem of "adversarial learning" has attracted significant interest in the machine learning and data mining community[1–7].

Dalvi et al. [1] modeled adversarial scenarios under the assumption that both the adversary and the data miner have perfect information of each other. In their formulation, the adversary is fully aware of the parameter settings of the classifier, and uses the classifier's decision boundary to undermine the classifier. In [2] the perfect knowledge assumption is relaxed by assuming that the adversary has the ability to issue a polynomial number of membership queries to the classifier in the form of data instances which in turn will report their labels. Globerson et al. [3] use deletions of features at test time to approximate the strategies of adversaries. However, a disadvantage of this feature deletion algorithm is that it fails to simulate scenarios where the adversary is more interested in adding features, or more generally applying a linear transformation of the features.

In addition, Kantarcioglu et al. [5] and Liu et al. [6] have proposed approaches that model the competing behavior between the adversary and the data miner as a sequential Stackelberg game. They use simulated annealing and genetic algorithms respectively to search for a Nash equilibrium as the final state of play. While [5] assumes the two players know each other's payoff function, [6] relaxes this assumption and only the adversary's payoff is required in achieving the equilibrium. But a common problem for [5] and [6] is that the strategies of the adversary are *stochastically* sampled (e.g., Monte Carlo integration in [5]) and then among the samples the best fit is selected (e.g., genetic algorithm in [6]). This *stochastic optimization* process is not realistic for rational adversaries in practice, since rational adversaries rarely make "random" moves, but instead always try to optimize their payoff at each step of play.

More recently, Liu et al. [7] formulate the adversarial learning problem into a maxmin problem where they relaxed the assumption of a normal distribution and forced adversarial transformations to be rational. Similarly, Bruckner et al. [8] formulate the maxmin problem by a different ordering of the players' movements. However, to solve these maximin problems the authors have to use an *iterative* algorithm that *solves a convex optimization problem in every iteration of their algorithms*, which is computationally very expensive. We refer to these existing maxmin optimization based methods (i.e., [7]) the "iterative methods".

In this study, we assert that simulations of adversarial transformations and solutions of Nash equilibria do not have to be modeled as an expensive iterative optimization process, and it is possible to discover the equilibrium state significantly quicker and cheaper by solving one optimization problem only. In contrast to the existing "iterative method", we call the method proposed in this paper the "one-step method". More specifically, the innovations and contributions we make in this paper are as follows:

1. We model malicious manipulations of an adversary as transformations on singular vectors of the training data matrix, and these transformed singular vectors determine distributions of subsequent malicious training samples.

2. We propose a novel payoff function for the adversary, which leads to an optimization problem whose solution achieves the final game state of Nash equilibrium.
3. We perform comprehensive empirical evaluations on spam email and hand-written digit data sets, and demonstrate that our method is able to produce comparative Nash equilibrium results while using significantly less computation time compared to the previous iterative maxmin approach.

2 Game Theory and Nash Equilibrium

In this paper we model the interactions between data miners and adversaries in Stackelberg games. In a Stackelberg game, two players are distinguished as a leader (L) and a follower (F), and it is the leader who makes the first move. In our case the adversary is the leader and the data miner is the follower, since it is always the adversary who proactively attacks her[1] opponent. We call an "attack" from the adversary and "defence" from the data miner as plays/moves of the game.

Each player is associated with a set of strategies, U and V for L and F respectively, where a strategy means a choice of moves available to each player. In this paper, strategy spaces U and V are finite dimensional vector spaces. The outcome from a certain combination of strategies of a player is determined by that player's payoff function, J_L and J_F. Rational players aim to maximize their corresponding payoff functions using their strategy sets. So given an observation v the best strategy of L is

$$u^* = \arg\max_{u \in U} \ J_L(u, v) \tag{1}$$

Similarly, if L's previous move is u, the reaction of F is

$$v^* = \arg\max_{v \in V} \ J_F(u, v) \tag{2}$$

As each player seeks to achieve as high a payoff as possible in each of their moves, they will arrive in a state of Nash equilibrium when their rational strategies interact: the state of **Nash equilibrium** means that simultaneously each player is using the strategy that is the best response to the strategies of the other player, so that no player can benefit from changing his/her strategy unilaterally [9]. Thus the problem reduces to efficiently determining the state of the Nash equilibrium.

2.1 The Maxmin Problem

In the formulation of the sequential Stackelberg game proposed in [7], a Nash equilibrium is the strategy pair (u^*, v^*) that simultaneously solves the optimization problems in Eq. 1 and 2. Because this Stackelberg game is also a

---

[1] For ease of interpretation, in this paper we call the data miner a male (i.e. "he/his") player, and the adversary a female (i.e. "she/her") player.

"constant-sum" game, we have $J_F = \phi - J_L$, where ϕ is a constant number standing for the total profit in the game. Then Eq. 2 can be rewritten as:

$$
\begin{aligned}
v^* &= \arg\max_{v \in V} \ \phi - J_L(u, v) = \arg\max_{v \in V} \ - J_L(u, v) \\
&= \arg\min_{v \in V} \ J_L(u, v)
\end{aligned}
\tag{3}
$$

where the constant number ϕ is ignored, and the equation is transformed into a minimization problem which removes the negative sign. By combining Eq. 3 with Eq. 1, the following maxmin problem is obtained:

$$
\text{Maxmin:} \ (u^*, v^*) = \arg\max_{u \in U} \ J_L(u, \ \arg\min_{v \in V} J_L(u, v))
\tag{4}
$$

The solution to the maxmin problem maximizes the leader's profit under the worst possible move of her opponent. To solve this maxmin optimization problem, the authors in [7] simulate two players of the data miner and the adversary iteratively, and solve one optimization problem (either the "minimization" or the "maximization") at a time. They discover Nash equilibrium when the adversary's payoff stops increasing through the iterating process. Since this iterative algorithm has to solve an optimization problem at every play of the game, it can be computationally expensive to find the final state of Nash equilibrium (which we show in the experiment section).

3   One-Step Method for Finding the Nash Equilibrium

We derive our efficient one-step equilibrium searching method by utilizing singular value decomposition (SVD) on the training data. Among many kinds of matrix factorization methods, SVD has the property that it gives bases for both the *row* and the *column space* of a matrix simultaneously. It also "orders" the information contained in a matrix so that it is possible to spot the "principle components" of that matrix. Given a $m \times n$ matrix A, it can be factorized such that

$$
A = U \Sigma V^T
$$

where $U \in \mathbb{R}^{m \times m}$ and $V \in \mathbb{R}^{n \times n}$ are orthogonal matrices whose columns are (left and right) singular vectors of A, and $\Sigma \in \mathbb{R}^{m \times n}$ is an diagonal matrix whose diagonal entries $\Sigma_{i,i}$ specify singular values of A.

In binary-class classification problems, given training data of positive instances $X^+ \in \mathbb{R}^{m^+ \times n}$ and negative instances $X^- \in \mathbb{R}^{m^- \times n}$, where m^+, m^- are the numbers of positive and negative instances, and n is the number of features, the label of a new instance x_{new} can be determined by using orthogonal basis vectors from SVD as follows.

We compute the SVD of each class of the instance matrix:

$$
X^+ = S^+ \Sigma^+ (V^+)^T; \quad X^- = S^- \Sigma^- (V^-)^T.
$$

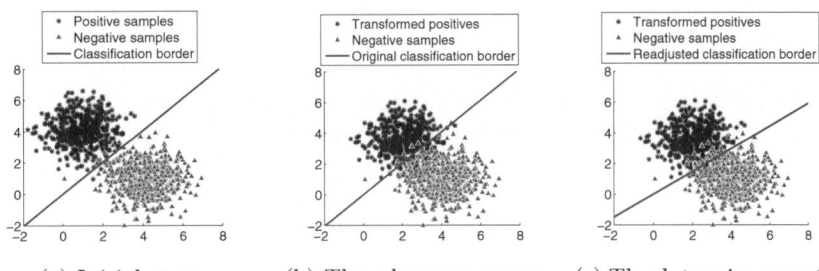

(a) Initial state.   (b) The adversary moves.   (c) The data miner reacts.

Fig. 1. An example of the interactions between a data miner and an adversary. The line in the middle of the data clouds represents the classification boundary. Based on the initial state of the game (subfig. a), the adversary moves positive instances towards negative samples and produces more false detections (subfig. b); the data miner then reacts by re-constructing (shifting) the classification boundary (subfig. c).

The instances of X^+ and X^- both span a linear space of $\mathbb{R}^n$, so their *right singular vectors* (i.e. column vectors of $V^+ \in \mathbb{R}^{n \times n}$ and $V^- \in \mathbb{R}^{n \times n}$) form an orthogonal basis of their corresponding type of class.

We characterize each type of class by the first k singular vectors of that class. If the new class-unknown instance x can be better represented in the basis of singular vectors of one class (e.g., the positive class) than in those of the opposite class, then x is more likely to belong to the former class (i.e., positive class). Then the classification process is equivalent to choosing the smaller residual vector generated from the representations of the two classes:

$$Label\ of\ x_{new} = \arg\min_{c \in \{+,-\}} || \sum_{i=1}^{k} \left(v_i^c \times ((v_i^c)^T \times x_{new}) \right) - x_{new}|| \qquad (5)$$

where v_i is the ith column vector in V^c, $c \in \{+, -\}$, $|| \cdot ||$ is the Euclidean norm, and we assume x_{new} and v_i^c are column vectors. This classification strategy forms the fundamental basis of many practical classifiers (e.g., [10, 11]). Now we proceed to analyze how manipulations from adversaries can degrade the performance of this SVD classification model.

3.1   Formulation of Adversarial Manipulations

The data miner's classification strategy in Eq. 5 (i.e., on the original data) constitutes the **initial state** of our game theoretical model when there are no moves made by the adversary. Fig. 1a shows an example of such an initial state: without malicious modifications on positive samples (blue asterisks), the (solid red) boundary line learned from Eq. 5 separates the two classes of data samples and defines the optimal initial classification boundary.

Although data miners are able to obtain correct singular vectors from solving Eq. 5, these initial singular vectors become ineffective when adversaries change the distribution of their input feature vectors. We assume the adversaries modify feature vectors by introducing a transformation vector α, so that positive instances "X^+" in the training phase are shifted to "$\alpha + X^+$" during the test phase. Moreover, in order to decrease the data miner's classification accuracy, a rational adversary will transfer positive instances[2] in a way that makes its distribution similar to that of the negative class, as shown in Fig. 1b. By denoting

$$\alpha + X^+ = S^\alpha \Sigma^\alpha (V^\alpha)^T$$

as the SVD of the positive instances transformed by an adversary, and $v_i^\alpha \in V^\alpha$ as the transformed positive singular vectors, the payoff function of an adversary can be stated as

$$J(\alpha) = \sum_{i=1}^{k} ||v_i^\alpha - v_i^-|| \, , \tag{6}$$

whose aim is to minimize the difference between the singular vectors of the negative instances and those of the (transformed) positive instances.

However, the further the original positive instances are transformed the higher the cost the adversary has to pay, and when positive instances are transformed to the same as negatives the adversary pays the highest cost, since such positive instances bring no profit to the adversary even if they are undetected by the classifier. For example, when the pattern of words in spams is modified such that it is the same to legitimate emails, these spams might not be detected by a spam filter but they also bring no profit at all to the spammer. Therefore at the same time of maximizing her payoff, a rational adversary also attempts to minimize the step size of transformations. So we propose that the adversary's optimal movement α^* is determined by the following optimization problem:

$$\alpha^* = \arg\min_{\alpha} \; J(\alpha) + \lambda ||\alpha||^2$$
$$= \arg\min_{\alpha} \; \sum_{i=1}^{k} ||v_i^\alpha - v_i^-|| + \lambda ||\alpha||^2 \tag{7}$$

Eq. 7 is our overall objective function. It reflects that a rational adversary wants to not only minimize the distance between distributions of negative instances and transformed positive instances (i.e., the first term of Eq. 7), but also minimize the transformation itself (i.e., the second term of Eq. 7). In contrast to the iterative method that solves Eq. 4, we aim to find the final equilibrium state of the players by solving one optimization problem, and hence we call the minimization problem in Eq. 7 the "one-step" method.

3.2   Solving the Minimization Problem

In this section, we describe how we solve the minimization problem in Eq. 7 via *trust region* methods – a powerful yet simple technique for solving convex

---

[2] In this paper, we assume it is the positive class which is of value to an adversary. For example, in spam filtering domain, we assume spam emails belong to the positive class, and legitimate emails belong to the negative class.

optimization problems[12]. The following unconstrained minimization problem is an abstraction of Eq. 7:

$$\alpha^* = \arg\min_{\alpha} f(\alpha) \tag{8}$$

Suppose we are at the point α_0 of function f, and we want to move to another point with a lower value of f. The main idea of the trust region method is to approximate f with a simpler function q, which mirrors the behavior of function f in a neighborhood Ω around the point α_0. This neighborhood is the so-called *trust region* [13]. Then instead of minimizing f on the unconstrained range as in Eq. 8, the trust region method minimizes q in the constrained neighborhood Ω:

$$s^* = \arg\min_{s \in \Omega} q(s) \tag{9}$$

and the next point is determined as $\alpha_0 + s^*$ if it has a lower f value. The approximation function q by convention is defined though the second order Taylor expansion of f at α_0, and the neighborhood Ω is usually a spherical or ellipsoidal in shape [12]. So the problem in Eq. 9 is reduced to:

$$s^* = \arg\min_{s} \frac{1}{2} s^T H s + s^T g \tag{10}$$
$$subject\ to\ \|Ds\| \le \bigtriangledown$$

where g and H are the gradient and the Hessian matrix of f, D is a diagonal scaling matrix, and $\bigtriangledown$ is a positive number. The problem in Eq. 10 is also known as the *trust region sub-problem*. While there are many ways to avoid the expensive computation on H, we reuse the straightforward subspace approximation [14], which restricts the problem in Eq. 10 to a two-dimensional subspace S. In this subspace, the first dimension s_1 is in the direction of the gradient g, and the second dimension s_2 is an approximated Newton direction (i.e., the solution to $H \cdot s_2 = -g$). Within the subspace S, Eq. 10 becomes easy and efficient to solve since it is always in a two-dimensional space.

4   Experiments and Analysis

We focus on comparing the difference between the equilibrium states generated from our *one-step* model, and the ones from the *iterative* process proposed in [7], in terms of their efficiency and the accuracy of the classifiers at equilibrium. Our experiments are carried out on a real email spam data set and a handwritten digit data set. To balance the two terms in our objective function (Eq. 7), we set λ to the number of singular vectors (i.e., k) used in each experiment.

4.1   Rational Behavior on Synthetic Data

We first carry out experiments on synthetic data, and examine whether the data miner and the adversary do behave in a *rational* manner under our one-step game model. We generated positive and negative class data from multivariate normal distributions with mean $[\mu_1^p, \mu_2^p] = [4, 1]$ and $[\mu_1^n, \mu_2^n] = [1, 4]$ respectively, and a common standard deviation I (the identity matrix). Note that the multivariate normal distribution has been used only to generate the data and not for the purpose of solving for the Nash equilibrium. We expect a rational adversary to transform the data so that the positive class elements are displaced towards the negative class, and at the same time to try to prevent the two classes from completely overlapping. Thus we expect that the transformation in the first dimension (f_1) to be in the range of $(-3, 0)$ and second dimension (f_1) in the range $(0, 3)$.

We put the synthetic data into our objective function with $k = 2$ (the data has only two features/dimensions), and obtain equilibrium transformation $\alpha^* = $ [1.67, -1.91]. In Fig. 2 we show the value of the objective function with respect to different settings of the transformation α on f_1 and f_2. As we can visually inspect from the figure, the obtained equilibrium transformation α^* is an effective minimizer of the objective function. This visualization of the objective function also confirms our expectations that a rational adversary would transform the first dimension by a value in the range $(-3, 0)$ and second dimension in $(0, 3)$.

Fig. 2. Values of the adversary's objective function (Eq. 7), with respect to different setting of transformations (α) on the two-dimension synthetic data. The arrow in the figure points to a minimizer of the objective function, generated by our one-step method.

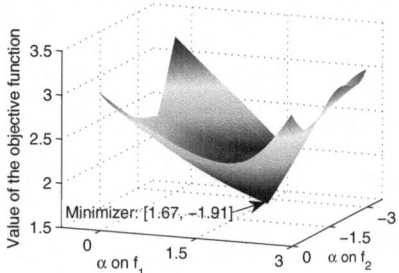

4.2   Email Spam Filtering

The objective of this experiment is to compare the performance of classifiers built on a normal training data set and on a training data set obtained at equilibrium after the application of an adversary's final optimal manipulation.

The spam data set consists of fifteen months of emails obtained from an anonymous individual's mailbox [15]. The first three months of data was used for training and the remaining twelve months for testing. We further split the test data into twelve bins - one for each month. Since at any given time spam can be received from diverse sources and spammers have different goals, the intrinsic nature of spam evolves over time. The data has 166,000 unique features. A feature ranking process using information gain was carried out and we selected the top 20 features to build the classifier.

To test the influence of k in terms of classification, we control k and vary it from 1 through 20, in testing all the twelve months' test data with 5-fold cross validation. With spam emails belonging to the positive class, the true positive rate (TPR), true negative rate (TNR) and overall accuracy is illustrated in Figure 3a. The overall accuracy stops increasing at around 16, which means the

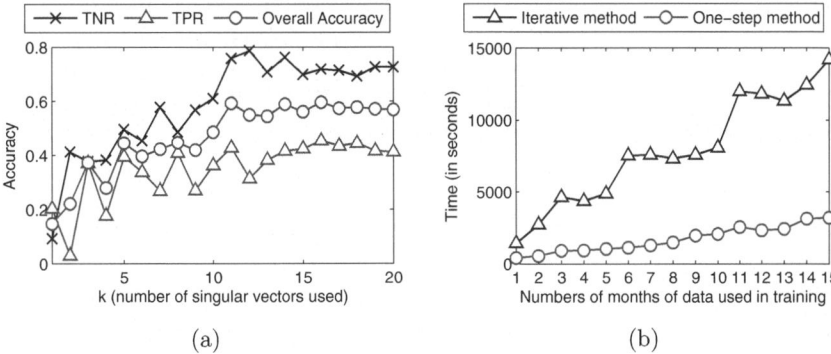

(a)   (b)

Fig. 3. Subfig.(a): Accuracy of SVD classifications on all test data with varying k. Subfig.(b): Comparisons on time (in seconds) between iterative processes and our one-step processes in finding Nash equilibria. To compare these two methods, in (b) we used varying amounts of training data indicated on the x-axis. We find that the one-step process substantially reduces computation time in searching for Nash equilibria, especially when the total amount of data is large.

Table 1. Comparisons on classification accuracy on spam data between iterative processes and our one-step processes, by using the data at Nash equilibria. Although the one-step method needs much less time compared against the iterative method, it is still capable of producing comparable equilibrium classification results.

Months	M1	M2	M3	Months	M1	M2	M3	Months	M1	M2	M3
Jan	.7686	.9179	.9195	May	.6803	.7655	.7439	Sep	.7648	.8277	.8187
Feb	.6256	.7258	.6817	Jun	.9249	.9671	.9882	Oct	.5169	.6046	.6490
Mar	.9071	1	.9991	Jul	.9384	1	1	Nov	.5915	.6597	.6946
Apr	.9150	.9892	.9534	Aug	.5527	.6032	.6795	Dec	.7950	.9323	.9146
Friedman test (M1 vs. M2): 5×10^{-4}											
Friedman test (M1 vs. M3): 8×10^{-5}											
Friedman test (M2 vs. M3): 0.7630											

training data can be well represented by the first 16 singular vectors. We choose 16 as the value of k in our following experiments on spam emails.

We first test the difference on time used in achieving Nash equilibrium between the previous iterative method and our one-step method. Since there are fifteen months of data available to us, we test the total time used in training one month, two months, ..., until all fifteen months. The total running time is shown in Figure 3b, where we can see that the one-step process has substantial savings in computation time on searching for Nash equilibrium, especially when the size of data set is large.

We then compared the one-step method with the iterative method on classification accuracy, where we used the first three months of data for training and the other twelve for test. We perform Friedman tests on the classification accuracy across all data sets, where p–values that are lower than 0.05 reject the hypothesis with 95% confidence that the classifiers in the comparison are not statistically different. The Friedman test is reported as the most appropriate method for validating multiple classifiers among multiple data sets [16]. In Table 1, "M1" uses the original data (i.e., X^+ and X^-), "M2" uses the equilibrium data generated by the iterative method (i.e., $X^+ + \alpha^*$ and X^-, where α^* is from the iterative method [7]), and "M3" uses the equilibrium data generated by our one-step method (i.e., $X^+ + \alpha^*$ and X^-, where α^* is from solving Eq. 7). As shown by the Friedman tests in Table 1, although one-step processes save a great amount of time in finding the Nash equilibrium, it can still generate comparable classification results compared against the iterative method (i.e., not significantly different under the Friedman test).

4.3   Handwritten Digit Recognition

In this section we examine the influence of equilibrium feature weights on the problem of feature selection. We use the classic US Postal Service (USPS) data set which was created for distinguishing handwritten digits on envelopes [17]. This data set consists of gray-scale images of digit "0" through "9" where each image consists of $16 \times 16 = 256$ pixels or features in the classification problem. We assume that the data was independent and identically distributed, and the objective of the data miner is to separate the digits while that of the adversary is to transform an image so that one digit can be confused with another.

Each digit has 2200 images, and we divide them equally into training and test sets. All combinations of pairs of digits from "0" to "9" are tested and we select the ones whose false positive rates are higher than 0.02 in the initial game state. The selected pairs are (2,6), (2,8), (3,8), (4,1), (5,8), (7,9), where we use the first digit of a pair as the class of interest for the adversary (i.e., the positive instances that the adversary manipulates).

Fig. 4. Comparisons on time (in seconds) between iterative processes and our one-step processes in finding Nash equilibria. Numbers on the x-axis represent indexes of selected digits pairs in the order of (2,6), (2,8), (3,8), (4,1), (5,8), (7,9). Similar to experiments on spam emails, here we also can see that the one-step process used much less computing time compared against the iterative method.

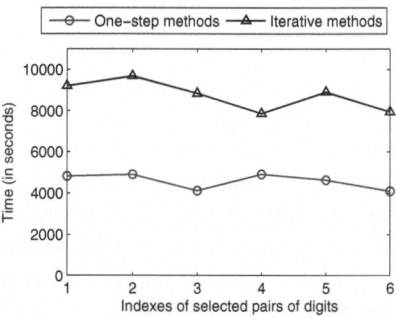

We first compare the total amount of time (in seconds) used for finding Nash equilibrium of these digit pairs, as shown in Figure 4. As expected, we can see from the figure that the one-step process used much less computation time compared to the iterative method in each of the six pairs of digits. More importantly,

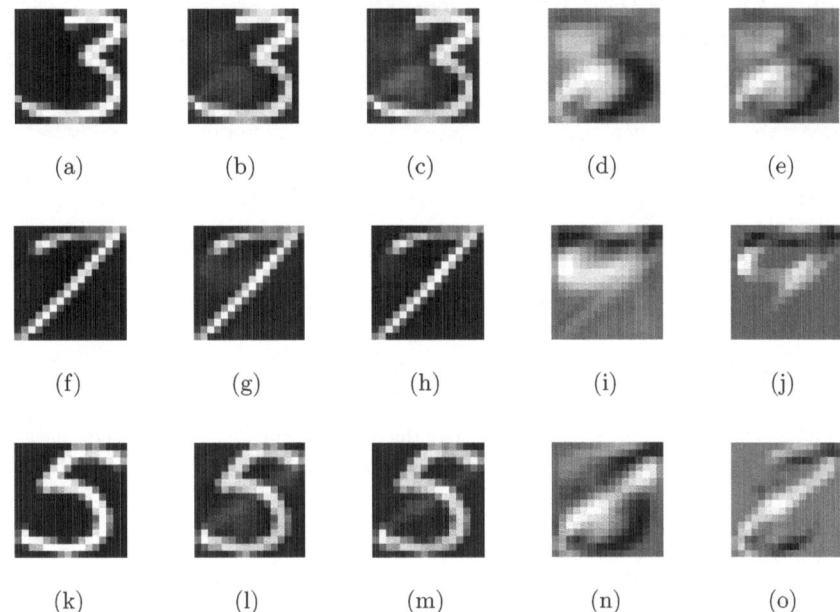

Fig. 5. Some example comparisons of transformed images in digit pair "3" vs. "8", "7" vs. "9", and "5" vs. "8", with the first digit being positive class. Subfig. (a), (f) and (k) show the original digit "3", "7" and "5"; (b), (g) and (l) show these digits transformed by the iterative method; (c), (h) and (m) are these digits transformed by our one-step method; (d), (i) and (n) are the equilibrium transformations generated by the iterative method; (e), (j) and (o) are the equilibrium transformations generated by our one-step method. Although our one-step method require much less computational time, it can still produce comparable equilibria results compared with the iterative method.

although the one-step method requires much less time, Nash equilibrium results obtained from the one-step method can still reasonably approximate adversarial manipulations on positive training data. As shown by some examples of our digit pairs in Figure 5, the adversary simulated by our one-step method increases or decreases values on some specific pixels on the positive images (i.e., digits "3", "7" and "5"), so that they look more like negative images (i.e., digits "8", "9" and "8") after the equilibrium play. Moreover, the close similarities of the final equilibrium adversarial transformations between the interactive method and the one-step method further confirm that the one-step model can perform comparably to iterative models in terms of finding correct Nash equilibria.

5   Conclusions and Future Research

In this paper we have studied the classification problem in the presence of adversaries. In this scenario data miners produce classification models and adversaries transform the data to deceive the classifier. We have modeled the interaction of a data miner and an adversary using a one-step game theoretical model, where the adversary aims to minimize both the difference between distributions of positive and negative classes and the adversarial movement itself. The solution to the minimization problem unveils the state of Nash equilibrium in the interactions between the data miner and the adversary. We have also demonstrated that our one-shot game significantly reduces computation time compared with iterative process used in the previous literature, while it can still generate comparable results in searching for Nash equilibria.

In the future we plan to investigate the use of coalition games to model scenarios where multiple adversaries exist and collaborate against the data miner.

References

1. Dalvi, N., Domingos, P., Mausam, Sanghai, S., Verma, D.: Adversarial classification. In: Proc. of KDD 2004, pp. 99–108 (2004)
2. Lowd, D., Meek, C.: Adversarial learning. In: KDD 2005, pp. 641–647 (2005)
3. Globerson, A., Roweis, S.: Nightmare at test time: robust learning by feature deletion. In: Proc. of ICML 2006, pp. 353–360 (2006)
4. Kołcz, A., Teo, C.: Feature weighting for improved classifier robustness. In: CEAS 2009: Sixth Conference on Email and Anti-Spam (2009)
5. Kantarcioglu, M., Xi, B., Clifton, C.: Classifier evaluation and attribute selection against active adversaries. Data Min. Knowl. Discov. 22(1), 291–335 (2011)
6. Liu, W., Chawla, S.: A game theoretical model for adversarial learning. In: Proceedings of the 2009 IEEE International Conference on Data Mining Workshops, pp. 25–30 (2009)
7. Liu, W., Chawla, S.: Mining Adversarial Patterns via Regularized Loss Minimization. Machine Learning 81(1), 69–83 (2010)
8. Brückner, M., Scheffer, T.: Stackelberg games for adversarial prediction problems. In: Proc. of KDD 2011, pp. 547–555 (2011)
9. Fudenberg, D., Tirole, J.: Game Theory, 1st edn. The MIT Press (1991)
10. Fortuna, J., Capson, D.: Improved support vector classification using PCA and ICA feature space modification. Pattern Recognition 37(6), 1117–1129 (2004)
11. Selvan, S., Ramakrishnan, S.: SVD-based modeling for image texture classification using wavelet transformation. IEEE Transactions on Image Processing 16(11), 2688–2696 (2007)
12. Byrd, R., Schnabel, R., Shultz, G.: Approximate solution of the trust region problem by minimization over two-dimensional subspaces. Mathematical Programming 40(1), 247–263 (1988)
13. Moré, J., Sorensen, D.: Computing a trust region step. SIAM Journal on Scientific and Statistical Computing 4, 553 (1983)
14. Branch, M., Coleman, T., Li, Y.: A subspace, interior, and conjugate gradient method for large-scale bound-constrained minimization problems. SIAM Journal on Scientific Computing 21(1), 1–23 (2000)
15. Delany, S.J., Cunningham, P., Tsymbal, A., Coyle, L.: Tracking concept drift in spam filtering. Knowledge-Based Systems 18(4-5), 187–195 (2005)
16. Demšar, J.: Statistical comparisons of classifiers over multiple data sets. Journal of Machine Learning Research 7, 1–30 (2006)
17. Hastie, T., Tibshirani, R., Friedman, J.: The elements of statistical learning (2001)

Signal Selection for Sleep Apnea Classification

Yashar Maali and Adel Al-Jumaily

University of Technology, Sydney (UTS)
Faculty of Engineering and IT, Sydney, Australia
Yashar.Maali@student.uts.edu.au, Adel.Al-Jumaily@uts.edu.au

Abstract. This paper presents a method for signals and features selection when classifying sleep apnea. This study uses a novel hierarchical parallel particle swarm optimization structure as proposed by the authors previously. In this structure, the swarms are separated into 'masters' and 'slaves' and access to global information is restricted according to their types. This method is used to classify sleep apneic events into apnea or hypopnea. In this study, ten different biosignals are used as the inputs for the system albeit with different features. The most important signals are subsequently determined based on their contribution to classification of the sleep apneic events. The classification method consists of three main parts which are: feature generation, signal selection, and data reduction based on PSO-SVM, and the final classifier. This study can be useful for selecting the best subset of input signals for classification of sleep apneic events, by attention to the trade of between more accuracy of higher number of input signals and more comfortable of less signals for the patient.

Keywords: Sleep apnea, Particle swarm optimization, Support vector machines, Parallel processing.

1   Introduction

Sleep Apnea (SA) is one of the most common and critical components of sleep disorders. SA is characterized by the repeated temporary cessation of breathing during sleep [1]. Clinically, apnea is defined as the total or near-total absence of airflow. This becomes significant once the reduction of the breathing signal amplitude is at least around 75% with respect to the normal respiration and occurs for a period of 10 seconds or longer. A hypopnea is an event of comparatively less intensity; it is defined as a reduction in baseline of the breathing signal amplitude to around 30–50%, also lasting 10 seconds in adults [2].

The SA has several short term and long term side effects[3]. Short-term effects lead to impaired attention and concentration, reduce quality of life, increased rates of absenteeism with reduced productivity, and increased the possibility of accidents at work, home or on the road. Long-term consequences of sleep deprivation include increased morbidity and mortality from increasing automobile accidents, coronary artery disease, heart failure, high blood pressure, obesity, type 2 diabetes mellitus, stroke and memory impairment as well as depression. Long-term consequences, however, remain open[4].

Unfortunately, as many patients are asymptomatic, sleep apnea may go undiagnosed for years [5, 6]. Usually it is patients' spouses, roommates, or family members who

M. Thielscher and D. Zhang (Eds.): AI 2012, LNCS 7691, pp. 661–671, 2012.

report the apnea periods alternating with arousals and accompanied by loud snoring [7, 8]. Symptomatic patients with SA are usually assessed by Sleep Medicine Specialists and diagnosed through an overnight sleep study in a sleep clinic. SA is diagnosed by a manual analysis of a polysomnographic record, an integrated device comprising of the EEG, EMG, EOG, ECG, and oxygen saturation (SPO2) [9]. The polysomnography also records the airflow through the mouth and nose, along with the thoracic and abdominal effort signals [10], and the position of the body during sleep. A sleep apnea event can also be classified into three groups as: central sleep apnea, obstructive sleep apnea, and mixed sleep apnea. In case of the first, sleep apnea is originated by the central nervous system. In the case of the second, the reason for the pauses in the breathing lie in a respiratory tract obstruction, while in the third case, both of these reasons may be present.

The conventional scoring of the polysomnographic recording is costly and time-consuming. Therefore, many efforts have been made to develop systems that score the records automatically [11-13]. For this reason several Artificial Intelligent (AI) algorithms are used in this area such as; fuzzy rule-based system [14], genetic SVM [15], and PSO-SVM [16] which have been proposed in our previous works.

Classification of apneic events to apnea or hypopnea is also so important for severity calculation of the sleep disorder. The classification of apneic events is also considered in many studies, such as [17-19]. But, up to the authors' knowledge, there has no publish work on impact and importance of different signals in sleep apnea classification. In this paper, we rank most important signals for the classification of sleep disorder events into apnea or hypopnea by a hierarchical parallel PSO-SVM[16]. The second section of this work covers details of the parallel model. We also introduce the PSO-SVM model in the third section of this paper, which is followed by experimental results in section four, and the conclusion in section five.

2   Parallel PSO

Particle Swarm Optimization (PSO), was introduced by Kennedy and Eberhart in 1995 [20, 21] based on the movement of swarms and inspired by the social behaviors of birds or fishes. Similar to the genetic algorithm, PSO is a population-based stochastic optimization technique. In the PSO, each member is named particle, and each particle is a potential solution to the problem. In comparison with the genetic algorithms, PSO updates the population of particles by considering their internal velocity and position, which are obtained by the experience of all the particles.

2.1   Proposed Parallel Structure

In this work, given the enormous size of the search space, a single PSO cannot perform well and may lead to the local optimum with low accuracy. Therefore, we have used a new PSO parallel structure[16], to perform better explorations and exploitations in the search space.

In the traditional multi-PSO models, all of the swarms are at the same level and exchanging information is just based on the definition of neighborhood [22]. But, in this structure, swarms are classified at two different levels as 'masters' and one (or more) 'slave(s)'. Master swarms have access to the best particle of other swarms but the slave swarms have no access to others' information, and actually just provide information for others. Sending the best local particle information among the masters and from the slave(s) to the masters can entail performing each iteration by a specified frequency.

In this hierarchical model, one of the master swarms is considered to be the centre swarm. All of the swarms, masters or slaves, send the local best particle to the centre swarm. The centre swarm computes the global best particle and sends it to the other master swarms. So all of the master swarms update their particles using the global best particle, but the slave swarms only use their own local best particles for updating themselves. The pseudo code for the hierarchical multi-swarm PSO is as follows.

Begin

Select the number of master and slave swarms, number of the particles for each sub-warm along with the frequency for the sending of the information. Select one of the master swarms as the centre.

 Initialize the position and velocity of each particle

Do in parallel until the maximum number of iterations has reached {

      Evaluate the fitness value of each particle

      Find out the local best particle in each sub-swarm

      If meet sending condition

          Sending the local best particle (lp_{best}) from each swarm to the centre swarm.

      Updating global best particle (Gp_{best}) in the centre swarm.

      Sending the global best particle to the master swarms.

      End If

      Calculate the new velocity of each particle in each sub-swarm

      Update the position of each particle in each swarm

   End Do}

Return the best solution (the global best particle) of the algorithm

End

To provide more information how the model work; figure 1 illustrate a sample of the proposed parallel structure with 4 masters and 2 slave swarm. In this implementation, master 1 is selected as the center swarm, so all of the swarms send their local best particles to this swarm. After computing the global best swarm, center swarm sends it to all of the master swarms. So in this structure, slave swarm provides information for other swarms, but not gets benefit from the other's information.

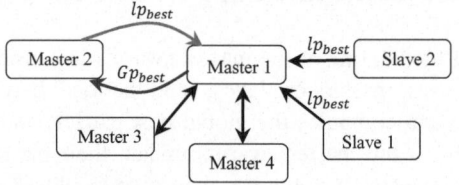

Fig. 1. Proposed parallel structure with 4 masters and two slaves

Indeed, fast convergence is one of the disadvantages of the PSO, which is heightened in the parallel structure. This hierarchical model tries to expand both of the exploration and exploitation abilities of the parallel PSO, by integrating the isolated swarms and the linked swarms. Slave swarm(s) in this model help prevent premature convergence. PSO parameters for the slaves and masters can be different. Therefore, it helps to have greater exploration abilities for the slaves and a greater local search for the masters.

3   Approach and Method

In this section, we present the proposed algorithm for the ranking of input signals by attention to their impact on classification of the sleep apneic events into apnea or hypopnea. The proposed methodology is as follows:

- Feature generation: this stage generates several statistical features for each event from the wavelet packet coefficients.
- Parallel PSO-SVM: this stage uses the PSO algorithm to select a best signal and features subset interactively with the SVM. PSO also is used for tuning the parameters of the SVM. In the process, SVM is used as the fitness evaluator. This PSO-SVM combination is applied in parallel by the new architecture to achieve better performance and avoid of the local optimal solutions.
- Final classification: the selected pattern is used for classification of the unseen validation data in this stage. The accuracy of this step is assumed as the final performance of the algorithm.

The details of these steps are as follows:

3.1   Features Generation

As mentioned previously, we used 10 biosignal from the polysomnographic record. Table 1 lists these signals and their frequencies.

Table 1. List of signals that are used in this study

	Signal	Frequency
#1	EEG C3A2	100
#2	EEG C4A1	100
#3	EEG A1A2	100
#4	EOG	100
#5	EMG chin	200
#6	ECG	200
#7	Air flow	10
#8	Thoracic movement	10
#9	Abdominal movement	10
#10	SPO2	1

For feature generation, First of all, 10 seconds after of each apneic event is selected from each signal. Then, we used wavelet package coefficients to generate features for each of these signals. For example for airflow, abdominal, thoracic movement, and SPO2, we generated the features by applying statistical measures from Table 2 to each coefficient of the 4 levels Daubechies wavelet packet with order 3 [23].

Table 2. List of statistical features, x is coefficients of wavelet packet

$\log(\text{mean}(x^2))$	$\text{kurtosis}(x^2)$	$\text{geomean}(|x|)$
$\text{std}(x^2)$	$\text{var}(x^2)$	$\text{mad}(x)$
$\text{skewness}(x^2)$	$\text{mean}(|x|)$	$\text{mean}(x^2)$
$\text{skewness}(x)$	$\text{kurtosis}(x)$	$\text{var}(x)$
$\text{geomean}(x^2)$	$\text{mad}(x^2)$	$\text{std}(x)$

The details of feature generation for other signals are as follows:

A. EEG

Based on [24], we applied the Daubechies order 2 (db2) wavelet transform. The frequency ranges of the EEG signal are broken down into Delta (below 3.5 Hz), Theta (4-7 Hz), Alpha (8-13 Hz), and Beta (14-30 Hz) bands [24]. Then, the following statistical features were used to represent the time–frequency distribution of the EEG signals:

1. Mean quadratic value or Energy of wavelet packet (WP) coefficients for each of the sub bands,
2. Total Energy,
3. Ratio of different Energy values,
4. Mean of the absolute values of the coefficients in each sub band, and
5. Standard deviation of the coefficients in each sub band.

Also more features are generated for EEG signals based on [25]. Given this reason, we apply a level 4 wavelet packet of Daubechies by order 20 and then, generate the features for each coefficient displayed in Table 2.

B. EOG

To generate the features from the EOG signal, we apply an 8 level Daubechies with order 3 wavelet packet. Then, we generate the features for each coefficient according to Table 2, for each of the left and right EOG signals. Also, we calculate the normalized correlation coefficient between the two EOG channels [26].

C. EMG

For the EMG signal based on [23], we generate features by applying statistical measures from Table 2 to the coefficients of level 2 Daubechies with the order 2.

D. ECG

For feature generation of ECG signals based on [27], first of all we apply an order 3 Daubechies wavelet packet with 8 level. Then, for each event by attention to the wavelet coefficients features are generated by the statistical measures from table 2.

By attention to these ten signals and described features, 205 features are generated for each apneic event. In next step the parallel PSO-SVM is used for feature selection to eliminate the irrelevant features and therefore improving the accuracy of the classification.

3.2   Parallel PSO-SVM Algorithm

After generating the features, we need to classify events as apnea or hypopnea. For this reason, we use the described hierarchical parallel PSO-SVM algorithm to initiate pattern selection and tune the parameters of the SVM.

SVM is used to evaluate each particle of the PSO. The fitness of each particle is computed as the accuracy of the SVM when classifying the test set with the selected pattern related to the particle.

In the first step, total data from all of the samples are integrated as Meta data. Then, the Meta data is separated into the train and the validation. The hierarchical parallel PSO-SVM is used using the 5*10 CV paradigms to select the best signals and features sets from the training data. Then, the selected signals and features are used to classify the validation set. Accuracy of classification of validation set by the tuned SVM and selected patters is considered as performance of the system.

3.3   PSO Structure

In this study, we use the constriction coefficient PSO [28]. In this approach, the velocity update equation is as (1),

$$v_{ij}(t + 1) = \chi \left[v_{ij}(t) + \phi_1 \left(y_{ij}(t) - x_{ij}(t) \right) + \phi_2 \left(\hat{y}_{ij}(t) - x_{ij}(t) \right) \right], \quad (1)$$

where y_{ij} is the particle best and $\hat{y}_{ij}$ is the global best particles. And,

$$\chi = \frac{2k}{|2 - \phi - \sqrt{\phi(\phi - 4)}|}, \quad (2)$$

with,

$$\phi = \phi_1 + \phi_2, \quad \phi_i = c_i r_i \quad i = 1,2.$$

Equation (2) is used under the constraints that $\phi \geq 4$ and $k, r_i \in [0,1]$.

The parameter k in the equation (2) controls the exploration and exploitation. For $k \sim 0$, fast convergence is expected and for $k \sim 1$ we can expect slow convergence with a high degree of exploration [28].

The constriction approach has several advantages over traditional PSO model such as; we do not need velocity clamping for constriction model and this model guarantees convergence under the given constraints[29].

By paying attention to the proposed parallel structure, for the slave swarms, k considered as 0.8 and $c_1 = 2, c_2 = 4$, and for the master swarms k considered as 0.2 and $c_1 = 4, c_2 = 2$.

3.4   Particle Representation

In this study, each particle consists of three arrays; the length of the first array is equal to the number of signals, which equal ten. Each cell can get a real number between 0 and 1 as importance of the relevant signal. Rank of each signal is computed by the rank of the corresponding cell.

The length of the second array is equal to the number of the features. Again each cell can get a real number between 0 and 1. Features, which their corresponding cells have values higher than 0.5, are selected for classification. The third array is related to the gamma and cost as parameters of the SVM, which can get a value between 2^{-5} to 2^5.

4   Results and Discussion

Experimental data consist of polysomnographic records from 20 subjects, which events of them are annotated by experts were provided by concord hospital in Sydney. In the parallel structure, 4 slaves and two masters are selected and each swarm contain 20 particles. The RBF kernel is selected for the SVM in both of the master and slave swarms. Frequency for changing information between swarms is set as 5 iterations.

Table 3. Diversity of classes in different runs

	Validation		Training	
	Apnea	Hypopnea	Apnea	Hypopnea
#1	833	636	1632	1309
#2	780	683	1685	1262
#3	865	701	1600	1244
#4	874	610	1591	1335
#5	787	601	1678	1344

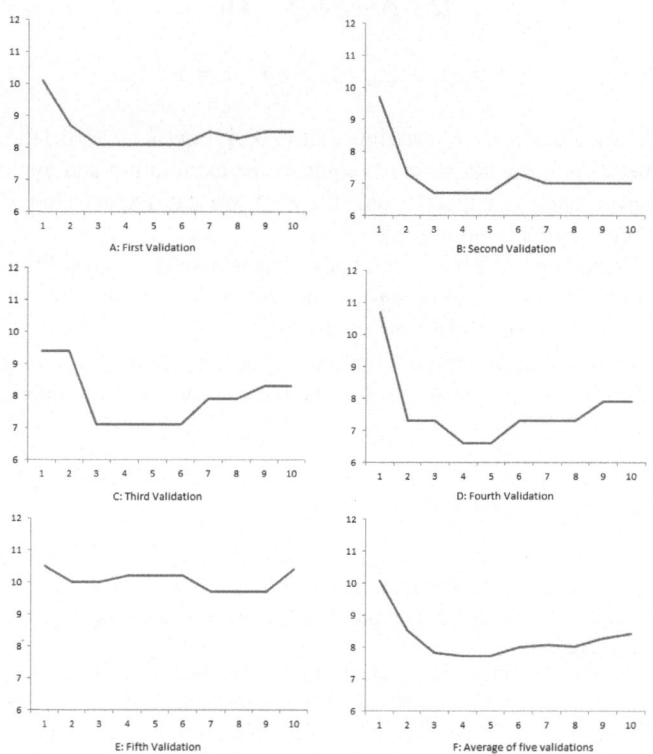

Fig. 2. Classification error curve using the signal selection method

In this experiment records from 5 subjects are considered as the validation and records from 15 subjects make the training data. It also take in consideration to overcome the impact of the validation sets on the final result, 5 independent experiments had validated. Table 3 tabulates the number of sleep apnea or hypopnea events in each of the validation set and the training in these 5 runs.

We investigated whether the best way to select signals for apnea or hypopnea classification. First we consider the best size for the input signals' set. The results are depicted in Figure 2. The first five plots, A to E, show the individual classification error for the five validations against the different numbers of signals chosen. The sixth plot, figure F, shows the classification error averaged over the five validations.

As can be seen in Figure 2, using irrelevant signals increased the classification error. For example, using 3 channels for validation 1, figure A, yields the least error. The result averaged over the five validations plotted in the last figure, figure F. This figure also shows that when removing channels iteratively the classification error decreases slightly until all irrelevant channels are removed. The average error rate (taken over all validations) of 7.84% using 3 signals is very close to the error of the baseline which is 7.74% using 5 signals. This can show that increasing the number of input signals from 3 to 5 has not high impact on the performance. Therefore, by attention to the cost of using more signals and on the other side slight improvement in the performance we can decide the preferred size of the input signals.

Table 4. Ranking of 10 signals

Rank	Validations				
	1	2	3	4	5
1	Airflow	Airflow	Airflow	Airflow	Airflow
2	Abdominal	Abdominal	Abdominal	Abdominal	Abdominal
3	Thoracic	EMG chin	Thoracic	Thoracic	Thoracic
4	EMG chin	Thoracic	EMG chin	EMG chin	EMG chin
5	EEG C4A2	ECG	EEG C4A2	ECG	EEG C4A2
6	EEG C4A1	EEG C4A2	ECG	EEG C4A1	ECG
7	ECG	EEG C4A1	EEG C4A1	EEG C4A2	EEG C4A1
8	EOG	EOG	SPO2	SPO2	EOG
9	SPO2	SPO2	EOG	EOG	SPO2
10	EEG C3A2	EEG C3A2	EEG C3A2	EEG C3A2	EEG C3A2

Table 4 contains signal rankings; as we have the three most common signals are airflow, abdominal and thoracic movement. For each validation we can obtain a heuristic estimate on the number of irrelevant signals from the classification error curves in Figure 1. We underlined one entry in each column of Table 4. The row number of that entry is an estimate for the ranks position of the best set of signals for classification of that validation set. For example in validation 4, the local minimum of the classification error happened by 4 signals. Thus, the best 4 selected signals can be used instead of the full data without increasing the error. Selecting 4 signals instead of the whole polysomnographic records is important because less signals means less recording cost and also more comfortable for the patients.

5   Conclusion

In this study we ranked the polysomnographic signals by attention to their impact on classification of sleep apneic events into apnea or hypopnea. We used a hierarchical parallel PSO-SVM for the signal selection. This study shows that it is possible to reduce the number of signals for a robust classification without an increase of classification error. Average of results from 4 different experiments shows, using 4 signals can provide the least classification error. But, the different between classification error of the best 3 signals and the best 4 signals is less than 0.10%. This comparison is important as using less signals means more comfortable for the patients. Therefore, trade-off between selecting more signals and it cost must be considered. The same study for detecting apnea events and also classification of apnea events to central, obstructive or mixed will be subject to future research.

References

1. Guilleminault, C., van den Hoed, J., Mitler, M.: Overview of the sleep apnea syndromes. In: Guilleminault, C., Dement, W.C. (eds.) Sleep Apnea Syndromes, pp. 1–12. Alan R Liss, New York (1978)
2. Flemons, W.W., et al.: Sleep-related breathing disorders in adults: Recommendations for syndrome definition and measurement techniques in clinical research. Sleep 22(5), 667–689 (1999)
3. Chokroverty, S., et al.: Sleep deprivation and sleepiness. In: Sleep Disorders Medicine, 3rd edn., pp. 22–28. W.B. Saunders, Philadelphia (2009)
4. Chokroverty, S.: Overview of sleep & sleep disorders. Indian Journal of Medical Research 131(2), 126–140 (2010)
5. Ball, E.M., et al.: Diagnosis and treatment of sleep apnea within the community - The Walla Walla project. Archives of Internal Medicine 157(4), 419–424 (1997)
6. Kryger, M.H., et al.: Utilization of health care services in patients with severe obstructive sleep apnea. Sleep 19(9), S111–S116 (1996)
7. Stradling, J.R., Crosby, J.H.: Relation between systemic hypertension and sleep hypoxemia or snoring- analysis in 748 men drawn from general-practice. British Medical Journal 300(6717), 75–78 (1990)
8. Hoffstein, V.: Snoring. In: Kryger, M.H., Roth, T., Dement, W.C. (eds.) Principles and Practice of Sleep Medicine, pp. 813–826. Saunders, Philadelphia (2000)
9. Penzel, T., et al.: Systematic comparison of different algorithms for apnoea detection based on electrocardiogram recordings. Medical & Biological Engineering & Computing 40(4), 402–407 (2002)
10. Kryger, M.H.: Management of obstructive sleep-apnea. Clinics in Chest Medicine 13(3), 481–492 (1992)
11. Cabrero-Canosa, M., Hernandez-Pereira, E., Moret-Bonillo, V.: Intelligent diagnosis of sleep apnea syndrome. IEEE Engineering in Medicine and Biology Magazine 23(2), 72–81 (2004)
12. Cabrero-Canosa, M., et al.: An intelligent system for the detection and interpretation of sleep apneas. Expert Systems with Applications 24(4), 335–349 (2003)
13. de Chazal, P., et al.: Automated processing of the single-lead electrocardiogram for the detection of obstructive sleep apnoea. IEEE Transactions on Biomedical Engineering 50(6), 686–696 (2003)
14. Maali, Y., Al-Jumaily, A.: Genetic Fuzzy Approach for detecting Sleep Apnea/Hypopnea Syndrome. In: 2011 3rd International Conference on Machine Learning and Computing, ICMLC 2011 (2011)
15. Maali, Y., Al-Jumaily, A.: Automated detecting sleep apnea syndrome: A novel system based on genetic SVM. In: 2011 11th International Conference on Hybrid Intelligent Systems, HIS (2011)

16. Yashar, M., Adel, A.-J.: A Novel Partially Connected Cooperative Parallel PSO-SVM Algorithm Study Based on Sleep Apnea Detection. IEEE Congress on Evolutionary Computation 2012, Brisbane, Australia (Accepted in, 2012)

17. Schluter, T., Conrad, S.: An approach for automatic sleep stage scoring and apnea-hypopnea detection. Frontiers of Computer Science 6(2), 230–241 (2012)

18. Aksahin, M., et al.: Artificial Apnea Classification with Quantitative Sleep EEG Synchronization. Journal of Medical Systems 36(1), 139–144 (2012)

19. Guijarro-Berdinas, B., Hernandez-Pereira, E., Peteiro-Barral, D.: A mixture of experts for classifying sleep apneas. Expert Systems with Applications 39(8), 7084–7092 (2012)

20. Eberhart, R., Kennedy, J.: A new optimizer using particle swarm theory. In: Proceedings of the Sixth International Symposium on Micro Machine and Human Science, MHS 1995 (1995)

21. Kennedy, J., Eberhart, R.: Particle swarm optimization. In: 1995 IEEE International Conference on Neural Networks Proceedings, vol. 1-6, pp. 1942–1948 (1995)

22. Fan, S.K.S., Chang, J.M.: Dynamic multi-swarm particle swarm optimizer using parallel PC cluster systems for global optimization of large-scale multimodal functions. Engineering Optimization 42(5), 431–451 (2010)

23. Kiatpanichagij, K., Afzulpurkar, N.: Use of supervised discretization with PCA in wavelet packet transformation-based surface electromyogram classification. Biomedical Signal Processing and Control 4(2), 127–138 (2009)

24. Ebrahimi, F., et al.: Automatic Sleep Stage Classification Based on EEG Signals by Using Neural Networks and Wavelet Packet Coefficients. In: 2008 30th Annual International Conference of the IEEE Engineering in Medicine and Biology Society, vol. 1-8, pp. 1151–1154 (2008)

25. Ebrahimi, F., et al.: Automatic sleep stage classification based on EEG signals by using neural networks and wavelet packet coefficients. In: 30th Annual International Conference of the IEEE Engineering in Medicine and Biology Society, EMBS 2008 (2008)

26. Kempfner, J., et al.: Automatic REM Sleep Detection Associated with Idiopathic REM Sleep Behavior Disorder. In: 2011 Annual International Conference of the IEEE Engineering in Medicine and Biology Society, pp. 6063–6066 (2011)

27. Gubbi, J., Khandoker, A., Palaniswami, M.: Classification of sleep apnea types using wavelet packet analysis of short-term ECG signals. Journal of Clinical Monitoring and Computing 26(1), 1–11 (2012)

28. Clerc, M.: The swarm and the queen: towards a deterministic and adaptive particle swarm optimization. In: Proceedings of the 1999 Congress on Evolutionary Computation, CEC 1999 (1999)

29. Engelbrecht, A.P.: Fundamentals of Computational Swarm Intelligence. Wiley (2005)

Minimum Message Length Inference and Mixture Modelling of Inverse Gaussian Distributions

Daniel F. Schmidt and Enes Makalic

Centre for MEGA Epidemiology, The University of Melbourne
Carlton, VIC 3053, Australia
{dschmidt,emakalic}@unimelb.edu.au

Abstract. This paper examines the problem of modelling continuous, positive data by finite mixtures of inverse Gaussian distributions using the minimum message length (MML) principle. We derive a message length expression for the inverse Gaussian distribution, and prove that the parameter estimator obtained by minimising this message length is superior to the regular maximum likelihood estimator in terms of Kullback–Leibler divergence. Experiments on real data demonstrate the potential benefits of using inverse Gaussian mixture models for modelling continuous, positive data, particularly when the data is concentrated close to the origin or exhibits a strong positive skew.

1 Introduction

A common approach to learning structure in complex data is through clustering, or more generally, finite mixture modelling. A finite mixture model with K classes models a probability distribution as

$$p(\mathbf{y}_i; \boldsymbol{\alpha}, \boldsymbol{\theta}_1, \ldots, \boldsymbol{\theta}_K) = \sum_{k=1}^{K} \alpha_k p_k(\mathbf{y}_i; \boldsymbol{\theta}_k), \tag{1}$$

where $\boldsymbol{\alpha}$ are the K mixing weights and $\boldsymbol{\theta}_i$ are the vectors of parameters that define the component distributions $p_i(\cdot)$. In general, $\boldsymbol{\alpha}$, K and $\boldsymbol{\theta}_i$ are all unknown and we are required to learn an appropriate mixture model using only the observed data. Unsupervised learning of finite mixture models has been one of the most successful applications of the information theoretic minimum message length (MML) [1–3] principle of inductive inference. Over the past forty years this work has been continuously improved, with refinements to the coding schemes and the addition of new distributions. This paper extends MML mixture modelling further by the inclusion of the inverse Gaussian distribution for positive, continuous data. We say that a variable $Y_i \sim IG(\mu, \lambda)$ if the probability density function for $Y_i = y$ is given by

$$p(y_i; \mu, \lambda) = \left(\frac{1}{2\pi\lambda y_i^3} \right)^{\frac{1}{2}} \exp\left(-\frac{(y_i - \mu)^2}{2\mu^2 \lambda y_i} \right), \tag{2}$$

M. Thielscher and D. Zhang (Eds.): AI 2012, LNCS 7691, pp. 672–682, 2012.

where $\mu > 0$, $\lambda > 0$. The inverse Gaussian is a flexible distribution for modelling continuous, positive data. This work therefore helps to fill a hole in the current MML mixture modelling literature. Previous work [4] has examined modelling this type of data using the gamma distribution. Unfortunately, the treatment of the prior distributions used in [4] is somewhat superficial, and the resulting criterion depends on arbitrarily chosen hyperparameters, which have a crucial effect on the estimation of the number of classes. This paper offers an alternative distribution modelling for continuous, positive data, and uses sensible, data driven choices for the necessary prior distributions. These ideas could easily be further adapted to alternative distributions such as the gamma and Weibull.

2   The Minimum Message Length Principle

Minimum message length (MML) [1, 3] is an information theoretic Bayesian principle for inductive inference. The fundamental idea is that compressing data equates to learning the structure in the data. Theoretical results support the argument that if we can substantially compress the data, then there is a high probability we have learned something about the underlying process that produced the data [5]. In contrast to more traditional statistical procedures for learning, such as those based on hypothesis testing, the MML principle generalises in a straightforward manner to cover estimation of both conventional continuous model parameters in addition to structural parameters, such as the number of components in a mixture model [3].

To learn a model from data $\mathbf{y}$ using MML, we must first posit a countable set of candidate models $\gamma \in \Gamma$, each with associated parameters $\boldsymbol{\theta}_\gamma \in \Theta_\gamma$. We then compare the models in terms of their ability to compress the data. To do this, we view the compressed data as a message composed of two components. The first component, or *assertion*, encodes the details of the model, such as the structural and continuous parameters; the length of the assertion, in base-e digits, is $I(\gamma) + I(\boldsymbol{\theta}_\gamma | \gamma)$. The second component, or *detail*, encodes the data with the aid of the previously stated model, and is of length $I(\mathbf{y} | \gamma, \boldsymbol{\theta}_\gamma)$. The total message length may then be used as a measure of quality of fit of a model to the data, which automatically takes into account the complexity of the model as well as its ability to explain the data. To estimate a model, including structural parameters, from observed data using MML, we solve

$$\left\{ \hat{\gamma}_{\mathrm{MML}}(\mathbf{y}), \hat{\boldsymbol{\theta}}_{\mathrm{MML}}(\mathbf{y}) \right\} = \underset{\gamma \in \Gamma, \boldsymbol{\theta} \in \Theta_\gamma}{\arg \min} \left\{ I(\gamma) + I(\boldsymbol{\theta}_\gamma | \gamma) + I(\mathbf{y} | \boldsymbol{\theta}_\gamma, \gamma) \right\}. \qquad (3)$$

Coding of the structural parameters is straightforward due to the equivalence of discrete codewords and probability mass functions, i.e., $I(\gamma) = -\log \pi_\gamma(\gamma)$, where $\pi_\gamma(\cdot)$ is a suitable prior distribution over Γ. The coding of the continuous parameters assertion is more problematic, as any single point of a probability density function has measure zero. It is therefore necessary to quantise the continuous parameters, rendering them essentially discrete. While there are a variety of ways in which the resulting codelengths can be computed [6–8], if the model is sufficiently regular it is most convenient to use the Wallace–Freeman (MML87) codelength approximation [7] for models with continuous parameters. For a model with k continuous parameters $\boldsymbol{\theta}_\gamma$, the MML87 codelength for $I_{87}(\mathbf{y}, \boldsymbol{\theta}_\gamma, \gamma) \approx I(\gamma) + I(\boldsymbol{\theta}_\gamma | \gamma) + I(\mathbf{y} | \boldsymbol{\theta}_\gamma, \gamma)$ is

$$-\log \pi_\gamma(\gamma) - \log p(\mathbf{y} | \boldsymbol{\theta}_\gamma, \gamma) - \log \pi_{\boldsymbol{\theta}}(\boldsymbol{\theta} | \gamma) + \frac{1}{2} \log |\mathbf{J}_n(\boldsymbol{\theta}; \gamma)| + c(k), \qquad (4)$$

with

$$c(k) = -\frac{k}{2} \log 2\pi + \frac{1}{2} \log k\pi + \psi(1),$$

where $p(\cdot)$ is the probability density function for the model, $\pi_{\boldsymbol{\theta}}(\cdot)$ is the prior distribution for $\boldsymbol{\theta}_\gamma \in \Theta_\gamma$, $\mathbf{J}_n(\cdot)$ is the Fisher information matrix for n samples, and $\psi(\cdot)$ denotes the digamma function. Under suitable regularity conditions, the MML87 approximation is within a term of order $o_n(1)$ of the exact message length. An extensive discussion of the MML principle, along with the associated coding procedures, can be found in the excellent book by C. S. Wallace [3].

2.1   Message Lengths of Mixture Models

This section summarises the message length expressions for general finite mixture models. For the purposes of simplicity, we restrict our discussion to the case of univariate data, though the ideas extend in a straightforward manner to the multivariate case. The treatment is necessarily brief, and for a much more complete discussion of the message lengths of mixture models in general, the reader is referred to [3], pp. 275–297.

From (1) it is clear that a mixture model consists of K classes, and models the probability density function of the observed data as a weighted sum of these K classes. We first require some notation. Let $\mathbf{y} = (y_1, \ldots, y_n)$ denote the observed data, let $\boldsymbol{\theta}_1, \ldots, \boldsymbol{\theta}_K$ denote the parameters of the distributions associated with each of the K classes, and recall that $\boldsymbol{\alpha} = (\alpha_1, \ldots, \alpha_K)$ denotes the mixing weights. An important quantity is the *degree of membership* of each datum to each class. Let $\mathbf{R} \in (0, 1)^{n \times K}$ denote the matrix of class memberships. The entries of this matrix are given by

$$r_{i,k} = \frac{\alpha_k \, p(y_i; \boldsymbol{\theta}_k)}{\sum_{j=1}^{K} \alpha_j \, p(y_i; \boldsymbol{\theta}_j)}, \qquad (5)$$

which can be interpreted as the posterior probability of data y_i belonging to class k, treating the mixing weights as *a priori* probabilities of belonging to the K classes. From this quantity we can derive the effective sample sizes associated with each class as

$$n_k = \sum_{i=1}^{n} r_{i,k}. \qquad (6)$$

The totality of parameters for a mixture model of inverse Gaussian distributions is then $\boldsymbol{\Phi} = \{K, \boldsymbol{\alpha}, \boldsymbol{\theta}_1, \ldots, \boldsymbol{\theta}_K\}$. The length of a message that encodes both the data given the mixture model parameters $\boldsymbol{\Phi}$, and the mixture model parameters themselves may be found using the lengths of the following message components:

1. A codeword for K. We chose a uniform distribution over $\{1, \ldots, K_1\}$ so that $I(K) = \log K_1$, with the choice of K_1 being essentially irrelevant.
2. A statement of the parameters $\boldsymbol{\alpha}$. This is done by treating these as the parameters of a multinomial distribution with cell counts n_k, yielding a codeword of length

$$I(\boldsymbol{\alpha}) = \left(\frac{K-1}{2}\right)\log n - \frac{1}{2}\sum_{k=1}^{K}\log\alpha_k - \log\Gamma(K).$$

3. A statement of the model parameters $\boldsymbol{\theta}_k$ for each class and variable. Appealing to the independence arguments in [3] (pp. 291–293) we can decompose the statement of this parameters into a sum of components of length $I(\boldsymbol{\theta}_k)$, the details of which depend on the particular distribution in question. For the inverse Gaussian, these are detailed in Section 3.2.
4. The data, given the previously stated mixture model parameters, which is given by

$$I(\mathbf{y}|\boldsymbol{\Phi}) = -\sum_{i=1}^{n}\log\sum_{k=1}^{K}\alpha_k p(y_i; \boldsymbol{\theta}_k). \tag{7}$$

One of the most interesting aspects of MML mixture modelling is that the above codelength of the data can be itself be broken down into two parts: a first part, stating which class each data point belongs to, and a second part in which the data is coded using that particular class. Due to the clever way in which the assignment to classes is coded the joint codelength for these two components reduces to (7).

Using these components, the total codelength for the mixture model with parameters $\boldsymbol{\Phi}$ is given by

$$I(\mathbf{y}, \boldsymbol{\Phi}) = I(K) + I(\boldsymbol{\alpha}) + I(\mathbf{y}|\boldsymbol{\Phi}) + \sum_{k=1}^{K}I(\boldsymbol{\theta}_k) + c(d), \tag{8}$$

where $d = (K-1) + \sum_{k=1}^{K}|\boldsymbol{\theta}_k|$ is the total number of continuous parameters in the mixture model. To estimate a mixture model using MML we seek the values of $\boldsymbol{\Phi}$ that minimise (8), which is usually done using the expectation-maximisation algorithm coupled with a suitable non-linear search for the structural components, the details of which lie outside the scope of this paper.

3   MML Inference of Inverse Gaussian Models

To compute message lengths for inverse Gaussian models, and therefore find MML estimates for the parameters μ and λ, we use the MML87 approximation (4). This requires the following ingredients: (i) a likelihood function, (ii) the Fisher information matrix and (iii) appropriate prior distributions. From (2) it is straightforward to see that the negative log-likelihood of data under an $IG(\mu, \lambda)$ model can be compactly written as

$$-\log p(\mathbf{y}; \mu, \lambda) = \frac{n}{2} \log(2\pi\lambda) + \frac{3}{2} \sum_{i=1}^{n} \log y_i - \frac{n}{\mu\lambda} + \frac{S_1}{2\mu^2\lambda} + \frac{S_2}{2\lambda} \qquad (9)$$

where

$$S_1 = \sum_{i=1}^{n} y_i, \quad S_2 = \sum_{i=1}^{n} \frac{1}{y_i},$$

are minimal sufficient statistics for the inverse Gaussian distribution. The maximum likelihood estimates for μ and λ are given by

$$\hat{\mu}_{\mathrm{ML}}(\mathbf{y}) = \frac{S_1}{n},$$

$$\hat{\lambda}_{\mathrm{ML}}(\mathbf{y}) = \frac{S_1 S_2 - n^2}{n S_1}.$$

The entries of the Fisher information can be found by noting that $\mathrm{E}[S_1] = n\mu$ and $\mathrm{E}[S_2] = n(1/\mu + \lambda)$. We then have

$$\mathbf{J}_n(\mu, \lambda) = \begin{pmatrix} \dfrac{n}{\mu^3\lambda} & 0 \\ 0 & \dfrac{n}{2\lambda^2} \end{pmatrix},$$

and thus

$$|\mathbf{J}_n(\mu, \lambda)| = \frac{n^2}{2\mu^3\lambda^3}. \qquad (10)$$

To perform MML inference we need priors on μ and λ. We assume the two parameters are *a priori* independent. We could use the conjugate priors (half-normal for μ, inverse-gamma for λ) [9], but instead choose to use simpler componentwise Jeffreys' priors (i.e., Jeffreys' priors for each parameter, assuming that all other parameters are known). This is the same procedure as is done in the MML treatment of the standard univariate Gaussian distribution. We then have

$$\pi_{\mu,\lambda}(\mu, \lambda) = \pi_\mu(\mu)\pi_\lambda(\lambda) \qquad (11)$$

$$\pi_\mu(\mu) = \frac{\sqrt{\mu_0}}{2\mu^{\frac{3}{2}}}, \qquad \mu \in (\mu_0, \infty),$$

$$\pi_\lambda(\lambda) = \frac{1}{\log(\lambda_1/\lambda_0)\lambda}, \qquad \lambda \in (\lambda_0, \lambda_1)$$

where sensible, data-driven choices for μ_0, λ_0 and λ_1 will be discussed later.

Substituting (9), (10) and (11) into (4), and minimising for μ and λ yields the MML87 estimates

$$\hat{\mu}_{87}(\mathbf{y}) = \frac{S_1}{n}, \qquad (12)$$

$$\hat{\lambda}_{87}(\mathbf{y}) = \frac{S_1 S_2 - n^2}{(n-1)S_1}.$$

It is clear that $\hat{\mu}_{87}(\mathbf{y}) = \hat{\mu}_{\mathrm{ML}}(\mathbf{y})$, and $\hat{\lambda}_{87}(\mathbf{y}) = (n/(n-1))\hat{\lambda}_{\mathrm{ML}}(\mathbf{y})$. Substituting these estimates into the message length yields the minimised message length, $I_{87}(\mathbf{y}, \hat{\mu}_{87}(\mathbf{y}), \hat{\lambda}_{87}(\mathbf{y}))$:

$$\left(\frac{n-1}{2}\right) \log\left(2\pi e \hat{\lambda}_{87}(\mathbf{y})\right) + \frac{3}{2}\sum_{i=1}^{n}\log y_i + \log\left(\frac{\sqrt{2}\,n\log(\lambda_1/\lambda_0)}{\sqrt{\mu_0}}\right) + \psi(1). \quad (13)$$

It is clear that the choice of the prior hyperparameters $(\lambda_0, \lambda_1, \mu_0)$ has no effect on the MML estimators of the μ and λ parameters. However, in the setting of mixture modelling, in which a model can potentially comprise several inverse Gaussian distributions, the choice of these hyperparameters will have a crucial effect on the message length. Section 3.2 addresses the use of inverse Gaussian distributions in the mixture modelling setting, and details a data driven way of selecting these hyperparameters.

3.1 Behaviour of the MML Estimates

Let μ^* and λ^* denote the true parameter values, i.e., $y_1, \ldots, y_n \sim IG(\mu^*, \lambda^*)$. It is well known that

$$\hat{\mu}_{\mathrm{ML}}(\mathbf{y}) \sim IG\left(\mu^*, \frac{n}{\lambda^*}\right), \quad (14)$$

and it follows immediately that $\mathrm{E}\left[\hat{\mu}_{\mathrm{ML}}(\mathbf{y})\right] = \mathrm{E}\left[\hat{\mu}_{87}(\mathbf{y})\right] = \mu^*$, i.e., both ML and MML87 yield unbiased estimates of μ^*. To explore the behaviour of estimates of λ^* we use the fact that

$$\left(\frac{n}{\lambda^*}\right)\hat{\lambda}_{\mathrm{ML}}(\mathbf{y}) \sim \chi_{n-1}^2, \quad (15)$$

where χ_ν^2 denotes a chi-squared distribution with ν degrees of freedom. Using this result, along with the fact that $\hat{\lambda}_{87}(\mathbf{y}) = (n/(n-1))\hat{\lambda}_{\mathrm{ML}}(\mathbf{y})$, it is straightforward to show that

$$\mathrm{E}\left[\hat{\lambda}_{\mathrm{ML}}(\mathbf{y})\right] = \left(\frac{n-1}{n}\right)\lambda^*, \quad \mathrm{E}\left[\hat{\lambda}_{87}(\mathbf{y})\right] = \lambda^*. \quad (16)$$

The maximum likelihood estimator exhibits a downward bias, while the MML87 estimator is unbiased. These results closely parallel those found in the case of the usual univariate Gaussian distribution.

Measures of estimator quality such as bias and expected squared error suffer from the fact that they are parameterisation dependent. This issue can be circumvented by examining the behaviour of the estimators in terms of measures that are invariant under reparameterisations. A common choice is the Kullback–Leibler (KL) [10] divergence. The KL divergence from the true, generating $IG(\mu^*, \lambda^*)$ to an approximating $IG(\hat{\mu}, \hat{\lambda})$ is

$$\Delta(\mu^*, \lambda^* \| \hat{\mu}, \hat{\lambda}) = \frac{1}{2}\log\left(\frac{\hat{\lambda}}{\lambda^*}\right) + \left(\frac{1}{\hat{\lambda}}\right)\left(\frac{\lambda^*}{2} + \frac{1}{2\mu^*} + \frac{\mu^*}{2\hat{\mu}^2} - \frac{1}{\hat{\mu}}\right) - \frac{1}{2}. \quad (17)$$

Estimators may be assessed in terms of their expected KL divergence, or *KL risk*, for a particular sample size n. Let $R_n(\hat{\mu}, \hat{\lambda}) \equiv \mathrm{E}[\Delta(\mu^*, \lambda^* || \hat{\mu}(\mathbf{y}), \hat{\lambda}(\mathbf{y}))]$ denote the KL risk for sample size n, the expectation being taken with respect to the generating model $IG(\mu^*, \lambda^*)$. It is of interest to compare the KL risks of the ML and MML87 estimators. This is done by examining the difference in KL risks. The risk difference is given by

$$R_n(\hat{\mu}_{\mathrm{ML}}, \hat{\lambda}_{\mathrm{ML}}) - R_n(\hat{\mu}_{87}, \hat{\lambda}_{87}) = \left(\frac{3\mu^*\lambda^* + n^2 + n}{2(n-3)n^2}\right) + \frac{1}{2}\log\left(\frac{n-1}{n}\right),$$

which is strictly greater than zero for all $n > 3$. This shows that for all $n > 3$, *the MML87 estimator has strictly lower KL risk than the maximum likelihood estimator*, irrespective of the model (μ^*, λ^*) that generated the data. In the case that the sample size $n \leq 3$, it turns out that both MML87 and ML estimators have infinite KL risk, and neither is demonstrably more accurate in terms of KL divergence.

3.2 Inverse Gaussian Distributions in MML Mixture Models

The minimised message length for inverse Gaussian models given by (13) is not exactly appropriate for the mixture model case, as it is based on complete membership of all the data to a single inverse Gaussian model. It is, however, straightforward to adapt the message length expressions to the mixture setting by appealing to the independence arguments outlined by Wallace in [3]. It can be shown that the appropriate negative log-likelihood for the k-th inverse Gaussian component in a mixture model is

$$\frac{n_k}{2}\log(2\pi\lambda) + \frac{3}{2}\sum_{i=1}^{n} r_{i,k}\log y_i - \frac{n_k}{\mu\lambda} + \frac{S_{k,1}}{2\mu^2\lambda} + \frac{S_{k,2}}{2\lambda} \tag{18}$$

where

$$S_{k,1} = \sum_{i=1}^{n} r_{i,k}\, y_i, \quad S_{k,2} = \sum_{i=1}^{n} \frac{r_{i,k}}{y_i},$$

are the appropriately weighted sufficient statistics. Due to the form of (18), the Fisher information is simply given by $\mathbf{J}_{n_k}(\mu_k, \lambda_k)$, with n_k being the effective sample size for class k given by (6). The prior distributions remained unchanged, and the MML estimates become

$$\hat{\mu}_k(\mathbf{y}) = \frac{S_{k,1}}{n_k},$$

$$\hat{\lambda}_k(\mathbf{y}) = \frac{S_{k,1}S_{k,2} - n_k^2}{(n_k - 1)S_{k,1}}.$$

As was previously noted, the choice of the prior hyperparameters μ_0, λ_0 and λ_1 becomes an issue in the mixture model setting, as the particular values chosen will have a crucial effect on the estimate of the number of classes unless the sample size is very large. To solve this problem, we use two simple, data driven choices for the hyperparameters. The μ_0 hyperparameter sets the lower-bound on the prior density for μ. From the form of the MML estimator $\hat{\mu}_k(\mathbf{y})$ we can easily determine that the smallest value the estimate may assume is equal to the smallest data point in $\mathbf{y}$. Therefore, we have

$$\hat{\mu}_0 = \min_i \{y_i\}.$$

The form of the estimate for $\hat{\lambda}_k(\mathbf{y})$ is complex, and determination of the smallest and largest values it may assume, given a particular dataset $\mathbf{y}$ is computationally intensive. To avoid this problem, we instead use the simple idea proposed by Rissanen to deal with the similar problem of infinite parametric complexity [11]. This involves setting $\lambda_0 = e^{-a}$, $\lambda_1 = e^a$, with $a \in \{1, 2, \ldots\}$ the smallest positive integer such that

$$e^{-a} \le \lambda_k \le e^a, \quad k = 1, \ldots, K.$$

Using this choice of priors, the quantity needed for mixture modelling is

$$I(\mu_k, \lambda_k) = \log n_k - \frac{1}{2} \log \hat{\lambda}_k(\mathbf{y}) + \log\left(\frac{2\sqrt{2}a}{\sqrt{\hat{\mu}_0}}\right). \tag{19}$$

For the resulting codelength of the entire mixture model to be valid it must also include the length of the codewords needed to state the hyperparameters $\hat{\mu}_0$ and a. The total codelength of a mixture model for inverse Gaussian distributions, using these empirical priors, then becomes

$$I(\mathbf{y}, \boldsymbol{\Phi}, a, \hat{\mu}_0) = I(\mathbf{y}, \boldsymbol{\Phi}) + I(\hat{\mu}_0) + I(a).$$

where $I(\mathbf{y}, \boldsymbol{\Phi})$ is given by (8). We note that $\hat{\mu}_0$ is a continuous parameter, and may be stated with a codelength of $I(\hat{\mu}_0) \approx (1/2) \log n$. The hyperparameter a is a positive integer, and following [11], we code this using the log-star code for integers, yielding a codelength of $I(a) \approx \log_*(a) + 2.86$, where $\log_*(x) = \log x + \log \log x + \ldots$, the logarithms iterating until they become negative.

4   Experiments

There have been a large number of previous simulation studies conducted demonstrating that MML is, in general, superior to commonly used asymptotic techniques such as Akaike's information criterion (AIC) [12] or the Bayesian information criterion (BIC) [13] in the context of estimating a finite mixture model (for example, [4, 14]). Given that the inverse Gaussian model satisfies the conditions for the MML87 approximation, and therefore yields sensible codelengths, there is no compelling reason to expect any significant departure from this trend.

Therefore, we conclude the paper by comparing MML inverse Gaussian mixture modelling against regular MML univariate Gaussian mixture modelling on the three real datasets: (i) "Enzyme", (ii) "Acidity", and (iii) "Galaxy" (see [15]).

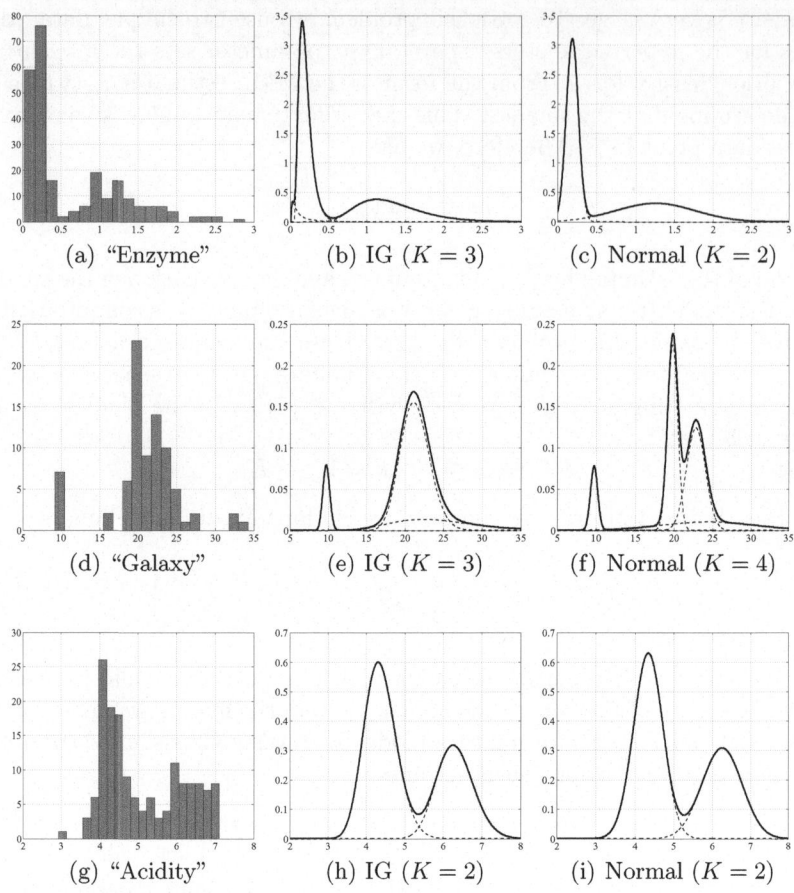

Fig. 1. Mixture Modelling using Inverse Gaussian (IG) and Normal Distributions

All three datasets are composed of non-negative data, and their histograms suggest that multiple modes are a possibility. For each dataset, two mixture models were estimated, one using inverse Gaussian distributions, and a second using univariate Gaussian distributions, univariate Gaussian mixture modelling being the standard approach to clustering of continuous variables used by most software packages. The histograms of the datasets, along with plots of the estimated Gaussian and inverse Gaussian mixture models are presented in Figure 1. The differences between the estimated models for each of the datasets are summarised below:

- **"Enzyme":** For this dataset the advantage obtained by using a positively skewed distribution for positive, continuous data was substantial. The estimated Gaussian mixture model was composed of two classes and had a total message length of 86.19 nits (base-e digits), while the inverse Gaussian mixture model was composed of three classes with a total message length of 69.34 nits. The large difference in message lengths suggests that the inverse Gaussian model offers a significantly better fit to the data than the regular Gaussian model; this is primarily due to the clustering of data near the origin, as well as the positively skewed nature of the data further away from the origin, both of which cause problems for Gaussian distributions.

- **"Galaxy"**: The estimated Gaussian mixture model contained four classes with a total message length of 236.16 nits, and the inverse Gaussian model was composed of 3 classes, with a message length of 235.5 nits. Both mixture models identify the small peak around $y = 10$ as a separate class, but differ in the way that they model the large cluster from $y = 15$ to $y = 30$. The inverse Gaussian mixture model has identified this cluster as unimodal, while the Gaussian mixture model has split the cluster into two separate classes. The difference in message lengths indicates a slight preference for the inverse Gaussian explanation, but it is not great enough to make any conclusive decision.

- **"Acidity"**: The estimated Gaussian mixture model was composed of two classes with a total message length of 209.4 nits, and the estimated inverse Gaussian mixture model also contained two classes, with a total message length of 210.57 nits. From Figure 1 we can see that the data is not close to the origin and appears to be reasonably tightly clustered around $y = 3$ through $y = 7$. Both mixture models are very similar, the primary difference being the height and width of the first peak. This similarity is also mirrored in the message lengths of the two models, which are very close, the Gaussian mixture model being slightly preferred.

The above analyses suggest that the mixture modelling with inverse Gaussian distributions can lead to big improvements over regular Gaussian mixture modelling if the data exhibit positive skewness or are clustered close to the origin. In both of these cases, the regular Gaussian distribution, being symmetric and defined over the entire real line, will be unable to provide an excellent fit to the data. Of course, the strength of MML mixture modelling is that the message length is comparable between mixture models of different distributions. This highlights an important property of MML mixture modelling: for a given dataset, we may use the message length to not only to select the number of classes, but also to select an an appropriate distribution for the classes themselves.

References

1. Wallace, C.S., Boulton, D.M.: An information measure for classification. Computer Journal 11(2), 185–194 (1968)
2. Wallace, C.S., Dowe, D.L.: MML clustering of multi-state, Poisson, von Mises circular and Gaussian distributions. Statistics and Computing 10(1), 73–83 (2000)
3. Wallace, C.S.: Statistical and Inductive Inference by Minimum Message Length, 1st edn. Information Science and Statistics. Springer (2005)

4. Agusta, Y., Dowe, D.: Unsupervised learning of gamma mixture models using minimum message length. In: Hamza, M. (ed.) Proceedings of the 3rd IASTED Conference on Artificial Intelligence and Applications, pp. 457–462. ACTA Press, Benalmadena (2003)

5. Grünwald, P.D.: The Minimum Description Length Principle. In: Adaptive Communication and Machine Learning. The MIT Press (2007)

6. Wallace, C.S., Boulton, D.: An invariant Bayes method for point estimation. Classification Society Bulletin 3(3), 11–34 (1975)

7. Wallace, C.S., Freeman, P.R.: Estimation and inference by compact coding. Journal of the Royal Statistical Society (Series B) 49(3), 240–252 (1987)

8. Schmidt, D.F.: A new message length formula for parameter estimation and model selection. In: Proc. 5th Workshop on Information Theoretic Methods in Science and Engineering, WITMSE 2011 (2011)

9. Banerjee, A.K., Bhattacharyya, G.K.: Bayesian results for the inverse gaussian distribution with an application. Technometrics 21(2), 247–251 (1979)

10. Kullback, S., Leibler, R.A.: On information and sufficiency. The Annals of Mathematical Statistics 22(1), 79–86 (1951)

11. Rissanen, J.: Fisher information and stochastic complexity. IEEE Transactions on Information Theory 42(1), 40–47 (1996)

12. Akaike, H.: A new look at the statistical model identification. IEEE Transactions on Automatic Control 19(6), 716–723 (1974)

13. Schwarz, G.: Estimating the dimension of a model. The Annals of Statistics 6(2), 461–464 (1978)

14. Bouguila, N., Ziou, D.: High-dimensional unsupervised selection and estimation of a finite generalized Dirichlet mixture model based on minimum message length. IEEE Transactions on Pattern Analysis and Machine Intelligence 29(10), 1716–1731 (2007)

15. Richardson, S., Green, P.J.: On bayesian analysis of mixtures with an unknown number of components. Journal of the Royal Statistical Society. Series B (Methodological) 59(4), 731–792 (1997)

A Probabilistic Least Squares Approach to Ordinal Regression

P.K. Srijith[1], Shirish Shevade[1], and S. Sundararajan[2]

[1] Computer Science and Automation, Indian Institute of Science, India
{srijith,shirish}@csa.iisc.ernet.in
[2] Yahoo! Labs, Bangalore, India
zensid@yahoo.com

Abstract. This paper proposes a novel approach to solve the ordinal regression problem using Gaussian processes. The proposed approach, probabilistic least squares ordinal regression (PLSOR), obtains the probability distribution over ordinal labels using a particular likelihood function. It performs model selection (hyperparameter optimization) using the leave-one-out cross-validation (LOO-CV) technique. PLSOR has conceptual simplicity and ease of implementation of least squares approach. Unlike the existing Gaussian process ordinal regression (GPOR) approaches, PLSOR does not use any approximation techniques for inference. We compare the proposed approach with the state-of-the-art GPOR approaches on some synthetic and benchmark data sets. Experimental results show the competitiveness of the proposed approach.

Keywords: Gaussian processes, ordinal regression, probabilistic least squares, cross-validation.

1 Introduction

Most of the works in machine learning have focused on the standard problems of classification and regression. Classification problems aim to label examples from a discrete unordered set, while regression problems aim to label examples from a real valued set. Recently some new classes of learning problems started emerging and the prominent among them is the ordinal regression problem [1]. This problem aims to provide labels to the examples from a discrete but ordered set. It differs from a multi-class classification problem in that the labels are ordered, and from a regression problem in that the labels are discrete. The problem arises in social sciences and information retrieval, where humans rate an item on an ordinal scale. In information retrieval, a user may grade the retrieved documents as highly relevant, relevant, irrelevant or highly irrelevant.

Formally, we define the ordinal regression problem as follows. We are given a sample of n labeled independent training examples, $\mathcal{D} = \{(x_i, y_i)\}_{i=1}^n$, where x_i is an element of a d dimensional input space X ($X \subseteq \mathcal{R}^d$) and y_i is an element of output space Y. The output space $Y = \{r_1, r_2, \ldots, r_q\}$ is a discrete set with an order among its elements, say $r_1 < r_2 < \ldots < r_q$. Our goal is to learn a decision

M. Thielscher and D. Zhang (Eds.): AI 2012, LNCS 7691, pp. 683–694, 2012.

function $h : X \rightarrow Y$, such that it generalizes well. We consider an ordinal regression problem with r ordered categories and without loss of generality, we denote them by r consecutive integers $\{1, 2, \ldots, r\}$. Ordinal regression problems have the property that the penalty for an incorrect prediction should be proportional to the deviation of the predicted label from the true label.

Most of the works on ordinal regression problems are based on the large margin framework [1,2,3]. A distribution independent learning approach based on a loss function between pairs of examples was used in [1] to perform ordinal regression. Fixed margin and sums of margin approaches [2] used the support vector machine framework to solve the ordinal regression problem. They learn $r - 1$ thresholds that divide the real line into r consecutive intervals for r ordered categories. However the thresholds learnt with this approach need not be ordered. Support vector ordinal regression [3] approach corrected this problem by explicitly specifying the ordering constraint on the thresholds. It also proposed a new formulation which implicitly takes into account the ordering constraint on the thresholds. Kernel discriminant ordinal regression [4] extended the Kernel discriminant learning for classification to the ordinal regression setting. In sparse Bayesian ordinal regression [5], the proportional odds model [6] for ordinal regression is extended using kernel methods, and a sparse solution is obtained by imposing a zero-mean Gaussian prior distribution over the weight vector.

Gaussian processes (GP) are non parametric Bayesian models which provide a probabilistic approach to learning in a kernel based framework [7]. The existing Gaussian process approaches for ordinal regression [8] use a non Gaussian likelihood function for modeling the ordinal labels. The use of non Gaussian likelihood forces it to use approximation methods like Laplace approximation [7] or expectation propagation [9] to obtain an approximate Gaussian posterior. The approach performs model selection by maximizing the marginal likelihood using either a maximum a posteriori approach (MAP-GPOR) or expectation propagation approach (EP-GPOR). MAP-GPOR and EP-GPOR are among the state-of-the-art approaches for ordinal regression.

In this work, we propose a simple approach, probabilistic least squares ordinal regression (PLSOR), to perform ordinal regression using Gaussian processes. In PLSOR, the predictive distribution of the latent functions is learnt as a Gaussian process regression (GPR) on ordinal variables. This results in a Gaussian distributed posterior which avoids the use of any approximation methods. The predictive distribution of ordinal targets is obtained by using a likelihood function which takes care of the regression nature of the latent function. In PLSOR, the model parameters are estimated using leave-one-out cross-validation (LOO-CV) [7]. The experiments on synthetic and benchmark data sets showed that the performance of the PLSOR approach is comparable with that of the MAP-GPOR and EP-GPOR approaches. This is also validated using a statistical significance test.

The rest of the paper is organized as follows. In Section 2, we discuss Gaussian process regression. The MAP-GPOR and EP-GPOR approaches are summarized in Section 3. Section 4 discusses the proposed approach, probabilistic least squares ordinal regression (PLSOR), in detail. Comparison of PLSOR with the MAP-GPOR and EP-GPOR approaches on synthetic and benchmark data sets is presented in Section 5. Finally, some conclusions are drawn in Section 6.

2   Gaussian Process Regression

A Gaussian process (GP) is a collection of random variables with the property that the joint distribution of any finite subset of which is a Gaussian [7]. It generalizes Gaussian distribution to infinitely many random variables. The GP is completely specified by a mean function and a covariance function. The covariance function is defined over function values of a pair of input and is evaluated using the Mercer kernel function over the pair of inputs. The covariance function expresses some general properties of functions such as their smoothness, and length-scale. A commonly used covariance function is squared exponential (SE) or Gaussian kernel

$$cov\big(f(x_i), f(x_j)\big) = K(x_i, x_j) = \sigma_f^2 \exp(-\frac{\kappa}{2}||x_i - x_j||^2). \tag{1}$$

Here $f(x_i)$ and $f(x_j)$ are function values associated with the inputs x_i and x_j respectively. σ_f^2 and $\kappa > 0$ are hyperparameters associated with the covariance function.

In a regression problem the output space Y is real valued, $i.e.$ $Y \subseteq \mathcal{R}$. We assume a noisy Gaussian process regression (GPR) approach in which the outputs lie around a latent function $f(x)$ with an additive, independently and identically distributed (i.i.d.) Gaussian noise ϵ with mean 0 and variance σ_n^2, $i.e.$ $y = f(x) + \epsilon$. The likelihood function for the noisy GPR approach follows a Gaussian distribution

$$p(y|f(x)) = \mathcal{N}(f(x), \sigma_n^2). \tag{2}$$

Let $\mathcal{D}$ be the set consisting of n training data points $\mathbf{X}$, the corresponding outputs $\mathbf{y}$ and n_* test data points $\mathbf{X}_*$. Let $\mathbf{K} = K(\mathbf{X}, \mathbf{X})$, $\mathbf{K}_* = K(\mathbf{X}, \mathbf{X}_*)$ and $\mathbf{K}_{**} = K(\mathbf{X}_*, \mathbf{X}_*)$. Here $K(\mathbf{X}, \mathbf{X}_*)$ is an $n \times n_*$ matrix of covariances evaluated at all pairs of training and test input data. The matrices $K(\mathbf{X}, \mathbf{X})$, $K(\mathbf{X}_*, \mathbf{X})$ and $K(\mathbf{X}_*, \mathbf{X}_*)$ are also defined similarly. The GPR approach imposes a zero mean GP prior over the training latent functions $\mathbf{f}$ and test latent functions $\mathbf{f}_*$. The predictive distribution for the test latent functions, $p(\mathbf{f}_*|\mathcal{D})$, is obtained by integrating the conditional distribution $p(\mathbf{f}_*|\mathbf{f}, \mathcal{D})$ over the posterior distribution $p(\mathbf{f}|\mathcal{D})$, $i.e.$ $p(\mathbf{f}_*|\mathcal{D}) = \int p(\mathbf{f}_*|\mathbf{f}, \mathcal{D})p(\mathbf{f}|\mathcal{D})d\mathbf{f}$. In GPR, both the conditional distribution and the posterior distribution are multivariate Gaussians. Hence the predictive distribution of the test latent functions is a multivariate Gaussian with mean (4) and covariance (5),

$$p(\mathbf{f}_*|\mathcal{D}) = \mathcal{N}(\bar{\mathbf{f}}_*, cov(\mathbf{f}_*)), \text{where} \tag{3}$$

$$\bar{\mathbf{f}}_* = \mathbf{K}_*^\top (\mathbf{K} + \sigma_n^2 \mathbf{I})^{-1} \mathbf{y}, \tag{4}$$

$$cov(\mathbf{f}_*) = \mathbf{K}_{**} - \mathbf{K}_*^\top (\mathbf{K} + \sigma_n^2 \mathbf{I})^{-1} \mathbf{K}_*. \tag{5}$$

The predictive distribution of the test outputs $\mathbf{y}_*$ is obtained by averaging the likelihood (2) over predictive distribution of $\mathbf{f}_*$, $p(\mathbf{y}_*|\mathcal{D}) = \int p(\mathbf{y}_*|\mathbf{f}_*)p(\mathbf{f}_*|\mathcal{D})d\mathbf{f}_*$. It is also a multivariate Gaussian with the mean same as that of $\mathbf{f}_*$ while the covariance is obtained by adding $\sigma_n^2\mathbf{I}$ to the variance of $\mathbf{f}_*$. Model selection (hyperparameter optimization) is done using either Bayesian techniques or cross-validation techniques [7].

Performing ordinal regression using GPR is simple and straightforward. It treats the ordinal outputs as real numbers and perform regression on the ordinal outputs. However, such an approach does not provide a valid probability distribution over the ordinal outputs. The Gaussian process ordinal regression (GPOR) approaches [8], maximum a posteriori GPOR (MAP-GPOR) and expectation propagation GPOR (EP-GPOR), provide a valid probability distribution over the ordinal outputs. The following section briefly summarizes the MAP-GPOR and EP-GPOR approaches.

3   Gaussian Process Ordinal Regression Approaches

MAP-GPOR and EP-GPOR use a zero mean Gaussian process prior. Under noisy observations, for an input x and the latent function f, the likelihood function for an ordinal output y is defined as [8]

$$p(y|f) = \Phi\left(\frac{b_y - f}{\sigma}\right) - \Phi\left(\frac{b_{y-1} - f}{\sigma}\right) \tag{6}$$

where σ is the standard deviation of the Gaussian noise and Φ is the Gaussian cumulative distribution function *i.e.* $\Phi(z) = \int_{-\infty}^{z} \mathcal{N}(\delta; 0, 1)d\delta$. The thresholds $b_0, b_1, \ldots, b_r \in \mathcal{R}$ ($b_0 \leq b_1 \leq \ldots \leq b_r$ where $b_0 = -\infty$ and $b_r = \infty$) are fixed so that the likelihood function represents a valid probability distribution over the ordinal outputs. The thresholds $b_1 \leq b_2 \leq \ldots \leq b_{r-1}$ divide a real line into r contiguous intervals. A real latent function value is mapped to a discrete ordinal output based on the interval in which it lies. The likelihood (6) is not a Gaussian and therefore the posterior, $p(\mathbf{f}|\mathcal{D})$, is also not a Gaussian. MAP-GPOR works by approximating the posterior as a Gaussian distribution using Laplace approximation while EP-GPOR uses expectation propagation (EP) [9]. The MAP-GPOR and EP-GPOR approaches perform model selection by maximizing the evidence $p(\mathcal{D}|\theta)$, where θ is the model parameter vector which includes the kernel parameter κ in the covariance function[1], the threshold parameters$(b_1, b_2, \ldots, b_{r-1})$ and the noise parameter σ in the likelihood function. In MAP-GPOR, model selection is done using maximum a posteriori approach with Laplace approximation while in EP-GPOR, it is done using expectation propagation approach with variational methods. Both MAP-GPOR and EP-GPOR take $\mathcal{O}(n^3)$ time for model selection as the optimization method requires inversion of an $n \times n$ matrix.

---

[1] GPOR approach uses a squared exponential covariance function with a single hyperparameter κ. $cov(f(x_i), f(x_j)) = K(x_i, x_j) = \exp(-\frac{\kappa}{2}||x_i - x_j||^2)$, where $f(x_i)$ and $f(x_j)$ are function values associated with the inputs x_i and x_j respectively.

Performing ordinal regression using MAP-GPOR and EP-GPOR is complicated since they use a non Gaussian likelihood. They have to use approximation methods like Laplace approximation or expectation propagation to obtain a Gaussian posterior. We propose a new approach, probabilistic least squares ordinal regression (PLSOR), which provides a simple and exact way to perform ordinal regression using Gaussian processes.

4   Probabilistic Least Squares Ordinal Regression

PLSOR extends probabilistic least squares approach for classification [7] to the ordinal regression setting. In PLSOR, the predictive distribution of test latent functions is learnt using Gaussian process regression on ordinal outputs. The predictive distribution of the test outputs is learnt by squashing a linear function of test latent function predictive probability through a sigmoid. Since the test latent function f_* is learnt using GPR on ordinal outputs it takes real values ranging from 1 to r (number of ordinal categories). We map f_* to a real line by using a linear map $(\hat{\alpha} f_* + \hat{\beta})$, where $\hat{\alpha}, \hat{\beta} \in \mathcal{R}$. The real line is divided into r contiguous segments using thresholds $b_1 \leq b_2 \leq \ldots \leq b_{r-1}$. The segment (b_{y_*-1}, b_{y_*}) is associated with the ordinal category y_* and maps the scaled latent function value to that category. In PLSOR, the following likelihood function is used to estimate the probability of an ordinal category y_* for the test data x_*:

$$p(y_*|f_*) = \Phi(b_{y_*} - (\hat{\alpha} f_* + \hat{\beta})) - \Phi(b_{y_*-1} - (\hat{\alpha} f_* + \hat{\beta})). \tag{7}$$

Here $y_* \in \{1, 2, \ldots, r\}$, $b_0, \ldots, b_r \in \mathcal{R}$ such that $b_0 \leq b_1 \ldots \leq b_r$ and Φ denotes the Gaussian cumulative distribution function i.e. $\Phi(z) = \int_{-\infty}^{z} \mathcal{N}(\delta; 0, 1) d\delta$. We fix $b_0 = -\infty$ and $b_r = \infty$, so that the likelihood function is a valid probability distribution. The predictive distribution of the test latent function f_* is Gaussian with mean μ_* and variance σ_*^2 given by (4) and (5) respectively. The predictive distribution of the test ordinal category y_* is obtained by averaging the likelihood (7) over the test latent function predictive distribution:

$$p(y_*|x_*, \mathbf{X}, \mathbf{y}, \theta) = \int \Phi(b_{y_*} - (\hat{\alpha} f_* + \hat{\beta})) \mathcal{N}(f_*|\mu_*, \sigma_*^2) df_*$$

$$- \int \Phi(b_{y_*-1} - (\hat{\alpha} f_* + \hat{\beta})) \mathcal{N}(f_*|\mu_*, \sigma_*^2) df_*$$

$$= \Phi\left(\frac{b_{y_*} - (\hat{\alpha}\mu_* + \hat{\beta})}{\sqrt{1 + \hat{\alpha}^2 \sigma_*^2}}\right) - \Phi\left(\frac{b_{y_*-1} - (\hat{\alpha}\mu_* + \hat{\beta})}{\sqrt{1 + \hat{\alpha}^2 \sigma_*^2}}\right). \tag{8}$$

The predictive distribution (8) is redefined as

$$p(y_*|x_*, \mathbf{X}, \mathbf{y}, \theta) = \Phi\left(\frac{\alpha\mu_* + \beta_{y_*}}{\sqrt{1 + \alpha^2 \sigma_*^2}}\right) - \Phi\left(\frac{\alpha\mu_* + \beta_{y_*-1}}{\sqrt{1 + \alpha^2 \sigma_*^2}}\right) \tag{9}$$

where $\alpha \in \mathcal{R}$, $\beta_0 = -\infty$, $\beta_r = \infty$, $\beta_1, \beta_2, \ldots, \beta_{r-1} \in \mathcal{R}$ such that $\beta_1 \leq \beta_2 \leq \ldots \leq \beta_{r-1}$. Here we have redefined the variables as $\alpha = -\hat{\alpha}$ and $\beta_i = b_i - \hat{\beta}$. θ

is a vector of model parameters which include α, thresholds $(\beta_1, \beta_2, \ldots, \beta_{r-1})$, kernel parameters $(\sigma_f^2$ and $\kappa)$, and noise parameter (σ_n^2). The parameters σ_f^2, κ, and σ_n^2 appear in (9) through the expressions for mean (μ_*) and variance (σ_*^2). Estimating the optimal model parameters (θ^*) (model selection) can be done using the leave-one-out cross-validation (LOO-CV) technique which we will discuss in Section 4.1. The prediction is made by selecting the ordinal category with highest probability, *i.e.* $\underset{1 \leq k \leq r}{\operatorname{argmax}} \, p(y_* = k | x_*, \mathbf{X}, \mathbf{y}, \theta^*)$.

4.1   Model Selection Using Leave-One-Out Cross-Validation

Model selection for the PLSOR approach is done using the leave-one-out cross-validation (LOO-CV) [7] technique. The log predictive probability of the ith training example x_i, when learnt using the remaining training examples, is

$$\log p(y_i | \mathbf{X}, \mathbf{y_{-i}}, \theta) = \log \left(\Phi \left(\frac{\alpha \mu_{-i} + \beta_{y_i}}{\sqrt{1 + \alpha^2 \sigma_{-i}^2}} \right) - \Phi \left(\frac{\alpha \mu_{-i} + \beta_{y_i - 1}}{\sqrt{1 + \alpha^2 \sigma_{-i}^2}} \right) \right) \quad (10)$$

where $y_i \in \{1, 2, \ldots, r\}$ is the output of ith training example x_i and $\mathbf{y}_{-i}$ is the output vector of the remaining training examples. The predictive distribution mean μ_{-i} and variance σ_{-i}^2 for the training example x_i are obtained by performing a Gaussian process regression on all training examples except x_i and are given by (4) and (5) respectively. Model parameters (θ) are estimated by optimizing the sum of the log leave-one-out (LOO) predictive probability (10) over all the training examples. The optimization problem is defined as follows

$$(\theta^*) = \arg \min_{\theta} \mathcal{L}(\theta) = \arg \min_{\theta} - \sum_{i=1}^{n} \log p(y_i | \mathbf{X}, \mathbf{y_{-i}}, \theta) =$$

$$\underset{\alpha, \beta_1, \Delta_2, \ldots, \Delta_{r-1}, \kappa, \sigma_f^2, \sigma_n^2}{\arg \min} \quad - \sum_{i=1}^{n} \log \left(\Phi \left(\frac{\alpha \mu_{-i} + \beta_{y_i}}{\sqrt{1 + \alpha^2 \sigma_{-i}^2}} \right) - \Phi \left(\frac{\alpha \mu_{-i} + \beta_{y_i - 1}}{\sqrt{1 + \alpha^2 \sigma_{-i}^2}} \right) \right)$$

subject to $\beta_1 \in \mathcal{R}$,

$$\beta_j = \beta_1 + \sum_{l=2}^{j} \Delta_l \quad \forall j = 2, \ldots, r - 1 \quad , \quad \Delta_l \geq 0 \quad \forall l = 2, \ldots, r - 1. \quad (11)$$

This problem minimizes the negative log predictive probability (NLP) measure over all the training examples. Note that the constraint, $\beta_1 \leq \beta_2 \leq \ldots \leq \beta_{r-1}$, is imposed by redefining the threshold variables as $\beta_j = \beta_1 + \sum_{l=2}^{j} \Delta_l$ using positive padding variables Δ_l. The optimal model parameter values are obtained by solving the optimization problem (11). The optimal model parameter values are used to make prediction using (9).

The proposed approach requires the computation of predictive mean and variance for n training examples. Computation of the predictive mean and variance for each training example involves inversion of an $(n - 1) \times (n - 1)$ covariance matrix which requires $\mathcal{O}(n^3)$ time. Therefore the complete LOO-CV procedure takes $\mathcal{O}(n^4)$ time which makes the method computationally expensive. But we get around this problem by noting that we need to perform inversion of only one covariance matrix, covariance matrix $\mathbf{K}$, formed by all training examples. It is then used to compute the predictive mean μ_{-i} and variance σ^2_{-i} for each leave-one-out case as [10]

$$\mu_{-i} = y_i - \left[\mathbf{K}^{-1}\mathbf{y}\right]_i / \left[\mathbf{K}^{-1}\right]_{ii} \tag{12}$$

$$\sigma^2_{-i} = 1/\left[\mathbf{K}^{-1}\right]_{ii}. \tag{13}$$

To evaluate the expressions for μ_{-i} and σ^2_{-i}, we need to perform inversion of the covariance matrix $\mathbf{K}$ and it takes $\mathcal{O}(n^3)$ time. Once we have $\mathbf{K}^{-1}$, we precompute $\mathbf{K}^{-1}\mathbf{y}$ and the computation of μ_{-i} and σ^2_{-i} for the leave-one-out case i is done in constant time using (12) and (13) respectively. The computational complexity of the entire LOO-CV procedure is dominated by the covariance matrix inversion and it is $\mathcal{O}(n^3)$.

The proposed approach, PLSOR, provides a simple and straightforward way to perform ordinal regression using Gaussian processes. In PLSOR, the model parameters are learnt using LOO-CV technique which is easier to implement than the Bayesian techniques employed in MAP-GPOR or EP-GPOR. The entire LOO-CV procedure takes $\mathcal{O}(n^3)$ time, and hence the computational complexity of PLSOR is the same as that of MAP-GPOR or EP-GPOR. In PLSOR, the predictive distribution of test latent functions is learnt using GPR, which in turn uses the likelihood (2) for the training outputs, while the predictive distribution of the test outputs is learnt using the likelihood (7). We call the former likelihood as the training likelihood and the latter as the test likelihood. PLSOR differs from MAP-GPOR or EP-GPOR in using distinct training and test likelihoods. Further PLSOR does not use any approximations unlike MAP-GPOR or EP-GPOR. A summary of the Gaussian process approaches to ordinal regression, MAP-GPOR, EP-GPOR and PLSOR, is given in Table 1.

Table 1. A Summary of the properties of the Gaussian process approaches to ordinal regression, MAP-GPOR, EP-GPOR and PLSOR

Property	MAP-GPOR	EP-GPOR	PLSOR
Training likelihood	$\Phi\left(\frac{b_y - f}{\sigma}\right) - \Phi\left(\frac{b_{y-1} - f}{\sigma}\right)$	$\Phi\left(\frac{b_y - f}{\sigma}\right) - \Phi\left(\frac{b_{y-1} - f}{\sigma}\right)$	$\mathcal{N}(f, \sigma_n^2)$
Test likelihood	$\Phi\left(\frac{b_y - f}{\sigma}\right) - \Phi\left(\frac{b_{y-1} - f}{\sigma}\right)$	$\Phi\left(\frac{b_y - f}{\sigma}\right) - \Phi\left(\frac{b_{y-1} - f}{\sigma}\right)$	$\Phi(b_y - (\alpha f + \beta)) - \Phi(b_{y-1} - (\alpha f + \beta))$
Inference	Laplace approximation	Expectation propagation approximation	Exact, no approximation
Model selection	Evidence maximization	Evidence maximization	NLP minimization
Computational complexity	$\mathcal{O}(n^3)$	$\mathcal{O}(n^3)$	$\mathcal{O}(n^3)$

5   Experimental Results

We perform the experiments on synthetic and benchmark data sets to compare the performance of the proposed PLSOR approach with MAP-GPOR and EP-GPOR approaches. First, we conduct experiments on the synthetic data set to visualize the behavior of the approaches and then, we study their generalization performance on several benchmark data sets.

5.1   Synthetic Data

We conduct experiments on a 1-dimensional synthetic data set with five ordinal categories. The training data set contains 20 points (marked by pluses in Fig.1) with two training data points in the interval $[2, 4]$ belonging to category 1, three in the interval $[4, 6]$ belonging to category 2, ten in the interval $[8, 14]$ belonging to category 3, five in the interval $[14, 18]$ belonging to category 4, and one in the interval $[18, 20]$ belonging to category 5. The test data consists of 200 points in the interval $[0, 20]$, each separated by a distance of 0.1. Fig.1(a) shows the mean and the confidence bound of the output predictive distribution for EP-GPOR on the synthetic data set. Similar plot for PLSOR is depicted in Fig.1(b). From Fig.1, we observe that the performance of both the approaches is similar.

5.2   Benchmark Data

We report the experimental results of our approach on 9 benchmark data sets [8]. Properties of these benchmark data sets are summarized in Table 2. These are regression data sets. The continuous target values are discretized into ordinal values using equal frequency binning. Here, we divide the range of target values into intervals of the same length. Target values are then relabeled according to the interval in which they fall. The ordinal target values thus obtained range from 1 to r, where r denotes the number of intervals. For each data set, we generate two versions, 5 bins and 10 bins, obtained by discretizing the target values in the original data set into 5 and 10 intervals respectively. We conduct experiments on both the versions of the data sets. Each data set is randomly

Table 2. Benchmark data sets and their properties

Data set	Attributes	Training Instances	Test Instances
Diabetes	2	30	13
Pyrimidine	27	50	24
Triazines	60	100	86
Wisconsin	32	130	64
Machine	6	150	59
AutoMPG	7	200	192
Boston	13	300	206
Stocks	9	600	350
Abalone	8	1000	3177

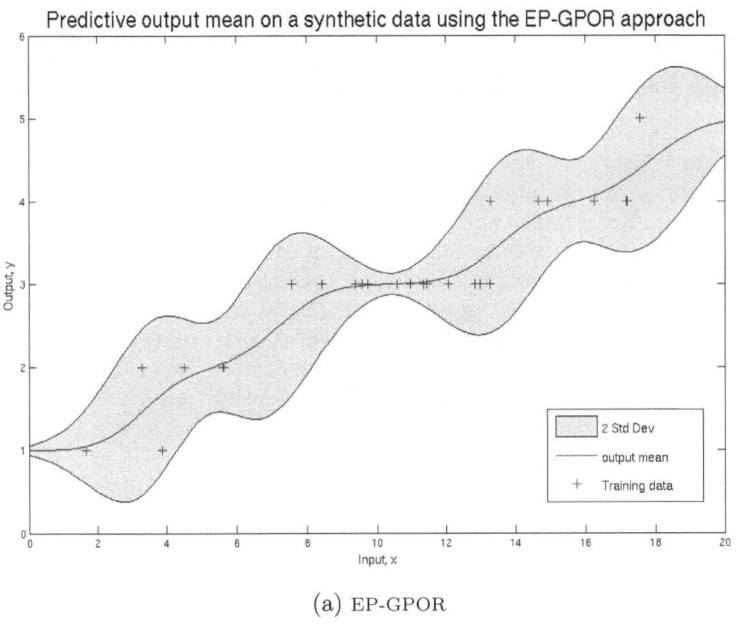

(a) EP-GPOR

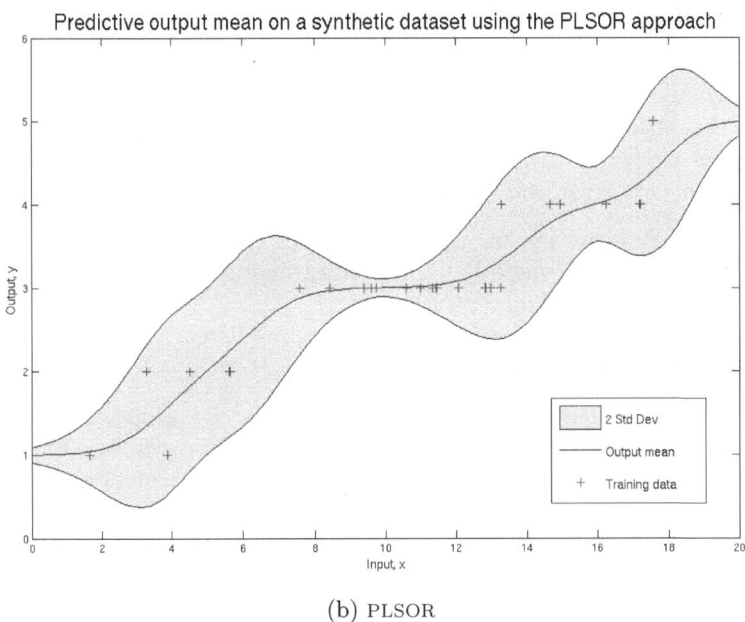

(b) PLSOR

Fig. 1. The mean value and the confidence bound of the output predictive distribution for EP-GPOR and PLSOR on an 1-dimensional synthetic data set

Table 3. Comparison of the results of PLSOR with MAP-GPOR and EP-GPOR on benchmark data sets for the 5 bins version. Mean zero-one errors are reported in percentage. Mean absolute errors are rounded off to 2 decimal places. Values in bold letters denote the lowest mean value among the three approaches.

Data	Mean zero-one error(%)			Mean absolute error		
	MAP-GPOR	EP-GPOR	PLSOR	MAP-GPOR	EP- GPOR	PLSOR
Diabetes	54.23±13.78	54.23±13.78	**48.46±11.2**	0.66±0.14	0.67±0.14	**0.62±0.16**
Pyrimidine	39.79±7.21	**36.46±6.47**	39.37±9.41	0.43±0.09	**0.39±0.07**	0.46±0.19
Triazines	52.91±2.15	**52.62±2.66**	54.42±3.43	**0.69±0.02**	0.69±0.03	0.74±0.063
Wisconsin	**65.00±4.71**	65.16±4.65	65.70±3.23	**1.01±0.09**	1.01±0.09	1.24±0.10
Machine	**16.53±3.56**	16.78±3.88	18.39±3.45	**0.19±0.04**	0.19±0.04	0.21±0.05
AutoMPG	23.78±1.85	**23.75±1.74**	25.76±2.19	0.24±0.02	**0.24±0.02**	0.26±0.02
Boston	24.88±2.02	**24.49±1.85**	24.59±2.57	0.26±0.02	0.26±0.02	**0.26±0.02**
Stocks	11.99±2.34	12.00±2.06	**10.70±1.66**	0.12±0.02	0.12±0.02	**0.11±0.02**
Abalone	**21.50±0.22**	21.56±0.36	22.05±0.30	**0.23±0.00**	0.23±0.00	0.24±0.00

partitioned into training and test data sets and 20 such training and test data set instances are generated by repeated independent partitioning. We use the Gaussian kernel (1) in all our experiments.

The model parameter values are obtained by solving the optimization problem (11). The optimization is run with random as well as fixed[1] initialization of optimization variables; we report the result for which the objective function value is the least.

We compare the generalization performance of PLSOR with MAP-GPOR and EP-GPOR on the benchmark datasets. We use two evaluation metrics to compare the performance, *zero-one error* and *absolute error* [8]. Let the actual test outputs be $\{y_1, \ldots, y_{n_*}\}$ and the predicted test outputs be $\{\hat{y}_1, \ldots, \hat{y}_{n_*}\}$. Then the *zero-one error* and *absolute error* are defined as follows.

zero-one error. gives the fraction of incorrect predictions on test data *i.e.* $\frac{1}{n_*} \sum_{i=1}^{n_*} \mathbb{I}(\hat{y}_i \neq y_i)$, where $\mathbb{I}(\cdot)$ is an indicator function which gives 1 when the argument is true and 0 otherwise.

absolute error. gives the average deviation of predicted test outputs from the actual test outputs *i.e.* $\frac{1}{n_*} \sum_{i=1}^{n_*} |\hat{y}_i - y_i|$.

For each data set, zero-one and absolute errors for the proposed approach is obtained on all the 20 instances of training and test data sets. The mean of the zero-one and absolute errors, along with their standard deviation, are used to compare the performance of various approaches. We prefer methods with low mean zero-one and mean absolute errors. Tables 3 and 4 compare PLSOR with MAP-GPOR and EP-GPOR for the 5 bins and 10 bins cases respectively.

We observe from Tables 3 and 4 that the results obtained with the PLSOR approach are comparable with those obtained with the MAP-GPOR and

---

[1] Fixed initialization is done as given in [8] where we choose $\sigma_f^2 = 1, \kappa = 1/d$, d being the dimension of the data set, $\beta_1 = -1, \Delta_l = 2/r$, r being number of ordinal categories.

Table 4. Comparison of the results of PLSOR with MAP-GPOR and EP-GPOR on benchmark data sets for the 10 bins version. Mean zero-one errors are reported in percentage. Mean absolute errors are rounded off to 2 decimal places. Values in bold letters denote the lowest mean value among the three approaches.

	Mean zero-one error(%)			Mean absolute error		
Data	MAP-GPOR	EP-GPOR	PLSOR	MAP-GPOR	EP-GPOR	PLSOR
Diabetes	83.46±5.73	83.08±5.91	**76.92±9.98**	2.14±0.33	2.14±0.33	**1.50±0.37**
Pyrimidine	55.42±8.01	**54.38±7.70**	55.63±8.47	0.88±0.18	**0.83±0.13**	0.89±0.18
Triazines	**63.72±4.34**	64.01±3.78	69.88±4.97	**1.20±0.07**	1.20±0.07	1.37±0.20
Wisconsin	78.52±3.58	78.52±3.51	**75.94±1.86**	**2.14±0.18**	2.14±0.18	2.94±0.13
Machine	33.81±3.91	**33.73±3.64**	35.17±3.64	0.48±0.07	**0.47±0.08**	0.53±0.08
Auto MPG	43.96±2.81	**43.88±2.60**	46.35±2.48	0.50±0.03	**0.50±0.03**	0.56±0.04
Boston	41.53±2.77	**41.26±2.86**	41.99±2.82	0.49±0.03	**0.49±0.03**	0.51±0.04
Stocks	19.90±1.72	19.44±1.91	**18.17±1.79**	0.20±0.02	0.20±0.02	**0.19±0.02**
Abalone	42.60±0.91	**42.27±0.46**	44.24±0.68	0.51±0.01	**0.51±0.01**	0.55±0.01

Table 5. Average rank of each of the ordinal regression approaches, MAP-GPOR, EP-GPOR and PLSOR, over all the data sets and the Friedman statistic computed over all the approaches

	5 bins		10 bins	
	zero-one	absolute	zero-one	absolute
MAP-GPOR	1.944	1.778	2.167	1.833
EP-GPOR	1.722	1.778	1.500	1.611
PLSOR	2.333	2.444	2.333	2.556
F_F	0.8266	1.3880	1.8449	2.5841

EP-GPOR approaches. PLSOR is found to perform better than MAP-GPOR and EP-GPOR on two data sets, Diabetes and Stocks. On other data sets, the PLSOR results are close to the MAP-GPOR and EP-GPOR results.

We use the Friedman test [11] to check if the performance of the proposed approach differs significantly from the existing GPOR approaches. Here we compare 3 approaches on 9 data sets. Therefore, the F distribution has 2 and 16 degrees of freedom[2]. For the level of significance $\alpha = 0.05$, the critical F value is 3.63. Table 5 reports the average rank of the ordinal regression approaches, MAP-GPOR, EP-GPOR and PLSOR, over all the data sets. It also reports the Friedman statistic F_F [11] computed over all approaches for 5 bins and 10 bins cases with respect to zero-one and absolute errors. In all the cases, the computed F_F values are less than the critical F value (due to the ranks being similar). Hence there does not exist any significance differences between various approaches. Thus, the proposed PLSOR approach is simple, easy to implement and gives competitive performance compared to the existing state-of-the-art GP based approaches for ordinal regression.

---

[2] For K approaches and N data sets, F distribution has $K - 1$ and $(K - 1)(N - 1)$ degrees of freedom.

6   Conclusion

In this work, we proposed a novel approach to solve the ordinal regression problem using Gaussian processes. The proposed approach, probabilistic least squares ordinal regression (PLSOR), provided an easy and exact way to perform ordinal regression using Gaussian processes. Here model selection is performed using leave-one-out cross-validation technique. Experiments on synthetic and benchmark data sets showed that the proposed approach is competitive with the state-of-the-art GPOR approach. In future, we would like to develop sparse models for the Gaussian process ordinal regression approaches so that the training time and inference time could be reduced considerably.

References

1. Herbrich, R., Graepel, T., Obermayer, K.: Large Margin Rank Boundaries for Ordinal Regression. In: Advances in Large Margin Classifiers. MIT Press (2000)
2. Shashua, A., Levin, A.: Ranking with Large Margin Principle: Two Approaches. In: Advances in Neural Information Processing Systems 15, pp. 937–944. The MIT Press (2003)
3. Chu, W., Keerthi, S.S.: New Approaches to Support Vector Ordinal Regression. In: Proceedings of the 22nd International Conference on Machine Learning, pp. 145–152. ACM (2005)
4. Sun, B.Y., Li, J., Wu, D.D., Zhang, X.M., Li, W.B.: Kernel Discriminant Learning for Ordinal Regression. IEEE Trans. on Knowl. and Data Eng. 22, 906–910 (2010)
5. Chang, X., Zheng, Q., Lin, P.: Ordinal Regression with Sparse Bayesian. In: Huang, D.-S., Jo, K.-H., Lee, H.-H., Kang, H.-J., Bevilacqua, V. (eds.) ICIC 2009. Part II. LNCS, vol. 5755, pp. 591–599. Springer, Heidelberg (2009)
6. McCullagh, P.: Regression Models for Ordinal Data. Journal of the Royal Statistical Society 42, 109–142 (1980)
7. Rasmussen, C.E., Williams, C.K.I.: Gaussian Processes for Machine Learning (Adaptive Computation and Machine Learning). The MIT Press (2005)
8. Chu, W., Ghahramani, Z.: Gaussian Processes for Ordinal Regression. J. Mach. Learn. Res. 6, 1019–1041 (2005)
9. Minka, T.: A Family of Algorithms for Approximate Bayesian Inference. PhD thesis, Massachusetts Institute of Technology (2001)
10. Sundararajan, S., Keerthi, S.S.: Predictive Approaches for Choosing Hyperparameters in Gaussian Processes. Neural Computation 13, 1103–1118 (1999)
11. Demsar, J.: Statistical Comparisons of Classifiers over Multiple Data Sets. J. Mach. Learn. Res. 7, 1–30 (2006)

Bagging Ensemble Selection for Regression

Quan Sun and Bernhard Pfahringer

Department of Computer Science
The University of Waikato
Hamilton, New Zealand
{qs12,bernhard}@cs.waikato.ac.nz

Abstract. Bagging ensemble selection (BES) is a relatively new ensemble learning strategy. The strategy can be seen as an ensemble of the ensemble selection from libraries of models (ES) strategy. Previous experimental results on binary classification problems have shown that using random trees as base classifiers, BES-OOB (the most successful variant of BES) is competitive with (and in many cases, superior to) other ensemble learning strategies, for instance, the original ES algorithm, stacking with linear regression, random forests or boosting. Motivated by the promising results in classification, this paper examines the predictive performance of the BES-OOB strategy for regression problems. Our results show that the BES-OOB strategy outperforms Stochastic Gradient Boosting and Bagging when using regression trees as the base learners. Our results also suggest that the advantage of using a diverse model library becomes clear when the model library size is relatively large. We also present encouraging results indicating that the non-negative least squares algorithm is a viable approach for pruning an ensemble of ensembles.

1   Introduction

The problem of constructing an ensemble from a library of base learners has always been of interest to the data mining community. Usually, compared with individual learners, ensemble strategies are more accurate and stable. In a typical regression setting, a given training set D consists of m instances, such as $D = \{(\mathbf{x_1}, y_1), ..., (\mathbf{x_m}, y_m)\}$, where $\mathbf{x_i}$ is an instance and y_i is a target, the task is to learn an approximate function $f : X \to \mathbb{R}$ of the true function f^0 from D. Let $f_j, j = 1...k$, be a set of base regression learners that output predictions $f_j(\mathbf{x_i})$. The output of a simple regression ensemble $F(\mathbf{x_i})$ for instance $\mathbf{x_i}$ can be expressed as:

$$F(\mathbf{x_i}) = \sum_{j=1}^{k} w_j f_j(\mathbf{x_i}), \qquad (1)$$

where w_j is the weight of base learner f_j. In this particular form, ensemble learning strategies can be seen as methods for calculating optimal weights for each base learner in terms of a regression goal. Since the mid-70s, many ensemble strategies have been proposed. We first review a few state-of-the-art ensemble

M. Thielscher and D. Zhang (Eds.): AI 2012, LNCS 7691, pp. 695–706, 2012.

strategies for regression. Gradient Boosting [9] is a classical ensemble learning algorithm. It produces an ensemble of base learners (e.g., decision trees) based on a stage-wise procedure to optimise an arbitrary differentiable loss function. Stochastic Gradient Boosting [8] is an extension of the Gradient Boosting algorithm, where at each iteration, a base learner trains on a subset of the training set drawn at random without replacement. Bagging (bootstrap aggregating) [2] is based on the instability of base learners, which can be exploited to improve the predictive performance of such unstable base learners. The basic idea is that, given a training set T of size n and a learner A, bagging generates m new training sets with replacement, T_i. Then, bagging applies A to each T_i to build m models. The final output of bagging is based on simple averaging [2]. For instance, in a regression setting using Eq. 1, the weight w_j for f_j is $\frac{1}{k}$. MultiBoosting [16] is an ensemble algorithm designed to reduce both variance and bias simultaneously, in which Boosting is used as the base learner for Bagging. For a more detailed review of recent developments on ensemble learning strategies please refer to [14,19]. Next, we discuss the motivations for proposing and studying the bagging ensemble selection (BES) strategy.

Before introducing the BES strategy, we briefly review the ensemble selection (ES) algorithm proposed in [6]. ES is a method for constructing ensembles from a library of base learners. Firstly, base models are built using many different machine-learning algorithms. Then a construction strategy such as forward step-wise selection, guided by some scoring function, extracts a well performing subset of all models. The simple forward step-wise model selection based procedure proposed in [6] works as follows: (1) start with an empty ensemble; (2) add to the ensemble the model in the library that maximizes the ensemble's performance using some given error metric on a hillclimb set; (3) repeat Step 2 until all models have been examined; (4) return that subset of models that yields maximum performance on the hillclimb set. One advantage of ES is that it can be optimised for many common performance metrics or even a combination of metrics. To exemplify this ability, a number of different metrics including mean absolute error, correlation coefficients, root mean squared error, and relative root squared error, will be used to present results in the graphs and tables of this paper. For variants of the ES algorithm, the reader is referred to [5,6].

Experimental results in [6,15] show that in the classification setting, the simple ES strategy sometimes overfits the hillclimb set, reducing its predictive performance. Our preliminary experimental results for employing ES on regression problems also identified a similar phenomenon. Figure 1 (a) shows an example of the hillclimb set overfitting problem of ES on the *Boston housing price* data. The red curve (top) is the hillclimb set performance; the blue curve (bottom) is the test set performance. We can see that as the size of the model library increases, the hillclimb set performance also improves gradually. However, the test set performance does not always improve. In this case, the local optimal performance is achieved when the model library size is about 700. Another practical issue is that users have to estimate the optimal hillclimb set ratio for a given data set. Figure 1 (b) shows an example on the *CPU* data based on cross-validation

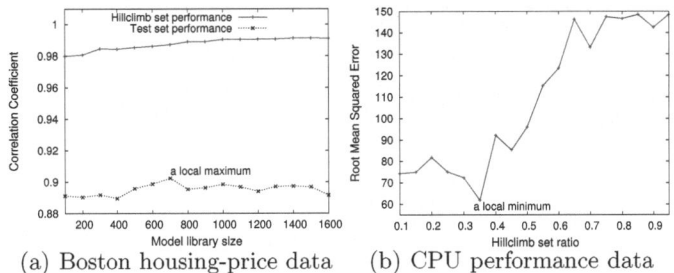

(a) Boston housing-price data   (b) CPU performance data

Fig. 1. Examples of the hillclimb set overfitting and the hillclimb set ratio problems of the Ensemble Selection strategy

based performance estimation. We can see that the local optimal performance is achieved when the hillclimb ratio is about 0.35; after that, the performance starts to drop. Although we could use cross-validation to estimate the hillclimb set ratio, this would substantially increase the practical training cost of ES. To overcome these problems and improve the predictive performance of the ES strategy, three BES strategies have been proposed in [15]. Experimental results show that, under the classification setting, the BES-OOB strategy is the most successful variant in terms of predictive performance. In this paper, we focus on examining the predictive performance of the BES-OOB strategy for regression problems.

2   The BES-OOB Strategy

The **BES-OOB** strategy uses the full bootstrap sample as the build set for model generation, and the respective out-of-bag sample as the hillclimb set for ensemble construction. The bootstrap sample is expected to contain about $1 - 1/e \approx$ 63.2% of the unique examples of the training set [1,2]. Therefore the hillclimb set (out-of-bag sample) is expected to have about $1/e \approx 36.8\%$ unique examples of the training set for each bagging iteration. Figure 2 shows the pseudocode for training the BES-OOB strategy. Please note that the term "classifier" in the pseudocode is used to refer to both classification and regression classifiers. An advantage of BES-OOB is that the user does not need to choose the size of the hillclimb set as in the ES algorithm. Bagging and ES are both generic strategies for supervised learning. When they are used for the regression setting, we can simply use regression algorithms as the base classifiers. BES-OOB combines the two strategies, therefore it is also a generic ensemble learning strategy for both classification and regression.

In the original ES algorithm, Step 6 in Figure 2 uses the forward step-wise selection method for ensemble construction. For the details of the method, we refer readers to [6]. In this paper, we also use the same method. Our emphasis here is to show that any "greedy" (active set) ensemble construction method that

---

BES-OOB(S, E, T)

S is the training set
E is the Ensemble Selection classifier
T is the number of bootstrap samples

```
1:  H ← empty ensemble
2:  for i ← 1 to T {
3:       S_b ← bootstrap sample from S
4:       S_oob ← out of bag sample
5:       train base classifiers in E on S_b
6:       E_i ← do ensemble selection based on
                    base classifiers' performance on S_oob
7:       add E_i to H
8:  }
9:  return H
```

Fig. 2. Pseudocode of the BES-OOB algorithm

utilizes the out-of-bag sample for performance estimation can be used in Step 6 of BES-OOB. Although in recent years, the ES algorithm has been highlighted in winning solutions of many data mining competitions [15], there is no theoretical work on explicitly examining the convergence property of the ES algorithm. Here we attempt to give a brief discussion on the theoretical aspect. If we see the forward step-wise method used in ES as a "greedy" feature selection algorithm, then the predictions of each base regression classifier can be seen as the "feature" values. Based on the theoretical work on forward feature selection [4], when certain conditions are met, such as sufficient conditions for convex optimization, use of squared error loss and in absence of noise, the theoretical convergence rate of the forward step-wise method used in ES is sublinear at $m^{-\frac{1}{2}}$, where m is the number of base classifiers. A comprehensive theoretical analysis of the ES algorithm is beyond the scope of this paper and we leave it for future research.

3   Experiments

In this section, we conduct a series of experiments and statistical tests to examine the performance of the BES-OOB ensemble strategy for regression.

3.1   Comparison to Other Ensemble Strategies

Firstly we compare BES-OOB to three state-of-the-art ensemble strategies for regression: Stochastic Gradient Boosting (SGB) [8], standard Bagging (BG) [2] and an ensemble of Bagging and Stochastic Gradient Boosting, denoted by BSGB. BSGB can be seen as a variant of the MultiBoosting algorithm [16], in which SGB is used as a base learner for Bagging. The experiments are based on 42 regression data sets from UCI repository[1] and StatLib[2]. We use 10 times 10-fold cross-validation to estimate the performance of each strategy. Then, several statistical significance tests are conducted, including the non-parametric *Friedman-test* and the *Bonferroni-Dunn test* as described in [7]. This approach utilises the

---

[1] http://archive.ics.uci.edu/ml
[2] http://lib.stat.cmu.edu

Table 1. Estimated correlation coefficients of BES-OOB, SGB, BG, and BSGB; and Win/tie/loss counts of *paired t-test*

Dataset	BES-OOB	SGB	BG	BSGB
quake	0.12	0.06 ●	0.12	0.12
cholesterol	0.19	0.07 ●	0.18	0.19
detroit	0.22	0.03 ●	0.24	0.24
breastTumor	0.22	0.16 ●	0.22	0.22
meta	0.38	0.14 ●	0.36 ●	0.38
veteran	0.42	0.26 ●	0.42	0.42
schlvote	0.45	0.10 ●	0.46	0.43
sensory	0.53	0.48 ●	0.53	0.52
longley	0.54	0.43 ●	0.54 ●	0.50 ●
strike	0.55	0.41 ●	0.55	0.55
kidney	0.55	0.38 ●	0.53 ●	0.58 ○
baskball	0.55	0.43 ●	0.55	0.56
newton-hema	0.57	0.54	0.58 ○	0.59 ○
pbc	0.57	0.52 ●	0.56 ●	0.58 ○
stanford	0.60	0.43 ●	0.63	0.63
sleep	0.64	0.52 ●	0.64	0.62
hungarian	0.65	0.63 ●	0.65 ●	0.66 ○
winequality-red	0.66	0.61 ●	0.66 ●	0.68 ○
echoMonths	0.67	0.69 ○	0.69 ○	0.68
winequality-white	0.68	0.62 ●	0.67 ●	0.70 ○
cleveland	0.69	0.63 ●	0.69	0.70 ○
pollution	0.75	0.51 ●	0.73 ●	0.75
vineyard	0.76	0.67 ●	0.75 ●	0.76
lowbwt	0.79	0.78 ●	0.79	0.79
elusage	0.82	0.81	0.82	0.84
vinnie	0.86	0.85 ●	0.86 ○	0.86 ○
bolts	0.86	0.83	0.83 ●	0.86
gascons	0.88	0.76 ●	0.84	0.83
cloud	0.91	0.84 ●	0.90 ●	0.91
autoMpg	0.91	0.92	0.91 ●	0.93 ○
servo	0.92	0.91	0.91 ●	0.93 ○
pwLinear	0.92	0.92	0.92	0.93 ○
housing	0.92	0.90 ●	0.91 ●	0.93 ○
boston	0.92	0.91 ●	0.92 ●	0.93 ○
socmob	0.92	0.92	0.91 ●	0.94 ○
autoHorse	0.93	0.91 ●	0.90 ●	0.93
autoPrice	0.93	0.92 ●	0.93 ●	0.94 ○
cpu	0.97	0.93 ●	0.96 ●	0.98
strikes	0.98	0.97 ●	0.96 ●	0.98 ●
fishcatch	0.98	0.96 ●	0.97 ●	0.97 ●
visualizing-galaxy	0.99	0.98 ●	0.98 ●	0.99 ○
bodyfat	0.99	0.98 ●	0.98 ●	0.98 ●

● ○, BES-OOB is significantly better or worse

	BES-OOB against		
	SGB	BG	BSGB
win/tie/loss	34/7/1	23/16/3	4/21/17

ranking information of each learner in comparison, which is suitable for comparing multiple learners on multiple data sets. The total numbers of win, tie and loss for the *paired t-test* (with significance level 0.05) are also recorded. To fairly compare the four strategies, REPTree (a CART-like regression tree) [10] is used as the base learner. The ensemble size is set to 1,500 for all these strategies. For SGB, the shrinkage parameter is set to 0.5 and the subsample size parameter is set to 50%. For BES-OOB, the number of base learners per "bag" is set to 30, and the number of bagging iterations is set to 50. Also, BES-OOB is set to optimise the correlation coefficient metric. For BSGB, the number of base learners for SGB (shrinkage is set to 0.5; subsample size is 50%) is set to 30, and the number of bagging iterations is set to 50. Table 1 presents the *paired t-test* results. Correlation coefficient scores are reported. Figure 3 is the graphical representation of the *Friedman-test* for the four strategies. We can see that both BES-OOB and BSGB significantly outperform BG and SGB, and BG significantly outperforms SGB. There is no significant difference between BES-OOB and BSGB's performance over the 42 data sets.

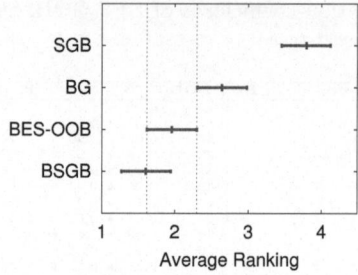

Fig. 3. Visualization of the *Friedman-test* results for BES-OOS, SGB, BG, and BSGB with REPTree as base learners over 42 data sets. The middle point of each bar indicates the average rankings, and the bars indicate the critical values of the *Bonferroni-Dunn test* (two-tailed test at significance level 0.05). Strategies having non-overlapped bars are significantly different.

3.2 Diverse Model Libraries

In the previous experiments, we have been testing on a single type base learner. However, one distinguishing feature of BES-OOB is that it can use different types of base learners. In this section, BES-OOB with a diverse model library consisting of three types of base learners (REPTree, SVM regression and M5P model tree [13]), denoted by BES-diverse, is compared to BES-OOB with only one of the three base learners, denoted by BES-reptree, BES-svm, and BES-m5p, respectively. Three different model library sizes are tested: 3, 30 and 300. The experimental setup is as follows: the number of bagging iterations for all BES strategies in comparison is set to 30; for BES-diverse, when the model library size is 3, only one of each type of base learners is used; when the model library size is 30, 10 of each type of base learners are used; so 100 of each type of the base learners are used for a model library size of 300. The correlation coefficient is set as the goal metric for all strategies.

Diversity is one of the key factors for ensemble learning. To simplify the procedure for generating diverse base learners, we adopt the "random subspace" idea [3] for each base learner in the library. That is, each base learner trains on a random subset (33% is used for all experiments) of the original variables. For REPTree, Weka default parameters are used, and we also randomly set its random seed; for SVM regression, we use the LibSVM default parameters for epsilon-SVM regression and RBF kernel, except the gamma value is randomly set to be between 0 and 1. We use the Weka default parameters for M5P model tree. Table 2 shows the *paired t-test* results of BES-OOB-diverse against BES-OOB-reptree, BES-OOB-svm and BES-OOB-m5p under three different model library sizes: 3, 30, and 300, respectively. Please note that the number of bagging iterations is set to 30. Therefore, the numbers of base learners that are allowed to be built for the three model library sizes are: 90, 900, and 9,000, respectively.

Figure 4 shows the average *Friedman-test* rankings of each strategy under the three model library sizes. We can see that the ranking of BES-OOB-diverse

Table 2. Win/tie/loss counts of *paired t-test* for BES-OOB-diverse against BES-OOB-reptree (A1), BES-OOB-svm (A2) and BES-OOB-m5p(A3).

Model library size = 3		
	BES-OOB-diverse against	
A1	A2	A3
win/tie/loss 4/20/18	32/8/2	5/13/24

Model library size = 30		
	BES-OOB-diverse against	
A1	A2	A3
win/tie/loss 19/15/8	34/6/2	9/20/13

Model library size = 300		
	BES-OOB-diverse against	
A1	A2	A3
win/tie/loss 5/37/0	14/28/0	4/38/0

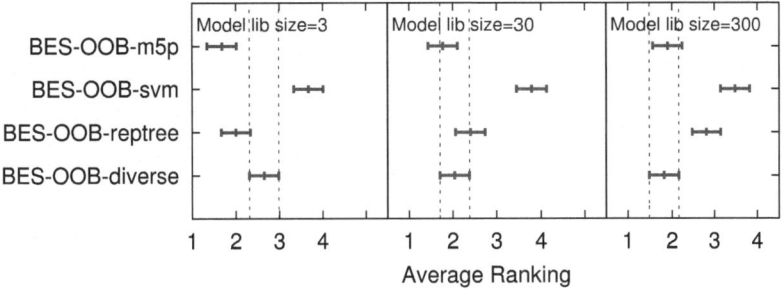

Fig. 4. Friedman average rankings under different model library sizes

improves (from the third to the second, and finally to the first) when the model library size increases. The result implies that the advantage of using a diverse model library becomes clear when the model library size is relatively large. To the best of our knowledge, this is a novel result in the regression setting.

3.3 Pruning an Ensemble of ES Ensembles

Until now, we have been using the standard output aggregation method for BES-OOB. That is, the final prediction of BES-OOB is simply the average of all individual ES learners. The final ensemble size of BES-OOB is therefore the number of bagging iterations. In this section, we consider methods for ensemble pruning. Usually, there are two main reasons for doing ensemble pruning. The first is to reduce the prediction cost (e.g., runtime or memory requirements) without sacrificing too much predictive performance. The second is to obtain a more accurate model. Based on the theoretical work of [20] in the study of neural networks, we know that theoretically "many could be better than all". This implies that the performance of an optimal subset of base learners may outperform the population average. Since the default BES-OOB strategy uses simple averaging, appropriate ensemble pruning may improve BES-OOB's performance in terms of both accuracy and prediction cost. We compare simple averaging to two pruning methods: pruning with the cocktail ensemble (CE) algorithm, and pruning with the stacking strategy using the non-negative least-squares (NNLS)

BES-OOB-CE(S, E, T)

S is the training set
E is the Ensemble Selection (ES) learner
T is the number of bootstrap samples

1: $H \leftarrow$ BES-OOB(S,E,T) // an ensemble of T ES
          ensembles
2: $f_1^c \leftarrow$ the ensemble in H with the smallest out-of-bag
          estimate of error
3: $e_{min} = +\infty$
4: for $i \leftarrow 2$ to T
5:     $f_i \leftarrow null$
6:     for each $f \in H$
7:         $e \leftarrow$ estimated error of combing f and f_{i-1}^c
8:         if $e < e_{min}$ then $f_i \leftarrow f$ and $e_{min} \leftarrow e$
9:     }
10:    if f_i is $null$ then $f_N^c \leftarrow f_{i-1}^c$ and $break$
11:    $f_i^c \leftarrow p_i f_{i-1}^c + (1 - p_i)f_i$, where p_i is obtained by
            Eq.2 for the mean squared error
12: }
13: return f_N^c

Fig. 5. Pseudocode of the CE method for BES-OOB ensemble pruning

algorithm as the meta-level learner. The three methods in this comparison are denoted by BES-OOB-avg, BES-OOB-ce, and BES-OOB-nnls, respectively. Next, we briefly introduce the BES-OOB-ce and the BES-OOB-nnls methods.

Cocktail ensemble (CE) [18], is a novel method of ensemble learning. One reason for using CE as an ensemble pruning method for BES-OOB is that the authors explicitly mentioned that the method is proposed for learning ensemble of ensembles. Since combination of multiple ensembles (equivalent to finding the optimal weights for each base learner) is an NP-hard problem [11], the authors of [18] proposed using the pair-wise combination for multiple ensembles. In addition, CE has an appealing mathematical foundation, which we will briefly discuss here. For a full account of the method, we refer readers to [18]. The basic idea is that, given two ensembles f_1 and f_2, a linear ensemble of ensembles f_1 and f_2 can be expressed as:

$$f^c = pf_1 + (1 - p)f_2, \quad wrt \ p \in [0, 1]$$

where p is the weight for f_1 and $1 - p$ is the weight for f_2. Then, the optimal weight of f_1 is:

$$p^* = \frac{E_2 - E_1}{2\triangle} + 0.5, \tag{2}$$

where E_1 and E_2 are the generalization errors of f_1 and f_2, and $\triangle = \mathbb{E}_x[(f_1 - f_2)^2]$ is the squared output difference of the two ensembles. Here E_1, E_2 and $\triangle$ can be estimated from data (in BES-OOB, we use the out-of-bag sample). Figure 5 shows the pseudocode for the CE method, which has been adapted for BES-OOB pruning.

Stacking, or stacked generalisation [17], is a popular ensemble learning strategy, where the weights of the base classifiers are the regression coefficients of the meta-level regressor. Usually linear regression (LR) is used at the meta-level.

Since our goal is to prune an ensemble, simply using LR would not reduce the ensemble size. Here, we propose using stacking with the NNLS algorithm. To the best of our knowledge, this is the first time that stacking with NNLS is considered as an ensemble pruning approach. Eq. 5 shows the basic form of the NNLS optimisation problem.

$$\min_{w \geq 0} \|Xw - y\|_2^2. \tag{3}$$

Here, X is the data matrix, w is the regression coefficient vector, and y is the target matrix. We can see that it is the same as the linear least-squares regression form, but with extra constraints on the values of the coefficient vector. For our experiment, we use the NNLS algorithm proposed in [12]. The BES-OOB ensemble strategy constructs an ensemble of ES ensembles. Each individual ES is trained on a corresponding bootstrap sample, and its ensemble selection is guided by its performance on the out-of-bag sample. The basic steps of using stacking with NNLS for BES-OOB pruning are as follows: Suppose S is the training set, and H is an ensemble of ES ensembles (same as line 1 in Figure 5). A meta-dataset can be constructed by using the predictions of each ES in H on S. The targets in S are used as the targets of the meta-dataset. Then, we use NNLS to build a model on the meta-dataset. The NNLS regression coefficients are used as the weights for each ES. Therefore, the final ensemble consists only of ES ensembles with greater than zero weight.

The experimental setup is as follows: the number of bagging iterations is set to 30 for all three methods (BES-OOB-avg/ce/nnls). For each bagging iteration, one REPTree-based ES learner is trained. The number of trees used for each ES is 10. As in the previous experiment, each REPTree is built using a random 33% of the original attributes. So in total 300 REPTree learners are built for each of the three methods in the comparison. At the individual bagging iteration level, all three BES-OOB methods are set to optimise the mean squared error (MSE) metric. At the pruning level, BES-OOB-ce is also set to optimise the MSE metric based on Eq. 2. Also, based on Eq. 5, we know that BES-OOB-nnls optimises square error by default. In total 42 data sets are used for this experiment.

Table 3 shows the *corrected paired t-test* results. The reported root relative squared errors are estimated from 10 times 10-fold cross-validation. The final ensemble sizes, and the final number of trees, are also reported. Figure 6 shows the *Friedman-test* results. Based on the *corrected paired t-test* results, we can see that both of the two pruning methods, BES-OOB-ce and BES-OOB-nnls, show competitive predictive performance compared to BES-OOB-avg, but with smaller final ensemble sizes and final number of trees. There are no significant *t-test*-based performance differences between BES-OOB-avg and the two pruning methods on most of the 42 data sets (39 for BES-OOB-ce; 37 for BES-OOB-nnls) in this experiment. Based on the *Friedman-test* and the *Bonferroni-test*, we can see that the performance of BES-OOB-avg and BES-OOB-nnls has no significant differences over the 42 data sets.

Table 3. The Root Relative Squared Error values, the ensemble sizes, and the number of trees in the final ensemble for BES-OOB-avg, BES-OOB-ce and BES-OOB-nnls, over 42 data sets

Data set	Root Relative Squared Error			Ensemble Size			Number of Trees		
	nnls	ce	avg	nnls	ce	avg	nnls	ce	avg
autoHorse	34.60	36.87	34.78	5.7	5.6	30	22.0	22.2	118.8
autoMpg	37.53	38.48	37.58	8.7	4.6	30	38.4	21.3	138.6
autoPrice	34.99	38.52	35.91	6.2	4.3	30	23.3	17.2	114.1
baskball	84.46	85.26	83.69	4.9	4.2	30	15.0	12.5	98.2
bodyfat	14.79 o	**27.53**	17.13	5.3	3.4	30	13.3	9.7	75.2
bolts	31.39	36.12	35.50	5.4	4.5	30	14.7	14.4	91.0
boston	41.85	44.99	43.02	7.4	5.3	30	28.7	23.4	124.9
breastTumor	97.40	97.75	96.50	4.5	4.1	30	15.9	15.7	104.2
cholesterol	101.31	100.47	99.15	3.7	3.9	30	13.6	15.0	108.1
cleveland	74.15	75.01	73.78	5.9	4.0	30	22.0	17.0	119.0
cloud	44.80	47.19	44.09	5.6	5.3	30	20.3	19.5	109.5
cpu	19.46 o	**29.41**	22.10	4.8	4.1	30	21.3	16.7	115.0
detroit	151.11	283.02	151.73	3.6	19.3	30	11.5	61.9	94.2
echoMonths	72.99	71.40	70.55	3.8	3.8	30	11.7	10.9	89.3
elusage	49.91	49.52	48.76	6.0	7.2	30	16.0	21.0	83.2
fishcatch	19.84	24.40	21.24	7.5	3.7	30	26.9	13.0	106.7
gascons	25.50	30.09	25.24	5.2	9.1	30	19.5	35.8	115.2
housing	41.57	45.03	43.16	7.3	5.2	30	28.5	21.2	123.7
hungarian	74.99	75.10	74.36	4.7	5.2	30	15.3	17.8	102.2
kidney	78.38	82.08	81.29	4.6	5.2	30	12.9	16.0	91.2
longley	47.35	61.70	49.97	5.0	12.5	30	16.4	39.8	102.1
lowbwt	63.02	64.00	61.62	4.4	3.9	30	13.8	11.6	92.3
meta	149.15	147.21	112.30	1.6	3.9	30	4.8	14.3	94.2
newton-hema	85.56	85.20	82.78	3.9	5.4	30	13.2	17.4	97.1
pbc	84.45	85.07	84.24	4.9	6.1	30	18.2	24.5	116.6
pollution	71.70	77.01	72.06	5.8	4.6	30	18.8	16.2	101.5
pwLinear	● **48.92**	55.53	53.93	5.0	3.8	30	14.0	12.9	96.8
quake	100.00	99.78	99.54	3.5	6.2	30	18.0	28.3	132.6
schlvote	84.32 o	110.16	79.01	2.9	12.6	30	8.4	36.4	84.8
sensory	● **84.82**	86.99	86.97	5.4	5.8	30	16.7	20.7	103.7
servo	37.66	44.59	43.44	3.9	7.0	30	10.9	23.3	94.0
sleep	82.01	80.57	77.49	4.3	4.5	30	11.9	13.3	90.0
socmob	● **37.24**	41.23	39.81	6.5	4.4	30	19.9	15.7	100.0
stanford	92.16	95.82	88.37	4.1	6.9	30	12.6	21.8	91.7
strike	88.44	87.79	80.79	3.3	4.8	30	11.8	16.9	111.8
strikes	● **0.41**	8.95	4.42	1.4	10.0	30	2.9	21.9	66.0
veteran	97.46	93.98	91.51	3.3	4.3	30	10.3	13.5	94.8
vineyard	62.82	63.97	62.57	4.5	8.1	30	14.2	24.1	95.1
vinnie	● **50.89**	52.39	51.30	7.7	4.5	30	23.5	13.3	88.4
visualizing-galaxy	15.60	16.31	15.65	10.5	5.7	30	42.7	23.6	126.0
winequality-red	77.08	77.98	77.39	7.4	9.8	30	40.2	57.8	166.1
winequality-white	76.13	76.75	76.39	9.0	15.4	30	63.4	106.1	215.1
Average	63.53	69.79	62.65	5.2	6.2	30	19.0	23.2	106.7

(win/tie/loss); avg vs. nnls: 0/37/5; avg vs. ce: 3/39/0;

● o, BES-OOB-avg is significantly worse or better, respectively; at significance level 0.05

The final ensemble size for BES-OOB-avg is 30 (equal to the number of bagging iterations). Over the 42 data sets, the average final ensemble size of BES-OOB-ce is 6.2, corresponding to a 70% reduction in terms of ensemble size; the average final ensemble size of BES-OOB-nnls is 5.2, corresponding to a 83% reduction in terms of ensemble size. The average final number of trees of BES-OOB-avg is 106.7, which is about 36% of the total 300 trees. The average final number of trees of BES-OOB-ce is 23.2, corresponding to a 78% ((106.7 - 23.2)/106.7) reduction in terms of number of trees; the average final number of trees of BES-OOB-nnls is 19.0, corresponding to a 82% reduction in terms of number of trees. Figure 7 shows the boxplot visualization for the ensemble sizes and the numbers of trees of BES-OOB-avg, BES-OOB-ce and BES-OOB-nnls. Notably, the BES-OOB-nnls method significantly outperforms the BES-OOB-avg method on 5 data sets (about 12% of the 42 data sets). This is a significant empirical result indicating that BES-OOB-nnls not only works well for ensemble pruning, but also could be used for further improving the predictive performance of the BES-OOB strategy.

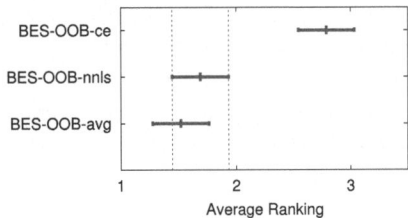

Fig. 6. The result of the *Friedman-test* over 42 data sets with two-tailed *Bonferroni-Dunn test* at significance level 0.05. Strategies having non-overlapped bars are significantly different.

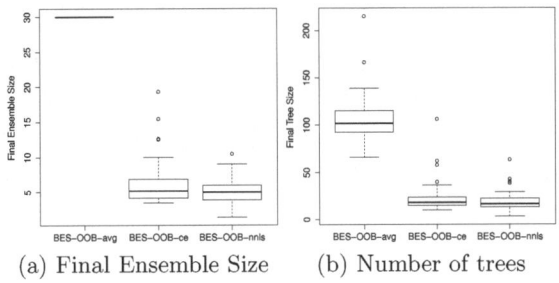

(a) Final Ensemble Size   (b) Number of trees

Fig. 7. The boxplot visualization for the final average ensemble sizes and the final average tree sizes

4   Conclusions

Bagging ensemble selection using the out-of-bag sample for hillclimbing (BES-OOB), is a relatively new ensemble learning strategy. In this paper, we studied the predictive performance of BES-OOB in the regression setting. The main contributions of this paper are:

- Previous studies focused on using BES-OOB for classification problems only. In this paper, through a series of experiments and statistical tests, we have shown that, in the regression setting, the BES-OOB strategy is competitive to MultiBoosting, and is superior to Bagging and Stochastic Gradient Boosting when using CART-like regression trees as the base learners.
- We have shown that using a diverse model library could further boost BES-OOB's predictive performance when the model library size is relatively large.
- Our results also have shown that both the cocktail ensemble and the stacking with NNLS methods work well for BES-OOB ensemble pruning. Particularly, the latter method can be also used to improve the predictive performance of the BES-OOB strategy.

One reason for the good predictive performance of the BES-OOB strategy is that it can optimise a user-specified error metric directly in the base learner selection stage. Out-of-bag samples seem to work well for ES's ensemble selection in practice. Another notable feature of BES-OOB is its simplicity and ease of implementation. The success of the BES-OOB ensemble strategy over a broad range of data sets examined in this study strongly suggests the applicability of the method to a wide range of problems.

References

1. Bauer, E., Kohavi, R.: An empirical comparison of voting classification algorithms: Bagging, boosting, and variants. Machine Learning 36(1-2), 105–139 (1999)
2. Breiman, L.: Bagging predictors. Machine Learning 24(2), 123–140 (1996)
3. Bryll, R., Gutierrez-Osuna, R., Quek, F.: Attribute bagging: Improving accuracy of classifier ensembles by using random feature subsets. Pattern Recognition 36(6), 1291–1302 (2003)
4. Buhlmann, P., van de Geer, S.: Statistics for High-Demensional Data: Methods, Theory and Applications. Springer (2011)
5. Caruana, R., Munson, A., Niculescu-Mizil, A.: Getting the most out of ensemble selection. In: Proceedings of the Sixth International Conference on Data Mining, ICDM 2006 (2006)
6. Caruana, R., Niculescu-Mizil, A., Crew, G., Ksikes, A.: Ensemble selection from libraries of models. In: Proceedings of the Twenty-First International Conference on Machine Learning, ICML 2004 (2004)
7. Demšar, J.: Statistical comparisons of classifiers over multiple data sets. Journal of Machine Learning Research 7, 1–30 (2006)
8. Friedman, J.H.: Stochastic gradient boosting. Computational Statistics and Data Analysis 38, 367–378 (1999)
9. Friedman, J.H.: Greedy function approximation: A gradient boosting machine. Annals of Statistics 29, 1189–1232 (2000)
10. Hall, M., Frank, E., Holmes, G., Pfahringer, B., Reutemann, P., Witten, I.: The weka data mining software: An update. SIGKDD Explorations 11(1) (2009)
11. Hernandez-Lobato, D., Martinez-Munoz, G., Suarez, A.: Pruning in ordered regression bagging ensembles. In: International Joint Conference on Neural Networks, IJCNN 2006, pp. 1266–1273 (2006)
12. Lawson, C., Hanson, R.: Solving Least-Squares Problems. Prentice-Hall (1974)
13. Quinlan, J.R.: Learning with continuous Classes. In: Proceedings of the 5th Australian Joint Conference on Artificial Intelligence, pp. 343–348 (1992)
14. Rokach, L.: Ensemble-based classifiers. Artificial Intelligence Review 33, 1–39 (2010)
15. Sun, Q., Pfahringer, B.: Bagging ensemble selection. In: Proceedings of the 24th Australasian Conference on Artificial Intelligence, pp. 251–260. Springer, Perth (2011)
16. Webb, G.I.: Multiboosting: A technique for combining boosting and wagging. Machine Learning 40(2) (2000)
17. Wolpert, D.H.: Stacked generalization. Neural Networks 5, 241–259 (1992)
18. Yu, Y., Zhou, Z.H., Ting, K.M.: Cocktail ensemble for regression. In: Seventh IEEE International Conference on Data Mining, ICDM 2007, pp. 721–726 (2007)
19. Zhou, Z.-H.: Ensemble Methods: Foundations and Algorithms. Chapman & Hall/CRC, Boca Raton, FL (2012)
20. Zhou, Z.H., Wu, J., Tang, W.: Ensembling neural networks: many could be better than all. Artificial Intelligence 137, 239–263 (2002)

Fixed Frame Temporal Pooling

John Thornton, Linda Main, and Andrew Srbic

Institute for Integrated and Intelligent Systems, Griffith University, QLD, Australia
{j.thornton,l.main}@griffith.edu.au, andrew.srbic@griffithuni.edu.au

Abstract. Applications of unsupervised learning techniques to action recognition have proved highly competitive in comparison to supervised and hand-crafted approaches, despite not being designed to handle image processing problems. Many of these techniques are either based on biological models of cognition or have responses that correlate to those observed in biological systems. In this study we apply (for the first time) an adaptation of the latest hierarchical temporal memory (HTM) cortical learning algorithms (CLAs) to the problem of action recognition. These HTM algorithms are both unsupervised and represent one of the most complete high-level syntheses available of the current neuroscientific understanding of the functioning of neocortex.

Specifically, we extend the latest HTM work on augmented spatial pooling, to produce a fixed frame temporal pooler (FFTP). This pooler is evaluated on the well-known KTH action recognition data set and in comparison with the best performing unsupervised learning algorithm for bag-of-features classification in the area: independent subspace analysis (ISA). Our results show FFTP comes within 2% of ISA's performance and outperforms other comparable techniques on this data set. We take these results to be promising, given the preliminary nature of the research and that the FFTP algorithm is only a partial implementation of the proposed HTM architecture.

1 Introduction

Recent work on action recognition has shown that general purpose unsupervised learning techniques can outperform more specialised approaches that rely on hand-crafted feature detectors. In particular, Le *et al.* [9] used independent subspace analysis (ISA) to learn invariant spatio-temporal features for action recognition, and produced the best pre-2012 bag-of-features recognition rates on a range of well-known benchmark datasets. Subsequently, several more sophisticated hand-crafted and supervised learning approaches have outperformed ISA on two of these datasets (e.g. see [16]). Nevertheless, ISA remains the state-of-the-art within the class of unsupervised learning algorithms that do not rely on additional higher-level information concerning the form of the input.

ISA is an extension of independent components analysis (ICA), and, like ICA, is able to learn receptive fields similar to those found in the V1 and MT areas of visual cortex [6]. This makes ISA a significant benchmark for the evaluation of any pattern recognition system that attempts to model the functioning of

M. Thielscher and D. Zhang (Eds.): AI 2012, LNCS 7691, pp. 707–718, 2012.
© Springer-Verlag Berlin Heidelberg 2012

visual cortex. One such system is the hierarchical temporal memory (HTM) architecture, originally proposed by Jeff Hawkins [4] and subsequently developed into a set of cortical learning algorithms (CLAs) [3].

In this paper we compare the performance of ISA with an adaptation of the latest version of the CLA spatial pooler. This pooler differs from ISA and ICA in being directly based on a biologically plausible learning model. The overall approach involves learning sparse distributed representations of the input by forming dendritic connections between functional units that model the minicolumns observed in human neocortex. These connections form in such a way that the column responses self-organise to produce sparse representations that have statistically interesting properties. A recent study has shown that an augmented CLA spatial pooler produces representations with significantly higher kurtosis values than those achieved by ICA on a well-known benchmark of greyscale images [15]. These higher values indicate a more evenly distributed response to the input data and a greater degree of statistical independence between the responses. Encouraging as such results are, they do not necessarily translate into better recognition rates. We therefore decided to compare this augmented spatial pooler with the state-of-the-art in the family of ICA algorithms: the ISA implementation of Le *et al.* [9].

To the best of our knowledge, no similar comparisons of the latest HTM cortical learning algorithms have been published. Instead, the majority of recent HTM papers still use the original NuPic implementation (e.g. [12]) made freely available by Numenta [2]. While some work has evaluated the question of parallelising the latest spatial and temporal pooler algorithms [11], there is no work we know of that tests these algorithms on standard vision processing tasks, such as action recognition.

The research here extends the previous statistical evaluation of the spatial pooler in [15], by adapting it to represent sequences of frames from movies. This is achieved by means of additively superimposing the responses to individual frames. Following the evaluation methodology used by Le *et al.*, we limited this superimposition to sequences of ten frames, producing a fixed frame temporal pooling (FFTP) algorithm that is considerably simpler than the temporal pooler proposed in [3]. We then compared the performance of FFTP to ISA on the well-known KTH action recognition data set. Our results show that FFTP comes within 2% of ISA's performance and outperforms the other directly comparable algorithms. We take this as a promising result given this is the first application of an HTM spatial pooler to the domain of moving images, and also given that the spatial pooler is only a single component within the HTM architecture. This means that the study is only a preliminary indication of the potential performance of a complete HTM implementation.

In the remainder of the paper we provide background on the original HTM spatial pooler and describe the enhancements proposed in [15]. We then introduce the fixed frame temporal pooling algorithm and evaluate its performance compared to ISA on the KTH dataset. These experiments follow the protocols developed by Wang *et al.* [17] that were used in the original ISA study [9].

2   Spatial Pooling

2.1   The HTM Architecture

The HTM model was originally introduced by Jeff Hawkins [4,5] and provides a framework within which the functioning of mammalian neocortex is understood in terms of a single algorithmic process. That process is a form of hierarchically-structured Bayesian-like predictive inference. The hierarchy itself consists of a set of regions, where each region consists of a set of columns. These columns correspond to the mini-columns observed within neocortex that Mountcastle identified as the basic functional units of neocortical processing [10]. Each column in turn consists of a set of neurons and their associated dendrites and synapses. According to HTM theory, these neurons control which columns in a region are currently active, and which columns are currently predicting they will become active.

Within each region, two functions are combined: a spatial pooler to form sparse representations of input, and a temporal pooler to learn temporal sequences. The two pooling functions form a single processing unit which is then replicated and arranged in a hierarchical structure. In this way, the HTM architecture is able to learn and exchange inferences about temporal sequences rather than just spatial patterns.

2.2   HTM Spatial Pooling

From the perspective of spatial pooling, a column can be considered as a unified entity with an associated set of proximal dendrites that synapse directly with the input (see [3]). These synapses are not associated with weights that multiplicatively determine the strength of the signal. Instead, each dendrite is associated with a potential synapse and each synapse is associated with a permanence value. If the permanence value of a synapse passes a certain threshold then the synapse is connected and the dendrite will directly relay the input to which it is connected, otherwise the synapse remains potential and inactive. The column then sums the inputs from all its connected synapses to determine its level of activity.

A spatial pooler learns on the basis of how well the synapses from a particular column match (or overlap) the input to which the synapses are connected. Instead of altering the relative weights of the synapses of neighbouring columns, a strongly activated column will compete with and inhibit its less active neighbours, implementing the function of short-range inter-columnar inhibition neurons [14]. At the end of this process, only the potential synapses belonging to the winning columns that best represent the current input will be able to learn. Here learning entails increasing the permanence values of potential synapses that are connected to active input and decreasing the permanence values of those connected to inactive input. This implements the forming and un-forming of synaptic connections discussed above.

2.3   Augmented Spatial Pooling

The augmented spatial pooler (ASP) introduced in [15] alters the learning algorithm of the original HTM spatial pooler in order that stable representations of greyscale images can be formed. The original spatial pooler was designed to encode binary input and failed to reliably converge on greyscale input. This original learning algorithm additively boosts the response of columns whose average *activity* falls below a predefined threshold (otherwise the boost value is set to one) and increases the permanence values of all potential synapses of columns whose *response* falls below the same threshold. The augmented spatial pooler will similarly boost the output of all columns whose activity falls below the threshold but only up to a predefined maximum boost value. Once that value is reached, the column boost is reset to one, and the closest disconnected column synapse with the largest permanence value has that value increased to the point where it becomes connected. This forcing of a connection significantly improves the convergence behaviour of the pooler on both binary and greyscale input.

Figure 1 shows a matrix of 16×16 ASP columns and their associated synapse connections after training on a set of greyscale images (see [15] for details). Here each of the 256 squares represents a column, and each of the 256 pixels in an individual square represents a synapse belonging to the associated column.

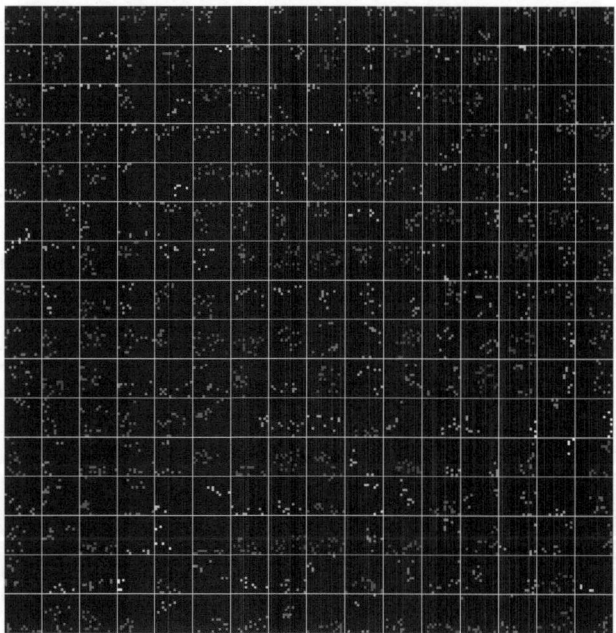

Fig. 1. Image filters for 256 ASP columns after training on a set of greyscale photographs of natural scenes (taken from [15]). Each square represents a column and each dot within a square represents a connected synapse.

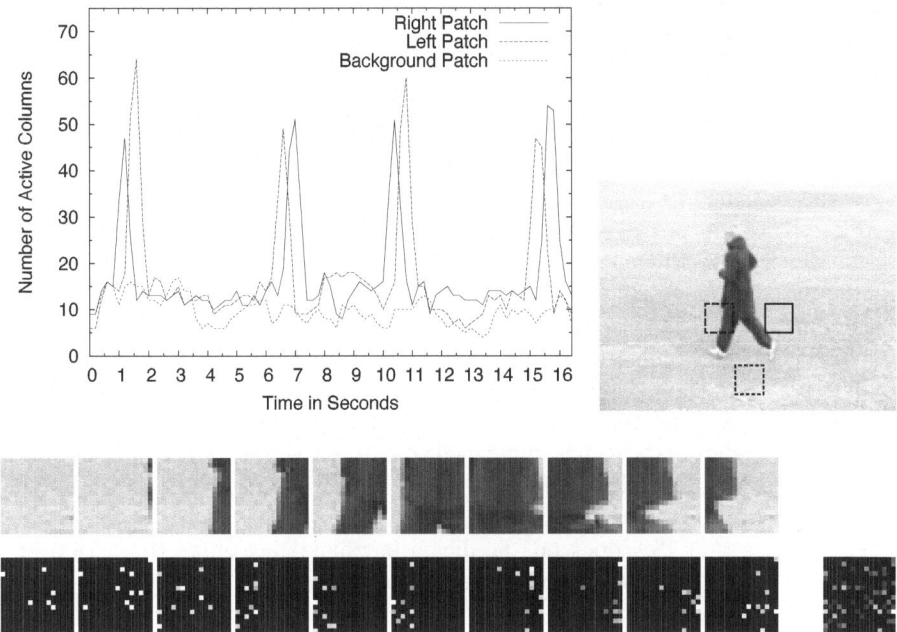

Fig. 2. Top left: Graph showing the number of active spatial pooler columns per unit time as the pooler processes a movie of a man jogging back and forth across a field. **Top right**: A full frame from the movie, showing the three patches from which the graph data is collected. **Second row from bottom**: a sequence of ten image patches taken from the left-hand patch position of the full frame image. **Bottom row**: Column responses of the FFTP algorithm where each response corresponds to the image immediately above the response. **Bottom right**: The superimposed stacked code produced from the ten preceding responses (this is the final output of the FFTP algorithm).

A disconnected synapse is represented by a black pixel, otherwise all non-black pixels represent connected synapses, where the intensity of a pixel represents the boost value of the associated column. This diagram illustrates the relative sparsity and simplicity of the image filters produced by a set of columns and should be contrasted with the correspondingly more complex filters produced by ISA (for example see Figure 2 from [9]).

3   Fixed Frame Temporal Pooling

The temporal pooler proposed in the most recent HTM technical report [3] implements a new column structure consisting of four cells, where each cell is laterally connected to other cells within the same region. These connections again consist of synapses whose permanence values are learnt according to the responses of the spatial pooler and the subsequent activity of the temporal pooler. The task of the temporal pooler is to predict the sequence of columns that will become active in the immediate future, according to the current and past activity of the columns. This prediction produces a pattern of responses where the currently active columns are co-active with the columns that are expected to become active in succeeding time intervals (see [3] for details).

In the current study we are interested in a direct comparison between the sparse representations produced by ASP and the responses of the ISA filters. Originally ISA was developed to handle static images, and was converted to handle moving images by altering the *form* of the input. This involved taking static image patches (typically 16×16 pixels) and arranging them in *temporal stacks*. These stacks consist of ten patches that represent a time 'tunnel' through a video, where the first patch is taken from location x_1, y_1 of the first video frame, the second patch is taken from location x_1, y_1 of the second video frame, and so on. These ten patches are then 'flattened' to form a single image that becomes the input to an ISA unit. The units themselves are convolved to overlap the entire video frame (see [9] for full details).

This means that ISA does not predict a particular action as the action unfolds. Instead it computes its responses retrospectively. In order to compute a comparable representation using ASP, rather than flattening a temporal input stack to form a single image, we decided to additively superimpose the ASP responses to each image patch in a ten patch stack, producing a single response for the entire stack (see the bottom right of Figure 2 below). This form of temporal pooling thereby combines the ASP responses to a *fixed* sequence of temporally ordered video frame patches (hence the name *Fixed Frame Temporal Pooling* or FFTP).

The FFTP algorithm is of a different and lower order of complexity compared to the full temporal pooler, in that FFTP performs no further learning, and simply combines the outputs of the spatial pooler in the temporal dimension. However, the representations of the two temporal poolers will still be similar. The main differences are that the full temporal pooler will *dynamically* predict a future sequence of frames and that the number of frames encompassed in that prediction will *vary* according to the strength of the learned connections. In contrast, FFTP firstly has the future data already available and so is not required to predict future input, and secondly, it has the time dimension of its representation fixed in advance (in this case to ten consecutive frames).

However, in combining the responses of the spatial pooler to form a temporal representation there are several possibilities in terms of how the column outputs are measured. Firstly, consider a spatial pooler comprising 16×16 columns arranged in a two-dimensional grid that corresponds to a 16×16 pixel input patch. Once the spatial pooler has converged it will produce stable responses to given input patches (i.e. the same set of columns will become active given the same input pattern). This response forms a sparse distributed representation of the original patch that then becomes the input for the temporal pooler. Given ten input patches we obtain ten corresponding sparse representations that are then combined to form a single 16×16 temporally pooled response (as per the diagram on the bottom right of Figure 2). There are now three possible ways we can combine these column activities:

1. Each column is represented using a binary code, where 0 indicates the column has been inactive during the entire ten frame sequence, and 1 indicates the column has been active at least once. We term this the *Binary* code.
2. Each column is represented according to a $0 - 10$ count of how many times it has been active during the entire ten frame sequence. We term this the *Count* code.
3. Each column is represented according to the *Count* code *multiplied* by the boost value for that column. We term this the *Boost* code.[1]

The pseudocode detailing the calculation of these three measures is shown in Algorithm 1. Here *code* specifies the measure and *pooledOutput* specifies the temporally pooled column outputs that form the input to Wang *et al.*'s pipeline (described in Section 4).

Algorithm 1 FixedFrameTemporalPooler(*columns, stacks, code, boost*)

---
for each c in *columns* **do** *pooledOutput*$(c) = 0$
for each s in *stacks* **do**
  for each *patch* in s **do**
    for each c in *columns* **do**
      if c is active in *patch* **then**
        if *code* is *Binary* **then** *pooledOutput*$(c) = 1$
        else *pooledOutput*$(c) = $ *pooledOutput*$(c) + 1$
      end if
    end for
  end for
  if *code* is *Boost* **then**
    for each c in *columns* **do** *pooledOutput*$(c) = $ *pooledOutput*$(c) \times$ *boost*(c)
  end if
end for
return *pooledOutput*

Figure 2 gives a pictorial illustration of the functioning of FFTP. The first ten images on the bottom row show the augmented spatial pooler's response to the static image patch appearing immediately above each response. For example, the bottom left response represents the outputs of the 256 columns, arranged in a 16×16 matrix. If a column is inactive it is represented as a black pixel, otherwise the boost activity is represented by the lightness of the pixel intensity. Note that

---

[1] The boost value for the column represents the amount the output of the column needs to be increased in order for it to exceed the activity threshold described earlier. It is this boost value in combination with the growth of new synapses that ensures the spatial pooler representations are distributed relatively evenly across all columns.

these images differ from those in Figure 1, in that now each pixel represents whether or not a *column* is *active,* whereas in Figure 1 each pixel represented whether or not a *synapse* for a particular column is *connected.*

The ten images on the second row up from the bottom of the figure form a stack of temporally consecutive instants taken from a KTH movie of a man jogging. A complete frame from this movie is shown in the top right of the figure. The ten images themselves show the man jogging through the patch appearing immediately to his left in the complete frame. The overall output of the FFTP algorithm for this image stack is represented in the eleventh image at the bottom right of the figure. This shows the summed value of the ten responses (using the *Boost* code). It is these summed values that become the input to Wang *et al.*'s pipeline in the experimental study.

The graph in the top left of Figure 2 shows how the number of active columns varies in proportion to the amount of activity that is occurring in the image. Here each point in the graph represents a count of the number of columns that respond to a particular stack of image patches. The stacks are ordered consecutively in time and represent what occurs in each of the three patches shown in the complete frame, i.e. as the man jogs across the field. Note the borders of the patches on the complete frame are the key to the graph plots. For example, the patch appearing at the bottom of the complete frame is represented by the dotted line in the graph that has the lowest column counts. These low counts show that very little change occurs in the corresponding patch as the man jogs across the field. In contrast, the peaks on the other two plots correspond to those portions of the movie where the man jogs through the patches that the plots are representing. More specifically, the plot shows the man jogging across the field four times, first from right to left, then left to right, and so on. The first graph peak therefore corresponds to the man first passing through the right patch, the second to his passing through the left patch, the third to his running back and passing through the left patch, then the right, and so on. This shows how the number of active columns is correlated to the number and degree of change occurring in the image pixels.

4   Experimental Study

In order to make direct comparisons between our FFTP encodings and previous work in the area, we decided to use Wang *et al.*'s pipeline [17][2] (the same pipeline is reported in the Le *et al.* ISA study). This pipeline takes the features determined by an external feature detection algorithm (e.g. ISA or FFTP), performs K-means vector quantisation, and finally classifies using a χ^2 kernel SVM for each action category.

---

[2] Available at http://au.stanford.edu/~wzou/

We further decided to evaluate our algorithm on the widely studied KTH dataset [13].[3] This set contains greyscale videos of six human action types (walking, jogging, running, boxing, handwaving and handclapping). The actions are performed several times by 25 different people, and recorded in four different settings; three outdoors and one indoors, making an approximate total of 600 videos, each containing an average of 484 frames. The videos are divided into a test set: (persons 2, 3, 5, 6, 7, 8, 9, 10, and 12) and a training set (the remaining 16 people).[4] We chose this dataset because it is one of the most widely reported in the literature and, as it is encoded in greyscale, it did not require any modifications to the existing augmented spatial pooler (see Figure 2 for an example KTH movie image).

Following the protocol used in [9] and [17], we trained the augmented spatial pooler on 200,000 randomly selected stacks of ten 16×16 pixel patches, densely sampled with a 50% overlap horizontally, vertically, and temporally (note: sampling was set to avoid selecting sequences that went over the end of a movie clip). The trained spatial pooler was then used to generate stacked responses to the full set of image patches, and these stacked codes became the input for Wang *at al.*'s pipeline. Within the pipeline, the K-means clustering algorithm was trained on 3,000,000 of the ASP stacked codes (generated from the original training split) to form 3,000 centroids (identical settings were used to generate the ISA results). Mean accuracy was then calculated by averaging the accuracy of six SVM classifiers (one for each action class), over three runs of K-means, using stacked codes generated on the original test set (again following the protocol used in [9] and [17]).

Table 1 presents the accuracy results for the three versions of FFTP tested, for ISA, and for the four other comparable techniques reported in Wang *et al.*'s study [17]. These results firstly show that FFTP (using *Boost*) comes close to matching ISA's performance (falling short by 1.7%). To verify this difference we performed a one-tailed independent two-sample t-test on the three accuracy results for FFTP *Boost* and for the three ISA results.[5] This confirmed the hypothesis that the mean accuracy of ISA is greater than the mean accuracy of FFTP *Boost* at a 1.5% level of significance.

It should be noted that in order to make a direct comparison between FFTP and ISA we did not test the second level hierarchy developed by Le *et al.* or use their norm-thresholding heuristic (see [9] for details). Nevertheless, we obtained slightly better results for ISA (94.5% versus 93.9%) in comparison to those reported in [9] (where both the hierarchy and the thresholding were employed).

Table 1 also shows that, of the three FFTP coding methods tested, *Boost* has the slightly better performance, followed by *Count*, with *Binary* coming third. This indicates that more fine grained information concerning the level of activity in each column provides useful information to the classifiers and contributes to better recognition rates. However, given the small sample sizes on

---

[3] Available at http://www.nada.kth.se/cvap/actions/

[4] This training/test set split follows the protocol defined in the Appendix of [9].

[5] FFTP *Boost* accuracy standard deviation was 0.3086 and ISA was 0.1782.

Table 1. Average accuracy on the KTH data set. The FFTP and ISA results were produced by us using Wang *et al.*'s pipeline. The other results (HOG3D [7], HOF and HOG [8]) were the comparable algorithms with dense sampling produced by Wang *et al.* in [17].

Algorithm	FFTP			Dense				ISA
	Boost	Count	Binary	HOG3D	HOG/HOF	HOG	HOF	
Accuracy %	**92.8**	92.7	92.4	85.3	86.1	79.0	88.0	**94.5**

which the average accuracy is based, these relative differences did not turn out to be statistically significant.

Lastly, FFTP shows notably improved performance over the four other comparable techniques that use dense sampling, reported in the Wang *et al.* study (HOG3D [7], HOG/HOF, HOG and HOF [8]). However, if we widen our consideration to include supervised learning techniques and techniques that employ interest point detectors, there have been some notable developments since the publication of Le *et al.*'s 2011 study. For example, Wang *et al.* [16] have developed a new supervised dictionary learning technique that outperforms ISA by 0.27%, meaning ISA is no longer the state-of-the-art on KTH. Nevertheless, it remains the best *unsupervised* learning technique that does not use interest point detectors, and so remains the most relevant technique for an evaluation of FFTP. This is because FFTP is also a pure unsupervised learning technique that plays the role of a *component* within an HTM architecture. The HTM architecture itself is designed to learn higher level features (without supervision) and then to feedback this higher level contextual information to the lower level spatial and temporal pooler representations. Following the principle of comparing like with like, it would not be equitable to compare an HTM component with Wang *et al.*'s new supervised learning architecture. Instead, it is the aim of this study to evaluate FFTP as a way of encoding image patches for *subsequent* recognition (hence the use of Wang *et al.*'s pipeline), rather than evaluate the recognition performance of an entire HTM. That task we leave for future work.

5   Discussion and Conclusions

The fact that FFTP produces results that are closely comparable with ISA is encouraging. Firstly, we should consider that this is the first application and evaluation of the new HTM spatial pooler on action recognition in the literature. FFTP is also unusual in not using a mathematical technique to optimise an objective function. It rather distributes the codes across columns according to a biologically inspired procedure of lateral inhibition and competition. This makes the system more adaptable than an optimiser, as it can adjust its representations in real time according to the input it receives (this kind of flexibility is also observed in the neurodynamics of natural systems [1]). In addition, unlike standard neural network algorithms, FFTP learns by forming and un-forming synaptic connections instead of adjusting the weights of those connections. This procedure receives support from the the observation that real synaptic transmission is too stochastic to provide the kind of fine distinction that many artificial neural network algorithms require [14].

It should also be remembered that the ISA algorithm is the result of nearly two decades of intensive research into the development of ICA related techniques. In contrast, the HTM spatial pooler was proposed in 2010 and is only now being applied to action recognition. We therefore have a reasonable expectation that the performance of the family of HTM poolers will improve over time.

Next, we should emphasise that FFTP is a partial implementation of the full temporal pooler proposed in [3]. As such it only combines the output of the spatial pooler according to an artificial boundary of ten frames. The full temporal pooler is designed to learn common sequences of actions of variable length, and thereby discover for itself when a particular sequence starts and stops (according to how often such sequences are repeated as input). This more natural encoding should be more efficient and more representative of the underlying structure of action events. If such encodings can be produced, it is again reasonable to expect a positive effect on event recognition rates.

In conclusion, the current study represents a preliminary evaluation of a promising new technology. In that context, our having nearly matched the performance of the state-of-the-art in general purpose unsupervised learning is a strong indication that it is worth developing the technology further. Clearly, the next step is to develop and test a full (*non*-fixed frame) temporal pooler on the action recognition data sets and, if that proves successful, to build a hierarchy of such poolers.

References

1. Freeman, W.J.: How brains make up their minds. Columbia University Press, New York (2000)
2. George, D., Jaros, B.: The HTM learning algorithms. Tech. rep., Numenta, Inc., Palto Alto (2007),
   www.numenta.com/htm-overview/education/Numenta_HTM_Learning_Algos.pdf
3. Hawkins, J., Ahmad, S., Dubinsky, D.: Hierarchical temporal memory including HTM cortical learning algorithms. Tech. rep., Numenta, Inc., Palto Alto (2010),
   www.numenta.com/htm-overview/education/
   HTM_CorticalLearningAlgorithms.pdf
4. Hawkins, J., Blakeslee, S.: On intelligence. Henry Holt, New York (2004)
5. Hawkins, J., George, D.: Hierarchical temporal memory: Concepts, theory and terminology. Tech. rep., Numenta, Inc., Palto Alto (2006),
   www.numenta.com/htm-overview/education/Numenta_HTM_Concepts.pdf
6. Hyvärinen, A., Hurri, J., Hoyer, P.: Natural Image Statistics: A probabilistic approach to early computational vision. Springer-Verlag New York Inc. (2009)
7. Kläser, A., Marszalek, M., Schmid, C.: A spatio-temporal descriptor based on 3D-gradients. In: British Machine Vision Conference, BMVC 2008, pp. 995–1004 (2008)
8. Laptev, I., Marszalek, M., Schmid, C., Rozenfeld, B.: Learning realistic human actions from movies. In: Proceedings of the 2008 IEEE Conference on Computer Vision and Pattern Recognition (CVPR 2008), pp. 1–8 (2008)

9. Le, Q., Zou, W., Yeung, S., Ng, A.: Learning hierarchical invariant spatio-temporal features for action recognition with independent subspace analysis. In: Proceedings of the 2011 IEEE Conference on Computer Vision and Pattern Recognition (CVPR 2011), pp. 3361–3368 (2011)

10. Mountcastle, V.B.: Introduction to the special issue on computation in cortical columns. Cerebral Cortex 13(1), 2–4 (2003)

11. Price, R.W.: Hierarchical Temporal Memory Cortical Learning Algorithm for Pattern Recognition on Multi-core Architectures. Master's thesis, Portland State University (2011)

12. Rozado, D., Rodriguez, F.B., Varona, P.: Extending the bioinspired hierarchical temporal memory paradigm for sign language recognition. Neurocomputing 79, 75–86 (2012)

13. Schuldt, C., Laptev, I., Caputo, B.: Recognizing human actions: A local SVM approach. In: Proceedings of International Conference on Pattern Recognition (ICPR 2004), p. 3361, 3362, 3366 (2004)

14. Stuart, G., Spruston, N., Häusser, M.: Dendrites. Oxford University Press, New York (2008)

15. Thornton, J., Srbic, A.: Spatial pooling for greyscale images. International Journal of Machine Learning and Cybernetics 2, 1–10 (2012)

16. Wang, H., Yuan, C., Hu, W., Sun, C.: Supervised class-specific dictionary learning for sparse modeling in action recognition. Pattern Recognition 45, 3902–3911 (2012)

17. Wang, H., Ulla, M., Klaser, A., Laptev, I., Schmid, C.: Evaluation of local spatio-temporal features for action recognition. In: British Machine Vision Conference, BMVC 2009, pp. 127–138 (2009)

DIKEA: Domain-Independent Keyphrase Extraction Algorithm

David X. Wang, Xiaoying Gao, and Peter Andreae

School of Engineering and Computer Science,
Victoria University of Wellington, New Zealand
{david.wang,xiaoying.gao,peter.andreae}@ecs.vuw.ac.nz

Abstract. This paper introduces a new domain-independent keyphrase extraction system (DIKEA). Keyphrase extraction is a challenging problem that automatically extracts or assigns keyphrases to documents and it can benefit many research areas such as information retrieval, particularly indexing, clustering, and summarization. A landmark research KEA (Keyphrase Extraction Algorithm) formulated the problem as a supervised machine learning problem and successfully applied a Naïve Bayes model to it, which showed great promise but the performance is not satisfactory. Its state-of-the-art extension KEA++ has a significantly improved performance but relies on a domain specific vocabulary which is often not available or not complete. This paper introduces a novel domain-independent approach and has three main contributions: utilising the largest online knowledge source—Wikipedia—for keyphrase candidate selection; presenting new features for keyphrase evaluation, including a Wikipedia-based feature–link probability; and evaluating a number of different learning algorithms, including multi-layer perceptrons, for keyphrase selection. Experiments show that our system clearly outperforms KEA and closely matches the performance of KEA++, without requiring any domain-specific knowledge such as KEA++'s vocabulary list.

1 Introduction

Keyphrases provide insight into the contents of a document. Similar in purpose to an abstract, they introduce the topic of the document but more concisely, and can be easily indexed. Such keyphrases are highly beneficial for large document collections such as the ACM Digital Library. They are also particularly useful for document retrieval systems, where they can be used as the basis for documents indexing; collection browsing, by creating a hierarchical structure of keyphrases; and document clustering, by representing documents as a weighted vector of keyphrases.

Usually, keyphrases are assigned manually by either the authors themselves or by professional indexers. The problem is that producing high-quality keyphrases manually is expensive and time-consuming as it requires individuals with knowledge of a document's subject matter. As a result, the great majority of

M. Thielscher and D. Zhang (Eds.): AI 2012, LNCS 7691, pp. 719–730, 2012.

documents such as web pages come without keyphrases, putting automatic keyphrase extraction techniques in great demand.

Automatic keyphrase extraction is a very challenging task. In fact, research has found that the agreement between even human labelling is low [1]. Many research fields are related to keyphrase extraction; for example, information retrieval systems typically weight all terms using TF.IDF, many feature selection methods such as Information Gain and Chi-square can be applied to select key terms for document representation, and keyphrase extraction may be considered as a kind of information extraction. However, keyphrase extraction as a separate field is not very well studied, probably due to the lack of testing data. In 1999, a landmark research KEA (Keyphrase extraction algorithm) [1] formulated keyphrase extraction as a supervised machine learning algorithm and successfully applied Naïve Bayes learning to this problem and provided the benchmark testing data. There has been much research to further improve KEA [2,3,4] and its state-of-the-art extension KEA++ [5,6] significantly improve its performance. However, KEA++ relies on a domain specific vocabulary which is supposed to include all the descriptive phrases for a particular domain. In reality, such a vocabulary is often either unavailable or incomplete, and in those cases where a vocabulary is available, it may not be updated with time.

Our research aims to introduce a new domain-independent approach to the problem that does not require a domain specific vocabulary. We have chosen to use Wikipedia as an external, domain-independent resource because it is currently the largest, reliable and keep growing source available online. Our main goal is to develop an efficient and effective system to exploit the knowledge in Wikipedia for domain-independent keyphrase extraction. Previously KEA and KEA++ used features such as Tf.Idf and phrase length, and applied a Naïve Bayes learning model. We investigate new features especially Wikipedia-based features, and apply a number of learning algorithms including linear regression and neural networks.

The rest of this paper is organised as follows. Section 2 outlines related work and details two existing systems KEA and KEA++. Section 3 provides an overview of our domain independent approach, while Section 4 provides details regarding the new features introduced and other learning algorithms applied. Methods for empirical evaluation and results are presented and analysed in Section 5. Finally, Section 6 concludes and discusses future work.

2   Related work

Wikipedia as one of the largest online information resource has been found helpful for query expansion[7], semantic relatedness analysis [8], document clustering [9], and information retrieval [10] and many other areas. Our research is motivated by Huang et al. [9] which introduces a Wikipedia-based concept representation for documents and shows it improves document clustering performance. It matches terms in a document with Wikipedia anchor texts to identify the concepts and then represents each document as a weighted vector of concepts. Our system is similar in that we use Wikipedia anchor texts to select the candidate keyphrases from a document. Giving the big size and great coverage of the vocabulary of Wikipedia anchor texts and its expanding nature, our Wikipedia-based approach is domain independent and it works uniformly for different domains.

There have been a number different approaches to automatic keyphrase extraction [11]. [12] is an early machine learning approach for keyword extraction. Liu et al. [13] uses clustering to find exemplar terms and it shows clustering is helpful to identify good phrases that is the centre of a group of terms. [14] is another statistical based approach that can extract keywords from each single document without a corpus, and its performance is comparable to TF.IDF. Our approach is a supervised machine learning approach and the most closely related systems are KEA [1] and KEA++ [5].

KEA (Keyphrase Extraction Algorithm) [1] formulates keyphrase extraction as a supervised machine learning problem, and it does not require any prior knowledge of the document's domain. KEA++ [5] is the current state-of-the-art version of KEA, but it does so at a cost to domain-independence.

The rest of this section will detail KEA and KEA++. The following three subsections will briefly cover the three key steps of both KEA and KEA++ and identify rooms for further improvements. The comparison results between our system and the two systems are given in section 5.

2.1   Candidate Identification

The Candidate Identification step extracts candidate keyphrases from the document being summarised. The original KEA algorithm simply extracts all possible unigrams, bigrams and trigrams within phrase boundaries that occur at least twice in the document. Phrase boundaries are defined to be brackets, punctuation marks or numbers. After this, candidates which start or end with a stopword are removed and those that only contain a single proper noun are also removed. Finally, candidates are converted to lower case and stemmed using a Lovins Stemmer [15].

KEA++ improves on this by comparing candidate phrases with a controlled vocabulary in the domain of the document which is known to be descriptive.

KEA's solution to this step is very simple, but will produce a huge number of candidate keyphrases (usually many times the amount of words there are in the document) and assumes that a descriptive keyphrase appears in the document as a consecutive sequence of words. KEA++ does much better, significantly reducing the number of extracted candidates. However, the controlled vocabulary used has to be tailored to the document's domain, which means the overall solution becomes domain-dependent.

2.2   Feature Calculation

Once candidate keyphrases have been selected, a series of features will be calculated for each candidate. KEA used two such features as follows.

TF.IDF – Term frequency multiplied by inverse document frequency. This measure gives an indication as to how often a term/phrase appears in the current document as well as how unique the term is among all documents.

First Occurrence – This measures when a candidate first appears in the current document. It is calculated as a ratio of how many words precede the candidate's first occurrence vs. how many words are in the entire document.

KEA++ introduces two additional features as follows.

Candidate Length – The length of a candidate in terms of number of words.

Node Degree – Represents the number of thesaurus links that connect a candidate to other candidates. If a document is on a particular topic, then it will likely cover most of the thesaurus terms from that topic. Therefore, candidates with higher node degree may be more significant.

There are several issues with the above features. The TF.IDF value is calculated based on documents in the training corpus, which may not work well if the corpus is not representative of the domain. Furthermore, TF.IDF is a product of two separate features – term frequency (TF) and inverse document frequency (IDF). We would like to explore whether more interesting results might be obtained by separating these features. Finally, the Node Degree feature uses the domain-specific vocabulary, again making the overall solution domain-dependent.

2.3   Training Model

The final step of KEA involves feeding all of this information (the features) into a Naïve Bayes model to learn a classifier. The trained model outputs the *goodness* of a particular candidate keyphrase from a previously unseen document. Candidates are then ranked by this value and a certain number of candidates are chosen from the top of the list to be the final extracted keyphrases.

Naïve Bayes assumes that each feature is independent from the rest, which we don't believe is true. We would like to investigate other learning algorithms, especially the algorithms that can directly use continuous data.

3   Domain Independent Approach

KEA++ outperforms KEA by over a factor of two in terms of both precision and recall [5]. However, it does so by sacrificing the domain-independent nature of KEA. Our aim is to create a new system which can match KEA++'s performance, while avoiding the need for anything domain-specific. To do so, we need to identify the key differences between KEA and KEA++.

One such key difference is the use of a controlled vocabulary to narrow down the number of candidates extracted in the initial step of the algorithm. Using the FAO dataset mentioned in Section 5.1, KEA++ extracts five times less candidates than KEA on average (2491 vs. 463). It does this with a minimal loss in **candidate recall**, which is the maximum recall obtained if all candidates are classified as keyphrases, in other words, the recall before machine learning is applied. This is achieved by only extracting candidates that are matched to a controlled vocabulary of approximately 27,000 terms which are known to be good descriptors of agricultural documents. Classifiers trained using this condensed set of candidates perform significantly better, because of the reduction in misleading non-sense phrases which are an artefact of extracting overlapping n-grams. Precision is also increased as a direct result of only having to filter a much smaller subset of candidates.

However, the KEA++ system will breakdown if it is supplied with a controlled vocabulary which does not represent a particular document's domain, or is only partially representative. This could happen if a document covers a topic that is broader than the vocabulary's domain, or there is simply no suitable vocabulary in existence. In the first scenario, candidate recall will be significantly lowered as a result of potentially good keyphrases being filtered out by the non-representative vocabulary. For the second scenario, the system will just revert back to KEA.

What we require is a vocabulary of phrases that do not conform to any particular domain, but rather represent descriptors of all topics known to humanity. DIKEA utilises Wikipedia to obtain this data, more specifically, it matches candidates to a vocabulary of Wikipedia anchor texts (with millions of terms). Anchor texts are internal hypertexts that link to Wikipedia articles, which is what makes them great descriptors for documents. Wikipedia Miner[16,17] is used to speed up this process, such that it barely slow down the system at all. While a broad vocabulary does not reduce the number of candidates as aggressively as one that is more specific, it still prunes out most non-sense phrases. Unlike KEA++, DIKEA treats documents from different domains in a uniform way. Furthermore, as new anchor texts are introduced to Wikipedia, our system will be able to update itself alongside the natural progression of human knowledge.

Another key difference between KEA++ and KEA is the addition of two candidate features – candidate length and node degree. The extra values gained from these features improve the trained classifier by 4 to 5 percent[5]. Node degree, while useful, relies on domain-specific data. Therefore, DIKEA will use all other candidate features from KEA++ except node degree, as well as a couple of new ones.

Standard deviation will be one of the new features. It measures the spread of a candidate phrase within the document. The motivation behind this is that a phrase which appears evenly throughout a document may hold a different significance (in terms of being a keyphrase) to a phrase which only appears in a single paragraph or section. Link probability [18] is the other new feature, which we use to measures the uniqueness of a phrase – in other words, how well a phrase can distinguish different documents. Link probability [18] is defined as the probability of a phrase being used as a link in all Wikipedia documents with the phrase. Equation (1) shows how link probability is calculated for a given phrase P.

$$LP(P) = \frac{|\{doc|doc \in Wikipedia, P \in doc, isLink(P)\}|}{|\{doc|doc \in Wikipedia, P \in doc\}|} \qquad (1)$$

In a way, link probability is similar to inverse document frequency. Both measure how well a phrase can distinguish different documents, but link probability is obtained through a corpus of all Wikipedia articles while inverse document frequency (at least in KEA's case) is calculated based on a much smaller training corpus.

The final set of candidate features are: Term Frequency, Inverse Document Frequency, Candidate Length, First Occurrence, Standard Deviation and Link Probability. Note how term frequency is separated from inverse document frequency, the reason behind this is discussed in Section 2.2.

The final improvement we made to KEA is to use a different classifier than simple Naïve Bayes. Two other classifier models, linear regression and multilayer perceptron network are tried and see Section 5.3 for experimental results.

4   DIKEA Details

This section introduces the implementation details of our system.

4.1   Obtaining Vocabulary and Link Probability

To be of any use, DIKEA needed to perform two aspects efficiently – matching candidate phrases to a vocabulary of Wikipedia anchor texts and calculating link probabilities. For both these steps, we employed a toolkit known as Wikipedia Miner[16,17] along with a data dump of Wikipedia as of 22nd July, 2011. A summary of the same data dump was also obtained from Wikipedia Miner's website. With both of these, the toolkit can then quickly match any given phrase to a known Wikipedia anchor text. If a match is found, the result is returned as a Wikipedia Label object, which contains a multitude of statistical data. One of which is conveniently link probability.

4.2   Candidate Pruning and Calculating New Features

After performing the initial candidate identification step using the original KEA system (see Section 2.1), Wikipedia Miner is used to attempt to match each candidate with a known Wikipedia anchor text. Those that fail to match are removed from the list of candidates. Link probabilities are calculated for the remaining candidates. At first, candidates with link probabilities less than a specified threshold (i.e. 0.005) were also removed in an attempt to further boost precision. While this method worked, the negative impact to recall was too great to justify its use.

When this step is performed on a large dataset of documents, the extra processing time taken by Wikipedia Miner is noticeable (See Section 5.3). However, we believe the slight sacrifice in speed is worth the increase in the quality of keyphrases extracted.

4.3   Calculating New Features and Training

When it comes to feature calculation, the four old features are done using the same method as KEA and KEA++. Link probabality is done in the first step. To calculate standard deviation, the different positions where a term occurs (number of words from the beginning) in the document is recorded during candidate identification. Each position is divided by the total document length and then the population standard deviation is calculated.

Using these six features, we trained a variety of classifiers to rank candidates in terms of their keyphrase-worthiness. These include the Naïve Bayes model used by both KEA and KEA++, linear regression and multilayer perceptron network. Since regression models readily accepts continuous data, the raw feature values could be used where Naïve Bayes requires an extra discretisation step. For the multilayer perceptron network, we tried many different number of layers and different number of hidden nodes. Our best multilayer perceptron network as shown in Figure 1 contains a single hidden layer and is trained for 250 epochs at a learning rate of 0.15. All training was done with the help of the Weka 3 data mining package[19].

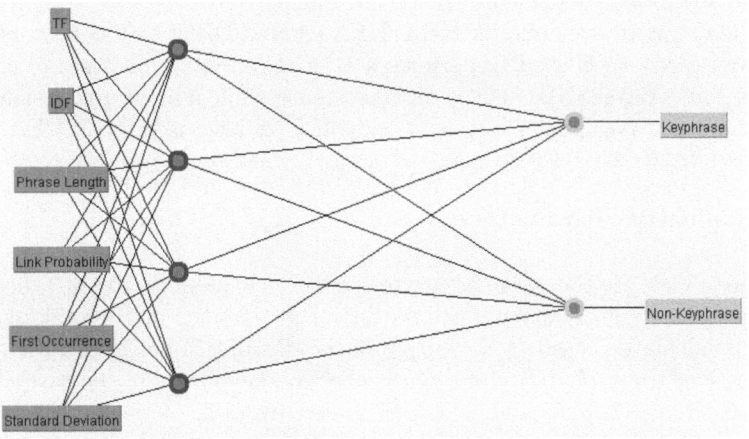

Fig. 1. Multilayer Perceptron Network model used by DIKEA

5   Evaluation

This section details our dataset, evaluation parameters and experimental results. Our results include a comparison of three different versions of our system with two existing systems KEA and KEA++, and an comparison of the contributions of different features.

5.1 Dataset

The data sets for evaluating keyword extraction are usually small and very hard to find because each document may contain hundreds to thousands of keyphrases which have to be manually labelled by professional indexers. Our dataset consists of 622 documents from the Food and Agriculture Organization of the United Nations (FAO), which are obtained from the Maui Indexer[20] project website. The original KEA and KEA++ papers test their system on a subset of this dataset with 25 and 200 documents respectively. We implemented the two existing systems and tested them on this relatively larger dataset.

These documents come with descriptive keyphrases which were manually assigned by professional indexers. All the assigned keyphrases are taken from a standardised vocabulary know as AGROVOC [21], which is the vocabulary given to KEA++.

Candidate keyphrases will then be extracted from these documents and their features calculated (see Section 4.3). Finally, each feature value will be either discretised or normalised (depending on the training model) and each candidate will be converted to a vector of either discreet integer or floating point values – each labelled as either a keyphrase or non-keyphrase according to the manually assigned keyphrases provided for each document.

The above steps are done for KEA, KEA++ and DIKEA. The vectors generated from each one is used to perform a 10-fold validation on a set of classifier models. Naïve Bayes (NB) is used on all systems; while a linear regression model (LR) and multilayer perceptron network (MLP) is also used for DIKEA.

5.2 Evaluation Parameters

In order to measure the performance of the trained classifier, the instances from each of the testing documents are fed into the classifier and a ranking of the phrase is calculated based on the output of the classifier, for example, the ranking of a phrase is the probability of a phrase being a keyphrase in the case of Naïve Bayes. Next, the top N instances are chosen by rank to be analysed. If two instances share the same rank (which can easily happen due to discretised feature values), the term frequency feature value will be used as a tie-breaker. Precision and recall is then calculated for each document and repeated for each fold to obtain an average.

Naturally, as N increases, precision will drop while recall rises. So in order to get a sense of the system's overall performance, N is tested at various values and a curve of precision and recall is plotted. We used two metrics to judge the performance. The first is the maximum F-Score over all recall intervals along the curve. The second metric involves plotting the best-fit curve of precision and recall on a graph and then taking the area under the curve.

We also consider three additional evolution criteria: Average Candidate Recall (Avg. C. R.) which is the maximum recall when all candidates are considered keyphrases; Average Candidates extracted per Document (Avg C/Doc) and Time.

5.3   Results and Analysis

The comparison results of KEA, KEA++ and three different versions of our system with Linear regression DIKEA(LR), Naïve Bayes DIKEA(NB) and multilayer perceptron networks DIKEA(MLP) are presented in Table 1.

Table 1. DIKEA's performance compared to KEA and KEA++

	KEA	KEA++	DIKEA(LR)	DIKEA(NB)	DIKEA(MLP)
Max. F-Score	0.210	0.301	0.267	0.273	0.281
Area	0.102	0.211	0.147	0.173	0.192
Avg. C.R.	0.671	0.629	0.619		
Avg. C/Doc	2491	463	1382		
Prep. Time	60 sec	116 sec	135 sec		

Our tests demonstrate clearly the significant improvement that DIKEA makes over KEA and how it comes close to matching the performance of KEA++ (as shown in Table 1). The first two rows are results gathered using the two metrics outlined in Section 5.2 – maximum F-Score and area under the curve. Both metrics reveal that DIKEA can closely match the performance of KEA++ (over 90%) when using a multilayer perceptron network for classification. By looking at Figure 2, which is the precision vs. recall plot for each system, it's even more apparent how similar DIKEA(MLP) performs to KEA++.

The next two rows of the table are the values for average candidate recall (Avg C. R.) and average candidates extracted per document (Avg C/Doc. As you can see, DIKEA can filter out a large number of candidate keyphrases while still maintaining almost the exact same candidate recall as KEA++. Also it is able to do so without having to know a document's domain. It is also obvious that DIKEA is much more conservative about which phrases are filtered out when compared to KEA++. This is expected as KEA++ knows beforehand exactly which phrases should be kept, thus making it perform slightly better than our system. It is also interesting to note that candidate recall(Maximum Recall) is only 0.671 for KEA, which doesn't filter candidates at all. The reason this value isn't simply 1.0 is because numerous documents in the dataset had manually labelled keyphrases that never appeared in the document.

The final row of the table presents the amount of time each system took to preprocess all 622 documents in the dataset. By using Wikipedia Miner and an efficient use of caching link probabilities, we were able to make our system run reasonably fast considering the heavy amount of processing that needs to be done – only 16% slower than KEA++.

We also wanted to know the exact contribution made by each of our chosen candidate features. The test was rerun on DIKEA system six times, with one of the six features excluded per run. By measuring the difference in performance with exclusion of each feature, we were able to determine their relative importance to the overall system – as shown in Figure 3. Our results reveals that term frequency and link probability contributes the majority of DIKEA's

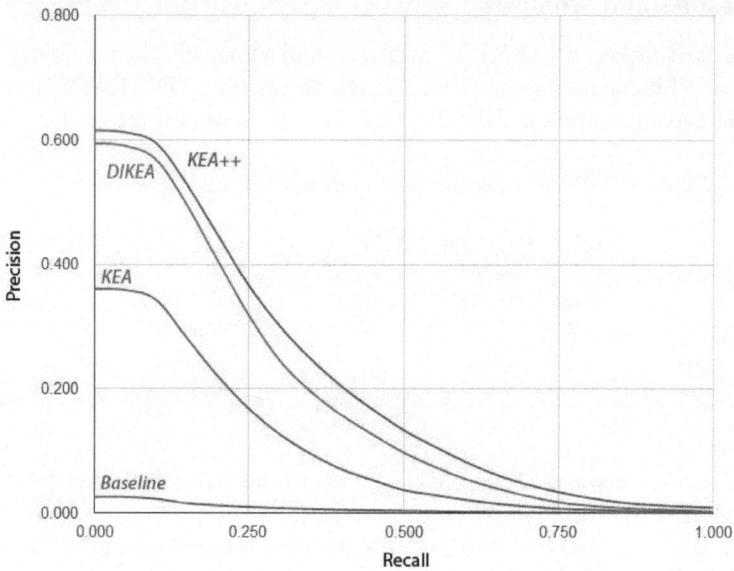

Fig. 2. Precision vs. Recall plot for KEA, KEA++ and DIKEA. Baseline only uses TFxIDF with no training.

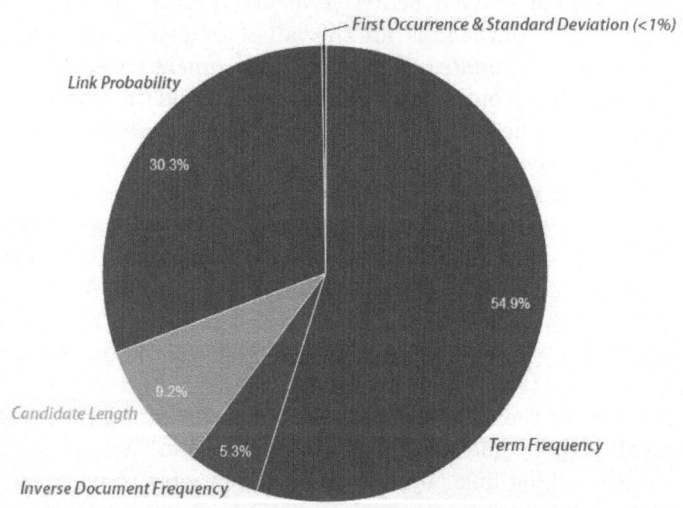

Fig. 3. Performance contribution of each candidate feature relative to each other

performance, at 54.9% and 30.3% respectively (relative to other features). Inverse document frequency only contributes a mere 5.3%, which confirms our theory that link probability is a much better alternative. What's surprising is the lack of importance from the standard deviation feature along with first occurrence.

This could either be an artefact of the dataset, or most likely, knowing the position and spread of a candidate within a document is of little use in determining its importance as a keyphrase.

6   Concluding Remarks and Future Work

Utilising Wikipedia, our DIKEA system provides a domain-independent solution to keyphrase extraction by processing all documents in a unified manner. Our system is able to closely match the performance of KEA++ without losing its domain independence. This is achieved by replacing the domain-specific vocabulary used by KEA++ with a vocabulary of Wikipedia anchor texts, adding new features and applying different learning algorithms. A further advantage of using our method is that our vocabulary can adapt to the natural evolution of human knowledge, as Wikipedia develops over time.

Although our approach is domain independent, out system is tested on domain-specific data. We will further evaluate our system on other datasets, for example, the recent datasets outlined in [11]. With the success of including link probability as a candidate feature (contributing over 30% of the performance in relation to other features), we intend to explore even more features to further improve DIKEA for future work. Another aspect of the system that can be improved is its low Candidate Recall: at just 62%, over one-third of human-labelled keyphrases could not possibly be identified by our system as they simply did not appear in the document. This is a problem common to KEA and KEA++ also, whose candidate recall is limited to 67% and 63% respectively. We will explore technologies to improve Candidate Recall. Another future work is to improve precision when only taking a relatively small portion of ranked candidates to be keyphrases (i.e. top ten to fifteen).

References

1. Witten, I.H., Paynter, G.W., Frank, E., Gutwin, C., Nevill-Manning, C.G.: Kea: practical automatic keyphrase extraction. In: Proceedings of the Fourth ACM Conference on Digital Libraries, DL 1999, pp. 254–255. ACM, New York (1999)
2. Turney, P.D.: Coherent keyphrase extraction via web mining. CoRR cs.LG/0308033 (2003)
3. Kelleher, D., Luz, S.: Automatic hypertext keyphrase detection. In: Kaelbling, L.P., Saffiotti, A. (eds.) IJCAI, pp. 1608–1609. Professional Book Center (2005)
4. Hulth, A.: Improved automatic keyword extraction given more linguistic knowledge. In: Proceedings of the Conference on Empirical Methods in Natural Language Processing (EMNLP), Japan (2003)
5. Medelyan, O., Witten, I.H.: Thesaurus based automatic keyphrase indexing. In: Proceedings of the 6th ACM/IEEE-CS Joint Conference on Digital Libraries, JCDL 2006, pp. 296–297. ACM, New York (2006)
6. Medelyan, O., Witten, I.H.: Domain independent automatic keyphrase indexing with small training sets. J. Am. Soc. Information Science and Technology (2008)

7. Xu, Y., Jones, G.J.F., Wang, B.: Query dependent pseudo-relevance feedback based on wikipedia. In: Allan, J., Aslam, J.A., Sanderson, M., Zhai, C., Zobel, J. (eds.) SIGIR, pp. 59–66. ACM (2009)

8. Gabrilovich, E., Markovitch, S.: Computing semantic relatedness using wikipedia-based explicit semantic analysis. In: Proceedings of the 20th International Joint Conference on Artifical Intelligence, IJCAI 2007, pp. 1606–1611. Morgan Kaufmann Publishers Inc., San Francisco (2007)

9. Huang, A., Milne, D., Frank, E., Witten, I.H.: Clustering Documents Using a Wikipedia-Based Concept Representation. In: Theeramunkong, T., Kijsirikul, B., Cercone, N., Ho, T.-B. (eds.) PAKDD 2009. LNCS, vol. 5476, pp. 628–636. Springer, Heidelberg (2009)

10. Egozi, O., Gabrilovich, E., Markovitch, S.: Concept-based feature generation and selection for information retrieval. In: Fox, D., Gomes, C.P. (eds.) AAAI, pp. 1132–1137. AAAI Press (2008)

11. Kim, S.N., Medelyan, O., Kan, M.Y., Baldwin, T.: Semeval-2010 task 5: Automatic keyphrase extraction from scientific articles. In: Proceedings of the 5th International Workshop on Semantic Evaluation, SemEval 2010, pp. 21–26. Association for Computational Linguistics, Stroudsburg (2010)

12. Turney, P.D.: Learning algorithms for keyphrase extraction. Inf. Retr. 2(4), 303–336 (2000)

13. Liu, Z., Li, P., Zheng, Y., Sun, M.: Clustering to find exemplar terms for keyphrase extraction. In: Proceedings of the 2009 Conference on Empirical Methods in Natural Language Processing, EMNLP 2009, vol. 1, pp. 257–266. Association for Computational Linguistics, Stroudsburg (2009)

14. Matsuo, Y., Ishizuka, M.: Keyword extraction from a single document using word co-occurrence statistical information. International Journal on Artificial Intelligence Tools 13(1), 157–169 (2004)

15. Lovins, J.B.: Development of a stemming algorithm. Mechanical Translation and Computational Linguistics 11, 22–31 (1968)

16. University of Waikato, N.Z.: Wikipedia miner, http://wikipedia-miner.cms.waikato.ac.nz/index.html (accessed March 25, 2012)

17. Milne, D., Witten, I.: An open-source toolkit for mining Wikipedia. In: Proc. New Zealand Computer Science Research Student Conf., NZCSRSC, vol. 9 (2009)

18. Mihalcea, R., Csomai, A.: Wikify!: linking documents to encyclopedic knowledge. In: Silva, M.J., Laender, A.H.F., Baeza-Yates, R.A., McGuinness, D.L., Olstad, B., Olsen, Ø.H., Falcão, A.O. (eds.) CIKM, pp. 233–242. ACM (2007)

19. Bouckaert, R.R., Frank, E., Hall, M.A., Holmes, G., Pfahringer, B., Reutemann, P., Witten, I.H.: Weka—experiences with a java open-source project. J. Mach. Learn. Res. 11, 2533–2541 (2010)

20. Medelyan, O., Frank, E., Witten, I.H.: Human-competitive tagging using automatic keyphrase extraction. In: Proceedings of the 2009 Conference on Empirical Methods in Natural Language Processing, EMNLP 2009, vol. 3, pp. 1318–1327. Association for Computational Linguistics, Stroudsburg (2009)

21. Leatherdale, D.: Food, Agricultural Organisation of the United Nations, Commision of the European Communities: AGROVOC: a multilingual thesaurus of agricultural terminology. Agrovoc : thesaurus multilingue de terminologie agricole. Apimondia by arrangement with the CEC (1982)

Evolving Event Detectors in Multi-channel Sensor Data

Feng Xie, Andy Song, and Vic Ciesielski

RMIT University, Melbourne, VIC 3001, Australia
{feng.xie,andy.song,vic.ciesielski}@rmit.edu.au
http://www.rmit.edu.au/compsci

Abstract. Detecting events of interest in sensor data is crucial in many areas such as medical monitoring by body sensors. Current methods often require prior domain knowledge to be available. Moreover, it is difficult for them to find complex temporal patterns existing in multi-channel data. To overcome these drawbacks, we propose a Genetic Programming (GP) based event detection methodology which can directly take raw multi-channel data as input. By applying it to three event detection tasks with various event sizes and comparing with four typical classification methods, we can see that those detectors evolved by GP can handle raw data much better than other methods. With features manually defined based on domain knowledge, our method can also be comparable with others. The analysis of evolved detectors demonstrates that distinctive characteristics of the target events are captured by these GP detectors.

1 Introduction

In a dynamic environment sensors continuously produce data when monitoring objects. The sequences of data can be viewed as time series. As the state of an object changes, certain variations would occur in this temporal space. For instance, heart failure may be reflected as a sudden decrease of blood pressure, a feeling of fear may be shown due to intensive muscle contractions. In reality multiple channels of sensors are often used, each being a time series of its own. For example in the field of Activity Recognition(AR), human locomotion, e.g. walking, sitting and standing, and gestures, e.g. drinking water and closing a door, can be identified by the fluctuations in a group of sensor readings. These temporal variations of interest can be viewed as events of which the duration is the event size. Detection of these events in time series input from sensors is obviously important in many areas, and it is also the goal of this study.

The interest in detecting patterns from sequential recordings has been increasing in the past few years. A common approach is to extract distinctive features of an event and then to "query" matching subsequences from incoming input stream. In domains that the features are well established, this approach is widely adopted due to its effectiveness and simplicity in implementation [17,18]. However when the underlying knowledge of an event remains unknown, finding good features for that event would be a challenge. Furthermore features suitable

M. Thielscher and D. Zhang (Eds.): AI 2012, LNCS 7691, pp. 731–742, 2012.

for one problem may not be appropriate for another problem since the knowledge is often domain dependent. There are no universal features.

In order to eliminate the requirements of priori knowledge, some researchers proposed to construct mathematical models based on original data. The objective then becomes detecting any significant changes of the model or the parameters of that model, therefore, it is also known as change detection problem [13,14]. This approach is highly effective for fields in which significant changes are unusual, for example astronomy. These change point detection techniques tend to use relatively simple models, for example linear models. It would be very difficult for such techniques to handle complex events which consist of not just a single changing point but a series of changing points. Moreover, this approach mainly aims at solving univariate time series problems and consequently not suitable for events occurring in multiple channels, for example a single sensor can hardly contain the information for recognizing a gesture.

To address the issues in these existing works, we propose a GP-based method that is capable of detecting events directly from raw time series data. The event can be simple as a change between two adjacent points or complex as variation in multiple variables during a period of time. The data we investigated in this study is time series stream. Each time step is labelled positive or negative indicating whether the event of interest occurred or not. Therefore, it is reasonable to use a supervised learning method. This approach seems similar to two-class time series classification [16]. However in time series classification the data has to be segmented into non-overlapped, fixed-length vectors in advance. On the contrary, our method receives continuous streaming input so it has to determine at which point an event occurs. The particular research questions are addressed here:

1. How can a suitable GP representation be established so event detectors for multi-sensor input can be evovled when features are not available?
2. How does the performance of GP working on raw data compare to typical classification algorithms when features are available?
3. How would GP-evolved programs detect events? Are there any insight to reveal their behaviours?

The performance of the proposed method is evaluated on three tasks, including both synthetic and real world data sets. Additionally, J48 decision tree classifier, Naïve Bayes classifier, IB1 nearest neighbour classifier and AdaBoost meta classifier are used for comparison due to their popularity in the area of classification.

2   Related Work

GP has been proven to be a powerful problem solving mechanism in many domains, especially in those where human knowledge is limited [1,2,3]. It is not surprising that GP has a long history of being adopted to handle time series data. A great number of works are devoted to prediction based on past observations [4,6,7], but few studies are on time series detection.

Previous work has shown that GP is capable of working on raw data, even in sophisticated domains such as Computer Vision, for example, texture segmentation [19], video shot detection [8,22] and motion detection [5].

Another related area is novelty detection [15] which is to find unseen time sequences. It uses a sliding window to examine through all the possible subsequences to identify the most distinctive ones from the rest of time series. It has some overlaps with our work since it essentially considers an abnormality as an event. Unfortunately, all novelty detection algorithms require parameters to be known beforehand, at least the length of a subsequence. Furthermore, only very limited of them are working on multi-channel time series.

3   GP Representations

We use tree-based GP in our study which requires a primary set of nodes including functions and terminals. Table 1 presents functions in GP representation. Apart from four basic mathematical operations, three extra functions are introduced to handle multi-channel sensor data. The two functions proposed for exploring temporal relationships are discussed in Section 3.1 and Section 3.2. Section 3.3 describes how to deal with multiple variables in time series. Terminals are listed in Table 2, each row presenting one terminal including its name, value ranges, return type and the specified functions it can be attached to. It should be noted that each terminal "Variable m" corresponds to one variable in time series, representing one channel input. The value of m is the index of that channel, which is within the range from 0 to total channel numbers minus 1.

Table 1. Function Set of GP

Function	Parameters	Return Type
+	Double, Double	Double
+	Double, Double	Double
*	Double, Double	Double
/	Double, Double	Double
Window	Double i, Int operation, Int temporal-index	Double
Temporal_Diff	Double i	Double
Multi-Variable	Int multivariable-operation, Int variable-index	Double

3.1   Window Function

A function named "Window" is defined to cover and analyse a collection of points as it moves along the stream data or data stream passes through it. The window size S determines the maximum number of data points within that window.

Table 2. Terminal Set

Terminal	Value	Return Type	Function
Variable m	Current value of channel m	Double	General
Random	A random value	Double	General
Operation	AVG,STD,DIF,SKEWNESS	Integer	Window
Temporal Index	$[1, 2^{window-size} - 1]$	Integer	Window
Variable Index	$[1, 2^{num-of-variables} - 1]$	Integer	Multi-Variable
Multivariable Operation	MED,AVG,STD,RANGE	Integer	Multi-Variable

This "Window" function takes three parameters. The first one is "i", the input of this function. Either a function or a terminal can be attached here as long as it returns a double value. The latest historical values of this input is stored in the function, denoted as $t_0, t_1, ..., t_{S-1}$ from the earliest value to the current one. The value of S is set to 8 in this study.

The second parameter is "Temporal Index" which returns a random integer falling in the range from 1 to $2^S - 1$. The binary equivalent of this decimal number is mapped to the window, one bit to one data point. A data point will be selected only when its corresponding bit is "1". Assume the value of "temporal index" is 11, of which the equivalent binary string is 00001011, it will select points t_4, t_6 and t_7 since bits at these three positions are "1". Similarly, a value of 255 will take in all 8 points in that window. This mapping mechanism enables flexible point selection within the window and consequently helps to find the event size.

The third parameter "operation" randomly applies one operation on values selected by the second parameter. It is assigned to an integer value from 1 to 4 inclusively. Each value corresponds one of four operations: AVG, STD, DIF and SKEWNESS. These operations calculate the average value, the standard deviation, sum of absolute differences and skewness of the selected points respectively.

3.2 Temporal_Diff Function

It is not difficult to see that temporal changes between two consecutive points are important to characterise an event. Function "Temporal_Diff" is proposed to capture such temporal information. It takes one parameter as its input and returns the difference between the last value and the current value, therefore it essentially behaves as a sliding window of size 2.

3.3 Functions for Multiple-variable Time Series

"Window" function is capable to handle the temporal relationships in one sequence of values, however, it is infeasible to capture events occurring in multiple variables. To address this issue, function "Multi-Variable" is introduced to select arbitrary variables and summarise characteristics of these variables. It takes two parameters: variable index and multiple-variable operation. The first parameter works similarly as temporal index in "Window" function, the only difference is the range of variable index is within the range of $[1, 2^M - 1]$(M is the total number of variables). The value of second parameter can be any integer value from 1 to 4, corresponding to four multiple-variable operations: MED, AVG, STD and RANGE which return the middle value, the average, the standard derivation, and the distance between the maximum and minimum values of the selected variables.

4   Experiments

As shown in Table 3, a standard GP setting was used in the experiments. Moreover, dynamic range selection [20] was adopted to help GP process classification problems. We applied GP on three event detection tasks including both synthetic and real world data, which are described in Section 4.1. We are interested in the best solution that can be found. Therefore, for each task, GP was run for ten times and the best result among these runs was then considered as the final outcome. In Section 4.2, We compare the performance of GP to four traditional classifiers.

Table 3. GP Runtime Parameters

Population	30
Generation	300
Maximum Depth	8
Minimum Depth	2
Mutation Rate	5%
Crossover Rate	85%
Elitism Rate	10%
Number of Runs	10

4.1   Data Set

One simulated and two real world data sets were investigated in this study. All of these problems are with multiple variables and varying event sizes. Table 4 presents numbers of positive instances, numbers of negative instances in both training and testing phases. As shown in this table, the number of instances used for training is twice than the number used for test. In the first data set the number of positives and negatives are close while the last two data sets are unbalanced.

Synthetic Data: Changes in Any Four out of Six. In many real world situations, it is expected that sensor data will be smooth and any temporal change beyond a normal range should raise an alarm. The task is to simulate such situation, of which the objective is to detect noticeable changes in a six-variable time series. A noticeable change occurs when the absolute difference between two adjacent points is larger than 5. The current time point is considered as positive when such a change just occurred in any four variables simultaneously. Therefore,

Table 4. Training and Testing Data of Three Data Sets(%)

Data Set	Training			Test		
	total	positives	negatives	total	positives	negatives
1. Synthetic Data: Changes in Any Four out of Six	400	206	194	200	108	92
2.Activity Recognition: Walking	11368	1322	10046	5647	855	4792
3.Activity Recognition: Lying Still	11368	229	11139	5647	147	5500

concurrent changes happened in more than four variables are positive as well. Otherwise, it should be negative. Since two consecutive time points defines the event, the time span of this event is 2. To produce the artificial time stream, first each variable is initialised with a random value. Then, six values for next time point are generated randomly. For each variable, the probability of a notice change occurring at next time stamp is 0.9.

Activity Recognition: Walking and Lying Still. As mentioned is Section 1, human locomotion can be detected in wearable sensor data. The data we used in experiment comes from OPPORTUNITY data set [23]. The data set contains recordings of four healthy subjects, two male and two female; for each subject, six daily activity sessions were recorded. Over one hundred sensors were located on the jacket, limbs and feet of the subjects. Four locomotion, including walking, standing, lying still and sitting, are manually labelled by at least two researchers and further validated by video-recordings. Beyond these four classes, there is a none class indicating any other locomotions, for example, running.

There are two tasks for this data set: walking detection and lying still detection. To simplify the problem, it is sensible that only data obtained from accelerometers located on feet are considered since movements of both feet are enough to distinguish the two actions from others. Finally, six channels are investigated in this study. The original data is sampled every 33 milliseconds. Considering that walking and lying are high level locomotion, a lower sample rate is suitable. Therefore, we take data every 0.1 second as inputs. It should be noted that neither cross-session nor cross-subject validation are studied in this research. We only use the data of the first session of one subject, two third for training and the rest for testing. It should be noted that the event size and optimal features are unknown in these two tasks.

4.2   Results

Four conventional classifiers were applied to each task. The first three are *IB1* [11], *Naïve Bayes* [10] and *J48* [9]. The best one among these classifiers was then selected as the base classifier for the ensemble classifier *AdaBoost* [12]. Since conventional classifiers have no built-in sliding window mechanism, we manually segment raw data according to the event size. Since in Task 2 and Task 3 the event sizes are not available, we use 8, which is the max window size of GP, to

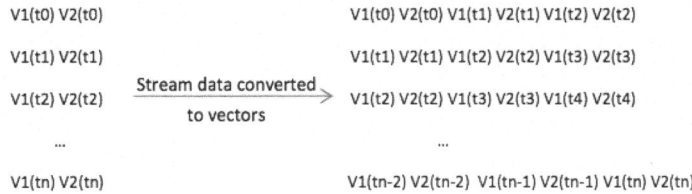

Fig. 1. Converting Raw Data Streams to Vectors for Conventional Classifiers

ensure that traditional classifiers receive the same amount of information as GP. Figure 1 illustrates the process of converting a two-variable time series stream into a six-attribute vectors, assuming an event size of 3.

Another group of experiments were conducted by applying the traditional classifiers to manually construct features. The features for all three data sets are the differences between two consecutive points of all variables. Given the same conditions in Figure 1, the extracted features can be shown in Figure 2.

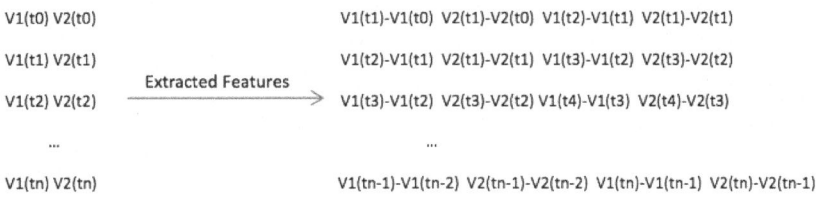

Fig. 2. Extracting Features for Conventional Classifiers

The results are presented in Table 5 and Table 6 which show the accuracies, true positive rates and true negative rates from test as test results are much more meaningful. With pre-defined features GP was slightly less effective but still comparable to other methods on Task 1. However, in the other two tasks GP can achieve better performance. As shown in Table 6, if the manually constructed features were not available, traditional classifiers suffered badly. On Task 1, J48 and Naïve Bayes classified all instances to be positive while IB1 and AdaBoost were not much better than random guessing (around 50%). In lying still detection task, traditional classifiers seemed to achieve similar accuracy as GP. However, it was because of the imbalance of the data that J48 and Naïve Bayes could appear accurate. The true positive rate were as low as 68.7% and 8.2% respectively. Only IB1 and Adaboost performed as good as GP. On Task 3, GP achieved the best performance as well. It should be noted here, in walking detection task, traditional classifiers gained benefits from features while in lying still detection task it was the contrary. With given features, classical classifiers can not successfully identify any positive instances except Naïve Bayes of which, unfortunately, the overall accuracy was only around 31%. The same set of features giving opposite results in two tasks further proves that an appropriate feature set are highly problem dependent.

Table 5. Comparing with Conventional Methods on Pre-defined Features(%)

Tasks	J48	Naïve Bayes	IB1	AdaBoost	GP
1. Changes in Any Four out of Six	89.95 TP : 91.7 TN : 87.9	92.46 TP : 90.7 TN : 94.5	**97.99** **TP : 100** **TN : 95.6**	97.49 TP : 99.1 TN : 95.6	95.34 TP : 95.28 TN : 95.4
2. Lying Still	97.4 TP : 0 TN : 100	31.27 TP : 83.7 TN : 29.9	96.97 TP : 0.7 TN : 99.5	96.97 TP : 0 TN : 99.5	**99.72** **TP : 99.32** **TN : 99.73**
3. Walking	88.05 TP : 48.7 TN : 95.1	86.08 TP : 51.3 TN : 92.3	89.08 TP : 53.1 TN : 95.5	88.16 TP : 53.2 TN : 94.4	**90.49** **TP : 52.28** **TN : 97.31**

Table 6. Comparing with Conventional Methods on Raw Data(%)

Tasks	J48	Naïve Bayes	IB1	AdaBoost	GP
1. Changes in Any Four out of Six	54.27 TP : 100 TN : 0	54.27 TP : 100 TN : 0	53.27 TP : 63 TN : 41.8	52.76 TP : 65.7 TN : 37.4	**95.34** **TP : 95.28** **TN : 95.4**
2. Lying Still	98.81 TP : 68.7 TN : 99.6	97.43 TP : 8.2 TN : 99.8	99.79 TP : 94.6 TN : 99.9	99.79 TP : 94.6 TN : 99.9	**99.72** **TP : 99.32** **TN : 99.73**
3. Walking	78.6 TP : 52.3 TN : 83.3	55.89 TP : 75.2 TN : 52.4	70.82 TP : 53.9 TN : 73.8	60.1 TP : 53 TN : 61.4	**90.49** **TP : 52.28** **TN : 97.31**

5   Discussion and Analysis

Some of the evolved detectors have been analysed to give us more understanding of the problem and of GP itself. Based on this analysis we discuss the aspects of GP on building reusable blocks, reducing dimensionality, and deciding event size.

It has been found that GP tend to build common blocks which can be reused in other parts of the same tree. We give two program trees as examples. The best individuals in Task 1 and Task 3 are shown in Figure 3 and Figure 4 respectively. The identical sub-trees are enclosed by dashed lines in the figures. The values of these repeated components are actually important to characterise events; therefore they can be considered as genuine features for those events.

In Task 1, the variable index 63 can be converted to binary string "111111", meaning that all variables should be taken into account. It is sensible since the

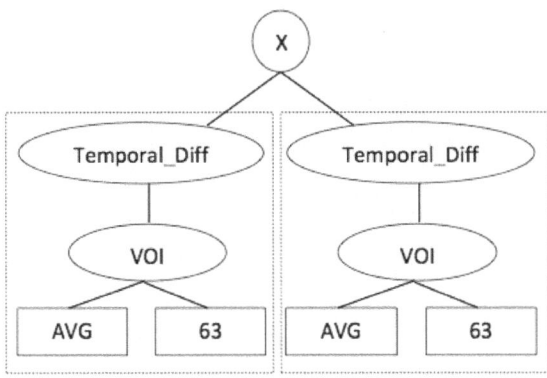

Fig. 3. Envolved Program(Task1)

changes may happen in sensor 1,2,3 and 4 as well as in sensor 1,3,5 and 6 or any combination of four. So no single sensor shall be ignored.

On detecting walking event, GP program took only 2 sensors among all six ones, the fourth and the sixth. However J48 classifier required all sensor inputs. Although only two channels were selected the performance of GP did not deteriorate. To verify the significance of these two channels of input, we applied feature extraction only on these two channels and fed the features to the traditional classifiers. The results are shown in Table 7. Comparing to all six features included, these two features still provided reasonable performance. It verifies that GP did find important inputs and was selective. It did not simply use all channels as other methods did.

Table 7. Conventional Methods on Dimensionality-Reduced Data of Task 3(%)

	J48		Naïve Bayes		IB1		AdaBoost	
Num of Channels	6	2	6	2	6	2	6	2
Accuracy	88.05	86.97	86.08	86.81	89.08	84.83	88.16	84.7
TP Rate	48.7	35.6	51.3	36.3	53.1	41.1	53.2	43.2
TN Rate	95.1	96.1	92.3	95.8	95.5	92.6	94.4	92.1

In addition, GP tries to identify the event duration as well. For example in Task 1, it is obvious that the event size of 2 was successfully captured by temporal function "Temporal_Diff" (see Figure 3). While in Task 3, "Window" functions were nested, suggesting data points more than the 8-point limit of a single window are needed (see Figure 4). GP found a way to go beyond that limit.

GP shows its flexibility on the choice of window size. To verify that, we applied GP to each task with different window size: 4,8,12 and 16. The results show that the performance deteriorated with a window size smaller than 8 while window

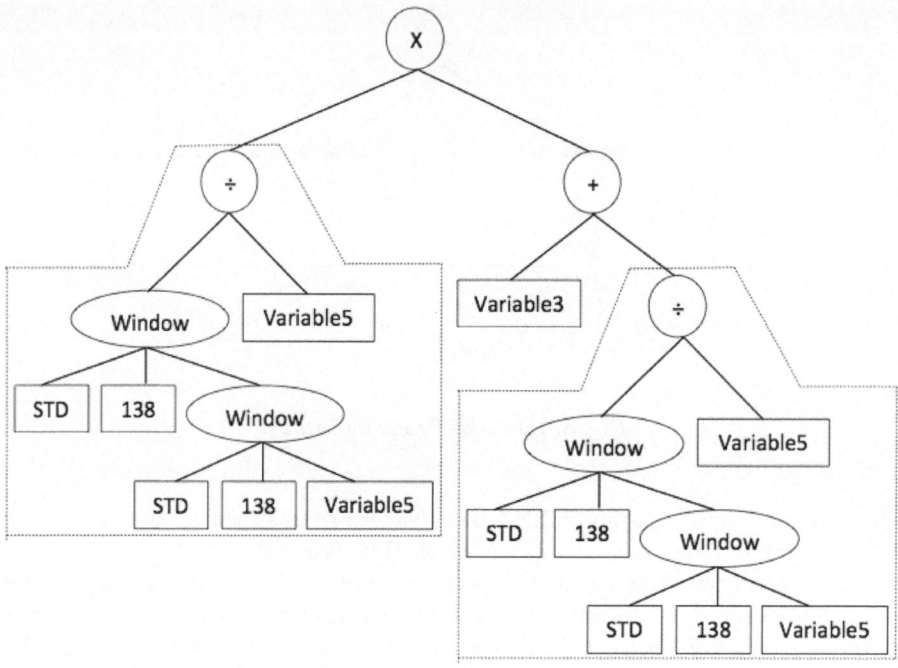

Fig. 4. Envolved Program(Task3)

sizes larger than 8 did not bring significant benefits in accuracy. GP is capable
to find reasonable solutions with these window sizes. However, how to find the
optimal window size is still an open question.

6   Conclusions and Future Work

In this study, we present a GP-based methodology for detecting event of interest
in multi-channel sensor data. A number of specialised representations are introduced to process multi-variable time series. The method was applied to a range
of detection tasks from changes in synthetic data to activity recognition problem
to verify its performance. The experimental results show that on manually constructed features GP can achieve comparable or even better performance when
comparing to the four traditional classifiers. Moreover when manually defined
features are unavailable, GP is far superior to the others. The analysis on evolved
event detectors demonstrates that GP successfully selected and extracted distinctive characteristics of the target events. On the synthetic data which is the
only case that we know the event size, GP evolved programs determined the
event size accurately.

At current stage, although intuitive analysis gives us some insights about
the behaviour of GP detectors, however, they can not be fully understood. On
the other hand, explanation of these models can be meaningful to the domain.

Therefore, in near future, we will further analyse the evolved programs. Another limitation of our work is that for window containing event boundaries, GP probably will make wrong decisions. In the next stage, we will try to address that issue. Additionally, as mentioned above, the system can be enhanced by enabling GP to search for the optimal window size in future.

References

1. Poli, R., Langdon, W., McPhee, N.: A Field Guide to Genetic Programming. Lulu.com (2008)
2. Koza, J.R.: Genetic programming I: On the programming of computers by means of natural selection. MIT Press (1996)
3. Lohn, J., Hornby, G., Linden, D.: An Evolved Antenna for Deployment on Nasa's Space Technology 5 Mission. In: Genetic Programming Theory and Practice II, pp. 301–315. Springer (2004)
4. Kaboudan, M.A.: Spatiotemporal Forecasting of Housing Price By Use of Genetic Programming. In: The 16th Annual Meeting of the Association of Global Business (2004)
5. Song, A., Pinto, B.: Study of GP representations for motion detection with unstable background. In: IEEE Congress on Evolutionary Computation (2010)
6. Hetland, M., Strom, P.: Temporal Rule Discovery using Genetic Programming and Specialised Hardware. In: Proceedings of the 4th International Conference on Recent Advances in Soft Computing (2002)
7. Wagner, N., Michalewicz, Z.: An analysis of adaptive windowing for time series forecasting in dynamic environments: further tests of the DyFor GP model. In: Proceedings of the 10th Annual Conference on Genetic and Evolutionary Computation, pp. 1657–1664 (2008)
8. Song, A., Xie, F.: Evolving automatic frame splitters. In: Proceedings of the 13th Annual Conference Companion on Genetic and Evolutionary Computation (2011)
9. Quinlan, R.: C4.5: Programs for Machine Learning. Morgan Kaufmann Publishers (1993)
10. George, H.J., Pat, L.: Estimating Continuous Distributions in Bayesian Classifiers. In: Eleventh Conference on Uncertainty in Artificial Intelligence, pp. 338–345 (1995)
11. Aha, D., Kibler, D.: Instance-based learning algorithms. Machine Learning 6, 37–66 (1991)
12. Freund, Y., Robert, E.S.: Experiments with a new boosting algorithm. In: Thirteenth International Conference on Machine Learning, pp. 148–156 (1996)
13. Guralnik, V., Srivastava, J.: Event detection from time series data. In: Proceedings of the Fifth ACM SIGKDD International Conference on Knowledge, pp. 33–42 (1999)
14. Preston, D., Protopapas, P., Brodley, C.: Event discovery in time series. In: Proceedings of the SIAM International Conference on Data Mining, pp. 61–72 (2009)
15. Keogh, E., Lin, J., Fu, A.: Hot sax: Efficiently finding the most unusual time series subsequence. In: Fifth IEEE International Conference on Data Mining (2005)
16. Ratanamahatana, C.A., Lin, J., Gunopulos, D., Keogh, E., Vlachos, M., Das, G.: Mining time series data. In: Data Mining and Knowledge Discovery Handbook 2010, pp. 1049–1077 (2010)

17. Hunter, J., McIntosh, N.: Knowledge-Based Event Detection in Complex Time Series Data. In: Horn, W., Shahar, Y., Lindberg, G., Andreassen, S., Wyatt, J.C. (eds.) AIMDM 1999. LNCS (LNAI), vol. 1620, pp. 271–280. Springer, Heidelberg (1999)

18. Shahabi, C., Yan, D.: Real-time pattern isolation and recognition over immersive sensor data streams. In: Proceedings of The 9th Intl Conference on Multi-Media Modeling, pp. 93–113 (2003)

19. Song, A., Ciesielski, V.: Texture Segmentation by Genetic Programming. In: Evolutionary Computation, pp. 461–481 (2008)

20. Loveard, T., Ciesielski, V.: Representing classification problems in genetic programming. In: Proceedings of the 2001 Congress on Evolutionary Computation, pp. 1070–1077 (2001)

21. Wagner, N., Michalewicz, Z., Khouja, M., McGregor, R.R.: Time Series Forecasting for Dynamic Environments: The DyFor Genetic Program Model. IEEE Transactions on Evolutionary Computation 11(4), 433–452 (2007)

22. Xie, F., Song, A., Ciesielski, V.: Event detection in time series by genetic programming. In: IEEE World Congress on Computational Intelligence, pp. 2507–2514 (2012)

23. Roggen, D., Calatroni, A., Rossi, M., Holleczek, T., Trster, G., Lukowicz, P., Pirkl, G., Bannach, D., Ferscha, A., Doppler, J., Holzmann, C., Kurz, M., Holl, G., Chavarriaga, R., Sagha, H., Bayati, H., del R. Milln, J.: Collecting complex activity data sets in highly rich networked sensor environments. In: Seventh International Conference on Networked Sensing Systems (2010)

Improving Classification Accuracy on Uncertain Data by Considering Multiple Subclasses

Lei Xu and Edward Hung

Department of Computing, The Hong Kong Polytechnic University
{cslxu,csehung}@comp.polyu.edu.hk

Abstract. We study the problem of classification on uncertain objects whose locations are uncertain and described by probability density functions (pdf). Though there exist some classification algorithms proposed to handle uncertain objects, all existing algorithms are complex and time consuming. Thus, a novel supervised UK-means algorithm is proposed to classify uncertain objects more efficiently. Supervised UK-means assumes the classes are well separated. However, in real data, subsets of objects of the same class are usually interspersed among (disconnected by) other classes. Thus, we proposed a new algorithm Supervised UK-means with Multiple Subclasses (SUMS) which considers the objects in the same class can be further divided into several groups (subclasses) within the class and tries to learn the subclass representatives to classify objects more accurately.

Keywords: classification, supervised UK-means, multiple subclasses, uncertain objects.

1 Introduction

While there has been a large amount of research on mining and queries on relational databases [15], the focus has been on databases that store data in exact values. In many real-life applications, however, the raw data (for example, in the case of sensor data) are not precise or accurate when they were collected or produced. Data uncertainty are classified into two types. One is existential uncertainty caused by not sure the existence of an object or a data tuple [1, 4, 5, 14]; The other is value uncertainty caused by not knowing the value precisely. In this paper, we focus on the second case (value uncertainty).

Classification is an important task in machine learning. [18,19] shows that the learning based similarity metrics can perform better in multimedia data classification and retrieval. Similarly to [18,19], we learn model based expected Euclidean distance used in UK-means. In previous work, we modified UK-means to supervised UK-means to classify uncertain objects in [21]. We considers the problem of classifying objects as a multi-dimensional uncertainty where an object is represented by an uncertain region over which a discrete probability distribution function (PDF), or a probability density function (pdf), is defined. Formally, we consider a training set of N labeled objects o_i, $1 \leq i \leq N$ in an m-dimensional

M. Thielscher and D. Zhang (Eds.): AI 2012, LNCS 7691, pp. 743–754, 2012.

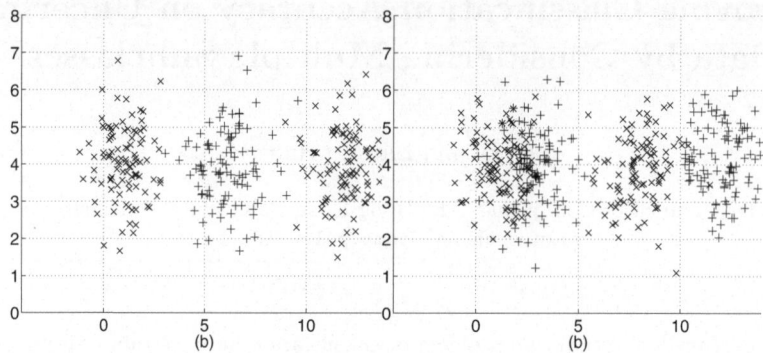

Fig. 1. (a) An example of one class ('x') divided by another class ('+') (b) Another example of one class ('+') divided by another class ('x')

space. An object o_i is represented by a pdf f_i: $IR^m \rightarrow IR$ (IR represents real number space) that specifies the probability density of each possible location of object o_i[1]. Thus, each object can be bounded by a finite bounding box. This assumption is reasonable because in practice the probability density of an object is high only within a very small region of concentration. o_i is associated with a class label $c_j(c_j \in L)$, where L is a class label set.

Supervised UK-means assumes the classes are well separated. However, in classification, the classes are often in arbitrary shape which makes the boundary between classes concave or convex but not a single line. In some cases, a class's objects are separated (disconnected) by objects of other classes. As Figure 1(a) shows one class (represented by 'x') is divided by another class ('+'). Figure 1(b) is another example showing that each class is divided by other classes and the boundary between classes is concave and convex. For the above cases, our solution is using a few class representatives to represent a class. We consider the problem as the estimation of the number of groups or subclasses (k) in each class. The key idea of estimation of k is to use splitting and/or merging methods to increase and/or decrease the number of clusters, which makes the model fit the data. Each subclass (cluster belonging to a class) can be considered as a Gaussian mixture model. Several algorithms have been proposed to determine k automatically [7, 8, 11, 20]. Most of them wrap around either K-means or Expectation-Maximization for fixed k. In a classification problem, training objects are labeled by class labels. When we consider objects from a class and further divide them into subclasses, we ignore their labels. In other words, objects are labeled during inter-class training, and in the process of the estimation of k (the number of subclasses in a class) during intra-class training, the labels of objects from the same class are ignored.

---

[1] The methods to be discussed in this paper require that for each object o_i, the uncertain region $UD(o_i)$ of each object o_i is finite, i.e. $\forall x \notin UD(o_i), f_i(x) = 0$.

2   Related Work

A large number of classification models have been proposed in the literature. However, few research focuses on the problem of classification handling uncertain data caused by value uncertainty. In [2], support vector machine is used to classify uncertain data. In this method, an uncertain object is assumed as a simple bounded geometric model. Support vector machine creates margins by using uncertain objects which lie on the boundary. In this model, the uncertainty (domain of uncertain objects) of objects are estimated. In our model, the maximum boundary of objects is fixed.

In [16, 17], an uncertain object is associated with a probability density function (pdf) and a finite region. The decision tree classifier is extended to handle uncertain data by using averaging or distribution-based approach. To improve the efficiency, some pruning techniques were proposed without affecting the results of decision tree. In [13], the uncertain model is the same as that in [16, 17]. In [13], Naive Bayes is used to classify uncertain data. Three approaches are proposed (averaging, formula-based, and sample-based) to calculate the probability of object label and assign it to the class with highest probability. In [12], uRule is proposed based on Rule-based algorithm to classify uncertain information. The difference between Rule-based and uRule is that the instances are partly covered by the rule in uRule. The key idea in uRule is that the algorithm computes which proportion of the instances is covered by a rule based on the uncertain attribute interval and probabilistic function. uRule considers to classify uncertain numerical and categorical data. Though some algorithms have been extended to classify uncertain information, the problem of building classifiers on uncertain data is still a challenge. The algorithms take quite a long time to classify uncertain objects because they are too complex.

Some work has been proposed to estimate the number of clusters during data clustering. X-means [11] is a regularization framework for learning k with K-means. X-means tries many values of k and obtains a model for each k value. Then X-means uses the Bayesian Information Criterion (BIC) to score each model and chooses the model with the highest BIC score. Other scoring criteria are also used in X-means. The drawback of X-means is that the algorithm assumes the cluster covariances are all spherical with the same width. X-means is likely to overfit the data when the clusters are non-spherical. Bayesian K-means [20] uses Maximization-Expectation (ME) to learn a mixture model. ME maximizes over the hidden variables (assignment of examples to clusters), and computes an expectation over model parameters (center location and covariances). The algorithm works well but it is time consuming. G-means (Gaussian means) [8] is a wrapper around the K-means algorithm. G-means uses projection and a statistical test for the hypothesis that the data in a cluster come from a Gaussian distribution. The algorithm grows k with a small number of centers. It applies a statistical test to each cluster and those which are not accepted as Gaussian are split into two clusters. Interleaved with K-means, this procedure repeats until every cluster's data are accepted as Gaussian. The method does not assume spherical clusters, but it works well when true clusters are well-separated.

It has difficulty when true clusters overlap since the hard assignment of K-means can clip data into subsets that look non-Gaussian. PG-means (Projected Gaussian means) [7] is proposed to handle difficult cases, such as non-Gaussian data, overlapping clusters, eccentric clusters, high dimension. Moreover, PG-means is faster than variational Bayesian K-means. PG-means is based on projections and statistical tests to determine whether a whole mixture model fits the data well. PG-means cannot been directly used in our UK-means classification, because PG-means is used to handle certain objects. In Section 3.4, we will describe how to modify PG-means for our problem.

3   Supervised UK-Means

3.1   Problem Definition

In the supervised model, there are a set of N training objects $o_1, o_2, ..., o_N$, and m numerical (real-valued) feature attributes $A_1, ..., A_m$. The domain of attribute $A_u (1 \le u \le m)$ is $dom(A_u)$. Each o_i is associated with a probability density function (pdf $f_i(x)$) and a class label c_j ($c_j \in L$, where L is the set of all class labels), where x is a possible location of o_i, and $UD(o_i)$ is uncertain domain of o_i. Each tuple x is associated with a feature vector $x = (\tilde{x}_1, \tilde{x}_2, ..., \tilde{x}_m)$, where $\tilde{x}_u \in dom(A_u)(1 \le u \le m)$. The goal of supervised UK-means is to find K (the number of labels, $|L|$) class representatives which can predict a testing object o_{test} to class c_k with the minimum expected Euclidean distance. The boundary between classes are sometimes in arbitrary shape (e.g. convex or concave). Also, the objects from the same class may be disconnected by other classes. It is obvious that one class representative is not enough for representing a class. In our model, we assume one class can be further divided into a number subclasses, and we try to estimate an appropriate number of subclasses of each class. Then, we find the subclasses' representatives to predict the labels of testing objects with the minimum expected Euclidean distance between objects and subclass representatives.

3.2   Expected Euclidean Distance

As Figure 2 shows, one way to approximate the calculation is to divide the uncertain domain into a number of grid cells. A sample is considered to be located at the center of each grid cell which represents a possible location of the uncertain object o_i. The expected Euclidean distance (EED) from object o_i (represented by a pdf f_i) to the cluster representative p_{c_j} is the weighted average of the distances between the samples in o_i and $\overline{p}_{c_j}$ (the mean vector of p_{c_j}), i.e. $EED(o_i, p_{c_j}) = \sum_{t=1}^{T} F_i(s_{i,t}) ED(s_{i,t}, \overline{p}_{c_j})$, where T is the number of samples in o_i, $s_{i,t}$ is the location (vector) of the t-th sample of o_i, p_{c_j} is a probabilistic object representing the domain of the cluster representative of cluster c_j, $F_i(s_{i,t}) = \int_{x \in cell_t} f_i(x) dx$ (F_i is a discrete probability distribution function over T grid cells, $cell_t$ is the grid cell that sample $s_{i,t}$ represents, x is

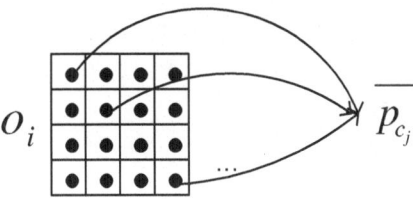

Fig. 2. Expected distance calculation from o_i to p_{c_j} in $[3, 9, 10]$

the possible location of sample $s_{i,t}$ in $cell_t$), and the metric ED is Euclidean distance used in $[3, 9, 10]$. In this paper, the mean vector $\overline{o_i}$ (expected value) of o_i, which is the weighted mean of all T samples (or possible locations), is calculated as Equation (1).

$$\overline{o_i} = \sum_{t=1}^{T} s_{i,t} \times F_i(s_{i,t}). \tag{1}$$

The mean vector $\overline{p}_{c_{j_k}}$ of k-th subclass representative $p_{c_{j_k}}$ of class c_j is obtained by Equation (2), where $|c_{j_k}|$ is the number of objects assigned to subclass c_{j_k}, and $C(o_i) = c_{j_k}$ means that object o_i is assigned to subclass c_{j_k}.

$$\overline{p}_{c_{j_k}} = \frac{1}{|c_{j_k}|} \sum_{o_i \in \{o_i | C(o_i) = c_{j_k}\}} \overline{o_i}. \tag{2}$$

3.3   Supervised UK-Means with Multiple Subclasses (SUMS)

Algorithm 1 shows Supervised UK-means with Multiple Subclasses (SUMS), where N is the number of training objects, K is the number of class labels, k_l is the number of subclasses of the l-th class. In Algorithm 1, the number of subclass representatives is estimated and the subclass representatives are trained by the objects of the same class. First, Algorithm 1 calculates the mean vectors of uncertain objects. Then the number of subclasses of each class is estimated by Algorithm 2. The subclass representatives are trained by UK-means based on the objects of the same class. The time complexity of the algorithm is decided by the time costing on estimation of k_i (the number of subclasses) and the calculation of subclass representatives. The time complexity of training subclass representatives is $O(NTKk_{max})$, where N is the number of training objects, T is the number of samples of object, K is the number of class labels, and k_{max} is the maximum number of subclasses of a class. The time complexity of estimation of k_i (the number of subclasses) will be discussed in Section 3.4.

3.4   Estimation of k_i

In [7], PG-means uses a statistical hypothesis test on one-dimensional projection of the data and model to determine if the examples are well represented by the

Algorithm 1. Supervised UK-means with Multiple Subclasses (SUMS)

Input: training set $\{o_1, o_2, ..., o_N\}$ with class labels c_j ($j \in \{1, 2, ..., K\}$)
Output: learner of sub-class representatives.

1: **for** $i = 0$; $i < N$; i++ **do**
2:     compute $\overline{o_i}$ of training objects by Equation (1);
3: **end for**
4: **for** i=0; $i < K$; i++ **do**
5:     Estimate the number of subclasses k_i by PG-means and get the subclass representatives $(p_{c_{i_1}}, p_{c_{i_2}}, ..., p_{c_{i_{k_i}}})$;
6: **end for**
7: **repeat**
8:     **for** m=0; $m < N$; m++ **do**
9:         **for** i=0; $i < K$; i++ **do**
10:             **for** j=0; $j < k_i$; j++ **do**
11:                 compute Expected Euclidean Distance by $EED(o_m, p_{c_{i_j}}) = \sum_{t=1}^{T} F_m(s_{m,t}) ED(s_{m,t}, p_{c_{i_j}})$;
12:             **end for**
13:         **end for**
14:         assign object o_m to the subclass with the minimum $EED(o_m, p_{c_{l_q}})$;
15:     **end for**
16:     update all subclass representatives by Equation (2);
17: **until** all subclass representatives converge

---

model. PG-means stands for Projected Gaussian and refers to the fact that the method applies the projections to the clustering model as well as the data, before performing each hypothesis test for model fitness. In [7], the standard Gaussian mixture model is used with Expectation-Maximization training. The key idea of PG-means is using the EM algorithm to learn a model containing k centers. When EM learning converges, PG-means projects both the data set and the learned model to one dimension, and then applies the Kolmogorov-Smirnov (KS) test to determine whether the projected model fits the projected data.

Assume some data X is sampled from a single Gaussian cluster with distribution $X \sim (\mu, \Sigma)$ in d dimension. $\mu = E[X]$ is the $d \times 1$ mean vector and $\Sigma = cov[X]$ is the $d \times d$ covariance matrix. Given a $d \times 1$ projection vector P of the unit length ($\|P\| = 1$), we can project X along P as $X' = P^T X$. Then, $X' \sim N(\mu', \sigma)$, where $\mu' = P^T \mu$ and $\sigma^2 = P^T \Sigma P$. We can project each cluster model to obtain a one-dimensional projection of an entire mixture along P. PG-means [7] repeats this projection and test step several times for a single learned model. If any test rejects the null hypothesis that the data follows the model's distribution, then it adds one subclass and starts with UK-means in our algorithm. If every test accepts the null hypothesis for a given model, then the algorithm terminates. The following are the two hypotheses:

H_0: The data around the center are sampled from a Gaussian.
H_1: The data around the center are not sampled from a Gaussian.

Algorithm 2. Estimation of k_i

Input: The mean vectors of objects X with the same label c_i,confidence α, number of projections J.

Output: the number of subclasses (k_i) of class c_i and subclass representatives $(p_{c_{i_1}}, p_{c_{i_2}}, ..., p_{c_{k_i}})$.

1: Let $k_i \leftarrow 1$. Initialize the class with the mean and covariance of X.
2: **for** $j = 0$; $j < J$; $j + +$ **do**
3:       Randomly generate a $d \times 1$ projection vector P.
4:       Project X and the model to P with the same projection.
5:       Use KS test at significance level α to test if the projected model fits the projected
       data set.
6:       **if** any test rejects the null hypothesis **then**
7:             break out of the loop.
8:       **end if**
9: **end for**
10: **if** any test rejected the null hypothesis **then**
11:       Initialize $k_i + 1$ subclasses as the k_i previously learned plus one new subclass.
12:       Run UK-means on $k_i + 1$ subclasses to learn $k_i + 1$ subclass representatives.
13:       Let $k_i \leftarrow k_i + 1$, and go to step 2.
14: **end if**
15: Every test accepts the null hypothesis; stop and return the model.

After projection, PG-means uses the univariate Kolmogorov-Smirnov (KS) test for model fitness. The KS test statistic is $D = max_X|F(X) - S(X)|$-the maximum absolute difference between the true cumulative distribution function (CDF) of $F(x)$ with the sample CDF $S(X)$. Algorithm 2 shows the algorithm more formally. PG-means uses UK-means to learn a model containing k_i centers. In our work, we use UK-means instead of EM training [7]. UK-means uses hard assignment (each example has membership in only one subclass). The worst case is that each object belongs to a subclass, and the time complexity of Algorithm 2 is $O(Jn^2T)$, where J is the number of projections, n is the number of objects of a class, T is the number of samples. In the algorithm, we use random projection [6] to project the data and the model. There are also other possible methods, e.g. principal component analysis which can be used to do projection. We wish to use a small but sufficient number of projections and tests to discover when a model does not fit data well. In [7], they followed Dasgupta's conclusion that c-separation[2] is the natural measure for Gaussian [6]. In [6,7], they gave the conclusion that if J random projections are performed, the probability that all J projections are 'bad'[3] is less than some ϵ: $Pr(J \ bad \ projections) = Erf(\sqrt{1/2})^J < \epsilon$, where Erf is the standard Gaussian error function. To find

---

[2] For any $c > 0$, assume the two cluster centers μ_1 and μ_2 are in d dimension and the spherical covariances Σ of the two clusters are the same for simplicity, c-separation is that the vector m connecting the two centers ($m = \mu_2 - \mu_1$) satisfies the condition $||m|| \geq c\sqrt{trace(\Sigma)}$.

[3] The probability that J is a 'bad' projection, i.e. that it does not maintain c-separation between the cluster means when projected.

a projection that keeps the two clusters means c-separated, approximately J is shown as $J < log(\epsilon)/log(Erf(\sqrt{1/2})) \approx -2.6198 log(\epsilon)$ follows [6, 7]. For example, if ϵ is 0.01, 12 projections are needed. In the experiments, we use $J = 12$ projections to estimate the number of subclasses in a class.

4   Experimental Evaluation

In this section, we evaluate Supervised UK-means with Multiple Subclasses (SUMS) by comparing it with supervised UK-means. We compare their classification results in this section. All algorithms were written in Matlab and were run on a Windows machine with an Intel 2.66GHz Pentium(R) Dual-Core processor and 4GB of main memory.

4.1   Synthetic Data Sets

We have done the experiments on the two typical data sets shown in Figure 1(a) and Figure 1(b). In Figure 1(a), the class ('x') is divided by the class ('+'). The number of objects in class ('+') is 100, and the number of objects in class ('x') is 200 with equally distribution on the two sides of class ('+'). We denote the data set by "Middle" which means that one class is divided in the middle. The centers of uncertain objects were generated from a Gaussian distribution, whose mean and standard deviation are equal to the class center and σ respectively. A set of uncertain objects represented by MBRs with size $S \times S$ were randomly generated in $2D$ space $[-100, 100] \times [-100, 100]$. An MBR is divided into $\sqrt{T} \times \sqrt{T}$ grid cells. Each grid cell corresponds to a sample. Each sample is associated with a randomly generated probability value. All probabilities in an MBR are normalized to have their sum equal to 1. For each data set, a set of K class representatives were trained by the labeled objects. Similarly, in Figure 1(b), the number of objects in class ('x') is 200, and the number of objects in class ('+') is 200. The class 'x' and the class '+' are divided into two subclasses by each other. We denote the example by "Side" with the meaning that each class being divided on two sides. Each subclass has 100 objects. The execution time is shown in Table 2. SUMS spends more time than supervised UK-means. Because in SUMS, PG-means is used to find the subclasses of class which costs extra time. The time of SUMS depends on the number of training

Table 1. Parameters for experiments using data sets

Parameter	Description	Baseline Value
K	number of classes	2
T	number of samples per object	49
w	maximum size of MBR, $S \times S$	0.25
D	number of dimensions	2
σ	standard deviation of Gaussian distribution	1

Table 2. Execution Time (Seconds)

Data Set	Supervised UK-means	SUMS
Middle	0.589	1.988
Side	0.704	3.215

objects, the number of samples and the number of projections. Table 3 shows that the accuracy is improved by SUMS compared with supervised UK-means. In Figures 3 and 4, the (symbol 'o' is the learned (sub)class representative of a class). In Figure 1(a), the center of class 'x' is $(1, 4)$ and $(12, 4)$, and the center of class ('+') is $(6, 4)$. As Figure 3(a) shows, in supervised UK-means, the learned mean vector of class ('x') is $(2.7931, 4.2881)$ while the learned mean vector of class ('+') is $(10.9975, 4.2332)$. Figure 3(b) shows, in SUMS, the learned class representatives of class ('+') is $(6.6879, 4.2589)$ while the learned class representatives of class ('x') is $(1.1130, 4.2304)$ and $(12.0707, 4.2947)$. In Figure 1(b), the subclass representatives of class ('x') is $(1, 4)$ and $(8, 4)$ and the center of class ('+') is $(3, 4)$ and $(12, 4)$. The learned subclass representatives of class ('x') are $(0.8984, 4.0726)$ and $(8.4050, 4.0098)$ while the learned subclass representatives of class ('+') are $(3.1032, 3.9298)$ and $(12.1603, 3.8576)$ (Figure 4(b)) in SUMS. In Figure 4(a), the supervised UK-means can only learn one class representative for each class (the class representative of class 'x' is $(1.8759, 4.0096)$ and the class representative of class '+' is $(10.2837, 3.9341)$). In Figure 3(a) and 4(a), the learned class representative is far from some objects from the same class which makes the accuracy of classifier low. In Figure 3(b) and 4(b), the learned

Table 3. Accuracy on synthetic data sets

Data Set	Supervised UK-means	SUMS
Middle	0.4667	0.9833
Side	0.5175	0.9067

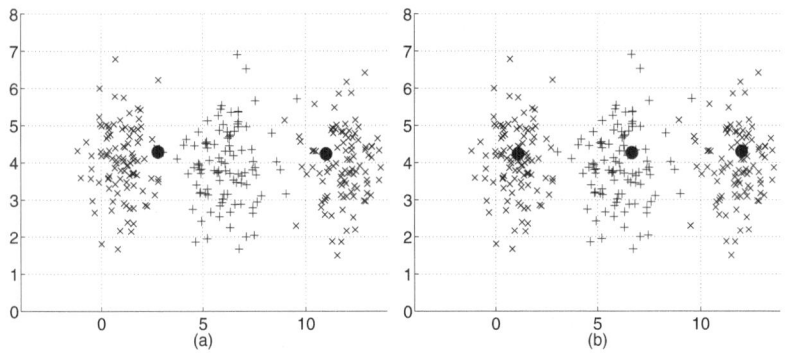

Fig. 3. (a) Class representatives of "Middle" learned by Supervised UK-means (b) Subclass representatives of "Middle" learned by SUMS

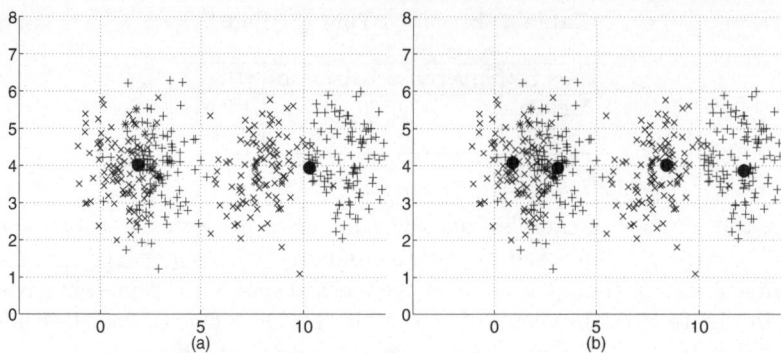

Fig. 4. (a) Class representatives of "Side" learned by Supervised UK-means (b) Subclass representatives of "Side" learned by SUMS

subclass representatives can improve the performance of supervised UK-means, because the subclass representatives are closer to their real class centers. From the experiments, the SUMS algorithm can learn more information compared with supervised UK-means. SUMS with PG-means can learn the subclasses of the synthetic data sets. SUMS improves the accuracy of supervised UK-means with more time cost. We also did experiments on other synthetic data sets which also show that SUMS can learn subclasses more accurately than supervised UK-means. From the experiments, if the number of subclasses (as well as classes, samples, objects, or dimensions) increases, the time of SUMS will increase. Because of space limitation, we will not show the figures.

4.2   Real Data Sets

We have also done experiments on real data sets. The parameters of the chosen data sets used for the experiments are summarized in Table 4. The attributes of all the data sets are numerical obtained from measurements. Classifiers are built on the numerical attributes and their "class label" attributes. For the chosen data sets, we use 10-fold cross validation to measure the accuracy. The 3 data sets contains "point values" without uncertainty. Similar to uncertainty generation of synthetic data sets, each object is represented by an MBR with size 0.25×0.25 in a multiple dimension space, which is divided into $\sqrt{49} \times \sqrt{49}$ grid cells. Each grid cell corresponds to a sample. Each sample is associated with a randomly

Table 4. Selected Data Sets from the UCI Machine Learning Repository

Data Set	Training Tuples	No. of Attributes	No. of Classes	Test Tuples
Iris	150	4	3	10-fold
BreastCancer	569	30	2	10-fold
Ionosphere	351	32	2	10-fold

Table 5. Accuracy on real data sets

Data Set	Supervised UK-means	SUMS
Iris	0.913	0.927
BreastCancer	0.843	0.895
Ionosphere	0.706	0.871

generated probability value. All probabilities in an MBR are normalized to have their sum equal to 1. From Table 5, SUMS with PG-means can classify the objects more accurately on real data sets compared with supervised UK-means. Supervised UK-means learns one class representative for each class. However, the objects of a class may be distributed nearer to other class representatives. Thus, the SUMS can train more than one class representatives for each class by PG-means. In SUMS, PG-means tries to estimate the number of subclasses of a class and learn local subclass representatives which may be closer to the objects belonging to the same class. The experiments on both synthetic and real data sets show that the Supervised UK-means with Multiple Subclasses (SUMS) can improve the accuracy of supervised UK-means.

5   Conclusion

In our work, we study the problem of classification on uncertain objects whose locations are uncertain and described by probability density functions (pdf). Though supervised UK-means algorithm is proposed to classify uncertain objects more efficiently, it assumes that the classes are well separated. In real data, subsets of objects of the same class are usually interspersed among (disconnected by) other classes. Thus, we consider the objects in the same class can be further divided into several groups (subclasses) within the class. We use PG-means (projected Gaussian) to estimate the number of subclasses in the class and train the subclass representatives by UK-means. Our experimental results demonstrated that our algorithm (SUMS) can overcome the limitation of supervised UK-means when a class is divided by other classes.

Acknowledgement. The work described in this paper was partially supported by grants from the Research Grants Council of the Hong Kong Special Administrative Region, China (PolyU 5182/08E, PolyU 5191/09E).

References

1. Barbará, D., Garcia-Molina, H., Porter, D.: The management of probabilistic data. IEEE Trans. Knowl. Data Eng. 4(5), 487–502 (1992)
2. Bi, J., Zhang, T.: Support vector classification with input data uncertainty. In: NIPS (2004)

3. Chau, M., Cheng, R., Kao, B., Ng, J.: Uncertain Data Mining: An Example in Clustering Location Data. In: Ng, W.-K., Kitsuregawa, M., Li, J., Chang, K. (eds.) PAKDD 2006. LNCS (LNAI), vol. 3918, pp. 199–204. Springer, Heidelberg (2006)
4. Cheng, R., Kalashnikov, D.V., Prabhakar, S.: Querying imprecise data in moving object environments. IEEE Trans. Knowl. Data Eng. 16(9), 1112–1127 (2004)
5. Dalvi, N.N., Suciu, D.: Efficient query evaluation on probabilistic databases. VLDB J. 16(4), 523–544 (2007)
6. Dasgupta, S.: Experiments with random projection. In: UAI, pp. 143–151 (2000)
7. Feng, Y., Hamerly, G.: Pg-means: learning the number of clusters in data. In: NIPS, pp. 393–400 (2006)
8. Hamerly, G., Elkan, C.: Learning the k in k-means. In: NIPS (2003)
9. Kao, B., Lee, S.D., Cheung, D.W., Ho, W.-S., Chan, K.F.: Clustering uncertain data using voronoi diagrams. In: ICDM, pp. 333–342 (2008)
10. Ngai, W.K., Kao, B., Chui, C.K., Cheng, R., Chau, M., Yip, K.Y.: Efficient clustering of uncertain data. In: ICDM 2006, pp. 436–445 (2006)
11. Pelleg, D., Moore, A.W.: X-means: Extending k-means with efficient estimation of the number of clusters. In: ICML, pp. 727–734 (2000)
12. Qin, B., Xia, Y., Prabhakar, S., Tu, Y.-C.: A rule-based classification algorithm for uncertain data. In: ICDE, pp. 1633–1640 (2009)
13. Ren, J., Lee, S.D., Chen, X., Kao, B., Cheng, R., Cheung, D.W.-L.: Naive bayes classification of uncertain data. In: ICDM, pp. 944–949 (2009)
14. Ruspini, E.H.: A new approach to clustering. Information and Control 15(1), 22–32 (1969)
15. Tan, P.-N., Steinbach, M., Kumar, V.: Introduction to Data Mining. Addison-Wesley (2005)
16. Tsang, S., Kao, B., Yip, K.Y., Ho, W.-S., Lee, S.D.: Decision trees for uncertain data. In: ICDE, pp. 441–444 (2009)
17. Tsang, S., Kao, B., Yip, K.Y., Ho, W.-S., Lee, S.D.: Decision trees for uncertain data. IEEE Trans. Knowl. Data Eng. 23(1), 64–78 (2011)
18. Wang, D., Kim, Y.-S., Park, S.C., Lee, C.S., Han, Y.K.: Learning based neural similarity metrics for multimedia data mining. Soft Comput. 11(4), 335–340 (2007)
19. Wang, D., Ma, X.: Learning Pseudo Metric for Multimedia Data Classification and Retrieval. In: Negoita, M.G., Howlett, R.J., Jain, L.C. (eds.) KES 2004. LNCS (LNAI), vol. 3213, pp. 1051–1057. Springer, Heidelberg (2004)
20. Welling, M., Kurihara, K.: Bayesian k-means as a "maximization-expectation" algorithm. In: SDM (2006)
21. Xu, L., Hung, E.: Distance-Based Feature Selection on Classification of Uncertain Objects. In: Wang, D., Reynolds, M. (eds.) AI 2011. LNCS, vol. 7106, pp. 172–181. Springer, Heidelberg (2011)

Hierarchical Multi-agent Distribution Planning

Tony Allard and Slava Shekh

Command, Control, Communications and Intelligence Division,
Defence Science and Technology Organisation, Adelaide, Australia
{tony.allard,slava.shekh}@dsto.defence.gov.au

Abstract. Logistics and distribution planning are an important element of military operational planning. The vast level of detail available during planning increases the difficulty in forming a complete solution within time constraints. Moreover, the consideration of multiple planning scenarios is paramount to successfully investigate all available contingencies. This paper presents a hierarchical multi-agent approach to distribution planning. The use of a multi-agent system enables a distribution problem to be logically separated, with each part being delegated to an independent agent. The application of hierarchy allows agent communication to be regulated, reducing redundancy in communication, as encountered in a flat multi-agent structure. Through multiple trials, it was found that the application of hierarchy vastly improved the computational performance of the system, without compromise to solution quality.

Keywords: distribution planning, multi-agent systems, agent hierarchy.

1   Introduction

A complete and robust distribution plan underpins a successful military operation. Logistics and distribution planning have become of central importance to operational planning. Logistics with respect to defence is defined as force projection and sustainment of forces [1] and distribution as the act of satisfying those logistical requirements. Therefore the distribution problem is defined as the satisfaction of deployment and redeployment activities (force projection) and the movement of sustainment stock (sustainment). A distribution plan is formed by constructing and assigning a schedule to each transport, collectively providing one possible solution to the distribution problem. Each schedule consists of a mapping of personnel, equipment and sustainment to movements conducted by a specific transport at a given point in time. The aim of a distribution plan is usually to achieve the movements required in the shortest time possible with the lowest cost. Solving the distribution problem is best described as the difficulty of managing cost and uncertainty [2].

The application of intelligent agents in software systems are becoming increasingly attributed as "capable of exhibiting flexible problem-solving behaviour" [3]. When the distribution problem is viewed with the mindset of employing an intelligent agent approach, one cannot help but see the possibility of using multiple agents [4]. This is because the problem can be easily viewed as a set of self-interested agents, some with

M. Thielscher and D. Zhang (Eds.): AI 2012, LNCS 7691, pp. 755–766, 2012.

tasks that require completion and others with resources to complete those tasks. In this paper we consider each transport as an individual agent with goals to complete distribution tasks in the shortest duration. A single agent handles task announcement and allocation using a bidding process, the details of which will be explained later. Through multi-agent negotiation, agents collaborate to formulate the distribution plan. As the number of agents increase so too does the communication overhead, increasing the time taken to produce a solution to the distribution problem. Since the agents themselves can be described by the transports they represent and the capabilities of those transports, we propose grouping the agents by capability. In this way a single agent can represent a collection of transports and a hierarchical structure of agents is developed. This paper presents a two-tiered hierarchical multi-agent approach to solving the distribution problem, modelling agents:

- at the micro level as individual transportation assets, and
- at the macro level as representations of homogeneous collections of transport capabilities

A hierarchical multi-agent system (MAS) is evaluated for the quality of the solution and the computational time taken to achieve the solution against a set of example scenarios. The distribution problem can be simplified to a Vehicle Routing Problem (VRP), which has been shown to be NP-Hard [5]. As a result, optimal solutions to the real-world scenarios considered in this paper could not be computed. However the solutions produced by the hierarchical MAS were compared to those produced manually and found to be of similar quality.

This paper focuses on the solution to the distribution problem from the point of view of efficient allocation of resources. Therefore force projection and sustainment are modelled as fixed time events. These events represent a quantity of personnel, equipment and sustainment (cargo) to be moved from one location to another by one or more transportation assets with set temporal constraints. The solution space of the distribution problem consists of transports, routes (modes) and bases (nodes) each with varying capabilities, as well as the possibility of unavailability time; such as maintenance. Therefore the logistical planner's job is one of data acquisition and analysis, resource allocation, risk mitigation and optimisation. This paper will discuss a solution to the resource allocation problem and optimisation, for an insight into risk analysis see [6].

2   Related Work

Multi-agent techniques have been used for planning and scheduling in a wide range of domains. Andreev, Rzevski et al. [7] used agents to model the drivers and vehicles of a Rent-a-Car company, while [8] applied multi-agent concepts to the newspaper industry. In these cases, a multi-agent system provided problem abstraction and efficiency in generating schedules, both of which would be difficult to achieve with a centralised approach. Agents provide a way of dividing responsibility among multiple entities and negotiation between agents can be used to formulate schedules. One negotiation technique is auction-based allocation, where tasks are allocated based on the best bids made by agents. [9] used this approach to model auctions with various trucking companies for deliveries in transportation logistics.

Military operations are generally very complex in nature, and modelling them is therefore a difficult task. Multi-agent systems provide an effective way of dealing with this problem. Agents can be used to represent various entities, such as transports, resources and units, including both friendly and hostile forces. The basic behaviours of these entities can then be modelled, which provides a platform for observing interactions between entities and utilising the resultant outputs. This approach has been applied to numerous types of military operations, including military combat [10], crisis management [11] and logistics [12]. The system described by [12], called UltraLog, utilises the interaction and collaboration of over a thousand planning agents to develop a military logistics plan.

Despite the ability of the MAS to provide problem abstraction, modelling a large system can result in a significant communication overhead. As the number of agents increases so does the number of communication channels and hence the effort required to search [13]. One strategy for dealing with this is to incorporate a predetermined hierarchy into the agent structure. [14] presents a hierarchical multi-agent approach for modelling work schedules on a construction site. The hierarchy consists of multiple tiers of agents, which task each other in building a structure, from the low-level agents that lay the bricks to the high-level agents that coordinate the construction. Similarly, the MAS presented in this paper uses a hierarchical structure (albeit not pre-determined) to allocate responsibility; high-level agents are responsible for broad planning through negotiation, while low-level agents perform detailed planning of their respective transportation requirements. The presence of fewer agents at the higher levels of the hierarchy results in less communication overhead.

A hierarchical agent structure was used by [15] to resolve conflicts amongst agents functioning as subject matter experts (SME). The agents were clustered together based on the data they used to make decisions; agents with common data were placed in similar clusters. The MAS was structured as a three-tiered hierarchy with each cluster headed by an agent that facilitated communication within the cluster and between different clusters. The top of the hierarchy was a single agent responsible for making the final decision based on the suggested decisions provided by each cluster. This implementation focused on reducing conflicts between agents and improving the accuracy of the system. While this reduced some communication overhead, if these SME agents are viewed as operating on similar capabilities, then this paper seeks to utilise the hierarchy to episodically filter agents whose capabilities are not suitable for a particular distribution problem.

Initial schedules formulated by agents can be sub-optimal, and improvements become more evident as the schedules are populated. Thus, our system incorporates techniques for schedule optimisation, similar to the transport load consolidation in the system described by [16]. Schedule optimisation allows cargo to be delivered quicker using fewer resources, which is an important factor given the limited transportation assets that are often available during military operations.

3 Problem Definition

The distribution problem defined in this paper is modelled as a finite set of jobs, $J := \{j_1, \ldots, j_n\}$, each with an amount of cargo requiring transportation from an origin to destination within fixed temporal boundaries. Let L be the finite set of geographical locations, which include the origin and destination of these jobs, $L := \{l_1, \ldots, l_p\}$. Each job, j_i, can then be represented by the tuple $\langle l_{j_i}^{origin}, l_{j_i}^{destination}, t_{j_i}^{start}, t_{j_i}^{finish}, C_{j_i} \rangle$ where, $t_{j_i}^{start}$ and $t_{j_i}^{finish}$ are the earliest time j_i can be started and the latest time j_i can be completed respectively. $l_{j_i}^{origin} \in L$ is the location of j_i's cargo at time $t_{j_i}^{start}$, while $l_{j_i}^{destination} \in L$ is the desired location of j_i's cargo at time $t_{j_i}^{finish}$. $C_{j_i} := \{c_{j_i 1}, \ldots, c_{j_i n}\}$ is the finite set of cargo for j_i; where, each element, $c_{j_i k}$, is the volume and mass representation of the kth cargo element.

Each geographical location is connected to other locations through zero or more routes. Let $R := \{r_1, \ldots, r_h\}$ be the finite set of routes for the distribution problem. Each of these routes can support a single mode of transportation within the fixed set $M := \{road, rail, air, sea\}$. Each route, r_b, is defined by the tuple $\langle l_{r_b}^{origin}, l_{r_b}^{destination}, m_{r_b}, d_{r_b} \rangle$ where, $l_{r_b}^{origin} \in L$ and $l_{r_b}^{destination} \in L$ are the start and end geographical locations of r_b; $m_{r_b} \in M$ is the mode of r_b and d_{r_b} is the distance of r_b. Two locations can be connected by a sequence of routes, where each route can potentially involve a different mode of transportation. Hence, a single job may involve traversing routes of multiple modes.

The distribution problem also models transportation assets as the fixed set $V := \{v_1, \ldots, v_m\}$. Each transport v_x is represented by the tuple $\langle \omega_{v_x}, d_{v_x}, m_{v_x}, c_{v_x}, \rangle$ where, ω_{v_x} and d_{v_x} are the maximum speed and distance v_x is capable of travelling respectively; $m_{v_x} \in M$ is the mode of transportation v_x can travel and c_{v_x} is the volume and mass representation of the amount of cargo v_x can carry.

Distribution planning is the allocation of transport assets to specific jobs. A job, j_1, is completed when its cargo C_{j_1} is transported from $l_{j_1}^{origin}$ to $l_{j_1}^{destination}$. Transportation of C_{j_1} cannot begin prior to $t_{j_1}^{start}$ and for j_1 to be successful all cargo must arrive at $l_{j_1}^{destination}$ no later than $t_{j_1}^{finish}$. A transport, v_1, can only participate in the completion of j_1 if there is some item in C_{j_1} that fits within the cargo capacity of v_1. When moving between two locations v_1 can only travel on the set of routes $R_\mu \subseteq R$, where $\forall y \in R_1, (m_y = m_{v_1}) \wedge (d_y \leq d_{v_1})$. v_1 can transport j_1's cargo directly to the $l_{j_1}^{destination}$ or partway to a new location, l_k. If v_1 transports the cargo partway, another transport, v_h, is required to transport the cargo the remaining distance (l_k to $l_{j_1}^{destination}$) or to another intermediary location (l_k to l_{k+1}). This cooperative style of transportation may be required if $l_{j_1}^{origin}$ and $l_{j_1}^{destination}$ are separated by routes of varying modes.

The distribution problem is solved when all jobs are completed successfully. It may not be possible to complete a job within a single trip, so a transport may need to perform multiple trips, or more than one transport may need to be used. Transports can also participate in multiple jobs at once.

4   Multi-agent Negotiation

We begin by looking at a non-hierarchical (flat) agent structure, which models agents as individual transportation assets. Let $A := \{a_1, \ldots, a_n\}$ be the fixed set of agents in the system. Each agent is aware of its capabilities as a transport, v_{a_i}; its current schedule, Δ_{a_i}; the locations it can travel, L_{a_i} and the other agents in the system with which it can communicate, A_{a_i}. Therefore an agent a_i can be represented by the tuple $\langle v_{a_i}, L_{a_i}, \Delta_{a_i}, A_{a_i} \rangle$. In this flat structure each individual agent is capable of communicating with all other agents in the system, meaning $A_{a_i} = \{a_i\}^c \cap A$.

The process of solving a distribution problem is coordinated by the Bid Controller (BC), with the goal of formulating an efficient allocation of transport resources. The BC has access to the set of jobs, J, and processes J in order of $t_{j_i}^{start}$, announcing each job to all agents in the system. The agents form their best bid for each job and submit that bid to the BC. This bidding process is illustrated in Fig. 1, and discussed in more detail below.

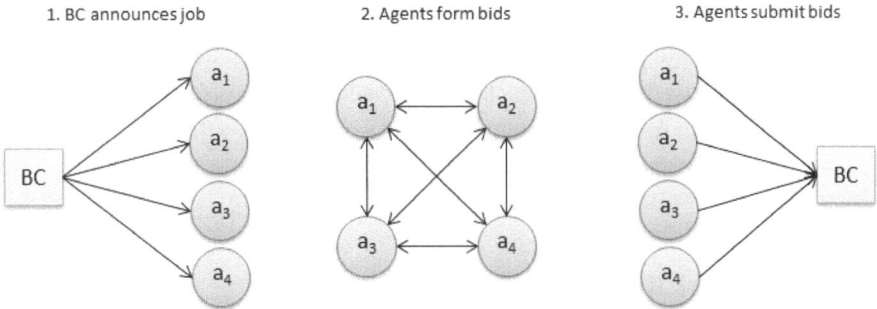

Fig. 1. The bidding process in the flat agent structure

When the BC announces a new job, j_1, the goal of each agent is to transport as much of C_{j_1} as possible from $l_{j_1}^{origin}$ to $l_{j_1}^{destination}$ before $t_{j_1}^{finish}$. To achieve this each agent computes a series of bids for j_1 and selects its most efficient bid to respond to the announcement.

A bid is a proposed movement or set of movements to complete j_1, either in part or in full. a_1 can form a bid to transport C_{j_1} directly from $l_{j_1}^{origin}$ to $l_{j_1}^{destination}$, or if it is unable to reach $l_{j_1}^{destination}$, it may transport C_{j_1} to an intermediate location l_k and subcontract the remainder of the journey. Once a_1 decides to subcontract, it will send a new sub-job announcement to A_{a_1} outlining the requirement to transport C_{j_1} from l_k to $l_{j_1}^{destination}$. The agents that receive the announcement will then undergo the same bidding process as described above with a_1. Concretely, each agent a_i in A_{a_1} will consider completing the sub-job themselves, or subcontracting further, depending on what is likely to result in the most efficient bid.

A bid that contains more than one movement is termed a composite bid. Composite bids are limited in size to no more than six movements or the number of transports in the problem, whichever is smaller. This means that for a bid to be valid it must complete the transportation of C_{j_1} from $l_{j_1}^{origin}$ to $l_{j_1}^{destination}$ utilising no more than six transportation assets. The imposition of a subcontract limit on the MAS limits the search space, preventing agents from pursuing intractable solutions. A subcontract limit of six was found to be a good compromise between computation time and solution quality.

Each agent, a_1, creates bids by iterating over L_{a_1} and A_{a_1} and attempts to move the maximum amount of cargo it can carry to each location, l_k, initiating subcontracting when $l_k \neq l_{j_1}^{destination}$. This follows a heuristic search which prunes branches of the search tree that can be seen to offer less efficient results.

Once all bids have been generated, a_1 responds to the job announcement with its most efficient bid. Efficiency is determined by the expected completion time of the job, according the bid. If two bids have the same expected completion time, the agent will use the bid with the lowest transport utilisation time. Bids that involve fewer transports for shorter periods of time will have lower utilisation times and are considered more desirable. The system itself maintains a set of bids received by agents and selects the best bid that satisfies the same efficiency criteria. All agents involved in the best bid will then have their schedules updated. If b_y does not transport all of C_{j_1} from $l_{j_1}^{origin}$ to $l_{j_1}^{destination}$, the system will create a new job announcement to transport the remaining cargo, at which point the bidding process begins again.

5   Benefits of Hierarchy

The MAS described above enables each agent to communicate or subcontract to any other agent in the system. This is termed a flat communication structure (FCS); meaning that for each agent in the system $A_{a_i} = \{a_i\}^c \cap A$. Therefore if N_a is the number of agents in the MAS, then each agent has $N_a - 1$ communication links. If ρ is the subcontract limit, then the worst case number of iterations of subcontracting is $\prod_{\varepsilon=1}^{\rho-1}(N_a - \varepsilon)$. If the MAS iterates over the set of jobs, J, and each job requires, at worst case, each agent to iterate over all locations, L, then the worst case computational complexity of the problem is $J \times L \times N_a \times \prod_{\varepsilon=1}^{\rho-1}(N_a - \varepsilon)$. Using this equation, two of the sets can be held constant while the other is increased. The effect of each set on the computational complexity is shown in Fig. 2. Computational complexity is modelled in computational units; an abstract unit representing a single iteration over any of the three sets. Fig. 2 shows that an increase in the number of jobs or locations in the system results in a linear increase in computational complexity. However as the number of agents in the system increases, the computational complexity increases exponentially. This exponential increase is not surprising, since N_a agents could have up to $N_a - 1$ communication links.

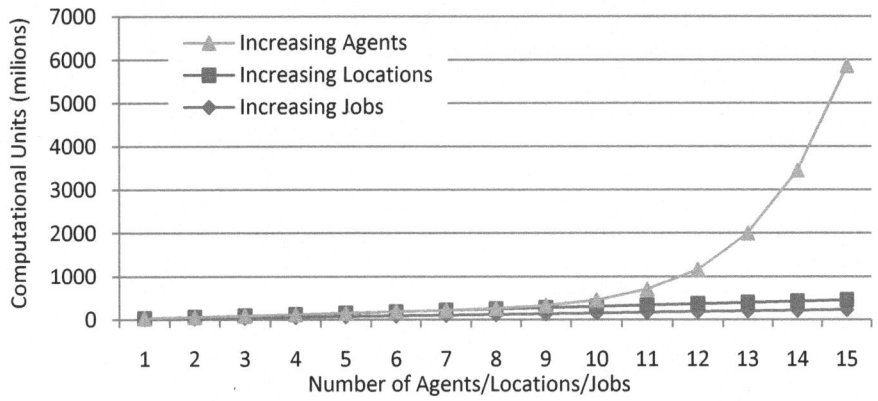

Fig. 2. Effect of system elements on computational complexity

It can therefore be said that the number agents in the MAS, or indeed the number of communication links between them, is the dominant factor affecting computational complexity. The most effective method for reducing computational complexity is to reduce agent communication or the communication overhead. This paper suggests logical grouping of agents to isolate communication between groups and the development of these groups into a hierarchical communication structure (HCS) to better direct communication. Agents were grouped based on the capabilities of the transport asset they were modelling, with similar capabilities grouped together. A new type of agent, transport agent T, models the head of an agent group and directs communication down the hierarchy. This hierarchy is illustrated in Fig. 3, providing an alternative communication structure to step 2 of Fig. 1.

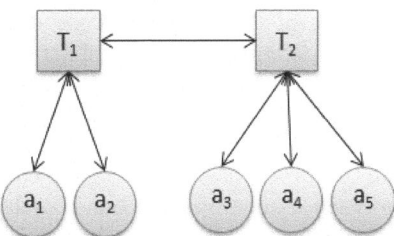

Fig. 3. The hierarchical agent communication structure

Bidding, communication and hence subcontracting are performed at the transport agent level. Transport agents select the most suitable agent in their group to participate in a bid. The original equation for worst case iterations of subcontracting thus becomes $N_t \times \prod_{\varepsilon=1}^{\rho-1}(N_t - \varepsilon)$ where N_t is the number of transport agents, and $N_t \ll N_a$. Each transport agent can be thought of as a different capability group within the MAS. The exponential growth of the computational complexity can now be limited by the ability to divide agents into capability groups. As will be shown in the next section the HCS results in a large reduction in computational complexity and hence computation time when compared with the FCS.

The HCS solution quality depends on the degree of similarity between transports within capability groups. When capability groups are characterised by specific platform type (e.g. C-130H aircraft, C-17 aircraft, etc.) the solutions of both MAS structures should be equivalent since the Transport Agent exactly represents its constituents. However when capability definitions are generalised (e.g. aircraft, ships, trucks, etc.) the solutions produced by the HCS tend to reduce in quality when compared to those produced by the FCS. As capability definitions become more abstract the quality of the HCS will continue to degrade with a corresponding increase in computational performance. This degradation in quality may require the use of an automated plan repair functionality to correct the errors introduced. This paper considers only specific transport capability groups, while abstract capability representations and plan repair techniques are areas for future work.

6   Results

Testing was completed in two parts; one assessing computational complexity and the other testing the quality of the solution.

Computational complexity was assessed using two distribution problem scenarios that were similar to circumstances faced by military planners. The two scenarios differed in their route network; the first was designed with a fully connected route network allowing each individual transport type to complete a problem in full. The second was designed with a partially connected route network where agents were required to subcontract to achieve their goals. Specifically, in the partially connected network, each location could only be reached, on average, by two routes. For example, Location C might only be reachable by sea from A, or by air from B. This created a need for agents to cooperate in the partially connected network, because most jobs could not be completed alone. Conversely, the fully connected network had no such restriction and each agent could operate independent of other agents.

Each distribution problem consisted of a set of fixed time events requiring the movement of supplies from multiple geographical locations. Three different transport asset capabilities were initialised in groups at random locations. The number of transports of each type was varied from one to 25 during testing with each amount tested 100 times. Both the HCS and FCS attempted to solve each of these distributions problems. When a solution was found, each communication structure produced the same solution however the time required to reach such a solution varied, especially when dealing with increasing instances of each transport capability. Solutions produced by both structures were of equal quality due to the use of specific transport capability groups in the HCS as described in Section 5.

The computation time for various problems is shown in Fig. 4 and Fig. 5 for fully connected and partially connected networks respectively. These graphs use a logarithmic time scale due to the rapid growth in computation time of the FCS. The vertical bars show the standard deviation of each result. Due to time constraints, the FCS was unable to complete instances of the problem comprising of more than four transports in each capability for a fully connected route network, and seven transports in each capability for a partially connected route network. These instances are therefore not shown in the graphs.

The quality of the solution was also tested against a centralised approach for distribution planning, known as the Greedy Distribution Algorithm (GDA) [17]. Instead of using a multi-agent system, the GDA contains a central entity that considers the constraints of the planning scenario and formulates a distribution plan by applying heuristics. The use of heuristics is driven by the inability of exact methods, such as integer programming, to scale effectively to larger problems [18].

The solutions produced by the HCS were compared to those produced by the GDA algorithm for the same problem set, as shown in Table 1. These problems are based on real world distribution scenarios faced by military planners, and for this paper have been labelled S1-S10. The quality of the solutions is measured by the makespan of the schedule generated by the algorithm. The makespan is the time difference between the start of the first movement and the end of the last movement. Shorter makespans are desired for a given distribution problem as it means the movements were completed in a shorter duration.

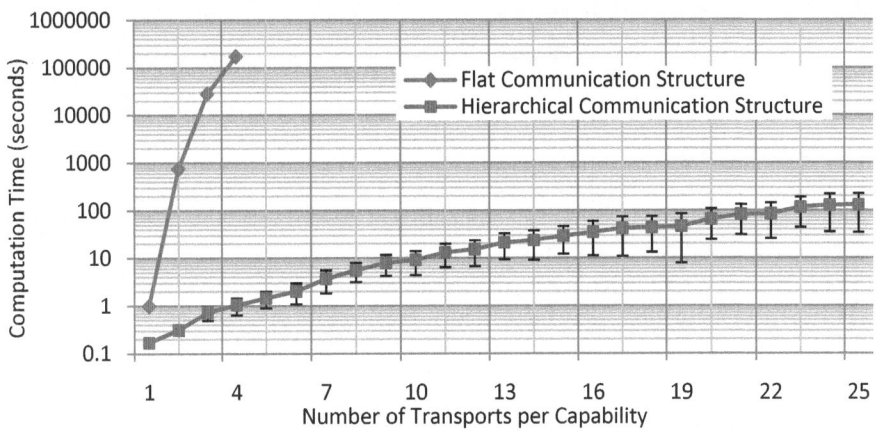

Fig. 4. Distribution problem computation time for a fully connected route network

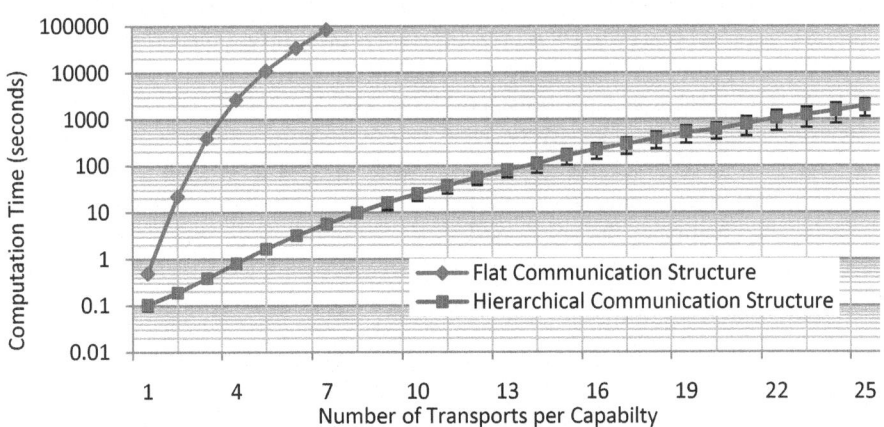

Fig. 5. Distribution problem computation time for a partially connected route network

Table 1. Distribution plan makespans for the HCS and GDA

Scenario	Hierarchical Communication Structure	Greedy Distribution Algorithm
S1	52 days, 14 hours, 41 minutes	68 days, 6 hours, 34 minutes
S2	21 days, 11 hours, 9 minutes	23 days, 21 hours, 32 minutes
S3	182 days, 5 hours, 51 minutes	199 days, 21 hours, 51 minutes
S4	10 days, 7 hours, 43 minutes	17 days 15 hours 40 minutes
S5	37 days, 4 hours, 12 minutes	37 days 12 hours 6 minutes
S6	121 days, 17 hours, 15 minutes	140 days 22 hours 9 minutes
S7	31 days, 8 hours, 9 minutes	31 days 12 hours 24 minutes
S8	70 days, 9 hours, 22 minutes	80 days 20 hours 25 minutes
S9	48 days, 8 hours, 46 minutes	50 days 11 hours 42 minutes
S10	21 days, 5 hours, 41 minutes	21 days 12 hours 36 minutes

7   Discussion

The results in Fig. 4 show a comparison of computation times for both communication structures in a fully connected route network. Fig. 5 shows a similar comparison for a partially connected route network. In both network configurations, the FCS performed poorly, growing at a near exponential rate. Due to this exponential growth, calculating a result became infeasible for transport quantities above four in fully connected networks, and seven in partially connected networks. For example, a fully connected network with four transports per capability using the FCS took approximately 48 hours to compute one solution. In contrast, the HCS demonstrated improved scalability, suggesting that it is better suited for handling the complexity of real-world scenarios. A solution could be found for route networks with up to 25 transports per capability in an acceptable timeframe, faster than the FCS could compute a solution for four transports per capability.

The poor computational performance of the FCS can be attributed to the large number communication links. Every agent can potentially communicate with every other agent, regardless of previous communications between agents of a similar capability. This leads to redundant communication that costs computation time without improving the quality of the solution. The HCS exhibits a distinct improvement in computational performance. This is due to the structure's logical isolation of similarly capable agents, thereby reducing redundant communication and allowing negotiation between agents to be better focused on improving the global solution. This is evident in Fig. 4 and Fig. 5 where the HCS consistently outperformed the FCS, despite both approaches producing solutions of equal makespan.

Fig. 4 displays a non-uniform computation time slope for the HCS, becoming increasingly evident as the number of agents per capability increases. This is caused by the lack of restriction in the route network. The ability of any transport to travel to any destination lends itself to many different solutions for the same problem. This requires a large number of samples for a statistically significant result. While the gathered data still reflects the scalability of the algorithm, a larger sample set could improve the uniformity of the computation time slope. Gathering more results and further investigating the progression of the computation time slope for the MAS implementation is an area for future research and is beyond the scope of this paper.

Table 1 shows the comparative performance of the HCS and GDA. The GDA utilises a greedy algorithm designed to produce solutions in a timely manner at the expense of solution quality. In contrast the HCS employs a more comprehensive search of the solution space enabling it to provide better quality solutions at the expense of computational performance. To overcome performance issues the HCS utilises hierarchy to logically group agents and reduce communication overhead. As a result the HCS was able to produce better quality solutions when compared with the GDA, while remaining comparable in computational performance.

8   Conclusion

This paper presents a hierarchical MAS for solving logistic distribution problems. From trials conducted against real-world distribution scenarios it was shown that the HCS dominates the FCS in its ability to produce efficient solutions in considerably less computation time. As the scenario size increases the FCS becomes intractable, while the HCS remains computationally efficient, without loss of solution quality. The efficiency of the HCS is the result of its ability to isolate similarly capable agents and better direct communication.

The hierarchical MAS presented was able to provide better quality solutions to distribution scenarios than algorithms developed with similar intent. When solutions from both the HCS and GDA were compared it was found that the HCS was able to produce on average better quality solutions with similar computational performance. This supports the claim that HCS can produce quality solutions to complex real-world problems within acceptable timeframes.

Future research is directed to further increasing the computational performance of the MAS, either through improved agent communication or applied heuristics. Another area of interest is the application of the MAS in dynamic replanning and plan repair as a computer-based decision aide for human planning.

Acknowledgements. The authors would like to acknowledge Don Gossink, Luke Marsh and Hing-Wah Kwok for their support, guidance and contributions to this research project.

References

1. Tuttle, W.G.T.: Defense logistics for the 21st century. Naval Institute Press, Annapolis (2005)
2. Simchi-Levi, D., Bramel, J., Chen, X.: The logic of logistics: theory algorithms and applications for logistics and supply chain management. Springer, New York (2005)
3. Jennings, N.R.: An Agent-Based Approach for Building Complex Software Systems. Communications of the ACM 44 (2001)
4. Perugini, D., Wark, S., Zschorn, A., Lambert, D., Sterling, L., Pearce, A.: Agents in Logistics Planning - Experiences with the Coalition Agents Experiment Project. In: 2nd International Joint Conference on Autonomous Agents and Multiagent Systems (2003)
5. Lenstra, J.K., Rinnooy Kan, A.H.G.: Complexity of Vehicle Routing and Scheduling Problems. Networks 11, 221–227 (1981)
6. Thiagarajan, R., Kwok, H., Calbert, G., Gossink, D., Shekh, S., Allard, T.: A simulation-based risk analysis technique to determine critical assets in a plan. In: 19th International Congress on Modelling and Simulation, pp. 503–509 (2011)
7. Andreev, S., Rzevski, G., Shviekin, P., Skobelev, P., Yankov, I.: A Multi-agent Scheduler for Rent-a-Car Companies. In: Mařík, V., Strasser, T., Zoitl, A. (eds.) HoloMAS 2009. LNCS, vol. 5696, pp. 305–314. Springer, Heidelberg (2009)
8. Böhnlein, D., Schweiger, K., Tuma, A.: Multi-agent-based transport planning in the newspaper industry. International Journal of Production Economics 131, 146–157 (2011)
9. Robu, V., Noot, H., La Poutré, H., Van Schijndel, W.J.: A multi-agent platform for auction-based allocation of loads in transportation logistics. Expert Systems with Applications 38, 3483–3491 (2011)
10. Malhotra, A.: Agent-Based Modeling in Defence. DRDO Science Spectrum, 60–65 (March 2009)
11. Kaddoussi, A., Zoghlami, N., Hammadi, S., Zgaya, H.: An agent-based distributed scheduling for military logistics. In: 11th International Conference on Intelligent Systems Design and Applications (ISDA), pp. 59–64 (2011)
12. Carrico, T., Greaves, M.: Agent Applications in Defense Logistics. In: Defence Industry Applications of Autonomous Agents and Multi-Agent Systems, pp. 51–72 (2008)
13. Perugini, D., Jarvis, D., Reschke, S., Gossink, D.: Distributed Deliberative Planning with Partial Observability: Heuristic Approaches. In: International Conference on Integration of Knowledge Intensive Multi-Agent Systems (KIMAS), pp. 407–412 (2007)
14. Molinero, C., Núñez, M.: Planning of work schedules through the use of a hierarchical multi-agent system. Automation in Construction 20, 1227–1241 (2011)
15. Wakulicz-Deja, A., Przybyla-Kasperek, M.: Hierarchical Multi-Agent System. In: Recent Advances in Intelligent Information Systems, pp. 615–628 (2009)
16. Baykasoglu, A., Kaplanoglu, V.: A multi-agent approach to load consolidation in transportation. Advances in Engineering Software 42, 477–490 (2011)
17. Marsh, L., Gossink, D.: Exploiting Symmetries in Logistics Distribution Planning. In: 19th International Congress on Modelling and Simulation, pp. 482–488 (2011)
18. Marsh, L.: A Study on Optimisation Techniques for Logistics Distribution. School of Mathematical Sciences. The University of Adelaide, Adelaide (2008)

Generating Project Plans
for Data Center Transformations

Amrit Lal Ahuja and Girish Keshav Palshikar

Tata Research Development and Design Centre (TRDDC),
Tata Consultancy Services Limited,
54B, Hadapsar Industrial Estate, Pune 411013, India
{amrit.ahuja, gk.palshikar}@tcs.com

Abstract. Operations of modern organizations critically depend on Data Centers (DC). Due to ad hoc additions from diverse business units over time, the IT resources in a DC get unwieldy and complex. Transformations of DC - server consolidation, migration, application/data simplification, technology standardization - are important for cost, efficiency and reliability. Even when a specific transformation is identified ("consolidate these 100 existing servers into these 48 new servers") it is difficult to generate a detailed optimal project plan for its execution. The project plan must identify all the tasks involved, identify an optimal team (size and expertise) and generate a detailed work schedule that meets the and respects the constraints and dependencies among the tasks. We present a methodology to generate such a plan automatically from given "high-level" IT transformation specifications ("as-is" and "to-be" states). We adopt a heuristic forward chaining metric temporal planner engine (SAPA) to generate a project plan that attempts to optimize the overall time and team-size. The idea is to capture the domain-knowledge as reusable planning action. This automation reduces the efforts and errors in manual project planning. The method can be extended to projects in other domains.

1 Introduction

Operations of modern organizations critically depend on *Data Centers* (DC), which consist of a large number of IT resources such as servers, storage, networks, OS, middleware, databases, business applications etc. Due to changing business requirements, changing workload patterns, new applications/users/customers/business partners and technology changes, the IT infrastructure in a DC keeps evolving. Due to *ad hoc* additions from diverse business units over time, the IT resources in a DC get unwieldy and complex. As a real-life example, a large bank has several DCs containing 30,000+ servers, 5+ OS with 20+ versions, 10+ database products, 25+ middleware environments, 2500+ app server instances, 10+ petabytes of storage, 35+ programming languages etc. As another example, the US Army has 800+ DCs which run 24,000+ servers and 9000+ applications, which they are planning to consolidate into 615+ DC by 2014, thereby hoping to save approx. $5 billion (http://www.army.mil/article/70991/ accessed on 04-July-2012).

M. Thielscher and D. Zhang (Eds.): AI 2012, LNCS 7691, pp. 767–778, 2012.
© Springer-Verlag Berlin Heidelberg 2012

Managing a DC consisting of such large, complex, heterogeneous and business critical IT resources is very difficult, leading to issues with performance, utilization, reliability, availability, costs (maintenance, license and power) and workload on support personnel. Thus DC transformations - e.g., server consolidations, application and data simplifications, technology standardizations - are important for cost, efficiency and reliability. Focus on green IT is another reason for DC transformations. DC transformations is an active area of research; e.g., [1,2,3,4,5,6] and much other work, most of which is primarily about problems and technologies related to DC transformations, including in cloud and other scenarios. Many IT organizations provide specialized services and products for DC transformations.

In this paper, we focus on two problems: (i) generating a detailed and reasonably good (not necessarily optimal) project plan for a given DC transformation project; and (ii) deciding the optimal team size for the project. Creating such a project plan is a complex and effort-intensive activity, as myriad details of identifying relevant tasks, interdependencies among IT resources as well as tasks, human resource related constraints etc. need to be taken into account. Manually creating such a plan is error-prone and time-consuming; ensuring that the plans are close to optimal is difficult.

In this paper, we propose an approach where detailed and reasonably good quality project plans for DC transformation projects are automatically generated using a standard temporal planner engine. The high-level details of the IT resources and their transformations are taken as input. The approach is based on a one-time activity of building a comprehensive library of transformation tasks, modeled as a set of actions (operators) in the domain file in PDDL. All the dependencies for each task as well as team-related constraints are built into the corresponding action. The transformation details are automatically translated to the problem file in PDDL. The planner engine then generates a location-wise plan (since a transformation project often includes multiple DCs) that includes start and end time for each task, along with the associated team member to carry it out. As far as we know, this is the first time a temporal planner is used to generate detailed project plans for DC transformation projects. The approach is extendible to projects of other kinds.

The paper is organized as follows. Section 2 defines the DC transformation task in detail along with a real-life case-study. Section 3 defines the approach and illustrates how it works for the case-study. Section 4 describes related work. Section 5 offers some conclusions and outlines future work.

2   DC Transformation Projects

2.1   Server Consolidation and DC Migration

We focus here on a particular kind of DC transformation strategy, called *server consolidation*. The task is to identify redundant, under-utilized, "small" or "old" servers in a DC and move all the data and applications on them to other "suitable" existing servers and/or on new servers, so that the new set of servers are "better" than the old set of servers (e.g., less power, less operating costs, better reliability, easier to manage etc.). Server consolidation is often coupled with *DC migration*, where all IT resources in a *source DC* are "consolidated" into resources in another *target DC* and the source DC is then closed, thereby saving on some capital costs. A server consolidation specification consists of one or more movegroups. A *movegroup* (MG) [1] often consists of a group of closely related servers along with related resources such as business applications (e.g., cheque processing or ATM transaction processing in a bank), databases etc. There are carefully designed strategies to form the MGs in a server consolidation project.

The MGs are disjoint i.e., any server in a source DC belongs to at most one MG. Each MG G is a unit of server consolidation project and consists of a finite set $S = \{s_1, s_2, \ldots\}$ of *source servers* from DC D, which need to be mapped or moved to a set T of *destination* (or *target*) *servers* in (possibly different) DC D'. We assume that $S \cap T = \emptyset$. Generally, $|T| \leq |S|$ i.e., target servers are fewer in number than source servers. For generality, we assume that source servers in all MG belong to the same DC D and target servers in all MG belong to the same DC $D' \neq D$. *MG specification* gives complete details of each source as well as target server in it; e.g., number of CPUs, memory, disk, OS, special-purpose HW devices connected to it, system software running on it, business applications running on it, old and new IP addresses etc. The MG specification also defines which source servers are mapped to which target servers and also the method of transformation (Section 2.2).

The MGs in a project may have dependencies among each other and so they need to be consolidated in a suitable order that "respects" these dependencies. However, we will ignore this issue and assume that we are given an MG which either has no dependencies on other MGs or all the MGs on which it is dependent are already consolidated in the target DC. This is not a serious limitation because our approach is designed to handle such dependencies.

If all the source servers in an MG were independent, then in principle they can all be consolidated in sequence, in parallel or in any combination of sequential and parallel steps. However, the source servers (and the applications running on them) within an MG may depend on each other in several ways:

- a source server may provide a shared service to other servers;
- a source server may host data (e.g., tables or files) shared by other servers;
- a source server may control access to a hardware resource (e.g., tape drive or communication link) by other servers.

Thus the dependencies among the source servers must be taken into account when preparing a project plan for an MG. In general, a server may run several business applications and there may be dependencies among these applications as well.

2.2 A Case-Study

We consider a real-life server consolidation and DC migration project, consisting of nearly 400 servers in source DC called DC1, which were to be consolidated and migrated to about 300 servers in target DC called DC2. This project was divided into 7 MGs. Figure 1 shows the specification for a particular MG consisting of 19 source servers (all in one DC) and 10 target servers (all in another DC). We have omitted some details such as source and target IP addresses etc. Servers marked as "shared" typically run common services or functionality (e.g., databases, user authentication etc.)

Source Server	Business Application Group	Server Function	CPU	Memory	Storage GB	SAN Boot	Target Server	Target State
1	Shared	App	1	8192	864.61	Yes	1001	LPAR
2	FRNA	App	2	767	20	Yes	1002	x86 V2V
3	FRNA	App	2	767	20	Yes	1002	x86 V2V
4	FRNA	App	2	2047	30	Yes	1002	x86 V2V
5	FRNA	App	2	1051	24.96	Yes	1002	x86 V2V
6	FRNA	App	4	3967	37.25	Yes	1003	new build on x86 P2P-M
7	FRNA	App	2	767	20	Yes	1003	x86 V2V
8	FRNA	App	2	767	20	Yes	1003	x86 V2V
9	FRNA	App	2	8191	33	Yes	1003	x86 P2V
10	Shared	Database	2	4096	157.24	Yes	1005	x86 P2V
11	FRNA	Database	2	3967	109.99	Yes	1006	new build on x86 P2P-S
12	Shared	Database	0.5	6144	615.25	Yes	1007	LPAR
13	Shared	Database	0.5	6144	598.03	Yes	1007	LPAR
14	GRPD_MFGPRO	MP	1	1023	8.43	Yes	1008	x86 P2V
15	FRNA	App	2	3967	50	Yes	1009	x86 P2V
16	GRPD_MFGPRO	App	2	2399	70	Yes	1008	x86 V2V
17	FRNA	Web	1	1563	20	Yes	1010	x86 V2V
18	STD	Web	2	3967	20	Yes	1011	x86 P2V
19	FRNA	Web	1	1563	20	Yes	1010	x86 V2V

Fig. 1. Specification of an MG

used by multiple applications. Here, LPAR indicates the process of migrating every-thing (OS, applications, data etc.) from a physical source server (IBM machine running AIX) to a virtual machine, which consists of a logical partition of hardware resources (e.g., CPUs, memory) on a physical target server from IBM running AIX. P2V indicates the process of migrating everything (OS, applications, data etc.) from a physical source server (Intel-based machine running Windows) to a virtual machine, typically emulating the same environment using virtualization software such as VMWare. Other transfor-mations can be similarly understood. We have assumed that shared servers within this MG need to be consolidated first and the business application groups (FRNA, STD, GRPD_MFGPRO) can be consolidated in any order. Within FRNA, the application servers can be consolidated in any order and the database server must be consolidated last; the system allows more complex precendece relations to be set among the servers in a business application group.

2.3 The Processes of Server Consolidation and DC Migration

Basic steps in server consolidation are about moving all the OS, database, middleware, application programs and other IT resources from a particular source server onto its tar-get server. These steps actually consists of several *tasks*, which depend on the specifics of the concerned server and the IT resources on it. Each task is executed either on the source server or on the destination server. Each task requires a particular skill and which generally takes a specific amount of time. In addition, the tasks themselves have depen-dencies among each other, which need to be respected when preparing a project plan. For example, suppose task A takes the backup of the data on source server, task B cre-ates the necessary tables, users and permissions on the destination server and task C restores this data on the target the server; clearly task A and B must be done before task C. In general, the tasks may be structured hierarchically i.e., a task may have sub-tasks and so forth. Even the time required for each task should ideally be treated as a random variable. However, for simplicity, we treat each task as an atomic unit which requires a specific skill and takes a fixed amount of time.

Any server consolidation and DC migration project typically involves some common tasks. The tasks can be divided into the following groups, where tasks within a group are functionally similar.

1. Source Server Handover: These tasks involve a formal handing over of a source server from the IT operations team to the server consolidation team.
2. Source Server Pre-migration: These tasks are related to system health checkup, installation checks and other tasks that need to be done before this server's consolidation can begin.
3. Server image: These tasks typically consist of creating an image (or a snapshot of the state) of the entire source server on a storage device, transferring this image to the target DC and copying the image onto the target server. Assuming that the target server has already been configured to have the system environment as the source server, the target server is then booted up and it starts in the same state as where the source server was stopped. Detailed specifications of these tasks are dependent on the type of the source and target servers. For example, AIX provides mksysb and related commands for non-SAN bootable servers.
4. Data Backup: This involves taking a backup of all the user files, tables etc. Detailed specifications of the tasks are dependent on the type of the source servers as well as the device on which the backup is taken (e.g., tape, USB, CD etc.). Also, the backup can be total or only incremental. Incremental backup is required if the source server is functioning during the server consolidation project.
5. Data Transfer: These tasks involve either physically shipping a storage device to the target DC or transferring the backed up data over a communication network, typically using ftp commands.
6. Server Shutdown: These tasks are related to shutting down a (source) server.
7. Target Server Startup and Data Restore: These tasks are related to starting up a source server, creating the same system environment on it (using virtualization if required) and ensuring that the required configuration parameters, environment variables, users, access permissions, devices etc. are correctly set. These tasks also include using a storage device to restore the backed up data from the source server into the target server and ensuring its completeness and correctness. The restored data may be part of a full or incremental backup. The business applications on the target are then started one by one and brought up "alive".
8. Target Server Go-Live and Handover: These tasks involve user acceptance testing of business applications in a live environment and a formal handing over of a source server from the server consolidation team to the IT operations team.

Detailed specifications of the tasks in each group are dependent on the type of the source server. The tasks have well-understood precedence relationships, which can be modeled as precedence graph or equivalently, a partial order. There are precedence relations even among the tasks in the same task group; thus the precedence graph is actually over all pairs of tasks and servers. However, in most cases, these dependencies are only for tasks to be performed on the same server; tasks on different servers are usually unrelated or unconstrained (i.e., there is parallelism among tasks across servers).

2.4   Project Plan

We focus here on creating a project plan for a particular MG. The approach can be extended easily to create a project plan for the entire server consolidation project (i.e., all the MG together). A project plan for an MG lists out all the tasks involved for consolidating each source server onto the destination server, along with start and end time for each task and assigns a specific person to carry out each task. Clearly, the requirement is to prepare a project plan that respects all server dependencies as well as task dependencies (which corresponds to the required domain knowledge), minimizes the overall time as well as minimizes the number of people required to execute the tasks. Additional people-related constraints need also to be taken into account while preparing the project plan; e.g., a person cannot work more than, say, 9 hours in a day and a person can work on exactly one task at any time (no "multiplexing" of tasks).

Clearly, creating such a detailed project plan manually (even for a single MG), is difficult, time-consuming and error-prone, particularly when the MG includes a large number of servers. It is difficult to ensure that the manually created plan is optimal in terms of delivery time and team size. Lastly, manually re-generating the project plan at some later stage during execution is even more difficult.

3   Using a Planner Engine to Generate Project Plans

3.1   The Approach

We propose an approach where a project plan for an MG is automatically generated by a planner engine from the given MG specifications. We maintain the required domain knowledge about the tasks and their dependencies, input pre-conditions and output effects (post-conditions), as a library of standard actions in the planner engine. Creating such a library is a one-time task, which is reused for generating project plans for multiple MGs as well as multiple server consolidation projects. This approach makes it easy to quickly generate optimal (or at least close to optimal) project plans. The steps in the approach are as follows:

1. Create a reusable library of tasks involved in server consolidation and DC migration as a domain file in PDDL; this is a one-time manual step.
2. Automatically generate a PDDL problem file from MG specifications
3. Automatically generate a detailed project plan from given problem file and the domain file, using a standard planner engine.
4. Automatically generate a Gantt chart and other project plan deliverables from the output plan.

3.2   Modeling Tasks as a Domain File in PDDL

Detailed specifications of these tasks specialized for each type of servers, including their precedence tasks and post facto effects, the skills required and expected duration for each task constitutes a reusable component of domain knowledge. We model each task as a durative action (or operation) in the planning domain and specify it using Planning Domain Definition Language (PDDL) 2.1 [7]. Briefly, a PDDL specification consists of:

1. *Objects*: in our case, these are the various IT resources such as servers, devices, operating system, system software, databases, middleware and business applications.
2. *Predicates*: Boolean properties of objects which can be TRUE or FALSE.
3. *Initial state*: in our case, these specify the initial conditions about the source and target servers.
4. *Goal state specification*: in our case, these specify the final conditions about the target servers.
5. *Actions/operators*: ways in which the objects can be manipulated to reach a goal state from the given initial state. Each action has a set of *parameters*, a *precondition* (which must beTRUE for the action to get executed and a *post-condition* (or *effect*, which is guaranteed to be TRUE after the action is executed. In our case, actions correspond to tasks. We encode the precedence relations for a task as part of the pre-conditions for the task. We use durative action facility in PDDL and associate a time duration with it; this means that we can only use temporal planner engines to generate the project plan.

In PDDL, the predicates and actions (operators) are defined in a *domain file* and objects, initial state and goal state specifications (for a specific instance of IT transformation) are defined in a *problem file*. This library (i.e., the domain file) of PDDL predicates and actions is reusable for generating project plans for multiple MGs and different server consolidation projects (i.e., for different problem files). If the given MG includes an unknown IT resource (e.g., a server with a previously unseen operating system) then we need to manually add the corresponding tasks to the domain file, including any changes to the precedence relations for all tasks.

Figure 2(a) shows PDDL specifications of one task. SERVER, BA, LOCATION and TEAM are (sets of) objects. Here, BA stands for a set of business applications, TEAM stands for a set of human beings involved in carrying out the tasks, LOCATION contains locations of the source and target DC. These objects have various Boolean properties, which are specified as predicates; e.g., each server has a type (predicate serverTypeIs) and a location (predicate at), each server contains one or more business applications (predicate partOfBA), each team member has a location (predicate available-at) and can be free or busy (predicate free) and so forth. This task depends on the shutdown task for the given server, which sets the flag shutdown-done for the given server. Note that a precondition for this action checks that the given team members is free to perform this task. The flag virtualReplica-done-at is set for the given server and location as a post-condition of this task, which the later tasks can check.

3.3 Modeling MG Specification as Problem File in PDDL

The actual MG is specified as a problem file in PDDL. The problem file contains a set of objects, the initial conditions and a specification of the goal state. In our case, the initial conditions correspond to the information about the source servers (e.g., their location is the old DC). The goal state specification corresponds to the facts that all source servers are moved to the target DC and are "working satisfactorily" i.e., all the tasks have been performed and the user acceptance testing is passed for each target server. We generate the problem file automatically from the MG specification (Figure 2(b)).

```
(:durative-action NetApp6060snapMirrorReplica_P2V         (define (problem server-consolidation-DC-migration)
  :parameters (                                             (:domain itInfraTrans)
      ?srvr - SERVER                                        (:objects
      ?ba - BA                                                  SharedServers STD GRFD_MFGPRO FRNA - BA
      ?loc1 - LOCATION                                         S1, S2, ..., s9, ..., s19 - SERVER
      ?tm - TEAM                                               DC1 DC2 - LOCATION
      ?loc2 - LOCATION                                         Legacy P2P V2V P2V LPAR - TARGET
  )                                                           Windows - SERVERTYPE
  :duration (= ?duration 4.0)                                 WEB DBA APP MFS - ITAPP
  :condition (and                                           )
      (over all (at ?srvr ?loc1))                           (:init
      (over all (partOfBA ?srvr ?ba))                          ...
      (over all (serverTypeIs ?srvr Windows))                 (nameOfBA FRNA)
      (over all (toBeMigratedTo ?srvr ?loc2))                 (baCurrentlyAt  FRNA DC1)
      (over all (toBeMigratedAs ?srvr P2V))                   (at s9 SVSDC)
      (over all (notTakeFromISONet ?srvr))                    (toBeMigratedTo s9 DC2)
      (at start (shutdown-done ?srvr))                        (partOfBA s9 FRNA)
      (over all (does-replica ?tm))                           (toBeMigratedAs s9  P2V)
      (over all (available-at ?tm ?loc2))                     ...
      (at start (free ?tm))                                 )
  )                                                         (:goal (and
  :effect (and                                                 (migrationDoneTo s9 DC2)
      (at start (not (free ?tm)))                              (UAT-done FRNA)
      (at end (free ?tm))                                      ...
      (at end (not (shutdown-done ?srvr)))                  )
      (at end (virtualReplica-done-at ?srvr ?loc2))         )
  )
)
```

Fig. 2. (a) PDDL specification for one task. (b) Problem file for MG specification in Figure 1.

3.4   Finding Optimal Team Size

In our formulation of the multi-agent planning problem, the optimal number of agents is unknown and the planner is expected to generate a plan that is not only optimal in terms of time but also in terms of number of agents required to carry out the plan. We are working to reformulate the planning problem accordingly. In the meantime, we take a simple approach: we run the planner several times, each time varying the team size and checking the overall turnaround time for the project. We then select the optimal team size as one that delivers the project in the shortest time. For the example MG, we have clubbed handover and pre-migration tasks into a single skill-group, shutdown tasks constitute a separate skill-group, data backup, data transfer, data restore and system image as two separate skill-groups (for Microsoft Windows and for AIX), and finally, handover and go-live tasks as a separate skill-group. For brevity, we report only the results where we have kept the team-size for 4 groups as fixed and only vary the team-size for the skill-group for Windows. Figure 3 shows how the project turn-around time varies with team-size for this skill-group; clearly, the team-size of 14 is optimalfor this skill-group. The overall team-size as per this optimal plan is 21 people and 5 skill-groups, with the following skill-wise and location-wise break-up: handover and pre-migration in DC1:1, shutdown in DC1:2, AIX in DC2:2, Windows in DC2:14, go-live and final handover (user acceptance testing) in DC2:2.

3.5   Project Plan for the Example MG

We use the metric temporal planner engine SAPA [8] to generate the plan using the domain file (which is fixed) and the given porblem file, which is specific to a particular MG. The generated plan for the example MG contains a server and task-wise schedule that spans 40 hours, which is well within the given upper limit of 48 hours (a weekend). The composition of the optimal team is already discussed. Our system also has facilities to convert the generated project plan into user-readable artifacts such as schedules (Gantt charts), team utilization summary and other auxiliary outputs which are useful

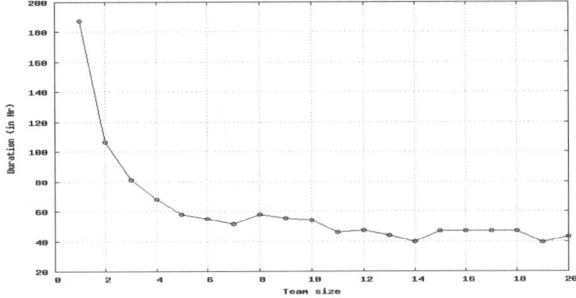

Fig. 3. Project turn-around time as a function of the team-size, for the example MG

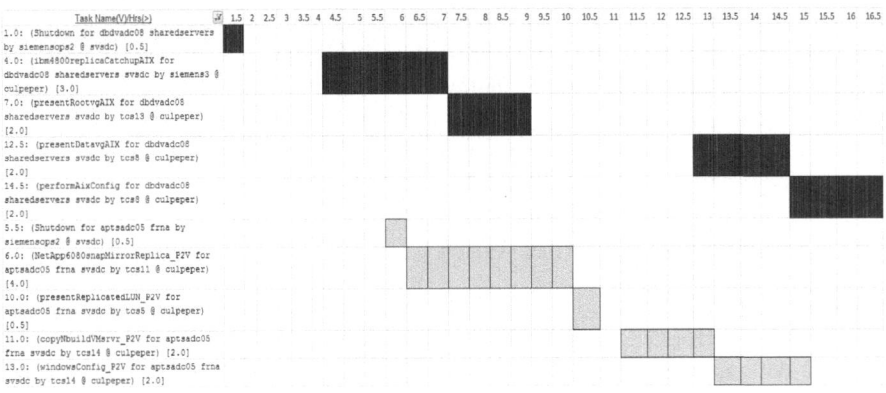

Fig. 4. Part of the Gantt chart produced for the example MG

for understanding the plan and during plan execution. Figure 4 shows a part of the Gantt chart for servers 9 and 12 in this MG. Even though 12 is a shared server, its consolidation overlaps in time with that of the server 9 in application FRNA. This is fine because there is no direct dependency between the two and the entire FRNA application does not go "live" untill all the shared servers are already consolidated. This part of the Gantt chart is not shown.

4   Related Work

Automated planning plays a significant role in a variety of demanding applications, ranging from controlling space vehicles and robots to playing bridge [9]. As in our work, planners have been used for generating workflows for IT infrastructure management which transform a given initial state to a desired final state and where the transformation actions are encoded as planning actions. [10] used a partial order planner for this purpose. [11] generates workflows for IT infrastructure reconfiguration projects, where each step in the workflow preserves global constraints, which are specified by the end-users "outside" of any particular actions. [12] develop propositional planners which use domain-specific heuristics to generate plans for the closely related problem of incremental transformations of a network topology so as to minimize service disruptions. In these papers, the actions are not durative and team size optimization is not considered. Planners are also used for somewhat similar problems of services software composition in business process management, which we do not review here; see [13].

A closely related planning problem formulation is called *multiagent planning*, in which the planner needs to create a plan taking into account concurrent actions of and dependencies of multiple autonomous agents, such as robots. Several approaches have been designed to create multi-agent plans; see, for example, [14,15,16,17,18,19,20,21,22] etc. The issues there are related to the nature of the planning process: dynamic or static, centralized or distributed, agents are truthful or not, nature of cooperation among agents etc. The focus is on coordination and control of agent actions. In this paper, we have considered a centralized, static project planning formulation, in the classical planning framework, where the tasks and their precedences are known and the time required for each task is also known. We have associated a specific skill with each task. The key difference is that the number of people required to execute the plan is not fixed and known; rather, we want to find the right plan along with the right team size. There are probabilistic planning approaches where quantities like task times can be treated as random variables to generate "most probable" plans; e.g., [17,23].

5   Conclusions and Further Work

In this paper, we use a standard temporal planner engine to automatically generate a detailed project plan for DC transformation projects, which takes into account the needed tasks and skills as well as various kinds of dependencies. The approach is based on one-time creation of a reusable library of DC transformation tasks in PDDL. We illustrated the approach using a real-life case-study.

A limitation of the current approach is scale: SAPA is unable to handle large projects involving 100s of servers. We currently do not take into account some precedence and priority constraints; e.g., FRNA and STD are treated as equal, without any precedence among them, except that shared servers are consolidated before both business applications. We do not take into account precedence among specific programs running on a server. The system is not currently usable to generate a partial plan, after some of the tasks are done and perhaps they have overshot their allocated time. End-users need a lot more information, summarized from the generated plan, such as utilization factors, workload measures etc. We are working on adding these features. A key aspect of our work is manually transforming the domain knowledge (for IT infrastructure transformations) into PDDL. For a planning problem with a large number of inter-related tasks and objects, this becomes complex and error prone; approaches like HTN to PDDL translation [24] can simplify this process and approaches like PDVer [25] can be used to verify the planning domain description. Planners which use PDDL3 [26] (with additions such as sometime, at-most-once etc.) can be exploited to make the generated plan more realistic. we need to generalize our approach by treating each task duration as a random variable (not as a constant) and then generate "most probable" plans. We are working on reformulating our planning problem to include team sizing and utilization as an integral part. A key aspect of project planning is identifying the risk factors, quantifying risks and creating a project plan that minimizes risks (e.g., by including risk mitigating actions), as well as suggests alternative workflows in case a risk materializes. We are working on including these aspects in the planning problem formulation.

Acknowledgements. We thank Prof. Harrick Vin for supporting this work, Rahul Kelkar, Anjali Gajendragadkar and Manish Sarda for their domain knowledge and Prerna and Arpit for working on the mPlan tool. We thank the reviewers for their insightful comments.

References

1. Gajendragadkar, A., Bhardwaj, R., Sarda, M., Malavade, C.: A systematic approach for data center migration analytics driven methodology. In: TACTiCS, TCS Technical Architects Conference 2010 (2010)
2. Ramakrishnan, K.K., Shenoy, P., Van der Merwe, J.: Live data center migration across wans: a robust cooperative context aware approach. In: Proceedings of the 2007 SIGCOMM Workshop on Internet Network Management, INM 2007, pp. 262–267. ACM (2007)
3. Hacking, S., Hudzia, B.: Improving the live migration process of large enterprise applications. In: Proceedings of the 3rd International Workshop on Virtualization Technologies in Distributed Computing, VTDC 2009, pp. 51–58. ACM (2009)
4. Clark, C., Fraser, K., Hand, S., Hansen, J.G., Jul, E., Limpach, C., Pratt, I., Warfield, A.: Live migration of virtual machines. In: Proceedings of the 2nd Conference on Symposium on Networked Systems Design & Implementation, NSDI 2005, vol. 2, pp. 273–286. USENIX Association (2005)
5. Nelson, M., Lim, B.H., Hutchins, G.: Fast transparent migration for virtual machines. In: Proceedings of the Annual Conference on USENIX Annual Technical Conference, ATEC 2005, pp. 25–25. USENIX Association (2005)
6. Bradford, R., Kotsovinos, E., Feldmann, A., Schiöberg, H.: Live wide-area migration of virtual machines including local persistent state. In: Proceedings of the 3rd International Conference on Virtual Execution Environments, VEE 2007, pp. 169–179. ACM (2007)
7. Fox, M., Long, D.: PDDL2.1: An extension to PDDL for expressing temporal planning domains. Journal of Artificial Intelligence Research 20, 61–124 (2003)
8. Do, M., Kambhampati, S.: Sapa: A multi-objective metric temporal planner. Journal of Artificial Intelligence Research 20, 155–194 (2003)
9. Ghallab, M., Nau, D., Traverso, P.: Automated planning theory and practice. Morgan Kaufmann Publishers (2006)
10. El Maghraoui, K., Meghranjani, A., Eilam, T., Kalantar, M., Konstantinou, A.V.: Model Driven Provisioning: Bridging the Gap Between Declarative Object Models and Procedural Provisioning Tools. In: van Steen, M., Henning, M. (eds.) Middleware 2006. LNCS, vol. 4290, pp. 404–423. Springer, Heidelberg (2006)
11. Herry, H., Anderson, P.: Planning with global constraints for computing infrastructure reconfiguration. In: Proceedings of the 2012 AAAI Workshop on Problem Solving Using Classical Planners. AAAI Press (2012)
12. Yoon, Y., Robinson, N., Muthusamy, V., Jacobsen, H.A., McIlraith, S.A.: Planning the transformation of network topologies. In: Proceedings of the 2012 AAAI Workshop on Problem Solving Using Classical Planners. AAAI Press (2012)
13. Hoffmann, J., Weber, I., Kraft, F.M.: Sap speaks pddl: Exploiting a software-engineering model for planning in business process management. Journal of Artificial Intelligence Research 44, 587–632 (2012)

14. Jonsson, A., Rovatsos, M.: Scaling up multiagent planning: A best-response approach. In: Proceedings of the Twenty-First International Conference on Automated Planning and Scheduling (ICAPS 2011), pp. 114–121. AAAI (2011)
15. Kvarnstrom, J.: Planning for loosely coupled agents using partial order forward-chaining. In: Proceedings of the Twenty-First International Conference on Automated Planning and Scheduling (ICAPS 2011), pp. 138–145 (2011)
16. Nissim, R., Brafman, R.I., Domshlak, C.: A general, fully distributed multi-agent planning algorithm. In: Proceedings AAMAS 2010, pp. 1323–1330 (2010)
17. Beaudryi, E., Kabanza, F., Michaud, F.: Planning for concurrent action executions under action duration uncertainty using dynamically generated bayesian networks. In: Proceedings of the Twentieth International Conference on Automated Planning and Scheduling (ICAPS 2010), pp. 10–17 (2010)
18. Larbi, R.B., Konieczny, S., Marquis, P.: Extending Classical Planning to the Multi-agent Case: A Game-Theoretic Approach. In: Mellouli, K. (ed.) ECSQARU 2007. LNCS (LNAI), vol. 4724, pp. 731–742. Springer, Heidelberg (2007)
19. Ephrati, E., Rosenschein, J.S.: Multi-agent planning as search for a consensus that maximizes social welfare. In: Castelfranchi, C., Werner, E. (eds.) MAAMAW 1992. LNCS, vol. 830, pp. 207–226. Springer, Heidelberg (1994)
20. Dimopoulos, Y., Moraitis, P.: Multi-agent coordination and cooperation through classical planning. In: Proceedings IAT 2006, pp. 398–402 (2006)
21. Cox, J.S., Durfee, E.H.: An efficient algorithm for multiagent plan coordination. In: Proceedings AAMAS 2005, pp. 828–835 (2005)
22. Bacchus, F., Ady, M.: Planning with resources and concurrency: a forward chaining approach. In: Proc. International Joint Conference on Artificial Intelligence (IJCAI 2001), pp. 417–424 (2001)
23. Mausam, Weld, D.: Planning with durative actions in stochastic domains. Journal of Artificial Intelligence Research 31, 33–82 (2008)
24. Alford, R., Kuter, U., Nau, D.: Translating HTNs to PDDL: A small amount of domain knowledge can go a long way. In: Proceedings of IJCAI 2009, pp. 1629–1634 (2009)
25. Raimondi, F., Pecheur, C., Brat, G.: PDVer, a tool to verify pddl planning domains. In: Proceedings of ICAPS 2009 Workshop on Verification and Validation of Planning and Scheduling Systems, Thessaloniki, Greece (2009)
26. Gerevini, A., Haslum, P., Long, D., Saetti, A., Dimopoulos, Y.: Deterministic planning in the fifth international planning competition: PDDL3 and experimental evaluation of the planners. Artificial Intelligence 173(5-6), 619–668 (2009)

Planning with Action Prioritization and New Benchmarks for Classical Planning

Kamalesh Ghosh*, Pallab Dasgupta, and S. Ramesh

Indian Institute of Technology Kharagpur and
GM India Science Lab Bangalore
{kghosh,pallab}@cse.iitkgp.ernet.in, ramesh.s@gm.com

Abstract. We introduce a new class of planning problems in which there is a separate set of actions with higher priority than regular actions. We present new planning domains to show that problems of practical interest may easily fit in this framework. We argue that though this framework is quite succinctly encoded in classical planning itself, existing planners are disappointingly inept at solving them. To demonstrate this, we have built a wrapper tool for planners which uses ad-hoc techniques to give far better results. Therefore, we also propose our encoded domains as new challenges for general-purpose planners.

Keywords: Planning, benchmarks, action priority.

1 Introduction

Automated planning is an important area of research in Artificial Intelligence. Not only is it a very interesting research problem, but it also has real-life usage in areas like logistics scheduling and spacecraft commanding. It is widely recognized that automated planning is a very difficult problem by itself and in general, no planners can give any reasonable guarantee on performance. However, through successive improvements over the years, general purpose planners have become highly capable of solving a wide range of problems.

It is expected from general purpose planners that they are able to solve a wide range of problems without specific bias to any special characteristics of the problems. Based on this belief, we translated some special verification problems from the automotive control domain to planning. These verification problems are marked in their similarity with the planning problem itself, so translation is trivial and good results were expected. To keep it simple, we consider the original verification problem itself to be outside the scope of this paper and discuss our problem entirely from a planning perspective. We present some planning domains in this paper which are sufficiently endowed with the special characteristics of our original verification problems.

Basically, our typical planning problem has two independent sets of actions. As in classical planning, an initial state and planning goal is given and we need

---

* This work is partially supported by a research grant under the General Motors Collaborative Research Lab, IIT Kharagpur.

M. Thielscher and D. Zhang (Eds.): AI 2012, LNCS 7691, pp. 779–790, 2012.

to find a sequence of actions that transform the initial state to a final state satisfying the goal. However, we have a special requirement which is to ensure during planning that we do not choose actions from the second set as long as any action from the first set is applicable. In other words, actions from the first set, which we term as the *control actions*, take an absolute priority over actions from the second set, termed as the *environment actions*. Additionally, the goal must be achieved in a state where no control actions are applicable.

As we show in this paper, this problem is easily reduced to classical planning so we can always encode and try to solve it with standard planners like FF[3] and LPG[4]. However, none of the planners that we have tried so far works well on our encoded instances. Consequently, we have formed the opinion that even domain-independent planners today have a bias towards solving some specific type of problems better than others. We believe that this bias has come because of an enthusiasm in the planning community with solving specific problems like the blocks world, logistics etc. In an attempt to help break off from this set pattern, we propose our encoded instances as new challenges for general purpose planners.

Our planning domains touch problems of practical interest in areas like power supply restoration [6] and functional model verification. Additionally, we argue that these problems are not as difficult to solve as the planners may make it appear because we are able to produce far better results through our own wrapper tool.[1]

Thus, our main contributions in this work are that (i) we introduce a new class of planning problems for critical appreciation by the planning community and (ii) our encoded domains and tools give an opportunity to compare, investigate and improve on the existing capability of general-purpose planners.

The rest of this paper is structured as follows. We describe the basic framework of our class of planning problems in Section 2. In Section 3, we describe the encoding mechanism to support this framework in standard planners. In Section 4, we present a primary analysis of the reason that this encoding fails to work well in most planners. In Section 5 and 6, we present two domains which are modeled in our framework. Finally, in Section 7 we describe our wrapper tool and compare its results with the results achieved from planners through direct encoding.

2   Planning with Action Prioritization (PAP)

Our problem formulation is primarily based on propositional STRIPS planning [1]. A *state* is given by a set of propositions (i.e. ground atoms) belonging to a finite superset $\mathcal{P}$. The presence of a proposition indicates that its value is assigned to true in the state (and false otherwise). The precondition and postcondition of an action α, denoted by the symbols $\text{pre}(\alpha)$ and $\text{post}(\alpha)$, are finite sets of literals. The action set, $\mathcal{A}$, in our case is the union of two disjoint sets $\mathcal{A}_e$ and $\mathcal{A}_c$. We

---

[1] Our planning domains and tools can be downloaded from the link
http://www.facweb.iitkgp.ernet.in/~pallab/paplan.tar.gz.

refer to $\mathcal{A}_e$ as the set of *environment actions* and $\mathcal{A}_c$ as the set of *control actions*. Thus an instance our problem, which we name as PAP, is actually a five-tuple $\langle \mathcal{P}, \mathcal{A}_e, \mathcal{A}_c, \mathcal{I}, \mathcal{G} \rangle$. As in propositional STRIPS planning, we are given an initial state $\mathcal{I}$ and a goal condition $\mathcal{G}$ (which is a set of literals) and we are required to find a sequence of actions which will transform the initial state to a state satisfying the goal condition. However, unlike in classical STRIPS planning, this sequence of actions (i.e. the *plan*) must have some special properties which we specify below.

A state is said to be a *control stable state* if and only if no control action is applicable in it. To keep things simple, we require that for each $\alpha \in \mathcal{A}_c$, there exists some $l \in \mathrm{pre}(\alpha)$ such that $\bar{l} \in \mathrm{post}(\alpha)$ (i.e., applying a control action makes it inapplicable). Now, considering the sequence of states that are visited as we apply the plan, we require the following:

1. Environment actions in the plan are applied only from control stable states.
2. The final state achieved by the plan is a control stable state.

There is one last issue that we must address before we can say that our problem is well defined. It is always possible that control actions are defined such that they form an inescapable loop in some states (meaning, we would keep applying control actions without any hope of reaching a control stable state). In this paper, we just assume that such situations are not allowed to occur.

Assumption 21. *In a valid PAP instance, a control stable state is always reachable from every reachable state.*

Unfortunately, this condition is not easy to verify. In practice, it may be possible to introduce stronger assumptions which are relatively easy to verify (e.g. disallowing any control loop, not just inescapable ones). As we intend to address PAP only in its most generalized form here, we consider this topic to be outside the scope of this paper.

2.1 Complexity of PAP

Finding whether a solution exists for a PAP instance is PSPACE-hard as an instance of the classical planning problem can be reduced to an instance of PAP by copying all the actions to the environment action set and leaving the control action set empty. On the other hand, we propose an algorithm in Section 3 which reduces PAP to classical STRIPS planning in polynomial time. This implies that the problem of checking whether a solution exists for a PAP instance is in PSPACE. Hence we deduce that PAP is a PSPACE-complete problem.

3 Compilation to Classical Planning

In this section, we show how PAP can be easily reduced to classical planning. The pseudo code of this reduction algorithm, named PAPLAN, is given in

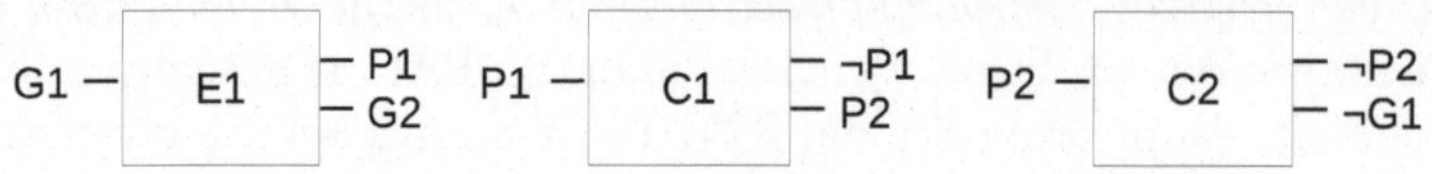

Fig. 1. Environment action E1 and control actions C1 and C2

Algorithm 1. We illustrate the working of this reduction algorithm on the set of actions shown in Figure 1.

The main emphasis of this reduction is on preventing the environment actions from being applied unless the state is a control stable state. In order to impose this restriction in a classical planning framework, we introduce one additional proposition $\text{dis}(C_i)$ for each control action C_i. The proposition $\text{dis}(C_i)$ is true only at states where C_i is not applicable. In order to express that an environment action applies only at a control stable state, we add all the $\text{dis}(C_i)$ propositions to its precondition (Algorithm 1, Line 6). For example, the precondition of E1 becomes $\{G1, \text{dis}(C1), \text{dis}(C2)\}$.

We say that an action α (environment or control) *triggers* a control action C_i if and only if the postcondition of the former contains one or more propositions that appear in the precondition of the latter. In our encoded instance, whenever we apply an action α which triggers a control action C_i, we set $\text{dis}(C_i)$ to false. The intent here is to prevent any environment action from being applied till we ensure that C_i is not applicable anymore. Therefore, we rewrite the postcondition of α to include $\neg\text{dis}(C_i)$ for each triggered C_i (Algorithm 1, Line 9). Using the shorthand $\langle\text{pre}(\alpha), \text{post}(\alpha)\rangle$ to express actions, the actions in our example in Figure 1 would finally become:

$$E1 = \langle\{G1, \text{dis}(C1), \text{dis}(C2)\}, \{P1, G2, \neg\text{dis}(C1)\}\rangle$$
$$C1 = \langle\{P1\}, \{\neg P1, P2, \neg\text{dis}(C2)\}\rangle$$
$$C2 = \langle\{P2\}, \{\neg P2, \neg G1\}\rangle$$

It is possible that C_i is not applicable after applying its triggering action α because some of the other propositions in its precondition are not true. Alternatively, C_i may later cease to be applicable after applying C_i or some other control actions. In both situations, we must be able to set $\text{dis}(C_i)$ back to true. For this, we introduce some new actions (for each C_i), each of which has the negation of a precondition of C_i as its precondition and $\text{dis}(C_i)$ as its postcondition (Algorithm 1, Line 12). For our particular example, they are:

$$M1 = \langle\{\neg P1\}, \{\text{dis}(C1)\}\rangle$$
$$M2 = \langle\{\neg P2\}, \{\text{dis}(C2)\}\rangle$$

The initial state and goal are modified suitably (Line 2, Line 3) and finally, we extract the plan by calling a classical planner (Lines 14-15). We do not argue the correctness of this reduction here due to space limitation, but believe that the reader will be readily convinced of it with a little effort.

Input: The propositions in the planning domain ($\mathcal{P}$), a set of environment actions ($\mathcal{A}_e$), a set of control actions ($\mathcal{A}_c$), the initial state ($\mathcal{I}$), and the goal state ($\mathcal{G}$).

Output: The generated plan (*plan*).

1   $\mathcal{P}' \leftarrow \mathcal{P} \cup \{\mathrm{dis}(a_c) \mid a_c \in \mathcal{A}_c\}$

2   $\mathcal{I}' \leftarrow \mathcal{I} \cup \{\mathrm{dis}(a_c) \mid a_c \text{ is not applicable in } \mathcal{I}\}$

3   $\mathcal{G}' \leftarrow \mathcal{G} \cup \{\mathrm{dis}(a_c) \mid a_c \in \mathcal{A}_c\}$

4   $\mathcal{A}_d \leftarrow \emptyset$

5   **foreach** $e \in \mathcal{A}_e$ **do**

6 | $\mathrm{pre}(e) \leftarrow \mathrm{pre}(e) \cup \{\mathrm{dis}(a_c) \mid a_c \in \mathcal{A}_c\}$

   end

7   **foreach** $a \in \mathcal{A}_e \cup \mathcal{A}_c$ *and* $a_c \in \mathcal{A}_c$ **do**

8 | **if** a *is a trigger for* a_c **then**

9 | | $\mathrm{post}(a) \leftarrow \mathrm{post}(a) \cup \{\neg\mathrm{dis}(a_c)\}$ /* To mark a_c as enabled */

     | **end**

   end

10   **foreach** $a_c \in \mathcal{A}_c$ **do**

11 | **foreach** $\ell \in \mathrm{pre}(a_c)$ **do**

12 | | $\mathcal{A}_d \leftarrow \mathcal{A}_d \cup \{\langle\{\neg\ell\}, \{\mathrm{dis}(a_c)\}\rangle\}$ /* To mark a_c as disabled */

     | **end**

   end

13   $\mathcal{A}' \leftarrow \mathcal{A}_d \cup \mathcal{A}_e \cup \mathcal{A}_c$

14   $plan' \leftarrow \mathrm{PLAN}(\mathcal{P}', \mathcal{A}', \mathcal{I}', \mathcal{G}')$

15   $plan \leftarrow \mathrm{RemoveMarkerActions}(plan', \mathcal{A}_d)$

16   **return** $plan$

Algorithm 1. PAPLAN

4   Our Encoding and Planning Graphs

Though all planners employ different heuristics and techniques, the most successful ones usually employ the planning graph [2] in some way or other. Since it is practically impossible for us to analyze the specific reasons of under performance for each and every planner, we focus on the planning graph and *mutex* relations to obtain a general picture. We assume that the reader is well aware of planning graphs and their construction method [5].

Let us again take the example in Figure 1 and assume that we are given the initial state $\mathcal{I} = \{\mathrm{G1}\}$ and goal $\mathcal{G} = \{\mathrm{G1}, \mathrm{G2}\}$. It is obvious that this goal is not achievable because as soon as we apply E1, we have to next apply control actions C1 and C2 which would then destroy the goal G1. Remember that by definition we are required to achieve the goal in a control stable state.

The above example represents a very common phenomenon in planning problems featuring our prioritized action framework (as the reader may appreciate better in the next two sections). We will informally refer to this phenomenon as the *distant destruction* of goals. Basically, achieving of one literal using an action may necessitate destruction of others through successive triggering of control actions. A planner which is aware of such inevitable consequences would probably perform better than others.

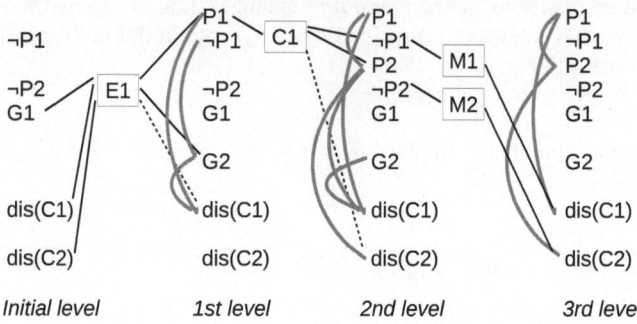

Fig. 2. Planning graph for encoded problem

Taking our encoded example, let us observe how the planning graph works. We partially depict the planning graph in Figure 2. Note that in order to prevent cluttering, we have only depicted those literals which are either goal literals or appear in some action's precondition. Persistence actions and some inconsequential actions have not been depicted either. A dashed line from the action to a literal indicates that the action destroys that literal.

At the first level, we are able to achieve G2 but it is mutex with dis(C1) (as E1 triggers C1). This mutex carries on to the second level. However, as C1 causes the deletion of the mutex between ¬P1 and G2 in the second level, we get no mutex between G2 and dis(C1) in the third level (M1 and persistence of G2 are no longer mutex). So the planning graph predicts no difficulty in achieving the goal set $\mathcal{G}' = \{G1, G2, dis(C1), dis(C2)\}$.

Quite clearly, as the goal literals are achieved together pairwise in the intermediate levels, the planning graph looses all information relevant to distant destruction. We believe that this is an important drawback to the efficiency of any planner using planning graphs and mutex relations. We are presently working on techniques to address this and look forward to any future inputs from the planning community on this.

5   The Power Supply Restoration Planning Domain

The Power Supply Restoration (PSR) domain [6] is known to the planning community as it was featured in the fourth International Planning Competition (IPC-4). As our first working example of PAP, we present a model of this domain in our framework. What we like about our version of PSR is that we basically express the domain in plain STRIPS syntax, yet it remains just as succinct and easy to understand as the versions from IPC-4. The models of PSR from IPC-4 invariably make use of advanced syntactic constructs such as derived predicates or conditional effects that become unreadable when compiled to plain STRIPS.

The PSR domain basically models an electrical power distribution system. The model of a small power distribution system is illustrated in Figure 3. It is composed of *power lines, switching devices* and *circuit breakers.* Each power line is connected to one or more switching devices. The main power station (not shown in the figure) distributes the power through the circuit breakers. A switching device connects two power lines. *Closed* circuit breakers and switching devices are darkened in the figure to help identify them. Whenever a *fault* appears in a line, it puts all its feeding lines and the main power station under risk. Therefore, any circuit breaker supplying power to it needs to be opened immediately. Subsequently, the switches and breakers need to be opened or closed in such an order that power can be safely restored to a given set of power lines.

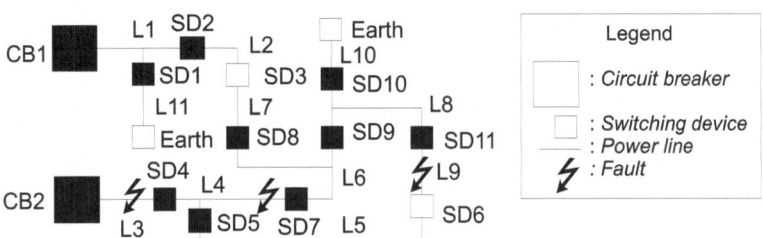

Fig. 3. Example of a Power Distribution System

To represent the logic of a power distribution system, we define a set of **control actions** which model the automatic flow of electrical power through the system. For example, some control actions for the system in Figure 3 are as follows:

$$\langle\{\text{closed(CB1)}, \neg\text{fed(L1)}\}\,, \{\text{fed(L1)}\}\rangle$$
$$\langle\{\text{closed(SD1)}, \text{fed(L1)}, \neg\text{fed(L11)}\}\,, \{\text{fed(L11)}\}\rangle$$
$$\langle\{\text{closed(SD1)}, \text{fed(L11)}, \neg\text{fed(L1)}\}\,, \{\text{fed(L1)}\}\rangle$$

The first control action above ensures that the line L1 is *fed* (meaning, powered) through a closed CB1. The second and third control actions ensure that the lines L1 and L11 feed each other through a closed SD1 (the third action is actually redundant for this particular example).

Further, if one side of a switching device or circuit breaker is connected to a faulty line, we mark the other side as *unsafe.* For example. we would define a control action for this as follows (the upper side called *side1*):

$$\langle\{\text{faulty(L9)}, \text{closed(SD11)}, \neg\text{unsafe(SD11, side1)}\}, \{\text{unsafe(SD11, side1)}\}\rangle$$

Additionally, if one side of a switching device or circuit breaker is connected through some line to the unsafe side of another switching device, the other side is deemed unsafe:

$$\langle\{\text{unsafe(SD11, side1)}, \text{closed(SD9)}, \neg\text{unsafe(SD9, side2)}\}, \{\text{unsafe(SD9, side2)}\}\rangle$$

Finally, if a circuit breaker has an unsafe side, then it is said to be *affected*:

$$\langle\{\text{unsafe(CB2, side1)}, \neg\text{affected(CB2)}\}, \{\text{affected(CB2)}\}\rangle$$

Next, we come to the **environment actions** which represent things that we can perform at will on the power distribution system, e.g. closing and opening of the switching devices. For example, we define the following two actions to represent the closing and opening of a switching device SD1, respectively:

$\langle$ { ¬closed(SD1), ¬affected(CB1), ¬affected(CB2)}, {closed(SD1)}$\rangle$

$\langle$ { closed(SD1), ¬affected(CB1), ¬affected(CB2)},

{ ¬closed(SD1), ¬fed(L1), ..., ¬fed(L11),

¬unsafe(SD1, side1), ..., ¬unsafe(SD11, side2),

¬unsafe(CB1, side1), ..., ¬unsafe(CB2, side2)}$\rangle$

Note that with each "open" action, we mark all the power lines as unfed and all the switching devices and circuit breakers as safe. This is because we intend to force a complete re-evaluation of the logic represented by the control actions in order to retain the correct values.

We have also have a "wait" action, quite similar to "open", to represent the opening of circuit breakers specifically when they are affected (note that we are not allowed to perform normal opening and closing in that case). These actions mark the circuit breaker as unaffected in addition to opening it.

In Figure 3, a number of faulty lines are fed through the circuit breaker CB2, hence we must apply "wait(CB2)" before anything. Following this, lines L3 to L10 are left without power. To solve this example, we may open SD7 and SD11 first and then close SD3 to safely restore power to all non-faulty lines except L5. Finding out this sequence can be quite a difficult problem for large distribution systems. The reader is encouraged to satisfy himself/herself of the fact that our prioritized action planning would allow us to do such reasoning correctly.

6   The GRID Domain

We present here another representative domain for PAP. The system we visualize is a grid of *processors* serving job requests from one or more external *dispenser* units. A processor in our domain has four communication channels each of which can be connected to a neighbouring processor or dispenser unit. Examples of such interconnected systems are shown in Figure 4.

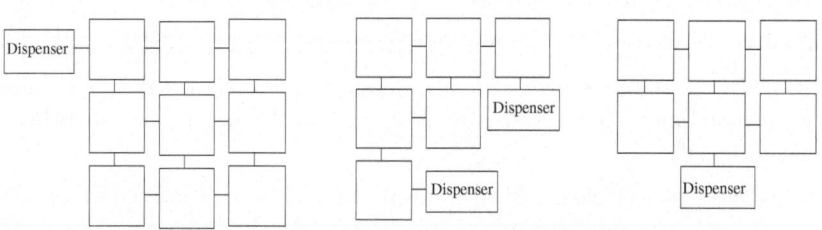

Fig. 4. Various configurations for a grid of processors

A dispenser unit creates new jobs and makes requests to one of its neighbouring processors to take them up. If the requested processor accepts, then it is instantly handed over the job. In the case of a reject, the dispenser waits till it eventually gets an accept signal from the requested processor. Though the dispenser receives an instantaneous response on its request, the internal allocation of the handling processor (or the collective decision to reject) happens through a non-trivial protocol which we clarify below.

Control Actions for GRID Domain. The processor allocation protocol dictates that each request be propagated through the grid in a distributed depth first manner. As soon as an available processor receives the request, it responds by giving an acceptance to the request. This acceptance is relayed back to the dispenser which then hands over the job description to be relayed back to the accepting processor. The communication channels allow the exchange of signals such as request, accept, reject, busy etc. and data such as job description between neighbours.

To make the problem more interesting, we assume that it is required that no processor handling a job should have more than two neighbours handling similar jobs. Also, no processor is allowed to handle two jobs simultaneously.

As a detailed description of the complete domain is beyond the scope of this paper, we just reproduce the English translation of some of the control actions below. Note that this is just a sample to illustrate the type of actions used and not a complete description:

- If any of the following three conditions hold, then mark self *unavailable*:
    1. The processor is *busy* handling a job.
    2. Three neighbours are busy with jobs.
    3. A busy neighbour has two busy neighbours.
- If none of the above conditions hold, mark self available.
- If a request for job processing is made by a neighbour and the current state does not have any outgoing requests (i.e., this is the first request to be processed in this round), then:
    1. If state of self is *unavailable*, make outgoing requests to all other neighbours besides the one making the request.
    2. If state of self is *available*, signal acceptance to the requesting neighbour.
- When transformed in to a state making outgoing requests to neighbours:
    1. If all requested neighbours signal reject or convey requests themselves (meaning that they cannot handle the job), then signal reject to requesting neighbours.
    2. If any requested neighbour indicates acceptance, then indicate acceptance to any requesting neighbour.
- If the processor (or dispenser) has a new job to dispense and a neighbour has indicated acceptance, hand over the new job to that neighbour and drop all outgoing requests and accepts.
- If the processor has received a new job description and is available itself, then get busy and drop outgoing accept signal.

- If state of self is such that requests have been made to three neighbours and the fourth neighbour (i.e. the original requester) has dropped its request, then drop all outgoing request and reject signals.

Environment Actions for GRID Domain. The main role of the environment in this domain is to submit and finish jobs. We maintain a total count of jobs at the system level (up to N, where N is the number of processors). The following environment actions are associated with each dispenser (there are N actions for each dispenser):

- If there are n jobs in the system and the dispenser is free, create a new job description in the dispenser and mark there to be $n + 1$ jobs in the system.

Likewise, the following environment actions are associated with each processor, representing the finishing of jobs (N actions for each processor):

- If there are $n + 1$ jobs in the system and the processor is busy, mark the processor to be not busy and the system to have n jobs.

Goals for Planning. Our planning goals typically represent some worst case scenario, very much like in verification problems:

1. Is it possible that the grid may not find a processor for the fourth job submitted?
2. Is it possible that the grid allows six jobs to run simultaneously?

7 Experiments

As the direct translation (Algorithm 1) fails to provide a satisfactory solution for our planning problems, we have created a wrapper tool which employs existing planners in an intelligent manner to solve these problems efficiently. This tool basically makes use of the same encoding as Algorithm 1, but in an incremental manner. The input language of this tool is the standard STRIPS subset of PDDL and we follow a simple naming convention to identify the control actions separately. We briefly explain the working of this wrapper tool here, and follow it with a comparison of the results achieved with it versus Algorithm 1.

There are basically four steps which our wrapper tool continuously iterates over till a solution is found:

Step 1, Compilation and planning. The original problem is translated partially and given to the classical planner, almost exactly as in Algorithm 1. By a partial translation we mean that many control actions do not have the dis(C_i) propositions added or instrumented for them. In the very first iteration, the input instance is actually passed verbatim to the planner. Further iterations keep including more and more control action instrumentation.

Usually, the incomplete translation allows for easier plan generation, albeit in violation of the action priority requirements. For example, our illustrative problem in Section 4 will have a solution plan consisting of only the action E1 in the first iteration, which achieves both G1 and G2. This, clearly, is not an acceptable solution as C1 becomes applicable after applying E1.

Step 2, Rectification. After we generate a plan, we *rectify* it by patching it with applicable control actions. The **rectify** procedure basically scans the generated plan in order and inserts as many pending control actions as possible before each environment action (and at the end of the plan as well). For example, the rectification would give us E1.C1.C2 for our illustrative example. This is a very simple procedure that works on brute-force principle.

Step 3, Control Action Selection. If the planning goal is not met by a rectified plan, we then select some new actions to be restored to their special status as control actions (as mentioned in Step 1). We have two alternative policies to select new control actions. Our first variant, which we call the *Fast Convergence* policy, restores the status of all the control actions that needed to be inserted during rectification. The second variant, which we call the *Slow Convergence* policy, takes a more selective approach: only the control actions which were critical to the missing of the goal are restored.

Step 4, Macro Generation. We exploit the information from previous runs by introducing some environment-control interactions from last runs as *macro environment actions* for future runs. For example, the sequence E1.C1.C2 could be introduced as one macro action $\langle\{G1\},\{\neg G1, G2, \neg P1, \neg P2\}\rangle$. By careful selection of macro environment actions, we are able to achieve great improvements in total solution time.

We compare the performance of direct compilation versus our wrapper tool. We use test cases of different sizes from the PSR and GRID domains and use three different planners FF, maxplan[7] and LPG to demonstrate the consistency of results. The scalability of different versions of the tool (that is, different combinations of optimization techniques and back-end planners) is illustrated by

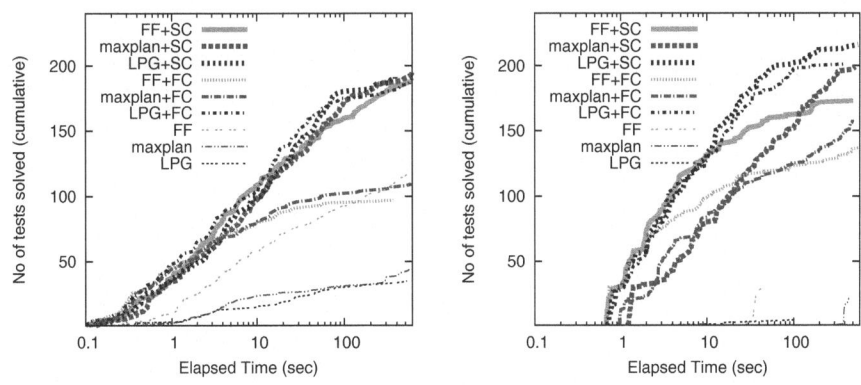

Fig. 5. No. of Tests Solved with Time for PSR and GRID domains

plotting the cumulative number of tests solved against elapsed time in Figure 5. We use a logarithmic scale for time as it gives a clearly visible and almost linear distribution of points. The curves for the versions of the tool using a direct compilation with a planner typically appear at the bottom, indicating that they solve fewer instances and take more time. The curves with the fast convergence policy (shown as +FC) appear in the middle while the best results are typically achieved by the slow convergence policy (+SC) for the same planners.

8   Conclusion

We strongly believe that the PAP formulation can prove useful for modeling many problems of practical interest. However, we realize that it may take much deliberation within the planning community to establish and treat it as a first class entity. For now, encoding it as classical planning seems to be the most legitimate solution but unfortunately, existing planners fail to satisfactorily solve it. We feel that the domains presented in this paper (i.e, their encodings) serve as a good challenge for general purpose planners as they may reveal some intriguing and commonly occurring features in difficult-to-solve planning problems which can be exploited by the planners.

References

1. Fikes, R., Nilsson, N.: STRIPS: A new approach to the application of theorem proving to problem solving. Artificial Intelligence 2(3/4), 189–208 (1971)
2. Blum, A., Furst, M.: Fast planning through planning graph analysis. Artificial Intelligence 90(1-2), 281–300 (1997)
3. Hoffmann, J., Nebel, B.: The FF Planning System: Fast Plan Generation Through Heuristic Search. J. Artif. Intell. Res (JAIR) 14, 253–302 (2001)
4. Gerevini, A., Serina, I.: LPG: a planner based on local search for planning graphs with action costs. In: Proc. ICAPS, pp. 12–22 (2002)
5. Russell, S., Norvig, P.: Artificial intelligence: A Modern Approach, 2nd edn., ch. 11. Prentice Hall of India Private Limited, New Delhi (2006)
6. Thiébaux, S., Cordier, M.: Supply restoration in power distribution systems: A benchmark for planning under uncertainty. In: Pre-Proc. 6th European Conference on Planning (ECP 2001), pp. 85–96 (2001)
7. Chen, Y., Zhao, X., Zhang, W.: Long-distance mutual exclusion for propositional planning. In: Proc. IJCAI, pp. 1840–1845 (2007)

Efficient Solution of Capacitated Arc Routing Problems with a Limited Computational Budget

Min Liu and Tapabrata Ray

School of Engineering and Information Technology,
University of New South Wales, Northcott Drive, Canberra, Australia
min.liu@student.adfa.edu.au, T.Ray@adfa.edu.au

Abstract. Capacitated Arc Routing Problem (CARP) is a well known combinatorial problem that requires the identification of the minimum total distance travelled by a set of vehicles to service a given set of roads subject to the vehicle's capacity constraints. While a number of optimization algorithms have been proposed over the years to solve CARP problems, all of them require a large number of function evaluations prior to its convergence. Application of such algorithms are thus limited for practical applications as many of such applications require an acceptable solution within a limited time frame, e.g., dynamic versions of the problem. This paper is a pre-cursor to such applications, and the aim of this study is to develop an algorithm that can solve such problems with a limited computational budget of 50,000 function evaluations. The algorithm is embedded with a similarity based parent selection scheme inspired by the principles of multiple sequence alignment, hybrid crossovers, i.e., a combination of similarity preservation schemes, path scanning heuristics and random key crossovers. The performance of the algorithm is compared with a recent Memetic algorithm, i.e., Decomposition-Based Memetic Algorithm proposed in 2010 across three sets of commonly used benchmarks (gdb, val, egl). The results clearly indicate the superiority of performance across both small and large instances.

Keywords: Capacitated arc routing problem, memetic algorithm, heuristic, random key representation, multiple sequence alignment.

1 Background

The capacitated arc routing problem (CARP) [12] can be described as follows: Assume a road network represented using a undirected graph $G = (V, E)$ with a set V of v nodes and a set E of e edges. The set of p tasks (required edges) $T = (t_1, ..., t_p)$ needs to be served by a fleet of vehicles which are associated with a same capacity C and located at a depot s ($s \in V$). Each edge is associated with a distance $d(i) \geq 0 (i = 1, 2, ..., e)$ and a demand $q(i) \geq 0 (i = 1, 2, ..., e)$. A demand of $q(i)$ equal to zero indicates that the edges do not need service. The objective is to find the set of vehicle trips using minimum total distance D, such that each vehicle trip starts and ends at the depot s, each required edge is serviced by one single trip, and the total demand handled by any vehicle must not exceed its capacity C. The distance of a trip includes the distance of its serviced tasks and the distance traveled through edges that are not serviced.

M. Thielscher and D. Zhang (Eds.): AI 2012, LNCS 7691, pp. 791–802, 2012.

Table 1. Mathematical Symbols used in this paper

Symbol	Meaning
Q	Population
w	Population size
S	Solution
N	Number of trips
C	Capacity of vehicle
e	Number of edges
d_i $(i = 1, ..., e)$	Distance of each edge
q_i $(i = 1, ..., e)$	Demand of each edge
T	A set of tasks
s	Depot of the vehicles
p	Number of tasks
D	Total distance, i.e., fitness of the solution

The symbols used in the paper are provided in Table 1.

Arc routing problems [7, 9, 10] are classic combinatorial optimization problems, wherein the aim is to find a route with minimum total distance subject to the set of predefined constraints. CARP is a practical form of an arc routing problem, in which a fleet of homogeneous (same capacity) vehicles needs to service the set of demands associated with the edges. CARP is known to be NP-hard and thus application of exact optimization methods are still limited small problems (20-30 edges) [12]. Although exact methods can solve some large instances of CARP, the computational cost is exorbitantly large, e.g., the branch-and-cut-price algorithm required around 20000 seconds [16] to solve a problem with 190 edges. In most real-world applications, it is necessary to obtain a solution within a given time budget. Different heuristic based approaches have been proposed over the years to deal with such problems, which include augment-merge [12], path-scanning [11, 21], construct-and-strike [19], Ulusoy's tour splitting [23], argment-insert [20] etc. Metaheuristic based approaches have also been proposed such as Simulated Annealing [8], Tabu Search [17], Variable Neighborhood Search [22], Guided Local Search [4], Genetic Algorithm [18], Evolutionary Algorithm (EA) [24], Ant Colony Optimization [1] and more recently hybrids such as Memetic Algorithm (MA) [13,22] which is an intelligent combination of a genetic algorithm and a local search.

A memetic algorithm with extended neighborhood search (referred as MAENS) [22] was introduced by Yi Mei *et al* in 2010 and is one of the most efficient algorithms developed till date. However, the number of function evaluations required (approximate from 4.0×10^7 to 3.0×10^9) are still far more than what can be afforded for practical problems such as for dynamic CARPs. The performance of any optimization algorithm is largely dependent on the mechanisms of parent selection, method of recombination and local search strategies. The proposed algorithm is realized using a memetic algorithm as its baseline form. The parent selection is based on a similarity measure inspired by multiple sequence alignment while the recombination process is a hybrid consisting of path scanning heuristics and random key crossovers. The performance of the proposed method has been evaluated on three sets of CARP instances (*gdb, val, egl*) that contain a total of 81 instances and compared with MAENS [22]. Section 2 describes the proposed Memetic Algorithm (MA) and Section 3 describes the numerical experiments and results. The conclusions are summarized in Section 4.

2   Proposed Algorithm

The algorithm maintains a population of solutions which are evolved over generations. Fitter individuals are paired with its partner based on a multiple sequence alignment inspired similarity measure. Such a scheme identifies pairs of solutions that have the maximum number of common vehicle trips which is then inherited by the child solution. Such a process is similar to inheriting good building blocks from parents in the context of genetic algorithms. As for the remaining set of demand edges, path scanning heuristic is used. Unique solutions are always maintained in a population and in the event, the number of unique solutions is less than the population size, solutions are generated using random key crossovers. In order to further improve a child solution, a neighborhood based local search is invoked with a given probability. The pseudocode of the algorithm is presented in Algorithm 1.

2.1   Solution Representation and Generation of the Initial Population

Firstly, the undirected graph of the road network is transformed to a directed graph, i.e., each edge is represented as two directed arcs in opposite directions and each of these arcs have the same edge ID. A solution(chromosome) for CARP is represented as a list of edge IDs. The set of w chromosomes are generated to form the initial population Q using a set of edge IDs using path-scanning (PS) heuristic without considering the capacity constraints (Rule 1: maximize the distance $dist(t, s)$ from task t to depot; Rule 2: minimize the distance $dist(t, s)$; Rule 3: maximize the yield $q(t)/d(t)$, i.e., the ratio of demand/distance for each task; Rule 4: minimize the yield $q(t)/d(t)$; Rule 5: use Rule 1 if the vehicle's capacity is less than half-full, else use Rule 2) [11]. Non-unique solutions are replaced with randomly generated chromosomes. Then the chromosomes are (split) using Ulusoy heuristic [13] which identifies the locations of the split that results in a minimum D while satisfying capacity constraints of the vehicles. This D is assigned as the fitness of the chromosome. The individuals of the population are sorted based on their fitness.

2.2   Multiple Sequence Alignment Inspired Selection

Parent selection is an important element in any population based search strategy. There are different variants of parent selection such as through the use of roulette wheel, binary tournament, random selection etc [24]. Fundamentally, all such processes aim to generate child solutions which inherit good building blocks from fitter parents. In the context of molecular biology [14], scientists are faced with the challenge of aligning multiple DNA sequences. Each DNA sequence is a set containing the base elements, i.e., A, C, T or G, and similarity between two sequences are sought via maximization

Algorithm 1. Proposed Algorithm

REQUIRE: Population size (w), Maximum number of function evaluations (MFE), Local search probability r_{LS}

1: Generate an initial population Q
2: **while** Number of solutions evaluated $\leq MFE$ **do**
3:    Apply MSA inspired selection operator to select $w/2$ pairs of parents
4:    Save the common trips of each pair of parents, keep the different part of each pairs, i.e., a set of edges that contains different trips, as $P*$
5:    w solutions P_c are generated by using path-scanning heuristic (PS) without considering capacity constraints on each edge in $P*$ twice
6:    Keep the unique solutions in P_c
7:    **if** Number of $P_c \leq w$ **then**
8:        **for** i = 1:w-Number of P_c **do**
9:            Apply roulette wheel to select two solutions P_{c1} and P_{c2} in P_c
10:           Apply Random Key Crossover on P_{c1} and P_{c2} to generate a child $Child$
11:           Insert $Child$ into P_c
12:       **end for**
13:    **end if**
14:    Sort P_c
15:    Select the best one in P_c as C_1 (if the best one is same (all generated solutions are worse than the best in P_c), using roulette wheel instead)
16:    **if** $m \leq r_{LS}$; m is a random number [0,1] **then**
17:        Apply local search to C_1 to generate C_3
18:        **if** C_3 is not a clone of any chromosome in Q **then**
19:            Insert C_3 into Q
20:        **else if** C_1 is not a clone of any chromosome in Q **then**
21:            Insert C_1 into Q
22:        **end if**
23:    **else if** C_1 is not a clone of any chromosome in Q **then**
24:        Insert C_1 into Q
25:    **end if**
26:    Sort the chromosomes in Q and keep the best w solutions in Q
27: **end while**

of the matching score. In the current context of a population of solutions sorted based on fitness, a partner of solution P_1 is the solution that has maximum number of vehicle trips in common. In the event there are multiple potential partners (i.e., with the same number of trips in common), a random partner is chosen among them.

2.3 Hybrid Recombination

A hybrid recombination scheme is used in this study. The recombination process identifies trips that are common in both the parents and maintains the same for the child solution. As for the remaining set of edges, a path-scanning heuristic without considering the capacity (PS) is used to generate the giant trip. By applying PS twice on the same set of remaining edges, two offsprings are generated. After all w child solutions are created, unique solutions are maintained and in the event the number of unique solutions is less than the size of the population, a random key crossover [2] is used to generate new solutions. From the set of w parent solutions and newly generated w child solutions, the best w individuals are maintained in Q.

The process of random key crossover is illustrated below for completeness. Two individuals P_{c1} and P_{c2} are identified using a roulette wheel based selection. Seven random numbers (one for each task in P_{c1}) are drawn uniformly from $(1, 3000)$ and for the discussion assume them as follows : $(2100, 569, 3, 888, 970, 1100, 30)$. The sorted list of random numbers is $(3, 30, 569, 888, 970, 1100, 2100)$. The original chromosome $(6, 1, 5, 4, 2, 3, 7)$ is encoded such that the element 3 in the sorted list of random numbers is inserted in location 6, 30 in location 1, 569 in location 5 and so on resulting in an encoded chromosome as $(30, 970, 1100, 888, 569, 3, 2100)$. The process is repeated for P_{c2}, the encoded form of which is $(90, 220, 457, 140, 1400, 700, 550)$. It is important to highlight that the random numbers used in P_{c1} and P_{c2} should be unique. Following the standard form of two point crossover in the encoded space, the child chromosomes R_1* and R_2* assumes the form $(30, 970, 1100, 140, 1400, 3, 2100)$ and $(90, 220, 457, 888, 569, 700, 550)$. A decoding of the chromosomes R_1* and R_2* back to the original space results in $(6, 1, 4, 2, 3, 5, 7)$ and $(1, 2, 3, 7, 5, 6, 4)$ respectively, where 6 denotes the position of the smallest random number in the encoded chromosome, 1 denotes the position of next smallest random number and so on. These offsprings generated by crossover via *random keys* are guaranteed to be feasible and a random one is selected. The pseudocode of the process is presented below.

Algorithm 2. Modifed Random Key Crossover

1: **for** $i = 1 \rightarrow w - Number of P_c$ **do**
2:     Apply roulette wheel to select two individual P_{c1} and P_{c2}
3:     **for** $j = 1 \rightarrow 2$ **do**
4:         Randomly select h numbers $\subseteq (1, 3000)$ {Number of total tasks in P_{cj}}
5:         Encode $P_{cj} \Longrightarrow R_i$
6:         Randomly select two integer numbers $m_{point1} \subseteq [1, h-1]$ and $m_{point2} \subseteq [1, h-1]$
        to split R_i
7:         **while** $m_{point1} = m_{point2}$ **do**
8:             Randomly select a integer number $m_{point2} \subseteq [1, h-1]$
9:         **end while**
10:        $R_i \Longrightarrow (part_i^1*, part_i^2*, part_i^3*)$
11:     **end for**
12:     Swap $(part_1^2* \Longleftrightarrow part_2^2*) \Longrightarrow R_1*, R_2*$
13:     **for** $j = 1 \rightarrow 2$ **do**
14:         Decode $R_j* \Longrightarrow Chr_j*$
15:     **end for**
16:     Randomly select Chr_1* and $Chr_2* \Longrightarrow C_1$
17: **end for**

2.4 Local Search

Apart from recombination, local search plays an important role in any hybrid or memetic forms. Firstly, the child C_1 is improved using a local search with a probability r_{LS}. Three move operators have been used to perturb the solution, i.e., *single insertion, double insertion*, and *swap*. The best chromosome C_2 with the shortest distance is the outcome of this phase. It is very important to highlight that if the top Q is still the same after a generation, a roulette wheel selection is used to identify C_1.

The best result S from *splitting* C_1 identified from phase 1 is now improved further using a larger search domain, wherein tasks of two vehicle trips are redistributed among them using five rules of path scanning respectively resulting in five candidate part-solutions. The best candidate part-solution is inserted into the rest of the S to result in the new solution S_C. Since there are C_N^2 combinations possible, the following condition is enforced, i.e., if $I:N!/2(N-2)! < 50$, $l_{times} = I$, else $l_{times} = 50$, where l_{times} denotes the number of attempts.

The solution identified through this second phase of local search is accepted if its distance is lower than the one obtained during the first phase of local search, else the local search phase is aborted and the best solution corresponds to the one obtained in phase one. In the event, the solution obtained from the second phase of local search is better than the one obtained from the first phase, the algorithm offers one more chance to the solution to improve while moving through phase one and phase two of the local search procedure. The best solution of this phase is denoted as C_3.

The pseudocode of the local search process is presented in Algorithm 3.

Algorithm 3. Local Search Algorithm

REQUIRE: Probability $\leq r_{LS}$

1: Perform *single insertion* operator to $C_1 \Longrightarrow C_1^1$
2: Perform *double insertion* operator to $C_1 \Longrightarrow C_1^2$
3: Perform *swap* operator to $C_1 \Longrightarrow C_1^3$
4: Keep the best one of C_1^1, C_1^2 and $C_1^3 \Longrightarrow C_2$
5: Apply *split* method to $C_2 \Longrightarrow S = (S_1, S_2, ..., S_N)$
6: $l_{times} = \min[I, 50]$
7: **for** $i = 1$ to l_{times} **do**
8:     Apply path-scanning to each pair of solutions to generate five different *part solutions*
9:     Select the best one of them $\Longrightarrow S_C$
10:    Combine S_C with the rest solutions $\Longrightarrow C_3$
11:    Apply *split* method to evaluate C_3
12:    Update the solution if C_3 is better than C_2, $C_3 \Longrightarrow C_{new}$
13: **end for**
14: **if** Found $C_{new} = $ true **then**
15:    Apply local search again on C_{new}
16: **end if**

---

3   Performance on Benchmarks

In this section, the computational experiments and results are discussed. The first benchmark set contains 23 instances (*gdb*) originally generated by DeArmon [6]. The second benchmark set is from Benavent *et al* [3] which contains 34 instances (*val* benchment) defined using 10 different graphs. In both these instance sets, all the edges of the graphs require service. The final benchmark set [8] consists of 24 instances with large number of edges constructed from winter gritting data of Lancashire. The road networks of all the instances are undirected. Although the proposed algorithm can deal with mixed networks, we still focus on these problems since there are no mixed graph data instances in public domain.

The performance of the proposed algorithm is presented in Tables 2 3 4 and compared with the state-of-the-art algorithm MAENS [22] using a limited budget of 50,000 function evaluations(FE). For each instance, the results reported are averaged over 20 independent runs. Population size (w) is set to 30. Local search is applied with a probability $r_{LS} = 0.2$. In each table, the number of vertices are denoted as $|V|$, edges as $|E|$, the number of tasks as $|T|$, the average computational time as $T_c(second)$ and low bound as LB [4, 5, 15]. The average distance, standard deviation of the distance, best distance and the number of vehicles corresponding to the solution with the best distance are indicated for all the problem instances. The value in column R_s indicates the number of runs in which the worst solution obtained by the proposed algorithm in 20 runs is better than the best obtained using MAENS. A value of 20 indicates that the results obtained in all the runs of the proposed algorithm is better than the best obtained using MAENS. The progress plot of the median run for one of each problem classes are presented in Figure 1. One can clearly observe the benefits of the initialization scheme and the efficiency of the proposed approach. Detailed comparison of results of MAENS with other approaches have appeared in [22] and hence have been omitted in this paper.

Table 2 presents the results of experiments on the *gdb* benchmark, which consist of small networks with no more than 55 tasks. It is clear that the proposed algorithm performs significantly better than MAENS in terms of the best, average and the standard deviation when the budget is limited to 50,000FE. Table 3 and Table 4 present the results for *val* and *egl* benchmarks which represent large size network instances. It can be observed that the proposed algorithm still performs significantly better than MAENS in all aspects, i.e., best, average and the standard deviation. While this study considered the performance of the proposed algorithm with limited number of evaluations (50,000), a quick comparison with the known lower bounds reported in [13] indicates that in 63 out of 81 instances, the best solution obtained by the proposed algorithm is within 20% of the lower bound. In order to observe the performance of the algorithm for higher number of function evaluations, the algorithm was allowed to use 250,000 function evaluations and in 71 out of 81 instances the best solution was siwthin 20% of the lower bound. One can observe a signifcant improvement in performance when the allowed number of function evaluatsiona are higher. In order to study the effect of MSA based parent selection, the same algorithm was run with random parent selection. The results of MSA based parent selection are signifcanltly better than the random parent selection scheme.

Table 2. Results on the set of *gdb* benchmark

Inst.	$|V|$	$|E|$	$|T|$	LB	MAENS(50,000FE)				R_s	With-MSA(50,000FE)					With-MSA(250,000FE)				Without-MSA(50,000FE)			
					$Average_1$	Std_1	D_1	N_1		$Average_2$	Std_2	D_2	N_2	$T_c(s)$	$Average_3$	Std_3	D_3	N_3	$Average_4$	Std_4	D_4	N_4
gdb1	12	22	22	316	397.9	18	372	5	30	323.5	5.6	**316**	5	20.2	319.3	4.3	316	5	329.2	6.3	316	5
gdb2	12	26	26	339	433.8	12.7	420	6	30	362.4	9.3	**345**	6	19.2	351.3	4.5	345	6	370	8.6	353	6
gdb3	12	22	22	275	394.3	7.9	382	6	30	288.1	5.6	**275**	5	18.5	281.4	4.9	275	5	294.8	7.7	281	5
gdb4	11	19	19	287	350	21.8	333	4	30	298.3	11.5	**287**	4	19.6	289.1	5.3	287	4	300	8.6	287	4
gdb5	13	26	26	377	495.9	10.7	481	6	30	400.2	9.7	**383**	6	19.8	387.2	6.6	377	6	405.6	11.3	383	6
gdb6	12	22	22	298	440.1	21.9	413	6	30	317.3	8.1	**298**	5	17.9	308.2	7	298	5	321.8	6.5	306	5
gdb7	12	22	22	325	413.5	9.3	405	6	30	333.2	7	**325**	5	19.5	328.1	3.9	325	5	341.1	9.6	325	5
gdb8	27	46	46	348	647.6	13.5	633	12	30	387.6	11.9	**364**	10	24.5	371	7.9	362	11	390.7	11.1	369	11
gdb9	27	51	51	303	568	16	541	13	30	363.8	14.8	**336**	11	22.3	343.3	7.8	331	11	374.4	18.7	339	11
gdb10	12	25	25	275	418.5	18.4	398	6	30	302.2	10.1	**288**	4	18.4	281.5	5.3	275	4	310.3	8.7	295	5
gdb11	22	45	45	395	781	15.8	756	6	30	495.4	23.4	**439**	6	20.1	446.2	17.9	419	5	503.6	21.1	444	6
gdb12	13	23	23	458	646.6	25.3	616	8	30	484	12.4	**462**	7	20.3	482.9	12.9	462	7	477.8	9.8	468	7
gdb13	10	28	28	536	626.4	7.3	617	8	30	553.5	4.8	**546**	7	20.3	548.6	1.7	544	7	557.6	5.8	548	7
gdb14	7	21	21	100	125	3.5	121	6	30	101.2	1.2	**100**	5	19.5	100.3	0.7	100	5	102.4	1.2	100	5
gdb15	7	21	21	58	67.3	2.3	66	4	30	58.5	0.9	**58**	4	20.2	58	0	58	4	58.9	1	58	4
gdb16	8	28	28	127	155.5	4.8	147	5	30	131	1.6	**129**	6	17.9	129.1	1	127	5	132.5	2	129	6
gdb17	8	28	28	91	107.6	3.1	105	5	30	91.7	0.9	**91**	5	18.1	91	0	91	5	93.3	3.1	91	5
gdb18	9	36	36	164	220.1	5.8	211	5	30	180.9	3.9	**173**	5	18.2	169.3	2.2	166	5	185	4.3	176	5
gdb19	8	11	11	55	55.4	0.5	55	3	30	55	0	**55**	3	22.8	55	0	55	3	55	0	55	3
gdb20	11	22	22	121	144.9	4.9	140	5	30	123.8	0.9	**123**	5	17.7	123	0	123	5	125.2	1.4	124	5
gdb21	11	33	33	156	218	7.1	209	8	30	165.9	3.4	**159**	7	18.4	159.4	1.5	156	6	168.9	4.5	160	7
gdb22	11	44	44	200	240.9	2.7	236	9	30	210.8	3.2	**204**	9	22	205.6	1.2	204	9	213.3	3.8	206	10
gdb23	11	55	55	233	293.5	4.2	290	13	30	253.3	4.3	**244**	12	30.3	245	2.8	237	11	258.6	6	248	13

Table 3. Results on the set of *val* benchmark

Inst.	$|V|$	$|E|$	$|T|$	LB	MAENS(50,000FE) Average₁	Std₁	D₁	N₁	Rₛ	With-MSA(50,000FE) Average₂	Std₂	D₂	N₂	Tc(s)	With-MSA(250,000FE) Average₃	Std₃	D₃	N₃	Without-MSA(50,000FE) Average₄	Std₄	D₄	N₄
val1a	24	39	39	173	327.5	11.8	316	2	30	215.8	12.4	**189**	3	24.4	197.9	10.9	180	3	213.9	10.11	**186**	3
val1b	24	39	39	173	324	10.8	312	4	30	216.2	9.1	**191**	4	21.7	192.2	6.2	183	4	214.3	9.6	192	4
val1c	24	39	39	245	369.3	6.7	359	11	30	267.4	6.9	**254**	10	20.3	256.6	4.1	250	9	275.6	9.2	258	10
val2a	24	34	34	227	369.8	11.9	355	2	30	300.1	26.3	**246**	2	22.6	247.9	7.4	231	2	299.8	15.7	269	2
val2b	24	34	34	259	410.8	13.1	398	4	30	315.8	16.6	**278**	3	19	282.4	7.7	264	3	319.5	17.4	278	3
val2c	24	34	34	457	589	13.3	572	10	30	499.1	11.9	**479**	8	20.3	488.2	10.7	473	8	501.6	12.9	**475**	8
val3a	24	35	35	81	137.8	4.2	133	2	30	104.6	7	**86**	2	22.8	89.6	3.4	84	3	104.7	6.5	91	2
val3b	24	35	35	87	162.5	7.2	154	3	30	112.7	7.1	**98**	4	20.2	98.2	4.2	93	3	114.9	4.3	108	3
val3c	24	35	35	138	218.7	6	210	8	30	151.3	3.6	**143**	7	17.4	148.1	2.9	144	7	155.2	5.2	146	8
val4a	41	69	69	400	796.6	7.2	788	4	30	551.9	21.4	**506**	7	31.6	539.9	20	495	7	549.3	21	507	4
val4b	41	69	69	412	844.1	15.8	827	5	30	570.3	19.3	**531**	5	38	557.6	23.8	495	4	569.4	18.6	**529**	5
val4c	41	69	69	428	778	8.7	768	7	30	596.7	21.4	**528**	6	31.2	573	18.9	528	6	598.8	16.9	557	7
val4d	41	69	69	530	922.6	16.3	907	11	30	671.2	25.4	**620**	10	33.2	638.6	19	601	9	678.7	20.7	630	9
val5a	34	65	65	423	736.1	16.2	720	5	30	590.5	18.1	**546**	5	27.6	576.4	21.6	539	4	588.5	23.4	**538**	3
val5b	34	65	65	446	808	14.2	793	5	30	613.1	22.8	**545**	5	36.4	601.6	20.8	549	4	611	17	573	5
val5c	34	65	65	474	831.3	9	822	6	30	643.5	17.7	**587**	6	27	621.3	15.9	571	6	647.6	19.5	612	6
val5d	34	65	65	577	943.7	10.5	930	12	30	729.4	22.3	**689**	9	28.1	703.3	12.3	676	10	730.2	18.6	689	10
val6a	31	50	50	223	430	11.8	412	4	30	289.8	8.3	**276**	5	26.9	275.5	13.4	253	4	292.9	9.8	**274**	4
val6b	31	50	50	233	422.7	11.3	409	5	30	300.7	12.9	**271**	5	22.1	274.1	12.9	253	5	303.1	9.6	281	5
val6c	31	50	50	317	542.2	7.9	531	11	30	372.7	10	**339**	10	24.7	346.3	8.9	330	10	373.5	12.9	354	10
val7a	40	66	66	279	638	14.5	620	4	30	363.1	12.7	**333**	4	35.3	354.6	10.4	335	4	365.1	11.4	343	4
val7b	40	66	66	283	553	12.2	540	7	30	356.2	16.1	**319**	5	27.5	339	10.6	316	5	363.1	11.5	339	5
val7c	40	66	66	334	602	14.6	586	11	30	403.6	14.4	**371**	10	27.6	381.7	11.8	362	9	421.9	18.1	385	11
val8a	30	63	63	386	783.1	16.8	762	5	30	548.1	18	**516**	3	29.2	527	16.9	501	4	554.8	15.6	524	5
val8b	30	63	63	395	721.7	13.5	706	5	30	568.9	24.1	**494**	4	28.5	536.3	26.2	474	4	581.9	16.2	547	5
val8c	30	63	63	521	895.3	14.9	878	12	30	678.7	23.1	**623**	11	33.7	636.5	14.1	610	10	686.3	28.5	635	10
val9a	50	92	92	323	748.8	16.7	726	4	30	431	15.7	**399**	4	54	405.6	10.1	392	4	435.1	12.5	402	4
val9b	50	92	92	326	785	16.6	761	5	30	443.8	12.1	**416**	6	58.1	431.1	9.6	402	6	441.7	10.4	416	6
val9c	50	92	92	332	666.1	13	652	6	30	453	11.9	**420**	6	58.2	423.3	10.1	399	6	456	8.4	436	6
val9d	50	92	92	391	815	15	795	6	30	519	16.3	**480**	12	50.2	483.5	12.1	457	12	520	15	481	11
val10a	50	97	97	428	855.6	16.4	841	5	30	584	12.1	**555**	4	61.6	577.9	12.9	555	4	580.7	11.5	556	3
val10b	50	97	97	436	712.6	12.9	697	6	30	598.6	12.5	**571**	5	73.4	595.8	17.8	554	6	600.8	10.8	575	5
val10c	50	97	97	446	993.7	11.3	987	7	30	611.3	15.5	**555**	5	61.4	590.5	18.2	534	6	612.9	11	585	6
val10d	50	97	97	531	926.3	13.3	911	12	30	696.6	14.8	**656**	10	58	681.9	14	653	10	692.5	15.8	**654**	11

Table 4. Results on the set of *egl* benchmark

Inst.	|V|	|E|	|T|	LB	MAENS(50,000FE)				R_s	With-MSA(50,000FE)					With-MSA(250,000FE)				Without-MSA(50,000FE)			
					$Average_1$	Std_1	D_1	N_1		$Average_2$	Std_2	D_2	N_2	$T_c(s)$	$Average_3$	Std_3	D_3	N_3	$Average_4$	Std_4	D_4	N_4
egl-e1-A	77	98	51	3548	7856	187	7618	6	30	3926	95.6	**3729**	5	20.7	3783	75.7	3672	5	4029	147	3766	5
egl-e1-B	77	98	51	4498	8274	194.1	8026	9	30	4852	78.3	**4681**	7	24.5	4728	78.9	4603	7	4945	158.4	4683	7
egl-e1-C	77	98	51	5566	8723	157.2	8563	10	30	5992	64.1	**5850**	10	24.5	5876	65	5742	10	6034	89.9	5896	10
egl-e2-A	77	98	72	5018	8335	100.2	8211	8	30	5800	150.9	**5486**	7	27	5499	128.3	5226	7	5763	161.5	5419	7
egl-e2-B	77	98	72	6305	8799	127.8	8630	10	30	6936	139.7	**6728**	10	26.6	6733	90.8	6563	10	7035	164.6	6743	10
egl-e2-C	77	98	72	8243	14433	102.9	13650	16	30	8959	100.9	**8716**	15	26.5	8778	86.4	8600	14	9024	190.8	8750	14
egl-e3-A	77	98	87	5898	12545	102	10960	9	30	6752	100.5	**6422**	8	43.6	6530	120.3	6297	8	7005	262.7	6462	8
egl-e3-B	77	98	87	7704	13720	142.1	12333	14	30	8659	127.4	**8267**	13	44.9	8767	263.9	8296	12	8383	111.9	8172	12
egl-e3-C	77	98	87	10163	16166	199.5	15930	18	30	11163	149.4	**10827**	17	44.2	10968	99.5	10793	17	11217	198.9	10827	17
egl-e4-A	77	98	98	6408	10381	162.2	10200	12	30	7532	234.9	**7024**	9	53.3	7319	184.9	7000	9	7589	228.2	7131	9
egl-e4-B	77	98	98	8884	15440	222	15201	15	30	10106	169.4	**9613**	15	55.3	9897	170.3	9562	14	10183	348.7	**9608**	14
egl-e4-C	77	98	98	11427	18577	206.6	18265	22	30	12735	201.5	**12210**	20	55.1	12521	178.9	12080	20	12811	222.9	12542	21
egl-s1-A	140	190	75	5018	8210	176.4	7964	8	30	5734	110.5	**5433**	7	41.6	5564	88.3	5368	7	5827	170.8	5449	7
egl-s1-B	140	190	75	6384	9823	177.3	9633	11	30	6940	124.7	**6721**	10	33.8	6854	81.9	6631	10	7081	163.1	**6718**	10
egl-s1-C	140	190	75	8493	14505	198.2	14212	14	30	8971	122.1	**8715**	14	33.9	8786	95.8	8668	14	9252	248.9	8792	15
egl-s2-A	140	190	147	9824	19136	176	18965	16	30	11752	152.2	**11372**	15	95.4	11545	181.2	10987	14	11920	153.1	11497	14
egl-s2-B	140	190	147	12968	20082	228.1	19869	22	30	15004	159.6	**14706**	21	102.7	14784	160.3	14387	21	15082	268.7	14744	21
egl-s2-C	140	190	147	16353	21523	142.5	21321	29	30	18645	194.4	**18291**	29	100.1	18404	179.5	18115	29	18765	258.8	**18249**	29
egl-s3-A	140	190	159	10143	19290	226.7	18927	16	30	12124	158	**11792**	15	116	12011	139.3	11654	15	12222	218.8	11802	15
egl-s3-B	140	190	159	13616	22565	145.3	20563	23	30	15900	189.3	**15505**	23	111.7	15739	179.9	15433	22	15893	223.7	15564	24
egl-s3-C	140	190	159	17100	25643	244	25362	31	30	19464	207.4	**19069**	30	108	19291	122.2	18909	31	19464	199.6	**18959**	30
egl-s4-A	140	190	190	12143	18733	210.1	18520	20	30	14956	247.8	**14334**	20	176.3	14771	317.5	13991	19	14966	264.3	14452	19
egl-s4-B	140	190	190	16093	24411	206.7	24122	30	30	19041	194.5	**18533**	28	173.9	18900	178.2	18449	29	19075	157.2	18621	28
egl-s4-C	140	190	190	20375	26730	167.9	26541	37	30	23669	263.1	**23240**	39	168	23489	275.4	22926	38	23618	174.4	23251	38

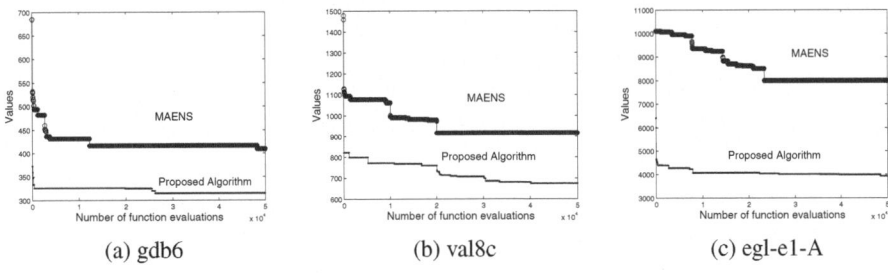

Fig. 1. The rate of convergence

4   Conclusion

In this paper, a memetic algorithm is introduced that relies on the use of multiple sequence alignment inspired parent selection scheme, a hybrid recombination strategy and a local search. Results on both small and large scale instances with limited number of solution evaluations indicate the applicability of the proposed algorithm for dynamic CARP problems, where one is interested in identifying an acceptable quality of solution within a short time. Although in reality, computational time is of primary interest, we focus here on a more objective performance indicator, i.e., number of function evaluations which is independent of the computing platform and skills of implementation. The proposed algorithm obtained high quality solutions to 81 well studied CARP instances within 50,000 function evaluations and all of which are better than the existing state-of-the-art approach based on MAENS. The performance of the algorithm is also presented for 250,000 function evaluations for further studies. Apart from the convergence observed in the objective function space, the detailed performance on its components are analyzed and discussed. In future, we would incorporate an adaptive strategy which allocates/redistributes function evaluations to local search and recombination strategies based on their success which is likely to further improve the effectiveness of the algorithm.

References

1. Bautista, J., Fernández, E., Pereira, J.: Solving an urban waste collection problem using ants heuristics. Computers & Operations Research 35(9), 3020–3033 (2008)
2. Bean, J.: Genetic algorithms and random keys for sequencing and optimization. ORSA Journal on Computing 6(2), 154–160 (1994)
3. Benavent, E., Campos, V., Corberán, A., Mota, E.: The capacitated arc routing problem: lower bounds. Networks-New York 22, 669–669 (1992)
4. Beullens, P., Muyldermans, L., Cattrysse, D., Van Oudheusden, D.: A guided local search heuristic for the capacitated arc routing problem. European Journal of Operational Research 147(3), 629–643 (2003)
5. Brandão, J., Eglese, R.: A deterministic tabu search algorithm for the capacitated arc routing problem. Computers & Operations Research 35(4), 1112–1126 (2008)

6. DeArmon, J.: A comparison of heuristics for the capacitated chinese postman problem. Master's thesis (University of Maryland, College Park, MD) (1981)
7. Dror, M.: Arc routing: theory, solutions, and applications. Springer, Netherlands (2000)
8. Eglese, R.: Routeing winter gritting vehicles. Discrete Applied Mathematics 48(3), 231–244 (1994)
9. Eiselt, H., Gendreau, M., Laporte, G.: Arc routing problems, part i: The chinese postman problem. Operations Research, 231–242 (1995)
10. Eiselt, H., Gendreau, M., Laporte, G.: Arc routing problems, part II: The rural postman problem. Operations Research, 399–414 (1995)
11. Golden, B., DeArmon, J., Baker, E.: Computational experiments with algorithms for a class of routing problems. Computers & Operations Research 10(1), 47–59 (1983)
12. Golden, B., Wong, R.: Capacitated arc routing problems. Networks 11(3), 305–315 (1981)
13. Lacomme, P., Prins, C., Ramdane-Cherif, W.: Competitive memetic algorithms for arc routing problems. Annals of Operations Research 131(1), 159–185 (2004)
14. Lecompte, O., Thompson, J., Plewniak, F., Thierry, J., Poch, O.: Multiple alignment of complete sequences (macs) in the post-genomic era. Gene 270(1-2), 17–30 (2001)
15. Longo, H., de Aragâo, M., Uchoa, E.: Solving capacitated arc routing problems using a transformation to the cvrp. Computers & Operations Research 33(6), 1823–1837 (2006)
16. Martinelli, R., Pecin, D., Poggi, M., Longo, H.: A branch-cut-and-price algorithm for the capacitated arc routing problem. Experimental Algorithms, 315–326 (2011)
17. Mei, Y., Tang, K., Yao, X.: A global repair operator for capacitated arc routing problem. IEEE Transactions on Systems, Man, and Cybernetics, Part B: Cybernetics 39(3), 723–734 (2009)
18. Morgan, M., Mumford, C.: A weight-coded genetic algorithm for the capacitated arc routing problem. In: Proceedings of the 11th Annual Conference on Genetic and Evolutionary Computation, pp. 325–332. ACM (2009)
19. Pearn, W.: Approximate solutions for the capacitated arc routing problem. Computers & Operations Research 16(6), 589–600 (1989)
20. Pearn, W.: Augment-insert algorithms for the capacitated arc routing problem. Computers & Operations Research 18(2), 189–198 (1991)
21. Santos, L., Coutinho-Rodrigues, J., Current, J.: An improved heuristic for the capacitated arc routing problem. Computers & Operations Research 36(9), 2632–2637 (2009)
22. Tang, K., Mei, Y., Yao, X.: Memetic algorithm with extended neighborhood search for capacitated arc routing problems. IEEE Transactions on Evolutionary Computation 13(5), 1151–1166 (2009)
23. Ulusoy, G.: The fleet size and mix problem for capacitated arc routing. European Journal of Operational Research 22(3), 329–337 (1985)
24. Xing, L., Rohlfshagen, P., Chen, Y., Yao, X.: An evolutionary approach to the multidepot capacitated arc routing problem. IEEE Transactions on Evolutionary Computation 14(3), 356–374 (2010)

Block-Structured Plan Deordering

Fazlul Hasan Siddiqui and Patrik Haslum

The Australian National University & NICTA Optimisation Research Group,
Canberra, Australia

Abstract. Partially ordered plans have several useful properties, such as exhibiting the structure of the plan more clearly which facilitates post-plan generation tasks like scheduling the plan, explaining it to a user, or breaking it into subplans for distributed execution. The standard interpretation of partial ordering implies that whenever two subplans are unordered, every interleaving of steps from the two forms a valid execution. This restricts deordering to cases where individual steps (i.e., actions) are independent. We propose a weaker notion of partial ordering that divides the plan into *blocks*, such that the steps in a block may not be interleaved with steps outside the block, but unordered blocks can be executed in any sequence. We present an algorithm to find such deorderable blocks, and show that it enables deordering plans in many cases where no deordering is possible under the standard interpretation.

1   Introduction

In AI planning, the process of *deordering* converts a sequential plan into a partially ordered plan, by removing ordering constraints between steps, such that the steps of the plan can be successfully executed in any order consistent with the partial order and still achieve the goal [1]. Partially ordered plans have two advantages: first, they afford execution flexibility, thus allowing plans to be scheduled for improved efficiency or robustness [2]; and second, they make the plan structure more accessible, which facilitates further analysis of the plan. However, current state space search planners, which produce totally ordered sequential plans, are far more efficient than the older partial order planners. Thus, deordering plays a useful role in that it enables more efficient generation of partially ordered plans.

The standard interpretation of a partially ordered plan is that it is valid if and only if every sequential plan that is a topological sort of the steps is valid (according to the semantics of sequential plan execution). This implies that for two subplans to be unordered, every interleaving of steps from the two must form a valid execution. This restricts deordering to only the cases where individual steps (i.e., actions) are independent and non-interfering. We examine a weaker notion of partial ordering: We divide a plan into *blocks*, such that the steps in a block may not be interleaved with steps outside the block, but unordered blocks can be executed in any sequence. The difference is illustrated in Figure 1. The restriction to non-interleaved executions allows "transient" dependencies and effects to be encapsulated within a block, and thus not cause

M. Thielscher and D. Zhang (Eds.): AI 2012, LNCS 7691, pp. 803–814, 2012.

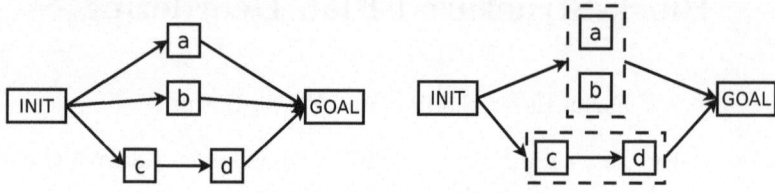

Fig. 1. A normal partially ordered plan (left) represents the set of all sequential plans that are topological sorts of the plan steps, such as *abcd*, *acbd*, *cbda*, etc. A block ordered plan (right) allows unordered blocks (shown with dashed outlines) to be executed in any order, but not steps from different blocks to be interleaved. Thus, *abcd*, *bacd*, *cdab* and *cdba* are the only linearisations of this plan.

interference with other blocks. This can enable deordering of blocks in some cases also when their constituent actions cannot be deordered under step-wise interpretation of partially ordered plans. (An example of this is shown in Figure 2.) We also present an algorithm to find block deorderings of plans, and show empirically that it deorders plans to a much greater degree than step-wise deordering.

Since unordered blocks cannot, in general, be executed concurrently, block deordering improves mainly on the second advantage of partial ordering, viz. making the structure of the plan explicit. We believe that the main benefit of this will be to facilitate post-plan generation tasks such as explaining the plan to a user, or breaking it into a set of subplans with minimal constraints between them, which is useful for reducing the coordination overhead if the plan is to be executed by a distributed team of agents [3], or for improving plan quality by local modifications [4].

2   Plans, Validity and Deordering

AI planning is model-based: a planner takes as input a description of available actions, in some formal modelling language, and the initial state and goal. Several modelling languages are in use (see, e.g., [5]). Because many details of the modelling language are not relevant for the purpose of plan deordering, we adopt Bäckström's [1] *producer-consumer-threat* model, which is general enough to encompas most common planning formalisms (e.g., STRIPS and SAS+).

A planning problem is defined over a set of *atomic propositions*. An action that makes a proposition p true is called a *producer* of p; an action that requires p to hold is called a *consumer* of p, and p is called a *precondition* of the action; and an action that makes p false is called a *threat* to p. (In the common propositional STRIPS formalism, producers are actions that add p and threats are actions that delete p.) A partially ordered plan is a set, S, of *steps*, where each step $s \in S$

is labelled by an action, $\mathrm{act}(s)$, and a strict (i.e., irreflexive) partial order $\prec$ over S. There is one *final step*, s_G in S, which represents the goal. If necessary, we can also include in S an initial step, which acts as the producer of initially true propositions. We use the terms producer, consumer and threat also for plan steps, referring to their associated actions. We use $\prec^+$ to denote the transitive closure of a partial order $\prec$. An element $(s_i, s_j) \in \prec$ (also $s_i \prec s_j$) is a *basic ordering constraint* iff it is not implied by other constraints and transitivity, that is, iff $(\prec -\{s_i \prec s_j\})^+ \subset \prec^+$. A *linearisation* of $\prec$ is a strict total order that contains $\prec$ (i.e., a topological sort). A partially ordered plan $(S, \prec)$ is *valid* iff for every step $s \in S$ and for every precondition p of $\mathrm{act}(s)$, there is a producer s_{p} of p that precedes s (i.e., $s_{\mathrm{p}} \prec^+ s$) and for every step s_{t} that threatens p, s_{t} is either ordered before s_{p} or after s (i.e., $s_{\mathrm{t}} \prec^+ s_{\mathrm{p}}$ or $s \prec^+ s_{\mathrm{t}}$). This is essentially Chapman's [6] modal truth criterion (without "white knights"), and equivalent to the standard notion that a partial order plan is valid iff every linearisation of it is valid under the usual sequential execution semantics [5].

There are three possible reasons for an ordering constraint $s_i \prec s_j$: (1) Step s_i produces a proposition p that s_j consumes. This relation is usually called a *causal link* from s_i to s_j [7]. (2) s_i threatens a proposition that s_j produces, and that is consumed by some later step. Note that it is not necessary to order a producer and threat if no step that may occur after the producer in the plan depends on the produced proposition. (3) s_j threatens a proposition that s_i consumes. It is easy to see that if every precondition is supported by a causal link, and no causal link is threatened by a possibly intervening step, the plan is valid in the sense defined above. We will use the labels $\mathrm{PC}(p)$ (producer–consumer of p), $\mathrm{TP}(p)$ (threat–producer) and $\mathrm{CT}(p)$ (consumer–threat) to denote the three reasons. Note that an ordering constraint can have several associated reasons (including several reasons of the same type but referring to different propositions). We denote the set of reasons for an ordering constraint $s_i \prec s_j$ by $\mathrm{Re}(s_i \prec s_j)$.

Let $(S, \prec)$ be a valid partially ordered plan. A (step-wise) *deordering* of the plan is a valid plan $(S, \prec')$ such that $(\prec')^+ \subset \prec^+$. That is, a deordering is the result of removing some basic ordering constraints without invalidating the plan. Deordering a sequential plan is simply a special case, since a total order is a special case of a partial order. Several algorithms for plan deordering have been proposed [8,9,10,11,12,13]. The complexity of optimal deordering depends on the planning formalism and the measure of optimality. To compute a deordering with a smallest (w.r.t. cardinality) ordering relation is NP-hard for almost every planning formalism [1]. We use a combination of two simple methods: Chrpa & Bartak's algorithm [14] for computing causal links (what they call "dependency"), with the difference that our version selects the earliest unthreatened producer whereas theirs selects the latest, and the PRF algorithm [1] for computing threat–producer and consumer–threat orderings. This procedure is essentially the same as the algorithm by Kambhampati & Kedar [11]. Although it does not guarantee optimality, a recent study found that it did produce optimal deorderings of all plans on which it was tested [13].

3   Block Decomposition and Deordering

3.1   Blocks and Their Semantics

A *block* is a part of the plan, i.e., a subset of steps, that must be executed without being interleaved with any step not in the block. Thus, there cannot be a step not in the block that is ordered in between two steps of the block.[1] The no-interleaving restriction affords us a simplified, "black box", view of blocks, in which only the preconditions and effects of executing the block as a whole are important. Thus, for the purpose of deordering we can ignore some dependencies and effects that matter only internally within the block.

A decomposition of a plan into blocks can be recursive, i.e., a block can be a strict subset of another block. However, blocks cannot be partially overlapping.

Definition 1. *Let $(S, \prec)$ be a partially ordered plan. A* block w.r.t. $\prec$ *is a subset $b \subset S$ of steps such for any two steps $s, s' \in b$, there exists no step $s'' \in (S - b)$ such that $s \prec^+ s'' \prec^+ s'$ or $s' \prec^+ s'' \prec^+ s$. A set B of subsets of S is a* block decomposition *of $(S, \prec)$ iff (1) each $b \in B$ is a block w.r.t. $\prec$ and (2) for every $b_i, b_j \in B$, either $b_i \subset b_j$, $b_j \subset b_i$, or b_i and b_j are disjoint.*

We omit the reference to the ordering relation when it is clear from context. A set consisting of a single step is always a block, but we do not consider such "trivial blocks" explicitly in the decomposition.

Formally, the semantics of a partially ordered block decomposed plan are defined by restricting its linearisations to those that respect the block decomposition, i.e., that do not interleave steps from disjoint blocks. The plan is defined to be valid iff every linearisation of it is valid, in the sense defined earlier.

Definition 2. *Let $(S, B, \prec)$ be a partially ordered and block decomposed plan. A* linearisation *of $(S, B, \prec)$ is a total order $\prec_{lin}$ on S such that (1) $\prec \subseteq \prec_{lin}$ and (2) every $b \in B$ is a block w.r.t. $\prec_{lin}$.*

The set of linearisations of a partially ordered and block decomposed plan is a subset of the linearisations under the same partial ordering without block decomposition, as illustrated by the example in Figure 1.

As mentioned above, the restriction on exections of a block decomposed plan allows us to ignore some dependencies and effects that matter only within the block. The following definition captures those preconditions and effects that are visible from outside the block, i.e., those that give rise to dependencies or interference with other parts of the plan. These are what we need to consider when deciding if two blocks can be unordered.

Definition 3. *Let $(S, B, \prec)$ be a partially ordered and block decomposed plan, and $b \in B$ a block:*

---

[1] Chrpa & Bartak [14] define the same concept, but call it a "subplan". We use the term "block" to emphasize the contiguous, "black box", nature of them, and to leave the term "subplan" free to refer to any part of a plan.

- b consumes p iff *there is a step $s \in b$ that consumes p such that there is no step $s' \in b$ with $s' \prec^+ s$ that produces p and for which either $s'' \prec^+ s'$ or $s \prec^+ s''$ holds for any $s'' \in b$ that threatens p, (In other words, there is a consumer s of p in the block, and there is no producer of p within the block from which we could draw a causal link to s that is not threatened by any step in the block.)*

- b produces p iff *there is a step $s \in b$ that produces p such that for any step $s' \in b$ that threatens p, $s' \prec^+ s$, and b does not consume p.*

- b threatens p iff *there is a step $s \in b$ that threatens p such that there is no step $s' \in b$ with $s \prec^+ s'$ that produces p.*

Whenever a block consumes, produces or threatens a proposition, there is at least one step within the block that does the same. We refer to this as the *responsible step*, and it plays an important role in the block deordering algorithm.

Note that if a block consumes a proposition, it cannot also produce the same proposition. The reason for this is that taking the "black box" view of block execution, the proposition simply persists: it is true before execution of the block begins and remains true after it has finished. If the steps within a block are totally ordered, the preconditions and effects of a block according to Definition 3 are nearly the same as the "cumulative preconditions and effects" of an action sequence, defined by Haslum & Jonsson [15], the only difference being that a consumer block cannot also be a producer of the same proposition.

3.2   Block Deordering

The process of block deordering is more complicated than standard deordering, which only involves removing constraints from the ordering relation. A block deordering involves adding new blocks to a plan decomposition, removing ordering constraints, and possibly also adding some explicit ordering constraints that were transitively implied by the removed constraints.

Let $(S, B, \prec)$ be a valid partially ordered and block decomposed plan. Consider a basic ordering constraint $s_i \prec s_j$, and the set $\mathrm{Re}(s_i \prec s_j)$ of reasons for this constraint. (We consider only basic ordering constraints, since removing a transitively implied constraint does not lead to any de facto deordering of the plan.) To remove $s_i \prec s_j$, we create two corresponding blocks, b_i and b_j, where s_i is the unique last step in b_i (that is, every step in b_i is transitively ordered before s_i) and s_j is the unique first step in b_j (that is, every step in b_j is transitively ordered after s_j). Note that one of the two blocks can be trivial, i.e., consist of a single action. Both blocks must be consistent with the existing decomposition, i.e., $B \cup \{b_i, b_j\}$ must still be a valid block decomposition, in the sense of Definition 1. We seek blocks that allow us to remove reasons from $\mathrm{Re}(s_i \prec s_j)$. Therefore, conditions on the blocks depend on what those reasons are:

- If $\mathrm{PC}(p) \in \mathrm{Re}(s_i \prec s_j)$, b_i must not produce p. Since s_i produces p and is the last step in b_i, and thus cannot be possibly followed by a threat to p within the block, this means b_i must consume p. Since the plan is valid, there must be some (unthreatened) producer, s', that necessarily precedes the step in b_i

that consumes p. If s' can precede every step in b_i, then adding the causal link $\mathrm{PC}(p)$ to $\mathrm{Re}(s' \prec s_j)$ (adding (s', s_j) to $\prec$ if not already present) allows $\mathrm{PC}(p)$ to be removed from $\mathrm{Re}(s_i \prec s_j)$. (Note that the added ordering constraint, even if not already explicitly in $\prec$, is transitively implied by $s_i \prec s_j$ and the conditions on b_i.)

- If $\mathrm{TP}(p) \in \mathrm{Re}(s_i \prec s_j)$, then b_j must include every step s' such that $\mathrm{PC}(p) \in \mathrm{Re}(s_j \prec s')$. Then $\mathrm{TP}(p)$ can be removed from $\mathrm{Re}(s_i \prec s_j)$.
- If $\mathrm{CT}(p) \in \mathrm{Re}(s_i \prec s_j)$, then either b_i must not consume p or b_j must not threaten p. Then $\mathrm{CT}(p)$ can be removed from $\mathrm{Re}(s_i \prec s_j)$.

The ordering $s_i \prec s_j$ can exist for several reasons (including several reasons of the same type, referring to different propositions). Only if blocks b_i and b_j can be found that meet the conditions above to remove every reason in $\mathrm{Re}(s_i \prec s_j)$ can the ordering be removed. Yet, even this does not guarantee the blocks will be unordered. If b_i contains some step other than s_i that is ordered before a step in b_j (s_j or another), the two blocks will still be ordered. Note that we must also check for new threats between steps in or before b_i and steps in or after b_j that become unordered as a result of removing $s_i \prec s_j$.

Theorem 1. *Deordering according to the rules above preserves plan validity.*

Proof. Let $(S, B, \prec)$ be a valid partially ordered and block decomposed plan, $s_i \prec s_j$ a basic ordering constraint, and b_i, b_j blocks that meet the conditions for removing $s_i \prec s_j$, and that are not ordered for any other reason. Let $(S, B', \prec')$ be the plan that results from deordering. Any linearisation of $(S, B', \prec')$ in which b_i precedes b_j is also a linearisation of $(S, B, \prec)$, and thus valid by assumption. Consider a linearisation in which b_j precedes b_i:

$$s_1, \ldots, s_m, b_j = [s_j, \ldots, s_{k_j}], s_{k_j+1}, \ldots, b_i = [s_{k_i}, \ldots, s_i], \ldots, s_n.$$

We examine each of the possible reasons for $s_i \prec s_j$: If $\mathrm{PC}(p) \in \mathrm{Re}(s_i \prec s_j)$, then the precondition p of step s_j is now supplied by the step s' (which is one among $s_1, \ldots, s_m$). b_j cannot threaten the causal link for p from s' to the step s'' in b_i that consumes p, since for it to do so, there must be some step $s \in b_j$ that threatens p, which would imply $\mathrm{CT}(p) \in \mathrm{Re}(s'' \prec s)$, making this linearisation inconsistent. Neither can any of the steps between b_j and b_i threaten p, since they can appear between s' and s'' also in a linearisation of the original plan.

If $\mathrm{TP}(p) \in \mathrm{Re}(s_i \prec s_j)$, then b_j includes every step s' such that $\mathrm{PC}(p) \in \mathrm{Re}(s_j \prec s')$. Thus, s_i does not threaten any causal link originating in s_j.

If $\mathrm{CT}(p) \in \mathrm{Re}(s_i \prec s_j)$, there are two possibilities: either b_i does not consume p or b_j does not threaten p. In the first case, this means that b_i constains a step s' that produces p, such that s' precedes s_i and the causal link is not threatened by any step in b_i; this means that the causal link is also unthreatened in the above linearisation, since no steps not in b_i appear between s' and s_i. In the second case, since b_j includes s_j, which does threaten p, b_j must also include a step s' that produces p and that is ordered after any step in b_j that threatens p. Since the original plan is valid, there is a step s'' that supplies an unthreatened causal link for p to s_i. Again, there are two cases: If s'' is one of the steps $s_1, \ldots, s_m$, then none of the steps between b_j and b_i can threaten p, since these steps can appear between s'' and s_i also in the original plan. Thus, we can now form an unthreatened causal link from the step s' in b_j to s_i. Otherwise, s'' is one of the steps between b_j and b_i, in which case the causal link from the original plan remains unthreatened.   □

3.3   The Block Deordering Algorithm

The previous subsection described the conditions under which block deordering is correct, in the sense that it preserves plan validity. Next, we describe the algorithm that we use to efficiently find block deordering possibilities in a plan.

We extend ordering to blocks: two blocks are ordered $b_i \prec b_j$ if there exist steps $s_i \in b_i$ and $s_j \in b_j$ such that $s_i \prec s_j$ and neither block is contained in the other (i.e., $b_i \not\subseteq b_j$ and $b_j \not\subseteq b_i$). In this case, all steps in b_i must precede all steps in b_j in any linerarisation of the block decomposed plan. We also extend the reasons for ordering (PC, TP and CT) to ordering constraints between blocks, with the set of propositions produced, consumed and threatened by a block given by Definition 3. Recall that a responsible step is a step in a block that causes it to produce, consume or threaten a proposition. For example, if b produces p, there must be a step $s \in b$ that produces p, such that no step in the block not ordered before s threatens p; we say step s is "responsible" for b producing p.

The core of the algorithm is the RESOLVE procedure (Algorithm 1). It takes as input two blocks, b_i and b_j, that are ordered (one or both blocks may consist of a single step), and tries to break the ordering by extending them to larger blocks, b_i' and b_j'. The procedure examines each reason for the ordering constraint and extends one of the blocks to remove that reason, following the rules given in the previous subsection. After this, the sets of propositions produced, consumed and threatened by the new blocks (b_i' and b_j') are recomputed (following Definition 3) and any new reasons for the ordering constraint that have arisen because of steps that have been included are added to $\mathrm{Re}(b_i' \prec b_j')$. This is repeated until either no reason for the ordering remains, in which case the new blocks returned by the procedure can safely be unordered, or some reason cannot be removed, in which case deordering is not possible (signalled by returning NULL). The function INTERMEDIATE(b_i, b_j) returns the set of steps ordered between b_i and b_j, i.e., $\{s \mid b_i \prec^+ s \prec^+ b_j\}$. Where Algorithm 1 refers to a "nearest" step s' preceding or following another step s, it means a step with a smallest number of basic ordering constraints between s' and s.

Applying the RESOLVE procedure to each basic ordering constraint we obtain a collection of blocks with which we can break some orderings. But this collection is not necessarily a valid decomposition, since some of the blocks may have partial overlap. To find a valid decomposition, we use a greedy procedure with some heuristic enhancements. We repeatedly examine each basic ordering constraint $b_i \prec b_j$ and call RESOLVE to find two extended blocks $b_i' \supseteq b_i$ and $b_j' \supseteq b_j$ that allow the ordering to be removed. In each iteration, constraints are checked in order from the beginning of the plan. If such blocks are found, and they are

---

Algorithm 1 Resolve ordering constraints between a pair of blocks.

1: **procedure** RESOLVE(b_i, b_j)
2:     Initialise $b_i' = b_i$, $b_j' = b_j$.
3:     **while** Re($b_i' \prec b_j'$) $\neq \emptyset$ **do**
4:         **for each** $r \in$ Re($b_i' \prec b_j'$) **do**
5:             **if** $r = \mathrm{PC}(p)$ **then**
6:                 Find a responsible step $s \in b_i'$ and a nearest $s' \notin b_i'$ that consumes p such that $s' \prec^+ s$.
7:                 **if** such s' exists **then**
8:                     Set $b_i' = b_i' \cup \{s'\} \cup$ INTERMEDIATE(s', b_i').
9:                 **else**
10:                     **return** NULL
11:             **else if** $r = \mathrm{TP}(p)$ **then**
12:                 Find a responsible step $s \in b_j'$ and a nearest $s' \notin b_j'$ that threatens p such that $s \prec^+ s'$.
13:                 **if** such s' exists **then**
14:                     Set $b_j' = b_j' \cup \{s'\} \cup$ INTERMEDIATE(b_j', s').
15:                 **else**
16:                     **return** NULL
17:             **else if** $r = \mathrm{CT}(p)$ **then**
18:                 Find a responsible step $s \in b_j'$ and a nearest $s' \notin b_j'$ that produces p, such that $s \prec^+ s'$.
19:                 **if** such s' exists **then**
20:                     Set $b_j' = b_j' \cup \{s'\} \cup$ INTERMEDIATE(b_j', s').
21:                 **else**
22:                     Find a responsible step $s \in b_i'$ and a nearest $s' \notin b_i'$ that produces p, such that $s' \prec^+ s$.
23:                     **if** such s' exists **then**
24:                         Set $b_i' = b_i' \cup \{s'\} \cup$ INTERMEDIATE(s', b_i').
25:                     **else**
26:                         **return** NULL.
27:         Recompute Re($b_i' \prec b_j'$).
28:     **return** (b_i', b_j').

---

consistent with the current decomposition, b_i and b_j are replaced. If b_i' or b_j' cannot be added to the decomposition (because one or both of them partially overlaps with an existing block), we consider all blocks ordered immediately after b_i, and check if all these orderings can be broken simultaneously, using the union of the blocks returned by RESOLVE for each ordering constraint. (Symmetrically, we also check the set of blocks immediately before b_j, though this is only very rarely useful.) As an additional heuristic, we discard the two blocks if there is a basic ordering constraint between a step that is internal to one of the blocks (i.e., that has both preceding and following steps within the block) and a step outside the block. If either possibility leads to a valid new decomposition, the ordering is removed. The inner loop then exits and the ordering relation is updated with any new constraints between b_i' and blocks ordered after b_j and between b_j' and blocks ordered before b_i. This is done by checking for the three reasons (PC, TP and CT) based on the sets of propositions produced, consumed and threatened by b_i' and b_j'. The inner loop is then restarted, with ordering constraints that previously could not be broken checked again. This is done because removing ordering constraints can make possible the resolution of other constraints, since removal of orderings can change the set of steps intermediate between two steps.

The main loop repeats until no further deordering consistent with the current decomposition is found. It is easy to verify that each iteration runs in polynomial time, but we currently do not have an upper bound on the number of iterations. Note, however, that the procedure is "any time", in the sense that if interrupted before running to completion, the result at the end of the last completed iteration is still a block deordering of the plan. Since the choice of deordering to apply is greedy, the result is not guaranteed to be optimal.

4   Results

We tested block deordering on a large set of plans generated by planners participating in past editions of the International Planning Competition (IPC). To measure the effect of deordering, we compare the *flexibility* [2], or "flex", of plans, after standard, step-wise, deordering (as described in Section 2) and after block deordering. The flex of a partially ordered plan is defined as the fraction of pairs of steps that are not (transitively) ordered. Thus, a higher flex value indicates a less strictly ordered plan, with a fully sequential plan having a flex of zero. We apply the same definition to block deordered plans. Recall that in a block deordered plan, all steps belonging to two ordered blocks are ordered by the requirement that blocks not be interleaved, even when there is no ordering between an individual pair of steps. This is taken into account when calculating the flex of a block deordered plan. Because of this, it is in fact possible for block deordering of a partially ordered plan to decrease its flex value. For example, assume the plan on the left in Figure 1 also had the ordering constraints $a \prec d$ and $b \prec d$, and that the block decomposition on the right removed only the first of these: it would then only have the linearisations $abcd$ and $bacd$, and have lower flex than the original plan (which has c unordered w.r.t. both a and b). However, we did not observe this happening in any of the plans analysed.

Results are summarised by domain in Table 1. For each domain, we report the number of plans analysed, the number of plans for which block deordering led to an increase in flex, and the average (over all analysed plans) flex values after step-based deordering and after block deordering. We imposed a 600 second time limit on the block deordering procedure; where the limit was reached ($\sim 8\%$ of all plans), we take the flex of the plan after the last completed iteration.

Note that several domains are purely sequential, and do not permit any deordering of individual steps. (These have an average flex of zero after step

---

[2] The term "flexibility" is used with different meanings by different authors. Nguyen & Kambhampati's [16] definition is equivalent to ours. Muise et al. [13] use it for the number of linearisations of a partially ordered plan.

Table 1. Comparison of step and block deordering. For each domain, the first column shows the number of plans analysed, and the second the number of plans in which block deordering increased the flex value above that achieved by step deordering. The average flex values after step and block deordering are over all plans in each domain.

Domain	#plans	#inc.	Average flex after deordering	
			step	block
Airport (IPC4)	563	262	0.1492	0.1562
Blocks (IPC2)	381	284	0.0	0.0479
Cybersec (IPC6)	109	109	0.0142	0.2476
Depots (IPC3)	234	183	0.1589	0.1951
Elevators (IPC6)	276	216	0.1543	0.1965
FreeCell (IPC2)	358	214	0.0516	0.0596
Logistics (IPC2)	534	437	0.2435	0.2629
Openstacks (ADL, IPC5)	109	109	0.0	0.0733
Openstacks (STRIPS, IPC5)	15	15	0.0	0.0353
Openstacks (ADL, IPC6)	312	312	0.0453	0.1298
Openstacks (STRIPS, IPC6)	488	487	0.0469	0.1347
ParcPrinter (IPC6)	252	218	0.0820	0.2747
Pathways (STRIPS)	113	85	0.2455	0.2683
PegSol (IPC6)	301	261	0.0	0.1018
Rovers (IPC3)	187	187	0.2003	0.3541
Scanalyzer (IPC6)	343	202	0.1201	0.2418
Sokoban (IPC6)	205	174	0.0	0.0144
Storage (IPC5)	185	117	0.0423	0.1119
Transport (IPC6)	243	156	0.2071	0.2340
Woodworking (IPC6)	277	5	0.4551	0.4551

Fig. 2. Visualisation of the execution of (part of) an example plan in the Sokoban domain. Arrows show the movements of the man; dashed outlines show the movement of boxes that he pushes. The blocks consisting of steps 3–4 and 5–28 can be safely unordered, as can the blocks 10–21 and 22–23.

deordering.) Yet, even in these domains, it is often possible to block deorder plans. As an example, Figure 2 visualises the execution of part of a plan from the Sokoban domain (the reference plan for problem #11 from the IPC6 satisficing track). Sokoban is a puzzle game, involving a man who must push boxes around on a grid, one at a time, to reach a goal configuration. The domain is sequential because actions in the planning encoding of the game move the man from one square to another; thus, every step has a causal link from the step immediately before, and no deordering of individual steps is possible. Block deordering, however, is: In the example plan, the blocks consisting of steps 3–4 and steps 5–28 are independent and can be unordered. As can be seen clearly from the visualisation, moving steps 3–4, as a block, to after step 28 does not invalidate the plan. There are also two blocks, consisting of steps 10–21 and 22–23, within the larger block 5–28, that can be deordered. Our algorithm found all these possibilities.

5   Conclusions

Deordering makes the structure of a plan explicit, showing us which parts are necessarily sequential (because of dependency or interference) and which are independent and non-interfering. Block deordering improves on this by creating an on-the-fly hierarchical decomposition of the plan, encapsulating some dependecies and interferences within each block. Considering blocks, instead of primitive actions, as the units of partial ordering thus enables deordering plans more, including in cases where no deordering is possibly using the standard, step-wise, partial order plan notion. We showed that using a simple greedy algorithm to find block decompositions we could substantially increase the flex of deordered plans across many planning domains.

Maximising flex is not an end in itself; we use it only as a way to measure the "amount of deordering" done. The ultimate significance of block deordering will be determined by how much we can exploit the additional structural information it provides to improve on various post-plan generation tasks, such as explaining the plan to a user, or minimising execution coordination. We are particularly motivated by the use of plan structure information to improve the quality of plans by identifying subplans that can be locally improved [4]. As a simple example, in Figure 2 it can be observed that if the block 3–4 is relocated to after the block 5–28, steps 4 and 29 become redundant and can be removed. We are currently developing plan optimisation methods based on block deordering.

Acknowledgements. This work was supported by the Australian Research Council discovery project DP0985532 "Exploiting Structure in AI Planning". NICTA is funded by the Australian Government as represented by the Department of Broadband, Communications and the Digital Economy and the Australian Research Council through the ICT Centre of Excellence program.

References

1. Bäckström, C.: Computational aspects of reordering plans. Journal of AI Research 9, 99–137 (1998)
2. Policella, N., Smith, S., Cesta, A., Oddi, A.: Generating robust schedules through temporal flexibility. In: Proc. 14th International Conference on Automated Planning & Scheduling (ICAPS 2004), pp. 209–218 (2004)
3. Cox, J., Durfee, E., Bartold, T.: A distributed framework for solving the multiagent plan coordination problem. In: Proc. 4th International Joint Conference on Autonomous Agents and Multiagent Systems (AAMAS 2005), pp. 821–827 (2005)
4. Chrpa, L., McCluskey, T., Osborne, H.: Optimizing plans through analysis of action dependencies and independencies. In: Proc. 22nd International Conference on Automated Planning and Scheduling, ICAPS 2012 (2012)
5. Ghallab, M., Nau, D., Traverso, P.: Automated Planning: Theory and Practice. Morgan Kaufmann Publishers (2004) ISBN: 1-55860-856-7
6. Chapman, D.: Planning for conjunctive goals. Artificial Intelligence 32, 333–377 (1987)
7. McAllester, D., Rosenblitt, D.: Systematic nonlinear planning. In: Proc. 9th National Conference on Artificial Intelligence (1991)
8. Pednault, E.: Formulating multiagent, dynamic-world problems in the classical planning framework. In: Reasoning about Actions and Plans (1986)
9. Regnier, P., Fade, B.: Complete Determination of Parallel Actions and Temporal Optimization in Linear Plans of Action. In: Hertzberg, J. (ed.) EWSP 1991. LNCS, vol. 522, pp. 100–111. Springer, Heidelberg (1991)
10. Veloso, M.M., Pérez, M.A., Carbonell, J.G.: Nonlinear planning with parallel resource allocation. In: Workshop on Innovative Approaches to Planning, Scheduling and Control, pp. 207–212. Morgan Kaufmann (1990)
11. Kambhampati, S., Kedar, S.: A unified framework for explanation-based generalization of partially ordered and partially instantiated plans. Artificial Intelligence 67(1), 29–70 (1994)
12. Winner, E., Veloso, M.: Analyzing plans with conditional effects. In: Proc. 6th International Conference on Artificial Intelligence Planning and Scheduling (AIPS 2002), pp. 23–33 (2002)
13. Muise, C., McIlratih, S., Beck, J.: Optimally relaxing partial-order plans with MaxSAT. In: Proc. 22nd International Conference on Automated Planning and Scheduling, ICAPS 2012 (2012)
14. Chrpa, L., Barták, R.: Towards getting domain knowledge: Plans analysis through investigation of actions dependencies. In: Proc. 21st International Florida AI Research Society Conference (FLAIRS 2008), pp. 531–536. AAAI Press (2008) ISBN 978-1-57735-365-2
15. Haslum, P., Jonsson, P.: Planning with reduced operator sets. In: Proc. 5:th International Conference on Artificial Intelligence Planning and Scheduling (AIPS 2000), pp. 150–158 (2000)
16. Nguyen, X., Kambhampati, S.: Reviving partial order planning. In: Proc. 17th International Conference on Artificial Intelligence, IJCAI 2001 (2001)

Ride-Sharing: A Multi Source-Destination Path Planning Approach

Jamal Yousaf[1], Juanzi Li[1], Lu Chen[2], Jie Tang[1], Xiaowen Dai[2], and John Du[2]

[1] Department of Computer Science and Technology,
Tsinghua National Laboratory for Information Science and Technology, Tsinghua
University, Beijing, 100084, China
[2] General Motors, China Science Lab, Shanghai
{jamalyousaf,ljz,jietang}@keg.tsinghua.edu.cn,
{lu.chen,xiaowen.dai,john.du}@gm.com

Abstract. Ride-sharing is considered as one of the promising solutions for reducing fuel consumption of fuel and reducing the congestion in urban cities, hence reducing the environmental pollution. With the advancement of mobile social networking technologies, it is necessary to reconsider the principles and desired characteristics of ride-sharing systems. Ride-sharing systems can be popular among people if we can provide more flexible and adaptive solution according to preferences of the participants and solve the social challenges. In this paper, we focus on encouraging people to use a ride-sharing system by satisfying their demands in terms of safety, privacy, convenience and also provide enough incentives for drivers and riders. We formalized the ride sharing problem as a multi source-destination path planning problem. An objective function is developed which models different conflicting objectives in a unified framework. We provide the flexibility to each driver that he can generate the sub-optimal paths according to his own requirements by suitably adjusting the weights. These sub-optimal paths are generated in an order of priority (optimality). The simulation results have shown that the system has the potential to compute multiple optimal paths.

Keywords: Ride-sharing, Path Planning, Dynamic Optimization.

1 Introduction

We are entering "a new era" enabled with new smart phone applications and more intuitive software that will help us find efficient and easy-to-use shared rides. Technology thus plays a major role in overcoming carpool barriers such as perceived ease-of-use and flexibility. As our society adapts to these new tools, our perception of carpooling will change as well. Apparently, there is plenty of room for improvements, for example, when considering the fact that on average cars carry 1.58 passengers, i.e., only an estimated 25% of emissions are caused by people traveling, and the rest by moving empty seats [6]. The growing ubiquity of mobile Internet technology has created new opportunities to bring together

M. Thielscher and D. Zhang (Eds.): AI 2012, LNCS 7691, pp. 815–826, 2012.

people with similar itineraries and time schedules to share rides on short-notice. Encouraging ride-share is, after all, an easy and cost-effective solution to helping reduce congestion and gas emissions.

Internet-enabled smart-phones allow people to offer and request trips whenever they want wherever they are. By dynamic ride-sharing, we refer to a system where an automated process employed by a ride-share provider matches up drivers and riders on very short notice [5], which can range from a few minutes to a few hours before departure time. Dynamic ride-sharing systems are developed to publicize formal ride-sharing in urban areas. Most of the current ride-sharing systems are covering formal requirements of users. Safety, security, flexibility, enough incentives for drivers and riders are the critical issues for users and it is also necessary to understand that riding and meeting with people are often related activities. Gathering enough participants is also major concern for web based and mobile ride-sharing systems. This paper addresses the following questions.

Q1) *How can we provide more flexibility to drivers in finalizing the path based on his own preferences?*

Q2) *Can we use social networking features like social strength or closeness in the path computation?*

Q3) *Could we provide a ride-sharing system that encourages the people and satisfying their demands in terms of safety, flexibility, privacy and convenience?*

In our approach for ride-sharing system, we particularly focus on encouraging people to use a ride-sharing system by satisfying their demands addressed above. We provide the flexibility to each driver that he can generate the sub-optimal paths according to his own requirements by suitably adjusting the weights. An objective function is developed which models different conflicting objectives in a unified framework, different objectives can be assigned with different weights.

With a GPS-enabled phone, a user can select his current location as the origin of the trip. For security purpose, the system will generate an auto pin number for the riders and also provides an option to see the complete description of the vehicle and the proposed path before finalizing the trip. The system allows the riders to rate the driver and the ride including the vehicle (zero to five stars), and optionally a comment just after the ride. Such ratings are converted into the feedback score. In addition, the driver could also rate participants by monitoring cancelations, no-shows and late arrivals. Such ratings are converted into a reliability score. Both the reliability and feedback scores are computed and recorded by the ride-sharing system and have great importance on the trust building of the system. If the driver and the rider both agree on the proposed arrangement, the driver picks up the rider at the agreed time and location.

The rest of the paper is structured as follows. In Section 2, we will introduce the related work. In Section 3 and 4, we will formulate the ride-sharing problem and discusses the route matching factors and finally the cost function is developed. In Section 5, we explain our approach to solve the dynamic ride-share problem and the simulation results are discussed in Section 6. Finally, in Section 7, we summarize our main insights in the form of conclusion.

2   Related Work

Many solutions concerning to the Ride-sharing System have been proposed in the literature and many of them were implemented and are used on the Web. In this section we will summarize the related work in cotext of ride sharing systems and the path planning.

Ride Sharing System: Real-time ride-sharing is becoming a new, mainstream mode of transport and a lot of work has already been done in this regard. In a recent work, Trasarti et al. [2] introduces a methodology for extracting mobility profiles of individuals from raw digital GPS traces. In his experiments, the impact of car pooling application based on profile matching is measured and showed as it may foster an intelligent car pooling service. In another work Kleiner et al. [3] presents an incentive compatible dynamic ride-sharing solution based on auctions. It also provides tradeoff the minimization of vehicle kilometers travelled with overall probability of successful ride-share.

Resnick [16] suggests to drop the concept of a few standardized pickup and drop off locations and replace them with dynamically chosen collecting points regarding the current position of the rider and driver. Kelley [11] introduces an automatic system by which needed information is retrieved by special RFID tags. Smart Jitney [12] is a slightly different system design approach. Murphy et al. suggests to equip every vehicle with identifiable and trackable hardware. Just as a cab, this device can be contacted to reserve a seat.

SafeRide [9] is a draft of a dynamic ride-sharing system for modern Smartphones. Morris proposes to use existing Web technologies such as Google Transit and combine them in order to facilitate user interaction. Further, he recommends the riders to rate the driver (and vice versa) in an also included eBay-like reputation system. With Ride Now! Kirshner [8] introduces a testable computer- and telephone-based dynamic ride-sharing system. The system finds a feasible driver for this request and informs the rider about the drivers contact details. Vanoutrive et al. [1] find that the most carpool-oriented sectors are construction and manufacturing and also in the wholesale and retail sectors carpool is popular. It is rather unpopular at universities, health sector and in public transport companies, and seems to be an alternative at locations where rail is no real alternative.

Multi Objective Path Planning: In this section, we will give a brief overview of some efforts directed towards solving the multi objective shortest path finding problem. There are of two main broad categories of multi objective shortest path problem. The first category is the deterministic (global optimal) approaches which are generalizations of the traditional single objective shortest path label setting and label correcting algorithms, and the second category is the approximation schemes, mainly evolutionary algorithms.

Herbwai et al. [4] presents evolutionay multiobjective route planning algorithm for solving the route planning problem in the dynamic multi-hop ridesharing. They have used the time expanded graph to represents the drivers offers. In another independent work, Martins et al. [18] have provided a detailed theoretical study for different types of labeling algorithms to solve the multi objective path problem. They have proved that it is bounded if and only if absorbent cycles are not present in the network. Müller-Hannemann and Weihe [17] have identified a set of key characteristics that exists in many applications of shortest path problem that makes the number of Pareto optimal paths at each visited node to be limited by a small constant.

Shad et al. [15] have analyzed and concluded that the genetic algorithm performs poorly on large size networks. However, Mooney et al. [14] have developed an evolutionary algorithm for the multi objective shortest path problem and showed its feasibility through a set of experiments over real road networks. Pangilinan et al. [13] have explored the behavior of a multi objective evolutionary algorithm when applied to solve the shortest path planning problem. The behavior of the algorithm is described in terms of the diversity and optimality of the solutions in addition to its computational complexity.

Summary: To summarize the literature review, the majority of the existing systems provides one fixed path to the driver and the rider based on their locations. The drivers do not have the flexibility to change or compute the path according to his own requirement. This is one of the main motivations of this work because the driver can be any person from any discipline of life therefore his choice of preferences are different at different times and on different days.

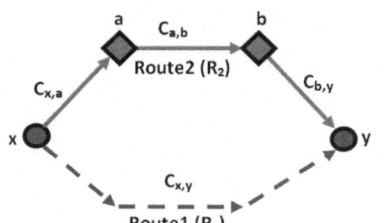

Fig. 1.   A   shared   trip   between
driver(circles) and rider(diamonds)

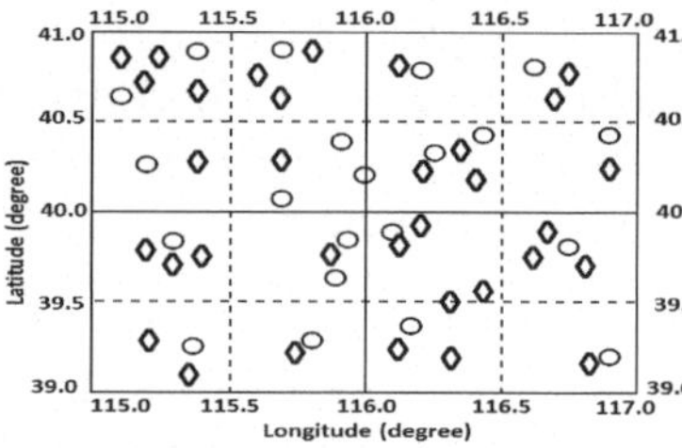

Fig. 2. A grid showing the drivers(circles)
and riders(diamonds)

3   Problem Formulation

The target system of our Ride-sharing System approach is a smart-phone application for dynamic ride-sharing, does not require pre-declared paths or pickup points, and can be used from virtually any location at any time. The system promotes ride-shares among people with connections within social networks (e.g., Facebook) in order to favor ride-shares among users that trust each other.

3.1   Ride Sharing

Ride-sharing system continuously receives a sequence Z of trip announcements over time from potential participants and stored this information in the database.

A trip announcement contains an origin and a destination location, and additional information that specify its potential timing. With this information, the provider automatically establishes ride-shares over time, matching potential drivers and riders. Now the goal of our system is twofold, on the one hand the system needs to minimize the distance or path length and on the other hand it increases the number of passengers for optimal utilization of the resource.

We suppose that the database has set of drivers $D = \{d_1, d_2, ., d_n\}$, a set of stations $S = \{s_1, s_2, ., s_m\}$ and a set of driver's offers $O = \{o_1, o_2, ., o_k\}$. Each offer consists of a starting station s_1, ending station s_2, departure time t_1 and arrival time t_2, and a cost c such that $\forall o \in O : o = \{s_1, s_2, t_1, t_2, c : s_1, s_2 \in S, \ s.t \ s_1 \neq s_2 \wedge t_1 < t_2\}$. We also have set of riders $R = \{r_1, r_2, ., r_n\}$ with request q for sharing a ride, it contains the source station s_1, destination station s_2, and the earliest departure time t_1 and the latest arrival time t_2. Similarly for all requests $\forall q \in Q : q = \{s_1, s_2, t_1, t_2 : s_1, s_2 \in S, \ s.t \ s_1 \neq s_2 \wedge t_1 < t_2\}$. Now we have the multiple drivers' and the riders' presents as agents in the system.

The basic motivation behind the ride sharing system usage is to reduce the travel cost. In this work, we focus on systems designed to enable users to share variable trip costs. When such costs are roughly proportional to distance traveled, cost reduction is only possible when the length of a ride-share trip is shorter than the sum of the lengths of the separate trips. We consider this as a first condition for a feasible match only if it provides positive cost savings: i.e a ride-share between driver d and rider r is feasible iff $C(P) > 0$, where

$$C(P) = C_{(x,y)} + C_{(a,b)} - (C_{(x,a)} + C_{(a,b)} + C_{(b,y)}) \tag{1}$$

3.2   Modeling Drivers' Offers

Here we will model the two sets of group to solve the route matching problem. We are using the geodetic grid (latitude/longitude) system with a resolution of 0.5 degree in each axes to efficiently map the drivers' offer and riders' request in each grid element as shown in the Fig. 2. Whenever a new request $r \in R$ and offer $o \in O$ comes from the rider and driver respectively, it will be first directly assigned to some grid element and then it is processed. Each grid element has its own local list of the drivers and riders based on the trip announcements. If there is no driver already present to any grid element or no successful match found then the respective grid element is expanded to neighboring eight grid elements to find suitable match for the ride-sharing. The request of the rider is evaluated with the driver's list based on the following factors as discussed below.

4   Route Matching

In this section we will discuss about the various factors which will be used in matching the new request $r \in R$ from the rider to each driver $d \in D$ present on the network.

4.1   Detour and Range Factors

At this stage we make use of the detour distance and the range factor as an initial measurement criteria of route matching and further it is used for calculating the relevancy rate. The ride request which has higher relevancy rate value will occupy the higher position in the recommendation list of drivers. The number of riders assigned to each driver depends upon the nature and capacity of vehicle. Moreover the detour distance and range factor between new request from rider and default paths of online drivers are computed in respective grid elements.

Definition (Detour and the Range Factor): Given two ride requests $R1$ and $R2$ which have start and destination locations $\langle a, b \rangle$ and $\langle x, y \rangle$ as shown in the Fig. 1. Now if $\mu(x, y)$ denotes the length of the shortest path of the driver from point x to y and $\mu(a, b)$ denotes the length of the shortest path of the rider. The detour factor is then defined as:

$$f_d(R_1, R_2) = \frac{(\mu(x, a) + \mu(a, b) + \mu(b, y) - \mu(x, y))}{\mu(x, y)} \tag{2}$$

and the range factor is defined as:

$$f_r(R_1, R_2) = \frac{mean(\mu(x, a), \mu(b, y))}{\mu(x, y)} \tag{3}$$

The value range of detour factor will be $[0, +\infty)$. Now we define a transformation $E : R^{[0, +\infty)} \to (0, 1]$ for uniform comparison of the values between driver and different riders. We define this transformation as relevancy rate:

$$E(R_1, R_2) = e^{-f_d(R_1, R_2)} \tag{4}$$

The range of the values of relevancy is between $(0, 1]$ and 1 means the maximum matching of the routes. The value of the range factor needs to be less than 0.5 as the first step for suitable match. The system determines drivers that are online and compatible for this ride based on the relevancy of both the paths, the value of the range factor, condition of the Eq. 1 and whether the deadlines will comply. In this way system assigns multiple riders to single driver based on these factors.

Graph Generation: From drivers' perspective, each driver may have single or multiple riders associated with him based on vehicle capacity. Now just before starting the drive, the driver computes the path for the whole ride. The system will generate a number of sub-optimal paths for the driver based on the multiple riders requests and the weights of the objective function set by the driver as shown in the Fig. 3.

Now each driver has its own local network, rider nodes are sorted in ascending order with respect to the distances, the drivers' initial point I and final point F are then inserted at the start and end of the list. Each start point node in this sorted vector is a candidate for connection to all start nodes ahead of it and no

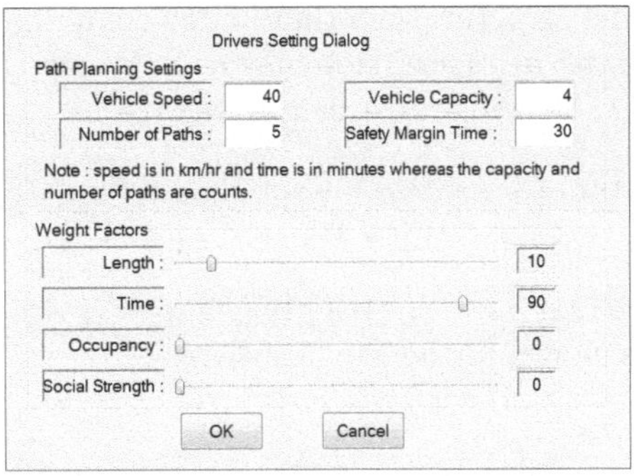

Fig. 3. The drivers' setting dialog

unrealistic edge (e.g inserting destination node without the source node and vice versa) is allowed into the grid. Therefore, the node N_i is connected to all source nodes and hence with their corresponding destination nodes $I, N_{i+1}, ..., N_N, F$. Each edge is evaluated under several constraints like length, time etc and assigned the edge cost based on the objective function as described below.

4.2   Cost Function

In the ride-sharing system, new riders and drivers continuously enter and leave the system. Some drivers want the shortest route and some may want the maximum riders on the weekends or holidays. Some people may only feel safe sharing rides with friends or acquaintances and possibly also with the friends of friends. The different objectives need to be considered when defining the edge cost. Often these objectives are conflicting, and thus there is a need to incorporate them into a single multi-objective function that satisfies route requirements. In this study the objectives considered are: **1)** *Minimization of the path lengths* **2)** *Minimization of the travel time* **3)** *Maximization of the available seats (occupancy)* **4)** *Maximization of social closeness.*

The first objective can be modelled as $\frac{L_E}{L_{max}}$, where L_E is the edge length and normalized by the maximum length L_{max}. The travel time is the time spent in the vehicle while actually traveling from origin to destination. The second objective of minimization of travel time can be transformed into an equivalent objective of minimizing the path length. It can be modelled by dividing the edge distance by the average velocity of the vehicle i.e $\frac{L_E}{Avg_{vel}}$. The third objective of maximum utilization of the available seats(i.e occupancy) can be modeled as $\frac{c}{(Sa)_{max}}$, where c is the constant usually taken to be 1 (the same for all the edges) and the $(Sa)_{max}$ is the maximum number of the riders used for the normalization of the cost. This objective may be beneficial for a ride-share provider whose revenues are linked to the number of successful ride-shares. In social closeness calculation, we adopt the same method as defined by Gilbert et al. [10]. From their method we consider some measures like social distance, demographic and some structural information to compute the social closeness. Finally we normalize the net social closeness as S. We assign the -S to the edge cost, where $0 \le S \le 1$. The edge cost can be written as:

$$E_{cost} = \frac{W_L \times C_1 + W_T \times C_2 + W_{Sa} \times C_3 + W_{Sd} \times C_4}{W_L + W_T + W_{Sa} + W_{Sd}} \tag{5}$$

Here E_{cost} is the edge cost and W_L, W_T, W_{Sa} and W_{Sd} are user defined weights for four objectives as shown in the Fig. 3. where

$$C_1 = \frac{L_E}{L_{max}}, C_2 = \frac{L_E}{Avg_{vel}}, C_3 = \frac{c}{(Sa)_{max}}, C_4 = -S$$

5   Path Planning

In this section we will discuss how we have exploited the greedy algorithm to compute a number of suboptimal paths available to the driver.

5.1   Path Optimization

Our goal is to select an algorithm that solves the minimum cost problem given in Eq. 5 above, furthermore we would like to work out a number of sub-optimal paths also. The edge cost components discussed above can be negative, the choice of the optimization algorithm therefore needs to be done accordingly. Since the Bellman-Ford algorithm works well with the negative edge costs and computes the shortest path between two given nodes in a weighted digraph. The Bellman-Ford algorithm in the process of finding the optimal path from the start node I to the final node F, also finds lowest cost paths from the start node to all other nodes. This feature of the algorithm is used here in the computation of a number of sub-optimal paths. We have extended the Bellman-Ford algorithm and incorporate the constraints directly into the runtime. In the algorithm, we have assigned the labels to nodes and the edges. Each label consists of three tags i.e cost, name and the time. The cost tag indicates the cost in going from the node I to that node and the name tag contains the name of edge that connects to the node I on the shortest path found so far and the third tag contains the time.

The algorithm can be divided into four parts. The graph generated in above section is a directed graph with an edge j starting from node b(j) and ending at node e(j) with cost E^j. Let C_I^i be the cost of the shortest path of the ith node from the node I, P_I^i is the edge previous to the ith node and T_I^i is the time to the ith node on that path.

1) During the initialization part, first assign a label (0,0,0) to the initial node I, and the labels $(\infty, 0, 0)$ to all other nodes and the edges respectively. The zero present in the name tag indicates that neither preceding edge assignment has been made, nor the edge originates from the initial node I.

2) The forward and reverse phase computations are done for generating the multiple paths. At the start of the algorithm we check if the start node of an edge is the initial node I, in which case the cost of the end node of the edge is compared with the cost of the edge itself. If the cost of the edge is smaller, the label of the end node and the time tags are updated accordingly. If an edge does not originate from the initial node I, we check if a preceding edge assignment for the edge start node exists. Then previously stored cost at the end node of the edge is compared to that accrued by going through this edge. In case of a lower cost, the end node label and the edge label are both updated whenever there is an end node assignment, there is also an edge assignment as the reverse is not possible. If however the cost at the end node while going through the edge is not lower, then this cost is compared with the cost stored in the edge label. In case of a lower cost, only the edge label is updated. This implies that this new path from I to e(j) via the jth edge results in a lower cost, and hence the label of the jth edge now contains this cost. During forward phase computation, we have traced for each edge j, the shortest path vector j2I from e(j) to initial node I by linking each node to preceding node as:

$$j2I = [e(j), b(j), b(P_I^j), b(P_I^{P_I^j}), b(P_I^{P_I^{P_I^j}}), ..., I]$$

The shortest path vector I2j from I to e(j) can be obtained by reversing this.

3) Similarly treatment is done in the reverse phase computation, we interchange the roles of b(j) and e(j)and also the nodes I and F, the shortest path vector from I2j from I to e(j) is obtained along with the corresponding cost C_I^j and the time T_I^j. The paths are generated in an order of priority if one path does not meet user satisfaction for some reason, the next path can be considered.

4) Now during the multiple path computation, we finds the corresponding list of the path vectors $[I2j \cup \overline{j2F}]$, where $\overline{j2F}$ is the shortest path vector from edge j to the final node F, computed during the reverse phase computation. This will give the multiple best paths in the order of priority defined by the driver that fulfils all the required constraints.

6   Simulation Results

The above algorithm is coded into a software application for generating the optimal paths from given set of offers and requests at any time t. We utilized the OpenStreetMaps (openstreetmap.org) data together with the MoNav planner that offers exact routing without heuristic assumptions at very little computational demand due to a routing core based on contraction hierarchies Vetter [7]. As a test bed for our experiments we used the following case study.

6.1   Case Study

In this section, we will discuss the different scenarios and monitors the performance of our algorithm. Optimal paths (satisfying all constraints) are computed using the above algorithm and the effect of varying the weights is studied here.

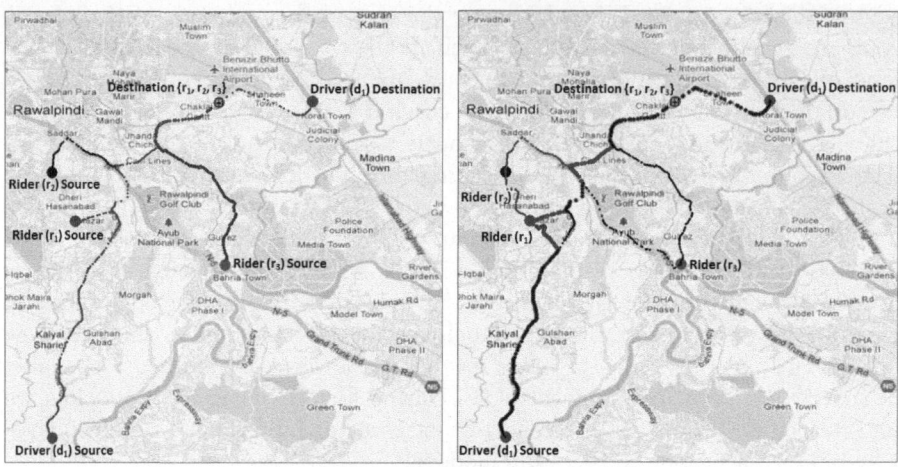

Fig. 4. Individual paths of driver and riders   **Fig. 5.** Shortest length paths

The case study considers a person (driver) who has uploaded his schedule of departure from home to the office with the route map. Similarly, numerous people, who intend to reach airport for catching a flight have also uploaded their schedule along with departure point. Based on the information uploaded by the riders, the riders are automatically assigned to a suitable driver as per defined criteria described in section 4. All the scenarios consider $r_1, r_2, r_3 \in R$ are three riders with requests $q_1, q_2, q_3 \in Q$ and one driver $d_1 \in D$ with offer $o_1 \in O$ and their default paths are shown in Fig. 4.

In the first scenario, the objective function is optimized for the shortest path with weight settings $W_L = 1$, assuming that all other weights are considered to be zero. Similarly in the second scenario, the objective function is optimized for the maximum occupancy by adjusting weight as $W_{Sa} = 1$. The third scenario is worked around optimizing the minimum time constraint, with the weight $W_T = 1$. In the fourth scenario, the paths are computed on the basis of the social closeness value by mining the riders social network. It can be achieved by setting the weight as $W_{Sd} = 1$. Finally we applied multiple constraints like time and social closeness by assigning the weights as $W_T = 0.4, W_{Sd} = 0.6$.

In all the five scenarios, the optimal paths are generated by the application based on priority settings adjusted by the driver and the paths which are not complying with the constraints are simply rejected. The path computed closest to the objective function will be ranked the highest and is shown in red, similarly the next path in green and the third path is shown in blue color as shown in figures Fig. 5, 6, 7, 8, 9 respectively. Moreover Fig. 9 shows that the shortest closeness path(red) comes as a first choice in comparison with Fig. 8 output.

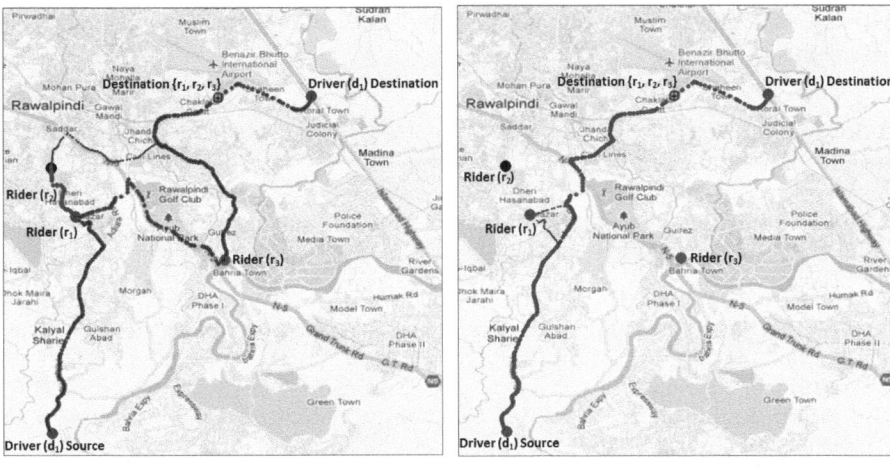

Fig. 6. Paths with maximum occupancy   **Fig. 7.** Paths with time constraint

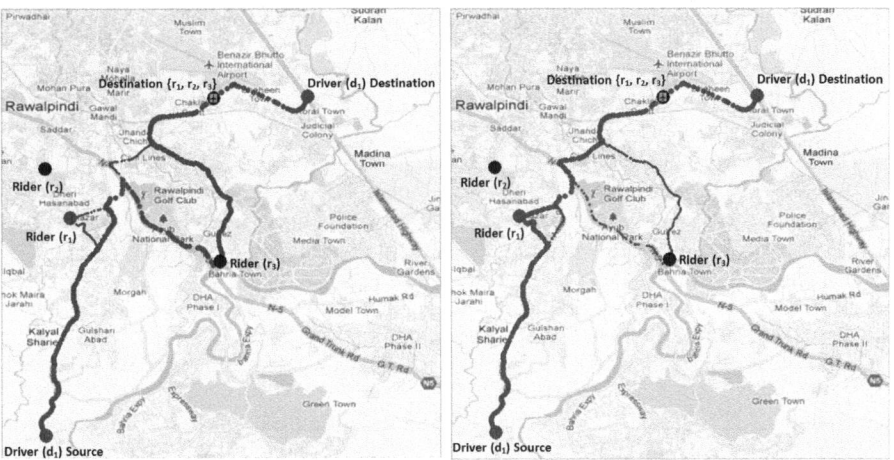

Fig. 8. Paths with Social Closeness   **Fig. 9.** Time constraint on Social Closeness

7   Conclusion

Internet-enabled mobile technology allows car travelers to announce trip requests and ride offer on short notice. In this paper we have presented a novel path planning approach that: 1) Allows more flexibility than state of the art system, as it gives more freedom to the users in the choice of ride sharing partner such as social interests matching and provides more security and convenience. 2) Furthermore it provides multiple feasible paths along with the ranking that minimizes a multi-objective cost function and weights of the factors can be specified by the driver to achieve the optimal objectives, such as the length, time, occupancy and social closeness. 3) Our simulation study results have shown that the proposed system may have the potential to compute that multiple optimal paths against different user defined objective function.

Acknowledgments. The work is supported by the General Motors, China Science Lab, Shanghai.

References

1. Vanoutrive, T., Van De Vijver, E., Malderen, L.V., Jourquin, B., Thomas, I., Verhetsel, A., Witlox, F.: What determines carpooling to workplaces in Belgium: location, organisation, or promotion? Journal of Transport Geography 22, 77–86 (2012)
2. Trasarti, R., Pinelli, F., Nanni, M., Giannotti, F.: Mining mobility user profiles for car pooling. In: KDD 2011, pp. 1190–1198 (2011)
3. Kleiner, A., Nebel, B., Ziparo, V.A.: A Mechanism for Dynamic Ride Sharing Based on Parallel Auctions. In: IJCAI 2011, pp. 266–272 (2011)
4. Herbawi, W., Weber, M.: Evolutionary multiobjective route planning in dynamic multi-hop ridesharing. In: Merz, P., Hao, J.-K. (eds.) EvoCOP 2011, pp. 84–95. Springer, Heidelberg (2011)
5. Agatz, N., Erera, A., Savelsbergh, M., Wang, X.: Sustainable passenger transportation: Dynamic ride-sharing. Tech. rep., Erasmus Research Inst. of Management (ERIM), Erasmus Uni., Rotterdam (2010)
6. Jeanes, P.: Can total car emissions be reduced enough by 2020? In: Traffic Engineering & Control. PA Associates (January 2010)
7. Vetter, C.: Fast and Exact Mobile Navigation with OpenStreetMap Data. Diploma thesis, Algorithmics II, University of Karlsruhe, Germany (2010)
8. Kirshner, D.: Ride Now (2010), http://www.ridenow.org
9. Morris, J.H.: SafeRide: Reducing Single Occupancy Vehicles. Carnegie Mellon school of computer science, Tech. Rep. (2009)
10. Gilbert, E., Karahalios, K.: Predicting tie strength with social media. In: CHI 2009, pp. 211–220. ACM, New York (2009)
11. Kelley, K.L.: Casual Carpooling - Enhanced. Journal of Public Transportation 10(4), 119–130 (2007)
12. Murphy, P.: The Smart Jitney: Rapid, Realistic Transport. New Solutions 12, 12 (2007)
13. Pangilinan, J., Janssens, G.: Evolutionary algorithms for the multi-objective shortest path problem. IJASET 4(1), 205–210 (2007)
14. Mooney, P., Winstanley, A.: An evolutionary algorithm for multicriteria path optimization problems. IJGIS 20, 401–423 (2006)
15. Roozbeh, S., Hamid, E., Mohsen, G.: Evaluation of route finding methods in GIS application. In: Map Asia 2003, Bejing, China, pp. 12–20 (2003)
16. Resnick, P.: SocioTechnical Support for Ride Sharing. University of Michigan, School of Information, Tech. Rep. (2003)
17. Müller-Hannemann, M., Weihe, K.: Pareto Shortest Paths is Often Feasible in Practice. In: Brodal, G.S., Frigioni, D., Marchetti-Spaccamela, A. (eds.) WAE 2001. LNCS, vol. 2141, pp. 185–197. Springer, Heidelberg (2001)
18. Martins, E., Santos, J.: The labeling algorithm for the multiobjective shortest path problem. Tech. rep., University of Coimbra, Portugal (1999)

A Novel Approach to Ball Detection
for Humanoid Robot Soccer

David Budden, Shannon Fenn, Josiah Walker, and Alexandre Mendes

School of Electrical Engineering and Computer Science
Faculty of Engineering and Built Environment
The University of Newcastle, Callaghan, NSW, 2308, Australia
{david.budden,shannon.fenn,josiah.walker}@uon.edu.au,
alexandre.mendes@newcastle.edu.au

Abstract. The ability to accurately track a ball is a critical issue in humanoid robot soccer, made difficult by processor limitations and
resultant inability to process all available data from a high-definition
image. This paper proposes a computationally efficient method of determining position and size of balls in a RoboCup environment, and compares the performance to two common methods: one utilising Levenberg-
Marquardt least squares circle fitting, and the other utilising a circular
Hough transform. The proposed method is able to determine the position
of a non-occluded tennis ball with less than 10% error at a distance of 5
meters, and a half-occluded ball with less than 20% error, overall outperforming both compared methods whilst executing 300 times faster than
the circular Hough transform method. The proposed method is described
fully in the context of a colour based vision system, with an explanation
of how it may be implemented independent of system paradigm. An extension to allow tracking of multiple balls utilising unsupervised learning
and internal cluster validation is described.

Keywords: Robotics, robotic soccer, computer vision, feature
extraction, object recognition, clustering.

1 Introduction

The problem of developing a team of humanoid robots capable of defeating the
FIFA World Cup champion team, coined "The Millennium Challenge" [9], has
been a milestone that has driven research in the fields of artificial intelligence,
robotics and computer vision for over a decade. One crucial skill of soccer, the
accurate, robust and efficient determination and tracking of ball size and location, has proven to be a challenging subset of this task and the focus of much
research [11–13, 16]. With the evolution of robot platforms and subsequent advances in processor performance over the last decade, from the 384 MHz RISC-
based processors of the Sony AIBO ERS-210 (2002) to the 1.6 GHz Intel Atom
processors of the Robotis DARwIn-OP [7] platform (2012), the temporal and
spatial complexity of feature extraction algorithms to solve this task has grown
accordingly.

M. Thielscher and D. Zhang (Eds.): AI 2012, LNCS 7691, pp. 827–838, 2012.
© Springer-Verlag Berlin Heidelberg 2012

With past research suggesting that colour-based algorithms are suboptimal for object recognition in a RoboCup environment [12, 13], particularly in the presence of varying lighting conditions, a paradigm shift from colour-based to shape-based feature extraction has been evident amongst RoboCup teams [12]. This shift has been amplified as a result of the evolution of RoboCup rules, with "colour-coded" objects, such as landmark beacons and uniquely-coloured goals, being phased out entirely from the Standard Platform League to facilitate convergence with the FIFA rules of human soccer [2, 9].

Despite this trend, it is important to note that the paradigm-shift from colour-based to shape-based feature extraction is not universal, with many Robo-Cup teams, including the University of Newcastle's *NUbots* and 2012 kid-sized humanoid league champions *Team DARwIn*, depending primarily on colour look-up tables (LUTs) to facilitate the process of feature extraction. With this in mind, this paper presents a method of ball detection which can be implemented independently of the adopted paradigm, requiring only a set of points marking the edges of potential salient features. The algorithm is very efficient, implementing only basic geometric operations, and yet effective at locating the ball from the opposite side of a SPL RoboCup field (up to 5 meters). This method, which was effectively utilised by the NUbots team at RoboCup 2012 (Mexico City), is demonstrated to be robust against both considerable levels of noise and occlusion, and can readily be extended to cater for a non-RoboCup environment with multiple present balls.

The remainder of this paper, firstly, presents a description of how a ball candidate can be determined in the context of a colour-based vision system. Extensions of this method to a shape-based system are described, in addition to detailing a method by which multiple candidates can be generated to facilitate tracking of multiple balls. The refinement of these candidates to calculate exact ball position and size is then described, for both ideal and occluded ball scenarios. Finally, the accuracy and efficiency of the algorithm is compared to previous ball detection approaches, including the previous NUbots system [1], implementing Levenberg-Marquardt least squares circle fitting [10]; and a circular Hough transform based method [16], similar to those implemented by many RoboCup teams [11, 15].

2   Ball Detection in Context

In computer vision, a mapping from an arbitrary 3-component colour space C to a set of colours M assigns a class label $m_i \in M$ to every point $c_j \in C$ [5]. If each channel is represented by an n-bit value and $k = |M|$ represents the number of defined class labels, then

$$C \to M,$$

where

$$C = \{0, 1, \ldots, 2^n - 1\}^3 \quad \text{and} \quad M = \{m_0, m_1, \ldots, m_{k-1}\}.$$

Where computational resources are limited, the colour segmentation process is performed off-line, with the resultant mapping represented in the form of a $2^n \times 2^n \times 2^n$ look-up table (LUT). This LUT can then be used for efficient, real-time colour classification [5], and as such colour-based vision systems utilising LUTs are still commonplace amongst RoboCup teams [1]. Specifically, the NUbots vision system, for which this ball detection method was initially developed, adopts the following methodology:

1. *Generate scan lines:* As current processor limitations do not allow complex operations over every pixel of a 2-megapixel image without significant framerate reduction, only the pixels along a set of vertical and horizontal *scan lines* are considered for candidate determination. This method is preferred over reduced camera resolution, as it provides the same performance increase (i.e. the same number of pixels are considered) whilst still allowing for small, high resolution portions of the image to be processed to resolve finer detail. Scan lines may be either equidistant on the image plane, or spaced in such as way as to be equidistant on the field plane (requires robot kinematics data).

2. *Determine field border:* Determination of the field border, or *green horizon*, allows for specific knowledge of the RoboCup environment to be applied to reduce the required image processing. For example, a ball and field lines should only ever be found beneath the horizon, whereas the majority of the goal post area will be found above. Starting at the top of the image, each pixel along each vertical scan line is inspected until a certain threshold of consecutive green pixels is exceeded, at which stage the top green pixel coordinates are added to a list of points. The green horizon then becomes the upper convex hull of these points, determined by a modified implementation of Andrew's monotone chain algorithm [3].

3. *Generate colour transitions:* Processing of the image to locate potential field object candidates is a *colour transition* level operation. To generate colour transitions, each pixel along each scan line is considered, and wherever the colour class label of a pixel differs from that of the previous adjacent pixel, a transition is generated. The information stored in each transition includes its (x, y) image coordinate, start colour class label and end colour class label.

4. *Determine candidates:* Colour transitions are considered to determine potential field object candidates. This process may or may not consider transitions of opposite direction or orthogonal orientation as equivalent (e.g. ball detection does, but goal detection does not).

5. *Refine candidates:* The area surrounding each candidate is processed at a pixel level to determine the exact location, dimensions and confidence of a particular field object.

Steps 1-3 simply describe one method by which a series of points, representing the positions of edges of various image features, may be generated. Any system capable of returning equivalent information, whether it be primarily colour, intensity gradient or shape-based, may be implemented as a substitute. As such, the ball detection method described may be implemented somewhat independently of the adopted paradigm.

Sect. 3 and 4 describe how steps 4 and 5 of the above list above are realised for the proposed ball detection method.

3   Determining Candidates

As outlined in Sect. 2, given a set of points corresponding approximately with edges of image features (herein assumed to be colour transitions, consistent with the NUbots vision system), the next step of ball detection is to determine the (x, y) image coordinates of potential ball candidates. The remainder of this section, firstly, describes a simple and computationally efficient method by which a single candidate may be determined. Finally, a generalised method is proposed, which utilises unsupervised learning to allow for the determination of any number of ball candidates.

3.1   Single Ball

Given a set of colour transitions, the first step of determining the ball candidate is to ignore all transitions which do not fulfill the following criteria:

- Must have a start or end colour class label consistent with the ball colour (typically orange).
- Must be located beneath the green horizon.

Transitions are considered independent of their direction, i.e. an orange-white transition is equivalent to a white-orange transition. Following this, the candidate position is calculated as the geometric mean of the transition coordinates. Concretely, given a set of transitions $\{t_1 = (x_1, y_1), \ldots, t_n = (x_n, y_n)\}$,

$$p_{cand} = \left(\left(\prod_{i=1}^{n} x_i \right)^{1/n}, \left(\prod_{i=1}^{n} y_i \right)^{1/n} \right).$$

To prevent arithmetic overflow in a noisy image, in which several hundred transitions may be present, the following observation is utilised:

$$\left(\prod_{i=1}^{n} x_i \right)^{1/n} = \left(\prod_{i=1}^{k} x_i \right)^{1/n} \times \left(\prod_{i=k+1}^{2k} x_i \right)^{1/n} \times \cdots \times \left(\prod_{i=n-k+1}^{n} x_i \right)^{1/n}.$$

Maximum computational efficiency is obtained by determining the largest value of k for which the data type chosen to store the intermediate value is guaranteed not to overflow. Concretely, for an image of width w pixels and a data type of length m bits,

$$k = \lfloor \log_w (2^m) \rfloor.$$

As an example, given a full HD image (1920 × 1080 resolution) and a C++ unsigned long long data type[1] ($n = 64$ bits), k is calculated to be 5.

---

[1] Increasing k will also reduce the average rounding error for integer data types.

3.2 Multiple Balls

Given a non-RoboCup environment with multiple balls, the process of ball detection can be extended simply by replacing the *determine candidates* module (see Sect. 2) by a generalised module capable of determining multiple candidate points. In an environment where the maximum number of balls is known a priori, this is accomplished via k-means clustering [8, 14]. Concretely, given a set of m data points $P = \{x^{(1)}, \ldots, x^{(N)}\}$ ($x^{(i)} \in \mathbb{R}^m$), k-means clustering attempts to partition P into K sets (known as *clusters*) $\mathbf{S} = \{S_1, \ldots, S_K\}$ such that the following objective function J is minimised.

$$J(c^{(1)}, \ldots, c^{(m)}, \mu_1, \ldots, \mu_K) = \frac{1}{m} \sum_{i=1}^{m} \|x^{(i)} - \mu_{c^{(i)}}\|^2,$$

where c^i is the index of the cluster $(1, \ldots, K)$ to which data point $x^{(i)}$ is currently assigned, μ_k is the *cluster centroid* of S_k ($\mu_k \in \mathbb{R}^n$), and therefore $\mu_{c^{(i)}}$ is the centroid of the cluster to which $x^{(i)}$ has been assigned [8, 14]. This is accomplished via the repeating the following two-step algorithm until convergence.

Step 1: Assignment step:

$$S_i^{(t)} = \{x^{(p)} : \|x^{(p)} - \mu_i^{(t)}\| \leq \|x^{(p)} - \mu_j^{(t)}\| \ \forall 1 \leq j \leq k\}.$$

Step 2: Update step:

$$\mu_i^{(t+1)} = \frac{1}{|S_i^{(t)}|} \sum_{x^{(j)} \in S_i^{(t)}} x^{(j)}.$$

The resultant *cluster centroids* form the ball candidates. The benefits of utilising k-means clustering for determining candidates are twofold. Firstly, compared to other common clustering techniques such as mean shift and expectation maximisation, k-means is computationally efficient, with time complexity $\mathcal{O}(Km)$ [4]. In addition, as clustering only takes place over the set of colour transitions and very few iterations are required, this method is able to be executed in real time on the DARwIn-OP platform [7]. Secondly, k-means utilises an implicit representation of the underlying probability distribution as a superposition of spherically symmetric distributions [14], which performs well given a set of colour transitions positioned approximately on the circular border of a ball.

For an image where the number of balls, b, is known a priori, the number of clusters, K, may simply be set to equal the number of balls. In general, for an environment where the number of balls is known but with no guarantee every ball is present in a given image, an *internal cluster validation criteria* (such as the *Dunn's based index* [5, 6]) is applied to the each cluster for $K = \{1, \ldots, b\}$, with the K value yielding the best results indicating the number of balls in the current image.

4   Determining Location and Size

As outlined in Sect. 2, once the ball candidate(s) have been determined, the final step in ball detection is to inspect each candidate point to calculate the exact location, dimensions and confidence of the ball itself. The remainder of this section, firstly, describes a computationally efficient method by which the position and size may be determined, assuming an occlusion-free ball. Next, a generalised version of this method is explained, which extends the functionality to deal with balls suffering from up to 50% occlusion, either from a direction parallel to the x or y-axes (4-*point occlusion detection*) or an arbitrary direction (*n-point occlusion detection*). Finally, systems of verifying the correctness of the ball detection results are described; this is particularly vital in a multiple candidate scenario.

4.1   Occlusion-Free

Given a candidate point p_{cand}, as determined by one of the two methods described in Sect. 3, the process of calculating the exact dimensions of an occlusion-free ball is a straightforward process that operates at a pixel level to maximise the detail which can be resolved. Concretely, given an image where each possible pixel value maps to some colour class label via a look-up table (LUT), each pixel along the x and y-axes (relative to origin p_{cand}) is inspected until a certain threshold, ϑ, of consecutive "non-ball" pixels is exceeded[2], at which time the last-considered pixel belonging to the ball is stored. The four resultant points, $p_1, \ldots, p_4$ (see Fig. 1), therefore correspond ideally with four points on the edge of circle.

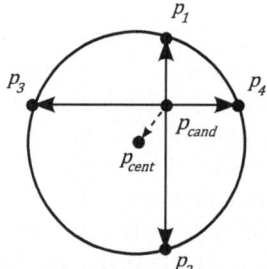

Fig. 1. *Center update* method for determining center of a non-occluded ball

As balls in images are rarely perfect circles (due to motion blur and pixel quantization) and LUT mappings are often noisy (due to variations in ambient illumination), the ball location and dimensions are not determined by substituting the above points into the equation of a circle. Instead, a single-iteration

---

[2] In the NUbots vision system, "non-ball" pixels are simply those which do not map to the orange colour class label.

center update method is applied to find the exact center of the ball. For a non-occluded ball, the center update consists of two steps:

1. *Determine center:* Considering the points $p_1 = (x_1, y_1)$, ..., $p_4 = (x_4, y_4)$ (see Fig. 1), the center of the ball, p_{cent}, is calculated as

$$p_{cent} = \left(\frac{x_3 + x_4}{2}, \frac{y_1 + y_2}{2} \right).$$

2. *Determine diameter:* Considering p_{cent} as the origin, each pixel along the x and y-axes is inspected until a certain threshold, ϑ, of consecutive "non-ball" pixels is exceeded, at which time the last-considered pixel belonging to the ball is stored. Considering the resultant points, p'_1, ..., p'_4 (labeled in the same orientation as p_1, ..., p_4, see Fig. 1), the diameter of the ball, d, is calculated as

$$d = \max \left\{ ||p'_1 - p'_2||, ||p'_3 - p'_4|| \right\}.$$

It can be demonstrated that, given a candidate point p_{cand} within some ideal circle C, this method is guaranteed to yield correct results[3]. An example is illustrated in Fig. 2a.

4.2 4-Point Occlusion Detection

Although the threshold parameter ϑ may be tuned to compensate for classification noise, the method presented in Sect. 4.1 is unable to deal with any ball occlusion. This is illustrated in Fig. 2a; any occlusion from any side of the ball will result in a shift of the ball center p_{cent} and reduction of diameter d. Fortunately, the process of *4-point occlusion detection* may be used to compensate

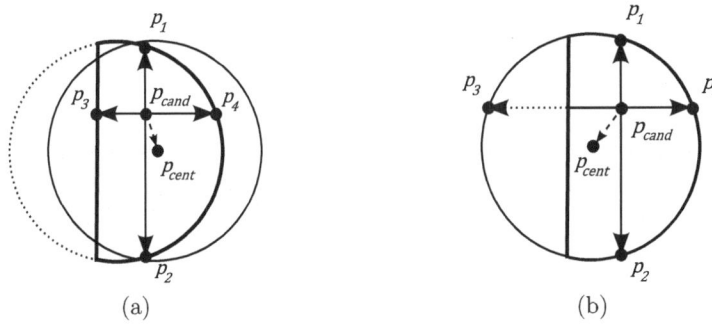

(a)   (b)

Fig. 2. Error in applying initial *center update* method to occluded ball (a), and the corrected result of applying *4-point occlusion compensation* (b)

---

[3] Proof omitted. Available at: http://www.davidbudden.com/research/ball-detection/

for occlusion of the ball from a single direction, as illustrated in Fig. 2b. This method requires the addition of the following three steps to those presented in Sect. 4.1:

1. *Detect occlusion:* Consider a ray, r_1, with initial point p_{cent} and passing through p_1. Starting at p_1, inspect φ pixels in the direction of r_1, where φ is the *occlusion sensitivity* parameter. If none of these are "field"[4] pixels, mark p_1 as occluded. Repeat for p_2, ..., p_4.

2. *Determine if correction is required:* If none of the points p_1, ..., p_4 are marked as occluded, no ball occlusion is detected, and the method of updating center and diameter reduces to that of Sect. 4.1. Likewise, if more than one point is marked as occluded, the ball is occluded from multiple directions; this is a scenario unable to be corrected by 4-point occlusion detection, so the method also reduced to that of Sect. 4.1 (with error).

3. *Correct points:* Assume p_3 is marked as occluded. The position of p_3 is updated such that its distance from p_4 becomes exactly $\max\{\|p_1 - p_2\|, \|p_3 - p_4\|\}$, as illustrated in Fig. 4.2b. An equivalent method is applied for all possible occluded points.

Although not guaranteeing correctness, this method presents allows for fast execution, whilst maintaining high accuracy in position determination. To function correctly, 4-point occlusion detection requires the direction of the occlusion source be parallel to either the x or y-axes. This limitation can be reduced by extending the method to *n-point occlusion detection*, where n points about the circle C are utilised, p_1, ..., p_n. Ignoring pixel quantisation and assuming an ideal ball, n-point occlusion detection yields accurate results for 50% occlusion as $n \to \infty$, independent of the direction and nature of the occlusion. The process of 4-point occlusion detection is illustrated in Fig. 2b.

4.3   Ball Verification

Although the proposed method is robust against both noise and ball occlusion, it does not inherently deal well with images where no ball is present; specifically, in an image with no ball, the algorithm will attempt to locate a ball in any appropriate transitions caused by noise or over-classification, such as in a shadowed yellow goalpost. This is corrected by the addition of a *ball verification* stage, where the distance to the potential ball is calculated by two different metrics:

− *Distance by width:* The distance between the robot and the ball is calculated directly from determined ball width:

$$d_w = \sqrt{\left(\frac{r_{cm}}{\tan{(\gamma_x r_{px})}}\right)^2 - h_{cam}^2} \,, \quad \gamma_x = \frac{\theta_x}{w_{img}} \tag{1}$$

---

[4] In the NUbots vision system, "field" pixels are simply those which map to the green colour class label.

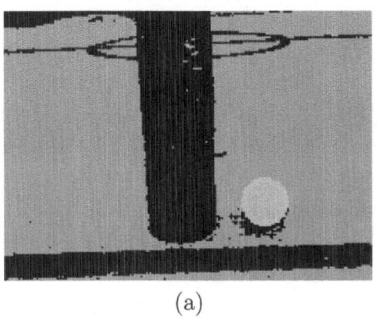 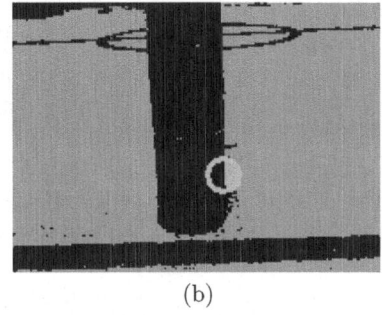

(a)   (b)

Fig. 3. Correct ball detection for a LUT-classified RoboCup image, for both non-occluded (a) and 50% occluded (b) ball scenarios (calculated ball represented by cyan circle)

where r_{cm} is the actual radius of the ball (cm), r_{px} is the radius of the ball located in the image (pixels) and h_{cam} is the current height of the camera from the ground (calculated from kinematics data). The *pixel angular width*, γ_x, is a conversion factor that approximates the relationship between horizontal field of view of the camera, θ_x, and the pixel width of the image, w_{img}. This approximation is most accurate at the center of the frame.

- *Distance to point:* This method utilises a ground-plane projection to calculate the distance to any point on the field, knowing only the (x, y) pixel coordinates, pixel angular width γ_x and height γ_y, and the kinematics data of the robot[5]:

$$d_p = \frac{h_{cam} \tan(\theta_{head} + \beta)}{\cos \alpha},$$

where θ_{head} is the robot head elevation and α and β, the point bearing and elevation, are defined as

$$\alpha = \gamma_x \left(\frac{w_{img}}{2} - x \right), \quad \beta = \gamma_y \left(\frac{h_{img}}{2} - y \right).$$

If the absolute difference between the two calculated distances exceeds a certain error threshold value, the ball is disregarded. This process prevents the detection of false balls, except in the scenario that the offending object is actually ball-sized. Additional checks, such as maximum ball distance and minimum orange pixel density, may also be applied such that false positives can only result from ball-sized, ball-coloured objects positioned on the field of play.

5   Computational Results

The performance of the proposed ball detection method was evaluated by calculating the distance to the ball from its pixel width, as described in Sect. 4.3

---

[5] γ_y is defined as per γ_x in (1), in terms of θ_y and h_{img}, the image pixel height.

(1). This distance was calculated at 0.5 meter intervals, from a distance of 0.5 to 5.0 meters, for non-occluded, 25% and 50% occluded balls[6]. The accuracy of the algorithm is compared to previous ball detection approaches, including the previous NUbots system [1], implementing Levenberg-Marquardt least squares circle fitting [10]; and a circular Hough transform based method [16] similar to those implemented by many RoboCup teams [11, 15].

Fig. 4 illustrates the experimental results, with the proposed ball detection method indicated by blue, the previous NUbots method by magenta and the Hough transform based method by red. It can be seen from Fig. 4a that, for a non-occluded ball, the proposed method yields the most accurate results for balls greater than 1.5 meters away. For closer balls, the Hough transform method performs best, although the error in both instances is very small. Increasing the level of occlusion from to 25% and 50% increases the distance for which the Hough method is most accurate, to 2.0 m and 3.5 m respectively. Overall, the proposed method produces the most consistently accurate results; the error is consistently less than 10% for non-occluded and 25% occluded balls, and less than 20% for 50% occluded balls. The previous NUbots method performed worst in all cases, and was incapable of detecting balls at a distance greater than 3.5, 3.0 and 2.5 meters for 0%, 25% and 50% occlusion respectively.

The dashed lines in Fig. 4 represent the mean calculated distance error over 100 frames of a stationary robot. To minimise error introduced by the approximated *pixel angular width* (see Sect. 4.3), all images were captured with the ball positioned in the center of the frame. As pixels are an inherently quantised unit, it follows that, for a fixed camera height, certain distances will be less susceptible to error than others. For example, at a distance of 4 meters, the optimal ball width is 4.94 pixels, whereas for 3.5 meters the optimal width is 5.64. As 4.94 is much closer to an integer value than 5.64, it is reasonable that some methods perform better at 4.0 meters than 3.5 (see the blue dashed line in Fig. 4a and c). As this *pixel quantization error* is a function of camera height, which varies as the robot walks, the solid lines (representing the current maximum error) are introduced to Fig. 4 to provide a better indication of the expected error at a given distance.

As robots in humanoid soccer typically suffer from significant processor constraints due to power consumption requirements, it is vital that any implemented algorithm is as computationally efficient as possible. Table 5 contains the execution times for the *refine candidates* module of the proposed ball detection system (see Sect. 2) and equivalent sections of the compared methods, as measured on the DARwIn-OP platform [7]. Results demonstrate that the proposed system executes 1.5 times faster than the previous NUbots system, and over 300 times faster than the Hough transform based system[7].

---

[6] The official kid size league match ball was utilised for all experiments.

[7] Performance overhead may have been introduced by the OpenCV C++ Hough transform implementation.

Fig. 4. Comparison of ball distance errors for the proposed ball detection method (blue), previous NUbots method (magenta) and Hough transform based method (red), for occlusion levels of 0% (a), 25% (b) and 50% (c). As finite camera resolution introduces a pixel quantisation error (demonstrated by the dashed lines), the solid lines are introduced to represent the expected performance considering variations in camera height (see Sect. 5).

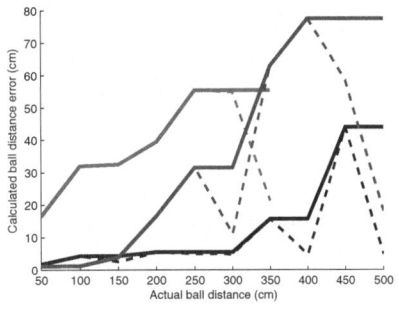

(a)

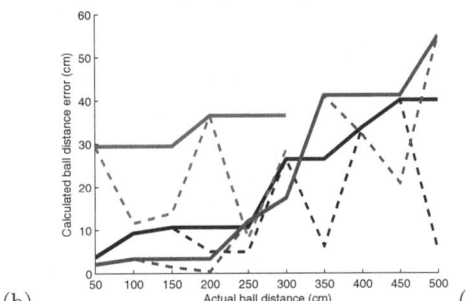

(b)

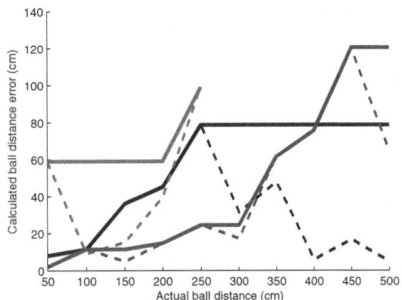

(c)

Table 1. Execution time mean μ and standard deviation σ for the proposed ball detection method, previous NUbots method and Hough transform based method

Method	μ (ms)	σ (ms)
Center update w/ 4-point occlusion detection	0.395	0.088
Previous NUbots (least squares circle fitting)	0.615	0.103
Circular Hough transform	128	18.4

6 Conclusion

The proposed ball detection method overall demonstrated the most accurate results, maintaining an error in calculated ball distance of less than 10% for non-occluded and 25% occluded balls, and less than 20% for 50% occluded balls, over a range of distances from 0.5 to 5.0 meters. The compared Hough transform method performed slightly better for balls closer than a certain distance, which increased from 1.5 to 3.5 meters as occlusion levels were raised. The previous NUbots ball detection method, which implemented Levenberg-Marquardt least squares circle fitting, performed worst for all distances and occlusion levels.

In addition to accurate performance, the proposed method executed over 300 times faster than the Hough transform based method on the DARwIn-OP platform [7]. Much of this performance gain was leveraged by utilising specific knowledge of the RoboCup environment, such as the ball size and quantity known a priori, in addition to the green field border. Future research will focus on dynamically identifying these salient features in real time, such that similar performance advantages may be leveraged in an arbitrary environment.

References

1. Nicklin, S.P., Bhatia, S., Budden, D., King, R.A.R., Kulk, J., Walker, J., Wong, A.S.W., Chalup, S.K.: The NUbots' Team Description for 2011, https://www.tzi.de/spl/pub/Website/Teams2011/NUbotsTDP2011.pdf
2. Robocup standard platform league (nao) rule book (online) (2012), http://www.tzi.de/spl/pub/Website/Downloads/Rules2012.pdf
3. Andrew, A.: Another efficient algorithm for convex hulls in two dimensions. Information Processing Letters 9(5), 216–219 (1979)
4. Bishop, C., En Ligne, S.S.: Pattern recognition and machine learning, vol. 4. Springer, New York (2006)
5. Budden, D., Fenn, S., Mendes, A., Chalup, S.: Evaluation of colour models for computer vision using cluster validation techniques. In: RoboCup 2012: Robot Soccer World Cup XVI. LNCS (LNAI). Springer (2013) (accepted)
6. Dunn, J.: Well-separated clusters and optimal fuzzy partitions. Journal of Cybernetics 4(1), 95–104 (1974)
7. Ha, I., Tamura, Y., Asama, H., Han, J., Hong, D.: Development of open humanoid platform DARwIn-OP. In: 2011 Proceedings of SICE Annual Conference (SICE), pp. 2178–2181. IEEE (2011)
8. Hartigan, J., Wong, M.: Algorithm as 136: A k-means clustering algorithm. Journal of the Royal Statistical Society. Series C (Applied Statistics) 28(1), 100–108 (1979)
9. Kitano, H., Asada, M.: The robocup humanoid challenge as the millennium challenge for advanced robotics. Advanced Robotics 13(8), 723–736 (1998)
10. Marquardt, D.: An algorithm for least-squares estimation of nonlinear parameters. Journal of the Society for Industrial and Applied Mathematics 11(2), 431–441 (1963)
11. Martins, D., Neves, A., Pinho, A.: Real-time generic ball recognition in robocup domain. In: Proc. of the 3rd International Workshop on Intelligent Robotics, IROBOT, pp. 37–48 (2008)
12. Murch, C., Chalup, S.: Combining edge detection and colour segmentation in the four-legged league. In: Proceedings of the Australasian Conference on Robotics and Automation 2004 (2004)
13. Seysener, C., Murch, C., Middleton, R.: Extensions to Object Recognition in the Four-Legged League. In: Nardi, D., Riedmiller, M., Sammut, C., Santos-Victor, J. (eds.) RoboCup 2004. LNCS (LNAI), vol. 3276, pp. 274–285. Springer, Heidelberg (2005)
14. Szeliski, R.: Computer vision: algorithms and applications. Springer-Verlag New York Inc. (2010)
15. Velthuis, D., Verschoor, C., Wiggers, A., Cabot, M., Keune, A., Nugteren, S., Egmond, H., Rossum, T., Molen, H., Rozeboom, R., Becht, I., Jonge, M., Prong, R., Kooijman, C., Slaap, R., Visser, A.: Dutch nao team, team description paper for robocup 2012 (2009)
16. Yuen, H., Princen, J., Illingworth, J., Kittler, J.: Comparative study of hough transform methods for circle finding. Image and Vision Computing 8(1), 71–77 (1990)

Analysis of Cluster Formation Techniques for Multi-robot Task Allocation Using Sequential Single-Cluster Auctions

Bradford Heap and Maurice Pagnucco

ARC Centre of Excellence in Autonomous Systems
School of Computer Science and Engineering
The University of New South Wales
Sydney, NSW, 2052, Australia
{bradfordh,morri}@cse.unsw.edu.au

Abstract. Recent research has shown the benefits of using K-means clustering in task allocation to robots. However, there is little evaluation of other clustering techniques. In this paper we compare K-means clustering to single-linkage clustering and consider the effects of straight line and true path distance metrics in cluster formation. Our empirical results show single-linkage clustering with a true path distance metric provides the best solutions to the multi-robot task allocation problem when used in sequential single-cluster auctions.

1 Introduction

We consider a team of autonomous mobile service robots operating in an office-like environment. These robots may be required to deliver mail between rooms, provide an escort to visitors, or complete cleaning tasks. In all of these situations a set of tasks is to be completed and it is our desire that the tasks are distributed amongst all available robots in a manner that seeks to optimise a global team objective.

Recent research has shown market-based sequential auctions can quickly generate good solutions to this class of problem. In particular, *Sequential single-item auctions* (SSI auctions) which allocate tasks to robots one task per auction round at a time provide solutions within guaranteed bounds [11,8]. Further refinements of this approach have considered various components such as considering complete task allocations with *rollouts* [20], changing the winner determination rules [10], and exchanging tasks post-initial allocation [19,14].

However, a drawback of allocating tasks one at a time in a market-based environment is that robots are generally greedy in their bidding strategies and will often only consider tasks that seek to minimise their overall cost, rather than the global team cost. For instance, it is common for two robots to be allocated one task each when the overall team cost would be lower if one robot completed these two tasks and the other robot was allocated and completed other tasks.

M. Thielscher and D. Zhang (Eds.): AI 2012, LNCS 7691, pp. 839–850, 2012.
© Springer-Verlag Berlin Heidelberg 2012

To overcome this problem, Koenig *et al.* [9] consider an extension of SSI auctions where robots form and bid for combinations of multiple tasks during each auction round. However, despite this approach improving the final task allocation, the calculations required to form the task bundles are very computationally expensive. Heap and Pagnucco considered the merits of this approach in their work on *Sequential single-cluster auctions* (SSC auctions) [5,6] which uses K-means clustering to form clusters of tasks that are allocated to robots as fixed bundles.

Furthermore, K-means clustering has also been used in a variety of other multi-robot task allocation problems. These include evenly balancing task allocation between robots [4], ensuring robots are spread out in the exploration of unknown space [17,15], and for map segmentation in RoboCup Rescue Agent Simulation [13]. However, few papers have considered alternative algorithms for the formation of task clusters. In this paper we use SSC auctions to compare K-means clustering to *single-linkage clustering* and consider both straight line distance and true path distance (which takes into consideration obstacles between tasks) as metrics in cluster formation.

In the remainder of this paper we define the multi-robot task allocation problem in the domain of auction-like algorithms, we define SSC auctions, outline each clustering technique, consider the time required for each clustering algorithm to complete, and report our empirical experimental results for each clustering techinque when used in SSC auctions for task allocation. Our key results show single-linkage clustering with a true path distance metric is the best performing clustering technique when used in SSC auctions to solve the multi-robot task allocation problem. However, we also show that the time required to form clusters using a true path distance metric is around 100 times slower than using straight line distances.

2   Multi-robot Routing

Multi-robot routing (Fig. 1) is considered the standard testbed for the multi-robot task allocation problem in which each task is represented as a location to visit [3]. We follow Koenig *et al.* [9] in their formalisation of the problem. Given a set of robots $R = \{r_1, \ldots, r_m\}$ and a set of tasks $T = \{t_1, \ldots, t_n\}$, any tuple $\langle T_{r_1}, \ldots, T_{r_m} \rangle$ of pairwise disjoint bundles $T_{r_i} \subseteq T$ and $T_{r_i} \cap T_{r_j} = \emptyset$ for $i \neq j$, for all $i = 1, \ldots, m$, is a partial solution of the multi-robot task allocation problem. This means that robot r_i performs the tasks T_{r_i}, and no task is assigned to more than one robot. To determine a complete solution we need to find a partial solution $\langle T_{r_1} \ldots T_{r_m} \rangle$ with $\cup_{r_i \in R} T_{r_i} = T$, that is, where every task is assigned to exactly one robot.

Robots have perfect localisation and can calculate the costs to travel between locations. We assume costs are symmetric, $\lambda(i,j) = \lambda(j,i)$ and are equal across all robots. The robot cost $\lambda_r(T_r)$ is the minimum cost for an individual robot r to visit all locations T_r assigned to it. There can be positive synergies between

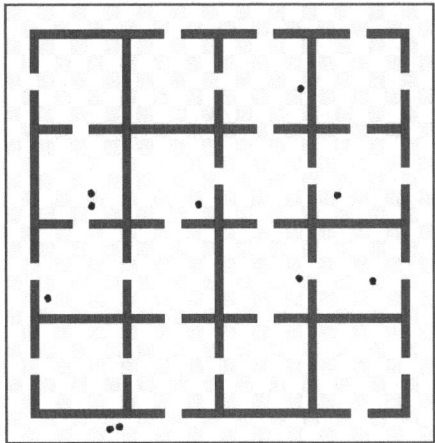

Fig. 1. Multi-Robot Routing

tasks where $\lambda_{r_i}(T_{r_i} \cup T_{r'_i}) < \lambda_{r_i}(T_{r_i}) + \lambda_{r_i}(T_{r'_i})$. Furthermore, we desire to find a complete solution that seeks to minimise a global team objective. In this paper we test with two common team objectives first introduced in [18]:

MiniMax $\max_{r \in R} \lambda_r(T_r)$, that is to minimise the maximum distance each individual robot travels.

MiniSum $\sum_{r \in R} \lambda_r(T_r)$, that is to minimise the sum of the paths of all robots in visiting all their assigned locations.

3   Sequential Single-Cluster (SSC) Auctions

SSC auctions [5] are an extension of SSI auctions and assign fixed clusters of tasks to robots over multiple bidding rounds. At the conclusion of each bidding round one previously unassigned task cluster $c = \{t_1, \ldots, t_o\}$ is assigned to the robot that bids the least for it so that the overall team cost increases the least. After all task clusters are allocated, each robot seeks to complete all its allocated tasks in as short a distance possible. Robots do not have to do all tasks in a cluster sequentially. When a robot is awarded a new cluster, the robot adds the tasks in this new cluster to its existing task assignment and replans its path to travel.

We formulate the algorithm for SSC auctions in Fig. 2. Each robot runs the algorithm independently of other robots and, with the exception of supplying the initial list of tasks and clusters to each robot, there is no centralised controller. Before the SSC auction algorithm begins, a clustering algorithm is used to allocate all tasks into task clusters and $C = \{c_1, \ldots, c_k\}$ is the set of all clusters. Each task is assigned to one, and only one cluster, and clusters can be of varying sizes. All robots are informed of all tasks and all clusters.

function SSC-Auction $(\bar{C}, C_r, r, R)$

Input: $\bar{C}$: the set of clusters to be assigned

$\qquad$ C_r: the set of clusters presently assigned

$\qquad$ r: the robot r

$\qquad$ R: the set of robots R

Output: C_r: the set of clusters assigned to the robot

1: **while** $(\bar{C} \neq \emptyset)$
2: $\quad$ /* *Bidding Stage* */
3: $\quad$ **for each** cluster $c \in \bar{C}$
4: $\qquad$ $\beta_r^c \leftarrow$ CalcBid(C_r, c);
5: $\qquad$ Send$(\beta_r^c, R) \mid B \leftarrow \bigcup_i$ Receive$(\beta_{r_i}^c, R)$;
6: $\quad$ /* *Winner-Determination Stage* */
7: $\quad$ $(r', c) \leftarrow$ arg min$_{(r' \in R, c \in \bar{C})}$ B;
8: $\quad$ **if** $r = r'$ **then**
9: $\qquad$ $C_r \leftarrow C_r \cup \{c\}$;
10: $\quad$ $\bar{C} \leftarrow \bar{C} \backslash \{c\}$;

Fig. 2. Sequential Single-Cluster Auctions

The SSC auction begins and continues while there are unassigned task clusters (Line 1). During the bidding stage (Lines 2-5) the robot calculates bids for every unassigned task cluster and submits its lowest bid to all other robots. Each bid calculation requires robots to provide a solution to the travelling repairman problem [1]. Because this problem is NP-hard, robots often use the cheapest-insertion and two-opt heuristics [2] to provide a close approximation to the optimal solution. Each bid is a triple $\beta = \langle b_r, b_c, b_\lambda \rangle$ of a robot b_r, a task cluster b_c and a bid cost b_λ. The function CalcBid takes the set of previously assigned clusters C_r to robot r and the cluster c being bid on and uses a bidding rule to calculate a bid cost (Line 4). The robots send their bids and receive all bids from other robots in parallel (Line 5). The winner-determination stage (Lines 6-10) consists of each robot choosing the task cluster with the lowest bid from the set of submitted bids. Ties are broken in an arbitrary manner. The robot with the winning bid has the winning task cluster assigned to it. All robots then remove the winning task cluster from the set of unassigned clusters and the next bidding round begins.

4 Clustering Techniques

We now consider two different models of cluster formation. K-means clustering is a form of centroid based clustering where each object is assigned to a single cluster based on the object's proximity to the centre of the cluster. Single-linkage clustering is a form of connectivity based clustering which recursively merges clusters by the minimum distance between two objects in each cluster. In this section we also compare the effects of using straight line distance and true path distance as metrics for both clustering models.

function K-means (T,k)
Input: T: the set of tasks to be clustered
$\qquad$ k: the number of clusters to form
Output: C: the set of clusters

1: $M \leftarrow$ InitialiseClusterCentres(T,k);
2: **while** *cluster centres have changed*
3: $\quad$ /* *Task Cluster Assignment Stage* */
4: $\quad$ **for each** task $t \in T$
5: $\quad\quad$ **for each** cluster centre $m_i \in M$
6: $\quad\quad\quad$ $\lambda^t_{m_i} \leftarrow$ CalcDistance(t,m_i);
7: $\quad\quad$ $C_{min_{(\lambda^t_{m_i})}} \leftarrow t$;
8: $\quad$ /* *Update Cluster Centres Stage* */
9: $\quad$ **for each** cluster $c \in C$
10: $\quad\quad$ $M_c \leftarrow$ CalcCentre(c);

Fig. 3. K-means Clustering

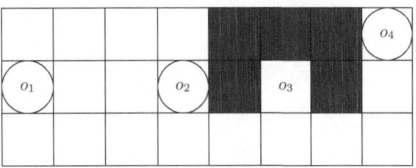

a. Initial Cluster Centres

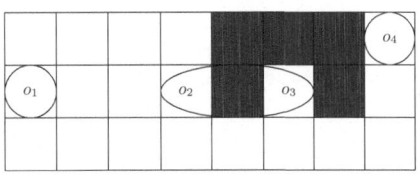

b. Stable Cluster Centres

Fig. 4. Formation of three clusters of four objects using K-means clustering with a straight line distance metric.

The standard K-means clustering algorithm [12] is given in Fig. 3 and an example cluster formation with a straight line distance metric is presented in Fig. 4. Before the algorithm begins the initial centres of all clusters must be selected (Line 1). A common approach for this is to randomly select k objects from the set of data to be clustered and use each of these objects as an initial cluster centre (Fig. 4a). The algorithm then alternates between two stages until the membership of all clusters is stable (Fig. 4b). During the task cluster assignment stage (Lines 3 - 7) every task is considered independently. The distance between the task and every cluster centre is calculated and the task is reassigned from its current cluster to the cluster with the minimum distance to itself. During the update cluster centres stage (Lines 8 - 10) the centre of each cluster is recalculated to reflect the changes in the membership of each cluster. The algorithm then repeats until no object moves between clusters.

We present an algorithm to perform single-linkage clustering [16] in Fig. 5 and give an example cluster formation with a true path distance metric in Fig. 6. The algorithm begins with each object being assigned to a cluster containing only itself (Lines 1 - 2) (Fig. 6a). Clusters are then repeatedly merged until the number of clusters is equal to k (Lines 3 - 10) (Fig. 6b). To merge clusters we calculate the distance between every individual object in each cluster and every object in every other cluster (Lines 4 - 6). The two clusters containing the two objects with the minimum distance between them are then merged (Lines 7 - 10). The algorithm then repeats until there are k clusters.

function Single-linkage (T,k)
Input: T: the set of tasks to be clustered
        k: the number of clusters to form
Output: C: the set of clusters

1: **for each** task $t_i \in T$
2:     $C_i \leftarrow t_i$;
3: **while** $|C| > k$
4:     **for each** cluster $C \supset C_i$
5:         **for each** cluster $C \backslash C_i \supset C_j$
6:             $\lambda_{C_j}^{C_i} \leftarrow$ CalcDistance(C_i,C_j);
7:     **if** $min(\lambda_{C_j}^{C_i})$ **then**
8:         $C_{merged} \leftarrow \{C_i,C_j\}$;
9:         $C \leftarrow C \cup \{C_{merged}\}$;
10:        $C \leftarrow C \backslash \{C_i,C_j\}$;

Fig. 5. Single-linkage Clustering

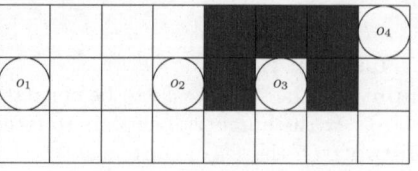

a. Initial Clusters

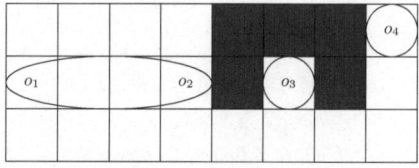

b. Final Merged Clusters

Fig. 6. Formation of three clusters of four objects using single-linkage clustering with a true path distance metric

In our experiments we expect that the differences in the design of these two algorithms will cause vastly different task allocations to robots. Due to K-means clustering focussing on 2-dimensional areas of tasks, we expect that each robot will be generally constrained to completing tasks within an isolated area. In comparison, task clusters formed using single-linkage clustering are more likely to see robot paths crossing over each other as the task formation is focussed on the 1-dimensional connection between any two tasks.

5   Cluster Formation Time Analysis

The length of time required to formulate clusters is crucial in finding a good solution to the multi-robot task allocation problem. The time complexity for K-means clustering is $O(|T|^{dk+1} \log |T|)$ (where d is the number of dimensions) [7] and for single-linkage clustering is $O(|T|^2)$. Generally speaking single-linkage clustering is much quicker than K-means clustering.

However, it is also important to take into account the time involved in the calculation of the distance metric. When we consider the calculation of a straight line Euclidean distance between objects the time required is minimal. Contrary to this is the time required to calculate the true path distance between two objects taking into account obstacles. Even in a two dimensional environment, such as the map presented in Fig. 4 and Fig. 6, two geographically close objects o_2 and o_3 have a true path distance that is greater than the distance between o_1 and o_2. To calculate the true path distance we are required to perform a search for the shortest distance between every object and every other object using an

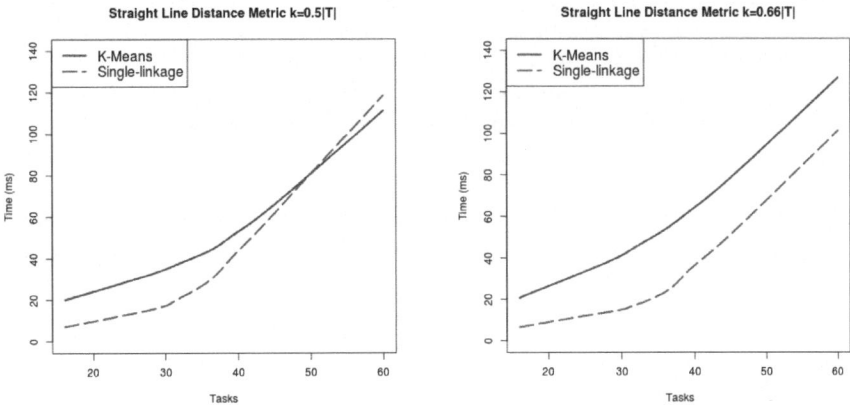

Fig. 7. Cluster Formation Time using a Straight Line Distance Metric

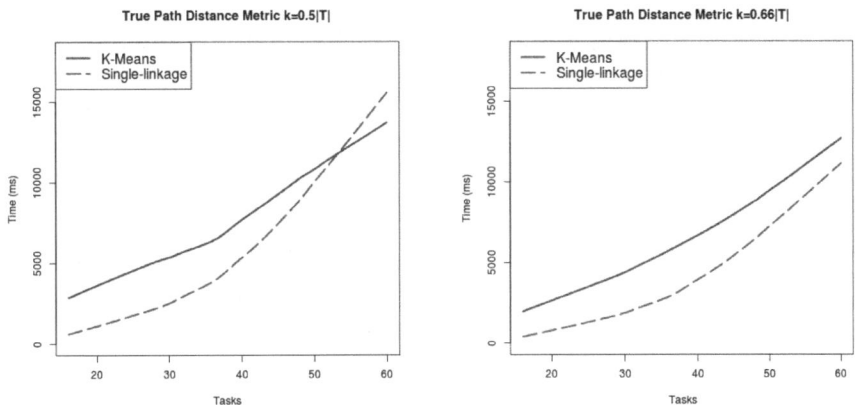

Fig. 8. Cluster Formation Times using a True Path Distance Metric

occupancy grid map. The number of true path calculations required for single-linkage clustering is constrained by the number of tasks. However, in K-means clustering every time a cluster centre is changed we are required to recalculate the distance from the centre to all objects.

To examine the real time requirements of each clustering algorithm we simulate an office-like environment with 16 rooms each containing four interconnecting doors that can be independently opened or closed to allow or restrict travel between rooms (Fig. 1). We test on 25 different fixed configurations of combinations of opened and closed doors. In each configuration we guarantee there is an open path between each room and every other room. For each configuration we test a wide range of total tasks to be clustered $|T| \in \{16, \ldots, 60\}$. For each task set we repeat the clustering process for two different values of k, $k = \frac{1}{2}|T|$ and $k = \frac{2}{3}|T|$. To calculate the true path cost between tasks we use an A* search on an occupancy grid map of each office environment with our heuristic being the straight line distance between the two tasks.

The results of clustering using a straight line distance metric are plotted in Fig. 7 and the results of clustering using a true path distance metric are plotted in Fig. 8. These plots show that generally, as expected, single-linkage clustering completes quicker than K-means clustering. However, when there are a large number of tasks and $k = \frac{1}{2}|T|$ single-linkage clustering takes a long period of time to complete. This is due to the large number of cluster merges required when k is small. We note that K-means clustering does not suffer this problem as the stablisation of clusters is independent of the value of k. Finally, we also observe that the use of a true path distance metric causes both clustering algorithms to perform about 100 times slower compared to the straight line distance metric.

6   Empirical Analysis Using SSC Auctions

We now test each of these clustering techniques with SSC auctions to solve the multi-robot task allocation problem for both the MiniMax and the MiniSum team objectives. Using the clusters formed in Sect. 5 we test homogeneous mobile robots in teams of varying sizes $|R| \in \{4, 6, 8, 10\}$. In each of the 25 office configurations robots are initially positioned in different random locations. Robots can only travel between rooms through open doors and they cannot open or close doors. We present the mean results of the maximum distance and the summation of all distances travelled for the two team objectives in Tables 1, 2, 3 and 4.

The results for SSC auctions with robots bidding according to the MiniMax team objective are shown for clusters formed with $k = \frac{1}{2}|T|$ in Table 1 and for clusters formed with $k = \frac{2}{3}|T|$ in Table 2. Both of these result tables show that generally the use of a true path distance metric results in task allocations that have lower mean maximum robot travel distances. Overall, single-linkage clustering with a true path distance metric produces the best task allocations for this team objective and K-means clustering with a straight line metric performs the worst.

To confirm the statistical validity of these results we perform *non-parametric one-sided Wilcoxon signed-rank tests* for each robot/task/cluster combination. We choose this statistical test as we cannot make distribution assumptions due to the differences in robot initial locations and the map configurations of opened and closed doors for each experiment. We seek to confirm that the use of a true path distance metric in cluster formation results in lower final travel distances than clusters formed using a straight line distance metric. Our null hypothesis is defined as $H_0 : \mu\lambda_{true\text{-}path} \geq \mu\lambda_{straight\text{-}line}$ and our alternative hypothesis as $H_0 : \mu\lambda_{true\text{-}path} < \mu\lambda_{straight\text{-}line}$.

For K-means clustering with $k = \frac{1}{2}|T|$ we get a significant difference with confidence greater than 0.90 for all robot/task/cluster combinations tested. However, for K-means clustering with $k = \frac{2}{3}|T|$ our results are not significant for all robot/task/cluster combinations. In particular, our mean results for the configuration of 4 robots, 24 tasks, and 16 clusters has true path distances resulting

Table 1. Mean Maximum Distance for MiniMax Team Objective with $k = \frac{1}{2}|T|$

			Straight Line Metric		True Path Metric	
Robots	Tasks	Clusters	K-means	Single-link	K-means	Single-link
4	16	8	995	954	906	874
6	24	12	983	963	816	777
8	32	16	895	921	773	690
10	40	20	823	870	677	636
4	20	10	1090	1084	989	932
6	30	15	1023	1032	888	833
8	40	20	898	918	802	776
10	50	25	814	883	745	679
4	24	12	1203	1174	1053	1027
6	36	18	1117	1094	965	913
8	48	24	988	983	863	810
10	60	30	887	886	805	690

Table 2. Mean Maximum Distance for MiniMax Team Objective with $k = \frac{2}{3}|T|$

			Straight Line Metric		True Path Metric	
Robots	Tasks	Clusters	K-means	Single-link	K-means	Single-link
4	16	11	910	873	864	874
6	24	16	810	874	750	713
8	32	21	830	840	727	671
10	40	27	718	746	669	617
4	20	13	1004	1043	991	917
6	30	20	932	941	841	826
8	40	27	818	831	762	731
10	50	33	752	753	698	652
4	24	16	1015	1154	1029	967
6	36	24	955	969	936	886
8	48	32	884	863	840	785
10	60	40	860	742	724	698

in a worst maximum distance travelled than the use of a straight line metric. We speculate that the cause of these non-significant results is due to K-means clustering seeking to form non-overlapping clusters of geographically close tasks, whereas robots, in seeking to minimise their path travelled, may not confine themselves to particular local geographic areas.

Our results for single-linkage clustering have much stronger statistical significance. For all robot/task/cluster combinations we obtain confidence 0.97 and greater for both $k = \frac{1}{2}|T|$ and $k = \frac{2}{3}|T|$. Finally, we compare our best and worst results of single-linkage clustering with true path distances to K-means clustering with straight line distances. Again for $k = \frac{1}{2}|T|$ we get a very significant result with confidence 0.99 and with $k = \frac{1}{2}|T|$ we get confidence 0.97. Overall, we can conclude that using true path distance metrics produces much better solutions to the multi-robot task allocation problem than straight line distances for the MiniMax team objective.

Table 3. Mean Summed Distance for MiniSum Team Objective with $k = \frac{1}{2}|T|$

Robots	Tasks	Clusters	Straight Line Metric		True Path Metric	
			K-means	Single-link	K-means	Single-link
4	16	8	2298	2231	2197	2140
6	24	12	2801	2701	2565	2489
8	32	16	3123	3061	2893	2806
10	40	20	3444	3301	3087	3000
4	20	10	2701	2621	2483	2464
6	30	15	3239	3083	2943	2850
8	40	20	3627	3504	3300	3211
10	50	25	3775	3741	3459	3409
4	24	12	3011	2864	2767	2715
6	36	18	3511	3464	3272	3258
8	48	24	3917	3821	3605	3541
10	60	30	4208	4059	3878	3786

Table 4. Mean Summed Distance for MiniSum Team Objective with $k = \frac{2}{3}|T|$

Robots	Tasks	Clusters	Straight Line Metric		True Path Metric	
			K-means	Single-link	K-means	Single-link
4	16	11	2232	2178	2142	2117
6	24	16	2642	2640	2519	2501
8	32	21	3090	3009	2896	2809
10	40	27	3105	3185	3045	2990
4	20	13	2636	2569	2495	2460
6	30	20	3101	3058	2897	2878
8	40	27	3329	3419	3241	3229
10	50	33	3626	3500	3446	3375
4	24	16	2839	2850	2783	2748
6	36	24	3339	3401	3268	3230
8	48	32	3813	3643	3551	3350
10	60	40	4160	3849	3850	3814

Our results for robots bidding according to the MiniSum team objective are likewise shown for $k = \frac{1}{2}|T|$ in Table 3 and for $k = \frac{2}{3}|T|$ in Table 4. This data mirrors our results for the MiniMax team objective with single-linkage clustering using a true path metric producing the best results and K-means clustering with a straight line metric the worst.

Again we perform *one-sided Wilcoxon signed-rank tests* to confirm the statistical validity of our data. For K-means clustering with $k = \frac{1}{2}|T|$ we confirm a very significant result with confidence 0.99. However, when tested with clusters of $k = \frac{2}{3}|T|$ K-means clustering again fails to deliver a strong statistical confidence. This is despite our overall means showing the use of a true path distance metric outperforming a straight line distance metric in all robot/task/cluster combinations.

For single-linkage clustering we again get strong statistically significant results. For clusters formed with $k = \frac{1}{2}|T|$ we measure a confidence result of 0.995 and for $k = \frac{2}{3}|T|$ a confidence of 0.95. Finally, we conclude by testing the significance of the difference between our best performing single-linkage clustering using true path distances and worst performing K-means clustering using straight line costs. Comparing $k = \frac{1}{2}|T|$ we get a confidence of 0.998 and for $k = \frac{2}{3}|T|$ a confidence of 0.95.

In summary, for both MiniMax and MiniSum team objectives tested, we have shown the power of using a true path distance metric in the formation of clusters to solve the multi-robot task allocation problem. Despite our cluster formation time measurements showing that the use of true path distance metrics is around 100 times slower than straight line calculations, we believe that the overall travel distance saved as a result of better clusters far outweighs the extra initial time spent on cluster formation. Futhermore, it can be argued that the cluster formation time with a true path metric will be much smaller than the expected execution time of the robots completing all allocated tasks.

7 Conclusions and Further Work

We have presented an analysis of clustering techniques to solve the multi-robot task allocation problem using SSC auctions. We have considered the time required using two different clustering models and the effect of calculating true path distances instead of straight-line distances in the formation of clusters. Our empirical results show the benefit of using single-linkage clustering with a true-path distance metric over other cluster formation techniques.

There remains much scope for future work. Finding a good value for k remains a challenge. A large k value results in clusters that contain few tasks and, as such, little inter-task synergy is considered. On the other hand, small k value results in clusters containing many tasks can lead to robots being allocated tasks and resultant paths that would be better suited to other robots. A clustering approach that sought a balance between these two challenges would be ideal, however, the time complexity may be much greater than our existing approaches.

In a related vein, disparity between the number of tasks contained in each cluster can lead to clusters containing few tasks being allocated in earlier auction rounds than larger clusters. Future work could consider the effects when robots take into account the size of clusters during the formation of bids. Allocating large clusters first may lead to better solutions than a series of small clusters being allocated in early auctions rounds.

Finally, we also wish to consider more complicated extensions to the multi-robot task allocation problem. Of particular interest is the *courier delivery problem* which requires robots to pick up and drop off objects. Auctioning clusters of tasks in this problem domain is much more difficult as we are required to consider both the pick up and drop off locations of objects when forming clusters.

References

1. Blum, A., Chalasani, P., Coppersmith, D., Pulleyblank, B., Raghavan, P., Sudan, M.: The minimum latency problem. In: Proceedings of the Twenty-Sixth Annual ACM Symposium on Theory of Computing, pp. 163–171 (1994)

2. Croes, G.: A method for solving traveling-salesman problems. Operations Research 6, 791–812 (1958)
3. Dias, M.B., Zlot, R., Kalra, N., Stentz, A.: Market-based multirobot coordination: A survey and analysis. Proceedings of the IEEE 94(7), 1257–1270 (2006)
4. Elango, M., Nachiappan, S., Tiwari, M.K.: Balancing task allocation in multi-robot systems using K-means clustering and auction based mechanisms. Expert Systems with Applications 38(6), 6486–6491 (2011)
5. Heap, B., Pagnucco, M.: Sequential Single-Cluster Auctions for Robot Task Allocation. In: Wang, D., Reynolds, M. (eds.) AI 2011. LNCS, vol. 7106, pp. 412–421. Springer, Heidelberg (2011)
6. Heap, B., Pagnucco, M.: Repeated sequential auctions with dynamic task clusters. In: Proc. AAAI 2012 (2012)
7. Inaba, M., Katoh, N., Imai, H.: Applications of weighted voronoi diagrams and randomization to variance-based K-clustering. In: Proceedings of the Tenth Annual Symposium on Computational Geometry, pp. 332–339. ACM (1994)
8. Koenig, S., Tovey, C., Lagoudakis, M., Markakis, V., Kempe, D., Keskinocak, P., Kleywegt, A., Meyerson, A., Jain, S.: The power of sequential single-item auctions for agent coordination. In: Proc. AAAI 2006 (2006)
9. Koenig, S., Tovey, C., Zheng, X., Sungur, I.: Sequential bundle-bid single-sale auction algorithms for decentralized control. In: Proc. IJCAI 2007, pp. 1359–1365 (2007)
10. Koenig, S., Zheng, X., Tovey, C., Borie, R., Kilby, P., Markakis, V., Keskinocak, P.: Agent coord. with regret clearing. In: AAAI 2008 (2008)
11. Lagoudakis, M., Markakis, E., Kempe, D., Keskinocak, P., Kleywegt, A., Koenig, S., Tovey, C., Meyerson, A., Jain, S.: Auction-based multi-robot routing. In: Proc. Int. Conf. on Robotics: Science and Systems, pp. 343–350 (2005)
12. Lloyd, S.: Least squares quantization in pcm. IEEE Transactions on Information Theory 28(2), 129–137 (1982)
13. Nanjanath, M., Erlandson, A., Andrist, S., Ragipindi, A., Mohammed, A., Sharma, A., Gini, M.: Decision and Coordination Strategies for RoboCup Rescue Agents. In: Ando, N., Balakirsky, S., Hemker, T., Reggiani, M., von Stryk, O. (eds.) SIMPAR 2010. LNCS, vol. 6472, pp. 473–484. Springer, Heidelberg (2010)
14. Nanjanath, M., Gini, M.: Repeated auctions for robust task execution by a robot team. Robotics and Autonomous Systems 58(7), 900–909 (2010)
15. Puig, D., Garcia, M., Wu, L.: A new global optimization strategy for coordinated multi-robot exploration: Development and comparative evaluation. In: Robotics and Autonomous Systems (2011)
16. Sokal, R., Sneath, P., et al.: Principles of numerical taxonomy. Principles of Numerical Taxonomy (1963)
17. Solanas, A., Garcia, M.: Coordinated multi-robot exploration through unsupervised clustering of unknown space. In: Proc. IROS 2004, pp. 717–721 (2004)
18. Tovey, C., Lagoudakis, M., Jain, S., Koenig, S.: The generation of bidding rules for auction-based robot coordination. In: Multi-Robot Systems. From Swarms to Intelligent Automata Volume III, pp. 3–14 (2005)
19. Zheng, X., Koenig, S.: K-swaps: Cooperative negotiation for solving task-allocation problems. In: Proc. IJCAI 2009, pp. 373–379 (2009)
20. Zheng, X., Koenig, S., Tovey, C.: Improving sequential single-item auctions. In: Proc. IROS 2006, pp. 2238–2244 (2006)

On-Line Model-Based Continuous State Reinforcement Learning Using Background Knowledge

Bernhard Hengst

University of New South Wales
Computer Science and Engineering
bernhardh@cse.unsw.edu.au
http://www.cse.unsw.edu.au

Abstract. Without a model the application of reinforcement learning to control a dynamic system can be hampered by several shortcomings. The number of trials needed to learn a good policy can be costly and time consuming for robotic applications where data is gathered in real-time. In this paper we describe a variable resolution model-based reinforcement learning approach that distributes sample points in the state-space in proportion to the effect of actions. In this way the base learner economises on storage to approximate an effective model. Our approach is conducive to including background knowledge to speed up learning. We show how different types of background knowledge can used to speed up learning in this setting. In particular, we show good performance for a weak type of background knowledge by initially overgeneralising local experience.

Keywords: Artificial Intelligence, Machine Learning, Reinforcement Learning, Robotics, Background Knowledge, Function Approximation, Continuous State, Model-Based.

1 Introduction

In robotics it is often the case that we wish to control a real, possibly non-linear, continuous dynamic system when the model is unknown. In principle reinforcement learning (RL) holds out the promise to solve this control problem by simply letting the learner interact with the system. By specifying a reward signal to guide the learner to the control goal the theory suggests that a policy can be learned over time given enough training experience. Unfortunately in practice the shear number of trials required to learn a good policy becomes prohibitive. It may take a long time to learn anything useful, the real system may break down before learning is complete, or it may be costly to run a system sub-optimally for the duration of the training phase. It is clearly desirable to have methods that can speed up learning by finding a good policy with as few trials as possible. Sometimes we have an approximate model of the system and would like to use this as a starting point. However, many reinforcement learning

M. Thielscher and D. Zhang (Eds.): AI 2012, LNCS 7691, pp. 851–862, 2012.

methods do not provide representations that are conducive to including background knowledge to help the learner. In this paper we describe a RL approach that:

- automatically changes the resolution of the representation based on the effect of actions. It stands to reason that the representation of the dynamics can be coarser where actions move the system over a greater distance. A sparser representation requires less trials to learn.
- is able to include background knowledge by generating or seeding the state transition dynamics in particular parts of the state space. We show how background knowledge can be introduced in a natural way to significantly speed learning.
- over-generalises local dynamics to larger parts of the surrounding state space to quickly find a working policy and then progressively refining the representation to improve performance over time.

RL has been studied and applied for well over a decade and we assume the reader has a basic understanding of its methods. Introductory material can be found in several AI texts, for example[1,2], or in specifically dedicated texts [3,4,5]. In brief, reinforcement learning involves an agent learning to take appropriate actions to maximise future reward by interacting with the environment. The reinforcement learning problem is usually couched in the form of a Markov decision problem $\langle S, A, T, R \rangle$, were S is a set of states, A is a set of actions, $T : S \times A \times S \rightarrow [0,1]$ is a stochastic state transition function and $R : S \times A \times \mathbb{R} \rightarrow [0,1]$ is a stochastic reward function. The transition function and the reward function define the *model* of the environment. The agent interacts with the environment by iteratively observing state $s \in S$, taking an action $a \in A$ and at the next time-tick receiving reward $r \in \mathbb{R}$, and observing the next state $s' \in S$. The aim is to learn an action *policy*, $\pi : S \rightarrow A$, to maximise a measure of future reward. This is usually achieved by learning an optimum value function, e.g. $Q^* : S \times A \rightarrow \mathbb{R}$ using *policy iteration*, from which follows the optimum policy $\pi^*(s) = \arg\max_a Q^*(s, a)$. So called *model-free* methods exist that learn the value function directly from environmental interaction, but we take the view in this paper that explicitly learning the model has advantages.

We will briefly review related work modelling continuous dynamic systems and methods for speeding up learning. We describe our approach to variable resolution modelling and how to include background knowledge. The presentation uses a simple cart to illustrate the concepts. Results for a cart showing that learning is speeded up by a factor of 2 and even more when more explicit background knowledge is provided.

2   Related Work

Sutton and Barto [4] show how reinforcement learning can be speeded up with the Dyna architecture. Transition experiences of the form $(s_t, a_t, r_{t+1}, s'_{t+1})$ are retained, thereby model-learning the dynamics of the system. The trick is to play transitions back as simulated experience interleaved with real-experience during Q-learning. The relatively slow interactions for a real robot may be interleaved with many simulated experiences that help converge the value function much faster. Related methods to help speed learning are the use of eligibility traces that store transition experience and back up recent experience along the trace, and prioritised sweeping that prioritises back-ups of the value function in the reverse direction to the directionality of state transitions. All these methods rely on storing the model to some degree. The approach in this paper is to incrementally store all novel transition experiences and run Q-Learning until convergence or until the next real experience becomes available.

As we are modelling continuous systems with an infinite number of states, and RL uses finite tables, we need a method for *function approximation* to generalise the value of learned points to nearby query points. Function approximation can use any supervised machine learning method. Here we use a non-uniform case-based lazy-learner approach, similar to methods by Santamaria, et al [6] in which neighbouring cases are chosen based on the Euclidian distance d_i between the i-th case point and query point. This linear function approximator is a nearest neighbour function that uses a Gaussian kernel, $K(d_i) = exp(-d_i^2/\tau^2)$, to weigh each i-th neighbour's contribution to the query point Q value, where τ is a smoothing parameter that controls the blending of values of the nearest neighbours. Gabel and Riedmiller further investigate the use of Case-Based Reasoning function approximation methods in reinforcement learning [7]. Where our approach differs is that we store the local model in each case and vary the resolution of cases in each dimension of the state space based on the effect of actions. We store separate cases for each action.

More recent work by Jong and Stone [8] also stores the model as a set of instances and uses kernel-based averages to approximate the value of a query state. Kernel-based averages are known to converge. We use a similar approach to represent the model and to approximate the value function. Our concern in this paper is how we incorporate and employ background knowledge about the dynamics of the system to help speed learning.

A different but related research topic is qualitative modelling and simulation [9]. Qualitative modelling reasons about continuous aspects of systems in logical form (without numbers). For example, the statement "acceleration increases velocity" imparts information about a system's dynamics without being specific about the numerical value about of the acceleration or the velocity. The objective is to reduce search time by reasoning and constraining the learner subject to the qualitative descriptions. We show how qualitative knowledge may be used to guide a RL by seeding the learner with compliant transitions. This suggests a method whereby qualitative modelling can bridge quantitative implementations in specific instances.

3   Approach

We start by introducing an intuitive example sufficient to illustrate the continuous modelling of a dynamic system. We then describe our model-based approach to RL and show how background knowledge can be incorporated.

3.1   Motivating Example

Our physical system consists of a frictionless wheeled 104kg cart moving in one dimension on a horizontal flat 40 meter table as shown in Figure 1. At a frequency of 6 Hertz the controller is able to sense the position and velocity of the cart and apply a positive force of 1000 Newtons through the wheels, a negative force of the same magnitude, or to let the cart coast under its own momentum. The aim of the reinforcement learning controller is to learn to bring the cart to rest at the goal position. We model the cart system as an instance of the PhysicsVehicle class in the open source real-time physics simulator jMonkeyEngine [10].

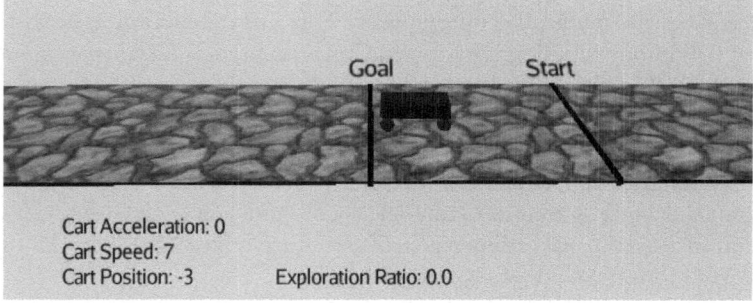

Fig. 1. The cart on a horizontal table as rendered by the real-time jMonkeyEngine 3D game and physics simulator. The positive direction is towards the left. The cart is started at random during learning and at -15 meters to periodically measure performance. The goal is to reach the origin in the middle of the table.

3.2   Method

As the reinforcement learner interacts with the environment it experiences the model of the system as successive tuples of the form (s, a, r, s') where taking action a in state s results in a reward r and a transition to the next state s'. The state s may be multi-dimensional, hence $s = (x_1, x_2, \ldots, x_n)$ for an n-dimensional state vector. In the case of the cart the state has 2-dimensions: $s = (position, velocity)$. We assume all dimensions are continuous.

Rather than throwing the experience away after updating the value function as one would in model-free RL, we store the model information as a *case*, subject to a resolution criterion. Experiencing similar transitions over and over again leads to diminishing information gain. We therefore only store new experiences when the state s is greater than a threshold distance from previously stored cases with the same action for any one of the dimensions. The threshold itself is variable (subject to a minimum value) throughout the state space and depends on the effect of the action recorded for the nearest neighbouring state. If the following isNeighbour function returns true for any existing case the experience is not added as a new case.

Algorithm 1. Tests if existing case, caseID, covers the experience (s, a)

```
isNeighbour(s[], a, caseId, spread){
    if(cases[caseId].a!=a) return false;
    for (int d=0; d<dimS; d++) {
        v1 = s[d];
        v2 = cases[caseId].s[d];
        delta = cases[caseId].threshold[d];
        if(Math.abs(v1-v2)>spread*delta) return false;
    }
    return true;
}
```

The parameter *spread* in the above function regulates the resolution of the cases representing the system. It can be used to increase the resolution if required, for example to better represent stochasticity. We set *spread* = 0.9. Figure 2 shows the transition cases stored for the cart after plying the RL with random transitions for a long period.

It is reasonable to reduce the number of cases in parts of the state-space where the effect of actions leads to greater transition distances. For the cart the density of cases is reduced along the position dimension with an increase in the magnitude of the velocity, as the cart moves further at higher speed.

At each time-tick we find the optimum policy by repeatedly iterating through all the cases stored so far using a temporal difference Q-learning method in the spirit of the Dyna architecture, halting only after convergence or in an anytime fashion when the next experience arrives. As the next state s' for each case is unlikely to be equal to a state s from another case, we approximate the Q-values of s' from the neighbouring cases using a Gaussian kernel. Figure 3 illustrates the estimation of the Q-value of s' for action a' using Algorithm 2.

Without enough experience the controller is unlikely to find a solution. Nevertheless it solves the problem with whatever cases are available and attempts an optimal policy. Early in the learning, when there are no neighbours, we set the next Q values optimistically high to encourage exploration. During Q-learning we use a discount rate of 0.99 to ensure the value function remains bounded while discovering the model, and a learning rate of 1.0, making the tacit assumption that the system is deterministic.

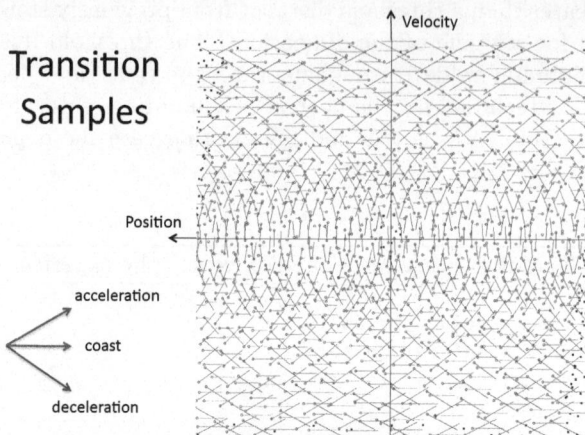

Fig. 2. Transition cases for the cart showing the effect of different actions in the position-velocity space. Note the reduction in resolution for position for higher velocity values. Solid dots indicate terminations cases - goal with reward 0, -100 otherwise.

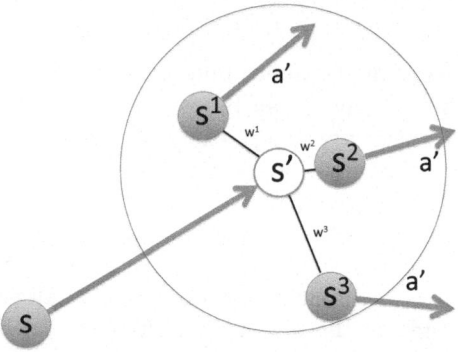

Fig. 3. Estimating successor Q-values from neighbouring cases. The red circle delimits the neighbourhood cases.

3.3   Inserting Background Knowledge in RL

Background knowledge includes all the assumptions, inductive bias (both representational and preference), parameter settings, and system dynamics provided to the learner beforehand. We focus here on background knowledge about the system dynamics. The language provided by the MDP model is used to describe this background knowledge, namely the state transition and reward function. With this representational approach it is possible to generate background knowledge as case samples and feed these to the learner beforehand, giving the learner a head-start. As an extreme example, if the dynamics of the system are known,

Algorithm 2. Estimate max Q-value of next state s' of case t from Neighbours

```
dimension estQneighbour[numA]; totWeight[numA];
ret = -100;
for(int n=0; n<numNeighbours(t); n++){
    tn = cases[neigbour(n)];
    dist = sharpness*distance(tn.s, s');
    weight = exp(-dist*dist);
    totWeight[tn.a] += weight;
    estQneighbour[tn.a] += weight*tn.Qvalue;
}
for(int nA=0;nA<numA;nA++) {
    if(totWeight[nA]<=0f)
        if(measuring) estQneighbour[nA] = -100; //act greedily
        else estQneighbour[nA] = 0f; //encourage exploration
    else estQneighbour[nA] /= totWeight[nA];
    if(estQneighbour[nA]>ret) ret = estQneighbour[nA];
}
return ret;
```

we could generate experience cases to cover the whole state-action space so that the learner would not require any training, effectively dynamic programming the optimal policy using the Q-Learner. In other situations, a qualitative description or an approximate model may be available that could be used to generate cases a priori to speed up learning.

It is also possible to generate additional cases from background knowledge during the learning process. For example when we know the system dynamics exhibits symmetry we could mirror experiences speeding up learning. In the following results we will show two other examples of the use of background knowledge to insert cases while learning. In one case we model common sense knowledge that physics is invariant to the inertial frame of reference, and in the other we over-generalise local experiences.

When we use background knowledge to insert approximate cases we label them as *provisional* and allow cases from real experience to progressively replace them. The objective is to quickly learn a satisficing [11] policy and improve it over time.

4   Results

In this section we show experiments with the cart that illustrate how background knowledge can be used to speed up learning.

We start the cart at a random position and velocity with the goal of coming to rest at the origin. We accept any position and velocity satisfying $|position| < 1$ meter and $|velocity| < 1$ meter/second as having reached the goal. For practical purposes we limit the position and velocity space to lie in a region ± 20 meters and ±20 meters/second and terminate a trial if the cart moves outside these limits, takes more than 50 time-steps to reach the goal, or reaches the goal. We administer a reward of −1 per time-step, implicitly setting the objective to reach the goal in minimum time. The minimum resolution for cases for both position and velocity is set at 0.9. The RL is initialised with optimistic Q values to encourage exploration. We periodically measure the performance of the controller by starting the cart at rest at position -15 meters as show in Figure 1. During this time we use the latest optimum greedy policy. Learning is turned off during performance measurement so that the results are not influenced by this observation process.

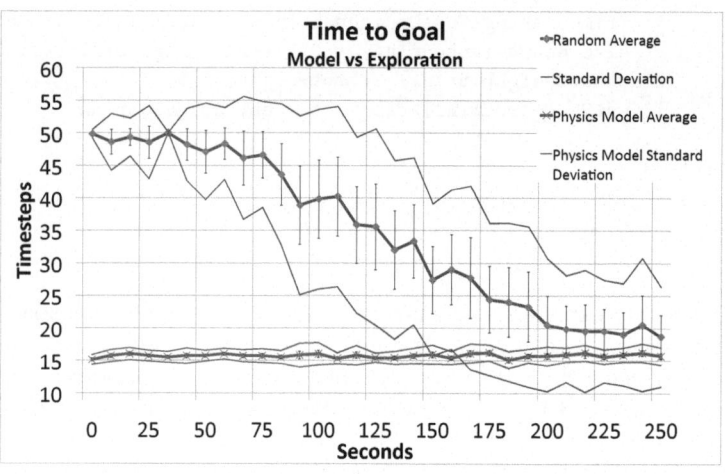

Fig. 4. The number of time-steps to reach the goal given the time in seconds of real-time training. The blue graph shows the results when learning without any extra background knowledge by taking random exploration actions. The red graph shows the results when the learner is given the physics model in the form of sample transitions that cover the state-action space and provides a benchmark of the best performance achievable with this controller i.e. 15.7 ± 1.1. The experiments are each run between 10 and 20 times and the graphs show the standard deviation and the standard error.

The first two experiments were designed to set upper and lower bounds on the RL's performance. We plot the number of time-steps to reach the goal vs the number of seconds of real-time training. In the first experiment the learner was given no additional background knowledge and required to explore and learn an optimum policy just from interaction with the simulated real-time system. As shown in Figure 4 (blue plots) the RL took over 4 minutes on average to learn a good policy. At the other extreme, if the learner was supplied with the exact physical model of the cart by seeding the RL with sample transitions prior to learning similar to that show in Figure 2, the RL was able to learn and execute an optimal policy without any real-time training (Figure 4, red plots).

The standard deviation in performance is much greater when learning in real-time due to the hit and miss nature of the random exploration actions taken by the RL. The error bars indicate that after about 4 minutes our confidence even at 68% cannot separate the two experiments[1].

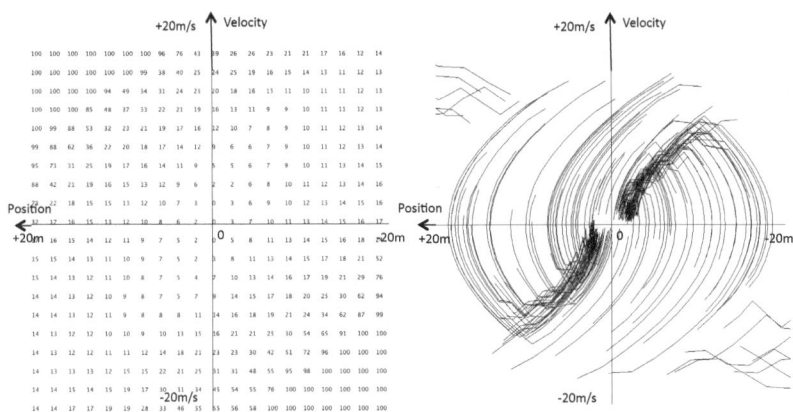

Fig. 5. RIGHT - $max|Q|$ values sampled uniformly over the state-space, LEFT - typical trajectories from random starting positions

Figure 5 gives some further insight to the working of the RL. The left of the Figure shows the maximum $|Q|$ values sampled over the relevant state-space. As the goal becomes unreachable from certain parts of the state space values start to approach the undesirable termination value set to 100. The right shows the trajectories after learning when the cart is started at random locations. The trajectory to reach the goal area is not a simple straight line in the position-velocity space, but usually requires a carefully timed 2-phased strategy involving acceleration and deceleration.

In the next experiment we include the qualitative background knowledge that the physics of the cart is invariant to position. Since the table is uniformly level, the effect of an action on velocity is the same for any position, and the cart's change in position is also be expected to be the same for any position.

To make use of this background knowledge, whenever we experience a transition at one position and velocity, we duplicate the experience and seed this transition for all positions for the same velocity. Figure 6, left shows the RL seeded with duplicated position invariant transition cases from just a few

---

[1] Both the standard deviation and the standard error were calculated assuming Gaussian distributed data. The termination of trials after 50 time-steps and the lower bound of the theoretical optimum policy means that the Gaussian assumption does not hold and the interpretation of the plot of these measures needs to take this into account.

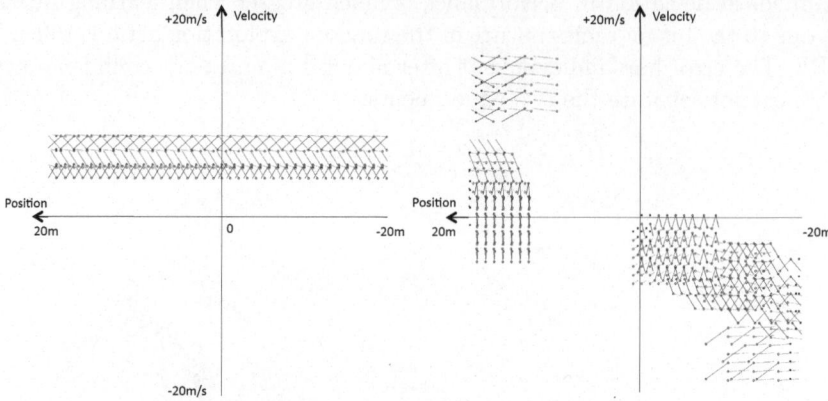

Fig. 6. RIGHT - The transition cases duplicated from background knowledge that physics is position invariant, and LEFT - Transitions seeded by overgeneralising from limited real experience

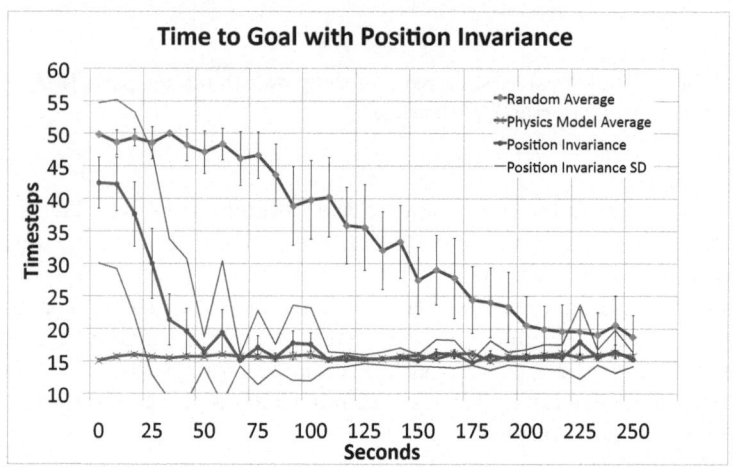

Fig. 7. The green graphs show the improvement in learning with the addition of the common-sense background knowledge, namely that the physics of the cart is the same at all positions on the table. Graphs from Figure 4 are retained for comparison.

real-time experiences. The improvement in learning is shown as the green plot in Figure 7. It is apparent that the inclusion of this background information has had a significant effect on learning time which is now reduced to less than a minute.

Position invariance may not always be appropriate background knowledge. It will not apply for example to the mountain car test-bed [12] where the surface is hilly. We tested a weaker form of background knowledge that would apply in many continuous dynamic systems. We assume that experienced transitions are a good approximation in a larger neighbourhood and seed the RL accordingly. While this approximation may not produce an optimal solution, it does nevertheless find a solution quickly that can later be refined when more real experiences come to hand.

Figure 6 (right) shows this generalisation applied to several cases in a rectangular neighbourhood around a real-experience. In this way the state-action space can be quickly filled with approximate transitions to allow the learner to find a path to the goal. Figure 8 (black plots) charts the performance of this overgeneralisation approach. Other experiments are retained on the graph to show the relative performance. Overgeneralisation for the cart results in a two-fold speed-up, learning an optimal policy in about 2 minutes, and even after one minute of training, the RL has made good progress.

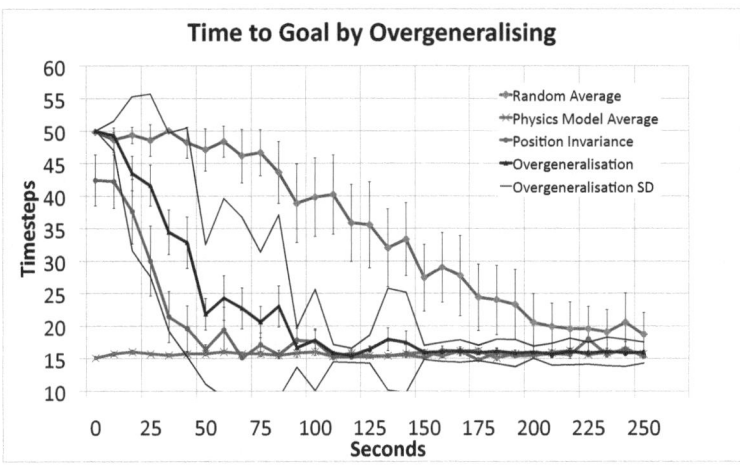

Fig. 8. The performance of the RL by over-generalising experience in a local neighbourhood. This weak type of background knowledge shows a significant speedup. The approximation is progressively improved with additional real experience over time.

5   Discussion

An advantage of learning the model of the system rather than just the value function is that the model can be reused to achieve alternate goals. For the cart, not only do we have a policy to bring the cart to rest from any position and velocity, but we can now set any (*position, velocity*) as a goal and the RL can use the stored experience to learn a new policy with minimal on-line learning.

While the implementation has been developed for a general multi-dimensional continuous system we have only tested the RL algorithm on the cart problem. We would next wish to test it on standard problems such as the 2-dimensional mountain-car and the 4-dimensional pole and cart. The latter provides an opportunity to add background knowledge in the form of the symmetry of the inverted pendulum. These problems are not expected to exhibit any surprises. The issue that will need attention is scaling the implementation to larger and higher dimensional spaces. For the current implementation neighbouring cases are precomputed and store as part of each case to make Q-Learning more efficient. For query points during execution we could use a kd-tree and for higher dimensions an approximate nearest neighbour algorithm. There are also several parameters that need setting, such as the minimum resolution and spread, that are problem dependent.

One application that we propose to tackle is bipedal walking that was previously reported using just a naive discretisation for function approximation and model-free learning [13]. In conclusion, we have outlined a variable-resolution model-based approach to tackle RL for continuous systems and have shown how to include various forms of background knowledge to help speed up learning.

References

1. Russell, S., Norvig, P.: Artificial Intelligence: A Modern Approach. Prentice Hall, Upper Saddle River (1995)
2. Mitchell, T.M.: Machine Learning. McGraw-Hill, Singapore (1997)
3. Puterman, M.L.: Markov Decision Processes: Discrete Stochastic Dynamic Programming. In: John Whiley & Sons, John Whiley & Sons, Inc., New York (1994)
4. Sutton, R.S., Barto, A.G.: Reinforcement Learning: An Introduction. MIT Press, Cambridge (1998)
5. Wiering, M., van Otterlo, M. (eds.): Reinforcement Learning: State of the Art. Adaptation, Learning, and Optimization, vol. 12. Springer (2012)
6. Santamaria, J.C., Sutton, R.S., Ram, A.: Experiments with reinforcement learning in problems with continuous state and action spaces. Adaptive Behavior 6(2) (1998)
7. Gabel, T., Riedmiller, M.: CBR for State Value Function Approximation in Reinforcement Learning. In: Muñoz-Ávila, H., Ricci, F. (eds.) ICCBR 2005. LNCS (LNAI), vol. 3620, pp. 206–221. Springer, Heidelberg (2005)
8. Jong, N.K., Stone, P.: Compositional Models for Reinforcement Learning. In: Buntine, W., Grobelnik, M., Mladenić, D., Shawe-Taylor, J. (eds.) ECML PKDD 2009, Part I. LNCS, vol. 5781, pp. 644–659. Springer, Heidelberg (2009)
9. Kuipers, B.: Qualitative simulation. Artificial Intelligence 29, 289–338 (1986)
10. jMonkeyEngine 3D Game Development SDK (2012), http://jmonkeyengine.org/
11. Simon, H.A.: Rational choice and the structure of the environment. Psychological Review 63(2), 129–138 (1956)
12. Moore, A.W.: Efficient memory-based learning for robot control. Technical Report UCAM-CL-TR-209, University of Cambridge, Computer Laboratory (November 1990)
13. Hengst, B., Lange, M., White, B.: Learning ankle-tilt and foot-placement control for flat-footed bipedal balancing and walking. In: 11th IEEE-RAS International Conference on Humanoid Robots (2011)

A Novel D-S Theory Based AHP Decision Apparatus under Subjective Factor Disturbances

Wenjun Ma, Xudong Luo*, and Wei Xiong

Institute of Logic and Cognition, Sun Yat-sen University, Guangzhou, 510275, China

Abstract. In real life, sometimes Multi-Criteria Decision Making (MCDM) problems are dealt with inevitably under the disturbance of subjective factors such as intuition, feeling and emotion. However, the existing work cannot handle the issue well. As a result, it is difficult for them to predict and give some decision support for MCDM problem of this kind. Thus, to address the issue, this paper constructs a novel Analytic Hierarchy Process (AHP) approach based on Dempster-Shafer (D-S) theory. More specifically, our model can: (i) handle the subjective factor disturbances by distinguish complete (there not exists any hidden subjective factors impact the decision) and incomplete (the converse of complete) criteria; (ii) differentiate incomplete and complete relative ranking of the groups of decision alternatives over a criterion; and (iii) handle the ambiguous criteria evaluations of the groups of decision alternatives. Moreover, we give two methods to reduce the subjective factor disturbances. Finally, we illustrated our approach with a real-life problem.

1 Introduction

In real-life, often a decision is influenced by different hidden subjective factors, such as intuition, feeling, emotion of the decision maker. For example, an investor wants to pick up a house from three options that an agency introduces to him. When he enters a house, if he feels very uncomfortable suddenly, although the agency tells him how nice this house is at the reasonable price, the investor may still hesitate to make a deal. Another example is that a man wants to buy a second-hand car. Although the car dealer offers a good price and shows many excellent aspects of his car, if the man feels that the dealer cannot be trusted, he would not buy. Apparently, in both two Multi-Criteria Decision Making (MCDM) problems, the final choice of the decision makers has been affected by their feelings or intuition. Therefore, subjective factor disturbances actually plays a vital role in real-life MCDMs [7]. Especially, when we need predict what will happen if subjective factors will indeed work, the factors have to be reflected in the decision model that is used to predict this case.

Actually, decision making problems with the effects of subjective factors have been an active area of research that obtain more and more attentions from researchers [1]. Some focus on eliciting the influence of subjective factors for the

---

* Corresponding author.

M. Thielscher and D. Zhang (Eds.): AI 2012, LNCS 7691, pp. 863–877, 2012.

decision making by psychological investigations [10,4,21] and experiments in behavioral economics [8,17,6]. All of these researches show that subjective factors
such as emotions and intuition are, in manifold ways, involved in process of decision making. However, all of these researches do not give a formal treatment
to this kind of decision problems, which is the main contribution of our model
proposed in this paper. Another line of research incorporating subjective factor
disturbances into models of decision making can be seen in the development of
prospect theory [9], regret theory [13], dual-process models [18], smooth ambiguity model [11], and so on. However, all of these models focus on the decision
making in single criterion, which means that they do not account the effect of
subjective factors as the criteria weights in MCDM problems. Moreover, because
of the subjective factor disturbances, it is difficult even impossible to elicit accurate evaluations for each decision alternative regarding each criterion in MCDM
problem [12]. As a result, to handle hidden subjective factors in MCDM problem
has to base on some uncertainties theory in MCDM. There are some important
methods have been developed to deal with uncertainty in MCDM problems. For
example, fuzzy sets approach [25] is used to model and solve fuzzy MCDM problems [16,22]. Beynon et al. [3] extend the AHP model to a DS/AHP method that
introduce the basic concepts of D-S theory based AHP model to deal with the
incomplete pairwise compare and the range of levels of uncertainty in MCDM
problem. Nevertheless, all of these models do not consider the effects of subjective factors for the finally decision. Also, these MCDM approaches are essentially
based on traditional evaluation methods, which cannot well handle uncertainty
of different kinds of ambiguity, such as missing, imprecise, and uncertain evaluations of multi-criteria.

In order to address these issues, we propose model extend Analytic Hierarchy Process (AHP), which is one of the most well-known MCDM techniques.
Also our extension is based on D-S theory, which is one primary theory to handle the ambiguity information. So, this paper actually proposes a novel method
that incorporates AHP method and D-S theory to handle MCDM problems under subjective factor disturbances. First, as the subjective factor disturbances
will impact the choices of a decision maker and change the criteria weights in
the given MCDM problems, we identify two situations of criteria by considering whether or not there exists subjective factor disturbances. Therefore, we
construct two comparison rules. (i) When the importance ordering of all criteria have been revealed (i.e., when subjective factor disturbances do not exist),
the decision maker will apply the complete relative ranking rule. (ii) When the
importance ordering of all criteria are incomplete (i.e., when subjective factor
disturbances do exist), the decision maker will apply incomplete relative ranking rule. Then, our new model employs the rules to set the preference degree of
decision alternatives. After combining the criteria weights and preference degree
of decision alternatives, our method can find the optimal decision alternatives.

Actually, compared with the DS/AHP method that is also based on the D-S
theory, our model can solve some problems of it while maintaining its advantage.
(i) The DS/AHP method cannot explain why the criterion weights established

by a pairwise comparison matrix is still constructed as in AHP, but not by identifying a especial group of focal elements (set of single element sets) as favorable from the frame of discernment (of all criteria), but our model can apply the same rules to set the criteria weight and the relative ranking of groups of decision alternatives against the each criterion. (ii) The DS/AHP method does not offer an approach to obtain the optimal decision alternative based on the final mass function of each decision alternative, but our model does. Moreover, we extend the DS/AHP method to deal with subjective factor disturbances and ambiguity information.

This paper advances the state of art in the field of MCDM in the following aspects. (i) Our model can deal with the influence of subjective factors of the decision maker, and discerning two types of the criteria: revealed and hidden ones. (ii) While remaining the advantages of the DS/AHP model, our model can handle the complete and incomplete relative ranking of all choices over a criterion. (iii) Our model can incorporate the ambiguity aversion principle of minimax regret [14,15,23,24] to handle three types ambiguity evaluations that are mentioned in [14,15]. And (iv) according to our model, we give two methods to reduce the influence of subjective factor disturbances to make decision more rationally.

The rest of this paper is organised as follows. Section 2 recaps D-S theory and the decision rule under ambiguity. Section 3 models the subjective factor disturbances. Section 4 discerns the relative ranking of groups of decision alternatives on each criterion and discusses how to combine the criteria's weights and the decision alternatives' relative ranking. Section 5 shows some properties of our method. Section 6 illustrates our model by a real-life problem. Finally, Section 7 conclude the paper with future work.

2 Preliminaries

This section recaps D-S theory [19] and the decision rule under ambiguity [14,15,23,24].

2.1 Basics of D-S Theory

Definition 1. *Let an exhaustive set of mutually disjoint atomic Θ be a frame of discernment.*

(i) *Function $m : 2^{\Theta} \to [0,1]$ is called a basic probability assignment or a mass function if $m(\phi) = 0$ and $\sum_{A \subseteq \Theta} m(A) = 1$.*

(ii) *Function $Bel : 2^{\Theta} \to [0,1]$, defined as follows, is a belief function over Θ:*

$$Bel(A) = \sum_{B \subseteq A} m(B). \tag{1}$$

If $m(B) > 0$, then B is said to be a focal element of Bel.

(iii) Function $Pl : 2^\Theta \to [0,1]$, defined as follows, is called a plausibility function over Θ:

$$Pl(A) = \sum_{B \cap A \neq \phi} m(B). \tag{2}$$

Moreover, D-S theory also provides a rule to combine different mass functions:

Definition 2 (Dempster combination rule). *Let m_1 and m_2 be two basic probability assignment over the discernment frame Θ. Then function $m_{12} = m_1 \oplus m_2$ is given by:*

$$m_{12}(\{x\}) = \begin{cases} 0 & \text{if } x = \emptyset \\ \dfrac{\sum\limits_{A_i \cap B_j = x} m_1(A)m_2(B)}{1 - \sum\limits_{A_i \cap B_j = \emptyset} m_1(A)m_2(B)} & \text{if } x \neq \emptyset \end{cases} \tag{3}$$

The following is the concept of a mass function's ambiguity degree, which is a normalised version of the generalised Hartley measure for nonspecificity [5].

Definition 3. *Let m be a mass function over discernment frame Θ, and $|A|$ be the cardinality of set A. Then the ambiguity degree of mass function m, denoted as δ, is given by*

$$\delta = \frac{\sum\limits_{A \subseteq \Theta} m(A) \log_2 |A|}{\log_2 |\Theta|}. \tag{4}$$

The point-valued expected utility can be extended to the interval one [20]:

Definition 4. *For choice a specified by mass function m over Θ, its expected utility interval is $EUI(a) = [\underline{E}(a), \overline{E}(a)]$, where*

$$\underline{E}(a) = \sum_{A \subseteq \Theta} \min(A)m(A), \tag{5}$$

$$\overline{E}(a) = \sum_{A \subseteq \Theta} \max(A)m(A). \tag{6}$$

In the above definition, if each $A \subseteq \Theta$ has only one element, $m(A)$ degenerates to probability and formulas (5) and (6) degenerate to the point-valued expected utility. In other words, the interval-valued expected utility is caused by $m(A) > 0$ where $|A| > 2$ (i.e., ambiguity).

2.2   Ambiguity Aversion Principle of Minimax Regret

In [14,15,23,24], we propose the following decision rule:

Definition 5 (The ambiguity aversion principle of minimax regret). *Let m be an initial mass function over a set of utilities $\Theta = \{x_1, ..., x_n\}$, $EUI(x) = [\underline{E}(x), \overline{E}(x)]$ be the expected utility interval of choice x and $\delta(b)$ be the ambiguity* *degree of choice b. Then the ambiguity-avoiding maximum regret of the choice a against choice b is defined as*

$$\Re_a^b = \varepsilon(b) - \underline{E}(a), \tag{7}$$

where $\varepsilon(b) = \underline{E}(b) + (1 - \delta(b))(\overline{E}(b) - \underline{E}(b))$, called the ambiguity-avoided upper expected utility of choice b. For any two choices a and b, the strict preference ordering $\succ$ is defined as follow:

$$a \succ b \Leftrightarrow \Re_a^b < \Re_b^a. \tag{8}$$

In [23], we prove that the binary relation $\succ$ defined in the above is a preference relation (asymmetric, acyclic and transitive) and so with the binary relation $\sim$ ($x \sim y$ if $x \not\succ y$ and $y \not\succ x$), we can compare any choices properly.

Also, in [14,15], we give a point-valued preference degree over a group of identified decision alternatives with the expected utility interval, which can induce a preference ordering equivalent to that in Definition 5. That is the following definition:

Definition 6. *Let $EUI(A, c) = [\underline{E}(A, c), \overline{E}(A, c)]$ be an interval-valued expected utility of the group of decision alternatives A against criterion c, and $\delta(A, c)$ be the ambiguous degree of $EUI(A, c)$, then the preference degree of A is given by*

$$\rho_c(A) = \frac{2\underline{E}(A, c) + (1 - \delta(A, c))(\overline{E}(A, c) - \underline{E}(A, c))}{2}. \tag{9}$$

Also, in [14,15], we present the following method to obtain the optimal decision alternative by the idea similar to that of the ambiguous aversion principle of minimax regret.

Definition 7. *Let $m(\{a_i\})$ is a mass function over $\Theta = \{a_1, a_2, \ldots, a_n\}$, where each a_i is a decision alternative , which induces belief function $Bel(\{a_i\})$ and plausibility function $Pl(\{a_i\})$, then the degree of preference of a_1 over a_2, denoted by $P_{a_2}^{a_1} \in [0, 1]$, is given by:*

$$P_{a_2}^{a_1} = (Bel(\{a_1\}) + \mu(\{a_1\})) - (Bel(\{a_2\}) + \mu(\{a_2\})), \tag{10}$$

where $\mu(\{a_i\}) = (1 - \delta_U(a_i))(Pl(\{a_i\}) - Bel(\{a_i\}))$ $(i = 1, 2)$ and $\delta_U(a_i) = \frac{\sum_{\{a_i\} \cap B \neq \emptyset} m(B) \log_2 |B|}{\log_2 |\Theta|}$.

Thus, the preference relation between two decision alternatives can be defined as follows:

Definition 8. *The preference relation between two decision alternatives a and b is defined as follows: (i) $a \succ b$ if $P_b^a > 0$; (ii) $a \prec b$ if $P_b^a < 0$; and (iii) $a \sim b$ if $P_b^a = 0$.*

The binary relation in Definition 8 is proved indeed a preference ordering [14,15].

3   To Model Subjective Factor Disturbances

This section will handle the issue of subjective factor disturbances in MCDM, which has two characteristics. (i) The subjective factors will change the criteria weights in a given problem. For example, although the apples quality is high and the price is reasonable, which should be the main concerns of a buyer, the buyer might still not buy if he feels that the salesman cannot be trusted. In this case, apparently the intuition of the decision maker weakens the importance of the revealed criteria (i.e., quality and price) in the final decision. (ii) The decision maker cannot tell how important the subjective factors are in affecting his decision. To reflect these two characteristics, we take the subjective factors as a hidden criterion, denoted as T with an imprecise value of weight. Therefore, we can distinguish two situations for criteria: (i) complete criteria, i.e., the decision maker is sure that he has considered all relevant criteria; and (ii) incomplete criteria. i.e., there is a hidden criterion T, which is caused by some subjective factors that might disturb his decision. Formally, we have:

Definition 9. *Let discernment frame $\Theta \subseteq \{c_1, \ldots, c_n\}$, which is the set of all the criteria of an MCDM problem. Then the criteria are said to be complete if $\Theta = \{c_1, \ldots, c_n\}$, while the criteria are said to be incomplete if $\Theta \supset \{c_1, \ldots, c_n\}$.*

In the situation of incomplete criteria, as the decision maker is uncertain about the weight of the hidden criterion T, the decision maker has no evidence about the weight of it. According to D-S theory, a belief degree should be assigned to the whole discernment frame. On the other hand, the complete criteria mean that the decision maker has the evidence to support the relative ranking of all criteria. So, we need not to assign any belief degree to the discernment frame to express the ignorance of the decision maker.

From the previous discussion, we can distinguish complete and incomplete criteria. First, in the case of incomplete criteria, when the relative ranking of some criteria weights are hidden, the decision maker adopts a frame of discernment to express his ignorance for the final relative ranking. These groups of decision alternatives and the discernment frame constitute a specific matrix. Through comparing a group of decision alternative with discernment frame Θ, the decision maker can express his preference ordering of the given criteria. So, our method satisfies the following theorem and corollary of [2]:

Theorem 1. *For $(d+1)$ by $(d+1)$ matrix*

$$A_{d+1} = \begin{pmatrix} 1 & 0 & \cdots & 0 & a_1 \\ 0 & 1 & \ddots & \vdots & a_2 \\ \vdots & \ddots & \ddots & 0 & \vdots \\ 0 & \cdots & 0 & 1 & a_d \\ 1/a_1 & 1/a_2 & \cdots & 1/a_d & 1 \end{pmatrix}, \quad d = 1, 2, \ldots, \tag{11}$$

where $a_1, \ldots, a_d$ are positive real values, the largest eigenvalue defined λ_{d+1}^L associated with matrix A_{d+1} is $\lambda_{d+1}^L = 1 + \sqrt{d}$.

Corollary 1 (Incomplete Relative Ranking Rule (IRRR)). *For $(d+1)$ by $(d+1)$ matrix A_{d+1} given in Theorem 1, the normalised values within the eigenvector defined by $(x_1, \ldots, x_{d+1})$ associated with the largest eigenvalue of the matrix A_{d+1} are as follow:*

$$x_j = \frac{a_j}{\sum_{i=1}^{d} a_i + \sqrt{d}}, \tag{12}$$

$$x_{d+1} = \frac{\sqrt{d}}{\sum_{i=1}^{d} a_i + \sqrt{d}}, \quad (j = 1, 2, \ldots, d). \tag{13}$$

In this situation, based on the belief interval obtained by Corollary 1, by the similar idea of Definitions 6 and 7, we can obtain the point-value weight for each criterion under the condition of hidden criteria disturbance:

$$\omega_i = m(i) + \frac{(1 - m(\Theta))(m(\Theta))}{2d}, \tag{14}$$

$$\omega_T = 1 - \sum_{i=1}^{d} \omega_i = \frac{m(\Theta)(1 + m(\Theta))}{2}. \tag{15}$$

Now we turn to the situation of complete criteria. In this situation, as the decision maker actually has sufficient evidence for ranking all given criteria, he can rank the criteria without hesitation. As a result, he needs not to use the discernment frame to express his ignorance. Using the idea behind DS/AHP, we can introduce a new measurement: in the complete criteria, any relative ranking made on given criteria is compared with empty set $\emptyset$, which means no elements can be chosen by the decision maker, he must accept even turn out to be worst or least important criterion. In this aspect, we consider that empty set $\emptyset$ reflects the least important criterion. As the DS/AHP method [3] constructed, by Theorem 1, Corollary 1, and Definition 1, we can obtain:

Corollary 2 (Complete Relative Ranking Rule (CRRR)). *For the complete criteria, let s_i be one of d focal elements of a criterion with scale values a_i, then the normalised value for the relative ranking value of the decision alternatives over the criterion is:*

$$m(s_i) = \frac{a_i}{\sum_{j=1}^{d} a_j}, \quad (i = 1, 2, \ldots, d). \tag{16}$$

Proof. By Definition 1, we have $m(\emptyset) = 0$ and $\sum_{A \subseteq \Theta} m(A) = 1$. And thus we have:

$$m(s_i) = \frac{\frac{a_i}{\sum_{j=1}^{d} a_j + \sqrt{d}}}{\sum_{A \subseteq \Theta} m(A)} = \frac{\frac{a_i}{\sum_{j=1}^{d} a_j + \sqrt{d}}}{1 - \frac{\sqrt{d}}{\sum_{j=1}^{d} a_j + \sqrt{d}}} = \frac{a_i}{\sum_{j=1}^{d} a_j}, \quad i = 1, 2, \ldots, d. \quad \square$$

It is straightforward that the weight of each criterion is the percentage of its importance value from the total importance value of all revealed criteria.

4   Discern the Relative Ranking Value on an Individual Criterion

Similar to Definition 9, we can also distinguish two situations for the relative ranking of the groups of decision alternatives with respect to a given criterion:

Definition 10. *Let $\Theta = \{a_1, \ldots, a_n\}$ be the discernment frame of all decision alternatives, and $A_1, \ldots, A_m$ ($A_i \cap A_j = \emptyset$ if $i \neq j$) be the groups of decision alternatives with respect to a given criterion that we can assign a preference scale value. Then the relative ranking of the groups of decision alternatives over a criterion is said to be complete if $A_1 \cup \ldots \cup A_m = \Theta$; and it is said to be incomplete if $A_1 \cup \ldots \cup A_m \subset \Theta$.*

Actually, we can also use the CRRR and IRRR rules to solve these two cases. When the relative ranking of the decision alternatives against a criterion is incomplete, then the relative ranking of some decision alternatives against the given criterion is completely ignorant. As a result, a belief degree should be assigned to the discernment frame. On the other hand, the relative ranking of the decision alternatives regarding a criterion is complete, which means that the decision maker has the evidence to support the relative ranking of all decision alternatives over the criterion. As a result, we need not to assign any support belief degree to the discernment frame to express the ignorance of the decision maker.

Formally, by CRRR and IRRR, the relative ranking value of the decision maker regarding a criterion can be counted by formulas (17) and (18). Notice here without loss of generality, this paper uses $1 - 6$ for discriminating levels of favourability, meaning *equal, strong, very strong, really strong, extremely strong,* and *absolutely strong,* respectively.

When the relative ranking is complete, it is

$$v(a_i) = m(s_i), \tag{17}$$

where $m(s_i)$ is given by formula (16). When the relative ranking is incomplete, it is

$$v_t(s_i) = x_j, \ v(\Theta) = x_{d+1}, \tag{18}$$

where x_j and x_{d+1} is given by formulas (12) and (13). As a result, our model can solve the complete evaluation ignorance problem by introducing two methods of pairwise comparison.

After obtaining the criteria weights and the relative ranking value of the decision alternative of each criterion, the next step is to combine these two values and apply Dempster combination rule (i.e., formula (3)) to obtain the overall mass function for each decision alternative. In the DS/AHP method, Beynon [3] suggests that the weight of each criterion is incorporated into their respective knowledge matrix. So, the preference scale value of each decision alternative is multiplied by the respective weight of the given criterion.

However, if we adopt the DS/AHP method in the case that the relative ranking of the groups of decision alternatives is complete, the relative ranking value of the groups of decision alternatives regarding a given criterion will not change no matter which weight we assign to the criterion. For this reason, we propose a new method to combine criteria weights and the relative ranking value of groups of decision alternative. Formally, we can set the mass function for the focal elements of each criterion as follows:

$$m(x) = \omega_i v(x), \; m(\Theta) = 1 - \omega_i + v(\Theta)\omega_i, \tag{19}$$

where $v(x)$ and $v(\Theta)$ is the relative ranking value of groups of decision alternatives against criterion i, Θ is the frame of discernment of all decision alternatives, and ω_i is the weight of criterion i. This method means that because of the influence of the weight for a given criterion, the result (the relative ranking value) obtained by the criterion is on the level of ω available for the final ranking. The other level of $(1 - \omega)$ is unknown because we do not have evidence about the relative ranking of the decision alternatives regarding other criteria if we just consider the preference scales of the criterion.

Finally, the decision maker can obtain the mass function of each criterion by formula (19) and then use Dempster combination rule (i.e., formula (3)) to aggregate the overall mass function. After that, the decision maker can apply Definition 8 to set the preference ordering over the belief intervals and finally set the optimal option.

Moreover, in [14,15], we have pointed out that there are five types of evaluation over the groups of decision alternatives regarding each criterion, i.e., point-valued, risk lottery, missing, interval-value, and ambiguous lottery ones. Actually, in our ambiguity aversion AHP method, when the preference degree is point-valued, we can apply the complete relative ranking rule (CRRR) and incomplete relative ranking rule (IRRR) to obtain the relative rank value (the mass function for each criterion). As a result, we can apply formulas (5) and (6) and Definition 6 to obtain point-valued preference degree for these five types of evaluation, and then handle the ambiguity information directly.

5   How to Reduce the Disturbance

In real-life, sometimes it is necessary to reduce the effects of subjective factor disturbances in decision making. For example, in business, although a manager hates some suppliers, he should put the interest of the company in the first place and consider the deals more rationally or less emotionally. So, we need consider how to reduce the effect of subjective factor disturbances according to our model. This section will discuss this issue. First, we will give a formal definition for the effect of this kind before showing the properties.

Definition 11. *For a MCDM problem with subjective factor disturbances with the relative ranking of already known criterion is a_i, suppose the overall mass function of each group of decision alternatives is $m_1(X_t)$ in the condition of complete criteria, and the the overall mass function of each group of decision alternatives $m_2(X_t)$ in the condition of incomplete criteria then the effect of subjective factors T is*

$$f_t = \sum_{j=1}^{2^\Theta} (m_1(X_j) - m_2(X_j))^2. \qquad (20)$$

This definition means that the effect of subjective factor disturbances are determined by the sum of difference of two sets of overall mass function about each group of decision alternatives, one of which consider the subjective factor disturbances and another is not. There are two reasons for this definition: (i) The effect of subjective factor disturbances is based on its impact for the final decision choice. For example, the feeling of uncomfortable for a house might change the final choice of decision maker. (ii) By Definitions 7 and 8, we can find that the preference ordering of the decision alternatives is determined by the value of $Bel(\{a_i\}) + \mu(\{a_i\})$. Moreover, because the ambiguity degree of the belief interval and $Bel(\{a_i\}) + \mu(\{a_i\})$ can be obtained by the overall mass function, we can just consider the change of overall mass function that considered the subjective factor disturbance or not to know the effect of subjective factors disturbances.

Now, we present a lemma as follows:

Lemma 1. *Suppose the mass function of the criteria's relative ranking is $m(i) = s$, $m(\Theta) = t$, where Θ is the discernment frame of each revealed criterion i and hidden criterion T. Then the higher the value of t, the higher the value of ω_T, vice versa.*

Proof. In this case, by formula (15), we can obtain the point-valued weight of each criterion:

$$\omega_i = s + \frac{(1-t)(t)}{2d}, \quad \omega_T = \frac{(1+t)(t)}{2}.$$

Since $0 \le t \le 1$, the higher the value of t, the higher the value of ω_T, *vice versa.* $\square$

Moreover, because the higher value of criteria weight of ω_T, the more effects the subjective factor disturbances will cause for the final decision, then by Lemma 1, we can derive:

Theorem 2. *The larger scale value (favourable degree) the decision maker uses as the basic for discriminating level of favourability, the less effects subjective factor disturbances will cause for the final decision, ceteris paribus.*

Proof. By formulas (15) and IPOR (Corollary 2), we have $\omega = 1 - \sum_{j=1}^{d} \omega_i = \frac{t(t+1)}{2}$, $t = \frac{\sqrt{d}}{\sum_{j=1}^{d} a_j + \sqrt{d}}$, where $t = m(\Theta)$. As a results, we can easily find that when the number of the revealed criteria does not change, and the decision maker uses the larger scale value (favourable degree) for the basic for discriminating level of favourability, which means that the value of $\sum_{j=1}^{d} a_j$ is higher, we find that the new weight of hidden criteria T: ω'_T is less than the old one. By Lemma 1, we can obtain the theorem directly. $\square$

This theorem means that to reduce the influence of subjective factor disturbances in an MCDM problem, the decision maker has to use large enough unit-scale to discriminate level of favourability on the criterion. This is consistent with our intuition that the more important (facourability level) the decision maker thinks the revealed criteria are, the more confident for him to insist on his choice. For example, the buyer might easily change his mind for buying some daily necessities, but in financial industry, it is hard for a CEO to change his mind, for example, when considering the feasibility of an equity financing project.

Theorem 3. *When the total preference degree of revealed criteria satisfies* $\sum_{j=1}^{d} a_j < 2d + 1$, *where d is the number of revealed criteria, the more criteria in consideration, and the less effects subjective factor disturbances cause upon the final decision, ceteris paribus.*

Proof. Let the number of the revealed criteria in an MCDM problem be d, T be the hidden criterion with weight ω_T. Now we add a new criterion that favourable degree compared with Θ is r (≥ 1). In order to prove that subjective factor disturbances will cause less affects for final decision, by Lemma 1 and Corollary 2, we have (noticing $\sum_{j=1}^{d} a_j = k$):

$$\frac{\sqrt{d}}{k + \sqrt{d}} > \frac{\sqrt{d+1}}{\sum_{j=1}^{d+1} a_j + \sqrt{d+1}} \Leftarrow \sqrt{d}(k + 1 + \sqrt{d+1}) > \sqrt{d+1}(k + \sqrt{d}) \text{ (when } r \geq 1)$$

$$\Leftrightarrow (\sqrt{d}k + \sqrt{d})^2 > (\sqrt{d+1}k)^2$$
$$\Leftarrow 2d + 1 > k > 0 \qquad \square$$

By Theorems 2 and 3, we find that according to our model, there are two ways for reducing the effects of subjective factor disturbances: (i) to make a larger scale value to capture the importance degree of the revealed criteria; and (ii) when the scale value is small enough ($\sum_{j=1}^{d} a_j < 2d + 1$), to consider more relevant criteria to make decision. This result satisfies our intuition well: the decision maker will be not hesitated for subjective factors when making the decision if he has firmness of will or considers the problem very rationally.

6   The Problem of House Investment

This section illustrates our model by a real life house investment problem, which decision tree is shown in Fig. 1. Suppose a decision maker wants to buy a house for investment. There are four different alternatives A, B, C, and D and two criteria. Moreover, when he comes to house A, suppose he feels very uncomfortable suddenly.

To set the preference ordering for the decision alternatives over all the criteria, by the ambiguity aversion AHP method, first we use a 6-unit scale to discriminate the preference degrees of the decision alternatives and obtain the favourable matrix for criteria *price*, *quality* and *hidden* (see Table 1). From Fig. 1, we can see that for criterion *price*, three groups of decision alternatives have been identified and the union of these set of decision alternatives is the same as the discernment

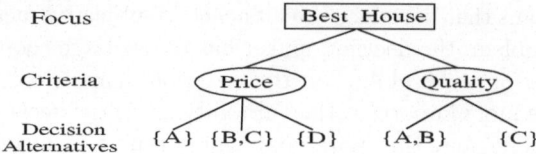

Fig. 1. Decision tree for the example of house investment

Table 1. Initial favourable matrix for price and quality criterion

Price	$\{A\}$	$\{B, C\}$	$\{D\}$	$\emptyset$	Quality	$\{A, B\}$	$\{C\}$	Θ	T	$\{A\}$	$\{B, C, D\}$	$\emptyset$
$\{A\}$	1	0	0	6	$\{A, B\}$	1	0	3	$\{A\}$	1	0	1
$\{B, C\}$	0	1	0	3	$\{C\}$	0	1	4	$\{B, C, D\}$	0	1	4
$\{D\}$	0	0	1	1	$\{\Theta\}$	1/3	1/4	1	$\emptyset$	1	1/4	1
$\emptyset$	1/6	1/3	1	1								

frame. So, by Definition 9, the relative ranking of decision alternatives over the price criterion is complete, which means that the distinct groups of decision alternative are compared with the empty set (this set stands for the worst choice according to criterion *price*). For criterion *quality*, the union of two identified groups of decision alternatives are real subsets of the discernment frame, which means that the relative ranking of decision alternatives over criterion *quality* are incomplete. So, the decision maker compares the groups of decision alternatives with the discernment frame to express his ignorance in the preference degrees over criterion *quality*. Finally, for hidden criteria T, the decision maker feels very uncomfortable with house A, meaning that all other decision alternatives are must better than A. In order to distinguish the situation of no subjective feeling from that of an uncomfortable feeling, we set other decision alternative in higher level, but the preference relation amongst these decision alternatives is uncertain. As the decision maker knows all situations of his feelings, the relative ranking of decision alternatives over the hidden criterion is complete, meaning that the distinct groups of decision alternatives are compared with the empty set. This is exactly the meaning of Table 1. Now the decision maker can obtain the relative ranking value of each criterion by formulas (17) and (18) as follows: (i) for criterion *price*: $v(\{A\}) = 0.6$, $v(\{B, C\}) = 0.3$, $v(\{D\}) = 0.1$; (ii) for criterion *quality*: $v(\{A, B\}) = 0.357$, $v(\{C\}) = 0.475$, $v(\Theta) = 0.168$; and (iii) for the hidden criterion: $v(\{A\}) = 0.2$, $v(\{B, C, D\}) = 0.8$.

After confirming the favourable matrix, the decision maker will set the criteria weights. In this example, the decision maker feels very uncomfortable for house A, which means that this kind of subjective factor disturbed his final decision. As a result, the decision maker thinks that his criteria weight may change by the disturbance of hidden criterion T, which stands for his feeling about the houses. After using a 6-unit scale to discriminate importance degrees of the criteria, by the importance degrees of the criteria that is compared with the discernment frame, we can obtain the favourable matrix as follow:

$$\begin{pmatrix} \text{Criteria} & \text{Price} & \text{Quality} & \Theta \\ \text{Price} & 1 & 0 & 3 \\ \text{Quality} & 0 & 1 & 1 \\ \Theta & 1/3 & 1 & 1 \end{pmatrix} \tag{21}$$

By formulas (12) and (13), we can obtain: $m(p) = 0.554$, $m(q) = 0.185$, $m(\Theta) = 0.261$. Therefore, by formulas (14) and (15), the point-valued weight for each criterion is: $\omega_p = 0.602$, $\omega_q = 0.233$, $\omega_T = 0.165$. Then, form the relative ranking value of each criterion and the criteria weight, by formula (19), we can obtain the basic probability assignment in the D-S theory, which stands for the priority value over each criterion as follows: $m_p(\{A\}) = 0.361$, $m_p(\{B, C\}) = 0.181$, $m_p(\{D\}) = 0.06$, $m_p(\Theta) = 0.398$; $m_q(\{A, B\}) = 0.083$, $m_q(\{C\}) = 0.111$, $m_q(\Theta) = 0.806$; $m_T(\{A\}) = 0.033$, $m_T(\{B, C, D\}) = 0.132$, $m_T(\Theta) = 0.835$.

By Dempster combination rule (i.e., formula (3)), we can aggregate the overall mass function for all criteria as follows: $m_h(\{A\}) = 0.322$, $m_h(\{B\}) = 0.021$, $m_h(\{C\}) = 0.07$, $m_h(\{D\}) = 0.053$, $m_h(\{A, B\}) = 0.031$, $m_h(\{B, C\}) = 0.158$, $m_h(\{B, C, D\}) = 0.047$, $m_h(\Theta) = 0.298$.

Thus, form the above mass function, by formulas (1) and (2) we have:

$$[Bel(A),\ Pl(A)] = [0.322,\ 0.651],\quad [Bel(B),\ Pl(B)] = [0.021,\ 0.555],$$
$$[Bel(C),\ Pl(C)] = [0.07,\ 0.573],\quad [Bel(D),\ Pl(D)] = [0.053,\ 0.398].$$

Hence, form the belief interval and overall mass function, by Definitions 7, we can obtain

$$P_B^A = 0.524,\ P_C^A = 0.435,\ P_D^A = 0.535,\ P_A^B = -0.524,\ P_C^B = -0.089,\ P_D^B = 0.011,$$
$$P_A^C = -0.435,\ P_B^C = 0.089,\ P_D^C = 0.1,\ P_A^D = -0.535,\ P_B^D = -0.011,\ P_C^D = -0.1.$$

Moreover, by Definition 8, we can set the preference ordering of the house investment problem as $A \succ C \succ B \succ D$. So, the decision alternative A is the optimal one over all the criteria.

7   Summary

This paper proposes a new MCDM method. (i) It can deal with the situation that the optimal option of decision maker is disturbed by some subjective factors (e.g., intuition, feeling, and emotion). (ii) It can differentiate two types of criteria that can consider the effects of subjective factors in MCDM problem. Moreover, our method offers two different rules (i.e., CRRR and IRRR) to deal with two criteria situations that distinguish by the existence of hidden criterion. (iii) It shows that actually the relative ranking values have two types that can be distinguished by the completeness of the information obtained. These two types can also be solved by CRRR and IRRR. And (iv) we identified two ways for reducing the effects of subjective factor disturbances to ensure the decision making is more rational. However, we still need to do some psychological experiments to check and improve our decision model in the future work.

Acknowledgements. This paper is partially supported by National Natural Science Foundation of China (No. 61173019), Bairen plan of Sun Yat-sen University, National Fund of Philosophy and Social Science (No. 11BZX060), Office of Philosophy and Social Science of Guangdong Province of China (No. 08YC-02), Fundamental Research Funds for the Central Universities in China, and major projects of the Ministry of Education (No. 10JZD0006).

References

1. Böhm, G., Brun, W.: Intuition and Affect in Risk Perception and Decision Making. Judgment and Decision Making 3(1), 1–4 (2008)
2. Beynon, M.J.: DS/AHP Method: A Mathematical Analysis, Including an Understanding of Uncertainty. European Journal of Operational Research 140(1), 149–165 (2002)
3. Beynon, M.J., Moutinho, L., Veloutsou, C.: A Dempster-Shafer Theory Based Exposition of Probabilistic Reasoning in Consumer Choice. In: Casillas, J., Martínez-López, F.J. (eds.) Marketing Intelligence Systems. STUDFUZZ, vol. 258, pp. 365–387 (2010)
4. Chua, H.F., Gonzalez, R., Taylor, S.F., Welsh, R.C., Liberzon, I.: Decision-Related Loss: Regret and Disappointment. Neuroimage 47(4), 2031–2040 (2009)
5. Dubois, D., Prade, H.: A Note on Measures of Specificity for Fuzzy Sets. International Journal of General Systems 10(4), 279–283 (1985)
6. Fenton-O'creevyi, M., Soane, E., Nicholson, N., Willman, P.: Thinking, Feeling and Deciding: The Influence of Emotions on the Decision Making and Performance of Traders. Journal of Organizational Behavior 32(8), 1044–1061 (2011)
7. Wenstøp, F.: Mindsets, Rationality and Emotion in Multi-criteria Decision Analysis. Journal of Muliti-Criteria Decision Analysis 13(4), 161–172 (2005)
8. Gollier, C.: Portfolio Choices and Asset Prices: The Comparative Statics of Ambiguity Aversion. Review of Economic Studies 78(4), 1329–1344 (2011)
9. Kahneman, D., Tversky, A.: Prospect Theory: An Analysis of Decision under Risk. Econometrica 47(2), 263–291 (1979)
10. Kahneman, D.: A Perspective on Judgment and Choice: Mapping Bounded Rationality. American Psychologist 58(9), 697–704 (2003)
11. Klibanoff, P., Marinacci, M., Mukerji, S.: On the Smooth Ambiguity Model: A Reply. Econometrica 80(3), 1303–1321 (2012)
12. Luo, X., Zhang, C., Jennings, N.R.: A Hybrid Model for Sharing Information between Fuzzy, Uncertain and Default Reasoning Models in Multi-Agent Systems. International Journal of Uncertainty, Fuzziness and Knowledge-Based Systems 10(4), 401–450 (2002)
13. Loomes, G., Sugden, R.: Regret Theory: An Alternative Theory of Rational Choice under Uncertainty. Economic Journal 92(4), 805–824 (1982)
14. Ma, W., Luo, X., Xiong, W.: Ambiguous DS/AHP Decision Making Approach with Missing, Imprecise, and Uncertain Evaluations of Multiple Criteria. Technique Report, Institute of Logic and Cognition. Sun Yat-Sen Univerisity (2012)
15. Ma, W., Xiong, W., Luo, X.: A D-S Theory Based AHP Decision Making Approach with Ambiguous Evaluations of Multiple Criteria. In: Anthony, P., Ishizuka, M., Lukose, D. (eds.) PRICAI 2012. LNCS, vol. 7458, pp. 297–311. Springer, Heidelberg (2012)

16. Magoč, T.J., Wang, X.J., Modave, F.: Application of Fuzzy Measures and Interval Computation to Financial Portfolio Selection. International Journal of Intelligent Systems 25(7), 621–635 (2010)
17. Martineza, L.F., Zeelenbergb, M., Rijsman, B.J.: Regret, Disappointment and the Endowment Effect. Journal of Economic Psychology 32(6), 962–968 (2011)
18. Reyna, V.F., Brainerd, C.J.: Dual Processes in Decision Making and Developmental Neuroscience: A Fuzzy-Trace Model. Developmental Review 31(2-3), 180–206 (2011)
19. Shafer, G.: A Mathematical Theory of Evidence. Princeton University Press, Princeton (1976)
20. Strat, T.M.: Decision Analysis Using Belief Functions. International Journal of Approximate Reasoning 4(5-6), 391–418 (1990)
21. Summerville, A.: The Rush of Regret: A Longitudinal Analysis of Naturalistic Regrets. Social Psychological and Personality Science 2(6), 627–634 (2011)
22. Tan, C.Q., Chen, X.H.: Induced Intuitionistic Fuzzy Choquet Integral Operator for Multicriteria Decision Making. International Journal of Intelligent Systems 26(7), 659–686 (2011)
23. Xiong, W., Ma, W., Luo, X.: An Expected Utility Interval Theory for Decision-Making under Uncertainty of Ambiguity: To Avoid Ambiguity and Minimise Regret. Technique Report, Institute of Logic and Cognition. Sun Yat-Sen Univerisity (2012)
24. Xiong, W., Luo, X., Ma, W.: Games with Ambiguious Payoff and Played by Ambiguity and Regret Minimising Players. In: The 25th Australia Joint Conference on Artificial Intelligence (2012)
25. Zadeh, L.A.: Fuzzy Sets. Information and Control 8(3), 338–353 (1965)

MML Logistic Regression with Translation and Rotation Invariant Priors

Enes Makalic and Daniel F. Schmidt

Centre for MEGA Epidemiology, The University of Melbourne
Carlton VIC 3053, Australia
{emakalic,dschmidt}@unimelb.edu.au

Abstract. Parameters in logistic regression models are commonly estimated by the method of maximum likelihood, while the model structure
is selected with stepwise regression and a model selection criterion, such
as AIC or BIC. There are two important disadvantages of this approach:
(1) maximum likelihood estimates are biased and infinite when the data
is linearly separable, and (2) the AIC and BIC model selection criteria
are asymptotic in nature and tend to perform well only when the sample size is moderate to large. This paper introduces a novel criterion,
based on the Minimum Message Length (MML) principle, for parameter
estimation and model selection of logistic regression models. The new
criterion is shown to outperform maximum likelihood in terms of parameter estimation, and outperform both AIC and BIC in terms of model
selection using both real and artificial data.

Consider the logistic regression model for explaining data $\mathbf{y} \in \mathbb{R}^n$ given a matrix
of covariates $\mathbf{X} = (\mathbf{x}_1', \mathbf{x}_2', \ldots, \mathbf{x}_n')'$

$$p(\mathbf{y}|\mathbf{X}, \alpha, \boldsymbol{\beta}) = \prod_{i=1}^{n} \left(\frac{1}{1 + \exp(-y_i(\alpha + \mathbf{x}_i'\boldsymbol{\beta}))} \right) \tag{1}$$

where the target variable $y_i \in \{-1, +1\}$, $\mathbf{x}_i \in \mathbb{R}^p$ $(i = 1, 2, \ldots, n)$, $\boldsymbol{\beta} \in \mathbb{R}^p$ is a
vector of logistic regression coefficients and $\alpha \in \mathbb{R}$ is the intercept parameter.
The p regression coefficients $\boldsymbol{\beta}$ and the intercept parameter α determine the
probability of the target variable $y_i = \pm 1$. The task in logistic regression is to
estimate the $(p + 1)$ parameters $\boldsymbol{\theta} = (\alpha, \boldsymbol{\beta})' \in \mathbb{R}^{p+1}$ and select a subset of the p
predictor variables that is associated with the target.

Logistic regression is the most commonly used model in epidemiology and
social science for analysis of data with a binary outcome. The parameter coefficients are often estimated by the method of maximum likelihood

$$\hat{\boldsymbol{\theta}}_{\text{ML}}(\mathbf{y}) = (\hat{\alpha}(\mathbf{y}), \hat{\boldsymbol{\beta}}'(\mathbf{y}))' = \arg\max_{\alpha, \beta} \left\{ \prod_{i=1}^{n} \frac{1}{1 + \exp(-y_i(\alpha + \mathbf{x}_i'\boldsymbol{\beta}))} \right\} \tag{2}$$

which effectively sets the free parameters to the values that maximise the likelihood or, equivalently, the log-likelihood of the observed data. However, the

M. Thielscher and D. Zhang (Eds.): AI 2012, LNCS 7691, pp. 878–889, 2012.

maximum likelihood estimates for logistic regression are biased and can be infinite in small samples and when the data is linearly separable. To select which predictors are associated with the target, one combines maximum likelihood with best subset selection or forward/backward regression and applies a model selection criterion, such as Akaike's Information Criterion (AIC) [1] or the Bayesian Information Criterion (BIC) [2].

This paper considers minimum message length (MML) [3] parameter estimation and model selection in logistic regression analysis. We derive a new Bayesian model selection criterion that is defined even when the data is linearly separable, requires no user specified parameters and exhibits good performance in small samples. A procedure for obtaining MML parameter estimates is introduced and the new estimates are shown to exhibit better prediction performance than the traditional maximum likelihood estimates. The new model selection criterion is then empirically evaluated against two popular criteria, AIC and BIC, and demonstrates excellent performance. This is a remarkable result. By minimising the MML codelength function we obtain parameter estimates that are superior to maximum likelihood and bias–corrected maximum likelihood estimates, especially in small samples with correlated covariates. Further, minimising the same codelength function yields a model selection criteria that outperforms both AIC and BIC.

1   Minimum Message Length (MML)

Minimum message length (MML) [4,5,6,3] principle of inductive inference states that the best model is one which results in the best compression, or shortest codelength, of the data. The compressed codelength comprises two parts: (1) the *assertion*, stating a model for the data from a set of candidate models, and (2) the *detail* which encodes the data using the model that was named in the assertion. The assertion and the detail are commonly denoted as $I_{87}(\boldsymbol{\theta})$ and $I_{87}(\mathbf{y}|\boldsymbol{\theta})$ respectively. The most commonly used form of MML is the Wallace–Freeman approximation [6], or the MML87 approximation, which states that the codelength, $I_{87}(\mathbf{y}, \boldsymbol{\theta})$, of model $\boldsymbol{\theta} \in \boldsymbol{\Theta} \subset \mathbb{R}^k$ and data $\mathbf{y} \in \mathbb{R}^n$ is

$$I_{87}(\mathbf{y}, \boldsymbol{\theta}) = \underbrace{-\log \pi(\boldsymbol{\theta}) + \frac{1}{2} \log |\mathbf{J}_{\boldsymbol{\theta}}(\boldsymbol{\theta})| + \frac{k}{2} \log \kappa_k + \frac{k}{2}}_{I_{87}(\boldsymbol{\theta})} \underbrace{- \log p(\mathbf{y}|\boldsymbol{\theta})}_{I_{87}(\mathbf{y}|\boldsymbol{\theta})} \qquad (3)$$

where $\pi(\cdot)$ denotes a prior distribution over the support $\boldsymbol{\Theta}$, $p(\mathbf{y}|\boldsymbol{\theta})$ is the likelihood function, $\mathbf{J}_{\boldsymbol{\theta}}(\boldsymbol{\theta})$ is the $(k \times k)$ Fisher information matrix and $\kappa_k > 0$ is a dimensionality constant. Following Wallace (p. 237, [3]), the dimensionality constant is well approximated by

$$\frac{k}{2}(\log \kappa_k + 1) \approx -\frac{k}{2} \log(2\pi) + \frac{1}{2} \log(k\pi) + \psi(1) \qquad (4)$$

where $\psi(\cdot)$ is the digamma function. MML is a Bayesian principle and requires stating a prior density over the free model parameters. Under MML87, the model

$\hat{\boldsymbol{\theta}}_{87}(\mathbf{y})$ which minimises (5) is chosen as the most a posteriori likely explanation of the data $\mathbf{y}$, in view of the chosen prior density $\pi(\cdot)$.

The Wallace–Freeman approximation is derived under the following assumptions: (1) the log-likelihood is approximately quadratic at the maximum, (2) the Fisher information matrix is positive definite over the support $\boldsymbol{\Theta}$ and (3) the prior density is locally continuous and 'slowly' varying around the region determined by $|\mathbf{J}_{\boldsymbol{\theta}}(\boldsymbol{\theta})|$. Assumptions (2) and (3) do not hold for logistic regression models with the priors selected in Section 2.1. This is because the chosen prior density has a singularity at the origin and the Fisher information is semi-positive definite; that is, the Fisher information tends to zero as the regression parameters tend to infinity. The combination of these two factors may result in a breakdown of the codelength approximation and hence nonsensical codelengths.

To alleviate these issues, we use the "small sample" codelength approximation suggested by Wallace ([3], pp. 235–236)

$$I_{87}(\mathbf{y}, \boldsymbol{\theta}) = \underbrace{\frac{1}{2} \log \left(1 + \frac{|\mathbf{J}_{\boldsymbol{\theta}}(\boldsymbol{\theta}) + \mathbf{I}_k| \kappa_k^k}{\pi(\boldsymbol{\theta})^2} \right)}_{I_{87}(\boldsymbol{\theta})} + \underbrace{\frac{k}{2} - \log p(\mathbf{y}|\boldsymbol{\theta})}_{I_{87}(\mathbf{y}|\boldsymbol{\theta})} \tag{5}$$

Further, we add an identity matrix to the Fisher information matrix to prevent the parameters from shooting off to infinity and prevent the codelength approximation from breaking down. This change to the Fisher information matrix makes little to no difference around the 'true' MML estimate, but significantly improves the codelength accuracy when the parameters are large (that is, the Fisher information is nearly singular). The new codelength is unfortunately no longer invariant under model transformation due to the modification to the Fisher information matrix. However, this violation appears minor since the models that actually minimise the codelength are virtually unaffected by the change to the Fisher information.

If the number of parameters is fixed and does not grow with the sample size, the MML87 estimates asymptotically converge to maximum likelihood as the sample size $n \to \infty$. Furthermore, the MML87 codelength is asymptotically equivalent to the Bayesian Information Criterion (BIC) as $n \to \infty$. In contrast to maximum likelihood, MML87 estimates are statistically consistent in certain difficult inference problems; for example, the Neyman–Scott problem [7] and the factor analysis model. The MML87 estimator also tends to improve upon maximum likelihood in problems where the data size is small to moderate. Thus, the MML criterion may be viewed as a small–sample version of BIC that also features improved parameter estimates.

2   MML Logistic Regression

Standard Bayesian inference of logistic regression models requires specifying a prior distribution over the parameters and sampling from the corresponding posterior distribution given the observed data. This has traditionally been done using Markov Chain Monte Carlo (MCMC) techniques with Gaussian approximations, some variant of the Metropolis–Hastings sampler [8] or numerical integration techniques. More recently, researchers have examined MCMC techniques with alternative representations of the logistic function and Gaussian scale-mixture priors [9]. A common representation of the logistic function is to model the data $\mathbf{y} \in \mathbb{R}^n$ as a thresholded version of some underlying continuous random variable. Examples include the the random-utility construction of the logistic model by Holmes and Held [10], the Z–distribution framework of Gramacy and Polson [11] and the Polya–gamma representation of Polson et al. [12].

In the Bayesian framework, the prior distribution hierarchy commonly follows the local/global shrinkage framework described by Polson and Scott [13]. The prior distribution over the regression coefficients is taken to be the Gaussian distribution with a prior variance hyperparameter, which is given a separate hyperprior. The functional form of the hyperprior allows the generation of several widely used distributions for the regression coefficients through Gaussian-scale mixtures; examples of distributions that may be generated in this setting include the Student t-distribution or the double exponential distribution used in Bayesian LASSO regression [14], among others.

Although the MML principle is Bayesian by design, the MML approximation (5) that is used in this paper does not require any sampling from the posterior distribution of the parameters. Instead, one must specify: (1) the negative log-likelihood function, (2) the determinant of the Fisher information matrix, and (3) a prior distribution over the free model parameters for the logistic regression model. The fully-specified model $\boldsymbol{\theta}(\mathbf{y})$ which minimises the codelength approximation given by (5) is then the best MML model in light of the chosen priors. The negative log-likelihood function and the Fisher information for logistic regression models are

$$-\log p(\mathbf{y}|\mathbf{X}, \boldsymbol{\theta}) = \sum_{i=1}^{n} \log(1 + \exp(-y_i(\alpha + \mathbf{x}_i'\boldsymbol{\beta}))), \tag{6}$$

$$|\mathbf{J}_{\boldsymbol{\theta}}(\boldsymbol{\theta})| = |(\mathbf{1}_n, \mathbf{X})'\mathbf{V}(\boldsymbol{\theta})(\mathbf{1}_n, \mathbf{X})|, \tag{7}$$

where $\mathbf{1}_n = (1, 1, \ldots, 1)'$ is an n-dimensional vector of ones, $\mathbf{V}(\boldsymbol{\theta}) = \operatorname{diag}(\mu_1(1 - \mu_1), \mu_2(1 - \mu_2), \ldots, \mu_n(1 - \mu_n))$ is an $(n \times n)$ diagonal matrix, $\mu_i = 1/(1 + \exp(-\alpha - \mathbf{x}_i'\boldsymbol{\beta}))$ and $\boldsymbol{\theta} = (\alpha, \boldsymbol{\beta})' \in \mathbb{R}^k$ denotes the $k = (p + 1)$ vector of free parameters. It remains to specify the prior distribution over the regression coefficients.

2.1 Prior Distribution

Almost all Bayesian approaches to logistic regression use a Gaussian prior distribution (or Gaussian-scale mixtures) over regression coefficients $\boldsymbol{\theta} \in \mathbb{R}^k$. This is done primarily out of mathematical convenience. However, the Gaussian distribution is not invariant under rotations and translations of the decision hyperplane implied by the logistic model. We argue that this is not desirable and seek a prior that is invariant under all translations and rotations of the decision hyperplane.

The decision boundary in logistic regression models is

$$\alpha + \mathbf{x}'\boldsymbol{\beta} = \tilde{\alpha}(1 + \mathbf{x}'\tilde{\boldsymbol{\beta}}) = 0, \tag{8}$$

which is a $(p-1)$-dimensional hyperplane embedded inside the p-dimensional data space induced by the predictor matrix $\mathbf{X}$, assuming $\mathbf{X}$ is full rank. Note that the logistic regression model is now parameterised in terms of $\tilde{\boldsymbol{\theta}} = (\tilde{\alpha}, \tilde{\boldsymbol{\beta}}')' \in \mathbb{R}^k$, where the parameter transformation function $F : \mathbb{R}^k \mapsto \mathbb{R}^k$ maps $\boldsymbol{\theta} \in \mathbb{R}^k$ to $\tilde{\boldsymbol{\theta}} = F(\boldsymbol{\theta}) = (F_0(\boldsymbol{\theta}), F_1(\boldsymbol{\theta}), \dots, F_p(\boldsymbol{\theta}))'$ and

$$\tilde{\alpha} = F_0(\boldsymbol{\theta}) = \alpha \tag{9}$$
$$\tilde{\beta}_j = F_j(\boldsymbol{\theta}) = \beta_j/\alpha \quad (j = 1, 2, \dots, p), \tag{10}$$

provided $\alpha \neq 0$. It is clear from (8) that $\tilde{\alpha} \in \mathbb{R}$ does not affect the location and orientation of the decision boundary which is solely determined by the regression coefficients $\tilde{\boldsymbol{\beta}} \in \mathbb{R}^p$.

A prior distribution over $\tilde{\boldsymbol{\beta}} \in \mathbb{R}^p$ that does not favor any orientation or position of the decision boundary is

$$\pi_{\tilde{\beta}}(\tilde{\boldsymbol{\beta}}) = \frac{\Gamma(p/2)r_0}{2\pi^{p/2}}(\tilde{\boldsymbol{\beta}}'\tilde{\boldsymbol{\beta}})^{-(p+1)/2}, \quad (\|\tilde{\boldsymbol{\beta}}\|_2 \geq r_0 > 0), \tag{11}$$

where $\Gamma(\cdot)$ is the gamma function and r_0 is a lower limit on the ℓ_2-norm of the parameter vector $\tilde{\boldsymbol{\beta}}$ (discussed below). The prior distribution was originally derived in the context of feed-forward multilayer perceptron networks [15]. Let $\mathbf{I}_p$ denote a $(p \times p)$ identity matrix. It is straightforward to show that $-\log \pi_{\tilde{\beta}}(\tilde{\boldsymbol{\beta}})$ is a strictly concave function of $\tilde{\boldsymbol{\beta}}$ since the $(p \times p)$ Hessian matrix

$$-\frac{\partial^2 \log \pi_{\tilde{\beta}}(\tilde{\boldsymbol{\beta}})}{\partial \tilde{\boldsymbol{\beta}} \partial \tilde{\boldsymbol{\beta}}'} = \left(\frac{p+1}{\tilde{\boldsymbol{\beta}}'\tilde{\boldsymbol{\beta}}}\right)\left(\mathbf{I}_p - \left(\frac{2}{\tilde{\boldsymbol{\beta}}'\tilde{\boldsymbol{\beta}}}\right)\tilde{\boldsymbol{\beta}}\tilde{\boldsymbol{\beta}}'\right) \tag{12}$$

has a strictly negative determinant

$$\left|-\frac{\partial^2 \log \pi_{\tilde{\beta}}(\tilde{\boldsymbol{\beta}})}{\partial \tilde{\boldsymbol{\beta}} \partial \tilde{\boldsymbol{\beta}}'}\right| = -\left(\frac{p+1}{\tilde{\boldsymbol{\beta}}'\tilde{\boldsymbol{\beta}}}\right)^p < 0, \quad \tilde{\boldsymbol{\beta}} \in \mathbb{R}^p. \tag{13}$$

The constant r_0 may be set to the radius of the minimum volume enclosing hyperball of the predictor matrix $\mathbf{X}$; this can be efficiently computed for moderate p using the fast algorithm in [16]. Alternatively, one may set $r_0^2 = 1/(\mathbf{t}'\mathbf{t})$ where $\mathbf{t} \in \mathbb{R}^p$ is the point closest to the origin through which the decision hyperplane passes. This procedure was recommended by Toussaint et al. ([15], Section 3.1). Section 2.2 discusses how to set the constant r_0 in the current paper.

It remains to specify a prior distribution over the parameter $\tilde{\alpha} \in \mathbb{R}$. We opt for the scale invariant prior

$$\pi_{\tilde{\alpha}}(\tilde{\alpha}) = \frac{a}{2\tilde{\alpha}^2}, \quad \tilde{\alpha} \in [a, \infty). \tag{14}$$

where $a > 0$. Note that Toussaint et al. ([15], Section 3.1) advocate a maximum entropy prior for $\tilde{\alpha}$ in neural networks using the maximal slope of the decision boundary as testable information. The maximum entropy prior however introduces an extra hyperparameter which is not easily eliminated. Since $\tilde{\alpha}$ is a common parameter to all models, the choice of prior is not expected to significantly alter the results and conclusions of this paper.

To summarise, the complete prior distribution over the k free parameters $\tilde{\boldsymbol{\theta}} = (\tilde{\alpha}, \tilde{\boldsymbol{\beta}}')'$ is

$$\pi_{\tilde{\boldsymbol{\theta}}}(\tilde{\boldsymbol{\theta}}) = \pi_{\tilde{\alpha}}(\tilde{\alpha})\pi_{\tilde{\boldsymbol{\beta}}}(\tilde{\boldsymbol{\beta}}). \tag{15}$$

where the prior distributions for $\tilde{\alpha}$ and $\tilde{\boldsymbol{\beta}}$ are assumed to be conditionally independent and are given by (14) and (11), respectively.

2.2   MML Logistic Regression Criterion

It remains to specify the complete MML codelength (5) for the logistic regression model as a function of the new parameters $\tilde{\boldsymbol{\theta}} = (\tilde{\alpha}, \tilde{\boldsymbol{\beta}}')' \in \mathbb{R}^k$ (see Section 2.1). The negative log-likelihood and the Fisher information are now given by

$$- \log p(\mathbf{y}|\mathbf{X}, \tilde{\boldsymbol{\theta}}) = \sum_{i=1}^{n} \log(1 + \exp(-y_i(\tilde{\alpha}(1 + \mathbf{x}'\tilde{\boldsymbol{\beta}})))) \tag{16}$$

$$|\mathbf{J}_{\tilde{\boldsymbol{\theta}}}(\tilde{\boldsymbol{\theta}})| = |\mathbf{J_T}'\mathbf{J}_{\boldsymbol{\theta}}(\boldsymbol{\theta})\mathbf{J_T}| = \tilde{\alpha}^{2p}|(\mathbf{1}_n, \mathbf{X})'\mathbf{V}(\tilde{\boldsymbol{\theta}})(\mathbf{1}_n, \mathbf{X})| \tag{17}$$

where $\mathbf{J_T}$ is the $(k \times k)$ Jacobian transformation matrix

$$\mathbf{J_T} = \begin{pmatrix} 1 & \mathbf{0}'_p \\ \tilde{\boldsymbol{\beta}} & \tilde{\alpha}\mathbf{I}_p \end{pmatrix}, \quad |\mathbf{J_T}| = \tilde{\alpha}^p \tag{18}$$

and $\mathbf{V}(\tilde{\boldsymbol{\theta}}) = \mathbf{V}(\boldsymbol{\theta})$ (see Section 2). The complete MML codelength for logistic regression is

$$I_{87}(\mathbf{y}, \tilde{\boldsymbol{\theta}}) = \frac{1}{2}\log\left(1 + \frac{|\mathbf{J}_{\tilde{\boldsymbol{\theta}}}(\tilde{\boldsymbol{\theta}}) + \mathbf{I}_k|\kappa_k^k}{\pi(\tilde{\boldsymbol{\theta}})^2}\right) + \sum_{i=1}^{n}\log(1 + \exp(-y_i(\tilde{\alpha}(1 + \mathbf{x}'\tilde{\boldsymbol{\beta}})))) + \frac{k}{2}$$

where the prior density and the Fisher information are given in (15) and (17) respectively. The constant κ_k^k is approximated using (4). We set the prior parameters a and r_0 to the parameter estimates that minimise the codelength. That is, we choose $a = \hat{\tilde{\alpha}}(\mathbf{y})$ and $r_0 = \hat{\tilde{\boldsymbol{\beta}}}(\mathbf{y})'\hat{\tilde{\boldsymbol{\beta}}}(\mathbf{y})$.

We have thus far ignored the important requirement for stating which of the p predictors are used in the model under consideration. In this paper, we choose a prior distribution that treats each possible subset of regressors of size q $(0 < q \leq p)$ as equally likely. The new prior adds a term of size

$$\log(p + 1) + \log\binom{p}{q}$$

to the codelength (19). The first term states the number $q(\leq p)$ of predictors which are in the model, while the second term names which of the p predictors are selected. Recall that a model with q predictors always includes an additional intercept term, represented by the parameter $\tilde{\alpha} \in \mathbb{R}$, and thus has $(q + 1)$ free parameters.

2.3   Parameter Estimation

It is well known that maximum likelihood parameter estimates for logistic regression (2) are biased away from the point $\boldsymbol{\theta} = \mathbf{0}_k$ and are infinite if the data is linearly separable [17]. In order to remove or lessen the bias, some amount of parameter shrinkage towards the origin is necessary. The bias arises due to the curvature and unbiasedness of the score function (that is, the derivative of the log-likelihood). A common method of reducing the bias is that of Firth [18] where, instead of maximising the log-likelihood, one maximises the penalized log-likelihood

$$\hat{\boldsymbol{\theta}}_{\mathrm{FR}}(\mathbf{y}) = (\hat{\alpha}(\mathbf{y}), \hat{\boldsymbol{\beta}}'(\mathbf{y}))' = \underset{\alpha, \boldsymbol{\beta}}{\arg\max} \left\{ \log p(\mathbf{y}|\mathbf{X}, \boldsymbol{\theta}) + \frac{1}{2} \log |\mathbf{J}_{\boldsymbol{\theta}}(\boldsymbol{\theta})| \right\} \qquad (19)$$

where the penalty is equal to the determinant of the Fisher information matrix. This penalized log-likelihood introduces bias into the score function by an amount that depends on the curvature of the log-likelihood. The end result for exponential families is the removal of $O(n^{-1})$ bias for the canonical parameter.

Firth's penalized log-likelihood estimates are not model space invariant, since bias itself is not invariant. Shen and Gao [19] extend the approach and add a second, ridge regression, penalty to the log-likelihood function to improve maximum likelihood estimates in case of highly correlated predictors. A potential disadvantage of both penalized likelihood estimates is that commonly used model selection criteria, such as AIC and BIC, are only derived assuming maximum likelihood estimates and may need modification for penalized regression procedures. In contrast, the MML approach allows parameter estimation and model selection within the same framework. The authors recommend [20] for an overview of other similar approaches to bias reduction in logistic regression models.

The MML parameter estimates, $\hat{\boldsymbol{\theta}}_{87}(\mathbf{y})$ can be obtained by minimising the total codelength (19) with respect to the parameters $\tilde{\boldsymbol{\theta}}$, that is

$$\hat{\boldsymbol{\theta}}_{87}(\mathbf{y}) = \underset{\tilde{\alpha}, \tilde{\boldsymbol{\beta}}}{\arg\min} \left\{ I_{87}(\mathbf{y}, \tilde{\boldsymbol{\theta}}) \right\}. \qquad (20)$$

The Fisher information term $\log |\mathbf{J}_{\hat{\boldsymbol{\theta}}}(\tilde{\boldsymbol{\theta}})|$ and the prior distribution $\pi_{\tilde{\boldsymbol{\beta}}}(\tilde{\boldsymbol{\beta}})$ are strictly concave functions and unbounded below. The negative log-likelihood function is strictly convex and bounded below. In this paper, the parameter estimates are obtained using the MATLAB `fminunc` optimisation function. Preliminary simulation experiments initially showed that minimising the codelength with respect to both $\tilde{\alpha}$ and $\tilde{\boldsymbol{\beta}}$ can sometimes result in numerical issues, especially as $\tilde{\alpha} \to 0$ and the parameter transformation becomes singular. A possible remedy is to fix $\tilde{\alpha}$ to equal, say, $\hat{\alpha}_{\mathrm{FR}}(\mathbf{y})$, and estimate the p regression coefficients by minimising the codelength. This removes all issues with numerical optimisation and yields valid codelengths provided the initial estimate of $\tilde{\alpha}$ is reasonable. The effect of the prior distribution $\pi_{\tilde{\beta}}(\tilde{\boldsymbol{\beta}})$ on the MML codelength is to shrink the maximum likelihood parameters towards the origin of the coordinate system. Given the tendency of maximum likelihood to overestimate the regression coefficients, we expect the MML estimates to exhibit less bias (see Section 3.1).

It is interesting to note that some penalized regression procedures can be interpreted within the MML framework. The bias correction suggested by Firth, for example, amounts to maximising the posterior distribution of the parameters assuming a Jeffreys' prior distribution. This is equivalent to using a constant Fisher information when computing MML87 estimates.

3   Results and Discussion

3.1   Parameter Estimation

This section compares the prediction performance of the maximum likelihood estimator $\hat{\boldsymbol{\theta}}_{\mathrm{ML}}(\mathbf{y})$, the MML parameter estimator $\hat{\boldsymbol{\theta}}_{87}(\mathbf{y})$ and Firth's penalized maximum likelihood estimator $\hat{\boldsymbol{\theta}}_{\mathrm{FR}}(\mathbf{y})$ in logistic regression models. The three estimators are defined in (2), (20) and (19) respectively. In the spirit of reproducible research, all MATLAB simulation code will be made available on the authors' web pages[1]. Recall that

$$\mu_i = \frac{1}{1 + \exp(-y_i(\alpha + \mathbf{x}_i'\boldsymbol{\beta}))} \quad (i = 1, 2, \ldots, n), \tag{21}$$

denotes the probability of datum $y_i = \pm 1$, and let $\hat{\mu}_i$ denote an estimate of μ_i inferred by one of the three aforementioned estimators. Similarly, let $\hat{y}_i$ denote the predicted class of the datum y_i. The estimates will be compared on the area under the receiver operating characteristic curve (AUC) and

$$\mathrm{CA} = \frac{1}{n} \sum_{i=1}^{n} \delta(y_i, \hat{y}_i) \tag{22}$$

$$\mathrm{KL} = -\frac{1}{n} \sum_{i=1}^{n} \left(\mu_i \log\left(\frac{\hat{\mu}_i}{\mu_i}\right) + (1 - \mu_i) \log\left(\frac{1 - \hat{\mu}_i}{1 - \mu_i}\right) \right), \tag{23}$$

where CA denotes classification accuracy, KL denotes Kullback–Leibler divergence [21] and $\delta(y_i, \hat{y}_i) = 1$ if and only if $(y_i = \hat{y}_i)$, otherwise $\delta(y_i, \hat{y}_i) = 0$. These three metrics will measure the prediction error of the estimators under consideration.

---

[1] www.emakalic.org/blog and www.dschmidt.org

Table 1. Parameter estimation performance measured by median classification accuracy (CA), area under the ROC curve (AUC) and KL divergence (KL) computed for maximum likelihood $\hat{\boldsymbol{\theta}}_{\mathrm{ML}}(\mathbf{y})$, penalized maximum likelihood $\hat{\boldsymbol{\theta}}_{\mathrm{FR}}(\mathbf{y})$ and minimum message length $\hat{\boldsymbol{\theta}}_{87}(\mathbf{y})$ estimators

n	ρ	$\hat{\boldsymbol{\theta}}_{\mathrm{ML}}(\mathbf{y})$			$\hat{\boldsymbol{\theta}}_{\mathrm{FR}}(\mathbf{y})$			$\hat{\boldsymbol{\theta}}_{87}(\mathbf{y})$		
		CA	AUC	KL	CA	AUC	KL	CA	AUC	KL
	0.0	72.16	75.01	8.72	72.45	81.11	0.58	72.43	83.10	0.57
	0.2	77.79	81.85	6.59	77.77	87.25	0.47	85.45	94.71	0.40
25	0.5	80.11	84.72	5.66	79.92	89.37	0.43	90.44	97.74	0.30
	0.7	81.00	85.51	5.39	80.46	90.10	0.41	91.92	98.45	0.26
	0.9	81.53	86.21	5.17	81.01	90.57	0.41	93.12	98.85	0.24
	0.0	78.11	85.54	0.87	78.48	87.60	0.49	77.50	87.69	0.52
	0.2	83.36	86.93	4.89	84.06	92.95	0.36	86.89	95.30	0.31
50	0.5	85.97	89.36	4.13	86.42	94.88	0.30	91.15	97.83	0.24
	0.7	86.99	90.39	3.78	87.24	95.44	0.29	92.63	98.48	0.21
	0.9	87.68	91.16	3.52	87.84	95.83	0.27	93.66	98.85	0.19
	0.0	81.47	90.30	0.44	81.47	90.31	0.41	81.50	90.39	0.40
	0.2	87.17	95.11	0.35	87.26	95.23	0.30	87.95	95.69	0.28
100	0.5	89.67	96.40	0.41	89.89	96.97	0.24	91.26	97.72	0.21
	0.7	90.35	95.16	1.33	90.69	97.45	0.22	92.69	98.38	0.18
	0.9	90.97	94.08	2.43	91.33	97.79	0.20	93.84	98.85	0.15
	0.0	82.94	91.49	0.38	82.93	91.49	0.37	82.95	91.50	0.37
	0.2	88.67	96.07	0.27	88.67	96.07	0.26	88.84	96.17	0.26
250	0.5	91.39	97.70	0.21	91.39	97.71	0.20	91.76	97.88	0.19
	0.7	92.30	98.16	0.20	92.33	98.17	0.18	92.85	98.40	0.17
	0.9	92.94	98.46	0.19	92.95	98.47	0.17	93.89	98.82	0.15

The test procedure for comparing the estimators is now described. For each test, a training data set comprising the predictor matrix $\mathbf{X} \in \mathbb{R}^{n \times p}$ was generated from a multivariate Gaussian distribution $\mathbf{X} \sim N_p(\mathbf{0}_p, \boldsymbol{\Sigma})$, where the entries of the variance–covariance matrix are $\boldsymbol{\Sigma}_{i,i} = 1$ for all $(i = 1, 2, \ldots, p)$ and $\boldsymbol{\Sigma}_{i,j} = \rho$ whenever $(i \neq j)$; that is, $\boldsymbol{\Sigma}$ is a variance–covariance matrix with ones on the diagonal and ρ everywhere else. This is expected to produce significant correlation in the covariates as $|\rho| \to 1$. The training data $\mathbf{y} \in \mathbb{R}^n$ was generated using the predictor matrix $\mathbf{X}$ and $(\alpha, \boldsymbol{\beta}) = (0', \mathbf{1}')'$ for the unknown parameters $\boldsymbol{\theta} = (\alpha, \boldsymbol{\beta}')' \in \mathbb{R}^{p+1}$. The maximum likelihood, penalized maximum likelihood and the MML estimators were then used to estimate the unknown parameters $\boldsymbol{\theta}$ given the training data. For the the MML estimate, $\hat{\tilde{\alpha}}(\mathbf{y})$ is set to the Firth estimate (see Section 2.3). The performance of the three estimators was compared using the three metrics CA, AUC and KL computed from a new test data set with sample size $(m = 10^5)$. In all tests, $(p = 10)$ predictor variables were used to generate the predictor matrices. The entire procedure was repeated for 2000 iterations for the following values of (n, ρ): $n \in \{25, 50, 100, 250\}$ and $\rho \in \{0.0, 0.2, 0.5, 0.7, 0.9\}$. The results are shown in Table 1.

It is clear that both the MML and Firth's penalized likelihood estimator substantially improve the prediction performance of maximum likelihood, especially when the sample size is small ($n < 100$). This is not surprising as such data is often linearly separable and maximum likelihood tends to estimate $\beta \to \pm\infty$. The MML estimator and Firth's penalized likelihood estimator exhibit similar prediction performance for larger sample sizes ($n \geq 100$) and for all values of correlation ρ. However, the MML estimator has significantly better prediction error as measured by all three metrics for $n = \{25, 50\}$, especially as $\rho \to 1$. This indicates that the MML estimator is able to better estimate the underlying 'degrees of freedom' of the model when the data is highly correlated. For larger sample sizes, all three estimators performed equally well under the metrics considered.

3.2   Model Selection

The MML logistic regression criterion is now compared against AIC and BIC in terms of model selection performance on five real data sets. The data sets were: pima (8 predictors, 768 samples), australian (15 predictors, 690 samples), wcbc (10 predictors, 683 samples), liver (6 predictors, 345 samples) and heart (13 predictors, 270 samples). The pima, wcbc and liver data sets were obtained from the UCI Machine Learning Repository, while the remaining data sets were downloaded from StatLOG.

For each data set, random samples of $n = 25$ and $n = 50$ data were used for training, while the remaining data was used for estimating prediction performance. Prior to each test iteration, the predictor variables were normalized to have zero mean and length $\mathbf{x}_j'\mathbf{x} = n$ for all ($j = 1, 2, \ldots, p$). Initially, all-subset selection was used to generate candidate models. However, the computational complexity of examining all 2^p models renders any kind of exhaustive empirical comparison extremely difficult. Consequently, the elastic net procedure [22] (function lassoglm in MATLAB with parameter $\alpha = 0.95$) was used to generate candidate models – the elastic net parameter estimates were ignored. Two metrics were computed from the test data: (a) classification accuracy, and (b) negative log-likelihood. The complete test procedure was repeated for 10^3 iterations for each data set. The results are shown in Figure 1. Note, the AIC score resulted in inferior performance in comparison to BIC in virtually all tests considered and was hence omitted.

In terms of median classification accuracy, both MML and BIC perform similarly across all data sets and sample sizes considered. However, the models selected by the MML criterion have significantly smaller variance in terms of classification accuracy than those selected by BIC. This is clearly visible for $n = 50$ training samples where the variance in classification accuracy of the MML models is approximately half of the BIC models. In terms of negative log-likelihood, the MML criterion has resulted in clearly superior models to BIC for both $n = 25$ and $n = 50$ training samples.

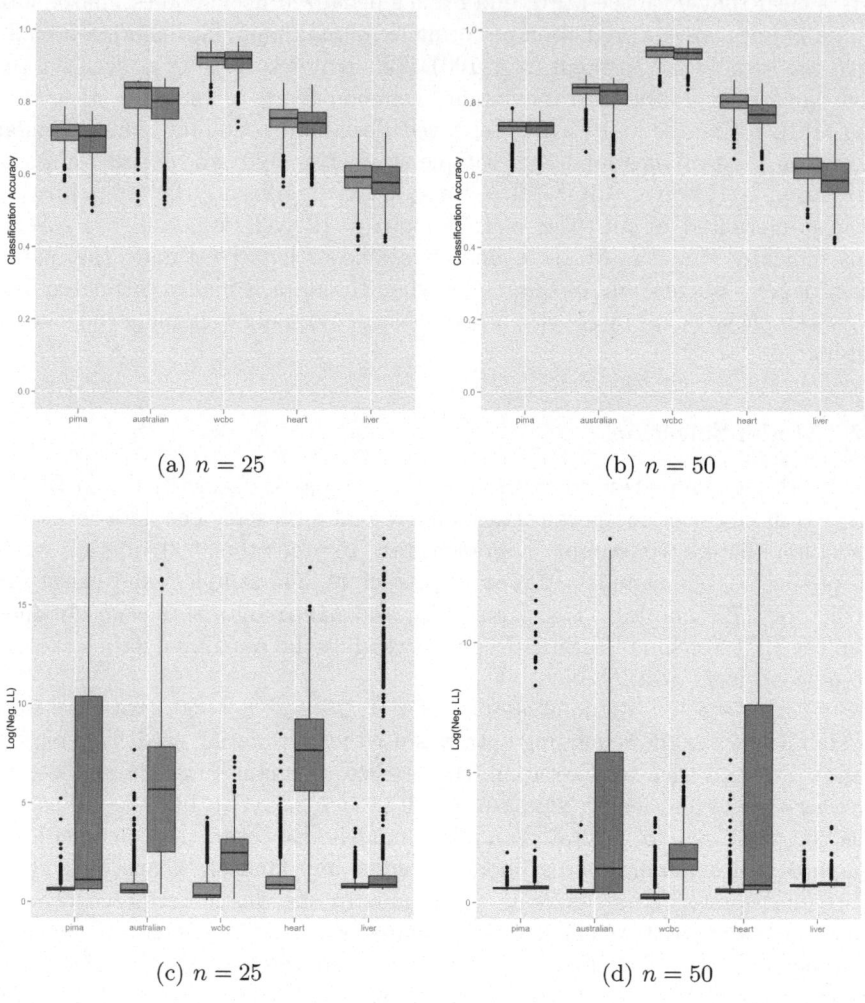

(a) $n = 25$ (b) $n = 50$

(c) $n = 25$ (d) $n = 50$

Fig. 1. Classification accuracy and negative log-likelihood computed from test data for MML (left boxplot) and BIC (right boxplot) for sample sizes $n = 25$ and $n = 50$

References

1. Akaike, H.: A new look at the statistical model identification. IEEE Transactions on Automatic Control 19(6), 716–723 (1974)
2. Schwarz, G.: Estimating the dimension of a model. The Annals of Statistics 6(2), 461–464 (1978)
3. Wallace, C.S.: Statistical and Inductive Inference by Minimum Message Length, 1st edn. Information Science and Statistics. Springer (2005)
4. Wallace, C.S., Boulton, D.M.: An information measure for classification. Computer Journal 11(2), 185–194 (1968)

5. Wallace, C., Boulton, D.: An invariant Bayes method for point estimation. Classification Society Bulletin 3(3), 11–34 (1975)
6. Wallace, C.S., Freeman, P.R.: Estimation and inference by compact coding. Journal of the Royal Statistical Society (Series B) 49(3), 240–252 (1987)
7. Dowe, D.L., Wallace, C.S.: Resolving the Neyman-Scott problem by minimum message length. In: Proc. 28th Symposium on the Interface, Sydney, Australia. Computing Science and Statistics, vol. 28, pp. 614–618 (1997)
8. Metropolis, A.W., Rosenbluth, M.N., Rosenbluth, A.H., Teller, E.: Equations of state calculations by fast computing machines. Journal of Chemical Physics 21, 1087–1092 (1953)
9. Andrews, D.F., Mallows, C.L.: Scale mixtures of normal distributions. Journal of the Royal Statistical Society (Series B) 36(1), 99–102 (1974)
10. Holmes, C.C., Held, L.: Bayesian auxiliary variable models for binary and multinomial regression. Bayesian Analsyis 1(1), 145–168 (2006)
11. Gramacy, R.B., Polson, N.G.: Simulation-based regularized logistic regression. Bayesian Analsyis 7(3) (to appear, 2012)
12. Polson, N.G., Scott, J.G., Windle, J.: Bayesian inference for logistic models using polya-gamma latent variables. arXiv:1205.0310
13. Polson, N.G., Scott, J.G.: Shrink globally, act locally: Sparse Bayesian regularization and prediction. In: Bayesian Statistics, vol. 9 (2010)
14. Park, T., Casella, G.: The Bayesian lasso. Journal of the American Statistical Association 103(482), 681–686 (2008)
15. van Toussaint, U., Gori, S., Dose, V.: Invariance priors for Bayesian feed-forward neural networks. Neural Networks 19(10), 1550–1557 (2006)
16. Gärtner, B.: Fast and Robust Smallest Enclosing Balls. In: Nešetřil, J. (ed.) ESA 1999. LNCS, vol. 1643, pp. 325–338. Springer, Heidelberg (1999)
17. Albert, A., Anderson, J.A.: On the existence of maximum likelihood estimates in logistic regression models. Biometrika 71(1), 1–10 (1984)
18. Firth, D.: Bias reduction of maximum likelihood estimates. Biometrika 80(1), 27–38 (1993)
19. Shen, J., Gao, S.: A solution to separation and multicollinearity in multiple logistic regression. J. Data Sci. 6(4), 515–531 (2008)
20. Bull, S.B., Mak, C., Greenwood, C.M.T.: A modified score function estimator for multinomial logistic regression in small samples. Computational Statistics & Data Analysis 39(1), 57–74 (2002)
21. Kullback, S., Leibler, R.A.: On information and sufficiency. The Annals of Mathematical Statistics 22(1), 79–86 (1951)
22. Zou, H., Hastie, T.: Regularization and variable selection via the elastic net. Journal of the Royal Statistical Society (Series B) 67(2), 301–320 (2005)

Probabilistic Model-Based Assessment of Information Quality in Uncertain Domains*

Steffen Michels, Marina Velikova, and Peter J.F. Lucas

Institute for Computing and Information Sciences
Radboud University Nijmegen, The Netherlands
s.michels@science.ru.nl

Abstract. In various domains, such as security and surveillance, a large amount of information from heterogeneous sources is continuously gathered to identify and prevent potential threats, but it is unknown in advance what the observed entity of interest should look like. The quality of the decisions made depends, of course, on the quality of the information they are based on. In this paper, we propose a novel method for assessing the quality of information taking into account uncertainty. Two properties – *soundness* and *completeness* – of the information are used to define the notion of information quality and their expected values are defined using a probabilistic model output. Simulation experiments with data from a maritime scenario demonstrates the usage of the proposed method and its potential for decision support in complex tasks such as surveillance.

1   Introduction

Information is collected virtually in any domain and task to increase our knowledge about reality and to provide bases for decisions. The quality of these decisions depends, of course, on the quality of the information they are based on and the estimation of the latter has been the focus of research for many years. Very early work can be found in the science of experimental measurement, where information is largely collected in a controlled setting with priorly defined expected outcomes, and information quality is typically quantified by statistical measures such as systematic and statistical errors. Later the field of information retrieval emerged based on survey studies and database management tasks, where measures such as precision and recall are used to determine the goodness of answers extracted with respect to a pre-defined question [8]. These measures are clearly defined with respect to ground-truth information, assumed to be provided by an expert or another information source with certainty [3]. Studies in information management have further defined information quality by a large variety of dimensions, e.g., completeness, accuracy, relevancy, timeliness, as summarised

---

* This publication was supported by the Dutch national program COMMIT. The research work was carried out as part of the Metis project under the responsibility of the Embedded Systems Institute with Thales Nederland B.V. as the carrying industrial partner.

M. Thielscher and D. Zhang (Eds.): AI 2012, LNCS 7691, pp. 890–901, 2012.

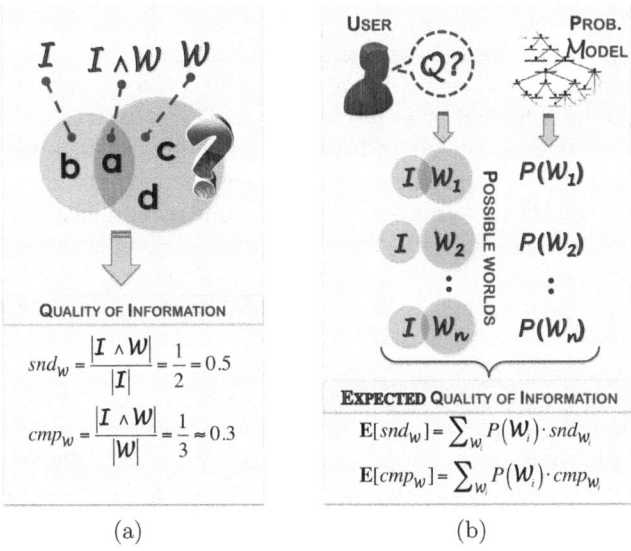

(a)   (b)

Fig. 1. Two approaches for estimating the quality of information $\mathcal{I}$ in terms of soundness (snd) and completeness (cmp): a) standard method used in information retrieval, assuming that the hypothetical true world $\mathcal{W}$ is known, and b) our model-based method yielding expected values based on probabilistic estimates of the possible true worlds $\mathcal{W}_i$ generated from a set of user queries Q

in [7]. The definitions of these dimensions include uncertainty but no methods for the practical assessment of the dimensions are provided.

In recent years, we observe wide availability and heterogeneity of information sources in new domains, such as security, surveillance and object recognition, where one has to handle a continuous stream of information and it is unknown in advance what the observed entity of interest should look like. This leads to *uncertainty* in the information obtained and in the estimation of its quality. Hence, new measures are required for defining and assessing information quality such that uncertainty is explicitly taken into account. The notions and probabilistic method we propose in this paper are a contribution in this direction.

The representation language of our method is based on first-order logic with binary predicates, which allow a straightforward expression of object-attribute-value relations, typically referred as facts in the information obtained from sources. We define the notion of "information quality" in terms of two properties – *soundness* and *completeness* – that are based on the estimation of set cardinalities. The conceptual idea is similar to the ones proposed earlier in [2,6], but we propose a novel formalisation and estimation of these properties taking into account uncertainty, as illustrated in Figure 1, namely:

– We define the intersection set of the information gathered and the ground-truth with respect to a set of user queries and not to a fixed database as done before. Hence, we consider "quality" as a dynamic property of the information, which depends on the questions at hand.

– Unlike the related studies, we do not assume that the true world is provided, for example by a human or a database, but we generate the set of possible true worlds based on the set of user queries. Then for each world we compute the probability for being true using a predefined model using domain knowledge and other information. The probabilities obtained are finally used to compute the expected value for soundness and completeness of the information gathered. Here, we do not restrict the structure or the nature of the model, as long as it provides a proper probability distribution of the possible world states.

The proposed method is general and can be applied to any domain where uncertainty of information plays a role, but its development was motivated by our research on estimating information quality in maritime surveillance. Therefore, we next present a scenario from the maritime domain to motivate this research. Section 3 presents the language and main notions used to define information quality. The main theoretical contribution–probabilistic method for assessment of information quality–is described in Section 4. Experiments described in Section 5 illustrate the application of the method. Section 6 concludes the paper.

2   Motivating Scenario

The detection of drug smuggling is one of the biggest challenges that maritime surveillance and the coast guard operators nowadays face. Typical hypotheses that increase the suspiciousness of a ship are falsified/missing ship identity information or the type of cargo that allows to hide drugs easily (e.g., bulk dry). The operators need to check the quality of information reported by the ship via the automatic identification system (AIS) or radio contact in their daily tasks to examine these hypotheses.

The Dutch bulk-carrier "Seaman" approaches the port of Rotterdam carrying cement, sand and stone, and sends the following AIS information to the coast guard:

i: ID = *23378*, name = *Seaman*, type = *bulk-carrier*, cargo = {*sand, gravel*}.

An intelligence report of the same day warns an operator that a bulk carrier, most likely carrying cement and registered in Bahamas, is expected to arrive within a day at the Rotterdam port and it is suspected for drugs smuggling. To decide whether the Seaman may be the suspected vessel, the operator wants to examine the quality of information reported by the ship with respect to various questions:

– Does *Seaman* carry cement?
– Is *Seaman* a bulk-carrier registered in Bahamas?

To get answers to these questions, the operator uses additional information from other sources such as a ship registry database and visual observations and finds out that the *Seaman* is a Dutch bulk-carrier carrying also cement and stone but not gravel on board.

Thus, the operator concludes that the *Seaman* has reported incorrect and incomplete cargo, prompting some attention for further monitoring.

Performing such manual check-ups in practice, however, would make the work of operators practically impossible. Furthermore, some sources may not be easily accessible or their information not fully trusted, thus making the conclusions uncertain. Therefore, an automated approach is needed to evaluate the quality of information inherent with uncertainty.

3   Preliminaries

3.1   Representation Language

We use *first-order logic* as a flexible way to represent information and formulate queries. This abstracts from how data is stored in an actual implementation which could for instance be in some kind of database system. Our logic consists of a countable set of *predicate symbols*. We do not use functions, only constants like seaman. This restriction is chosen to ensure that domains are finite, as is common in probabilistic logics. We use upper case labels for variables, like X. We further use the common logical connectives $\forall$, $\exists$, $\wedge$, $\vee$, $\implies$ and $\iff$ to build up formulas.

We assume that information consists of logical facts described as object-attribute-value relations, which are represented as binary predicates in the form $a(O, V)$, where a refers to an attribute of object O and V is the attribute value. We do this without loss of generality as binary predicate logics is as expressive as full predicate logic. In the paper we use the name of objects, like seaman, as object labels for better readability. Adding new information means taking the conjunction of the previous and the new one. Instantiation of O and V means assigning a value to them. We explicitly do not use a *closed world assumption*, but distinguish wrong information from not reported information which is true in the real world.

3.2   Information Quality

In Table 1 we define the notions for representing information used in the rest of the paper. Although (sets of) queries and the true world also represent information, for the remaining of the paper we will use the term *information* only for what has been reported, thus defining and estimating its quality. For the meta properties we use to define information quality we use upper case labels for variables, like X and lower case labels for instantiations (x). We use bold notation for variables and instantiations representing sets ($\mathbf{X}$ and $\mathbf{x}$). We finally use logic entailment, denoted by $\models$, to indicate that a query is positively answered by given information.

Ideally, all queries positively answered by the information one has are true in the real world, too. The other way around, everything true in the real world should be derivable from the information. So we consider information quality as

Table 1. Definition of notions for representing information

Notion	Definition	Scenario examples
Information I	A self-contained statement about the world that can be expressed by a logical ground sentence (a formula without free variables).	$i_1 = type(\text{seaman}, \text{tanker})$ $\wedge name(\text{seaman}, \text{seaman})$ $\wedge id(\text{seaman}, 23378)$ $i_2 = cargo(\text{seaman}, \text{sand})$ $\wedge cargo(\text{seaman}, \text{gravel})$ $i = i_1 \wedge i_2$
Query Q	A logical ground sentence, representing a question, which is positively answered if it is entailed by the information	$q_1 = cargo(\text{seaman}, \text{sand})$ $q_2 = type(\text{seaman}, \text{bulk-carrier})$ $\wedge flag(\text{seaman}, \text{Bahamas})$
Set of queries $\mathbf{Q}$	It can be abbreviated by a formula with a free variable, if all possible groundings of the variable are known.	$\mathbf{q}_1 = \{q_1, q_2\}$ $\mathbf{q}_2 = cargo(\text{seaman}, \mathbf{TYPE})$ $\mathbf{q}_3 = \{cargo(\text{seaman}, \text{cement}),$ $cargo(\text{seaman}, \text{sand}),$ $cargo(\text{seaman}, \text{stone})\}$
World $\mathcal{W}$	The information representing the state of the real world.	$\mathcal{W} = \{flag(\text{seaman}, \text{NL}),$ $type(\text{seaman}, \text{bulk-carrier}),$ $cargo(\text{seaman}, \text{cement}),$ $cargo(\text{seaman}, \text{sand}),$ $cargo(\text{seaman}, \text{stone}), \ldots\}$

a two dimensional property. We introduce measures of how much those desired meta properties are true, referred to as *soundness* and *completeness* of information I with respect to a set of queries $\mathbf{Q}$ and they are formalised as follows:

$$snd_{\mathcal{W}}(\mathbf{Q}, I) \equiv \frac{\left|\left\{Q \in \mathbf{Q} \mid I \models Q \wedge \mathcal{W} \models Q\right\}\right|}{\left|\left\{Q \in \mathbf{Q} \mid I \models Q\right\}\right|} \tag{1}$$

$$cmp_{\mathcal{W}}(\mathbf{Q}, I) \equiv \frac{\left|\left\{Q \in \mathbf{Q} \mid I \models Q \wedge \mathcal{W} \models Q\right\}\right|}{\left|\left\{Q \in \mathbf{Q} \mid \mathcal{W} \models Q\right\}\right|} \tag{2}$$

In the case the denominator is 0 the soundness or completeness becomes 1. The values for soundness and completeness range from 0 to 1, where 0 is the worst and 1 the best possible quality. The soundness intuitively measures how much of what the information tells is actually true, the completeness measures how much of what is true is included in the information. In the special case that the set contains one query only, the result is always 0 or 1. The completeness never decreases when additional information $\mathbf{I}'$ is added to the information $\mathbf{I}$, whereas for soundness such a general property cannot be stated.

Example 1. The soundness and completeness of i_2 given $\mathbf{q}_3$ defined in Table 1 are:

$$snd_{\mathcal{W}}(\mathbf{q}_3, i_2) = \frac{1}{1} = 1 \qquad cmp_{\mathcal{W}}(\mathbf{q}_3, i_2) = \frac{1}{3} \approx 0.33$$

The definitions in (1) and (2) are closely related to the notions of precision and *recall* in information retrieval, and soundness and completeness as defined in [2,6], which are also based on the comparison of set cardinalities. The main difference in our definitions is that we construct the sets with respect to the set of queries. In other words, the elements of the sets depend on whether a query is entailed by the information and/or the true world, instead of directly comparing the information and the true world as done in the other approaches.

4   Probabilistic Method for Assessing Information Quality

In practice the entire state of $\mathcal{W}$ is often not known, especially in the domain we deal with. Previous work [2] for instance solves this by using data for which the world is assumed to be true, for example based on expert evaluation. There are two problems with this approach. First, the quality of received information cannot be assessed instantaneously in an automated way. Second, it cannot deal with uncertainty about how the world looks like.

Therefore, instead of requiring hard decisions of what is true or not in the real world, we construct a set of all possible worlds, which is restricted only to the relevant part given by all groundings of predicates relevant for the set of queries $\mathbf{Q}$. We denote this set of possible worlds by $\mathbf{W_Q}$.

Example 2. The possible parts of all relevant worlds given $\mathbf{q}_3$ are:

$$\mathbf{w_{q_3}} = \{ \ \mathit{cargo}(\text{seaman}, \text{cement}) \wedge \quad \mathit{cargo}(\text{seaman}, \text{sand}) \wedge \quad \mathit{cargo}(\text{seaman}, \text{stone}),$$
$$\mathit{cargo}(\text{seaman}, \text{cement}) \wedge \quad \mathit{cargo}(\text{seaman}, \text{sand}) \wedge \neg \mathit{cargo}(\text{seaman}, \text{stone}),$$
$$\ldots \ \}$$

Now for every possible world $W \in \mathbf{W_Q}$ we want to compute the probability for being true. To achieve this, we use a probabilistic model $\mathcal{M} = \langle \mathcal{S}, P \rangle$, where $\mathcal{S}$ denotes the structure of the model and P is a probability distribution such that $P : \mathbf{W_Q} \longrightarrow [0,1]$. The probability of a possible world is denoted by $P(W)$ and we have $\sum_{W \in \mathbf{W_Q}} P(W) = 1$. In general, P is the joint probability distribution of the specific grounding terms in W.

Building such a probabilistic model can itself be a complex task, but there is a largo body of work about how to build such models by incorporating expert knowledge or learning from data. Here we do not restrict the structure of the model, as long as the model produces a valid probability distribution, but in Section 4.2 we discuss some possible alternatives. A strong point of our approach is that once such a model is build, it can be reused for different vessels and sets of queries.

4.1   Expected Information Quality

We can then use $\mathcal{M}$ to derive the *expected soundness* and *completeness* of a set of queries, as defined in (1) and (2). For this we sum over all possible worlds and parametrise snd and cmp with a possible world. We use the notation snd_W and cmp_W replacing $\mathcal{W}$ by the possible world W in (1) and (2), respectively:

$$\mathbf{E}\Big[snd_{\mathcal{W}}(\mathbf{Q}, I)\Big] \equiv \sum_{W \in \mathbf{W_Q}} P(W) \cdot snd_W(\mathbf{Q}, I) \tag{3}$$

$$\mathbf{E}\Big[cmp_{\mathcal{W}}(\mathbf{Q}, I)\Big] \equiv \sum_{W \in \mathbf{W_Q}} P(W) \cdot cmp_W(\mathbf{Q}, I) \tag{4}$$

Note that if the probability distribution P gives a probability of 1 for a possible world then the formulas for the expected values of soundness and completeness reduce to those in (1) and (2), respectively.

Example 3. In this example we use i_2, $\mathbf{q_3}$ and $\mathcal{W}$ from Table 1. Given $\mathbf{q_3}$, we generate the set of all relevant possible worlds $\mathbf{W_{q_3}}$ and we assume that a probabilistic model gives the probability $P(W)$ of each possible world W being true; see the table below. This probabilities could for instance be frequencies obtained from past observations. We abbreviate the possible world by only giving the cargo the Seaman is carrying instead of giving the full predicates. To compute the expected values of soundness and completeness we count the number of queries $q \in \mathbf{q_3}$ satisfying $i_2 \models q \wedge W \models q$, $i_2 \models q$ and $W \models q$, shortly abbreviated as $|i_2 \wedge W|$, $|i_2|$ and $|W|$.

W	$P(W)$	$|i_2 \wedge W|$	$|i_2|$	$|W|$	$snd_W(\mathbf{q_3}, i_2)$	$cmp_W(\mathbf{q_3}, i_2)$
$\neg$cement $\wedge$ $\neg$sand $\wedge$ $\neg$stone	0.56	0	1	0	0	1
$\neg$cement $\wedge$ $\neg$sand $\wedge$ stone	0.06	0	1	1	0	0
$\neg$cement $\wedge$ sand $\wedge$ $\neg$stone	0.07	1	1	1	1	1
$\neg$cement $\wedge$ sand $\wedge$ stone	0.1	1	1	2	1	1/2
cement $\wedge$ $\neg$sand $\wedge$ $\neg$stone	0.04	0	1	1	0	0
cement $\wedge$ sand $\wedge$ $\neg$stone	0.09	1	1	2	1	1/2
cement $\wedge$ $\neg$sand $\wedge$ stone	0.05	0	1	2	0	0
cement $\wedge$ sand $\wedge$ stone	0.03	1	1	3	1	1/3

Using (3) and (4) the expected soundness and completeness are then:

$$\mathbf{E}\Big[snd_{\mathcal{W}}(\mathbf{q_3}, i_2)\Big] = 0.29 \qquad \mathbf{E}\Big[cmp_{\mathcal{W}}(\mathbf{q_3}, i_2)\Big] = 0.735$$

We notice that the estimations are not close to the actual qualities computed in Example 1, as $P(W)$ is based on prior distributions and does not account for additional information, for instance, that the vessel is a bulk-carrier.

An advantage of our approach is that it allows for a lot of flexibility in what one is interested in. One could for instance ask whether two types of cargo are on board of the Seaman or at least one of them.

Example 4. Some examples for more complex queries are given, together with the true and estimated qualities of $\mathbf{i_2}$, given the estimates of Example 3:

$\mathbf{Q}$	$snd_W(\mathbf{Q}, i_2)$, $cmp_W(\mathbf{Q}, i_2)$	$\mathbf{E}[snd_{\mathcal{W}}(\mathbf{Q}, i_2)]$, $\mathbf{E}[cmp_{\mathcal{W}}(\mathbf{Q}, i_2)]$
$\mathbf{q_4} = \{cargo(\mathsf{seaman}, \mathsf{cement}) \wedge cargo(\mathsf{seaman}, \mathsf{sand})\}$	1.0, 0.0	1.00, 0.88
$\mathbf{q_5} = \{cargo(\mathsf{seaman}, \mathsf{cement}) \vee cargo(\mathsf{seaman}, \mathsf{sand})\}$	1.0, 1.0	0.19, 1.00

4.2 Probabilistic Model

Although in this paper we do not restrict ourselves to a particular type of a probabilistic model, below we discuss some alternatives for estimating the probability distribution of the set of possible worlds depending on available information.

No Information–Uniform $P(\mathbf{W_Q})$. When no knowledge and information about the domain is given, the simplest assumption is that all possible worlds are equally likely:

$$\forall_{W \in \mathbf{W_Q}} : P(W) = \frac{1}{|\mathbf{W_Q}|} \tag{5}$$

Example 5. Consider again Example 3. Given the assumption in (5), the expected soundness and completeness are $\mathbf{E}\Big[snd_W(\mathbf{q_3}, i_2)\Big] = 0.5$ and $\mathbf{E}\Big[cmp_W(\mathbf{q_3}, i_2)\Big] \approx 0.42$.

In practice, this assumption is most likely violated, making the estimation of information quality less reliable.

Estimate $P(\mathbf{W_Q})$ Using Prior Distributions. Information is often available as statistics over a population, which can be used as prior distribution for estimating $P(\mathbf{W_Q})$, when no other specific information is available. For example, in Example 3, one can derive the distribution by taking the fraction of vessels carrying the particular set of cargoes out of the bulk dry vessels documented at a particular port.

Although prior distributions could be a good first step for estimating $P(\mathbf{W_Q})$, we note that this may be suboptimal since the quality of information about unlikely cases will be considered low, even if the quality is good; this is illustrated in the examples in Section 5.2.

Update $P(\mathbf{W_Q})$ Using New Information. If new information becomes available, in terms of probability theory, we can condition on this information to update the estimate of $P(\mathbf{W_Q})$.

Example 6. Continuing Example 3, the prior distribution estimate can be improved by using the type of the vessel. Next to the type adding also information obtained from a visual observation that the vessel definitely carries sand, further updates the probability distribution of the possible worlds, as shown in the table below:

W	$P(W)$	$P(W|\texttt{bulk\_carrier})$	$P(W|\texttt{bulk\_carrier}, \texttt{sand})$
¬cement ∧ ¬sand ∧ ¬stone	0.56	0.06	0.00
¬cement ∧ ¬sand ∧ stone	0.06	0.02	0.00
¬cement ∧ sand ∧ ¬stone	0.02	0.08	0.10
¬cement ∧ sand ∧ stone	0.15	0.04	0.05
cement ∧ ¬sand ∧ ¬stone	0.04	0.05	0.00
cement ∧ sand ∧ ¬stone	0.09	0.03	0.0375
cement ∧ ¬sand ∧ stone	0.05	0.07	0.00
cement ∧ sand ∧ stone	0.03	0.65	0.8125

How the probabilities are updated depends on the model, which is not the focus in this paper but we note that the probabilities of $P(W|\texttt{bulk\_carrier}, \texttt{sand})$ can be derived from the probabilities for $P(W|\texttt{bulk\_carrier})$. This example demonstrates that more relevant information contributes to getting a distribution closer to the true world. Below are shown the actual qualities together with the expected ones using the different distributions:

Model distribution	$snd_W(\mathbf{q_3}, i_2) = 1$ $\mathbf{E}[snd_W(\mathbf{q_3}, i_2)]$	$cmp_W(\mathbf{q_3}, i_2) = 0.33$ $\mathbf{E}[cmp_W(\mathbf{q_3}, i_2)]$
$P(W)$	0.29	0.735
$P(W\|\text{bulk\_carrier})$	0.8	0.392
$P(W\|\text{bulk\_carrier}, \text{sand})$	1	0.415

This shows that having more specific information leads to better estimates of the expected values of information quality.

Derivation of $P(W_Q)$ Using Independence Assumptions. Learning the probabilities for all possible worlds may quickly become impractical because their number grows exponentially with the number of queries. One way to tackle this is to assume that the probability $P(g)$ for a grounding g of a predicate, representing a query in $\mathbf{Q}$, is true is independent of all the others. In this case, only one estimated probability is needed for each query to define the model. The probability that a possible world is true can then be defined as:

$$P(W) \equiv \prod_{W \models g} P(g) \cdot \prod_{W \models \neg g} (1 - P(g)) \qquad (6)$$

Example 7. Consider again Example 3. Suppose that the model cannot give a probabilistic estimate of each possible world as before but only to the grounding of each predicate in the queries, i.e.,

$P(cargo(\text{seaman}, \text{cement}))$	$P(cargo(\text{seaman}, \text{sand}))$	$P(cargo(\text{seaman}, \text{stone}))$
0.21	0.29	0.24

Here, the probabilities are computed as the marginals for the sake of comparison. Now using (6) and the three probabilities above, we compute the probabilities for each possible world. Then $\mathbf{E}\left[snd_W(\mathbf{q_3}, i_2)\right] = 0.29$ and $\mathbf{E}\left[cmp_W(\mathbf{q_3}, i_2)\right] \approx 0.66$. The expected soundness is still the same, while the expected completeness changes.

Although in practice, the independence assumption may be too strict for all variables, it can still help reduce complexity while providing useful estimations.

Typical examples of probabilistic models that are able to incorporate domain knowledge, manage dependencies, and provide prior and posterior (joint) probability distributions include probabilistic graphical models such as Bayesian networks [5] and probabilistic logic [4,1].

5   Experiments

We perform two experiments to show that (i) the queries matter for estimating information quality (Exp-1), showing that our flexible approach to define queries is necessary, and (ii) a distribution conditioned on observations of the actual world is needed to give proper estimates (Exp-2).

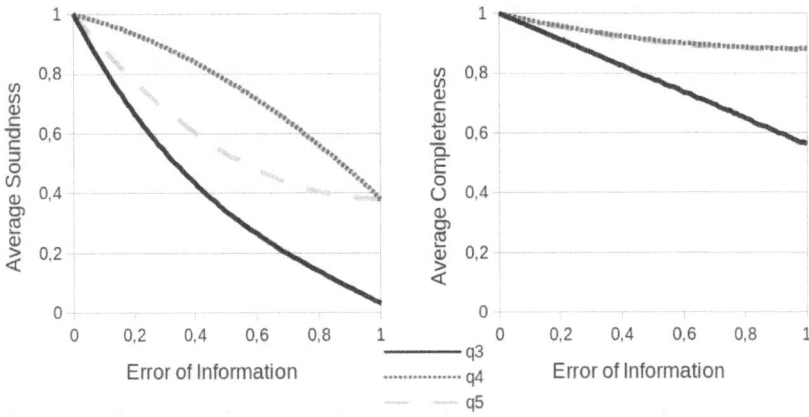

Fig. 2. The effect of the query on the soundness and completeness of information

For both experiments we generate N samples using the distribution given in the table of Example 3. Each sample $S_1, \ldots, S_N$ therefore consists of three Boolean values indicating whether the ship carries cement, sand or stone. We fix $N = 100000$ for all experiments. We simulate pieces of information $I_1, \ldots, I_N$ by observing whether a type of cargo is present in the actual world or not. The information can be wrong, which we simulate by introducing an error ϵ, i.e. there is a probability ϵ that the observation is wrong, which means that the cargo is reported while not present or the other way around. In the dynamic domain we deal with the actual error rates are unknown. We therefore vary ϵ from 0 to 1 in steps of 0.01 in the experiments to get results for various error rates.

5.1 Exp-1: Effect of Query on Information Quality

The information quality decreases with more discrepancies between the information and the actual world, i.e., with increasing ϵ. The rate of change of soundness and completeness given the error, however, depends on the query, as demonstrated in this experiment.

We compare the different sets of queries: $\mathbf{q_3}$ from Table 1 and $\mathbf{q_4}$, $\mathbf{q_5}$ from Example 4. For the different queries we determine the actual soundness and completeness $snd_{S_i}(\mathbf{Q}, I_i)$ and $cmp_{S_i}(\mathbf{Q}, I_i)$ for each sample and compute the averages. We repeat this for different ϵ. Figure 2 shows the average soundness and completeness for the different queries against ϵ.

The quality of information obviously decreases as the error increases. If there is no error the quality is perfect, but it is interesting that it never goes to 0 even if the reported information is completely wrong. For instance, the mean completeness for $\mathbf{q_3}$ and $\epsilon = 1.0$ is above 0.5. This is because according to the distribution in 56% of the cases none of the three cargo types is on board of a ship. The reported completely wrong information reports all three kinds of cargo, which is per definition complete. This is true for soundness in an analogous way.

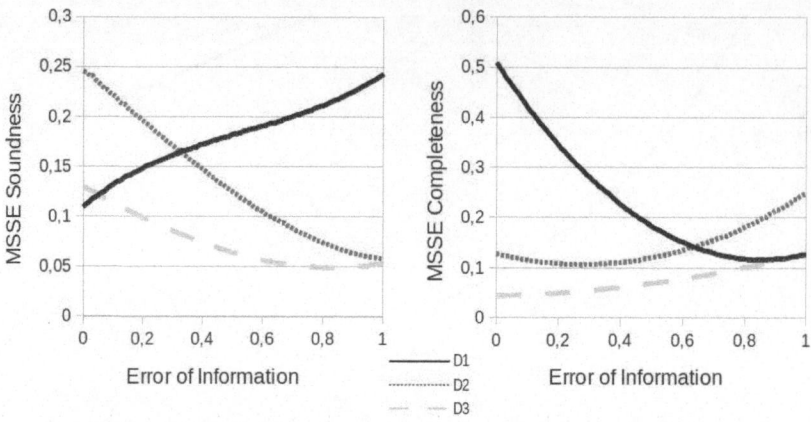

Fig. 3. The effect of the distribution used to estimate information quality on the MSSE

The set of query containing the conjunction q_4 has a better soundness, as in less situations the query can be positively answered. In this case the soundness is 1.0. The difference between the completeness of q_4 and q_5 is very small. This is not a general property of the queries, but changes with a different distribution used to generate the samples.

5.2   Exp-2: Comparison of Different Distributions for Prediction

In this section we compare how different distributions perform when used to estimate the information quality. This shows that as already shown in Example 6 conditioning on some knowledge about the actual world is needed to get proper estimates. We only use q_3 and use the following distributions:

- $\mathcal{D}_1$: the uniform distribution (Equation 6)
- $\mathcal{D}_2$: the distribution used to generate the data (table of Example 3)
- $\mathcal{D}_3$: the distribution used to generate the data conditioned on the observation whether the ship is carrying sand ($P(W|\text{sand})$ or $P(W|\neg\text{sand})$)

For the different distributions we determine for each sample the actual and estimated soundness and completeness and compute the *mean sum of squared errors* (MSSE). We repeat this for different ϵ; see Figure 3.

   The result clearly shows that using a distribution which is dynamically conditioned on information from the actual world, outperforms fixed distributions in nearly all cases. It might be surprising that the uniform distribution for some ϵ works better than the one used to generate the data. We focus on the soundness for the case $\epsilon = 0$ to give a better insight of why this is the case. In the following table we give for each pair of estimated and actual soundness the frequency of how often this pair occurs for all samples $S_1, \ldots, S_N$:

$snd_\mathcal{W}(\mathbf{q_3}, I)$	$\mathcal{D}_1$		$\mathcal{D}_2$	
	$\mathbf{E}[snd_\mathcal{W}(\mathbf{q_3}, I)]$	frequency	$\mathbf{E}[snd_\mathcal{W}(\mathbf{q_3}, I)]$	frequency
1.0	1.0	0.562	1.0	0.562
1.0	0.5	0.438	0.247 ± 0.026	0.438

For the cases where no information is reported the information is always sound, so the difference is in the other cases. Using $\mathcal{D}_1$ for those cases all predictions are 0.5 and for $\mathcal{D}_2$ it is always smaller. Since 0.5 is close to the actual soundness 1.0, $\mathcal{D}_1$ performs better for this case. This shows that a fixed distribution is not sufficient even if the actual distribution is perfectly known.

6   Conclusions

We propose a novel methodology for systematically representing and assessing the quality of information obtained from various sources in uncertain domains such as maritime surveillance. We give a concise, formal definition of information quality based on logical entailment and two sub-properties–soundness and completeness–indicating the goodness of answers derived from information compared to the ground truth. Unlike previous work the definition allows to consider information quality as a dynamic property of the information, which depends on the questions at hand. Also we do not require certain knowledge about reality and allow to deal with uncertainty, by proposing method to estimate information quality using a probabilistic model. An application on a maritime scenario demonstrated basis properties of the proposed method.

In future, we plan to study the effect of the estimates from the probabilistic model on the quality of information by developing a realistic model based on the maritime domain.

References

1. Laskey, K.B.: MEBN: A language for first-order bayesian knowledge bases. Artif. Intell. 172(2-3), 140–178 (2008)
2. Motro, A., Rakov, I.: Estimating the Quality of Databases. In: Andreasen, T., Christiansen, H., Larsen, H.L. (eds.) FQAS 1998. LNCS (LNAI), vol. 1495, pp. 298–307. Springer, Heidelberg (1998)
3. Naumann, F., Leser, U., Freytag, J.C.: Quality-driven integration of heterogenous information systems. In: Proc. of the 25th Int. Conf. on VLDB, pp. 447–458 (1999)
4. Nilsson, N.J.: Probabilistic logic. Artif. Intell. 28(1), 71–87 (1986)
5. Pearl, J.: Probabilistic reasoning in intelligent systems: networks of plausible inference. Morgan Kaufmann (1988)
6. Peim, M., Franconi, E., Paton, N.W.: Estimating the quality of answers when querying over description logic ontologies. Data & Knowl. Eng. 47(1), 105–129 (2003)
7. Pipino, L.L., Lee, Y.W., Wang, R.Y.: Data quality assessment. Communications of the ACM 45(4), 211–218 (2002)
8. Salton, G., McGill, M.J.: Introduction to Modern Information Retrieval. McGraw-Hill (1983)

Causal Discovery of Dynamic Bayesian Networks

Cora Beatriz Pérez-Ariza[1], Ann E. Nicholson[2], Kevin B. Korb[2],
Steven Mascaro[2], and Chao Heng Hu[2]

[1] Dept. of Computer Science and Artificial Intelligence
University of Granada
Granada, 18071, Spain

[2] Clayton School of IT
Monash University
Clayton, VIC 3800

Abstract. While a great variety of algorithms have been developed
and applied to learning static Bayesian networks, the learning of dynamic networks has been relatively neglected. The causal discovery program CaMML has been enhanced with a highly flexible set of methods
for taking advantage of prior expert knowledge in the learning process.
Here we describe how these representations of prior knowledge can be
used instead to turn CaMML into a promising tool for learning dynamic
Bayesian networks.

Keywords: Learning dynamic Bayesian networks, causal discovery,
dynamic Bayesian networks.

1   Introduction

Bayesian networks (BNs) have become a valuable tool for applied Artificial Intelligence, where they are effective in reasoning about and under uncertainty,
managing uncertainty, and providing better information for planning. Bayesian
networks have been widely and successfully applied across the sciences, including economy, biology, and medicine. In simpler cases, a Bayesian network can
be built by expert elicitation. However, for many real world applications, BNs
are too complex to be fully specified by experts, requiring learning from observational data. A great amount of effort has been spent on research on learning
Bayesian networks from data, with many successful programs and algorithms the
consequence (see Daly et al., 2011, for a recent review). While the generalization of static to dynamic Bayesian networks (DBNs), representing both "static"
causal relations (within one time slice) and dynamic causal relations (across time
slices), is relatively straightforward, the generalization of static BN learners to
dynamic BN learners is a bit trickier. Here we present some preliminary results
applying a static learner, the CaMML causal discovery program (causal discovery via Minimum Message Length), to learning dynamic BNs structure from
data.

M. Thielscher and D. Zhang (Eds.): AI 2012, LNCS 7691, pp. 902–913, 2012.

2   Bayesian Networks

A *Bayesian network* is a directed acyclic graph where each node represents a random variable, and the topology of the graph encodes the independence relations among the variables, according to the *d*-separation criterion (Pearl, 1988). Given the independencies implied by the graph, the joint distribution is determined by the condiional probability tables (CPTs) associated with each node; thus, for a Bayesian network with variables $X_1, \ldots, X_n$:

$$p(x_1, \ldots, x_n) = \prod_{i=1}^{n} p_i(x_i | pa(x_i)), \qquad (1)$$

where $pa(x_i)$ denotes a configuration of values of the parents of variable X_i in the network.

2.1   Learning Bayesian Networks

There are two fundamental difficulties in learning Bayesian network structures. One is the complexity of learning Bayesian network structures. The space of Bayesian networks is super-exponential in the number of variables, and the learning problem has been proven to be NP-hard (Chickering, 1996). The other difficulty is that given observational data there is usually no unique Bayesian network that represents observed joint distribution over a set of variables. Various approaches have been developed to make the problems tractable, which can be categorized into constraint-based methods and metric-based methods.

Constraint-based methods aim to discover causal models using conditional independences from statistical tests on data, incorporating heuristic search to find the best structure over the Markov equivalence classes.

Metric-based learners use metrics that score candidate structures embedded in a search procedure aiming to maximize or minimize that score. The Bayesian Information Criterion (BIC) score (**?**) and the Bayesian Dirichlet (BDe) score (Cooper and Herskovits, 1991) are two popular metrics that have been used in many BN learning techniques. Wallace and Korb (1999) used Minimum Message Length (MML) metric for learning BN in the casual discovery program CaMML.

2.2   The CaMML Learner

CaMML (Causal discovery via Minimum Message Length) attempts to learn the best causal structure to account for the data, using a Minimum Message Length (MML) metric (Wallace, 2005) with a two-phase search over the model space, simulated annealing followed by Markov Chain Monte Carlo (MCMC) search. CaMML has been developed at Monash University over the past 16 years (see Korb and Nicholson, 2011, Ch 9, and O'Donnell, 2010 for a full description). We used the most recent open-source version of CAMML,[1]. CaMML supports multiple ways of describing prior information about relationships between variables

---

[1] https://github.com/rodneyodonnell/CaMML

(O'Donnell et al., 2006), each of which can be accompanied by a confidence level. The types of priors are:

- Full structure. An expert may supply a fully specified network for all or subnetwork.
- Direct causal connections between variables may be indicated (e.g., $A \rightarrow B$).
- Direct relation ($A - B$). I.e., there is an arc between two variables, but the direction is unknown.
- Causal dependency ($A \Rightarrow B$). One variable is an ancestor of the other.
- Correlation ($A \sim B$). There is some connection between the nodes, which may be a causal dependency in either direction or via a common ancestor.
- Temporal order ($\{A_1, A_2, ...A_m\} \prec \{B_1, B_2, ...B_n\}$). This sorts variables into tiers, a partial ordering based on the notion that tiers separate the variables on a timeline and that causality only occurs in the forward time direction. This is the most commonly allowed prior constraint in BN learning (e.g., Tetrad IV and K2). Thus $\prec$ means that the A_i occur before the B_j; for CaMML this becomes the structural constraint that the A_i cannot be descendants of B_j.

The expert may provide CaMML with any combination of the priors above, together with the confidence in each (expressed as a probability).[2] CaMML then combines these into an MML code for a prior probability distribution over the model space, as explained, for example, in Korb and Nicholson (2011, Chap 9).

3   Dynamic Bayesian Networks

A *dynamic Bayesian network* (DBN) represents a system that changes over time. A static model over the variables $X_1, \ldots, X_n$ is repeated for each time slice T_i.[3] To distinguish between corresponding variables across time slices, we will denote them $X_n^{T_i}$, meaning variable X_n during time slice T_i. The time slices are connected through *temporal links*, that are the same for every consecutive pair of time slices. Usually the temporal links only connect one time slice with the next (so, the order 1 Markov assumption holds). Finally, the conditional probabilities don't change over time (the system is assumed to be stationary). A DBN can be specified very compactly:

- Set of node names, defined as $\Omega_X = \forall n \forall i X_n^{T_i}$
- Intra-slice links, that connect variables in the same time slice
- Temporal (inter-slice) links
- CPTs for the first time slice
- CPTs for the second time slice (when parents may be either from T_i or T_{i+1} time-slices)

---

[2] Some other BN learners also support the use of structural knowledge, but they have been limited to specifying one or two of these kinds of priors.

[3] I.e., DBNs are stationary systems. The flexibility of CaMML would allow us also to look at learning *non-stationary* dynamic models, which we may do in the future.

3.1   Learning Dynamic Bayesian Networks

Friedman et al. (1998) were the first to look at automated learning of DBNs, extending both the BIC score and the BDe score to apply them to DBNs. They decomposed the learning problem into learning first the static network, representing time slices, and then the transition network relating one time slice to the next, applying Friedman's structural EM algorithm to the learning tasks. Tucker and Liu (1999, 2003) applied evolutionary algorithms with an MDL score to DBN learning. Other techniques that have been applied include branch-and-bound (de Campos and Ji, 2011) and greedy search (Van Berlo et al., 2003).

Comparison with these methods is made difficult by the lack of a common set of learning problems and lack of access to the programs used (although the EM MDL approach is available in Murphy's BNT). Here we will simply explore using CaMML for DBN learning in comparison with the PC algorithm in GeNIe. We chose CaMML because, not only are we familiar with it, but it has the widest and most flexible range of representations for prior learning constraints of the available BN learning programs (see §2.2), allowing DBN constraints to be readily incorporated.

4   Examples of Dynamic Bayesian Networks

To explore the possibilities of learning DBNs with CaMML, we have taken two Bayesian networks from the literature, modified to represent stationary models with two time slices. The CPTs were handcrafted.

4.1   eMilk Dynamic Bayesian Network

Milk from a cow may be infected. There is a test to detect whether the milk is infected, which may give either a positive or a negative test result. The test is not perfect. It may give a positive result on clean milk as well as a negative result on infected milk (Jensen and Nielsen, 2007).

We have added some weather conditions that may affect the milk, namely temperature and humidity. These two variables are summarized in a weather variable, that affects directly the quality of the food eaten by the cow and indirectly the probability of an infection in the milk. In our model high humidity increases the probability of an infection, and the temperature has an impact on the accuracy of the test, with extreme temperatures increasing the chances of a malfunction. The model can be extended over time to observe this situation over time. We duplicated the original structure to obtain two time slices, with some *temporal links* between them. The full model is shown in Fig.1.

4.2   eMetCancer Dynamic Bayesian Network

Metastatic cancer is a possible cause of brain tumors and is also an explanation for increased total serum calcium. In turn, either of these could

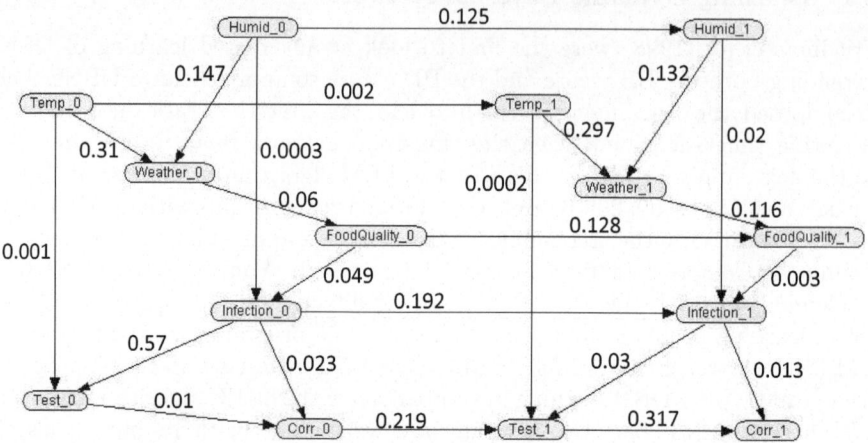

Fig. 1. Handcrafted extended milk model (eMilk)

*explain a patient falling into a coma. Severe headache is also associated
with brain tumors. (Cooper, 1984)*

This situation can also be observed over time. For example the presence of a
brain tumor at one time may be due to an earlier tumor metastasizing. We have
expanded this model into two time slices by duplicating the original structure
and adding five temporal links to it. Note that the model has not been checked
with an expert and so it may not represent the medical reality. The resultant
model is shown in Fig. 2.

4.3   Sensitivity Analysis

We performed sensitivity analysis on the models in order to determine the *connection strengths* of the links in the dynamic Bayesian networks (Jitnah, 1999;
Boerlage, 1992). This allowed us to check the strengths of the links that CaMML
was not able to detect. We obtained the mutual information between each pair
of connected nodes using Netica's M.I. function.[4] These strengths are specified
in Fig.1 and Fig.2 as links weights. As shown, we designed both examples to
have a mixture of weak and strong arcs.

---

[4] See www.norsys.com. More specifically, the Netica M.I. measure is over all paths
between two nodes; we limited it to the direct connection path by d-separating the
nodes on any other paths, by averaging over the Markov blanket (excluding the path
in question).

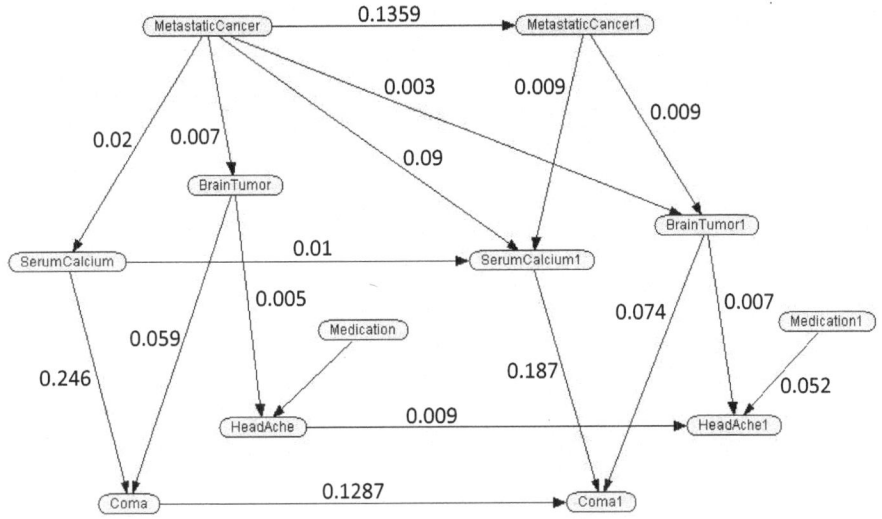

Fig. 2. Handcrafted extended Metastatic Cancer model (eMetCancer)

5 Experimental Evaluation

5.1 Methodology

In order to learn dynamic Bayesian networks with CaMML, we incorporated as prior knowledge constraints that define DBNs. The most obvious such constraint is to group variables within a time slice in a tier, so all the variables of one time slice must precede all those in the next. Thus we define the temporal order: $\{X_1^{T_0}, X_2^{T_0}, ... X_i^{T_0}\} \prec \{X_1^{T_1}, X_2^{T_1}, ... X_i^{T_1}\}$.

A more elaborate approach to learning DBNs is shown in Algorithm 1. The idea here is to learn a static Bayesian network for a single time slice; duplicate it, identifying it as the subnetwork for both time slices, by fixing its causal arcs as prior constraints with confidence 1 (as CaMML allows us to do); learn the temporal links connecting the two tiers.

We used three sample sizes for most of our experiments: 1000, 10000 and 100000 cases. CaMML was run with the default of $201n^3$ iterations in its search (where n is the number of variables).

For comparison, we also learned models using the version of the PC algorithm implemented in GeNIe,[5] employing both tier priors and Algorithm 1. GeNIe permits the incorporation of certain types of prior information, in particular temporal tiers and the hard constraint of arcs that can or can't be in the model. Since PC does not direct all arcs learned, when measuring the quality of these

---

[5] From the Decision Systems Laboratory of the University of Pittsburgh http://dsl.sis.pitt.edu/.

models, we penalized undirected arcs (when present in the original model) with half the penalty used for standard errors.

Algorithm 1: Learn a DBN with CaMML using learned prior information

Input: A database D
Output: $\mathcal{DBN}_D$, a DBnet for D

1 **begin**
2 $\quad$ // Divide D into D^{T_1} and D^{T_2}
3 $\quad$ Let $D^{T_1} =$ data from variables in T_1
4 $\quad$ Let $D^{T_2} =$ data from variables in T_2
5 $\quad$ Let $X_1...X_n$ be the generic variables in a time slice
6 $\quad$ Change variables in D^{T_1} and D^{T_2} for their equivalents in $X_1...X_n$
7 $\quad$ // Note that $D_{generic}$ will have twice as much data as D^{T_1} and D^{T_2}
8 $\quad$ Make $D_{generic} = D^{T_1} \cup D^{T_2}$
9 $\quad$ Learn $G_{generic}$ from $D_{generic}$ using CaMML
10 $\quad$ **foreach** *time slice* T_k, $k = 1, 2$ **do**
11 $\quad\quad$ **foreach** *pair of variables* X_i, X_j *in* T_i **do**
12 $\quad\quad\quad$ **if** $X_i \rightarrow X_j \in G_{generic}$ **then**
13 $\quad\quad\quad\quad$ set the intra-slice link $X_i^{T_k} \rightarrow X_j^{T_k}$ as prior with confidence 1
14 $\quad\quad\quad$ **else**
15 $\quad\quad\quad\quad$ set the intra-slice link $X_i^{T_k} \rightarrow X_j^{T_k}$ as prior with confidence 0
16 $\quad$ Set tier for the temporal order $(\{X_1^{T_1}, X_2^{T_1}, ...X_n^{T_1}\} \prec \{X_1^{T_2}, X_2^{T_2}, ...X_n^{T_2}\})$
17 $\quad$ Learn temporal links with CaMML using the priors defined in steps 10-15 and the tier defined in step 16, using database D
18 $\quad$ Set the result as $\mathcal{DBN}_D$
19 $\quad$ **return** $\mathcal{DBN}_D$

5.2 Evaluation

To evaluate the different approaches to learning we measured how close learned structures were to the original networks used to generate the data using edit distances. For learning static BNs, this can be as simple as counting the minimal number of arc deletions, additions and reversals to go from one model to the other.[6] DBNs require some adjustment to the edit distance, however.

Edit Distance for DBNs (eED). In a stationary DBN, all time slices have the same structure, so if during the learning process this restriction is violated, the traditional computation of the edit distance does not detect it. We modify

---

[6] Even for static BNs this is too simple, ignoring the difference between reversals that leave models Markov equivalent and those that don't. In any case, however, edit distance will remain crude compared to Kullback-Leibler divergence and other measures. For a discussion see Korb and Nicholson, 2011, Sec 9.8.

this metric by counting the errors in just the second slice and the errors in the temporal links separately. These links suffice to reconstruct the entire DBN, excepting the first time slice, whose importance disappears in a sufficiently large expansion of the DBN. Thus we used:

$$eED(N, N') = w_t E(N_t, N'_t) + w_s E(N_s, N'_s)$$

where N, N' are the original and learned networks respectively, $E(\cdot, \cdot)$ measures static BN edit distance, w_t is the weight assigned to temporal links and w_s that for static links, N_t is the original network restricted to temporal links, N_s is the same restricted to static links in the second tier, and N'_s and N'_t the corresponding learned subnetworks. For this work we set $w_t = w_s = 1$.

5.3   Results and Discussion

Some of our results are shown in Table 1. A more detailed view of results for eMilk without priors is given in Table 2. If we look only at the outcome of the experimentation with no priors and with tier priors, an inspection of the learned BNs for eMilk (e.g., Figure 3) shows that when arcs are missing, these arcs are the ones with the lower M.I. score, e.g., $Temp\_0 \rightarrow Test\_0$, $Temp\_1 \rightarrow Test\_1$ and $Humid\_0 \rightarrow Infection\_0$. In the case of the eMetCancer model, the errors are always found in the temporal link set.

While we have a general expectation that learning with more samples will reduce errors, interestingly this is not always the case. For example, GeNIe no priors, the eED for eMilk goes from 4.25 to 7.5 from 1000 to 100000 sample points. In such cases, the increase in the eED is commonly due to errors of commission, with spurious arcs being added. This happens for both networks and for learning with and without priors, suggesting that especially GeNIe's PC is overfitting its data. For a detailed comparison of PC and CaMML's learning performance, see Dai et al. (1997).

Tier priors for GeNIe reduced the eED in all cases. For CaMML, priors, whether with tiers or Algorithm 1, eliminated errors with eMetCancer, but did

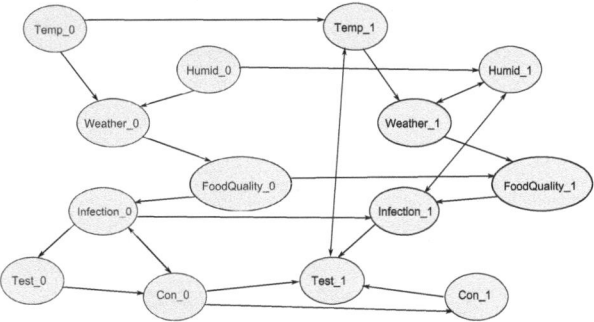

Fig. 3. Extended milk model learned with the PC algorithm, with a database of 10000 cases

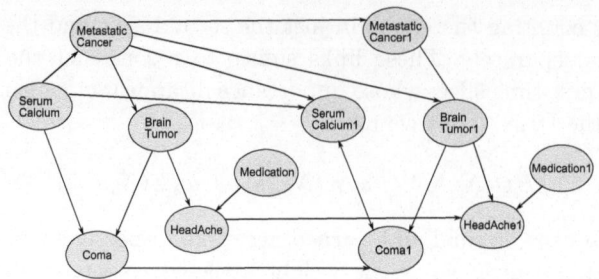

Fig. 4. Extended Metastatic Cancer model learned with the PC algorithm, with a database of 10000 cases and the temporal tier

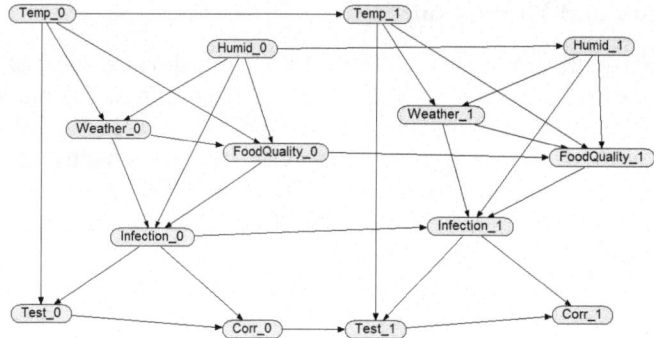

Fig. 5. Extended milk model learned by CaMML with Alg. 1 using a 100000 cases database

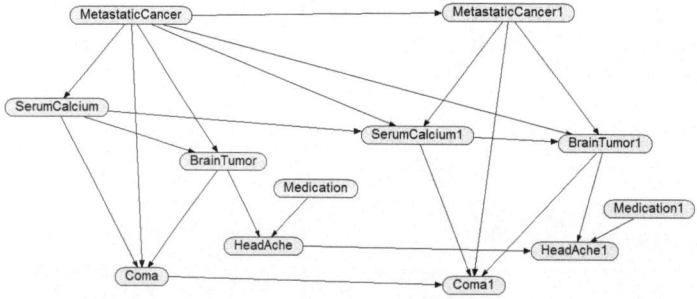

Fig. 6. Extended Metastatic Cancer model learned by CaMML with Alg. 1 using a 100000 cases database

Table 1. Edit distance for DBNs (eED) obtained for the different models learned

		CaMML		GeNIe	
		eMilk	eMetCancer	eMIlk	eMetCancer
no priors	1000	0.95	2.6	4.5	4.5
	10000	0	0.5	2	4.5
	100000	0	0.5	7.5	1
tier	1000	0.975	2.4	3.5	2.5
	10000	0	0	3	1.25
	100000	0	0	4.5	0.25
Algorithm 1	1000	1.5	0	5.5	5
	10000	0	0	4.5	3
	100000	0	0	9	4.5

Table 2. Mean errors (omissions, commissions, reversals) and edit distances (eED) for eMilk without priors (reporting standard deviations for CaMML over twenty runs; PC is deterministic)

		CaMML				GeNIe			
		om	com	rev	eED (sd)	om	com	rev	eED
no priors	100	4.2	0	1.65	3.425 (0.43)	9	2	0	5.5
	1000	1.9	0	0	0.95 (0.15)	4	4	1	4.5
	10000	0	0	0	0 (0.0)	2	1	1	2

not make a difference for eMilk, where the learning is exact given 10k or larger samples. Both the use of tiers and Algorithm 1 appear to provide a satisfactory basis for learning dynamic networks.

Table 2 shows the results for eMilk without priors in more detail (other cases show similar results). In order to examine variation, we ran CaMML twenty times and estimated its mean and standard deviation in eED (PC is deterministic). The results show differences in performance between CaMML and PC at all sample sizes that are statistically significant.

6   Conclusions and Future Work

In this paper we have shown how a static BN learner with structural priors can be adapted to learn dynamic Bayesian networks, which explicitly model changes over time. We have presented experimental results applying two such learners, CaMML (a metric-based learner) and GeNIe (which uses conditional independence learning). Applying temporal tiers can result in networks with different structures in each time slice. An alternative two-stage algorithm ensures the connections within a slice remain the same, but may lead to other errors in the network structure. Our results also show that CaMML clearly outperforms GeNIe PC.

The obvious next step is to compare the performance of the static learners used with priors and Algorithm 1 with tailored DBN learners such as that provided with Murphy's BNT software (Murphy, 2001). There are further opportunities for using CaMML's flexible priors to boost DBN learning. Finally, CaMML's scoring metric may be enhanced to deal with DBN features intrinsically. While this work is very preliminary, it clearly points out a promising direction for future research.

Acknowledgments. This work has been partially funded by the FPI scholarship programme (BES-2008-002049).

References

Boerlage, B.: Link Strengths in Bayesian networks. Master's thesis, University of British Columbia (1992)

Chickering, D.M.: Learning Bayesian networks is NP-complete. In: Fisher, D., Lenz, H.-J. (eds.) Learning from Data: AI and Statistics V, ch. 12, pp. 121–130. Springer (1996)

Cooper, G.: NESTOR: A Computer-Based Medical Diagnostic Aid That Integrates Causal and Probabilistic Knowledge. Ph. D. thesis, Stanford (1984)

Cooper, G., Herskovits, E.: A Bayesian method for the induction of probabilistic networks from data. Technical Report Stanford KSL 9 (June 1991)

Dai, H., Korb, K., Wallace, C., Wu, X.: A study of causal discovery, with weak links and small samples. In: International Joint Conference on Artificial Intelligence, vol. 15, pp. 1304–1309 (1997)

Daly, R., Shen, Q., Aitken, S.: Learning Bayesian networks: Approaches and issues. The Knowledge Engineering Review 26, 99–157 (2011)

de Campos, C., Ji, Q.: Efficient structure learning of Bayesian networks using constraints. Journal of Machine Learning Research 12, 663–689 (2011)

Friedman, N., Murphy, K., Russell, S.: Learning the structure of dynamic probabilistic networks. In: Cooper, G.F., Moral, S. (eds.) Proceedings of the 14th Conference on Uncertainty in Artificial Intelligence (UAI 1998), July 24-26, pp. 139–147. Morgan Kaufmann, San Francisco (1998)

Jensen, F.V., Nielsen, T.D.: Bayesian networks and decision graphs. Springer (2007)

Jitnah, N.: Using Mutual Information for Approximate Evaluation of Bayesian Networks. Ph. D. thesis, Monash University (1999)

Korb, K.B., Nicholson, A.E.: Bayesian Artificial Intelligence, 2nd edn. Chapman & Hall/CRC, Boca Raton (2011)

Murphy, K.: The Bayes net toolbox for MATLAB. Computing Science and Statistics 33, 1024–1034 (2001)

O'Donnell, R.: Flexible Causal Discovery with MML. In: Faculty of Information Technology (Clayton), Monash University, Australia 3800 (2010)

O'Donnell, R.T., Nicholson, A.E., Han, B., Korb, K.B., Alam, M. J., Hope, L.R.: Causal Discovery with Prior Information. In: Sattar, A., Kang, B.-H. (eds.) AI 2006. LNCS (LNAI), vol. 4304, pp. 1162–1167. Springer, Heidelberg (2006)

Pearl, J.: Probabilistic reasoning in intelligent systems. Morgan Kaufmann, San Mateo (1988)

Schwarz, G.: Estimating the dimension of a model. Ann. Stat. 14, 461–464 (1978)

Tucker, A., Liu, X.: Extending evolutionary programming methods to the learning of dynamic Bayesian networks. In: Banzhaf, W., Daida, J., Eiben, A.E., Garzon, M.H. (eds.) Proceedings of the Genetic and Evolutionary Computation Conference (1999)

Tucker, A., Liu, X.: Learning Dynamic Bayesian Networks from Multivariate Time Series with Changing Dependencies. In: Berthold, M., Lenz, H.-J., Bradley, E., Kruse, R., Borgelt, C. (eds.) IDA 2003. LNCS, vol. 2810, pp. 100–110. Springer, Heidelberg (2003)

Van Berlo, R., Van Someren, E., Reinders, M.: Studying the conditions for learning dynamic Bayesian networks to discover genetic regulatory networks. Simulation 79, 689–702 (2003)

Wallace, C.S.: Statistical and Inductive Inference by Minimum Message Length. Springer, Berlin (2005)

Wallace, C.S., Korb, K.B.: Learning linear causal models by MML sampling. In: Gammerman, A. (ed.) Causal Models and Intelligent Data Management, pp. 89–111. Springer (1999)

Author Index